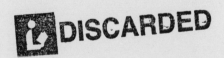

THE
GLADSTONE
DIARIES

Gladstone aged sixty-nine, photographed in Lenbach's studio in Munich on
13 October 1879

THE
GLADSTONE
DIARIES

WITH
CABINET MINUTES
AND
PRIME-MINISTERIAL
CORRESPONDENCE

VOLUME IX
JANUARY 1875–DECEMBER 1880

Edited by

H. C. G. MATTHEW

CLARENDON PRESS · OXFORD
1986

Oxford University Press, Walton Street, Oxford OX2 6 DP
Oxford New York Toronto
Delhi Bombay Calcutta Madras Karachi
Kuala Lumpur Singapore Hong Kong Tokyo
Nairobi Dar es Salaam Cape Town
Melbourne Auckland
and associated companies in
Beirut Berlin Ibadan Nicosia

Oxford is a trade mark of Oxford University Press

Published in the United States
by Oxford University Press, New York

British Library Cataloguing in Publication Data
Gladstone, W. E. (William Ewart)
The Gladstone diaries: with Cabinet minutes and
prime-ministerial correspondence.
Vol. 9: January 1875–December 1880.
1. Gladstone, W. E. (William Ewart)
2. Prime ministers—Great Britain—Biography
I. Title   II. Matthew, H. C. G.
941.081'092'4   DA563
ISBN 0-19-822775-2

Typeset by Joshua Associates Limited, Oxford
Printed in Great Britain
at the University Printing House, Oxford
by David Stanford
Printer to the University

PREFACE

This volume of Gladstone's diaries continues the pattern of the previous two volumes, that is, in addition to the complete publication of the daily diary text, all of the relevant Cabinet Minutes and an extensive selection of Prime-Ministerial correspondence have been included.

The Archbishop of Canterbury, the owner of the diaries, is to be thanked for permission to publish them, as is Sir William Gladstone both for permission to publish material from the collections in the British Library and St. Deiniol's Library, Hawarden, and for his generous assistance to the editor and the edition. The editor is also grateful to the Duke of Devonshire, the Countess of Rosebery, the Hon. Simon Howard, and Mr. Keith Adam for permission to publish papers or illustrations in their possession.

The editor continues to be much obliged for support to the *ad hoc* committee which superintends the publication of this edition. Lord Blake is its chairman, its other members being Mr. E. G. W. Bill, Lord Bullock, Dr. J. F. A. Mason, Mr. C. H. Stuart, and Mr. A. F. Thompson, with Dr. I. Asquith of the Oxford University Press as secretary and Dr. C. Peach of St. Catherine's College (the project's academic sponsor) its treasurer. The editor would like to thank the members of this committee for their encouragement.

The research for this volume has been financed by the Archbishop of Canterbury, by the Gladstone Memorial Trust, by Dr. Anthony Henfrey, and especially by the Rhodes Trust, whose assistance has permitted the continuation of the edition.

Gladstone's college of Christ Church, Oxford, has very generously continued its support of the edition by providing accommodation, by maintaining the editor as Lecturer in Gladstone Studies, and by supplying, directly or indirectly, most of the membership of the committee.

The editor's debts continue unabated. Mrs. Francis Phillips has done much very accurate transcription and typing, and has laboured to identify the vast mass of Gladstone's reading, in this volume probably the heaviest of any. Her calm self-reliance is a great asset to the edition. Mrs. Jean Gilliland has been most generous with her time, vastly speeding the editing by taking on a large number of routine chores, and assisting in research and transcription at the British Library. Others who have generously assisted have been Dr. Richard Brent, Miss Catherine Morshead, Mrs. Vicky Phillips, Miss Karen Puddephatt, and Mrs. Theresa Webber. The edition could hardly have proceeded without their energetic and expeditious help. Miss Margaret Jacobs gave useful information about Lenbach material in Munich.

Dr. John Mason and Mr. John Wing (the Librarian and Assistant Librarian at Christ Church Library), Mr. Geoffrey Bill of Lambeth Palace Library, and their respective staffs, have all been most helpful. The Clwyd Record office at Hawarden, which produces the Gladstone family papers deposited at St. Deiniol's Library, has continued, under its Archivist, Mr. Geoffrey Veysey, to be of enormous assistance. In particular, all Gladstone scholars are obliged to Mr. Christopher Williams, whose knowledge of the family papers is unsurpassed.

Thanks must also be given to the staff of the History Faculty Office and Library at Oxford, to the staffs of the Bodleian Library, the Public Record Office, the National Library of Scotland, Glasgow University Library, the Library of Congress, and the Public Record Office of Northern Ireland.

Professor H. W. Lawton's typescript of the daily journal continues to be of exceptional accuracy, despite the gradual decline in the diarist's legibility. The marginalia written on it by Professor M. R. D. Foot have solved a number of tricky problems. Mrs. Vera Keep, who has set this and the previous two volumes, has by her good humour made the production of the volume an enjoyable process for the editor and has put readers in her debt by her skill in setting a complex and awkward text.

For assistance in particular points of research, the editor is especially obliged, among the many he has bothered with his query-sheets, to Dr. Agatha Ramm for advice, encouragement, and suggestions, to Mr. Peter Parsons, Mr. Keith Thomas, and the Very Reverend Eric Heaton for eclectic information, and to Mr. Denis Mack Smith, Dr. Theo Hoppen, Dr. Kenneth Morgan, Professor Sir Dimitri Obolensky, and Dr. Stephen Ashby for information, respectively, about Italy, Ireland, Wales, and Bulgaria. Mr. Mark Curthoys, Dr. John Davis, Mr. Peter Ghosh, and Dr. Brian Harrison have helped me with their wide knowledge of Britain in the 1870s. Dr. Alban Krailsheimer assisted with Gladstone's French, and Mr. Paul Foote with Madame Novikov's Russian. To its profit, the Introduction was read by Lord Blake, Mr. Peter Ghosh, Dr. Boyd Hilton, Dr. Ross McKibbin, Professor Peter Pulzer, and Mr. A. F. Thompson, and I am much obliged to these for their time and trouble. Any mistakes in the edition remain my responsibility.

The writing of the Introduction and the final preparations before printing took place in a Sabbatical term; I am most grateful to the Governing Body of St. Hugh's College, Oxford for releasing me from my college duties and to my colleagues there for allowing me a clear run.

I first became aware of Gladstone and the Midlothian Campaigns when as a child in Edinburgh I heard from our neighbour, a retired physician, how when a medical student he had run with his friends—for many Edinburgh doctors were Liberals in those days—behind Gladstone's carriage as it made its way (almost certainly during the 1892 campaign) from the West End along the Queensferry Road to Dalmeny, a distance of some seven miles. On arrival at Dalmeny, he told me, the gates closed behind the carriage, but Gladstone got out to make a short speech of thanks to his perspiring supporters.

This volume takes us to within sixteen years of the end of the diary. If the 1840s has been intrinsically the most interesting decade to edit so far, the 1870s has been the most remarkable and the most puzzling. As the diarist ages, as what may be called the 'King Lear factor' looms, so the problems of sympathy and imagination increase.

In November 1878, Dr. Wilde of Plymouth sent Gladstone his splendidly entitled *Brainfag from mental worry and overwork*, with the hope that he would not suffer from the disease. The reader who cares to read these diaries in detail—and they yield their secrets only when read in detail—may find Dr. Wilde's volume needful. Certainly, I have been rescued from its symptoms by my wife, Sue, and by my children, David, Lucy, and Oliver; to them I am most grateful for that, and for so much else.

COLIN MATTHEW

Oxford
December 1984

CONTENTS

LIST OF ILLUSTRATIONS

Gladstone aged sixty-nine, photographed in von Lenbach's studio in
Munich, 13 October 1879   *Frontispiece*

between pp. 350 and 351

Millais' first portrait of Gladstone, 1878–79
  in the National Portrait Gallery

Gladstone by F. von Lenbach
  in the Scottish National Portrait Gallery

Gladstone resting while felling a tree at Hawarden, 1877

Gladstone watching a steam saw, 1878
  Reproduced from The Graphic

Facsimile of 4–6 April 1880
  Lambeth MS 1447, f. 115

Notes for the opening speech of the first Midlothian Campaign, 1879
  Add MS 44666, f. 63

Sketch of Gladstone in 1879 by George Howard, M.P.
  *From the Castle Howard Collection, reproduced by courtesy of the
  Hon. Simon Howard*

The house party at Dalmeny during the first Midlothian Campaign, 1879
  Reproduced by courtesy of the Countess of Rosebery

ABBREVIATED CHRISTIAN AND SURNAMES

in diary text of Volume IX

(*prefixed or suffixed to a name in a footnote indicates an article in the *Dictionary of National Biography*)

A.	Agnes Wickham, *daughter, or* the duke of Argyll
A., D. of	duke of Argyll
Agnes	Agnes Wickham, *daughter*
A.K.	A. Kinnaird
A.L.	Alfred Lyttelton
Arthur	A. Gordon
Arthur, Ld	Clinton
B., Lord	Lord Beaconsfield
B. Mr.	A. J. Balfour
B., Mrs.	Mrs. Bennett, *cousin*, or Mrs. Birks, *neighbour*
B. & B.	Bickers & Bush, *booksellers*
C.	Catherine Gladstone, *née* Glynne, *wife*
C., Ld F.	Lord Frederick Cavendish
C., Lucy	Lady Frederick Cavendish, *née* Lucy Lyttelton
C.G.	Catherine Gladstone
C.N.G., Lady	Lady Charlotte Neville Grenville
D.	B. Disraeli
D., Ld	Lord Derby
E.	Elizabeth Honoria Gladstone, *née* Bateson, *sister-in-law*
E.C.	Edward Cardwell *or* Elizabeth Collins *or* Emma Clifton
E.M.P., Lady	Lady Elizabeth M. Pringle
E.W.	Edward C. Wickham, *son-in-law*
E.T.	Edward Stuart Talbot
F., Mr.	W. E. Forster
F.E., Ld or Ly	Lord *or* Lady F. Egerton
F.C., Ld	Lord Frederick Cavendish
Ff., Archd.	Archdeacon Ffoulkes
F.H.D.	Sir F. H. Doyle
F.L.	Frank Lawley *or* F. Leveson [Gower]
Frank	Frank Lawley
G.	George Lyttelton, *wife's brother-in-law, or* Lord Granville

Gertrude	Gertrude Pennant, *née* Glynne, *or* Gertrude Gladstone, *née* Stuart
G.L.	George Lyttelton
H.	(Bishop) W. K. Hamilton *or* Helen Jane Gladstone, *sister*
H., Lord	Lord Hardinge
H., Lady	Lady Herbert of Lea
H., Mr. and Mrs	Mr. and Mrs. Hampton, *the butler and his wife*
Harry	Henry Neville Gladstone, *son*
Helen	Helen Jane Gladstone, *sister*, *or* Helen Gladstone, *daughter*
Herbert	Herbert John Gladstone, *son*
H.G.	Helen Jane Gladstone, *sister*
H.J.G.	*the same*
Hs., the two	Harry and Herbert, *sons*
J.	John Neilson Gladstone, *brother*, *or* Johnnie Gladstone, *nephew*
J.L. & co.	Johnson, Longden & Co., *stockbrokers*
J.M., Lord	Lord John Manners
J.M.G.	James Milnes Gaskell, *or* John Murray Gladstone, *cousin*
J.M.G.(R.)	J.M.G. Robertson, *cousin*
Johnnie	John Gladstone, *nephew*
J.R.	J. M. G. Robertson, *cousin*
J.S.W.	James Stuart-Wortley
K.	A. Kinnaird *or* Lord Kimberley
Kate *or* Katie	Catherine Glynne, *wife's niece*, *or* Katherine Gladstone, *niece*
L.	Lyttelton *or, occasionally* Marquis of Lorne
L., Lord	Lord Lansdowne
Lavinia	Lavinia Glynne, *née* Lyttelton, *wife's sister-in-law*
Lena	Helen Gladstone, *daughter*
L.L.	Lucy Lyttelton
Ln	Lord Lyttelton *or, occasionally* W. H. Lyttelton
Louisa	Louisa Gladstone, *née* Fellowes, *sister-in-law*
Lucy	Lady Frederick Cavendish
M.	Meriel Sarah Lyttelton, *wife's niece*
M., Dr.	Dr. Moffatt
Mary Ellen	Mrs. Robertson Gladstone, *née* Jones, *sister-in-law*
May	Mary Lyttelton, *wife's niece*
Mazie *or* Mary	Mary Gladstone, *daughter,* *or* Mary Lyttelton, *wife's niece*
M.E.	Mrs. Robertson Gladstone, *sister-in-law*
Meriel	Meriel S. Lyttelton, *wife's niece*
M.G.	Mary Gladstone

Molly	Mary Glynne, *wife's niece*
Mr. G.	J. A. Godley
N., D. of	duke of Newcastle
N.	N. G. Lyttelton, *wife's nephew*
Neville *or* Nevy	*the same*
Nina	Helen Gladstone, *daughter*
Nora	Honora Glynne, *wife's niece*
P., Col.	Col. Ponsonby
R.	Robertson Gladstone, *brother*
R., Lord	Lord Ripon *or* Lord Russell
R.G.	Robertson Gladstone, *brother*
Rn (G.)	*the same*
Robn	*the same*
Ronald	Ronald Leveson-Gower
R.P.	Robert Phillimore
S. of A.	Lord Stanley of Alderley
S.E.G.	Stephen Gladstone, *son*
S.G.	*the same*
Stephy	*the same*
Sybilla	Sybella Lyttelton
T.	(Sir) Thomas Gladstone, *brother*
T., Mrs. *or* Th., Mrs.	Laura Thistlethwayte
T. & B.	Townshend & Barker, *solicitors*
T.G.	Sir Thomas Gladstone, *brother*
Tom	*the same*
V. Mr.	J. S. Vickers, *Hawarden agent*
W.	William Henry Gladstone, *son*
W., Lord	Lord Wolverton
Willy	William Henry Gladstone, *son*
Winny	Lavinia Lyttelton, *wife's niece*
W.H.L.	William Lyttelton
W.L.	*the same*
W.W., Sir	Sir Watkin Williams Wynn
Xt	Christ

ABBREVIATED BOOK TITLES, ETC.

Used in Volume IX

Add MS(S)	*Additional Manuscript(s), British Library*
Argyll	Eighth Duke of Argyll, *Autobiography and memoirs*, 2v. (1906)
Arnstein	W. L. Arnstein, *The Bradlaugh Case* (1965)
Autobiographica	J. Brooke and M. Sorensen, eds., *The prime minister's papers: W. E. Gladstone*. I–IV (1971–81)
Bahlman, *Hamilton*	*The diary of Sir Edward Walter Hamilton 1880–1884*, edited by Dudley W. R. Bahlman, 2v. (1972)
Bassett	A. Tilney Bassett, ed., *Gladstone to his wife* (1936)
Bassett, *Speeches*	A. Tilney Bassett, ed., *Gladstone's speeches: descriptive index and bibliography* (1916)
Bew	P. Bew, *Land and the National Question in Ireland 1858–82* (1978)
BFSP	*British and Foreign State Papers*
Blake	Robert Blake, *Disraeli* (1966)
Boase, *M.E.B.*	F. Boase, *Modern English Biography*, 6 v. (1892–1921)
Brand MSS	Papers of H. B. W. Brand, Lord Hampden, in the House of Lords Record Office
Brown, *Metaphysical Society*	A. W. Brown, *The Metaphysical Society* (1947)
Buckle	W. F. Monypenny and G. E. Buckle, *Life of Benjamin Disraeli*, 6v. (1910–1920)
Buxton, *Finance and Politics*	Sydney Buxton, *Finance and politics: an historical study, 1783–1885*, 2v. (1888)
CAB	Prime Minister's letters to the Queen, on film in the Bodleian Library
Cambridge University Library	Papers of Sir J. D. Acton, first Baron Acton, in the Cambridge University Library
Chamberlain MSS	Papers of Joseph Chamberlain in Birmingham University Library
Chamberlain, *Political memoir*	J. Chamberlain, *A political memoir 1880–92*, edited by C. H. D. Howard (1953)
Chatsworth MSS	Papers of Lord Hartington at Chatsworth House
Checkland	S. G. Checkland, *The Gladstones: a family biography, 1764–1851* (1971)
Conzemius	*Ignaz von Döllinger: Lord Acton. Briefwechsel 1850–1890*, edited by Victor Conzemius, 3v. (1963–71)
Cowper	*Earl Cowper, K.G. A memoir by his wife* (1913)
Crewe, *Rosebery*	Marquess of Crewe, *Lord Rosebery*, 2v. (1931)

DLFC	J. Bailey, ed., *Diary of Lady Frederick Cavendish*, 2v. (1927)
D.N.	*Daily News*
D.N.B.	*Dictionary of National Biography*, 71v. (1885–1957)
D.T.	*Daily Telegraph*
E.H.R.	*English Historical Review* (from 1886)
Elliott	A. R. D. Elliott, *Life of G. J. Goschen*, 2v. (1911)
Fitzmaurice	Lord E. Fitzmaurice, *Life of Earl Granville*, 2v. (1905)
F.J.	*Freeman's Journal*
F.O.C.P.	Foreign Office Confidential Prints, PRO
Gardiner	A. G. Gardiner, *Life of Sir William Harcourt*, 2v. (1923)
Garvin	J. L. Garvin, *Life of Joseph Chamberlain*, 3v. (1932–4)
Gleanings	W. E. Gladstone, *Gleanings of past years*, 7v. (1879)
Goodfellow	C. F. Goodfellow, *Great Britain and South African Confederation 1870–1881* (1966)
Gopal, *Ripon*	S. Gopal, *The Viceroyalty of Lord Ripon, 1880–1884* (1953)
Guedalla, *Q*	P. Guedalla, ed., *The Queen and Mr Gladstone*, 2v. (1933)
Gwynn and Tuckwell	S. L. Gwynn and G. M. Tuckwell, *Life of Sir Charles Dilke, Bart.*, 2v. (1917)
H	*Hansard's Parliamentary Debates*, third series (1830–91)
Hammond	J. L. Hammond, *Gladstone and the Irish Nation* (1938)
Harrison, *Drink and the Victorians*	B. H. Harrison, *Drink and the Victorians* (1971)
Hawn P	Hawarden Papers (deposited in St Deiniol's Library, Hawarden)
Holland	B. Holland, *Life of Spencer Compton, eighth Duke of Devonshire*, 2v. (1911)
Hughenden MSS	Papers of B. Disraeli in the Bodleian Library
Knaplund, *Imperial policy*	P. Knaplund, *Gladstone and Britain's imperial policy* (1927)
Lathbury	D. C. Lathbury, *Correspondence on church and religion of W. E. Gladstone*, 2v. (1910)
LQV	A. C. Benson, Viscount Esher, and G. E. Buckle, *Letters of Queen Victoria*, 9v. (1907–32) in three series: 1st series 1837–61; 2nd series 1862–85; 3rd series 1886–1901
Liddon Diary	Diary of H. P. Liddon, in Liddon House, London
Magnus	Sir Philip Magnus, *Gladstone* (1954)
Magnus, *Edward VII*	Ibid., *King Edward the Seventh* (1964)
Masterman	C. F. G. Masterman, ed. and abridged J. Morley, *Life of Gladstone* (1927)

Matthew, 'Vaticanism'	H. C. G. Matthew, 'Gladstone, Vaticanism and the Question of the East' in D. Baker, ed., *Studies in Church History*, xv (1978)
Medlicott	W. N. Medlicott, *Bismarck, Gladstone, and the Concert of Europe* (1956)
Millman	R. Millman, *Britain and the Eastern Question, 1875–1878* (1979)
Morgan, *Wales in British Politics*	K. O. Morgan, *Wales in British Politics 1868–1922* (1963)
Morley	J. Morley, *Life of William Ewart Gladstone*, 3v. (1903)
Mundella MSS	Papers of A. J. Mundella in Sheffield University Library
Newman	*The Letters and Diaries of John Henry Newman*, edited by C. S. Dessain and T. Gornall (1961ff.)
N.L.S.	National Library of Scotland
Ornsby	R. Ornsby, *Memoirs of J. R. Hope-Scott*, 2v. (1884)
Phillimore MSS	Papers of Sir R. J. Phillimore in Christ Church Library, Oxford
Political Speeches (1879)	W. E. Gladstone, *Political Speeches in Scotland, November and December 1879* (1879)
Political Speeches (1880)	Ibid., *Political Speeches in Scotland, March and April 1880* (1880)
Ponsonby	A. Ponsonby, *Henry Ponsonby* (1943)
PP	*Parliamentary Papers*
Purcell	E. S. Purcell, *Life of Cardinal Manning*, 2v. (1896)
R.A.	Royal Archives, Windsor Castle
Ramm, II	Agatha Ramm, *Political Correspondence of Mr Gladstone and Lord Granville 1876–1886*, 2v. (1962)
Reid, *F*	(Sir) T. Wemyss Reid, *Life of... William Edward Forster*, 2v. (1888)
Reid, *G*	Sir T. Wemyss Reid, ed., *Life of W. E. Gladstone* (1899)
Rome and the newest fashions	W. E. Gladstone, *Rome and the newest fashions in religion. Three tracts* (1875)
Rosebery MSS	Papers of 5th Earl of Rosebery, in the National Library of Scotland
Rossi, *T.A.P.S.*	J. P. Rossi, 'The Transformation of the British Liberal Party: a study of the Tactics of the Liberal Opposition, 1874–1880', *Transactions of the American Philosophical Society* (1978)
Schreuder	D. M. Schreuder, *Gladstone and Kruger. Liberal Government and Colonial 'Home Rule' 1880–85* (1969)
Selborne MSS	Papers of 1st Earl of Selborne in Lambeth Palace Library

Selborne, II	Earl of Selborne, *Memorials Personal and Political 1865–1895*, 2v. (1898)
Seton-Watson	R. W. Seton-Watson, *Disraeli, Gladstone and the Eastern Question* (1935)
Shannon	R. T. Shannon, *Gladstone and Bulgarian Agitation 1876* (1963)
Stead, *M.P. for Russia*	W. T. Stead, *The 'M.P. for Russia'. Reminiscences and Correspondence of . . . Olga Novikoff*, 2v. (1909)
Sumner	B. H. Sumner, *Russia and the Balkans 1870–1880* (1937)
Tait MSS	Papers of A. C. Tait in Lambeth Palace Library
T.A.P.S.	*Transactions of the American Philosophical Society*
Thomas, *Gladstone of Hawarden*	I. Thomas, *Gladstone of Hawarden* (1936)
T.T.	*The Times*
Walling, *Diaries of Bright*	R. A. J. Walling, *The Diaries of John Bright* (1930)
Ward, *Victorian Oxford*	W. R. Ward, *Victorian Oxford* (1965)
West, *Recollections*	Sir Algernon West, *Recollections 1832 to 1886*, 2v. (1899)
Wilberforce	A. R. Ashwell and R. G. Wilberforce, *Life of the Right Reverend Samuel Wilberforce*, 3v. (1880–2)
Wilberforce MSS	Papers of S. Wilberforce in the Bodleian Library
Wolf, *Ripon*	L. Wolf, *Life of the first Marquess of Ripon*, 2v. (1921)

OTHER ABBREVIATIONS

ab.	about
abp.	archbishop
acct.	account
aft(n).	afternoon
agst. or agt	against
amdt.	amendment
appt.	appointment
apptd.	appointed
arr.	arrived
aut.	autograph
b.	book *or* born *or* brother
bart.	baronet
Bd.	board of trade
B.I.R.	board of inland revenue
Bkfst.	breakfast
B.N.A.	British North America
B. of T.	board of trade
bp.	bishop
B.P.	Book Post *or* Book Parcel
br.	brother
B.S.	Bedford *or* Berkeley Square
B.T.	board of trade
ca.	*circa*
C.G.	Carlton Gardens
Ch.	church *or* Chester
Ch. of Exchr.	Chancellor of the Exchequer
C.H.T.	Carlton House Terrace
C.L.	Civil List
C.O.	colonial office
commee.	committee
commn.	commission
cons.	conservative
cr.	created
ctd.	continued
cttee.	committee
cum	with
d.	died
da.	daughter
deb.	debate
deptn. or dpn.	deputation

dft.	draft
div.	division
do.	ditto
Dowr.	Dowager
Dr.	doctor *or* dowager
E.	Earl
eccl.	ecclesiastical
ed.	edited *or* edition *or* editor *or* educational
E.I.	East Indies *or* East Indian
Ep.	epistle
evg.	evening
f.	father *or* folio
fa.	father
ff.	folios *or* following
F.O.	foreign office
1°R	first reading
G. & co.	Gladstone and company
gd.	granddaughter
gf.	grandfather
Gk.	Greek
gm.	grandmother
govt.	government
gs.	grandson
H.C.	holy communion
Hn.	Hawarden
Ho.	house of commons
H.O.	home office
H. of C.	house of commons
H. of L.	house of lords
H.S.	holy scripture *or* Harley Street
Ibid.	*ibidem*, in the same place
I.O.	India office
K.	killed
l.	letter
Ld.	lord
lect.	lecture
lib.	liberal
Ln.	London
Lpool	Liverpool
Ly.	lady

m.	married *or* mother, *or, with figures*, mille (a thousand)
ma	*ma* ('but' in Italian)
Made	Madame
M.D.R.	Metropolitan and District Railway
mem.	memorandum
mg.	morning
m͡ʟ	a million
Nk.	Newark
N.S.	National Society
N.S.W.	New South Wales
nt.	night
n.y.n.	not yet numbered
N.Z.	New Zealand
No. 11	11 Carlton House Terrace
No. 15	15 Grosvenor Square (Mrs. Thistlethwayte)
No. 42 P.P.	42 Portland Place (Lytteltons)
No. 73 H.S.	73 Harley Street
p., pp	page(s)
P.O.	post office
pr. or priv.	private
pt.	part
rec(d).	receive(d)
Rector, The	Stephen Gladstone
resp.	respecting
Rev(d)	reverend
R.R.	railway
2ºR	second reading
s.	son *or* series *or* sister
Sact.	sacrament
Sec. Euch.	Secreta Eucharistica
sd. or shd.	should
S.K.M.	South Kensington Museum
soc.	society
Sol. Gen.	solicitor-general
sp.	speech
S.P.G.	Society for the Propagation of the Gospel
succ.	succeeded
T.	Treasury
T.P.	Temple of Peace
tel.	telegram
3ºR	third reading
tr.	translated or translation

Univ.	university
v.	verso *or* very *or* volume
V.C.	vice-chancellor
vol.	volume
vss.	verses
vy.	very
w.	wife
wd.	would
wh.	which
W.I.	West Indies
W.L.	Wine Licences
Xtn	Christian
yesty.	yesterday

Signs used by the diarist

X	rescue work done this day
+	prayer, usually when on a charitable visit
m̂	million
ma	'but'
(B.P.)	Book Post or Package

Signs inserted into the text editorially

[R]	follows names of subjects of diarist's rescue work
⟨ ⟩	words written by diarist and then deleted

INTRODUCTION

The year [1875] has been an important one, & not only on account of its great abundance, as usual, in opportunities & in failures. In the great business of unwinding the coil of life & establishing my freedom I have made some progress by resigning the leadership, selling my House (needful for pecuniary reasons) and declining public occasions. But more has yet to be done. To minimise my presence in London is alike needful for growth, for my work, for the great duty & business of solemn recollection & preparation.

I hope my polemical period is over. It has virtually occupied over a twelvemonth: but good has been done, especially in Italy.[1]

And now I am writing in the last minutes of the seventh decade of my life. This closing is a great event. The days of our life are three score years and ten. It is hardly possible that I should complete another decade. How much, or how little, of this will God give me for the purposes dear to my heart? Ah what need have I of what I may term spiritual leisure: to be out of the dust and heat and blast and strain, before I pass into the unseen world.

But perhaps this is a form of selflove. For the last 3½ years I have been passing through a political experience which is I believe without example in our Parliamentary history. I profess it [*sic*] to believe it has been an occasion, when the battle to be fought was a battle of justice humanity freedom law, all in their first elements from the very root, and all on a gigantic scale. The word spoken was a word for millions, and for millions who themselves cannot speak. If I really believe this then I should regard my having been morally forced into this work as a great and high election of God. And certainly I cannot but believe that He has given me special gifts of strength, on the late occasion especially in Scotland. But alas the poor little garden of my own soul remains uncultivated, unweeded, and defaced. So then while I am bound to accept this election for the time, may I not be permitted to pray that the time shall be short? Three things I would ask of God over and above all the bounty which surrounds me. This first that I may escape into retirement. This second that I may speedily be enabled to divest myself of everything resembling wealth. And the third—if I may—that when God calls me He may call me speedily. To die in Church appears to be a great *euthanasia*: but not a time to disturb worshippers. Such are some of the old man's thoughts, in whom there is still something that consents not to be old. Though I am well aware that my wonderful health is contingent on the freedom of my actual position, and that I could not bear the strain of anxiety. All this I ought to have written on my knees: from which indeed were I never to rise.

> Last among the last
> Least among the least
> Can there be a place for me
> At the marriage feast?[2]

I

In every decade of these diaries, the theme has been the same: the yearning for retirement from political life. With the decisive defeat of the Liberal Government

---

[1] 29 Dec. 75 (cross references to the diary text are all in this abbreviated form).   [2] 28 Dec. 79.

in 1874, the moment had come. Though declining a peerage and not resigning his seat in the House of Commons, Gladstone made a series of purposeful steps, adumbrated in the extract quoted above, to distance himself from political affairs. He reckoned without the exigencies of his times and of his character. Hoping to stand outside political events, Gladstone found himself increasingly enclosed by them. After 1876, only extreme old age was to offer an escape.

If Gladstone had died, as Disraeli did, a year after the end of his chief administration, the teleological force of his career would have been emphasised, especially with respect to his fiscal policies. Even allowing for the uncertainties of the 1850s, his evolution as the most effective exponent of the 'minimalist state', rising from the ashes of his Coleridgian Idealism, would have had an obviously defined framework. His political career, had it ended in 1875, would have seemed relatively straightforward, with a beginning, a middle, and a prime-ministerial climax.

The fact that he died politically only briefly in 1875, and resurrected for a second political career, does not, of course, deny the force of this teleology, but it blurs its focus. It also makes the treatment of this second career uncertain, for Gladstone himself was uncertain, not about its rightness, but about its scope. He himself used the image of death with respect to his formal resignation as party leader in 1875, but the 'better life' that followed was political retirement.[1] Whereas up to the early 1870s, Gladstone had been self-consciously attempting a 'reconciliation between Christianity and the conditions of modern thought, modern life and modern society',[2] seeing himself as a chief agent in this process and seeing his career as the exemplar of its partial achievement in public affairs, from the mid-1870s onwards his position was more defensive. He found it hard to justify to himself as 'Godly'—as he had since the 1840s—the usual round of public business. As a consequence, his political activity after 1875 took the form of a series of 'campaigns', each with its peculiar justification. Having retired once and turned away from the party battle, future intervention had to be explained, to himself and to the public, in terms of unusual crises and special causes.

As a younger man, Gladstone had pursued a political career which, if it could hardly be described as normal, was not unusual in its marriage of idealism and ambition. After 1875, Gladstone's emphasis on 'exceptional circumstances' as his political *raison d'être* made the self-admission of ambition in any usual sense impossible. Hence he found himself discovering the abnormal, formulating policies in such terms, and orchestrating politics around him as if he was solving the last 'special' crisis and preparing for a final departure.[3] In such an atmosphere, political planning both for himself and for his colleagues became difficult, almost impossible, and the view of politics as a normal process was suspended. By investing politics with something of a millenarian tone, and by turning policy debate within the Liberal Party to some extent into the question,

---

[1] 16 Jan. 75; 'I seem to feel as one who has passed through a death, but emerged into a better life.'

[2] To Manning, 16 Nov. 69. References to letters printed with the diary text are given in this form; a note on editorial procedure will be found above, vii. 521.

[3] For a useful discussion of this, see T. A. Jenkins, 'Gladstone and whiggery: a study in Liberal leadership and politics 1874–86' (Cambridge Ph.D., 1984).

'Will he go?', Gladstone was helping to write the script for his own continuation, for the supposed normality of the 1860s was never restored, and his position as the coping stone of the delicately balanced arch which was the Liberal
Party meant that he could never simply absent himself, leaving other things and
beings equal.

There is no suggestion in the journal that Gladstone developed the idea of
'exceptional circumstances' as a way of justifying a return which he intended
anyway; all the evidence from a reading of the journal suggests the opposite,
that his return to politics was reluctant, was intended to be short, and was
unselfconsciously genuine in its motivation. To us, the nature of the 'return' of
1876 may indicate a lack of self-awareness, but there are dangers of anachron-
ism here. The political ethos within which Gladstone worked emphasised
Godly calling and service to an extent unknown since the seventeenth century.
Faced with conviction of this sort, understanding is probably more fruitful than
explaining, for explaining in this sort of case too easily becomes explaining
away. A brisk, dusting-down explanation of Gladstone as an ambitious
hypocrite or, alternatively, as a self-deceiver, is, at least at first glance, an easy
enough exercise; the problem with it is that it leaves the phenomenon curiously
unexplained and more mysterious, both as to its interest for historians and its
fascination for contemporaries.

The *mentalité* of the Victorian is perhaps more foreign to the twentieth-
century mind than any since the Reformation. Gladstone's diary, now sprawling
across the century, is emerging as one of the central private documents of that
strangeness and as one of the keys to its understanding. The diary's relentless
mixture of religion, duty, and materialism, as unselfconsciously presented as is
possible in such a document, helps the reader to penetrate the hard surface of
an age which wished to live by abstract principles but found itself living by
experience.

'It has been experience which has altered my politics', Gladstone very truly
told Sir Francis Doyle in 1880.[1] This 'experience', which under the influence of
Bishop Butler Gladstone elevated to a principle, had from the early 1840s to
the early 1870s shifted him, sometimes subconsciously, towards liberal positions in a movement *pari passu* with the dominant intellectual tendencies of the
age. These tendencies were now beginning to take a different direction.[2] Much
of the interest of the last twenty years of Gladstone's public life comes from the
observation of a powerful, dominating, and resourceful personality, increasingly
out of temper with its times, struggling to maintain right and order, resorting to
means regarded by many contemporaries as revolutionary, in order to sustain
the United Kingdom as a Christian, united, free-trading, non-expansionist
political community in the comity of nations.

After the self-confident beginning of the early years of the 1868 Government,
the 1870s turned out to be a decade of fears, alarms, and disappointments,
partly redeemed by the domestic success of a great crusade, which was moral
and religious as well as political in tone and intention. The Declaration of

---

[1] To Sir F. Doyle, 10 May 80; this letter offers an interesting contrast to that to Manning just
quoted.
[2] J. P. C. Roach, 'Liberalism and the Victorian intelligentsia', *Cambridge Historical Journal*, xiii. 58.

Infallibility by the Vatican Council of 1870, Gladstone's delayed but explosive reaction to it, and his consequent second estrangement from H. E. Manning, have been dealt with in volumes vii and viii,[1] but the Council's decision continued to cast its shadow, for it raised general questions of the nature of authority, the history of the Church and the role of Anglicans within it, which could not be quickly or easily answered. At a personal level, it caused intense concern about his sister Helen's beliefs until her death in 1880: had she died a Roman Catholic, or had she seen light in 1870 and at the least died an Old Catholic?[2]

If the reasonableness of the European mind had been betrayed by the Papacy, so also did it seem to be assaulted by the brutality and inflexibility of the Ottoman Empire, as a new phase of the 'Eastern Question' was launched in 1875–76, a development which in Gladstone's view was grossly mishandled and misused both internationally and domestically by the Conservative Government. The resurgent conservatism of the 1870s which the Disraeli Government of 1874–80 represented coincided with the first general awareness of the ending of Britain's economic hegemony, and a general crisis in European agriculture which was to encourage the politics of protection and cartelization in most Continental states. Though Gladstone remained optimistic about the future of free trade, his restatement of the concept of the Concert of Europe was thus to be attempted in the context of economic dislocation and tariff reconstruction rather than that of the free-trade comity which he believed to have been one of the chief advances of the century.

The opening months of this volume describe political retirement rather than any general decline in activity. Gladstone retired from the leadership of the Liberal Party first informally, in February 1874[3] following his Government's defeat, and then formally, in the face of his wife's opposition, by publication of a letter to Granville following a meeting of the ex-Cabinet in January 1875.[4] Little is known about general social attitudes to retirement in the Victorian period. For the landowner with other than local interests, educated in the rural values of Virgil and Horace, it probably represented a return from public or commercial life to the management of his estates; that is, 'retiring' meant not much more than the absence of appointments 'in town'.

This was not the case with Gladstone, Horatian enthusiast though he always was. In the early months of his retirement, he briefly owned the Hawarden estates when his brother-in-law, Sir Stephen Glynne, died in June 1874. But, in a move very unusual among the landed families of the time, he made over the estates to his son Willy when the latter married in 1875.[5] Gladstone complained when it was generally assumed, as, for example, by G. C. Brodrick in his *English Land and English Landowners* (1881), that he was the owner of the Hawarden estate.[6] Thus, although he continued to play an

---

[1] See above, vii. cxi–cxiii.
[2] Helen Gladstone's death is discussed at the end of this introduction.
[3] See 17 Feb., 5–11 Mar. 74. [4] 14 Jan. 75.
[5] See 28 Sept. 75.
[6] To Brodrick, 8 Dec. 80.

important role in the estate's development, he passed by the opportunity to play to the full the role of landowner. He was not the master of the estate and never presented himself as such. He did not 'play the squire', except, perhaps, in church. 'I love them not' was his comment as he tried to stop the annual Hawarden bazaar.[1] He never held any local office of the sort to which the considerable size of the Hawarden estates would have entitled him had he been the squire, such as Justice of the Peace or Deputy Lord Lieutenant, though his son Willy was both.[2] Retirement for Gladstone, therefore, was not simply a matter of a return to country life, and there was always a certain unease about his role at Hawarden, exemplified in this volume by the long debate within the family over whether Willy Gladstone should, after his marriage, live in the Castle or build his own house.[3] Gladstone in the mid-1870s addressed the odd local gardening society and the like, but Vickers, the agent, dealt with most of the business of the estate.

The journal does not suggest that Gladstone saw Hawarden affairs as any more central to his life than they had been; his great effort for the estate had been in the opposition years 1846–52, when he had prevented its bankruptcy. Hawarden's great attraction was that it was literally a 'Temple of Peace', removed from London and, with the exception of the Duke of Westminster's estate nearby, remote from fashion.

II

Retirement, in Gladstone's view, meant retirement from political life to the study, but it was certainly not intended to mean inactivity. Indeed, it cleared the way for the proper pursuit of 'my work'.[4] Politics was always for Gladstone a second-order activity with second-order expectations, in which it was important not to become excessively immersed: one must avoid 'sinking into a party man . . . into a politician, instead of a man in politics'.[5] Partly to satisfy his wife, Gladstone in March 1875 described a programme of intellectual activity which only 'exceptional circumstances' could suspend:

I endeavoured to lay out before C[atherine] my views about the future & remaining section of my life. In outline they are undefined but in substance definite. The main point is this: that, setting aside exceptional circumstances which would have to provide for themselves, my prospective work is not Parliamentary. My tie will be slight to an Assembly with whose tendencies I am little in harmony at the present time: nor can I flatter myself that what is called the public, out of doors, is more sympathetic. But there is much to be done with the pen, all bearing much on high & sacred ends, for even Homeric study as I view of it [sic] is in this very sense of high importance: and what lies beyond this is concerned directly with the great subject of belief. By thought good or evil on these matters the destinies of mankind are at

[1] 5 Aug. 79.
[2] Sir Stephen Glynne was Lord Lieutenant of Flintshire until his death in 1874; W. H. Gladstone was J.P. from 1863 and Deputy Lieutenant from 1866.
[3] See, e.g., 12–13 and 27 Apr., 1 May 76, 9 Aug. 77, 3 Aug., 1 Nov. 78.
[4] 29 Dec. 75.
[5] See above, iii. xxiv–xxv.

this time affected infinitely more than by the work of any man in Parliament. God has in some measure opened this path to me: may He complete the work.[1]

After completing his short book, *Homeric Synchronism*, in the autumn of 1875 and making some further progress on the often-delayed Homeric Thesaurus, Gladstone turned, as he had intended, to the 'great subject of belief'. The first- order work which he saw as a chief calling of his retirement was the service of the Church, and his actions show that the Church was to be served chiefly by the pen. In considering the activities of his retirement, we therefore plunge with him into the complexities of theological debate.

'Future Retribution. *From this I was called away to write on Bulgaria*': John Morley's memorable quotation of Gladstone's docket at the opening of his chapter on the Bulgarian Atrocities cannot but raise a twentieth-century smile.[2] Yet 'Future Retribution', 'Eternal Punishment' or, more simply, hell-fire, was a central intellectual concern of the day,[3] and a frequent talking-point at the week-end houses of the more highminded of the aristocracy. The unreasonableness of an all-powerful God who condemned his creatures to permanent torment was a formidable argument for the secularists against Christianity—an argument at least as much deployed as evolution—and it was met chiefly by a variety of Broad-Church defences, from 'Universalism' (the doctrine that all free moral creatures will ultimately share in the grace of salvation) to the more moderate position put forward by the Anglican head-master, F. W. Farrar, in his *Eternal Hope* (1877). Both the arguments of the secularists and the defences of the Broad-Churchmen were instinctively upsetting to Gladstone, whose theological inclinations (if not his eventual intellectual position) were always profoundly conservative.

Gladstone deplored the fact that 'A portion of Divine truth, which even if secondary is so needful, appears to be silently passing out of view, and ... the danger of losing it ought at all costs to be averted.'[4] None the less, he published nothing in the 1870s directly on the controversy. Gladstone was not at his best on abstract or speculative topics. In religious matters he profoundly mistrusted Broad-Church philosophising and his instinct (at any rate after his youthful attempt at Idealism in *The State in its Relations with the Church*) was always for the practical and the historical aspects of a subject. He also seems to have thought that the theme of retribution could best be approached in stages.

He thus cleared the way for future work on the subject not by developing the notes written privately on 'Future Retribution' between 1876 and 1879,[5] but by publishing the exposition of the views of the eighteenth-century bishop, Joseph Butler, 'Probability as the guide of conduct', which he had

[1] 30 Mar. 75.

[2] Morley, ii. 548; see 13 Aug. 76.

[3] See the *symposia* in *Contemporary Review*, xxxii. 156, 338, 545 (April–June 1878) and *Nineteenth Century*, i. 331 (April 1877).

[4] W. E. Gladstone, *Studies subsidiary to Bishop Butler* (1896), 199, which uses material from the 1870s; quoted in G. Rowell, *Hell and the Victorians* (1974), 3. See also Lathbury, ii. 123 and 20, 23 May 75.

[5] Add MS 44698, ff. 367–491. For his difficulties in dealing with the subject, see the letter to G. W. Potter, 22 October 1878, in Lathbury, ii. 105.

written in 1845 during his first period of resignation from politics.[1] The argument from probability, in Gladstone's view, recaptured the initiative for Christianity; 'The maxim that Christianity is a matter not abstract, but referable throughout to human action, is not an important only, but a vital part of the demonstration, that we are bound by the laws of our nature to give a hearing to its claims.'[2] 'Human action' meant human co-operation, institutions, local customs and traditions, without an understanding of which both the observer and participant would be without firm moorings. This 'human action' would be worked out within the concept of 'religious nationality', Gladstone's starting-point as an ecclesiastical thinker. He did not look for complete uniformity of ecclesiastical authority or practice but rather saw an apostolic system based on a degree of variety and a degree of local legitimacy as being natural, necessary, and desirable. The Papacy's increasingly strident absolutist and universalist claims clearly cut straight across this view.

Much of Gladstone's contribution to the religious debate of the 1870s therefore took the form first of the anti-Vatican pamphlets of 1874–75, and then of quasi-historical articles designed to analyse the development of Christianity in England since the Reformation, notably 'Is the Church of England worth preserving?'[3] and 'The courses of religious thought'.[4] Even when writing on a more abstract theme, a review of a reprint of the essay 'On the influence of authority in matters of opinion' (1849) by Sir George Lewis, his successor as Chancellor of the Exchequer in 1855, the thrust was the same: Lewis, though right in thinking 'that the acceptance of Christianity is required of us by a scientific application of the principle of authority', had been too narrow and too theoretical: he should have been not merely 'moral and symbolic' but concerned with the 'living and working system not without the most essential features of an unity'.[5]

It was the notion of unity which emerges as the central theme of Gladstone's religious preoccupations in these years. If the glory of Christianity was the unique representation of Revelation and moral truth in a 'living and working system', then the harmonious interaction of the different parts of that system must be of central concern to any of its participants.

Gladstone's concern for ecumenism manifested itself at several levels, European, British, occidental and transatlantic, international and local. There were two chief stimuli to ecumenical thinking among Anglicans in the nineteenth century; the *via media* of J. H. Newman, which saw the Church of England as the balancing point, and perhaps the broker between Roman Catholicism and Nonconformity, and the rather more cosmopolitan 'branch church' theory of William Palmer of Worcester College, Oxford, which saw the Apostolic Churches—Roman, Anglican, and Eastern— forming three branches, each with its own legitimacy and traditions, from one central Apostolic trunk.[6]

---

[1] 26 June 45, 9 Mar. 79.   [2] *Gleanings*, vii. 180.
[3] 4 June 75.   [4] 1 Apr. 76.   [5] *Gleanings*, iii. 151.
[6] See J. H. Newman, 'Introduction' to *Lectures on the Prophetical Office of the Church* (1837), 8 and W. Palmer, *Treatise on the Church of Christ*, 2v. (1838); Gladstone's interest in Palmer, important at the time of the writing of *The State in its Relations with the Church* in 1838 and its later editions, continued; see his mem. of 1885, Add MS 44769, f. 77; Palmer was in frequent correspondence in 1875, see Add MS 44446. Gladstone played some part in the *Treatise*'s re-publication, see letter to Döllinger,

THE GLADSTONE DIARIES

Rather characteristically, Gladstone made use of both these approaches simultaneously: 'The Church of England appears to be placed in the very centre of all the conflicting forms of Christianity, like the ancient Church between the Arians and the Sabellians.'[1] This Anglican centrality was to provide the basis for interest and activity in two rather different spheres. First, if a strictly Anglican based 'religious nationality' had ceased to be a practical possibility, then something of its quality might be saved by a broader-based alliance of religious and ethical organisations which could at least agree on second-order principles in the United Kingdom context. Second, the Church of England might play its part in recovering 'the visible unity' of the Church at an international level.

In what may be called domestic religion, Gladstone developed links with prominent Nonconformists such as the Wesleyan J. H. Rigg and the Congregationalists Baldwin Brown and Newman Hall;[2] he attended a number of the Moody–Sankey revivalist meetings in 1875;[3] and when writing about recent religious developments he attempted to stress points of agreement rather than of fault. Thus in 'The course of religious thought', published just before the start of the Bulgarian Atrocities campaign in 1876,[4] in attempting to classify 'multitudes of aimless or erratic forces, crossing and jostling one another',[5] he went out of his way to incorporate 'the Protestant Evangelical' school in a tone not at all characteristic of the 'high Church party' to which he gave the chief place and of which he was in most respects a member. Gladstone even praised Newman Hall's nondenominational Surrey Chapel, and also found some positive points in Unitarianism,[6] the belief held by his friend, the Belgian economist, de Laveleye. Although in no way conceding his own position, he showed considerable interest in the 'Ramsgate Tracts' series published by Thomas Scott, 'an ardent, unswerving Theist',[7] and engaged in a good-natured controversy with him about the value of prayer, sending him a series of 'Propositions on Prayer'.[8]

This enthusiasm for integration was given practical effect in Gladstone's quite frequent attendance at the Metaphysical Society, at which he sometimes took the chair.[9] This society, founded by James Knowles of the *Contemporary Review* and the *Nineteenth Century*,[10] brought together leading intellectual figures of the day and for a time provided a remarkable forum for discussion, if not agreement. It was a last attempt at a Coleridgian clerisy, a national intelligentsia—from Manning to Martineau and Huxley—and its disintegration mirrored the gradual waning of Liberal intellectual hegemony, with its eclectic

1 September 1882, in Lathbury ii. 321. Gladstone gave John Morley a concise description of the High-Church localist position when the latter argued in the *Pall Mall Gazette* that High-Churchmen should logically join Rome; see to Morley, 27 Oct. 80.

[1] W. E. Gladstone, *Church Principles considered in their results* (1840), 507.
[2] 16 Feb. 75.   [3] 25 and 29 Apr. 75.
[4] 1 Apr. 76.   [5] *Gleanings*, iii. 95.
[6] *Gleanings*, iii. 112–21. He had been re-reading Newman's *Arians of the fourth century* in the midst of the Vatican controversy; see 24 Jan. 75 and, for Martineau, 12 Feb. 75.
[7] Holyoake's description, in G. J. Holyoake, *Sixty years of an agitator's life* (1892), ii, chapter lxxii. I am obliged to Mr Brian Carter for this reference.
[8] See 9 and 15 Dec. 75.
[9] See 9 Mar., 8 June, 9 Nov. 75, 14 Feb., 9 May, 13 June 76, 9 Apr. 78.
[10] See Brown, *Metaphysical Society, passim* and P. Metcalf, *James Knowles, Victorian editor and architect* (1980), chs. 6–8.

span, best achieved in the 1860s, from Roman Catholic to secularist. In all of this, Gladstone's approach was less like that of a High-Churchman than of a Broad-Churchman, with his stress on areas of agreement. Much though he disliked Broad-Church anti-dogmatism and much though he held personally to rather rigid doctrinal positions, *in practice* Gladstone owed much more to the Broad-Church tradition than he cared to admit.[1] He found himself working in ecclesiastical affairs and indeed, as will be shown, in politics also, towards that 'unity of action' despite differences of belief which had been for Thomas Arnold the key to the development of a community.[2]

Gladstone's eirenic approach to domestic religion represented an attempt to find an alternative to that youthful ideal of 'religious nationality' whose failure to be realized on High-Church terms had caused such pain in the 1840s. He had never abandoned the ideal in principle, and he continued to believe, perhaps more in the 1870s than in the *dénouement* of the crisis in the later 1840s, in what J. H. Rigg aptly called 'the plastic quasi-secularism—for, after all, Gladstone does not in principle take his stand on secularism proper in any sphere—of his later years'.[3]

The other great ideal of the youthful Gladstone had been the 'visible unity' of the Church: 'when the mind recurs to that most solemn prayer of the Saviour, at that most solemn hour, for the visible unity of his Church, I feel how impossible it is to wrench away the hope of this (however distant and however difficult) achievement from the heart of all true belief in Christ'.[4] Impracticality and the realities of politics had broken the hope of 'religious nationality'; the Roman Catholic Church increasingly spoiled any immediate prospect of 'visible unity' with a series of developments: the definition of the Immaculate Conception in 1854, the *Syllabus Errorum* in 1864, and the Declaration of Infallibility in 1870. Any possibility of even tentative soundings towards Anglican–Roman union, of the sort proposed in the 1860s by Ambrose Phillipps de Lisle, were hardly worth practical consideration, and the sense of betrayal consequent upon this infused the writing of the second and third Vatican pamphlets with which this volume opens.[5]

As an alternative—and here Gladstone worked within an identifiably High-Church group—negotiations were begun with the Bonn Reunion Conferences of 1874 and 1875. These were sponsored by Gladstone's old friend Johann Ignaz von Döllinger, perhaps the only man of his contemporaries whom Gladstone regarded as heroic, whose opposition to the Declaration of Infallibility led to his excommunication. These conferences involved the Old Catholics, of whom so much was expected and who in the eyes of many High-Churchmen including Gladstone had taken on the mantle of true Continental Catholicism, the Anglican High-Churchmen (particularly H. P. Liddon, Malcolm MacColl, Christopher Wordsworth, and E. S. Talbot, Catherine Gladstone's nephew-by-

---

[1] Though in his handling of the Education Act in 1869–70, Gladstone had followed a clear High-Church line in wanting either full doctrinal teaching, or none at all; see above, vii. lxvi.

[2] Thomas Arnold, 'Appendix' to his 'Inaugural Lecture' in *Introductory lectures on modern history* (1845), 39.

[3] J. H. Rigg, 'Mr Gladstone's Ecclesiastical Opinions', *London Quarterly Review*, xliii. 385 (January 1875); a perceptive review both on *A Chapter of Autobiography* and on *Vaticanism*.

[4] *Church Principles*, 507.   [5] See 2–3 Jan. 75.

marriage) and representatives of the Eastern Orthodox Churches, particularly
the Greeks. The aim of the conferences, Gladstone believed, was in line with his
own preoccupation with the nature of authority; it was that 'of establishing the
voice of the individual Church as the legitimate traditional authority'.[1] The
conferences were thus simultaneously anti-Vatican and constructive in their
own right. Gladstone was asked to attend the 1875 Conference, but declined;[2]
he was none the less kept in close touch with developments.

The presence of the Orthodox representatives he found particularly gratifying. Orthodoxy represented the achievement of 'religious nationality' in
perhaps its most successful form, an almost complete blending of Church and
nation. Gladstone had with some success gone out of his way while Prime
Minister to encourage Anglican-Orthodox contacts.[3] Disagreements over the
Filioque clause of the Creed made progress difficult; on this issue Gladstone,
in marked difference with E. B. Pusey and most of the High-Church group,
conceded the Eastern Churches' case and hoped that the conferences would
lead 'swiftly to the door of *action*'.[4] He encouraged Döllinger and Lycurgus,
Archbishop of Syros and Tenos, whom he had entertained at Hawarden in
1870,[5] to further action. Some hoped for a further round of talks in 1876 or
1877, but the crisis over the rebellion of Serbia and the atrocities committed
by the Turks in Bulgaria destroyed these hopes, as the British Government
watched passively.

The resurgence of the Eastern Question broke these tentative ecumenical
roots: the Orthodox Slavs would not attend a conference with Anglicans while
the British Government was the chief defender of their Turkish persecutors. It
also broke the unity of the High-Churchmen: Gladstone, H. P. Liddon, and
Malcolm MacColl led the campaign; most Tories would not follow. A conference in 1878 was impossible, Liddon told Döllinger: 'so many good Churchmen (—for instance Mr. Beresford Hope—) are political allies of Lord
Beaconsfield'.[6] Beaconsfieldism thus helped to spoil a promising and important
ecumenical initiative, just as Pius IX, on a grander scale, had set back Church
unity by a century in 1870. The inner force of a Gladstonian pamphlet was
always religious, and these failures of ecumenism must be borne in mind as the
more political aspects of the Eastern Question are examined.

Gladstone's retirement had thus involved him in a complex series of theological and ecclesiastical debates and discussions, far removed, perhaps, from
modern expectations of the retirement interests of a former Liberal Chancellor
of the Exchequer and Prime Minister. This disjunction highlights the danger of
trying to extrapolate from a fundamentally religious mind those features of

[1] Letter to Döllinger, 29 August 1875, in Lathbury, ii. 62.
[2] Letter to Döllinger, 24 July 1875, in Lathbury, ii. 312.
[3] See Matthew, 'Vaticanism', 438.
[4] Letter to Archbishop Lycurgus, October 1875, Lathbury ii. 63; see 29 Sept., 1 Oct. 75. Gladstone
was also in touch with the Greek community in London, especially Mavrogordato, who organised a
Greek presence at the Bonn Conference and communicated with Döllinger; Add MS 44447, f. 109.
[5] 10 Jan. 70; see also 20 May 76n.
[6] Liddon to Döllinger, Trinity Sunday 1878, Liddon MSS, Keble College, Oxford; a conference in
1876 was prevented by disagreements over the *Filioque*, and a conference in 1878 by the Eastern
Question; see J. O. Johnston, *Life and letters of H. P. Liddon* (1904), 190.

Gladstone's opinions, writings, and actions which fit the categories of twentieth-century secularism.

The years 1874–76 form no incidental interval, nor were the issues small-scale or peripheral. The existence of hell and the unity of Christendom were hardly marginal themes: 'By thought good or evil on these matters the destinies of mankind are at this time affected infinitely more than by the work of any man in Parliament.'[1] Work 'with the pen' in his study in 1875 had brought him to focus considerably, though not uniquely, on the area of Orthodox Christianity which was shortly, for partially though not wholly different reasons, to be the centre of dramatic political controversy. These studies and activities serve as a warning against explaining his subsequent behaviour too much in terms of party or domestic politics. Moreover, interest in the Levant had been further increased by Gladstone's classical studies which, building on his earlier *Studies on Homer*, linked Egypt and Homeric Greece with Hebrew sources and the book of Genesis. The activities of retirement from political life thus ironically pointed Gladstone in precisely the direction of his political return.

III

It cannot be said that the Bulgarian Atrocities of 1876 burst upon Britain, or Gladstone, from a clear sky. War and revolution in the Balkans, widely reported in the press from the autumn of 1875, already raised the possibility of the collapse of Turkey-in-Europe and of a consequent partition by the powers. There were two questions, partly but not inseparably joined: the stability of Turkish power, and the lot of the Christian subjects of the Porte, as the Turkish Government was technically known. There were also two aspects to the subsequent campaign, its content, and its presentation.

From the autumn of 1875, when at Chatsworth he expressed alarm at 'the amazing news of a purchase outright of the Suez Canal Shares', fearing 'grave consequences' 'if not done in concert with Europe',[2] Gladstone became increasingly preoccupied with imperial affairs, whether in the form of the Canal share purchase, the Roman overtones of the Queen's new title (eventually announced as 'Empress of India'), the issue of slavery, and the position of Christians in Turkey. Seven of his ten substantial speeches in the Commons in 1876 were on these topics, opening with a brief 'vindication of our concern in the case of the Christian subjects of Turkey'.[3] These interventions were much more critical of the Government's Royal Titles Bill and of the Suez Canal purchase than they were of its Turkish policy, though hostility to the purchase partly reflected alarm at a much more direct and uniquely British involvement in Eastern Mediterranean affairs.

During the first six months of 1876, Gladstone's interest in Ottoman affairs certainly increased, with briefings from Stratford de Redcliffe[4] and Lady

---

[1] 30 Mar. 75.
[2] 26 Nov. 75. Gladstone came to have some personal interest in Egyptian affairs, for he bought £45,000 of Egyptian Tribute Loan at 38, probably in October 1876; see 12 Oct. 76.
[3] 8 Feb. 76.
[4] 27 June, 26 July 76.

Strangford and her son,[1] a reading of Serbian poetry, and assistance to a distressed gentlewoman destitute through the fall of the 1854 Turkish loan stock,[2] but he was also preoccupied with his very important review of Trevelyan's *Macaulay*,[3] and the suicide of his wife's brother-in-law, George Lyttelton.[4] The tone of his speeches on Eastern affairs was as much retrospective as admonitory. He spoke as 'the only person [in the House] who has been officially connected with this great question in its historical character, who is responsible for the proceedings connected with the Crimean War, and not only so, but who says now, in a day when the Crimean War is in a very different state of popularity from that which it enjoyed and elicited a quarter of a century ago, that he does not wish to shrink from that responsibility'.[5]

None the less, while admitting the difficulties of the Government, he asserted the general 'moral right of interference' of the 'European concert', and emphasised the essential need for the Government to accept the criterion of joint action abandoned in its unilateral purchase of the Suez Canal shares. He argued first, that Turkish territorial integrity should be, if possible, in principle maintained;[6] second, that Turkey had failed as a governor of Christian peoples ('The principles of civil society as they are understood in Europe are not understood in Turkey, are not embraced in the Ottoman faith'). Consequently 'measures conceived in the spirit and advancing in the direction of self-government' were required: 'if we can get rid of the difficulties of local administration by a Power which is wholly incompetent to conduct it', especially from Constantinople, 'we may attain the very practical object of good government'.[7] A solution of Turkish suzerainty over devolved local governments, rather than partition or independence for the provinces, was to be Gladstone's preferred position throughout the crisis. Even before the popular agitation had really begun, Gladstone had by the end of July 1876 measured out the ground and the arguments which were, in language much more strident, to be the essence of his position in subsequent years.

The campaign of 1876–80 is one of the great set-pieces of Victorian history, and both Gladstone and Disraeli realised it to be such. That sense of wonder and even of innocence which Victorians brought to their revivalist crusades and to their theatre-going and which Henry Irving, whose performances Gladstone eagerly attended in these years,[8] so astutely played upon, was an essential element of the politics of the time, and in the decaying days of Western representative government it is a quality which is hard to recapture.

Disraeli and Gladstone both played their parts to the full and both had a strong sense of the dramatic. The first, world-weary and ill, rallied his energies to achieve, at the least, the extraordinary personal triumph of the

[1] 18 Mar., 26 May, 6 July 76; the Strangfords were involved in organising relief for Bulgarians.
[2] 7 and 25 Apr. 76.   [3] 23 Mar. 76n. *et seq.*
[4] 17 Apr. 76.   [5] *H* 231. 174, 31 July 76.
[6] As Prime Minister, Gladstone had pressed Clarendon to prevent Egyptian independence from the Porte; see e.g., 4, 5 Nov. 69.
[7] *H* 231. 186, 198–9.
[8] See, e.g., 16 Apr. 75, 19 Feb., 8 May 76, 4 May 77, 5 and 22 Mar. 78, 19 Feb., 24 Mar. 79 (two visits to *Hamlet*), 19 June 79, 28 Feb. 80. For reading Kean's *Memoirs*, see 7 May 75.

Congress of Berlin, and to set the terms of Conservative imperial rhetoric for almost a century. Recognising the power of symbol, Disraeli created for the new electorate the myth of the imperial party with its 'patriotic' under-pinnings of Queen, Church, and Empire.[1] The corollary of this, the portrayal of the opposing party as unpatriotic, sketched in the 1872 Crystal Palace speech, entered the heart of Conservative electoral methodology in Beacons-field's 'manifesto' issued during the 1880 General Election, significantly for the future uniting constitutional change in Ireland with anti-Imperialism:

There are some who challenge the expediency of the imperial character of this realm. Having attempted, and failed, to enfeeble our colonies by their policy of de-composition, they may perhaps now recognise in the disintegration of the United Kingdom a mode which will not only accomplish but precipitate their purpose.[2]

Though hardly successful in 1880, this attempt at Conservative pre-emption of patriotism was, appropriately modified to suit the occasion, to have a long and effective life. Disraeli knew it to be a myth in the sense that he knew that his Government's policies were not intended to amount to a thorough-going 'Imperialism', but he also seems to have recognised that for certain sections of the electorate quite a wide discrepancy between rhetoric and policy was acceptable and perhaps even expected.

Gladstone brought to bear all his formidable powers of analysis, ethical power, and rhetoric to turn the crisis to encourage a national debate on national objectives, attempting to rally the electorate to the support of a wide range of policy positions. There was, therefore, an implied rationalism about his approach which contrasted markedly with the Conservatives' symbolism. Ironically, he too created a myth, but he differed from Disraeli in not knowing it to be such: the myth that the direction of British imperial policy could be more than marginally affected either by individuals or by popular opinion.

Few stories can be better known, or better documented, than the Eastern Question crisis and its aftermath, and it has called forth a distinguished literature which reflects the kaleidoscopic nature of the crisis, involving as it did foreign and imperial policy, religion, finance, and the form and organisation of domestic politics.[3] Only the Irish Question which replaced it rivalled it for drama, passion, and its capacity to act as a prism for the refraction of national and international attitudes.

---

[1] This is, considering its importance, a curiously understudied phenomenon; the survey in chapter 2 of R. T. McKenzie and A. Silver, *Angels in Marble* (1968) shows the unchanging essence of Con-servative propaganda from the late 1870s to the 1950s.

[2] Buckle, vi. 514–6.

[3] R. W. Seton-Watson, *Disraeli, Gladstone and the Eastern Question* (1935) still holds its place as an outstanding work of research and interpretation, as does B. H. Sumner, *Russia and the Balkans 1870–1880* (1937); the pathology of the campaign is well analysed in R. Shannon, *Gladstone and the Bulgarian Agitation 1876* (1963), with a gem of an introduction by G. Kitson Clark; R. Millman, *Britain and the Eastern Question 1875–1878* (1979) is a detailed survey; W. N. Medlicott, *Bismarck, Gladstone and the Concert of Europe* (1956) deals with the ideology and the negotiations of the late 1870s; 'Gladstonian foreign policy. The contradictions of morality' in A. J. P. Taylor, *The Trouble Makers* (1957) is a sparkling indictment. More sympathetic to the Porte is B. Jelavich, *The Ottoman Empire, the Great Powers, and the Straits Question, 1870–1887* (1973).

This is not the place to offer a detailed account of its very complex narrative.[1] Viewed retrospectively from Gladstone's point of view, the reader may care to bear in mind that the period 1876-80 fell into three general phases. First, from August 1876 to the spring of 1877, the 'atrocities campaign' attempted to rouse public attention and to force the Government and also the Liberal Party to respond to the atrocities in Bulgaria. The campaign in its early months was necessarily entirely extra-parliamentary in form, as Parliament did not sit between August 1876 and February 1877. Action was demanded through the Concert of Europe to end atrocitarianism by the Porte and to achieve a resettlement of the relations between the Porte and its Christian provinces. The Conference of Constantinople early in 1877, followed by Turkish rejection of its requirements and by British failure to respond to this rejection marked the end of this phase.

The second phase was that of the Russo-Turkish war and the subsequent settlement at the Congress of Berlin in 1878. It began when Russia cut the knot of inactivity in April 1877 and invaded Turkey on behalf of the Christian subjects. Gladstone reacted by moving Resolutions in the Commons in early May 1877. These Resolutions were designed to achieve 'a vital or material alteration of the declared policy of Her Majesty's Government', namely, the abandonment of the policy of 'remonstrances and expostulations only' and its

[1] It may be of use to give here a brief *résumé* of some of the main events:
1869 Suez Canal opened
1870 Start of establishment of Bulgarian Exarchate
1871 London conference ratifies changes in the Black Sea clauses of 1856 Paris Peace Treaty
1875 July Insurrection in Bosnia and Herzegovina
    November Britain buys Suez Canal shares
    December Andrassy Note calls for reforms for Bosnia and Herzegovina.
1876 April-May Bulgarian insurrection viciously repressed
    May Berlin Memorandum: plan for armistice and pacification of the Balkans not accepted
      by Britain
    Revolution in Constantinople regains power for the reformers
    June-July Serbia and Montenegro declare war on Turkey
    July Reichstadt agreement between Austria and Russia anticipates Turkish partition
    September 'Bulgarian Horrors' published
    December Constantinople Conference meets
      Midhat Pasha's constitution
1877 January Turkey rejects the Conference's demands
    March Ignatiev's mission to Western capitals
    April Russia declares war on Turkey
    May Gladstone's 'Resolutions' in the Commons
    December Fall of Plevna to Russia
1878 January British fleet despatched to Constantinople, but recalled: Carnarvon resigns
      Turkish-Russian armistice
    February British fleet reaches Constantinople
    March Treaty of San Stephano
      Derby resigns
    April Indian troops brought to Mediterranean
    May-June Secret Anglo-Russian and Anglo-Turkish agreements: Bulgaria reduced and
      Cyprus British
    June-July Berlin Congress
1879 October German-Austrian alliance
      Russia evacuates Roumania and Bulgaria.

replacement by participation in the 'united action of Europe' presently represented by Russia alone.[1] The failure of the 'Resolutions' and their weak
support by the Liberal Party in the Commons—the Government had a
majority of 131 on the only vote—perforce gave way to an attempt to ensure
right behaviour by Britain at the peacemaking Congress to gain a lasting
settlement of the problem of the instability in the Turkish Empire and of
injustice to its subject peoples. In the third phase, the question of Britain's
world role widened. The iniquities of the activities of Beaconsfield and
Salisbury in 1878 with respect to Turkish and Mediterranean affairs—'an
astounding announcement of the new Asiatic Empire'[2]—merged with imperial
crises in Southern Africa and the North-West frontier of India to produce a
general condemnation of 'a whole system of Government'.[3]

During the third phase, as the end of the seven-year Parliament neared,
Gladstone moved from attempts to influence and redirect Government policy
to a determination to defeat the Government at the coming General
Election, a determination publicly signalled by his agreement early in 1879 to
stand for Midlothian.

It must, of course, be remembered that these phases were hardly apparent
at the time. If Government policy was uncertain and divided, the task of
those in the Opposition attempting to influence it was made the more
complex and uncertain. However, once his attention was engaged upon
Balkan affairs, Gladstone at least had no doubts of the scale of the drama:

> My desire for the shade, a true and earnest desire has been since August [1876]
> rudely baffled: retirement & recollection seem more remote than ever. But [it] is in a
> noble cause, for the curtain rising in the East seems to open events that bear
> cardinally on our race.[4]

This Introduction will not attempt to take the reader through the narrative
of Gladstone's involvement in the details of the developing crisis in the East
and its *dénouement*. Rather, it will offer a discussion of the terms in which he
analysed the question and which led him to make a wholesale denunciation
of 'Beaconsfieldism' in the Midlothian Campaigns of 1879 and 1880.

Gladstone's behaviour in these years cannot be seen simply in terms of
party politics or personal ambition, though these factors no doubt played
their part. His approach reflected the theological preoccupations of the
previous eighteen months of retirement: it was High Church in conception,
Evangelical in conviction, and Broad Church in presentation. It will be
convenient to look at these three aspects of his reaction and contribution
very generally in such terms. This analysis will then be set in the context of
the party politics of the day, and of the structure of political communication
within which politicians were coming to work and which the campaign over
the Eastern Question in certain respects dramatically extended.

---

[1] *H* 234. 404, 416.
[2] 8 July 78.
[3] *Political speeches* (1879), 50.
[4] 29 Dec. 76.

IV

The High-Church ideology of the Concert of Europe is stated in essence in the opening sentence of the four volumes of *Commentaries upon International Law* written by Sir Robert Phillimore, Gladstone's High-Church friend and confidant: 'The necessity of mutual intercourse is laid in the nature of States, as it is of Individuals, by God, who willed the State and created the Individual.'[1] The Concert of Europe as it had operated between 1814 and 1871 had rested on the principle of reconciling the interests of the Great Power states through congresses (occasionally), conferences (frequently), and co-ordinated pressure upon deviant members.[2] Membership of it conferred and confirmed status and in turn expected responsibility, and its members were ready to go to considerable lengths to maintain the framework of Concert and Conference. It thus had a practical and a theoretical justification. It recognised the differing interests of states, it accepted that some states were more powerful than others, and it worked through the existing social structure of Europe, the continuing power of the aristocracy exemplified in its control of the embassies and chancelleries through which the Concert system was worked.

Of all this, the High-Churchman in Gladstone approved: the Concert could be seen as the Branch Church theory in action. It provided in the affairs of this world a means of co-operation without proselytisation between Protestant, Roman Catholic, and Orthodox. Unlike the Pope in 1864 and 1870, it was not inherently anti-national, and the new Italy and the new Germany were assimilable within its structure; 'Religious nationality' of the Gladstonian sort obviously required nations. The Holy Alliance powers of the Concert had, of course, been strongly opposed to the recognition of nationalism as a basis for legitimacy, but Britain and, spasmodically, France, had not been.

In looking to nationalism, Gladstone found himself apparently on common ground with the liberals, though his nationalism was primarily religious rather than liberal in origin; he had been a nationalist before he had been a liberal. He also shared, to a considerable extent, the Liberal belief in the benefits of free trade in promoting international harmony, and he saw free trade as the partner of the Concert. When he took the chair on the occasion of the centenary of the publication of *The Wealth of Nations*, he reminded his fellow members of the Political Economy Club and their distinguished guests that 'The operations of commerce are not confined to the material ends; that there is no more powerful agent in consolidating and in knitting together the amity of nations; and that the great moral purpose of the repression of human passions, and those lusts and appetites which are the great cause of war, is in direct relation with the understanding and application of the science which you desire to propagate.'[3] Free-trade commerce would provide the underlying drive towards amity; the Concert would work at the political level to prevent irresponsible acts by its

---

[1] R. Phillimore, *Commentaries upon International Law* (1854–7), i. v.

[2] See C. Holbraad, *The Concert of Europe. A study in German and British international theory 1815–1914* (1970).

[3] *Revised Report of the proceedings at the dinner of 31st May 1876 held in celebration of the hundredth year of publication of the 'Wealth of Nations'* (1876), 42–3.

members. The Concert was, therefore, reactive rather than anticipatory in its actions.[1] In advocating both free-trade commerce and the Concert as the means towards the avoidance of war, Gladstone stopped short of the classic Liberal position, well stated by F. H. Hinsley: 'The belief that progress was destined to replace inter-government relations by the free-play of enlightened public opinion between societies.'[2] Gladstone's sense of sin was married to his realism and his executive experience in preventing such thoroughgoing optimism.

None the less, Gladstone was optimistic. In advocating a view of inter-national society which had both an economic and a political dimension—free trade the regulator of the one, the Concert of the other—Gladstone at the least offered a wide vision which came to incorporate in British politics both the Manchester radicals, suspicious though they were of external obligation and intervention, and the Whigs, cautious though they were becoming about popu-lar influences on foreign policy. In bringing together Adam Smith and Canning, Gladstone based his position on the precedent and eirenicism of the past, but he also found himself offering, and newly associating with a popular campaign, a vision of international legitimacy and order which, as later developed and institutionalised in the League of Nations and the United Nations, represented the best hope of twentieth-century Liberalism.[3] Gladstone was, therefore, an important part of that process by which an international order of conservative, monarchic, origin was given a popular base in the era of the extended franchise.

The case of Turkey represented an example of the type of instance with which the Concert, in Gladstone's view, should deal. Since 1856 Turkey had been a member of the Concert, albeit on sufferance; if Turkey had, in the words of Sir Robert Phillimore, 'acquired the Rights, she has also subjected herself to the Duties of a civilised Community'.[4] These duties had in the 1860s and early 1870s been to a considerable extent fulfilled by the Tanzimat movement, with its leaders Ali Pasha and Fuad Pasha. The failure of their programme in 1871–72, and the consequent Islamic reaction, marked the end, at least for the time being, of expectations of a Europeanised Porte.[5] None the less, the atrocities in Bulgaria in May 1876 occurred within an area now expected to be subject to the usual European conventions and standards of civic behaviour. The scale of the atrocities was thought to be large: 12,000–15,000 killed either by the Turks or

[1] Thus Gladstone emphasised in his speech on 7 May 1877 that during the 1868–74 Liberal Government 'there were no events in Turkey on which we could take our stand. There was, so to speak, no point of departure'; *H* 234. 430.

[2] F. H. Hinsley, *Power and the Pursuit of Peace* (1963), 111. See also Deryck Schreuder, 'Gladstone and the Conscience of the State' in P. Marsh, ed., *The Conscience of the Victorian State* (1979), esp. 96ff.

[3] See J. L. Hammond, 'Gladstone and the League of Nations mind' in *Essays in Honour of Gilbert Murray*, ed. J. A. K. Thomson and A. J. Toynbee (1936), 95; see also P. F. Clarke, *Liberals and Social Democrats* (1978), 276ff. Hammond stressed the role of Homer in Gladstone's thoughts about the European comity; classicism offered a bridge between Gladstone and the Murray–Hammond group which crossed the chasm created by his High-Churchmanship.

[4] R. Phillimore, *Commentaries upon International Law* (1857), iii. iv.

[5] See R. H. Davison, *Reform in the Ottoman Empire 1856–1876* (1963), chs. vii and viii. As Prime Minister, Gladstone seems to have taken little interest in the dramatic change of mood in Turkey in 1872–74, although it was well reported by Elliot, the ambassador. In view of his attitude to Turkey from 1876 onwards, it is this absence, rather than his expectations in the 1856–70 period, which is strange.

by their local agents, the Bashi-Bazouks, was the usual contemporary estimate.[1] But it was not simply the number of dead which was important, large though this was by nineteenth-century standards, but rather that the slaughter had occurred within the boundaries of 'civilization'. Turkey was responsible for ensuring minimum standards of order and justice; thus the Concert was obliged to intervene in her internal affairs if it was shown that these standards had been grossly contravened.[2] The Concert had acted in 1854 to prevent Russia behaving irresponsibly towards Turkey; it must now act again to censure Turkey for her proven misbehaviour towards her Christian subjects. The solution, Gladstone thought, must be 'local liberty and practical self-government in the disturbed provinces of Turkey' while at the same time preserving the principle of Turkish sovereignty and thus avoiding partition, 'the imposition upon them of any other Foreign Dominion'. The precedent was the action of the Concert, under Canning's leadership, in the Greek crisis of 1826-27,[3] a precedent publicly recalled by Gladstone (following Earl Russell) at quite an early stage of the campaign.[4]

Gladstone's view of the Concert was by no means democratic. The Concert was essentially monarchic—in 1876 even France had a nominal monarchic majority in the Assembly—and its machinery was that of the overwhelmingly aristocratic structure of European embassies. Gladstone offered no structural proposals to improve or advance upon the Concert's effectiveness. He did not even go as far as those theorists such as J. C. Bluntschli who advocated limited machinery for codifying international law,[5] though he quoted Bluntschli in his pamphlet 'Lessons in Massacre' to justify intervention and described him as 'the greatest authority on international law of the present day'.[6] Although he could certainly point to his own Government's use of arbitration in 1872 to settle the 'Alabama claims' of the United States Government, to its value in drawing the United States towards the framework of the European Concert, and to its importance as a precedent, he none the less did not personally suggest means of institutionalising such procedures.

Gladstone's position was thus essentially conservative, in the straightforward meaning of that term, and also in its details rather cautious, though it also pointed, in the long term, towards a restored international order. He represented in international affairs what was fast coming to seem, for a generation, an apparently old-fashioned view of harmony obtainable through Concert and

---

[1] The actual number of dead remains uncertain; the evidence is surveyed in Millman, *op. cit.*, chapter 10.

[2] The bearing of the 1856 Treaty on this issue was a very vexed question; as Phillimore pointed out in 1857, Article ix contained 'the most singular provision, which might almost seem intended at once to recognise and to prohibit the Right of INTERVENTION by the powers of Christendom on behalf of their co-religionists'; *Commentaries upon International Law*, iii. iv.

[3] Gladstone's third and fourth Resolutions of 7 May 77; only the first Resolution was formally moved but Gladstone made it clear that, despite the reservations of other members of the ex-Cabinet, he stood by all five; see 27 Apr.-7 May 77.

[4] In 'The Hellenic Factor in the Eastern Problem'; see 13 Nov. 76.

[5] For Bluntschli's realistic recognition of the role of the Great Powers, and for his proposals, see Hinsley, *op. cit.*, 134-5 and Holbraad, *op. cit.*, 66-70.

[6] Though without naming him directly, in 'The Sclavonic Provinces' (1877), 8; see 16 Jan. 77. See also, for a similar named tribute, H 234. 432 (7 May 1877).

open Conferences, buttressed by free trade, a view soon to be undercut by secret alliances, protectionism, cartelisation, and all that Bismarck's *Reich* represented. As with all Gladstone's political initiatives, his conservatism had radical overtones, in this case, as so often, as much in the nature of its presentation as in its content. As applied in the circumstances of the day, it seemed, especially to Conservatives, dangerous and even revolutionary in its implications.

The aim of the Concert was to promote amity, but this promotion need not necessarily be pacific. The use of arms, though its slaughter was regrettable and its cost undesirable, was a legitimate weapon in the establishment of right. In Gladstone's view, Britain had been right to join other members of the Concert in armed resistance to Russia in 1854, and Russia was right forcibly to impose a solution upon Turkey in 1877–78. Within the context of the Concert, coercion by arms was, in its appropriate context, a proper instrument of policy which would in most cases achieve its result without war. 'Coercion by menace, justly and wisely used, need not lead to war.'[1] Gladstone sent the Concert's fleet to Smyrna in 1880 for a show of force against the Porte with no intellectual embarrassment.[2]

The point of departure of the popular phase of the Eastern Question campaign—the denunciation of Turkish atrocities—should not, therefore, be allowed to give the impression that Gladstone, and most of those involved in the campaign, were pacifists. The difference between types of killing lay in the authority for the action. The Concert had that authority, in Gladstone's view, because it represented the best available institutional representation of Christian morality in international affairs. In 1877, arguing that there was 'an authority that proceeds both from experts and from the race', Gladstone turned naturally to St. Augustine's majestic maxim, 'Securus judicat orbis terrarum', which he had quoted with such force at the height of the Franco-Prussian war in 1870.[3] Just as in the extra-European world the 'prolific British mother ... with her progeny, may also claim to constitute a kind of Universal Church in politics',[4] so, in the European context, the Concert linked Gladstone's longing for ecumenicity with his perception of authority in the world of affairs.

This elevated analysis was accompanied by a hard-headed view of Britain's interests. Gladstone dissented from what was becoming the conventional wisdom of the time, that the route to India must be the defining factor in British policy, and he attacked head on the view that the occupation of Egypt should be 'only a question of time'.[5] India detracted from rather than added to Britain's military strength; it was held only as long as 'the will of the two hundred and forty millions of people who inhabit India' wished it to be held. A world view which placed Indian defence as 'a high doctrine ... is humiliating and even

---

[1] *H* 234. 965 (14 May 1877). The criticism of the Government, therefore, was not its use of force to support a political demand, but its willingness to act alone, and in what Gladstone saw as the wrong cause.

[2] See 19 Sept. 80ff.

[3] In his dispute with James Fitzjames Stephen on the nature of authority; *Gleanings*, iii. 211.

[4] 'Kin beyond Sea', *Gleanings*, i. 205.

[5] 'Aggression on Egypt and Freedom in the East', *Nineteenth Century* (August 1877), a dispute with Edward Dicey, mostly reprinted in *Gleanings*, iv. 341, from which quotations in the rest of this paragraph are taken. See 21 July 77.

degrading. . . . The root and pith and substance of the material greatness of our nation lies within the compass of these islands; and is, except in trifling particulars, independent of all and every sort of political dominion beyond them.' Egypt, besides the route through the Canal which was less important than made out, was also implicitly dangerous. In a remarkable passage, Gladstone anticipated the events of the next eighty years, but in order to deplore them:

> Our first site in Egypt, be it by larceny or be it by emption, will be the almost certain egg of a North African Empire, that will grow and grow until another Victoria and another Albert, titles of the Lake-sources of the White Nile, come within our borders; and till we finally join hands across the Equator with Natal and Cape Town, to say nothing of the Transvaal and the Orange River on the south, or of Abyssinia or Zanzibar to be swallowed by way of *viaticum* on our journey. And then, with a great Empire in each of the four quarters of the world, and with the whole new or fifth quarter to ourselves, we may be territorially content, but less than ever at our ease; for if agitators and alarmists can now find at almost every spot 'British interests' to bewilder and disquiet us, their quest will then be all the wider. . . .

The Eastern Question, reinforced by the subsequent difficulties of the Tory Government in Southern Africa and on the Indian frontier, thus brought Gladstone to a bold and prophetic analysis of Britain's possible position in the future world order. He freely and without regret accepted the natural relative decline of Britain's industrial supremacy, and the ending of her unique position, especially through the growth of the U.S.A., which would 'probably become what we are now, the head servant in the great household of the World, the employer of all employed'. While 'we have been advancing with this portentous rapidity, America is passing us by as if at a canter'.[1] Since Britain's power rested on the strength of her domestic economy, and since that power would in the long run be relatively declining, imperial expansion, justifiable though it might be in particular instances, must be resisted. Otherwise a position would be reached where a relatively declining power sought vainly to defend and control a vast Empire whose new acquisitions would each multiply the points of danger, conflict, and potential crisis. An anxious Edwardian could hardly have put it better.

Gladstone thus held that an independently British policy towards the Straits, separate from the Concert's concern at civilised standards of behaviour in Turkey, was unnecessary, undesirable, and dangerous. There was no unique 'British interest', and there should therefore be no unilateral British action. Indeed, the assertion of a British interest independent of that of Europe played into the hands of Russia, for it left Britain the prisoner of the Turks, while allowing the Russians to appear as the sole champions of Christians in the Balkans, a role which they had, in Gladstone's view, been permitted by the Treaty of Küchük Kainardji (1774), but which they had ceded to the Concert at the end of the Crimean War in 1856.[2] To have allowed the Russians to reclaim, by default, their pre-1854 position, was a further danger. The Conservative Cabinet's policy in 1876 had allowed Russia to 'associate all Europe with her',

[1] 'Kin beyond Sea' (see 21 June 78) contains the discussion of the rise of the U.S.A., and continues together with 'England's Mission' (see 9 Sept. 78) the analysis developed in 'Aggression in Egypt'.
[2] This was a strongly contested point; see *H* 234. 433, 967 (7, 14 May 77).

with the danger of a Russo-Turkish agreement, settling 'matters in such a way as to leave all Europe out of account'.[1]

Gladstone was by no means an out-and-out Russophile. *The Bulgarian Horrors* pamphlet was quickly translated into Russian by K. P. Pobedonostsev, later the famous Procurator of the Holy Synod, and soon sold 20,000 copies,[2] but its author remained very cautious about Russian intentions. Gladstone recognised Russia's 'special temptations'[3] in the Near East; he had seen Russia disrupt Europe in 1854; he condemned her behaviour in Poland and towards Hungarians; his first Government had, at least to his own and Granville's satisfaction, dealt with Russian expansionism towards Afghanistan and her attempt at unilateral disruption of the 1856 Black Sea clauses in 1870 (eventually ratified, but with careful safeguards, by a conference in London in 1871). Moreover, Russia's role in ecclesiastical developments in the Balkans was, at the least, questionable. Gladstone's church contacts with the Balkans in the early 1870s were all with Orthodox Greeks and he had quite extensive links with the Greek community in London.[4] He had already been involved polemically in arguing that the Russian Orthodox Church was in spirit narrower than the Greek Orthodox.[5] The Greeks had reached an accommodation with the Porte by which Greek Orthodox religious supremacy over much of Turkey in Europe, and especially in Bulgaria, was until 1870 supported by the Turkish secular power. Gladstone was reluctant to play 'the game of Russia' to see this situation changed.

Russian influence, through the Panslavist Ignatiev, had encouraged the schism against Greek dominance which led to the Bulgarian Exarchate (separate ecclesiastical province) permitted by the Turkish Government's Firman (decree) of 1870. This independence from Greek ecclesiastical authority encouraged Bulgarian nationalism, a development anticipated by the Foreign Office at the time,[6] and it was the Turkish reaction to this consequence of their own Firman which developed into the massacres of 1876. Gladstone regarded the Bulgarians' ecclesiastical action as undesirable, though originally prompted by 'a genuine aspiration of nationality'.[7] The reason was that the Bulgarians, instead of accepting the old Christian principle of 'local distribution', beloved of High-Churchmen, demanded jurisdiction 'wherever there were Bulgarians', thus going against the tradition of the Ante-Nicene Church and making 'a plain

[1] Liddon's account of Gladstone's views; see 17 Jan. 77n.

[2] See 8 Sept. 76. The translation was arranged 'to redeem British honour' by L. C. Alexander, founder of the Royal Historical Society; Gladstone and Alexander wanted the proceeds to go to Balkan Slavs, but they went instead to Russian Panslavists. See R. F. Byrnes, *Pobedonostsev. His Life and Thought* (1968), 125, 433.

[3] *H* 234. 415 (7 May 77).   [4] See, e.g., 15 Mar. 75.

[5] See 13 Jan., 9 May 75.

[6] H. P. T. Barron, Chargé at Constantinople, to Clarendon, 22 March 1870, F.O.C.P. 3578: 'The question originated in the Hellenizing tendencies of the Greek clergy, which produced a reaction on the part of the Bulgarians in favour of their national clergy . . . it became aggravated by the obstinate resistance of the Patriarch to the originally modest demands of the Bulgarians, and has now become fraught with difficulty . . . the part taken by the Government in favour of the Bulgarians must have the effect of alienating the Greeks . . . it is very doubtful whether this policy is not playing into the hands of the so-called Panslavist party. . . .'

[7] 'The Hellenic Factor in the Eastern Problem'; see 13 Nov. 76.

violation of the first principles in any religious society'.[1] These reservations about the Bulgarian schism, expressed in 1872 and 1875,[2] may in part account for Gladstone's delay in August 1876 in involving himself with the rising agitation until the scale of Turkish atrocities became quite certain. Certainly, it is an aspect of Balkan affairs and Gladstone's reaction to them hitherto almost entirely disregarded.

The Bulgarian schism had broken the 'harmony between the Ottoman Porte and the Christian Churches within its dominions', important for 'the peace of the Levant' which Gladstone had encouraged in 1872, as well as being a further blow to ecumenicity. For a man who had looked in the early 1870s to 'a firm union, founded on common interest, between the Porte & its dependent provinces'[3] to switch to regarding the Bulgars and their grievances as the focal point of Balkan affairs required caution and confirmation. This, the sheer shock of the atrocities provided. Even when he had made the switch, Gladstone showed himself keen to broaden the question quickly, and he did so in his article 'The Hellenic Factor' which stressed the importance of remembering 'Greek as well as Slav grievances'.[4]

'Religious nationality' in the Balkans had thus by no means necessarily implied political independence from the Porte and, in advocating the half-way house of suzerainty, Gladstone believed that, at least for the medium term, he was, in contrast to the Conservative Government, offering the policy most likely to provide stability in the Near East. As so often in his career, he accepted change to achieve stability. Care must be taken in ascribing to him any full-blown theory of political nationalism. His view of political nationality was not an *a priori* one, but rather the application of 'experience' to situations given by history. Not surprisingly, as the former Colonial Secretary and Prime Minister

---

[1] Ramm I, ii. 359.

[2] See letters to Archbishop Lycurgus of 18 August 1872 and October 1875 in Lathbury, ii. 304, 63; that of 1872 is of especial interest as it anticipates the dangers of a religious dispute leading to Russian exploitation of political crisis. See also Ramm I, ii. 327, 337, 359, 368. See T. A. Meininger, *Ignatiev and the Establishment of the Bulgarian Exarchate, 1864–1872* (1970) which on the whole bears out Gladstone's reading of the case.

[3] To Sir H. Elliot, 9 May 71.

[4] See 13 Nov. 76. Gladstone reinforced his position in a letter replying to a request for comment by Negropontis, a Greek merchant in Constantinople (see 9 Jan. 77): 'For me the question of the East is not a question of Christianity against the Porte and the governing Ottomans; because all the grievances of the Mussulman and Jewish subjects—and such, without doubt, there are—ought to disappear in the act of applying an efficacious and well-considered remedy to the grievances of the Christians, who form the mass of the oppressed. I do not, then, recognise any plurality of causes; for me the cause is one only, and I cannot commend either Greeks, who refuse their moral support to the Slavs, or Slavs who refuse it to the Greeks. That efficacious remedy I find in the development of the local liberties of all such Provinces as are proved to be suffering. . . . The equitable delimitation of Slav and Hellenic Provinces is a question difficult and grave enough; but it is an ulterior question such as cannot, in my opinion, be adjusted in a satisfactory manner unless when Greek and Slav alike shall have imparted to one another, on the basis of a plan of local liberties, the reciprocal sympathy which will be alike generous and wise.' The *Daily Telegraph*, supposedly briefed by Layard, the Ambassador at Constantinople, reported this and a second letter as a call by Gladstone that the Greeks should attack the Turks. A prolonged wrangle between Gladstone, Layard and Levy-Lawson, proprietor of the *Telegraph*, followed, culminating in Ashley's motion in the Commons of 'regret' at Layard's behaviour, which was defeated in 132:206. The correspondence and newspaper reports are mostly printed in *H* 238. 1156 (12 March 1878) and *PP* 1878 lxxxi.

of the world's most extensive Empire, his point of reference was not the ruled, but the behaviour of the imperial power, whether Turkish, Russian, or British. It was the moral failure of Turkish rule, not the inherent virtue of her 'subject races' or 'subject peoples' (the terms are used interchangeably), which constituted his starting point.

Gladstone's instinctive interest, outside the sphere of religion, lay in factors preventing amalgamation rather than in those preserving or promoting national identity. In the case of Turkey, generations of rule had not led to that amalgamation of peoples essential to long-term stability, a failure exemplified in the events of 1876–78. In part, the absence of 'an organic union' in Turkey had a 'racial' cause:[1]

> There is, in fact, a great deal of resemblance between the system which prevails in Turkey and the old system of negro slavery. In some respects it is less bad than negro slavery, and in other respects a great deal worse. It is worse in this respect, that in the case of negro slavery, at any rate, it was a race of higher capacities ruling over a race of lower capacities; but in the case of this system, it is unfortunately a race of lower capacities which rules over a race of higher capacities.

More important than this, however, was the failure of the Turks to develop beyond the 'government of force' which they had originally been. Without the influence of law and individual political responsibility, the military genius of the Turks was corrupted and depraved.

> The Turks are what circumstances have made them, and depend upon it that if a lot of us were taken and put in their circumstances we, either individually or as a race, would soon cease to do even the limited credit to the Christian name that we now bring to it. They exercise a perfectly unnatural domination over their fellow-creatures; and arbitrary power is the greatest corruptor of the human mind and heart. There is nothing that can withstand it. Human nature requires the restraint of law. There is, unfortunately, no restraint of law in Turkey, and in the sight of God and man, much as these Christians are to be pitied, perhaps the Turks, who are the victims of that system, are to be pitied still more. The very worst things that men have ever done have been done when they were performing acts of violence in the name of religion. That has been the unfortunate position of the Turks, as a race that not only has conquered, but has conquered in the sacred name of religion. The corruption that results from such a system as that is deep and profound. Mahometans, where they manage their own affairs, and have not got the charge of the destinies of other people, can live in tolerable communities together, and discharge many of the duties of civil and social life. In certain cases, as for instance, in the case of the Moors of Spain, they have exhibited many great and conspicuous merits. It is not the fact, that their religion is different from ours, which prevents them from discharging civil duties. Do not suppose that for a moment. It is not because they are in themselves so much worse than we are. God forbid that we should judge them. It is that this wretched system under which they live puts into their hands power which human beings ought not to possess, and the consequences are corruption to themselves and misery to those around.

The consequence of this analysis, in many respects classically Liberal in its view of political corruption, was that, although there remained important

---

[1] 'The Sclavonic Provinces of the Ottoman Empire' (1877), 8; further quotations in this paragraph are taken from this lecture. See 16 Jan. 77. Gladstone read widely in the extensive literature on 'race'; see, e.g. 9 Sept. 77 where he renders *Types of mankind* as 'Indigenous Races'.

strategic attractions in Ottoman suzerainty as a solution, a 'clean arrangement' was necessary 'to remove all future occasions of collision and contention between her and the vassal community'.[1] The Turks had shown their inability to incorporate fully in their Empire 'races of men who were, before the days of Turkish domination, on the same level of civilization as was northern and western Europe, and who carry in them the instincts, and the materials, of freedom and progress'. The self-awareness of the Balkan peoples, chiefly preserved by the Orthodox churches, thus pre-dated the Turkish conquest. The Turks had had their chance and they had failed. Thus, 'let the daily power of the Turk in Bulgaria be destroyed'; even in his advice about the form of the Treaty of San Stephano in 1878 Gladstone stopped short of advocating outright political independence. 'A clean arrangement' did not necessarily mean a clean break.

This appreciation of the difficulties of the process of amalgamation clearly raised rather general questions, going beyond the affairs of the Porte and beyond 'religious nationality'. In a fragment almost certainly written in 1877, Gladstone noted:

> That no conquest can be legitimate unless it be marked by the introduction of superior laws, institutions, or manners among the conquered. No conquest has been permanent unless followed by amalgamation
>
> Saxons ⎫
> Normans ⎭ in England
> Franks in France
> Lombards in Italy.
>
> The very least that can be expected is that the conquerors should be able to learn civilisation from the conquered as Romans from Greeks.[2]

If amalgamation was the criterion, how stood the British Empire? England was a splendid example of success—'we have all happily settled down into one homogeneous whole'[3]—but Ireland and India were obvious subjects of question. Gladstone made glancing remarks about both in his comments on the Balkans, referring to Ireland as 'the far slighter case . . . a vastly milder instance', but none the less admitting an analogy. What was to be compared was Turkey's 'domination', which was 'incurable', with the 'Protestant ascendancy in Ireland', also incurable. Neither case had been in principle hopeless: 'The thing is incurable, but not the men who have to do with the thing. To make them curable, you have to take them out of a position which is false, and leave them in a position which is true, sound and normal.'[4]

This the Turks had failed to do, this his own first Government's Irish legislation had attempted to achieve, and this must be the motto for the governance of India, where amalgamation in the Saxon/Norman sense was never attempted. The containment and accommodation of 'subject peoples' within an Imperial structure was thus an essential part of the art of government. It might be 'the business of every oppressed people to rise upon every reasonable opportunity against the oppressor'; it might be that 'it was the duty of Bulgaria to rise and to fight';[5] but the implication of Gladstone's position was that it was the art

---

[1] 'The Peace to Come', *Nineteenth Century*, iii. 216 (February 1878); see 9 Jan. 78.
[2] Add MS 44763, f. 96; this paper was used in preparing for 'The Sclavonic Provinces'.
[3] 'The Sclavonic Provinces', 5.   [4] 'The Peace to Come', 216, 219.   [5] Ibid., 221.

of government to see that peoples did not feel themselves to be oppressed and that reasonable policies would remove the 'reasonable opportunity' for a rising. The notion of reasonableness was to prove hard to sustain in the context of late-nineteenth century nationalism.

To draw together the underlying theme of state organisation: imperial structures were not inherently unstable or undesirable, but they would become so if local traditions were not accommodated. The notion of suzerainty—an 'infinitely elastic' concept[1]—offered a means of allowing both local development and the maintenance of large units for the purpose of stability in international relations. If the 1870s saw moves towards both political nationalism and integrative imperialism, Gladstone offered a solution which gave a commitment to neither, and which was to be developed in the context of Southern Africa and Ireland, though events largely superseded it as a solution to the problems of the Ottoman Porte.

The mark of the successful imperial power would be the ability to strike a balance between the requirements of strategic security and the encouragement of local institutions which would preserve local liberties and ventilate local enthusiasm, customs, and traditions. Gladstone did not use the word 'nationalism' in the 1870s—indeed he very rarely used 'ism' as a suffix—and his preferred term, nationality, was applied always in particular cases except when used in conjunction with religion. It would be fair to say, therefore, that Gladstone did not think in terms of nationalism, outside the established nation-states, either as a general phenomenon or as an organising principle. In keeping with his general anti-metropolitanism in the 1870s, his articles and speeches certainly seemed to reflect important aspects of it, but, as so often, his position was in fact more metropolitan and less 'advanced' than many of his supporters supposed.

IV

There lay behind Gladstone's critique of the Eastern Question a coherent argument by no means radical, although coming to seem so in contrast to the strident jingoism of the late 1870s. None the less, the conviction with which he took part in the campaign was exceptional. Between July and September 1876, Gladstone experienced a conversion of Evangelical intensity. The end of his first ministry and the ecclesiastical legislation of 1874 had seen him politically estranged from all but a small group of Liberal High-Churchmen.[2] His resignation as party leader had occurred among a welter of negatives which went well beyond his own wish for an end to political activity: 'out of harmony' was the key-note phrase.[3] However, he had from the first privately reserved his position on a possible return, as he bore in mind 'cases where there is some great public cause for which to contend' which might constrain the immediate reasons for

---

[1] Described thus in 'The Hellenic Factor', *Gleanings*, iv. 301: 'what it implies is a practical self-management of all those internal affairs on which the condition of daily life depends, such as police and judiciary, with fixed terms of taxation, especially of direct and internal taxation, and with command over the levy of it'.

[2] See above, vii. cxiii.

[3] See 25 Feb., 5 and 7 Mar. 74, 14 Jan. 75.

retirement.[1] The Vatican pamphlets of 1874–75 had been an 'expostulation'; they were intended to make a point, and encourage *others* to action. By the end of 1875, Gladstone hoped 'my polemical period is over';[2] others had been exhorted, but on the whole they had not acted.[3] 1876 was to require a different attitude.

As the outcry against the Turkish atrocities developed, especially in the North of England, in late July and throughout August 1876, Gladstone was silent. No-one reading his journal between 1 and 27 August would imagine that his speech of 31 July was about to be followed by the most famous of all his publications, *The Bulgarian Horrors and the Question of the East*, begun on 28 August in bed at Hawarden, during a lumbago attack, and finished in London on 5 September.[4] On 3 September, before leaving for London, he committed himself to a speech in his constituency of Greenwich on the atrocities.[5] Various reasons for the delay can be offered—uncertainty about the extent of the atrocities, doubt about the Bulgarian position, unwillingness to embarrass Granville and Hartington, unease about his relationship with the Liberal Party, reluctance to commit himself to what was bound to be, at the least, as in the case of Vaticanism, a series of publications[6]—but with no clear conclusion. The reader of the journal after 28 August 1876 can however have no doubt about the depth and range of Gladstone's involvement with Balkan affairs.

Though the policy prescriptions remained, as has been shown, precise, cautious, and conservative, the passion which urged them was of a new dimension. Reading, correspondence, writing, speaking, all the habitual Gladstonian pursuits bore on a single theme. Moreover, Gladstone recognised he was in for a long haul: the tense used in his retrospect on 29 December 1876, by which time some thought the chief force of the agitation was passed, is significant: 'the curtain rising in the East seems to open events that bear cardinally on our race'. Quite suddenly, in late August 1876, the true nature of Turkish rule had been revealed. As Gladstone put it in his second pamphlet, *Lessons in Massacre* (originally to have been entitled *Who are the Criminals?*), published in March 1877:

> The Bulgarian outrages, though they are not the Eastern Question, are a key to the Eastern Question. They exhibit the true genius of the Turkish Government. Externally an isolated though portentious fact, they unlock to us an entire mystery of iniquity. Vast as in their intrinsic importance, they are yet more important for what they indicate, than for what they are.... As in individual life, so in the life of Governments, it is the great crisis that searches nature to its depths, and brings out the true spirit of the man.[7]

[1] 25 Feb. 74.   [2] 29 Dec. 75.

[3] Ironically, in Ulster Irish disestablishment produced a lowering of sectarianism, so that Orange orators 'did not like to follow Mr. Gladstone and give him any credit for No Popery zeal'; T. Macknight, *Ulster as it is* (1896), i. 331.

[4] It should be remembered that Gladstone's journal very rarely notices newspaper reading, for which see Shannon, 98ff.

[5] See 3 Sept. 76n.

[6] See Shannon, ch. 3.

[7] 'Lessons in Massacre', 73–4. See 26 Feb., 1 Mar. 77 for the titles. A second pamphlet was originally planned immediately after the first; see below, p. 1.

As the revelations had been dramatic, so the reaction must be passionate, even if the means of redress be moderate and carefully calculated. This combination of Evangelical enthusiasm and atonement with shrewd and controlled analysis is best seen in Gladstone's article, 'The Paths of Honour and of Shame', written at the height of the crisis in February 1878 as the British Fleet entered the Dardanelles without the permission of the Porte and the Russians halted just short of Constantinople.

The article opens with a classic Evangelical statement—'If this age has pride, and if its pride requires a whipping, the needful discipline is perhaps not far to seek'—and moves on through Bishop Butler to a sharp analysis of what ought to be the policies of Britain at 'the Conference or Congress, be it which it may, that is partly to record, and partly to adjust, the settlement of the great question of the East'.[1] Evangelicalism involved and implied not only enthusiasm, but a heightened sense of sin and obligation, a commitment to atonement, a crushing of pride, an acute awareness of the penalties for wickedness and, especially among Anglican Evangelicals, an application of these senses to the nation as well as to the individual. Gladstone's refurbished interest in Evangelicalism and its contribution to Anglicanism was reflected in his article of July 1879, which emphasised the close interplay between Evangelicalism and Tractarianism, by which the best features of the former, 'the juice and sap', permeated the latter and thus Anglicanism generally. It did this in part by an 'unseen relation' between the two: 'Causation, in the movements of the human mind, is not a thing single and simple. It is a thing continuous and latent.'[2]

In a true Evangelical spirit, Gladstone believed himself to have been called 'for a purpose', a call carrying 'the marks of the will of God'. This was a sober analysis of his position. Usually his service to the will of God in politics took the form of the application in particular instances of a general set of beliefs or precepts, carried through with a strong awareness of Godly support. But on this occasion he came to feel that he was the direct recipient of a specific call. Gladstone was conscious of the dangers of such a claim. He was fully aware 'that language such as I have used is often prompted by fanaticism'. He guarded against this 'by tests', that is, he interpreted what he believed to be a Providential calling within a well-established Evangelical context of analysis. The remarkable passage in the diary in which he describes this conviction is of an intensity not experienced since the extraordinary crisis of the 1840s and early 1850s.[3]

It is, of course, true that Gladstone saw any situation in religious terms, and that, like J. H. Newman and H. E. Manning and other Tractarians and High-

---

[1] 'Paths of Honour and of Shame', 1, 17; see 20 Feb. 78; see also 'The Peace to Come', 9 Jan. 78. A discussion of Gladstone's evangelicalism and Bishop Butler will be found in Boyd Hilton's article, the most original piece on Gladstone written in recent years, 'Gladstone's Theological Politics', in M. Bentley and J. Stevenson, *High and Low Politics in Modern Britain* (1983).

[2] 'The Evangelical Movement; its parentage, progress and issue', published in the Congregationalist *British Quarterly Review*; see 14 May 79.

[3] 29 Dec. 78. For the crisis of the 1840s and early 1850s, see above, Introduction to volume iii, xliv–xlix. I am much obliged to Dr. John Walsh for showing me his unpublished paper, 'Experience and Enthusiasm', which powerfully illuminates Evangelical self-awareness, a phenomenon on which there is much contemporary literature, but virtually none since.

Churchmen of Evangelical origin, he continually found the religious experiences of his youth a source of strength in later years when, theologically, he had moved beyond them. None the less, the personal commitment which the Eastern Question called forth from him was self-confessedly of a new order: 'When have I seen so strongly the relation between my public duties and the primary purposes for which God made and Christ redeemed the world?'[1]

It is significant that, despite the intensity of his personal involvement, Gladstone was careful, both in private correspondence and in his journal, to avoid personalising what is often seen as his dispute with Disraeli. Publicly, Gladstone was on record as stating his view of Beaconsfield's peculiar responsibility for his Government's Eastern policy, and his deliberate and persistent efforts to bring him to book.[2] Privately, however, Disraeli was not personally denounced in the strident terms used for the Sultan, 'a bottomless pit of iniquity and fraud' who had a fair chance of defeating Satan in a competition for the fathership of liars.[3] Phillimore noted that 'G. was careful to restrain the expression of his private feelings about Lord B. as he generally is',[4] and the introspective passages of the journal have the same reticence. There are two substantive comments on Disraeli. On 21 May 1879, Gladstone records: 'Went to afternoon tea with Lady Derby. Found myself face to face with Lord Beaconsfield & this put all right socially between us, to my great satisfaction.' In May 1880, after returning to office, Gladstone closely studied the recently published biography of Beaconsfield by George Brandes, the Danish critic and historian. He commented on it: 'His description of Beaconsfield's mind as metallic & mine as fluid, has merit.'[5] How far this reticence reflects the sort of self-control required by Gladstone's interpretation of Christian behaviour, and how far it suggests that Gladstone may actually have disliked Disraeli's policies rather than his person, cannot now be known.

The powerful impulses which brought Gladstone back to the centre of British politics in the autumn of 1876 were to lead, eventually, to his second Government in 1880. It took some time, both for Gladstone and for others, before it became clear what was to be the nature of the process which the Bulgarian Atrocities campaign had begun. Privately driven eastwards constantly, as the journal shows, Gladstone was reluctant to accept what were to be the full public implications of his position. Two days after the great meeting at Blackheath on 9 September 1876, he records telling Granville 'how pleasant it would be to me if he could publicly lead the present movement',[6] Gladstone seeing his own role, perhaps, as a writer of pamphlets and articles (he began a second pamphlet a few days after his talk with Granville, but converted it, 'I think under a right instinct', into a long letter to the newspapers).[7]

Gladstone was surprised to find a significant section of public opinion, especially non-metropolitan opinion, as anti-Turkish, or more so, as himself. πήγη (spring, fountain) was the docket he wrote on the letter of Alfred Days,

[1] 29 Dec. 78.
[2] Speech at Oxford, see 30 Jan. 78n.; Beaconsfield's relations with the Queen and with his Cabinet did raise a hypothetical personal condemnation; see 17 Jan. 78n.
[3] To Argyll, 26 Oct. 80; see also to Acton, 19 Sept. 80.
[4] Phillimore's Diary, 26 January 1878.
[5] 29 May 80; an extract from Brandes' text is given at that day's note.
[6] 11 Sept. 76.
[7] 14 Sept. 76.

secretary of the Workmen's Hyde Park Demonstration Committee in August 1876.[1] On a tour of Northumbria late in September 1876, he found himself pressed to speak wherever he went. Though his visits to villages were 'without notice', 'the same feelings were again manifested as we went along our route'.[2] Even when attending the theatre in Liverpool he found that 'I was never so well received in that town'.[3]

He had good cause to be wary of public opinion. It had thrown him out of South-East Lancashire in 1868; it had rewarded his first Government with the first Conservative electoral majority since 1841; it had failed to respond to 'Vaticanism'; it had begun a legal assault on High-Church ritualism. 'The People's William' had certainly had his popular successes, but they had not led to real warmth or popular affection. Gladstone's differences from his followers had always been as obvious as the common ground between them. In the years 1876–80 this was to change. A real empathy seemed to develop among the very different groups which made up the campaign;[4] a genuine fusion seemed to occur between certain sections of the Victorian ruling classes and 'labouring men'.[5]

By the end of 1876, Gladstone had become the central figure of the campaign, rather than the valuable extra asset which his *Bulgarian Horrors* pamphlet had made him appear in September. The Resolutions which he moved in the Commons in May 1877 showed him to be not merely the Government's most effective opponent on the Eastern Question but also the dominant figure in the Opposition, whether formally leader or not. In the initial phase of the campaign, Gladstone had resisted speaking (a speech being regarded by contemporaries as much more directly a political act than a pamphlet), because to make speeches while formally in retirement made him 'seem a rogue and imposter'.[6] A 'rogue and imposter' he may well have continued to seem to the embattled Lord Hartington, nominally and, in terms of day-to-day business, actually the leader of the Party in the Commons, but to Gladstone it was clear that, at the least, he was back in action for as long as the iniquities of the Government continued. The initiative thus lay with the Cabinet and the Prime Minister, as it always must for a government with a comfortable majority,[7] including the initiative of deciding on the date of the final reckoning, the dissolution. As Gladstone moved again to the centre of the political stage in 1876–77, he could not foresee that to the central errors of 'Turkism' were to be added the buttresses of South Africa and Afghanistan, which taken together, would lead to a general condemnation of 'Beaconsfieldism'.

Since Gladstone did not have the political initiative—a novel experience for a man hardly out of office since 1859—and since it was in no way clear that the Eastern Question Campaign implied an eventual return to office, he continued to try to draw a distinction between 'the part assigned to me in the Eastern

[1] 23 Aug. 76n.   [2] 5 Oct. 76.   [3] 17 Nov. 76.
[4] Well analysed in Shannon, *passim*.
[5] 29 Sept. 76.   [6] 23 Sept. 76.
[7] In Gladstone's previous period of opposition, 1866–8, the initiative had lain almost equally between the Government and the Opposition, for the Government was in a minority should the Opposition reunite, as it did over Gladstone's Irish Church Resolutions and over the abolition of compulsory Church Rates.

Question',[1] and a return to systematic political activity across the board. He described his position in a letter in October 1876 to W. P. Adam, the Liberal chief whip:

> I hope you will discourage the idea of any banquet to me in Edinburgh or elsewhere. I am a follower and not a leader in the Liberal party and nothing will induce me to do an act indicative of a desire to change my position. Any such act would be a positive breach of faith on my part towards those whom I importuned as I may say to allow me to retire, and whom I left to undertake a difficult and invidious office. True I have been forced, by obligations growing out of the past, to take a prominent part on the Eastern question; but I postponed it as long as I could, and have done all in my power, perhaps even too much, to keep it apart from the general course of politics & of party connection.[2]

During 1877 there are some indications that he realised this was beginning to be an untenable position. His reaction to the three large parties of Liberals which visited Hawarden in the summer of 1877 suggests a little movement. The first, a band of Liberal pilgrims from Bolton which collected splinters from the axe as relics, was greeted with some irritation—'we were nearly killed with kindness'—and Gladstone tried to avoid speaking.[3] But on the third group, from Bacup, he merely comments, 'It is the *reporting* that makes the difficulty in these things.'[4] 'Piracy in Borneo', written in the summer of 1877, marked a widening of the area of political controversy.[5] In November 1877 he decisively defeated Northcote, the Chancellor of the Exchequer, for the Lord Rectorship of Glasgow University, confirming the strength of Liberalism among the youth of Glasgow—the Rectorship campaigns were highly political and very seriously contested—and to some extent also confirming his own return to popularity among the Scottish university classes—he had been defeated for the Edinburgh Chancellorship in 1868. (Not too much should be made of this, however, since, ironically, the Tory Duke of Buccleuch, father of Lord Dalkeith, his opponent in Midlothian in 1880, was elected Chancellor by the Glasgow graduates in 1878.)[6]

On the one hand, 'quivering hopes' were held that a return to sustained work on the Homeric Thesaurus would be possible and a good deal of work on it was done.[7] On the other, no attempt at a birthday retrospect was made on 29 December 1877, and only a brief comment was noted on the 31st—usually both days for introspective writing—and this may indicate an unusual degree of uncertainty about the future.

Too much should not be read into such straws in the wind. It is clear that through 1877 and the first part of 1878, Gladstone was holding back to see what events would bring. His position was consistent, if inconvenient to the Party leadership: he was active in the Eastern Question Campaign, for which the leadership had shown little enthusiasm, and which was unlikely to last in

---

[1] 31 Dec. 77.   [2] To W. P. Adam, 4 October 1876, Blair Adam MS 4/431.
[3] 4 Aug. 77.   [4] 20 Aug. 77.   [5] 26 May 77.
[6] Gladstone declined to stand for the Rectorship of Aberdeen University; see 13 Feb. 75. Rectors were elected by the undergraduates, Chancellors by the graduates. Unfortunately, these hard-fought and fascinating contests have as yet no historian. For the Edinburgh contests, see above, v. xxxix. For Glasgow, see 19 May 76, 11 Apr. 77, 3 Dec. 77n.
[7] 13 Aug. 77.

full flood until the dissolution, but otherwise he was an independent force, as he had been in 1875. As the Liberal Party had no formal structure, and hardly even informal rules, his behaviour was difficult in Party terms either to condemn or to justify.

Gladstone developed 'five reasons' to support his position, describing them for the first time in an important conversation with Sir Robert Phillimore in March 1879,[1] and maintaining them even after the first Midlothian Campaign clearly committed him to some sort of return to office, should the Liberals win. When Hartington tried to resign as Liberal leader in the Commons in December 1879, Gladstone effectively forced the Whig leaders to continue their Party leadership, while maintaining his own freedom of action.[2] There were good political as well as personal reasons for this. Gladstone's campaign worked outwards from what the young H. H. Asquith described as 'the extreme left' of the Liberal Party[3] (the left/right dichotomy was just entering common usage in British political vocabulary), a position now apparently broadened and, in Whiggish eyes, confirmed by his comments on land while in Midlothian: 'compulsory expropriation is a thing which for an adequate public object is in itself admissible and so far sound in principle'.[4] Having Granville and Hartington as leaders to an extent kept on ice awkward questions about Gladstone's relationship with the Whigs on foreign, imperial, and land policy and perhaps also with nonconformists on English disestablishment and education. As Wolverton, the former Liberal chief whip and Gladstone's envoy in negotiations about the leadership, remarked in 1879: 'many of our weak kneed ones, would feel some alarm if H[artington] went from the front *now*'.[5]

V

'The great sabbath dawning in the East' in February 1878[6] marked the sharpest point of political conflict since 1876, as Carnarvon resigned and the Cabinet backed its sending of the fleet to Constantinople with a Vote of Credit of £6 million for a possible military expedition, and, a little later, by the calling out of the Reserves. Tension mounted in London as well as in Constantinople. The police defended Gladstone's house in Harley Street from a mob thought to have been organised by the Tory high command: 'there is strange work behind

---

[1] 30 Mar. 79. He repeated the 'five' to Rosebery verbally, and to Bright by letter, during the first Midlothian Campaign; see 28 Nov. 79. He discouraged Knowles from including a passage in an article by J. Guinness Rogers proposing his formal return, see 7 July 79.

In the footnotes to this volume, I have quoted quite extensively from Robert Phillimore's diary. The holograph of this was not found among Phillimore's papers at The Coppice, Henley, though a note referring to it was found, along with his wife's extensive diary; it must, unfortunately, now be supposed lost. The quotations are from a copy of extracts referring to Gladstone made by one of Phillimore's sons for Morley at the time of the writing of the biography; this copy is in the Phillimore MSS now in Christ Church, Oxford. The dates all coincide with Gladstone's notes of the conversations, and it is reasonable to suppose that the copy is accurate.

[2] The crisis is described in Morley, ii, ch. vii and Rossi, *T.A.P.S.*, lxviii, part 8, 103ff.

[3] [H. H. Asquith] 'The English Extreme Left', *The Spectator*, 12 August 1876; see *Bulletin of the Institute of Historical Research*, xlix. 150.

[4] *Speeches in Scotland* (1879), 102.

[5] Wolverton to Gladstone, 20 December 1879, Add MS 44349, f. 121.

[6] 10 Feb. 78.

the curtain if one could but get at it. The instigators are those really guilty: no one can wonder at the tools.'[1] Soon after this 'the news of the Peace arrived. It seems scarcely to leave openings for future quarrel.'[2] None the less, the Gladstones still could not walk to their house,[3] and royalty became notably hostile, the Duke of Cambridge (the Commander in Chief), 'black as thunder, did not even hold out his hand'.[4]

In the face of a 'dissolution which might be summary', Gladstone announced the end of his connection with his Greenwich constituency. His relationship with his Greenwich constituents had always been uneasy, and in November 1875 he had told Phillimore: 'Certainly, if it is in my option, I shall not stand again for Greenwich to be hustled between Boords and Liardets [the Tory M.P.s for the three-member constituency]. But this please mention to *no one*.'[5] In October 1876 he had privately informed Adam, as Liberal chief whip, of his decision: 'I am desirous you should know what may not yet have been directly stated to you that if a Dissolution were to occur nothing would induce me again to stand for Greenwich.' He told Adam this 'because Dissolution is at present among those remote possibilities which a new turn of the wheel *might* any day bring within the realm of the probable'. At that time—shortly after the start of the atrocities campaign—Gladstone was 'in two minds whether if this were disposed of I should incline to stand again *at all* or not: but in any case I am limited to an extremely small number of seats'.[6] Since the Eastern question was clearly not 'disposed of', his public announcement in 1878 of his decision not to stand again in Greenwich carefully left open the option of standing elsewhere.[7]

Gladstone's response to San Stephano and the Jingo outburst of the early months of 1878 was thus to open the process of finding another seat, for that was what his announcement to Greenwich implied. Various prospects, including Leeds, quickly presented themselves; these were set aside, rather than rejected outright.[8] Moreover, there is an indication that Gladstone was beginning to see himself as a political tribune of the people—a moral tribune, the Atrocities Campaign had already made him—representing right behaviour against a Court and a Prime Minister seen as increasingly unconstitutional in their behaviour. He comments at this time, after being snubbed by members of the Court,[9] on Prothero's Whiggish account of Simon de Montfort: 'What a giant! and what a noble giant! What has survival of the fittest done towards beating, or towards reaching him?'[10] In such a mood, choice of a seat would be an awkward business.

[1] 24 Feb. 78; see also 25 Feb. 78 for Gladstone's involvement with medical student jingoism, and 10 Mar. 78. London was the chief 'Jingoborough'; see Hugh Cunningham, 'Jingoism in 1877-88', *Victorian Studies*, xiv. 429 (June 1971). The rowdyism was reminiscent of Tory anti-popery riots earlier in the century, with the aristocracy cynically exploiting xenophobia; see G. A. Cahill, 'The Protestant Association and the anti-Maynooth agitation of 1845', *Catholic Historical Review*, xliii (October 1957).

[2] 4 Mar.78.   [3] 10 Mar. 78.   [4] 11 Mar.78.

[5] To Sir Robert Phillimore, 7 November 1875; Phillimore MSS.

[6] To W. P. Adam, 'Private', 30 October 1876; Blair Adam MS 4/431.   [7] 7, 23 Mar. 78.

[8] 11-13, 28 Mar. 78. The predominantly Nonconformist tone of Liberal politics in Leeds probably encouraged Gladstone's caution.   [9] 11 Mar. 78.

[10] 12 Mar. 78; Gladstone shared the general non-Tory alarm that, first, Disraeli was excessively acting as the Queen's minister, betraying Cabinet colleagues to her, and second, that there were threats to Cabinet control of foreign policy through the intervention of the Court. Carnarvon was the chief inside source for his fears; see 26 Jan., 14 Feb., 26 May, 31 Oct. 78.

Rosebery, the Narcissus of Scottish Liberalism, and one of the wealthiest men in Whig politics, seems to have taken the initiative together with Adam, the Liberal chief whip and a lowland Scottish M.P.: 'Lord Rosebery *cum* Mr Adam' waited on Gladstone in London in May 1878 and 'the Midlothian case' was opened, with further discussion in June.[1] The initiative was probably taken by the Scots, encouraged by Gladstone's easy success in the Glasgow Rectorial in 1877, so as to try to strengthen the Liberal cause in the Forth–Clyde valley. Rather characteristically, for all his suspicion of the 'classes', Gladstone talked this over, not with a Whig or a Liberal, but with his old Tractarian crony, Sir Walter James, a Conservative M.P. in the 1840s.[2] By January 1879, the case was closed: Gladstone was committed to campaign for the seat, and he opened his prosecution with a powerful letter accepting the Liberal nomination.[3]

The character of the constituency will be discussed shortly; but this must be set in the context of a campaign which broadened gradually and sometimes hesitantly from the relatively limited issue of 'the Bulgarian Horrors' to the wholesale condemnation of innovative Toryism. A former Prime Minister leading a great popular crusade was a new phenomenon in European politics, and before examining the substance of the objections to Beaconsfieldism, which lead us into the policies of Gladstone's second Government, some comment on the nature of the campaign is necessary. From the start, Gladstone saw the movement of protest as founded 'on grounds, not of political party, not even of mere English nationality, not of Christian faith, but on the largest and broadest ground of all—the ground of our common humanity'.[4] At a time when Continental political parties were increasingly narrowly based in terms both of class and doctrine, Gladstone's appeal was for a Broad-Church movement which stressed integration and comprehension. This was to be a Popular Front of moral outrage, a coalition ranging from the Roman Catholic ecumenist Ambrose Phillipps de Lisle to the secularist Charles Bradlaugh, a campaign ranging from the dignified splendour of the St. James's Hall meeting in December 1876 (chaired by the Duke of Westminster) to a 'Coffeehouse Company Meeting in Seven Dials' in April 1878,[5] a resurgence on a new humanitarian footing of the old Liberal spectrum of the 1860s which had disintegrated over the religious squabbles of 1873–74. Ironically, given the intense religious feeling invested in it by Gladstone personally and by many of its participants, the Midlothian Campaign—with the issue of Scottish disestablishment neatly side-stepped[6]—pointed the way towards the secular humanitarianism of twentieth-century Liberalism.[7]

Hitherto, Gladstone's public career had been in large measure a working out of the consequences of his changing view of the means of achieving 'religious nationality'. The religious 'expostulation' of the Vatican pamphlets seemed anomalous, even anachronistic, to many contemporaries and from the

---

[1] 16 May, 24 June 78.   [2] 17 May 78.   [3] To Cowan, 30 Jan. 79.
[4] Speech at Blackheath, 9 Sept. 76.   [5] 8 Dec. 76, 9 Apr. 78.
[6] See 2 Nov. 78n., 23 May 79n. Privately, Gladstone had noted: 'Spoke on the Scottish Established Church: which, in that character, has not I think another decade of years to live'; 18 June 78.
[7] As G. M. Young observed (*Portrait of an Age* (1960 ed.), 166): 'The mind of 1890 would have startled the mind of 1860 by its frank secularism.'

mid-1870s Gladstone came to recognise that his personal religious opinions had to remain personal if he hoped to achieve political results. The acceptance of the Midlothian nomination emphasised this, for Gladstone became a candidate in a country where, as an Episcopalian, he was a nonconformist. Whereas in his years as M.P. for Oxford University he had represented the heart of the Anglican national establishment, he now aspired to represent constituents most of whose religious views, however ecumenical his tone, he privately regarded as in schism from the Episcopalian Church, which he believed to be the true Church in Scotland. He saw the Church government of the Kirk and the Free Church as deficient in apostolicity. Though he attended afternoon and evening service in Established and Free Churches in Edinburgh, he would have communicated in neither.

Gladstone's isolation on religious questions in his own party and his need subsequently to subordinate his own religious priorities, bold though they were, to a political world increasingly secular in tone and language, reflected a general losing of the initiative by the Anglican Church. That church's hegemonic political, cultural, and intellectual claims of the 1830s had given way, partly in their political dimension under Gladstone's leadership, to the pluralism of the 1850s and 1860s. But that pluralism had been a pluralism of Christian denominations; paganism had been a regret but not an intrusion. Now, as the 1880s dawned, pluralism linked Anglicans not merely with Scottish Presbyterians, Methodists, Congregationalists, and Roman Catholics, but increasingly with agnostics and secularists, and public language began to assume not merely the latter's existence but their integration.

'I seemed to see the old dream of organic unity surviving where moral unity is lost' wrote Manning in 1865 of the 1840s.[1] As that dream faded, Gladstone attempted to reconstruct 'moral unity' through the humanitarianism of the party of progress; his religious objectives, once the prescription for the conscience of the nation, became private aims, pursued discreetly by a public figure accepting the religious reserve required for the preservation of 'moral unity' over a wide front—a tacit acceptance of secularism. 'Religious nationality' of the Coleridgian Idealist sort found its replacement in the more explicitly political ideology of a progressive citizenship. None the less, the clerisy which conditioned this political nation, though socially more broadly based, remained surprisingly unchanged, with Gladstone, even at seventy, still its rising hope.

The successes of the Liberals in the 1860s had taken place in the context of the pre-1867 franchise. Could the spectacular result of 1868, when the extended electorate had not had time to form a pattern, be repeated in more settled electoral conditions? By what means could a movement of protest become a parliamentary majority? The extended but still limited electorate in the boroughs greatly exercised politicians generally. The old, 'face-to-face' communitarian politics of the 1832–67 period, supervised by solicitors with generous bribes, were ending. With the secret ballot of 1872, the poll-book—the briber's book of reckoning—was no more. The Liberal Party, at least most of it and certainly Gladstone, was committed to introducing household suffrage in

---

[1] H. E. Manning, *The Temporal Mission of the Holy Ghost* (6th ed., 1909), 31.

the counties in addition to the boroughs,[1] thus prospectively compounding the difficulties.

Politicians' reactions to the problems of political communication and control fell into two categories, organisational and rhetorical. Gorst for the Tories and Chamberlain and others for the Liberals developed the first, through the Conservative Central Office (*ca.* 1870) and the National Liberal Federation (1877) respectively. Bureaucratic developments of this sort were by no means completely welcome to political leaders: political machines might have a life of their own, and tended, especially in the nineteenth century, greatly to increase the power and influence of politicians with strong regional bases. Joseph Chamberlain was the most effective of these caucus politicians, but he was by no means unique.

Gladstone became the supreme exponent of the rhetorical alternative, and he is to be seen in this volume of the diaries developing this role both self-consciously and unselfconsciously, both the deliberate developer of a method, and at the same time the unaware prisoner of a media-structure. As a public figure, Gladstone had few assets save his words and his personality expressed in words. He was the epitome of G. C. Brodrick's category of politicians who rose by 'brains and energy'.[2] The Whigs had money, and they used it; the local and regional politicians sat at the centre of a complex structure of interlocking business, local governmental, and charitable interests. Gladstone hardly spent a penny on elections; his personal patronage extended to two Church of England livings; and he had in opposition no secretary, let alone a political machine. While Whigs and caucus men dealt in leases, rents, contracts, donations, and votes, Gladstone and those like him dealt in words. When Gladstone did not speak or write, his political force disappeared. 'The word in man is a great instrument of power', Gladstone told a conference on preaching in 1877.[3] Words could be spoken or written or, as was the case with many of Gladstone's words, they could be simultaneously both spoken and written, the first by the speaker, the second by the shorthand reporter.

Words could be written in pamphlets or periodical articles, the traditional way of making one's point among the educated élite, a method by the 1870s much more personalised as the *Contemporary*, *Fortnightly* and *Nineteenth Century*, and other periodicals offered signed rather than anonymous articles. Gladstone certainly took full advantage of this medium, as the Appendix of his published works 1875–80 shows,[4] and he was careful to orchestrate the publication of his pamphlets and articles with releases to the newspapers about their preparation and their contents. The publication of a Gladstone pamphlet was a political event in itself, and Gladstone saw to it that the maximum effect was achieved.

Words could be spoken in the House of Commons, and read in Hansard and the reports in the newspapers. As parliamentary business became more complex and more clogged, this was a less effective and less used means of political communication, though it remained, of course, the most regular forum

---

[1] See letter to Forster, 23 July 73; also 11 Mar. 76n., 30 May 76.
[2] G. C. Brodrick, 'Liberals and Whigs', in his *Political Studies* (1879), 249.
[3] 22 Mar. 77.   [4] See below, pp. 659–60.

for political speaking. As early as 1870 Alex Ritchie of the *Leeds Mercury* told the Press Association, the telegraphic agency through which from 1868 the provincial press gained much of its material, that his paper 'would rather not have long Parliamentary reports, except on very special occasions, such as that on which Mr Gladstone introduced his Irish Church Bill. It would, as a rule, be a great inconvenience to me to give more than two columns of a [parliamentary] debate. Gentlemen like to peruse their newspaper at breakfast time, and they will not always care to wade through four or five columns of Parliamentary matter.'[1] Certainly, Gladstone used this means of communication throughout 1875-80, and a number of his speeches in the Commons were reprinted as pamphlets.[2] But the number of occasions, such as the debate on the Resolutions of 7-14 May 1877, when public attention could be easily focused on a parliamentary debate was limited. Moreover, the Resolutions affair showed the limited use of the Commons to Gladstone when he was not in a position to dictate Party business: 'This day I took my decision [to move Resolutions]: a severe one, in face of my not having a single approver in the *Upper* official circle.'[3] To avoid humiliation in the vote, he had to agree to move only the first Resolution,[4] a 'nominal' concession, given the way that he treated the debate,[5] but none the less an incident that highlighted what Gladstone felt to be the wide discrepancy of passion between the Liberal leadership and the campaign in the country.

The conjunction of pamphlet and extra-parliamentary speech in September 1876 marked the way of the future, though Gladstone was slow to take it. Extra-parliamentary speechmaking by cabinet-level politicians was not altogether new, though it was still rather unusual. Palmerston had been an effective exponent of it to an extent little recognised by historians.[6] Gladstone had distanced himself from the parliamentary Party by his use of it in the 1860s, and shown himself aware of its potentiality,[7] though during his first ministry he had, for several reasons, used the public speech sparingly. Disraeli's famous speeches at the Crystal Palace and in Manchester in 1872 had been an important element in confirming his position in the Tory leadership and in seizing the political initiative for the Conservatives. In the 1870s the number of extra-parliamentary speeches reported in the press markedly increased, because the means of making speeches nationally available through the telegraph networks became technically more sophisticated. After the Telegraph Act of 1868, with its clauses favouring the use of the telegraph by newspapers, the Press Association and Exchange Telegraph became the chief agents of political communication in Britain.

A political speech by a major politician now had two audiences; the audience

---

[1] G. Scott, *Reporter Anonymous. The story of the Press Association* (1968), 41.

[2] See, e.g., 30 July, 3 Aug. 78. A further disadvantage of the Commons was the lateness of its sittings; speeches after midnight could not be fully reported in next day's papers, as H. W. Lucy explained to Gladstone at the time of the Resolutions debate; see 14 May 77n.

[3] 27 Apr. 77.   [4] 5 May 77.   [5] Ibid.

[6] See David Steele, 'Gladstone and Palmerston, 1855-65', in P. J. Jagger, ed., *Gladstone, Politics and Religion* (1985), 117. I have tried to set the phenomenon of platform speaking in a general context in 'Rhetoric and Political Communication in Britain, 1860-1970', to be published in P. Pombeni, ed., *La trasformazione politica nell'Europa Liberale 1870-1890* (Bologna, 1986?).

[7] See above, v. xl-xlvi.

present at the meeting, and the readership of the next day's newspapers.[1] Gladstone's campaigns for the Midlothian seat made excellent use of both, but it
was the second that was the more important. When he spoke at the inaugural
meeting of the National Liberal Federation in 1877, he noted: 'A most intelligent orderly appreciative audience: but they were 25000 and the building of no
acoustic merits so that the strain was excessive.'[2] This, however, by no means
diminished the success of the occasion, for the speech was nationally available
next morning, *verbatim* in several columns. Gladstone had discovered—and
swiftly in the late 1870s moved to exploit—the central feature of modern political communication: the use of one medium to gain access to another (in this
case, the use of a political meeting to gain access to the national debating
society made possible by the popular press). Gladstone was not, of course,
alone in speaking on 'The Platform'; it was common form by the late 1870s for
Ministers and members of the ex-Cabinet. It is hard to say how much others—
for example Hartington who spoke publicly in 1880 much more often than
Gladstone[3]—were performing in response to his lead. But it would be true to
say that his speeches had that element of danger combined with breadth which
gained them pre-eminence in their time.

The dual nature of the audience for the late-Victorian political speech is very
well illustrated by the Midlothian Campaign. Early in 1879 Gladstone accepted
a requisition to run for Edinburghshire, or Midlothian as it was popularly
known. Gladstone did not agree to run until he knew that he could win. He
knew that he could win because Midlothian was an old-style county constituency, about as far removed in character from the new, household-suffrage
post-1867 borough seats as could be found; only about 15% of the adult males
in the constituency were registered to vote, in contrast to the average of about
55% in the boroughs. There were 3,260 registered electors for Edinburghshire,
contrasted with 49,000 in Leeds, the other constituency for which Gladstone
was returned in 1880.[4]

J. J. Reid and Ralph Richardson, the Edinburgh lawyers who ran the Midlothian Campaign under Rosebery's superintendence, organised the questioning of each registered voter and precise analyses of the expected vote were
produced. Adam confidently and accurately told Gladstone in January 1879:
'The return ... will shew a Liberal majority of about 200 after giving *all*
the doubtfuls (251) to the Conservatives.'[5] As Granville told Adam, 'I was
against Midlothian when Gladstone first mentioned it to me, but was converted by you and Roseberry [*sic*] on the ground of the stimulus it would give
to the Scotch Election, and of its being a certainty.'[6] Gladstone made the

---

[1] The point is well demonstrated by the illustrations above, vii. 206; the engraving clearly shows
the engraver's, and Gladstone's, awareness of the importance of stenographers.

[2] 31 May 77.

[3] In the 1880 campaign, Hartington made twenty-four major speeches, Gladstone fifteen, and
W. H. Smith, Bright, and Northcote six each, according to W. Saunders, *The New Parliament, 1880*
(1880), 38; see also H. Jephson, *The Platform* (1892), ii. 522.

[4] See F. W. S. Craig, *British Parliamentary Results 1832–1885* (1977) and H. McCalmont, *The
Parliamentary Poll Book of All Elections* (1910).

[5] W. P. Adam to Gladstone, 10 January 1879, Add MS 56444, f. 123.

[6] Granville to W. P. Adam, 17 January 1879, Blair Adam MS 4/431.

same point publicly when accepting the nomination: 'You have ... been kind enough to supply me with evidence which entirely satisfies my mind that the invitation expresses the desire of the majority of the constituency.' His observation was not an exhortatory hope but a fact.[1] The energetic creation of 'faggot votes' by the Tories, and by the Liberals in response, was the characteristic manoeuvre of the traditional pre-1867 political organiser; 'faggots' only worked when the numbers were small and the pledges well-known and reliable.[2] On the other hand, it was accepted that these forecasts would only be accurate if the campaign was vigorous. As Gladstone observed when he agreed to be nominated: 'if this thing is to be done at all it must be done thoroughly and you may rely upon it that I will not do it by halves.'[3]

The Midlothian Campaign thus had little to do with winning the Edinburghshire seat. It had everything to do with establishing Gladstonianism as the dominant force in Liberal politics and in winning the unknown and unpredictable new electorate in the boroughs. It was essentially a campaign not in or for Midlothian, but from Midlothian. The Campaign used an old-style seat as a base for new-style politics; it was bold, but it was not risky.

The real audience of the campaigns of 1879 and 1880 was the newspaper-reading public, whether Liberal, doubtful, or Tory. With the defection of its flag-ship, the *Daily Telegraph*, in 1876–77,[4] the Liberal press had begun the slow slide towards Conservatism which in the mid-1880s became an avalanche, but one advantage of the political speech was that it negated the political complexion of the newspaper, for Conservative papers reported the Campaign as energetically as Liberal ones. However stridently a leader-writer might reply, the speech constituted a four-column advertisement in a hostile paper, as well as being a large exhortation in a friendly one.

The speech of a first-rank politician appeared *verbatim* and with little in the way of accompanying report. There was no mediator between the speaker at the meeting and the reader of his words next day in his house, railway carriage, public house, or club. The reporter's job was to transcribe the speaker's words

[1] To J. Cowan, 30 Jan. 79.

[2] Reid told Rosebery (26 January [?1879], NLS 10075, f. 13): 'the chief matter really has been the unbounded creation of faggots, but I really think they have not done *at most* more than 100 in this way, and the largeness of the margin together with the natural increase of the constituency (now that Edinburgh is getting beyond its Parliamentary Boundary) ought to be quite sufficient'. W. P. Adam briefly felt alarmed: 'The Tories have attempted to *garotte* the real constituency by choking them with faggots. What they have been able to do up to the present time does not *really* affect the position, but if the general election be delayed till after next November (which is possible) and they *succeed* in their garotting ... the Committee will have to consider the propriety of your seat being risked and will have to say whether or not you should withdraw stating fully the reasons. In order to neutralise the present majority *and* the natural Liberal increase of the constituency they will have to create faggots to a disgraceful extent but they are not troubled by scruples of conscience' (Adam to Gladstone, 4 February 1879, Add MS 56444, f. 135). These fears were not realised and the Midlothian Liberals were as confident under the 1880 register as they had been under that of 1879: 'I consider Midlothian is ours till 1 Nov. 1881, & I hear the other side now admit Mr. Gladstone will win' (Richardson to Rosebery, 3 February 1880, NLS 10075, f. 188).

[3] To W. P. Adam, 11 January 1879, Blair Adam MS 4/431.

[4] See S. Koss, *The Rise and Fall of the Political Press in Britain* (1981), i. 211ff. The row over the Negropontis affair (see above, p. xliv, n. 4) between Gladstone and Levy-Lawson exemplified the split at a personal level.

accurately, not to interpret to the readers what he thought the speaker had meant. The audience actually present was important for local politics but nationally it could be redundant. Walter Hepburn, known as 'Mr. Gladstone's Fat Reporter'—he was the Press Association reporter with special responsibility for Gladstone's speeches—took down on the moving train a speech intended for a local deputation but not delivered because the train left the station before Gladstone had time to speak.[1] It is interesting that the young Gladstone, in one of his first pieces of journalism, chose to write 'On Eloquence'; he noted that eloquence was usually discussed in terms of the Senate, the Pulpit, and the Bar; he broadened the discussion to include 'less celebrated kinds of oratory' and among these was 'Advertising . . . Eloquence'.[2] A sharp awareness, not merely of the ideological importance of rhetoric, but also of the mechanics of its presentation in the context of nineteenth-century technology, thus characterised Gladstone's approach to public speaking.

At a more mundane level, whether the occasion was a major speech or a brief (i.e. half-an-hour) address to a cookery or gardening society, Gladstone was, at the least, a tremendous old trouper, giving a good performance even when ill. He himself used an acting metaphor to describe how he coped with a major occasion: 'Spoke $2\frac{1}{2}$ hours [on the Congress of Berlin]. I was in body much below par but put on the steam perforce.'[3] It was partly this ability to 'put on the steam' which ensured that he always had a full house, even for a matinée.

The great orations whether on the platform or in the Commons were, like all Gladstone's speeches, delivered from only the briefest notes. The speech was never written out in advance.[4] In one of the most tumultuous of the debates recorded in this volume, the Resolutions debate of May 1877, after 'over two hours . . . assaulted from every quarter', a speech of two and a half hours was delivered perforce without a note. Characteristically, the diary entry gives a short but accurate summary of the effect of the speech, and notes his 'wormlike' feeling, but does not draw attention to the personally dramatic element of the evening: 'I could make little use of them from having forgotten my eyeglass' reads the docket on the bundle of redundant speech notes.[5] An example of Gladstone's speech notes, those used for part of the opening Midlothian speech, is reproduced below (these notes are, perhaps, a little fuller than those for a more usual occasion). The brevity of the notes did not, however, mean an absence of preparation, indeed perhaps the reverse, as the triumph of the 'forgotten eyeglass' speech suggests. But the condensation of the preparation into a few short headings was deliberately designed so that the speech would exemplify the character of the speaker:

there cannot be too much preparation if it be of the right kind. No doubt it is the preparation of matter; it is the accumulation and thorough digestion of knowledge; it is

---

[1] G. Scott, *Reporter Anonymous. The story of the Press Association* (1968), 77–8, which also gives an example of Gladstone dictating a speech to Hepburn for telegraphing in advance of its actual delivery: 'the train did not stop as it had been scheduled to do; Gladstone did not make his speech; but the report of it was published just the same'.

[2] [W. E. Gladstone], 'On Eloquence', *The Eton Miscellany*, ii. 110 (1827); see 1, 10 Oct. 27.

[3] 30 July 78.

[4] Consequently, the speaker relied on the newspaper report to assemble a final version of what was said; see 3 Aug. 78.

[5] 7 May 77.

the forgetfulness of personal and selfish motives; it is the careful consideration of method; it is that a man shall make himself as a man suited to speak to men, rather than that he should make himself as a machine ready to deliver to men certain pre-conceived words.[1]

The extemporary speech had always been required in the House of Commons. Gladstone now used it as the basis for the development of a national debate through the columns of the national and provincial press.

The development of the phenomenon of 'the Platform' coincided with the high noon of Victorian religiosity. This was not accidental. The tradition of long sermons, especially in Scotland, had accustomed audiences to expect addresses of an hour and more, and had trained them to concentrate over such a long period. These great addresses thus sprang from and dovetailed into the natural habits and expectations of a churchgoing society. Many of the Midlothian speeches were given in churches, and on one occasion Gladstone spoke from the pulpit.[2] The Midlothian speeches were in a direct sense Gladstone's Bampton Lectures.

The Midlothian Campaign represented the flowering of a new style of politics, long in germination. As politics became more bureaucratised, extra-parliamentary speech-making provided the means for the Liberal intelligentsia to preserve its influence in British political life, and in doing so it linked the intellectual force of Liberal politics to a particular form of media-presentation. The full force of the popularisation of the Liberal ethos rose with the political press of the 1860s and died with it in the 1920s. Max Weber, in a justly famous analysis, argued that Gladstone's campaign represented the arrival of 'a Caesar-ist plebiscitarian element in politics—the dictator of the battlefield of elections', the natural concomitant to the caucus system which had 'arisen in the Liberal party in connection with Gladstone's ascent to power'.[3] Certainly Gladstone encouraged the caucuses and the National Liberal Federation in a way alarming to the 'notables' ('Honoratioren') of the Party, as Weber called them. Merely to address the N.L.F.'s inaugural meeting was seen by them as a radical act. But this introduced no new element into Gladstone's political position, which, from the 1860s, had always been one of careful distance from Party organisation. He was equally careful not to be drawn into the affairs of the N.L.F., or of the Marylebone Liberal Assocation, the caucus which came to run Liberal politics in his area of London, even though as respectable a figure as G. J. Goschen was its first chairman.[4]

[1] See 22 Mar. 77n.

[2] See W. Saunders, op. cit., 143–4.

[3] 'Politics as a vocation', a lecture given in 1918, translated in H. H. Gerth and C. Wright Mills, From Max Weber (1948), 106; the German reads: 'Ein cäsaristisch-plebiszitäres Element in der Politik: der Diktator des Wahlschlachtfeldes, trat auf den Plan' (Max Weber, Gesammelte Politische Schriften (1958), 523). Clearly Weber was wrong in his view of the rise of the caucus, which related to Gladstone more through opposition to his Cabinet's Education Bill in 1870 than through concern for his return in 1877.

[4] He did however referee a dispute between rival candidates there, see the series of letters from Gladstone to S. Chick, its secretary, read to its inaugural meeting: 'I feel it to be my especial duty at the present juncture to avoid taking a prominent part in any demonstrations bearing on politics generally with respect to which I can exercize an option, however sincerely I may wish them well', a position consistent with his statements about the leadership; St Pancras Guardian, 26 January 1878, 3a.

The Midlothian Campaign was more a counterweight to the caucus system than a development from it. As Gladstone had used extra-parliamentary oratory against the 'notables' in the 1860s, so he and his successors used the platform to outflank and to control local organisations rather than to represent them. Weber was right to point to 'the firm belief in the masses in the ethical substance of his policy'—this, we shall see, was exactly was Gladstone believed himself to be appealing to—and to 'their belief in the ethical character of his personality'. Gladstone had been aware since the 1860s of this charismatic element, of his own ability to exploit it, and of its dangers.[1] The phenomenon of being 'Gladstonised' while attending a meeting is well attested.[2] But Weber ignored the means of communication: the huge majority of electors met Gladstone on the column of a newspaper page, in a *verbatim* report of a two-hour speech, remarkably unadorned with ancillary description of the occasion, and with virtually no comment about the speaker himself. The absence of photographs in the daily newspapers reporting the speech was not compensated for by descriptions of dress or of facial expressions, or even by engravings, which were the prerogative of the weeklies such as *The Graphic* and *The Illustrated London News*, neither of which reached a really popular audience. There was the occasional cartoon, but usually only in the London evening papers or the cartoon weeklies.

A general impression of enthusiasm was given in the daily papers, but in such brief, dry tones as to be quite non-visceral. For most electors contact with the political leader was made through the rationalistic activity of the reading of his words as printed, without headlines and in small print, in the austere columns of the daily press. For a national leader, only a tiny proportion of the electorate—and that by custom within his own constituency—could have experience of the presence of the speaker personally or of the powerful harmonies of his voice.

The content of these speeches was, Gladstone fairly concluded, 'something like a detailed exposition of a difficult and complicated case'.[3] Planning the campaign in 1879, Gladstone intended 'to show up' the Tories by dealing with 'some given question in each place'.[4] Such demagogy as there was in Midlothian was the demagogy of a popular rationalism. No series of speeches intended to fill four columns of a serious newspaper for several days could be demagogic in the German sense: the medium of communication imposed literary and rationalistic standards upon the orator. The Midlothian speeches were popularly presented, but they contained much detailed argument and evidence. They presupposed considerable political knowledge on the part of their hearers and readers, and were addressed to an electorate assumed to be highly politicised. It is interesting that the most emotional section of the speeches— 'Remember the rights of the savage, as we call him'—was addressed to a special

[1] See, e.g. 14 Oct. 64.

[2] See 13 Mar. 80n. and Lloyd, *General election of 1880*, 152.

[3] *Political Speeches* (1879), 211; Weber called this 'the technique of apparently "letting sober facts speak for themselves"' (Gerth and Mills, 107); the translation softens Weber's perjorative tone ('der ein Techniker des scheinbar nüchternen "Die-Tatsachen-sprechen Lassens" war').

[4] To W. P. Adam, 14 November 1879, Blair Adam MS 4/431.

meeting of women, by definition non-voters (and in Gladstone's view rightly so) who, he told them he believed, had little taste for 'the harder, and sterner, and drier lessons of politics'.[1]

Although Midlothian emphasised a pattern of speeches, if not of meetings, which was to become normative in the 1880s, Gladstone saw the years of the campaign of the late 1870s as, at the time, unique, 'a crisis of an extraordinary character'.[2] He believed that Disraeli's Government had been 'vexing and alarming' an electorate not usually interested in the details of politics.[3] In an 'age of greater knowledge, man ought to grow more manly; to keep a sterner guard over passion', but the Disraeli Cabinet's policies had encouraged 'this want of sobriety, this loss of moral equilibrium', especially in 'large portions of what is termed society'.[4] 'Strange excesses' required exceptional explanations. Gladstone offered one in the form of an anecdote about Bishop Butler, who

> walking in his garden at Bristol . . . asked of his chaplain, Dean Tucker, whether, in the judgement of that noble man, it were possible that there could be in nations or kingdoms a frame of mind analogous to what constitutes madness in individuals? For, said the Bishop, if there cannot, it seems very difficult to account for the major part of the transactions recorded in history. Evidently he had in view the wars and conflicts, of which the blood-stained web of history has been usually woven.[5]

Only by a belief in such abrogations of reason could a theory of natural law be sustained. It was the duty of 'the leisured classes',[6] whose function was the government of the country, to 'soothe and tranquillize the minds of the people, not to set up false phantoms of glory'.[7] Gladstone thus saw the context of his return to sustained politics as being the failure in their duty of 'the classes', and especially those of metropolitan society. Gladstone had come to see certain sections of London society and its press as corrupted by money: 'if it be true that wealth and ease bring with them in a majority of cases an increased growth in the hardening crust of egotism and selfishness, the deduction thereby made from the capacity of right judgment in large and most important questions, may be greater than the addition which leisure, money, and opportunity have allowed'.[8]

Corruption by money is a constant theme in these years, most fully described in Gladstone's Address, delivered at the end of the first Midlothian Campaign, as Lord Rector of Glasgow University.[9] Among the wealthy classes, he told the undergraduates, rapid progress—'in itself a good'—had not been balanced by development of 'mental resources or pursuits'. The consequence was an unbalanced moral system among such people: 'disproportioned growth, if in large degree, is in the physical world deformity; in the moral and social world it is

---

[1] *Political Speeches* (1879), 90, 94. [2] Ibid., 18.
[3] Ibid., 22. [4] 'Paths of honour and of shame', 8.
[5] Ibid., 9. This anecdote was related by Josiah Tucker, the political economist, in the context of explaining war expenditure ('And all, alas! for what!!!!'); J. Tucker, *An humble address and earnest appeal . . . [on] a connection with, or a separation from the continental colonies of America* (1775), 20.
[6] 'Postscriptum on the county franchise', *Gleanings*, i. 193.
[7] *Political Speeches* (1879), 37.
[8] 'Postscriptum on the county franchise', *Gleanings*, i. 200.
[9] The Glasgow rectorial of 5 Dec. 79 is reprinted in *Political speeches* (1879), 229ff. from which quotations in this paragraph are taken.

derangement that answers to deformity, and partakes of its nature'. These bad qualities, distortions of nature, were most easily seen in 'the growth of a new class—a class unknown to the past, and one whose existence the future will have cause to deplore. It is the class of hybrid or bastard men ... made up from the scattered and less considerate members of all classes', united by 'the bond of gain; not the legitimate produce of toil by hand or brain', a class sustained by the cushion of limited liability, 'not fenced off from rashness, as in former times, by liability to ruinous loss in the event of failure, but to be had without the conditions which alone make pecuniary profits truly honourable'.

This was an analysis similar in conclusion, if not in tone, to Trollope's description of corrupt financial capitalism in *The way we live now* (1875). It was a view of society quite common in the 1870s, shared, ironically—given Gladstone's view of its political consequences—by the Queen. Gladstone did not succeed in showing how this class affected the policies of the Cabinet. He argued that the political system was being subverted and corrupted by the failures of moral education to match the progress of capitalism, but he did not succeed in showing how, or why, this should immediately be reflected in government policy, or why its effect was on the Tory rather than the Liberal Party.

The consequence of this analysis was the very non-Liberal view that 'intellectual forces', represented politically through the old property-based franchise and to some extent corrupted, must be counterbalanced by a popular vote which would be moral and ethical rather than intellectual in character: 'As the barbarian, with his undeveloped organs, sees and hears at distances which the senses of the cultured state cannot overpass, and yet is utterly deficient as to fine details of sound and colour, even so it seems that, in judging the great questions of policy which appeal to the primal truths and laws of our nature, those classes may excel who, if they lack the opportunities, yet escape the subtle perils of the wealthy state.'[1] Here was a curious paradox: Midlothian exemplified the use of rationalist rhetoric in an extended franchise system, yet its stimulus was profoundly conservative, echoing exactly those arguments which had been used by the ultra-Tories in the 1828–30 period to support parliamentary reform—that, for example, enfranchised popular Protestantism would never have permitted Catholic Emancipation.

The paradox is resolved by the self-selection of the electorate through the excluding power of the register. As Gladstone remarked when discussing the political sense and capacity for judgment of 'the masses', 'I have never heard of an attempt, as yet, to register those who sleep under the dry arches of Waterloo Bridge',[2] i.e. 'the residuum', as those were designated who were excluded from the franchise by the lack of stable residence, by the failure to be male or the head of a household, or by the want of civic competence which pauperism was taken to imply. The 'masses' were in fact sifted so that, in general, it was mainly 'capable citizens' who achieved the status of being placed upon the parliamentary register; in the post-1867 franchise, large though it had relatively become, voting remained a privilege to be earned rather than a right to be claimed.

[1] 'Postscriptum on the county franchise', *Gleanings*, i. 199, 201.
[2] Ibid., i. 197.

Though 'intellectual qualifications alone' were insufficient to form a right political judgment, the tone of Gladstone's speeches suggests that they were none the less assumed. Even the Waverley Market speech, addressed to those who 'do not fear to call yourselves the working men of Edinburgh, Leith and the district', though short, made no more concession in vocabulary to the audience than middle-class ministers of religion were wont to do in their sermons.[1]

The distancing from the caucus and the 'notables' allowed Gladstone— despite the fact that the Campaign was planned by 'notables' such as Rosebery and W. P. Adam—to present himself in 'my Northern Campaign' as a man apart, a peacemaker come from afar, almost as an Aristotelian law-giver.[2] The special train, the journey 'really more like a triumphal procession',[3] the image of physical and moral movement towards a new beginning, the torchlight processions through Edinburgh—'a subject for Turner'[4] with 'no police visible'[5]—would, if not limited and controlled by the means of communication and by the objectives of the campaign, foreshadow disturbing comparisons. In their context, they merely gave that most austere of cities some fun, though not, of course, frivolity.

Ignoring the many family links with Edinburgh which could have allowed his presentation as a home-comer, Gladstone began the campaign by emphasising his separateness: 'I am come among you as a stranger',[6] a man called by the requisitioning electors to pacify and to redress. His ally in this process would be a betrayed people, their morals and their prosperity alike defrauded by 'a series of surprises, a series of theatrical expedients, calculated to excite, calculated to alarm':[7]

> Do not let us suppose this is like the old question between Whig and Tory. It is nothing of the kind. It is not now as if we were disputing about some secondary matter—it is not even as if we were disputing about the Irish Church, which no doubt was a very important affair. What we are disputing about is a whole system of Government, and to make good that proposition that it is a whole system of government will be my great object in any addresses that I may deliver in this country.[8]

The attack was thus two-pronged: first, exposing 'a catalogue of expedients': second, denouncing 'a new method of government'.[9]

It may be noted that Gladstone's personalisation of Government policy in the 1876–78 period, when Disraeli was held largely responsible, broadens in 1878–80 into a more general denunciation, as Salisbury, at first exonerated by his behaviour at the Constantinople Conference, became tarnished by the secret negotiations with Russia and Turkey in 1878, by which Bulgaria and the Armenians were sacrificed and Cyprus obtained.

The content of the Midlothian Campaign was thus by no means that of a simple political raid. It represented, as Gladstone said at its beginning, an

---

[1] *Political speeches* (1879), 158.   [2] 21 Nov. 79.
[3] 24 Nov. 79.   [4] 4 Dec. 79.   [5] 8 Dec. 79.
[6] *Political speeches* (1879), 26. The emphasis on strangeness was premeditated; see the speech-notes reproduced in the illustrations below. For the campaign generally, see Lloyd, *General Election of 1880, passim.*
[7] Ibid., 36.   [8] Ibid., 50.   [9] Ibid., 36, 22.

indictment made 'many times elsewhere against her Majesty's Government'. It was, in a gathered and comprehensive form, the indictment stated in the vast range of pamphlets, articles, speeches, and letters issued since September 1876 whose preparation much of the journal for these years is devoted to describing.

Building on the basis of the Eastern Question, 'the question out of which almost every other question had grown collaterally',[1] Gladstone attacked the Government's record in an analysis in part geographic—its blunders in Cyprus, Egypt, South Africa, and Afghanistan; in part moral—its abandonment of justice, and liberty and communality as the criteria for British action; and in part financial—its abandonment of the strict canons of Peel–Gladstone budgetary finance and its coquetting with protectionism. This broad denunciation still reads formidably. It was carefully orchestrated across six major speeches and the Glasgow rectorial in the first campaign in November 1879, and repeated with variations and extra material supplied particularly by P. W. Clayden's well-researched *England under Lord Beaconsfield* (1880)[2] in fifteen major speeches during the second campaign following the dissolution in March 1880.

The breadth of his condemnation enabled Gladstone to broaden the rather narrow base which the initial subject of the Eastern Question had given him. In particular, while many had seen his concern with Turkish iniquities as obsessive, financial and fiscal policy—to which about a third of the first Midlothian Campaign was devoted—allowed him a much more generally acceptable appeal. Gladstone on finance was a call for the restoration of mid-Victorian values in the face of their corruption by profligate, careless, and irregular Tories.

This successfully tweaked a raw Conservative nerve. The presentation of a policy of prestige and patriotism was, in terms of finance, difficult to combine with the claim to be the heir of Peel.[3] As the bills came in,[4] the deficit rose and the political problems increased. When Beaconsfield intervened to prevent a rise in indirect taxation to meet some of the costs, a member of his Cabinet noted, 'the Chief suggested another course [to Northcote's proposal]—not so good financially but almost essential politically'.[5] However much Beaconsfield might privately suspect the competence of his satraps in South Africa and India, publicly he was hoisted on the petard of his own rhetoric. Once he presented himself, however off-handedly, as the proponent of the Roman virtues of '*Imperium et Libertas*',[6] the financial costs of '*Imperium*' could not be explained away with a nod of regret as the consequence of separate, local crises of the sort that Gladstone and other contemporaries accepted as inevitable. '*Imperium*' implied metropolitan control, direction and responsibility.

The new electorate might have its jingo element, but it also had its respectable, cautious citizens, a generation accustomed to Peel–Gladstone finance,

---

[1] Ibid., 39.   [2] Begun on 23 Feb. 80.

[3] For a discussion of Disraeli's self-presentation as 'an aggressive patriotic *and* imperial minister' in the late 1870s and for his financial policy generally, see P. Ghosh, 'Disraelian Conservatism: a financial approach', *E.H.R.*, xcix. 268 (1984).

[4] Literally in this simple form on one occasion, as an underestimate of £4 million on the cost of the Afghan war was discovered in March 1880; see N. E. Johnson, *The diary of Gathorne Hardy* (1981), 447.

[5] Ibid., 418 (entry for 30 July 1879). Northcote wanted to increase the tea duty.

[6] As, e.g., at Guildhall on 10 November 1879, in Buckle, vi. 483.

with its emphasis on balanced budgets, proper procedures, and minimal expenditure. The large deficit of £8 million, at a time when central government's annual revenue was about £81 million, gave Gladstone an easy target, given the assumptions of the time. As long as Conservative governments had been minority governments, he told the electors, 'we got on very decently with them', but now, let loose by a majority, 'the extravagance of expenditure ... bubbles up everywhere',[1] with the consequence that regular, balanced budgets, the centrepiece of Gladstonian finance, had been eclipsed by a series of back-door devices: 'the elementary duty of the Government in the right management of finance has been grossly neglected',[2] and Northcote's finance was 'truly ignoble'.[3] The exhortation to moral rectitude in government was thus stiffened by a call for a return to fiscal probity, Gladstone, as always, personally seeing the two as inherently related, as was indicated by his taking the Chancellorship of the Exchequer as well as the Premiership in 1880.

Governmental fiscal irregularity and profligacy and the flaunting of wealth by the 'plutocracy' would endanger the social order and disturb the willingness of the poor to accept their lot. As the theme of the Midlothian Campaign was a condemnation of innovations, so Gladstone defended the welfare assumptions of the 1834 Poor Law as the depression of the late 1870s deepened. Midlothian was no call to a new Jerusalem in this world, but its moral rectitude might lead to one in the next. Gladstone's thinking about poverty and the rising concern about what was soon to be called 'unemployment' is well shown in his talk to the 'old folks' of the St. Pancras Workhouse in August 1879.[4] Accepting that there were 'dark and gloomy skies that have overspread the land' with the onset of depression, Gladstone none the less reasserted the principle of 'less eligibility' of the 1834 Poor Law, buttressing it with Christian social quietism which, he said, would be 'an act of the basest guilt' unless 'conviction of the truth ... lay at the very root of my understanding and at the very bottom of my heart'. 'Indulgences by rule and under system' were unacceptable:

> It is not because the receiving of such indulgences would be dangerous or mischievous to yourselves. It is the effect ... that would be produced upon the community at large if those establishments, which are maintained out of the labour of the community and at its charge, were made establishments of luxury living. It is necessary that the independent labourer of this country should not be solicited ... by thinking he could do better for himself by making a charge upon that community. There is no more subtle poison that could be infused into the nation at large than a system of that kind. ... We live in an age when most of us have forgotten that the Gospel of our Saviour Christ ... was above all the Gospel of the poor ... from His own mouth proceeded the words which showed us in reference to temporal circumstances that a time will come when many of the first shall be last and many of the last first ... blessed are the poor who accept with cheerfulness the limited circumstances and conditions in which they have to pass those few fleeting years.

1880 was to be the last General Election at which the holding of such opinions by the leader of the party of progress could be regarded as unexceptionable.

[1] *Political speeches* (1879), 136–7.
[2] Ibid. (1880), 94.   [3] 6 Aug. 78.
[4] 21 Aug. 79; report in *T.T.*, 22 August 1879, 8d.

Taking politics to the electorate as directly as Gladstone did in Midlothian was, in the context of the day, highly controversial. *The Times* gave its verdict on the first Midlothian Campaign:

> In a word, everything is overdone.... Does it [the country] wish the conduct of public affairs to be at the mercy of excitement, of rhetoric, of the qualities which appeal to a mob rather than to those which command the attention of a Senate?[1]

Gladstone had anticipated such criticisms in 1877, when replying to Tory objections to the early phase of the Bulgarian Atrocities campaign, which was perforce carried out during the long Parliamentary recess:

> I suppose it may be said that the House of Commons represents the country; but still it is not the country, and, as people have lately drawn a distinction between the country and the Government, so there might be circumstances in which they might draw a distinction between the country and the House of Commons.[2]

The restoration of the natural harmony between Commons and electorate had been one of Gladstone's aims since his return in 1876. Such a harmony was represented, in Gladstone's view, by a Liberal majority. The Midlothian Campaign exemplified the drive to achieve it, for while its means were novel, its message was restorative.

The Midlothian Campaign has its obvious importance in late-Victorian politics. But it has a wider significance also. Various means have been developed through various media to attract the votes of the extended franchises common to the nations of Europe and North America since the 1850s: speeches, pamphlets, organisations, slogans, advertisements, bribes, and intimidations direct or implied. At a constituency level, the Midlothian election of 1880 involved all these. At a national level, however, the Midlothian Campaign speeches offered a remarkable solution to the problem of marrying a representative system to a large-scale franchise. Within the context of the given materials—the nature of the franchise and the nature of the media—Gladstone had squared the circle: he had formulated a politics that was both charismatic and rational. The serious discussion of a great national issue can never be simple or easy, but in the conditions of an extended franchise it must at least be widely articulated, and the quality of the articulation will have much to do with the general quality of national political life. Given the difficulties of expounding the complexities of an intricate series of principles, policies, and events, the Midlothian speeches were of international importance in encouraging a new and high standard of political awareness, discussion, and citizenship. The concept of the active citizen, so central to the ethos of Liberalism, was given fresh life and a larger definition by the new means of political discussion and communication.

VI

Thus in Midlothian did Gladstone 'hammer with all my little might at the fabric of the present Tory power'.[3] The result of the General Election of 1880

---

[1] Leader in *T.T.*, 29 November 1879, 9a.
[2] *H*. 232. 120 (9 February 1877).   [3] 2 Apr. 80.

was a Liberal majority over the Conservatives of 137, with the Irish Home
Rulers winning 65 seats, an even more spectacular victory than the majority of
between 56 and 76 which Gladstone had calculated in November 1878 as likely
from the evidence of by-elections.[1] Elected comfortably, as predicted, in Midlothian, and, without visiting the constituency, overwhelmingly in Leeds,[2] Gladstone went secretly from Edinburgh to Hawarden, rejecting plans for a
triumphal entry into London—mindful perhaps of his trenchant condemnation
of the Roman triumph of Beaconsfield and Salisbury in 1878[3]—and soon began
an article on the Tory débâcle.[4] Lord Wolverton (i.e. Glyn, the banker and former Liberal Chief Whip) arrived at Hawarden and 'threatens a request from
Granville and Hartington. Again I am stunned: but God will provide.'[5]

Through Wolverton, Gladstone made it clear that in 'the great matter of all'[6]
he remained in the position which he had tenaciously held, at least in principle,
since September 1876. He was not Party leader, '[my] labours as an Individual
cannot set me up as a Pretender', but a recognition of the needs of 'public
policy' might require suspension of the usual procedures.[7] He would be seen to
be invited back by the Party leaders who had been so reluctant to support the
Campaign especially in its Bulgarian days; his moral and political authority
would be seen to be derived from the size of the Liberal majority; his earlier
behaviour would be justified.

Hartington, for whom the Queen sent after her return from the Continent,
recognised that Gladstone was indispensable, being 'the chief personage & a
most powerful influence in the Liberal Party', and ceded the political initiative
to the former Prime Minister.[8] Granville and Hartington came together bearing
the Queen's command that Gladstone should go to Windsor.[9] When Gladstone
kissed hands for the second time he did so on his own terms: the Whigs were
seen to accept his authority which, he was careful to get Granville and Hartington explicitly to accept, rested on a recognition of 'public advantage'.[10] It was
the policy as much as the personage which the Queen and the notables had to

---

[1] 'Electoral Facts', *Nineteenth Century*, iv. 967 (November 1878); see 29 Sept. 78n., 9 Oct. 78.

[2] In 1874, Leeds, a three-member constituency, returned a Liberal and two Conservatives, the
other two Liberal candidates not being elected; in 1880, the Liberals ran two candidates only, Gladstone coming top, Barran (a Liberal) second, both with over 23,000 votes, and one of the two Tory
candidates third, 10,000 votes behind.

[3] '. . . the well-organised machinery of an obsequious reception, unexampled, I suppose, in the
history of our civilians; and meant, perhaps, to recall the pomp of the triumphs which Rome
awarded to her most successful generals'; 'England's Mission', *Nineteenth Century*, iv. 560 (September
1878).

[4] 13 Apr. 80.

[5] 10 Apr. 80. For the general surprise at the size of the majority and for the subsequent political
manoeuvres, see T. A. Jenkins, 'Gladstone, the Whigs and the leadership of the Liberal Party',
Historical Journal, xxvii. 337 (1984).

[6] 11 Apr. 80.

[7] To Wolverton, 13 Apr. 80. This position was already belied by many small signs; for example, it
was Gladstone who on 11 Mar. 80 answered Northcote's stop-gap budget after the dissolution was
announced; *H* 251. 834.

[8] Hartington's memoranda in preparation for his audience; two of these are in Holland, ii. 273ff.
and another in Chatsworth MSS 340. 940.

[9] 23 Apr. 80. Gladstone anticipated some manoeuvre of this sort as early as March 1879; see
30 Mar. 79n.   [10] Ibid.

recognise. Gladstone may have been 'stunned' by the notion of a return to the premiership, but he played his cards very carefully and shrewdly in April 1880. More was at stake than the acquiring of power: his authority over the Party and especially over the Whigs within it needed to be clearly established if his power was to be maintained.

Despite this careful distancing from the Party hierarchy, 1880 was the first occasion on which Gladstone had taken office as a 'liberal' (in 1868 he had still been a 'liberal conservative'). This was reflected in a marked shift of tone with respect to the history of his own times. Hitherto, Gladstone had seen progress in the nineteenth century as essentially the achievement of a beneficent governing class: franchise extension had been a necessary process to buttress the legitimacy of the ruling élite, but its cost had been a slowing down of legislative and administrative reform. In some respects he continued to hold this essentially Peelite view, arguing that the pre-1832 Parliament was 'intrinsically more favourable to the public interest than our present system'; early parliamentary reform would have prevented Roman Catholic emancipation in 1829, and had delayed Corn Law Repeal until 1846.[1] On the other hand, 'popular judgment was more often just than that of the higher orders', and the 'instances' of this— abolition of slavery, parliamentary reform, fiscal reform, trade union reform, a freedom-directed foreign policy, and others—were now regarded as making up 'nearly the whole history of the Country since the peace of 1815'.[2] The election victory of 1880 was seen *a fortiori* as a vindication of this view of popular judgment, giving joy 'to the large majority of the civilised world. The downfall of Beaconsfieldism is like the vanishing of some vast magnificent castle in an Italian romance'.[3]

Although he had allied himself very closely with the aspirations of the Liberal movement in the constituencies by publishing 'shopping lists' of outstanding legislation,[4] Gladstone saw his particular duty as Prime Minister as ensuring that the vanished castle did not reappear. The remnants of the Conservative Government's policies were to be tidied up as quickly as possible, in particular the implementation of the 1878 Berlin Congress's decisions about the Greek–Turkish border, the rounding off of the withdrawal from Afghanistan, and the restoration of correct financial procedures:

> I am decidedly of opinion that the proceedings of this Government in finance and expenditure, and in foreign Indian & colonial policy will find the first work to do for a Liberal Government & Parliament when we have them.[5]

Though he saw himself as representing the rightness of 'popular judgment' expressed through the Liberal movement (as distinct from the parliamentary Liberal Party), he does not seem to have seen his restorative task as lengthy.

Admittedly the process would 'probably take *time*'[6] but Gladstone seems to have believed grass would grow over the flattened foundations of Beaconsfieldism after a session or two, and that he could then resume retirement. He

---

[1] 'The county franchise, and Mr. Lowe thereon', *Gleanings*, i. 136; see 9 Oct. 77.

[2] 'Last words on the county franchise', *Gleanings*, i. 178; see 10 Dec. 77.

[3] To Argyll, 12 April 1880, Morley, ii. 615.

[4] See, e.g., in 'England's Mission', 560.

[5] To W. P. Adam, 12 April 1879, Blair Adam MS 4/431.   [6] Ibid.

continued, in fact, in his view that his return to active politics was a temporary
necessity, the result of an exceptional crisis. The whole episode from September
1876 onwards would soon become in the nation's memory a Butlerian fit of
insanity whose end had brought relief and joy. Writing to India to his son Harry
in 1881, Gladstone commented on his preparations for retiring as prime-
minister:

> As to public affairs, we have the utmost cause to be thankful in regard to the difficult
> and painful matters which had for some time confronted us before the present Govt.
> was formed. Montenegro & Greece have got in the main what they were entitled to—
> Afghanistan is in the main evacuated—the Transvaal is restored. Also we have at home
> I hope re-established the proper balance between Income & Charge which is the
> essential condition of all good finance. But two other subjects have sprung up, even
> more urgent in their character: the condition of Ireland, and the loss of capacity in the
> House of Commons under its present rules to discharge its legislative duties. I came
> into office with the view & intention of retiring from it, so soon as the questions I have
> named were disposed of: that would have been in the autumn of the present year
> [1881]. But my hopes were dashed. . . .[1]

Gladstone took office to right the wrongs of Beaconsfieldism. He did not personally have a programme for a Parliament. His condemnation of the Tory
Government lay partly in its incumbrance of parliamentary business as a result of
'new fangled' external policies, and in its consequent abandonment of 'all idea of
living . . . by great measures of legislation addressed to the national benefit'.[2] But
Gladstone did not now see himself as the legislative fountain, as in his first
Government. His preparation for office was therefore not idle, but it was limited.

That he thought Beaconsfield's 'Imperialism'—Gladstone first used the word
in 1878,[3] though he did not use it often—could be righted in a year or so shows
the essentially liberal cast of his thought. Although he believed Disraeli had
begun the construction of a new 'system of government', Gladstone also
believed a new man with the right morality could dismantle it quite quickly: 'I
form a very high estimate of the power still possessed by individuals.'[4] No
general critique of Disraelian 'Imperialism' was offered, only the analysis of a
series of wrong moral choices. Thus Britain's 'influence is assured by special
causes, and can only be destroyed by particular errors of judgment, or by a disposition to domineer, or by an unwise self-seeking: whether these be the result
of panic or of pride'.[5] The domestic, parliamentary, and financial consequences
of these were coherently worked out, and when Gladstone referred to a new
'system' it was usually these internal consequences that he meant. The British,
he thought, were inherently imperial—this their history and their character
obviously showed: 'It is part of our patrimony: born with our birth, dying only
with our death; incorporating itself in the first elements of our knowledge, and
interwoven with all our habits of mental action upon public affairs. . . . The

---

[1] To H. N. Gladstone, 2 Dec. 81; a more diffuse version of the same points was sent to him on 21
Apr. 81; Hawn P.

[2] 'England's Mission', 563.

[3] Ibid., 571. Koebner and Schmidt comment, 'Once the Liberal leader had given the cue, Imperialism became an anti-Disraeli slogan'; R. Koebner and H. D. Schmidt, *Imperialism* (1964), 148.

[4] 'The county franchise', 161.

[5] Undated fragment (1878?) in Add MS 44764, f. 44.

dominant passion of England is extended empire.'[1] It was an expansionism that had brought much good, moral and physical, but it was also an expansionism which should and could be limited by will, by 'the exercise of moral control over ambition and cupidity'.[2] The 1880–85 Government was to show in full measure the difficulties of this position.

Not surprisingly, the early months of the 1880 Government show Gladstone giving his first attention to these Beaconsfieldian priorities, as may be traced easily enough in the daily diary text, the cabinet minutes, and the letters quoted below. The Midlothian Campaign had been a campaign for restoration, not innovation. The restoration of what Gladstone saw as correct political relationships and policies chiefly involved the rounding off of Turkish frontier affairs (successfully achieved after a sharp crisis in which Gladstone led the Concert in sending the fleet against the Sultan),[3] the winding-up of Afghan expansionism, and the re-establishment of correct financial behaviour (not simply a matter of restoring the annual budget to its place of priority, but also of resurrecting the creative side of Gladstonian finance, as is shown by the plans for the repeal of the malt tax and the reconstruction of the death duties).[4] All these constitute what might be said to be Gladstone's regular, normative activities in the first months of his Government. They were expected activities, and on the whole they went to plan. They were complemented by the usual careful disposal of ecclesiastical, legal, and political patronage. Beyond this, Gladstone seemed reluctant to go. He received deputations on the Employers Liability Bill, but showed little interest in that important measure.[5] As Chancellor of the Exchequer, Gladstone led his contemporaries in the view that the central Government had no responsibility for ameliorating the severe depression which had played an important if unquantifiable part in returning the Liberals to power. This was fully in keeping with the Midlothian maxim, taken from Cobden and echoing though not mentioning Adam Smith, 'that public economy was public virtue'.[6] Only with respect to Ireland was the possibility of setting aside the canons of fiscal orthodoxy to be considered, and then most reluctantly.

The fascination of these first months of government in 1880 is to watch the restorative, soothing Gladstone being driven at first slowly, reluctantly, hesitantly, to accept for a second time a high-profile, legislatively-oriented leadership. Instead of a straightforward session in which he, as Leader of the House and Chancellor of the Exchequer, would pass the usual Finance Bill and sundry other measures such as the Burials Bill, controversial, no doubt, but controversy containable, he found himself superintending the complexities of the Charles Bradlaugh affair, and the Irish Compensation for Disturbance Bill, whose importance will be discussed shortly.

[1] 'England's Mission', 569–70.   [2] Ibid., 570.
[3] 6 Sept., 1–12 Oct., 10 Nov. 80, and letters in September and October 1880.
[4] An early priority, see 4 and 7 May 80; see also 2 Oct. 80.
[5] 2 and 3 June 80; see also to Dodson, 9 May 80.
[6] *Political speeches* (1880), 233. The Midlothian Campaign discussed various bills to improve the position of tenant farmers, especially in Scotland, but in the short Session of 1880 it was the 'Hares and Rabbits' Bill—dealing with game rights, important and contentious but hardly of fundamental economic significance—which formed the Government's chief rural measure with respect to mainland farmers.

Under the strain, Gladstone's health gave way at the end of July. This was not the brief 'diplomatic' sort of illness quite often seen in the first Government, but a real crisis. For the first time in half a century, death seemed possible, though not imminent: 'On Sunday I thought of the end—in case the movement [of temperature] had continued—coming nearer to it by a little than I had done before: but not as in expectation of it. C. read the service.'[1] The possibility of resignation and the subsequent succession was discussed.[2] Convalescence took the form of a speedy round-Britain cruise on Donald Currie's *Grantully Castle*, during which a brief stop was made, amongst other places, at Dublin, 'in time to land suddenly & go to Christ Church'.[3] Thus almost the only visit to Ireland by a Prime Minister in office between the Act of Union and 1914 was to attend an Anglican church service.[4]

Of the stated remnants from the Tory Government, it was the Transvaal which, unexpectedly, posed much the greatest problem. The bold imperatives stated in Midlothian were, if not ignored, held in abeyance; Sir Bartle Frere was retained until August 1880, and the Gladstone Government set out on the Beaconsfield–Carnarvon road of Confederation and the maintenance of sovereignty over the Transvaal,[5] combined with a statement of 'desire that the white inhabitants of the Transvaal should without prejudice to the rest of the population enjoy the fullest liberty to manage their own affairs'.[6] By December, the Transvaal was in armed rebellion and the Gladstone Government committed to repressing it.

Gladstone operated from an unusually narrow base with respect to South African policy. Against his usual custom, he seems to have had no private information with which to balance the departmental view. His reading shows little interest in Southern African works, though he did read some.[7] He knew a great deal about the war-like characteristics of the Montenegrins, but little of the Boers. Donald Currie, chairman of the Castle shipping line (later Union-Castle), who sponsored Kruger on his visits to London in 1877 and 1878 and who took Gladstone on cruises on his steamers in 1878 and 1880, might have filled the role of confidant, especially during the convalescence voyage in August 1880, but does not seem to have done so. The links with Sir Garnet Wolseley, now in charge of South African forces, which had been quite close in the later years of the 1868–74 Government, were not maintained. Wolseley would have alerted Gladstone to the complexities and dangers of the Transvaal situation.[8] The 'official mind'—such as it was—of the Colonial Office thus had exceptional authority and, very unusually—probably without precedent in Gladstone's premierships—drafted a vital letter for him, the letter to Kruger and Joubert on the future of the Transvaal.[9]

More surprising is what is, at first glance, Gladstone's uncertainty in his handling of Ireland. He was, of course, by no means ignorant of Irish affairs

[1] 31 July 80.   [2] 23 Aug. 80.
[3] 29 Aug. 80; the cruise lasted from 26 August to 4 September.
[4] Lord John Russell made a short visit in 1848.
[5] See 3, 12 May 80 and Schreuder, 60ff.
[6] To Kruger and Joubert, 15 June 80.
[7] 27 Jan., 3 July, 6 Aug. 77, 26 Apr., 5 Aug. 78.
[8] See Schreuder, 62.   [9] 15 June 80; Gladstone amended the draft.

generally, or of its agricultural problems. By December 1880, he noted 'The state of Ireland in particular' as the chief concern of the year.[1] Yet the view that Ireland came to Gladstone like a cloud from the west unheralded is well borne out by the journal and its ancillary material. Gladstone came to see Ireland as he had seen its famine in 1845, as a divine retribution, 'a judgment for our heavy sins as a nation'.[2] But the revelation of the punishment was sudden, certainly not anticipated during his visit to Ireland in 1877, when he spent almost a month in County Wicklow and Dublin. This visit turned out, against his intentions, for the most part to be a holiday; for political reasons plans to extend it to Ulster and perhaps Killarney were abandoned.[3] What seems to have been designed as a wide-ranging visit became more limited: 'the larger parts of my project gradually fade from view, & my movements must be in a small[er] circle'. As Gladstone noted, he was in 'the least Irish part of Ireland'.[4]

This was true, for the Fitzwilliam estates at Coollattin, where Gladstone stayed, were a model of high capitalization and benificence, generous treatment of tenants and a low rate of return to the landlord (about 1%). Finlay Dun, *The Times* journalist who discussed Irish land with Gladstone at Hawarden at an important moment of the discussions in December 1880,[5] described the Fitzwilliam estates as exceptional: 'prosperity, peace and progress, spread through a wide area'.[6] It would be wrong to see this visit as simply a tour of great houses. Gladstone was diligent about visiting 'farms, cottages, & people' and holding conversations, 'turning my small opportunities to account as well as I could'.[7] Undoubtedly there were difficulties about doing this, and Gladstone shows some irritation at a day spent with the potentates of the English establishment in Dublin: 'not enough of *Ireland*'.[8] He did, however, succeed in visiting a number of farms, including one on Parnell's estate.[9] The tour included a visit, on Guy Fawkes Day, to Maynooth College, the Roman Catholic seminary whose extended grant had been the cause of his resignation from Peel's Cabinet in 1845: 'It produced on the whole a saddening impression: what havock have we made of the vineyard of the Lord!'[10]

Such might be Maynooth, but this was not the general impression of Ireland in 1877 on Gladstone. The burgeoning Home Rule movement he was well aware of, and on receiving the freedom of Dublin, 'treading on eggs the whole time', he could not 'be too thankful for having got through today as I hope without trick & without offence'.[11] His comments in Dublin on local government anticipated the paper on 'Devolution' which he presented to the Cabinet in 1880,[12] but they were not offered with any great urgency. Ireland generally, such as he was able

[1] 31 Dec. 80. For the Cabinet's Irish policy, see A. J. Warren, *The Irish policies of the Second Gladstone Government, 1880–1885*, Oxford D. Phil., 1974.

[2] Ibid.; there are several echoes of the famous 'cloud in the west' letter of 1845 (see Bassett, 64) in 1880; see 12 Dec. 80.

[3] See 17 Oct.–12 Nov. 77.

[4] 18 Oct. 77.

[5] 4 Dec. 80.

[6] Chapter iv of Finlay Dun, *Landlords and tenants in Ireland* (1881), a reprint of earlier reports for *The Times*, describes the Fitzwilliam estates.

[7] 25 Oct. 77.

[8] 20 Oct. 77.

[9] 26 Oct. 77.

[10] 5 Nov. 77.

[11] 7 Nov. 77.

[12] 23 Oct. 80.

to see of it, did not disturb him. This was not surprising, for Ireland was not yet disturbed; 1877 was the lowest year of the decade for evictions.[1] What is surprising, is that Gladstone does not appear to have anticipated the effect on Ireland of the agricultural crisis of the late 1870s. He was well aware of its causes, both long-term, through the Ricardian comparative advantage effects of the expansion of the American and Canadian wheat lands,[2] and immediate, through the disastrous wet summer of 1879, carefully observed in the journal. Hawarden estate rents were reduced by 15% in 1879 ('It is to be 15% and as a rule in kind') and by the same again in 1880 to meet the emergency.[3] However, what was a crisis in English and Welsh agriculture could hardly be less than a catastrophe for Ireland and Scotland, even allowing for their smaller proportion of cereal production.

On the other hand, the founding of the Land League in October 1879 did not make its success nor the scale of its ultimate demands inevitable. When the Liberal Government took office, the Land League was still 'basically a Connaught phenomenon', and its programme still uncertain.[4] In April 1880, Parnell was still thinking in terms of a mere revival of Butt's limited Bill of 1876.[5] The new Liberal Government was faced with suffering and confusion in Ireland, but not yet with systematised disorder. Initially the Cabinet moved quickly, though without Gladstone playing more than a co-ordinating role. The early Cabinets of the administration discussed both 'Peace Preservation' and an extension of the Bright Land Purchase clauses of the 1870 Land Act. The Cabinet's assessment was that it was not necessary to renew the Peace Preservation Act, due to expire on 1 June, 'but general duty to be recognized'[6] (so little impact had the Land League as yet made), and that, the 1880 Session being short, 'Amendment by extension of the Bright Clauses. Too complex for this year.'[7] Consideration of the Bright clauses referred to the long-term pattern of land tenure in Ireland: 'We never considered the question of ejectments connected with the present distress in Ireland.'[8] By June 1880, the question of these had been forced upon Gladstone and his Cabinet: 'I *was* under the impression that ejectments were diminishing, but I now find from figures first seen on Saturday [12 June] that they seem rather to increase.' Hence 'the duty of enquiring, where I had not previously known there was urgent cause to inquire'.[9]

The consequences were two-fold. First, the Bessborough Royal Commission on the working of the 1870 Land Act was set up in June 1880 parallel to the Royal Commission on agricultural distress earlier set up by the Tories for the United Kingdom as a whole.[10] The Bessborough Commission could hardly take evidence and report before January 1881 at the earliest, and clearly looked to some general development of the 1870 settlement. Second, the immediate

---

[1] See the table in P. Bew, *Land and the national question in Ireland 1858–82* (1978), 36.
[2] See *Political Speeches* (1879), 95ff. and 'Kin beyond Sea', *Gleanings*, i. 203. See 23 July, 9 Sept. 79.
[3] 5 Nov. 79; see *T.T.*, 17 July 1880, 10c.
[4] See Bew, op. cit., chapters 5 and 6.   [5] Ibid.
[6] The position respecting the Act (a watered-down version of the liberal Acts of 1870 and 1871) was complex because of the time-table in the Commons and the Tory Cabinet's failure to renew the Act before dissolving; see Selborne II, ii. 7. The act, as it stood, would have been of little use against the Land League, but the failure to renew made the Irish land-lord class feel the more isolated.
[7] 14 May 80. See also 5 May 80.   [8] To Argyll, 14 June 80.   [9] Ibid.
[10] See 19, 26 June 80. Bessborough was made chairman when Devonshire declined.

crisis was to be met by taking over the private member bill of the Parnellite O'Connor Power and replacing it by a Government-sponsored Compensation for Disturbance Bill. This was eventually lost in the Lords in August 1880, its legitimacy destroyed by the Government's uncertainty about its own statistics.[1] As a consequence of the landowning interest's bitter opposition to even this rather modest initiative, the first resignations from the Government had to be accepted.[2]

'Is the non-payment due to *distress or to conspiracy?*'[3] The Compensation for Disturbance Bill assumed it was '*distress*': the dénouement, as the Land League gained support and confidence in the second half of 1880, suggested to Gladstone that it was both. '*Conspiracy*' was to be met by the prosecution of Parnell, Dillon, Biggar, and others, agreed in principle at the Cabinet of 30 September 1880 subject to the Law Officers' advice, with the hope of showing that the Land League's policy of combination to encourage breach of contract was illegal,[4] and, if it was not, opening the way for an Act that would make it so. Gladstone hoped for much in the way of 'moral effect' from the trials.[5] He also hoped they would make a suspension of Habeas Corpus unnecessary, for he regarded such a measure as futile, since 'Parnell Biggar & Co' were not intending to commit crimes, but to incite others 'by speech': if prosecution could not 'enforce silence', no more could Habeas Corpus suspension.[6]

The prosecutions announced on 2 November 1880 failed in January 1881 because the jury in Dublin could not agree. Gladstone had personally intervened to ensure a fair trial,[7] and the probability of a stalemate does not seem to have occurred to him, only the possibility that the law might not be sufficiently extensive. The prosecutions at least gained enough time to make impossible an emergency pre-Christmas Session for Habeas Corpus suspension.

'*Distress*', in the rising tension following the Lords' rejection of the Compensation for Disturbance Bill, would have to be met by 'remedial legislation' to balance the demand for coercion which by late autumn was becoming hard to resist.[8] By 'remedial legislation' Gladstone did not mean merely a Land Bill, and, until a late date in 1880, perhaps not a Land Bill at all. Only with extreme reluctance did he come to accept the need for another Land Bill. He saw the problem in much wider terms. After reading various works on the 'closure' and after studying the speeches of Grattan and Pitt on the Irish Union,[9] he wrote a long paper on 'Obstruction and Devolution'.[10] This paper met what Gladstone saw as the long-term corruption of the British legislature, clogged with detail and arrears even before the Irish and others began 'obstructing'.

This corruption, unworthy of a great Empire and possibly fatal to it, had been a major theme of his articles and speeches in the late 1870s, reinforcing views expressed since the 1850s, and had Gladstone anticipated being Prime Minister for a full term, he might well have worked more on his plan before the ministry

---

[1] To Forster, 14 July 80. [2] To Zetland, 16 Aug. 80. [3] 12 June 80.
[4] To Kimberley, 21 Oct. 80. [5] Ibid., and to Forster, 25 Oct. 80.
[6] To Forster, 25 Oct. 80. Gladstone saw Parnell as a new phenomenon in Irish history, willing to incite to violence but not to take the responsibility for it; in the late 1870s, Gladstone revised his opinion of O'Connell, so hostile in the 1830s; see 17 Nov. 77n. [7] To Forster, 9 Dec. 80.
[8] To Forster, 25 Oct. 80. [9] 18–19 Oct. 80.
[10] See 19, 25–26 June 80. Bessborough was made chairman after Devonshire's refusal was assumed.

began, and presented it to his Cabinet in more normal circumstances. As it was, one of the chief legislative corollaries to the Midlothian Campaign came before the Cabinet in the context of the Irish emergency. Devolution would restore the capacity of Parliament, and in the Irish context it would have a direct political advantage:

> I must add that besides the defeat of obstruction, and the improvement of our attitude for dealing with arrear, I conceive that Devolution may supply the means of partially meeting and satisfying, at least so far as it is legitimate, another call. I refer to the call for what is called (*in bonam partem*) Local Government and (*in malam*) Home Rule.

Circulated among ministers, and discussed without enthusiasm in Cabinet—only Chamberlain and Bright showing strong interest—the scheme was, for the time being, largely lost in the exigencies of the 'sheer panic' in Ireland[1] though it was still on the agenda, as 'measures of self-government', bracketed with Irish land, at the extraordinary Cabinet held on 31 December 1880. It showed, none the less, the natural tendency of Gladstone's mind towards a political and constitutional initiative and solution.

Even with this constitutional initiative effectively frustrated, Gladstone was unwilling to be launched on a new Land Bill, preferring instead a new bill to defend contracts between landlord and tenant.[2] He looked to the Tories' Royal Commission on agricultural distress to countervail the unexpectedly radical proposals of the Liberals' Bessborough Commission whose report, known to the Government by December 1880, was to Gladstone's alarm tantamount to endorsing the 'three Fs' of fair rents, fixity of tenure, and free sale.[3] Angry at what he saw as the 'unmanliness', the 'astounding helplessness' of the landlord class in failing to resist the Land League, and at the 'cupidity' in assisting the League which he ascribed to various institutions and individuals,[4] he moved towards a Land Bill only when it became clear that coercion was becoming politically unavoidable and that a positive political act would be needed to balance it.[5] Even then, Gladstone was 'very desirous to keep if possible on the lines & basis of the [1870] Land Act'.[6] 'The three Fs ... in their popular meaning ... will I fear break the Cabinet without conciliating the Leaguers.'[7] Yet it had to be recognised that support for the three Fs was strong: 'evidence comes in, rather more than I should have expected, of a desire for a measure such as the brewers call treble X'.[8] The final Cabinet of 1880, on 31 December, left the situation open-ended: 'Irish Land 1. To stand on the principles of the Land Act of 1870. 2. To propose measures of self-government.' Forster passed a note across the Cabinet table: 'To what does this conversation pledge us?';

[1] 11, 15 Nov., 31 Dec. 80. Cabinet replies included encouraging comments from Childers and Forster, and a dampening one from Hartington; Add MS 44625, f. 8. See also to Forster, 9 Dec. 80.
[2] To Selborne, 14 and 22 Dec. 80.
[3] Gladstone attempted to lean heavily upon the Commissioners; see to Forster, 7, 9 Dec. 80.
[4] To Harcourt, 12 Dec. 80, to the duke of Devonshire, 20 Dec. 80, to Selborne, 22 Dec. 80; see also to Forster, 9 Dec. 80, to Clonmell, 12 Dec. 80.
[5] See letters to Forster in November and December 80, and 13 Dec. 80.
[6] To Forster, 29 Nov. 80. See the memorandum at 9 Dec. 80 spelling out Gladstone's view of what the 1870 Act intended.
[7] To Forster, 3 Dec. 80.
[8] To Forster, 4 Dec. 80.

Gladstone replied, 'We are pledged to take Land Act for starting point and develop it. Each man his own interpreter.'[1]

Gladstone's 'development' in 1881 was, in the light of his comments and correspondence in 1880, to be startling. There is, to posterity, a striking feature about these comments and letters. At this stage Gladstone made no analogy between the Montenegrins and the Land League. That crisis of Balkan nationalism which had subsumed his energies and his sympathies in the mid-1870s and which had led as has been shown to some Irish analogies, seems to have offered him, despite a conscientious reading of Gavan Duffy's *Young Ireland*,[2] no insight into the phenomenon with which he now had to deal. His reading gave him information about Irish land reform proposals, but his opinion of Parnell's intentions ('curious, perhaps hopeful')[3] came from the newspapers.

Gladstone was less well informed about the objectives of the Land League leaders than he was about Balkan nationalism. He was already cautiously in touch with Captain O'Shea; he was supplied with the views of the Ulster Liberals, and with those of some of the older tenant-right campaigners, but he was unable to support his opposition to Habeas Corpus suspension with any inside information save that supplied, usually late and inadequately, by Dublin Castle and various members of the Irish aristocracy.

In 1880 Gladstone regarded the Land League simply as a criminal conspiracy, 'a fit object for permanent and effective prohibition'.[4] But, at the least, 'Parnell & Co.' had upset the reasonableness of British politics. The two measures, 'both most reasonable',[5] which in the summer of 1880 had seemed sensible within the usual practices of Cabinet government—the application and testing of the existing law, and a Royal Commission to inquire into possible changes—had led the Government not only into a timetable trap, though one which Gladstone manipulated in the November cabinets very adroitly to play for delay, but had made its response, looked at from any angle, seem inadequate, unimaginative, and feeble.

As with the household suffrage in 1866-67, Gladstone held out in 1880 against a 'radical' solution until it became irresistible. When it became so, all his resourcefulness, his speed of movement, and his control of detail were to enable him in the early months of 1881 very swiftly to regain the initiative, take the lead, and drive towards a legislative triumph.

VII

Thus far, this introduction has looked at the start and early development of Gladstone's second political career. But there was also much change in the Gladstones' personal life in these years. The loss of office in 1874 had led, as we have seen in an earlier volume,[6] to a sharp fall in income and a shortage of ready cash. This, allied to the announcement of formal retirement in 1875, resulted in

---

[1] 31 Dec. 80.   [2] 6 Nov. 80, read throughout this month.
[3] To Forster, 11 Nov. 80.
[4] To Bright, 23 Dec. 80. See K. T. Hoppen, *Elections, Politics, and Society in Ireland 1832-1885* (1984), 473ff. for the League's success in achieving a farmer–agricultural labourer alliance.
[5] To Forster, 3 Dec. 80.   [6] See above, vii. cviiiff.

a major change in domestic arrangements, a move from the plush fashion of the Carlton House area to a—relatively—cheaper and less grand house in Harley Street. The move was complex. In February 1875, following the announcement of retirement, the lease of 11 Carlton House Terrace, the Gladstones' house since July 1856, was sold for £35,000 to Sir Arthur Guinness.[1] William Gladstone then took 23 Carlton House Terrace, a 'small & rather quaint house just 50 yards from our own' for the season.[2] From the autumn of 1875, Arthur Balfour's house at 4 Carlton Gardens, just round the corner from Carlton House Terrace, was used as a London base. It was not until 8 February 1876 that 73 Harley Street was leased for thirty years, the assignment being executed on the same day that Gladstone 'spoke briefly in vindication of our concern in the case of the Christian subjects of Turkey':[3] a secure London base thus ironically being obtained exactly as the start of the long process of political return began, though at the time of the move Gladstone told Phillimore the house was 'for his wife's sake ... exclusively'.[4]

Gladstone does not seem to have taken much to the Harley Street house. When the family was away, he usually dined with Mrs. Birks, his next door neighbour, about whom little is known: Mary Gladstone describes her in a Pre-Raphaelite context, at Burne-Jones's house at North End, as having a 'scarlet shawl and gold lockets',[5] but she also seems to have had brewing connections.[6]

The move out of Carlton House Terrace was physically and emotionally exhausting, Gladstone doing much of the donkey work himself. There was a further sorting and destruction of papers, and part of the library appears to have been sold to the omnipresent Lord Wolverton.[7] The considerable art and china collections assembled since the 1830s (and by the 1870s housed partly at Carlton House Terrace and partly at the Brown Museum in Liverpool) were sold by Christie, Manson and Woods in a sale lasting four days in June 1875.

The sale was described by the catalogue as of 'English and foreign pottery and porcelain, bronzes, marbles, decorative furniture, silver-gilt tankards, cups and dishes, Camei, carvings in ivory, jade and wood, water-colour drawings, and pictures of the Italian, Spanish, Dutch and English schools.' It made £9351. 0s. 6d. The best price was for the last item of the sale, £483 for Bonifazio's 'Virgin',[8] the next best, £420, for William Dyce's beautiful portrait, 'Lady with the coronet of Jasmin', in fact a portrait of the rescue case, Miss Summerhayes, commissioned by Gladstone in 1859 and reproduced above, in volume five.[9] The large number of Continental paintings and artefacts, so carefully chosen and brought back from the various Continental tours, raised little (£85 for a 'Giorgione',[10] 11 guineas for a 'Murillo'). H. N. Gladstone

[1] 25 Feb. 75n.
[2] 17 Mar. 75. See also *T.T.*, 8 April 1875, 5f.
[3] 8 Feb. 76.   [4] 6 Feb. 76n.
[5] Mary Gladstone, *Diaries and letters* (1930), 191.
[6] See letter to her on the Malt Duty, 26 June 80.   [7] 24 Mar. 75.
[8] The whereabouts of this picture are unknown; it is probably not by Bonifazio and may be by Girolamo da Sta Croce (information from Sir Ellis Waterhouse).
[9] See above v. 328 and 6 Aug. 59.
[10] Both the 'Giorgiones' in the Gladstone sale were bought by Agnew's and given in 1926 to the Detroit Institute of Art; they are now ascribed to Palma Vecchio.

attempted to reassemble the collection in 1910, but few of the items could be traced.[1]

The whole business was embarrassing—'two huge Auctioneers' Bills today adorn the doorposts of the portico'[2]—and upsetting: 'Visited my room at No 11 for the last time as the proprietor. . . . The process as a whole has been like a *little* death. . . . I had *grown* to the House, having lived more time in it than in any other since I was born; and mainly by reason of all that was done in it. Sir A. G[uinness] has the chairs and sofa on which we sat when we resolved on the disestablishment of the Irish Church in 1868.'[3] As always, Gladstone extracted a moral lesson from unpleasantness: 'I am amazed at the accumulation of objects which have now, as by way of retribution, to be handled, & dispersed, or finally dismissed.'[4] Marx and Engels (the latter lived across the Park from the Gladstones' new house, in Regents Park Road) would have been amused at this Evangelical reaction to commodity-fetishism.

The result of these various sales was the end of the immediate cash crisis which had been worrying Gladstone since 1872, when he began to note concern about being 'pinched'.[5] He was, of course, a wealthy man. His 'approximate sketch' of his property in 1878 showed a total value of £280,522, which included £176,032 in land and £92,870 in stocks and shares.[6] But he was also the father of seven children, most of them, in some degree, still dependent on him. Agnes was married, and the Gladstones enjoyed visits to her and her husband, the headmaster of Wellington College, whose reputation Gladstone successfully defended in the Commons.[7] Willy, the oldest son, forty as this volume ends, at last married, to Gertrude Stuart, daughter of Lord Blantyre, whose wife was a daughter of the Duchess of Sutherland, Gladstone's female confidante in the 1860s.[8]

Willy, although technically since 1875 the owner of most of the Hawarden estates, still received an allowance from his father. Stephen, the second son, was prosperously settled in the wealthy rectorship of Hawarden. Harry, the third son, went into the family firm in Calcutta, but his difference with James Wyllie, who ran it, led to a long and bitter wrangle which surfaces several times in this volume.[9] His spasmodic lack of employment left him from time to time dependent on his father. Mary and Helen, the unmarried daughters, were completely dependent on their father, as was Herbert until he was elected to a lectureship in Modern History at Keble College, Oxford, following his First in the Modern History School in 1876.[10] His entry into politics as M.P. for Leeds in 1880

---

[1] The St. Deiniol's copy of Christie's catalogue of the sale is marked with the prices and the names of the buyers, mostly dealers. In 1929 H. N. Gladstone docketed a letter from Christie's of 31 August 1910: 'Messrs. Christie found it impossible to trace the collection.'

[2] 5 Apr. 75.   [3] 15 Apr. 75.
[4] 2 Apr. 75.   [5] 2 Sept. 72.
[6] In 'Rough Book B', Hawn P.   [7] 1 Apr. 79.

[8] 30 Sept. 75. At almost the same time Gertrude Glynne married into the ultra-Tory Douglas Pennant family, Barons of Penrhyn, a marriage which soon involved Gladstone in family rows (see 18 Jan. 76). There are thus two married 'Gertrudes' in this volume; it is sometimes unclear which is being discussed.

[9] 25–7 Nov. 75, 25 Mar. 76.
[10] See 19 June 76, 30 Apr. 79.

(taking the seat won by his father at that election) deprived him of even that modest stipend.

The children therefore still constituted a considerable financial obligation. Only Stephen and Agnes could be described as off the parents' hands. Financial dependence had, of course, from the father's view-point its advantages as well as its obligations. Increasingly the family could be used as a secretariat. Once Helen had gone to Cambridge, first to study, then to teach with Millicent Fawcett at what became Newnham College, Mary found herself manning the post, helped by Herbert when he was at home. Copies of letters in their hands begin to be quite frequent in the late 1870s. Mary's role as her parents' companion—into which she seems to have been drawn unselfconsciously on their part and only partly reluctantly on hers—was beginning to be quite well defined. 'I lost good company in Helen and Herbert; but Mary is all-sufficing in point of society.'[1]

The letters form a major theme and complaint of the years covered by this volume. The correspondents, together with people met, are listed each day, almost always without comment, save for titles and the occasional geographical identification; 'Mr James (U.S.)' turns out, for example, to be the young Henry James, whose own account of the meeting was less cryptic.[2] As a glance at the text and the *Dramatis Personae* at the end of this volume will show, their number is legion. The correspondence drove Gladstone near to despair: 'It is a terrible oppression.'[3] He made the strategic decision early in his retirement not to employ a secretary. Many times in the late 1870s he wondered if this decision had been right, but he did not go back on it, even despite various applications from would-be secretaries, one from S. Stringer Bate who worked under the pseudonym of 'Walter Raleigh',[4] although J. A. Godley from time to time helped out.

Pamphlets, speeches, and the campaigns from September 1876 until the return to office in 1880 produced a deluge of mail, a considerable proportion of which was from correspondents hitherto unknown to Gladstone. Fifty or so letters a day reached Hawarden or Harley Street, many more at a time of political crisis, and a few days away brought huge accumulations of arrears. Family help in their answering was never regularised: Gladstone did most of the work himself, perfecting the use of the post-card as cheap, polite, but enforcing a convenient word limit.[5] He showed considerable interest in the introduction of the telephone to London, attending several demonstrations of its powers.[6] In 1880 a telephone was apparently installed at Hawarden, probably one of the first political houses to have one. Gladstone found it 'most unearthly'[7] and does not seem to have used it, at least in the early 1880s. In any event, and fortunately for the historian, too few of his correspondents would have had a machine for the chore of letter writing to be alleviated.

[1] 5 Jan. 77.   [2] 28 Mar. 77.
[3] 12 Dec. 79.   [4] 28 Nov.–2 Dec. 75.
[5] The costs of the correspondence were carefully noted, in that '(B.P.)' is put after a correspondent's name when a pamphlet or book was sent by Book Post. In the later years of this volume '(O)' is also quite commonly placed after a correspondent's name; unfortunately, no satisfactory explanation of its purpose has yet been found.
[6] 18 Mar. 78; 30 Apr. 79.
[7] Probably used in its Glynnese sense of gnomish or nasty; see 27 Nov. 80.

Burdensome though Gladstone undoubtedly felt his correspondence to be, it enabled him to indulge his passion for order. The same almost physical pleasure that he gained from a neat solution to a difficulty in compiling the national budget is to be seen in his enthusiasm for reducing a confusion of letters or books or trees to an orderly sequence, catalogued—or, in the case of the trees, distanced between each other—in an intellectually satisfying form. It would be going too far to say that Gladstone was obsessed with order for its own sake—attacks on 'chaos' were responses to undeniable problems—but the activity of the bringing of order stemmed restlessness and justified possession, whether of goods such as letters and books, or of places such as libraries and estates, or even of the right to existence. The form of the daily diary entry, so remorselessly repeated, reflected the same preoccupation and offered a similar satisfaction.

The random element in the correspondents listed in the journal text has made identification complex. Some, but not a great proportion, of the casual letters survive in the 'minor correspondents' files at St. Deiniol's Library. These files are an important supplement to the main political correspondence which forms the bulk of the Gladstone Papers in the British Library. Gladstone did not set out to retain all his incoming mail, and Tilney Bassett, the family archivist in the early twentieth century, is known to have destroyed a certain amount of the minor correspondence.[1] For these opposition years in the 1870s, a rough estimate, made while trying to identify correspondents, suggests that only about twenty per cent of the incoming mail has survived, though even that is a very considerable number of letters.[2] The difficulties of identification are increased by Gladstone's increasingly eccentric spelling of names[3] and by his egalitarian listing of his correspondents. There is no ranking; a grocer in Nairn is likely to fall between two ex-cabinet ministers. Experience in successful identification by way of the surviving minor correspondence at St. Deiniol's suggests that what seems to be the name of a well-known correspondent in London is often in fact a name-sake in Penzance, Thurso, or Iowa.

Many of the letters were invitations to further political action. Gladstone resented this, and on one occasion tabled in considerable irritation the number of invitations turned down that day.[4] His irritation is perhaps surprising, given the extent to which he was already involving himself in public activity. It

---

[1] *Autobiographica*, iv. 124.

[2] The same procedure has been followed for unidentified correspondents as is described above, vii. xcixn.

[3] The spelling in the text of the names of correspondents and authors continues to be as faithful as possible to the holograph. [*Sic*] has been added in some instances of striking abberation, but to have attempted to add it each time Gladstone mis-spells a name would have swamped the text. Common but not consistent abberations in this volume are Schenk (for Schenck), Sirmoneta (for Sermoneta), Mochler (for Mockler), Irvin or Irvine (for Irving, the actor), Sybilla (for Sybella Lyttelton); Kandahar is randomly spelt with a 'K' and a 'C'. Increasingly Gladstone lists the names of correspondents in columns, without writing out prefixes though sometimes suggesting the prefix by a ditto mark. In such cases, where initials have been given, the prefix 'Mr.' has not been supplied, though 'Rev.', 'Dr.', and 'Lord' have been supplied where so indicated; where Gladstone notes no initials, the prefix 'Mr.' has been supplied; an example of this can be seen from the facsimile of the diary text reproduced below.

[4] 8 July 78.

represents, perhaps, the general unawareness of politicians at this time of that large degree of public exposure which democratic politics was going to expect of its chief practitioners. Correspondence in these non-governmental years took up as much time as it had when in office, perhaps even more. Together with Church and meals, it dictated the rhythm of the day. It allowed Gladstone, sitting in the Temple of Peace at Hawarden, to maintain contact with the political world and to agitate its nerves by letters and postcards: such was the efficiency of the Victorian Post Office[1] and the attention given to the written word.

The daily routine at Hawarden involved Gladstone in a good deal of exercise: the early morning walk through the Park to the Church and back (along a specially built path to ensure privacy), walking in the surrounding countryside and, of course, silviculture, felling and planting trees. Gladstone always used an axe, and in these years many were presented to him. It became almost a totem among his admirers. Margaret de Lisle, daughter of the convert to Roman Catholicism, always wore an axe to indicate loyalty to Gladstone, until Gordon's death in 1885, when she took it off.[2] He visited Ransome and Sons' factory to watch an exhibition of the powers of a steam saw in felling a tree;[3] the expression on his face in the illustration printed in this volume reflects the conflict of utility *versus* pleasure.

The rest of the day was often spent in reading or writing. The reader who wishes to penetrate the mind of the 1870s could do worse than to read through all the books, pamphlets, and periodical articles which Gladstone notes reading in the course of a month. It would be an arduous but illuminating task, for it would show a curious blend of modernity and religiosity. In a month taken at random—June 1879—Gladstone read twenty-eight books and seven periodical articles. The books range from sustained study of W. E. H. Lecky's *History of England in the Eighteenth Century* (which prompted Gladstone's article on the history of evangelicalism, finished during this month) and of J. R. Green's *A Short History of the English People*, to a number of works on popular science, of which Gladstone in the late 1870s became quite a keen student. Literature is represented by Hannah Swanwick's *Egmont* and the poetry of Coleridge, Goethe, and Tennyson, the classics by a paper on 'Homeric Doubts', and contemporary affairs by L. Kong Meng's *The Chinese Question in Australia* and a number of pamphlets in French, Italian, and English. Sunday reading, spilling over into the rest of the week, was a biography of Alexander Duff, the Scottish missionary, the frequently read Thomas à Kempis, and a number of sermons, tracts, lectures, and addresses.

The selection is a fair representation of Gladstone's reading habits. He liked to have a substantial religious and a substantial secular book 'on the go', and to buttress these with an eclectic bundle of material, increasingly selected from the contributions posted to him by authors and publishers. With a good deal of this latter material he was personally involved, in that the works were often dedicated to him, or attacking him, or requesting by covering letter a public response, quite often given in a letter subsequently released by the recipient to

---

[1] This efficiency explains how a letter and its reply are often dated the same day, even though the correspondents may be in different cities.

[2] 20 Feb. 78n.   [3] 2 Feb. 78.

the press. For example, the private remarks he made on the first volume of Duff's biography became the basis of an assessment of Duff quoted in the second volume published later in the year, and his letter approving of Fagan's *Life of Panizzi* was immediately printed in the biography's second edition.[1]

Gladstone's reading was in part a self-education, but even this private act was in fact public, part of the process of 'putting his mind into the common stock'. This was most directly done by the writing which sprang from the reading. There is hardly a month in these years when an article or a pamphlet is not in progress. Between 1875 and 1880, Gladstone wrote almost sixty articles and published two books of new material, *Homeric Synchronism* and *Primer of Homer*, the latter in J. R. Green's popular series for Macmillan (the forerunner of the Home University Library),[2] and 'a treat' rather than a duty.[3] He produced several books of speeches and recently written articles, and he edited his selected collected articles—'rather a daring measure'[4]—in seven volumes entitled *Gleanings of Past Years*,[5] published by John Murray.

In 1879, he noted that his total literary earnings to date were about £10,000 gross;[6] £5009 was earned between 1876 and 1880.[7] The largest item was the income from the pamphlets and subsequent book on the Vatican controversy 1874-75 (£2800), one of the smallest items the £58 received from the Clarendon Press of Oxford University for *Studies on Homer* (1858), the work which undoubtedly cost the most thought and effort.

By the 1870s, Gladstone was, obviously enough, an author much in demand, and able, on the whole, to call his own tune. James Knowles carried articles such as 'The Slicing of Hector' (£52) in the *Contemporary Review* and later in the *Nineteenth Century* so as to be able to publish great contemporary pieces such as 'England's Mission' (£100). Gladstone's literary work was thus lucrative but not money-directed. He wrote *gratis* for the Congregationalist *British Quarterly Review* and for almost nothing for the Tractarian *Church Quarterly Review*. Had he been writing chiefly for money, he would have written much more for the United States market. His 'Kin beyond Sea', *inter alia* a curious elaboration of Bagehot's *The English Constitution* written for the *North American Review* in 1878, brought a shoal of invitations to write and lecture, all of which were turned down, including an invitation from Harvard for a series of lectures on Political Economy for which he was preferred as a speaker to Jevons, Marshall, and Fawcett.[8]

The articles and other writings reflected Gladstone's eclectic interests, covering a vast range of subjects from a cautious introduction to de Laveleye's Weberesque thesis in *Protestantism and Catholicism* (1875), through anonymous and on certain occasions unpublished notices and reviews for Cazenove's new *Church Quarterly Review* to his notable series of comments on affairs of the day

---

[1] See 22 Oct. 80.   [2] 24 Sept., 20 Nov. 77.
[3] 29 Apr. 78.   [4] 6 Nov. 78.
[5] 6 Sept. 77, 6 Nov. 78.   [6] See the 'Testamentary Memorandum' at 1 Jan. 79.
[7] Account book for 1878-94, Hawn P, from which subsequent figures are taken. This book estimates total literary earnings to the end of 1880 as £10,239. If £450 is subtracted for articles from the 1876 total of £1790, this would give £1340 for the 'Bulgarian Horrors' pamphlet in that year.
[8] 15 Aug. 78. See also 20 Aug. 79n. for an offer of £4000, and see 15 Jan. 79 for an invitation from Phi Beta Kappa at Harvard.

in the *Contemporary Review* and the *Nineteenth Century*, for which James Knowles captured him after Knowles's row with Strahan, the publisher of the *Contemporary*. To assist the reader in finding and correlating these pieces, they are listed in an Appendix in chronological order of first mention in the diary.

Though all these writings are of interest, and most show Gladstone to be much terser and sharper with the pen than is often thought, there can be little doubt that of the literary pieces the best is his anonymous review in the *Quarterly* of G. O. Trevelyan's *Life and Letters of Macaulay*. In view of the savage attack which Macaulay had made on Gladstone's first book in 1838, it shows generosity as well as understanding. Gladstone's literary output would have made him an important Victorian figure even if his political activities were discounted, but his essay on Macaulay suggests rather more than this. It is a model retrospect, still holding a place on its own merits in the study of Macaulay. Gladstone took a great deal of trouble with the essay, which he began on 13 April 1876 and finished on 12 June, the writing being interrupted by George Lyttelton's suicide and various family illnesses: 'It is a business made difficult by the utter want of continuity in my application to it. And really the subject is beyond the common order.'[1]

From the point of view of our understanding of Gladstone, the essay is interesting for the qualities it praises and condemns: 'As the serious flaw in Macaulay's mind was want of depth, so the central defect . . . is a pervading strain of more or less exaggeration . . . amidst a blaze of glory, there is a want of perspective, of balance, and of breadth.' To demonstrate this defect, Gladstone offered the examples of Macaulay's exaggerated treatment of Milton and Bacon in the *Essays*, and, drawing on Churchill Babbington, of the Restoration clergy in the *History*. But he recognised that to show that Macaulay was 'wrong' was essentially beside the point, which was that Macaulay had written an English romance, 'his whole method of touch and handling are poetical'. The transcendent quality which redeemed his weaknesses and made Macaulay's works 'a permanent addition to the mental patrimony of the human race' was his nature, best seen in his poems which 'possess the chief merits of his other works, and are free from their faults': the *History* is essentially a poetic romance, 'and greater and better yet than the works themselves are the lofty aims and conceptions, the large heart, the independent, manful mind, the pure and noble career'.[2]

We can see here how it was that with his low view of his own nature, his persistent self-abasement, Gladstone never completed a major work after his *Studies on Homer* (1858), the product of his earlier years of extended opposition, and how it was that he concentrated on short pieces making limited points. The mass of his scholarly effort went into the Homeric Thesaurus, never published as such though sections of it appeared from time to time in the periodicals. Gladstone had in mind a volume on Olympian religion but, apart from fragments for the periodicals, chips from a Hawarden workshop, little was achieved in the way of a book-length plan.

These short pieces, fervent though many of them are, were always fair. Within the traditions of his age, and certainly compared with any twentieth-

---

[1] 10 June 76.   [2] Quotations from *Gleanings*, ii. 265ff.

century political figure, Gladstone was an erudite, scrupulous commentator and combatant. Even as a politician in retirement, he knew the Blue Books as well as any government spokesman, and the diary continues to testify to the energy of his ephemeral reading. Yet this sort of speaking and writing made him more aware of his weaknesses as an author. Commenting on his letters to Samuel Wilberforce as he re-read them in preparation for their extensive use in Wilberforce's biography, he observed of them, 'they are curiously illustrative of a peculiar and second-rate nature',[1] and, revising his review of Tennyson's *Maud* for republication in *Gleanings*, he noted: 'The fact is I am wanting in that higher poetical sense which distinguishes the true artist.'[2] The persistent emphasis on control, balance, holding things in check, might not have seemed obvious to a Tory opponent in this period, but it was of the very essence of Gladstone's character. His nature was poetic, but his character, as he had forged it, was captive.

VIII

This captivity, not always successfully enforced but always strenuously pursued, was contained by religion, for from regular religious observance, particularly of the Eucharist, Gladstone gained an element of peace, a redress to his restlessness. In terms of his personal life, the years covered in this Volume were relatively tranquil. He was on good terms with his wife and family. Catherine Gladstone differed sharply with him over his retirement in 1875[3]— one of the few occasions on which she intervened politically to disagree—and there were difficulties about the sale of the London house,[4] but these were not long-term differences. Like her husband, Mrs. Gladstone retained her exuberance and her energy: 'At 64 she has the vigour & freshness of 34.'[5] She continued her work for her charitable homes, and her care for the many members of the Gladstone–Lyttelton connection. She was an important contributor to the management and personal success of the Midlothian Campaign, her regular appearances with her husband on the political platform being widely noticed in the contemporary press.

Gladstone's 'rescue work' with London prostitutes continued in a routine way. An occasional 'X' is placed after his meetings with Laura Thistlethwayte,[6] the evangelical ex-courtesan who had been the focus of the major emotional crisis of 1869-70, but in general his relationship with her seems to have become less charged. The very intense tone of the correspondence of the early 1870s—an intensity surely unsustainable—gives way to a calmer, easier exchange. They were both guests at a house party given by Lord Bathurst at Oakley Park in 1875, but, despite the absence of Catherine Gladstone and three specifically itemised conversations, nothing of the crisis at Boveridge in 1869 was repeated.[7]

As Arthur Thistlethwayte's financial and sexual life became ever more complex, Gladstone acted as an adviser to Laura, especially when she was

---

[1] 3 Sept. 79.   [2] 25 Nov. 78.
[3] 7 Jan. 75.   [4] 30 Mar. 75.
[5] 6 Jan. 76.   [6] See, e.g., 13 Feb. 77.
[7] 1-3 Oct. 75; for 1869, see Introduction above, vii. civ and 'Appendix' to volume viii.

summoned to the debtors' court by Henry Padwick, a well-known race-horse
owner, gambler, and money-lender. In 1878 Captain Thistlethwayte was in
court in dispute with Padwick, and for a time in 1879 it looked as if an action
would be brought by Padwick directly involving Laura. The case would have
been, at the least, very awkward for Gladstone. Since the late 1860s he had
accepted from her gifts 'which in aggregate must have cost hundreds'.[1] He had
protested against their receipt and had clearly been embarrassed by them, but
he had not put a stop to the practice. When Mrs. Thistlethwayte's financial
position became serious, in 1878, he attempted without success to return the
presents, and he tried again and failed again in 1879. But the difficulty if the
case became public would have gone well beyond the gifts. Padwick's case was
that Captain Thistlethwayte refused to honour his wife's debts. Thistlethwayte's defence was that his wife ran them up by entertainment and munificence given without his knowledge. A subpoena was issued to Gladstone to
appear as a witness.[2] He was definitely alarmed. The witnesses, he told Laura,

> will probably be asked *whom* they met at your table. . . . The witnesses would probably
> be asked whether they had partaken of your hospitality—I should have to reply yes;
> especially at luncheons from time to time where I used to meet some greatly esteemed
> friends. . . . I would probably be asked who were the guests I had met at your table. It
> would be most offensive to me to detail their names as if charging them with some-
> thing discreditable. . . . I doubt whether either you or Mr. T. is at all aware of the
> amount & kind of mischief done by the trial of last year: It was exceedingly great, and
> rely on it that by any similar trial now repeated it would be aggravated tenfold.[3]

Fortunately for Gladstone, for the guests were not all of his usual circle, the
case was settled out of court.[4] The Gladstone–Thistlethwayte correspondence
for the later 1870s contains the odd political and religious comment, but it con-
sists mostly of arrangements for meals and of family news: Laura Thistlethwayte saw to it that she was well-informed about the doings of the Gladstone
children, although her exigency was not always successful. Increasingly, the
initiative in the correspondence came from her, with Gladstone responding
cordially but often also cautiously, wary of being drawn in further than polite-
ness and his sense of duty required. He felt obliged, even bound to her, as he
saw her bravely facing her difficulties, but he also found her importunity on
occasions irritating.

One of the guests at the Thistlethwayte table was Olga Novikov, the 'M.P. for
Russia'. Several important meetings on Russo-Turkish affairs took place at Mrs.

[1] Letters to 'Mrs Thistlethwayte' of 3 May 1879, Lambeth MSS. In letters on the court case, Gladstone reverts to 'Dear Mrs Thistlethwayte' as the form of address, instead of 'Dear Spirit', the form
used since 1869. Lack of space prohibits in this volume an Appendix of letters to Laura Thistlethwayte; a future volume will contain a selection of letters to her for the years after 1870. See above,
viii. 557ff., for letters to her in 1869–70.

[2] 1 Apr. 79n.

[3] To Mrs. Thistlethwayte, 10 April 1879. Gladstone discussed the case with Rosebery, by no
means an intimate, in April 1879, which may indicate alarm about its consequences in Midlothian;
19 Apr. 79.

[4] 'So now Padwick abandons the idea of getting more than his due, while his due will be offered to
him. Good'; letter to Mrs. Thistlethwayte of 3 July 1879. For a court appearance in a quite different
case in 1879, see 13 Sept. 79.

Thistlethwayte's house in Grosvenor Square, notably Gladstone's meeting with
Shuvalov in December 1876 on the evening of the great St. James's Hall meeting on the Bulgarian atrocities.[1] Gladstone saw Olga Novikov as a Russian
rather than a woman. The sentimental paternalism characteristic of his letters
to women on politics is absent from his correspondence with Madame Novikov.[2] Her views, as an enthusiastic Pan-Slavist, did not fit precisely with Gladstone's, but she was a well-informed source of information about Russian affairs
and a useful link for him with the Russian community in London, Paris and
beyond. He carefully distanced himself from her on becoming Prime Minister,
but maintained a spasmodic correspondence.[3] It may be that Madame Novikov
thought she was using Gladstone, and this was a common view at the time, and
indeed later;[4] but there is no indication in the journal that he found himself in
her thrall.

Laura Thistlethwayte was also a link with the theatre. It is striking that in
this, one of the most Evangelical periods of his life, Gladstone when in London
became almost a theatrical devotee. He was, in private relaxation, 'enthusiastic'
rather than 'earnest'.[5] Phillimore noted, as the Eastern Question reached its
climax: 'I was amused to hear him defend plays & the Theatre—on no subject
have his opinions undergone a more complete revolution.'[6] He went to one of
the first London performances of *Lohengrin*, at Covent Garden,[7] but for the
most part his theatre-going was to the fashionable West End with its comedies
and farces, or to Shakespeare in Irving's productions at the Lyceum.[8] He
sampled the increasingly popular Music Hall ('the show was certainly not

[1] 8 Dec. 76.

[2] The remnants of the Novikov Papers, now in Christ Church, Oxford, unfortunately do not
include Gladstone's letters to her; many of these were published by W. T. Stead in *The 'M.P. for
Russia'*, 2v. (1909).

[3] 4 May 80.

[4] A remarkable letter from R. B. D. Morier to L. Mallet, 20 May 1880 (copy made from the
Wemyss MSS now in Balliol College, Oxford, amongst which this letter is no longer to be found; I
am obliged to Dr. Ramm for the copy) reflects this view: 'As regards Gladstone's action it is most
interesting to me from a merely psychological point of view. The real motive powers necessarily
escape the mass because they are to be detected only in a word or a sentence dropped here and
there which only the initiated can comprehend. But if for instance you read his review of that strum-
pet Madame Novikoff's book you will see much. The first thing to note is the influence that woman
has over him and the way quite unconsciously to himself, that he sees everything through *her* eyes.
Now I have often told you that I am convinced no one really understands Gladstone unless he notes
that very much of his ways are the result of what I call suppressed priapism! I maintain that at least
one third of human action is determined by the too much or too little of the sexual intercourse that
has fallen to the lot of the actor. Of course in the case of Gladstone it is a case of too little. I am convinced that he came into the world with the most tremendously virile powers, that his strongly
ascetic religiosity has kept them down—that Mrs G. has been the only flesh he has ever tasted! consequently that there is even at his time of life a lurking desire within him seeking unconsciously to
himself to be assuaged. Madame N. who is an extremely accomplished whore will have seized this at
a glance. She will have been far too cunning to play on this instrument directly but she will have
known exactly how to utilize her knowledge. . . .' The rest of the letter contains equally strident anti-
semitic comments about Rosebery's wife and Beaconsfield, Morier being incensed at rumours of
'outsiders' being appointed to embassies and at Montagu Corry's peerage; Morier admitted 'I am
not just now a perfectly impartial judge.'

[5] Walter Houghton's distinction is used to good effect in Boyd Hilton, art. cit., 48–9.

[6] Phillimore's diary, 26 January 1878.

[7] 8 May 75.

[8] For attendances at Irving's performances, see above, p. xxxiv, n. 8.

Athenian' was Gladstone's cryptic comment),[1] and the ballet at the Alhambra.[2] He attended a private performance by Sarah Bernhardt at the house of Mrs. Ralli, another of his theatre-going companions,[3] he saw her as Phèdre at the Gaiety ('⅔ full')[4] and with his family he went to the Théâtre Français season in Paris.[5] His famous appearance at the Haymarket Theatre with Hartington and Granville on the night of the publication of the 'Bulgarian Horrors' was thus by no means idiosyncratic.[6] Unfortunately, it is not now possible to know whether this theatre-going extended Gladstone's range as a speaker. But it is not unreasonable to suppose that his observation of theatrical occasions contributed to his skills in moving an audience, skills which in a large hall required every resource of voice and gesture. An interesting by-product of this theatre-going was his letter to *The Theatre* in 1878 which formed a focal point for one of the early campaigns for a National Theatre.[7] In this Gladstone touched English life characteristically, for one of the most striking aspects of his long career is the astonishing range of his activities. Rare is the Victorian archive or institution without a Gladstonian dimension.

IX

Gladstone had always seen Laura Thistlethwayte in a Pre-Raphaelite or Tennysonian light; in this volume he several times notes reading Tennyson to her, notably 'Guinevere' following their visit to the Alhambra ballet.[8] Anything that he tried to see nobly, particularly in women, he saw through the categories of mediaeval chivalry, as softened and made Victorian in Tennyson's poems and plays.[9] The years covered by this volume record considerable contacts with what may be called the respectable elements of Tennysonian Pre-Raphaelitism. These were encouraged by a very different influence from Laura Thistlethwayte, his daughter Mary, who was friendly with the Burne-Jones circle.

In particular, Hawarden was visited by two of the great potentates of Victorian aesthetics: Tennyson and Ruskin.

Tennyson came in October 1876. The visit was not altogether a success, though it was probably more of a success than it might have been if Newman had accepted Gladstone's invitation to join the party.[10] Tennyson had finished, but not yet published, his play *Harold* and was nervous about its success. Gladstone noted politely: 'Tennyson read to us his Harold: it took near 2¼ hours';[11] he did not mention that the family thought that he nearly fell asleep, and that his son Willy had a fit of suppressed giggles.[12] The next day Gladstone encouraged conversation on his favourite topic of the time, the decline in the belief in hell. Not surprisingly, although Arthur Hallam had been in a sense the inspirer of both, the author of *Church Principles* found himself on different

[1] 21 July 77.   [2] 25 Sept. 77.
[3] 23 June 79.   [4] 9 June 80.
[5] 17 and 20 Oct. 79.   [6] 5 Sept. 76.
[7] 9 Mar. 78. See also 14 June 79.
[8] 25 Sept. 77. See above v. lxiv and vii. cvi.
[9] See M. Girouard, *The Return to Camelot. Chivalry and the English gentleman* (1981), ch. xii.
[10] See 29 Oct. 76n.   [11] 1 Nov. 76.
[12] See R. B. Martin, *Tennyson. The unquiet heart* (1980), 516.

ground from the composer of *In Memoriam*: 'Conversation with Tennyson on Future Retribution, and other matters of theology: he has not thought, I conceive, systematically or thoroughly upon them, but is much alarmed at the prospect of the loss of belief. He left me at one.'[1] Tennyson and Gladstone were to clash with increasing vigour in the 1880s, but their public face in these years was harmonious: Tennyson's sonnet extolling the virtues of the Montenegrins immediately preceded Gladstone's article, 'Montenegro', in the third number of the *Nineteenth Century*.[2]

Gladstone was always an enthusiast for respectable art, as shown at Agnew's, Colnaghi's, and the Royal Academy exhibition—an enthusiasm marked by his election in 1876, in the room of Connop Thirlwall, as Royal Academy Professor of Ancient History. But he also began visiting the Grosvenor Gallery,[3] the show-place of the avant-garde—immortalised by W. S. Gilbert's lines in *Patience* (1881): 'a greenery-yallery, Grosvenor Gallery, foot-in-the-grave young man!'— and his correspondence with Oscar Wilde, inaugurated by the latter while an undergraduate, went beyond mere formality.[4]

Gladstone to some extent patched up his differences with John Ruskin, the Pre-Raphaelites' patron, who deplored Gladstone's fiscal liberalism, by two successful visits to Hawarden, though this did not prevent Ruskin, in his campaign to succeed Gladstone as Rector of Glasgow University, observing that he cared no more for Gladstone and Disraeli than he did for two old bagpipes.[5] With Henry Scott Holland also present at Hawarden, the company had a distinctively Christian Socialist flavour.

On the second visit, Ruskin 'developed his political opinions. They aim at the restoration of the Judaic system, & exhibit a mixture of virtuous absolutism & Christian socialism.'[6] In response, Gladstone delighted Ruskin by declaring 'I am a firm believer in the aristocratic principle—the rule of the best. I am an out-and-out *inequalitarian*.'[7]

Ruskin charmed Gladstone, but his view of government and political economy can hardly have appealed to him. As to Gladstone's declaration, it is hard at first glance to know whether it is odder that it should have been made by a free-trade Chancellor of the Exchequer, or applauded by a Christian Socialist. At second glance, it can be seen that it is consistent with Gladstone's view that free trade would confirm rather than topple the social order of the nation, and that Ruskin's Christian Socialism was profoundly hierarchic.[8]

Ruskin's visits to Hawarden were followed by one from Burne-Jones, who was active in the Atrocities campaign and who 'left good memories behind him'. Burne-Jones, recovering from an illness, certainly bore the brunt of Gladstonian enthusiasm; 'Read my chapter on Judaism in the "Studies [on Homer]"

---

[1] 2 Nov. 76.   [2] 14 Apr. 77.
[3] 9 May 77, 30 Apr. 79, 30 Apr. 80.   [4] 15 May 77.
[5] 12–15 Jan. and 12–15 Oct. 78. For the Glasgow campaign and correspondence, see L. March-Phillipps and B. Christian, *Some Hawarden letters 1878–1913* (1917), 62ff.
[6] 14 Oct. 78.
[7] Morley, ii. 582: rendered as '*inegalitarian*' in Magnus, 257, without a reference.
[8] See R. Hewison, *John Ruskin* (1976), 182ff. Mary Gladstone noted: 'the experienced Ch. of Ex. and visionary idealist came into conflict'; L. Masterman, *Mary Gladstone* (1930), 142.

& inflicted it on Mr Burne Jones' and, next day, 're-read my Chapter [1858] on the Jews and gave it to Mr Burne Jones who approved'.[1]

Gladstone was also in contact with Pre-Raphaelites, or former Pre-Raphaelites, through the portraits painted of him in these years. G. F. Watts began his third portrait of Gladstone in May 1874.[2] It was commissioned by his Oxford college, Christ Church. The sittings continued through the 1870s, prolonged by gossiping on both sides. In 1876 Gladstone noted 'Delightful conversation, but little progress on the picture'; and in 1878 'Sat to Watts from 12 to 4. He would but for courtesy willingly have had more. This length of time is really a national vice in English artists.'[3] The picture was hung in Christ Church Hall, but opinion at the annual Gaudy feast rejected it. It was sent back to Watts in 1879 who 'partially defaced it in the hope of making it a more satisfactory likeness'; further sittings in 1881 proved impossible and Watts returned his fee, retaining the picture.[4] One can see why the portrait was turned down. It is not a good likeness and lacks the authority of Watts's earlier efforts. No comment from Gladstone on the picture or on its rejection has been found.[5]

Millais was a different case. Like Watts, he was now largely a society portrait-painter, but, unlike Watts, he did not agonise. Millais took the initiative in a businesslike manner: 'I have often wished to paint your portrait ... one hour at a time is all I would wish.'[6] In fact the sittings were sometimes of two hours, but the portrait was finished in under a month in five sittings.[7] After a touching-up sitting, Gladstone noted that Millais's 'ardour & energy about his picture inspire a strong sympathy'.[8] The portrait, now in the National Portrait Gallery and reproduced in this volume, is often regarded as one of Millais's finest, but it is effeminate compared with his second portrait of Gladstone, painted in the 1880s, which eventually filled the gap in Christ Church left by the rejection of the Watts. Gladstone showed considerable interest in artists and in art, but none at all in portraits of himself. He was genuinely lacking in vanity: 'a dull and slow judge of all works of art, I am a particularly bad one of any representation of myself'.[9]

X

Reading, writing, meetings, and visits, quite apart from the extraneous intrusions of politics, left Gladstone in retirement as busy as he had ever been. The diary reflects this. Its form remains that of a man of action. Gladstone liked to be busy. The diary was usually written each day, with never a day missed in this volume, except during the acute illness of July–August 1880 when its declining

[1] 10–15 Aug. 79.

[2] From the sittings beginning on 14 June 59, Watts painted two portraits, now at Hawarden and the National Portrait Gallery.

[3] 16 May 76, 1 June 78.

[4] Christ Church Governing Body minutes, i. 298, 301.

[5] There is a small photograph of the portrait in the Watts Museum near Guildford. Mary Gladstone noted: 'To see the Watts picture of Papa, couldnt bear it—a weak, peevish old man; quite wretched over it'; Masterman, *Mary Gladstone*, 143.

[6] 18 Mar. 78n.

[7] See 26 June, 24 July 78.

[8] 6 Aug. 78.

[9] To Laura Thistlethwayte, 12 November 1875.

legibility shows the onset of the fever and several days were written up later *en bloc*. Occasionally, internal evidence suggests that the writing was done a day or so late, but this did not lead to more reflective entries. But if there is no major change in the nature of the journal, there is a minor one. Entries became longer, for two reasons. First, there are more names of correspondents to be noted. Evidence in the archives shows that not all the correspondents' names are mentioned, but that about two-thirds of them are for the period up to May 1880; in government, almost all of the names of the correspondents to whom Gladstone wrote personally are mentioned. Second, the amount of comment is slightly increased, with the result that, if the names are discounted, the diary becomes a rather more readable and accessible document.

The comments, telegraphic though they usually are, are unmistakably clear to the experienced reader, curiously sharp emotionally, considering their brevity. None the less, Gladstone did not write the diary with readability in mind, even though he sometimes used the earlier volumes for reminiscences.[1] It is essentially a record of achievement in time spent, and time spent on a day-to-day basis. In earlier years he had drawn up lists which sometimes spanned a decade; in the 1870s, his view of time seems to have been more limited. Though there are quite frequent references to his age, there is no reflection on what it means to be old rather than young. The rebelliousness against growing old, the 'resistance to the passage of Time',[2] quite a feature of Gladstone in his fifties, has by his late sixties apparently gone, with the exception of a brief remark in December 1879, 'there is still something that consents not to be old'.[3] Rather, there is surprise and thanks that, at seventy, he is functioning as effectively as he had been at forty. Age thus became a weapon rather than a fear. Angry though he was about developments in public life, equanimity seems to characterise Gladstone's view of himself far more than in any earlier decade. To have held the great offices of state and to have retired, however briefly, from the political scene allowed Gladstone to see himself as outside the usual confines of political time and ambition. This status was to become a terrible weapon, used ingeniously and systematically against opponents and colleagues alike.

XI

A break from the stresses and strains of writing and especially from corresponding was gained by various expeditions. The visit to Ireland in 1877 has already been discussed. There was also a trip with some of the children to the Isle of Man,[4] and a continental journey in 1879, a break before the first Midlothian Campaign, and the subject of a short separate travel diary, now tipped in to the relevant volume of the journal.[5] This trip took the Gladstones first to stay with Acton and his wife at Tegernsee in the Bavarian Alps, where Dr. Döllinger was also of the party. This visit was of particular importance for Mary Gladstone, for from it sprang her intimacy with Acton.[6] The Gladstone party then travelled through the Dolomites—at that time an unusual and unfashionable

[1] See, e.g. 27 July 79.   [2] 29 Dec. 59.   [3] 28 Dec. 79.
[4] 1–7 Oct. 78.   [5] 14 Sept.–21 Oct. 79.
[6] Described in the fine study by Owen Chadwick, 'Gladstone and Acton' (1976).

route—to Venice, where Lady Marian Alford acted as hostess, organising trips and meetings with the members of English society in Venice, such as Robert Browning. Acton rejoined them by a different route.

The stay in Germany and Italy confirmed the rather cautious relationship between Gladstone and Acton, which had been to some extent damaged by the Vatican pamphlet of 1874.[1] Gladstone felt Acton willing to wound, but afraid to strike the Papacy: 'Walk & long conversation with Ld Acton: who seems in opinion to go beyond Döllinger, though in action to stop short of him.'[2] There is not much indication of intimacy, at least on Gladstone's side. The real enjoyment, for him, was the talks with Döllinger, whom the party visited in Munich on the way home. The references to Döllinger in the diary are always warm, positive, and enthusiastic, those to Acton, usually neutral. It was during this visit that Lenbach, the Munich artist, painted the portrait reproduced below and had the photograph taken which is used as the frontispiece to this volume. A few days in Paris completed the holiday, with a Republican dinner organised by de Girardin as a result of which he became particularly interested in the writings of the critic Edmond Scherer, a diplomatic dinner organised by Waddington—'He did not open on the Eastern question and I thought it would be bad taste in me'—an incautious interview on British foreign policy with the *Gaulois* newspaper, and shopping, churches, and the theatre.

This was the Gladstones' longest continental journey since 1866–67. On that previous journey, Gladstone had been well known in certain sections of Continental society. He was now famous. This made the Continental journey much more a public event, a tour of the great, but visits to 'Book & curiosity shops' were still possible.

XII

Not surprisingly for a man who was seventy-one when this volume ends, the death of contemporaries was a quite frequent experience, often producing an optimistic comment in the diary on the probable state of the dead person's soul at the moment of death. Physically, the most immediate was the death of the Duchess of Argyll, who had a seizure while sitting down next to Gladstone at dinner; he attended her funeral in Scotland, finding the Presbyterian burial service more pleasing than in earlier years.[3] Another notable death was that of Antonio Panizzi, architect of the expansion of the library of the British Museum. As Panizzi's health declined, Gladstone tried to ensure that he died in a state of grace. Gladstone recorded the scene as Panizzi lay dying: 'I said to him, as I have done of late: Shall I say our little prayer now before I go? He looked at me and said "What the devil do you mean?" I said: I mean our prayer, the Lord's prayer: that is right, is it not? He said "Yes". (He had asked it shd be in Latin).'[4] Gladstone

[1] See 30 Oct. 74n., 9 Nov. 74n.

[2] 2 Nov. 76. On this occasion, Acton was part of the party to entertain Tennyson; he was also of the party during Ruskin's first visit in 1878; see 14 Jan. 78.

[3] 24 May–5 June 78.

[4] 7 Apr. 79; Panizzi died next day. See also 6 Mar. 79. For an account of Gladstone's concern for him, see M. R. D. Foot, 'Gladstone and Panizzi', *British Library Journal*, v. 48 (1979).

assisted in the preparation of Panizzi's biography, and was pleased by the result, commenting on it: 'Panizzi had long acquired a stronghold upon my feelings, and the way in which he has dwelt upon my mind since his death shows me that it was even stronger than I knew of during his life-time.'[1]

A number of family deaths are noted in this volume. The most important were those of George Lyttelton, Catherine Gladstone's brother-in-law, of Robertson Gladstone, and of Helen Gladstone. Mentally ill for several years, Lyttelton broke away from his attendant and killed himself by falling into the stair-well in 18 Park Crescent. Gladstone inspected the site in order to be able to contradict to his own satisfaction the view that it was not an accident, but 'intended: intended not by him but by that which possessed him'. He went with his wife 'to observe the fatal stair. Its structure is dangerous; & it confirmed the notion I had previously entertained of the *likelihood* that he [Lyttelton] never meant at all to throw himself over, but fell in a too rapid descent, over the bannisters.'[2] The whole incident is Gladstonianism in miniature: the implied deductive proposition, inductively demonstrated by probability.

George Lyttelton's death was a shock, but caused little lasting distress. The death of Robertson Gladstone, the third of the four brothers, and the only one with whom William had retained much intimacy, was more disturbing and more difficult, for his slow decline had left his affairs in chaos, and cost his brother William a considerable amount on the family's property at Seaforth.[3] But a searing death, despite their rare meetings since her conversion to Roman Catholicism in 1845, was that of his sister Helen. Her death in the hotel in Cologne where she had lived for many years as 'Mrs. Gladstone' (a conventional Victorianism) was, Gladstone convinced himself, at the least that of a non-Roman Catholic and almost certainly that of an 'Old-Catholic' (i.e. a Döllingerite). Her last painful illness, with suffering possibly compounded by a shortage of her habitual morphia, was watched by her two living brothers, Tom and William, together with Louisa, Tom's wife.

To William Gladstone the death brought back all the memories of the 1840s, the extraordinary 'Self-Examination' of October 1845 occasioned by his bizarre Continental search for his apostasised sister, when sex, religion, and politics intermingled to produce a nervous crisis which all but shook his moral foundations:[4] 'immediately upon the death followed a rush of thoughts & cares'.[5] Gladstone made 'an examination of all the books of devotion: it was very interesting & set forth the whole history of her mental transition since [the declaration of Infallibility in] 1870.... They show she died at one with us as before.'[6] Gladstone and his brother took the body to the family vault at Fasque, where it was buried according to the rite of the Episcopal Church of Scotland.

Helen Gladstone brought out an otherwise nonexistent trait in her brother: he bullied her. Her attempts at independence, exemplified in her conversion to

---

[1] To Fagan, 22 Oct. 80.
[2] 19 Apr., 14 May 76. Lucy Cavendish, Lyttelton's daughter, noted: 'we shall never know if it was in any degree accidental or not, but we *do* know he was as unaccountable as if a lightning stroke had fallen on him'; *D.L.F.C.*, ii. 196.
[3] 23 Sept. 75.
[4] See 26 Oct. 45.
[5] 16 Jan. 80.
[6] 18 Jan. 80.

Rome, seem to have affronted his code of how women should behave, especially when contrasted with the memory of his evangelical sister Anne, who died in 1829, her birthday still commemorated in the diary in 1878. Apostasy always distressed Gladstone, but apostasy in a sister riled him. Despite his public yearning for ecumenicity, he found it very hard to practise in the family context, as was also seen in the case of his apostate cousin and co-translator, Anne Ramsden Bennett.[1]

In his dealings with his sister, Gladstone was not fully in control of himself. Much of his correspondence with her is uncharacteristically harsh, unfeeling and petty, culminating in a brutal letter written in 1878, when Helen Gladstone had failed to repay a loan of £20 and to send a promised £50 for the Bulgarian refugee fund. The former Prime Minister's letter continues:

> A parcel arrived from you a few days ago. It contains I have no doubt a gift or gifts kindly intended by you for me, or for us. *It remains unopened, and at your disposal*; I have paid the charge upon it, but I can have no other concern with it while matters remain as they are. I did not wish to subject you to the further charge upon it for carriage back to you. It is most painful for me to write this letter, which I do without the knowledge of any one, but with a perfectly fixed purpose.[2]

Usually magnanimous and generous—perhaps particularly so—to those with whom he had differed, Gladstone behaved to his sister as if they were still in the nursery. No biography of this sad woman has yet been written; when it is, one of its major themes will be how her strong-willed brother, usually so careful in control and respect, ground her down and, if he did not 'break' her (the word he used of his own children), at the least exiled her, emotionally and morally as well as physically.

Helen Gladstone's death in January 1880, shortly before the General Election which brought him back to power, came at an appropriate time for her brother. With Hope-Scott already dead and Manning hopelessly estranged by the row over Vaticanism, it broke the last links with the emotional Church–State crisis of the 1840s. That crisis had confirmed Gladstone in his move towards fiscal liberalism whose development had taken thirty years and whose *finale* had been, in his view, the Government of 1868–74. He had seen his return to political life in 1876 in limited and restorative terms, fighting 'a consecutive battle against ideas & practices neither Liberal nor Conservative'.[3] But that return had led him to add a much more pronouncedly political liberalism to his fiscal and ecclesiastical beliefs. It had brought him, despite himself, to a new position in British political life, the epitome of a new form of political communication, the harbinger of a revived political liberalism. At an advanced age he had become in politics, that art of the second-best, what he described Macaulay as being in literature, 'a meteor, almost a portent'. Launched upon a second political career, Gladstone concludes this volume, as the year 1880 ends, with buoyant zest: 'I plunge forward into the New'. He did so reminded 'of the great lesson "onward"'.[4]

[1] See above, 8 June 71.
[2] To Helen Gladstone, 5 January 1878, Hawn P.
[3] To Doyle, 10 May 80.
[4] 29–31 Dec. 80.

Indeed, the capacity to move 'onward', to shift a generation as the times change, is one given to very few politicians, and to none completely. Gladstone had already made this shift once. It was not his intention, but it was to be his calling, to do so again.

Friday. Circumcision.

Rose late. It fights off my cold. Wrote to Bp of Winchester—Mrs Hamilton—Mr Melly—Williams & Norgate—Mrs Th.—Mrs Buckler—Mr Knowles—M.W. Womack—Mr Redford—Rev. S.B. Gould—Mr B. Scott[1]—Rev J.M. King[2]—H. Hampton—Dr H. Macnaghton Jones.[3] Read Butler's Memoirs of Engl. Catholics[4]—Protest agt Vade Mecum[5]—Slater's Letters[6]—Cath. Petri.[7] Conversation with E. Wickham. Made out Annual of Property, Debts, and Income.[8]

2. Sat.

Rose at 11. Wrote to Bp of New York—Mr J.P. Adams—Sir Thos G.—Mr. A.W. Peel—Mr Ouvry—Mr Tarbet. Considering matter for the next Tract.[9] Walk with E. W[ickham]. Read Fessler on Infallibility[10]—Decrees of Councils of Const[ance] and Basle[11]—Milman's History—Jenkins on Infallibility[12]—M'Naghton Jones on the Study of Life.

3. S. aft Circ.

Ch 11 AM (& H.C.) and 6½ P.M. Wrote to Mrs Abraham[13]—Mr Murray—Mrs Th.—Mr Levy. Read Br.Q.R. on Bismarck[14]—Jenkins on Priv. Petri—Fessler on Infallibility—Milman's History—Döllinger's History.[15] Corrected some proofs for the Q.R.[16]

4. M.

Ch. 8½ AM. Wrote to Bp Vaughan—Rev. Polwhele[17]—E. Hamilton—Lady A. Ewing[18]—Rev Dr Allon—Ld Aberdare—Rev R.C. Jenkins—Ld Wolverton—Mr

[1] Benjamin *Scott, 1814-92; social reformer and Chamberlain of the City of London 1858-92.

[2] John Myers King, 1804-87; vicar of Cutcombe-cum-Luxborough since 1832; classicist.

[3] Henry Macnaughton Jones, physician and author, had sent his *The study of life* (1874); see 2 Jan. 75.

[4] See 26 Nov. 74.   [5] Not found.   [6] See 24 Nov. 74.

[7] By T. Greenwood, see 25 Sept. 58.   [8] His annual statement of accounts; Hawn P.

[9] i.e. 'Vaticanism: an answer to *reproofs and replies*' (February 1875), reprinted in *Rome and the newest fashions in religion* (1875); planned earlier, see 12 Dec. 74. Most of the diarist's reading in early January 1875 is in preparation for this pamphlet.

[10] J. Fessler, 'The true and false infallibility of the Popes. A controversial reply to ... Dr Schulte' (1875).

[11] i.e. the Councils of 1414 and 1431 which reaffirmed the authority of a General Council over the Pope; F. Palacky, *Monumenta Conciliorum Generalium Seculi Decimi Quinti* (1857 ff.).

[12] R. C. Jenkins, *The papal infallibility in the light of the Council of Basle* (1872).

[13] Ellen, wife of Rev. T. E. Abraham, corresponded on bp. Patteson's *Life*, Add MS 44446, f. 39.

[14] *British Quarterly Review*, lxi. 168 (January 1875).

[15] J. J. I. von Döllinger, probably his *The Church and the Churches, or the Papacy and the temporal power*, (1862).

[16] i.e. for his article 'Speeches of Pope Pius IX', published anon. in the *Quarterly*; see 9 Dec. 74.

[17] Robert Polwhele, 1810-77; vicar of Avenbury 1867-77; s. of the author, see 6 May 75n.

[18] Lady Alice Louisa, da. of 18th earl of Morton, m. 1862 bp. A. Ewing.

Simpson[1]—Dr Dollinger (Tracts)—Messrs Clowes (Revises)—Dean of Lincoln—Dean of Chester. Finished correction of Revises & sent off for Press. Read Lectures of Bishop Vaughan[2]—Cranford[3]—Discorsi di Pio IX.[4] The E. Talbots came. Conversation on Inspiration with E.W.

5. Tu.

Ch. 8½ AM. Wrote to Bp of Winchester—Mr Blandford—Dr Rigg—Editor of Echo[5]—Ld Sydney—Mr Parker—Messrs T[ownsend] & B[arker]—Mr Potts—Dr Badenoch—Mr Kingston—Housekeeper at 11 C.H.T.—Mr Tennyson—Ld L[yttelto]n—Authors of Aurora.[6] Saw C.G. on House Establishments.[7] Wrote a little on Vatican. E.W. & E.T. on Univ. Reforms—Mrs Stume, on her affairs. Spoke at Rent dinner with reference to Stephen—his history—and the present prospects.[8] Read Cranford—Pref. to Sydow.[9]

6. Wed.

Epiph. Ch. 8¾ AM. Wrote to Ld Wolverton—Ld Granville—Ld Cardwell—Messrs Clowes—Wms & Norgate—Mr Levy—Dean of St Paul's—Sir R. Phillimore—Mr Goschen—Mr Morier—Mr Grogan—Mr Legge[10]—Mr Westell. Saw Mrs Stume on her matters. Worked on Roman Theol. Worked on Vatican: sent queries to Dr Döllinger.

Dearest C.s birthday—It is wonderful to see her power: what a blessing she is, and to how many!

Felling trees in afternoon. Read Hallam on Eccl. Power[11]—Cranford.

7. Th. [London]

Ch. 8½ A.M. Wrote to Ld Granville—Dean of Raphoe—Messrs T. & B.—Mrs Malcolm. Conversation with C. on the question of leadership in which she urges me in the sense of the politicians.[12] Off at 11. Shopping in Chester—C.H.T. at 6¼. Dined at 15 G[rosvenor] S[quare].[13] Saw Mr Levy—Lady

---

[1] Richard *Simpson, 1820–76; liberal Roman Catholic journalist and friend of *Acton; corresponded on Vaticanism; see J. Altholz, *The liberal catholic movement in England* (1962), appendix.

[2] H. A. Vaughan, *Pastoral letters* (3 December 1874, reprinted with appendices, 1875); see *Rome and the newest fashions*, 124.

[3] By E. C. *Gaskell (1853).

[4] See 9 Dec. 74.

[5] Not published.

[6] Alaric Alfred Watts and Anna Mary Howitt, authors of *Aurora: a volume of verse* (1875).

[7] Plans for sale of 11 Carlton House Terrace through Grogan, the house agent (see 26 June 54); see 25 Feb. 75n.

[8] No report found.

[9] Perhaps C. L. A. Sydow, 'Preface' and 'Introductory remarks' to his *Scottish Church Question* (1845).

[10] Alfred A. K. Legge, a guest at Hawarden in November 1874.

[11] H. *Hallam, 'History of ecclesiastical power' in *View of the state of Europe during the Middle Ages*, 2v. (1818).

[12] i.e. she opposed his resignation of the liberal party's leadership; for diarist's exchange of letters with his wife during this London visit, see Bassett, 206 ff.

[13] Laura Thistlethwayte's.

Strangford[1]—Mrs Fenn. Saw two [R]. Read Fessler—Engl. & Prussia[2]—Curry's Reply.[3]

8. Fr.

Wrote to C.G.—Ld Cardwell—Mr Leeman—E. Hamilton—Mr Layman—Mrs Malcolm. Saw Rev. R.R. Suffield—Count Münster—Mr Grogan—Mr MacColl—Mr Ouvry—Mr Murray. Read Fessler—Engl. Cath. on Papal Infallibility[4]—Greville's Memoirs.[5] Conversation with L[yttelton?] on Vatican & on the Leadership.

9. Sat.

Wrote to C.G.—Dean of St Pauls—Sir J. Lubbock—Mr Huske[6]—Saw Mr Kin-naird—Mr Simpson—
Ld Cardwell ⎫ each on the
Ld Granville ⎭ Leadership
Ld Acton (2)—Miss Wright, Impostor?[7] Sat to Mrs Th. for bust—or to M. Goflowski.[8] Saw Bp of Winchester—Mr Noble. Read Fessler.

10. 1 S. Epiph.

Savoy Chapel mg—Temple aftn. Wrote to Sir R. Phillimore—Duchess of Argyll. Saw Dean of St P[aul's] & Dr Liddon on Vatican & kindred matters $1\frac{3}{4}$-3—Granville & Cardwell on the Leadership $5\frac{1}{4}$-$7\frac{1}{4}$—Dr Clark in evg: examined me. All are against me. Dr Coghlan dined. Read Fessler. Re-wrote drafts of letters to G.[9]

11. M.

Wrote to Mrs Helen G.—Ld Hartington—D. of Argyll—Mr Hankey—Mr Suffield—Bp of Winchester—C.G.—Ld Granville—Mr Hayden. Saw Ld Granville (2)—Ld Cardwell—Ld Acton—Dean of St Paul's—Mr Cooke—Count Münster (2)—Dr Clark (who examined me further & reported very well)—Mr Kinnaird—Mr Levy[10]—Sir A. Panizzi. Dined at No 15 G.S.—Saw Mrs Th. X. She is I believe generous & noble in the base of her character. Finished Fessler.

12. Tu.

Wrote to Count Cadorna—Mr Redford—C.G.—Sir W. Palmer—and. . . . Read Greville's Journals. Saw Seymour [R]. Saw Ld Hartington—Sir J. Lubbock—Mr

[1] Emily Anne *Smythe, d. 1887; widow of 8th Viscount Strangford; organised fund for relief of Bulgarian peasants 1876-7, and team of nurses at the front in the Russo-Turkish War 1877.
[2] *Prussia in relation to the foreign policy of England* (1875).
[3] J. Curry, *Catholicity, liberty, allegiance; a disquisition on . . . Gladstone's 'Expostulation'* (1875).
[4] *Papal infallibility and persecution . . . By an English Catholic* (1870).
[5] C. C. F. Greville, *The Greville memoirs*, ed. H. Reeve, 4th ed., 3v. (1875); see Ramm I, ii. 466.
[6] Reading uncertain.   [7] Obscure; a rescue case?
[8] Or Geflowski (see 9 Nov. 74); bust untraced.
[9] On resignation; see 27, 31 Dec. 74, 14 Jan. 75.
[10] Of the *Daily Telegraph*, who at this meeting pressed Gladstone to resign as leader; Bassett, 209.

Goschen—Mr Knowles—Mr Grogan—Mr MacColl—Scotts—Shopping. Saw Sybella [Lyttelton] recovering well.[1] Dined as President at the dinner of the Metaphysical Soc. Manning did *not* come. Discussion on Mysteries as defined by Newman until after 10.30.[2]

13. Wed.

Wrote to Mr Edwards—Sir R. Anstruther—C.G.—Sir W. Harcourt—Archbishop of Syra (French).[3] Dined at Gen. Malcolm's. Saw Count Cadorna—Mr MacColl—Mr Noble. Luncheon at 15 G.S. Read Greville Journals—An Engl. Catholic on Capel[4]—Harcourt's Speech[5]—Catholicismus.[6] Saw Seymour & gave £5 [R].

14. Th.

Saw Lady Strangford—Mr G. Richmond—Mr Motley—Mr MacColl—Mr Levy 6 P.M.—Ld Granville—Sir A. Panizzi 5 PM. Dined with the Wortleys: told him & Sir F. Doyle what had been accomplished. Wrote to Bp of Winchester—Mr Leeman—Mr Balfour[7]—C.G.—Sec. G.E.R.R.—Ld Granville: *the* letter of retirement finally written out (But at his wish it was published with the date 13th.)[8]— Ld Wolverton—Mrs Th.—Dr A. Clark—Mr Levy. Read Newman's Reply (part only).[9] His admissions are [blank]. About two my old colleagues, except Bright and Argyll, assembled at Granville's: I explained the matter briefly & read the papers. There was argument & expostulation & much kindness: but all was settled before four o'clock: & the terms of Granville's reply were agreed on.

Memoranda read to late Colleagues Jan. 14. 75[10]

1. The question of the Leadership of the Liberal Party is full of difficulty—apart from the collateral question who is to be leader.
    My impression is that it can only be managed at present by broaching very few points, selected mainly with a view to avoid division & scandal. Many things must be passed by. It is not easy for me as leader to pass these things by. It is far easier for younger & less committed men.

[1] From giving birth to Hester Margaret, her third child and George Lyttelton's fourteenth.

[2] Gladstone was chairman for the year; J. F. *Stephen led the discussion; Brown, *Metaphysical Society*, 327; see also Bassett, 209.

[3] Stating, *inter alia*, that the spirit of the Russian church was more narrow than that of the Greek; the Russian *Ecclesiastical Messenger (Tzerkovny-Vestnik)* published a rebuke, to which Athens replied; see 9 May 75.

[4] *A criticism on Monsignor Capel's Reply to . . . Gladstone's pamphlet. By an English Catholic* (1875).

[5] Sir W. V. Harcourt, 'A speech addressed to his constituents . . . at Oxford on December 21, 1874' (1875); an attack on Gladstone's Vatican pamphlet.

[6] Fr. A. von Hartsen, *Der Katholicismus und seine Bedeutung in der Gegenwart* (1874).

[7] Sending him a paper on spiritualism; see Add MS 44446, f. 102.

[8] This, and Granville's reply (dated 14 January), in Ramm I, ii. 464 and *The Times*, 15 January 1874, 9 f.

[9] J. H. Newman, 'A letter to . . . the Duke of Norfolk on the occasion of Mr Gladstone's recent Expostulation' (1875).

[10] Holograph docketed: 'Confidentially read to the members of the late Cabinet at Lord Granville's Jan. 14. 75'; Add MS 44762, f. 162. Printed in M. Temmel, 'Gladstone's resignation of the liberal leadership, 1874–1875', *Journal of British Studies* (1976).

2. Reflection convinces me more & more of the *solidity* of the difficulty I have mentioned with regard to the internal controversies of the English Church.

My object is to labour for holding together the Church of England. This purpose has involved & probably will involve pleadings for sufferance as to what cannot be defended on its merits, & what is intensely unpopular with the constituents of Liberal members.

I cannot expect or ask from the Liberal party hearty co-operation in such a purpose.—It is rather the proper work of the other side.—I am profoundly reluctant to come into that conflict with the party which my function as leader might involve.

3. In the present blank state of the horizon we must judge by probabilities & the question most likely to come to the front, most for the interest of the Tories to bring to the front, is that of denominational education.

On this question I cannot concur in what I plainly see to be the dominant tendencies of the Liberal party.

4. Of the objects for which I have been accustomed to labour actively in public life I see none which I can effectively promote as leader.

I am out of harmony with the younger generation of men on the questions on which both parties are agreed and which will almost certainly form a large part of the subject matter of Parliamentary business. It is the known & admitted purpose of the Govt. to give prominence to this class of question.

On the other side is the inconvenience of changing the leader. This is an inconvenience which in any case (except that of breach with him) would at any time be felt. There is no prospect that, were I to engage now in a service of undefined duration that inconvenience would be smaller at a future period.

[Notes written by Gladstone, apparently in February 1874, and circulated or referred to by him at the meeting on 14 January 1875][1]

I shall not continue to discharge the duties of leader of the Liberal Party.

No one will remain under any tie or obligation to me. It will be for the members of the party to consider whether & when other arrangements should be made. Those members of the party who have most largely claimed & exercised the right of individual judgment, action, & criticism, will be the first to acknowledge their duty to promote whatever may be requisite for cohesion and efficient maintenance of old & good political traditions & sound principles & for the promotion of good legislation.

I shall not now resign my seat in Parliament: but after the labours of the last years I require rest particularly mental rest, and my attendance will be only occasional.

There are at this time gnawing if not burning questions, on which the Liberal party is not in accord with itself: I have no solution to suggest on which it could be likely at present to agree: and I stand publicly pledged not to take part in an intestine war of sections. Neither is there any great purpose, or any marked and clear policy which the Party is at this juncture unitedly resolved or disposed to pursue.

I do not conceal my hope and expectation that this first step of retirement into the shade will be followed by others accomplishing the work. Still, though not meaning to oppose for opposition's sake, or even to take part in the ordinary duty of watching & controuling the Government from day to day, I do not forget that I am in debt to the Party generally for kindness, indulgence, & confidence, much beyond what I have deserved.

[1] All undated holographs, each docketed later in diarist's hand 'ab.F.12' [1874], and kept by him with the resignation memorandum; a docket by Bassett reads 'Retirement from Leadership 1875'; Add MSS 44762, ff. 167-71. See Temmel, art. cit. and Ramm I, ii. 463-5.

Deeming myself unable to hold it together from my present position in a manner worthy of it I see how unlikely it is that I should hereafter be able to give any material aid in the adjustment of its difficulties. Yet if such aid should at any time be generally desired with a view to arresting some great evil or procuring for the nation some great good, my willingness to enter into counsel for the occasion would follow from all I have said. But always with the understanding that as between section & section I could not become a partisan, and that such interference even in the case of its proving useful would entail no obligation whatever on those accepting it, and carry with it no disturbance of any arrangement subsisting at the time.[1]

1. The absence of any great positive aim (the late plan having failed) for which to co-operate.
2. The difficulty of establishing united & vigorous action in the Liberal party for the purposes of economy.
3. The unlikelihood of arriving at any present agreement respecting Education.[2]

1. The desire of rest bodily and mental.
2. Experience convinces me that I cannot with effect lead the Liberal party as a whole, and as at present minded, in Opposition, for the ordinary purposes of Opposition.
3. Were I to keep the place, discharge formal duties now and then, and wait the future, this would check all spontaneous movement from within the Liberal party towards better organisation, & discipline.
4. There are at least two special questions of great importance on which my personal views would constitute at present serious difficulties in the way of union. One is public economy: the other, & this is very pressing, is the question of Education. I am a de-nominationalist and favour Voluntary Schools: while I have no hatred & fear of secularism.

15. Fr. [Hawarden]

Wrote to Mr Levy—and . . . Calls and shopping. Saw Ld Granville—Ld Lyttel-ton—Mr Murray—Mrs Th. (luncheon)—Mr Murray Gladstone (RR). Finished Newman. Packed my things & off at 2.45: reached Hawarden 8.15. All well. C. I think rather low as [to] what has happened.

16. Sat.

Wrote to Mr Peck MP—Mr Adam—Ld F. Cavendish—Sir Thos G.—Mr Goschen—Robn G. Church 8½ AM. Read Ullathorne's (able) Reply 'Mr G. &c. unravelled'.[3]—Nardi Tentativo Anticatolico[4]—Hayward's Art, on the Greville Journals.[5] Walk with C. & then some of the young ladies. I seem to feel as one who has passed through a death, but emerged into a better life.

[1] Part in Morley, ii. 498.   [2] This note in Morley, ii. 498.
[3] W. B. Ullathorne, 'Mr Gladstone's expostulation unravelled' (1875).
[4] F. Nardi, *Sul tentativo anti-cattolico in Inghilterra e l'opuscolo dell' Sig. Gladstone* (1875).
[5] A. Hayward, *Quarterly Review*, cxxxviii. 1 (January 1875).

17. 2 S. Epiph.

Hn Church at 11 A.M. with H.C. and [blank.] Wrote to Earl Granville—Dr Newman[1]—Rev R.R. Suffield—Mrs Hampton—Mr M. Gladstone. Read Baur's book on the Vatican Council[2]—Paget's Student Penitent.[3] Conversation with C. on the situation—with Mr Temple on speculative matters.

18. M.

Ch. 8½ AM. Wrote to The Speaker—Mr Bright—Mr Grogan—G. Howard—H. Sewell Stokes—Rev. A. Watson[4]—Rev. E. Haskins.[5] Saw Mr Barker. Conversation with C. on the 'situation'. Worked on Vaticanism. Read Nardi's Reply—Baur's Work on The Council—Q.R. on Life of P. Consort.[6] Felled a tree with W.

19. Tu.

Ch. 8½ A.M. Wrote to Ld Tenterden—Mr English—Mrs Wynne—Mrs Hampton—Sir Thos G.—Earl Stanhope—Robn G.—Rev. W. Newick[7]—Mr Levy—Mr Sherlock[8]—Dr Smith—Mr Leeman MP—Mrs Sharp—Rev. E.G.S. Browne—Mr F. Shum. Our good nieces Annie & Mary (T.G.) went. Worked on Vaticanism. Read Abp Kenrick[9]—Pickering on Friendship[10]—The Pope's Allocutions[11]—and finished Nardi.

20. Wed.

Ch. 8½ A.M. Wrote to Ld Hatherley—Sir A. Gordon—Ld Halifax—Dr Dollinger—Scotts—Col. Wilbraham—Mr Cook—Mr Benjamin—Miss Neville—Sec. Soc. Gardeners[12]—Sec. Soc. Musicians—Rev. Mr Brameld. Felled an alder. Read Kenrick—Baker's Three Personal Authorities[13]—L'Etat Religieux en Belgique[14]—Review of Dr Newman's Apology—Account of Grain.[15] Worked on Vaticanism.

21. Th.

Ch. 8½ AM. Wrote to Gen. Ponsonby—Sir Aug. Paget—The Queen—Mr Johnstone—Mr Vincent—Mr Handyside[16]—Mr Robinson—Mr Annsberg—H.N.G.—

---

[1] In *Newman*, xxvii. 193.
[2] F. C. Baur, probably his *Geschichte der christlichen Kirche*, 5v. (1863-77).
[3] F. E. Paget, *A student penitent of 1695* (1875).
[4] Probably Albert Watson, fellow and librarian of Brasenose, Oxford.
[5] Edmund Henry Haskins, rector of Stow, Lincolnshire from 1865.
[6] *Quarterly Review*, cxxxviii. 107 (January 1875).
[7] Apparently a nonconformist.
[8] Oliver Sherlock wrote regretting his resignation, sending a paper on Vaticanism; Add MS 44446, f. 66.
[9] P. R. Kenrick, probably *The validity of Anglican ordinations examined* (1841).
[10] P. A. Pickering, *An essay on friendship* (1875).
[11] *Two Allocutions of . . . Pope Pius IX*, tr. W. H. Anderdon (1867).
[12] See 19 Aug. 75.
[13] J. Baker, *The three personal authorities by divine right* (1874).
[14] Not found.
[15] Untraced.
[16] Peter David Handyside, physician in Edinburgh; Hawn P.

Mrs Putnam[1]–Mr Vickers–Rev. O'Keeffe–E. Randolph Clay–Mr Sidney Smith.[2] Walk & much conversation with Dr Cazenove. *Inter alia* on his forth-coming Review.[3] We all dined at the Rectory. Worked on Vaticanism. Read Etat Rel. en Belgique–O'Keeffe on Ultramontm.[4]

22. *Fr.*

Ch. 8½ A.M. Wrote to Mr R. Warburton–Rev R R Suffield–Rev Dr Schaff–Rev A. Gurney–Rev J.D. Copeland[5]–Mr Macray–Mr Godley–Mr J.F. Lloyd–Mr J. Cook. Felling trees. Worked on Vaticanism. Finished Baur's Book–Etat Relig. en Belgique. Read Cranford.

23. *Sat.*

Ch. 8½ AM. Wrote to Mr A.J. Balfour–Mr Layard–Sir A. Gordon–Mr Morier–Mr T.B. Hall[6]–Mr Stoneham–Mrs Th. Felled an Alder with W. Worked on Vaticanism. Read Cranford–Reperused Newman. Dined at Mr Johnson's. Conversation with Dean of Chester.

24. *Septa S.*

Ch. 11 A.M. and 6½ P.M. Wrote to Mr Witherspoon[7]–Mons. V. Oger–Ld Ebury–Rev. N.S. Bullock[8]–Mr Hatton–Dean of Chichester–Mr Baverstock. Read Tosti's Council of Constance[9]–Du Chastenet's do[10]–Newman's Hist. Arians.[11]

25. *M. Conversion of St Paul.*

Ch. 8¾ AM. Wrote to Sir J. Watson & Smith–Sir J. Watson–Mr King–Percy M. Hart[12]–Dr M'Corry–Mr F.B. Watkins[13]–Mr Johnston–Mr Planché. Saw Mr Townshend–Mrs Stume (her affairs)–Mr Noble[14] respecting the monument to Stephen in the Church. Felled an alder with W.H.G. Read Allocutions of Pius IX[15]–Newman on the Arians–Cranford–Watkins, Tranl. Hermann & Dor.–with original. Worked on Vaticanism.

---

[1] Gertrude A. Putnam; on dedication to diarist of M. A. Mignaty's *Sketches of the past of Italy* (1876); Hawn P.

[2] Of the Liberal Registration Association; see 13 July 61.

[3] The *Church Quarterly Review*, edited by J. G. Cazenove (see 30 Dec. 54), to which Gladstone contributed; see 26 Apr., 16 July 75.

[4] R. O'Keeffe, *Ultramontanism versus civil and religious liberty* (1875).

[5] Probably George Dale Copeland, anglican priest in Walworth.

[6] Thomas B. Hall of Truro; on diarist's resignation; Hawn P.

[7] Joseph Witherspoon of Chester-le-Street; sent press cuttings.

[8] A nonconformist.

[9] L. Tosti, *Storia del Concilio di Constanza*, 2v. (1853).

[10] H. Bourgeois du Chastenet, *Nouvelle histoire du Concile de Constance*, 2v. (1718).

[11] J. H. *Newman, *The Arians of the fourth century* (1833); see 9 Mar. 34.

[12] Correspondent on Vaticanism; Hawn P.

[13] Frederick B. Watkins, had sent his tr., *Goethe's Hermann und Dorothea* (1875); Hawn P.

[14] i.e. the sculptor; see 20 Mar. 54.

[15] See 19 Jan. 75.

26- Tu.

Ch. 8½ A.M. Wrote to Millikin & Lawley[1]—Ld Tenterden—Mr Murray—Mr Shaw Stewart—Mr J. Henderson—Sec. Railway Duty Assoc.[2]—Sec. Charity Orgn Assoc.—Rev. C.J. Elliot. Worked on Vaticanism. Felled a Sycamore with W.H.G. Read Newman's Arians—Cranford—Fleury's Hist. Eccl.[3]—Milman, do[4]—Slater on R.C. Tenets.[5]

27. Wed.

Ch. 8½ AM. Wrote to Ld Granville—Mrs Alexander (Victoria B.P.)[6]—Mr Collinson—Mr Fetherston[7]—Mr Ponsford—Mr Book (Blackheath)[8]—Mr Martin—Mr Davies—Mr Jos Rhodes.[9] Walk with C: called at Hurst's. Read Newman, Arians—Flanagan, Hist. of Church[10]—Cranford, finished. Delightful. Worked on Vaticanism.

28. Th.

Ch. 8½ AM. Wrote to Watson & Smith—Mr Geo. Harris—Robn G.—Rev. W.P. Ward[11]—Mr R. Dunn—Mr Geo. Johnston. Worked on Vaticanism. Felled a tree with W.H.G. Read Bossuet & his Contemporaries.[12]

29. Fr.

Ch. 8½ AM. Wrote to Sir A. Gordon—Rev. E. Jenkins[13]—Mr C. Dickinson—Mr T. Greener—B.C. Young[14]—Messrs Vandyke & Brown.[15] Found the outer circuit of the Lancashire walk 1¾ miles. Worked on Vaticanism. Read Newman's Arians—Read The Medecin malgré lui.[16] The wit and fun are admirable. But it is less decent than I had thought. Read also Mailfer.[17]

30. Sat.

Ch. 8½ AM. Wrote to Mr Braithwaite—M. Mailfer—Mr J. Wood. Cleared & sorted Vatican & retirement correspondence. Worked on Vaticanism. Read Newman—Le Tartuffe.[18]

---

[1] Surgical instrument makers in the Strand.

[2] Association working for repeal of railway passenger duty imposed by Gladstone in 1840s; see G. Alderman, *The railway interest* (1973), 85.

[3] C. Fleury, *Historia Ecclesiastica Latine*, 87v. (1758-94).

[4] See 27 Aug. 54.   [5] See 24 Nov. 74.

[6] Possibly Mrs. Cecil Frances *Alexander 1818-95; hymnist; wife of William Alexander, abp. of Armagh, with whom Gladstone corresponded.

[7] F. M. Fetherston had offered to sell portraits of diarist in Huddersfield for £20; Hawn P.

[8] i.e. a constituent.

[9] Josiah Rhodes of Liversage sent an election guide; Hawn P.

[10] See 17 Apr. 59.   [11] See 21 June 42.

[12] *Bossuet and his contemporaries*, by H. L. Farrer, afterwards Lear (1874).

[13] Evan Jenkins, rector of Flint from 1865.

[14] Of Coseley; had sent a pamphlet; Hawn P.   [15] Photographers in Liverpool.

[16] By Molière, first published 1666; see 7 Nov. 25.

[17] H. C. Mailfer, *De la Démocratie en Europe. Questions religieuses et juridiques* (1874).

[18] By Molière (1664); see 18 Feb. 26.

31. Sexa S.

Ch. 11 AM and 6½ P.M. Wrote to Ld Granville—Sir A. Gordon—Mr Morier—
Rev. Dr Gordon—Mr Knowles—C.G.—Mr Nash—Mary G. (to send to Baroness
de Hugel, ex-Mary Herbert)[1]—Bp of Winchester. Worked a little on Vaticanism: rather late: & suffered for it. Read Newman's Arians—Bp of Winchester's
Sermons and Appendix.[2] Conversation with Mr Parker on Oxford.

Hn. Mond. Feb. One 1875

Ch. 8½ A.M. Wrote to Dean of St Paul's—German Ambassador—Rev. Mr Gill—
Mr Murray—Mr Macray. Worked on Vaticanism. Saw Mr L. Barker. Conversa-
tion with Mr Parker on Aristoph.—Socrates—Grote. Woodcutting. Read Le
Tartuffe.

2. Tu. Purification

Ch. 8¾ AM. Saw Mrs Hampton. Wrote to Lord Hartington—Archbp Manning—
Mr Ouvry—Rev Mr Scrivener—Mrs Helen G.[3]—Rev Sir W. Palmer—C.G.—Rev.
Newman Hall—Mr J. Gill—Mr J. Wood. I spent the whole morning in reading
up the Councils of 863 (Roman) & 1869, Baronius & the historians, to track
Manning in his devious ways. At least such I fear they are. Woodcutting. Con-
versation with Mr Parker on Vaticanism. Received, & began, Abp Manning.[4]
Read Tartuffe.

3. Wed.

Ch 8½ A.M. Wrote to Ld Granville—Sec. Syrian Patronage Fund—Mr J.R.
Jolly[5]—Mr Levy—Rev Mr M'Coll—Sir A. Gordon—Vicar of St Martin's—Sir F.A.
Steele[6]—Rev. A. Roberts—Ed. Dublin Review—Mr H.H. Murphy[7]—Sec. Inter-
natl Exhibition—Sec. Met. Dist. RR. Farm calls with M. Again busy with
Archbp Manning's references, in Gerson.[8] Read Abp M. (finished)—Dublin
Review on Expostn[9]—Tartuffe (finished).

---

[1] Letter untraced.

[2] E. H. Browne, 'The strife, the victory, the kingdom. Three sermons . . . with an appendix' (1872).

[3] i.e. his sister Helen.

[4] H. E. *Manning, 'The Vatican decrees in their bearing on civil allegiance' (1875), answered by
Gladstone in Appendix H of *Vaticanism*, some of whose comments were modified in later impressions; see *Rome: newest fashions in religion*, 128-9.

[5] Thanking J. R. Jolly, chairman of the Greenwich Liberal Association, and liberals generally for
resolutions on his retirement and admitting 'shortcomings with respect to local duty, which it
[Greenwich] has ever regarded with so much indulgence'; printed, dated 4 February, in *T.T.*,
5 February 1875, 8a.

[6] Sir Frederick Ferdinand Armstead Steele, 1787-1876; 5th bart. 1872.

[7] Of Sheffield; sent press cuttings; Hawn P.

[8] J. Gerson's *De potestate ecclesiae*, quoted in Manning, op. cit., 60.

[9] [W. G. *Ward], 'Mr Gladstone's *Expostulation*', *Dublin Review*, xxiv. 170; answered in *Rome,
newest fashions in religion*, 109.

4. Th.

Ch. 8½ AM. Wrote to Dr Döllinger—Abp Manning—Mr Grogan—Ly Strang-
ford—Mrs Th.—J. Nash[1]—J. Martin—S. Langley—J. Macdonald—Mrs Gilby—
C.G. Saw Mann (Gl[ynne] Arms)—Mrs Hancock. Worked on Vaticanism. Read
Dryden: in his remarkable Theological Poems[2]—Moliere, Le Sicilien—Collier
Eccl. Hist.[3]—Pickering on Friendship (finished).[4]

5. Fr.

Ch. 8½ AM. Wrote to Mr P.A. Pickering—Mr Newdegate—Mr Liardet[5]—Mrs
Grote—Rev. N. Hall—Rev. H.G. Edwards[6]—Mr Bentley—Mr Girdlestone[7]—
Messrs Painter—Sir T. Briggs B.P.[8] Worked on Vaticanism. Read Dryden Hind
& P[anther][9]—Newman's Arians. Calls—Johnson—Stume. Saw Mr Johnson—Mr
Vickers.

6. Sat.

Ch. 8½ AM. Wrote to Mr H.H. Murphy—Mr A. Kinnaird—C.G.—Rev. Archer
Gurney—H.J.G.—Mr E. Boardman[10]—S. Faber—Mr F.S. Relling. Worked hard
on Vaticanism: I see daylight as to finishing—the *job* is to keep down bulk. Read
Dryden—Clarke's Sermon (Boston).[11] W.H.G. returned—Woodcutting.

7. Quinqua S.

Ch. 11 AM and H.C. 6½ PM. Wrote to Mr Richardson—Rev. Mr Scrivener—Mr
Grogan—Rev. Dr Quarry[12]—Mr G. Newman[13]—Mrs Williams. Read Newman,
Arians—Burgon on the Study of [blank][14]—Mr G. Newman, Poems. Worked on
Vaticanism.

8. M.

Ch. 8½ A.M. Worked on Vaticanism nearly all the day, and (an exception to my
rule) late at night. Wrote to Mr Murray—Mr James Lord. Saw Mr Townshend.
Visit at Aston Hall.

[1] Of London; occasional correspondent; Hawn P.
[2] Discussed in *Vaticanism*; see *Rome: newest fashions in religion*, 43.
[3] J. Collier, *An ecclesiastical history of Great Britain*, 2v. (1708-14).
[4] See 19 Jan. 75.
[5] J. E. Liardet, tory candidate at Greenwich, defeated in 1874 election by diarist; see 3 Feb. 74n.
[6] Henry Grey Edwards, perpetual curate of Llandinorwig, Carnarvon, from 1856.
[7] See 18 Jan. 29.
[8] Sir Thomas Graham Briggs, 1833-87; prominent Barbadian; cr. bart 1871. 'B.P.' indicates
diarist sent a 'Book Parcel'.
[9] See 4 Feb. 75n.
[10] Of Dumfries; sent a French work on the papacy; Hawn P.
[11] Sent by James Freeman Clarke, 1810-88; minister of the Church of the Disciples, Boston, Mass.
[12] John Quarry, D.D., anglican priest in co. Cork.
[13] George Newman of Gravesend, had sent his *Wayside Lyrics* (expanded ed. 1874); Hawn P.
[14] J. W. Burgon, *A plea for the study of divinity in Oxford* (1875).

9. Tu.

Ch. 8½ A.M. Steady work till four finished my 'Rejoinder': and it went off. Wrote to Mr MacSweeney—Lord Blantyre—Capt. Moger[1]—Sir Jas Watson. Woodcutting with W.H.G. Saw my nieces on the investment of their money: & on the agreement about their house. Began Mr Austin's Tower of Babel[2]—Nixon on Theism[3]—Gloag on Bauer.[4]

10. Ash Wed.

Ch 11 AM. Wrote to Ld Granville—Mrs Pigot (B.P.)—Mr M'Sweeney (B.P.)—Sir Jas Watson—Mr J.H. Parker—Robn G.—Mr A. Austin—Mr Harris—Ld Harrowby—Mrs Th.—Mr Murray—Ld Acton—Rev. Mr Shawcross[5]—Mr J. Lord—Mr R. Simpson—Mr Ward—Rev. N. Wilson[6]—Mr H. Syce—Mr Newdegate—Mr Banner—Mr Bright—Mr Vurtis.[7] Read Newman's Arians—Austin's T. of Babel. Woodcutting with W. C.G. came back for a day: relieved, thank God, from anxiety about May Lyttelton's illness.

11. Th.

Ch. 8½ AM. Wrote to Dr Döllinger (& BP.)—Mr Macray (BP.)—Mr Grogan—Mrs Bennion—Mr F. May—Rev. R. Suffield—Rev. N. Hall—Messrs Tangye[8]—Rev Dr Irons—Mr G. Richardson—Mr G. Newman. Yesterday & today I had to work in Waifs & Stray's of Vaticanism. Also much work in sorting & arranging letters, pamphlets, papers of all kinds. Felled an ash with W. Finished Newman's Arians. Read A. Austin—Richardson's Lecture[9]—Pax[10] Vobiscum Bamberg 1863—Ueber romanisirende tendenzen Berlin 1870—Stahl, Lutherische Kirche u. die Union.

12. Fr. [London]

Ch. 8½ AM. Wrote to Col. Ackroyd—Mr Macray—Messrs Watson—Mr A. Banner—Mr Collingwood.[11] Read Martineau on the Church and on God in Nature.[12] Setting my room in order mg: Off at 11. Reached C.H.T. at 5.45. Two hours of conflict with the chaos of letters parcels &c. there. Dined at Lady

[1] Perhaps George Moger of St. Stephen's Road, London.

[2] Alfred *Austin, 1835-1913; Roman catholic and versifier; made poet laureate by *Salisbury 1896; had sent his *The Tower of Babel* (1874).

[3] B. Nixon, 'Theism. An address' (1875).

[4] P. J. Gloag, *Introduction to the Pauline Epistles* (1874).

[5] Richard Shawcross, vicar of Ellerburne from 1866.

[6] Nathaniel Wilson, vicar of Ingham from 1873.

[7] Might read 'Curteis'.

[8] Hydraulic engineers in Birmingham, owned by (Sir) Richard *Tangye, 1833-1906, liberal and Cromwellian; kt. 1894.

[9] B. W. Richardson, *On alcohol; a course of six Cantor Lectures delivered before the Society of Arts* (1875).

[10] Rest of day's entry inserted on a slip of paper, now missing.

[11] Possibly William Gershom Collingwood, 1854-1932; Ruskin's secretary and biographer; contemporary of Herbert Gladstone at University college, Oxford.

[12] J. Martineau, *The pretensions of the Roman Catholic Church* (1874); *The place of mind in Nature* (1872).

Strangford's. Conversation with her on G. Smythe—With Ld C. on the Vatican, Bp Ullathorne, Abp Manning. Saw Mrs Th. afr. X.

13. Sat.

Renewed labours for order. Visited Christie's. Wrote to Mr Don & others, Aberdeen Univ.[1]—Mr Don & others, ibid.—Mr Heinemann[2]—Mr W. Smith—Mr Hertslet—Mr Gurdon—The Speaker—C.G.—Mr De Lisle. Saw Mr MacColl—Ld Granville—Ld Acton—Ly Waldegrave—Mr Grogan—Ld Carlingford—Scotts—Sir A. Panizzi—Mrs Th.—Mr Cooke (Mr Murray's).[3] Read D. Grant on Liberal Politics[4]—Hartsen, Catholicismus, began.[5] Luncheon at 15 G.S. Dined with the Wortleys. Conversation on Judicature.

14. 1 S.L.

Chapel Royal 10 AM. St James's, Prayers, 7 P.M. Wrote to Mr Hill (D. News) Eight hours work on my proof sheets. Read Hartsen—Digby Campbell[6]—Bancroft U.S.[7]—M'Clellan's New Transl. NT.[8] Luncheon 42 P.P.[9]—Conversation with Lyttelton.

15. M.

Wrote to Dr Bennett—Messrs Clowes—Sir Jas Watson—Lord Acton—Sir Jas Hudson—Mr C. Hill[10]—Mr D. Campbell—Mr D. Gooch[11]—Mr Planché—Ld Southesk—C.G. Two more hours on the proofs. Went through Acton's corrections & notes on my proofs.[12] Saw Ld Granville—Mr Murray—Mr Adam—Mr Kinnaird—Mr Bright—The Speaker—Ly Strangford—Ld J. Manners—Sir T. May—Mr Dodson—Ld Hartington—and others. H of C. $4\frac{1}{2}$-7.[13] Dined at 15 G.S. (Mr Singleton). Read Catholicismus.[14]

16. Tu.

Wrote to Ld Tenterden—Ld Lyttelton—Sir A. Paget—Sir A. Gordon—Mr Macrae—C.G.—Mr Murray. Read Catholicismus. Saw Mr A. Dennington—Mr

[1] An invitation from a cttee. led by Alexander Birnie Don, a third year undergraduate, to stand for the Rectorship; Gladstone replied 'intimating that he does not feel himself to be in a position to allow his name to be brought forward'; *Aberdeen Journal*, 17 February 1875.

[2] Perhaps Arnold Heinrich Heinemann, wrote in London on German affairs.

[3] Robert Cooke, *Murray's cousin and partner.

[4] D. Grant, *On the policy of liberalism* (1875).   [5] See 13 Jan. 75.

[6] Probably an untraced work by Alexander Digby Campbell of Cranbrook; Hawn P.

[7] See 15 July 48.   [8] J. B. McClellan, *The New Testament. A new translation*, 2v. (1875).

[9] i.e. the Lytteltons in Portland Place.

[10] Charles Hill, of the Working Men's Lord's Day's Rest Association; corresponded on Sabbatarianism; Hawn P; see 13 Jan. 76.

[11] John Gooch of Kingsland had written on religion; Hawn P.

[12] He was also to be assisted in proof-reading by Henry Nutcombe Oxenham, anglican priest converted to Roman catholicism 1857; See J. L. Altholz, *The liberal catholic movement in England* (1962), appendix.

[13] Artizans Dwellings Bill, *H* 222. 335; 'I . . . came down to the House and took my seat nearly in the same spot as last year, finding Bright my neighbour, with which I was very well pleased. Granville and Hartington both much preferred my continuing on the Front Bench to my going elsewhere'; Bassett, 212.   [14] See 13 Jan. 75.

MacColl—Mr Gurdon—Sir Jas Watson—Ld Acton—Sir Thos G. (the J.N. G[lad-stone] Trust)—Mr Levy. At 8 drove to Hampstead with Mr Glanville[1] and met a large conclave of leading Nonconformists, lay & ministers, chiefly the latter. We had much interesting conversation until 12: on Vaticanism, Disestablishment, Moody & Sankey,[2] & other matters: & in answer to Mr N[ewman] Hall my host I expressed my grateful feeling to the Nonconformists for their most hand-some, most indulgent treatment of me. The Scotch Patronage Act was also included in our conversation.[3] Home at 1.

17. Wed.

Wrote to Mrs A. Sted—Mr Jas Martin—Watsons—Mr J.E. Liardet—Mr S.E. ODell.[4] Sat to Mr L. Dickinson 3-5 and caught some chill.[5] Conversation with M. respecting Helen. Saw Ld Cardwell—Mr Bright—Sir A. Gordon—Sir W. James. Dined with the Jameses. H of C. $12\frac{1}{4}$-1.[6] Read Ld Russell, Recollections[7]—Sicherer, Eherecht.[8]

18. Th.

Wrote to Helen G. H of C. $4\frac{1}{2}$-$8\frac{1}{4}$. Much disgusted with the conduct of the Liberals to Hartington in the Division.[9] Luncheon at 15 G.S. Dined with the Lytteltons. Read Ld Russell—Sicherer. In bed until 1. Saw Ld Hartington—Mr Murray—Mr Grogan—Mr A. Peel & others at H. of C.

19. Fr.

Wrote to C.G. Again confined to bed—until the evening. Dr Clarke came, spon-taneously. Conversation on Vaticanism. Worked on Revises. Read Sicherer, finished—Catholicismus, finished. Began Ld Southesk.[10] Worked much in even-ing on finishing up my Tract, Dr Döllinger's final criticism having arrived. By midnight I had the Revises ready with the corrections, mainly from Sicherer who has been of great use. Evening with M.G. who is such good company.

[1] Possibly James Glanville, chartered accountant in London; fa. of H.J. Glanville, later a liberal M.P.

[2] See 25 Apr. 75.

[3] For this meeting, see C. Newman Hall. An Autobiography (1898), ch. xviii.

[4] Stackpool Edward O'Dell, phrenologist in Birmingham, sent article analysing diarist's head; Add MS 44446, f. 200.

[5] Portrait exhibited at Royal Academy 1875, now in Liverpool College.

[6] Scottish Wild Animals Bill; H 222. 422.

[7] Lord Russell, Recollections and suggestions 1813-1873 (1875); on p. 344 Russell accused Gladstone of 'a want of plain speaking' and of a foreign policy which had 'tarnished the national honour, injured the national interests, lowered the national character'.

[8] H. von Sicherer, Ueber Eherecht und Ehegerichtsbarkeit in Bayern (1875).

[9] Many liberal M.P.s failed to support Hartington on the question of a select cttee. on the case of J. Mitchel, elected M.P. for Tipperary but a convicted felon: H 222. 536.

[10] J. Carnegie, Lord Southesk, Jonas Fisher. A poem (1875).

20. Sat.

Wrote to Messrs Clowes (2)—Dr von Döllinger—C.G.—Mr Todd. Breakfast party. Saw Mr Agnew—Mr Bevan—Sir A. Gordon—Mr Bevan—Mr M'Coll—Mr N. Hall—Mr Godley—Mr Hayward—Ld Stanhope—Sir G. Jessell—Sir T.E. May—Mr A. Peel—German Ambr—Ld Granville—Mr Noel—Musurus Pacha. Luncheon at Mr Grahams.[1]

Inserted one or two references and wrote *Press* on the 2d Revises. May the power and blessing of God go with the work. For every word shall I have to answer at the last day: and I desire it to be such as I can *then* gladly acknowledge.

Worked at London Library. Read Purcell's Essay (1867)[2]—Schäfer's Non Possumus.[3] Dined at Sir C. Forster's—Ly Granville's party after.

21. 2 S.L.

Chapel Royal mg, and H.C.—which was most seasonable after the important act of yesterday. It is my sincere desire that this work be united with the All holy Sacrifice. Arranged my Presentation List: nearly 150 strong. Wrote to Dr Von Döllinger—Mr Morier—Mr Murray—Mr Poynder[4]—Dr Angus. Read Hooks Abps Cant. Vol. X[5]—Langdon, Letters to Ricasoli[6]—The Paraclete[7]—Introduction to Germ. Theology.[8] Saw Lady Derby—Miss Talbot. Sir C. Lambson. Tea with the Wortleys. Litany afternoon at Abp Tennison's Ch.

22. M.

Wrote to Mrs R. Rayner—Lord Acton—Mr E. Davis—Rev A. Anderson—Rev J.[E.]N. Molesworth[9]—Rev S. Naish—Mr T. Collins—T. Sinclair—J. Boughey—J.S. Mills—Mr F. Adams—Mrs Heath—C.G.—German Ambassador—Rev. R. O'Keeffe—Mr Jas Lord—Mr A.H. Greenhow—Mr G. Jackson. Saw Ld Granville—Consul White[10]—American Minister[11]—Eton Master on Buchholz &c.[12]— A. Kinnaird. Dined at Mrs Th.s H of C. $4\frac{1}{2}$-7 and $10\frac{1}{2}$-$12\frac{1}{4}$. Voted in 185:282: a weak division on a strong cause.[13] Attended Committee Meeting on Hawtrey Memorial.[14]

[1] Perhaps Charles James Graham, London barrister.

[2] E. S. Purcell, *On church and state* (1867).

[3] A. Schaeffer, *Non Possumus* (1869).

[4] Perhaps Clement Poynder, 1835-1929; rector of Wyck-Rissington 1872-85.

[5] W. F. *Hook, *Lives of the archbishops of Canterbury*; this v. is on the reformation.

[6] Untraced work by W. C. Langdon, active in the reform movement in the Italian Church, to which Baron Ricasoli was sympathetic.

[7] [J. Parker], *The Paraclete: an essay* (1874).

[8] Probably *Aids to the study of German theology* (n.d.).

[9] John Edward Nassau Molesworth, 1790-1877; vicar of Rochdale from 1840; novelist and theologian.

[10] Probably William Arthur White, British consul at Danzig.

[11] i.e. Schenck.   [12] Not found.

[13] Regimental Exchanges Bill: *H* 222. 714.

[14] Memorial in Eton Chapel to E. C. Hawtrey, completed 1878; see F. St. J. Thackeray, *Memoir of E. C. Hawtrey* (1896), 214.

23. Tu.

Wrote to Mr Suffield—Prof. Reynolds—Dr Benisch[1]—Messrs Townshend—Mr Wheeler[2]—Miss Whitfield—Mr M'Coll—Mr Harrington—C.G.—Signor Valletta.[3] Worked on arrangement of tracts papers & letters, wh are in chaotic arrear. Saw Sir R. Phillimore—Mr Cartwright—Mr Grogan—Mr Murray—Mrs Th.—3 PM. & late—Sir A. Panizzi—German Ambassador. Read Reynald Hist. Angleterre.[4]

24. Wed.

Wrote to Sig. Minghetti—Emperor of Brazil—Ld Lyons—Mr Whitty—Sir A. Paget—Dr Mackenzie—C.G.—Mr Marshall. Saw Sir R. Blennerhassett—Mr Bentley—Mr Grogan—Sir A. Panizzi –S.E.G. (on Vaticanism)—Ld Kensington[5]— Mr Bright. Dined at the Speakers. Read Spiritualism explained[6] and [blank.]

25. Th.

Wrote to Mr Arthur—Dr Parker—Messrs Clowes (2)—Archbp Manning (2)—Ld Camoys. Luncheon at 15 G.S. Saw Mrs Th. Late X. Dined at Mr Lowe's. Conclave at Ld Granville's 3.15 P.M. Saw Mr Knowles—Mr Vivian—Mr Lowe—Ld Hartington—Mr Murray—Mr Grogan—Sir A. & Lady Guinness: with whom I am on the point of concluding for the sale of this house.[7] Read Neville's Reply.[8]

26. Fr.

Wrote to Messrs T. & B.—Abp Manning—Miss Glynne—Messrs Clowes— C.G.—Mr Locke King—Mr White—Mr C. Parker—Watsons—Ld Hartington. Saw Mr E. Hamilton—Mr Strahan—Mr Grogan (2)—Sir A. Gordon—Mr Murray—Rev Mr Molesworth—Ld F. Cavendish—Mrs Th.—Lady E.M. Pringle. Corrections of Pamphlet still going on. Luncheon at 15 G.S. Dined at Sir C. Forster's. Finished Canon Neville's not very important Reply. Visited a house in St G. Terrace with Mr Grogan.

27. Sat. [Hatfield House]

Wrote to Count Cadorna—Miss Holland[9]—Mr J. Weymouth[10]—Mr Ouvry—E. Hughes[11]—Dean of Chichester—Gweirydd ap Rhys[12]—Rev. W. Denton—T.M.

---

[1] Abraham Benisch, 1811-78; ed. the *Jewish Chronicle*; sent his *Judaism Surveyed* (1874); Add MS 44446, f. 211.   [2] Of the *Central News*; see 5 Mar. 75n.

[3] S. J. Valetta, friend of duke of Sermoneta; on Dante; Hawn P.

[4] H. Reynald, *Histoire de l'Angleterre depuis la mort de la reine Anne jusqu'à nos jours* (1875).

[5] William Edwardes, 1835-96; 4th baron Kensington (Irish peerage) 1872; liberal M.P. Haverfordwest 1868-85; household office 1873-4, 1880-5, 1886.

[6] Perhaps [E. S. G. Saunders], *Spiritualism. What is it?* (1864).

[7] The lease of 11 Carlton House Terrace was sold for £35,000 (contract signed on 12 April 1875, with completion on 15 April) to Sir Arthur Edward Guinness, 1840-1915, 2nd bart 1868, cr. Baron Ardilaun 1880, and his wife Lady Olivia Charlotte, da. of 3rd earl of Bantry.

[8] H. Neville, *A few comments on . . . Gladstone's Expostulation* (1875).

[9] Caroline, da. of Sir H. Holland, 1st bart., sent one of her fa.'s works; Hawn P.

[10] John Francis Weymouth, London solicitor.

[11] Probably Charles Hughes, liberal in Wrexham and occasional correspondent; Hawn P.

[12] Pseudonym of Robert John Pryse, 1807-89, Welsh literary and historical author; under his real name, tr. *The Vatican Decrees* and *Vaticanism* into Welsh.

Gemmell[1]—Rev. M. Mayne—Sir J. Lacaita—G. Harris—T. Edwards—J. Dougal[2]—
W. Fawens—J. Green—Robn G. Luncheon at 15 G.S. Went with Grogan to see
two houses. Read C. Greville. Dined at Ld Dartrey's: went down by midnight
train to Hatfield.

28. 3 S. Lent.

Hatfield Ch mg. Chapel evg at 6. Walk with the party. Conversation with Mr
Hayward—Mr Brewer—Ld Shrewsbury—Mr Balfour—Lady Salisbury—Sir [H.]
D[rummond] Wolff (Public Worsh. Bill).[3] Read N. Hall on Prayer[4]—Mill on
Religion—Reynolds on St Joh. Baptist[5]—Harmony in Religion.[6] Wrote to C.G.—
Mrs Th.

Monday Mch One 1875. [London]

Wrote to Messrs Watson—Ld Wolverton—and [blank.] Read Shelburne's
Memoirs[7]—Staat u. Kirche[8]—Pattison's Casaubon.[9] Lady Salisbury drove me to
St Albans & we went through the noble Church. Saw Panizzi—Mr Herbert—
Dined at 15 G.S.

2. Tu.

Wrote to Dr Bennett (2)—A.P. de Lisle—W.T. Tippet—E. Hanan[10]—R.
Mullan[11]—H.P. Powell[12]—Rev. R. OKeeffe—Rev. M. M'Coll—Rev. A.B.
Grosart—Miss Scott—C.G. Saw Mr Salkeld—Ld Aberdeen—Ld Wolverton—Mr
Bright—Mr E. Ashley. H. of C. $4\frac{3}{4}$-$7\frac{1}{4}$: a doubtful motion made on Educn by Mr
Fawcett.[13] Saw three: one with some hope [R]. Dined at Ld Lyttelton's. Read
Spiritualism explained—The Dying Priest[14]—Divers Tracts.

3. Wed.

Wrote to Mr Pryse (my Welsh Translator)[15]—Dean of St Paul's—Mr Applegarth
& Mr Edwards[16]—Dr Rigg—Mr Bramwell—Mr E. Ellis—Ld Russell—Mr
Murray—Rev Mr Davey[17]—Mr J.O. [Halliwell] Phillipps—Mr Ashton—Rev Mr

---

[1] Thomas M. Gemmell of Ayr; on diarist's resignation; Hawn P.
[2] John Dougal on the staff of *Witness*, of Montreal; Hawn P.   [3] See 3 Nov. 58.
[4] C. N. Hall, *Prayer; its reasonableness and efficacy* (1875).
[5] H. R. Reynolds, *John the Baptist* (1874).
[6] [T. O'Malley], *Harmony in religion* (1872).
[7] Lord E. G. P. Fitzmaurice, *Life of William, Earl of Shelburne*, 3v. (1875-6).
[8] Probably E. Bauer, *Der Streit der Kritik mit Kirche und Staat* (1843).
[9] M. Pattison, *Isaac Casaubon 1559-1614* (1875); notes at Add MSS 44792, f. 53, 44794, f. 186; see
18 June 75.
[10] E. H. Hannan of Liverpool; on anti-popery; Hawn P.
[11] Robert Mullan, published in Belfast (1874) his ed. of J. S. Knowles, *The elocutionist*.
[12] Henry Pryor Powell, London merchant.
[13] On desirability of children in rural areas receiving same amount of education as town children:
H 222. 1067.
[14] *The dying priest and the cleansing blood. With a prefatory note by . . . J. H. Wilson* (1875).
[15] See 27 Feb. 75.
[16] Probably Thomas Edwards of Islington, in correspondence on Vaticanism; Hawn P.
[17] William Harrison Davey, vice-principal of St David's, Lampeter.

Scrivener. Dined at Mr Kinnaird's. Saw Count Cadorna—Mr Murray—Scotts—
Ld Wolverton—Ld F.C.—Lady E.M.P. and Mrs Th.—Mr Graham. Saw Hamilton
X some hope. Read Greville's Mem. Vol. II.

4. Th.

Wrote to Messrs T. & B.—J. Watson & S.—C.G.—W.D. Wolff.[1] H. of C. $4\frac{1}{2}$-$7\frac{1}{2}$
and 11-1.[2] I now forget sometimes to put down the House among the items of
my day's work. Eight to breakfast 10-11$\frac{3}{4}$. Saw Mr Benjamin—Mr E. Joseph—
Mr Rigg—Mr Bramwell—W.H.G.—Ld Hartington—Mr Ellice—Mr Whitbread—
Mr Bright—Lady Minto—Mrs Ellice—Mr Grogan. Read Tracts. Dined at Mr
Ellice's.

5. Fr.

Wrote to German Ambassr—Prince Bismarck[3]—Dr Schaff—Mr Saunders[4]—Mr
E. Jones—Mr Hudson & others—Rev W.T. Perry[5]—Mr A. Dowling—Rev Mr O.
Keeffe (B.P.) Dined with the Farquhars. Lady Waldegrave's afterwards. Saw Mr
Gurdon—Mr West—Mr Ouvry—Mr Herbert *cum* Mr Gassiot.[6] Conclave at Ld
Granville's 3.15 on Reg. Exchanges Bill Amendments.[7] Peel Memorial Commit-
tee $4\frac{1}{4}$. H of C. 5-$7\frac{1}{4}$.[8] Much conversation on the Reur [*sic*] business[9] with Sir W.
Farquhar—Mr Leeman—& others—

Ld O Hagan ⎱ on Judicature Ap-
Ld Cork   ⎰   peals
Ld Carlingford ⎱
Mr Newdigate   ⎰ Vatican.
Lady Romilly.
Read Ld Russell Recollections[10]—Prize Essay on Art. Some Minor House
arrangements.

6. Sat.

Wrote to Sir J. Lacaita—Avvocato de Giovanni[11]—Rev. Jas Wall[12]—J. Watson &
S.—Rev. A. Jones[13]—C. Nosotti—Corresp. Independance Belge[14]—Abbé
Michaud—Mr H. Clark[15]—Mr Toorley—Mr Jas Orton[16]—Rev. Mr M'Lennan—

---

[1] Henry W. Wolff, ardent protestant, had written on Vaticanism; Hawn P.

[2] Voted against Regimental Exchanges Bill: *H* 222. 1270.

[3] Thanking him for his letter on receiving *Vaticanism*; Add MS 44446, f. 294; see Matthew,
'Vaticanism', 436.

[4] William Saunders (1823-95; owned Central News agency; liberal M.P. Hull 1885-6, Walworth
1892-5) complained at early publication of *Vaticanism* in the *Telegraph*, Add MS 44446, f. 299.

[5] i.e. T. W. Perry, see 13 Aug. 51.

[6] i.e. the art dealer (see 14 June 75) and J. R. Herbert.

[7] Hartington this day announced further amendments: *H* 222. 1288.

[8] Irish education: *H* 222. 1289.

[9] Probably the start of the 'Is war in sight' crisis; the Berlin *Post*'s article of that title published on
9 May.

[10] See 17 Feb. 75.   [11] Untraced.   [12] A nonconformist.

[13] Perhaps Ambrose Jones, vicar of Stannington from 1867.   [14] Untraced.

[15] Henry William Clarke; unbeneficed priest in Liverpool; Hawn P.

[16] Had sent verses on Vaticanism; Hawn P.

Herr Neuhaus[1]—C.G.—Ld Provost of Glasgow—Mr A. Elliot—Dr Shirtwant[2]—
Sec. Science & Art Dept—Messrs Clowes—Mr Tritten.[3] Saw Mr Salkeld—Mr
Murray—Mr Grogan—Consul White—Dean of Westmr—Baron L. Rothschild—
Baroness L. Rothschild (conversation on state of belief). Dined with the Pem-
brokes: they, and the party, were very pleasant. Luncheon at 15 G.S. Read U.S.
Congr. Quart. on Ch & St.[4] and [blank].

7. 4 S. Lent

Chapel Royal 10 AM and St Paul's Kn. 7 P.M. Saw Mad. Ralli: with her a Greek
gentleman[5] with whom I had much conversation on Döllinger & Church
matters. Read Fraser on Laud[6]—Contemp. R. on Life at High Pressure[7]—Satan
and Sabbath[8]—Wallace on Prayer[9]—Bp Potter's Address[10]—Hook's Life of
Grindal—and tracts.

8. M.

Wrote to Mr W. Bartlett—Rev. A. Hall—Dr Littledale—LNW Goods Supt Chester—Messrs T. & B.—M. Ch. Lucas[11]—M. Ch. de Franqueville—Mr Heneage[12]—
Mr Wright—Mr R. Lilburne[13]—C.G.—Mr Wilshere.[14] H of C. $4\frac{1}{2}$-$5\frac{1}{2}$.[15] Saw Ld
Granville—Gen. Ponsonby—Mr Joseph—Ld Bathurst—Sir W. Harcourt. Dined
at 15 G.S. Read Greville's Journals—Torelli, Poter Temporale.[16] Saw one X.

9. Tu.

Wrote to Mr Plimsoll MP—Rev. Mr MacClennan—Mr Heard—Count
Cadorna—C.G.—Dr Angus. H of C. $4\frac{1}{4}$-$6\frac{3}{4}$ P.M.[17] Dined (as Pres.) at the Metaphysical Society.[18] Saw Mr Courroux—Mr Owen (S.K.M.)[19]—Mr Murray—Mr

[1] Perhaps Johann Christoph Neuhaus, German author of *Die Sagen von der Götten und Helden der Grieschen und Römer* (1873).
[2] *Sic*; unidentified.
[3] Perhaps Joseph Tritton, treasurer of the Baptist Missionary Society.
[4] Anon. review of 'The Vatican Decrees' in *Congregational Quarterly*, xvii. 321 (Boston, 1875).
[5] Emanuel Antonio Mavrogordato, of Westbourne Terrace, prominent member of the Greek community in London; Add MS 44446, f. 318. See 15 Mar. 75.
[6] Probably a pamphlet by William Fraser.
[7] *Contemporary Review*, xxv. 623 (March 1875).
[8] R. A. Proctor, 'Satan and the Sabbath of the Jews', *Contemporary Review*, xxv. 610 (March 1875).
[9] H. Wallace, *Prayer in relation to natural law* (1875).
[10] H. C. Potter, *Shams in Lent; or, the real and false in Lenten duties* (1875).
[11] Possibly Charles Lucas, French architectural historian.
[12] Edward Heneage, 1840-1922; liberal (unionist) M.P. Lincoln, 1865-8, Grimsby 1880-92, 1893-5; cr. Baron 1896; chaired liberal unionist council 1893-8.
[13] Richard Lilburne, editor of the *Belfast Newsletter*, on church matters; Hawn P.
[14] Charles Willes Wilshere, 1814-1906; Hertfordshire J.P. and D.L.; Hawn P.
[15] Army: *H* 222. 1413.
[16] Count L. Torelli, *La questione del potere temporale del Papa considerata nel 1845, nel 1853 e nel 1870* (1870).
[17] Education Code: *H* 222. 1508.
[18] W. K. Clifford led discussion on the scientific basis of morals; Brown, *Metaphysical Society*, 328.
[19] (Sir) Francis Philip Cunliffe *Owen, 1828-94; director of South Kensington Museum 1873-93; kt. 1878.

Wortley—Mr Goschen—Mr Grey—Mr Knowles—Mr ----- (Ld Spencer's Solr)—
Mr Raikes MP—Dr Acland. Finished Torelli, Poter Temporale—Heresy &
Sham[1]—Exposition of The Church.[2] Saw Temple X & another.

10. Wed.

Wrote to Rev. M. Hughes[3]—Mr H. Farquhar—C.W. Collette[4]—
Gam. Bradford[5]
W.A. Stephens[6] } U.S. & Canada
W.H. Tivy[7]
Mr T. Ogilvy—Chairman Leeds Exhibn.—Rev. G.P. Ottey[8]—Rev. A. Schaeffer.[9]
Saw Mr Grogan—Sir Geo. Bowen—Ld Granville—Ld Rosebery. Dined with Sir
D. Marjoribanks. Attended Speaker's Levee. Marlb. House Ball after. Read Rey-
nald.[10]

11. Th.

Wrote to Messrs Clowes—R.A. Martin[11]—E. Spender—J.L. Bowes—E. Good-
burn—C.G.—Mr Ouvry—C. Cowen—Scotts. Fifteen to breakfast. Conclave at Ld
Granville's 3 PM. Nat. Portr. Meeting 3.30. House 4.30-6.[12] Saw Mr Froude—
Mr Herbert—Mr A.B. Hope—Christie's—Consul White—Mr Martineau—Ld
Kimberley. Packed a box for Hawarden. Dined at D. of Bedford's.

12. Fr.

Wrote to Dr Döllinger—A. Kinnaird—Mr Murray—Bp of London—Watsons—
Mr P.J. Blake[13]—C.G.—Ld Wolverton—Robn G.—Lady Cowper—Messrs
Barker—Messrs T. & B.—Mr Owen. Kept my bed till 11 AM with a cold. Saw Sir
A. Gordon—Ld Hartington—Ld Granville. Dined at 15 G.S. Packed two boxes
of books. Read N.A. Rev. on Currency.[14]

13. Sat.

Wrote to Mr J.C. Hoey—Lady Strangford—C.G.—Archbishop of Lydda.[15] Dined
at Count Münster's. Attended Mrs Wilson's play in aftn. Packed another box of

[1] D. Buchanan, *Heresy and sham of all the leading so-called Christian sects* (1875).
[2] Anon., *An exposition of the Church in view of recent difficulties* (1875).
[3] Morgan Hughes, Vicar of Bettws, Llanelly, from 1865.
[4] Perhaps Charles Hastings Collette, protestant propagandist.
[5] Gamahil Bradford had written on Vaticanism; Hawn P.
[6] Of Ontario, sent pamphlets on Vaticanism; Hawn P.   [7] Unidentified.
[8] George Philip Ottey, 1824-91; inspector of schools in London 1871-86.
[9] Adolphe Schaeffer, theologian and protestant pastor at Colmar, Alsace; see 20 Feb. 75 and
Hawn P.
[10] See 23 Feb. 75.
[11] R. A. Martin of Horsham, had sent artistic designs; Hawn P.
[12] Income tax; navy: *H* 222. 1615.
[13] Of Cork; on Vaticanism; Hawn P.
[14] *North American Review*, cxx. 84 (January 1875).
[15] Domenico Panelli, whose *Cenni biografici documati* Gladstone reviewed in 'Italy and her church'
(see 16 July 75).

books: examined Plato. Lady Granville's in evg. Saw Ld Halifax—Scotts. Read
Epist. Obsc. Vir.[1]—Scott's 'Since I was a Student'.[2]

14. 5 S.L.

Chapel Royal at 10. St James's at 7. Saw Lady Herbert. Read Benisch on Development of Judaism: Most interesting[3]—Dublin Rev. on Atheism & the Kensington College(!)[4]—Van Ryn on Disestablt[5]—and other Tracts.

15. M.

Wrote to J.M. Cowper—Dean of St Pauls—C.G.—Rev Mr Bingham[6]—Robn G.—
Mr W.J. Stillman[7]—Mr Tracey[8]—Mr A.J. Ritchie[9]—Lady Cowper. Luncheon at
15 G.S. Conversation with Lady E. P[ringle]. Saw Mr Mavrocordato with Rev
Mr Myriantheus[10]—Mr M'Coll—Mr W. Cowper—Mrs Knowles—Mr Noble.
Dined at Ld F.C.s. H of C. $5\frac{1}{2}$-8 and $9\frac{3}{4}$-12: on Reg. Exchanges Bill.[11] Read Still-
man, Cretan Insurrection—Rogers's Address.[12]

16. Tu.

Wrote to J. Murray—H. Merritt—J.C. Wylie[13]—F.B. Barton[14]—Rev. Dr Blaikie[15]—
T.W. Mossman—R. Yonge—Sec. S.K. Museum—Pres. Lpool Chamb. Commerce—Gen. Ponsonby—Dr Bennett. Dined at Madame Ralli's. Saw Mr
Grogan—Mr Cartwright—Mr Goschen—Count Beust—Ld Hartington—Best of
all C.G. who came in evg home from her blessed work.[16] Read Spiritualism
explained—Blaikie on Scots Churches. H of C. $2\frac{1}{2}$-$6\frac{1}{2}$. Spoke on Regimental
Exchanges Bill.[17]

17. Wed.

Wrote to Robn G.—Messrs Barker—Rev. Mayow—Adm. Hamilton—Ld Wolverton. Worked, as I now do all days, on packing sorting or arranging books &

---

[1] *Epistolae obscurorum virorum de S.S. Concilio Vaticano*, and *Novae Epistolae virorum obscurorum S. XIX conscriptae* (1860).
[2] Untraced; perhaps one of T. Scott's 'Ramsgate tracts'.   [3] See 23 Feb. 75.
[4] By [W. G. Ward], *Dublin Review*, xxiii. 441 (October 1874).
[5] J. G. van Ryn, *Disestablishment a duty: an appeal to the conscience* (1875).
[6] Probably William Philip Strong Bingham, vicar of Berwick Bassett from 1872.
[7] William James Stillman, had sent his *The Cretan insurrection of 1866-8* (1874); Hawn P. See 29 Sept. 79.
[8] Matthew Tracey of Kingstown, Ireland, had written on Vaticanism; Hawn P.
[9] Of Greenwich; sent synopsis of work on the Creation; Hawn P.
[10] Archimandrite Hieronymos Myriantheus, new clergyman for the Greek community.
[11] *H* 222. 1808.
[12] Perhaps J. G. Rogers, 'The age and our work in it. An address' (1874).
[13] Jonathan C. Wylie, a schoolmaster; see Add MS 44436, f. 251.
[14] Frederick Bolton Barton; positivist; corresponded on the bible and science; Hawn P.
[15] William Garden *Blaikie, 1820-99; professor of theology, New College, Edinburgh, 1868-97; wrote 'Letter to Lord Polwarth on the union of churches in Scotland' (1875).
[16] Nursing at Hagley; see 21 Mar. 75.
[17] On aftermath of abolition of purchase: *H* 222. 1904.

other effects. Divers interviews with Mr Grogan: & in the afternoon we agreed to take Mr Tod Heatley's small & rather quaint house just 50 yards from our own: having both gone over it.[1] H. of C. $12\frac{1}{2}$-$2\frac{1}{4}$ and 4-$5\frac{1}{2}$. Spoke on Goschen's Banker's Bill.[2] Saw Ld Granville—Ld Grey—Ld & Lady Egerton. Dined at Sir A. Bannerman's.[3] Lady Beauchamp's party afterwards. Read Mr Noel's poem on Livingstone.[4]

18. Th.

Wrote to Mr Mortimer—Mr Weld Blundell—Messrs T. & B.—Messrs Fresh-fields—Mr Bartley—Mr Grogan. Dined at Mr Beresford Hope's. An agreeable evg. Twelve to breakfast. Sent off my ivories to S[outh] K[ensington] M[useum]. Saw M. Gavard—Ld Overstone. Conclave at Granville's $2\frac{1}{2}$-$4\frac{1}{4}$. Read Hist. Cretan War. The meeting at Granville's was of about 14 on the Judicature Bill. Harcourt urged having a great debate before the Easter recess. The older heads were for awaiting the Govt's initiative. Sir W. H[arcourt']s counsel seemed to be unconsciously prompted in the main by a sense of the necessity of a speech from himself on the subject without more delay.[5]

Conversation with C. on House matters. They involve more than would at first sight appear. I at least am loath to contemplate a new *home*, as apart from a new house, in London. C. slept so well and seemed to be making up for her long watches. Saw Baroness L. de R[othschild] on Dr Benisch's Book:[6] and the Baron on the Currency question, which I think he does not know.

19. Fr.

Wrote to Mr Hertslet—Messrs Harper[7]—Mr Corbett[8]—Robn G.—Mr Murray—Chancr of Exr—C.G.—Mr Grogan—Mr Edgecumbe[9]—Ld Lorne—Mr Wilber-force—Scotts. My conversation with Ld Overstone yesterday was very characteristic: as with Sir R. Peel on Monday. He was enthusiastic on my Tracts respecting the Vatican.[10] Worked on packing and preparing books & other effects. Luncheon at 15 G.S. H. of C. at $4\frac{1}{2}$.[11] Dined at Mr Graham's. After several days of much improving prospects, Catherine was today most sadly called away to Hagley, with Lyttelton & Sybella, in consequence of a telegram announcing the inability of the chest to find relief by expectoration. Saw the Jameses. Read Cretan War.

[1] 23 Carlton House Terrace, which the Gladstones took for the season.
[2] Explaining principles of 1844 Bank Act: *H* 222. 1984.
[3] Sir Alexander Bannerman, 1823-77; 9th bart. 1851.
[4] R. B. W. Noel, *Livingstone in Africa* (1874).
[5] The govt.'s bill to amend the 1873 Supreme Court of Judicature Act was withdrawn on 8 March; a second bill introduced on 9 April, eventually passed; the chief contentious issue was the 1873 ending of the Lords as the final court of appeal; Harcourt spoke, reasonably moderately, on 10 June; *H* 224. 1642.
[6] See 23 Feb. 75.
[7] Harper, Boulton & Co., London wine merchants.
[8] Charles Joseph Corbett, London architect.
[9] Perhaps Frederick J. S. Edgecomb of Brompton.
[10] As he had been earlier; D. P. O'Brien, *Correspondence of Lord Overstone* (1971), iii. 1271.
[11] Probably for Dilke's motion for select cttee. on elections: *H* 223. 82.

Sat 20.

All Saints Ch. at 5 P.M. Wrote to Dr Bennett—Mr Salkeld—C.G.—Mr Lehmann.[1] Twelve to breakfast. Saw Ld Wolverton—Mr Agnew—Mr MacColl(?)—Sir A. Panizzi—Mr Lowe *cum* Mr Childers. Dined at the Duke of Cambridge's. We were cheered in the morning by a somewhat improved Telegram but there followed a call for F.C. & J. Talbot to go down. In the evg again a very faint improvement.

At the Duke's, Ripon rather evaded me: once, & again after I had made a marked effort. Of course *he* did not do it rudely.[2]

21. *Palm S.*

(Such a dreary sky & wintry wind, biting the chest!) Chapel Royal at 10 and H.C. when after my most poor manner I bare up that dear sad sufferer in the Holy Sacrifice before the Eternal Throne. All Saints afternoon. On return from St James's found a message of death immediately impending.[3] Wrote to Mr Weld Blundell—Sec. Fishmongers Co.—Mr R. Lehmann. Read Keble's Letters[4]—and a considerable number of Tracts. Dined at Argyll Lodge with the family.

22. *M.*

Parting service and H.C. at King's Coll Chapel 11 A.M. A congregation of Arthur Gordon's friends.[5] All remained. It was so timely, & so soothing. Surely she[6] is gone to rest: and may her peace and light abound.

Wrote to Ld Lyttelton—Ld Wolverton—C.G.—P. Williams—Robn G.—Rev R. Wilson[7]—Mrs Th.—Jos Elliot jun.—Mr Joseph—R. Russell—Mr Adam—Sir G.B. Airy—Mr Grogan—Rev W. Nevin[8]—Mr Ouvry—Mr Stibbs—Ed. Internat. Rev. N. York.[9] Worked on books. Read Greville—Internat. Rev.—Account of Bernese movement. Saw Mr Salkeld—Mr Hodge—Made Ralli.

23. *Tu.*

All Saints 5 PM. Wrote to Mr Morier. Worked on arranging books for valuation, also packing books & papers. Saw Mr Grogan—Mr Joseph—Mr Phillips. Luncheon at 15 G.S. Much said of Sir W.H. Read Greville's Journal—Account of Berne Movement[10]—Miller—Christine.[11] We enjoy having Agnes with us: she falls in just as of old.

[1] Rudolph Lehmann of Campden Hill Road.

[2] For *Ripon's conversion to Roman catholicism, see 21 Aug. 74.

[3] Death this day of Mary Catherine Lyttelton, aged 25, Catherine Gladstone's niece.

[4] J. *Keble, *Letters of spiritual counsel and guidance* (3rd ed. 1875).

[5] Gordon was leaving to govern Fiji, just annexed.

[6] i.e. Mary Lyttelton.

[7] Robert Francis Wilson, once Keble's curate, now vicar of Rownhams; on Keble's letters; Hawn P.

[8] Probably H. W. Nevins; see 8 July 75.

[9] Not published; perhaps on R. Payne Smith's article on the supernatural; *International Review*, ii (March 1875).

[10] Not found.   [11] S. Punot, *Christine or the Bible girl* (1875).

24. Wed. [Hagley]

Engaged for some mornings past in fighting off a cough. Rose at 9.15. Wrote to W.H.B. Hutchins[1]–Ld Granville–Mr Agnew–Rev Mr Lewis–Mr J.E. Reeve– Messrs Barker–Miss Wing[2]–Sec. Liberal Association–Mrs Burnett–Mrs Ralli–Mr Weld Blundell. Saw Ld Wolverton & arranged finally with him for the transfer of my library to the satisfaction of both. Saw Messrs Sotheby & their Expert who valued the books Hansard £150; the rest £670. Saw Mr Christie, took him over the House and made the necessary arrangements for removal with a view to the sale. More packing & putting away. Off before 6 with W.H.G. Reached Hagley past 11. Found poor George [Lyttelton] & his sons still up. Slept at Mr Harrison's.

25. Th.

Church at 10 AM for H.C. and soon after eleven for the funeral. It is hard to believe, with a real belief, that that bright life is extinct and that fine form wasted and still. Thy kingdom come. It was very touching to see Mr Graham.[3] Also Mr A. Balfour came; an act like him, not like others. In the afternoon I walked with George and F.C. The Father grieves profoundly but as a Christian & a man.

And now three times, at three spots, from three houses, within the last eight months or little more have I, now 65, walked in the funeral procession of nephews or nieces cut off in their opening bloom. Thy kingdom come!

It were best

That we should rest, that all should rest.

Wrote to Mr Grogan–Sir R. Phillimore. Read Ld Russell's Recollections– Philosophismus u. Christenthum (C. Frank).[4]

26. Good Friday.

Church 10½ AM and 7½ PM. Wrote to Ld Russell–Wms & Norgate. Read Philos. & Christenthum: finished: a notable Tract–Todd Martin's Impersonal God[5]– Gillmor's Sermons[6]–Comizio Popolare (Geneva).[7] Walk with G. to the top of Walton Hill. Conversation with C., on Agnes's coming confinement & our little 'den' *inter alia*.

27. Easter Eve.

Church 10½ A.M. and 7½ P.M. Wrote to J. Watson & Smith–Mr T.M. Wyatt–Rt Rev. Dr Döllinger–Mrs Warner. Read Comizio Popolare (finished)–Ld Russell Recollections. Walk with G. & his family party.

---

[1] Packing case manufacturer in London.
[2] Louisa Wing of Windsor requested help in selling her drawings; Hawn P.
[3] Perhaps Malcolm Richard Graham, 1846-1927; curate at Sedgley, not far from Hagley.
[4] C. Frank, *Philosophismus und Christenthum* (1875).
[5] W. T. Martin, *The doctrine of an impersonal God in its effects on morality and religion* (1875).
[6] W. Gillmor, 'The Public Worship Regulation Act. Two sermons' (1875).
[7] See 23 Mar. 75?

28. *Easter Day.*

Ch 11 AM. H.C.—Edw. Talbot preached admirably. Ch. 6½ P.M. Wrote to Mrs Hampton—Rev A.J. Ingram[1]—Mr Grogan. Read Chillingworth, Life—Do, Religion of Protestants[2]—Thomas a Kempis—Buchner's Gottesbegriff.[3] Walk with G. & party in aft. Took his opinion on republication of my three pamphlets jointly.[4]

29. *Easter M. [London]*

Ch. 10.30 AM. Wrote to Messrs Christie—E. Joseph—W. Purdy—J. Watts[5]—Grogan—Scotts—Rev W. Jagoe[6]—Mr W. Logan. Left Hagley 1.50—11 C.H.T. at 8. Read Buchner (finished)—Ld R.s recollections (finished)—Art. in Indian R.C. Rev. on Vatican Decrees.[7]

30. *Tu.*

St And. Wells St 5 PM. Wrote to Ld Wolverton—Rev. Mortlock—Sir R. P[hillimore]—Mr Baverstock[8]—Mr Gurdon—Mr King—Mr Knowles—Bp of Guildford—Messrs Freshfield—and Miss Gilby.[9] Saw Mr Grogan—Sir A. Panizzi.

Several conversations with C. We have rubbed a good deal about the contract of sale wh she naturally regards with discomfort & reluctance. The habit of my life makes me turn my eyes off a disagreeable resolution when once adopted it [*sic*], and go to work on giving it effect as if taking physic.

Also I endeavoured to lay out before C. my views about the future & remaining section of my life. In outline they are undefined but in substance definite. The main point is this: that, setting aside exceptional circumstances which would have to provide for themselves, my prospective work is not Parliamentary. My tie will be slight to an Assembly with whose tendencies I am little in harmony at the present time: nor can I flatter myself that what is called the public, out of doors, is more sympathetic. But there is much to be done with the pen, all bearing much on high & sacred ends, for even Homeric study as I view of it [*sic*] is in this very sense of high importance: and what lies beyond this is concerned directly with the great subject of belief.[10] By thought good or evil on these matters the destinies of mankind are at this time affected infinitely more than by the work of any man in Parliament. God has in some measure opened this path to me: may He complete the work.

---

[1] Arthur John Ingram, 1840-1931; curate in London 1871-2; rector of St. Margaret's, Lothbury, 1882-1921.

[2] P. Des Maizeaux, *An historical and critical account of the life and writings of William Chillingworth* (1725); *The religion of Protestants* (1638).

[3] By F. C. C. L. Büchner (1874).

[4] Published with a preface dated 7 July 1875 as *Rome and the newest fashions in religion. Three tracts* (1875).

[5] Perhaps James Watts, curate at Crundall.

[6] William Jagoe, anglican priest without benefice.

[7] Untraced.

[8] Edwin H. Baverstock, senior clerk in the National Debt Office; Hawn P.

[9] Miss E. M. Gilbey of Cheltenham, corresponding on Troy; Hawn P.

[10] Version of previous five sentences in Morley, ii. 523.

Read Sir W. Palmer (Umbra Oxoniensis) on Vaticanism[1]—G. Smythe's Novel.[2] Six hours on classing china, & other effects, with packing & the rest, tired me out.

31. Wed.

Wrote to Mr Owen Morgan[3]—Mr Geo. Harris—Watsons—Mrs Burnett—Mr Adam—Ld Wolverton—Mr Agnew—Capt. Kinloch[4]—Mrs Th.—Mr Thomson—Dowager Lady Strangford. Four or five hours work on collections furniture & house arrangements. Read Angela Pisani—Rev. Morton Shaw on the Eastward position.[5] Saw Mr Merritt—Mr King—Mr Woods—Murrays—Sir A. Panizzi—Dowager Duchess of Somerset. Dined with the Wortleys.

11 C.H.T. Thurs. Ap. 1. 75.

Wrote to Sec. Statistical Society—Sec. S.K. Museum—Sec. Brown Free Museum[6]—Rev W. Jagoe—Scotts—Dean of Chichester—Rev G.C. Hutton[7]—Messrs Minton—Rev R. Suffield—Sir A. Panizzi—Mr Weld Blundell. Saw Mr Gurdon—Mr Woods. Luncheon at 15 G.S. Saw Dickie—inq. for Seymour, Graham & saw mother [R]. Read Morton Shaw—Angela Pisani. Continued work on preparations and removals.

2. Fr.

Wrote to Mr Agnew—Ed. Guardian—Mr Merritt—and [blank]. China removed. Various packing and directing. Saw Mr Merritt—Mr Woods—Sir A. Panizzi—Mr Quaritch. Read Greville's Memoirs—Morton Shaw's Pamphlet—P. Consort, Speeches & Introdn.[8] Dined with the Lytteltons. I am amazed at the accumulations of objects all of which have now, as by way of retribution, to be handled, & dispersed, or finally dismissed.

3. Sat.

Wrote to Sec. G.P.O.—Ed. Guardian—Christies—Mr Alexander—Watsons—Sir Geo. Prevost—J.K. Aston[9]—Bp of Bath & Wells—Mr Hurn—Sir Jas Hogg—Robn G. More packing, directing, & removing. Visited briefly three galleries, Pall Mall, M'Lean, & British Artists. More work, work, work, on the great flitting operations. Saw Mr Grogan—Baron L. de Rothschild—Baroness L. de R. Dined at No 15 G.S. Finished Mr Morton Shaw's able pamphlet.

---

[1] Sir W. Palmer, *Results of the 'Expostulation' in their relation to the unity of Roman catholicism* (n.d., 1875).

[2] G. Smythe, Lord Strangford, *Angela Pisani: a novel*, 3v. (1875); with Lady Strangford's memoir of Smythe.

[3] Also known as 'Morien', 1836?-1921; journalist on *Western Mail* and author on druids.

[4] Probably of the Kinloch of Kinloch family, where Mrs Thistlethwayte stayed.

[5] M. Shaw, 'The position of the celebrant at the holy communion' (1874).

[6] Brown Museum in Liverpool where the diarist's porcelain collection, soon to be sold, was on deposit.

[7] George Clark Hutton of the United Presbyterian Synod; on Scottish church patronage bill, Add MS 44446, f. 364.

[8] Sir A. Helps, ed., *Principle speeches and addresses* (1875).

[9] Joseph Keech Aston, secretary to Queen Anne's Bounty.

4. 1 S.E.

Chapel Royal mg—St James's evg. Saw Ld Wolverton—Also we dined with them. Long and very interesting conversation with Lady Lothian. Saw Sir C.T. A modicum of flitting operations: but on the whole a great rest. Wrote to Mr Grogan—And a long letter, on grave matters, to WHG.[1] Read Dr Lee on the Public Worship Act[2]—Sir H. Moncreiff on the Free Church claims—&c.[3]

5.

Wrote to Prof. Hillebrand[4]—Mr Higgins—Sir A. Paget—Mr Parker—Mr T.B. Potter—Bp of Winchester—Mrs Dickie: and reviewed my letter to W.H.G. Luncheon at 15 G.S. Saw Mr Grogan—Mr Lowe—Sir W. James—Sir Thos G. (on Bowden affairs &c.) Dined with the T.G.s. H of C. at 4.30.[5] Many hours of labour at clearing. Read Kavanagh's Reply.[6] Christie's men completed their labours: 3 or 4 other sets are at work in the unfortunate house: & two huge Auctioneers' Bills today adorn the doorposts of the portico. But the worst of the wrench is over: & thankful should I be that we have a comfortable place of sojourn to receive us.

6. Tu.

Wrote to Mr Salkeld—Dr A. Clark—Mr Picton—Mrs Th.—Mr Fagan—Dr Kavanagh. Dined at Mr Hankeys. Saw Ld Wolverton—Mr M'Coll—Mr Walter—Mr Hankey—Mr Nash. Saw two [R]. H of C. $4\frac{1}{2}$-$7\frac{1}{4}$. Spoke briefly on Brewer's Licences.[7] Finished Kavanagh. Continued the work of dislocation & dispersion. The poor house looks dismal indeed.

7. Wed.

Wrote to Mr Higgins—Watsons—Robn G. Hours on hours more in poor desolate No 11, and hard work. Saw Sir G. Prevost—Mr Grogan—Mr Salkeld—Mr Bright. Dined at Ld Egerton's. H of C. $12\frac{1}{2}$-2: on Woman's Suffrage Debate.[8] Read Greville—Lawley's new & very interesting pamphlet.[9]

8. Th.

Wrote to W.H.G. (2)—Dr Döllinger—Watsons—Messrs T. & B.—Sup. Goods Camden—Miss M. Watson. Dined with the James's. Work at No 11 continued.

---

[1] On the history of the estate and the duties of a landed proprietor, printed in full in Morley, i. 344, dated (as on the holograph in Hawn P) 5 April 1875.

[2] F. G. Lee, 'The repeal of the Public Worship Regulation Act' (1875?).

[3] Sir H. W. Moncreiff, 'The identity of the Free Church claim from 1838 till 1875' (1875).

[4] Karl Arnold Hillebrand, German author now resident in Italy, friend of Guerrieri-Gonzaga; Add MS 44447, f. 5.

[5] Service affairs: H 223. 297.

[6] James B. Kavanagh, president of St. Patrick's College, Carlow, sent a work on religion; Hawn P; see 29 Oct. 77.

[7] H 223. 388.

[8] He did not vote: H 223. 455.

[9] Probably an untraced pamphlet by Frank Lawley.

Our possession is now virtually contracted to my sitting room: which I will not utterly leave till the last moment. H of C. 4½-6½.[1] Saw Mr Newdigate [*sic*]—Mr Bright. Dined with the Jameses. Read Mr Neale on Maryland[2]—Statement on Honduras Loan—Capecelatro's Reply.[3]

9. Fr.

Wrote to H.N. Gladstone—Mr Ouvry—Mr Freshfield (2). Conclave at Granville's 3-4½. H. of C. & H. of L. 4½-7.[4] The Talbots & F.C. to dinner. Read Johnstone's Reply[5]—Greville's Memoirs. Luncheon with Baroness Meyer de Rothschild. Saw Ld Acton—Mr Grogan. More sorting and arranging.

10. Sat.

Wrote to Rev. E. Mason[6]—Mrs Savile—Mr Varnish[7]—Mr Barclay MP[8]—Col. P. Cameron—T.C. Smith[9]—M. Emile de Laveleye—Kate Gladstone—Sir Thos G.—Col. C. Gordon[10]—T.W. Brown—F. Morse—L. Lewis[11]—J. Graham—Mr Billson—Mr Arthy.[12] Saw Mr Murray. Dined at Sir J. Sebright's.[13] Conversation with D. of Cambridge on P. of Wales's meditated journey to India.[14] Read C. Lamb's Memorials[15]—Capecelatro's Reply.

11. 2 S.E.

Chapel Royal 10 A.M.—All S. 4 P.M. Wrote to Sir W. Palmer—Scotts. Wrote Preface for the Collected Anti-Vatican Tracts.[16] Dined with the Lytteltons. Read M'Coll on Ritualism[17]—Umbra Oxoniensis (finished)—&c.

12. M.

Wrote to W.H.G.—Messrs Robn & Nicholson—Messrs Phillips—General Pringle Taylor.[18] Saw Mr Salkeld—Messrs Freshfield—Sir Thos G.—Lady

[1] Merchant shipping: *H* 223. 473.
[2] E. D. N[eale], 'Maryland not a Roman Catholic colony' (1875).
[3] Cardinal A. Capecelatro, *Gladstone e gli effetti de Decreti Vaticani* (1875).
[4] In Commons, the navy, in Lords, amndt. of 1873 Supreme Court Act: *H* 223. 574.
[5] J. Johnstone, *A few days on the Continent embracing a reply to . . . Gladstone's 'Vaticanism'* (1875); see Add MS 44447, f. 28.
[6] Perhaps Edmund Thomas Mason, anglican priest without benefice.
[7] Henry Varnish, London silk manufacturer.
[8] Alexander Charles Barclay, 1823-93; liberal M.P. Taunton 1865-80.
[9] Perhaps Thomas Charles Smith of Oxford Square, London.
[10] Colonel Charles Alexander Boswell Gordon of 60th Rifles, in correspondence on the Gordon marriage case (see 3 May 75n.); Add MS 44447 *passim*.
[11] Lewis Lewis, rector of Denbigh; on its church funds; Add MS 44446, f. 343.
[12] Probably John Arthy, rector of Caistor, Norwich, from 1842.
[13] Sir John Gage Saunders Sebright, 1843-90; 9th bart. 1864.
[14] Just being arranged, despite the cost; Magnus, *Edward VII*, 132; see 15 July 75n.
[15] M. A. Lamb, *Mary and Charles Lamb . . . Poems, letters and remains* (1874).
[16] Unclear; the preface to *Rome and the newest fashions* was written in July (see 2, 5 July 75); perhaps a discarded draft.
[17] M. MacColl, *Lawlessness, sacerdotalism and ritualism discussed in six letters addressed to . . . Lord Selborne* (1875).   [18] Pringle Taylor, 1796-1884; retired general.

Cowper—Mr Bright.—London Libr. Committee at 4¼. Made my arrangements as to completion, and disposal of the money on Thursday: & executed the deeds. H of C. 6½-8.[1] Today the Sale of furniture at No 11 took place. Read Capecelatro (finished)—Beard on the Vatican Contr.—MacColl on Ritualism.

13. Tu.

Wrote to Mr Morier—Sir H. Moncrieff—Herbert J.G.—Mr Rawlinson—Mr Woodall—Col. C. Gordon—Rev. C. Beard.[2] Saw Col. C. Gordon—Mr MacColl—Mr Kinnaird—Mr Knowles—Mr Grogan—Mr Murray—Sir W. James—Ld Cardwell. Dined with the Jameses. Read Greville—MacColl. Saw Wilmot [R].

14. Wed.

Wrote to Mrs Burnett—Dean of St Asaph—Dr Angus—Messrs T. & B.—Mr Scully—Dean of Westminster—W.F. Batley—T.C. Smith—R. Greenwood—Mr Phillips. Saw Ld Stanhope. Luncheon with Baroness Meyer R. and party to Sir A.P.s to examine lift with a view to her having one. Saw Wilmot X. Dined with the Lytteltons and arranged for the Translation of Laveleye's Tract into English.[3] Men, and final arrangements for moving out of No 11. Saw M.G. on social calls—W.H.G. on Hn matters. Read Justine[4]—M'Coll on Ritualism—Renan on IV Esdras.[5]

15. Th.

Wrote to Bp of Ripon—Barclays—T. Ryder—Mr Adare—Mr Rutherford—Mr Batigann—Watsons—Robn G.—Mrs Barnes—C.G. H. of C. 4½-8½. Prittlewell petition. Bright spoke: right in substance: the House delighted: he was dissatisfied, & rightly: there was not enough measure.[6]

Visited my room at No 11 for the last time as its proprietor: & made some parting arrangements. The process as a whole has been like a *little* death. In the afternoon I went into the city and completed the transaction. I had *grown* to the House, having lived more time in it than in any other since I was born; and mainly by reason of all that was done in it. Sir A.G.[7] has the chairs & sofa on which we sat when we resolved on the disestablishment of the Irish Church in 1868.[8]

Saw Mr Grogan—Mr Freshfield—Sir A.G.s Solr *cum* do—Barclays—Scotts—Mr Murray—Mr Bright. Dined with the F.C.s. Read MacColl's Book.

---

[1] Artizans Dwellings Bill: *H* 223. 732.

[2] Charles Beard, unitarian minister, had sent his *The soul's way to God, and other sermons* (1875).

[3] E. L. V. de Laveleye, *Protestantism and Catholicism, in their bearing upon the liberty and prosperity of nations*, with an introductory letter by Gladstone (1875); see 26 May 75.

[4] Possibly *Notice sur la vie de la Révérende Mère Sainte-Justine* (1865).

[5] An early version of J. E. Renan, *Histoire des origines du Christianisme*, v. chapter xvi (1877).

[6] Petition from Prittlewell on Regina v. Castro (a consequence of the Tichborne case) discharged, with Bright's support, because of 'baseless insinuations' about the Speaker; *H* 223. 1004.

[7] i.e. Sir Arthur Guinness, purchaser of the lease, see 25 Feb. 75.

[8] See 24 Feb. 68.

16. Fr.

Wrote to Mrs Heath (B.P.)[1]—Mr Du Boulay[2]—Ld Rosebery—Rev Morton
Shaw—Mr Spencer—Bp of B. & Wells—Mrs Prynne. H. of C. $4\frac{1}{4}$-$5\frac{3}{4}$. Short conclave on the silly mess.[3] Saw Mr De Lisle—Mr Theodore Martin—Sir R. Phillimore—Col. [J. S.] North. Dined with Sir C. Forster & went afterwards to the
play. Irvine's [sic] Hamlet though a work of ability is not good: but how marvellous are the drama and the character.[4] Saw Mrs Tollemache. Read Hope on
Ritual[5]—MacColl on do.

17. Sat.

Wrote to Mr Collman—Mrs Tollemache with incl.—Ld Caithness—Watsons.
Dined at 15 G.S. Making arrangements & gradually settling down into our new
& humble nest.[6] Read Hope—MacColl—Q.R. on Vatican Controversy.[7] Saw Ld
F. Cavendish—Mr Thistlethwayte.

18. 3 S.E.

Chapel Royal 10 AM—St Paul's 3.15—We fell upon a *function* as well as a service
of high order.[8] Saw the Dean. Dined at 42 P.P. Wrote to Messrs Freshfield (cancelled)—Mr MacColl—Mr Painter—Sir A. Guinness—Sec. Incorp. Law Soc. Read
Hope—MacColl—D. of Argyll on Anthropomorphism.[9]

19. M.

Wrote to Mr Coleman—Dean of Chichester—Dean of Windsor—Mr Beresford
Hope—Helen G.—Ld F.C.—Mr G. Mitchell. Eight to dinner: our first party
except family. Read MacColl (finished)—Hope on Ritual—Mrs Cravens article
in Correspondent: disappointing.[10] Saw Sir A. Panizzi—Mr Childers—Sir R.
Phillimore. H of C. $4\frac{1}{2}$-$5\frac{3}{4}$.[11]

20. Tu.

Wrote to Dr Killen[12]—Mr Grant Duff—Mr Murray—Mr Forster—Mr Falle (of
Jersey, and others)[13]—Mr J. Ross—Dr Marsh. Saw Col. Gordon—Mr Murray—Sir

---

[1] Formerly of Greenwich, now of Ontario; assisted by Gladstone; Hawn P.

[2] John Du Boulay, 1811-95, of Shaftesbury; Dorset J.P.; some of his family became Roman
catholics; corresponded on Vaticanism; Hawn P.

[3] Privilege issue involving *The Times* and the *Daily News* and the Tichborne case; *H* 223. 1112.

[4] At the Lyceum Theatre. Sir Henry *Irving, 1838-1905, kt. 1895; his incisive Hamlet
stressed failure through tenderness rather than weakness of will.

[5] A. J. B. Hope, *Worship in the Church of England* (1874).　　　　　[6] See 17 Mar. 75.

[7] [W. C. Cartwright], *Quarterly Review*, cxxxviii. 459 (April 1875).

[8] No special occasion noted in St. Paul's registers.

[9] G. D. *Campbell, duke of Argyll, *Anthropomorphism in theology* (1875).

[10] Probably P. M. A. A. Craven, 'Deux incidents de la question Catholique en Angleterre ... M.
Gladstone et les catholiques anglais' (1875).

[11] Artizans Dwellings and Public Health: *H* 223. 1231.

[12] William Dool Killen, Irish church historian.

[13] Josue George Falle, 1820-1903; jurat and leader of the conservatives in Jersey, successfully leading a deputation to London to enlist support against the Jersey Bill. Gladstone did not speak on the
Bill, which was withdrawn.

W. Miller[1]—Mr Leveson—Mr Murray—Mr Bright—Mr Goflowski—Mr Agnew—
Mr Dodson—Mr Woolner—Mr Balfour. H of C. $4\frac{1}{4}$-$5\frac{1}{2}$.[2] Nine to dinner. Read
Hope (finished)—Dean of Bristol (2°)[3]—Q.R. on Macready. Nine to dinner.

21. Wed.

Wrote to Mr M'Coy—M. Michel Chevalier—Sir C. Trevelyan—Mr Ouvry—Mr
Jas Wilson—Dean of Chester—Mr Tallerman.[4] H of C. $12\frac{1}{4}$-2 and 5-6. Spoke
briefly on Burials Bill & voted in 234:248.[5] Read Knight of Kerry on Ch. of I.[6]—
Q.R. on Macready (finished)—Wilkins on Future Punishment[7]—Michaud's
Eglise en France.[8] Saw Sir Gibt. Lewis—Sir W. James—Ld Hartington. Dined
with Ld Hartington.

22. Th.

Wrote to Ld Hatherley—Messrs T. & B.—Mr Strachan—Dined at the Duke of
Cleveland's. Read Michaud's Eglise en France—and saw the Marine[?] Gallery[9]
under the guidance of Mr Agnew. Ten to breakfast. Saw Bp of Winchester—Mr
Oxenham—Mr Beresford Hope—Mr MacColl—Mr Beard—Greenwich Peti-
tioners[10]—Dean of St Paul's. Saw Seymour—other inquiries [R].

23. Fr.

Wrote to Dr Allon—Mr Edwards (Birm)[11]—Captain Chatterton[12]—and [blank].
Dined with the Malcolms. H. of C. $4\frac{1}{2}$-$7\frac{1}{2}$ and $10\frac{1}{2}$-1 (Kenealy-Tichborne).
Bright's speech and Disraeli's were in marked & illustrative contrast, much to
B.s advantage. But D.s was extremely clever.[13] Read Pomponio Leti.[14] Saw Mr
Acland—Mr Stansfeld—Mr Bright. $2\frac{1}{2}$-4. Attended conclave at Devonshire
House.

24. Sat.

Wrote to Ld Ln—Ld Stanhope—Mr Wheeler—Rev. Mr Bennett. Dined with Mr
Rathbone.[15] Read Renan on Esdras IV—D'Alviella's Catholicisme Liberal.[16] Saw

[1] Sir William Miller, b. 1809; liberal M.P. Leith district 1859-68, Berwickshire 1873-4.
[2] Army recruiting: H 223. 1287.
[3] Gilbert Elliot, probably his 'The Reformation and the Counter-Reformation' (1874).
[4] Daniel Tallerman of Quadrant Road, Islington.   [5] H 223. 1375.
[6] P. Fitzgerald, 'The Knight of Kerry', 'Two letters on the Irish church' (1875).
[7] N. G. Wilkins, *Errors and terrors of blind guides* (1875).
[8] E. Michaud, *De l'état présent de l'Église Catholique Romaine en France* (1875).
[9] Just opened in New Bond Street.   [10] No account found.
[11] Thomas Edwards of Smith and Edwards, tool-makers.
[12] Perhaps Hedges Eyre Chatterton, 1819-1910; Irish barrister and legal officer; a tory.
[13] Case of *The Queen v. Castro*: H 223. 1513.
[14] Pomponius Leti [i.e. Marchese F. Nobili-Vitelleschi], 'Otto Mesi a Roma, durante il Concilio
Vaticano' (1873), reviewed in 'Italy and her church', see 16 July 75n.
[15] Grant Duff, another guest, noted: 'It ought to have been extremely brilliant, but it was one of
the dullest functions at which I ever assisted'; *Notes from a diary 1878-1889* (1898), i. 91.
[16] E. Goblet, Count d'Alviella, *Le catholicisme libéral autrefois et aujourdhui* (1875); friend and biographer of de Laveleye.

Lady E.M. Pringle—M. Michel Chevalier—Ld Granville—Mr Bright—Visited Mrs Warner, now widowed.[1] Luncheon at 15 G.S.

25. 4 S.E. & St Mark.

Chapel Royal 10 A.M. Tennison's Chapel 3½ PM. Islington Hall 7¼ P.M. with A. K[innaird]. The sight was wonderful, & touching in a high degree: also the earnestness of Mr M. whom I saw for a moment.[2] Wrote to Rev. Mr Macmillan—Rev. M. MacColl—Rev. N.G. Wilkins[3]—Mr Ellaby[4]—M. Victor Oger—Col. C. Gordon. Read Pomponius Leti—Spurgeon's Sermon[5]—many tracts—Finished Wilkins & Dalviella.

26. M.

Wrote to Sir F. Hincks—M. Wolowski—Robn. G.—Mr Jenkins MP.[6]—Ld Devon—Mr Meyrick—Mr Greenwood. Luncheon at 15 G.S. A kind of Sermon from Mr Th. Saw Lady (& Ld) Westmoreland. H of C. 4½-6.[7] Saw Ld Granville—Ld Halifax. Ten to dinner. Read Pomp. Leti. Wrote a little of the Prince Consort Article.[8]

27. Tu.

Wrote to Sec. Gen P.O.—Mr Newdigate—Mr Watt—Ld Granville—Mr Shepherd—Scotts. Dined at Mr Pender's, to meet the R.A.s. Saw Lord Young—German Ambassador—Mr Ward. Saw Seymour—Scott—& two more—X. Mr Pender showed me his pictures. A most beautiful, almost wonderful, Turner. Worked on Article 'Prince Consort's Life'. Read Mr Th. Martin—Trevor on Ritual.[9]

28. Wed.

Wrote to Mr Gurdon—The German Ambassador—Mr Wylie (of Belfast)—Mr E. Lilley[10]—Mr Grogan—Mr Harris—Robn G.—Dr Hayman—Mr Downing—Mrs Th.—Scotts. Conclave at Granville's 4-5¾ on Finance. Worked a little on the Prince. Dined with the Misses Holland. Saw Mr Holland—Sir F. Doyle—Miss Stanley (an assault)[11]—Mr Lecky—Scotts. H. of C. at 2.30.[12] Read Dr Trevor (finished)—Blair on Ritualism.[13]

[1] Maria, widow of Edward Warner, M.P.; see 25 July 60.
[2] A. Kinnaird, with Q. Hogg, organized the Moody and Sankey meetings; this one, at the Agricultural Hall, Islington, was addressed by Moody alone.
[3] Nathaniel George Wilkins had sent his book, see 21 Apr. 75.   [4] R. Ernest Ellaby.
[5] C. H. Spurgeon, *A double knock at the door of the young* (1875).
[6] Edward Jenkins, 1838-1910; anti-slaver radical M.P. Dundee 1874-80; later a tory imperialist.
[7] Ireland: *H* 223. 1640.
[8] Review of the first volume of Martin's *Life*, published anon. in the *Contemporary*; see 21 Dec. 74n.; the review was originally intended for the first number of Cazenove's *Church Quarterly Review*, but its delay caused the switch to the *Contemporary*.
[9] G. Trevor, *On the disputed rubrics, and the Public Worship Regulation Act* (1875).
[10] Not traced.
[11] i.e. Mary Stanley; but the occasion not further recorded.
[12] Scottish affairs: *H* 223. 1736.   [13] W. T. Blair, *A lecture on ritualism* (1873).

29. Th.

Wrote to Rev H. Clark—Bp of Winchester—Mr Graham—Mr G.M. Ward[1]—Mr Rothwell—'Brother Henry'[2]—Mr Ellaby—Mr Th. Martin—Mr A. Ince—The German Ambassador—Ld Hatherley—Sir W. Anderson. Read Mahony's Reply.[3] Thirteen to breakfast. Saw M. Wolowski—Mr Murray—Mr Knowles. H of C. 4-5.[4] Attended the Aitken meeting at the Opera House in evg. About 1500 present.[5]

30. Frid.

Wrote to Mr Jackson—Parcel Supt LNW. Chester—Mr Suffield. Wrote on P. Consort. Saw Mr Oxenham—Duke of Argyll. Worked on papers. Breakfast with Ld Granville 10-12 when we discussed & settled the terms of Mr Fawcett's motion.[6] Dined at Argyll Lodge. Read Q.R. on Jesuits—Tract on Bp of Peterborough's Bill.

Sat. May One 1875. [*The Deanery, Windsor*]

Wrote to Mr W. Downing[7]—Mr Macmillan. 9½-11½. Breakfast & conversation on the 'situation' as to ritual with Bp of Winchester—12-1. Discussion finance with Sir W. Anderson. Saw Shoreditch Deputn.[8] 2-5 at the Academy surveying the pictures: there are many of interest, few of great interest. Acad. Dinner 6½-9½. Then to Windsor. Stiff conversation with Ld Selborne.[9] Read Martin's Essays.[10]

2. 5 S.E.

St George's Chapel mg and aft. Much conversation with the Dean [Wellesley], & two walks. Satisfactory, as ever. Conversation with Mr Holland. And with Gen. Ponsonby. Saw Pr. Leopold: much recovered. Wrote on P. Consort: the religious phase. Read Brooke's Preface[11]—Guicciardini on Papal Power & Introdn[12]—Christie's Answer to WEG.[13]

3. M. [*London*]

Wrote to Mr Freeland—Rev Mr Fosbery—Mr T.C. Smith—The O'Conor Don. Visited the Wolsey Chapel: & the Norman Gate Chambers: each of extreme

---

[1] Of Ebbw Vale, had sent details of his finances; Hawn P.

[2] Secretary of the English Benedictines, about a subscription for Father Ignatius; Hawn P.

[3] D. P. M. O'Mahony, *Rome, semper eadem* (1875).   [4] Ireland: *H* 223. 1828.

[5] William Hay Macdowell Hunter Aitken, curate in Everton, 1871-5, was one of the assistants at the Moody and Sankey meetings at the Opera House, Haymarket. See 25 Apr., 16 May 75.

[6] Fawcett's amndt. on local taxation to the Public Works Bill, moved on 24 May; *H* 224. 802.

[7] Perhaps Arthur Matthew Weld Downing of the Royal Observatory.

[8] No account found.

[9] Selborne feared Gladstone would come out for disestablishment generally; Selborne, II, i. 359-61.

[10] T. Martin, *Essays on the drama* (1874).

[11] S. A. Brooke, perhaps *Sermons*, 2nd series (1875).

[12] F. Guicciardini, *The temporal and spiritual power of the Pope*, tr. J. Fowle (1860).

[13] T. W. Christie, 'A reply to Mr Gladstone's "Ritual and Ritualism" ' (1875).

though very diverse interest. Back to London at 11.20. Saw Sir W. Anderson (on Finance)—Mr Childers (do)—do cum Mr Holms (do)—D. of Argyll (Gordon case)[1]—Mr Bouverie—Sir J. Lacaita. Worked on Hansard & Parl. papers at H. of C. H. of C. at 4.30.[2] Ten to dinner. Read Bray on Toleration[3]—Pearson on Newman.[4]

4. Tu.

Wrote to Col. Gordon—Mr MacColl. Worked on Prince Consort & made some real progress with the Article. Six to dinner: Lady M. Alford came in. Luncheon at 15 G.S. H of C. early and $10\frac{3}{4}$-$1\frac{1}{2}$: an unsatisfactory scene.[5] Saw Ld Wolverton—Rev. Mr Aitken.

5. Wed.

Wrote to Mr Annett[6]—Mr Whidelington—Rev. Mr Polwhele—Bp of Lichfield—Mr Mavrocordato. H. of C. $12\frac{1}{2}$-$1\frac{3}{4}$ and 4-6. Spoke briefly on the Irish Sunday Closing Bill.[7] Worked on Pr. Consort Article. Saw Sir R. Phillimore—Ld Granville—Ld Hartington—Chancr of the Exchequer—Bp of Chester—Mr Th. Martin. Read Pr. Consort's Speeches. Dined with the Warrens.

6. Th. Ascension.

Chapel Royal at noon. Wrote to Dean of Ely—German Ambassador—Mr C. Sharp—Mr Ouvry—Sir J. Lacaita. Dined at Lady Stanley's: much conversation on Italy & Vaticanism. Saw Lord Moncreiff—Mr Ouvry—Ld Granville. Read Pr. Consort's Speeches—Scott's Letters to Polwhele[8]—Abbott's Serm. on Nous of the Church.[9] Wrote on P. Consort: & in substance finished. H of C. $4\frac{1}{2}$-6. Said a few words on Dizzy's strange escapade.[10]

7. Fr.

Wrote to S.E.G.—Dean of Durham—Helen G.—Rev. Dr Cazenove—H.N.G.—Rev. Mr Wilkinson—Miss [E. M.] Gilbert—Dr Liddon. Worked on Finance

[1] Complex marital affairs of G. J. R. Gordon (see 22 May 52), whose case implied Vatican denial of the validity of protestant marriages; discussed, without naming Gordon, in preface to *Rome and the newest fashions*. Mrs Gordon's mem. for the Pope, January 1875, is at Add MS 44446, f. 4 and other mem. and correspondence in Add MS 44447 and Duke University MSS. Capt. W. E. A. Gordon (see 9 May 75) told Gladstone next day: 'I understand . . . that it is your intention to take means for bringing into public notoriety the deplorable case of my brother Mr Gordon of Ellon's Roman Catholic marriage at Manchester. I strongly protest against this action on your part . . . the only result which can ensue from the fulfilment of your intentions, will be a prosecution of my brother for bigamy. . . .' Add MS 44447, f. 110. Gladstone replied he acted on Sir A. Gordon's suggestion; ibid., f. 112. See 14 July 75.   [2] Ireland; *H* 223. 1980.
[3] C. Bray, *Toleration: with some remarks on Professor Tyndall's address at Belfast* (1875).
[4] S. Pearson, *Conscience and the Church in their relations to Christ and Caesar* (1875).
[5] Strangers excluded for part of a debate on Hartington's motion on publication of debates and exclusion of strangers; *H* 224. 89.   [6] Of Simpson and Annett, decorators.
[7] Supporting the bill of the O'Connor Don and others; *H* 224. 144.
[8] Sir W. Scott, 'Letters . . . addressed to the Rev. R. Polwhele' (1832).
[9] E. A. Abbott, probably 'The signs of the Church' from *Cambridge Sermons* (1875).
[10] Attacking Disraeli's handling of govt. business: *H* 224. 171.

Papers. Saw Ld Wolverton—Ld Granville. Luncheon at 15 G.S. H of C. 4¼-7.
Spoke 1¼ h. criticising this very guilty Budget.[1] Also 11-12½. Dined with the
Jameses & went to Salvini in Gladiatore: manifestly an actor of real greatness.[2]
Read Kean's Memoirs.[3]

8. Sat.

Wrote to Col. C. Gordon—German Ambassador (2)—M. Idromenos[4]—Mr
Grogan—Sir A. Guinness—Dr Stuart—Dean of St Paul's—Rev Mr Pease—Mr
Polwhele. Revised good part of my MS for Dr Cazenove's Review.[5] Luncheon at
15 G.S. Saw Mr Christie—London & Westmr Bank—Mrs Grote—Sir Jas Watson—Rector of Lincoln Coll. *cum* Mrs Grote. Dined at Mr Balfour's: then with
Mrs Ralli to Covent Garden for Wagner's Lohengrin:[6] on which there is much
to say.

9. S. aft Ascension.

Chapel Royal 10 AM—St Paul's aft. A very able Sermon from Dr Lightfoot.
Finished revision of article on Prince Consort. I am considering whether to take
pains to keep the authorship secret.[7] Wrote to Editor of Eklektiké[8]—Prince
Rhodokanaki[9]—Sec. to People's Café Co.[10]—Mr Johnson—Capt Gordon RN[11]—
(Packet to Dr Cazenove). Saw Ld Granville—Ld Wolverton—Ld F. Cavendish
(then on Finance)—Dean of St Paul's—Ld Blachford—Mr M'Coll—then on
Rubrics—Gordon Case—R.C.s—&c. Read Tracts, various.

10. M. [Nottingham]

Wrote to Mr Johnson—Messrs Christie—Dr Döllinger—Mr . . . (U.S., Texas) B.P.
Packed and off at 9.30 for Nottm.—Met the Museum Committee at luncheon.
Went over the Castle grounds & discussed the questions now open.[12] Went
over the Park property: took another view of the 'Monks' Holes'. Dined with
the Yeomanry in the Evg. Read Pattison's Casaubon[13]—And The Skeleton at
the Plough.[14] Saw one [R].

11. Tu. [Clumber Park, Worksop]

Wrote to C.G.—Mrs Th. Visited the Museum—The Mayor's Lace Factory—
Wollaton Hall: a remarkably fine exterior, except the added top. Before

---

[1] Attack on Govt.'s handling of income tax, brewers' licences and the debt: *H* 224. 290.
[2] Tommaso Salvini, 1829-1916, Italian actor and colleague of Ristori, in Soumet's *Il Gladiatore* at
the Theatre Royal, Haymarket.
[3] F. Phippen, *Authentic memoirs of Edmund Kean* (1814).
[4] Andreas M. Hidromenos, Greek author.   [5] See 26 Apr. 75n.
[6] The first British performance (in Italian) of Wagner's opera.   [7] See 25 May 75n.
[8] Thanking him for his defence of his views about the narrowness of the Russian church; printed
in *T.T.*, 5 June 1875, 12a. See 13 Jan. 75n.
[9] Prince Demetrius Rhodocanakis; see Add MS 44448, f. 119.   [10] Not found.
[11] William Everard Alphonso Gordon, 1817-1906, captain R.N., admiral 1887; involved in the
Gordon marriage case.
[12] i.e. in his capacity as a trustee of the Newcastle estate.
[13] See 1 Mar. 75.   [14] Untraced pamphlet.

breakfast I cut down a Siberian Elm in the Park, bad axe but soft tree 4 f. 6 ord. meas. 5.6 when cut. It took 50 m. At 4 PM. by rail to Mansfield & carriage to Clumber. The last ten of the fifteen miles were just such as Lancelot might have traversed when bringing Guinevere. We were received by Housekeeper & servants in state at 7¼ P.M. The place seems to be beautifully kept: which in one way makes it sadder. Read Casaubon—Skeleton at the Plough—Beranger Procès.[1]

12. Wed.

Wrote to Ld F. Cavendish—W.H.G.—Sir A. Panizzi—C.G.—Edr Devonshire Paper. Read Steele on Expression by signs of measure & melody in Language[2]—Hogarth Analysis of Beauty[3]—Skeleton at the Plough (finished). Saw Mr Williams—Mr Hanley (Worksop)—Mr Cookson (W. Manor)[4]—Mr Lister.[5] We set out at 11½ for 7 hours of inspection at Worksop—the Manor (especially the dismounted Stone) and in the Woods. The Manor Hill Woods were admirable.

13. Th.

Wrote to Mr Th. Woods—Dr Cazenove—C.G.—Sir Thos Acland—Robn G.—Ld F. Cavendish (Tel.)—Ld De Tabley. Another lengthened circuit over the property. The Gardens—Decoy Wood & Decoy—Mr Brameld's Chapel—Markham Clinton Church—The Aviary. Saw Mr North—Mr [G. W.] Brameld. Back between 5 & 6. Read Politique Très Chretien—Isaac Casaubon—Crimes des Jesuites.[6]

14. Fr. [Courthey, Liverpool]

Wrote to C.G.—W.H.G. We went over the house, seeing the Pictures, Porcelain, state of the fabric &c. The moveable wealth here may touch ¼ million. Saw the old people—and off at 12¾ with Mr Ouvry. Reached Liverpool 4.40. Courthey before 6. Saw Robn G. Conversation with his son Robn on the internal condition of the Firm. Read Casaubon—Crimes des Jesuites (finished).

15. Sat.

Wrote to S.E.G.—Townshend & Barker—Dr Smith—Mrs Hope: a statement—Ld De Tabley. Spent the morning, in writing, & on Pattison's remarkable Life of Casaubon.[7] To Lpool in aftn. Conversation with Robn. Attended the afternoon service in the Catholic Apostolic Church.[8] It was somewhat impressive. About 50 present. Examined their Liturgy a little.

---

[1] P. J. de Beranger, *Chansons inédites, suivies des procès* (1828).
[2] J. Steele, *An essay towards establishing the melody and measure of speech* (1775).
[3] W. Hogarth, *The analysis of beauty* (1753).
[4] William Isaac Cookson of Worksop Manor.
[5] Probably George Spoforth Lister, J.P., of Bawtry.
[6] Not found.
[7] See Add MSS 44792, f. 53, 44794, f. 186.
[8] i.e. a branch of the Irvingite church in Catherine Street; no permanent minister.

16. *Whits.*

To Lpool with Robn. I went to Mr Aitkens Ch but he was not there as he had said.[1] A good sermon, & H.C.—In the afternoon I heard Mr Hurditch[2] at the building in Victoria Street. The notes of Mr Aitken's Church were curious; its general arrangements "low" but 30 & 40 years ago Mr Wilson was drummed out of Liverpool for less. Walk & bus out to C. Hey. Read Thornton on Doctrine Old & New[3]—Cazenove on D. of Somerset—Do on Reformation[4]—Newman, Occl Sermons.[5] In a singular conversation at night Robn showed an excitement I had not expected, on the subject of the late Government.

17. *M.* [*Hawarden*]

Wrote to Sec. G.P.O.—Capt Gordon RN—Mr F. Adam—Rev Mr Warleigh[6]—C.G.—Sec. Guy's Hospital—Mr Knowles—Rev. Mr Mayow—Mr Griffith—Mr J.F. Robertson—Prof. Cazenove. Read Mr Richards on Moral and brute force[7]—Pattison's Casaubon. Conversation with Walter G. Reached Hawarden at one. Hours of work among letters & papers.

18. *Tu.*

Ch. 8 AM & H.C. Wrote to Mr Oxenham—Mr Knowles—Mr Banister—Mr Hayward—Mr Stansfeld jun.[8]—A. White—C.G.—Mrs Grote—Mr Ikin—Mr Oxley—Mrs Th. Long confabulation with Messrs T. & B. on Residuary Estate affairs—& on my own Estate. Some woodcutting with W. Conversation with S. & his Curates on Ultramontanism. Examining rooms with a view to the planting out of my Library.

19. *Wed.*

Ch. 8¼ AM. Wrote to J. Watson & Smith—Capt. Gordon RN—C.G.—J. Murray—C. Finlay[9]—W. Aronsberg[10]—J. Macray—Mr Potter MP—Rev R. Polwhele—W.T. Thornton.[11] Saw Mr Stewart whom the D. News has dismissed.[12] Further examn ab. rooms. Cut part of a large oak. Read Fortnightly on Ch.—Austin—Contemp. on Covenanters—Pattison's Casaubon.

20. *Th.*

Ch. 8¼ AM. Wrote to Mr Cowper Temple—Dowr Lady Westmoreland—Mr J. Hamilton—Mr R. Harrison—Rev. R.W. Dale—Rev T. Adair—Mr Murray

[1] i.e. the revivalist; see 29 Apr. 75.

[2] Apparently not an anglican; perhaps 'Hebditch' (see 22 May 75) is intended.

[3] W. T. Thornton, perhaps *Old-fashioned ethics and common-sense metaphysics* (1873).

[4] J. G. Cazenove, *Modern theism* (1872); comments on Somerset's *Christian theology* (1869); see also 18 July 69.

[5] J. H. Newman, probably *Sermons preached on various occasions* (1857).

[6] Henry Smith Warleigh, moral theologian and rector of Ashchurch; Hawn P.

[7] Not traced.

[8] Apparently the cabinet minister, whose father had the same name.

[9] Charles Finlay, J.P., Belfast linen manufacturer; Hawn P.

[10] Woolf Aronsberg, Manchester instrument manufacturer; corresponded on politics; Hawn P.

[11] William Thomas Thornton, had sent his book; see 16 May 75.   [12] Not further identified.

Gladstone—Mr G. Johnston—Mr Hine—C.G.—H.N.G.—Sig. Dassj. Saw Mr
Roberts. Attended Meeting of Hawarden School Feofees.[1] Finished the Oak
with WHG. Read Tracts on Vivisection—Dale on the Atonement[2]—Casaubon's
(noble and instructive) Life (finished)—Literature & Mission of the Plymouth
Brethren[3] (If this is a representative Tract, they will not fail from pitching their
merits and claims too low.)—Jukes on Restitution.[4]

21. Fr.

Ch. 8½ AM. Wrote to Mr Kinnaird—Mr R.M. Stuart—C.G.—Rev. Dr Belcher—
Mr G. Swindells. Worked hard on setting up bookcases in the supplemental
T[emple of] P[eace], unpacking bookboxes, & placing books. Read Dale on
Atonement—Burns' Poems—Byron Painted by Compeers[5]—Method. Mag. on
Vatican Controversy[6]—Jukes on Univ. Restitution—Johnstone on W.E.Gs
Pamphlets.[7]

22. Sat.

Ch. 8½ AM. Wrote to Mr Hebditch[8]—Mr J. Knowles—Mr E. Sturges—Mr W.F.
Smith—Mr Strahan (proofs). Corrected Proofsheets of my Article on the Prince
Consort. Worked on books. Read Arthur on the Popes Discourses[9]—Burns's
Poems—Delitzsch, Lehrsystem[10]—Jukes on Restitution. Cut down a Spanish
Chestnut at the Rectory with W. & S.

23. Trin. S.

—H.C. 8 AM. Morning Ch 10½, Evg 6½. Wrote to Marq. of Hartington—C.G.—
Capt. Gordon RN.—Mrs Hope—An Artist. Walk with Stephy: spoke of W.
Finished Jukes on Restitution: the testimonies in the Appendix are remark-
able.[11] Read also Passages from the Diary of an Artist[12]—Bp Browne on
O.C.s[13]—Meade on Ath. Creed[14]—Harper on Nat. Church[15]—and other Tracts.

24. M. [London]

Ch. 8½ A.M. Wrote to Mr Hamilton—Mrs Th. Arranging matters for departure—left at 2.30—business in Chester. Read Arthurs Modern Jove—Johnson's

[1] i.e. the trustees. [2] R. W. Dale, *The atonement* (1875).
[3] Possibly D. Macintosh, *Brethrenism, or the special teachings of the ... Plymouth Brethren* (1875).
[4] A. J. Jukes, 'The second death and the restitution of all things' (4th ed. 1875); see 23 May 75; important text in the Future Retribution debate.
[5] *Byron painted by his Compeers; or, all about Lord Byron* (1869).
[6] *Wesleyan-Methodist Magazine*, xxi. 433 (May 1875).
[7] J. Johnstone, 'A few days on the continent ... a reply to Gladstone's "Vaticanism"' (1875); reprinted from the *United Kingdom Anti-Papal League Magazine*.
[8] S. Hebditch, nonconformist minister first met at the rally on 15 Feb. 75; Hawn P.
[9] W. Arthur, *The modern Jove; a review of the collected speeches of Pio Nono* (1873).
[10] J. Delitzsch, *Das Lehrsystem der römischen Kirche dargestellt und beleuchtet* (1875).
[11] See 20 May 75; the 4th ed. has appendices on patristics and death.
[12] Anon. (1875).
[13] E. H. Browne, *The Old Catholic movement on the continent of Europe* (1875).
[14] J. F. Meade, *The Athanasian Creed and legislation thereon* (1875).
[15] F. W. Harper, *Dialogues on National Church and National Church Rate* (1861).

Starry Haven[1]—Dodd on the Land question.[2] London at 11. H. of C. $11\frac{1}{4}$-1.[3] Long meeting in Chester with Messrs T. & B.—and B. and H. saw Ld Harting-ton. Saw Mr Lowe. Sat late with arrears.

25. *Tues.*

Wrote to S.E.G.—Mr F. Knowles—Rev. R. Suffield—Messrs Cassell—Messrs Hayden (Guildford).[4] Saw Mr Bayley Potter—Lady Stradbroke—Mr R.M. Stuart—Sir Thos G.—Mr C. Parker—Mr F. Lawley—Dr Playfair—Princess Louise. Corrected Revises of Article on P. Consort.[5] 5-$6\frac{3}{4}$ Mrs Malcolm's Private Theatrical. Dined with the [Baldwyn] Leightons. Saw Wilson X. Read Hist. Maryland.

26. *Wed.*

Wrote to Bp of Ely—Mr Lynian—Mr Barnett—Mr Mackay—Mr Bayley Potter MP.—Rev. R. Yonge—Rev. W. Sinclair—H. Fawcett—Ld Ripon—Mr Strahan—Robn G.—Miss M'Ghee[6]—Mr Murray—Mrs Malcolm, and wrote my letter to M. de Laveleye which is to accompany the Version.[7] Saw M. Bourgeois[8]—Mr Knowles (bis)—Mr F. Lawley—Prof. Blackie—Mr Murray—Sir W. Farquhar—Mr E. Ashley—Scotts. Luncheon at No 15 G.S. Dined with the Farquhars. Re-perused M. de Laveleye's pamphlet in order to work upon it.

27. *Th.*

Wrote to Mr Mitchell—Sir W. Farquhar—Christie's—Lieut. Bacon—Mr Abbott—Mr Wolff—Gulielmus.[9] Short dinner at Mr Parkers. Breakfast with the Cowper-Temples to meet Mr & Mrs Pearsall Smith.[10] *He* made a very interesting statement of his work. Saw Sir R. Phillimore—Mr S. Morley—Mr Graham. 7 hours in H of C: fighting the Savings' Banks Bill.[11] We ran our heads against the brick wall of the majority with more effect than usual. Read The Statute Dogm. Discipl.[12]

[1] Not traced.

[2] G. Dodd (& others), *The land we live in* (1854).

[3] Fawcett on local taxation (see 30 Apr. 75): *H* 224. 802.

[4] Haydon and co., bankers in Guildford.

[5] See 26 Apr. 75. Report of publication and denial of authorization by diarist in *T.T.*, 26 and 27 May 1879, 9f, 9d.

[6] One of the three daughters of bp. M'Ghee.

[7] Introductory letter (cautious and noncommital) to the translation of E. L. V. de Laveleye, *Protestantism and Catholicism, in their bearing upon liberty and prosperity of nations* (1875); see 23 July 70n., 14 Apr. 75. Draft at Add MS 44447, f. 167.

[8] Probably Paul Bourgeois, deputy in the National Assembly 1871-1906; supported de Broglie.

[9] Possibly the author of *The canon of scripture* (1878).

[10] Robert Pearsall Smith, 1827-98, nondenominational evangelist, and his wife; parents-in-law of Bertrand Russell; for this meeting see B. Strachey, *Remarkable Relatives* (1980) 45; Add MS 44447, f. 147 gives Smith's views on the German religious situation.

[11] Spoke several times: *H* 224. 987.

[12] See 6 Oct. 75.

28. Fr. [Holmbury][1]

Wrote to Mr Knowles—Sir A. Panizzi—Robn G.—Mr Mavrocordato—Mr de Lisle. Luncheon at 15 G.S. Saw Mr [Thomas] Woolner's Studio—Mrs Hope—Do *cum* Duchess of N.—and others. Off at 4.25 to Holmbury. Walk with Mr Leveson Gower. Read Dublin Review on W.E.G.[2]—Jew's letter to Bp of Manchester.[3]

29 Sat.

No letter written: a day of liberty. Conversation with Granville—C. Howard—H. Cowper—K. Hodgson. Walk on the hills: & drive. Worked on correcting my Tracts for new Edition.[4] Read Brook's Reports—Dublin Review—and various Tracts.

30. 1 S. Trin.

Ch (Mr Powell)[5] at 11 A.M.—Aftn walk. Wrote to Ld Hatherley. Read Brook—Lightfoot on Colossians[6]—Spalding's Pastoral[7]—Denison's Charge[8]—and other Tracts.

31. M. [London]

Wrote to Mr Murray. Read Mr Th. Martin's Essays on the Drama.[9] $10\frac{3}{4}$-$1\frac{1}{4}$: back to town. H of C. 5-$7\frac{3}{4}$.[10] Dined with the Cowpers—conversation with both Lady C.s. Saw Mr Browning—Ld Granville—Rev. Mr Suffield—Mr Bright—Ld Cowper (Old Catholicism).

Tues. June One. 1875.

Wrote to Ld Hartington—Mr Wood (of Nottingham)—Mr Ouvry—Mr Burton—Rev. Mr Wilkinson—Mr Bond Hughes. Saw Messrs Christie—Irish Sunday Bill Secretaries[11]—Ld De Tabley—Mr Joseph—Mrs Hope. Saw Tollemache—Chapman X. Read Th. Martin—Scott's Letters to Polwhele[12]—Contemp. Rev. on Religion in France.

2. Wed.

Wrote to Sir J. Lacaita—Miss M'Ghee—Rev Mr Hobling[13]—Registrar of Charterhouse[14]—Mr E. Wallace—Rev Mr Prescott[15]—Dean Keating[16]—and. . . .

---

[1] Leveson-Gower's house near Abinger, Surrey.   [2] *Dublin Review*, xxiv. 454 (April 1875).
[3] Not found.   [4] i.e. *Rome and the newest fashions in religion*.
[5] John Welstead Sharp Powell, rector of Abinger.
[6] J. B. Lightfoot, *The Epistles of St Paul* (1865).
[7] M. J. Spalding, *Pastoral letter on the papal infallibility* (1870).   [8] By G. A. Denison (1875).
[9] See 1 May 75.   [10] Publication of debates: *H* 224. 1148.
[11] Perhaps with respect to Sullivan and Pease's Intoxicating Liquors (Ireland) Bill, withdrawn 1 July.   [12] See 1 May 75.
[13] W. B. Hobbling, nonconformist minister at Gerrard's Cross; had sent a resolution; Hawn P.
[14] See 16 June 75.
[15] Oliver Sherman Prestcott, historian of Maryland; Add MS 44447, f. 122.
[16] Michael J. Keating, dean of Kilfenora.

Saw Mr Tollemache—Mr Ouvry—Mr T.B. Potter—Ld Wolverton—Sir J. Lacaita—Mr Th.—Mrs Malcolm—Mrs Th.—and others. Read Investigator.[1] H. of C. 3½–6.[2] Dined with the Sydneys. Devonshire House after.

3 Th.

Wrote to Watsons—Mr Murray—Mr Brookes—Rev. G. Macaulay[3]—Mr Lander[4]—Charterhouse Brothers[5]—Bishop [Reginald] Courtenay—Mr Cavendish—Mr Petrie—Sir S. Scott & Co.—Ly Burrell. Saw Mr Herbert—Mr Keightley—Mr Parker—Dowager Lady Westmoreland—Mr Sanders (Dentist)—Mr de Lisle. Luncheon at 15 G.S. Read Martin's Essays—Callard on Antiquity of Man[6]—Investigator.

4. Fr.

Wrote to Mr Strahan—Robn G.—Rev Mr Dodds—Mr Th. Wood—Prof. Blackie—Sec. Soc. Arts—Mr G. Whale[7]—E. Williams—Mr Gardner—Mr James & Mr King. Saw Sir A. Panizzi—Sir R. Phillimore. Read Ought we to Obey in Contemp. Rev.[8]—Bp of Bombay's (noble) Charge[9]—Martin's Essays—Bp Ullathorne's Synodal Discourse.[10] Began my trial efforts at a paper on Ritualism.[11]

5. Sat.

Wrote to D.C. Link—Dr Von Döllinger—L'Abbé Portaz Grassés[12]—German Ambassador—Messrs Clowes—Rev. R. Smith—R. Fergusson—Rev E.H. Haskin—Mr Grogan—Rev G.H. Forbes—Supt Lost Prop. Office Euston—Mr Cowper Temple. Mr Tollemache drove us (4 inh[and]) to Dulwich where I refreshed my unpardonably dim recollections of the charming gallery. Saw Mr Roundell—Mr M. Bernard—Sir W. James. Wrote on Pr. Consort. Dined with the Jameses. Duchess of Cleveland's afterwards. Read Martin's Essays on Drama.

6. 2 S. Trin.

Chapel Royal 10 A.M.—St James's 7 AM. [sic] Saw Ld Clanwilliam—Lady Ashburnham—Mr Prescott Hewett—long conversation about Pembroke &

---

[1] *Revelation of science in Scripture . . . By Investigator* (1875).
[2] Bill to amend 1870 Irish Land Act: *H* 224. 1295.
[3] Free church minister in Edinburgh, had sent a book; Hawn P.
[4] Of Landor and Bedells, architects.
[5] See 16 June 75.
[6] T. K. Callard, *The geological evidences of the antiquity of Man reconsidered* (1875).
[7] George Whale, liberal organizer and solicitor in Woolwich; Hawn P.
[8] *Contemporary Review*, xxvi. 123 (June 1875); on church discipline.
[9] H. A. Douglas, 'Charge delivered . . . 12th January 1875' (1875).
[10] By W. B. Ullathorne (1875).
[11] Published as 'Is the Church of England worth Preserving?', *Contemporary Review*, xxvi. 193 (July 1875), reprinted in *Gleanings*, vi. 143.
[12] To Abbé Portaz-Grassis of Naples, declining direct correspondence on Vaticanism; Add MS 44447, f. 201.

especially about the N. family & the boy's leg.[1] Read B. Brown on Future Punishment[2]–Droop on the Rubrics[3]–Baroness Rothschild's very touching volume of prayers.[4]

7. M.

Wrote to Mr Vere Bayne–Bp of Kingston–Pr. Rhodokanakis–W.E.C. Smith[5]–Rev. Mr Wilkinson–Rev. Provost of Eton. Dined at Mr Rathbone's. Arr. papers & pamphlets. Saw Mr Godley–Ld Lanerton[6]–Mr Rathbone–Bp of Peterborough–Mr W. Graham–Sir J. Lacaita. Luncheon at Prince Lucien Bonaparte's: he described the method of his Library and in part showed it. H of C. 4½-7½. Spoke on Savings Banks.[7] Read Theodore Martin's Essays–finished.

8 Tues.

Wrote to Robn G (Tel)–Sec. London Library–W.S. Scurr–D. Harvey–W.A. Lindsay[8]–F.J. Dishman–Rev Dr Myriantheus–Earl Derby [sic]–Rev P. Schaff–Mr Matthews. Saw Mr Lawley–Mr Knowles–Dr Clark–Mr K. Hodgson. Luncheon 15 G.S. Attended Baptism of our first Grandchild:[9] at the same font, & in the same dress, as our children. H of C. 3½-7: opposing the mischievous financial manipulations, but for the moment in vain.[10] Read Claudian.[11] Dined with Metaphys. Soc. and discussed Vivisection.[12]

9. Wed. [Christ Church, Oxford]

Wrote to Mr Price–Prince Rhodokanakis–J. Maitland–Mr M'Kechnie[13]–Mr Setter–Mr Murray–R. Main. Read 'Claudian'. Saw Dr Clark. Correcting Proofs of the Vatican Tracts for collective reprint. Off at 3 to Oxford. Ch.Ch. Prayers on arrival. Heard the oration in Hall: attended the Banquet, and spoke vice Lord Granville.[14] It was an occasion of real interest. Saw Dean [Liddell] of ChCh.–Ld Rosebery–Prof Stubbs[15]–Dr Acland–Sir Thos G.–and others.

---

[1] Possibly Newcastle family health; for Hewett at Wilton, see 9 Aug. 61.

[2] J. B. Brown, The higher life. Sermons (n.d.).

[3] H. R. Droop, The Edwardian vestments. An investigation into the history and construction of the ornaments-rubric (1875).

[4] Probably Hester Rothschild, Prayers and meditations (1856).

[5] Possibly W. E. Smith, secretary of the Evangelization Society.

[6] Edward Granville George Howard, 1809-80; admiral; cr. Baron Lanerton January 1874.

[7] H 224. 1477.

[8] William Alexander Lindsay, 1846-1926; barrister and tory candidate; m. 1870 Harriet, da. of 5th earl of Aberdeen.

[9] Agnes' daughter, Catherine Mary Lavinia Wickham, later head of Bishop Creighton House, Fulham.

[10] Attacking proposals for a sinking fund: H 224. 1544.

[11] Perhaps L. T. Hodgkin, Claudian; the last of the Roman poets (1875).

[12] Lord Arthur Russell led the discussion; Brown, Metaphysical Society, 329.

[13] C. M. McKechnie of Darlington; sent a press cutting; Hawn P.

[14] At the Christ Church Gaudy. The oration (given by a recent graduate) was by Francis *Paget, 1851-1911; dean of Christ Church 1892.

[15] i.e. the historian; see 16 Apr. 58.

10. Th. [London]

Ch.Ch. Prayers 8 AM. Off at 9. C.H.T. at 11¼. Saw Sir A. Guinness—Dr A. Clark—Mr Morley—Dean of Ch.Ch.—Mr Bryce—Dr Acland—Capt. Burton[1]—Sir J. Lubbock. Wrote a little on ritual. Finished Claudian: read the two Artists. Wrote to Rev. Dr Parker—J. Parker—J. Wilkie—T. Shea[2]—Dr Myriantheus— J. Bowen—Mr Oxenham—Prof. Reynolds[3]—Baldwin Brown. Dined at Ld Houghton's.

11. Fr. St Barnabas.

Wrote to Ld Mayor's Sec.—Mr A. Strahan—H.J.G.—Dr Nixon B.P.—Mr Watson—Mr Morgan. Wrote on Ritualism. Seven to dinner. H of C. 4½–5¾.[4] Twelve to breakfast. Saw Abp of Dublin—Mr de Lisle—Mr Bright—Mr Dalby (aurist)[5]—Rev. Dr Case[6]—long conversation on his position & on Antivaticanism. Revised partially Christie's Proof of Catalogue.[7] Read Swainson on Rubric.[8] Saw Sir R. Phillimore on Rubrical Laws—Kate G. on her Father's will.

12. Sat.

Wrote to Dr Schliemann—L. Morris—W.H. Groser[9]—E. Gardner[10]—Ld Granville—Count Münster—Robn G. Went at 3 to B. Square to see the young Newcastle boys. Also conversation on business with Mrs H. & the Duchess. Wrote on Ritualism. To Christie's with C. to see Porcelains and revise Catalogue. Saw Mr M'Coll on the Rubrics. Saw Miss Stanley—Tea at Lady Stanleys. Read Edinb. Rev. on Vatican controversy.[11]

13. 3 S. Trin.

St James's mg—St Mary le Strand evg. Wrote much on Ritualism. Read Swainson on Rubrics—Allg. Zeitung on Vaticanism and [blank]. Walk & calls with C.

14. M.

Wrote to Barker & Hignett—Messrs G. & Co.—Mr T.B. Potter—Rev. Mr James—Mr Wells Gardner[12]—Mr Humphrey. Wrote on Ritualism. Expedition to Tooting to see Mr Gassiot's Gallery:[13] also the Dyce Pictures at Mr Brand's.

---

[1] Captain Henry Burton of N. Audley Street, London.
[2] Gladstone arranged for him to hear a debate; Hawn P.
[3] Henry Robert *Reynolds, 1825–96; congregationalist and principal of Cheshunt college.
[4] Supreme Court Bill amending 1873 Act: *H* 224. 1631.
[5] (Sir) William Bartlett Dalby, 1840–1918; ear specialist; kt. 1886.
[6] George Case, Roman catholic priest.
[7] For the sale on 23 June.
[8] C. A. Swainson, *The rubrical question of 1874* (1874).
[9] Of Banbury; Hawn P.
[10] Edward Gardner, a town commissioner of Downpatrick, Ireland, in correspondence on tenants' rights; Hawn P.
[11] *Edinburgh Review*, cxli. 554 (April 1875); author unknown.
[12] William Wells Gardner, bookseller and publisher.
[13] Charles Gassiot, art dealer, later a major benefactor of the Guildhall Art Gallery.

H of C. 5-6¼.[1] Dined at F.C.s. Saw F.C.—Mr Herbert. Went to Christie's & delivered over the Proof Catalogue for Printing. Read 'The Democratic Party'.[2] Saw three [R].

15. Tu.

Wrote to Mr Harris—Rev. Mr Naish B.P.[3]—Rev. T.W. Carr[4]—Mrs Owen—Mr C. Barton—Ld Stanhope—Ld Craufurd—Mr H.W. Leman. Luncheon at 15 G.S. H of C. 2¾-4½.[5] Saw Dr Schliemann—Ld Granville—Ld Shaftesbury—Ld Camperdown—and others. Dined at Ld Abercrombie's. Sir[?] Matthew Ridley's afr. Wrote on Ritualism.

16. Wed.

Wrote to Mr Byrom[6]—Mr A. Murray—Sir Thos G.—Mr J.E. Gladstone. Charterhouse 11-2: Committee on the (Hyett) grievance memorial.[7] Correcting article on Ritualism. Saw Digby X. Saw Bp [Browne] of Winchester respecting my Article. Dined at Bp of Winchester's. Saw Bp [Goodwin] of Carlisle. Read Stuart's Italian Tale.[8]

17. Th.

Wrote to M. Victor Oger—Dep. Mayor of Liverpool—W. Hill—T. Elliot—W. Scott—G. Redford—Rev. A. Lendrum—Miss A. Cowper—Mr E. Lynch—C.K. Watson—A. Strahan—Baptist Ch of Llanfyllin. Fourteen to breakfast 10-12. Saw Mr Humphrey—Dr Schaff—Dr Case—Ouvry (Clerk)—Sir Thos G. *cum* J.E.G. on the Bowden Affairs[9] & prospects. Finished correcting, & sent off to press, my Essay on Church Affairs.[10] Dined at [blank]. Read Tracts and [blank.]

18. Fr.

Kept my bed for influenza until 6. Then got up & went to dine at Mr Parker's. Interesting conversation on the Canons & Church Law: Dean Stanley, Mr [C.] Bowen, Ld Cardwell. Saw Mr Knowles—W.H.G. Read Borderlands of Insanity[11]—Peacock, with Mema[12]—Casaubon, with do.[13]

---

[1] Supreme Court Bill: *H* 224. 1815.
[2] Not found.
[3] Francis Clement Naish of St. Andrew's mission, Gravesend.
[4] Thomas William Carr, rector of Barming from 1865.
[5] Misc. business: *H* 224. 1900.
[6] William Byrom, Liverpool accountant, sent press cuttings; Hawn P.
[7] He was a governor of the Charterhouse.
[8] R. M. Stuart, *Fiesole* (1871).
[9] i.e. his brother John's house.
[10] See 4 June 75.
[11] By A. Wynter (1875).
[12] E. Peacock, *English church furniture* (1875); diarist's digest at Add MS 44762, f. 181.
[13] See 1 Mar. 75n.

19. Sat

Rose at 12. Luncheon at 15 G.S. Saw Mr Redford. Visited Christie's. Saw Agnew—Baron L. de Rothschild—Ar. & E. Lyttelton dined. Read Borderlands of Insanity—J. Miller's Ship in the Desert[1]—and divers Tracts. Saw Mrs Grote.

20. 4 S. Trin.

Conversation with C. on W.s matters. Chapel Royal 10 A.M. St And. Wells St 4 PM: a great crowd—for the Duchess of Edinburgh. Corrected proofsheets of my article on the Church: & wrote to Mr Strahan. Read Manning's Sermons on the Internal Work of the Holy Ghost[2]—They have life in them. Read Morton Shaw[3]—and various Tracts.

21. M.

Wrote to Mr A.M. Stewart[4]—Mr Hatherley[5]—Mr W. Clark—Mr M. Bensusan[6]—Robn G.—Rev. F. Humphrey[7]—Mr M. Mayow—Mr W.J. Douse—Mr E. Arnold[8]—Mr Cartwright. Dined at Lady Aberdeen's. Saw Mr A. Kinnaird—Mr Herbert—Scotts—Mr Baillie Cochrane—The Speaker—Mr Wyndham. Went at 8.30 to Christie's with Mr Herbert, to survey. Conclave at Granville's $2\frac{3}{4}$-$4\frac{1}{2}$. H. of C. after.[9] Mrs Goldschmidts[10] music at $5\frac{1}{2}$-7. Delightful. Conversation with C.G. on W.s matters. The Teck[11] musical party after dinner. Saw D. of Edinb.—Ld Shrewsbury—Mr Sturt & others.

22 Tu.

Wrote to Lady Stanley (Ald.)—Mr Ouvry—E. Chilver—J.P.R. Morris—T. Skaife[12]—T.W. Hancock[13]—S. Massett[14]—Sir R. Alcock—J.K. Aston—W. Graham—Jas Coffey—Scotts—Sir R. Ph. Saw Mr Palgrave. Further conversation with C.G. on W.s matters; most embarrassing to her, he is so much *in request*.[15] It does him honour, but I fear runs the risk of pain to some. May he be wholly leal & true. Arranging my papers & letters: I am in

[1] By J. Miller (1875).

[2] H. E. *Manning, *The internal mission of the Holy Ghost* (1875).

[3] See 31 Mar. 75.

[4] A. M. Stewart of the West of Scotland Protestant Association; diarist's letter supporting its meeting on ultramontanism printed in its *Annual Report* (1876).

[5] Perhaps the Orthodox convert; see 2 Jan. 70.

[6] Manuel Bensusan, London stockbroker.

[7] Francis Humphrey, rector of Belaugh 1873.

[8] Regretting his retirement as editor of the *Echo*, *T.T.*, 28 June 1875, 7b.

[9] Misc. business: *H* 225. 257; the 'conclave' was perhaps on trade union legislation or on the state of business; statements on both made by govt. next day; ibid. 290.

[10] i.e. Jenny *Lind; see 28 May 47.

[11] Prince Francis Paul Charles Louis Alexander of Teck and his wife Mary, da. of the duke of Cambridge.

[12] Thomas Skaife, artist and photographer in Croydon, on Moody and Sankey; Add MS 44447, f. 226.

[13] Thomas William Hancock of Llanrhaiadr; see 28 Sept. 75n.

[14] Stephen Massett of London; Hawn P.

[15] See 21 July 70.

unexampled arrear. Dined at Sir C[outts] Lindsay's: interesting discussions on history & Scepticism: the play afterwards at Mr Freak's,[1] admirably got up. Read MacColl's Preface[2]—Stansfeld's Speech on Cont. Dis. Acts[3] & other Tracts. Saw Scotts—Ld Wolverton—Mr Murray.

23. Wed.[4]

Wrote to Mr [R.]A. Arnold—Sir J. Lacaita—Rev Mr Mossman—Rev J.B. Brown—Mr Newton—J. Rhodes—E. Peel. H. of C. 4¼-6. Voted in minority agt Cont. Diseases Acts.[5] Again with C. on W's matters: which by degrees converge. Saw Mr J.K. Aston—Christies—Mr Agnew—Ld F. Cavendish—Mr Bright—Mr Graham—Mr Levy—Ld Hammond—C. Münster—Sir R. Phillimore. Dined at Mr Levy's. The Palace Concert afterwards.

24 Th. St Joh. B.

Wrote to Messrs Barker & Hignett—Master of Charterhouse—Mr Roundell. H. of C. 4¼-6½.[6] Read Queen Mary.[7] Fourteen to breakfast. Corrected Revises of Art. on Ch. of England. Further conversation with C.G. on W.s matters. Saw Mr Christie & went with him to separate the wrongly inserted articles. Saw Dr Pantaleone—Mr Oxenham—Mr Schwerz[?]—Sir Thos Acland—Mr F. Lawley—Dr Myriantheus—Mr Bright—Mr Richardson—Sir J. Lacaita. Dined with Ld Stanhope: then to the Soc. of Antiquaries where Dr Schliemann lectured 1¼ hours. I had to speak.[8] Then took Dr S. to Lansdown [*sic*] House & introduced him to many. Then to Ly Ripon's ball: where *he* avoided me.[9] Saw three [R].

25. Fr.

Wrote to Count Münster—Freshfields—Mr A.H. Black—Sir Wm Knollys. Luncheon at 15 G.S. Calls. Sent Ch. Article to Press. Saw Ld Granville—Mr B.H. Cooper—Mr Knowles—Mr Newton—Scotts—L & W. Bank. Fourteen to breakfast: ten of us a Schliemann party: we had a long Homeric discussion. 4-6. Council of King's Coll. [London] on the admission of a-Churchmen to emoluments.[10] We dined at Ld Derby's: *most* kindly received by both: an agreeable dinner, *between* Ly Salisbury & Delane who was very gracious: saw Mr Badger—

---

[1] See 25 Feb. 70.

[2] M. MacColl, *My reviewers reviewed in a preface to the third edition of Lawlessness, Sacerdotalism and Ritualism* (1875).

[3] J. Stansfeld, 'Substance of the speeches ... on the Contagious Diseases Acts' (1875).

[4] This day, and next three days, diarist's pottery, porcelain, artifacts, furniture, watercolours and pictures, 'removed from his Residence in Carlton House Terrace; and the Brown Museum at Liverpool', sold in Christie's Rooms in King Street.

[5] i.e. supporting Stansfeld's bill to repeal the Acts; bill rejected in 126 : 308; *H* 225. 421.

[6] English agriculture: *H* 225. 497.   [7] By Tennyson (1875).

[8] He questioned Schliemann's dating of Troy; *Proceedings of the Society of Antiquaries*, 2nd series, vi. 423.

[9] See 21 Aug. 74, 20 Mar. 75, for Ripon's conversion to Roman catholicism.

[10] i.e. whether students not attending theology lectures could win bursaries etc.; King's College Council Minutes.

Capt. Burton—Saw one [R]. Read Queen Mary. Corrected proofs of Remarks on Thursday evg.

26. Sat. [*Windsor*]

Wrote to Sir R. Phillimore—Mr Knowles—Mr Lornie—Mr Evers—Mr Tabor[1]— Captain Battersby—W.H.G. (& draft)—Robn & Nichn—Princ. Librarian—Mr Laird—Sec. Trin House. Calls & business. Saw Mr Woods: after considering with WHG about 'reserves' on the Pictures. Saw Sir A. Panizzi. Charterhouse 2-3¾ on the Poor Brothers' case.[2] To Windsor at 5. Much & really harrowing conversation with C. on Lady A.F.[3] and her feeling for W. Read Queen Mary.

27. 5 S. Trin.

St George's mg—Eton Chapel aft.—Conversation with Dr Lightfoot—Ld Cowley. Walk with the Dean. Read Tracts on The Apocalypse—Moody & Sankey—Gonzaga's Parroci Eletti[4]—Villari, Discorso[5]—Ashe, Origin of Xty.[6] Further conversation with C. on W.s case—we are quite agreed.

28 M. [*London*]

St George's Chapel mg. Wrote to Ld De Tabley—Mr Ouvry—H.J.G. Helen's birthday: age creeps on her—would she could be again among us. Went over St George's with the Dean & Ld Wrio.[7] Off at 12: with the Tankerville's: much conversation: on his cattle *inter alia*.[8] To Mr Roundell's for luncheon: fine etchings. Various calls. Finished Queen Mary. Dined at Sir Thos May's. Saw Ld Wolverton—Ld Cardwell.

29. Tu.

Wrote to Sir R. Collier—Dss of Newcastle—Rev Mr Jenkins—G.S. Drew—Capt. Graham—Mrs A. Cooper—Pellet—Boyd—Lyne. Saw two X. Saw Mr Ouvry (bis)—S.E.G. on Hawarden matters—Mr Christie—Mr Agnew (jun.)—Duke of Buckingham—Mr Beresford Hope—Ld Selborne—Sir J. Lacaita. 2-3½ Radcliffe Trust Meeting. We dined with the Salisbury's: & I had interesting conversations with Lady Derby, Lady Cairns (Moody & Sankey) and Miss Alderson.[9] Read Minghetti's Speech[10]—Peacocks Vol.[11]—The Ship in the Desert.[12]

---

[1] Perhaps Robert Montagu Tabor, London barrister.
[2] In his capacity as a governor of the Charterhouse.
[3] Probably Lady Alice Mary Fitzwilliam, d. unmarried 1922, da. of 6th Earl Fitzwilliam; see 9 July and 30 Nov. 75.
[4] C. G. Gonzaga, *I parroci eletti e la questione ecclesiastica* (1875).
[5] P. Villari, *Discorso del deputato Villari sulle relazione dello stato colla Chiesa* (1875).
[6] I. Ashe, *The divine origin of Christianity* (1875).
[7] Reads *sic*; perhaps Wrottesley.
[8] His herd of wild, white cattle at Chillingham, Northumberland.
[9] A relative of Lady Salisbury, *née* Alderson.
[10] M. Minghetti, 'Discorsi . . . 7 e 8 Maggio 1875' (1875).
[11] See 18 June 75n.   [12] See 19 June 75.

30. Wed.

Wrote to Mr Lindsay—Sir A. Panizzi—Italian Chargé d'Affaires—Mr Murphy—Mr Wilmot—Mr Mendham—Mr Tennyson—Col. H. Fuller—Ld Hartington—Robn G. Dined at Mr Beaumont's. Conversation with Queen of N[etherlands][1]—Mr Fowler—Mrs Vaughan—Mr Manners—Ld Camperdown. Saw Ld Granville cum Ld Hartington.—Mr Lindsay—on Gordon case—Duke of Argyll on Ritual—Bp of Winchester. Duchess of Argyll's garden party in afternoon. Luncheon at 15 G.S. Read Grueber on Ritual.[2] Saw Creagh X with hopes.

Th. Jul. One. 1875.

Wrote to Dowr Lady Waterford—Rev Mr Henderson—Rev Mr W.W. Malet—Rev Mr D.P. Alford[3]—Gen. Bainbrigge[4]—H. Williams—J. Melvill. Saw Thornton X with hope. Dined at Ld Lytteltons. Arranging letters and papers. Twelve to breakfast. Saw Mr Barton (Natal)—Rev. B. Brown—Sir T. May—Sir J. Lacaita—Mr Bromhead—Sir A. Panizzi. Further conversation with C. on W. & the matrimonial prospects. Read Alford's 'Retreat'.

2. Fr.

Wrote to Sir J. Lacaita—T.B. Potter—Golightly—Weld Taylor[5]—W. Hart—Sir A. Guinness—Herr Haug[6]—Rev. Hugh Baker—Rev R. Leslie[7]—J. Burston—W. White—W. Penrose—Rev. A. Murdoch[8]—Mr Kinnaird—Capt. Gordon. Lady Egerton's in evg: a long conversation with the Queen of the Netherlands. C. went off to Hn. Saw Mr MacColl—Sir C. Trevelyan—Ld Stanhope—Mr Bromhead.[9] At Mrs Ralli's concert. And the Archaeol. Socs meeting to hear Mr [J. H.] Parker on the Coliseum.[10] Calls.—Saw Lloyd (80) X. Read Holyoake on Cooperation[11]—The Retreat.[12] Wrote the chief part of a Preface for my reprint of Tracts on Vaticanism.[13]

3. Sat.

Wrote to Capt W. Gordon—Dr Cazenove—Dr Schliemann—'A Looker On'[14]—Mr Freeland—Mr Ouvry—C.G.—Herbert J.G.—Mr Strahan—Mrs Schwabe—Rev

---

[1] See 16 Mar. 70.

[2] C. S. Grueber, 'Three recent decisions. A letter' (1875); on ritual cases.

[3] Daniel Pring Alford, vicar of Tavistock from 1869; see 2 July 75n.

[4] Probably General Philip John Bainbrigge, a constituent.

[5] Perhaps of the Roman catholic Weld family.

[6] Perhaps Martin Haug, German orientalist.

[7] Robert Tronson Leslie, curate in Toxteth 1855-7, then chaplain of W. Derby workhouse, Liverpool.

[8] Alexander Drimmie Murdoch, episcopalian incumbent of All Saints', Edinburgh.

[9] Perhaps Joseph Crawford Bromehead, formerly barrister, now apparently gentleman and nonpracticing priest. See 17 June 48.

[10] See *Archaeological Journal*, xxxii. 275 (1875).

[11] G. J. Holyoake, probably *The logic of co-operation* (1873).

[12] D. P. Alford, *The retreat and other poems* (1874).

[13] i.e. the preface (printed version dated 7 July 1875) to *Rome and the newest fashions in religion*.

[14] *Some reflections on the Public Worship Act and ritualism*, by 'a looker on' (1875).

Mr Greer.[1] Breakfast with Sir J. Lacaita & a long & interesting conversation on Italian Ch. matters (till noon) in which Marchese Vitelleschi[2] took the lead. Saw Mr Cooke (Murray)—G. Hampton—Mr Paterson (US).[3] Dined at Sir T. Acland's. Saw Sir R. Gerard—Lord Greville—Lord Stratford. Read Pomponio Leti[4]—Roussel on Protm & Cathm.[5]

4. 6 S. Trin.

St James's 10 A.M. Curzon St Chapel(Mr Aitken)[6] 6.45 PM. Saw The Farquhars—The Wortleys—Mrs Grote on the MSS. & the Church. Read Bp of Carlisle's Charge—Laurs Bossuet u. die Unfehlbarkeit[7]—Peacock on Church Ornaments (Lincoln)—Roussel—Sermon.

5. M.

Wrote to Mr S. Mayer[8]—Mr Murray—L. Thornton—Mr Agnew. 4-8½. To the Prince's party at Chiswick: with mournful recollections.[9] Finished Peacock, with my notes from this curious work.[10] Saw Sig. René Martino[11]—Col. N. Sturt—Ld De Tabley—Mr Knowles—Duke of Marlborough—Sir R. Collier & Dean Church—Lord Beauchamp—Belgian Minister—The Queen of Holland— again!! Manning was at Chiswick: I fear I looked black at him: he not natural at me. Finished & sent off to Murray my Preface.[12] Read Senior's Journal of 1849[13]—Peacock's Inventory, finished—The Retreat.

6. Tu.

Wrote to Mr T.B. Potter—Benj. Potter—Ed. Guardian[14]—Sir A. Gordon. Searching Journals & Statutes of Charles I. H of C. 3-5.[15] Dined with Ld Halifax. Read Memoir of J. Meadows[16]—Senior's Journal (finished)—Pomponio Leto. Saw Ld Granville—Mr Playfair—Mr Childers—Ld Carnarvon—Mr [blank] (Head of Bombay Police)[17]—Ld F. Cavendish—Ld Crawford—Ld Wimmersley[18]—Ld St Germans. Lady Crawfords in evg. Saw Wilmot X.

[1] William Benjamin Greer, originally from Ireland; curate in Hardingham, Norfolk, 1875-7.
[2] Marchese Francesco Nobili-Vitelleschi, 1829-1906; m. Amy, da. of Lord Lamington; senator 1871; published his anti-infallibilist views in Italian and English, often using the pseudonym 'Pomponio Leti'; see 23 Apr. 75.
[3] Unidentified; probably for an autograph.   [4] See 23 Apr. 75.
[5] N. Roussel, *Différence entre Catholicisme et Protestantisme* (1845).
[6] Probably the revivalist, see 29 Apr. 75.
[7] E. Laur, *Bossuet und die Unfehlbarkeit* (1875).
[8] Samuel Mayer, London porcelain dealer.
[9] See above, v. lv.   [10] See 18 June 75n.
[11] *Chargé d'affaires* of the Italian embassy.
[12] See 2 July 75n.   [13] See 30 Dec. 50.
[14] Not published; its leaders of 7 and 14 July discussed his views on ritualism; *The Guardian* (1875), 852, 888.
[15] Central Asia: H 225. 1034.
[16] E. Taylor, *The Suffolk Bartholomeans; a memoir of John Meadows* (1840).
[17] (Sir) Frank Henry Souter, d. 1888 was commissioner of Bombay police from 1864; but he was probably in Bombay at this time.
[18] *Sic*; *sc.* Winmarleigh (Wilson-Patten).

7. Wed.

Wrote to Mr Bromhead—Mr Campbell—Mr MacColl—Mr G. Harris—Mr Knowles—Mr Morier—Mrs Creagh. Dined at Ld Cardwell's. Calls. Saw Wilmot—Creagh [R]. Saw Ld De Tabley—Mr Murray—Mr S. Morley—Sir T.E. May—Mr Howard—Mr Bright—Mr Leeman. H of C. 3¾-6 to vote in favour of Trevelyan's County Household Suffrage Bill.[1] Read Meade on Polynesia[2]—Be ye therefore Perfect(!!)[3]—Memoir of J. Meadows.

8. Th.

Wrote to Ld Ripon—Mr T. Routledge[4]—Mr Baulf—Mr T. Macnab[5]—Canon Lane[6]—Sec. [Additional] Curates' Fund—Lord Huntley. Dined at Ld Ebury's. Lady Dudley's concert afterwards. 13 to breakfast. Saw Sir Thos Acland—Dean of Durham—Mr Godley—Christies—Rev. Dr Nevins[7] who gave me most interesting tidings from Rome—Ld Camoys—Ly Ebury (D of W)—Dr Abbott[8]—Ld Lisgar. Saw L. Creagh who goes home on Saturday [R]. Saw May. Read Pomp. Leto. Finished Meadows's Memoirs. Distributed copies of my Church Article ab. 2 dozen; one half to Bishops.

9. Fr. [Windsor Castle]

Wrote to Bp of London—Mr Ouvry—Mrs Grote—Mr F. Burrell[9]—Rev J. Rowlands[10]—Mr Weld Taylor—Lady Alice Fitzwilliam (& draft)[11]—Mrs Th.—Messrs Townshend & Barker. Saw Mr MacColl—Mr Grogan—General Ponsonby—Dean of Windsor—Dean of Westmr. Luncheon with the C. Murrays[12] & saw their objects: 5 miles off. Then to Windsor. We dined with the Queen. She was kind as usual but evidently under restraint with me. I judge that she has not faced reading my article, which the Dean of W. gave her. Read The Retreat—Pomponio Leto.

10. Sat. [London]

Prayers at 9 A.M. Wrote to Bp of London—Mr Bartlett. ⟨Saw H.M.s portrait (& others) by Angeli with infinite pleasure.⟩ Left the Castle 10.25. Saw May.

[1] Bill was withdrawn after a procedural defeat: *H* 225. 1124. See 23 July 73.

[2] H. Meade, *A ride through the disturbed districts of New Zealand; together with some account of the South Sea Islands* (1870).

[3] Untraced.

[4] Thomas Routledge, had sent his work, see 13 July 75.

[5] Thomas Macnab of Montreal; on Quebec law on ultramontanism; Hawn P.

[6] See 18 May 53n.

[7] Henry Willis (Probyn-) Nevins, d. 1896; ordained anglican priest 1871; wrote on Rome, and Anglican-Russian relations.

[8] Edwin Abbott *Abbott, 1838-1926; headmaster of City of London school 1865-89; rabbinical scholar.

[9] Probably Frederick William Burrell of Vincent Street, London.

[10] John Rowlands, d. 1919; rector of Hope, by Mold, 1875-91.

[11] Thanking her for a gift; Add MS 44447, f. 269; see 26 June 75.

[12] Sir Charles Augustus *Murray (1806-95, author and retired diplomat) and his wife Edith; lived in Wimbledon, latterly in Windsor.

Corrected proofs for the collected reprint of Tracts respecting Vaticanism. Saw Scotts—Mr Duckworth. Saw Angeli's admirable portraits. The Queens is truly historical & of great value.[1] Saw Dean of Windsor. Eleven to dinner: conversation with Mr Martin—Mrs Martin—Lady Herbert—Mr Goldsmidt—last but not least Mrs Goldsmidt. Read Pomponio Leto—The Battle of Pluck.[2]

11. 7 S. Trin.

Chapel Royal 10 A.M. and Tenison's Chapel (Mr Knox Little) at 7 P.M. Wrote to Bp of Edinburgh—Dr Cazenove—Rev. H. Dixon. Read Pomponio Leto—Hopgood on Disestablishment[3]—and divers Tracts.

12 M.[4]

Wrote to Mrs C.S. Petrie—J. Stuart Wortley (2)—Rev. T. Keane[5]—Messrs Clowes—Mr Gurdon. Luncheon at 15. G.S. Dined with the F.C.s. H of C. $5\frac{1}{4}$-8 and $10\frac{1}{2}$-12.[6] Lond. Libr. Comm. at $4\frac{1}{4}$-5. Read the MS History of the Atlantic Telegraph Co. & enterprise[7]—Pomp. Leto—Life of Ld Shelburne.[8] Saw Ld Stanhope—Ld Hartington—Mr Howard—Mr Bright—Bp of Ely.

13. Tu.

Wrote to Rev Mr Howard—Gen. Cesnola—Mr Richardson—Mr A. Williams—Mr E. Levy—Mr G.H. Reid[9]—Mr G. Bramwell—Mr W.A. Carter[10]—H.N.G. (B.P.) Read Don Pasquale's case—Zone to Lord Bute[11]—Pomponio Leto—Routledge on Paper Trade.[12] Saw Mr Whitwell—Dr Schliemann, & Mrs S.—Ld Shrewsbury—Abp of Canterbury. Attended meeting of Nat. Portr. Gall. Trustees. Dined with the Murrays at Wimbledon: saw the Rector.

14. Wed.

Wrote to Ld R. Browne[13]—Mr Gurdon—Mr A. Fawcett[14]—Mrs Th.—Rev Mr Henderson. Read Pomp. Leto—Castle Daly.[15] Dined at Ld Hatherley's. Saw Sir

[1] Now in Buckingham Palace; Victoria in a black dress with a fan, by Heinrich von Angeli, 1840-1925.   [2] Untraced.

[3] J. Hopgood, *Disestablishment and disendowment of the Church of England* (1875).

[4] *T.T.* this day published a long letter from Dean Howson on diarist's views on the eastward position.   [5] Thomas Keane of Irvine had sent an address; Hawn P.

[6] Diarist and ex-cabinet voted with govt. against liberals on Protection of Property Bill; *H* 225. 1331.

[7] Perhaps an untraced work by A. Marcoartu; see 17 Sept. 75n.

[8] See 1 Mar. 75.

[9] (Sir) George Houston *Reid (1845-1918; Australian federationalist and free-trader; prime minister of Australia 1904-5) had sent his *Five essays on free trade* (1875); this letter, encouraging Australian free-trade, printed in Sir G. H. Reid, *My Reminiscences* (1917), 25 and *T.T.*, 18 November 1875, 8b.

[10] Perhaps William Allan Carter, Scottish sanitarian.   [11] Neither found.

[12] T. Routledge, *Bamboo considered as paper-making material* (1875).

[13] Lord Richard Howe Browne, 1834-1912, s. of 2nd marquis of Sligo; soldier.

[14] Possibly Andrew Robert *Faussett, 1821-1910; theologian and Homeric scholar.

[15] A. Keary, *Castle Daly*, 3v. (1875).

A. Panizzi—Rev. M. MacColl—Mr Murray—Rev. C. Miller—Mr Bonamy Price—Ld Hatherley. Further corrected my Preface, & had much consideration & conversation as to the further proceeding about the Gordon case, with the possibility, tho' it be no more, of an action.[1] On the whole I think I have bound myself in honour to go forward.

15. Th.

Wrote to Mr Barker—Mr Cross—Mr Beaumont—Sir A. Panizzi—Robn G.—W.B. Gurdon. H of C. $4\frac{1}{2}$-$8\frac{1}{2}$ & $10\frac{1}{2}$-12. Spoke on P. of Wales grant.[2] Eleven to breakfast. Saw Marquis Vitelleschi—Count Corti—Mrs Schwabe—Sir J. Lacaita—Mr Probyn—Mr Goschen—Mr Coxe (B. Libr.)[3]—Mrs Grote. Ten to dinner. Read Pomponio Leto—Castle Daly.

16. Fr.

Wrote to Count Münster—Rev Mr Mossman—Mrs Grote—Bp of Carlisle—Mr W. Setter—Professor Villari—Mr J. Wyld—Sec. LSW. RR.—Lord Coleridge. H of C. $3\frac{3}{4}$-$6\frac{1}{4}$. Delivered a protest on behalf of Economy.[4] Saw Sir G. Bowen—Miss Darby Smith[5]—Mr Knowles—and others. Read Pomp. Leto—Castle Daly. Began Article on Religious affairs of Italy.[6] Dined at [blank]. Luncheon 15 G.S.

17. Sat. [Hatfield]

Wrote to Mr Kimber[7]—Mr Boulting—Sir W. Trevelyan[8]—and. . . . Finished Pomp. Leto. Read Sir R. Phillimore's Judgment. Read Thornton on Settlement of New England[9]—& Rigg on Natural Development of public Education.[10] Saw Sir Jas Lacaita—and others. Off at 5 to Hatfield; where we were received with all the usual kindness. Much conversation with Ld Carnarvon.[11]

---

[1] Discussion in his preface (see 2 July 75) of the Gordon divorce case (see 3 May 75) produced much controversy; see *The Guardian* (1875), 1086.

[2] Supporting govt. grant (opposed by some liberals) for his Indian visit: *H* 225. 1497; see 10 Apr. 75.

[3] Henry Octavius *Coxe, 1811-81; Bodley's librarian from 1860.

[4] Respecting, especially, employment of judiciary: *H* 225. 1596: 'He was never very proud of the achievements of the late Government in the matter of public economy.'

[5] She had requested criticism of a book; Hawn P.

[6] 'Italy and her church', published anonymously despite the editor's request, in Cazenove's *Church Quarterly Review*, i. 1 (October 1875), reprinted in *Gleanings*, vi. 193. See 21 Jan. 75.

[7] Greenwich solicitor, had challenged diarist to public debate on the Tichborne case; this letter, declining, in *T.T.*, 29 July 1875, 8c.

[8] Sir Walter Calverley *Trevelyan, 1797-1879; 6th bart.; naturalist.

[9] J. W. Thornton, *The historical relation of New England to the English Commonwealth* (1874).

[10] J. H. Rigg, 'The natural development of national education in England' (1875).

[11] 'I have had a good deal of talk with Gladstone who seems to me somewhat softened & quieter since I last saw him to talk with—now nearly a year ago. Theology & ecclesiastical controversy are the subjects on which his mind is mainly moving. I spoke to him also of Pembroke & Lady P.' Carnarvon's Diary, 17 July 1875, Add MS 60907.

18. 8 S. Trin.

Hatfield Church 11 A.M. and H.C.—Chapel service 6 PM. Wrote to Miss Monro. Read Q.R. on Church matters—Swainson on Act of Uniformity[1]—and divers Tracts. Walk with the party.

19. M. [London]

Wrote to S.E.G.—J. Murray. Off at 11.25.—Saw May X and two. Saw Gen. Ponsonby—F. Cavendish. H. of C. 4½-8.[2] The F.C.s dined. Read The Royal Academy—Bossuet u. die Unfehlbarkeit.[3]

20. Tu.

Wrote to Mr Gurdon—Miss Darby Smith—Mr Dyer—Mr Whitfield—Mr Freeland. Luncheon at 15 G.S.—Various calls—Dined at Ld Stratford's: Played host at dinner but saw him afterwards and had a notable conversation. H. of C. 4-6¾.[4] Read Q.R. on Queen Mary—Castle Daly—Flower on Sacerdotalism[5]—Thornton on N. England. Saw Ld Hartington—Sir Thos Acland—Prince Humbert:[6] whom I found above the reports I had heard of him. Ld Wolverton's in evg.

[The inside back cover contains, in pencil:—]

The Hollies Clapham Common	*19.7*
J.R.—33 Montagu Pl. R. Square	*13.10*

Mr [G. F. H.] Foxton Hurstpierpoint vacancy
May 160 Piccadilly
Mad. Novikoff care of Rev E. Popoff 32 Welbeck St

Rev. Winslow
    Winterbotham[7]
Rev. M. M 12 Chester Terrace SW
Dr Saville W. Lodge W. End Lane Stamford
5 Catherine Road W. Brn
Cl. Orphan W L Cavan, A W Cavan
Cambridge ⎫
Big Offord ⎬ 129 11 162
Warwick ⎭

[End of Volume XXX.]

[1] C. A. Swainson, *The Parliamentary history of the Act of Uniformity* (1875).
[2] Agricultural Holdings Bill: *H* 225. 1668.
[3] See 4 July 75.
[4] Agricultural Holdings Bill: *H* 225. 1751.
[5] J. E. Flower, 'Sacerdotalism. What and whence is it. An address' (1875).
[6] Crown Prince Umberto of Italy, 1844-1900; king 1878 (assassinated).
[7] Perhaps L. W. Winterbotham; see 23 Dec. 73.

[The inside front cover contains:—]

Private.

No 31

July 21. 1875–March 15. 1877.

ἐγὼ μὲν, ὦναξ, πρεσβύτερός τε ἤδη εἰμί,
καὶ βαρὺς ἀείρεσθαι · σὺ δὲ τινα τῶνδε
τῶν νεωτέρων κέλευε ταῦτα ποιέειν.[2]
Herod[otus] IV. 150.

21. *Wed.*

Wrote to Mr Browne—Marquis Gonzaga[3]—Rev. Mr Flower[4]—Wolfe[5]—[D. Baxter] Langley—Hogg[6]—Ld Cottesloe—Rev Mr Molesworth—Librarian Lond. Libr.—Rev. Mr Drew—Mr R. Williams—Mr Hussey[7]—Mr Downing—Mr Kinnaird—Mr Wade—Mr H. Jowett[8]—Mr J. Haslam[9]—Mr Murray—L. Thornton. Nine to dinner: a few in evg. Much conversation with C. on Matrimonial matters. Saw Mr A. Strahan—Sig. René Martino—Ld Houghton—Mr Grogan—Sir R. Phillimore—Mr [R. H.] Dana jun. This day our dear son Willy proposed to and was accepted by Miss Gertrude Stuart.[10] We have every reason to believe that this will under the favour of God be a happy marriage.

22. *Th.*

Wrote to Mr D. Burns—Mr Robbins (aut.)[11]—Mr J. Gason—Mad. Novikoff—Mr N. Capra—Rev Mr Portman[12]—Mr Parsons—Ld Brownlow—Mr Matthews—Dr Schliemann. Discussed the provision to be made for Willy & his wife and

---

[1] Lambeth MS 1445.

[2] 'Lord, I am old now, and do not travel easily; tell one of these young men to take over the task.'

[3] Marchese Carlo Guerrieri Gonzaga, Italian deputy; tr. *Vaticanism* into Italian; corrected proofs of 'Italy and her Church'; Add MS 44448, f. 131. See 1 Aug. 75. See also 27 June 75n.

[4] James Edward Flower, had sent his book; see 20 July 75n.

[5] Arthur Wolfe, d. 1892; rector of Farnham 1862–91; hymnist.

[6] Probably George Robert Hogg, curate in Holborn.

[7] Henry L. Hussey had sent a book on Homer; Hawn P.

[8] Possibly Henry Jowett, who published later on Byron; apparently not a relative of B.*

[9] Accountant for the Newcastle estate.

[10] Daughter of Lord Blantyre; see 5 Oct. 58n. and 30 Sept. 75.

[11] i.e. an autograph hunter. Possibly an early interest by his biographer, (Sir) Alfred Farthing Robbins, 1856–1931, journalist and historian.

[12] Fitzhardinge Berkeley Portman, rector of Staple-Fitzpaine; Hawn P.

engaged myself to Ld Blantyre that it should not be under £2000 p.a. But understanding through C. that she will have £20000 I think the income will be more. Saw Mr F. Lawley—Ld Spencer—Mr Grogan—Mr Ouvry (Clerk)—Ld Wolverton—Col. N. Sturt. Seven to breakfast. Dined at Sir C. Forster's. Ld Wolverton's afr. Saw Graham—& another X. H of C. $4\frac{3}{4}$-$7\frac{1}{4}$.[1] Charterhouse 2-4.

23. Fr.

Wrote to Messrs T. & B.—Messrs Barclay—Mr Eastlake—Robn G. Tel. & l.—H.N.G.—Baron Tauchnitz[2]—Ld Blantyre. 2-4. Luncheon at Lord Blantyre's. The bride [to be] dined with us: also the F. C[avendishe]s. Saw Dr Schliemann—Christies (bis)—Ld Dufferin—Mr Murray. H of C. $5\frac{1}{2}$-7. 9-$10\frac{1}{2}$.[3] With Panizzi, who opens his heart much to me. Then Marlborough House party, when Prince and Princess were most kind. A long conversation with Lord B[lantyre] on Hawarden and the marriage arrangements. Then another with the bride; I am greatly pleased with her. Read Tract on [blank].

24. Sat.

Wrote to J. Murray—Dr von Döllinger—Director of Ecole des Sc. Politiques[4]—C. Harris—R. Cowtan—J.H. Meister—W.B. Adams[5]—Christies—Mr Maskelyne[6]—Mrs Th.—Sir H. Cole—Mr Westropp.[7] Dined with Mrs Th: & staid after X. Read Ayton on Ward's pamphlet. Arranging books & pamphlets. Saw Mr Tennyson—Mrs Monk (aet. over 90)[8]. . . . Calls.

25. St James & 9. S. Trin.

Chapel Royal mg and St Paul's aft. Saw Ld Clanwilliam—Mr MacColl—Mrs Church. Dined with the Wortleys. Read Humes Christian Hour[9]—Baur's Bossuet (finished)—Remarks on Orthodoxy—Newman's New Tracts[10]—and other Tracts.

26. M.

Wrote to Dr Kennedy—Mrs Grote—Dean of St Pauls—Mr Praed[11]—Dr Dollinger—Sir Thos G.—Mr W. Williams. Dined with the F.C.s and then to see 'Money':[12] some really good acting. Packed two boxes of books. Saw Mr Russell—Mr Ouvry—Miss Darby Smith—Mr Leeman—Mr Barrington. H of C. 4-7.[13]

---

[1] Deb. on *Plimsoll's suspension put off a week: H 225. 1824.
[2] Baron Christian Bernhard von Tauchnitz, 1816-95, German publisher. Facsimile of this letter, on the Tauchnitz ed. of *Rome and the newest fashions* (n. 1524, 1875), in B. Tauchnitz, *The harvest* (1937), 52.
[3] Misc. business: H 225. 1905.   [4] Business untraced.
[5] Perhaps William Bartholomew Adams, London stationer.
[6] Mervyn Herbert Nevil *Story-Maskelyne, 1823-1911; keeper of minerals at British Museum 1857-80; liberal (unionist) M.P. Cricklade 1880-92.
[7] Hodder Michael Westropp, wrote on archaeology; see 10 Aug. 75.
[8] See, perhaps, 12 Feb. 73.   [9] By A. Hume (1875).   [10] See 5 Apr. 74.
[11] Probably Charles Tyringham Praed, 1833-95; banker and tory M.P. St. Ives 1874-80.
[12] Lord Lytton's play at the Prince of Wales' theatre.
[13] Misc. business: H 226. 43.

Devonshire H[ouse]—12¼ to consider the Merchant Shipping Bill.[1]—Saw Graham X.

27. Tu.

Wrote to Dr Dollinger—A. Tennyson—Duke of Argyll—Herr Laur[2]—Dr Delitzsch[3]—Mr Wood—General Schenk (& copy)[4]—Dr Eckenbrecher[5]—Mr Adams—Rev. O. Rodway[6]—Rev. E. Chapman[7]—Rev. J.B. Sweet—Rev. Dr Kennedy[8]—Abp Panelli—Sig. A. Carrara.[9] Saw Mr Russell—Mr F. Lawley—Ld Blantyre (also W.H.G. on the money arangements)[10]—Ld Hartington—Ld F.C. Calls. Read Peacock's Works. H of C. 11½-2 AM.[11]

28. Wed.

Wrote to Sir P. Braila—Avv. Prof. P. Barbari—Mr W. Thomas—Ld Stanhope—Lady Russell—. . . . Wrote on Italian Ch. Saw May & another [R]. H of C. 12½-2 and 3-5.[12] Dined at Mr Hankeys. A pleasant party, marvellously balanced: 5 Tories, 5 Liberals, 2 Officers of H. of C., 2 at home. Read Hist. of Farnham Castle.[13] Saw Campbell—Stuart [R]. Saw Sir T.D. Acland—Mr Gibson—Count Münster (bis).

29. Th.

Wrote to Mr E. Herford—Ld Blantyre—Provost of Eton—Miss G. Stuart—Bp of Winchester—Mr Strasser—Mr Maynard—Helen G.—Mr Dana. Eight to dinner. H of C. 4¼-7¼.[14] Saw Campbell X & others. Saw Mr Knowles. Read Tracts—Castle Daly.

30. Fr.

Wrote to Mr Murray—Mr Walpole—Mr Farnfield—Mrs Scott—Mr Ouvry—Scott & Co. Saw Bennett X: a strange, unequalled narrative. Conversation with C.G. on House plans—WHG on Settlements—Mr Newton—Lady Russell and Lord Russell at Richmond 12-5. 9-11 with Panizzi: much interesting conversa-

---

[1] The *Plimsoll incident (see 22 July 75n.) and the government's Unseaworthy Ships Bill, introduced on 28 July.

[2] E. Laur of Heidelberg; see 4 July 75.

[3] Johannes Delitzsch, German writer; see Add MS 44446, f. 321.

[4] Calling his attention to his earlier letters of 20 February and 10 December 1874; Add MS 44447, f. 319.

[5] C. Gustav von Eckenbrecher, German classical author; see 25 Sept. 75.

[6] Clergyman in Brighton; sent a sermon; Hawn P.

[7] Probably Edward Martin Chapman, vicar of Low Toynton, Lincolnshire, from 1862.

[8] Benjamin Hall *Kennedy, 1804-89; regius professor of Greek, Cambridge, 1867-89; author of the famous *Latin Primer*.

[9] Unidentified.   [10] See 30 Sept. 75.

[11] Misc. business: *H* 226. 91.

[12] Unseaworthy Ships Bill introduced: *H* 226. 145.

[13] Not found.

[14] *Plimsoll (see 22 July 75n.) apologised; Agricultural Holdings Bill: *H* 226. 181.

tion: & a sad goodbye for 2 months. Read Convent Experience[1]—Gent. Mag. on Ultramontanism in Ireland—and. . . .

31. Sat

Wrote to Mr A. Taylor Innes—E.G. Porter[2]—M.J. Barry[3]—Messrs Barker—N. Lubbock[4]—Rev. E.D. Neill—Mr J.P. Jackson—Mr Grogan—Mr Jones (aut)—H.A. Brown[5]—J. Murray. Saw Mr F. Palgrave—Mr Murray—Mr Ouvry—Mrs Th. X—Ld Blantyre—Mr Newton. Read Foreign Loans Report[6]—Castle Daly.

10 S. Trin. Aug. One. 75.

Chapel Royal mg St James's Evg. Read Guerrieri Gonzaga's inclosures on It. Ch. affairs[7]—Dr Adolph Kohut on Obedience[8]—Bp of Oxford's Charge—and Tracts. Wrote to Mrs Thornton—Mrs Creagh—Dr Döllinger—for the Bonn Conference. Saw Dowager Duchess of Somerset—Mrs Th.—L. Thornton—Mrs Morison—Interviews singular enough.

2. M.

Wrote to Dr Dollinger—Bp of Winchester—Mr Smyth and Mr Grogan—Mrs Butler—Mrs Ingham—Rev F. Meyrick—Rev W. Malet—Messrs Freshfield—Mr Ouvry—Mr Wylie—Dr A. Kohut—Ld Blantyre—Bp of Oxford—S. Barns. Ld F. Cavendish dined. Arranging papers & effects for departure. Saw Mr MacColl. Sat to Mr Noble.[9] H of C. $5\frac{1}{2}$–$7\frac{3}{4}$.[10] Read Castle Daly—Meyrick Correspondence.[11] Saw divers [R].

3. Tu.

Wrote to Mr MacColl—Marquis Guerrieri Gonz[aga]—Lady F. Cavendish—Mr Holyoake—Mr Calderwood—Dr Gialussi[12]—Dean of Chester—Miss Bennett (B.P.)—Miss Hart (B.P.)—Helen G.—Mr J. Nixon. Saw Mr MacColl—Scotts. Saw Mrs Stuart X with interest: also Campbell. C. came back with an attack of what may be erysipelas: I hope not. Busy in sorting and packing papers & books. Conversation with Willy on his mission to Clumber. Saw Stuart X promised to

---

[1] Miss A. F. B[arlow], *Convent experiences* (1875).
[2] Rev. Edward G. Porter, of Lexington, U.S.A., had sent a history of Lexington; Hawn P.
[3] Michael Joseph Barry, 1817-89; Irish poet and nationalist; Hawn P.
[4] (Sir) Nevile Lubbock, 1839-1914, br. of 1st Lord Avebury; insurance broker; kt. 1899.
[5] Henry Alvin Brown, U.S.A. congressman specialising in sugar tariffs; Hawn P.
[6] On Ottoman loans; *P.P.* 1875 lxxxiii. 459.
[7] Copies of his speeches, quoted with approval in *Gleanings*, vi. 224. Cazenove sent him proofs of the Italian article; Add MS 44447, f. 369.
[8] Adolph Kohut, 1848-1917, German historian and biographer, had sent his *Was lehrt die Bibel über den Gehorsam gegen Staat und Obrigkeit?* (1875).
[9] To Matthew *Noble, for an untraced bust; Hawn P.
[10] Unseaworthy Ships Bill: *H* 226. 379.
[11] F. Meyrick, *Correspondence between the secretaries of the Friends of Spiritual Enlightenment and the Anglo-Continental Society* (1875).
[12] Aristide Gialussi, French philologist working on Greek.

return some time hence. Read Capital & Labour[1]—Bagwell on Irish Educn[2]—
Castle Daly—heavy.

4. Wed.

Wrote to Rev Mr Mertens[3]—Mr F. Oxenham—W.H.G.—Ed. Dubl. Ev. Post[4]—
Mr Thos Wood. Much work in packing, shopping, & arranging for departure. C.
better. Saw Dr Clark. H of C. $12\frac{1}{2}$-2[5]—Saw Mr Dodson—Mr Ward Hunt. Wrote
on Ital. Ch. question. Read Castle Daly—Arnold, Lives of Bps & Deans.[6]

5. Th.

Wrote to Mr Lightfoot. The last hours of removal, full of trouble as usual. Saw
Stuart [R]. Saw Mr M'Coll—Mr Beresford Hope. In evg went to see the revived
Ticket of Leave Man.[7] Its aim is good, & the good passages are appreciated.
Read Lenormant, Magie Chaldéenne &c.[8]—Castle Daly—Scott's Marmion—
Browning's Aristophanes.[9]

6. Fr.

Wrote to Sec. P.M.G.—Mr Skeffington—Mr J. Murray—Count Krasinski[10]—Mr
Hayter. $12\frac{1}{2}$-$1\frac{1}{2}$. B. Museum with Mr Poole & Mr Gardner examining coins. Saw
Mr Newton—Mr Murray—Ld Granville—Mr Adam—Sir A. Panizzi *cum* Sig.
René Martino—Mr Beresford Hope—and Dr A. Clark who finds me (and
himself) guilty of gout. Read Lenormant. H of C. $5\frac{1}{2}$-7 and 11-$12\frac{3}{4}$. Hartington
did his work well; and he develops. Dizzy was good in his kind. I am not sure
that the *move* was politic: but I did not read the Mansion House Speech which
provoked it.[11]

7. Sat. [Hawarden]

Wrote to Watsons. Wrote on Italian Church. Saw Ld Granville—Scotts. Read
Lenormant, on Chaldean Magic—And various Tracts. 2.45 train. Reached
Hawarden in evg & went fiercely to work on the accumulations of the Post.

---

[1] Possibly the National Federation of Associated Employers' newspaper.
[2] R. Bagwell, *A plea for national education, in answer to Mr Butt's proposal for its destruction* (1875).
[3] Frederick Montgomery Dirs Mertens, headmaster of Ardingley College.
[4] Not published.
[5] Supply: *H* 226. 571.
[6] F. Arnold, *Our bishops and deans*, 2v.(1875).
[7] At the Royal Olympic theatre.
[8] F. Lenormant, *Les sciences occultes en Asie. La magie chez les Chaldéens*, 2v. (1874-5).
[9] R. Browning, *Aristophanes' apology* (1875).
[10] Count Henry Krasinski, d. 1876; Polish novelist and historian of the Cossacks.
[11] Attack by Hartington on Disraeli's self-vindication at the Mansion House, arguing the govt.
'have established no principle, grappled with no difficulty, solved no problem'; *H* 226. 655.

8. *11 S. Trin.*

Ch 11 AM & 6½ PM. Wrote to Dr Döllinger—Mrs Heywood—Mr Edwards—Archdeacon Matthias[1]—Rev. J. Skinner—Mrs Laird—Rev. J.H. Wood[2]—Mr C.R. Finlay—Jas Watson & Smith—Scotts—Rev. A. Trench (B.P.)—Rev. A.E. Evans.[3] Wrote on Ital. Church question. Read a series of Voysey's Sermons:[4] they suggest & show much. And many tracts.

9. *M.*

Ch. 8¼ A.M. Wrote to Major Byng Hall[5]—T. Turner—E.W. Eyles[6]—R.B. Austin—W.T. Moore[7]—R. Nicholson—Rev. J. Withington[8]—Messrs Barker—Dr Hayes[9]—Mrs Th. Made my computations for new bookcases on the usual plan: 2500 to 3000 volumes: and arranged with Bailey.[10] Read Byng Hall's Bric a brac—Lenormant, Magic &c.—Herodotus: commenced anew to read through.[11]

10. *Tu.*

Ch. 8¼ AM. Wrote to Manager Ch. Bank—Dr Liddon—H.J.G.—G.T. Edwards[12]—F. May & Co.[13]—Mr Downing—Mr Grogan—Messrs Garrard. Wrote on Ital. Ch. The Miss Balfours came.[14] Read Lenormant—Westropp on Prehistoric age[15]—Herodotus B.I. Unpacking.

11. *Wed.*

Ch. 8½ AM. Wrote to Mr Westropp—Mr Morier—Sir Thos G.—Rev A.E. Evans—H.J.G.—Sec. G.P.O. 12½-4½. Journey to Chester. Saw Mr Hignett. Shopping. Read Herodotus—Lenormant—Byng Hall's Bric a brac.

---

[1] John Mathias, archdeacon of Colombo.

[2] Nonconformist minister in Warwickshire, on Vaticanism; Hawn P.

[3] Alfred Eubule Evans, rector of Kirk-Hallam; corresponded on church affairs; Hawn P.

[4] C. Voysey, probably 'The Gospel of adversity. A sermon' (1875).

[5] Herbert Byng Hall, 1805-83; soldier and author; had sent his *The adventures of a bric-a-brac hunter* (1868).

[6] Edward Wells Eyles of the Office of Woods and Forests.

[7] William Thomas Moore, 1832-1926; minister of the Disciples of Christ in Cincinatti; in England 1878-81; had sent an article; Hawn P.

[8] J. S. Withington, methodist minister in Leeds, had sent a resolution supporting the Vatican pamphlets; Hawn P.

[9] Probably Thomas Crawford Hayes, physician at King's College Hospital. Treating Catherine Gladstone (see 3 Aug. 75)?

[10] The joiner; see 17 Apr. 74.

[11] See quotation on fly-leaf at 21 July 75.

[12] George T. Edwards of Windermere; corresponded on church affairs; Hawn P.

[13] Booksellers in Piccadilly.

[14] Two of A. J. Balfour's sisters: Eleanor Mildred, principal of Newnham, Cambridge and suffragist, m. 1876 H. *Sidgwick, and Alice Blanche; Hawarden Visitors Book. Helen Gladstone was Eleanor Sidgwick's pupil and later her colleague.

[15] H. M. Westropp, *Prehistoric phases* (1872).

12. Th.

Ch. 8½ AM. Wrote to Mr [C.] Knight Watson—Mr A. de Lisle—Mrs R. Lawley—Mr A. Taylor—Mr G. Howard—Mr W. Grogan. Wrote on Ital. Ch. question. Resumed moving & arranging papers: I must now give to this business, & my library, 2 to 3 hours per diem. Wrote on Ital. Ch. question. Read Herodotus—Lenormant on Chaldea & Accadians (finished)—Westropp—Hall's Bric a brac.

13. Fr.

Ch. 8½ AM. Wrote to Messrs Barker & H.—Mr Downing—Mr Griffin—Messrs Watson & Smith—Ld Tenterden. Wrote on Italian Ch. 2½ hours in papers & unpacking books. Cut down a yew-tree. Read Herodotus—Cosmo de' Medici.[1] Mr Pennant came: on the great business.[2]

14. Sat.

Ch. 8½ AM. Wrote to Rev Mr Edwards—Mr Blomfield—Mr Strangways. Read Herodotus—Dexter on Govt of London[3]—Westropp. Arranged papers & correspondence on Vaticanism: a mighty mass. Walk with Mr Pennant.

15. 12 S. Trin.

Ch. 11 AM & H.C.—and 6½ P.M. Wrote to Mr J.E. Alexander—Mr MacColl—Mrs Scott—Dr Harvey—Mr Lynch. Read Lloyd on Suppression of Popery (1677)[4]—Bryson on Preaching[5]—Perceval's Sermons[6]—Divine Afflatus (Shakers)[7]—Norwood & many other Tracts.[8]

16. M.

Ch. 8½ A.M. Wrote to Mr Mavrocordato—Capt. Helbert (B.P.)—Dr Bryson—Rev Mr Suffield—Mr Gurdon. Mr Pennant went: to return on Thurs. We like him much. His marriage with Gertrude Glynne is virtually settled. Wrote on It. Ch. question. Three hours on my papers. Cut away a holly stump. Saw Mr Townshend. Conversation *inter alia* on Agric. Holdings Act. Read Herodotus—Bric a Brac.

17. Tu.

Ch. 8½ AM. Wrote to Messrs Farrer & Ouvry—'Spes' P.O.[9] We cut down a large sycamore now worth 2/6 a foot. Wrote much on Italian Church question. Read Herodotus—Canning on Toleration.[10]. Arranging papers.

[1] Perhaps L. Cantini, *Vita di Cosimo de Medici* (1805).
[2] G. S. G. Douglas-*Pennant, later 2nd Baron Penrhyn (see 24 Sept. 50) who married Gertrude Glynne as his second wife on 21 October 1875.
[3] J. T. Dexter, *The government of London* (1875).
[4] W. Lloyd, *Papists no Catholicks and Popery no Christianity* (1677).
[5] J. Bryson, *The preacher and pulpit orator* (1875).
[6] A. P. Perceval, *Sermons preached chiefly at the Chapel Royal, St James* (1839).
[7] [D. Fraser], *The divine afflatus; a force in history* (Boston, 1875); on the millenarian sect.
[8] i.e. tracts from T. *Scott of Ramsgate and Norwood.
[9] Perhaps E. P. *Shirley (see 29 July 56), who used 'Spes' as his pseudonym.
[10] A. S. G. Canning, *Christian toleration. An essay* (1874).

18 Wed.

Ch. 8½ AM. Wrote to Mr Macnulty[1]—Rev. W. Wallace[2]—Rev J. Baillie—Canon Blomfield—Mr Burke. Finished Paper on It. Ch. Read Herodotus—Canning on Toleration (finished). Cutting with W. in Nurs. Wood.

19. Th.

Ch. 8½ A.M. Wrote to Prese. Soc. Reale di Napoli[3]—Mr Downing—Mr T.E. Holland[4]—Mr Gregory—Dr Cazenove—Rev W. Gordon[5]—Mr T.W. Parsons. Revised Art. on Ital. Church, and rewrote a lost leaf. Attended Horticultural Meeting & spoke.[6] Read Hall's Bric a brac—Mr Holland on Alb. Gentilis[7]—Herodotus (finished Clio)—Westropp Hist. Phases (finished). Today the marriage of Gertrude to Mr Pennant was settled. God prosper it: as we trust He will. Woodcutting with W. & H.

20. Fr.

Ch. 8½ AM. Wrote to Hon A.S.G. Canning[8]—Sir F. Doyle—Messrs Watson—Mr M. Lynch—Mr Grove—Mr M'Laughlin—Dr Gatty[9]—Mr A.R. Dinnen—Mr H. Stone.[10] Read Herodotus—Doyle's Nearnet & Noam[11]—Snape's Essay on Swinburne[12]—Hall's Bric a Brac (finished). Woodcutting. Arranging papers & effects.

21. Sat.

Ch. 8½ AM. Wrote to Marq. C. Guerrieri—Mr Williams—H.J.G.—Mr T.W. Hancock—Mr Boord MP. Read Herodotus—Cosmo de' Medici. *Resumed Homer*—in a small way: & wrote on Hymn to Delian Apollo. Arranging papers &c. Walk with Mr Pennant, to explain to him in outline the financial history of the family, and G[ertrude] G[lynne]'s position. Walk with E. Talbot after.

22. 13 S. Trin.

Ch. 11 AM and [blank]. Wrote to Mr J.C. Earle[13]—Mr Beresford—Mr H.W. Hall[14]—Rev. Dr Cazenove—Sir W. Stephenson—J. Murray—Mrs Finnie—

---

[1] B. McNulty, a supplicant; Hawn P.

[2] William Baillie Wallace, priest and master at Wrexham grammar school.

[3] Business untraced; probably a resolution supporting Vaticanism.

[4] (Sir) Thomas Erskine *Holland, 1835-1926; professor of international law, Oxford, 1874-1910; kt. 1917.

[5] Perhaps William Gordon, curate in Huddersfield.

[6] On virtues of working-class gardening, at show held in Castle grounds; *The Guardian*, 25 August 1875, 1069.

[7] T. E. Holland, 'An inaugural lecture on Albericus Gentilis delivered at All Souls College' (1874).

[8] Albert Stratford George Canning, 1832-1916, 2nd s. of 1st Baron Garvagh; Irish J.P. and author; see 17 Aug. 75.

[9] Perhaps William Gatty, physician in Market Harborough.

[10] Henry Stone of Banbury, on Church and State; Hawn P.

[11] A poem, printed in Sir F. Doyle, *Lectures on poetry* (1877), 239.　　　[12] Not found.

[13] John Charles Earle, barrister, on religion; Hawn P.　　　[14] *Sc.* H. B. Hall.

H. Davey[1]—S.R. Lawley. Conversation with E. Talbot. Read Horbery on Future Punishment[2]—Jesuit's reply . . True Jesuit![3]—De Boulay's Evidences[4]—and other Tracts.

23. M.

Ch. 8½ A.M. Wrote to Rev Dr Pusey—Ld Cottesloe. Saw Mr Pennant—on G.G.s affairs—Mr Townshend. Woodcutting. Wrote on Delian Hymn. Read Herodotus—Mirabeau's Letters in Engl.[5]

24. Tu.

Wrote to Farrer & Ouvry—Mr H. Sotheran—P[ost] Master H of C.—Saw Mr Williams *cum* Mr Morton. Wrote on Delian Hymn. Arranging my effects. Read Herodotus—Mirabeau—Cosmo de' Medici.

25. Wed.

Ch. 8¾ AM. Wrote to Bp of Winchester—Sig. Alagna[6]—Mr Ord[7]—Mr Milliken—Mr J. Thomas—Dr MacCulloch—Robert Gladstone. Finished my chapter on Delian Hymn. Woodcutting, with W. Arranging my effects & papers. Read Herodotus—Alagna, Vero ed Unico Sistema—Cosmo de' Medici (finished)—Mirabeau's Letters.

26. Th.

Ch. 8½ AM. Wrote to Mr J. Murray jun.—Mr Camden[8]—Mrs Th.—Robn G. Woodcutting with W. Arranging papers &c. Read Herodotus—Hesiod's Theogony—Mirabeau's letters. The Wenlocks came: conversation on Dee Estuary &c.

27. Fr.

Ch. 8½ AM. Wrote to Mr Mavrocordato—M. Victor Oger—Mr Whalley—Rev. W. Wallace—Mr Croggan—Mr W. Downing—W.H. Worth—H. Kilgour—W. Martin jun.[9]—Rev J. Baillie—Rev Mr Williams. 1½-5. Went with Wenlock over the River to examine the Dee Embankment—Saw Mr Green—Mr Potts. Read Herodotus—Zincke on Egypt[10]—Mirabeau's Letters—Layman on the Vestments.[11]

[1] (Sir) Horace *Davey, 1833-1907; barrister; liberal M.P. for Christchurch 1880-5, Stockton 1888-92; solicitor general 1886; kt. 1886; appeal judge 1893; cr. Baron 1894.

[2] M. Horbery, *An enquiry into the Scripture doctrine concerning the duration of future punishment* (1744).

[3] Untraced.

[4] J. Du Boulay, *The evidences of rational evangelism* (1875).

[5] *Mirabeau's letters during his residence in England [1784-85]* (1832).

[6] G. A. Alagna had sent his *La Sicilia e l'Italia, Ossia Esposizione del vero ed unico sistema finanziario* (Florence, 1875).

[7] Benjamin Thomas Ord, printer in Hartlepool, had written on a legacy dispute; Add MS 44447, f. 378.

[8] G. J. S. Campden of Chester sent pamphlets on Vaticanism; Hawn P.

[9] Perhaps William Martin of Sidmouth, correspondent in 1874; Hawn P.

[10] See 29 Dec. 71.

[11] *"The Vestments" illegal, or, the rubric: its history and meaning. By a Layman* (1867).

28. Sat.

Off at 8¾ to my Cousin Murray's funeral at Penmaenmawr.[1] Returned at 7. Saw Mr Darbishire—Dr [J.G.] Risk—Mr T.S. Gladstone—The respect shown was very marked. Read Herodotus—Scott's Monastery.

29. 14 S. Trin.

Ch. 11 A.M. and 6½ P.M. Wrote to Dr Dollinger (2)[2]—Mr M'Coll—T.S. Gladstone—Bp of Winchester—Bp of St Asaph—Editor of "Catholic Times".[3] Read Horbery on Future Punishment[4]—Wallace & Wright on Bible Wine[5]—Etat Relig. du Belgique—Relig. of Rome by a Roman[6]—Reports of Bonn Conference.[7]

30. M.

Ch. 8½ AM. Wrote to Rev. Mr Paterson—Mr Grogan—Mr Wilshire—Mr Reg. Wilberforce[8]—Mr Jas Rowcliff—Rev. Dr Cazenove—Rev. H. Lomas.[9] Some new bookcases set up: worked on papers. Read Herod—Finished II—Rawlinson Anc. Hist.[10]—Scott, The Monastery. We dined at the Rectory. Saw Mr Thompson *cum* Mr Buddicorn.

31. Tu.

Ch. 8½ A.M. Wrote to Ed. Cath. Times & copy[11]—Ld Blantyre—Mr Whitfield—Dr Sanderson[12]—Mr H. Pease—Mr Ryan—Mr Dalton—Mr Rimmer.[13] Farm calls: & cut a Spanish Chestnut. Worked on books & papers. Read Herodotus—The Monastery.

Wed. Sept. One. 1874 [sc. 1875] [St Asaph]

Ch. 8½ AM. Wrote to Messrs T. & B. (B.P.)—Ld Bathurst[14]—Ld Cardwell—Prof. Monier Williams[15]—Miss Doyle—Rev Mr Dowding—G. Hazard[16]—G.T. Boyd—

[1] Murray Gladstone, 1816-75, 6th s. of Robert, Sir John's br.; Manchester merchant; drowned while fishing at Penmaenmawr on 23 August. He was fa. of the Murray Gladstone, b. 1848, who m. E. A. Wynn (see 12 Aug. 74n.).

[2] One in Lathbury, ii. 62.

[3] Asking for documentary support for its account of the French Assembly's deb. on the banning of *Vaticanism*; Add MS 44447, f. 389.   [4] See 22 Aug. 75.

[5] *Yayin; or the Bible wine question. Testimony by ... Professors Watts, Wallace and Murphy ... and the reverend W. Wright* (1875).

[6] *The religion of Rome described by a Roman* (1873).

[7] The second conference (1875) on reunion organized by Döllinger.

[8] Reginald Garton Wilberforce, 1838-1914, 2nd s. of the bp., whose biography he was preparing; for negotiation on use of Gladstone's letters, see 22 Nov. 80.

[9] Holland Lomas, S.P.G. organizer in Liverpool.

[10] G. Rawlinson, probably *A manual of ancient history* (1869).   [11] See 29 Aug. 75n.

[12] Robert Edward Sanderson, 1828-1913; headmaster of Lancing college, of which Gladstone was a governor; on Vaticanism; Hawn P.

[13] Alfred Rimmer of Broughton, wrote on the Pope; Add MS 44448, f. 4.

[14] William Lennox Bathurst, 1791-1878; 5th Earl Bathurst 1866; formerly clerk of the privy council. See 1 Oct. 75.

[15] (Sir) Monier *Monier-Williams, 1819-99; professor of Sanskrit at Oxford 1860; kt. 1886.

[16] Perhaps of Hazard and Boucher, London printers.

O.H. Schon (aut). Off at 2½ to St Asaph: where we were most kindly received by the Bp[1] & his family. Went over the Cathedral. Geological walk by the River. Read Padelletti on Italian Ch. policy and Cavour[2]—Herodotus—Worked on papers.

2. Th. [Hawarden]

Cathedral H.C. at 8.15—and the Opening ceremonial 11½-1¾. Luncheon at the Dean's. Saw Bp of Rochester—Duke of Westminster—Bp of St Asaph—& examined some records of the Diocese. Home about 7. Finished Padelletti. Read The Monastery—D of Argyll on Instinct.[3]

3. Fr.

Ch. 8½ AM. Wrote to Messrs B. & H.—J. Murray jun—C.G.—Rev. C. Tondini[4]— W. Brough[5]—Dr Hayman—Bp of Winchester. Woodcutting alone. Worked on books & papers. Read Herodotus—The Monastery—Mr Tondini's Reply to me—Senex Rusticus.[6]

4. Sat.

Church 8½ AM. Wrote to Mr Grogan—Mrs Th.—C.G. Read Herodotus—The Monastery—Senex Rusticus—Rawlinson, Excursus.[7] Continued my work on a large tough sycamore nearly dead. Also on books & papers. Corrected proofs of my Article on Italian Church.

5. S.

Ch. 11 AM & H.C.—6½ P.M. Walk with E. W[ickham]. Read Curci, Ragione dell'Opera[8]—Fortn. Rev. on W. Law—Dowding on Coming Days[9]—Stanley's S. on Kingsley, fine: the quotations finer yet[10]—Corresp. on Xtn dogma.

6. M.

Ch. 8½ AM. Wrote to Sir R. Phillimore—S. Gilgrass[11]—C.G. 3½ hours work on books, carrying & arranging. 2¼ hard work on getting my tree down. Rather overtired. Conversation with E. W[ickham]—and with Sir R. Phillimore on the

---

[1] Joshua Hughes.

[2] Work sent to diarist by Guido Padelletti, 1843-78, Italian author.

[3] G. D. Campbell, 'On animal instinct, in its relation to the mind of man', *Contemporary Review*, xxv. 352 (July 1875).

[4] Cesario Tondini d'Quarenghi, 1839-1909?; Italian theologian; had sent his *Anglicanism, Old Catholicism and the union of the Christian episcopal churches* (1875), an attack on Vaticanism.

[5] William Brough, printer and stationer in Holborn.

[6] *Truth and candour vindicated from the assaults . . . of Dr Parker. By Senex Rusticus* (1875).

[7] See 30 Aug. 75.

[8] C. M. Curci, *Ragione dell'opera premessa alle lezioni esegetiche e morali sopra i quattro Evangeli* (1874).

[9] W. C. Dowding, *The coming of the Church of England: with a glance at Scarborough* (1875).

[10] A. P. Stanley, 'Charles Kingsley: a sermon preached in Westminster Abbey on January 31, 1875' (1875).

[11] Samuel Gillgrass of Leeds; on reports in *Leeds Mercury* of diarist's ritualism; Add MS 44448, f. 16.

M.G. & G.G. matters[1]—he came in evg. Read Herodotus—The Monastery—
Aylmer Ward's Reply—I hope the last! It is quite unedifying[2]—'Oppression et
Delivrance'.[3]

7. *Tu.*

Ch. 8½ AM. Wrote to Mr E. Freshfield—E. Eastham—P. Parry[4]—R. Galloway.
Three hours on books. Kibbling with E. Lyttelton. Saw the two Mr Hignetts
with Sir R.P.—We were all agreed as to what Gertrude should do for her sister.
Read Herodotus—The Monastery. 11 to dinner.

8. *Wed.*

Ch. 8½ A.M. Wrote to Sir T. Bateson (B.P.)—Prof. M. Müller—Watson & S.—Rev.
J.R. Gregg.[5] 1-6½. Went to Chester to luncheon with the Dean—gathering at the
Town Hall. Speech at the laying the Foundation Stone of the new King's
School.[6] Saw Messrs Barker & Hignett. Shopping. We brought out the Bp of
Winchester[7] & Mrs Browne. Twelve to dinner. Conversation with Bp of
Chester—Mr Dodson. Saw Mrs Hampton—E. Lyttelton & Helen on the move-
ment of unbelief, & uniformity of laws. Read Herodotus—Three hours on my
library. Read Tracts.[8]

Th. S. 9.

Ch. 8½ AM. Worked again on my books, i.e. arranging them.

10. *Fr.*

Ch. 8½ A.M. Morning walk with The Bp & Mr Dodson. Afternoon with the Bp
& Mrs B[rowne]. Also much conversation with him on the *Filioque* & other-
wise. Read Mr Gowen's Arg. on the Phil. & R. Railway (finished)[9]—The
Monastery—Worked a little on books. Wrote to R. Bulgin—P. Paston. Read Mr
Gowen.

11. *Sat.*

Ch. 8½ A.M. Wrote to Robn G.—Count Cadorna. The Bp. & Mrs B[rowne]
went. We like them much. Visited Hawarden's Hayes[10] & saw the young wife
(d. in law) there, evidently dying. Worked on books as usual: there is yet much
to do. Read the Monastery—The Lost Continent.

[1] i.e. Mary and Gertrude Glynne.
[2] A. Ward, *Rationalism and its relation to Mr Gladstone's expostulation* (1875).
[3] Not found.
[4] Parton Parry, see 23 Sept. 75.
[5] John Robert Gregg, vicar of Deptford 1875.
[6] See *T.T.*, 11 September 1875, 5e.   [7] E. H. *Browne; see 28 Nov. 41.
[8] The last two sentences of this entry, and the entries for 9-11 September, appear in a curious
order, rearranged by lines, suggesting that these days were written up late.
[9] *Argument of F. B. Gowen in the cases of the Philadelphia and Erie rail road company vs. the Catawiosa
railroad etc.* (1866); Gowen prosecuted the Molly Maguires.
[10] Farm of Thomas Davies and his son John near the village.

12. 16 S. Trin.

Ch. 11 A.M. and [blank]. Wrote to Sir A.H. Gordon—A.E. West—C. OShaugh-
nessy—Rev. Mr Wilkinson—Mrs Thistlethwayte—Prof. L. Levi—Robn G.—Thos
Beck.[1] Read Roussel, Nations Catholiques et Protestantes[2]—Evang. Quarterly
on Homeric Religion—Origin of Phoenicians[3]—Dubl. Rev. on Bp Pecock [*sic*]—
Tracts.

13. M.

Ch. 8½ AM. Wrote to Messrs B. & H. (on Draft Settlement)—Mr Jas Taylor—
Robn G.—Principal Librarian Br. Mus.—J. Watson & Smith. Read Herodotus—
The Monastery—Key to the Creeds[4]—Watson on Q. Elis. & R.C.s.[5] 2 h. on
arranging books. Woodcutting. Conversation & arranging with SEG respecting
the Institute. Saw Mr Townshend.

14. Tu.

Ch. 8¼ AM. Wrote to Messrs B. & H. (G.J.G.)—Ld Blantyre—Sir Thos G.—Mr P.
Parry—Rev. E. Lewis[6]—T.E. Manners—Mr Pease MP. 2½ h. on books. Felled an
ash in M. Lane. Read The Monastery—Butler Johnstone on the Eastern Question.[7] Also examined Eden & other books for the evg assembly. Examined the
Institute & grounds with S. 7½-9 at the Meeting where I made an Address of ¾
hour on behalf of the Institute.[8] It was a true parish meeting, with many of the
Colliers present. Our evg meal at the Rectory.

15. Wed.

Ch. 8¼ AM. Wrote to Mr Middlehurst—Dr Cazenove—Mr Brough—M. Victor
Oger. Corrected the revises of my art. on 'Italy & her Church' and dispatched
them. Two hours on my books. Woodcutting. Conversation with C. on marriage arrangements. Read Herodotus—Monastery.

16. Th.

Ch. 8½ A.M. Wrote to Rev R. Suffield—Messrs B. & H.—H.N.G.—Mrs Frampton—Rev. J.A. Moody[9]—Mr Cunnington.[10] Three hours on books. A little woodcutting. Dined at the Rectory. Saw Mr Hurlbutt[11] [on] direct communication
with Liverpool. Read Herodotus—The Monastery—Casaubon v. Perron.[12]

[1] Perhaps Thomas Snow Beck, London physician.
[2] See 3 July 75.
[3] See 16 June 63.
[4] *The keys of the Creeds* (1875).
[5] See 21 Oct. 73.
[6] Perhaps Edward Lewis, d. *ca.* 1879; rector of Harescombe 1867-78.
[7] H. A. M. B. Johnstone, *The Eastern question (1875)* reprinted from the *Pall Mall Gazette*.
[8] 'On mental culture' *T.T.*, 15 September 1875, 5e.
[9] Perhaps James Leith Moody, anglican chaplain to the forces at Warley.
[10] John Cunnington of Oakley Square, London, had sent a speech; Hawn P.
[11] Henry Hurlbutt of Wold House, Hawarden.
[12] *Isaaci Casauboni . . . Ad epistolam . . . Cardinalis Perronij responsio*, ed. F. Meyrick (1875).

17. Fr.

Ch. 8½ AM. Wrote to Messrs B. & H.—Sig. A. de Marcoartu[1]—General Cesnola (B.P.)—Mr R. Williams—Rev. T.H. Jones[2]—Mr Buckmaster—Williams & Norgate—Sec. Wrexham Luncheon.[3] Three hours on my books. Woodcutting with H. Read Herodotus—The Monastery—Cath. Religion in Scotland[4]—and Casaubon v. Perron.

18. Sat.

Ch. 8½ AM. Wrote to Walter Gladstone (Tel. on his disquieting letter about his Father)[5]—Mr Edwards—Mr Vaughan—T.W. Russell[6]—E. Williams—R.S. Poole—T. Scott—Watsons. Read Herodotus—Letter on Cardplaying—The Abbott.[7] Three hours again on my books, and at last got through the *gros* of the operation. Woodcutting with Herbert.

19. 17 S. Trin.

Ch. 11 A.M. with H.C. and 6½ PM. Read the Lessons. Wrote to the King of the Belgians—Sir F. Seymour—R. Mackay—Bishop of Moray[8]—Mrs Conolly—Mr O. Williams—Mrs Lamont—Rev. J. Williams—Mr Murray (B.P.). Read Report of Abp of Syra[9]—Baring Gould on Difficulties[10]—Pater on Renaissance[11]—Letters on Primitive Xty[12]—Braund on Hist. & Revelation.[13] Conversation with J. Talbot on H. of C.

20. M.

Ch. 8½ AM. Wrote to Bp of Zululand[14]—Williams & Co.—A.M. Stewart—Rev. H. Harrison—Mr Braund—Sec. 27th Kent Volunteers[15]—The Viceroy of India.[16] Read Herodotus—The Abbott—God's Trial by Fire.[17] Wood cutting with WHG. Saw Mr L. Barker—Mary Glynne—on her affairs—W.H.G.—on his.

21. Tu. St Matthew.

A day for thankfulness, from 1847.[18] Ch. 8¼ AM. Wrote to Dean of Rochester—Mr Greenhill—Ld Bathurst—M. Jules Favre[19]—Mrs Th.—Rev. Mr Downing—Mr

---

[1] Arturo de Marcoartu; Spanish senator and international law reformer; published on telegraphs.
[2] Thomas Hughes Jones, rector of Rhoscolyn, Holyhead.
[3] Presumably declining an invitation.   [4] Not found.
[5] See 23 Sept. 75; Walter Longueville, 1846-1919, 5th s. of Robertson Gladstone.
[6] Thomas Wallace Russell, 1841-1920; Irish temperance organizer; liberal M.P. S. Tyrone 1886-1910.
[7] By *Scott (1820); see 18 Aug. 52.
[8] R. Eden; see 25 Dec. 41.   [9] See Add MS 44448, f. 5.
[10] S. B. Gould, *Some modern difficulties; nine lectures* (1875).   [11] See 3 Aug. 73.
[12] [J. Walker], *Letters on primitive Christianity* (ed. of 1874).
[13] James H. Braund had sent his *History and revelation*, 3v. (1870-5).
[14] Thomas Edward Wilkinson, 1837-1914, bp. of Zululand 1870-86, of Europe 1886-1911.
[15] Business untraced.   [16] *Northbrook; business untraced.
[17] By W. Rowton (1870).   [18] Agnes's erysipelas; see 20-4 Sept. 47.
[19] Jules Gabriel Claude Favre, 1809-81; French minister for foreign affairs 1870-1 (see 23 Dec. 70n.).

Rimmer—Rev. G.B. Howard.[1] Woodcutting with H. Supplemental work on books. A little also on Homer.[2] Read Herodotus—Greenhill's Letter[3]—Eichthal on Site of Troy[4]—The Abbott.

22. Wed.

Ch. 8½ A.M. Wrote to Mr A. Sandilands[5]—W.S. Lindsay—H.J. Morton—S. Williams—Bennett—Messrs T. and B.—Robn G.—A.E. Evans—A.J. Ritchie—O. Williams. Woodcutting with H. Read Eichthal on Site of Troy—Herodotus—The Abbott. Worked on Homer.

23. Th. [Courthey]

Ch. 8½ A.M. At 9½, an alarming Telegraph from Courthey caused C. & me to repair thither. We arrived at one, and found my very dear Brother Robertson in his death-struggle. At five o'clock he expired. Last evening he went downstairs, sat in the drawing room, and looked so that no one from his appearance would have known him to be ill. The approach of Death was most rapid: the struggle sharp: but a little before the end all was peace. Catherine read the Commendatory prayers. His countenance, after dying, was calm and noble; a stranger would have supposed him under rather than over fifty.[6]

Wrote to Professor Stubbs[7]—Mr Parton Parry—W.H.G.—Ld Penrhyn—D. Puseley—Mr Mavrocordato—Mrs Upher [sic]—Dr MacCulloch.[8] Read Eichthal on Schliemann and Chevalier—Williams, Defence of Welsh People.[9]

24. Fr. [Hawarden]

After making arrangements for next week, I left at 10¼ for Hawarden—arrived at 1¼. C. remained, to see Dr Waters.[10] Wrote to Mr Farncourt—Mr Salkeld—Mr Jones. Read Eichthal (finished)—Began Otto Keller, Entdeckung Ilion's[11]—And read the very interesting Notices & Memoirs of my dear brother in the Liverpool Post, Mercury, & Courier—Read The Abbott—Dr Waddell's Ossian.[12] Cut some trees with H. Tea at the Cottage. M. G[lynne] so very well.

[1] George Broadley Howard, 1827-1913; anglican priest and author; wrote 'The supply of clergy ... a letter to ... Gladstone' (1875).
[2] Start of final work on *Homeric Synchronism*; see 6 Nov. 75.
[3] Perhaps A. Greenhill, 'Is it so? or the logic of the Pope in his claim to infallibility' (1871).
[4] G. Nikolaides, *Topographie et plan stratégique de l'Iliade*, ed. G. d'Eichthal (1867).
[5] Alan Sandilands of Buxton; Hawn P.
[6] He was 68. Diarist's verse on his deathbed appearance at Add MS 44762, f. 193.
[7] Thanking him for the first volume of his *Constitutional History*; printed in W. H. Hutton, *Letters of William Stubbs* (1906), 94; see 22 Nov. 75.
[8] John Murray MacCulloch, presbyterian minister and educationalist.
[9] J. Williams, 'A defence of the Welsh people against the misrepresentations of their English critics' (1869).
[10] Thomas Houghton Waters, Liverpool physician and alderman.
[11] O. Keller, *Die Entdeckung Ilions zu Hissarlik* (1875).
[12] P. H. Waddell, *Ossian and the Clyde* (1875).

25. Sat.

Ch. 8½ A.M. Wrote to Earl Bathurst—Sir Thos G.—Mr Nevin—Mr MacColl. Read Schliemann's Troy[1]—P. Smith's Introduction &c.[2]—Otto Keller (finished)—Eckenbrecher (began)[3]—Sir J. Lubbock Prehist. Times[4]—The Abbott—Smith's Poems.[5] Woodcutting with H.

26. 18 S. Trin.

Ch. 11 AM & 6½ P.M.—Saw Mr Temple. Wrote to Helen G.—Dowager Duchess of Somerset—C.G., and. . . . Read B. Gould on 'Some Mysteries'[6]—Sadler on the Bible[7]—D'Alembert's Dialogue &c.[8]—Account of Máhabhárata[9]—Routon, God's Trial by Fire[10]—M'Bean, right of Priv. Judgt.[11]

27. M.

Ch. 8¼ AM. Wrote to Mr Viner[12]—Rev. Dr Waddell[13]—W.H.G.—Mrs Th.—Dr Eckenbrecher—C.G.—Miss Hart—Rev. F. Meyrick. Read Eckenbrecher Lage des Hom. Troja (finished)—Carlisle on Troic Plain—Schliemann's Introduction—The Abbott. Preparation for journey. A little woodcutting.

28. Tu.

Wrote to Herr F. Eysenhardt[14]—Rev. Mr Porter—Ld Wolverton—Rev D.T. Gladstone—Mrs Heywood—W.H.G.—C.G.—Ld Cardwell—A Brown—J.G. Jones—S. Pearce—J. Kerr. Shortly before eleven, we proceeded to Knotty Ash Church where the remains of my dear brother were laid in their last home amidst remarkable tokens of general esteem and affection. I had some conversation with Robertson, & with Walter, in the afternoon: & at night Arthur gave me the Will (of 1865) to read. I joined with Tom in thinking it very faulty as to the relative positions of the brothers in particular: and I wrote to Mrs Heywood to express this feeling.[15] Began translating the Preface to the Welsh Bible.[16] Much conversation with Sir T.G. Saw Mr Kelso[17] on the imputation about the

---

[1] See 9 Mar. 74.

[2] Introduction to P. Smith's ed. of H. Schliemann, *Troy and its remains* (1875).

[3] C. Gustav von Eckenbrecher sent his *Die Lage des Homerischen Troja* (1875); Hawn P.

[4] See 6 July 66.

[5] W. F. Smith, *Poems* (1864).

[6] S. B. Gould, perhaps *Yorkshire Oddities; incidents and strange events*, 2v. (1874).

[7] M. F. Sadler, *Scripture truths* (1874).

[8] J. Le R. d'Alembert, *Dialogues* (1847 ed.).

[9] Probably M. Williams, *Indian epic poetry . . . with a full analysis of the Maha-Bharata* (1863).

[10] See 20 Sept. 75.

[11] Untraced.

[12] Probably George Barber Peregrine Viner, Canadian priest in London.

[13] Peter Hately Waddell; seceded from the Free Church; literary historian; see 24 Sept. 75.

[14] Unidentified.

[15] Letter untraced; her reply agreed the 'property is left in a rather complicated state'; Hawn P.

[16] At the request of T. W. Hancock, Gladstone tr. the Latin dedication by bp. W. *Morgan, 1540?-1604, to his tr. of the bible into Welsh; Add MS 44447, f. 233.

[17] Archibald Kelso, Liverpool broker.

Slave Trade. Such were today's occupations: yesterday I signed the marriage settlement, and the Deed constituting Willy absolute owner in law of the Hawarden Estate.

29. Wed. St Michael [London]

Tom & I went off to Edgehill at 8.45. I reached 4 C[arlton] Gardens[1] at 2.45. Worked on heaps of letters. Wrote to W. Higham (Tel.)—Mr Powell—Sig. Ferrari[2]—Mr Child[3]—Mr W. Saunders—Mr J. Graham—Manager Parcels Express and German letter in draft to Archbishop of Syra.[4] Worked on Translation of Preface to Bible. Read Ed. Hartmann.[5] Saw Sir Thos G.—Sir A. Panizzi—Ld Wolverton (dined). Shopping. Saw L. Hart and found with joy that a good life has taken the place of an evil one [R].

30. Th. [The Coppice, Henley]

At 11 AM we went to St George's & the marriage[6] service began soon after the half hour, Stephen assisting Francis Grey[7] who was unhappily almost inaudible. Both behaved well. A little tremor was perceptible in Willy's hand: but his words were very distinct. Some friends came with very special kindness and there was a public. I went to [41] B[erkeley] Square to *bless*: & remained until the luncheon, at their desire, as it was wholly informal. May it be a holy living union & may the bride learn the noble ways of her mother in law to which I trust she is much inclined. There were two very special thoughts of the absent: one of her mother, the other of her grandmother.[8]

Conversation with *her* upstairs—and with Mr Stuart the Minister[9]—The Master of Blantyre[10]—Mr Noble—Lord Ronald Gower—Mr [W. B.] Ferrand (most agreeably softened)—Ld Lyttelton—and afterwards—Scotts—Lord Granville—Mrs Tyler. Much shopping. Off by 5 PM Train to Phillimore's most hospitable, most homelike abode at the Coppice [Henley]. Much conversation with him. Read Père Hyacinthe's first letter.[11] Wrote to L. Creagh [R]. Copied out my German letter to Abp Lycurgus (how bold!)

Frid. Oct. One 1875. [Oakley Park, Cirencester]

Wrote to King of the Belgians—Mrs Begbie—Abp Lycurgus—part of a long letter in English.[12] My German letter passed the ordeal of Sir R. & Lady

---

[1] A. J. *Balfour's London house.   [2] See 7 Oct. 51?
[3] William S. H. Child of Greenock had requested employment; Hawn P.
[4] German version not found; see 1 Oct. 75.
[5] C. R. E. von Hartmann, *Die Selbstzersetzung des Christenthums und die Religion der Zukunft* (1874).
[6] Of W. H. Gladstone to Gertrude Stuart, daughter of Lord Blantyre.   [7] See 21 Feb. 52.
[8] Her mother, Evelyn, had died in 1869; her grandmother was Harriet, duchess of Sutherland, Gladstone's confidant in the 1860s.
[9] Probably *sc.* Stewart, a relative of the bride's aunt, Margaret Stewart.
[10] Walter Stuart, 1851-95, the bride's brother; styled Master of Blantyre; W. B. Ferrand was also of the connexion.
[11] C. J. M. Loyson, *Catholic Reform. Letters . . . with a preface by A. P. Stanley* (1874).
[12] On Old Catholics and Anglican-Orthodox relations, in Lathbury, ii. 63.

P[hillimore] so it will go. Walked with R.P. about his nestlike home. Off at 2.15 for Oakley Park.[1] Arrived before six: Ld Bathurst there, and a crowd in the Station. Worked on Translation of Morgan's Epistle. Read Hyacinthe's Second Letter—Hartmann, Selbstzersetzung des Christianthums.

2. Sat.

Lord Bathurst at 85 spent full six hours in taking me to the Museum of Roman antiquities—the Agricultural College, which we surveyed with much interest—and driving to Pinbury & Satterton [*sic*], and to all the interesting points of this vast & noble Park. Saw Mrs Th. Visit 1. Conversation with Hayward—Dr Miller.[2] Read Hartmann. Wrote to [blank].

3. 20 [*sc. 19*] *S. Trin.*

Cirencester Ch (a very fine Perpendicular—large congregation) 11 A.M. (and H.C.) and 3 P.M. (Ld B[athurst] bis) Wrote to Père Hyacinthe—Mr Dorn[3]—C.G.—and Helen. Read Hartmann—much. Saw Roman Museum. Read Hymns, aloud—in evg. Mrs Th. No 2.

4. M.

Wrote to C.G.—Helen G. Long drive to the Chedworth Roman Villa. Ch. at 8.30 A.M. Read Hartmann. Whist in evg. Mrs Th. No 3. It was worth remembering; she gained I trust a victory.

5. [*Hawarden*]

Expedition to Gloucester and Worcester Cathedrals. After 50 years! Both most interesting—Worcester sumptuous. Farewell to Oakley and its most kind hospitable Master. Went on to Hawarden. At Gloucester we had most of the service & saw Canon Harvey.[4] At Chester went to the Theatre for a spell—short but long enough.[5] Read Hartmann (finished)—Among our ain folk[6]—Events of Geneva.[7]

6. Wed.

Ch. 8½ A.M. Wrote to Lord Lyttelton—Mr Ouvry—Mr Palgrave—Rev Mr Theed—Miss Goalen—Thorn & Co[8]—Mrs Th.—Miss Ponsonby (B.P.)[9]—Rev. J.M. Capes—Mr Gobert[10]—Mr Gallaghan[11]—C.G.—Mr S. Byrne. Spent the

[1] Lord Bathurst's place near Cirencester; Laura Thistlethwayte was another of the guests.
[2] i.e. J. Cale *Miller (see 1 Apr. 51), arranging the Greenwich visit; see 11 Nov. 75.
[3] Possibly Heinrich Ludwig Egmont Dorn, who published on the German Academy of Art in 1875. [4] Richard Harvey; see 30 Mar. 34.
[5] Mrs. Vandenhoff's entertainment at the Theatre Royal.
[6] [W. Alexander], *Sketches of life among my ain Folk, by the author of Johnny Gibb* (n.d.).
[7] Perhaps Père Hyacinthe's letter on Genevan affairs in *Evangelical Christendom*, xvi. 237 (August 1875). [8] London bookbinders.
[9] Perhaps Alberta Victoria (Betty), da. of Sir H. F. Ponsonby.
[10] *Sic*; perhaps *sc.* Gobat.
[11] John Gallagher of Belfast, correspondent on religion; Hawn P.

morning chiefly in opening & reading the accumulated arrivals. Woodcutting with Herbert. Read the Abbott—Prota Giurlio[1]—Bp Thirlwall's last Notes[2]—and divers pamphlets.

7. Th.

Ch. 8½ AM. Wrote to Reeves & Turner—Walter Gladstone—R. Quain[3]—Rev G.B. Howard—C. Smith—Mr J.W. Barclay[4]—S.C. Hall—R.M. James. Also finished my long letter to the Archbishop of Syra. Woodcutting with Herbert. More work on the accumulations. Read The Abbott—Howard on Numbers of Clergy[5]—Hesiod Theogony—Bp Sandford's Sermon[6]—Austin's Tower of Babel.[7]

8. Fr.

Ch. 8½ AM. Wrote to Abp of Syra (sent)—Rev. G.H. Sumner—Archimandrite Myriantheus—A. Kinnaird—Sig. Piselli[8]—Sig. Sbarbaro[9]—Creswicks—Mr Wall— Mr Highton—Sir C. Wood—Mr Williams—St. D'Aloz—Robertson & Nicholson. Woodcutting with H. Saw G. Glynne & settled her matters on the Executorship account. Saw Mr Williams—Conversation with C.G. on the coming festivities. Read Tower of Babel—Tulloch on Religion & Theology[10]—Tom & his Grandfather[11]—Corresp. with Eastern Churchmen.

9. Sat.

Ch. 8½ AM. Wrote to Jas Watson & Smith—Messrs Barker (per Messrs T. & B.)—Rev. N. Woodard—Mrs Th.—Jas Latimer—Mrs Bellairs—J.G.E. Astle[12]— A. Wilson—Mr Reverdy Johnson—W.G. Ross.[13] Read Guttmann on Homeric Hymns[14]—Ross's Poems—The Abbott. Mr Pennant came again.

10. S. 20 aft. Trin.

Ch 11 AM and 6½ A.M. Wrote to Duke of Argyll—Arthur G.—Ed. Scottish Guardian[15]—Messrs Murray—Rev Mr Colley[16]—Dr Cazenove—G.B. Howard—

---

[1] L. Prota-Giurleo, *Statuto dogmatico-organico-disciplinare della Chiesa cattolica nazionale italiana* (1875).

[2] See *Contemporary Review*, xxvi. 703 (October 1875).

[3] (Sir) Richard *Quain, 1816-98; physician; cr. bart. 1890.

[4] James William Barclay, 1832-1907; liberal (unionist) M.P. Forfarshire 1872-92.

[5] G. B. Howard, *On the future supply of clergy* (1875).

[6] C. W. Sandford, 'The duties of the clergy as minister of the National Church. A sermon' (1875).

[7] See 9 Feb. 75. [8] Unidentified.

[9] Pietro Sbarbaro of Macerata University; involved in international law reform; an earlier letter from Gladstone had been printed in *Gazette d'Italia*, 8 August 1875; see Add MS 44447, f. 363.

[10] J. Tulloch, 'Religion and theology. A sermon' (1875). [11] Not found.

[12] John George Edmund Astle, later historian of Merthyr Tydfil.

[13] W. B. Ross had sent his *Occasional verses* (1875).

[14] A. Guttman, *De Hymnorum Homericorum historia critica* (1869).

[15] Appreciation of A. P. *Forbes: 'of devoted life and labour, of wide learning, of balanced mind, uniting with a strong grasp of Catholic principles the spirit of a true historic student and a genuine zeal for literary culture . . .'; *Scottish Guardian*, 15 October 1875, 192.

[16] Thomas Colley, curate in Portsmouth 1875-7; later archdeacon of Pietermaritzburg.

W.H.G.—Dr Cooke.[1] Read Luthardt on St John's Gospel[2]—Narrative of French Convert.[3] Set about rendering into Latin the beautiful Hymn 254.[4]

11. M.

Ch. 8¼ A.M. Wrote to Robertson & Nichn—Sig. Luigi Morelli[5]—Rev. Cav. Prota Giurlio[6]—Dr Adolph Kohut (B.P.)—Canon Rawlinson—Mrs Gilbert—Gen. Seager (Morocco, B.P.)[7] Saw Mr Barker—on the festivities. Cut down a beech. Worked on Homer. Revised & wrote out my version of the Responsory Hymn. Read R. Johnson's Speech—The Abbot—The Tower of Babel (finished).

12. Tu.

Ch. 8¼ AM. Wrote to Rev. D. Gladstone—Fletcher & Co.—Mr H. Jones—Earl of Glasgow. Wrote on the Nekuia[8]—Read Nitzsch on do—The Abbott—Tom & his Grandfather. Herbert & I had a tough job with a large hornbeam embedded into a wall.

13. Wed.

Ch. 8¼ AM. Wrote to Marquis C. Guerrieri—Watson & Smith—Mr Bullock—Dr Max Lossen[9]—Rev. T. Wallace[10]—B. Porter—Mr Hills—Mr Neall—P. Parry—J. Latimer. Worked on the Nekuia. We got the hornbeam down & set to kibbling. Read Nitzsch on Nekuia—Tom & his Grandfather—The Abbott. Dr Marshall dined.[11] Much conversation chiefly on Newman.

14. Th.

Ch. 8¾ A.M. and 7 P.M. Harvest Service, good, hearty, & crowded. Wrote to Lord Lyttelton—Watsons (Tel.)—Mr Hancock. Dean of Manchester dined[12]—conversation in evg. Woodcutting with Herbert. Finished revising & copied out my Translation of Bp Morgan.[13] Read The Abbott.

15. Frid.

Ch. 8¼ A.M. Wrote to Sir James Watson—Mr Gurdon—Mrs Fleming—Sir G. Prevost—Mr Parker—Messrs Bickers—W.H.G.—Mr Collings—Sir C.A. Wood.

[1] William Cooke, protestant tract-writer; on Vaticanism; Hawn P.

[2] C. E. Luthardt, *De compositione Evangeli Joannei* (1852).

[3] Perhaps *The French convert*, a ballad (1790?).

[4] 'Art thou weary?'; tr. at Add MSS 44762, f. 248, 44770, f. 53; for publication, see 3 Dec. 75.

[5] Professor Luigi Morelli of Naples presented diarist with diploma of the Circolo d'incoraggiamento (society to promote 'perfection in women'); Hawn P.

[6] Cavaliere Luigi Prota-Giurleo, Neapolitan priest; see 6 Oct. 75n.

[7] Dixon Seager, residing in Morocco, had asked for copies of *Vaticanism* for the English community there; Hawn P.   [8] Book xi of the *Odyssey*.

[9] Max Lossen, 1842-98; private scholar and historian living in Munich (see Conzemius, *Döllinger*, iii. 468); tr. the Vatican pamphlets and *Rome and the newest fashions in religion* into German (1875, 1876).

[10] Thomas Wallace, nonconformist minister in Bath, on R. Gladstone's death; Hawn P.

[11] Peter Marshall; D.D. 1872; rector of Hulme from 1858.

[12] B. M. Cowie; see 10 Oct. 72.   [13] See 28 Sept. 75.

Worked on Homer. Kibbling & clearing wood. Arranging books (Poetry). Read
The Abbott: finished—The Chapters where Mary [Stuart] appears cannot (I
think) as a rule be surpassed. Read Stimmen aus der Scharof-Kirche[1]—Tom and
his Grandfather. Worked on Homer.

16. Sat.

Ch. 8½ AM. Wrote to Reeves & Turner—Messrs Clowes (BP.)—Miss Marsh—Mr
J. Darley—Mr J.B. Smith—Ld Harrowby—Rev. Mr Rees[2]—Sig. Luigi Centola [sc.
Cesnola]—Rev Mr Grosart. Felled an oak with H. Saw Mr Villiers. Read Q.R. on
the Govt—De Vere's Mary Tudor[3]—Tom & his Grandfather—and [blank].
Worked on Homer. Lady Brownlow came.

17. 21 S. Trin.

Ch. 11 AM and (H.C.) and [blank]. Wrote to Cocks & Biddulph—Capt.
Spiller[4]—Watsons—J. Cunnington—Rev T.W. Shaw—J.E. Thomas—Miss M.
Elliot—Sir G. Prevost. Conversation with Lady Brownlow who is as good as she
is beautiful, & that is saying much. Read Bp of Gloucester's Lecture on Difficulties[5]—White on Life in Christ[6]—Finished Tom & his Grandfather.

18 St Luke.

Ch. 8¾ A.M. Wrote to Mr T.B. Potter MP—Mr E.W. OBrien[7]—Mrs Th.—Mr P.
Parry. Worked on Homer. Kibbling & tidying with H. Read Mary Tudor—
Duprat on African races.[8]

19. Tu.

Ch. 8½ A.M. Wrote to Mr J. Wilson—Mr G.H. Palmer—Mr Morier—Dr
M'Cosh[9]—Ld Odo Russell—Rev W. Nevins—Sir A. Paget—Capt. Spiller. And
sent out the spare or separate copies of my Church Article to Germany Italy
&c. Worked on Homer. Read Nevins on Vaticanism[10]—Mary Tudor—Duprat
Races d'Afrique and [blank].

20. Wed.

Ch. 8½ A.M. Wrote to Miss F. Garland—Mr Sweeney—Mr Housden—Mrs
Fleming—Mr Cunnington—Rev Mr Richards. Worked on Homer. Read Mary
Tudor. Out with Herbert at the Mill Dam: expectations of a dangerous

---

[1] Not found.   [2] Perhaps Charles Davies Rees, vicar of Llanwrthwl.
[3] A. T. de Vere, *Mary Tudor; an historical drama*; in his *Works* (1875 ed.).
[4] Probably of the Volunteers, involved in the marriage celebrations.
[5] Probably early version of C. J. Ellicott, 'What is the real distinction between England and
Rome?' (1876).
[6] See 3 Aug. 50.
[7] Edward William, s. of W. Smith *O'Brien; landowner in co. Limerick; liberal on the land question.
[8] P. Duprat, *Essai historique sur les races anciennes et modernes de l'Afrique septentrionale* (1845).
[9] James *McCosh, 1811-94; president of Princeton university 1868-88; inductivist philosopher.
[10] W. P. Nevins, *The Jesuits and other essays* (1874).

flooding from the immense rains. The marriage guests arrived. Eighteen to dinner.

21. Th.[1]

Ch. 8½ A.M. The Marriage Service at 10.45.[2]—It was very impressive. Gertrude retained perfect self-command. I conducted her: George gave her away. W. Lyttelton officiated, the Rector assisting. The day just fair until 4 or 5. Showed Lord P[enrhyn] the Park. Torrent of rain night & morning: but a remission came (nothing more) in time for the entry of the newly wedded. They were received with affection & enthusiasm: Willy made an excellent speech, I added a few words. The village was a long line of triumphal arches flags & other manifestations. Straightway after, the rain resumed. Yesterday & today G[eorge Lyttelton] helped me with excellent criticisms and suggestions on my version of 'Art thou weary'.[3]

Wrote to Canon [J. Cale] Miller—Cocks & Biddulph—Dr Wade—Watson & Smith—Mrs Kirkby—Mr S. Cox[4]—Mrs Th. Walk with Ld P[enrhyn]—Our party continued large. Conversation with Lady P[enrhyn]—with W. Lyttelton. Went to the fireworks in evg and tea at Mr Hurlbutt's. The rain was savagely obstructive. Read Mary Tudor. Worked on Homer.

22. Fr.

Ch. 8½ AM. Wrote to W.L. Gladstone—Mr J. Roberts—Jas Beal—E.F. Burton—G.D. Tomlinson—Rev Dr Gregg—Rev Dr Badenoch. Walk to Buckley with Ld Lyttelton: saw Mr Torr.[5] The *gros* of the party broke up. Worked on Homer: settled the mutton matter. Read Mary Tudor—L [blank] on Egyptian Finance—Professor [blank']s Address.

23. Sat.

Ch. 8½ AM. Wrote to Cocks & Biddulph—Capt. Page—Mr Hertslet—Sir C. Wood—Rev. Jas Hook[6]—Mr A. Cooper[7]—Mr J. Brownlees—Mr S. Gass[8]—Mr W. Rusbridge—Mr W.W. Clark—J. Watson & Smith (Tel. & l.). Worked on Homer. Felled a tree with W. Saw Ld F. Cavendish—Mr Raikes. Read Mary Tudor—Gass on Ultramontanism.

---

[1] This day's entry written in two columns.
[2] Marriage as his second wife of Gertrude Jessy Glynne to G. S. G. Douglas-*Pennant, tory M.P. and 2nd Baron Penrhyn 1886 (see 24 Sept. 50n.). See 18 Jan. 76.
[3] See 10 Oct. 75.
[4] Perhaps Samuel *Cox, 1826-93; Baptist minister in Nottingham; ed. *The Expositor* from 1875.
[5] John Torr, 1813-80; Liverpool merchant; Cheshire J.P.; tory M.P. Liverpool from 1873.
[6] James Hook, 1837-77, s. of W.F.*; vicar of Moreton 1869-77. See 11 Nov. 75.
[7] Not traced.
[8] Matthew Gass of Glasgow had sent his 'Ultramontanism in morals and theology' (1875); Hawn P.

24. 22 S. Trin.

Ch. 11 AM. and 6½ P.M. Wrote to Rev. F.N. Oxenham[1]—Messrs Clowes (B.P.)—Mr Macmillan—Rev. J. Matheson.[2] Began Allies's Remarkable Book on the Formation of Christendom P.III[3]—Read F. Oxenham on Future Punishment—Ritualism & the Divine Word.[4] Walk with F.C.

25. M.

Ch. 8½ AM. Wrote to Mr Cunnington—Rev. Dr Miller—Mr McColl—Mr Palgrave—P. Parry (& copy). Worked on Homer. Woodcutting with W. & F.C. Feast to 900 children. What a mass of happiness was there: and the apparatus pretty simple. Read Joanna Baillie—Preface, and part of Orra—Phallic worship[5] and [blank].

26. Tu.

Ch. 8¼ AM. Dinner to 400. Carving and speaking. Ball in evening: Ann Thomas, over 80 danced like a ball of India Rubber, and never tired.[6] All watched & loud cheers continually burst out. A sad day. Wrote to Mr Jas Knowles—Mr R. Wilson—and Rev Mr Mountfield.[7] Worked on Homer. Finished Orra—Read Major on O.C. Persecution.[8] Finished revision of Lamb.[9] Cut a tree with W.

27. Wed.

Ch. 8¼ AM. Wrote to J. Watson & Smith—Rev. Th. Mills[10]—Mr T.B. Potter. Woodcutting, a little. Worked on Homer. Read Grote's Greece[11]—The Dream (Baillie)—Duprat, Races d'Afrique. 450 to dinner: the same process (nearly) of carving, toasts, & speaking: a second ball afterwards. We have now nearly touched 2000 guests young & old this week.

28. Th. SS. Simon & Jude.

Ch. 8¾. Wrote to Mr Macmillan—Mr Bentley—Mr Dalton—Manager B. of Scotland—Dean of Rochester. Worked on Homer. Read Eckenbrecher—Hook's Preface[12]—The Standard of Israel on the Tribe of Dan[13]—Miss Baillie's 'The

---

[1] Frank Nutcombe Oxenham, d. *ca.* 1892; curate of St Alban Holborn 1873-5, later unbeneficed; had sent his 'Everlasting punishment: a letter to . . . Gladstone' (1875).

[2] A nonconformist.

[3] T. W. Allies, *Formation of Christendom*, part 3 (1875).

[4] 'Ritualism in its treatment of the Divine Word: by a member of the General Council of the University of Edinburgh' (1873).

[5] J. Baillie, *Orra: a tragedy* and *The Dream*, in her *Works* (1851).

[6] Report of speeches in *T.T.*, 27 October 1875, 7a.

[7] David Mountfield, 1827-87; theologian and rector of Newport, Salop, 1864-86.

[8] Untraced work on the Old Catholics, possibly by R. H. Major.

[9] i.e. in Homer; see 22 Oct. 75.

[10] Declining invitation of Thomas Mills, vicar of St Jude's, Dublin, to attend a meeting on behalf of O'Keeffe; *T.T.*, 30 October 1875, 10a.

[11] See 19 Mar. 47.

[12] See 21 Feb. 75.

[13] Untraced.

Siege'.[1] Corrected Articles on Ritual for reprint.[2] Tonight the scene changed to a more formal ball for the Upper Tenants & their families with some neighbours. It lasted till late. Sir C.A. Wood came to discuss the Mersey Tunnel.

29. Fr.

Ch. 8½ AM. Wrote to Mr W. Saunders–Mr French–Mr Philips–Mr Holingworth. Finished correction of Articles on Ritual. Worked on Homer: but spent the morning principally with Sir C.A. Wood & Mr Williams on the subject of the Mersey Tunnel & communication with Liverpool.[3] A servants' ball this evening closed at length our part of the marriage festivities. Our guests have been nearly 2500: one third children.

30. Sat.

(Not called) Church in evg 7 P.M. Wrote to Mr Hofland–Mr Salkeld–W.A. Lindsay–T.B. Green[4]–Bp of Winchester–Sir R. Phillimore–C.J. Herries– Watsons–Mr King–A. Harris[5]–E. Phillips. Wrote reply to Q.R. *note* on Ritual.[6] Felled a tree with W. Further conversation with C.A. Wood. Read Miss Baillie's 'The Tryal' [*sic*]–Greens Fragments of Thought–St James's Mag.

31. 23 S. Trin.

Ch. mg & aft. Wrote to Supt Telegr. Dept.–Rev. C.P. Clarke[7]–Miss Applegate–Mr Nugent–Mr Rusher–Mrs Th.–Mr Crawley–J. Knowles–Sir J. Watson–Chamberlain of the City[8]–Rev E. Bickersteth. Read Allies Formn of Xtndom–Harrison, Charge & Notes[9]–Bickersteth on Eternal Punishment, & Poem[?] B.XI.[10]

Mond. All S. Nov. 1. 75.

Wrote to A.H. Louis–Rector of Athenian University[11]–L. Henner–F. Barber– J. Slagg[12]–Rev. M. MacColl–Arthur R. Gladstone–Mrs Grote–Watsons–Mr H. Clark–Mr Dobson. Church 8¾ AM. Read Mr Louis's Pamphlet Letter[13]

---

[1] From her *Works* (1851); see 25 Oct. 75.

[2] 'Ritual and Ritualism' and 'Is the Church of England worth preserving?' were reprinted, with a preface dated 12 November 1875, as 'The Church of England and Ritualism'.

[3] Work on the tunnel was begun 1866, frequently suspended, renewed 1880, completed 1885; no financial involvement by Gladstone has been traced.

[4] Thomas Bowden Green had sent his *Fragments of Thought* (1875); Hawn P.

[5] Possibly Andrew Harris, later a correspondent; Hawn P.

[6] An unpublished and untraced reply to a note on MacColl in *Quarterly Review*, cxxxix. 577 (October 1875).

[7] Charles Pickering Clarke, rector of Thornham 1875.

[8] See 1 Jan. 75n.

[9] B. Harrison, 'Prospects of peace for the Church in the Prayer Book' (1875).

[10] E. H. Bickersteth, probably part iii of his *The shadowed home* (1875).

[11] Emmanuel Ch. Kokkinos, on death of Abp. Lykourgos; Add MS 44448, f. 130; printed in *Allgemeine Zeitung*, reprinted in *T.T.*, 20 November 1875, 9e.

[12] John Slagg, free-trade propagandist; published on the Cobden treaty (1870).

[13] Perhaps A.H. Louis; see 13 Mar. 67.

—Miss Baillie's Basil—Xtn Quarterly (U.S.) on Vaticanism.[1] Cut & kibbled—alone.

2. Tu.

Ch. 8½ AM. Wrote to Archbp of Dublin—Rev Canon Easton [*sic*][2]—Mrs Th.—Mrs Gutteridge—Dr Bennett—Le Baron de Wolffert [*sic*][3]—Miss Colentrof (Autogr). Felling & marking trees with W.H.G. Worked on Homer. Read Basil (finished)—The Critic—Birdwood on Frankincense.[4]

3. Wed.

Ch. 8¼ AM. Wrote to Mr Blackwood (P.O.)—Mr Ouvry—Dr Bennett—Rev W. Price—Ld Granville—A.S. Dyce[5]—A.R. Gladstone—Admiral [A. P.] Hamilton—Sec. Great Eastern RR. Co—Mr J. Williamson. Worked on Homer. Felling and kibbling. The Bishop[6] came. Long conversation with him on plans of Welsh & especially Welsh clerical Education. Read The Queen of Connaught.[7]

4. Th.

Ch. 8¼ AM. & again 12-1 for the latter portion of the Confirmation service: a beautiful spectacle. Wrote to Watson & Smith—Sir Jas Watson—Mr W. Williams—Sir C.A. Wood—Rev Mr Bellairs—Mrs Heaphy[8]—Mr John Watson—Dr Smith—Mr A. Balfour—Rev. Dr Tremlett—Mr H.A. Bright[9]—Dr Döllinger. Worked on Homer. Felling and kibbling. Read The Queen of Connaught—Renan's Introductory Discourse.[10]

5. Frid.

Ch. 8½ A.M. Wrote to Ed. Greenwich Paper—Mr Macmillan—F. Harman—Dean [J.] Nicolson—Messrs Hoare[11]—Rev. W. Luke[12]—Dr Hancock—Rev. G. Bulstrode[13]—Mr Rusher (B.P.) Woodcutting with W. The Westminsters came to see Gertrude & staid a while. Conversation on Land Act. Worked on Homer—reading Schliemann the while—The material is valuable but chaotic. Read Bellairs, Nuneaton[14]—Queen of Connaught.

[1] Not traced.
[2] Thomas Eaton, 1805-89; rector of W. Kirby 1860-89; canon of Chester.
[3] Baron Fr. von Wolffers had sent his book, see 1 Dec. 75.
[4] Untraced work by Sir G. C. M. Birdwood.
[5] Possibly Alexander Stirling Dyce, a cousin of the artist.
[6] i.e. Joshua Watson, bishop of St Asaph.
[7] [H. Jay], *The Queen of Connaught, A story*, 3v. (1875).
[8] Perhaps the rescue case; see 4 Oct. 73.
[9] Henry Arthur Bright, 1830-84; Liverpool shipowner; wrote on Romanism; Add MS 44448, f. 144.
[10] E. Renan, perhaps *An essay on the age and antiquity of Nabathaean agriculture, to which is added an inaugural lecture on the position of the Semitic nations in the history of civilization* (1862).
[11] London bankers.
[12] William Henry Colbeck Luke, d. 1895; rector of Elmswell from 1863.
[13] George Bulstrode, 1824-97; vicar of Ely from 1868.
[14] H. W. Bellairs, *Traditions of Nuneaton and its neighbourhood* (1860?).

6. Sat.

Ch. 8½ A.M. Wrote to Marq. C. Guerrieri—Mr Hofland—S. Langley—E. Falney—J. Bell—Messrs Spottiswoode—Rev. F. Meyrick—Rev Dr Miller—M. Mason—W. Allom.[1] Woodcutting in aft. Finished the rough MS of my little book on Homer.[2] Read Queen of Connaught.

7. 24 S. Trin.

Ch. 11 A.M. and H.C.—Also 6½ PM. Wrote to Sir R. Phillimore—Canon Miller—Mr Clodds—Ld Lyttelton—Mrs Herring—Mr Montgomery—Sir Geo. Prevost. Also finished and dispatched in proof the reprint of my Articles on Ritual.[3] Read Report Anglic. Soc.—Allies, Formation of Xtendom—Chester Dioc. Conf.—Ritualist Treatment of H.S.[4]

8. M.

Ch. 8¼ A.M. Wrote to Mr A. de Lisle—Mr Chambers—Sir Thos G.—Mr F.T. Paris[5]—Mrs Grote—G.S.C. Swinston (Autogr)—Mr T. Winston—Mr J. Gason (Rome)—Mr R.L. King.[6] Corrected for press several Sections of my work on 'The Time & place of Homer'. Arranging papers &c. for journey to London. Cutting & kibbling with W. Dined at the Rectory. Read Sermon Directory.

9. Tu. [London]

Up early and off at 8. Euston 2.30. Wrote to Watsons—Helen G. Saw Mr Johnson—Mr L. Barker[7]—Mr Knowles—Ld Lyttelton—Scotts—Ld F. Cavendish—Sir R. Phillimore. Grappled with the London accumulations, to prepare for clearing them. Dined at Metaphys. Socy.[8] Agreed to fill the Chair again. Discussion on miracles is to be resumed. Saw Stewart—& another [R]. Read Lady of the Lake[9]—Conze on Schliemann[10]—Mr F. Stephen's Essay.

10. Wed.

Very busy. Wrote to Mr Plumptre—C.G.—Mr Russell (U.S.)[11]—Mr Freeland—Mrs Bathurst[12]—Mr Sturton[13]—Mr Reverdy Johnson—Mr Pope Hennessy—Mr

---

[1] W. T. Allom, apparently a nonconformist; see 17 Nov. 75.
[2] *Homeric Synchronism: an enquiry into the time and place of Homer* (1876).
[3] See 28 Oct. 75.
[4] See 24 Oct. 75.
[5] Perhaps of the London wine merchants.
[6] Robert L. King, secretary of the Hackney Liberal Club; Hawn P.
[7] R. Longueville Barker, a guest at the Castle.
[8] As chairman; J. F. *Stephen led a discussion on his 'Remarks on the proof of miracles' (1875); Brown, *Metaphysical Society*, 329.
[9] By *Scott (1810); see 22 Mar. 75.
[10] One of A. C. L. Conze's many works on the Homeric period.
[11] Not further identified.
[12] Not traced.
[13] Perhaps Thomas Sturton of Deptford, a constituent.

Fosbroke. Saw M. Victor Oger (on the incredible conduct of the French Government)[1]—Mr Newton and Dr Birch on Homeric questions—Sir A. Panizzi—Mr Murray—Mr Louis—Mrs Grote—Mr Macmillan—Director of Cheque Bank, & Sir R. Phillimore (with whom I dined) on many matters. Shopping. Read Gilbert on Disestablishment.[2]

11. Th.

Wrote to Mrs Gordon—Dr Burnett(Tel)—H. Jones—Ld Granville—J.R. Baird—J. Pisani[3]—Mr Thomson—and others (autographs &c). Saw Bp of Rochester—Sir W. Farquhar—Mr Beresford Hope—Rev Mr Meyrick—Hook Committee Meeting 1 PM.[4] Shopping, letters, & accounts. Read Sermon & Art papers. Off to Greenwich 4¾. Dined at Dr [J. Cale] Miller's. Much pleased with Sir Cooper Key.[5] To the meeting at 8. Address ab. 1¼ hour.[6] The people followed to the Station. 'Three cheers for (i.e. agt) the Vatican Decrees'. Read Watkiss Lloyd, Age of Pericles.[7] Saw Three [R].

12. Fr. [Hawarden]

On my way down turned Tennyson's Epitaph on Franklin into an Alcaic Stanza.[8] Conversation with Mrs Howson[9] on the degeneracy of Liverpool. With the Dean on the King's College School. Wrote to Sir W. Farquhar—Mr Murray—Mrs Th.—Mad. Novikoff. After a busy morning, off at 11.30. Reached Hawarden 6.30. Saw Mr Edwards—Mr Ouvry—Sir G. Prevost—Mr MacColl—Mr Barker. Read [blank].

13. Sat.

Ch. 8½ AM. Wrote to Mr A.G. Williams[10]—Ld Lyttelton—Mr F.T. Davis—Rev G. Mather[11]—Rev Dr Robinson (Warden T.C.)[12]—Rev H. Solly—Mr A. Grainger[13]—Mr Strahan (Revises)—Rev Dr Case. Revising my C.R. art on Homer and Egypt.[14] Company in aft. Conversation with Ld Selborne[15] on Oxford—And on Burials Bill and Disestablishment. Read Queen of Connaught.

[1] In September 1875 the French government banned the sale at railway stations of the French translation of Gladstone's Vatican pamphlets.
[2] W. Gilbert, *Disestablishment from a Church point of view* (1875).
[3] Probably of Maclean and Pisani, manufacturers in Birmingham and London; but see 22 Dec. 75.
[4] Planning memorial to W. F. *Hook.
[5] Sir Ashley Cooper Key, 1821-88; sailor; planned R.N. college, Greenwich; its president 1872-6.
[6] Presenting prizes to students from 'the schools in a large district of the South of London', *T.T.*, 12 November 1875, 10a. Published as a pamphlet 'Science and Arts, Utility and Beauty', with introduction dated 21 December 1875.
[7] W. W. Lloyd, *The age of Pericles*, 2v. (1875).
[8] Add MS 44762, f. 194.
[9] Mary, wife of J. S. Howson (see 8 Mar. 50).
[10] Of Worksop; sent an axe; Hawn P.
[11] George Mather, 1833-92; curate of St Chad's, Freehay, 1847-87; had sent a pamphlet; Hawn P.
[12] William Percy Robinson, 1836-81; warden of Trinity College, Glenalmond, from 1873.
[13] Allerdale Grainger of Kilburn sent *Labour News* and details of clerical unemployment; Hawn P.
[14] See 4 May 74n.
[15] His only visit; see Selborne, II, i. 366.

14. S. 25 Trin.

Ch. 11 A.M. and 6½ P.M. S.E.G. excellent. Wrote to Prof. Cassania (B.P.)[1]—Mr H.J. Rollo—Mr S. Barnes—Mr R.M. Stuart—Mr J.R. Beck[2]—Rev. G. Elder.[3]— Read Bp of Down's Charge—Scott on Ritualism[4]—Dr Perry's Sermon[5] . . . &c. Conversation with Sir G. P[revost] on Miracles & Future Punishment.

15. M.

Ch. 8½ A.M. Wrote to Bp of Chichester—Bp of Rochester—Sir Thos G.—Mr Goflowsky—Sir T.E. May—Rev. R. Jenkins—Mr W. Smith—Mrs Gordon—Mr Jeans—Ld Lyttelton. 2-6. The marriage dinner.[6] Beautifully got up. The N. School quite full. W. spoke well: G. still better: Selborne made a beautiful speech, though much too laudatory: all was interesting. Long conversation with S. on the Newcastle matters. Also on Slave Trade Circ.[7] And on R. Dee Lands. Worked on Homer. Read Queen of Connaught. Conversation with Sir G. Prevost. Company out, & in.

16. Tu.

Ch. 8½ A.M. Wrote to Mr Tennyson sending him a batch of six versions of his Franklin Epitaph[8]—Mr Knowles—sending him the Latin Hymn[9]—Watsons— Rev Dr Case—Mr Tinsley—J. Jones—Canon Miller—Lord Lyttelton—Mr Cunnington—R.L. Barker—R.G. Sweeting[10]—Shaw Stewart. Walk with Sir C. Anderson. Made a 2d & better Version of the Epitaph. Finished revision of the Latin Hymn & dispatched it. Conv[ersation] of [sc. on] Parl. Retrospect with the party.—The Selbornes went. He has been very genial. Read Queen of Connaught.

17. Wed.

Ch. 8½ A.M. Wrote to Macmillan (B.P.)—Watsons—Mr W. Sears[11]—J.S. Mills[12]— Rev. F. Sterry[13]—Mr A.J. Ritchie—Rev W.T. Allom—W. Denton—F.J. Perry. With a good many hours of work, finished revising the MS of my little Homeric

---

[1] Giacomo Cassani of Bologna, wrote *Delle principali questioni politiche-religiose*, 3v. (1872-6).

[2] Perhaps of C. H. Beck of Nördlingen, publishing the German ed. of *Rome and the newest fashions*; see Max Lossen to diarist, 11 October 1875; Hawn P.

[3] Perhaps George Alder, d. *ca.* 1882; unbeneficed anglican priest.

[4] Probably one of T. *Scott's tracts.

[5] W. S. Perry, 'Anglo-American sympathy with continental reform. A sermon' (1875).

[6] Report of speeches in *T.T.*, 16 November 1875, 10a. Selborne called Gladstone 'for many years . . . the greatest honour, the ornament and the example of that Assembly [the Commons]'.

[7] See Buckle, v. 396.

[8] On Sir John Franklin, arctic explorer; Add MSS 44448, f. 246, 44762, f. 194.

[9] See 13 Oct. 75.

[10] An artist, attempting to set up 'the Gladstone Exhibition' to by-pass 'Dealers and other fraudulent gamblers'; Hawn P.

[11] William Sears, printer's compositor in Greenwich; see Add MS 44448, f. 208.

[12] James Smith Mills, public notary in Dundee, sent verses; ibid., f. 265.

[13] Francis Sterry, rector of Poltimore from 1869.

Volume, & dispatched it, as above. Read Q. of Connaught—Mr Moody's case of Intolerance.[1] A mild attack of diarrhoea.

18. Th. [Chatsworth]

Kept my bed till 10.30. Wrote to Mr T. James—Rev. A. Wright[2]—Rev S. Bentley[3]—Rev J. Gott—R. Grant & Sons—S.D. Ashby—J. Robertson—Mr Beresford Hope—Ld Lyttelton—Rev. S.E.G.—Rev Dr Lowe (Lpool)[4]—C.A. Hardy[5]—L. Henner—J.W. Julian—Woolner—E. Trimmer[6]—Dr Hooker—Mr Salkeld—Mrs Wickham. Off at 12.50. Reached Chatsworth at six. Read Deramey, Précis du Mouvement Cath. Liberal[7]—Farley on decline of Turkey.[8]

19. Fr.

Wrote to Mr Ouvry—Walter Gladstone—Mr W. Forbes—Sir Thos Gladstone. Walk with the Duke & party. Conversation with Sir J. Lacaita[9]—Ld Hartington (political)—and [blank.] Read The Caxtons[10]—Arnobius Adv. Gentes[11]— Finished Farley on Turkey.

20. Sat.

Wrote to Ld Lyttelton—Mr Lavis. Walk with the party. Read Arnobius (with Anal.—More's Answer to Frith[12]—Deramey's Précis. Conversation with Hartington. Conversation with the duke on the Land Bill: with Mr [T. E.] Welby.

21. Preadvent S.

E[de]nsor Ch mg. Service in Chapel 6 P.M. Wrote to Sir T.G.—Rev. S.E.G. Read Arnobius—Sir T. More Apology[13]—Harrison in C.R. on Positivism—Ch. Qu. on Th. of Mopsuestia.[14] Walk with the Party.

[1] Probably one of the moral tales told by D. L. Moody, the American evangelist, in his *London Discourses* (1875).

[2] Arthur Wright, 1836–1909; rector of Coningsby 1873–1913; Tennyson's wife's cousin, on the translations of his verse; see 16 Nov. 75 and Add MS 44448, f. 217.

[3] Samuel Bentley, 1823–1908; rector of St Mary's, Bridgnorth, 1860–79; vicar of Bosbury 1879–97; sent his *Sermons*; Hawn P.

[4] Josiah Beatson Lowe; D.D. 1860; vicar of St Michael, Toxteth, 1875–6; then unbeneficed.

[5] Charles Atwood Hardy had written on the Greenwich address; Add MS 44448, f. 189.

[6] Edward Trimmer, secretary to the Royal College of Surgeons.

[7] J. P. Deramey, *Précis du mouvement Catholique-libéral dans le Jura bernois 1873–74* (1875).

[8] J. L. Farley, *The decline of Turkey financially and politically* (1875); Farley was one of the leaders of the 1876 agitation.

[9] Librarian at Chatsworth; see 13 Nov. 50.

[10] *The Caxtons. A family picture*, 3v. (1849); by *Lytton.

[11] Arnobius, *Adversus Gentes* (1542); Gladstone probably read the 1871 ed. by Bryce and Campbell.

[12] T. More, 'A letter . . . impugnynge the erronyouse wrytyng of John Frith' (1533).

[13] *The apologye of syr Thomas More knyght* (1533).

[14] *Church Quarterly Review*, i. 115 (October 1875), 'Theodore of Mopsuestia and modern thought'; the issue contained his own article, see 16 July 75.

22. M.

Wrote to M.G.–W.L. Gladstone–Lyttelton. Conversation with Hartington. Walk with the party. Read Arnobius–The Caxtons–Foreign–Stubbs Constit. Hist.[1]–La Roumanie.[2]

23. Tu.

Wrote to A. Strahan–Went to Haddan: a second & more careful visit. Back with Mr Welby & Mr Doyle: infinite ambages: arrived just in time to arrest alarm.[3] Conversation with F.C. on politics, respecting electoral systems–With Mr Welby, Turkish Repudiation & Loan of 1855. Read Arnobius–Stubbs Const. Hist.

24. Wed.

Wrote to Watsons–A. Tennyson–Ld Halifax–A. Beresford Hope–Mr Harris– Bp of Chichester. Walk with Duke & Ld Lovelace.[4] Read Arnobius–Fergusson's Tree & Serpent Worship[5]–King on Gems & Precious Stones[6]–Stubbs Const. Hist. Conversation with Mr Gurdon.

25. Th.

Wrote to Mr Jas Wylie[7]–Mr Knowles (Tel.)–Mr A. Strahan–Mr J.T. Bunce. Conversation with C.G. on the Wyllie letter. On the whole I cannot think my son Harry has up to this time been very well used or any great desire shown to redeem the promises expressly or virtually given him. The subject has cost me more care than any other of a temporal nature since the smash of 1847. Walk with the Duke & Lord G. Read Arnobius (finished)–Fergusson Introdn &c.– Stubbs Const. Hist.

26. Fr.

Wrote to Rev F. Caudwell[8]–Mr Jas Lord. Read Fergusson (finished)– Marchese del Cigno[9]–Lord on the British Crown.[10]

In the forenoon we received the amazing news of a purchase outright of the Suez Canal Shares.[11] If true as it seems to be, & if not done in concert with

[1] See 23 Sept. 75n.

[2] Perhaps *Les Principautés Roumaines et l'Empire Ottoman* (1858).

[3] Search parties were preparing; *T.T.*, 26 November 1875, 7f.

[4] See 27 Mar. 41n.

[5] J. Fergusson, *Tree and serpent worship* (1868).

[6] C. W. King, *The natural history of gems and decorative stones* (1867).

[7] The Liverpool merchant (see 23 Jan. 71n., since R. Gladstone's death, in control of Gladstone & Co.) insisted on H. N. Gladstone's recall from India; Thomas, *Gladstone of Hawarden*, 68.

[8] Francis Caudwell, vicar of St Peter's, Hoxton Square, London.

[9] *Sic*; untraced.

[10] J. Lord, *The protestant character of the British Constitution* (1847).

[11] Purchase agreed 23-4 November; 'you have it, Madam', Disraeli told the Queen on 24 November; Buckle, v. 448.

Europe, I fear grave consequences: & I am not in the least degree moved by the storm of approval wh seems to be rising.

2¼-6. To Hickleton: where Halifax took much the same view: also G. Grey.

27. Sat.

Wrote to Mr J. Wyllie, & draft: an anxious letter[1]—Mr Beresford Hope. Much conversation with Halifax & G. Grey chiefly on Suez Canal affair: & with H. on Land Act. Walk with C. Wood: conversation on O[ld] C[atholics]—Public Worship Act—Ld Courtenay. Read March. del Cigno—finished Lord on the British Crown.

28. Adv. S.

Ch 11 AM & 3 P.M. Wrote to Bp of Chichester—Ld Granville—Mr Rickart—Sir J. Watson—Mr Raleigh[2]—Mr E. Levy. Read Mr Main's (admirable Sermon)[3]—The Unseen Universe[4]—Dr Bright's Hymns &c.[5] Hymn-music in evg. Conversation with H. on Land Act. Walk with C.W. & C.G.

29. M.

Wrote to Rev R. Main—Manchr (V. Road) St. Master—Wms & Norgate. Walk with C. Wood & Helen. Read Marchese del Cigno—Stubbs—Raleigh's Wolsey. Whist in evg. Conversation with Ld H.—Mr Church—Lady Grey—Mr C. Wood.

30. Tu. St Andrew. [Hawarden]

Holy Communion at 8.30. We went off at 11 after a warm farewell. At the last moment we changed our route, for particular reasons, on an invitation from Wentworth:[6] and spent three hours there, in active seeing. Both deeply interested in Lady Alice. She & Lady Alb. accompanied us to Wortley. We reached Hawarden at 11½. Rather embarrassed in Manchester by the kindness of friends. Began to open letters.

Wed. Dec. One 1875.

Ch. 8½ A.M. Wrote to Ed. Scottish Guardian—A.H. Louis—Mr Ouvry—Mr Rollo—G. Harris—E. Levy—Mr Cornish—Rev. A. Wright—Rev Mr M'Coll—Rev Mr Dampier[7]—Ld Lyttelton—Ld Wolverton—A. Tennyson—W.L. Gladstone.

---

[1] Final attempt to persuade Wyllie not to recall H. N. Gladstone: 'My father put you on the first step of the ladder; you have put my son into the street'; Thomas, *Gladstone of Hawarden*, 68.

[2] 'Walter L. Raleigh', pen name of S. Stringer Bate, of Newcastle had written, unsuccessfully, to apply to be diarist's private secretary, sending his *Cardinal Wolsey and the love of the poets* (1874); Hawn P.

[3] R. Main, 'A sermon ... preached ... during the meeting of the British Association for the Advancement of Science' (1875).

[4] [P. G. Tait and B. Stewart], *The unseen universe; or, physical speculations on a future state* (1875).

[5] W. Bright, *Hymns and other poems* (1866).

[6] Near Rotherham, seat of the whiggish 6th Earl Fitzwilliam; Alice and Albreda were his unmarried daughters; for Alice and Willy Gladstone, see 26 June, 9 July 75.

[7] Probably William James Dampier, d.1878; vicar of Coggeshall 1841-76.

Worked on opening letters until one—I think in all, with packets, they were 300. Read Green's Hist. Engl. People (began)[1]—The Interior[2]—Turkey & England (Wolfferts)[3]—Wolsey (finished).

2. Th.

Wrote to Harry—on his affairs—J. Allbron[4]—W. Scott—R.G. Sweeting— H. Major[5]—Watsons—Author of 'Qu. of Connaught' [H. Jay]—Lady Herbert— Mrs Heywood—G.M. Mansfield (Autogr.)—W.L. Raleigh—P.E. Eyton—Thos Scott—W. Chevalier[6]—S. Smith. Worked on proofsheets of 'The Time & place of Homer'. Read March. del Cigno—Green's History—Began. Walk & kibbling.

3. Fr.

Ch. 8½ AM. Wrote to W.L. Gladstone—Mr Macmillan—Ld Lyttelton—Bp of Rochester—Capt. of Lancing School[7]—Mr Ouvry—Mr Marsh—Watsons. And sent off a number of copies of the translated Hymn 'Scio te lassum'.[8] Saw Dr Cathie—Jenkins—respecting assault[9]—Roberts, Wellhouse, on the Land Act &c. Read March. del Cigno—Proposal for a new Service.[10]

4. Sat.

Ch. 8½ AM. Wrote to Ed. Reynolds's Newsp.[11]—S.S. Bate = W.L. Raleigh— Messrs T. & Barker—Miss Kortright—Ld Granville—Mr Levy—Mr Pascoe—Mr Brion—Mr F. Scott. Went over the newsp. &c to get through my absence accumulations. Worked on Proofsheets, & wrote on Art in Homer.[12] Read March. del Cigno—Memorial on Turkish Debt—Working Men on Ritualism.[13] Dined at the Rectory.

5. 2 S. Adv.

Ch 11 AM with H.C. and 3 P.M. Wrote to D. of Argyll. Read Bp of Andrews's Speech (all wrong)[14]—E.B. Smith's Appeal[15]—Manning & Redesdale Corresp[16]

---

[1] J. R. Green, *A short history of the English people* (1874).
[2] Perhaps *An interior [a tract on prayer]* (1876).
[3] Baron Fr. von Wolffers, *Turkey's fall the decline of England. A suggestion and a warning* (1875).
[4] John Allbeson, Manchester grocer, on religion; Hawn P.
[5] See 26 Oct. 75.
[6] William Chevalier of Camden Town; an admirer; Hawn P.
[7] C. E. M. Sanderson, d. 1877, s. of the headmaster; probably subscribing to the boys' gymnasium fund.
[8] In the *Contemporary Review*, December 1875, 160.
[9] Incident untraced; perhaps Joseph Jenkins, tenant at Pentrobin.   [10] A tract (1875).
[11] Denying he appointed Stephen Gladstone to the Hawarden living or misused Crown patronage; printed in *T.T.*, 14 December 1875, 7c.
[12] Further work on the *Homeric Thesaurus*, fragments of which were published in the *Contemporary Review*, xxvii. 632, 803 (March–April 1876).   [13] Untraced tract.
[14] C. Wordsworth, 'The General Synod. Why it should be convened at the present time' (1875).
[15] E. B. Smith, 'Appeal ... to the General Assembly of the Presbyterian Church [of the U.S.]' (1875).
[16] J. T. T. Mitford, Lord Redesdale, *The infallible church and the holy communion of Christ's body and blood. Correspondence... with Cardinal Manning*, 2 pt. (1875).

—Debary on Sectaries[1]—Smith on Sponsorship—Prayer—([T.] Scott)—& wrote Propositions.[2] To bed early, for cold.

6. M.

Remained in bed to 3 P.M. Wrote to Mr Townshend—Watsons—Mr de Lisle—Mrs Th.—Mr H.P. Smith[3]—Mr Youngman. Read Boscawen on the Assyrian Inscriptions[4]—Marchese del Cigno. Got up to receive the Jubilee Singers[5] whom we entertained 3½-6 and who richly repaid us by offering to sing. Their John Brown is still noble, almost sublime.

7. Tu.

Again kept bed till 3½. Wrote to Mr Shaw Lefevre—Gen. P. Taylor—Mr Main—Bp of Rochester—Mr Vightoller—Mr J.K. Cross[6]—Messrs Macmillan (Sheets)—Scotts—Mr MacColl. Read March del Cigno—Mr Freeland's Translation &c.[7] Worked on Proof Sheets.

8. Wed.

Rose at 1.30.—C. & H. also were better. Got out a little. Wrote to Mr W.L. Raleigh—J. Canbrough—W.W. Wynne—C.K. Watson—Herbert J.G.—Rev E. Wilberforce—Rev H. Roberts—Sir Thos G.—Mrs M.G. Grey—Dr A. Clark—Rev Mr Holland. Read Green, English History—Marchese del Cigno—Milton on MacColl[8]—Wynne, Corresp. of Great Rebellion.[9]

9. Th.

Rose at 11¼. Out in aft: a few strokes of the axe. Saw Mr Townshend[10] 11½-1½ on Agr. Holdings Act & much else. I am more & more pleased with him. Wrote to Ld Lyttelton—W.L. Gladstone—Messrs G. & Co—Rev. F. Caudwell—Mr Thos Scott—Dean of Windsor—May & Co—Watsons—W.G. Ross.[11] Finished Marchese del Cigno. Read Valussi on Ch. question It.[12] and divers Tracts.

---

[1] T. Debarry, 'Our sectaries. How shall we meet them? A letter to the bishop' (1875).

[2] See 9 Dec. 75.

[3] Henry Percy Smith, vicar of Great Barton, Suffolk, sent his work on sponsorship; Hawn P.

[4] Untraced work by W. St. Chad Boscawen, Assyriologist.

[5] See 14, 29 July 73.

[6] John Kynaston Cross, 1832-87 (suicide); Bolton cotton spinner; liberal M.P. Bolton 1874-85.

[7] H. W. Freeland's tr. of A. Fischhof, *On the reduction of the continental armies*, (1875).

[8] W. Milton, *Fancies and fallacies of the opponents of the Purchas Judgment* (1875).

[9] W. W. E. W[ynne], 'Correspondence during the Great Rebellion', *Archaeologia Cambrensis* (1875), 307.

[10] His agent.

[11] W. G. Ross of Glasgow, who published as Herbert Martyne, had sent his *Poems* (1876); Hawn P.; see 31 Dec. 75.

[12] P. Valussi, *La Parte dello Stato nelle questioni chiesiastiche e specialmente dell'Italia* (1875).

Propositions on Prayer

1. There is One, who foresees.
2. *All* things are foreseen: both the acts of the free agents, and the performances of the unfree.
3. The workings of the unfree, and lower or mechanical agents are adapted and adjusted, to the training of the free (and higher) agents.
4. Prayer in all its parts, sorrowful, trustful, joyful, is, when normally offered according to its idea, healthy and improving for him who prays.
5. Why should not such an exercise enter into the dispensations of God for the creatures, whom He has to train?
6. Why should we be told that God will not alter His modes of action because we wish and ask it?
7. It is not a question of *impromptu* alteration, but of fore-ordered adaptation.
8. In the present, to see a thing is not to cause it. So in the future the simple act of fore-seeing it has nothing to do with bringing it about.
9. If it be said this doctrine of prayer is 'unthinkable' I admit it. But this is only saying that God is greater, and greatly greater, than we are. "His ways are not as our ways, nor His thoughts as our thoughts."
10. To us, who are so little, much is 'unthinkable' or inconceivable that is also matter of daily experience. And (the truly great, even of our own race, such as Homer and Shakespeare, are unthinkable, at least to me) few indeed are the things of which we have any full comprehension.

I submit these propositions for examination.[1]

10. *Fr.*

Rose at 11. Wrote to Rev. H.O. Battenbury[2]—Ld Granville—Ld Halifax—Mrs H. Green—Rev R.W. Deane[3]—Rev W. Arthur[4]—Rev E. Cravath—Mr Macmillan P.S.—Mr J. Wyllie—Mr Hollis—Mr Boscawen[5]—A. Balfour—Mr Mannheimer[6]—Wms & Norgate. Worked on Proof Sheets. Saw Dr Moffatt who reported well of C.s tedious influenza. Read many Tracts.

11. *Sat.*

Rose at one. Wrote to Mr De Lisle B.P.—Vicar of St Martin's B.P.—Edr of British Architect—Archd. Ffoulkes—Sir Thos G.—D. Hillock—W.W. Hunter[7]—S.T. King—R.S. Knight—J.T. Hayes[8]—Reeves & Turner—Rev Mr M'All[9]—Archdn Ewell[10]—C.H. Lake[11]—H. Bembury. Made a walk: but am not yet

---

[1] Initialled and dated 9 December 1875, Add MS 44762, f. 254. Sent to Thomas Scott of Norwood, who sent replies; Add MS 44448, f. 291. See 15 Dec. 75.

[2] Possibly Henry Charles Batterbury, curate in Hillingdon.

[3] Richard Wallace Deane, unbeneficed anglican priest living in Dover, sent Latin hymns; Hawn P.   [4] William Lihon Arthur, curate in Torquay.

[5] William St. Chad Boscawen had sent his book; see 6 Dec. 75n.

[6] Gustav Mannheimer of Schiller & Co., London commission agents.

[7] (Sir) William Wilson *Hunter, 1840-1900; historian of British India; sent his *Life of the Earl of Mayo*, 2v. (1875).

[8] Probably John Thomas Hayes, London publisher of works on church affairs.

[9] Samuel McAll, 1807-88; principal of Hackney college, London, 1860-80; had sent his *Delivery* (1875).

[10] *Sic*, but none of this name traced in Britain or the colonies.   [11] Not traced.

strong. We saw Dr M[offatt]. Read Hunter's Ld Mayo—Hypatia (began)[1]—Misunderstood (began)[2]—Warring's Miracle of Today.[3]

12. 3 S. Adv.

Ch. in mg only. Saw Dr M[offatt] (for C.G.) again. Wrote to Messrs Thomson—Dr Macdonald—Dr Butler—Dr Gordon. Read Dean Howson's strange Book[4]—Bp of Winchester's excellent Pastoral Letter[5]—and [blank.]

13 M.

Rose at 12. Wrote to Ld Hartington—Ld Halifax—M. Valussi[6]—T.N. Barker—R. Martin—E.A. Mavrocordato—Lady Selborne—Rev Mr Milton[7]—Rev Mr A. Wright—Rev Mr W.L. Nichols.[8] Read Misunderstood—Dean Howson's Before the Table—Warring's Miracle of Today. The [J. A.] Godleys came: much conversation with him & examination of verses &c. Felled the tree.

14. Tu.

Rose at 12. Sharp Lumbago in the night: much better, & walked with Godley. Wrote to Walter L. Gladstone—Mr Heywood—Mr J. Wyllie—Mayor of Chester—Dean of do—Bp of Winchester—Rev. C.T.E. Roberts[9]—Rev. Mr Prescot[10]—Mr Pratter—Mr Macmillan—Mr D. Peat—Reeves & Turner—Mr J. Caird—Farrer Ouvry & Co. Read Misunderstood—finished Dean Howson—read Warrings Miracle of today. Walk & much conversation with Godley.

15. Wed.

Rose at 12. Lumbago still hangs about me. Wrote to Mr [T.] Scott of Norwood[11]—Ld Granville—Mr Chesney—Mr Whibley—Messrs Macmillan—Marquis C. Guerrieri Gonzaga—Sir Thos G.—Mr Childers. Walk & divers long conversations with Godley: on Homer: on my answers to Scott's objections respecting Prayer. Read Macmillan's Mag. on Turkish Repudiations—Warring, Miracle—Morgan, Fairy Tales—Misunderstood, finished: very clever, far from satisfactory. Saw S.E.G. on Church matters.

---

[1] C. *Kingsley, *Hypatia. A romance* (1863).
[2] F. Montgomery, *Misunderstood. A tale* (1869).
[3] C. B. Warring, *Strike but hear me . . . the miracle of today* (1875).
[4] J. S. Howson, 'Before the table. An inquiry' (1875).
[5] E. H. Browne, 'The position and parties of the English Church. A pastoral letter' (1875).
[6] Pacifico Valussi, Italian author; see 9 Dec. 75.
[7] Thanking William Milton, vicar in Sheffield, for his book (see 8 Dec. 75), and criticizing his conclusions on the Eucharist; Add MS 44448, f. 288.
[8] William Luke *Nichols, 1802-89; vicar of Buckland-Monachorum; antiquarian.
[9] Charles Edward Thornes Roberts, schoolmaster and vicar of Brinsley.
[10] George Frederick Prescott, 1827-1917; vicar of St Michael, Paddington, 1864-1913.
[11] i.e. the free-thinker; see 16 May 55, 5 Dec. 75.

Proposition on Prayer. Reply to objections.

a. Unquestionably No 1 is an assumption: viz. of what I believed we had in common. It seemed therefore our proper starting point: & as legitimate as my assumption of the laws of grammar. I likewise assume free agency: for the present.

b. I take to myself the whole blame of the mistakes on which the rest of the Paper of objections is founded: they must be due to the faults of expression and arrangement in the Propositions, they predicate universal fore-seeing. They predicate foreordering of all that is produced by an unfree instrumentality. They predicate nothing except fore-seeing as to the acts of the free agents. They nowhere suggest that God may alter His modes of action: but rather they complain of the charge which imputes such suggestion to the Argument for Prayers. They assume I admit a moral Governor, a foreordering, as well as a foreseeing God: and upon the like ground.

c. There remains the objection, that it is better to hear a preacher than to pray. Why not both? To lay a philosophical basis for prayer I must show it to be reasonable, useful: I am not bound to show it to be the only thing reasonable and useful, or even to point out all its reasons and uses. Nor do I undertake, in exhibiting adequate ground of Prayer, to cover[?] *obiter* all the difficult problems of our state & destiny. I think it best to exhibit a narrow front; and will not now touch the origin of Evil.[1]

16. Th.

Rose at 11.30. Wrote to J. Watson & Smith—Mr Heywood—Mr Kelso—G. Harris—J. Wyllie—Mr Strahan—Macmillans (P. sheets)—H.N. Gladstone—Miss Morgan[2]—Lady Bell[3]—Dean of Chester—Mr Jermyn—Mr Ouvry. Kibbling a little. Read Morgan's Fairy Tales—The Unseen Universe—Dublin Rev. on Anglicanism—scurrilous braggadocio.[4] Began Correcting Greenwich Address.[5] Worked on Homeric Proofsheets.

17. Fr.

Up at 11.15. Wrote to Lord J. Manners—C.F. Whale[6]—Mr Tennyson—C. Lyttelton—Mr Mavrocordato—Mr Macmillan—Rev. Mr Milton—Rev Mr Churton[7]—Mr W. Brough. Worked on Greenwich Address & read on the subject of it. Dr A. Clark came. Conversation as usual on questions of philosophy. Mr Wilberforce came.[8] Read Morgan—Dean Howson—The Unseen Universe—The Miracle of today.

18. Sat.

Down to breakfast. Wrote to Mr Shaw—Sir Thos G.—Mr Hopwood—Mr Kelso. Worked on Greenwich Address. Wrote Mem. on Harry's Case.[9] Walk with Mr Wilberforce—Dr Clark—Mr Godley—and made conversation with Dr Clark.

[1] Initialled and dated 15 December 1875, Add MS 44762, f. 255. See 9 Dec. 75.
[2] Had sent her book, see 15 Dec. 75.
[3] Perhaps the wife of Sir Sydney Smith Bell, 1805–75; judge at the Cape 1868–79; kt. 1869.
[4] [T. W. M. Marshall], *Dublin Review*, xxv. 342 (October 1875).
[5] See 11 Nov. 75.
[6] Perhaps a relation of the Greenwich liberal; see 4 June 75.
[7] Henry Burgess Whitaker Churton, author and vicar of Icklesham from 1844.
[8] Probably E. R. Wilberforce.
[9] Hawn P; see 25 Nov. 75.

Read Miracle of today—Dean Howson Before the Table—MacColl, Preface to 3d Edn.[1]

19. 4 S. Adv.

Ch mg & H.C. Prohibited in evg. Wrote to Mr Strahan—Mr Thos Scott—Lady Bell—Mr A. Kelso—Mr Rigeston—Mr MacColl. Read MacColl's Pref. (finished)—S.E.G.s Letter—Bp Mackarness's Charge[2]—Miracle of Today—The Unseen Universe.

20. M.

Down to breakfast. Wrote to Mr MacColl—Mr Heywood—Mr F. Ouvry—Mr Stubbings—Mr Mills. Our guests went: Dr A. C[lark] & Mr G[odley] no common ones. In the woods with Willy. Worked hard & long on my Proofs of Greenwich Address, and on the Additional Matter. Read Ariston[3]—Miracle of Today—and Guido and Lita.[4]

21. Tu. St Thomas

Ch. 8¾ AM. Normal! Wrote to Mr K. Jagger[5] (B.P.)—Watsons (B.P.)—R. Martin—T.W. Hancock—J.A. Bourne[6]—Jas Foley[7]—R. Martin—W.T. Vincent[8]—Jas Tennant—E.A. Mavrocordato—Mr Grothin B.P.[9]—Messrs Strahan—Maj. Donnelly[10]—J.B. Winsor—R.H. Dunbar—H.M. Gilbert—Ld Granville—Mr A. Kelso—Dr Cazenove BP.—Mr Robson. Finished Greenwich Proofs for Mr Strahan. Cutting with Willy. Read Green, Engl. People—Miracle of Today—finished—Ariston.

22. Wed.

Off at 8 to Liverpool. Wrote to Sir Thos G.—Mr [W.] Hepworth Dixon—Mr F. Monk. Saw Bishop of Chester—Mr Kelso—do *cum* Mr Heywood—Mr Harris—Walter G.—Robn G. I went away from Lpool at 2 with much sadness on many grounds.[11] Saw Mayor of Chester & Mr Kelly. Read Deane on Serpent Worship[12]—R.C. on Vaticanism[13]—Pisani, Religioni e Stati.[14]

[1] See 22 June 75.
[2] By G. R. Mackarness (1875).
[3] *Ariston. A tragedy in five acts* (1870).
[4] Untraced.
[5] Newcastle estate affairs.
[6] Perhaps John Robert Bourne, London solicitor.
[7] Perhaps Joseph William Foley, d. 1890; Dublin solicitor; home rule M.P. New Ross 1880-90.
[8] Perhaps William Thomas Vincent, registrar in Plumstead.
[9] Reading uncertain.
[10] Major John Donnelly of Onslow Crescent, London.
[11] H. N. Gladstone's affairs; see 25, 27 Nov. 75.
[12] J. B. Deane, *The worship of the serpent* (1830).
[13] *Papal infallibility... by a Roman Catholic* (1876).
[14] Untraced work, probably by C. Ferri-Pisani.

23. Th.

Ch. 8½ A.M. Wrote to Harry—after consideration—Mr Wyllie—(& copy to H.)—Mr Macmillan—Mr Newton—Mr Veasey—Watsons (B.P.)—Bp of Chester (BP.)—Ferrier—Peek—Mr Girard. Finished correction of proofs of Homer's Date & Place. Treecutting with W. Read Bölticher Baumcultus der Hellenen[1]—Deane on Serpent Worship—R.C. Layman on Def. of Vatican Council.

24. Fr.

Ch. 8½ A.M. Wrote to Sec. Reform Club—Sec. Statistical Society—Duke of Westminster—Rev Mr Henderson—Rev Dr Cazenove—Lord J. Manners—Mr C.D. Cobham[2]—W. Regester[3]—Mr Powell—W.S. Aldis—J.A. Godley—Vickers. Wrote 'Notice' for C.Q.R.[4] Read Watts on Working Man[5]—St James's Mag. on Suez Canal & Falk Laws[6]—Trabucco's Address[7]—Deane's Serpent Worship—Jackson Bampt. Lecture I.[8] W. & I brought down a large Wych Elm.

25. Sat. Xm. Day.

Church 11 A.M. & H.C.—Also 7 P.M. Wrote to Q. Mast. Serj. Phippen[9]—Mr Lawrence—Mr Tirner—G. Brooks—Mr Middlehurst—P.M. General[10]—Dr Butler—Mrs Th. Saw Mr Prince. Conversation with Herbert on his future destination. Read Jackson on Retribution—Hancock's very notable Vol. Christ & the People[11]—Report of Oxford Delegacy[12]—Robinson on the Apocalypse.[13]

26. S. aft Xm.

Ch 11 AM & 7 PM. Wrote to Countess of Beauchamp[14]—Mr C.M. Gaskell—Mr Jackson—Mr A. Strahan (BP.)—Mr M'Coll—Ed. Architect.[15] Read Hancock's Vol.—Irons on [blank]—Roussel Nat. Cath. et Prot.[16] Corrected Revises of Paper on Beauty & Utility.

---

[1] C. G. W. Boetticher, *Der Baumkultus der Hellenen* (1856).

[2] C. Delavel Cobham of Honiton, on Venetian dialect; Hawn P.

[3] Not traced.

[4] Probably the anon. notice of a 'Roman Catholic' on *Papal infallibility* (which he had just read, see 22 Dec. 75), in *Church Quarterly Review*, i. 509 (January 1876).

[5] J. Watts, 'The working man: a problem. A lecture' (1875).

[6] Not found; British Library copy destroyed by Hitler's bombs.

[7] By G. Trabucco to the Societa Toscanà di Scienze Naturali; *Atti*, xiii (1875).

[8] W. Jackson, *The doctrine of retribution. Eight lectures* (1875).

[9] Business untraced.

[10] Lord John Manners.

[11] T. Hancock, *Christ and the people. Sermons* (1875).

[12] *Annual report of delegacy of non-collegiate students* (1875).

[13] W. Robinson, *Exposition of the Book of Revelation* (1875).

[14] Mary, *née* Stanhope, wife of 6th Earl Beauchamp; she d. 1876.

[15] Presumably a reply, not found published, to letter of C. P. Thomas of Chicago attacking Gladstone's remarks on American taste in the Greenwich address (see 11 Nov. 75); *The Architect*, 25 December 1875, 373; see also ibid. 15 January 1876, 36.

[16] See 3 July 75.

27. M. St John

Ch. 8¾ A.M. Wrote to Prof. Sheldon Amos—Professor Stubbs[1]—Sir Thos G.—Mr Middlehurst (Telegr.)—Mr Godley of Newark[2]—Duke of Argyll—Wms & Norgate. Worked on Revises of new Homeric Volume or Volumet. Saw the Grosvenors: she is really charming in manners. Tea with Mrs Burnett. Wood cutting. Read Lyte's Hist. Eton[3]—Brzoska de Hom. Mundi Imagine.[4]

28. Tu. H. Innoc.

Ch. 8¾ AM. Wrote to M. Vladimir Jovanovics[5]—Rev. J. Mason[6]—Mr Macmillan—T.B. Potter MP—Mr Hussey Vivian MP—Mr Strahan—L. Fry.[7] Framed Table of Contents for my new Vol. Read 'Temperance'—Lyte's Hist. Eton.—Deane on Serpent Worship. Wood cutting with W.

29. Wed.

Ch. 8½ AM. Wrote to Prof. Timotheus Thea[8]—Anon. at D. Mail O. Brighton[9]—Mr T.B. Potter—Mrs Caithbell—Rev. Mr Ingram—Mr S. Wulff[10]—Mr W.S.H. Child—Mrs Th.—Mr Vickers. Fourteen to dinner. Felled a tree. Read Lyte's Hist. of Eton—and sorting tracts and papers.

The year has been an important one, & not only on account of its abundance, as usual, in opportunities & in failures. In the great business of unwinding the coil of life & establishing my freedom I have made some progress by resigning the leadership, selling my House (needful for pecuniary reasons) and declining public occasions. But more has yet to be done. To minimise my presence in London is alike needful for growth, for my work, for the great duty & business of solemn recollection & preparation.

I hope my polemical period is over. It has virtually occupied over a twelvemonth: but good has been done, especially in Italy. Benedictus benedicat: Benedicto benedicatur. Ita ero peccatorum semper miserrimus.[11]

30. Th.

Ch. 8½ AM. Wrote to Mr Macmillan (BP)—Watsons—Ld Granville (BP)—H.J.G.—Williams & Co—Mr [G.] Grove[12]—Townshend & B.—Ld Halifax—Mr

---

[1] Thanking him for the second volume; Hutton, *Stubbs*, 95.
[2] George Godley; sending reminiscences of the 1832 campaign, later read out to Newark bellringers; *T.T.*, 17 November 1876, 9b.
[3] H. C. M. Lyte, *A history of Eton College, 1440–1875* (1875).
[4] H. G. Brzoska, *De geographia mythica specimen I. Commentationem de Homerica mundi imagine* (1831).
[5] See 1 Apr. 63.
[6] Perhaps John Mason, vicar of Fir Tree, Darlington.
[7] Architect of Tunbridge Wells, on architectural guilds; Hawn P.
[8] Of Patras, on the death of Abp. Lykourgos; Add MS 44448, f. 251.
[9] Obscure.
[10] Had written on a project to 'retry the faith of Christendom'; Gladstone advised against it; Add MS 44448, f. 349.
[11] 'So I go on, always the most wretched of sinners.'
[12] Who had unsuccessfully asked him to review Lyte's *Eton* in *Macmillan's Magazine*; Add MS 44448, f. 345.

Doherty—Mr Manry—Mr Hubbard. Saw Mrs Peake—Mr B. Potter. Walk with Mr Morgan (of Rhyl). Read Brodrick on Univ. Reform[1]—Lyte's History of Eton—M [blank] on Dante.[2] Arranging papers & letters.

31. Fr.

Ch. 8½ AM. Wrote to Mr Grove—Mr Wynn BP—Messrs Pears Logan & Co—Mrs Swift—Mr Pullen[3]—Dr Birch—Rev Mr Gill—Mr Engstrom[4]—Mr Macmillan—Dean of Canterbury—Sir Thos G.—and, on Harry's affairs, to J. Wyllie (& copy)—A. Kelso. Saw Mr Barker sen. Kibbling with Herbert. Read Lyte's Eton—Herbert Martyne's Poems.[5]

And so I bid farewell to the year. May the next be of purer & holier Retrospect.

Drew roughly my annual sketch of Property & Debts.[6] The position last year was indifferent. The measures lately taken have materially improved it.

[1] See 17 Feb. 66.

[2] Perhaps L. Marii, *Dante e la libertà moderna* (1865); the name of this day's correspondent is uncertain.

[3] Arthur Giles Pullen sent his 'Notes on a journey to Australia and round the world . . . a lecture at High Cross, 5 November 1875' (1875); Hawn P.

[4] Charles Robert Lloyd Engström had sent his *The claim and the claimant* (1875).

[5] See 9 Dec. 75n.

[6] Hawn P.

Sat. Jan 1. 1876. Circumcision.

Ch. 8¾ AM. Wrote to Sir Geo. Prevost—Mr Ouvry—H.J. Ladd[1]—Jas Caird—A. Jervise[2]—Gen. Schenck[3]—Mr Hursley—Dr M. Guastalla[4]—J. Fraser. Read Lyte's Eton—Lesseps's Lecture on Suez Canal[5]—and Babington on Macaulay.[6] Wood-cutting with W. & H.

2. 2 S Xm.

Ch 11 A.M. with H.C. and 6½ PM. Wrote to Mr J.E. Alexander—M. Victor Oger—Dr MacGill—Robert Gladstone—Archbp of Armagh. Read Abp of A. Charge—Babington on Macaulay (finished)—Jackson B. Lecture IV (I really can go no further)[7]—Stoughton's Hist Ch. of Eng.[8]—and Tracts. Long & stiff conversation on Prayer with E. Wickham.

3. M.

Ch. 8¼ AM. Wrote to Miss Marsh (*and* BP)—T.B. Potter—Ld Lyttelton—E.K. Hamilton—Mr Aronsberg—Mr Macmillan (B.P.)—J.S. James—E. Wirz[9]—Watsons. Worked on revises &c. Also on arranging papers: alack very partially. Kibbling.—Worked on Revises. W. & G. had 5 PM tea with me. Read Deane on S. Worship[10]—Ancient Symbol Worship[11]—Pullen, Austral. Lecture.[12]

4. Tu.

Ch. 8¼ AM. Wrote to Mr Max Freund[13]—J.R. Herbert—J.A. Godley—C.A. Hardy (Belief)[14]—Rev. Mr M'Coll—Rev. Mr Milman. Worked on Revises. Rent dinner 3¾-5¼: & spoke, principally on Agric. Holdings Act.[15] Long conversation with Mr

[1] Possibly Henry Ladd, published on temperance.

[2] Andrew Jervise, Scottish antiquarian; see 24 Jan. 76.

[3] Expressing desire to get, with Fish's support, his 'explanation' of the events of the 1860s published in America (see 28 Nov. 72, 19 Aug. 76); Add MS 44449, f. 3.

[4] Marco Guastalla, Italian living in London, had written on Vaticanism; Hawn P.

[5] F. M. de Lesseps, 'The history of the Suez Canal . . . from a lecture in April 1870' (1876).

[6] C. Babington, *Mr Macaulay's character of the clergy in the latter part of the seventeenth century considered* (1849).

[7] See 24 Dec. 75.

[8] See 5 Apr. 74.

[9] G. E. Wirz corresponded on tr. of English hymns into German; Hawn P.

[10] See 22 Dec. 75.

[11] Perhaps [T. Carlyle, Q.C.], *On symbols in worship* (1853).

[12] See 31 Dec. 75.

[13] Of Gower Street, London, sent E. Koppel's *Savonarola*; Hawn P.

[14] On Bp. Butler, Lathbury, ii. 101.

[15] No account found.

Townshend. Read Deane, Serp. Worship—Russell on Macbeth[1]—Cry for National Harbours.[2]

5. *Wed.*

Wrote to Mrs Pennant—Mr Ouvry—Sir Thos G.—Mrs Owen—Mr Cove—Mr Hopkey—Duke of Argyll—Mayor of Leicester[3]—Marquis Guerrieri—The Speaker—Mr Edwards. Wood chopping in aft. Worked on Revises. Read Deane, Serp. Worship—Symbol Worship—Napper on Ritual.[4]

6. *Th. Epiph.*

& dearest C's birthday. At 64 she has the vigour & freshness of 34. Ch. 8¾ P.M. Wrote to Dr Birch—Mr Knowles—Mr Barber—Mr Werninck[5]—Rev. J.M. Ashley[6]—Rev. G. Purcell[7]—Rev. A.J. Ingram. Dined at the Rectory. Worked on revises of "The Date & place of Homer". finished them. Read Deane—Barber on Education[8]—Butt on Home Rule[9]—Theod. Martin's Catullus, & Preface.[10]

7. *Fr.*

Ch. 8½ A.M. Herbert's birthday: God bless him, a fine fellow, most lovable. Wrote to Ld Lyttelton—J.C. Cox[11]—Mr Merrill—F. Ouvry—Mr Beresford Hope—Sir W. Stephenson—The Rector—Mrs Jackson—Rev. A. Bolland[12]—A. Von Studnitz[13]—Watsons. Saw Lizzie Waters[14] on her affairs. Went to Aston Colliery to see the new operations. Worked on Homer. Read Deane on S. Worship—Purcell on the Church[15]—Queen Elisabeth's Injunctions[16]—Formby's Lectures.[17] Mr Gurdon came: political conversation with him.

8. *Sat.*

Ch. 8½ AM. Re-corded my axe. Wrote to Archbp of Dublin—Rev. C. Tondini— Mr Sampson—Rev. J.R. Gregg—M. d'Eichthal—Mr Theodore Martin. Woodcutting with W & H. Worked on Homer. Read Hist. Guibord Case[18]—Deane on Serpent Worship—Purcell, Stone upon Stone.

[1] E. R. Russell, 'The true Macbeth. A paper' (1875).   [2] Untraced pamphlet.

[3] William Barfoot; on a speech; Hawn P; see 18 May 76.

[4] Perhaps W. Napper, *An exposition of the doctrine of the united Church of England concerning regeneration and baptism* (1843).

[5] Perhaps Henry Werninck of Leipzig; international stamp dealer.

[6] John Marks Ashley, 1828-1909; vicar of Fewston 1873-1900; wrote on theology and science.

[7] Goodwin Purcell, curate of Charlesworth.

[8] W. C. Barber, *The religious difficulty in national education* (1875).

[9] I. Butt, *Home government for Ireland. Irish federalism* (1874).

[10] T. Martin, *The poems of Catullus* (1861).

[11] John Charles Cox, 1843-1919; anglican (later Roman) priest; ecclesiastical historian.

[12] Arthur Bolland, d. 1889; vicar of St. Thomas', Leeds 1859-77.

[13] Arthur von Studnitz, German economist; his *Gold* was tr. (1876).

[14] Of the household.

[15] G. Purcell, *Stone upon stone and Church management in the present day* (1874).

[16] Perhaps *Queen Elizabeth's opinion concerning Transubstantiation* (ed. 1688).

[17] H. Formby, probably *Sacrum Septuarium; or the seven gifts of the Holy Ghost* (1874).

[18] J. Guibord, *History of the Guibord Case* (1875).

9. 1 S. Epiph.

Ch. 11 A.M. and 6½ P.M. Wrote to Mr Grogan—Mr Worsley—Messrs Barker—
Mr G. Wilberforce. Read Lea on Spiritualties Oath[1]—Engstrom on the Claim[2]—
Abp of Dublin's Charge—Pearce on the Diaconate[3]—and Scott Tracts.

10. M.

Ch. 8½ AM. Wrote to Mr C. Townshend (2)—Miss Linskill[4]—Mr Maitland—
Messrs MacDougall (Canada).[5] Long conversation with Mr T[ownshend] on
divers matters: ending in an instruction to offer 25 m[ille] for the Spencer or
Queensferry property.[6] Worked on Executorship affairs. Read Guibord Case
(finished)—Morehead on Dante[7]—Life of Sachs[8]—Deane's Serpent Worship
(finished). Worked a little on Dante Translation. And a little on Hom[eric]
Thes[aurus].

11. Tu.

Ch. 8½ AM. Wrote to Mr Strahan—Mr Hooper—Mr Slack—Mr Ouvry—Mr
Thorne—Rev. C. Mortlock[9]—Sir Thos G.—G. Moffatt—F.H. Fowler.[10] Read
Pamphlets—Ross, Experience of an Abolitionist.[11] Worked on Thes. Hom.
Felled a beech with W. & H. at Hawarden's Hayes. Dinner party. (Toothach).

12. Wed.

Ch. 8½ AM. Wrote to Baroness Burdett Coutts—Mr Gledhill[12]—Mr Grogan—J.
Griffiths—F.H. Fowler—Scotts—Rev A. Wright—Rev H.R. Baker[13]—Mr Kil-
patrick—Mr Dickinson. Saw S.E.G. on divers matters. Mrs Stume on her affairs.
Walk with E.W. Conversation on Homer, and Oxford. Worked on Thes. Hom.
Read Experiences of Abolitionist—Purcell on Church work. The Grosvenors
dined. Hoarseness in evg.

13. Th.

Kept my bed till dusk. Wrote to Macmillans (B.P.)—Mrs Th.—Mr C.T. Newton—Mr C. Hill[14]—Messrs Hoare—Mr Grogan—Mr Marcy Solr. Read Mr Heron

---

[1] J. W. Lea, *The Bishops' "Oath of homage"* (1875).
[2] C. R. L. Engström, *The claim and the claimant* (1875); on Tichborne.
[3] Z. Pearce, probably *The Dean of Winchester, his character of the English clergy* (1742).
[4] Mary Linskill, 1840-91; novelist; had sent her *Cleveden*; Add MS 44449, f. 23.
[5] Business untraced.
[6] Apparently an unsuccessful offer; the estate was auctioned in Chester on 9 and 10 August 1876.
[7] R. Morehead, *Poetical epistles and specimens of poetical translation, particularly from Petrarch and Dante* (1864).
[8] Perhaps H. Leupold, *Hans Sachs aus Nürnberg* (1876).
[9] Charles Mortlock, d. 1906?; vicar of Pennington 1851-1903.
[10] Francis H. Fowler, member for Lambeth of the Metropolitan Board of Works.
[11] A. M. Ross, *Recollections and experiences of an abolitionist from 1855 to 1865* (1875).
[12] Perhaps James Tidswell Gledhill, London wool factor.
[13] Hugh Ryves Baker, curate in Woolwich.
[14] See 15 Feb. 75; on sabbatarianism, reported in *T.T.*, 15 January 1876, 9f.

on Suez Canal[1]—Purcell's Church Work (finished)—Ross's Exp. of Abolition-ist—Chamberlain on Burials Bill[2]—Russell's 'True Macbeth'.[3] Finished work on Revises.

14. Fr.

Rose at 11½. Wrote to C.G.—Watsons—Hon A.M. Ross (Can)[4]—Mr Brough—Reeves & Turners—Mr Ouvry—Mr E.R. Russell—Mrs Th.—Mr Dowland—Mr Lawson. Read Gregson Lanc Fragments[5]—Ross's Recollections &c. (finished)—The Old Bible (ἀ ... ὡ)[6]

15. Sat.

Rose same time: but out in the afternoon. Read Grote, Essays on Mor. Phil.[7]—Gallenga, Italy revisited.[8] Played Gobang in evg. Wrote to Mr Newton (B. Mus.)—Mr Jackson—Mr Joy (Seul poss [sic])—Watsons—Mr Baverstock—C.G.—Mr Brandis[9]—Mr Thorne—Mr Cox.

16. 2 S. Epiph.

Ch 11 AM with H.C. and 6½ P.M. Wrote to Mr Macmillan—Mr W. Mason—Mr De Lisle—Mr Brownlee[10]—Captain Battersby—Lord De Tabley—Mr Sandys—Mr MacGregor—Rev. Mr Hobson[11]—Rev. W.T. Nicholson.[12] Read Hook's Life of Abp Laud[13]—Sursum Corda X[14]—Hobson on Vestments—Nicholson on Sources of Unbelief—Formby on Rome[15]—and other Tracts. Preparing for departure.

17. M. [Hagley]

Off at 8½. Hagley at 1¼. A large party: & concert in the evg. In aftn we attacked the great dead elm. Conversation with E. Talbot on E.W.s view of Prayer: on which we agreed. Wrote to Mr Grogan—Mrs Th. Read Eichthal on Genesis[16]

---

[1] R. M. Heron, 'The Suez Canal question ... a letter' (1875).

[2] W. Chamberlain, 'The case against the Burials Bill ... a paper' (1875).

[3] Sent (see 4 Jan. 76) by Edward Richard Russell, 1834-1920, formerly reporter on the *Star* (see 26 Feb. 69); ed. *Liverpool Daily Post* from 1869; liberal M.P. Glasgow (Bridgeton) 1885-7; published widely on Shakespeare; kt. 1893; cr. Baron 1919.

[4] Alexander Milton Ross, Canadian naturalist, had sent his book; see 11 Jan. 76.

[5] Possibly S. Gregson, 'Speech ... at the Royal North Lancashire Agricultural Society' (1855).

[6] E. Wynne, *The Old Bible, Martyr's gift* (1875).

[7] A. Bain, ed., *Fragments on ethical subjects by the late George Grote* (1876).

[8] A. C. N. Gallenga, *Italy revisited*, 2v. (1875).

[9] Presbyterian minister in Göttingen, had written at length on Vaticanism; Hawn P.

[10] William Brownlie of the Y.M.C.A. in Glasgow; had sent pamphlets; Hawn P.

[11] William Francis Hobson, d. 1892; chaplain of Faversham almshouses 1870-81; had sent his *Vestments and Law* (1875).

[12] William Trevor Nicholson, vicar of St. Benedict, Norfolk, had sent his *Thoughts on the remoter sources of modern unbelief* (1876).

[13] See 21 Feb. 75.　　　　　　　　[14] Perhaps F. E. Paget, *Sursum Corda* (1859).

[15] H. Formby, *The little book of the martyrs of the city of Rome* (1876?).

[16] One of various essays on the Pentateuch by G. d'Eichthal, ed. posthumously as *Mélanges de Critique Biblique* (1886).

—Chambers on Edinburgh[1]—Life of Bp. Gray[2]—Lns Address to the Young Men.[3]

18. Tu.

Wrote to Mr O. Hart[4]—Messrs T. and B.—Mr Hine—Sir A. Panizzi. Read Life of Bp. Gray—Chambers—Eichthal. Walk & conversation with G. Music. Worked on Hom. Mythol. Much disturbance & consultation upon an extraordinary letter to C. from G. Pennant.[5] We brought down the great elm: 15 or 16 feet round, by the usual measurement. A grand fall.

19. Wed.

Wrote to Helen G.—Mr M'Coll—Ld Granville—Mr Knowles—Mr Ouvry Tel.—Mr A. Peel—Rev. Mr Mountain[6]—Mr G. Douglas Pennant, (and draft): not without much consideration and counsel on a subject very painful & if possible yet more strange. Conversation with E. Talbot. He is excellent: & will make a mark. Walk with G. We felled a tree. Read Life of Bp Gray—D'Eichthal on Genesis.

20. Th. [London]

Wrote to . . . DC—Captain Donnithorne.[7] Off at 12.45. Suffolk St at 7.[8] Journey & talk of old Eton times with Sir G. Lewis. Dined with Mrs Th. Saw Mr Hayward. Saw divers. Read Bp Gray—Chambers Edinb.—finished D'Eichthal.

21. Fr.

Wrote to C.G.—Townshend & Barker. A long round. Went with Mr Grogan to Houses in Albemarle St—Dover Street—Harley Street.[9] Saw Miss Balfour—Sir W. Farquhar—Mr Irvine—Ld Granville—Ld Acton—Sir A. Panizzi—Scotts—Mr Macmillan—Mr Ouvry—Mr Stansfeld—do *cum* Mr Mason. Dined with the Wortleys. In G[rosvenor] Square after. Read Chambers—Memoirs of D. of Cumberland.[10]

22. Sat. [Hawarden]

Wrote to Mr Aston—Madam Minghetti—Baroness Burdett Coutts. Worked on Chaos of papers at 4 C[arlton] G[ardens].[11] Saw Mr Knowles—Lady Lyttelton—

[1] R. Chambers, *Traditions of Edinburgh* (1869 ed.).
[2] H. L. Farrer, *Life of R. Gray, Bishop of Cape Town*, 2v. (1876).
[3] G. W. Lyttelton, 'Address to young men . . . November 1875' (1875).
[4] John O'Hart of Dublin sent his book; Hawn P; see 29 Jan. 76.
[5] While staying at Penrhyn Castle, Mrs Gladstone inquired of the maid whether her niece, Gertrude Pennant, was pregnant (she was); Pennant sent a letter containing what Gladstone called 'contemptuous vituperation'; Gladstone's strong reply elicited an explanation of the Pennants' desire for secrecy and the incident was smoothed over; Hawn P.
[6] Probably James Mountain, Free Church hymnist and writer.
[7] Edward George Donnithorne, 1842-1906; of the Scots Greys.
[8] Probably Grieve's Hotel in Suffolk Street.
[9] See 8 Feb. 76.
[10] *Historical memoirs of William Augustus, Duke of Cumberland* (1767).
[11] A. J. Balfour's house; Balfour was abroad.

Sir A. Panizzi. Read Ed. Rev. on Suez Canal—Memoirs of Duke of Cumberland. Saw Miss Balfour. Left by 5.10 Train. Hn at 11¾. Worked on papers accumulated.

23. 3 S. Epiph.

Ch. 11 AM & Wrote to Hon & Rev. W. Lyttelton—Rev D. Howell—Rev J. Dawson[1]—Mrs Th. (B.P.)—Mr Morrell—Mrs Robertson—Watsons—Mr Douglas Pennant—after consideration and conference with C. & Mary. Read Father Damen's Lecture[2]—Misgivings & Convictions[3]—Rowton on Science & the Bible[4]—Clarke on Maryland Toleration—Byles on Principles of Religion[5]—Moral der Jesuiten[6]—Popery weighed &c.[7]

24. M.

Ch. 8½ AM. Wrote to R.C. Publn Socy (N. York)[8]—Rev. Mr Nicholson—Rev. Mr Symington[9]—Canon Ashwell[10]—Ld Granville—Sir Jas Watson—Mr Macdonnell—W.B. Gurdon—F.E. Abbot[11]—Mr Shirreff[12]—Jas Whyte—A. Kelso—G. Moffatt. Saw Mr Townshend on Q[ueen's] F[erry] offer, Resid. Estate account, Estate Deficit, &c.—Mr [C. S.] Parker[13] on Harry's predicament. Worked on arranging papers & Bills. We felled a tree in aftn. Read Walker on Egypt[14]—Jervise Scottish Epitaphs.[15]

25. Tu. Conv. St Paul.

Ch 8¾ AM. Wrote to Mr Macmillan—Mr Boothroyd—Mr Skinner (U.S.)[16]—Bp Mackenzie—Rev. Mr Blakiston—Rev. H.N. Oxenham—Dr Nicol[17]—Ivall & Large—Mr Dauval—Mr Hoyle[18]—Mr West. Conversation with Mr P[arker] on Land Laws. We felled an ash at C. Orchard. Read Ital. Version of Clodds:[19]

---

[1] John Dawson, d. 1913; vicar of St Peter's, Bristol, 1876-80.

[2] A. Damen, 'Lecture . . . the Catholic Church the only true Church of God' (1875).

[3] Pamphlets on catholicism published as 'No I Misgivings' 'No II Convictions' (1876).

[4] W. Rowton, 'Science's quarrel with the Bible. Two lectures' (1876).

[5] J. B. Byles, *Foundations of religion in the mind and heart of man* (1875).

[6] Perhaps a German ed. of S. J. du Cambout de Pont-Château, *La morale pratique des Jésuites* (1669).

[7] Anon., *Popery weighed in the balances and found wanting* (1840?).

[8] Founded 1866 by Isaac Thomas Heckley (1819-88, Roman catholic convert and pro-Infallibilist) for proselytizing Mass among Protestants.

[9] Alexander Macleod Symington; published for the Religious Tract Society.

[10] Arthur Rawson Ashwell, 1824-79; canon of Chichester; co-author of *Life of S. Wilberforce*.

[11] Francis Ellingwood Abbot, 1836-1903; Unitarian theologian, living in Boston, U.S.A., from 1873; see 3 Mar. 76.

[12] W. M. Shirreff, clerk of the Turner's Company; see 16 Feb. 76.

[13] Staying at the Castle; Hawn. Visitors Book.

[14] A. D. Walker, *Egypt as a health resort* (1873).

[15] A. Jervise, *Epitaphs and inscriptions from burial grounds and old buildings in the north-east of Scotland*, 2v. (1875-9).

[16] Edward J. Skinner, of First National Bank, Baltimore, had written on Vaticanism; Hawn P.

[17] Physician in Hanover, had written on ultramontanism; Add MS 44449, f.63.

[18] William Hoyle, criminologist, had sent his book; see 29 Jan. 76.

[19] E. Clodd, *L'infanzia del mondo* (1875); 'a new sign of rampant infidelity'.

a new sign grassantis ἀπιστίας–'L'Infanzia del Mondo'. Read Goldsmith on the Horse[1]–Smith on Canal Boat Population.[2]

26. Wed.

Ch. 8½ AM. Wrote to Miss A. Wilberforce–Rev. L.M. Hogg[3]–Rev. H.O. Coxe–Rev. W.J. Dampier–Rev. F. Caudwell–Messrs Blackburne[4]–Mr Grogan–Mr Pigot[5]–Capt. Lawley. Worked on Homer 'The Horse'. Conversation with Mr Parker on Homer. Kibbled a tree with W. Conversation with him & Gertrude on Estate matters, which she has a healthy anxiety to learn. Read Statistical Acc. of Scotland[6]–Mr S.J. Watson's Poem[7]–Q.R. on Sainte Beuve.

27. Th.

Ch. 8½ AM. Wrote to Townshend & Barker–Sir Jas Watson–Mr O'Donoghue–Mr Lockhart Gordon[8]–Mr Baverstock. Worked on Homer. Felled an ash with W. Read Watson's Poems–Q.R. on Hatfield House.

28. Frid.

Ch. 8½ AM. Wrote to Mr W.H. Lyttelton–Mr Grogan–S.J. Watson–Mr Pears–Mr Sharman–Mr Pillans–S. Smith–Sir S. Scott & Co.–Ld Hartington–A. Balfour–Mr Mavrocordato–A. Harris–Librarian Lond. Lib. Kibbled an Ash with W. Worked on Homer. Read Watson's Drama–Balfour on Gothenburg Law[9]–Meade on Ath. Creed Legislation.[10]

29. Sat.

Ch. 8½ AM. Wrote to Mr Salkeld (& B.P.)–W.B. Gurdon–Mr J.B. Taylor[11]–Mr Whitaker–Rev. Mr M'Coll–Rev. W. Nevins–and a long letter to H.J.G. once more, and strongly, endeavouring to rouse her. Dined at the Rectory. Farm calls–and walk. Worked on Homer: Aiolos &c. Read Hoyle on Crime[12]–O'Hart on Irish Pedigrees.[13]

30. 4 S. Epiph.

Ch 11 AM & 6½ PM. Wrote to Mr Beresford Hope–Rev. E. Talbot–Mr Grogan–Mr Durnchey–Mr Salmond–Mrs Th. Read Armstrong's Solomon[14]–

[1] O. Goldsmith, *A history of the earth and animated nature*, probably in J. F. Walker's ed., 2v. (1876).

[2] G. Smith, *Our canal population* (1875).

[3] Lewis Maydwell Hogg, wrote on Italian church affairs.

[4] Perhaps H. J. and W. Blackburn, London accountants.

[5] Perhaps Alfred Pigot of Milner Street, Islington.

[6] From Sir J. Sinclair, *Statistical account of Scotland*, 21v. (1791-9).

[7] Had sent some verses; not found published.

[8] Abercrombie Lockhart Gordon, Scottish educationalist.

[9] One of the many temperance tracts by Clara L. Balfour.

[10] See 23 May 75.   [11] James Bayard Taylor, poet and traveller.

[12] W. Hoyle, *Crime in England and Wales in the nineteenth century* (1876).

[13] J. O'Hart, *Irish pedigrees*, 2v. (1876-8).

[14] George Francis Armstrong had sent his 'King Solomon' from *The tragedy of Israel*, 3v. (1872-6).

W. Lyttelton on Future State[1]—Salmond on German Ch. controv.[2]—Byles, Foundations of Religion[3]—and various Tracts.

31. M.

Ch. 8¼ A.M. Wrote to Walter L. Gladstone—G. Harris—G. Gwilt—F. May—D. Pusely—Sir J.B. Byles[4]—Sir Kingston James[5]—Capt. F.B.O. Cole—Ed. Guardian[6] —Sir Jas Watson—Bp of Salisbury.

Examining accounts at some length 1. of Residence with C.G. 2. Of Estate with Mr L. Barker and W.H.G., Gertrude also present. Also revised some particulars of my Will; and amended paper of Directions. Felled & kibbled an ash. Read Armstrong's King Solomon—Ariston (finished)—Bp Moberly's Pindar[7]— Puller's Lectures[8]—Tracts.

Tues. Feb. One. 1876.

Church 8¼ A.M. Wrote to Earl Granville—Sir Jas Paget—Mr J.T. Carr—Hon Caroline Lyttelton (B.P.)—Mr E.R. Russell—Thos Caught[9]—Professor Armstrong—Mr Pears (B.P.) Again worked upon settlement of accounts. Packing & putting away much for departure. Walk with the Rector: saw Schools, cottage visits. Read Armstrong's Solomon—Watson's Drama (finished)—and [blank]. Worked on Homer.

2. Wed. Purifn. [London]

Ch. 8¾ AM. Wrote to Sir Chas Forster—Mr Stevens U.S.[10]—Mr Jeffery—Mr Moore[11] Canada—Mr C.S. Parker. Saw Mr Hayward—Mr Kinnaird. Much preparation. Off at 10.15. Saw Townshend & Barker in Chester on the accounts. Entered 4 C. Gardens as our temporary home at 5¼. Worked on letters & papers. Read Hoyle on Crime—Sheldon Amos on Suez Canal—Do on Slave Circular.[12] Dined at Mr Th's. Saw Divers [R].

3. Th.

Wrote to Messrs T. & B.—Mr L. Gordon—W.F. Boyd—G. Whale. Saw Sir A. Panizzi—Mr Salkeld—Scotts—Mr Murray—Mr MacColl—Mr Tomlinson.

---

[1] W. H. Lyttelton, *Scripture revelations of the life after death* (1875).
[2] C. A. Salmond, *Exposition and defence of Prince Bismarck's anti-ultramontane policy* (1876).
[3] See 23 Jan. 76.
[4] Sir John Barnard *Byles, 1801-84; barrister and author; see 23 Jan. 76.
[5] Sir John Kingston James, 1815-93; 2nd bart. 1869.
[6] Not found published; probably on need for replacement adjective for 'clerical'; see *The Guardian*, 2 February 1876, 154.
[7] G. H. Moberly, *The odes of Pindar* (1876).   [8] See 3 Jan. 76.
[9] Thomas Caught of Chiswick, on Sabbatarianism; Hawn P.
[10] Possibly John Austin Stevens, 1827-1910; American financier and historian.
[11] Perhaps Dennis Moore, 1817-87; steel manufacturer and liberal politician in Hamilton, Ontario.
[12] S. Amos, *The purchase of the Suez Canal shares, and international law* (1876) and a speech or letter on the slave circular (see 4 Feb. 76).

Shopping. Dined at J.S. Wortley's. Worked much on arranging papers. Read Mr Jebb on Attic Oratory[1]—Burgess on Disestablishment.[2]

4. Fr.

Wrote to Messrs T. & B.—Sec. Statist Soc.—Mr Falloon[3]—Mr T.B. Potter—Mr Gurdon—Mr Banbury—Dr Burgess—Mrs Pennant—Maveg[4] Worked on papers books &c. Went with C. to 73 H[arley] St and further considered the alterations & arrangements there. Saw Ld Granville—Warden & Sec. Turner's Co.[5]—Scotts. Read Jebb, Attic Oratory—James on U.S. Institutions.[6] 3-5¼. Meeting at Granville's on Slave Circular, Suez Canal, &c.[7]

5. Sat.

Wrote to Messrs T. & B.—Mr Planché—Mr Scales (B.P.)—Mr Morgan—Rev. Dr Allon—Ld Granville—Dr Acland—Mather & Co[8]—Rev. Mr Neville—Rev. Mr Pocock. Round of shops, to pay bills &c. Read Studies on Homer—Suez Canal & Slave Circ. Papers—and [blank]. Saw Mr Tomlinson—Mr Godley—Mr Chapman—Mr Knowles—Mr Quaritch—Lord Granville.

6. 5 S. Epiph.

St Anne's mg & Chapel Royal aft. Saw Ld Granville—Sir D. Wolff. Dined with the Phillimores: two hours conversation with him on Church, public, & family matters.[9] Read Contemp. Rev.—M. Arnold—Sir G. Bowyer—Jas Gairdner—Mr Oxenham—Armstrong's King Solomon.

7. M.

Wrote to Mr Chrysovoloni[10]—Mr Jas Lord—Rev Mr Cather—Mrs Th.—Ed. of Guardian.[11] 4½-7. Meeting at Ld G.s on the Slave Circular motion. The whole question returned upon us when we heard the Speech & Commission: and we had two more hours when Hartington's dinner was over.[12] Dined at Devonshire House. Worked on Homer (Apollo). Read Armstrong. Saw Dashwood, & another [R]. Saw Mr Macmillan—Mr MacColl—Ld Granville—Mr Tomlinson.

---

[1] R. C. Jebb, *The Attic Orators, from Antiphon to Isaeos*, 2v. (1876).
[2] H. Burgess, *Disestablishment and disendowment* (1875).
[3] Perhaps William Marcus Falloon; priest in Liverpool; rector of Ackworth 1875.
[4] This name written in pencil; a rescue case?
[5] See 16 Feb. 76.
[6] Probably Henry James *père*, 'The social significance of our institutions' (1861).
[7] For the circular on fugitive slaves, apparently reversing British policy, see Buckle, v. 396.
[8] William Mather & Co., royal surgical instrument suppliers.
[9] Phillimore noted in his diary: 'G's dined here. Both well. He talked upon many subjects—chiefly the connection with the Ch[urch]—but also on the Slave Circulars for wh. he thought the F.O. under various Govts. to blame—rather scoffed at Suez Canal. Has taken a house in Harley St for 30 years—for his wife's sake as he puts it exclusively'; Phillimore MSS.
[10] M. J. Chrysoveloni, Liverpool merchant; had sent a work on the Greek church; Hawn P.
[11] Sending his new London address.
[12] i.e. the eve-of-Session dinner when the Queen's speech was discussed.

8. Tu.

Wrote to Messrs T. & B.—Ld Granville—Rev. Mr Brewer—Sir Jas Watson—
Principal Librarian of B. Museum. Saw Mr Knowles (Contemp. R. & Chron. of
Ultramontane movement)[1]—Mr Moffatt respecting Harry—Mr Grogan
(executed the H[arley] St Assignment)[2]—Mr W. Cowper—Ld Granville (Slave
Circular)—C.G. on Mrs Hampton's affairs—Mr B. Hope on The Döllinger
Address—Ld Wolverton. Read Armstrong (finished). Saw one X. H of C. 4¼-9.
Spoke briefly in vindication of our concern in the case of the Christian subjects
of Turkey.[3] Dined with Sir Chas Forster.

9. Wed.

Wrote to Mr C.B. Waring[4]—Mr J. Rawlinson—Helen G.—Mr G. Ellis. Worked
on arranging papers &c. Saw Mrs Dalton: heard sundry things X. Saw Ld
Granville—M. Neville—Mr Gurdon—Mr Knowles—Mr Godley. Family party to
see Rip Van Winckle:[5] good scenery & acting, play most immoral re drink. Read
Youatt on The Horse[6]—M. Harvey on Irish Finance.[7]

10. Th[8]

Wrote to Mr Chadwick—Mr W.S. Lindsay—Rev. Dr Rowsell—Rev. Mr Wood—
Rev. Mr Houseman[9]—Mr King—Mr Dowgill—Mr Scratchley. Saw Mr Mac-
millan—Lady Waldegrave & Lord Carlingford—Mr Kinnaird—WHG &
G.G.—Ld Hartington—Mr Bright—Sir Thos Acland—Mr Lefevre. Round of
shopping. Eleven to breakfast. Twelve to dinner. House of C. at 4.30.[10] Read
Mrs Jerningham's Journal.[11] Worked on Apollo.

11. Fr.

Wrote to Mr Bayley Potter—Mr Richardson—Mr Huntley—Mr Penny—Miss
Marsh—Mr Bradlaugh—Mr Hartley. Read Mrs Jerningham—Brewer's Introduc-
tion. 3-4. Small conclave at Ld Granville's. Saw General Ponsonby—Mr
Lawson—Mr Knowles—Ld R. Gower (and his works)—Mr Macmillan—Mrs
Grote. Nine to dinner.

[1] See 3 Apr. 76.
[2] Leasing 73 Harley Street for 30 years; in Gladstone's 'sketch of property', 31 December 1876, it
is valued at £3,500, including improvements; Hawn P.
[3] Warning that 'integrity and independence of the Turkish Empire . . . can never be effectually
maintained unless it can be proved to the world that . . . the Government of Turkey has the power to
administer a fair measure of justice to all its subjects alike, whether Christian or Mahomedan'; H
227. 106.
[4] C. B. Warring of New York; Hawn P. See 11 Dec. 75.
[5] At the Royal Princess's theatre.
[6] W. Youatt, The horse (1831).
[7] Not traced.
[8] T.T. this day (9e) published an authorized statement that Gladstone was not 'engaged upon a
theological work', but was preparing his Homeric Thesaurus.
[9] Thomas Houseman, d. 1898; vicar of Whenby 1867-85.
[10] Questions: H 227. 132.
[11] See 26 Aug. 70.

12. Sat.

Wrote to Bp of Winchester—Mr Mogford[1]—Mr Grogan—Mr Carlisle—Mr Jas Orton—Mr J.W. Barnes[2]—Sir Francis Grant P.R.A.—Mr W. Reynolds—Rev. Mr Sparling[3]—Mr Jos Hollar—R. Handsley—E. Hanson—Jas Knowles. Dined at Sir W. James's. Saw Mr Fitzmaurice—Sir Francis Grant. Visited the Doulton Pottery Exhibition: greatly interested.[4] At Dalton's,[5] conversation with [blank] on engagements &c. Read Mrs Jerningham finished—and [blank]. Worked on Homer (Apollo).

13. Septa S.

Chapel R. mg & aft. Saw Sir W. Farquhar—Mr E. Hamilton. Wrote on Mr Fitz-James Stephen's Miracle Paper for Tuesday.[6] Read Introd. to Rig Veda[7]— Martensen Dogmatic Theol.[8]—Rhode Island Hist Soc on R[oger] Williams[9]— MacColl on Future Punishment[10]—Longridge Church case.

14. M.

Wrote to Sec. M. Dist. R.R.—Mr W.T. Vincent—Mr B. Moore—Messrs T. & B.— Rev B. Brown—Ld Hartington. H. of C. $4\frac{1}{4}$-$7\frac{1}{2}$. Spoke on Adjt of Suez Debate.[11] Saw Mr C. Bradlaugh—Mr Ouvry *cum* Ld De Tabley—Mr T.B. Potter— W.H.G.—Mr St George Mivart[12]—Mr Knowles—Mr Adam—Mr Otway. Dined at Sir C. Forster's. Read The Soldier of Fortune[13] and Fortnightly on Suez Purchase.

15. Tu.

Wrote to Ld Hartington—C. Hind—J.C. Jones—P. Walmesley—J.A. Keatinge— Mayor of Northampton—Rev. J. Penleaze[14]—Rev. W. Arthur—Dr Acland. Read D'Urfey's Pills to Purge Melancholy.[15] (What a picture!)—Soldier of Fortune— Macmillan on Univ. Reform. Saw Lady Bell—Mr Knowles. 7-11$\frac{1}{2}$. Attended Metaphysical Society: made my observations on Mr Stephen's paper, long debate, all *verifying* Bp Butler.[16] Luncheon at 15 G.S. Worked on Homer (Apollo).

[1] Perhaps Robert Mogford, London lithographer.
[2] Perhaps John Wickman Barnes, of Gower Street, London.
[3] Probably Philip William Sparling, 1844-1921; headmaster in Gloucester.
[4] A collection of Doulton's china to be sent to the Philadelphia Exhibition, discussed in his speech on 16 February.
[5] A rescue case; see 20, 23 Feb. 76.   [6] Add MS 44763, f. 1; see 15 Feb. 76.
[7] See 25 Sept. 59.   [8] H. L. Martensen, tr. W. Urwick, *Christian dogmatics* (1865).
[9] *Proceedings of the Rhode Island Historical Society* (1875-6), 53.   [10] See 21 July 72.
[11] Demanding details of govt.'s position as shareholder: *H* 227. 291.
[12] St George Jackson Mivart, 1827-1900; convert to Roman catholicism 1844; published widely on evolution. See 28 Sept. 73, 14 May 76.
[13] J. B. L. Warren, later Lord De Tabley, *The soldier of fortune* (1876); a tragic play.
[14] John Penleaze, rector of Black Torrington from 1834.
[15] T. D'Urfey, *Wit and mirth; or Pills to purge melancholy*, 5v. (1719).
[16] Discussion of Stephen's paper of 9 November 1875, as well as further discussion of Huxley, both on miracles; Brown, *Metaphysical Society*, 329-30; diarist's notes on Stephen, F. Harrison, etc. at Add MS 44763, f. 18.

16. *Wed.*

Wrote to Rev. Dr Miller—Mr W.P. Adam—Mr Firth—Rev W. Rogers—Ld R. Montagu—Messrs Barker & Hignett—Hon. Mrs G.D. Pennant—Rev. Mr Bellairs—Ld Lyttelton—Mrs Jackson—Mr Anthony. Dined with the Wests. Saw Mr Hanson (Leg. & Succ. Duties)—Mr Williams (Vet. Surgeon)—Hon. Mr Canning—Baroness Burdett Coutts—Mr Kirkman Hodgson— Dalton: readings, Longfellow and Shakespeare [R]. Read Tracts on Canal Purchase &c.—Soldier of Fortune. 2-5. In the City to be admitted Turner: spoke 40 m to the best audience I ever had within those precincts.[1]

17. *Th.*

Wrote to Sec. M. Dist. R.R. Co—Mr B. Freeman[2]—Rev. A. Pownall (B.P.)[3]—Mrs Ralli—Mr Chapman. Saw W.H.G. (on Agency)—Mr Lowe (after his speech)—Mr Bright—Mr C. Parker—Rev. Mr M'Coll—Rev. Mr Brewer—Rev. Mr Oxenham. Ten to breakfast: much conversation. Worked on Homer. Read Ashley's Palmerston.[4] H. of C. $4\frac{1}{2}$-$7\frac{1}{4}$.[5]

18. *Fr.*

Wrote to Ed. Bible Echo[6]—Mr Ouvry (Doc[uments])—Mr France—Mr May—Mr T. Meek—M. Bennall—Ed. Scottish Guardian[7]—Mrs Wilkinson—Ld Granville—Mr Chappuis[8]—Mr Cuthbertson—Mr Ewera(?)—Mr Collyns Simon[9]—Dr Badenoch—Mr Clode—Ld Hartington 2—Mr Knowles. Worked on Homer: finished Apollo. Saw Sir A. Panizzi—Gen Schenk—Mr E. Ashley—Sir W.R. Farquhar. Dined with the Farquhars. Read S[uez] Canal Papers[10]—D'Urfey X[11]—Soldier of Fortune—Life of Lord Palmerston.

19. *Sat.*

Wrote to Messrs B. & H.—Mr Poynter—Mr Rob. Gladstone—Mr Jas Grant. Saw Othello at the Lyceum: Mr Irving's a remarkable study: Iago good. Saw Mr Grogan—Mr Godley—Mrs(?) Herbert. Saw Scott—with dissatisfaction [R]. Read Suez Canal papers—Soldier of Fortune—Belaney on W.E.G.[12]

---

[1] *T.T.*, 17 February 1876, 10a, later printed as a pamphlet; see also A. C. Stanley-Stone, *History of the worshipful company of Turners* (1925), app. N. The company was pronouncedly liberal in tone.

[2] Probably Bellingham Freeman, of Canonbury Lodge, Islington.

[3] Assheston Pownall, d. 1886; rector of S. Kilworth from 1847.

[4] A. E. M. Ashley, *The life of... Viscount Palmerston 1846-1865*, 2v. (1876).

[5] Lowe opposed the introduction of the bill making Victoria Empress of India: *H* 227. 410.

[6] W. Kellaway, thanking him for tracts sent; *Bible Echo*, iv. 285 (March 1876).

[7] Not found published.

[8] Possibly P. E. Chappuis, London merchant, 'sole patentee of the Luminarium ... to supercede gas in day-time'.

[9] Thomas Collins Simon, philosopher; sent copies of his books; Hawn P.

[10] *PP* 1876 lxxxiii. 131.

[11] One of the salacious verses or plays by T. *D'Urfey, restoration poet, see 15 Feb. 76.

[12] R. Belaney, *Mr Gladstone himself reviewed and analysed* (1876); attack on 'Vaticanism', accusing diarist of being 'virtually' a Freemason.

20. Sexa S.

Chapel Royal & H.C. 10 AM. St James's 7 PM. Wrote to Mrs Th.—W.H.G. Saw Dalton: a long conversation & much insight into class-life [R]. Read Belaney (finished)—Norris, Rudiment of Theology[1]—Burgon on Mark XVI[2]—Simon on St Peter.[3]

21. M.

Wrote to Miss A. Peake—Sec. Metrop. Dist. RR. Co. Saw Mr Knowles—Lord F. Cavendish. Read (long) the Suez papers—and prepared Notes and Queries for Speech. Read Dr Cotton Smith on my Homer.[4] H of C. $4\frac{1}{2}$-$8\frac{3}{4}$ and $10\frac{1}{2}$-1. Spoke 1 h. 20 m. on Suez Canal case.[5] Saw Ld Hartington.

22. Tu.

Wrote to Dr Cotton Smith—J.B. Wright—J.W. Schofield—J. Belleley[6]—J. Thompson—Mr T. Harriot—Rev. Canon Norris.[7] H. of C. $4\frac{1}{2}$-$8\frac{1}{2}$.[8] Saw Ld Granville—Mr Lyte—Mr Grogan (assistant)—Mr J. Talbot. 2-4. Luncheon at Bss Burdett Coutts's. Saw Mr Irving—M. Renaud[9]—Rev. Mr Holland—Rev. Mr Sinclair.

23. Wed.

Wrote to Mr Harris—Principal Librarian B.M.—Mr Webb. Read Dr Cotton Smith—Schulte, Cölibat[10]—Life of Ld Palmerston. 12-$1\frac{1}{2}$ Meeting at Ld Granville's on Queen's Titles Bill. Luncheon at 15 G. Square. Saw Dalton [R]. Calls. Dined at the Speaker's. Saw Ld Kensington—Mr Grant Duff—Sir C. Anderson—Mr Newdigate. Corrected proofs of Apollo for Contemp. Rev.[11]

24. Th.

Wrote to Secy Grocers Co.—Mr C.E. Wallis (2)[12]—Mr Dinnen—Mr H. Hill—Mr Thos Gray[13]—Mrs Farnall—Rev. R. Main—Rev. M. M'Coll—Rev. J.H. Smythe[14]—Mr E. Bailey—Mr Annandale[15]—Mr W.A. Gibbs[16]—D. of Argyll. 12 to breakfast.

---

[1] By J. P. Norris (1876).

[2] J. W. Burgon, *The last twelve verses of the Gospel according to S. Mark* (1871).

[3] T. C. Simon, *The mission and martyrdom of St. Peter* (1852).

[4] John Cotton Smith, 1826-82, American episcopalian divine and social reformer; favourable review of *Studies on Homer* in his *Miscellanies old and new* (1876).

[5] *H* 227. 584.

[6] *Sic*, but probably Robert Belaney, 1804-95; anglican priest, convert to Rome 1857; Gladstone had just read his outraged pamphlet, see 19 Feb. 76.

[7] John Pilkington *Norris, 1823-91; canon of Bristol from 1864; archdeacon there from 1881. See 20 Feb. 76.

[8] Slave circular affair: *H* 227. 685.

[9] Perhaps Edward Renault of Holland Villas, London.

[10] J. F. von Schulte, *Der Cölibatzwang und diesen Aufhebung* (1876).

[11] The first three articles on 'Homerology' in the *Contemporary Review*, xxvii. 632 (March 1876).

[12] Perhaps C. Woodward Wallis, London barrister.   [13] Assistant secretary in board of trade.

[14] Nonconformist minister.   [15] Possibly Thomas Annandale, surgeon in Edinburgh.

[16] William A. Gibbs of Gillwell Park, Essex; sent books and invited diarist (unsuccessfully) for a visit; Hawn P.

Saw Ld Granville—Warden of Keble—Mr Knowles—Dr Rowsell—Dr Acland—
Ld Blachford—Mr Leighton—Ld A. Russell—Ld H. Lennox. Dined with the
Cartwrights. H. of C. 4½-7 and 10½-2¾: voted in two minorities each of 45, on the
Slave Circular.[1] Read Gibbs.

25. Fr.

Wrote to Messrs Macmillan—Mr Balfour MP.—A. Jervise—Mr Watts—Mr T.
Ogilvy—H.F. Jones—E.H. Straw—Dr Schulte[2]—Dr Brandis—Rev Dr Burgess—
Rev Dr Barry—Baron Tauchnitz—President B.T. Saw Ld Granville—Mr
Agnew—Ld Napier—Mr Motley—Mr Eaton—Ld Hartington—Dowager Dss of
Somerset. Dined at General Malcolm's. Read Mr G. Duff's answer to Greg[3]—Ld
Palmerston's Life. Visited Collection of Old Masters.

26. Sat.

Wrote to Sec. Royal Acad.—Duchess of Sirmoneta—Mr Napier—Mr Robin
Allen[4]—Mr C.A. Roberts—Professor Jebb.[5] Walk with C. Saw Mr Williams Vet.
S.—Dean of Wells—Mr L. Stanley. Saw Dalton X. Read Macbeth (aloud)—
Stanley on Univ. Reform[6]—Weingarten, Revolutionskirchen Englands.[7] Dined
at Lady Waldegrave's.

27. Quinqua S.

Chapel Royal 10 A.M. and 5.30 P.M. Wrote to Rev. R.R. Suffield—Mr Hill
(D[aily] N[ews]) Walk with C. Read Burgon on St Mark—Suffield's Croydon
Episode[8]—Schulte, Aufhebung des Cölibats—and many Tracts.

28. M.

Wrote to Sir C. Trevelyan—Rev. R. O'Keeffe—Rev. S.E.G.—Mr J.G. Gifford—
Rev. Hiram Carleton[9]—May Gladstone. Dined with the F.C.s. H. of C. 4½-7½ and
10½-1¼ on the Admiralty business or mess.[10] Read Tunbridge Correspondence[11]—Black Book of Calcutta[12]—Memnon on Suez Canal[13]—Clark's Address

[1] H 227. 899.

[2] Johann Friedrich von Schulte, German theologian and religious historian; see 23 Feb. 76.

[3] M. E. Grant Duff, 'Must we then believe Cassandra', Fortnightly Review, xxii. 581 (November 1874); reply to Greg's Warnings of Cassandra.

[4] Robin Allen, 1820-99; sec. to Trinity House 1867-81.

[5] Richard Claverhouse *Jebb, 1841-1905; professor of Greek at Glasgow 1875-89; regius professor at Cambridge 1889; tory M.P. Cambridge from 1891. See 3 Feb. 76.

[6] E. L. Stanley, Lord Sheffield, 'Three letters on Oxford University reform' (1876).

[7] H. Weingarten, Die Revolutionskirchen Englands (1868).

[8] R. R. Suffield, A Croydon episode (1876).

[9] Hiram Carleton, American divine; sent his Treatise on the meaning of the derivatives of the Greek root βαφ (1875).

[10] Loss of H.M.S. Vanguard: H 227. 1026.

[11] Statement and correspondence . . . concerning a proposed new church at Tonbridge (1875).

[12] [C. J. O'Donnell], The black pamphlet of Calcutta. The famine of 1874 (1876).

[13] 'Memnon', The 'Edinburgh Review' and the Suez Canal (1876).

on Iron Trade[1]—Bernard on Burials Bill[2]—Rev. H. Carleton on Βαφ. Took M. & H. to the Exhibition of Old Masters. Saw Mr Macmillan—Ld F.C.

29. Tu.

Wrote to Mr Lyulph Stanley—Mr D. Robertson—Mr Jellicoe[3]—Mr J.N. Block[4]—Mr W.R. Smith.[5] Saw Sir A. Panizzi—Master of the Rolls—Sir John Rose—Mr Reeve—Mr Bagehot—Sir W.V. Harcourt. Luncheon with the W.H.G.s. Dined at No 15 G.S. Read The Soldier of Fortune—Ducamp, Emplacement d'Ilion[6]—Cobbe on Vivisection[7]—The Catholic World for Mch.

Ash Wed. Mch One 76.

Wrote to Miss F.P. Cobbe[8]—Mr Murray—Mr Grogan—Mr Gurdon—Master of Magd. Coll. Camb.—Rev. T. Sissons[9]—Mr Chadwick—Mr Bramwell—Sir Thos G.—Miss Lyell[10]—Rev. Mr Malet—Mrs Th.—Mr Hayman—C.R. Reed. Saw Mrs Th. X. Church St Martin's 11 AM. Saw Sir D. Lange—Ld F. Cavendish—Mr Law—Mrs Talbot—Mr Goschen. H. of C. 3-5½.[11] Read Ducamp—Carvell Williams on Burials.[12]

2. Th.

Wrote to Sir S. Northcote—Rev. Dr Allon—Rev. R. O'Keeffe BP.—Gov. Pope Hennessy—M. Maxime Du Camp[13]—Sir D. Lange—Mr Hellyer.[14] Dined with the F.C.s: much conversation. Saw Ld Granville—Professor Huxley[15]—Rev. Dr Barry—Rev. Mr Baldwin Brown—Mr Mivart. Read Ducamp (finished)—Duke of Argyll on Land & T. Bill[16]—and Tracts.

3. Fr.

Wrote to Mrs Fitzpatrick—G.R. Jellicoe—Jas Wyllie—L.W. Dixon—T.F. Figes—Rev. A.J. Street[17]—Bp of Argyll—Mrs Bennetts—Mr Newton. Saw Ld Granville—

---

[1] Untraced.

[2] T. D. Bernard, perhaps *The rites of sepulture and memorials of the dead* (1854).

[3] George Rogers Jellico, barrister, on legal proceedings at St. Alban's, Holborn; Add MS 44449, f. 146.

[4] Perhaps of Block, Grey, and Block, London wine merchants.

[5] Perhaps William Richard Smith, London auctioneer.

[6] By Maxime Du Camp; see 2 Mar. 76.

[7] F. P. Cobbe, probably 'The moral aspects of vivisection', reprinted from *The New Quarterly Magazine* (1875).

[8] Frances Power Cobbe, philanthropist; see Add MS 44449, f. 276, and 29 Feb. 76.

[9] Congregationalist minister in Woolwich.

[10] Miss Katherine M. Lyell, the previous tenant of 73 Harley Street, sent a cheque for work on the house; Hawn P.

[11] Irish municipal franchise: *H* 227. 1164.

[12] J. C. Williams, *Religious liberty in the churchyard; or the case for the Burials Bill restated* (1876).

[13] Maxime Du Camp, French biographer, essayist and traveller; see 29 Feb. 76.

[14] Thomas Hellyer of Ryde had offered to send pictures; Hawn P.

[15] At breakfast; see Grant Duff, *Diary*, i. 167.

[16] In *Contemporary Review*, xxvii. 497 (March 1876).

[17] Arthur Joseph Street, d. 1901; vicar of Whittlebury 1873-86.

Mr A. Balfour—Mr Knowles—Mr Lowe—Ld F.C. Dined at Pol. Econ. Club & discussed S[uez] Canal Purchase. The Club was generally adverse.[1] H. of C. 9¾-1½—Burials Resolution, & Sir D. Lange.[2] Read Abbott on "The Catholic Peril in America".[3]

4. Sat.

Wrote to Sig. Guidicini[4]—Rev. Mr Ganini[5]—Mr Jenkins—Mr J. Morley[6]—Mr G. Harris—Mr W.L. Gladstone—Mr Ouvry. Saw Mr Jellicoe—Mr Hopwood—Mr Grogan. Saw Denton = Phillips: reading Hamlet [R]. Read also J. Warren.[7] Sixteen to dinner: & evening party. The Hardys came & we exchanged all manner of congratulations.[8] Luncheon with Baroness B. Coutts. Took C. to the Old Masters.

5. 1 S. Lent.

Chapel Royal 10 A.M. and 5.30 P.M. Wrote to Mr Reynolds Fox[9]—Mr Constable—Mr Lawson—Mr G. Potter—Rev M. M'Coll—Mrs Th. Read Gass, Symbolik der Gr. Kirche[10]—Plumptre, Religion &c. of Shakespeare[11]—Lectures on Bpric for Lpool.[12]

6. M.

Wrote to Barker & Hignett—Rev. Mr Hughes—Mr J. Morgan. Read Ld Palmerston's Life and.... Attended the Queen's Levee. Ten to dinner. Saw Sir A. Panizzi—Duke of Argyll—Mr Forbes—Rev Mr M'Coll—Mr Ouvry—Mr Goschen. Surveyed the Harley Street House and gave divers directions. H of C. 4½-7. Spoke on Lange & the Commn for Egypt![13]

7. Tu.

Wrote to M. Tallichet[14]—Col. Lawrie[15]—W.R. Leslie—B.G. Jenkins[16]—A.S. Murray—Dr Max Lossen—Sir Jas Watson—Watson & Smith—Mr H.C. Burdett. Saw

---

[1] Discussion introduced by E. *Chadwick; *Political Economy Club ... Proceedings* (1882), 256; 'Chamberlain' dined as a guest.

[2] Spoke on govt.'s unauthorized publication of Lange's correspondence with Granville in 1871 on Suez Canal; *H* 227. 1401.

[3] F. E. Abbott, 'The Catholic peril in America', *Fortnightly Review*, xxv. 385 (March 1876).

[4] Probably Giuseppe de Giovanni Battista Guidicini, wrote on Bolognese affairs.

[5] Possibly Francis Cecil Gallini, Roman catholic priest in Cardiff.

[6] Possibly his future biographer (see 10 Mar. 77), but unconfirmed.

[7] See 14 Feb. 76.

[8] John Hardy, 1809-88, tory M.P. S. Warwickshire 1868-74, was cr. bart. on 23 February 1876; his son, Reginald m. Lucy Marion, da. of J. N. Gladstone, on 29 April 1876.

[9] R. Reynolds Fox of Plymouth, on church affairs; Hawn P.

[10] W. Gass, *Symbolik der griechischen Kirche* (1872).

[11] C. J. Plumptre, 'The religion and morality of Shakespeare's works' (1873).

[12] Untraced.

[13] *H* 227. 1423.

[14] Perhaps E. Tallichet, wrote on Swiss railways.

[15] See 23 June 77?

[16] On Homer; Hawn P.

Ld Granville–Mr Bright–Mr Hardy–Mr Samuelson–Lady Westmoreland–
Mrs Th. & Miss Vernon–Mr Cartwright–Mr Cooke (Murray). Read Howard
on Meat Supply[1]–The Soldier of Fortune. Dined at Mad. Ralli's. Sir Rob. Phillimore's afterwards. H. of C. 4½-7.[2]

8. Wed.

Wrote to Sir Thomas G.–Sir A. Panizzi–Rev. A. Anson[3]–W.T. Pears–F.W.
Lowndes[4]–C.B. Warring. N. Portrait Gallery Meeting 3½-4½. We framed a
tribute to the memory of Lord Stanhope. Small Conclave at Granville's on the
[Royal] Titles Bill.[5] Dined at Sir H. Verney's: much pleased with Madame
d'Harcourt.[6] Read Palmerston's Life–Magniac on Suez Canal.[7] Saw Adm.
Yelverton–Sir John Hardy–Kate G. on his [i.e. Hardy's] conv. & the marriage
arrangements.[8]

9. Th.

Wrote to Sir Jas Watson–Rev. F.R. Smith–Mr W.T. Pears–Dr Baxter
Langley–Mr Phil. Reade[9]–Mons. D. Freck[10]–Mr R.R. Rae.[11] Ten to breakfast.
Attended Lady A. Stanley's Funeral 11½-1½. The Dean[12] gave the blessing, with
astonishing force of lungs: a brave and touching act. Saw Rev. Mr Suffield–Miss
Cobbe–Sir W. Harcourt–Lord F. Cavendish–Mr Murray–Sir W. James–Mr
A.S. Murray. H. of C. 4½-8¼. Spoke on Queen's titles: an attentive House.[13] Saw
three: two at least of them not unhopeful [R]. Read Ld Palmerston–Soldier of
Fortune–Leben Dante's.[14]

10. Fr.

Wrote to Messrs T. and B.–Herbert J.G.–Helen J.G.–M. Cernuschi[15]–Rev. Mr
Rodwell[16]–A. Macmillan–Mr Strahan–Sir W. Anderson–Mr J.H. Dart–Mrs
Th. Read Ld Palmerston's Life–Voysey on Religion.[17] Saw Messrs Bunn–Sir

[1] Untraced.   [2] Misc. business: H 227. 1569.
[3] Adelbert John Robert Anson, 1840-1909; rector of Woolwich 1875; bp. in Canada 1884-92.
[4] Frederick Walter Lowndes, physician, published The extension of the Contagious Diseases Acts to
Liverpool (1876).
[5] Bright, Forster, Gladstone, Granville, Hartington and Lowe; Walling, Diaries of John Bright, 377.
Disraeli the previous day had refused to say what the new title would be.
[6] Wife of the French ambassador.
[7] Untraced article by C. Magniac; see Nineteenth Century, xv. 13 (January 1884).
[8] See 4 Mar. 76n.
[9] Of Co. Clare; later wrote on Irish politics; Hawn P.
[10] Possibly H. D. Freck, published in French on India.
[11] Robert R. Rae of Brixton; corresponded on Homer; Hawn P.
[12] i.e. A. P. *Stanley, the deceased's husband.
[13] Arguing that the title of Emperor was normally associated with elective rather than hereditary
succession: H 227. 1736.
[14] Perhaps F. X. Wegele, Dante's Leben und Werke (1852).
[15] Henri Cernuschi, French economist; wrote Bi-Metallic money and its bearings on the monetary crises
in Germany, France, England and the United States (1876).
[16] John Medows *Rodwell, 1808-1900; anglican priest and orientalist; involved in Mrs Gladstone's
convalescent homes.
[17] C. Voysey, perhaps his 'The influence of dogma upon religion' (1872).

Erskine Perry—Mr Moffatt, respecting Harry—Mr Samuelson—Mr Bright—Mr Goschen—Lady Egerton—Ld Grey—Ld Overstone. Dined with the Wortleys. Ld Overstone's in Evening. H. of C. 4½-5.[1]

11. Sat.

Wrote to Ld Granville (2)—Mr G. Mitchell[2]—Rev. H. Brancker[3]—Mr Geo. Simpson—A. Wallis—Dr Mackay—Dr Bennett—Mr Lowe. Read Hamlet—Life of Ld Palmerston. Luncheon with Count Münster. Dined at Lord A. Russell's. Saw Dalton = Phillips [R]. Conversation with Count Münster—Dr Hooker—Lord Acton.

12. 2 S. Lent.

Chapel Royal 10 A.M. & 5.30 P.M. Saw Mr Forster. Wrote to Dr Nicoll. Read Sterling to Coningham[4]—Moeurs des Fourmis[5]—Montalembert on Spain III[6]— Clerk on Stone Age—Wood on Instinct & Reason[7]—Saecula Catholica—&c.

13. M.

Wrote to Dalton = Phillips. Sir Jas Watson (Tel.).—Saw Mr Ouvry—Sir A. Panizzi—Ld Hartington—Dean of Westmr—Sir W. Harcourt—P. Ralli—Mr Noel—Mr Anderson—Mr Irvine—Mr Christie. Eleven to dinner. Luncheon with Baroness Coutts. H. of C. 4½-5½.[8] Mr Sturge's in evg. Read Pietrement on Horses.[9]

14. Tu.

Wrote to Rev. Mr Oxenham—Dr Bendan[10]—Mr Geo. Wells.[11] Read Pietremont on Horses—Lord Palmerston's Life—Cossham Case[12]—Calvert on Educn.[13] Saw Mrs Th.—Ld Hartington—Dr Smith—Sir W. Harcourt—Mr Knowles—Ld F. Cavendish—Ld Granville—Dr W. Smith. H. of C. 4½-5½.[14]

---

[1] Misc. business: *H* 227. 1795.

[2] Declining invitation of George Mitchell, proprietor of a marble gallery in Brompton Road, London, to address a meeting of agricultural labourers: 'I need hardly add that I continue to be heartily favourable to his [the agricultural labourer's] political enfranchisement'; and defending the anglican clergy; Bodley MS Don. d. 137, f. 45; *The Guardian*, 15 March 1876, 342 and *D.T.*, 15 March 1876.

[3] Henry Brancker, vicar of Thursley from 1857.

[4] J. Sterling, *Twelve letters [to W. Coningham]* (1851).

[5] Untraced.

[6] Probably Montalembert's *Juan Donosa Cortès, marquis de Valdegamas* (1853), reprinted in *Oeuvres*, v. 189 (1860).

[7] Perhaps one of H. H. Wood's numerous articles.

[8] Admiralty affairs: *H* 227. 1873.

[9] C. A. Pietrement, *Les Origines du Cheval domestique* (1870).

[10] David Bendan of Dresden; tr.*Homeric Synchronism* into German (1876).

[11] George Wells of Yeovil; on the clergy; Hawn P.

[12] Probably Handel Cossham, 1824-90; temperance advocate.

[13] F. Calvert, *Denominationalists and secularists* (1876).

[14] Animal diseases; *H* 227, 2017.

15. Wed.

Wrote to Mrs Devereux—Mr Sewell—A.E. Smith—S. Benfield—F.J. Jeffery[1]—W.H. Clark—C.S. Roundell—Sec. National Dwellings Soc.—Herr Beck (Nordlingen)—Rev. Dr Gregg—C. Rowley—Rev. J. Oakley (BP)—Sir J.W. Kaye[2]—Mr G.E. Murray. Saw Mr Macmillan—Professor B. Price—Rev. Mr Oakley [*sic*] & Mr Passbridge[3]—Ld Granville—Ld Halifax—Mr Kinnaird & others. Saw Dalton = Philips. Dined with the Airlies. Speaker's Levee afterwards. H of C. at 1. Concert (Miss Robertson) 3-4½.[4] Read Ld Palmerston's Life—M. Pietrement.

16. Th.

Wrote to Rev. J. Ingram—F. Moore—T. Buckle—B.J. Willats—R.H. Baynes—F.H. Johnstone—P. Pearson—Thos Adcock. Read Pietrement on the Horse—Ld Palmerston's Life. Saw Ld Granville—Mr Brodrick—Rev. J. Rodwell—Ld Hartington. Thirteen to breakfast. Dined with Ld Halifax. An interesting after dinner conversation on Lord Palmerston. H of C. 4½-7½ and 10¾-1¾. Voted in 200 : 305 on Ld H.s amendment: one of the strangest divisions I ever knew: at any rate until explained.[5]

17. Fr.

Wrote to Prof. Price (Rev) B.P.—Rev. H. Bacon[6]—Rev W. Lethaby[7]—Mr Travis—Deptford Vestry Clerk—Mr Jas Boielle[8]—Mr J. Hilton B.P.—Rev. Mr Wallace—A. Kelso. Saw Ld Hartington—Mr Alg. West—Ld Granville *cum* Ld Halifax—Ld Hartington—Sir R. Phillimore—Mr W. James. Conclave on Amendments to R. Titles Bill at H of Commons 5½-6½.[9] Attended at Chamberlain's office Guildhall to receive the Freedom:[10] & saw curious old City MSS. Corrected proofs of Turner Speech.[11] Dined with Sir W. James. Read Ld Palmerston—Soldier of Fortune.[12]

18. Sat.

Wrote to Mr J. Hicklin—Miss H. Gladstone—T. Fifoot[13]—Mrs H. Gladstone and draft for her to sign—Rev. A. Blomfield—Ld De Tabley. Finished Article on

[1] Frederick John Jeffery of Liverpool; genealogist and numismatist.
[2] Sir John William *Kaye, 1814-76; secretary in India Office until 1874; historian of India.
[3] Business untraced.   [4] Not further identified; see 22 Mar. 76.
[5] Hartington's amendment allowed a change of royal title, but declared 'Emperor' inexpedient: *H* 228. 75, 160. Disraeli later remarked: 'we owe it to that Opposition that our majority appears almost to have doubled that which a generous country accorded to us at the last Election'; *H* 229. 462. Division list analysis in *T.T.*, 18 March 1876, 10b.
[6] Probably Hugh Bacon, rector of Baxterley from 1854.
[7] Nonconformist divine.
[8] James Boïelle, French scholar, translator and lexicographer.
[9] See 20 Mar. 76.
[10] Acquired by redemption on presentation of the Turners' Company, consequently a private occasion, though reported in *City Press*, 18 March 1876, 4d. He consequently could not be made an Honorary Freeman in 1881; see *London's Roll of Fame* (1884), 345.
[11] See 16 Feb. 76.   [12] See 4 Mar. 76.
[13] Thomas Fifoot, secretary of the [Anglo-]Catholic Clergy Sustentation Fund, asked support for the fund; Hawn P.

Hippos & Diphros, and corrected proofs. Saw W.H.G. (Estate matters)—The T.G.s—Lady Strangford (Ottoman affairs)—Lord Cork—Ld Halifax & Ld Cardwell. Dined with the Duke of Cambridge. Read Memoirs of Ld. P.—and. . . .

19. *3 S. Lent.*[1]

Chapel Royal mg and H.C.—H. of Charity Chapel aftn. Wrote to Rev. Mr Suffield—Rev. Mr Voysey[2]—Rev. Mr Oxenham. Read Montalembert on Spain (which in part disappoints me)[3]—Moeurs des Fourmis—Baynes's Sermon[4]— Proverbs of Aphobis[5]—Several Scott Series Tracts.[6]

20. *M.*

Wrote to Mr W. Morrison—Rev. Mr Heath (B.P.)[7]—E. Walker—Professor Bryce—H.J.G. (Telegr.). H. of C. $4\frac{1}{2}$-$7\frac{3}{4}$ & $8\frac{3}{4}$-$11\frac{1}{2}$ on Queen's Titles' Bill.[8] Wardour Street with C.G. Saw Mr James—Sir A. Gordon—Ld Hartington—Sir A. Panizzi—Mrs Th. Read Life of Dr N. Macleod[9]—Bryce on H.R. Empire.[10]

21. *Tu.*

Wrote to Mr R.P. Jeffery—Mr Wheatley—Mr Muir—Mr Guy Roslyn[11]—Mr Ffoot—Mr Hain Friswell[12]—Dr Cameron—Dr B. Langley—Rev. N. Hall—Ld Hatherley. Dined at Mr Hamilton's. H of C. $11\frac{1}{2}$-1.[13] Worked on Homer. Saw Lewis: not much gain [R]. Read Ashley's Palmerston—Soldier of Fortune.

22. *Wed.*

Wrote to J.K. Aston—J.H. Crellin—G. Loosley. Seventeen to dinner. Miss Robertson sang wonderfully afterwards. Saw Sir F. Doyle—Lord Granville—Mr E. Ashley—Mr Beresford Hope—Mr Pease—Mr Stuart Wortley. Luncheon at Sir Coutts Lindsay's. Meeting of Portrait Gallery Trustees afterwards, and went through the Gallery. Evening party till 12. Finished Ld P.s Life—Read Laveleyes 'L'Avenir Religieux'.[14]

---

[1] And wrote to R. Abbott on royal titles; *T.T.*, 27 March 1876, 11f.
[2] Charles *Voysey, 1828-1912; lost his living for unorthodoxy 1871; promoted theism in London; see 10 Mar. 76.
[3] See 12 Mar. 76.
[4] R. H. Baynes, perhaps 'Man, being in honour, abideth not. A sermon' (1865).
[5] *A record of the Patriarchal Age; or the proverbs of Aphobis*, tr. D. I. Heath (1858).
[6] i.e. tracts by *Scott of Ramsgate.
[7] Perhaps Charles Heath, curate of St. Margaret, Birmingham.
[8] Spoke several times on it: *H* 228. 272.
[9] D. Macleod, *Memoir of Norman Macleod*, 2v. (1876), reviewed by diarist in *Church Quarterly Review* (July 1876), reprinted in *Gleanings*, ii. 343.
[10] See 30 Mar. 66.
[11] Pseudonym of Joshua Hatton, Derbyshire poet, author of *George Eliot in Derbyshire* (1876).
[12] James Hain Friswell, 1825-78; novelist and essayist.
[13] Misc. business: *H* 228. 349.
[14] E. V. L. de Laveleye, *L'avenir religieux des peuples civilisés* (1876).

23. *Th.*[1]

Wrote to Ld Houghton—Mr Newdegate—W.T. Pears—J.T. Stitt—J. Smith—H. Edmonds—Messrs Hoare—Messrs Watson—Sir A.T. Galt—Mr H.A. Parry. Twelve to dinner: Mrs Brand's afterwards. Fourteen to breakfast. Saw Professor Reynolds—Mr Palgrave—Dr W. Smith—Mr Roundell—Sir A. Gordon—Mr Ellice. Saw Graham [R]. H. of C. 4½–7½. Interesting debate on Titles' Bill: of evil omen.[2] Read Trevelyan's Memoirs of Macaulay.[3]

24. *Fr.*

Wrote to Père Hyacinthe—Mr Swallow—E.C. Trott—Mr A. Strahan (B.P.)—Miss Jacobs[4]—Mr Rodwell—Sir F. Doyle. Dined at Sir B. Leighton's: much conversation with her.[5] Corrected Revises of Hippos. Saw Ld F. Cavendish—Herbert J.G. (profession)—Ld Hartington—Scotts—Mr Cartwright—Mr Barclay—Mr Murray.

25. *Annunciation. Sat.*

St Peter's E. Square at 5 P.M. Wrote to W.L. Gladstone—Rev. Dr Allon—Rev. R. Gordon[6]—Mr Pears (B.P.)—O.B. Cole—Freshfields—Herr Studniz—Miss Talbot—B. Pickard—N. Godden—W. Bristow[7]—F.A. Austin—Mr Willcox—A. Strahan. Long conversation with my dear son Harry who returned home last evening on his painful & most undeserved position.[8] Finished Soldier of Fortune. Read Trevelyan's Macaulay. Tea at Baroness Rothschild's. Saw Conte . . . there.

26. *4 S. Lent.*

Ch. Royal 10 AM and [blank]. Wrote to M. Emile de Laveleye—Mrs Dalton—Mr Mather. Saw Harry on his affairs—W.H.G. on Agency—H.N.G. on his affairs. Read Dupanloup's Letter to Minghetti[9]—Allon's Introd. to Binney[10]—and divers Tracts.

27. *M.*

Wrote to Canon Norris—A.J. Balfour[11]—E. Crane[12]—Miss M'Kenzie[13]—Remington & Co.—Rev. S.E.G.—Sir Thos G.—Mr Phillips. Saw Ld Granville—Harry on

[1] He also made a speech at the House of Charity, Greek Street, annual meeting; *T.T.*, 24 March 1876, 7f.

[2] Disraeli answered Gladstone with an amusing and sardonic speech; *H* 228. 484.

[3] G. O. Trevelyan, *The life and letters of Lord Macaulay*, 2v., just published; reviewed by diarist in *Quarterly Review*, cxlii. 1 (July 1876), one of his best literary pieces, and one of the finest critiques of Macaulay. See Introduction above, section vii.

[4] Jemima Jacobs of Bath, 'a Hero Worshipper'; Hawn P.   [5] See 25 Oct. 55.

[6] Perhaps Richard Gordon, vicar of Elsfield, Oxford.

[7] Perhaps John William Bristow, Cumberland gentleman.

[8] Back from India—the result of the dispute with Wyllie following Robertson Gladstone's death; Thomas, *Gladstone of Hawarden*, 68.

[9] F. A. P. Dupanloup, 'Second letter to M. Minghetti on the new Italian military law' (1876).

[10] H. Allon, 'A memorial of the late . . . Thomas Binney' (1874).

[11] Sending £300 as rent for Carlton Gardens; Add MS 44449, f. 227.

[12] Ebenezer Crane, marine store dealer and constituent.

[13] Miss F. M. MacKenzie of Edinburgh; Hawn P.

his affairs—Ld Hartington *cum* Mr Fawcett—do *cum* Mr Cartwright—Lady Waldegrave—Sir A. Panizzi—Mrs Th. Long conversation with Mrs Hope on the distressing state of the Newcastle family. Dined at Sir T. May's. Read Trevelyan's Macaulay—Jenkins on the Queen's Head.[1] H. of C. 4½-6½.[2]

28. *Tu.*

Wrote to Dr Plumptre—Rev G. Butler—Mr G.M. Joy. Dined at Sir E. Perry's. Packed box of books for Hawarden. Saw Harry on his affairs—Sig. Coscia[3]—Mr Weguelin MP.—Sir E. Perry. H of C. 4½-7½ and 10½-12½. Voted in 166 : 179 on Irish Franchise.[4] A sort of triumph. Read Macaulay's Life. Spoke at Mansion House Meeting for C.s convalescent Home.[5] Laid up with tightness on the chest at night.

29. *Wed.*

In bed all day. Saw Dr Clark. Read Trevelyan's Macaulay: a good spell. Finished Vol. 1.—Thornton on E.I. Public Works[6]—Our Work in Palestine.[7]

30. *Th.*

Wrote to J. Watson & Smith—Mr Wylrow[8]—John Grant—D. Grant—J. Knowles—J. Ross—Dr O. Webster (B.P.)—Mr C.S. Palmer[9]—Mr Hugessen—Mr Girdlestone—Mr Mooney—Mr Chance—Mr Myers—J.C. Earle.[10] Saw Ld Granville—Ld Hartington—Ld F. Cavendish—Rev. Mr Denton—Mr Murray—Rev. Mr Suffield—Mr Eaton. Twelve to breakfast. Dined at Mr Murrays. A fight with my softened cough. Read Earle Spiritual body—Ld S. de Redcliffe's Appeal[11]—Trevelyan's Macaulay (II).

31. *Fr.*

Rose at ten. Wrote to Mr A.C. Radnor—S. Dowell—W.A. Davison—M.J. Barry—Mr Newdegate—Rev Mr Jones—Miss White—Mr Medley. Dined with the F.C.s. Saw Ld Granville—Mr Knowles—Scotts—Mr Grogan (anr)—Sir W. Harcourt—Ld Lyttelton: who rallied a good deal this evening. Much preparation for departure from No 4 C.G. which we have liked so much. Also it is a departure from a *neighbourhood* where I have lived for forty years, & where I am the 'oldest inhabitant'. Truly one onward step in life. Read Trevelyan's Macaulay.

---

[1] [J. E. Jenkins], 'The blot on the Queen's Head' (1876); satire on Royal Titles Act.

[2] Merchant Shipping Bill; *H* 228. 627.

[3] Perhaps F. C. Coscia, later published on education in London (1885).

[4] Resolution to make the Irish borough franchise in line with the English: *H* 228. 763.

[5] *T.T.*, 29 March 1876, 12e.

[6] E. Thornton, *A summary of the history of the East India Company* (1833).

[7] Untraced tract.

[8] Could read 'Wytrow'.

[9] Possibly Cornelius Stocker Palmer, London clockmaker.

[10] John Charles Earle, b. 1850; London barrister and historian; author of *The spiritual body* (1876).

[11] Probably Stratford de Redcliffe's letter to *T.T.* of 31 December 1875 on the Balkans, reprinted in *The Eastern Question by the late . . . Stratford de Redcliffe* (1881), 6.

Sat. Ap. One 1876. [*Wellington College*]

Wrote to Mr Hyatt—Mr Phillips (Windsor). Packing, & off at 11 to Wellington College. Walk & conversation with E. Wickham. Mr Penny & Mr Tibbs dined: Mr Toye with his violin in evening.[1] Agnes D.G. so well and happy: Baby beautiful, does not now like my old face. Read Trevelyan's M—Contemp. Rev.— Spedding on Abbot—Sidgwick on Fellowships—Hunt on Newman.[2]

2. 5 S. Lent.

College Chapel at 12 and 8 P.M. Much conversation with E.W. Walk in afternoon. Wrote to Mr Knowles—To do, as Ed. of C.R.—Draft of do[3]— Algernon West—Ld F. Cavendish. Read C.R., Oxenham on Future Punishment[4]—Hymns (with Mr & Mrs W.)—Oakeley on Creation[5]—Several Tracts of Scott series.

3. M.

Chapel at 4 & 8 P.M. A confirmation: really edifying. Conversation with Bp of Oxford on Sisterhoods—And on the Keble [College] consecration.[6] Wrote to Duchess of Sirmoneta—Rev. Edw. Talbot—H.N.G. Made beginnings on Macaulay Review & Religious Thought Article.[7] Read Trevelyan.

4. Tu. [*London*]

Back to London at 10¾. Wrote to Mr G. Fletcher—Rev. C.F.S. Money—Rev. R.J. Simpson[8]—H.W. Hall—Dr W. Smith—Col. Neville. Saw Ld Wolverton—Ld F. Cavendish—Mr Balfour—Dr Benson—Ld Hartington *cum* Mr Forster. Attended Miss E. Balfour's marriage at 11.30 and the breakfast at 1.30.[9] H of C. at 4½. Ld H. was led by Disraeli into a trap.[10] We dined and slept at Kensington with the Wests. Read T.s Macaulay.

5. Wed.

Wrote a little on Macaulay.—C. laid up. Saw Sir A. Panizzi—Mrs Th.—Scotts —Ld Kimberley (on Edn)—D. of Argyll—Duchess of Argyll. Conclave at

---

[1] C. W. Penny, S. N. Tebbs, W. J. Toye: all members of staff.

[2] Articles by J. Spedding, H. Sidgwick and J. Hunt in *Contemporary Review*, xxvii. 653, 679, 764 (April 1876); Hunt's article led to Gladstone's 'Courses of religious thought'; see 2 and 3 Apr. 76n.

[3] On J. H. Newman, Wesley, and anglican secessions in *Contemporary Review*, xxviii. 168 (June 1876).

[4] Four articles by H. N. Oxenham, *Contemporary Review*, xxvii. 222, 425, 615, 724 (January-April 1876).

[5] F. Oakeley, *The voice of creation* (1876).

[6] A row between Keble college and the bp.; Gladstone offered to mediate; Add MS 44449, f. 247.

[7] For Macaulay, see 23 Mar. 76n.; 'The courses of religious thought' for Knowles' *Contemporary Review*, xxviii. 1 (June 1876); Add MS 44695, f. 1; *Gleanings*, iii.

[8] Robert James Simpson, unbeneficed priest living in the Strand.

[9] Marriage of Eleanor, A. J. Balfour's sister, to Henry *Sidgwick; see 10 Aug. 75.

[10] On the order of business and the Royal Titles Bill: *H* 228. 1181.

Granville's 3¼-5. Dined with the Ducies.[1] Read T.s Macaulay—Arnold on Ch. of Engl.[2]

6. Th.

Wrote to Ld Hartington—Ld A. Russell—Watsons (B.P.)—Warden of Keble—Dr Croce[3]—Hon C.L. Wood. Dined at Lady Stanley's. Saw Deputation from Greenwich on Income Tax.[4] Saw Rev. Mr West—Sir Harcourt Johnstone—Sir W. Harcourt—Warden of Keble—Mr Jenkins—Mr Lowe—Mr [E.]L. Stanley. Read Masson on Mrs Thrale[5]—Trevelyan's Macaulay.

7. Fr.

Chapel 8.30 AM. Wrote to Surveyor of Taxes—Mr Knollys—Mr Hindley[6]—Mr Ireland—Mr Macmillan—Ed. D. Telegraph[7]—Ed. Times—Mr Hart—Sec. G.P.O.—Mrs M'Laren. Wrote on Macaulay. H. of C. 4½-6¾.[8] Dined with the Argylls. Read Life of Macaulay—Servian Poetry.[9]

8. Sat. [Hawarden]

Chapel 8½ AM. Wrote to Mr Adam. Walked into town & transacted business in Harley Street where progress is but slow. Wrote on Chart of Religion. Read Life of Macaulay—Servian Poetry & Preface. Off to Hawarden 2.15. Arrived at the Rectory 8.30. The best of welcomes.

9. Palm S.

Ch. 11 AM & 6.30 P.M. Read Divers Tracts—Hist of St George's Church[10]—Oakeley's Lectures on Creation.[11] Wrote on Chart of Religion.

10. M.

Church 8¾ AM. Wrote to Mr Goodeve Mabbs[12]—Sir B. Leighton—Sir Jas Watson—Mr Hubbard—Mr Peddle—E. Watkin—Mr Jas Knowles—C. Mill—R. Eykyn—Pickett. Saw Mrs Peake and Helen G. on business. Arranging papers &c. Read Account of Robroy[13]—Life of Macaulay—Grote's History of Greece.[14] Wrote Chart of Religion.

[1] Lord Ducie (see 10 Dec. 68) and his wife Julia.

[2] M. Arnold, *Saint Paul and Protestantism; with an introduction on puritanism and the Church of England* (3rd ed. 1875); see 14 Nov. 69.

[3] Enrico Croce, Italian author; see Add MS 44449, f. 232.

[4] No account found, but see 19 Apr. 76n. Hubbard this day moved a motion on income tax: *H* 228. 1331.

[5] R. O. Masson, 'Mrs. Thrale', *Macmillan's*, xxxiii. 524 (April 1876).

[6] Charles Hindley, London carpet-maker.

[7] Letters to *T.T.* and the *Telegraph* announcing departure from London.

[8] Spoke on a petition from 'Inhabitants of Boulogne', deb. on Woolwich arsenal; *H* 228. 1413.

[9] J. Bowring, *Servian popular poetry* (1827).

[10] Untraced.   [11] See 2 Apr. 76.

[12] Goodeve Mabbs of Nottingham, author of *The Churches in Derbyshire* (1876).

[13] *An account of the life, transactions and death of Rob Roy M'gregor* (1810?).

[14] See 19 Mar. 47.

11. Tu.

Ch. 8.45 AM. Wrote to Mr Batchelor[1]—Mr J.A. Godley—Mr Best—Rev. S. Smith.[2] Read Trevelyan's Macaulay (finished)—Selwyn's Pastoral Colloquies[3]—Ancient Symbol Worship[4]—Macaulay's Bacon.[5] Wrote Chart of Religion.

12. Wed.

Ch. 8:45 AM. Wrote to W.H.G.—Dean of Chester—Mr Stone and Maj. Whisk of Boulogne[6]—Mr Newmarch—Edw. Smith. Walk with Herbert & conversation on points of history. Conversation with C.G. also with Willy on the proposal to establish a house at Penmaenmawr. Both C. & I press *strongly* for residence. Read Macaulay's Bacon. Wrote Chart of Religion.

13. Th.

H.C. at 8. Morning prayer as usual afterwards. Wrote to Rev. Canon Ashwell—Rev Mr Davis—Mr J.R. Martin—C.S. Palmer. Finished Macaulay's Bacon. Read Q.R. on Green's History.[7] Wrote Chart of Rel.—And on Macaulay. We made progress by conversation in the matter of W. & G.s residence. It will be *on the ground*.

14. Good Friday.

Church at 7 A.M.—11 A.M.—& 7 P.M. Read Lee on Inspiration[8]—Macaulay on Milton[9]—Hist. St George's Congregn Edinb.—Heygate's Why am I a Christian.[10] Wrote Chart of Religion. Walk with C.

15. Sat.

Easter Eve. H.C. at 8 AM. and Evg prayer 8½ PM. Wrote to Edw. Talbot—Watsons (for Helen G.)—Sec. M. Dist. Co for me, for d[itt]o. Read Ch. Quart. R. on Oxford—Macaulay's Milton (finished)—Milton on Divorce—on Toleration—& on Polygamy—Plumptre's Sermons[11]—Selwyn's Dialogues (finished)—Life of Norman Macleod. Wrote on Macaulay. Walk & hist. conversation with Herbert.

16. Easter Day.

H.C. at 8 AM Morning Pr. 11 AM. Evg 6½ PM. Read Ch. [Quarterly Review?] and Life of Norman Macleod. Conversation with S.

[1] Perhaps George Andrew Batchelor, India merchant.
[2] Perhaps Samuel Smith, anglican priest helping the deaf and dumb.
[3] W. Selwyn, *Pastoral colloquies on the South Downs* (1875).
[4] See 3 Jan. 76.
[5] In Macaulay's *Essays*, iii.
[6] Business arising from his speech; see 7 Apr. 76n.
[7] *Quarterly Review*, cxli. 285 (April 1876).
[8] W. Lee, *The inspiration of holy scripture* (1854).
[9] In Macaulay's *Essays*, i.
[10] By W. E. Heygate (1876).
[11] E. H. Plumptre, 'Respice, aspice, prospice. Two sermons' (1876).

17. *Easter M.*

H.C. at 8 A.M. Evg prayer at 7 P.M. Wrote to Ed. Journal of Amusement[1]—Mr Jas. Barnard—Rev. E. Talbot—Mrs Bennett—Mr Raeburn—Rev. Sir G. Prevost—Mr Pitman[2]—Mr Macveigh. Worked on my projected article for Q.R. about Trevelyan's Macaulay. Recommenced the Life, making notes. Read N. Macleod's Life. Conversation with Harry on his affairs. Four hours on Exorship and Estate affairs, principally with Messrs T. & B.

18. *Easter T.*

Ch. 8¾ AM. Wrote to Mr Knowles (MS of Aiolos)[3]—Mr Downing (Brmm)—Watsons—Rev. Dr Rees. Conversation with the Rector. Saw Ld Blantyre. Began work on Athenè. Read N. Macleod's Life—Trevelyan's Macaulay.

19. *Wed.*[4]

Ch. 8¼ AM. Wrote to Dr W.C. Bennett[5]—Lawrence Talbot—Mrs Hampton. Worked on Athenè. Read Dr Macleod's Life—Trevelyan's Macaulay.

In the morning C. called me while I was dressing, & I knew the tone portending evil. Letters from P[ark] Crescent announced that George [Lyttelton], rushing away from his attendant had begun violently to descend the stairs, then went over the bannisters from the landing and was taken up at the foot insensible. He remained so at post time. About eleven came a Telegram to announce that he died soon after midnight, still insensible. The letters justified our believing the fall an accident. Only after two days did it come before us that it was intended: intended not by him but by that which possessed him.[6] How deep are the mysteries of God. This is horrible. But let us trust, & adore. With how clean a scroll is he gone before the Eternal.

20. *Th.*

Ch. 8¼ A.M. Wrote to W.L. Gladstone—Mr Warwick Brookes—Agnes Wickham—Mr Jas Wilson—Mrs M. Slack—Mr G.J. Holmes—Dean of Elphin—Mr Godfrey Wedgwood.[7] Worked on Athenè. But all is out of course. Also worked with my sons on the great Beech Tree. Read Macaulay 2°, & made notes. Read Life of N. Macleod.

---

[1] Not found published; *Whitaker's journal of amusing and instructive literature* only ran January-June 1876.

[2] Perhaps Frederick Pitman, London publisher.

[3] Part of his *Contemporary Review* article of 1874 was used for *Homeric Synchronism* (1876).

[4] This entry is surrounded by a black line.

[5] Of Greenwich, on income tax, for a public meeting; *T.T.*, 21 April 1876, 9f.

[6] See 14 May 76.

[7] Godfrey Wedgwood, 1833-1905; master potter of Etruria; supporter of Chamberlain, but remained free trader.

21. Fr.

Ch. 8½ A.M. Wrote to Editor of Observer[1]—Gen. Ponsonby—Station master Chester (2)—Rev. C. Finch[2]—Sir J. Maclean[3]—Mrs Hampton—Mr Lowe—Mr Knowles—Mr Bramwell—Mr Abahall.[4] Worked on Athenè. Finished Life of Macleod. Lucy arrived, with F., in deep grief. Our journey was put off by message from H[agley] till tomorrow. The great tree, begun upon before the sad news, was brought down today: when one subject pressed hard upon every other. I had to attend the Dee Trust Meeting 12-1¼ and then to go through the Residuary Executorship and Succession Duty accounts with Mr Hignett.

22. Sat. [Hagley]

Off by the early train. Wrote to J. Watson & Smith—Sir J. Watson—Prof. Curry[5]—Sir S. Scott & Co—Ly Herbert—Mr Lowe—Mr Morrison—Mr De Lisle— Capt Clark.

We arrived at 1.30: amidst what mourning! The funeral at two. A very large number attended in & outside the Church: full of grief and reverence. Conversation with Herbert on History—Harry, on his prospects—F. Cavendish— Mr Marcy respecting Will &c.—Bp of Oxford—Mr Archer Clive[6]—J. Talbot.

23. 1 S.E.

—Holy Communion 8 AM. Ch. at 11 when Bp of Oxford preached admirably. Bp of Rochester in evg. Wrote to Messrs Freshfield—Rev. Mr Crawley[7]—Rev. Mr Olden[8]—Canon Oakeley—Mr Callcott[9]—Mr Lewis—Mrs Th.

Great crowds in Church; almost all in mourning. Much conversation especially with F. C[avendish] who shows better than ever in this sad hour. After much conversation & consideration went to work upon the very difficult duty of writing a notice to The Guardian,[10] which I executed but not to my satisfaction. However they were pleased: & we discussed & disposed of the doubtful points. Read Dickinsons Quarterly on St Luke's Gospel (finished)[11]—Oakeley's Lectures (finished). Every morning as we wake the 'blot in heaven' rises on the eye.

24. M. [Hawarden]

Wrote a very long letter to C. Lyttelton on the family matters, & a covering note. Also to W.L. Gladstone—Sir Thos G.—Marion G.—Sir F. Grant—W.N. Marcy—Rev. W. Nevins—Mr Adam. Also much conversation on the Notice for

[1] On royal titles; *The Guardian*, 26 April 1876, 537.
[2] Frederick Charles Finch, anglican priest; on Lyttelton's death; Hawn P.
[3] Sir John *Maclean, 1811-95; antiquarian and genealogist.
[4] May read 'Ahahall'; both untraced.
[5] Professor M. Currie, apparently an American, requested an autograph; Hawn P.
[6] Archer Anthony Clive, 1842-77, Lyttelton's br.-in-law by his second marriage; see 29 July 61n.
[7] Perhaps Henry Owen Crawley, chaplain of Melksham Union 1862-81.
[8] Thomas Olden, anglican incumbent at Ballyclough.
[9] Perhaps William Hutchins Callcott of Campden House Road, London.
[10] *The Guardian*, 26 April 1876, 540-1, printed an obituary and a leader signed 'W.E.G.'; draft at Add MS 44763, f. 19. Reprinted in *Brief memorials of Lord Lyttelton* (1876).
[11] By D. S. Gregory, in *Dickinson's Quarterly*, xi. 228 (April 1876).

the Guardian, & the family prospects. Especially with Sybella;[1] who is excellent. We went off at four; and reached Hawarden before nine. Curious conversation with an R.C. at Wolverhampton Station. Read T's Macaulay (2°)—Todhunter on Whewell[2]—Q.R. on the Herschels.

25. Tu. St Mark.

Ch. 8.45 AM. Wrote to Messrs T. & B. Mr E. Conolly[3]—Canon Ashwell—Mrs Mochler[4]—Miss Kortright—Ld Carnarvon—Creswicks[5]—Rev. H. Lansdell[6]— Rev. D.T. Gladstone—Mr Vickers—Sir Thos G.—Mr Parker—Mr Lawrence—Mr Elwell[7]—Mr Kernahan. Saw Harry on his matters—W.H.G. on the question of residence. Much conversation with C.G. Worked on Dr N. Macleod. Read Whewell Hist. Ind. Philosophy.[8]

26. Wed.

Off at 7¾ to Liverpool. Saw Mr Balfour—Robn Gladstone—Mr Heywood—W.L. Gladstone—Mr Stone—Mr Hignett—Mr Townshend—Two hours & a half with Mr Harris[9] on Seaforth management, income, accounts, & agency: on House matters & respecting Harry. Saw Mrs Dunn. Home at 6. Conversation with Lord Blantyre—Also with W. & C. on the Agency. Wrote to Ld Hartington—Mr Townshend. Read Catullus: he is really wonderful—Whewell, Inductive Phil.

27. Th.

Ch. 8½ AM. Wrote to Mr Hitchman—Sir Thos G.—Rev. I. Taylor (BP)—Mr Downing—Barker & Hignett—Mr Jones (Cross Tree)—Rev. F.C. Finch—Mr E.L. Lawson—Watsons—Mr Turner—A. Clark[10]—C.E. Giles—J. Whitaker.

I had a long conversation with Gertrude on the question of residence & all that has grown out of it, including the general view of life, on which I spoke plainly, & she took it most amiably. Then went over the subject with C; and we called on Mrs Burnett. Worked on N. Macleod: but family business encroaches largely. Conversation with Harry. Promised to find for him 12 m[ille], on which he should pay me two per Cent per ann. The same for Herbert when he is ready. Read Rees on Wales[11]—Clergyman's Mag (Ryle).[12]

[1] Lyttelton's widow.
[2] I. Todhunter, *William Whewell. An account of his writings* (1876).
[3] Edward Conolly, London barrister; corresponded on Latin hymns; Hawn P.
[4] Clara Isabella Mockler (sometimes spelt Mochler by Gladstone) of Teignmouth; had lost money on the 1854 Turkish bonds, and was being assisted by Gladstone; Hawn P. She also appears in F.O.C.P. 4250, f. 93.
[5] London silversmiths.
[6] Henry Lansdell, unbeneficed anglican priest living in Blackheath.
[7] Perhaps Francis Richard Elwell, London photographer.
[8] W. Whewell, *History of the inductive sciences*, 3v. (1837).
[9] George Harris managed the Seaforth property; Hawn P.
[10] Archibald Clarke; see 29 Apr. 76, otherwise unidentified.
[11] T. Rees, probably *History of Protestant nonconformity in Wales* (1861).
[12] *Clergyman's Magazine*, xi. 240 (April 1876); 'Simplicity in preaching' by J. C. Ryle.

28. Fr.

Ch. 8½ A.M. Wrote to Duke of Argyll—Mr G. Harris—Mr Knowles—Mr T. Ellis. Finished Macleod. Treecutting with W. More agency conversations: That question does not seem to close up yet. Read Hist. Isle of Man.[1] Worked a little on Athenè.

29. Sat.

Wrote to C.G. Lyttelton—Ld F. Cavendish—Mr Archie Clarke—Mr Morison—Rev. S. Taylor—Rev. W. Nevins—Rev. H. Overy—Mrs H. Ward.[2] Worked on Athenè. Further discussion on the Agency. Read Hist. Isle of Man—'He that overcometh'.[3] Read De Maistre[4] & Biogr. Univ. on Bacon.

30. 2 S.E.

Ch. 11 AM and 6¼ P.M. Wrote to Ld Hartington—Mr C.E. Lewis[5]—Mrs M.J. Heath (B.P.) Read 'He that overcometh'—Seccombe on Science &c.[6]—Mrs Alexander's beautiful Children's Hymns[7]—and divers tracts. Conversation with the Rector[8] on his projected trip to America: it is to be tested as being or not being a recreation. Walked with Mr Zwinckenbart.[9] Worked on Chart of Rel. Thought. Sent off papers on Dr Macleod to Canon Ashwell.[10]

Mon. May One 76. SS. Ph. & James.

Church H.C. at 8 A.M. Wrote to Rev. H.S. Thompson—Rev G.F. Boyle[11]—Miss Doyle—Mr J. Smith jun.—Watsons—Mr T. Turnerelli.[12] Worked on Athenè & on accounts. Settled a draft to T. & B. on Agency. Examined sites: the Burnett house was decided on.[13] Read Ld Crawford's Argo[14]—'He that overcometh' Vol. II.

2. Tu.

Ch. 8¼ AM. Wrote to Mr Hodgson Pratt—Jas Knowles—E. Davison—Mr F. May.[15] Willy & I finished a large oak of the Rector's, which we began yesterday.

---

[1] A complete history of the Isle of Man (1821).

[2] Perhaps Mary Augusta *Ward, née Arnold, 1851-1920; m. 1872 Thomas Humphry Ward, leader writer on T.T.; Gladstone reviewed her Robert Elsmere (1888) at great length; he could have been in contact with her earlier on charitable works.

[3] By F. A. Kortright, 2v. (1876).

[4] J. M. de Maistre, Examen de la philosophie de Bacon, 2v. (1836).

[5] (Sir) Charles Edward Lewis, 1825-93; tory M.P. Londonderry 1872-86; cr. bart. 1887.

[6] J. T. Seccombe, Science, theism and revelation (1875).

[7] C. F. Alexander, Hymns for little children (1848), including 'Once in royal David's city'.

[8] i.e. his son, Stephen.

[9] Not identified; did not sign the Visitors Book.   [10] See 20 Mar. 76n.

[11] To George David Boyle (1828-1901; vicar of Kidderminster 1867-80; dean of Salisbury from 1880) on Lyttelton's death: he was curate at Hagley 1859-60.

[12] See 11 June 77.

[13] i.e. the deceased agent's house to be occupied by W. H. Gladstone.

[14] A. W. C. Lindsay, Lord Crawford, Argo: or the quest of the golden fleece (1876).

[15] Probably Frederick May, the Queen's newsagent.

Worked much on Athenè. And somewhat on the Chart of Thought touching religion. Read Ld Crawford's Argo—He that overcometh.

3. Wed.

Ch. 8¼ AM. Wrote to Chester Stationmaster—Ed. Times[1]—Ed. Telegraph—Mr Warwick Brookes—J.W. Pickersgill[2]—A.R. Edwards—Jas Knowles—Ld Granville (Tel.)—Messrs B. & H.—W.H.G. Walk with S.E.G. to Shotton cottages. Advised him not to let secular reading drop. Wrote on Chart of Religion—& corrected Homeric papers. Finished 'He that overcometh' and read. . . .

4. Th. [Hagley]

Ch. 8½ A.M. Wrote to J. Watson & Smith—Rev Dr Butler—Sir Thos G.—Mr Hitchman—M. Mailfer[3]—Miss Kortright—Mr Earp—Ld Granville—Mrs Th.—Mr J.G. Talbot—Messrs T. & B. A very busy morning in arranging & preparing. Saw Mrs Griffiths—Mrs Stume—E.W. Waters—on their business.[4] Read Dean of Bristol on the Iconoclasm.[5] Off at 3.30. reached Hagley at 8; & found all as well as could be hoped.

5. Fr.

Four or five hours conversation with Charles, Mr Marcy, & Mr Mathews, gave me for the first time a view of the situation of things here, and enabled me to say to Charles such things as occurred, especially as to the need of some farther margin than is supplied by the present arrangements. Read Whewell's Letters[6]—Chillingworth's Works[7]—Dr Butlers Homeric Verses.[8] Wrote to Scotts—Mrs Hampton.

6. Sat. [London]

Wrote to Helen G.—Dr Seccombe[9]—Barker & Hignett. Worked on Macaulay. Read (½) Macaulay's Bacon—Chillingworth—& accounts of Turkish Loans. Some further examination of the facts here, & maps. Off at 5¾. Saw Harry at Oxford & settled about some letters to be written. 21 C.H.T.[10] at 11.15 and long conversation with F. & the party.

7. 3 S.E.

Chapel Royal at 10 A.M. St James's 7 PM. Walked with C.G. Saw Terry [R?]— Ld Granville—Ld Wolverton. Read Ch. Quart. divers Articles—Carter on the

---

[1] Details of movements.
[2] Possibly John William Pickersgill, author of *Lays of my youth* (1857).
[3] N. Mailfer of Paris had sent a book, perhaps H. C. Mailfer (see 29 Jan. 75); Hawn P.
[4] Of the Hawarden household.
[5] G. Elliot, *Bristol Cathedral* (1876); on its statues.   [6] See 24 Apr. 76.
[7] W. Chillingworth, *Works* (probably the 10th ed. 1742).
[8] H. M. Butler, *Six translations from the Old and New Testaments into Homeric verse* (1876).
[9] John Thomas Seccombe, physician in King's Lynn, had sent his book; see 30 Apr. 76.
[10] Lord F. Cavendish's.

Passion.[1] Wrote to Ld Wolverton—Mr G. Browning[2]—Mr Harrison—and Mr Lambert.[3]
[A thick black line is drawn across the column here. Underneath it, as follows:—]
Dined with J. Wortley. He talked boldly, largely, and most sympathetically, over the circumstances of Lyttelton's death.
[Text continues at top of next column:—]

8. M.

Saw Mr West (Mrs Croker)—Sir A. Panizzi—Sir Thos G. (family)—Scotts—F.C. & L.C.C. (Hagley)—Mrs H[ampto]n (at No 73 [Harley Street])—Ld Wolverton. 3-6. Mr Irvine [*sic*] read Hamlet at Ld Ducie's. It was full of interest. Read Keppel Memoirs.[4]—Saw two X.

9. Tu.

Wrote to W. Chaffers—Herbert J.G.—F. Lambert—Miss Sindarn—G.O. Garey—Emile Laveleye—W.E. Swain—W.L.G. (draft)—C. Farley—G. Battensberger. Conversation with Harry on his affairs—Mr Moffatt on d[itt]o—W.H.G. on Hn affairs—Mr Goschen—Mr Bright—Mr Knowles—Mr Murray & Dr Smith at great length on the Q.R. Croker and Macaulay matter.[5] H. of C. $4\frac{1}{2}$-$7\frac{1}{4}$. Spoke (reluctant to reenter this arena) on the Royal Academy.[6] $7\frac{1}{2}$-$10\frac{1}{4}$. Metaphysical Society. Discussion of considerable interest on Ld A. Russell's paper.[7] Worked on Chart of Religion.[8] Saw Phillips: & one—X.

10. Wed.

Wrote to Mr Spedding—Robn & Nichn—Rev. Dr Barry—W.L. Gladstone (draft corrected and dispatched)—J.A. Walker—J.A.R. Morison. Saw Phillips—Mr Godley—Scotts—Mr Herbert R.A. Saw Harry (enlarged draft)—W.H.G. on Agency—Mr Knowles—on papers in preparation. Luncheon at 15 G.S. Dined with the Jameses. Read [Tennyson's] Guinevere—aloud: & with undiminished admiration. Worked on Chart of Religious Thought.

11. Th.

Wrote to Town Clerk of City—Prime Warden of Fishmongers—Clerk & Registrar of Guy's Hosp.—Miss L. Lloyd[9]—J. Parker—G. Smith—E. Goodburn—

[1] By T. T. Carter in his *Manual of devotion*, 2v. (1868).
[2] George Browning of Berkeley Chambers, Bruton Street, London.
[3] Frederick Lambert, an active lay Anglican and br.-in-law of W. Heygate, had written on ritualism; Hawn P.
[4] G. T. Keppel, earl of Albemarle, *Fifty years of my life*, 2v. (1876).
[5] Macaulay's celebrated dispute with Croker over the latter's edition of Boswell's *Johnson*; W. *Smith, the editor of the *Quarterly*, to which Croker had been a prominent contributor, dealt with the topic in an article in the same number as the diarist's review of Trevelyan's *Macaulay*: 'the controversy relating to this work is too important to be dismissed with a passing notice' (*Gleanings*, ii. 298). See also West, *Recollections*, ii. 74.   [6] H 229. 294.
[7] On 'The persistence of religious feeling'; Brown, *Metaphysical Society*, 330.
[8] See 3 Apr. 76.   [9] Perhaps the rescue case; see 2 July 75.

Major Chiene—Mr Strahan—Mr Watts—Mr Ouvry—Sig. E. Rossi.[1] Dined with the W.H.G.s. Visited 73 H[arley] St, still chaotic. Shopping with C. H of C. $5\frac{1}{2}$-$7\frac{3}{4}$ and $10\frac{1}{4}$-$1\frac{1}{2}$. Voted in 226:334 on Royal Titles' Proclamation.[2] Read Bp Phillpotts and Macaulay Correspondence[3]—Harrison on Positivism.[4] Finished MS. of Chart of Religious Thought.

12. Fr.

Wrote to Dean of Rochester BP.—C.W. Meikle—Sir T. Dakin—P.H. Rathbone—Dr Peterson[5]—Rev Mr Cookesley. Saw General Menabrea—Sir Thos G.—Sir W. Farquhar—Lord Wolverton—Mr Dodson—Mr Childers—Sir Drummond Wolff. Worked on Athenè. H. of C. $4\frac{3}{4}$-$7\frac{1}{2}$ and $10\frac{1}{4}$-$12\frac{3}{4}$. Spoke on Irish Sunday Closing, and voted in 224:167.[6]

13. Sat.

Wrote to Council Alb[ert] Hall—Rev. Mr Andrewes[7]—Mr Bryce—Mrs Brackenridge—Dr Bartling[8]—Mr J. Macveigh—Mrs Barrett[9]—Duke of Argyll. Worked on Athenè. Saw Phillips & read Hamlet [R]. Saw Mr Newmarch—The Duke of Argyll. Moved into Harley Street. Dined with [blank]. Found a chaos of letters papers & parcels.

14. 4 S.E.

All Souls Ch. mg & aft. Read Mozley's Sermons (admirable)[10]—Dr Mellor on Priesthood[11]—Mivart on Development[12]—and Tracts.[13]

C. & I went to No 18 Park Crescent to observe the fatal stair. Its structure is dangerous; & it confirmed the notion I had previously entertained of the *likelihood* that he [i.e. George Lyttelton] never meant at all to throw himself over, but fell in a too rapid descent, over the bannisters.[14]

Dined with the Wenlocks.

15. M.

Wrote to Sir Thos G.—Messrs T. & B.—Ld Granville—Sir W. Knowles—Jas Lord—T.B. Green—Mr G. Harris—Consul Crowe[15]—Rev. Mr Hales—

[1] Perhaps Ernesto Rossi, Italian Shakespearean actor and author.
[2] Vote of censure moved by Sir H. James: *H* 229. 470.
[3] See *Gleanings*, ii. 317.   [4] F. Harrison, *Order and progress* (1875).
[5] R. E. Peterson of Maida Vale had sent some axes; Hawn P.
[6] i.e. voting with most Irish members in favour of Sunday closing: *H* 229. 570.
[7] Probably Nesfield Andrewes, 1844-1916; vicar of Southwater 1873-94.
[8] Or Barkling, see 15 May 76.
[9] Perhaps Elizabeth Barrett of Park Street, London.
[10] J. B. Mozley, *Sermons preached before the university of Oxford* (1876).
[11] E. Mellor, *Priesthood in the light of the New Testament* (1876).
[12] St. G. J. Mivart, *Contemporary evolution* (1876).
[13] Next sentence added, with a cross-reference, two pages later.
[14] This paragraph surrounded by a thick black line.
[15] (Sir) Joseph Archer Crowe, 1825-96; consul in Dusseldorf, doubtless on Helen Gladstone's affairs.

J. Macveigh—Mr Bromfield—Mr Annett—Mr Mumford—Mr Ramwell—Mr Willans—H. Clark—Mr Cayley—G. Mabbs. Dined with the F.C.s. Luncheon at 15 G.S. to meet the Breadalbanes.[1] H. of C. 4½-7¾ and 10½-12¾: voted agt Govt expenditure.[2] Saw Mr Ouvry—Dr Barkling. Worked on papers books &c. in a vague & distant hope of order.

16. Tu.

Wrote to Mr Mavrocordato—Mr Allingham[3]—Miss Edwards[4]—Sir J. Shuttleworth—Rev. Mr Molesworth—Dr Miller—Dr Vaughan—Leverett & Frye[5]—Mr Bencke—Mr Hilton—D.D. Hill—Mr Gühler—M. Pressensé.[6] Sat to Watts 12¼-2. Delightful conversation, but little progress in the picture.[7] Luncheon at A[rgyll] Lodge. Saw the Duke of Argyll. Saw Elford [R]. Dined with the Jameses. Worked much on arranging papers and effects. Read Spedding No II in C.R. on Bacon—Mayor on Oxenham.[8]

17. Wed.

Wrote to D. of Argyll B.P.—Gertrude Pennant—Helen G.—Mr J.E. Tugman[9]— Mr Marcy—Supt LNW Goods Station Chester—Archd. Harrison—Messrs Kelly—Mr T.B. Vernon[10]—Mr Constable[11]—Rev. Mr Grosart—Mr West. Saw Scotts—Ld Wolverton—Sir C.A. Wood. Agnes & Edward came: our first dinner at home. Corrected Aiolos for press: and worked on proofs of 'Religious Thought'.[12] Saw one [R]. We now make some progress towards order. Shopping with C.

18. Th.

Wrote to Ed. Leisure Hours—Rev. T.S. Jones[13]—Rev. Mr Meredith—Dr Harris— Mr D. Carnegie[14]—A. Austin—Mr Strachan—G. Hickson—E. Owen—Mr Pryce—

---

[1] Gavin Campbell, 1851-1922; 6th earl of Breadalbane 1871; household office as a whig 1873-4, 1880-5, 1892-5; cr. marquis 1885. He m. 1872 Alma, da. of 4th duke of Montrose.

[2] H 229. 753.

[3] William *Allingham, 1824-89; ed. Fraser's Magazine; asked, unsuccessfully, for a contribution; Add MS 44449, f. 314.

[4] Amelia Ann Blanford *Edwards, 1831-92; novelist and Egyptologist; see Add MS 44449, f. 308 and 29 Dec. 76.

[5] London grocers; on grocers' licences; in T.T., 19 May 1876, 10b.

[6] Edmond Déhault de Pressensé, 1824-91; French historian and theologian.

[7] This portrait (see 19 May 74) was commissioned by subscribers for Christ Church; H. L. Thompson of the college had written to request its completion by the summer Gaudy (see Add MS 44449, f. 317); it was shown at the Gaudy in 1878, but was 'not liked'; in May 1879 Dean Liddell took it back to Watts, who painted out the face; Gladstone then refused to give further sittings except at Hawarden; Watts abandoned the picture and returned the money; instead, after an unsuccessful attempt by W. B. Richmond, the second of Millais' portraits found its way to Christ Church 1885; see R. Lane Poole, Catalogue of Portraits in Oxford (1926), iii. 104 and Introduction above, section ix.

[8] J. Spedding and J. B. Mayor in Contemporary Review, xxvi. 821, 886 (May 1876).

[9] James E. Tugman, tr. works from Portuguese.

[10] Thomas Bowater Vernon, of Randolph Gardens, London; business untraced.

[11] Henry Constable, anglican priest in Hackney; in correspondence on eternal punishment; Hawn P.   [12] See 3 Apr. 76.

[13] Thomas Simpson Jones, curate at Stoke Newington.

[14] Probably David Carnegie, temperance advocate; wrote on the Gothenburg system (1873).

J.C. Earle. Saw Mayor of Leicester[1]–Sir A. Panizzi–Sir C.A. Wood–Sir Jas Watson–Mr West–Mr Spedding–Mr Knowles–Rev. N. Hall–Ld Wolverton– Mr Palgrave–Dr Smyth. Finished proofs of paper on Religious Thought. Read Martineau's Articles in Reply to Tyndall.[2] Dined with Ld Wolverton. H. of C. 9¾-1¼: spoke against the new Exemptions.[3]

19. Fr.

Wrote to Mr Macmillan–Mr J.F. Daly[4]–H.P. Gilby–W. Grogan–Sir A. Galt– Sec. Antislavery Society[5]–Robert Gladstone–Mr Eddy (LNW)–Rev. T. Vere Bayne. Dined with Mr Spottiswoode and attended Mr Newton's Lecture on Olympia. Saw Dr Clark. Saw Hallett [R]? Corrected proofs of Article on Dr N. Macleod. Conversation with H. on his matters. Began La Liberté comme en Belgique.[6]

20. Sat.

Wrote to Mrs Amadou–Morris Moore jun.–Rev. E.L. Murphy[7]–Rev. Canon Norris–Rev. A.H. Black–Miss Skene[8]–Ld De Tabley–Mr Strahan (Proofs &c.)–A. Burt–J.C. Earle–F.S. Turner–W. Smith–J. Alehurst. Saw Mr Macmillan–Mr [E. H.] Palmer (Dep. Gov. Bank)–Field on his sad affair[9]–Phillips + Bishop [?R]. Read Romeo & Juliet. Worked on Athenè. Dined with the Cowpers. Much pleased both with Père Hyacinthe and with Madame.[10]

21. May. 5 S.E.

Parish Ch mg & St James's–Chapel Royal 5½ PM. Heard two preachers in the Park. Saw Ld Wolverton–Ld Hanmer–and [blank]. Read Mozley's Sermons[11]– Arthur Leigh's Poems[12]–and divers Tracts. Wrote on the Greek Triad.

22. M.

Wrote to Mr Ouvry–Mr Heyworth–Mr Phelps. Saw Ld Granville–Ld Field –Mr Goschen–Sir H. Johnstone–Ld F. Cavendish–Mr Knowles–Sir R.

[1] See 5 Jan. 76.
[2] J. Martineau, *Modern materialism* (1876), replying to J. Tyndall.
[3] Opposing new income tax exemptions; *H* 229. 986.
[4] John Fairley Daly (later a Free Church minister), undergraduate at Glasgow University and president of the Glasgow University Liberal Association, inviting diarist to stand for the next Lord Rectorship; 'our University, which has so long been a Tory Stronghold, is beginning to yield to Liberal influences, & the Committee feels that very much depends upon the candidate that is secured at next election, whether this beginning be confirmed'; Hawn P. He agreed to nomination in Spring 1877; see 11 Apr. 77n.
[5] Aaron Buzacott, its secretary 1875-8; business untraced.
[6] Untraced.
[7] Eustace L. Murphy, Roman catholic priest in Dublin, on Vaticanism; Add MS 44450, f. 53.
[8] Felicia Mary Frances Skene, author, requested help with her memoir of Abp. Lycurgos; Add MS 44450, f. 94. See 3 Aug. 77.
[9] See 30 Oct. 76.
[10] Loyson's marriage, while nominally a Roman catholic priest, had caused a scandal in Paris; see 28 Nov. 70, 24 May 76.   [11] See 14 May 76.
[12] A. Leigh, *New Minnesinger and other poems* (1875).

Knightley—Sir Jas Watson. Dined at the Bp of Winchester's.[1] Conversation with him. Read Skene's Autobiography.[2] Worked on unpacking and arranging books.

23. Tu.

Wrote to Mr R. Stewart—Rev. Mr M'Cheane[3]—Rev. H. Solly—Mr Strahan (B.P.)—Sec. City Lib. Club.[4]—Sec L.N.W. Company—Dr W. Smith—Sir Thos G.—Mr F. May. Saw Sir Jas Watson—Mr Newmarch—Mr Leeman—Mr Trevelyan. Dined at Mr Hankey's where we met Mr [blank] a Cingalese Lawyer and I was greatly pleased with him. Read Austin's Human Tragedy.[5] H of C. $4\frac{1}{2}$-7. Spoke briefly on W. James's motion.[6] Saw Lockitt X.

24. Wed.

Wrote to Ld Selborne—Rev. Dr Miller. Again dined with W. Cowper: long conversation with Père H[yacinthe Loyson] on his views & plan.[7] H. of C. 3-4.[8] Read Life of Ld Althorp.[9] Saw Mr Freakes—Ld Granville. Attended Meeting of Commission of 1851. Saw Prince of Wales after, and gave him some information about Lyttelton. Worked on Athenè.

25. Th. Ascension Day.

All Souls Church at 11 AM and H.C. Wrote to Mr Knowles—Mr Watts R.A. Dined with the Leightons. Finished & sent off Athenè. Saw Ld Granville—Mr Russell Gurney—Mr Cartwright—Mr Forster. H of C. $4\frac{1}{2}$-$7\frac{1}{4}$.[10] Saw two X: A strange form of life. Read Life of Ld Althorp—Forster's Preface to Penn.[11]

26. Fr.

Wrote to Rev. J. Davies—Rev. E. Blenkinsopp[12]—Duke of Argyll—R. Morris—T.E.C. Leslie—J.B. Tomalin—Miss Phillips—Helen G. Saw Mr Freshfield

[1] E. H. Browne.

[2] Probably [F. M. F. Skene's] autobiographical novel, *Hidden depths* (1866); see her *D.N.B.* entry.

[3] Henry Dalgety McCheane; lived in Portland Place, involved with the Lytteltons.

[4] Wykeham T. Deverell; the club laid a foundation stone on 29 May, but Gladstone was not present.

[5] By A. Austin (1876).

[6] Inquiring into City of London companies; *H* 229. 1144.

[7] Gladstone told Döllinger, 29 May 1876: 'Père Hyacinthe is in London, and thinks of holding one or more Conferences (in which I believe nobody confers) on the "religious question". He asked my opinion and I recommended this. He seems a man of upright mind and his wife is a pleasing and sensible woman, with a good deal of apparent energy, and a real religious character—though many, and I am among them, think he made a serious mistake in dispensing himself from his vows to marry her. His ecclesiastical position seems to be that of the Old Catholics'; Lathbury, ii. 314. See 21, 28 June 76, 11 Dec. 78.

[8] Macdonald's Employers Liability Bill: *H* 229. 1154.

[9] Sir H. D. Le Marchant, *Memoir of John Charles, Viscount Althorp, 3rd Earl Spencer* (1876).

[10] Customs Bill: *H* 229. 1197.

[11] W. E. Forster, *William Penn and T. B. Macaulay* (1849).

[12] Edward Clennell Leaton Blenkinsopp, rector of Springthorpe; had been chaplain to the army in Turkey 1855-6.

(representative)[1]—Lord Stratford: a long conversation on Turkey & the East[2]—Rector of Lincoln[3]—Mr Farrer. Dined at Mrs Grotes small & pleasant party. Read Memoirs of Lord Althorp—and [blank.]

27. Sat.

Kept my bed a little. Wrote to Principal of King's Coll.—Mr Smalley—J. Drew Gay[4]—Lady Russell—Mrs Th.—Rev Mr. Kelly—Duke of Argyll—Watsons. Dined with the Cowper Temples; and had further conference with Père Hyacinthe on his plans. Saw one [R]. Saw Sir A. Panizzi. Read Memoirs of Ld Althorp, and Q.R. on Macaulay & his School (1868).[5]

28. S. aft Asc.

Vere Street mg, & Chapel Royal aft.—Walk with C. Wrote to Herbert J.G. Saw Ld Shrewsbury—Mr Bowman—Dr A. Clark. Read Mozley's Sermons—Mivart on Development.[6]

29. M.

Wrote to Herbert J.G.—Dr Döllinger—Mr Hitger[7]—Treasurer Lincoln's Inn—do Temple. Went to Richmond to see Ld Russell. In a conversation of $\frac{3}{4}$ hour I found him not fatigued, full of interest in affairs, now & then a puzzled head or failure of memory, but only now & then. I thought there was still vigour & life in him, as well as kindness. Conversation with Lady R. H. of C. $4\frac{3}{4}$-$6\frac{3}{4}$. The Irish debate prevented me from saying some words on finance.[8] Saw Dr Cameron[9]—Mr Childers—Mr Grant Duff—Ld Hartington—Sir T. Acland—Mr Cowper Temple. Nine to dinner: including a very interesting visitor, the blind Mr Warburton.[10] Some progress in restoring order.

30. Tu.

Wrote to J. Watson & Smith—W. Goalen—Mr H.C. Hines[11]—J. Croker[12]—W. Williams. Dined with Ld Selborne. H of C. $4\frac{1}{4}$-6 and 11-1. Voted for County Household Suffrage.[13] Read Ld Althorp's Memoirs. $12\frac{1}{4}$-2. Sat to Watts.

[1] Unclear of what; E. Freshfield was much involved in Bulgarian church affairs (see 13 Nov. 71) and probably saw Gladstone as representing the Eastern Churches Association; Freshfields, the solicitors, also dealt with family affairs.
[2] A meeting urgently and suddenly requested by Stratford; see Shannon, 93. News of atrocities in Bulgaria was reaching London, see *T.T.*, this day, p. 8.
[3] i.e. Mark Pattison.
[4] J. Drew Gay, had sent his book *From Pall Mall to the Punjaub, or with the Prince in India* (1876).
[5] By [A. Hayward], *Quarterly Review*, cxxiv. 287 (April 1868).
[6] See 14 May 76.
[7] Could read 'Hitzer'; unidentified; see 6 June 76.
[8] Imperial taxation on Ireland; *H* 229. 1357.
[9] Probably (Sir) Charles Cameron, 1841-1924; physician and liberal M.P. Glasgow 1874-95, Bridgeton 1897-1900; cr. bart. 1893.
[10] i.e. the poet, R. E. E. *Warburton; see 3 Sept. 42.
[11] Perhaps Henry Hines of Northumberland Terrace, London; or see 10 Aug. 76.
[12] Not traced.
[13] On Trevelyan's resolutions; *H* 229. 1442.

Luncheon at Argyll Lodge. At 3 went over the Grant Palace Kensington House[1] with Mr Knowles. What lessons does it not suggest: how it preaches!

31. Wed.

Wrote to Ld Shrewsbury—Mrs Mochler—Watsons—Lord Spencer—Mr Parker— Mr J.B. Anderson[2]—Mr W. Deanes—Mrs Cowper Temple. $6\frac{3}{4}$-$11\frac{1}{2}$. Dinner at the Pol. Econ. Club, and Speeches: to celebrate the 100th anniversary of A. Smith's great book.[3] Finished the Memoirs of that admirable man Lord Althorp.[4] Saw Gray [R]. Saw Jas Wortley.

Thurs. June One. 1876

Wrote to Baroness Burdett Coutts—Watsons (B.P.) Fourteen to breakfast. A conversation on Endowments. Then to the Lecture of Prof. Donders,[5] a remarkable & very pleasing person, on his instruments for measuring the times of thought. Saw Ld Northbrook—Lady E. Pringle (luncheon at 15 G.S.)—Ld Cottesloe. We dined with the Ralph Nevilles.—H of C. afterwards.[6] Saw Russell; & another [R]. Read Gibbs on Franchise[7]—Liberté comme en Belgique—Lewins on Matter & Mind[8]—and other tracts.

2. Fr.

Wrote to Mr Strahan—Dr Von Döllinger B.P.—Mrs Mochler B.P.—Hawarden Institute B.P.—Rev. H. Lansdell—Dr Winn[9]—Mrs Wagne—Sec. Lord Mayor—Mr Thrupp—T. Bradshaw—F. Cortazzi—J. Kaspari[10]—Ferd. Howe.[11] Dined with Ld Winmarleigh, & much conversation with him and Warburton. Some unpacking & arranging. Calls. Read Paget on Macaulay: also Vindications.[12]

3. Sat.

Willy's birthday: God bless and guide him. Wrote to Dr Haig Brown— Rev. W. Cadman[13]—Rev. S.E.G.—Rev. J.T. Roberts[14]—Messrs Hamilton—Mrs

---

[1] Old Kensington Bedlam, bought by Albert *Grant, the financier (see 16 Apr. 66) and converted for him by James *Knowles, an architect as well as editor; auctioned but bought in in 1878, eventually sold off 1882 and demolished by creditors.

[2] Perhaps John Bennett Anderson, temperance advocate.

[3] Gladstone took the chair and made two short speeches; see Introduction above, section iv.

[4] His speech this day included a eulogy of Althorp.

[5] Frans Cornelius Donders, 1818-89; Dutch physiologist and ophthalmologist; the first to measure the reaction time of a psychical process.

[6] Prisons Bill; H 229. 1536.

[7] E. J. Gibbs, *The county franchise and rural municipalities* (1876).

[8] R. Lewins, *Life and mind* (1873).

[9] James Michell Winn, London physician, practising in Harley Street.

[10] Joachim Kaspary had sent the proofs of his essay on 'Natural Laws' attacking J. S. Mill; Hawn P.

[11] Ferdinand Howe of Gray's Inn; Hawn P.

[12] J. Paget, *An inquiry into the evidence relating to the charges brought by Lord Macaulay against William Penn* (1858).

[13] William Cadman, 1815-91; church reformer; rector of Marylebone from 1859.

[14] A nonconformist?

Newberry—A.W. Inman[1]—W. Talmadge[2]—E. Wright. Read Paget on Macaulay—Grote on Switzerland.[3] Worked on Macaulay. Calls.

4. *Whits.*

Trin. Ch. 7 H.C. with Mary 11-2. St Andr. Wells St at 5. Wrote to Rev. Dr Mozley. Saw Miss Talbot. Read Mozley's 5th Sermon[4]—Mivart Contemp. Evolution (finished): and Tracts. Wrote a *piece* on Macaulay's Religious character.[5]

5. *M.*

St Andr. 5 P.M. Wrote to Rev Mr MacColl—Père Hyacinthe—H.N.G.—Mr Weeks (Philadelphia)[6]—Mme Agstado?[7] (B.P.)—Rev Mr Hopps and [blank.] Worked a good deal on Macaulay. Luncheon at 15 G.S. Saw Lady *E.* Pringle. Ci baciammo, congedandoci![8] Saw Mr & Mrs Heywood. Read Abbott on Bacon.[9]

6. *Tu.*

Wrote to Earl of Devon—Rev. A. King—F.R. Statham[10]—Jas Lindsay—Mr Hitzer. Worked on Macaulay Art. Dined at Ld Acton's. Walk with C.—Calls. Saw Mr McColl—Lady Stanley (Conversation on Macaulay)—Mr Murray do—Lord Acton do. Read Cooper on Horus Myth.[11]

7. *Wed.*

Wrote to Mad. Loyson—Mr Cowper Temple—Mr Skeffington—Mrs Hunter U.S. (BP)—Mr Hutchinson—Rev. Mr M'Coll—Rev. J. Cotter[12]—Mr White. Worked well on Macaulay. Dined with the Wests. Saw Sir A. Panizzi—Mr Welby—Lady Grey (conversation respecting Lyttelton). Read the Month on Macaulay[13]—Cornhill Mag. on do.[14]

8. *Th.*

Wrote to Messrs T. & B.—Rev. J. Parry Morgan[15]—A.H. Jupp—Bishop of London—W. White—Mr G. Bellis.[16] Worked on Macaulay. Dined with Kate & her

---

[1] Perhaps of the Cheshire family.   [2] See 19 July 59.

[3] G. Grote, *Seven letters on the recent politics of Switzerland* (1847).

[4] See 14 May 76.

[5] Paragraphs 26 and 71-96 in *Gleanings*, ii deal with Macaulay's religion and his treatment of the anglican clergy.

[6] A. M. Weeks, student at Boston university, unsuccessfully asking diarist to contribute to his magazine, *The Centennial Eagle*; Hawn P.

[7] Perhaps *sc.* Azelasto; two men of that name lived in London.

[8] 'We kissed one another, in taking leave of one another.'

[9] E. A. Abbot, 'The latest theory about Bacon. A reply to … Spedding', *Contemporary Review*, xxviii. 141 (June 1876).

[10] Probably Francis Reginald Statham, journalist; went to Natal 1877; see Add MS 44469, f. 47.

[11] W. R. Cooper, *The Horus myth in its relation to Christianity* (1877).

[12] Probably James Laurence Cotter, curate of St Paul's, Liverpool.

[13] *The Month*, viii. 129 (June 1876).   [14] *The Cornhill Magazine*, xxxiii. 563 (June 1876).

[15] John Parry Morgan, vicar of Holywell, near Hawarden.

[16] Of the Chester family; see 15 Jan. 57.

sisters. House before & after: *Saeva indignatio*, at S.H.N.[1] Six to breakfast. Saw Ld Wolverton. Read the Horus Myth—Fraser (Froude) on Macaulay.[2]

9. Fr.

Saw Mr Strahan—Ld Hartington. Wrote to Ld Granville—Mr Robin Allen—and Mr H. Jones. H of C. $4\frac{1}{4}$-$5\frac{1}{2}$.[3] Dined with J. Wortley. Read Count M.s Travels.[4] Worked much on Macaulay: but it is a Chaos.

10. Sat.

Wrote to Mr MacColl—Mr Macadam—F. Cortazzi—G. Howe B.P.[5]—G. Scott B.P.—Mr Knowles—Rev. Mr Kingsmill[6]—Mr R. Huntley—Mr Delane—Mad Loyson. Saw Mr MacColl—Sir James Lacaita. Worked much on Macaulay. It is a business made difficult by utter want of continuity in my application to it. And really the subject is beyond the common order. C. slept at Mrs Talbots: the illness is formidable. C.G. in George St. Mrs T[albot']s illness having assumed an alarming character. Saw Rev. Mr Fremantle[7]—Mr Knowles. Visited the sick & sad house.

11. 1 S. Trin.

St James's 10 A.M. Westmr Abbey 7 P.M: Mr Stopford Brooke,[8] very noteworthy, a little perilous. Twice in G. St—a formidable crisis. Read Mozley—Dr Mellor—Rev. A. King[9]—and other tracts—Rev Mr Savile. Saw Mr Levy—Mr Arnold—& the D. Tel. machinery.[10]

12. M.

Finished work on Macaulay MS and sent it to press. Nine to dinner. Wrote to Mr C.M. Walker—Mr C. Fletcher—Mr Macmillan—and Mr Molesworth. Luncheon at 15 G.S. Saw Mrs Th.—also Mr Th. on P[addington] Estate.

In George St at noon. Mrs Talbot[11] was in the last struggle: and died at four. We seem ever to hear the funeral bell. Read Langham Mag.[12]

13. Tu.

Wrote to Mr Macmillan—Sec. Free Library Birmm.—J. Carvell Williams—T. Grahame—J.W. Hanson[13]—Robt Gladstone—and Dr Smith. 12-2. Sat to Watts.[14]

[1] Presumably Northcote, though his only duty this day was to 2°R a Friendly Societies Bill; *H* 229. 1597.

[2] By J. A. Froude, *Fraser's magazine*, xci. 675 (June 1876).

[3] Gladstone was privately indignant at Disraeli's easy evasion of Hartington's half-hearted attempt to extract information about the state of affairs in the Balkans; *H* 229. 1606; Shannon, 93.

[4] Possibly *The travels and surprising adventures of Baron Munchausen* (1868 ed.).

[5] Gerald Howe of London; assisted by Gladstone; Hawn P.

[6] Probably Charles Kingsmill, anglican curate in East London.

[7] W. R. Fremantle (see 9 Aug. 28); much involved with Balkan Christians.

[8] See 24 Nov. 67.   [9] A. King, *Protestantism and the Church of Rome* (1876).

[10] *The Telegraph*, still a liberal paper, was printed at 135 Fleet Street; no report of this visit found.

[11] Caroline Jane, wife of J. C. Talbot; see 2 Feb. 52.

[12] First number of the *Langham Magazine*, ed. C. Voysey.

[13] Relative of E. Hanson of Aston Hall colliery; see 3 June 74.   [14] See 16 May 76.

Again we vowed not to talk & again talked ad inf. and that on matters of deep interest, religious, & other. Saw Duke of Argyll—Mr Kinnaird—Mr Mivart—Ld F. Cavendish. Dined with Metaphysical Society. We discussed Mr Mivart's paper on truth: which seemed to have a Roman twist in it.[1] Read Kuklos on Opium Trade.[2]

14. Wed.

Laid from disturbance of the bowels. I could not discern any physical cause. Much conversation with Harry on his affairs. With Mrs H[ampto]n on her brother's. Read Half the Vol. of Lady Lyttelton's Letters.[3] A wonderful development of character, with great talents. Also read Paget on Nelson & on Sarah Stout.[4]

15. Th.

Rose at noon. Wrote to Mr Macadam—Rev. Dr. Cazenove—Rev. B.W. Savile— Rev. Thos Brown—Rev. Moncure Conway[5]—Rev. N. Hall—Messrs Daldy & Co[6]—J. Carvell Williams—Jas Saunders (U.S.)[7]—Rev. R.B. Drummond[8]—J. Lewis—W.E. Feilding[9]—H.D. Seymour—Jas Ram[10]—E.A. Nüth—B. West—F. Ouvry—Dr D. Bendan. H. of C. $5\frac{3}{4}$-$7\frac{1}{2}$.[11] Saw Mr Murray & Dr Smith—Scotts—Mr Newdigate—Sir W. Harcourt—Mr Hubbard—Mr B. Hope—Mr Russell Gurney. Read Lady Lyttelton's Letters—Paget on E. Canning: and on Lord Byron.

16. Fr.

Wrote to Rev. W. Sharman[12]—H. Roberts—W. Newmarch—A.W. Clement— T.C. Hine—Strahan (B.P. Athenè)—F. Cortazzi—D.H. Saunders. Saw Elford: & again fined [R]. Corrected report of Speech at Pol. Economy Dinner[13]—Also of Speech at Shirwalls[14]—Also of Athenè & Aiolos. Read Lady Lyttelton's letters. Saw Lord Wolverton—Sir A. Panizzi.

---

[1] Paper by St. George Mivart, 'What is the good of truth?'; Brown, *Metaphysical Society*, 330.

[2] Kuklos [J. Harris], *The Church of England, the British Empire and the Chinese* (1876).

[3] Presumably a bound volume of MSS; the letters were published in Mrs. H. Wyndham, *Correspondence of... Lady Lyttelton, 1787-1870* (1912).

[4] J. Paget, *Paradoxes and puzzles* (1874), 213, 387; also read next day.

[5] Moncure Daniel Conway, 1832-1907; American unitarian; minister in Finsbury 1867-91; active in the atrocities campaign; see J. M. Davidson, *Eminent Radicals* (1880), 200.

[6] Dalby, Isbister; London publishers.

[7] Probably an autograph hunter.

[8] Robert B. Drummond of Edinburgh, on Unitarianism; Hawn P.

[9] Possibly William Henry Adelbert Feilding, 1836-95; later colonel in Coldstream guards.

[10] James Ram, London barrister; wrote on philosophy of war (1878); Hawn P.

[11] Elementary Education Bill; *H* 229. 1897.

[12] William Sharman, unitarian minister in Plymouth.

[13] See 31 May 76.

[14] *Sic*; in Nottinghamshire; probably Snaresbrook, Mrs Gladstone's Home, is intended; see 28 Mar. 76.

17. Sat. [Albury Park]

Wrote to Mrs Potter—Messrs Williams—Mr Cowper Temple—Messrs Towns-hend & Barker. Off at 10.30 to Falconhurst: where in persistent rain we buried the excellent Mrs Talbot. Saw Ld Shrewsbury—Ld F. Cavendish—W.H.G.—Ld Hatherley. Read Murray's Mythology[1]—Lady Lyttelton's Letters. At 6 we reached Albury[2] & were most kindly received. Conversation with Père Hyacinthe—Mr Thiersch.[3]

18. 1 S. Trin.

Parish Ch mg & evg. Mr Dundas's[4] Sermon excellent. A day of much conversa-tion with Ld Percy—Père Hyacinthe—The Duchess [of Northumberland]—Mr Cappadon—Mr Seaton—Mr Caird. Wrote to Sir J. Lacaita—Mr Strahan—Sir Ph. Egerton. Read Earle's Sonnets[5]—Taylor Lewis on H.S.[6]—Dante Purg. canto 4 with close comparison of Engl. Version MS for E.W.

19. M.

Wrote to dear Herbert on his Class,[7] a success which his modesty forbade him to anticipate. It was a joyous surprise; and may be a great fact in his life; I feel confident it will be a good one. God be praised. Wrote also to D[uke] of Northumberland. Drive & walk with the party in the very beautiful woods & glade. Saw Mad. Hyacinthe (on the C[atholic] A[postolic] worship yesterday)—M. Gähring (Swiss religion)[8]—M.F. Tupper (who called)[9]—The Duchess—Lady L. Percy.[10] Read Lady Lyttelton—Edinb. Rev. on Bp Thirlwall—Ld Albemarle's 50 Years.[11]

20. Tu. [London]

Wrote to Mons. Lombard—Mr Cortazzi—Rev. J.G. Rogers[12]—Rev. R.C. Jenkins—Rev. Dr Allon—Mrs H. Rawson—Mrs Th.—Mr Pain—Mr Strahan—Bp of Moray—Mr Ouvry. Dined at Mr Beaumont's. Visited Mr Brock's Studio to see the Canning Statue.[13] Saw Ld Granville—Lady Marg. Beaumont. Came up from

---

[1] A. S. Murray, *Manual of mythology* (1872-4).
[2] Seat of the Irvingite Lord Percy; see 13 May 56.
[3] Probably Heinrich Wilhelm Josias Thiersch, German theologian and historian.
[4] Robert James Dundas, rector of Albury.
[5] J. C. Earle, *Light leading into light; a series of sonnets and poems* (1875).
[6] Tayler Lewis, *The Light by which we see light* (1875).
[7] One of two Firsts in modern history at Oxford; he had been given a Third in classics in 1874.
[8] Not further identified.
[9] Tupper lived nearby; see 16 May 56n.
[10] Lady Louisa Percy, d. 1883; da. of 5th duke of Northumberland.
[11] *Edinburgh Review*, cxliii. 281, 455 (April 1876).
[12] James Guinness *Rogers, 1822-1911; congregationalist minister in Clapham 1865-1900; strong Gladstonian, prominent in the atrocities campaign, at this time setting up a 'Vigilance Committee'; Rogers had earlier met Gladstone at Newman Hall's and at Penmaenmawr (see 15 Aug. 74); J. G. Rogers, *An autobiography* (1903), 210, 216, 223.
[13] (Sir) Thomas *Brock, 1847-1922; completed J. H. *Foley's statue of Canning for Calcutta; his statue of Gladstone (1902) is in Westminster Hall.

Albury at 2 PM. Read Ld Albemarle—Murray's Mythology—Lady Lyttelton's letters.

21. Wed.

Wrote to Herbert J.G.—Rev Mr Mason—Dr W. Smith—Mr Aspinall—*and others*. 8½-10. Royal Academy with Agnes and Harry. 10-12¼. Breakfast at Sir J. Lacaita's. H. of C. at 4½.[1] Hyacinthe's Lecture at 3½.[2] He is a great orator. Dined with Benchers of Lincoln's Inn. Saw Ld Hartington—Captain Beaumont[3]—Ld Acton—Ld Hatherley—Ld OHagan. Finished Lady Lyttelton's letters. How fair a picture of a human soul!

22. Th.

Wrote to Rev. J. Watt—W.D. Seymour—Rev. R. Suffield—Mr Hayter MP.—T. Montgomery—T. Constable[4]—J.R. Hamilton. Thirteen to breakfast. Saw Bps of Moray and Edinburgh on Panangl[ican] Congr.[5]—Mr Roger Eykyn—Mr Bright—Mr Holyoake—Mr Knowles—Mr Herbert—Mr Grove—Mrs Mochler— Dr Clark—Mr Newdigate—Mr Russell Gurney—W.H.G. on Hn matters. H of C. at 4¼-6 and 10-11½.[6] Meeting at Ld Granville's 3-4.[7] Read Divers Scots Tracts— Barclay's Ship of Fools.[8]

23. Fr.

Wrote to Mr Marple—Rev. N. Woodard—Ld Acton—Rev. Mr Johnstone—Mr B. Brown—Messrs Clowes. Worked hard on proofs of Macaulay: and returned them. Read Pref & Life of Barclay[9]—Westmr Rev. on Theology. Saw W.H.G. (Memorial Gates)[10] & Mr Roundell.

24. Sat. St Joh. Bapt.

Wrote to Mrs Weldon—Canon Ashwell—Rev. J. Malcolmson[11]—Dr Myrian- theus—R.C. Jenkins—J. Jones—T.N. Roberts—Mr de Lisle—Mrs Th.—Miss Allworth—J. Gregory—F. Lyne—A. Balfour. Dined with the Jameses. Fourteen to breakfast for Père Hyacinthe. Corrected Revise of N. Macleod. Saw Mr A. Balfour (MP.)—Scotts—Bp of Carlisle—Père Hyacinthe—Sir A. Panizzi. All Saints Church 5 PM. Read Rev. N. Loraine[12]—Life of Barclay—and Howson.

[1] Irish and Scottish affairs; *H* 230. 179.

[2] His second lecture on 'Prospects of Christiandom' at St James's Hall attracted a fashionable audience, with Argyll in the chair; *T.T.*, 22 June 1876, 7f.

[3] Probably Frederick Edward Blackett Beaumont, 1833-99, Royal Engineers; liberal M.P. S. Durham 1868-80.

[4] Thomas *Constable, 1812-81; printer and publisher; on the Macleod article (see 24 June 76).

[5] Preparations for the second Pananglican synod, known as the Lambeth conference, of July 1878.

[6] Statement by Disraeli on Turkish affairs; later, Prisons Bill: *H* 230. 265.

[7] On the Turkish question; Shannon, 93.

[8] A. Barclay's tr. of Brandt's *Narrenschiff* as *The ship of fools* (1874 ed.).

[9] T. H. Jamieson, *Notice of the life and writings of A. Barclay* (1874).

[10] Memorial for G. W. Lyttelton.   [11] James Malcolmson, vicar of St Luke, Deptford.

[12] N. Loraine, *The church and liberties of England* (1876); anon. short notice of it by Gladstone in *Church Quarterly Review*, ii. 565 (July 1876); see 26 June 76.

25. 2 S. Trin.

Vere St 11 A.M. and H.C.—Chapel Royal 3½ PM. Wrote to Bp of Manchester—Mrs Thistlethwayte: this may close a correspondence affording much matter of reflection. Read N. Loraine (finished)—Rogers on Anglican Dignitaries[1]—Mozley's Sermons[2]—Memoirs of Mrs Bathurst[3]—Barclay Life & Ship of Fools. Dined with the Godleys. Saw Ld Wolverton—Mr Richmond—Mr Laing (Merton).[4]

26. M.

Wrote to Serjeant Cox—Mr Hamilton Fish (& copy)[5]—Canon Ashwell—Rev A. Campbell[6]—J.H. Parker—Mr Palgrave—J. Macveigh—R.H. Hogg—Ld Acton. Wrote a short paper for Church QR on Loraine. Saw Lord Granville—Prince Rhodokanaki—Count Menabrea—Mr Forster—Mr [blank] U.S.—Mr Adam. Saw Mr Cox—Mr Palgrave jun. Saw two [R]. Wrote on Hom. Mythol. Dined at Argyll Lodge. Read Ship of Fools.

27. Tu.

Wrote to Mr Grant Duff—Rev Mr Henderson—Helen G.—Mr A. Stear—Ld Acton—Ld Granville—Sir Jas Paget. Dined at Ld Tollemache's. Saw Fredin X—Temple. Ah! Saw Mr Ouvry—Mr Sandys[7]—Ld Stratford de Redcliffe.[8] Corrected (in part) Revises of Macaulay. Luncheon at Ld Houghton's. Bookbuying. Read Ship of Fools.

28. Wed.

My sister Helen's birthday: I wrote her a line of benediction & stimulus. Wrote also to Rev Mr Millson[9]—Ld Acton—Mr Stearn[10]—Mr Lewin—Mr Gough—Miss Jackson—E. Williams—Mr Harington—Messrs Clowes. Finished my work on Revises of Macaulay. Presided at Père Hyacinthe's last Conference, a brilliant assembly, a brilliant & a most honest Speech.[11] Attended the concert: & conversed with divers Royalties.[12] Read Skene on Ancient Scotland.[13] H of C. at 5.

[1] J. G. Rogers, *Anglican church portraits* (1876).

[2] See 14 May 76.

[3] Perhaps *Truth vindicated by the faithful . . . writings of Elizabeth Bathurst* (1705).

[4] Presumably Andrew *Lang, 1844-1912, author and Homerist; fellow of Merton 1868, but moved to London 1875.

[5] On the publication of the 'explanation' (see 28 Nov. 72, 19 Aug. 76); Add MS 44449, f. 99 (misplaced).

[6] Perhaps Arthur Bruce Knight Campbell, d. 1881; chaplain to his fa., bp. of Bangor, 1876-81.

[7] Perhaps R. H. Sandys, London barrister.

[8] On Turkey; see Ramm I, ii. 487.

[9] F. E. Millson, Unitarian minister in Halifax, aggrieved at diarist's comments in 'Course of Religious Thought'; Hawn P.

[10] Probably David de Stearn, commissioner of lunacy; probably involved in the Lyttelton affair.

[11] *T.T.*, 29 June 1876, 12f.; see also Grant Duff, *Diary*, i. 192.

[12] State concert at Buckingham Palace.

[13] W. F. Skene, *Celtic Scotland; a history of ancient Alban*, 3v. (1876-80).

Voted for Intestacy Bill.[1] Saw Père Hyacinthe—Sir W. Farquhar—D of Argyll—
Ld F. Cavendish—Harry on his affairs—
Ld Hartington (2) }
Mr Forster[2]   } Turkish matters.

29. Th.

Wrote to Prof. Rhomi—Sir W. Farquhar—Mr Jacobs—Mr Copeland Borlase[3]—
Rev. Mr Dampier—Sir R. Cunliffe—Mr Merz[4]—Mrs Greig. Read The Magician.[5]
Ten to breakfast. Saw Mr Stanley Leathes[6]—Mr De Lisle—Mr N. Pocock—Mr
Parker—Lady Lyttelton (on S. L[yttelton])—Ld Hartington—Ld Acton—Ld
Granville—Mr Irving. Dined at Ld Ducie's. H. of C. $4\frac{1}{4}$-$6\frac{1}{4}$ and 11-2: voted agt Mr
Butt's [Land Tenure] Bill.[7]

30. Fr.

Wrote to Mr Robin Allen—Mr Ouvry—Messrs Clowes—Helen G.—Messrs
Daldy & Isbister—Mr G.W. Mason[8]—Rev. Dr Littledale—Rev. Mr Millson—Lady
Lyttelton. Saw Mr W.E. Forster—Sir A. Panizzi—Lady Lyttelton (S.L.)—Mr
Davis—Ld Hartington—Ld Granville—Mr Bright. H. of C. 11-$1\frac{3}{4}$ (Home Rule).[9]
Dined with Sir J. Hardy. Read Caesar in Egypt[10] & other works: to reject them.

Sat. July One. 1876.

Wrote to Mr F.H. Hangar—Rev. Dr Newman[11]—Canon Ashwell—Rev. C.C.
Grimes[12]—Rev. R. Peaton[13]—Rev. N. Hall—Rev. S.K. Stothart[14]—Mrs Th.—Sir B.
Leighton—Mr J.R. Palmer[15]—Mr Phillips—Mr Fredin.[16] Read Afranius[17]—Ship of
Fools—and various. Did a little for order. Evg at home.

2. 3 S. Trin.

Marylebone Old Ch at 11—Chapel Royal at 5.30. Walk with C. Wrote to Ld
Granville—Canon Ashwell—Rev. Jas Davis—Rev. C. Voysey—Rev. R.R. Suffield—
Mr R. Bosworth Smith—Mr Wood—Mr Cruikshank.[18] Read Wood MS.[19]—Voy-
sey & Unitn Tracts[20]—Mozley's Sermons—Oxenham's Eschatology.[21]

---

[1] T. B. Potter's bill, which was defeated; H 230. 606.

[2] Forster was encouraging Hartington to action on the atrocities; Shannon, 93.

[3] William Copeland Borlase, 1848-99; liberal M.P. E. Cornwall 1880-5, St Austell 1885-7; bankrupt 1887.   [4] Theodore Merz of Gateshead; on religion; Hawn P.   [5] Untraced.

[6] Stanley *Leathes, 1830-1900; theologian; Warburtonian lecturer at Lincoln's Inn 1876.

[7] H 230. 713.   [8] Of Retford; on Homeric mythology; Hawn P.

[9] Voted against P. J. Smyth's amndt. to Butt's motion for a select cttee. on Home Rule;
H 230. 820.   [10] J. Ellis, Caesar in Egypt... and other poems (1876).

[11] In Newman, xxviii. 82.   [12] Apparently a dissenter.

[13] Dissenting minister in Great Yarmouth; sent press cuttings; Hawn P.

[14] See 19 Feb. 58; had considerable Turkish experience.

[15] Of Cannock; had expressed gratitude; Hawn P.   [16] Relative of the rescue case.

[17] Probably O. Ribbeck's ed. (1852) of Lucius Afranius.

[18] Alfred Hamilton Cruikshank, a scholar at Winchester; taught there from 1886; had written on
Homer; Hawn P.

[19] John Wood, Sir A. T. Galt's br.-in-law, had sent his essay on 'Geological Antiquity'; Hawn P.

[20] Sermons by C. Voysey given in 1873, published in the Index and reprinted as The Mystery of pain,
death and sin and discourses in refutation of atheism (1878).

[21] H. N. Oxenham, Catholic eschatology and universalism (1876).

3. M.

After looking at letters &c. off at ten on expedition to the Docks & Warehouses. A laborious but instructive day; seeing many & much. Back at 5¼. Went to Lady Ossington's to see the Duke of Sirmoneta: rather volcanic. H of C. in evg.[1] Read Yonge on Marie Antoinette.[2]

I was greatly struck, returning Holborn way, with the now really great beauty of the City, as well as its astounding stir.

4. Tu.

Wrote to Ld Hammond—Messrs Beechend—Sir F.C. Knowles[3]—G. Sanders— A. Sinclair—E.H. Currie[4]—Walter Wood[5]—Ld H. Scott—Ld Wolverton—Rev. Mr Blair[6]—Mr Lyte[7]—Sir D. Lange—Mrs Th. Saw Dr Liddon. Luncheon at 15 G.S. Dined with Lady L. Cotes.[8] Saw Mr Cotes—Sir Phil. Egerton. Saw Howard [R]. Read C.R. on Strauss—On Restitution—Patridge's Narrative[9]—Col. H. Smith on Horses.[10]

5. Wed.

Wrote to Dr Moffatt (Bills)—Dr W. Smith—Mr W. Downie—Rev. Mr Robjohns[11]—Rev. C. Voysey. Dined at Trinity House with Harry: & proposed the Toast of the Corporation.[12] Saw Rev. Mr Rodwell--Mr Hayward—Ld Granville—Mr Milner Gibson—Sir R. Phillimore. Read Patridge (finished)—Skene's Hist. of Scotland[13]—and [blank].

6. Th.

Wrote to Dr Döllinger—Sir Thos G.—Mr N. Macleod—Rev. A. King. Twelve to breakfast. Saw Lord Acton—Mr Otway—Lord O. Russell—Lady Strangford. Delivered the Prizes at King's Coll. & an Address of 40 minutes.[14] H. of C. 4¼-6 and 11-1.[15] Read Clarendon (Crimean) Speeches in Hansard[16] and [blank].

[1] Prisons Bill, missing an exchange between Bright and Disraeli on Turkey; *H* 230. 885; see *H* 231. 175.

[2] C. D. Yonge, *The Life of Marie Antoinette*, 2v. (1876).

[3] Sir Francis Charles Knowles, 1802-92; 3rd bart. 1831; barrister.

[4] Edmund Hay Currie, London distiller.

[5] London solicitor.

[6] Probably Robert Hugh Blair, headmaster of the school for the blind, Worcester.

[7] Perhaps John Maxwell-Lyte; curate in Biggleswade 1874-7, at St Peter's, Eaton Square 1877.

[8] Lady Louisa Cotes, 1814-87, da. of 3rd earl of Liverpool, widow of J. Cotes, M.P.

[9] *Sic*; perhaps J. A. Partridge, *Citizenship versus secularists and sacerdotalists* (1873), or one of the astrological forecasts of John Patridge or Partridge, 1644-1715.

[10] Could read 'Horus'; both untraced.

[11] Henry J. Robjohns, dissenting minister in Hull; Hawn P.

[12] *T.T.*, 6 July 1876, 8a.

[13] See 28 June 76.

[14] *T.T.*, 7 July 1876, 11a.

[15] Oxford and Cambridge affairs; *H* 230. 1050.

[16] *H* 130. 568, quoted by Gladstone on 31 July 76 to refute Bright's claim that Clarendon said Britain drifted into war in 1854.

7. Fr.

Wrote to Mr G. Levick—Lady Stratford de R.—Mr Long—Mayor of Ports-
mouth—Mr Hargood. Dined at Mr Magniac's. At Lady May's Tea party. Saw
Rev Mr Cadman—Ld Granville—Mr Murray—Mrs Lowe—Sir T.E. May. Saw
Mrs Phillips X. Read Tracts: Croker Corresp.

8. Sat.

Wrote to Mr Murray—Messrs T. & B.—Sir H. Elliot[1]—Dr Schliemann—Sir J.
Lacaita—Messrs Tatham. Dined with the Goschens. Duke of Sirmoneta & a
small party came to tea. Read Ship of Fools and saw Mr M. Arnold—Ld Acton.
Arranging papers.

9. 4 S. Trin.

Chapel Royal 10 A.M: and 5.30 P.M. Wrote to Bp of St Asaph. Saw Ld Clan-
william—Sir W. & Lady M. Farquhar. Walk with C. Read Ch. Qu. on Educn—Bp
Hughes on do in Wales[2]—Mr Wright on Div. School[3]—Divers Tracts—Mozley's
Sermons: that on the Atonement admirable, even beyond others.

10. M.

Wrote to Mr Paull—Hon. & Rev. L. Neville—Ed. International Rev. N.Y.[4]—Mrs
Grote. Saw Mr Palgrave—Sir A. Panizzi—Mr Cadman—Ld Blachford—Mr
Forster—Ld Granville. Luncheon at 15. G.S. Attended Childrens Flower Show
at Grosvenor House, & spoke.[5] H. of C. 6-7.[6] Bookbuying. Read Ship of Fools—
Report of Committee on Silver.[7]

11. Tu.

Radcliffe Trust Meeting 2-3. Then to the H. of C. till 6½.[8] Dined with Mr & Mrs
Theodore Martin. Read Austin's Human Tragedy[9]—Eastern question Papers.[10]
Saw Mr Sayward[11]—Mr Grogan (we decided on the House & Stable plans)—
Lady Egerton—Mr Th. Martin.

---

[1] Asking for assistance for Schliemann; Elliot replied on 5 August offering such as could be found,
adding 'I see from what you say that you are rather an advocate for autonomy in the Insurgent
Turkish Provinces, but I do not think that those who brought forward that view have properly
viewed the practical difficulties'; Add MS 44451, f. 21.
[2] See 27 Feb. 70.
[3] See 12 Mar. 74.
[4] Not found published; perhaps on the article on Ionia, *International Review*, iii. 499 (July 1876).
[5] *T.T.*, 11 July 1876, 5f.
[6] Thus probably being too late for exchanges between Forster and Disraeli on Turkey;
H 230. 1180.
[7] Report of Select Cttee. on depreciation of silver, *PP* 1876 viii. 217.
[8] Misc. business; *H* 230. 1279.
[9] See 23 May 76.
[10] Probably the Blue Book on Bosnia of 27 April; *PP* 1876 lxxxiv. 137.
[11] Involved in the Bulgarian campaign.

12. Wed.

Wrote to Mr Milroy—A. Arnold—A. M'Culloch—A.A. Corfe—T. Newman[1]—
E. Tolson. Calls. H of C. 12½-5. Spoke shortly on Irish Sunday Closing Bill.[2]
8½-12½. Attended a Nonconforming Conclave at Mr N. Halls: with much
interest & advantage. Saw Mr Gregory—Mr Forster—Mr D. Currie[3]—Mr
Hope—Mr Proctor. Saw Mrs Bishop X. Read Mr de Vere's Introdn to Thomas a
Becket,[4] and Papers on Eastern Question.

13. Th.

Wrote to Messrs Coutts—Mr Thos Fraser—Gen. Bowie—Mr M.R. Sharp—Mr
Bramwell—Bp of Edinburgh—Mr H. Jowett—Mr Ohlson—Dr Newman—Messrs
Harper—& others, B.P.—Rev. Mr Bellairs—Rev. T. Smith—Mr A. Austin. Twelve
to breakfast. Saw Mr Palgrave—Count Münster—Mr Forster—Lady M. Alford +
—Ld Wolverton—Mr Newdigate. H. of C. 11-11¾.[5] Dined at Lady Ashburton's: a
first conversation with the Princess Teano,[6] which pleased me much. Delivered
Prizes & an Address at Lond. Hospital.[7]

14. Fr.

Wrote to Mrs Lowe BP—Mrs H. May—Mrs Black—Mrs Loverdo—Mrs Cross—
Dean of Christ Church—E. Chambers—Ld Cardwell—Baden Powell[8]—Rev. R.S.
Scott[9]—Rev. Mr Harrison—Rev. Mr Stanley Leathes. Dined at Ld Aber-
crombie's. H of C. 3½-6.[10] Saw Mr MacColl—Mr Warwick Brookes—Mr
Trevelyan—Lord Granville—and others. Read Eastern Papers 1856[11]—A. de
Vere's St Thomas—Life of Marie Antoinette.[12]

15. Sat. [Strawberry Hill]

Wrote to Miss Walker—Mrs Th.—Rev. Mr Main BP—Messrs Brown & Barnes—
J.L. Taylor—J. Cashel Hoey—Rev. J. Foxley[13]—J.J. Parker—B. Wed[14]—Mr
Sparkes—O. Lewis[15]—G.W. Moon[16]—Mr Congreve—H. Banff—C. Wilkes—S.
Kimber—G. Dyer[17]—J. Penrose.[18] Mr Woolner's Studio at 1. Saw Mr A. Arnold—
Ld Carlingford—Lady Waldegrave—Count Beust—Sir T.E. May—Mr Hayward.

---

[1] Perhaps Thomas Newman of Old Brentford, poet.   [2] H 230. 1340.
[3] (Sir) Donald *Currie, 1825-1909; ship owner; encouraged contacts between Transvaal and U.K.
in 1870s; liberal (unionist) M.P. Perthshire 1880-5, 1886-1900; organized several cruises for diarist,
see e.g. 26 Aug. 80.
[4] A. T. de Vere, St Thomas of Canterbury. A dramatic poem (1876).
[5] Questions; H 230. 1389.   [6] See 12 Nov. 66n.
[7] Spoke on medical education and Aristotle; T.T., 14 July 1876, 6f.
[8] (Sir) George Smyth Baden-*Powell, 1847-98; author and imperialist; tory M.P. Kirkdale
1885-98.
[9] Robert Selkirk Scott, Presbyterian minister.   [10] Education Bill; H 230. 1435.
[11] Christian privileges in Turkey, etc., PP 1856, lxi. 353.   [12] See 3 July 76.
[13] Joseph Foxley, 1827-1911; rector of Market Weighton 1857-86; disciple of F. D. Maurice.
[14] Reading uncertain.
[15] Henry Owen Lewis, 1842-?; liberal M.P. Carlow 1874-80.
[16] George Washington Moon had sent some of his books defending Queen's English; Hawn P.
[17] Perhaps George Dyer, London goldsmith.
[18] Perhaps John Penrose, priest in Uffculme; formerly fellow of Lincoln College, Oxford.

Read Patterson on Rome[1]—Q.R. on J.W. Croker. Went down to Strawberry Hill[2] in afternoon. Suffocating heat. 92° in the shade I hear.

16. 5 S. Trin.

Tw[ickenham] Green Ch and H.C. mg. Five only went: a wretched contribution from this large party. φεῦ φεῦ. Prayers with the servants in afternoon. Read Mozley's Sermons—Voysey Reply No IV[3]—Congreve Positivist Lectures[4]—Q.R. on the Age of the World. I fled the afternoon gathering by a visit to old General Peel[5] who was most kind. Saw Malcolm Khan[6]—Mr Milner Gibson—and others.

17. M. [London]

Wrote to Rev. J. Christie—Mr M. Moir—Mr Thicke[7]—Mr Colman—Mrs Brand— Mr C. Knight Watson. Saw Ld Granville—Ld Hartington—Mr Hayward—Mr Trevelyan—Mr Bright—Ralph Neville: sadly changed. Dined with the F.C.s. Saw Newton [R]. Luncheon at 15 G.S. Home at noon. Read Ld Amberley on Rel. Belief[8]—De Vere's St Thomas—Q.R. on Orkneys. H of C. $4\frac{1}{4}$-$6\frac{1}{4}$.[9]

18. Tu.

Wrote to Mr J.D. Taylor[10]—Mr Bartout Van der Fan[11]—A. Austin—A. de Vere— Rev. Sir G. Prevost—Rev. Mr Suffield—Mrs Mockler—Dr W. Smith—F. Young— Mrs Th. H. of C. $5\frac{1}{4}$-$6\frac{3}{4}$.[12] Saw Mr Knowles—Mr J.K. Aston—Mr Grogan—Mr Bright. Saw Phillips X. Read De Vere—and [blank].

19. Wed.

Wrote to Mr Pears—Bp of Tasmania BP.—Mr Marchant—Mr Cattell[13]—Mr Urquhart—Mr Rollason. Breakfast with Sir S. Northcote. Saw M. Lesseps—Mr Drummond Wolff—Sir S. Northcote—Mr Russell Gurney—Mr Forster— W.H.G.—Mr Leeman—The Speaker. H of C. $3\frac{1}{2}$-6.[14] [Queen Anne's] Bounty Board $2\frac{1}{2}$-$3\frac{1}{2}$. Tea at No 11 C.H.T.—Lady O.[15] kind & simple. Went over the altered rooms. Read Forsyth's Sclavonia[16]—De Vere's St Thomas—Railway Clearing House.

---

[1] J. L. Patterson, 'Rome and Italy. A letter to . . . the Duke of Norfolk' (1876).
[2] Lady Waldegrave and Lord Carlingford's place at Twickenham.
[3] See 10 Mar. 76.
[4] R. Congreve, 'Human Catholicism. Two sermons delivered at the Positivist School' (1876).
[5] The prime minister's br. Jonathan (see 8 Jan. 35n.) who lived at Marble Hill, Twickenham.
[6] Prince Malcolm Khan, the Persian ambassador.
[7] Perhaps J. Thick, office keeper of Somerset House.
[8] J. Russell, Lord Amberley, *An analysis of religious belief*, 2v. (1876).
[9] Unclear whether he was in the House for Disraeli's statement on Bulgaria; *H* 230. 1486.
[10] Perhaps John Daniel Taylor, London china dealer.
[11] Reading uncertain.
[12] Elementary education; *H* 230. 1528.
[13] Probably Christopher William Cattell, London solicitor.
[14] Contagious diseases; *H* 230. 1556.
[15] i.e. Lady Olivia Guinness.
[16] W. Forsyth, *The Slavonic provinces south of the Danube* (1876).

20. Th.

Wrote to Mr S. Kimber[1]—Mr W.B. Gurdon—Mr O. Lewis. Dined at Miss Leslies,[2] whom I liked much. P. of Wales's Ball afterwards. 1½ hour of conversations. Eleven to breakfast. Saw Bp of Lichfield—Mr Suffield—Dr W. Smith—The King of the Hellenes[3]—H.N.G. (whose immediate destination is now decided: his behaviour in very trying circumstances has been admirable)[4]—Lady H. Forbes—Mr Murray. Read de Vere's St Thomas.

21. Fr.

Wrote to D. of Sutherland. Kept my bed until evg. Went down & spoke on the case of the Loan of 1854.[5] Read Life of A. Barclay &c.[6]—Church Q.R.—finished de Vere's St Thomas.

22. Sat.

Rose at 11. Wrote to Sir Jas Watson—Messrs T. & B.—Mr Hilskin—Rev. H.P. Goodridge[7]—Signor Ruiz[8]—Mr Kimber—Mr J. Wilkinson (B.P.)—Mr S. Stephen—Miss Kislingbury.[9] Dined at Ld Northbrooks. Saw Digby & another [R]. Saw Sir Aug. Paget—Capt. Clark—Sir A. Panizzi—Ld Napier of Magdala—Col. Napier Sturt (Newc.)—Baroness L. Rothschild (Dr Benisch &c). Read [blank.]

23. 6 S. Trin.

All Souls mg, Chapel Royal aft. Read Mozley's Sermons—Ch. Quart. on Bp Gray—do on Scepticism—Spiritualist Prize Essays[10]—and [blank.]

24. M.

Wrote to Mr O. Crauford—Ld Rosebery—Mrs Th.—Mr Horsley Palmer.[11] H of C. 4¼-5¼.[12] Lady Ossington's at 5½ to meet Duke of Sermoneta. Meeting at Ld Granville's on Eastern Affairs 12½-2½. Read Eastern Papers[13]—Imperial Federation[14]—The Human Tragedy[15]—Life of M. Antoinette.[16] Saw Ld F. Cavendish—Sir C. Trevelyan—Mr Nevins.

---

[1] On Plumpstead Common; T.T., 29 July 1876, 9f.
[2] Perhaps of 2 Davies Street, Berkeley Square.
[3] George I, 1845-1913; king of the Hellenes 1863.
[4] H. N. Gladstone returned to India, to work for Gillanders, Arbuthnot and Co. in Calcutta.
[5] H 230. 1741.
[6] See 22 June 76.
[7] Henry Painter Goodrich, chaplain in the navy.
[8] M. F. Ruiz, Spanish publisher working in London; Hawn P.
[9] Emily Kislingbury; sent copy of an essay; Hawn P.
[10] Untraced.
[11] Probably John Horsley Palmer, s. of the economist and relative of Lord Selborne.
[12] Education; H 230. 1853.
[13] PP 1876 lxxxiv. 255; the Turkey N. 3 papers, published on 21 July.
[14] F. Young, Imperial federation of Great Britain and her colonies (1876).
[15] See 23 May 76.
[16] See 3 July 76.

25. Tu. St James

Our wedding day 37 years ago, and my eldest & now only brother's birthday. *Benedicto benedicatur*.
Wrote to Countess of Ashburnham—Mr Parker Snow[1]—Sir Thos G.—Cav. de Martino—Mrs Th.—Messrs B. & H.—Mr C. Powell[2]—Messrs Barnes & Co—Rev. N. Hall—Rev. T.R. West—Mr. T. Best—M. Cernuschi—Mr Murray. Read Palmer's Statement[3]—Salonica Papers No 4[4]—Turkey No 3 Papers. Breakfast and conversation with Sir Salar Jung,[5] who asked me much. Saw Phillips: bad is my best; but there is good material [R]. Ten to dinner. Conversation with Harry on whom a new opening dawns.

26. Wed.

Wrote to Ld Granville—M. D'Eichthal (BP)—Sir W. James—Mr W. Thompson— Mr Veitch[6]—Dr Stoughton[7]—Mr Walkerston—Prof. Monier Williams. Dined at Mr Lawson's. Luncheon at 15 G.S. Saw Harry on his matters. Saw Ld S. de Redcliffe on Eastern question—D. & Dss of Sermoneta—Scotts—Mr R. Eykyn—Mr Adam—Mr Lawson—Mr Hayward—Master of the Rolls.[8] Dined at Mr Lawson's. Read papers on Turkey. Saw one who is to return [R]. Read [blank.]

27. Th.

Wrote to Amn Minister[9]—M. de Laveleye—Mr Orr[10]—Mr Bramwell BP.—Ld Granville. Saw Ld E. Fitzmaurice—Ld F. Cavendish—Mr Forster—Ld Kimberley—Mr Adam—and others. Read Turkish Papers—Life of Marie Antoinette. Lord Tollemache drove us to the Crystal Palace for Circus & Fire works. H of C. $4\frac{1}{4}$-$5\frac{3}{4}$ & after midnight.[11] Ill in the night: deranged liver & diarrhoea.

28. Fr.

Kept my bed till $4\frac{1}{2}$. Then rose to attend meeting at Ld Granville's on the Eastern Question. Read (for many hours) & finished the Blue Book on E. question[12]—also Q.R. on Ticknor—and on Engl. & America.

29. Sat.

Wrote to Mr Salkeld—Mr Kimber—Principal of Lancing Coll.—Messrs Macmillan—D. Aristarchi Bey[13]—Mr Flamdy[14]—Countess Russell—Rev. J.W. Joyce—

[1] William Parker *Snow, 1817-95; geographer and explorer.
[2] Charles Powell of the London Working Men's Committee; sent details of progress; Hawn P.
[3] See 7 Mar. 37, or document sent by Horsley Palmer.   [4] *PP* 1876 lxxxiv. 705.
[5] Sir Salar Jung, 1829-83; formerly Dewan of Hyderabad; in Britain to receive honorary degree at Oxford.
[6] William Veitch, minister and grammarian in Edinburgh, on Homer; Hawn P.
[7] John *Stoughton, 1807-97; congregationalist and church historian.
[8] Sir G. Jessel.   [9] Edwards Pierrepoint, Schenck's successor, recently arrived.
[10] Perhaps John Bryson Orr of Westcombe Park; active liberal.
[11] Argued with Disraeli about the delaying of debate on Turkey; *H* 230. 1975.
[12] See 24 July 76n.
[13] Probably Demetrios Aristarches, published on Turkish legislation 1873-8.
[14] May read 'Flanedy'; neither identified.

Messrs B. & H.—Mr Farnfield—Mr E. Arnold—Mr Salkeld. Breakfast & much conversation with U.S. Minister. Greatly pleased with him & Mrs T. Saw Chev. de' Martini—Prof. Caffarelli[1]—Lord Edm. Fitzmaurice—Dr Elam[2]—on *the* question—Sir A. Panizzi—Mrs Tyler—Dowager Duchess of Somerset (Newcastle affairs). Dined with Agnes & E. at 21 CHT. Read Sweetman[3] & divers Tracts. Trevelyan, Pesth to Brindisi.[4]

30. 7 S. Trin.

Chapel Royal mg. St James's Evg. Saw Dr Elam—Mr Nevins. Dined with the Wortleys. Saw Ld Granville. Wrote to Mrs Th. Read Congreve's Addresses[5]— Trinity in Man[6]—and many tracts.

31. M.

Wrote to Miss Hawkins—Mr Lattimer—G. Harris—W. Mason—Mr Marvin— Mrs Lindsay—Mr Westell. Dined at Ld Wolverton's. Saw Ld Wolverton (H.N.G.)—Sir C. Dilke. Much sorting & preparing for departure. Got up the Turkish papers and question. H. of C. $4\frac{1}{2}$-$7\frac{3}{4}$ and $9\frac{1}{4}$-$1\frac{1}{2}$. Spoke over two hours on this wide and difficult subject.[7]

Tues. Aug. One 1876

Wrote to Lady Strangford—Mr Farnfield—Mr P. Girard—Prof. M. Williams—Mr Scudamore—Mr D. Whitley—Countess Russell—W. Bishop—W. White—Mrs Davidson—Messrs J. Watson—J. Burton[8]—Mr Whitfield—S.L. Low. Dined at Mr Hubbards. Saw Mrs Th.—Mr Ouvry—Mr Harris—Mr Bramwell—Lord Gran- ville—Leeds Deputation[9]—Lady Lechmere.[10] Much packing & preparation.

2. Wed. [Hawarden]

Wrote to Ed. D.T. (P.C.).[11] Saw Mr Bright—Scotts—Mr Forster—Mr Knowles— Mr Harris. H. of C. $12\frac{1}{2}$-$3\frac{1}{2}$.[12] Packing & preparing. Off at $4\frac{3}{4}$. Hn at $11\frac{1}{2}$. Read Fitzgerald's Suez Canal.[13]

---

[1] Unidentified; Francesco di Caffarelli published on music in Milan in 1894.

[2] Charles Elam, 1824-89; physician; published *Winds of Doctrine* (1876); see 23 Dec. 76.

[3] W. Sweetman, probably *A few thoughts on the infallibility of the Pope* (1870).

[4] Sir C. E. Trevelyan, *From Pesth to Brindisi in the autumn of 1869* (1870).

[5] See 16 July 76.

[6] T. Boys, *Trinity of Man* (1876).

[7] Reviewing British policy at the time of the Crimea, and arguing for 'by far of all the elements in this question—namely, the principle of the common concert of Europe'; 'the real question . . . is not whether the supremacy of the Porte can be established in its ancient form . . . but whether its politi- cal supremacy in some improved form can be—as I hope it may be—still maintained. . . What is this concert to be for? I say, without the least hesitation, it must be for measures conceived in the spirit and advancing in the direction of self-government'; *H* 231. 182.

[8] Perhaps John Burton, Wesleyan minister, wrote *The Christian Sabbath* (1876).

[9] No account found.

[10] Louisa Katherine, wife of Sir E. A. H. Lechmere.

[11] i.e. a post card, probably to announce departure from London.

[12] Drink in Ireland; *H* 231. 330.

[13] P. H. Fitzgerald, *The great canal at Suez*, 2v. (1876).

3. Th.

Wrote to R.K. Hutchinson—Mr J. de Morgan[1]—Mrs Hampton—Mr A.C. Sellar[2]—Dr Ward—Mad. Walterer. Unpacking & sorting books for some hours. Read Fitzgerald on Suez Canal—Laing on Caithness Remains.[3] Ch. 7 P.M.

4. Fr.

Ch. 8½ AM. Wrote to Professor Stubbs[4]—Dr Döllinger B.P.—Sir Jas Watson, and [blank.] Read Fitzgerald, Suez Canal—Curtius Hist of Greece[5]—Laing, Caithness Remains—Ld Russell Foreign Policy.[6] Drive with C. Worked on books & papers.

5. Sat.

Ch. 8½ AM. Wrote to Very Rev. Dr Newman[7]—Lady L. Grant[8]—Lady Lechmere—A. Piper—F. Pope—Rev. G. Wiseman—Rev. Churchill Babington[9]—Rev. S. Osborne. Read Curtius—Fitzgerald—Hélie, Rome des Papes[10]—M. Morris, Il Falcone.[11] Axe work.

6. 8 S. Trin.

Kept my bed till evg for tightness in the chest. Took the usual measures. Wrote (for H.G.) to T. & B. Read Foxley's MS.[12]—Constable on Future State[13]—Edw. White on do[14]—Report on Conditional Immortality[15]—Speeches on Bonn Conference[16]—Rowsell's Sermon.[17]

7. M.

Wrote to Ld Shaftesbury—Rev. Dr Newman—Rev. J. Foxley—Ld Granville—Scotts—Herbert J.G.—Mrs Th.—Baroness L. de Rothschild—Managing Director

[1] John de Morgan of the Commons' Protection League, campaigning for commoners' rights in Woolwich; D.T., 3 July 1876, 3f.

[2] Alexander Craig Sellar, 1835-90; Scottish advocate; liberal (unionist) M.P. Haddington 1882-5, Partick from 1885; liberal unionist whip 1886-8.

[3] S. Laing, Prehistoric remains of Caithness (1866).

[4] Thanking him for his Lectures (1876), which he read this day, sending them on to Newman and Döllinger; W. H. Hutton, William Stubbs (1906), 96 and Newman, xxviii. 99.

[5] E. Curtius, The history of Greece, tr. A. W. Ward, 5v. (1868-73).

[6] John, Earl Russell, The foreign policy of England 1570-1870 (1871).

[7] In Newman, xxviii. 99.

[8] Lady Lucy Grant, da. of 7th earl of Elgin, widow of J. Grant of Kilgraston; she d. 1881.

[9] Churchill *Babington, 1821-89; priest and antiquarian. Gladstone relied heavily in his review of Trevelyan's Macaulay (see 23 Mar. 76n.) on Babington's defence of the restoration clergy.

[10] A. Hélie, La Rome des Papes (1861).

[11] Untraced; perhaps an early work of Mowbray Walter Morris, poet and critic.

[12] Sent by J. Foxley (see 15 July 76); Hawn P.

[13] H. Constable, Hades; or the intermediate state of man (1873).

[14] E. White, Life in Christ (1846, 2nd ed. 1876), which denied natural immortality, confining it to the regenerate; see 3 Aug. 50.

[15] Untraced.

[16] Report of Bonn Reunion Conference 1875 (1876).

[17] T. J. Rowsell, 'A sermon on Matt. xi 28' (1874).

Nat. Prov. Bank—Mr Grogan. Read Fitzgerald Vol. II—Tchihatchef, Chances de Paix et de Guerre.[1] I give about two hours a day to sorting and righting my books & papers: a heavy job. The 'clergy' dined here.

8. Tu.

Attended the Cathedral opening service at Chester 3-5½. Bp Claughton preached a fine Sermon:[2] but actually let in the phantasm of the Liberationists! We had a public luncheon with the Mayor at one. And dined at Sir Thos Frost's. Saw the Dean—Mr Holland—The Bishop—Mr Townshend—Col. Gillespie.[3] Read Arnold's Indian Song[4]—Freeman Clarke's Xtn Doctrine of Prayer.[5]

9. Wed.

Ch. 8½ AM. Wrote to Finlay Brothers[6]—Mr Babington—A. Seymour—Keeper of Books Br. Mus. Read Suez Canal (finished Vol. II)—Behr's Origines Biblicae and Pref. to Father Paul's L.[7] Dined at the Rectory. Worked on Books. Two hours conversation with Mr Holland[8] on Oxford, state and studies.

10. Th.

Ch. 8½ AM. Wrote to Bp of Winchester—Duke of Argyll—Mrs Wheeler—Lady Strangford—J.L. Hanley[9]—Mr Hedderwick. Worked on arranging books & pamphlets. Read White's Life in Christ[10]—Hine's Nottingham Castle[11]—Relations of Landlord and Tenant[12]—E. Arnolds Song of Songs. Saw Mr D. Melville—Mr Dunn.

11. Fr.

Ch. 8½ AM. Wrote to Dr Von Dollinger—E. Arnold—T.C. Hine—W. Wilson—F. May—T.T. Hayes. Read E. Arnold (finished)—White's Life in Christ—Hélie, Rome des Papes[13]—Bear on Landlord & Tenant. All these days I have to give about two hours daily to moving & arranging books tracts & papers.

12. Sat.

Ch. 8½ AM. Wrote to Mr Wash (after consultation with Harry)[14]—Mr Middlehurst—Miss Smith B.P. Drove into Chester to dine with the Bp & see Bp of

[1] P. A. Chikhachev, *Chances de paix et de guerre* (1875).
[2] Reopening of Chester Cathedral; *The Guardian*, 16 August 1876, 1083.
[3] Perhaps Robert Rollo Gillespie, 1830-90; lieut. col. 1873; served in Egypt in 1882.
[4] E. Arnold, *The Indian Song of Songs. From the Sanskrit* (1875).
[5] J. F. Clarke, *The Christian doctrine of prayer. An essay* (1854).
[6] Liverpool merchants.
[7] Probably A. G. Campbell, *The life of Fra Paolo Sarpi* (1869).
[8] Henry Scott *Holland; Hawarden Visitors Book.
[9] J. Laffan Hanley, ed. *Le Journal Stamboul* at Constantinople and sent information on the atrocities; Add MS 44451, f. 38.
[10] See 6 Aug. 76.
[11] Thomas Chambers Hine had sent the 1st volume of his *Nottingham Castle*, 2v. (1876-9).
[12] W. E. Bear, *The relations of landlord and tenant in England and Scotland* (1876).
[13] See 5 Aug. 76.   [14] His arrangements for India.

Salisbury. First day of the Bazaar. A world of labour & little fruit. Worked on books & letters. Read White—Van Ryn on Disestablishment[1]—Laws on Prostitn—and other Tracts.

13. 9 S. Trin.

Hn Ch. mg and Chester Cathedral (Bp [Moberley] of Salisbury, crowded from end to end) evg. Tea at Bp of Chester's. Wrote to Mrs Th.—Mr Salkeld—and Captain Jones. Read White's Life in Christ—Donaldson on Sacrifice Symbolism.[2] Wrote on Future Punishment.[3]

14. M.

Kept my bed in mg. Wrote to Ld Blachford—Sir T. Bateson (papers)—Dr Donaldson—D. of Argyll—Professor Sbarbaro—Mr Mugford. Second day of the bazaar. A greater failure than Sat. We shall not I hope be tempted to repeat a very questionable experiment. *I* could not properly have done it. But it is trying for C. who has worked very hard. Read Donaldson (finished)—Life in Christ—Turner's Reply to Dodwell[4]—Johnson's Letters. Saw Mr [blank.]

15. Tu.

Ch. 8½ A.M. Wrote to Bp of St Andrew's—Col. Napier Sturt—Dr Dunbar—Mr Richard MP—Mr Lowndes—Bp of Moray—F.A. Frost.[5] Wrote on Future Punishments. Finished Turner's Reply. Read S. Clarke's Reply[6]—White's Life in Christ—Johnson's Letters. Inspection of the Effigy of our dear Stephen [Glynne] with a view to proper placing in the Church. Long conversation with Mr [Benjamin] Webb on questions of belief.

16. Wed.

Ch. 8½ AM. Wrote to Miss E.R. Howe (BP)—Ld Dufferin—Mrs Th.—Sir A. Gordon—Mr Lewis—Rev. D. Melvill—Mr Thicke—Mr A. Wash. Read White—Whitby's Reply to Dodwell[7]—Bp of St Andrews' Charge—Reply to Bp of St Asaph[8]—Okely's Letter to Southey.[9] Conversation with Mr Webb. Saw Bp of St Andrew's.

---

[1] J. G. Van Ryn, *Disestablishment, a duty* (1875).

[2] Probably J. W. Donaldson, *The theatre of the Greeks* (new ed. 1875).

[3] The skeleton of a book, never published (but used in *Studies subsidiary to Bishop Butler* (1896)), deriving in part from the Clarke-Dodwell controversy of 1706; it was these papers that Gladstone later docketed 'From this I was called away to write on Bulgaria'; Add MS 44698, 367ff.

[4] J. Turner, *Justice done to human souls, in a short view of Mr Dodwell's book* (1706).

[5] Of the Chester family.

[6] S. Clarke, *A fourth defense of an argument made use of in a Letter to Mr Dodwell* (1708).

[7] D. Whitby, *Reflections on some assertions and opinions of Mr Dodwell* (1707).

[8] Untraced reply to J. Hughes, see 9 July 76.

[9] W. Okely, 'A letter to ... Southey on his life of the late Mr John Wesley' (1820).

17. Th.

Ch. 8½ A.M. Wrote to Bp of Winchester—Dr Gialussi—Rev. Mr Gedge[1]—Mr M'Garel—Mr Strahan. Saw Mr Vickers. Attended the Horticultural Fete: & spoke, for C.[2] Conversation with Mr Webb. Conversation with Jack on his studies. Read White—Whitby (finished)—Johnson's Letters—Parker's Speeches NSW.[3]

18. Fr.

Ch. 8½ AM. Wrote to Mr Bradley (Tel.)—Mr Weill (U.S.)[4]—R. Frost—J. Evans— Mrs Th.—C. Knight[5]—Sir Thos G. Read White—Dodwell, Praemonition[6]—Bear, Landlord & Tenant—Rapport de Edib Effendi[7]—Johnson's Letters—Clevedon Hall.[8] Walk with Mr Webb: saw Broughton Church. We were all photographed. I took a written engagement as to my *carte de visite*.

19. Sat.

Ch. 8½ AM. Wrote to Messrs Harper N. York (& sent them my M.S.)[9]—also copy—Mr H. Wilson—Messrs Ouvry—Mr G. Redford—T. Martineau.[10] Corrected & prepared for press my letter of Nov 72 to Gen. Schenk. Read White—Dodwell—Hagenbach on Doctrines[11]—Story, Dietetic Error[12]—Locke, Reasonableness of Xty.[13]

20. 10 S. Trin.

Church 11 A.M. (H.C.) and 6½ PM. Wrote to Lord Blachford—Mr Redford. Read White—Dodwell—Bartle on Hades[14]—Eternal Suffering as Privation: Cutting on Baptists:[15] Dr Horbery.[16]

---

[1] Perhaps John Wycliffe Gedge, school inspector.
[2] On cottage gardening; *T.T.*, 18 August 1876, 9f.
[3] H. Parker, *Speeches ... connected with New South Wales* (1876).
[4] Probably for an autograph.
[5] Charles Knight, a Greenwich elector, had written asking if diarist intended to speak in the constituency; Gladstone's reply prevaricated; *T.T.*, 22 August 1876, 9f.
[6] H. Dodwell, probably *Epistolary discourse [on the immortality of the soul]* (1706).
[7] *Traduction du Rapport présenté, par ... Edib Effendi ... sur l'enquête ordonnée ... dans de Vilayet d'Andrinople* (1876).
[8] See 10 Jan. 76n.
[9] Arranging publication in *Harper's* of the vast letter to Schenck on diarist's attitude to the American civil war; printed at 28 Nov. 72; see above, vii. xlvii and 1 Jan. 76.
[10] Giving Thomas Martineau, niece of Harriet,* permission to include letters from Gladstone on her pension in her biography; Add MS 44451, ff. 63, 73.
[11] C. R. Hagenbach, *A textbook of the history of doctrines*, tr. C. W. Buch, 2v. (1871).
[12] Untraced.
[13] See 3 June 27.
[14] See 11 Jan. 74.
[15] Perhaps S. S. Cutting, *A discourse on the application of the epithet Evangelical* (1843).
[16] See 1 Sept. 72.

21. M.

Ch. 8½ A.M. Wrote to Dr Buchholz (& B.P.)[1]—Sir E. Watkin—Mr Tallack.[2] Wrote on Future punishments. Read White—Dodwell—Bp Butler on Future Life[3]—Johnson's Letters & Thrale.[4]

22. Tu.

Ch. 8½ AM. Wrote to Sir A. Buchanan—Mr MacColl—Mr G. Potter—Mons. E. Belleroche[5]—Mr ACourt (B.P.)—Mr G.M. Walker—Mr A.Austin (BP). Read White—Dodwell—Johnson's Letters—Gardner on River Worship.[6] We began a new piece of walk round part of the Old Castle Walls. Wrote on Future Punishments.

23. Wed.

Ch. 8½ AM. Wrote to Mr A. Austin B.P.—Rev. E. White[7]—Rev. J. Simpson[8]—Earl of Carnarvon—Miss C. Aird—A. Days[9]—R.J. Pike[10]—Mr Vickers. Read White (finished)—Dodwell (finished)—Chishull on Dodwell[11]—De la Voye on The Word[12]—Gorman, Xtn Psychology.[13] Worked at the walk, & much worsened my lumbago at night by it.

24. Th.

Did not rise early. Wrote to Mr T.B. Potter MP—Mr Price—Mr Walker—Mr O'Brien—Mr Hitchman—Mrs Forbes—Dean Torry—Dr Petavel.[14] Read Chishull against Dodwell[15]—Presbyter for Dodwell[16]—Petavel on Future Punishment—Johnson's Letters. I was a cripple today. Long conversation with Mr Hignett on the Succession & Residuary accounts.

[1] Eduard August Wilhelm Buchholz, 1825-87; German classical scholar; published, as did Gladstone, on Homeric geography.

[2] William Tallack, writer on penal reform; see Add MS 44431, f. 239.

[3] See 8 Oct. 31.

[4] H. L. Piozzi, *Letters to and from the late Samuel Johnson*, 2v. (1788).

[5] Edward Belleroche, Huguenot friend of de Laveleye living in London; sent de Haulleville (see 29 Aug. 76); Hawn P.

[6] Perhaps the entry on rivers in J. Gardner, *The Christian Cyclopaedia* (1865), 575, 786.

[7] Edward White, 1819-98; congregationalist minister in London, and friend of C. N. Hall; see 6 Aug. 76n.

[8] Perhaps John Simpson, d. 1899?; curate at Neenton 1874-91.

[9] Alfred Days, secretary to the 'Workmen's Hyde Park Demonstration Committee' on the atrocities, had asked for help; Gladstone sent a message of support, read out to the working men's meeting in Hackney on 29 August; *T.T.*, 30 August 1876, 7f. and Tauchnitz, 1631. Days' letter is docketed by Gladstone 'πήγη' (spring, or fountain); Hawn P.

[10] Of Nottingham, on working-class investment in the Post Office Savings Bank; Hawn P.

[11] E. Chishull, *A charge of heresy* (1706); against Dodwell.

[12] M. J. G. de La Voye, *The Word!* (1868).

[13] T. M. Gorman, *Christian psychology* (1875).

[14] Emmanuel Pétavel (-Olliff), 1836-1910; French theologian; R. W. Dale's tr. of his *Struggle for eternal life* just published.

[15] See 23 Aug. 76.

[16] *The Holy Spirit the author of immortality, proved by a Presbyter of the Church of England* [J. Pitts] (1708).

25. Fr.

Ch. 8½ AM. Wrote to Mr Gorman[1]—Messrs Barker & Hignett—Mr Macmillan—Rev. Mr Denton. Arranged letters & papers on matters of business (private & family). Conversation with Mrs Hampton respecting her son W. Read Chishull (finished)—Petavel—Johnson's Letters. Wrote on Future Punishment. Lumbago much better.

26. Sat.

Ch. 8½ AM. Wrote to Lady Russell—Mr de Lisle—Mrs Manning[2]—Mr A. Days. Wrote on Future Punishment. Read Chishull on Justin Martyr—Autel contre Autel[3]—Pitts' reply to Clarke—Oxenham[4]—Jukes[5]—St Irenaeus—Justin—finished Johnson's Letters. Walk with Herbert & conversation on his reading.

27. 11 S. Trin.

Ch 11 AM: and 6½ P.M. Wrote to Mr J. Rawlinson—Ld Carington[6]—Sir W. James—Ld Granville—Mr Macmillan—T.B. Potter MP—Mr McGarel (B.P.)—A.S.Wilson.[7] Read Bp Conybeare, Defence of Revealed Religion[8]—Wilson, Creed of tomorrow—Pitt, Reply to Clarke on Future Punishment—Began 'The Salvation of all Men'.[9]

28. M.

Ch. 8½ AM. Worked on a beginning for a possible pamphlet on the Turkish question.[10]

I stupidly brought on again my lumbago by physical exertion. Was obliged to put off my post. Read The Salvation of All Men—Dr S. Clarke on the Soul[11]—& his Adversary—Gifford against Priestly.[12]

29. Tu.[13]

Kept my bed long. Wrote to Ld Granville—Mr MacColl—Mrs Winn—Lady Russell—Mrs Th.—Edr of Times[14]—Mr Bailie—Mr Burbidge[15]—Mr Brough.

---

[1] Probably Thomas Murray Gorman, curate in Campden; Swedenborgian.

[2] Perhaps a relative of the custom official; see 26 Feb. 45.   [3] Untraced.

[4] See 2 July 76.

[5] A. H. Jukes, *"Catholic eschatology" examined. A reply to Oxenham* (1876).

[6] Charles Robert Wynn-Carrington, 1843-1928; a liberal; 3rd Baron Carrington 1868; office 1881-5, 1892-5; governed N.S. Wales 1885-90; in Edwardian cabinets; cr. marquis of Lincolnshire 1912. On the by-election consequent on Disraeli's peerage, see Ramm, I, ii. 490 and 11 Sept. 76.

[7] Alexander Stephen Wilson sent his *Creed for tomorrow* (1872).

[8] J. B. Conybeare, *A defence of revealed religion* (1732).

[9] Perhaps E.J.H., *Salvation: what it is and who it is for* (1875).

[10] See 5 Sept. 76. Extracts from entries until 5 Sept. in Morley, ii. 551.   [11] See 15 Aug. 76.

[12] R. Gifford, *Outlines of an answer to Dr Priestley's Disquisitions* (1781).

[13] For an account of Gladstone apparently at this time (though the visit is unmentioned in diary or visitor's book) see J. Wordsworth, *The episcopate of Charles Wordsworth* (1899), 210. The bp. was a strong ecumenist.

[14] Details of correction to his speech of 31 July, respecting Baring's mission; Add MS 44451, f. 103.   [15] Possibly John Burbidge, poet.

Read The Soul controversy—Salvation of All Men—De Haulleville's Reply to Laveleye[1]—and as a treat began Waverley once more. Lumbago bad: aggravated by trying to walk and by writing, which (oddly) works the *back*.

30. Wed.

Much bed: forswore all writing: rubbed &c: some improvement. Read St Thomas Aquinas on the Soul—The Clarke Controversy—De Haulleville—Salvation of all Men (finished)—Teape's Letter to Close[2]—Waverley. A snug evening with M. and H. in the Temple of Peace.

31. Th.

Wrote to Mr M'Coll—Bp of Rochester—Lady Strangford—Ld Granville—Rev F. Clarke[3]—Mr Bromham.

Kept my bed till four & made tolerable play in writing on Bulgarian Horrors: the back is less strained in bed, where I write against the legs.

Read the Clarke Controversy on the Soul—Waverley—No 3 of Parl. papers on Turkey.[4] History conversation with Herbert.

Frid. Sept 1–76.

Wrote to Bp of St Andrew's (BP)—Keeper of Pr. Books B. Museum[5]—Mr Murray tel. and letter—W. Russell[6]—R. Law—E.J. Collings[7]—Ld Granville—Dr [J. H.] Gladstone—Mess. Pears & Logan B.P.—Mess. Farrer & Ouvry B.P.—Mrs Winn—Rev. J. Owen[8]—Rev. C. Babington—Sir J. Watson—Messrs Clowes—Ed. Daily News.[9] Again worked hard in bed: and sent off more than half to the Printer. Read Waverley. Short drive with C.

2. Sat.

Wrote to Rev. Mr Morgan—Bp of St Andrews—Mr Wenkirten—Ld Granville Tel. This day I wrote again a good piece of the pamphlet in bed but improved considerably by the aid of two hot baths. Rose at 4. Read Waverley in evg.

3. 12 S. Trin.

Hn Ch (and H.C.) 11 A.M. and 6½ PM. Wrote to Newc. Estate Agent—Sir H. Elliot—Mr G. Whale[10]—Messrs Clowes—Mr Delisle—Gen. Cesnola—Mrs

---

[1] Baron de Haulleville, probably his articles in *Révue Générale* in reply to de Laveleye's *Protestantism and Catholicism*, tr. (1878) as *Social aspects of Catholicism and Protestantism*; see 22 Aug. 76n.

[2] Apparently *sic*; untraced.

[3] Perhaps Frederick Kent Clarke, d. 1920; rector of Orcheston St Mary 1876–88.

[4] See 24 July 76n.   [5] Arranging to work there; see 4 Sept. 76.

[6] William Russell of Onslow Gardens, London; Hawn P.

[7] Edward J. Collings of the Bristol School, Bolton, on free libraries; Hawn P.

[8] John Owen, rector of Erryrys, Mold.

[9] Announcing publication and asking for details of its Bulgarian reports; Add MS 44451, f. 102 and Shannon, 108. The acting editor was Peter William *Clayden, 1827–1902; unitarian minister; worked on *Daily News* 1868–96; historian. Gladstone used his *England under Lord Beaconsfield* (1880) in preparing for the 1880 Midlothian Campaign.

[10] Accepting invitation to attend a meeting in Greenwich on Bulgaria; *D.T.*, 5 September 1876, 3a.

Wynn—Chairman B.I.R.—Mrs Th.—Mr J. Fraser—Dr Sieveking[1]—Mr H.R. Taylor—Rev. M. M'Coll—Mr A. Giles[2]—Mr T.B. Potter MP.—Mr Harry Wilson.[3] Preparing for departure. Read but a little, of Winn (Materialism)[4] and Haulleville. Off at 10.15 for London.

4. M. [London]

Reached 18 C.H.T.[5] at 5 by Limited Mail and bed till nine. Wrote to C.G.[6]— Rev. Newman Hall. Saw Ld Granville—Mr Delane—Sir A. Panizzi—Mr Clowes—Mr V. Murray—The American Minister.

In six or seven hours, principally at the B. Museum I completed my MS making all the needful searches of Papers and Journals: also worked on proof sheets.

Granville had a small very pleasant dinner party.

5. Tuesday.

Wrote to C.G.—Messrs Murray (list)[7]—Mr E. Davis[8] Greenwich. Saw Ld Granville—Ld Hartington—Mr Clowes—Ld Chief Baron—Mrs Th.—General Cesnola and Mr [C. T.] Newton, to examine the very beautiful objects from Kurium & Amathus.

Finished the correction of revises before one: discussing the text with Ld G. & making various alterations of phrase which he recommended. At seven I received complete copies.[9]

We went to the Haymarket Theatre.[10] Arranged my papers after this 'skrimmage': & sent off copies in various directions. Saw Phillips aftn X.

6. Wed.

Wrote to C.G.—Ld Carington—Mr E. Davis—Canon Venables—Mr Tilley—Gen. Manager Euston—Ld Stratford de Redcliffe—Messrs Murray—Messrs Clowes. Saw Mr Newman Hall (& discussed the subject)—Mr A.E. West—Mr Knowles (2)—Mr Palgrave—Mr Davies [sc. Davis]—Ld Granville—Sir J. Hudson & Sir J. Lacaita—Mr Bartlett.[11] Saw A. Seymour: now about to be married [R]. Dined

---

[1] Henry Sieveking, London physician.

[2] Declining to join J. Alfred Giles's cttee. on the atrocities: 'my own personal exertions must lie in other directions for the same end'; D.T., 5 September 1876, 3a. See 24 Sept. 76n.

[3] Of West Bromwich; correspondence on religion in Hawn P.   [4] By J. M. Winn (1875).

[5] Granville's house.   [6] Letters until 7 September in Bassett, 217ff.

[7] For the pamphlet's complimentary copies, including Disraeli, whose papers contain two copies, one of them uncut; Hughenden MSS, Bodleian Library. Millman, 181, 524 mentions the uncut copy only.

[8] Ebenezer Davis, acting secretary of the Greenwich Liberal Association; arranging the meeting with him next day; D.T., 7 September 1876, 3c.

[9] 'The Bulgarian Horrors and the Question of the East', published by Murray, printed by Clowes, dedicated to Stratford de Redcliffe; reprinted in the Tauchnitz series (1631) together with his review of Schuyler, the Blackheath speech and sundry letters; Add MS 44695, f. 376. The early completion caught the newspapers unready, publication being expected on the 7th; Bassett, 219. The first printing of 2,000 was supplemented to 24,000 by 7 September; ibid. See also 8 Sept. 76n.

[10] i.e. Gladstone, Granville, and Hartington, to see 'The Heir-at-Law', a farce.

[11] (Sir) Ellis Ashmead *Bartlett, 1849-1902; then a school inspector; tory imperialist converted briefly on the atrocities by Liddon; visited Balkans 1877-8; M.P. Eye 1880-4, Eccleshall from 1885. See Shannon, 62, 104.

with Mrs Th. & read her some passages. Better than usual. Read Eastern Pamphlets.

7. *Th.*

Wrote to Mr Potter (Tel.)—Messrs Clowes (2)—C.G.—Liberal Depn (Tel.)[1]—Countess of Sydney—Mr Congreve[2]—Mrs Th.—Mr R. de Broc—Ld Granville. Read Ticknor's diaries.[3] Saw Mr Cooke (Murray 2)—Ld Carington—Scotts—Mr West—Greenwich Deputn to make arrangements:[4] I wrote out a draft of Address. Went to Harley St to arrange books & papers. In evg saw M. Phillips X: I might put down much.

8. *Fr.*

Wrote to Ed. Daily News—Mr Whale—Mr Batty[5]—Mr Anderson—Mr Read—P. Parry—Mr De Broc—Geo. Harris—Mr Gurdon—Mr Corke[6]—Mr Marvin—Editor of Times[7]—Mr Delane—Mr Vavassour—Mr Alexander[8]—Jas Ford[9]—J. de Morgan—Ly Russell. Saw Sir W. James—Mr F. Leveson—Rev. Mr Birley—Sir A. Panizzi—Sir F. Doyle. Saw Graham: with hope of a betaking to refuge [R]. Read Ticknor's Diaries—Westmr R. on Macaulay—Rev. Deux Mondes on India & on the East. Dined with Mrs Th. Saw C.G. in evg just come up.

9 *Sat.* [*Frognall, Foot's Cray, Kent*]

Wrote to Rev. Mr Mayow—Ld Carington—Mr Solly—Mr Rushbrooke[10]—Mr Anderson[11]—Jas Ford. Packed up. Saw Ld Carington—Mr West—Sir W. James. Read D News Pamphlet[12]—Various tracts.

Thought over my subject for Blackheath. Off at two. A very large meeting. The most enthusiastic by far that I ever saw. Spoke over an hour.[13] We were then carried off by the kind Sydneys to their charming place at Frognall. A party came to dinner.

[1] Arranging meeting later this day.

[2] Richard *Congreve, 1818-99; physician and positivist; his article 'England and Turkey', *Fortnightly Review* (October 1876) opposed the agitation; Shannon, 217.

[3] G. Tickner, *Life, letters and journals*, 2v. (1876).

[4] See *D.T.*, 8 September 1876, 3a; Gladstone 'inclined to an indoor meeting'.

[5] Councillor Batty, active in the atrocities campaign.

[6] Perhaps John Corke, active liberal in Sutton.   [7] In Tauchnitz, 1631.

[8] Giving permission to L. C. Alexander (founder of Royal Historical Society, just leaving for St Petersburg) to have 'Bulgarian Horrors' translated into Russian; this was done by K. P. Pobyedonostsev and K. N. Bestuzhev-Ryumin, with a preface by Alexander, who on 6 October reported 20,000 copies printed; Hawn P.

[9] Had requested a copy; Hawn P.

[10] W. G. Rushbrooke, Highgate liberal, of the City of London school, had appealed to diarist to break silence on the atrocities; Hawn P.

[11] George Anderson, 1819-96; liberal M.P. Glasgow 1868-85; on the atrocities; Add MS 44451, f. 146.

[12] Containing Schuyler's report on Bulgaria, sent by Clayden, 'just out'; Add MS 44451, f. 148.

[13] *The Times* recorded he spoke 'exactly one hour', calculating the audience at about 10,000; *T.T.*, 11 September 1876, 10a; published as a pamphlet together with the letters to Days (23 Aug.) and to *T.T.* (14 Sept.). Speech notes—three sides of brief points—at Add MS 44664, f. 60. See also W. T. Stead, *Gladstone. A character sketch* (1898), 13.

10. 13 S. Trin.

The near Church at 11 AM: Chiselhurst Ch, reviving all the dear recollections of the place, at 3.45. Wrote to Gen. Manager Euston—Miss L. Lowe—Mr de Lisle—Canon Venables—Mr Lush[1]—Earl Granville—Ed. of Guardian. Much conversation with Ld Sydney, on the Queen, & the Newcastle family. Read Haulleville—and various Tracts.

11. Monday. [Wycombe Abbey, High Wycombe]

Back to London after breakfast. Saw Ld Granville & reviewed his draft letter which he strengthened at my instance.[2] I told him how pleasant it would be to me if he could publicly lead the present movement: though I could not urge him to do it against his own view and in his position relatively to the party. Corrected my speech of Sat. for the Guardian.[3] Wrote to Mr E. Davis—Mr Merriman (& two Tel.)[4]—Mr V. Fitzgerald—Mrs Potts—Also draft reply to the High Wycombe Liberal Assocn.[5] Off at 4.50 to High Wycombe & the Abbey:[6] the town gave me an enthusiastic reception, of course with relation to the present circumstances. We discussed the Election & particular voters in the course of the evening. Read D'Haulleville.

12. Tu. [Hawarden]

We left High Wycombe Station soon after ten. Wrote to Sir J. Bennett[7]—Rev. Mr Swayn—Mr Jolly. Shopping in London. Saw Sir A. Panizzi—Lady Granville—Mr Grogan—Sig. Farini (companion)[8]—Mr Payne (Murray). Wrote out & sent Reply to H.W. Liberal Association. Finished correcting Speech. Worked on books & papers: off from H[arley] St at 4¾. Reached Hn at 11½. Read Ld Derby's Speeches[9]—Reply to W.E.G.[10]—Baron d'Haulleville.

13. Wed.

Ch. 8½ AM. Wrote to Mr Merriman (2 Tell)—Ld Granville—D. of Argyll—Ld Carington—T.B. Potter MP—A.W. Pet (MP)[11]—Capt. Healy[12]—Miss Kort-

[1] Perhaps Samuel Clarence Lush, London solicitor.

[2] Granville's open letter, dated 10 September, to the cttee. for the City meeting in Guildhall on the atrocities; *T.T.*, 13 September 1876, 8a.

[3] In *The Guardian*, 13 September 1876, 1213.

[4] Arthur P. Merriman, secretary to J. J. Merriman, chairman of the City meeting.

[5] Invitation and draft reply (not found published) at Add MS 44763, f. 33.

[6] Lord Carrington's house; his br., Rupert, narrowly failed on 22 September to win the seat in the by-election following Disraeli's peerage, but greatly narrowed the tory majority of 1874; he held it 1880-5. See R. W. Davis, *Political change and continuity* (1972), 204.

[7] Sir John *Bennett of Greenwich, 1814-97; br. of W.C.; watch manufacturer; active in London liberal politics; stood for Greenwich 1873. Gladstone sent £100 for his fund for Balkan relief; *D.T.*, 14 September 1876, 5a.

[8] Domenico Farini, friend of Panizzi, son of L.C. (whose book Gladstone translated, see 27 Nov. 50, 3 Mar. 59), and Italian parliamentary deputy; Hawn P.

[9] *The Eastern Atrocities. Lord Derby's defence* (1876).

[10] See 15 Sept. 76?

[11] *sc.* A. W. Peel.

[12] R. C. Healy of Victoria Street, London, on the atrocities; Hawn P.

right[1]—Mr Morgan MP—Mr Harry Wilson—Capt. Drummond[2]—Rev. Mr Cookesley—Mrs Th.—Mr Cornish—Mr Laing MP—T. Grey BP—J. Thomas BP.—J. Roberts—Mrs Kenrick—Mrs Helen G.—Mr Davis—Mr Burnard. Read Mr Carterets Llewellyn:[3] and more of Baron de Haulleville.

14. Th.

Ch. 8¼ AM. Wrote to Ed. of Daily News (2)—Rev. Mr Denton (Tel. B.P.)[4]—J.W. Thompson[5]—Sig. Farini—Messrs Clowes (B.P.)—Mr Miller—Mr Fergusson—Duchess of Cleveland—Mr Watt—Mr Stark—Mr Knowles—Ed. Times.

I began the writing of what might have become a new pamphlet on Lord Derby's Speeches: but I gave it up, I think under a right instinct, and I composed instead of it a letter to the D. News and Times, endeavouring to sum up the whole.[6] It goes by the day post tomorrow. Walked with Mr Warwick Brooks.[7] A party of fifteen to dinner. Conversation with Mr Murray—Mayor of Chester—The Dean.

15. Fr.

Ch. 8¼ AM. Wrote to Maj. Gen. Bowie—Mr A. Austin—Mr [W.] Rayner Wood—Sec. to Ld Mayor—Rev. E. Johnson[8]—Mr R. Payne—Mr Wilson B.P.—Miss Walker.

Six gentlemen came down to ask me to attend the City Meeting. I persisted in saying no, with reasons: & took them about the place.[9] This journey is a remarkable indication of the state of public feeling.

Saw Mr Vickers—Mr Murray. Walk & conversation with Lord Rayleigh. Read Mr Austin's Reply[10]—Mr Carteret's Llewellyn (finished). The London Press seems now up to the mark. All goes well. Oh what should be our gratitude!

16. Sat.

Ch. 8¼ AM. Wrote to Rev. E. Coleridge—Ld Granville—Aldn Bickerton—Councr Batty—Rev. F. Meyrick—Rev. Dr Allon—Mons. H. Passy[11]—Mr Dobson—Mr Drew—Mr Storr—Mr Davis—Mr Brown—Mr Carteret—W.H. Green. Walk with H. & H. which I much enjoy. Read Mr Freeman's powerful article on the

---

[1] The novelist (see 31 Jan. 70), organizing Ladies' Memorial to the Queen on the atrocities; *D.T.*, 15 September 1876, 3a.

[2] Arthur Hay-Drummond, 1833-1900; captain R.N.; Perthshire landowner.

[3] A. E. Carteret, *Llewelyn: a tragedy* (1876).

[4] W. Denton (see 13 June 51), one of the chief organizers of protest in London.

[5] Joseph William Thompson of Cardiff; see Add MS 44451, f. 178.

[6] *T.T.*, 16 September 1876, 5d. and Tauchnitz, 1631.

[7] See 17 July 66.

[8] Edward Ralph Johnson, d. 1911; archdeacon of Chester 1871-6; bp. of Calcutta 1876-98. See 20 Nov. 76.

[9] Deputation led by J. J. Merriman; *D.T.*, 16 September 1876, 3c.

[10] A. Austin, 'Tory horrors or the question of the hour. A letter . . . to Gladstone' (1876).

[11] Hippolyte Philibert Passy, political economist; see Add MS 44127, f. 33.

Turks[1] (I am now again & perforce immersed in the Newspapers.) Newman's Historical Sketch.[2] Strong neuralgia came on at night.

17. 14 S. Trin.

Ch. 11 AM with H.C. and 6½ P.M. Wrote to Messrs Murray—Mr A. Days. Read Maurice, Theological Essays[3]—Newman's Hist. Sketch. Walk with Ld R[ay-leigh] & Mr [J. H.] Parker. Neuralgia continues: from overpressure.

18. M.

Did not venture to Church in mg. Wrote to Count Ricciardi[4]—Ld Granville—F. May & Co—Mr J. P[assmore] Edwards—Mrs Thorpe—Mr Hayden—Messrs B. & H.—Rev. Mr Tucker.[5] 2 hours on arranging books and papers. Read Outline of History[6]—Newman on the Turks—Finlay, Byzantine Empire[7]—Adye on British Army.[8] My neuralgia took itself off in the afternoon.

19. Tu.

Ch. 8½ AM. Wrote to Ld Carington—Mr Wilson—Mr Bikela[9]—Mr Walters—Mr Hagopian[10]—Mr Murray—Hon & Rev. J. Grey—F.J. Jeffery—H.P. Owen—J. Bland—Rev. J. Macdona—W. Brough—E. Davis—W.H. Stokes[11]—Jas Wyld—D.M. West—Rev. R.R. Suffield—Miss Patteson[12]—Capt. Brady.[13] Saw Rev. (Brahmin)[14] Worked on books: arranging &c. Mr Parker explained to me his book & views on the Forum. Read Newman on the Turks (finished)—Finlay's Byzantine Empire. Walk & conversation with Herbert: tried to give a view of Turkish &c. History. Attended the St John's Meeting & spoke on presentation to Mr Barnes.[15] It was very pastoral.

20. Wed. [Raby Castle, Darlington]

Wrote to Hon F. Lawley (BP)—Ld Carington—Mr Dobson—Mr Kitchin—Mr Lemon—Messrs Clowes BP. Off at 9.15. Reached Raby[16] 6.15. We were most

---

[1] E. A. Freeman, 'The Turks in Europe', *British Quarterly Review*, lxiv. 441 (October 1876); see Shannon, 31.

[2] [J. H. Newman], *Lectures on the history of the Turks in its relation to Christianity* (1854): 'the Turks are simply in the way. They are in the way of the civilization of the nineteenth century.'

[3] J. F. D. Maurice, *Theological essays* (1853).

[4] Acknowledging his telegram reporting a Neapolitan meeting on the atrocities: 'the Bourbon government which once seemed to him so black, now seems almost immaculate in view of the horrible deeds perpetrated by the Turks'; *D.T.*, 25 September 1876, 5d.

[5] Henry William Tucker, assistant secretary, later secretary, of S.P.G.

[6] Perhaps *Outline of ancient history* (1830).

[7] See 10 July 54.   [8] See above, vii. xcv.

[9] D. Bikelas, 1833–1909; prosperous Greek trader in London; tr. Shakespeare into Greek, giving diarist a copy; see L. Politis, *History of Modern Greek Literature* (1975), 164.

[10] Garabet Hagopian, Armenian living in Shepherd's Bush, in correspondence on Armenian churches and education.

[11] William Haughton Stokes, 1802–84; fellow of Caius, Cambridge; rector of Denver from 1852.

[12] Of Torquay; had sent a walking stick; Hawn P.

[13] Perhaps John Brady, surgeon, magistrate and liberal M.P. Leitrim 1852–80.

[14] This phrase in pencil.   [15] No account found.

[16] Duke of Cleveland's castle near Darlington.

kindly received. Conversation with Lady M. Alford—M. Hübner[1]—Dean of Durham. Corrected the proofs of the new Pamphlet on the Railway.[2] Read Dante—Othello (in Germ. & Mod. Greek (began)—Argyll's Speech of 1867 on Crete.[3]

21. Th.

Castle Prayers at 9.15. (A clergyman officiated: very short.) Wrote to Mr Granville Vernon—Sig. Sella[4]—Mr S.G. Rathbone—Sir A. Gordon—Sir John Adye[5]—Hon & Rev J. Grey. Read Dante Inferno—Othello (as before)—and Book of Forrain Travel 1650.[6] We went to see the strange edifice built for a Museum[7] beyond Barnard Castle: I walked back. Conversation with the Duke—Lady Marion [Alford].

22. Fr.

Prayers 9.15. Wrote to Mr H. Wilson—Mr Craggass[8]—Mr Macmillan Tel.—Mr Read—Mr Bailey. Saw Mr Halliday—endeavouring hard to fight off a meeting & speech at Staindrop. Walk with the Duke: who has much knowledge of his own greatly extended affairs, and of other things: The park *very* fine. Began the cutting of a great *porcupine* beach [*sic*] near the Castle. Read Dante—Memoirs of Mad. du Barri.[9] Conversation with Lady M.—Baron Hübner.

23. Sat.

Prayers 9.15. Saw Mr Pease M.P.—Professor Hunter respecting Glasgow Election.[10] 1½ hour on the Beech, & conversation with the Forester. Went down to Staindrop and was forced to go into the Hall and make a speech[11] sorely against my will for if this sort of thing goes on I shall seem a rogue and impostor. Read Dante—Mad. Dubarri's Life: certainly a most repulsive & most instructive relation.

[1] Count Joseph Alexander Hübner; friend of Lady Herbert; published on his tours of the British Empire.
[2] See 9 Sept. 76n.
[3] G. D. Campbell, duke of Argyll, 'The Eastern Question. Speech . . . on the conduct of the Foreign Office during the insurrection in Crete in 1867' (1876).
[4] See 22 Jan. 63 and Add MS 44450, f. 98.
[5] Sir John Miller *Adye, 1819-1900; war office reformer; governor of Woolwich 1875-80; second in command in Egypt 1882. See 18 Sept. 76.
[6] J. Howell, *Instructions for forreine travell* (1642), collated with 2nd ed. of 1650 by E. Arber (1869).
[7] The French renaissance-style Bowes museum.
[8] Thomas Cruddass, Staindrop liberal; Hawn P.   [9] See 9 Oct. 48.
[10] By-election for the Aberdeen and Glasgow university seat, held by the tories on 14 November. William Alexander Hunter, 1844-98; of Aberdeen; professor of law in London 1869-82; liberal M.P. N. Aberdeen 1885-96; secured free education for Scotland 1890. See Ramm II, i. 12.
[11] Gladstone had told the deputation on 22 Sept. that he would not make a speech, but he 'stated he would be driving down from the Castle on Saturday afternoon to inspect the church, when he would be happy to shake hands with any of his friends'. 'About a dozen gentlemen from Darlington and a few from Barnard Castle got private intimation of the event. . . . It rained at the time, and at the suggestion of Mr Pease, M.P., the hon. gentleman permitted the carriage to be driven to the public hall . . . the proceedings which took place were quite informal and impromptu'; *D.T.*, 25 September 1876, 3d and *T.T.*, 25 September 1876, 6c.

24. 15 S. Trin.

Staindrop Ch mg: Prayers in Castle (short) 10 PM. Wrote to Editor of Echo—
Duke of Argyll—Mary G.—Mr Schnadhorst[1]—Mr Murray—Sir J.E. Bennett—Mr
J.A. Giles[2]—Rev. Mr Tucker—Scotts—Rev. A. Jenkins[3]—Mr West—Mr ODonnell—Mrs Th.—Mr Morison—Dr Protich[4]—Mr Bromskill—Mr Fraser—Ld
Houghton. Saw the Staindrop Monuments. Read Dante—Sir B. Frere on Indian
Missions[5]—Voysey in answer to W.E.G.[6]

25. M. [Durham]

Off at 8.45. Reached Durham before 11. What a view on the approach. What a
glorious interior! The paring[7] on the outside murderous. But the remains of what
has been here are still noble and inspiring, in a high degree. Went over the Deanery—Priory—Castle—the grounds, & the School. The dean[8] sent us in afternoon to
Houghton Le Spring. A very pleasant evening with the Greys. Ch. conversation
with him: & mining, with Mr Morton.[9] Church Prayers at 6. AM. [sic]. (A crowd
greeted me, & followed me in).[10] Wrote to Ld Carington—Lady Waterford[11]—
Stat. Master Coldstream. Read Dante—began Freeman's Lectures.[12] Saw Lady
Canning's remarkable drawings.

26. Tu. [Ford Castle, Coldstream]

Visited the town: a beautiful 16th Cent. House. Most warm greetings here and
everywhere. Reached Ford at 3.30. Lady W[aterford] took us through the
grounds. A pleasant party especially Lady M. A[lford]. Read Dante—Freeman.

27. Wed.

Wrote to Duchess of Northumberland—Mr Bright—Mr Alden (N.Y.)[13]—Mr Murray—Mr Lush—Landlord (Coldstream)—Mr Melrose (ibid.)[14] We went in afternoon over Flodden hill: Lady W[aterford] walking all the way with much grace
and vigour. Visited the School filled with her paintings: so great in colour, feeling,
invention, & much of the execution. She & others sang at night. Miss

[1] Francis Schnadhorst, 1840–1900; secretary of Birmingham Liberal Association 1873, of
National Liberal Federation 1877; loyal to Gladstone and the party 1886.

[2] Declining the invitation of J. Alfred Giles (another secretary of the Workmen's Demonstration
Committee, see 23 Aug. 76n.) to preside at a meeting at St James's Hall in October; Hawn P.

[3] Perhaps Alfred Augustus Jenkins, episcopalian minister in Galashiels.

[4] Staying in London, wrote on the atrocities; Hawn P.

[5] Sir H. B. E. Frere, *Indian Missions* (1870).

[6] See 10 Mar. 76.

[7] The outer stonework was pared down in 1780; the interior had just been restored.

[8] W. C. Lake, Gladstone's host in Durham and later his nephew-in-law; see 4 Mar. 40n.

[9] Probably Henry Thomas Morton of Biddick Hall, Durham.

[10] In fact, a deputation from the Liberal Association; he made a short speech; *D.T.*, 26 September
1876, 3f.

[11] Louisa, Lady Waterford (see 7 July 53), owner of Ford castle.

[12] See 5 June 74? Or some of E. A. Freeman's speeches on the atrocities.

[13] Henry Mills Alden, ed. *Harper's Magazine*, arranging details of publication of the 1872 letter, for
which Gladstone received £20; see 19 Aug. 76 and Add MS 44451, f. 118.

[14] Thomas Melrose, Coldstream liberal; declining to speak there; Add MS 44451, f. 256. But see
30 Sept. 76.

Lindsay recited. Saw Lady M. Alford's remarkable work: & conversation with her in its character. Read Dante—Israel in Britain.[1]

28. Th.

Wrote to Ly M. Alford—Lady E.M. Pringle—Mr R. Ramsay[2]—Mr J. Freeman[3]—Rev. Mr Tucker—Landlord (Coldstream)—Editor of Daily News[4]—Miss J.C. Robertson. Drive to Ld Durham's.[5] Walk back: interesting information from a young Scotch Labourer. Music in evg: some of Lady Waterford's singing was, as I thought, perfect. Conversation on 'Israel in Britain'. Read Dante—Haxthausen on Transcaucasia[6]—Freeman's Lectures.

29. Fr.

Prayers 9.45. Wrote to Mr Dalgleish—Warden of Cav. Coll. Cambridge[7]—Rev. Mr Baring Gould—Mr A. Atkinson[8] (D. & D). Saw Rev. Dr Duff:[9] conversation on Indian Missions. Planted a tree: & cut down part of one: with a considerable and very hearty concourse of labouring men. Music in evg. Read Dante—Swinburne's Bothwell[10]—and [blank.] Music in evg.

30. Sat.

Wrote to Mr Melrose—Ed. Northern Echo[11]—Mr Sparkin. Prayers as usual. Again visited the School. Read Dante—Bothwell—Bulgaria—Fashion & Passion.[12] A reluctant goodbye. We went off at 2.30 by Coldstream. Arrived 2.30. Great warmth all the way. Was obliged to say a few words to the people at Coldstream. Dinner party at Langton.[13] Lady E. Pringle went through the evening wonderfully.

Oct 1. 16 S. Trin.

Dunn[s] Episc. Ch (H.C.) mg. House prayers evg: the Parish minister officiated.[14] Read Frere on Missions—Fashion & Passion—Bulgaria. Conversation with Mrs Hamilton. Wrote to Mrs Th.—Mr E. Vivian[15]—Mr. . . .

[1] Untraced work sent by a correspondent, see 15 Oct. 76.
[2] Robert Ramsay, secretary of anti-atrocitarian meeting at Blaydon, sent its resolutions; Add MS 44451, f. 248.
[3] Not traced. [4] See Shannon, 132.
[5] George Frederick D'Arcy Lambton, 1828–79; 2nd earl of Durham 1840; seat at Lambton Castle, Durham. [6] Baron A. von Haxthausen, *Transcaucasia*, tr. J. E. Taylor (1854).
[7] Thomas James Lawrence, 1849–1919, sent details of the college, which opened in late October; *The Guardian*, 1 November 1876, 1436; Add MS 44451, f. 226.
[8] Possibly Amos Atkinson of Newcastle. [9] Alexander *Duff, missionary; see 16 May 79n.
[10] A. C. Swinburne, *Bothwell; a tragedy* (1874).
[11] William Thomas *Stead, 1849–1912; led campaign on the atrocities as ed. *Northern Echo* (of Darlington) 1871–80; assistant ed. *Pall Mall Gazette* 1880–3, ed. 1883–90; his campaigns led to the navy 'scare' 1884, dispatch of Gordon 1884 and Criminal Law Amndt. Act 1885. This letter is in Stead, *M.P. for Russia*, i. 258.
[12] [Duke de Medina-Pomar], *Fashion and passion; or life in Mayfair*, 3v. (1876).
[13] Lady Elizabeth Pringle's house, 2 miles from Duns.
[14] William D. Herald, minister at Duns from 1873.
[15] Perhaps Edward Vivian, wrote on social questions.

2. M. [Alnwick Castle]

Prayers at 10: Parochial Minister officiated. Wrote to Messrs Pears & Logan—Mr Jas Allan[1]—Mr Murray—Mr Jas Moncreiff[2]—Mr Govan. In the forenoon we went up the hill: and I surveyed the fine pictures gathered here. In the afternoon we went to see the Church: a model for the Presbyterian worship, built by the munificence of Lady E. Pringle. Then I had to plant some trees. We were summoned away at 5 from a sudden change of trains: reached Alnwick[3] at 10.30. Early in the day I had to receive a deputation & address from Dunn. In Berwick I attended the meeting of the Museum society, went over the objects, & had to speak a little.[4] At every point on the road there were keen expressions of the public feeling, which it was impossible to escape. I never saw the like on any former occasion. Langton, Dunn, Berwick, Alnwick, all the same. Read Fashion & Passion—Freeman's Lectures. Conversation with Major Hamilton[5]—Lady E. Pringle—Capt. M. Home.[6]

3. Tu.

Wrote to Earl Granville—Rev. S.E.G.—J. Greig—Mr Rae Brown—Mr Horsburgh—Mrs Blake—Sir H.H. Campbell—Sidney Smith. The day being hopeless we saw but little indoors except the library. In the afternoon we drove to Howick.[7] Saw Mr Lehmann's drawings.[8] Read Dante. Began Life of Thos Ld Lyttelton.[9]

4. Wed.

Wrote to Mr Rowe—Mr Whigham[10]—Mr [W. P.] Adam—Hartlepool Committee[11]—Mrs Hamilton. We went over the interior & the pictures. In the afternoon we drove to Birsley Tower & Hulne Abbey: walked back by the beautiful Alnwick Tower. The vale is beautiful and the place is on the whole the stateliest in all points that I have seen. The Duke reads prayers in the Chapel mg & evg. Read most of the Life of Thomas Lord L. I think that on the whole he deserved his title: and the biographer's tone is bad. Conversation with Mr Lehmann—Mr Martin—Host & Hostess.

5. Th. [Jervaux Abbey]

Wrote to Mr Knowles—Mr Ouvry—Mr Downie—Mr Aldis—Col. Hood.[12] 10–5½. To Jervaux Abbey:[13] I went over the ruins twice, by day and by moonlight. The

---

[1] Possibly James Allan of Mid Calder; later a correspondent; Hawn P.
[2] James William Moncrieff, 1845–1920; W.S. in Edinburgh.
[3] Duke of Northumberland's seat.   [4] *T.T.*, 4 October 1876, 6d.
[5] Probably a relative of George Hans Hamilton, vicar of Eglingham, Alnwick.
[6] David Milne-Home of Wedderburn (1838–1901; soldier and tory M.P. Berwickshire 1874–85) was chairing the Museum annual meeting when Gladstone entered.
[7] Earl Grey's house.   [8] Probably Rudolph Lehmann, artist.
[9] T. Frost, *The life of Thomas, Lord Lyttelton* (1876).
[10] Perhaps James Whigham, county court judge.   [11] Not found published.
[12] Perhaps Arthur Wellington Alexander Nelson Hood, 1839–1924; soldier and tory M.P. W. Somerset 1868–80.
[13] Lord Ailesbury's seat near Leyburn.

buildings must have been very fine. The same feelings were again manifested as we went along our route though it was without notice. Read Bright's Speech[1]— Dante Inferno—S. Smith's Falkland.[2]

6.

Wrote to Ed. of Echo—O. Williams—Rev. Mr Clark—Sig. Caivano[3]—Mr Middlemas—Mr Gluckstein[4]—Mr De Lisle—Mr Kennedy. Ld Aylesbury [sic] gave H. & me a charming ride up to the moor. But the day was thick. The Abbey was illuminated at night by tar barrels & the like. Read Dante—Nestorian Appeal.[5] Wrote a long letter on the Eastern question for consideration. Much conversation with Ld A. who is much over par in political questions.

7. Sat. [Castle Howard]

I revised and considered my letter to Mr Giles:[6] and wrote one to Granville on the general subject.[7] Read Dante—Falkland. 11½ 4½. To Castle Howard:[8] we went to the Minster during the interval at York. Before starting we again heard the extraordinary singing of Gen. Macdonald's daughter aged 11. At Castle Howard we were enthusiastically drawn in by a large number of most hearty people. Our reception at this noble place was most kind. We found a party of friends: and assisted at an evening practice in the Chapel, which is of extraordinary beauty.

8. 17 S Trin.

Church at Welburn mg: aftn service in the Chapel. Excellent, & a large flock. Conversation with F. C[avendish][9] on letter to Mr Giles: & dispatched it, with a covering letter. Wrote to Ed. Daily Telegraph:[10] and privately to Mr Lawson. Also to [blank.] Read Drummond on Revealed Religion[11]—and [blank.]

9. M.

Wrote to Miss Doyle—Dr Baxter Langley. Saw the Pictures, & went over most of this noble House. Read Dante—Freeman's Lectures—Vitruvius Britannicus[12]

[1] At Manchester, cautious about British involvement in the Balkans; *T.T.*, 3 October 1876, 5a.

[2] Not by Sydney *Smith; perhaps by Sidney Smith, political agent, see 13 July 61, 3 Oct. 76; but see 30 Mar. 77.

[3] F. Caivano, Neapolitan advocate; Hawn P.

[4] Leopold Glückstein had sent his pamphlet, *The Eastern Question and the Jews* (1876); Gladstone wrote: 'I have always had occasion to admire the conduct of English Jews in the discharge of their civil duties, but I deeply deplore the manner in which what I may call Judaic sympathies, beyond as well as within the circle of professed Judaism, are now acting on the question of the East'; *The Guardian*, 18 October 1876, 1356.

[5] Not found.

[6] J. A. Giles (see 24 Sept. 76); draft in Add MS 44452, f. 37; read out to working men's meeting in St James's Hall on 8 October; see *D.N.*, 10 October 1876, 3a and Tauchnitz, 1631.

[7] Ramm II, i. 13 and Morley, ii. 556.   [8] Seat of Lord and Lady Lanerton.

[9] See his account of diarist's attitude in Holland, i. 181.

[10] Denying its statement that he 'would have no more to do with public meetings'; *D.T.*, 10 October 1876, 5d.

[11] See 13 Mar. 45.   [12] By C. Campbell, 3v. (1717–25).

—Forster's Speech. He should not have thrown me over *nominatim*.[1] Conversation with Mr John Grey—Mrs Meynell Ingram[2]—Ld Halifax. Drive about this noble place: and walk home with Ld L[anerton].

10. Tu.

Wrote to Mr Mottershead[3]—Editor of Echo—Mr Hayward—MM. Zanckoff & Balabanoff[4]—and.... Read Dante—Freeman on the Saracens—Schuyler's Turkistan.[5] Conversation with Mrs M. I[ngram]—Ld F.C. Drove to Slingsby, and saw the Church and Ruin, as well as more of the Park. Also went through other portions of the palatial House: there is too much to see at once.

11. Wed. [Hawarden]

Wrote to Mr Vickers. Bid goodbye with much regret. $9\frac{3}{4}$-$6\frac{1}{4}$. To Hawarden, more than an hour in York: & a good sight of the Cathedral. Read Freeman (finished)—Schuyler—and worked through a heap of papers.

12. Th.

Ch. $8\frac{1}{2}$ AM. Wrote to Sir Thomas G.—Herbert J.G.—Author of Turkey & India[6]—Rev Mr M'Coll—J. Turner—Mr Newman Hall[7]—W.B. Gurdon—E.R. Russell—W. Saunders—J. Murray. Read Milman, Latin Ch.—Schuyler's Turkistan—"S" on Turkey and India. Examined accounts of Tribute Loan purchases (45 m. stock).[8] Mr Knowles came: long conversation with him[9]—conversation with S.E.G.

13. Fr.

Ch. $8\frac{1}{2}$ AM. Wrote to Robn G.—Harry Wilson—Miss Doyle B.P.—Scotts—Lady Lanerton B.P.—Mr Ouvry—Madame Novikoff[10]—Mr Hancock—Sir Ch. Elton[11]—Lady M. Alford—Sig. Ruiz—Mrs Chambers. Much conversation with

[1] 'Mr. Gladstone's proposal that the Turkish officials, bag and baggage, should go out of Bulgaria and Bosnia (loud applause) would be without doubt a great and glorious result.... But to merely hurry out the officials without putting in ... a foreign army would leave them in a very awkward position'; Forster at Bradford, *D.N.*, 9 October 1876, 2d. Forster's solution—a constitution on the Cretan model—caused a radical furore; Reid, *F*, ii. 146.

[2] Halifax's da., Emily Charlotte, widow of H. F. Meynell Ingram, M.P.

[3] Thomas Mottershead, 1826–84; trade-unionist and anti-atrocitarian working with J. J. Merriman; contested Preston 1874.

[4] Dragan Kiryak Zankof and Marco D. Balabanow, Bulgarian politicians sent to publicize their cause; see *D.N.*, 10 October 1876, 3a.

[5] E. Schuyler, *Notes of a journey in Russian Turkistan, Khokand, Bukhara and Kuldja*, 2v. (1876); for diarist's review, see 19 Oct. 76.

[6] Published and evidently sent anon. by 'S'.

[7] In C. Newman Hall, *An autobiography* (1901), 272.

[8] Gladstone bought £45,000 of Egyptian Tribute Loan of 1871 at 38; Annual statement of accounts; Hawn P.

[9] Knowles arranged the *Contemporary* article, see 19 Oct. 76.

[10] Renewal of contact with her (see 14 Feb. 73) and start of her supposed 'influence'; see Seton Watson, 102, 115ff.; this letter in Stead, *M.P. for Russia*, i. 260.

[11] *Sic*; Sir Charles d. 1853; perhaps his s., Arthur Hallam Elton, 1818–83, is intended.

Mr Knowles. Read Schuyler's Turkistan—Turkish Dog &c.[1]—Glückstein on Jews & the East.[2] We cut down a tree for the edification of Mr K[nowles].

14. Sat.

Ch. 8½ A.M. Wrote to Mr O'Shaughnessy[3]—Mr Hutcheson—Mr Appleby—D.B. Chapman—Baron Tauchnitz[4]—Dean of Chester—Col. Chester[5]—Mrs R. Smith B.P.—Mrs Rocke B.P.—Mr Fisher—Mr Mozley—Mr Freis—Mr Waters[6]—Mr Jordan—[C.]E. Searle. Saw Mr Knowles. He went. Saw Mrs Hampton. Read Schuyler: (finished Vol. 1.) Worked through some part of my accumulations.

0. 15. S. Trin. 18.

Ch 11 AM (H.C.) and 6½ P.M. Read the Lessons. Wrote to Earl Dufferin—MM Zankow et Balabanow—T. Moore—Mr Chesson[7]—Mr Maclellan—A.F. Merriman—Mrs Swift—H.N.G. Read Horsley's Sermon[8]—Maclellan on Israel in England—Ch. Quart. on Abp Lycurgus &c. Walk with C.

16. M.

Ch. 8½ AM. Wrote to Ld Stratford de Redcliffe—Ld Acton—Mr G. Harris—Mr Skynner—Ld Acton [sic]—Mr Newmarch—Mr Saunders—Mr Davis—Mr Berger. Saw Mr Thompson (D & Ms)—W.H.G. on Estate affairs. Read Schuyler in all my available time.

17. Tu.

Ch. 8½ AM. Wrote to Ld F. Cavendish—Made Novikoff[9]—Rev. Mr Lawrence—Rev. Mr Tucker—Rev. A.T. Waugh[10]—Mr Hulme[11]—Mrs Noble—Dr Liddon—Mr Falton—Mr Farley.[12] Began cutting a large ash. Read steadily Mr Schuyler. Also on Scanderbeg.[13]

18. Wed. St Luke.

Ch. 8.45 AM. Agnes's birthday: *benedicat benedictus*. Wrote to Ed. Northern Echo—Ld Granville—Rev. R. Ellis[14]—Mr Tennyson[15]—R.S. Knight[16]—Ed. Daily

[1] Untraced pamphlet on the atrocities.   [2] See 6 Oct. 76n.
[3] Richard O'Shaughnessy, 1842-?; liberal M.P. Limerick 1874-83.
[4] Arranging publication; see 5 Sept. 76n.
[5] Joseph Lemuel Chester, 1821-82; known as 'colonel'; transcribed university and ecclesiastical registers; had sent diarist those of Westminster Abbey; Hawn P.
[6] Ernest E. Waters, author of *Servia's History* (1876).
[7] Frederick William Chesson, 1833?-88; sec. of Aborigines Protection Society from 1863; active in the atrocities campaign.
[8] See 4 Dec. 31.   [9] Stead, *M.P. for Russia*, i. 262.
[10] Arthur Thornhill Waugh, 1842-1922; vicar of St Mary's Brighton, 1873-95.
[11] Perhaps Alexander Hume of the Christian Emancipation League, wrote to Gladstone in September; Hawn P.
[12] James Lewis *Farley, 1823-85; formerly banker in Turkey; a leader of the atrocities campaign; published *Turks and Christians* (1876).
[13] Perhaps earlier version of G. T. Petrovich, *Scanderbeg* (1881); see 15 June 77n.
[14] Perhaps Robert Ellis, curate of Birdsall, Yorkshire.   [15] Inviting him; see 31 Oct. 76.
[16] Perhaps Robert Skakel Knight, wrote *Exercises in English composition* (1876).

News[1]—Mr V. Oger—Mr [J. T.] Leader—Mr L.C. Alexander—C.H. Hamilton[2]—Mr Mottishead—Mrs Th. Read Schuyler, Turkistan—Waters Hist. of Servia. Harry & I brought the ash down. Conversation with S.E.G.

19. Th.

Ch. 8½ A.M. Wrote to Mr Leader—Mr Griffiths—G. Harris—Mr Humphrey—Mr Sinayberger[3]—Elihu Burritt[4]—L.C. Alexander BP—C. Taylor BP—Rev. C. Babington—Rev. R.J. Blake[5]—Rev. T. Ashcroft[6]—Watsons—Mad. Novikoff. Began Art. on Schuyler for C.R.[7] Read Q.R. on the East—Schuyler's Turkistan (finished). Saw Mr Ward—Rev. Mr Bateman.[8] Walk with S.E.G.

20. Fr.

Ch. 8½ A.M. Wrote to Made Novikoff[9]—Mr F. Hill—Mr De Morgan—Jas Knowles—Mr Trotter—Mr Crawford—Mr Leader—Mrs Th.—London Library—Ld Halifax—Rev. J. Adams[10]—Messrs Murray—Dr A. Benisch—C.H. Hamilton—H.P. Owen—Thos Ffoulkes. Wrote on Russia in Turkistan and sent off the first batch. We saw in evg a Deputation from Hawarden respecting the proposed Church Yard Gates. Kibbled the fallen ash. Read Evans on Bosnia.[11]

21. Sat.

Ch. 8½ AM. Wrote to Herbert J.G.—Dr D. Bendan—Ld Acton—Mr N. Burnand—Mr T. Moore[12]—Rev. H. Lansdell—Canon Liddon B.P. Saw Mr Selby—Mr Douglas—Parish Deputn. Worked much on Russia in Turkistan. Read Evans's Bosnia. We began felling an Alder.

22. S. Trin 19.

H.C. 8 AM when we were all gathered with dear Harry. Then 11 AM. 6½ P.M. Wrote to Mad. Novikoff—Baron Tauchnitz—Mr Knowles—Ld Granville—Mr F. Hill—Mr G. Curtis (B.P.)—Mr Gurdon. Worked hard to finish my paper & sent it off. Criminal justice on Sunday! But it is for peace. Read Bp Wordsworth's Serm[13]—Davenport do[14]—Maclaren do.[15]

[1] See 25 Oct. 76.
[2] Secretary of the cttee. on the atrocities in Liverpool; Hawn P.
[3] M. Sinayberger wrote from Liverpool on the atrocities; Hawn P.
[4] Elihu Burritt, 1810-79; American philanthropist; see Add MS 44452, f. 35.
[5] Apparently a nonconformist.
[6] Nonconformist minister in Accrington; on the atrocities; Hawn P.
[7] Signed article, 'Russian Policy and Deeds in Turkistan', *Contemporary Review*, xxviii. 873 (November 1876); Add MS 44695, f. 187.
[8] Christian Henry Bateman, newly arrived as incumbent of St John's, Mold.
[9] Stead, *M.P. for Russia*, i. 298; on information sent by Gorlov (see 24 Oct. 76n).
[10] James Adams, anglican priest living in Greenwich.
[11] A. J. Evans, *Through Bosnia and the Herzegovina on foot* (1876).
[12] Thomas Moore of Hanley, on the atrocities and Sir C. Adderley, Add MS 44452, ff. 81-7.
[13] See 26 Nov. 76.
[14] J. S. Davenport, 'The dispensation of the Parousia' (1876).
[15] A. MacLaren, 'Time for thee to work' (1874).

23.

Ch. 8¼ AM. Wrote to Bulgarian Deputies[1]—Ld Granville—Ld Halifax—Ld Acton—Mad. Novikoff—Sig. Placidi[2]—Messrs Murray—R. Bushnell—Mons. J. D'Istria[3]—L.C. Alexander—Ld Wolverton—Sir P. Braila (B.P.)—Mrs Th—Mrs Adams—A. Evans—W. Evans—Mr Bird—A. M'Leod[4]—J.L. Farley—T. Moore—Mr Dobson. Corrected part of proofs. Arr. books & papers. Read Q.R. on Turkish Empire. We brought the alder to the ground.

24. Tu. [London]

8-2½. to London. Thrown nearly out of my Hansom & my keys lost. Wrote to Phillips—Mr [T.] Bowater Vernon—C.G.—Mr Chappuis—Mr J. Wood—Mr Winter—Mr Merton—Mr Wood—Mr ... of Ladywell. Worked on letters & papers. Saw Mr Knowles (C.R.)—Mr Gurdon—Mr Hayward—Made Novikoff—Made N. *cum* Gen. Gorlof[5]—Police in Scotland Yard—Mr Kinnaird—Mr Webster—Mr [J. T.] Knowles jun.—Sir A. Panizzi—Mr Herbert R.A. Dined at Mrs Th.s: a party. Read Farley, Cross & Crescent[6]—Mason, Silver in India[7]—MacGahan, Campaigning on the Oxus.[8]

25. Wed.

Wrote to C.G.—Mr Halliday Jones—Mr Harris—Mr Boulmere—Mr Puseley—Mr D. Grant—and. . . . Saw Dr Benisch—Mr Leader & conclave—Col. Maciver[9] *cum* Mr Farley—Mr Gurdon—Mr F. Hill[10]—The Wortleys—Dr Elam—Scotts. Saw Moon—Phillips [R]—Mr Murray. Breakfasted with Mrs Burke[11] who also bid me to dinner. Read MacGahan.

26. Th.

Wrote to Mr Knowles (Proofs)—Messrs Murray—W.H.G. Saw Madame Novikoff—Mr Alexander—Mr Knowles—The Bulgarian Deputies—Mr Westell—Mr Jones—Dr Clark—Mr Harrison—Dr Fraser. Read MacGahan—finished. Read the Gorloff MS—and corrected all my proofs adapting them to the revised MS.

[1] See 10 Oct. 76.

[2] Miagio Placidi; president of the 'Comitato di Soccorso per la Causa Slava' in Rome; Hawn P.

[3] President of the cttee. on the atrocities of the European diplomats (apart from Britain) at Philippolis; E. Schuyler, author of the report on the atrocities, was its vice-president; Hawn P.

[4] Alexander Macleod, Church of Scotland minister and supporter of Gladstone; on crofters' deprivations; Hawn P.

[5] Russian military attaché in London; see 26 Oct. 76 and Stead, *M.P. for Russia*, i. 296ff. for his influence. Gladstone proposed to the *Daily News* on 30 October that it should publish Gorlov's MS; Add MS 44452, f. 93.

[6] Probably J. L. Farley, *Turks and Christians* (1876); see 17 Oct. 76.

[7] Untraced comment on silver depreciation (see 10 July 76).

[8] J. A. MacGahan, *Campaigning on the Oxus and the fall of Khiva* (1874).

[9] Henry Ronald H. Douglas Maciver, colonel in the Serbian army, dedicated his 'Experiences of the Servian war' (1876) to diarist; Hawn P.

[10] Meeting with ed. of *Daily News*, proposed by Gladstone, to discuss Eastern affairs; Add MS 44452, f. 49.

[11] Mrs Birks, his neighbour at 71 Harley Street; often made him breakfast or dinner. She had brewing connections, see 26 June 80.

Breakfast—and dinner with kind Mrs Burke. Shopping. Harry came at six. We went at eight to see Peril:[1] very well acted, but a denouement of really bad *morale*.

27. Fr.

Wrote to C.G.—Mr Knowles. Up at 6. Went with Harry to Dover. Saw him off,[2] on board the packet, & from the Pier. God & His angels ever guard him. He is very dear. Drove over to Walmer: reviewed the place: saw Ld Granville—Sir W. James—Mr Hugessen. Returned to London at 5.45. Saw Madame Novikoff—Mr F. Hill. Dined with Mrs Th: & went at 9.30 to the Gaiety: saw a miserable burlesque,[3] of which she had heard a most inviting but false account. Read Records of the Past.[4]

28. Sat. [Hawarden]

Wrote to Lady Russell—Marquis of Hartington.[5] Read Records of Past Life (finished) Return to Hn at night. 4.45-11¼. Saw N. Moon & friend [R]. Saw Madam Novikoff—Mrs Th.—Mr Knowles—Mr S. Morley—do *cum* Mr Knowles—Dr Allon—Mr N. Hall. At a breakfast of 12 or 14 next door we discussed largely the Eastern question on which these men (of influence) were all sound.

S. 21. Trin.

Ch. mg & evg: excellent Sermons. Wrote to Mr Maclaren—Ld Shaftesbury—Dr Newman[6]—Dr Benisch—C.G.—Dr A. Clark—Ld Acton—Miss Downes. Read Christian Apologist (Mr Nevins) No 2[7]—Lignana's striking Lecture[8]—Dr Allon Sermon I[9]—Döllinger's Hippolytus.[10]

30. M.

Ch 8½ A.M. Wrote to Mrs Dalrymple (B.P.)—Madam Novikoff—Rev. Mr Bibby[11]—Rev. Mr Kingsmill—Rev. Mr Fagan[12]—German Ambassador—Mr Mavrocordato—Mr Merriman—Mr Bartlett—Mr Ouvry—Mr Grogan—Mr Adam MP—Mr Knowles. Saw Mr Thompson on the sad Moffatt & Field affair—

---

[1] At the Prince of Wales Theatre.

[2] To India, again.

[3] Farren in 'Little Don Caesar de Bazan'.

[4] Egyptian texts in vol. VI of *Records of the past* (1876); see 28 July 74.

[5] Just back from his tour of Turkey.

[6] Asking him to join the Tennyson house party (see 31 Oct. 76); Newman regretfully declined; *Newman*, xxviii. 131.

[7] *Christian Apologist*, ii (October 1876); 'Jesus is the Christ, or else?'.

[8] Giacomo Lignana, professor in Rome, had sent his 'Letter on Rome and the Slavs' (1876); Hawn P.

[9] H. Allon, *The vision of God and other sermons* (1876).

[10] J. J. I. von Döllinger, *Hippolytus and Callistus*, tr. A. Plummer (1876 ed.).

[11] Probably Isaac Henry Bibby, curate in Guildford.

[12] Probably Henry Stuart Fagan, vicar of St Just 1870.

C.G. on do.[1] Read Döllinger's Hippol.—Denton, Xtns of the East[2]—Ritual of Old Catholics—Evans's Bosnia. Walk with C.

31. Tu.

Ch. 8½ A.M. Wrote to Govr Hennessy (B.P.)—T.J.C. Dun—J. Murray—G. Bentley—Ld Acton—Rev.H. Fountain[3]—Bulkeley Hughes—T.A. Stimpson—T. Moore—D. Ross—General Cesnola—Mr H. Thompson—Messrs Rivington—Mr Macmillan—Messrs Wms & Norgate—A.M. Silber. Saw Mr Vickers *cum* W.H.G.—Mr Evans of Holywell. Long conversation with Ld T. Woodcutting with WHG. Tennyson[4] & H[allam] T. came. Dinner party. Read various Turkish Tracts.

Hawarden Wed. Nov. 1. 76.

Church 8¾ AM. (All S.) Wrote to Baron Tauchnitz & B.P.—Herbert J.G. & B.P.—Rev. Mr Bussell[5]—Mr Mottershead—Messrs Murray—Prof. Lignana B.P. & Letter[6]—Mr Ouvry—Geo Bet—W. Evans—R. Earle. Tennyson read to us his Harold: it took near 2¼ hours.[7] Walk with him & a party. Worked on the tree half cut. Read Fortnightly on Eastern Q.—MacColl in C.R. on do.

2. Th.

Ch. 8½ A.M. Wrote to Ld Stratford de Redcliffe—Ld Granville—Rev. T.E. Gibson[8]—Rev. T. Russell[9]—Rev. W.P. Roberts[10]—Mr Hitchman—Harry N G (BP)—Willsons. Read Gibson on Lydiate Hall—Bagehot on Lord Spencer's Life: very clever, very imperfect.[11] Conversation with Tennyson on Future Retribution, and other matters of Theology: he has not thought, I conceive, systematically or thoroughly upon them, but is much alarmed at the prospect of the loss of belief. He left us at one. Walk & long conversation with Ld Acton: who seems in opinion to go beyond Döllinger, though in action to stop short of him. We met on the question of a Woodard School.

---

[1] Apparently a dispute between Moffat, the Hawarden doctor, and Field, possibly a nurse; Gladstone wrote to his wife, 25 October 1876, Hawn P.: 'Thompson's note is singular—Field tells me that the other side have got hold of some woman who is at Manchester to give evidence on their side—I did not ask what'; Field assisted in treating face-ache.

[2] W. Denton, *The Christians in Turkey* (1863).

[3] Probably Henry Thomas Fountaine, curate at Bulwell, Nottinghamshire.

[4] For this visit, see H. Tennyson, *Alfred Lord Tennyson* (1897), ii. 214 and R. B. Martin, *Tennyson* (1980), 516.

[5] Perhaps Frederic George Bussell, curate in Birmingham.   [6] See 29 Oct. 76.

[7] *Harold* was published in December 1876. According to R. B. Martin, *Tennyson* (1980), 516, 'Gladstone struggled to keep awake, his son Willy had a fit of suppressed giggles, and his daughters worried that their father would fall fast asleep. . . . The fact that he read aloud for so long was probably an indication of nervousness, for Tennyson seldom did so during the day.' Gladstone was awake enough to quote from *Harold* in his article, 'The Hellenic factor'; *Gleanings*, iv. 262.

[8] Thomas Ellison Gibson had sent his *Lydiate Hall* (1876).

[9] Thomas Russell, presbyterian minister in Croydon; Hawn P.

[10] Probably William Page Roberts, 1836-1928; vicar of Eye 1864-78; curate of St Peter's, Marylebone, 1878-1907.

[11] In *Fortnightly Review*, xxvi. 573 (November 1876).

3. Fr.

Ch. $8\frac{1}{2}$ A.M. Wrote to Madame Novikoff—J. Knowles—F. Ouvry—E. Bailey—J. Lord—M. Rolin Jacquemins l. & BP[1]—Dr A. Martelaos[2]—Mr de Lisle (B.P.)— Miss Hawtrey—Rev. G. Coates[3]—W.D. Stead[4]—Mr Murray BP.—Mr G. Best BP. Much conversation with Ld Acton who went at $12\frac{1}{2}$. Read Rolin Jacquemins— Evans's Bosnia.

4. Sat.

Ch. $8\frac{1}{2}$ AM. Wrote to Ld Shaftesbury—C.M. Gaskell—J.W. Bosanquet—S.C. Salmon—Sig. G.D. Canala[5]—Rev. F.E. Warren[6]—Sig. Aurienna B.P.[7]—M. Escaud Volta B.P.[8]—J. Momby—J. Lewis—C. Pascoe[9]—Sir J. Adye BP—M. Reinach BP[10]—Mr Mackenzie. Finished felling an ash with W.H.G. Saw Mr Bateman. Read Evans's Bosnia—Mons. R. Jacquemins (finished).

5. 22 S. Trin.

Ch 11 A.M. with H.C. and $6\frac{1}{2}$ P.M. Wrote a long letter in French to Bishop Strossmayer.[11] Read Bp Conybeare[12]—Divers Tracts of the Scott series[13]—Glass on Advance Thought.[14]

6. M.

Ch. $8\frac{1}{2}$ AM. Corrected & sent l. to Bp S.—also B.P.—Wrote also Made Novikoff—Herbert J.G.—Mr Derry—Mr Mundella—Mr Lefevre. Read Evans's Bosnia—Th. Martin's P. Consort[15]—Diplomatic Review Octr—Morier's[16] & other Tracts on the Eastern question. Arranging letters & papers. Kibbled the cut ash with W. Urged W. to handle the Eastern question.

7. Tu.

Ch. $8\frac{1}{2}$ AM. Wrote to Barker & Hignett—Mr Knowles (2)—R. Simon—W. Smith—P. Hewitt—Baron Tauchnitz—Ld Kenmare (B.P.)—Mrs P. Ralli—

---

[1] Gustave Rolin-Jaequemyns, Belgian author of 'Le droit international et la question d'Orient' (1876). Add MS 44452, f. 95.

[2] Of Athens, on the atrocities; Hawn P.

[3] George Alexander Augustus Coates, rector of Earl's Combe.

[4] Sc. W. T. Stead.   [5] On poetry translations; Hawn P.

[6] Frederick Edward Warren, fellow of St John's, Oxford; published on Old Catholics.

[7] Francesco Auriemma, Italian advocate; see Add MS 44448, f. 33.   [8] Unidentified.

[9] Charles E. Pascoe, London agent of D. Appleton, publishers in New York, asking apparently unsuccessfully, for American rights on any further pamphlets; Hawn P.

[10] Perhaps Salomon Reinach, French archaeologist and anthropologist.

[11] Jošif Juraj Strossmayer, 1815-1905; Croat patriot and bp. of Bosnia, Slavonia and Sirmium; his correspondence with Gladstone (Strossmayer writing in German, Gladstone in French) intr. and printed in R. W. Seton Watson, *The Southern Slav Question* (1911), app. xvii.

[12] See 27 Aug. 76.

[13] i.e. tracts by Thomas *Scott, the freethinker.

[14] C. E. Glass, *Advance thought* (1876).

[15] Volume ii of Martin's *Prince Consort*, reviewed anon. in *Church Quarterly Review* (January 1877); in *Gleanings*, i. 63; see 21 Dec. 74.

[16] D. R. Morier, *Turkey and the Christian powers* (1876).

Scotts—Mrs A. Parker. Long *sederunt* on accounts and Estate arrangements with Mr Vickers & W.H.G. Correcting Tracts for the Tauchnitz Edition.[1] Part cut a large ash with W. Read Lorimer on the Eastern question[2]—Compte Rendu (Athens)[3]—Evans's Bosnia—Finlay's Greece.[4]

8. Wed.

Ch. 8¼ AM. Wrote to Mr W. Mackenzie—Col. Maciver (Tel.)—Earl Granville—Made Novikoff—Rev J. Dawson—A. Merriman—Mr Whittle—Mr Godley—Mr Knowles—Mr Salkeld BP.—Mr Gilmour—A. Smith—G. Duffey.[5] Worked on the Ash. Read Evans's Bosnia—Hobhouse's Albania &c.[6]—Borders of Xdom & Islam[7]—Life of Prince Consort. Read aloud the Debate of the First Iliad, from Pope.[8]

9. Th.

Ch. 8½ AM. Wrote to Ed. Northern Echo—Baron Tauchnitz—Scotts—Sir S. Northcote—Mr Godley—Mr Jas Taylor *BP.*—Herr Landi[9]—Rev. T. Ashcroft—Mr Catherall. Prepared additions for the Tauchnitz Volume. W. & I brought down the ash: a very fine fall. Read Ashcroft's Lecture[10]—Byron: life, and Poems[11]—Hobhouse's Albania—Evans's Bosnia. Also read aloud my version of the Assembly of Il. I.

10. Fr.

Ch. 8¼ A.M. Wrote to Made Novikoff—Mr Delevigne[12]—J.R. Godley[13]—Archdn Jones—Rev. R. Kerr (U.S.)[14]—Mr Shaw—T. Price—Mr Hamilton. Arranging Tracts &c. Part kibbled the tree. Read Hobhouse's Albania—Finlay Hist. Greece—Various authorities on the History: Pichler, Kirchliche Trennung[15]—Evans's Bosnia. Read aloud Ld Derby's and Cowper's Versions of the Assembly of Il. I.

---

[1] See 5 Sept. 76n.
[2] J. Lorimer, *On the denationalisation of Constantinople and its devotion to international purposes* (1876).
[3] 'Compte Rendu de l'Assemblée' (Athens, 1876); see *Gleanings*, iv. 259.
[4] See 21 May 72; much quoted in 'The Hellenic factor', see 13 Nov. 76.
[5] See, probably, 29 Dec. 71n.
[6] See 14 June 48.
[7] J. Creagh, *Over the borders of Christendom and Eslamiah*, 2v. (1876).
[8] *Pope's translation, first published in 1750.
[9] Possibly Salvatore Landi, Italian art historian; but no German link traced.
[10] T. Ashcroft, 'The Turko-Servian War. A lecture' (1876).
[11] Quoted in *Gleanings*, iv. 303.
[12] Harry Brunning Constant Delevingne, d. 1888; taught at Shrewsbury 1875-8, at Woodbridge 1878-80.
[13] Gladstone got Godley to consult unavailable books; Kilbracken, 109.
[14] Perhaps Robert Pollok Kerr, 1850-1923; American presbyterian minister and author.
[15] See 20 Sept. 74.

11. Sat.

Ch. 8½ A.M. Wrote to Mr Potter M.P. l. & B.P.—Dr Lang B.P.[1]—Mr Skelton[2]—M. Kokkinos[3]—Mr Sweeny—Dr Caldburies—Dr Collie[4]—Messrs B. & H.—Scotts—Rev. Mr Rodwell—S.E.G. Saw Mr MacColl—Major Robertson—Sir Thos Frost. Small dinner party. Kibbling the ash. Read Hobhouse's Albania—Finlay's Greece—England & the Dardanelles[5]—Waddington's Greek Church[6] and Ld Derby's Dispatch.[7]

12. 23 S. Trin.

Ch 11 AM and 6½ P.M. Mr M'Coll preached for the Eastern Christians with ability & effect. Wrote to Ld Stratford de Redcliffe—Countess Russell—A. Atkinson—Mr Salusbury—Mr Pennington[8]—Professor Thea[9]—Mr Holmes MP—J. Knowles—Miss Allen. Read Finlay's Greek Revolution—Boukharov, Russie et Turquie[10]—The Supremacy of Man[11]—Thring on a Weekly Ch Newspaper.[12]

13. M.

Ch. 8½ A.M. Wrote to Mr R.H. Hutton—Robertson & Nicholson—Mrs Wynne—Dr Wardell[13]—Archdeacon Jones—Dr Reynolds. Walk with Mr MacColl. Began to write my article on Hellenes.[14] Read Gordon's Greek Revolution[15]—Finlay's ditto. Walk with Mr MacColl. Fourteen to dinner.

14. Tu.

Ch. 8½ AM. Wrote to Made Novikoff[16]—Sir W. Farquhar—Mr Collinson—Mr Salusbury—Rev Mr Torre B.P.—Mr Godley—Mr Lefevre—Mr Fergusson. Saw

---

[1] Perhaps James Thomason Lang, d. 1923; fellow of Corpus, Cambridge, 1867-97.

[2] John Skelton, alias 'Shirley', sent a work on Mary, Queen of Scots; Add MS 44452, f. 111.

[3] Emmanuel Ch. Kokkinos of Athens, a contributor to the 'Compte Rendu'; see *Gleanings*, iv. 261 and 7 Nov. 76.

[4] Alexander Collie, physician at Homerton, near Mrs Gladstone's 'Home'.

[5] *The Dardanelles for England. The true solution of the Eastern question* (1876).

[6] G. Waddington, *The condition and prospects of the Greek or Oriental Church* (1854).

[7] Instructions to Elliot, published on 21 September; Shannon, 130.

[8] See 17 Nov. 76.

[9] Timotheus Thea of Patras; see Add MS 44449, f. 88.

[10] D. N. Bukharov, *La Russie et la Turquie depuis le commencement de leurs relations politiques jusqu'à nos jours* (1877).

[11] *The supremacy of man. A suggestive inquiry* (1876).

[12] Untraced.

[13] J. R. Wardell, M.D., on compulsory vaccination; *T.T.*, 16 November 1876, 10c.

[14] 'The Hellenic Factor in the Eastern Question', *Contemporary Review*, xxix. 1 (December 1876), reprinted in *Gleanings*, iv. 259 and, together with the 'Letters to Aberdeen' and sundry reviews, in the Tauchnitz series, 1646.

[15] T. Gordon, *History of the Greek revolution*, 2v. (1832).

[16] In Stead, *M.P. for Russia*, i. 268.

Mr MacColl—W.H.G. (for Vickers). Read Finlay—Gordon—Maciver's Pamphlet—The Olympian part of Il. I. in Pope's version aloud, then my own.

15. Wed.

Ch. 8½ Wrote to Made Novikoff—Arthur G.—J. Cleeve—J. Derry—J. Lewis—Rev. J.G. Henderson (& *B.P.*)—Rev. R. Yonge—Supt L.N.W.RR.—Miss Higinbotham—J. Catherall[1]—F. Cotgreave—Rev. J. Davis.[2] Wrote on the Hellenic matter. W. & I felled the alder. Read Russell on Shakespeare[3]—do on Home Life—Finlay's Hist. Long conversation with Lieut. Salusbury[4] on Servia & the War.

16. Th.

Ch. 8½ A.M. Wrote to D. of Westminster—Mrs Th.—Scotts—Mr Marcy—Mr Vickers—Mr Bennett—L. Levi—D. of Argyll—Ld Stratford de R.—Mr Tennyson—Mr Stillman—Dr Reynolds—Ed. Lpool Merc. Hawarden matters with W. Also kibbling. Worked on Hellenic paper. Read Tricoupi Hist Gk Rev.[5]—Joyneville, Alexander I.[6]

17. Fr. [Courthey, Liverpool]

Ch. 8½ AM. Wrote to Dr Forbes Winslow—Mr. Bunbury[7]—Mr Mitchell—Mr Ford—Mr Browning—Mr Ouvry—Rev. T. Wodehouse[8]—Ld Granville—Mr Lovinbeck. Walk with C. Finished draft MS on Greek element. Walk with C. We went off before 5 to Liverpool where we attended the Theatre to see Pennington in Hamlet.[9] It was really excellent.—I never was so well received in that town. We slept at Courthey: an important part of our object to see our nephews since their bereavement.[10]

18. Sat. [Hawarden]

Wrote to Mr Ouvry—Duke of Westminster—Raees Uddin Ahmed[11]—Mr W.H. Pennington—Mr E. Pennington[12]—Mr Geo. Potter. Left at 9¼: business in Liverpool: home at 1¼. Kibbling with W. Read Hamlet (the Ghost &c.) aloud in evg. Gordon, Greek Revolution—Grant Duff's Lecture on Eastern question (qy on Grant Duff?)[13]

---

[1] Of the Hawarden family.
[2] Perhaps John Davis, celtic scholar and vicar of Llandeloy.
[3] See 4 Jan. 76.
[4] Philip H. B. Salusbury served with the Christian forces in the Balkans; see 7 June 77n.
[5] S. Tricoupis, *Hellenikè Epanastasis*, 4v. (1853-7); discussed in *Gleanings*, iv. 278ff.
[6] C. Joyneville [C. L. Johnstone], *Life and times of Alexander I*, 3v. (1875); see *Gleanings*, iv. 274.
[7] Perhaps Henry Mill Bunbury, gentleman, of Marlston House, Newbury.
[8] Thomas Wodehouse, curate of Christ Church, St Giles, London.
[9] A benefit performance; Gladstone was cheered on entering the theatre; see Ramm, II, i. 22.
[10] i.e. death of his brother, Robertson; see 23 Sept. 75.
[11] On the Indian Civil Service and the syllabus for its examination; *T.T.*, 22 November 1876, 5f.
[12] Presumably a relative of the actor; see 23 Sept. 70, 17 Nov. 76.
[13] Sir M. E. Grant Duff, 'The Eastern question. A lecture' (1876).

19. *24 S. Trin.*

Ch. 11 AM with H.C. and [blank.] Wrote to Ld Granville—Lady Russell—Hon. A. Herbert—W. Lethaby—Mr Homersham Cox—J.H. Bell[1]—J. Knowles—J.M. Stark. Long conversation with Herbert on his prospects & studies at O[xford]. Conybeare on Revealed Religion[2]—Dr Aveling's Address[3]—Hird on Scripture names[4] and Döllinger's Hippolytus.[5]

20. *M.*

Ch 8½ AM. Wrote to Rev. Dr Angus—Mr Halcomb[e]—Mr Cooper. Worked on my MS for C.R. and sent off the greater part.[6] Read Life of Prince Consort. 1-6. Went off to the Wrexham Exhibition: a remarkable indication of the wealth of this country in precious things, appearing as it does in a provincial corner. Archdeacon [E. R.] Johnson, Designate for Calcutta, dined. Long conversation with him. He seems very good & sound.

21. *Tu.*

Ch. 8¼ AM. Wrote to Lord Granville—W.H. James MP[7]—Rev. Mr Jenkins—Dr Seaton[8]—Dr Pole[9]—G. Harris—A. Imrie—D. Ker. Finished revision of my MS 'The Hellenic Factor in the Eastern Problem' & sent it to press. Kibbling with W. Read Tricoupi's Helleniké Epanastasis—La Russie et la Turquie[10]—Winslow on Spiritualism[11]—& Bravo case[12]—[Pope's] Rape of the Lock, I & II, aloud—Life of Prince Consort.

22. *Wed.*

Ch. 8½ AM. Wrote to Madame Novikoff[13]—Mr A. Herbert (2)—Deputés Bulgares—Dr Greenhill—Rev. Mr Legeyt[14]—H.J. Johnson[15]—Ed. Northern Echo—W.H.G.—Mr Wybrov—Mr Murray—Mr Rigby. Walk with C., & wood-

---

[1] Of the *Northern Echo*, on arrangements for meeting; Hawn P.
[2] See 27 Aug. 76.
[3] T. W. B. Aveling, 'Why we keep the Sabbath' (1876).
[4] W. G. Hird, *Scripture names and their relation to ancient history* (1875).
[5] See 29 Oct. 76.
[6] See 13 Nov. 76n.
[7] Walter Henry James, 1846-1923; liberal M.P. Gateshead 1874-93; 2nd Lord Northbourne 1893.
[8] Edward Cator *Seaton, 1815-80; medical officer to L.G.B. 1876.
[9] Perhaps William *Pole, 1814-1900, engineer and musician.
[10] See 12 Nov. 76.
[11] L. S. F. Winslow, 'Spiritualistic madness' (1876).
[12] *The Balham mystery, or the Bravo poisoning case* (1876); the inquest declared Bravo murdered, but no murderer was found.
[13] In Stead, *M.P. for Russia*, i. 270.
[14] Charles James Legeyt, vicar of Stoke Newington.
[15] A nonconformist.

cutting. Read Evans's Bosnia—Pamphlet by Bulg. Deputies[1]—Life of Pr. Consort—Rape of the Lock, III–V aloud.

23. Th.

Ch. 8½ AM. Wrote to Mr E.A. Mavrocordato—Lady Russell—Rev. Mr Shutes[2]—Mr J. Knowles—H.D. Seymour—President Labour Repr. League[3]—Ld Provost of Glasgow[4]—Mr Lethaby (Frome)[5]—F. Joseph—J. Sangster—F. Ouvry—G. Griffiths. Read Evans's Bosnia (finished)—Attention aux Balkans[6]—Between Danube & Black Sea[7]—Life of the Prince Consort. Cut part of an Alder.

24. Fr.

Ch. 8½ A.M. Wrote to Ld Wolverton—Mr Knowles—Dr Farrer—Ld Stratford de R.—Rev. A. Brodrick—Messrs M'Corquodale BP.[8]—Messrs Hughes & Edwards—Mr Knowles Tel.—Mr W. Smith. Felled the Alder. Walk with C. Corrected proofs of 'The Hellenic Factor'. Read 'Why did Gladstone fall from Power?'[9]—Life of Prince Consort—Tennyson, Morte d'Arthur, and other pieces, aloud.—Lettres Nerbiennes.[10]

25. Sat.

Ch. 8½ AM. Wrote to Miss A. Besant—Lady Lisgar—Mr W. Pollard[11]—Mr E.R. Russell—Mr W. Agnew—Mr [R.] Bosworth Smith. Walk with C. Read divers Turkish Tracts—Richard on Crimean War[12]—Between Danube & Black Sea—Life of Prince Consort—and Milton, aloud.

26.

Preadvent S. Ch. 11 AM and 6½ PM. Wrote to Mr Mundella—Ld Granville—Sir A. Panizzi—Bp of Manchester. Read Bp Lincoln's Sermon[13]—Bp of Manchester's Charge[14]—Lay Preaching for Ch. of E.[15]—Tunbridge Correspondence[16]—and various Tracts.

---

[1] See 10 Oct. 76n.

[2] Perhaps Albert Shadwell Shutte, d. 1901; vicar of Mortlake 1865-95.

[3] Thanking him for its Resolution; *T.T.*, 27 November 1876, 6c.

[4] John Bain, lord provost 1874-7, unsuccessfully invited Gladstone to unveil a statue to Burns; see Add MS 44452, f. 208.

[5] On the Frome by-election, a gain for the liberals next day.

[6] *Attention aux Balkans!* (1876), quoted, on the Bulgarian schism, in 'The Hellenic factor'.

[7] H. C. Barkley, *Between the Danube and the Black Sea, or five years in Bulgaria* (1876).

[8] Printers of the *Contemporary Review*, whose affairs were in turmoil; see P. Metcalf, *James Knowles* (1980), 270.

[9] Pamphlet sent by the author, Annie *Besant, 1847-1933, radical and theosophist; her pamphlet pleased Gladstone on the Eastern question, but he complained at her comments on Hartington and Granville; see Ramm II, i. 23 and Add MS 44452, ff. 157, 179.   [10] *Sic*; untraced.

[11] William Pollard, 1828-93; secretary of Manchester Peace Society 1872-91.

[12] H. Richard, *History of the origin of the war with Russia* (1876).

[13] C. Wordsworth, 'The Mohammedan woe and its passing away. A sermon' (1876).

[14] By J. Fraser (1876).   [15] *Lay preachers in the Church of England* (1877).

[16] See 28 Feb. 76.

27. M.

Ch. 8½ A.M. Wrote to Ld Stratford de R.—W.B. Hughes—Mr Kinnear—J. Knowles—A.R. Davies[1]—Dr F.W. Lowndes—J. Marrant jun. Read Tricoupi, Epanastasis—Life of Prince Consort—Skelton on Bolingbroke.[2] Cut an ash. Tea with M. Rigby.

28. Tu.

Ch. 8½ A.M. Wrote to Messrs M'Corquodale—W.H.G.—Scotts—Ld Acton—Mr Vickers—Mr Knowles—R. Hay jun.—Geo. Harris—Ld Wolverton (Tel.)—Jas Atkinson[3]—A.O.M. Jay[4]—L. March—J. Harrison—A. de Lisle—Miss Peake (and draft for her to Sec. M. Distr. Co.) Made corrections for revises of my Article in C.R. Walk & drive with C. Tea with Peake & settled her a/c. Read Life of Pr. Consort (finished)—Skelton's St John (finished)

29. Wed.

Ch. 8½ A.M. Wrote to D. of Argyll B.P.—Mr Papautonopulos B.P.[5]—H.N. Gladstone B.P.—Rev. Mr Johnson—Th. Martin—Mr Goschen—Mrs Abraham—Dr Bendan—Mr Talley—Messrs King—Rev F.C. Finch—Ld Crewe. Wrote a Mem. on the Peelites in 1852.[6] Began to cut an Alder. Read Skelton's Qu. Mary[7] and [blank.]

30. Th. St Andrew

Ch. 8¾ AM. Wrote to Mr de Lisle—Mr Planché—Mr Bryce—Rev. Mr Coling[8]—Ld Wolverton—Marchioness of Salisbury—Rev. F. Hammond[9]—Rev. Mr Wardale[10]—Mr Richmond B.P.—Mr Mundella. Read Month on Eastern qu.— Macmillan on do—Bryce in Fortnightly on do. Off at 2½ for Crewe: business in Chester. Saw Mr L. Barker.

Friday Dec. One. 1876. [Arley Hall, Cheshire]

Wrote to C.E. Parsons—Mr Godley BP.—Mr Hamilton B.P.—Baron Tauchnitz BP.—Chester P. master—Rev. R. Balgarnie[11]—Rev. G. Foxton—Rev. R. Jones. Conversation with Mr Melville—Ld Hanmer—Mr [blank]. Walk with the party. Read Between Danube & Bl. Sea. Wrote on Mr Martin's 2d Vol.[12] Off at 4½ to

[1] Of Everton, assisted by Gladstone; Hawn P.
[2] Sir J. Skelton, 'The great Lord Bolingbroke, Henry St John. An Address' (1868).
[3] Of Bethnal Green; Gladstone earlier sent him books; Hawn P.
[4] Nonconformist clergyman in Shoreditch; Hawn P.
[5] Giving S. Papautonopoles permission to print 'The Hellenic Factor' in Clio, a Greek newspaper published in Trieste; Hawn P.
[6] Not found; probably incorporated in his review of Martin which had sharp comments on the Peelites; see 6 Nov., 1 Dec. 76.
[7] Sir J. Skelton, The impeachment of Mary Stuart (1876).
[8] Probably James Coling, 1819-88; rector of Maldon from 1868.
[9] Frederick Hammond, vicar of Talland 1876.
[10] Charles Bradford Wardale, d. 1903; vicar of Bowes from 1870.
[11] A nonconformist; Hawn P.
[12] Beginning his review; see 6 Nov. 76n.

Arley[1] & very old friends. Warburton is now blind, a fine specimen indeed of the English country gentleman, the intelligent & devout Christian, adding to this much accomplishment, singular taste, & an uncomplaining patience which makes him a living lesson, & recalls Lady H. Forbes. We played a little whist in evg.

2. Sat.

A musical service in the beautiful Chapel at nine. Wrote to Mrs Hampton—Dr Newman—a venture![2] Walk to Budworth: a fine Church & the village full of W.s handiwork. Wrote on Mr Martin. Read MS. Letters aloud to W.—also in evg, Tennyson's Morte d'Arthur, & Guinevere—Between Danube & Bl. Sea.

3. Adv. S.

H.C. at 8. Morning prayers 10.30—Aftn 3. Walks with W. & with his son. Read Bp Strossmayer's Letter (in German)[3]—Life of Bp Feild.[4] Mr Yates[5] the Chaplain dined: a man greatly above par & who wears well his office. Conversation on the Irish Succession &c. Wrote to Sec. Conjarada.[6]

4. M.

Chapel at 9. Wrote to Mrs Hampton—Mary G.—D. of Westminster—Mrs Th.—Mr Guillard—Mr Scott Robertson[7]—Mr Bartlett—Rev. Canon Ashworth. Saw Lady Egerton NB. Wrote on Martin's Vol. III [*sc*. II]. Walk with Mr W[arburton]. Much conversation with him. In this visit we are I hope of some use. Read G. Smith on Babylonian Antiquities.[8]

5. Tu. [London]

Off at 8¼ to N.wich Crewe & London. In H[arley] St. at 2.30. Saw Mr Knowles—Mr Stuart Wortley—Sir A. Panizzi—Mad. Novikoff (& Mr Kinglake, Count Beust). Dined with Mrs Th. Long conversation with *Conclave* on the Conference & next Friday. Wrote on Mr Martin. Read Between Danube & Black Sea (finished). Let fly at the Chaos I found awaiting me.

6. Wed.

Wrote (*B.P.*) to Ld Stratford de R.—Arthur G.—Madam Ralli—Mr Jackman—Mr Cowper Temple—Ld Russell—Rev. R. Johnson—and letters to Ld Granville—P.A. Taylor M.P.—Mr Rathbone MP—Robin Allen—Rev. Mr Green—C.G.—Dr

[1] Seat of R. E. Egerton-*Warburton; see 3 Sept. 42.
[2] Asking him to allow his name to be linked with the conference on 8 December; Newman declined; *Newman*, xxviii. 142.
[3] See 5 Nov. 76n.
[4] By H. W. Tucker (1876).
[5] William Yates, chaplain at Arley 1872-80; vicar of Worleston, Cheshire, 1881.
[6] Presumably an institution in Spain, but not traced.
[7] William Archibald Scott Robertson, d. 1897; antiquarian; rector of Elmley 1866-84, of Throwley 1884-92.
[8] G. Smith, *The Chaldean account of Genesis* (1876).

Barry—Mr Hodson—Mr Young. Spent several hours on my Chaos & worked nearly through. Saw Mr Bartlett (at much length on all the points)[1]—Sir W.R. Farquhar—Scotts—Mr Knowles—Mr T. Hughes—Mr Trevelyan—Mr Wortley. Dined at Mr Wortleys. Saw Bailey X 45. Read Fraser on Eastern Qu.

7. Th.

Wrote to Mr MacColl—Ld Stratford de R.—Messrs Harper—M. Papengouth[2]—Mr Whitfield—C.G.—Mr Godfrey—Mr Howlett.[3] Dined at Mr G. Howard's. Saw Madame Novikoff—Duke of Westminster—Mr E. Ashley—Mrs Th.—Mr C. Howard—Dr G. Smith. Read Hansard—Sir G. Campbell on Eastern Qu[4]—Harrison on do.[5]

8. Fr.

Wrote to C.G. Made notes & extracts for speech. Attended the meetings at St James's Hall 12 1½ and 4 8. Spoke (I fear) 1½ hour, with some exertion, far from wholly to my satisfaction.[6] The meetings were great, notable, almost historical. Dined at Mrs Th.s.[7] Saw Count Schuvaloff (at 15 G.S.)[8]—Mr Hayward—Mr Torrens—Ld Bathurst—Mr Hagopian—Made Novikoff. Read Siljeström on Vaccination.[9]

9. Sat. [Hawarden]

Wrote to A. Arnold—C.B. Cayley[10]—Ed. Daily News—Mrs Helen G.—J. Hodges—O. Chambers—A. Buzacott. Saw Mr Salmon—Sir A. Panizzi—Sir W.R. Farquhar—Mr Harvie Farquhar. Off at 4¾ to Hawarden. Amusing rencontre with an Irish Passenger. Read Die Orientalische Frage.[11] Found Ld Wolverton at Hawarden: sat late.

[1] i.e. E. Ashmead *Bartlett, one of the conference organizers.
[2] Sic; unidentified.
[3] Edmund Howlett, active liberal in Beckenham.
[4] Sir G. Campbell, A handy book on the Eastern question (1876).
[5] F. Harrison, 'Cross and crescent', Fortnightly Review, xxvi. 209 (December 1876).
[6] The duke of Westminster and Lord Shaftesbury took the chair at the two sessions, Gladstone speaking in the afternoon; T.T., 9 December 1876, 8a.
[7] Novikov and W. T. Stead both claimed that Gladstone escorted her to Claridge's thus making himself late for a dinner with Ambassadors; Herbert Gladstone used this as a disprovable 'Credulity', remarking, 'the infallible record of Mr Gladstone's own Diary shows that subsequently he dined quietly at the house of a friend', but, not surprisingly, he did not give that friend's identity; After Thirty Years, 35-6. The presence of Shuvalov at Mrs Thistlethwayte's may account for Stead's version in Stead, M.P. for Russia, i. 294.
[8] i.e. at Mrs Thistlethwayte's; Count Petr Andreievich Shuvalov, 1827-89; Russian ambassador in London 1874-9; introduced to Gladstone by Novikov.
[9] P. A. Siljeström, Vaccinationsfrågan (1874).
[10] Charles Bagot Cayley, 1823-83; tr. the Iliad 1877.
[11] Probably Oesterreich und die orientalische Frage (1875).

10. 2 S. Adv.

Ch mg & evg. Wrote to Mrs Hampton—Mr Goschen. Long conversation with Canon [R.] Gregory on the Education question, & on possible Ritual judgments. Read Service[1]—Wilkinson[2]—& sundries.

11. M.

Ch. 8½ A.M. Wrote to Ld Cottesloe—Mr A. Austin—Mrs Weldon[3]—Ld R. Montagu—Mr Turrell—Rev. J. Service—Mr W. Stampert. Much conversation with Ld Wolverton. Read Clarke's Travels[4]—Austin's Russia before Europe[5]—Waverley. Walk with Ld W[olverton].

12. Tu.

Ch. 8½ AM. Wrote to Mrs B. St J. Mathews[6]—Messrs Harper BP—Strahan BP—Scott—Cassell & Co—Lt Col. Dickson[7]—Mrs Beke—Mr Briggs—Mr Yates—Mr Jerred. We drove to Eaton[8] and went over all the new works: bid goodbye to Ld Wolverton there. Read Dr Garth Wilkinson—Norwood Tracts[9]—Waverley. The F. Cavendishes came.

13. Wed.

Ch. 8¼ A.M. Wrote to Madame Novikoff—Mr Oates[10] B.P.—Mr Ouvry B.P.—Messrs Bean—Miss Pearce—Rev. Mr Rowley—Rev. W. Awdry[11]—Rev. Dr Eversham. Made out statements of my Tribute Loan Purchases. Walk with F.C.s & cut down an evergreen. Read Burnaby's Ride to Khiva[12]—Siljeström on Vaccination Laws—Waverley.

14. Th.

Ch. 8¼ A.M. Wrote to Ed. Daily News—D[itt]o Private—Mr Lethaby—Mr Secales—Mr Oldham—Mons. Chrysoveloni (l. & BP)—Chester Postmaster—Earl Russell—Rev. Dr Parker—Miss Doyle—Mr Anchetell. Walk with C. Howard & F.C. Read Siljeström (finished)—Miss Irby on Slav Provinces[13]—Bright's Speech—Waverley.

---

[1] John Service, minister in Glasgow, had sent his *Salvation here and after* (1876).

[2] J. J. G. Wilkinson, *On human science* (1876).

[3] Further problems about litigation with the Rawlings family; Add MS 44452, f. 221; see 5 Oct. 71.

[4] See 15 May 27.   [5] By A. Austin (1876).

[6] Wife of Benjamin St John Mathews of Pontrilas Court, Herefordshire.

[7] Lothian Sheffield Dickson, D.L. of Tower Hamlets; lived in Brighton; dismissed from the army in 1859.   [8] Westminster's house in Cheshire; see 10 Dec. 61.

[9] i.e. by Thomas *Scott, the free-thinker.   [10] Wilfred Oates; Hawn P.

[11] William Awdry, 1842–1910; headmaster of St John's, Hurstpierpoint, 1873–9; principal of Chichester college 1879–86; bp. of Southampton 1895.

[12] E. H. V. Burnaby, *A ride to Khiva* (1876).

[13] See 14 Mar. 67 (though he told Granville (see Ramm I, i. 28) he had not read the book earlier, probably a slip of the memory, possibly a wrong attribution); a second ed. under the title *The Slavonic Provinces of Turkey in Europe* was published in 2v. with a preface by Gladstone in 1877; see 7 Apr. 77.

15. Fr.

Ch. 8½ AM. Wrote to Bp Strossmayer (Fr.)—Mr Herbert—Mr Peel MP.—G. Smith—Mr Clark—Mr Cornwallis West—Mr Newland—Made Ralli—Capt. Lumley—Dr Lewin.[1] Walk with C.H. & F.C. Read Irby on Slav. Provinces— Tracts on Eastern Quest.—Waverley.

16. Sat.

Ch. 8¼ A.M. Wrote to Ed. Daily News—Selim Effendi (French & Transl)[2]—Wms & Norgate—Dr W. Smith—Made Novikoff—Mr J.C. Kelly—Mr Ouvry B.P.—Sir F. Doyle—Rev Dr Parker—Mr G. Macewen. Walk with F.C. & S.E.G. Conversation with C. Howard;[3] who left us. A sterling man. Read Waverley—Moltke on the War of 1828-9[4]—Miss Irby on Slav Provinces and [blank.]

17. 3 S. Adv.

Ch 11 AM (with H.C.) and 6½ P.M. Wrote to Rev. Mr Bickersteth. Copied & dispatched l. to Selim Effendi. Read Hutton on Romanism &c.[5]—Bp Hooper on Ch. of Rome & Infallibility[6]—Oxenham in Xtn Apologist[7]—Smith on the Soul[8]— &c.

18. M.

Ch. 8¼ A.M. Wrote to Duke of Argyll—Prof. Thea B.P.—Mr Adams B.P.—Herr Krüger[9]—W.G. Hird[10]—Reeves and Turner—Rev. W. Pound—Rev. Th. Wood[11]—Rev. Mr Crawley.[12] Wrote on Martin's P. Consort. Read Ld Waveney's Rome & Italy[13]—Waverley. The Warburtons (and Ushers)[14] came: 12 to dinner.

19. Tu.

Ch. 8¼ A.M. Wrote to The Persian Minister[15]—Lord Granville—Dr A. Harawitz [sic]—Dr Lawrie[16]—Mr Bosworth Smith—Messrs T. & B.—Mrs Th.—Mr Binney—Mr Knowles—Mr Stanford—C.W. Jones. Wrote on Martin's P. Consort.

---

[1] Friend Lewin, physician at St Mary's hospital.

[2] Of the Turkish embassy in London; letter and reply in Add MS 44452, f. 253, later published in the *D.N.*

[3] See 28 Jan. 42.

[4] See 3 June 54.

[5] V. W. Hutton, *Church authority* (1875).

[6] G. Hooper, *A fair... discussion concerning the infallible guide* (1689).

[7] H. N. Oxenham, 'Jukes' defence of universalism', *Christian Apologist*, i. 87 (October 1876).

[8] J. Smith, *Food for the soul* (1873).

[9] Perhaps Carl Ludwig Krüger, German classicist.

[10] See 19 Nov. 76.

[11] Thomas Wood, d. 1894; curate, then rector, of Northbourne from 1874.

[12] Perhaps Henry Crawley, rector of Stow from 1849.

[13] R. A. S. Adair, Baron Waveney, *Forty years since; or, Italy and Rome* (1876).

[14] John Ussher of co. Waterford, d. 1907; m. 1865 Mary, R. E. E. Warburton's da.

[15] See Ramm II, i. 27.

[16] Perhaps John Douglas Lawrie, physician in Bradford.

Walk with Mr Warburton; & conversation as much as I could. He is so good & unselfish. Cut two Alders. Conversation with Mr Usher who knows the East. Read Forsyth's Sclavonia[1]—Stanford's Ethnography of Turkey[2] and Dillon's Account of The Ld M.s visit to Oxford:[3] aloud for Mr W.

20. Wed.

Ch. 8¼ AM. Wrote to Pears & Logan B.P.—Cyrus Field—Herbert Spencer[4]—Selim Effendi (supplem.)—S. Martin—G. Harris. Walked with Mr Warburton. H. & I. then cut an alder. Read Forsyth's Sclavonian Prov.—Mr Parsons on the condition of Clerks[5]—Waverley. Conversation with F.C. who went. Conversation with Mr Usher & looked up the Irish Succession in Palmer & Mant.[6]

21. Th. St Thomas

Ch. 8¾ AM. Wrote to Lady G. Fullerton—Marchese Vitelleschi—Mr C. Howard—Mr C.E. Palmer[7]—Mr G.F. Lutticke.[8] Wrote on Martin's Life of P.C. Sat to Mr Miller.[9] Cut down a beech with H. The Warburtons went: it is good to have had them. Read Forsyth's Slavonia—Missionaires Moscovites[10]—Waverley (finished). The two Carlisle Chapters are *grand*.[11]

22. Fr.

Kept my bed for a couple of hours to fight off cold. Wrote to Madame Novikoff[12]—M. Victor Oger—Mr Watkinson—Mr Balfour (BP)—Rev. Mr Jackson—Rev. Mr Harrison—Messrs Jones Lloyd & Co[13]—Capt. Walker[14]—Mr Worth—Mr Wren—Mr Lewis. Wrote Inscriptions on Dr Dillon's ridiculous work.[15] Walk with C.G. & Mr Miller. Sat to Mr Miller. Read Rob Roy[16] (afresh)—Missionaires Moscovites (finished)—and tracts.

---

[1] See 19 July 76.

[2] Edward Stanford sent his Ἐθνογραφικος χρατης της εὐρωπαικης Τουρκιας και Ἑλλαδος (1877).

[3] R. C. Dillon, *The Lord Mayor's visit to Oxford* (1876).

[4] Had sent the first v. of *Principles of Sociology*; Add MS 44452, f. 263.

[5] C. E. Parsons, *Clerks; their position and advancement* (1876).

[6] i.e. R. Mant, *History of the Church of Ireland* (1840), and W. Palmer, *The apostolical jurisdiction and succession of the episcopacy in the British Churches* (1840).

[7] Perhaps Charles Edward Palmer, d. 1889; classicist and chaplain of Great Torrington Union 1857-89.

[8] London commission agent.

[9] Possibly William E. Miller, painted portraits in Britain 1873-1903; but this work untraced, not recorded on his list of sittings in Hawn P.

[10] 'Les Missionaires Muscovites chez les Ruthenes Unis' sent by Lady G. Fullerton; see Stead, *M.P. for Russia*, i. 313.

[11] Chapters 68 and 69 on the executions of Fergus MacIvor and Evan Dhu Maccombich.

[12] In Stead, *M.P. for Russia*, i. 313.

[13] Liverpool accountants.

[14] Oliver Ormerod Walker, 1833-1914; captain in militia; tory M.P. Salford 1877-80.

[15] Verses at Add MS 44763, f. 35. See 19 Dec. 76.

[16] By *Scott.

23 Sat.

Again rose late. Wrote to Rev. A.T. Gregory[1]—Messrs Edmonston & Douglas[2]—Herr Wieler[3]—Mr A.C. Tiley—Mr J. M'Donald—Mr A.G. Austin. Sat to Mr Miller. Walk with C. & felled two alders. Read Elam, Winds of Doctrine[4]—Seebohm, Xtn Hypothesis[5]—Print Room of Br Museum—Forsyth's Slavonia (finished)—Robroy—Letter to Bp of Lichfield.

24. 4 S. Adv.

Ch. 11 AM 3 PM. Read De Lisle on the Prophecies[6]—Seebohm, Xtn Hypothesis—Black Book of Russia[7]—and Tracts.

25. Xm D.

The most solemn I have known for long: see that Eastward sky of storm, and of underlight!

Ch. 11 AM (H.C.) and 7 PM. Wrote to Lady C. Neville Grenville—Made Novikoff—Miss Collet[8]—Mr A. de Lisle—Mr Louder—Mr Geo. Whale—Mr Harris. Read De Lisle on Prophecy—Elam, Winds of doctrine—Formulary of Theistic Devotions—and Tracts. Conversation with S.E.G.

26. St Stephen.

Ch. 8.45 AM. C.G. went off at 8.30 to attend & await Agnes at No 73 H[arley] St. Wrote to Prof. Cav. Ginuti—Mr G.W. Smith—Mr A. Pitt—Mr Jas Toulson—Mr G.A. Norris—Mr Jas Morrison. Wrote on Martin's P. Consort. Cut an Alder. Read Irby & Mackenzie's Slavonic Provinces—Wordsworth on Apocalypse[9]—Old New Zealand[10]—Robroy. Cut some alders.

27. Wed. St Joh.

Ch. 8¾ AM. Wrote to Mr Mundella MP—Mr B. Langley—Rev. Mr Bickersteth l. & B.P.—C.H. Payne[11]—C.N. Hall—C.G.—Mrs Ward—Miss Howan BP. Read Pym on Ireland[12]—Lysias, Oration against Eratosthenes[13]—Irby & Mackenzie on Slavonia—Robroy. Finished Art. on P. Consort. H. & I cut down an ash.

[1] Arthur Thomas Gregory, rector of Trusham, Devon.
[2] Edinburgh printers and publishers.
[3] Possibly William Julius Wieler, published on financial affairs.
[4] C. Elam, *Winds of doctrine* (1876).
[5] F. Seebohm, *The spirit of Christianity: an essay on the Christian hypothesis* (privately printed 1876).
[6] E. J. L. M. P. De Lisle, *A comparison between the history of the Church and the prophecies of the Apocalypse* (1874).
[7] By E. de Prokopovich (1876); sent him by 'an anonymous lady'; see Stead, *M.P. for Russia*, i. 315; it attacked the Novikov family.
[8] Sophia Dobson Collet, 1822-94; journalist and biographer; sent her *Theistic devotions* (1876), Add MS 44452, f. 269. She ed. the *Brahmo Year Book* which Gladstone read annually at this time.
[9] C. Wordsworth, *The Apocalypse* (1849).
[10] [F. E. Maning], *Old New Zealand. By a Pakeha Maori* (1863).
[11] Possibly H. S. Payne, Congregationalist minister in Nantwich.
[12] Perhaps J. Pim, *The Land question in Ireland* (1867).
[13] Lysias, *Oratio in Eratosthenem* (1835).

28. Th. H. Innoc.

Ch. 8¾ AM. Wrote to Mad. Novikoff BP.—Canon Ashwell—Mr Agnew—Mr A. de Lisle—C.G.—Rev H.S. Cooke[1]—Mr S. Harris—Rev C.E. Butler.[2] Corrected my Article for Ch. of E. Quarty & dispatched it.[3] Kibbling & cutting with H. Read Irby & Mackenzie—Cooke on Disestablishment—Robroy—Letter to Rev. [blank.]

29. Fr.

Ch. 8½ AM. Wrote to Lady G. Fullerton—Made Novikoff—C.G.—Rev. A. Herring[4]—Mrs Th.—Mr Alexander—Capt. Gibson—Stationmaster Q. Ferry—Mr Bramwell. Read Mackenzie & Irby—Freeman in Fortnightly—Havelock in do(!)[5]—Robroy—Hahn Alban. Studien[6]—Miss Edwards on Egypt.[7] Visited the Manor tenants with H in pouring rain.

In the retrospect of this year I have no marked or cheering advance to report to myself. The gap continues to be wide between my measure of perception and my standard of action. The day of death seems to make its approach felt with a sense of great solemnity. That He will fix both as to time & manner: be it in His hands.

My desire for the shade, a true and earnest desire has been since August rudely baffled: retirement & recollection seem more remote than ever. But [it] is in a noble cause, for the curtain rising in the East seems to open events that bear cardinally on our race.

30. Sat.

Ch. 8½ AM. Wrote to Ld Hatherley—Mrs Bennett l. & B.P.—Sir H. Taylor—Capt. Helbert—Mrs Mochler—Mr Dudgeon[8]—Mary G.—Sir Thos G.—S. Harris—C.W. Jones—J.P. Jones. Cutting with Herbert. Read Irby & Mackenzie—Acksahoff's Speech[9]—Old New Zealand—Robroy.

31. S. aft Xm.

Ch. 11 AM and 6½ P.M. Wrote to Mr Wilson (Birmm)[10]—Mr Sands—W.H.G.—Scotts—C.G. Read Benrath's Ochino[11]—Thiersch on the Church.[12]

---

[1] Henry Salkeld Cooke, curate of St James's, Whitehaven, had sent an untraced work on disestablishment.

[2] Charles Ewart Butler, chaplain at Dieppe 1875-7; vicar of Tealby 1877.

[3] See 6 Nov. 76n.

[4] Armine Styleman Herring, 1831-96; vicar of St Paul's, Clerkenwell, 1865-96.

[5] Sir H. Havelock, 'A national training to arms', *Fortnightly Review*, xxv. 430 (March 1876).

[6] J. G. von Hahn, *Albanesische Studien*, 3v. (1853).

[7] A. B. Edwards, *A thousand miles up the Nile* (1876).

[8] William Dudgeon, active in liberal affairs in London.

[9] I. S. Aksakov, 'Condensed speech of . . . Aksakov, Vice-President of the Slavonic Committee of Moscow, October 1876' (1876).

[10] See 3 Sept. 76.

[11] C. Benrath, *Bernardino Ochino von Siena* (1876).

[12] H. W. J. Thiersch, *On Christian Commonwealth* (1876).

So passes over the year to join its fellows in eternity: laden with marks and with sins. O that I could but live my personal life even as I live my public life which however speckled with infirmity is upright in intention & less unfit to be offered up through Christ to the Most High.

Mond. Jan 1. 1877. Circumcision

Church 8¾ AM. Wrote to Made Novikoff—Mr Fairbrother—C.G.—Duchess of Argyll—Mr Dickson—Rev. B. Martin.[1] Tea at Miss Scotts. Cutting alders with H. Worked on my year's account and survey of property and income:[2] for the ease I hope of those who are to come after me. Read Mackenzie & Irby—Life of Ochino—Robroy.

2. Tu.

Ch. 8½ A.M. Wrote to Mr Mundella—Made Novikoff (& copy)—Mr A. Nicholson—C.G.—Miss C. Marsh—Scotts—Mr B. Clarke (autogr). Walk with the Rector. Read Mackenzie & Irby—Benrath's Ochino—Old New Zealand—Robroy.

3. Wed.

Ch. 8½ AM. Wrote to Dr Karl Benrath[3]—Messrs Nisbet—C.G.—Canon Ashwell—Miss Hooper—Mr Lloyd Pratt—Walter L.G.—Hon. R. Stewart—Mr F. Wright—Mons. T. de Thöner[4]—Mr G.F. Wills. Wrote a paper on Benrath's Life of Ochino for Ch. Qu. R. Read Benrath's Ochino (finished)—Irby & Mackenzie—Turkish Eg. Loans Bill—Robroy.

4. Th.

Ch. 8½ AM. Wrote to Spottiswoode's (BP)—G. Whale—A. Strahan—R.T. Morris—Scotts—C.G.—Mr Baldwin. Corrected proofs of article on Pr. Consort for Ch. Q.R.[5] Cutting alders. Read Regaldi, Arte dell'antico Egitto[6]—Mackenzie and Irby—Young respecting Vittoria Colonna & others[7]—Robroy.

5. Fr.

Ch. 8½ AM. Wrote to Dr Humphry Sandwith—Made Novikoff—C.G.—J. Watson & Smith—Mr B.H. Watt[8]—Mr Knowles. Read (in Le Nord) The Turkish Constitution!!![9]—Misses M'Kenzie & Irby—Thiersch on Xtn Commonwealth[10]—Kinglake's Preface[11]—Robroy. I lost good company in Helen and Herbert; but Mary

[1] Benjamin Martin, presbyterian minister in Fife, had sent his *Messiah's Kingdom* (1876).

[2] Hawn P.

[3] Karl Benrath, 1845-1924, historian of the reformation; Gladstone's notice of his *Bernardino Ochino* for the *Church Quarterly* was not published, a change of editors producing two notices, Gladstone's arriving second and too late; Ashwell to Gladstone, 13 April 1877, Add MS 44454, f. 47.

[4] Had written from St Petersburg, on religion; Hawn P.

[5] See 6 Nov. 76n.   [6] G. Regaldi, *L'Egitto antico e moderno* (1882).

[7] i.e. ch. XV on Vittoria Colonna and other chapters from M.Young, *The life and times of Aonio Paleario*, 2v. (1860).

[8] Perhaps Basil H. Watt, edited devotional works.

[9] Account in *Le Nord*, 1-3 January 1877 of Midhat's constitution, promulgated the day the Constantinople Conference began; for it, see R. H. Davison, *Reform in the Ottoman empire* (1963), ch. X.

[10] See 31 Dec. 76.

[11] To the 6th ed. (1877-8) of his *Crimea*, with comments on the death of Novikov's br., N. Kiréeff.

is all-sufficing in point of society. Cut an alder—in the rain, which hardly ever intermits: & then only as if to rest itself. Arranging letters.

6. Sat. Epiph.

Ch. 8.45 AM. Dearest C.s birthday: God prosper & complete the training of that noble soul. Wrote to Mr Mundella—Mr J. Murray—Scotts—Sir Chas Reed—Mr F. Ouvry—Miss Skene—Mr A. Joy—Professor Meiklejohn[1]—Mons. Tzwiet.[2] Saw Mr Vickers. Read Robroy (finished)—Thiersch—Mackenzie & Irby. Dined at the Rectory.

7. 1 S. Epiph.

Ch. 11 AM with H.C. 6½ P.M. with congregational practice afr. Wrote to Herbert J.G. (on the dear fellow's birthday)—Mr Knowles—Mr E. Jones—Mr Fremont—C.G. Read Wilkinson on Materialism[3]—Bp of Gibraltar's Charge[4]—Mr Reichel's Sermon[5]—Ramière on 'Courses of Rel. Thought'.[6] Walk with Charles [Lyttelton] who went off.

8. M.

Ch. 8½ A.M. Wrote to Mr M. Anchetill—Dr Schliemann—Mr Dunbar l. + BP—Ld Granville—C.G.—Mr D. Puseley—Sir S. Peto—Mrs Nicholson. Saw Miss Scott. Alder-cutting. Arrivals. Read Mackenzie & Irby—Thiersch, Xtn State—Lewis on Authority.[7] Began (tentatively) a paper on that subject.

9. Tu.

Ch. 8¼ AM. Wrote to Mons. Negropontes (Fr.)[8]—Madame Novikoff—Sir Arthur Gordon—Scotts—Messrs Pears BP.—C.G.—Mr Geo. Howell—W. Grogan—Mr W. Westell—Redacteur Publ. Blätter.[9] Attended the Rent dinner and spoke. Saw Mr L. Barker on the accounts: & made a fresh Exors payment of £600: sent by Alfred [Lyttelton] to Mr Marcy. Read Mackenzie & Irby.

10. Wed.

Ch. 8½ A.M. Wrote to Messrs Farrer (B.P.)—Gen. Cesnola—H.N.G. (BP)—Ed. Northn Echo—Sir J. Phillips[10]—Canon Liddon B.P.—Quartermaster King[11]—

---

[1] John Miller Dow Meiklejohn, d. 1902; professor of education at St Andrews 1876.
[2] Or Ćwiek, pseudonym of K. Cieszkowski, a leader of the Polish revolution 1863.
[3] See 10 Dec. 76.   [4] By C. W. Sandford (1876).
[5] C. P. Reichel, 'The nature and origin of episcopacy. A sermon' (1877).
[6] Probably H. Ramière's article in *Dublin Review*, xxvii. 215 (July 1876).
[7] New ed. (1875) by Sir Gilbert Lewis of G. C. Lewis, *Essay on the influence of authority in matters of opinion* (1849) (see 11 Sept. 71) reviewed by Gladstone as the inaugural article of Knowles's *Nineteenth Century*, i. 2 (March 1877), reprinted in *Gleanings*, iii. 137. The review led to a dispute with Sir J. F. Stephen; *Nineteenth Century*, i. 270; see 14 June 77.
[8] M. J. Negropontis, a merchant in Constantinople, on Greek-Slav relations. Draft in French of 9 January, with English tr. of 18 September, at Add MS 44453, f. 18. The correspondence led to a prolonged row with the *Telegraph*, see 19 Sept. 77n., 12 Mar. 78n., all printed in *PP* 1878 lxxxi. 687.
[9] Untraced.
[10] *Sic*; probably Sir James Erasmus Philipps, 1824-1912; vicar of Warminster 1859-97; 12th bart. 1873.   [11] Untraced.

Marquis Guerrieri Gonzaga—Rev. Mr Wilkinson—Rev. F. Randolph.[1] Saw Mary Glynne (£600). Cutting Alders with W. Read Mackenzie & Irby—Pickering on Vaccination[2]—Tennyson's Harold.[3] Conversation with Alfred & Mr Austin Leigh[4] on Scott & literature.

11. Th.

Ch. 8½ A.M. Wrote to Mad. Novikoff BP.—Ed. Chester Chronicle[5]—Bp of Chester—H.N.G.—Mr G.F. Turner—Mr Jas Long—Wms & Norgate. Saw Mr Vickers. Walk with the Rector:[6] and a conversation on marriage and other matters. The idea does not gain any increased hold on him. Called at St John's. Wrote on 'Authority'. Read Harold—Thiersch—Lewis on Authority.

12. Frid.

Ch. 8¼ A.M. Wrote to Made Novikoff—Mr J. Murray—Mrs Th.—Mr S. Hewitt—Helen J.G.—Ed. Northern Echo—Ld Rob. Montagu—Mrs Butler. Saw Mr Vickers & WHG. Cut down a sycamore with H. Read Wallace on Russia[7]—Longridge, War Fever[8]—Reinach on Montenegro[9]—Harold (finished)—and Neale on Montenegro.[10] Twelve to dinner.

13. Sat.

Ch. 8½ A.M. Wrote to Mr Cornwallis West—T. Panchaud[11]—Mr Grogan—F. Fuller—Bp Bath & W.—Mrs Butler BP.—Messrs Miles—Watsons—Rev. Mr Mossman—Rev. T.B. Dover.[12] Began cutting a large Ash. Tea party at five. Read Reinach on Montenegro—Fuller on the Exhibition[13]—Rodwell & Sale's Koran[14]—Auriemma, Questione d'Oriente[15]—Creagh, Xtendom & Islamiah.[16] Set to work on tidying books & papers.

14. 2 S. Epiph.

Ch 11 AM and 6¼ P.M. Wrote to Rev. E. Wickham—Mr H. Wright jun.—Ed. N. Echo—Miss Doyle—Rev Mr Stephens—Mr Tattersall (autogr). Read Day's

---

[1] Francis Randolph, d. 1898; vicar of Brent Pelham from 1876.
[2] J. Pickering, 'Anti-vaccination. A letter' (1876).
[3] See 1 Nov. 76.
[4] William Austen Leigh, 1843-1921; fellow of King's from 1864; Clerk of the Journal of the Lords; a friend of the Lytteltons; Hawarden Visitors Book.
[5] Notice of his lecture on 16 January.
[6] i.e. his son Stephen.
[7] Sir D. M. Wallace, *Russia*, 2v. (1877).
[8] Untraced work by J. A. Longridge, authority on artillery.
[9] J. Reinach, *La Serbie et le Monténégro* (1876).
[10] J. M. Neale, *Notes . . . on Dalmatia, Croatia, Istria, Styria, with a visit to Montenegro* (1861).
[11] Possibly Édouard Panchaud, author of *La Bible et la Science moderne* (1854).
[12] Thomas Birkett Dover, vicar of St Agnes, Kennington Park, London.
[13] F. Fuller, 'Plan for opening and developing the Alexandra Park and Palace' (1870).
[14] Tr. G. Sale (1734), J. M. Rodwell (1876).
[15] Untraced work by T. Auriemma.
[16] See 8 Nov. 76.

Russia & the East[1]—Stephen's See of Chichester[2]—Pritchard's Sermon[3]—Creagh on Montenegro—Abp Vaughan 'Hidden Springs'[4]—Dr Baxendale on Popular Mortality.[5] Wrote on 'Authority'. Conversation with E. Talbot on pending crisis in the Church. He can hardly be too much prized.

15. M.

Ch. 8½ A.M. Wrote to Baron Tauchnitz—Spottiswoode's—Ed. Echo—Archdn Allen—Mrs Stance—Mr Mundella—Mr Webster—Mr Steward. Wrote on the Turks—for tomorrow. Read Denton on E. Xtns[6]—Warring on Spiritualism[7]—Lyttelton & Baker Corresp. on Vaccination.[8] Finished Mackenzie & Irby. Wrote on Authority.

16. Tu.

Ch. 8½ A.M. Wrote to Rev. W.W. Merry[9]—Mr Murray—Mr Gostwick[10]—R.H. Dunbar[11]—Mr Rathbone MP.—Mr Gennadios[12]—T. Ingle[13]—L. Lloyd—Herr Karoly [sic]—Mr Haig—Mr Vickers. Worked much on preparations for departure. Also prepared citations &c. for Lecture—Lecture 7-8¼.[14] Yesterday we cut the large walnut: today kibbled it. Read Koran—Mackenzie & Irby.

17. Wed. [Longleat, Wiltshire]

Rose at 7. Finished packing. Worked through post. Wrote to J. Watson & Smith. Off at nine. Reached Longleat[15] at 8¾: visited Bristol Cathedral on the way. Read Q.R. on Milton—And on Mohammed.[16] A large party of Eastern sympathisers.[17]

---

[1] W. A. Day, *Russia and the Eastern Question* (1877).

[2] W. R. W. Stephens, *Memorials: South Saxon See and Cathedral of Chichester* (1876).

[3] C. Pritchard, probably 'The continuity of the schemes of nature and of revelation. A sermon' (1866).

[4] R. B. Vaughan, *Hidden springs* (1876).

[5] J. Baxendell, *On changes in the rates of mortality* (1876).

[6] See 30 Oct. 76.   [7] See 11 Dec. 75.

[8] T. Baker, *Letters to and from . . . Lord Lyttelton, on vaccination* (1877).

[9] William Walter Merry; fellow of Lincoln, Oxford, 1860; ed. Homer for schools.

[10] Joseph Gostwick, constituent in Dulwich; Hawn P.

[11] Robert Haigh Dunbar of Sheffield sent a cutting; see Add MS 44453, f. 39.

[12] Ioannes Gennadios, Greek minister in London.

[13] Perhaps Thomas Ingle, London solicitor.

[14] Published as 'The Sclavonic Provinces of the Ottoman Empire', *Eastern Question Association Paper*, 5 (1877); on Mackenzie and Irby's *Slavonic Provinces*; *T.T.*, 17 January 1877, 10a; notes at Add MS 44664, f. 79.

[15] Seat of John Alexander Thynne, 1831-96; 4th marquis of Bath; powerful supporter of the agitation, though a tory. The south-west had 'by far the most frequent proportional incidence of agitation'; Shannon, 150.

[16] *Quarterly Review*, cxliii. 186, 205 (January 1877).

[17] Liddon's account this day reads: 'After dinner Mr G. said that he thought Russia would be in as good a position as anybody after the conference: that by associating all Europe with her she had quite changed the situation created by the Moscow speech: that Ignatieff might intrigue on Russia's own account with Turkey, & settle matters in such a way as to leave all Europe out of account' (Liddon Diary).

18. Th.

Chapel at 9. A.M. Wrote to Mr Ingle (Tel)—Mr Selby—Bp of Philippopoli (French and draft)[1]—Mr Mundella. Went over the House. Read Q.R. on Eastern Question.[2] Walk. Our large party included Mr Freeman, Dr Liddon & others. Much conversation in the common interest.[3]

19. Fr.

Chapel at 9. Wrote to Mr Rawlings—F. May & Co—Mr MacColl—Mr Warne— Mr Suffield—Mr Anderson. Read Freeman on Horses[4]—Singer on Cards[5]— Remarkable Characters[6]—and [blank.] Walk to Shirewater. Our conversation on Eastern matters continues. Also with Dr Liddon on Ch & belief.

20. Sat.

Chapel 9 AM. Wrote to M. Contostavlos (Gk Min For. Aff)[7] in French—Dean Howson—Mr Jackson—Mr Hastings. Saw Mr Rawlings—Mr Lethaby. Walk about place & park in forenoon:[8] beautiful drive in afternoon to Sir R. Hoare's.[9] This is a noble place: with a host & hostess who are admirable.

21. 3 S. Epiph.

Mg service in Chapel at 11. Parish Ch. at 3. Walk with Ld Bath. Copied l. to M. Contostarlos. Sent Art. on P. Consort to Baron Tauchnitz.[10] Wrote covering l. to M. Gennadios. Read Dean Howson on Eastward position: anew[11]—Mahony on Hamlet[12]—Elam on Evolution[13]—Mozley on Sacrifice of Isaac.[14]

22. M. [The Bishop's Palace, Wells]

Chapel 9. A.M. Wells Cathedral 3 P.M. Wrote to Made O. Novikoff—U. Sec. for War[15]—Mr [C.] Knight Watson—Mr Luttiche—P. Hewitt—Boyd Kinnear—Rev.

[1] Neophytos; bp. of Philippopolis 1872-80; involved in the Bulgarian schism; patriarch of Constantinople 1891; see Add MS 44453, f. 10.

[2] [W. Smith and A. H. Layard], *Quarterly Review*, cxliii. 276 (January 1877).

[3] Liddon noted: 'Mr Gladstone said that he thought the theory of several pairs of human beings less difficult of belief in accordance with revelation than that of a *greatly elongated Antiquity*' (Liddon's Diary).

[4] S. Freeman, *The art of horsemanship* (1806); or one of E. A. Freeman's many articles, some on field sports.

[5] S. W. Singer, *Researches into the history of playing cards* (1816).

[6] Perhaps *Astonishing characters* (1820?).

[7] M. Kontostavlos, foreign minister since 1875; letter untraced.

[8] Liddon noted: 'Walk with Mr Gladstone & Lord Bath. Mr G. thought that the infamous charge against the Greek Bishops in the current number of the Quarterly ought to be exposed' (Liddon Diary).

[9] *Sc.* Sir H. Hoare, 5th bart; Stourhead House, Wiltshire, with magnificent gardens.

[10] For Tauchnitz n. 1646.

[11] J. S. Howson, 'The Lord's table, vestments and Eastward position' (1875).

[12] J. W. Mahony, *Hamlet's mission* (1875).   [13] See 23 Dec. 76.

[14] J. B. Mozley, *Ruling ideas in early ages* (1877).

[15] George Henry Cadogan, 1840-1915; 5th Earl Cadogan 1873; under-secretary for war 1875-8; this letter untraced.

W. Denton—Mr Grove—H. Reeve—W. Harriss—M. Moses—A. Strahan. 10¾-1. To my old Friend the Bishop at Wells:[1] stopping at Frome ½ hour for an Address and Speech.[2] In afternoon saw the grounds & buildings, Vicar's Close and other objects of interest. Large dinner & evening party. Saw Ld Cork: many of the Clergy: Mr (Burrell?) the Papermaker. Read part of Schuyler's Report as now sent.[3] Finished Memoires de la Corse.[4]

23. Tu.

Cathedral at 10 AM. Bps Chapel 10 P.M. Wrote to Rev. G.F. Magorne[5]—Pres. Bath Liberal Assocn[6]—Pres. Young Men's Liberal Assocn[7]—Lord Acton—Mr de Lisle. After service we went over the beautiful Cathedral, Chapter House, & Library. Off at one to luncheon at Summerlease, Mr [E. A.] Freeman's: a large party, health drunk & speech. Then drove to the very remarkable Cheddar Cliffs, almost unique I think. Back at 6¼. Large dinner party. There could not be greater hospitality: but for privacy, alas! Conversation with the Bp on the Public Worship Act. Read Schuyler.[8] Another dinner party. In the evening read the passage in Barrow which Macaulay so highly prized. I set up against it a line and a half from J. Collier.[9]

24. Wed. [Dunster Castle]

Bps Chapel 8 AM. Wrote to Mr A. Deans & others: Miss Scott—Mr Strahan— Mr Kimber—Mr Roberts[10]—Mr J. Murray—Mr Hardcastle—Mr Hebdike[11]—A. Groom. Visited St Cuthberts & set out for Taunton. There amid much popular demonstration we visited St M. Magd. The Vicarage, Castle, & Museum. Arrived at Dunster Castle[12] at 4. Most beautiful. A large party. Much conversation on Eton with Bp Chapman. Finished Schuyler—read Cobden on R. & Turkey.[13]

25. Th. Conversion St Paul

Kept my bed till noon. Saw the fine Church, so admirably restored by Mr L[ut-trell] and drove to St Mary's Abbey Cleeve, where all the details of monastic life

[1] Lord Arthur Hervey; see 8 Oct. 25.

[2] Arranged by S. T. Rawlings of Frome liberal association; T.T., 22 January 1877, 6f, 23 January 1877, 6b.

[3] E. Schuyler, Mr Baring's and Mr Schuyler's Report on the atrocities committed upon the Christians in Bulgaria (1876).

[4] Probably earlier version of Mémoires historiques sur la Corse, . . . 1774-1777 (1889).

[5] A nonconformist.

[6] W. Hunt; declining invitation to speak there; T.T., 27 January 1877, 5d.   [7] Not found.

[8] Rest of entry apparently written later, hence the dinner party repeated inadvertently.

[9] Not found; Macaulay's reference to Barrow untraced; Jeremy *Collier is mentioned in Macaulay's essay on Leigh Hunt.

[10] Christadelphian lecturer at Birmingham; had sent a tract; T.T., 27 January 1877, 5d.

[11] Sic; probably sc. Hebditch.

[12] Elizabethan seat near Taunton of George Fownes-Luttrell, 1826-1910; Eton and Christ Church, Oxford.

[13] R. Cobden, 'Russia' (1836), reprinted in The political writings of Richard Cobden, 2v. (1867); Ch. I is the anti-Turkish 'Russia, Turkey and England'.

are visibly exhibited in the buildings, & the scene was very melancholy. Again a large party. Sir Thos Acland came. Much conversation with him. Wrote to Mr Jos Samuelson[1]—Mr Geo. Whale (for consideration)[2]—Mr Adam. Read Schuyler finished—Cobden on Turkey & Russia—The House of Aspen.[3]

26. Fr.

Ch. at 10 A.M. Wrote to Mr G. Harris—Mrs Th. A long day on the hills here & at Holnicote[4] where we had luncheon & saw a fine district. Back at 6¾. Tree notes taken. A large party. Conversation with Acland. Read Hist. of Somersetshire[5] &c.

27. Sat. [Orchard Neville, Somerset]

Wrote to Ld Hartington—J. Gould King—J.H. Bell—W.S. Gover[6]—W. Whitbourn—Mr Chevalier—Rev. Mr Rodwell—Rev. W. Preston. After an early breakfast & planting a tree we bid farewell to this fine place. Our kind host came with us as did Acland. There was at Taunton a very warm reception. I spoke pr. about 50 min.[7] All along the road one & the same feeling prevailed about the Eastern question, of which I am made the local symbol. At Glastonbury above all the sympathy was enthusiastic. A triumphal expression escorted us through rain & mud. I could not but get out and thank them in a few sentences. At two o'clock we were safely housed at Orchard Neville.[8] Lady C.N.G.s health & vivacity are wonderful and there is a light as if of heaven on her face. Read Q.R. on the Cape[9]—Hillocks, a crambé.[10]

28. Septa S.

Parish Ch. at 11 A.M. and 6½ P.M. Wrote to Ld Granville—Stationmaster Glastonb.—Hotel Master do—Mr Dix Sadler do—Mr Crouch do.[11] Wrote on Authority.[12] Read Freeman Lect. I. on Wells[13]—Elam, Winds of Doctrine. Conversation with F. Neville: whose language on Disestablishment was remarkable. I had also much discourse with Lady Charlotte. She presents a picture I think the most remarkable in ripeness of all the aged persons I have ever known.[14]

[1] Chairman of Birkenhead working men's liberal association, regretting his inability to speak there; T.T., 2 February 1877, 9f.
[2] i.e. to Greenwich liberals.
[3] Untraced.
[4] Seat near Selworthy of Sir T. D. Acland.
[5] Perhaps J. Stuckey, A compleat history of Somersetshire (1742).
[6] Perhaps W. Sutton Gover, who tr. E. Reboul, The Duty of Life Assurance (1871).
[7] T.T., 29 January 1877, 10b.
[8] Home of Lady C. Neville-Grenville; see 11 July 39, 17 Aug. 66.
[9] Quarterly Review, cxliii. 105 (January 1877).
[10] James Inches Hillocks had sent his Life Struggles (1876).
[11] i.e. George Dix, a Glastonbury saddler and Henry Crouch, jeweller.
[12] See 8 Jan. 77.
[13] E. A. Freeman, History of the cathedral Church of Wells (1870).
[14] She died 15 June 1877.

29. M. [Bowden Park, Wiltshire]

Balsb. Ch. 8½ AM. Wrote to Consul Schuyler—Bp Claughton—G.H. Powell[1]—J. Armstrong—H. Swainson—Rev. J. Hillocks—Rev. S.E.G.—Bear, Devizes—Mr Ouvry—Mr Bryce—W. Money[2]—A. Barbosa—P. Sheridan[3]—E. Law—W. Smith. We set out at 12.30: not without hope that this visit may not be the last. Reached Bowden Park 3.30.[4] Found all in the usual good & seemly state. Saw Bp of B. & W.—Mr Rogers jun.—John Gladstone (T.S.G's). Read Dr Elam—Freeman on Wells.

30. Tu.

Ch. 10¼ A.M. Wrote to Hon C.L. Wood—Jas Knowles—Jas Elliot—Rev. W.R. Clark[5]—Rev. T.M. King—J. Bett[6]—W.H.G. Wrote on Authority. Walk with John G. & Constance. Saw Mr Palmer. Read Dr Elam—Butt's Speech on Repeal (1843)[7]—Symonds on Italy & Greece.[8]

31. Wed. [Savernake, Marlborough]

Ch. 10½ A.M. Wrote to Pears & Logan (deeds)—Rev. Mr Lawrence—Miss Gawne—Mrs de Ruvignés—Mr R.J. More—Mr Westgarth—Rev. Mr M'Callan.[9] Visited Mr Merewether's[10] family and place. Off at 2.30: reached Savernake[11] 4.45 seeing Devizes on the way: (St John's Ch). Read Hist. of Devizes[12]—Dr Elam, Winds of Doctrine. A large party & a most kind welcome. Conversation with Mr Kingsbury.[13]

Thurs. Feb. One. 1877.

Wrote to Mr Collings—Mr Stillman—Mr Knowles—Mr Jas Bayne—Rev. Morton Shaw. Finished, revised, and dispatched my paper on Authority. 3½-6. Ride in the beautiful Forest. The Duke's Vame is a most noble wreck. Acting in Evg. Read Klaczko, The Two Chancellors.[14] Acted charade in evg: very good. Conversation yesterday with Ld A[ilesbury], today with Lady Dunmore[,] the Newcastle daughters, so strangely circumstanced.

---

[1] George Henry Croxden Powell, secretary of liberal agents' association and of S.W. Lancashire liberal association.

[2] Walter Money, wrote on local history.

[3] Peter Sheridan, a home-ruler; this post card in *T.T.*, 6 February 1877, 5f.

[4] Seat of his nephew, J. E. Gladstone; see 23 Jan. 57.

[5] William Robinson Clark, d. 1912; church historian and vicar of Taunton; professor in Toronto from 1880.

[6] Probably John Bett, Scottish liberal activist.

[7] I. Butt, *Repeal of the union* (1843), defending the union against O'Connell.

[8] J. A. Symonds, *Sketches and studies in Italy and Greece* (1874).

[9] John Ferguson McCallan, vicar of New Basford, Nottingham.

[10] Of Bowden Hall, near Chippenham.

[11] Seat of marquis of Ailesbury, a strong supporter of Gladstone's position on Bulgaria; see Shannon, 129.

[12] *A history, military and municipal, of the ancient borough of the Devizes* (1857).

[13] Thomas Luck Kingsbury, 1822-99; chancellor of Salisbury from 1875.

[14] J. Klaczko, *The two chancellors: Prince Gortchakof and Prince Bismarck* (1876).

2. Fr.

Wrote to M. Gennadios—Rev Mr Teignmouth Shore—Ld Granville—Scotts—
W.H.G. Examining the old books with Mr Jackson & Mr Kingsbury. Saw the
Church, & the saving barn. Walk with Ld A. Read La Causa de' Slavi[1]—The two
Chancellors.

3. Sat.

Wrote to Cav. Landai—Rev. Mr Pritchard.[2] Luncheon with the Mayor of
Marlborough. Conversation with Mr [blank]. Saw the College. Addressed the
boys.[3] Then briefly the Foresters:[4] and home. Conversation with Mr Kingsbury.
Read The two Chancellors.

4. Sexa S.

St Kath. Ch. mg at 11 and H.C: aft $3\frac{1}{2}$. Walk with Ld A. & conversation on E.
question. Read The two Chancellors—Winds of Doctrine (finished)—Life of
King David.[5] Wrote to Dr Elam—Mr E. Chambers—Ed. Echo—Mr F. Gibbs.
Conversation with Mr Kingsbury.

5. M. [London]

Wrote to Mr Forster—Lady G. Fullerton—Mr Fox (of Devizes). Read Klatzko
(finished)—Lukis on Breton Remains[6]—Questione d'Oriente[7]—Tennyson. Off at
$12\frac{3}{4}$ from our most kind hosts. Saw Phillips X & another. Dined at Ld Granville's.
We sat to 12: about the possible course on Thursday.

6. Tu.

Wrote to Mr A. Makaroff[8]—Mad. Novikoff—Mr L. Drucker[9]—Mrs Malcolm—
Mrs Baxter—Mr Woodward—Mr Rowell—Mr Jas Moxon[10]—Mr Waylen—Sec. S.
Kens. Museum. Luncheon at 15 G.S. Dined with C.G. & the Hardy[11] party. Saw
Ld Granville—Do cum Ld Hartington—Sir R. Phillimore—Mr Hayward—Ld
Wolverton. Worked upon my chaotic arrear of papers.

[1] Untraced work sent by Luigi Landa of Naples, supporting the atrocities campaign; Hawn P.

[2] Probably Charles *Pritchard, 1808-93; wrote on astronomy and relation of science to religion;
see 14 Jan. 77n.

[3] On duties of public schools, with critical remarks about Eton; 'the constant influx of the
wealthy, and the tendency of wealth and large money indulgences among boys ... to corrupt and
lower the tone of the School'; T.T., 5 February 1877, 10a.

[4] i.e. the local branch of the Friendly Society.

[5] G. Smith, Life and reign of David, King of Israel (1867).

[6] W. C. Lukis, On the class of rude stone monuments (1875).

[7] See 13 Jan. 77.

[8] A well-known Russian name; not further identified.

[9] Louis Drucker, published Quelques documents relatifs aux emprunts Helléniques contractés à l'étranger
(1874).

[10] An Essex liberal, connected with Joseph Arch; Hawn P.

[11] See 4 Mar. 76n.

7. Wed.

Renewed struggle with Chaos. 12-2. Meeting at Granville's. Tone rather good. $2\frac{1}{2}$-$4\frac{1}{2}$. Working in H. of C. Library on Papers of 1853-4 &c. Read Stillman[1]—A. Arnold on Liquor & Licensing.[2] Dined at Ld Hartington's (Dev. H.) Saw Mr Forster—Ld Wolverton—Mr Adam—Lady Wenlock—Sir W. James—Ld F.C. & Mr Trevelyan. Saw Morton X & another.

8. Th.

Wrote to Mr C. Cowan—Sec. Exeter Reform Assocn.[3]—Rev. H.L. Greaves[4]— S.E.G.—Mr Rothery—H. Whitton[5]—F. Gray—C. Laflin[6]—W. Lane—W. Cousens.[7] Read Stillman on Turkish Provinces. Saw Mr Goldwin Smith—Mrs Anson—Sir W. James—W.H.G. H. of C. $4\frac{1}{2}$-$9\frac{1}{2}$. Dinner at Sir W. James's afterwards. In H. of C. the feeling was good, and the Session opened well. Northcote was not up to his new work. Hartington excellent. I spoke briefly to *fix* certain points & end the debate.[8]

9. Fr.

Wrote to S.T. Rawlings—A. Edwards[9]—J. Catherall—F.W. Evans[10]—E. Trimmer—Ld Acton B.P.—Admty (cover)—Dr Belcher[11]—Mr Boord. Long conversation with D. of Argyll. Also with Ld Granville. Saw Ld Houghton—Mr Moffatt—Mr Adam—Sir A. Panizzi (at length beginning to fail)—Ld Hartington—Mrs Th. Began the Blue Books.[12] Read Stillman. Dined at Sir C. Forsters. H. of C. $4\frac{1}{2}$-$5\frac{1}{2}$.[13]

10. Sat.

Wrote to Rev. S.E.G.—M. Gennadios—Mr Cooper—Mrs Th.—Rev. Dr Hornby. Saw Mr Cooper—Mr Strahan—Mr Knowles—Sir H. Elliot (a Turk indeed!)—Mrs Belcher—D. of Argyll. Dined with the Hardys. Read Wallace's Russia—Eastern Bluebooks. Tea at Argyll Lodge. We were grieved to see the Duchess on a decidedly lower level after the late attack.

[1] W. J. Stillman, *Herzegovina and the late uprising* (1877).

[2] Sir R. A. Arnold, *English drunkenness and Swedish licensing* (1877).

[3] Letter untraced.

[4] Henry Ley Greaves, 1846-99; episcopalian priest at Inverness cathedral, later in Aberdeenshire.

[5] Henry Whitten of Newcastle corresponded on Bulgaria; Hawn P.

[6] Christopher Laflin of Lower Norwood, wrote in admiration; Hawn P.

[7] Perhaps William Henry Cousins, 1833-1917; registrar of joint-stock companies 1871-83; secretary to Inland Revenue from 1883.

[8] *H* 232. 113. Northcote succeeded Disraeli as Leader of the Commons.

[9] Arthur Edwards; on charitable works; Hawn P.

[10] Perhaps the letter on disestablishment in *T.T.*, 13 February 1877, 5f.

[11] Thomas Waugh Belcher, 1831-1910; vicar of Stoke Newington 1871-86; published on science and religion; m. 1860 Mary M. Bunting.

[12] *PP* 1877 xc and xci, both published on 8 February.

[13] Prisons Bill; *H* 232. 132.

11. *Quinqua S.*

Parish Ch. mg and Chapel Royal aft. Corrected proofs of Article on Authority. Read Blue Book—Mozley on O.T.[1]—Rothe, Leben und Briefe.[2] Saw Ld Cardwell.

12. *M.*

Wrote to Mr Knowles BP.—Messrs T. & B. Worked on Blue Books. Read Gardner's Montenegro.[3] Saw Mr Wood (Hon)—Sir Wm James—Mr Ouvry. Saw Gerald [R]. H of C. 4-6$\frac{3}{4}$ (Irish S. Closing).[4]

13. *Tu.*

Wrote to Mr R. Cooke—Mr Marshall. Radcliffe [Trustees] Meeting 12-1. Hunterian Museum 3-4 for Sir J. Paget's Oration.[5] Saw Duke of Argyll—Dr Parker—Mr Knowles—Ld Granville—Mr Morley—Sir W. Harcourt—Sir Jas Paget—Ld Gilford.[6] Dined at Hunterian Museum, & proposed the health of Sir James Paget. Saw Mrs Th. X. Much to think & say thereon. Worked on Blue Books.

14. *Wed. (Ash)*

All Souls at 11 A.M. Wrote to Rev. N. Woodard—Dean Church[7]—Mr J. Catherall—Vestry Clerk Plumst.—H.N. Cox—Mr Rylett[8]—R. Watkin—J.F. Lloyd. Mrs Th.—Mrs Gerald—Mr [blank.] Saw Ld Hartington—Ld Selborne—Mr Pym[9]—Ld Granville. Worked on Blue Books much. Read Sir G. Wilkinson.[10] Further corrected Art. on Authority.

15. *Th.*

Wrote to Mrs Th.—Mr Denton—Mr Knowles BP. Meeting at Ld Granville's 2.30. H of C. 4-5$\frac{1}{2}$.[11] Dined with the Wests. Worked hard on Blue Books. Read B. Brunswick [*sic*].[12] Saw Plumstead Deputation[13]—Mr Murray.

16. *Fr.*

Wrote to Messrs Pears BP. Worked much on Blue Books. Examined Treaty papers &c. Saw Ld Granville—Ld Shaftesbury—Ld F. Cavendish—and [blank.]

[1] See 21 Jan. 77.

[2] Probably the life of Richard Rothe by E. Achelis (1869).

[3] J. D. Gardner, *The Ionian Islands in relation to Greece, with suggestions for advancing our trade with the Turkish countries of the Adriatic and the Danube* (1859).

[4] *H* 232. 183.   [5] *T.T.*, 14 February 1877, 11a.

[6] Richard James Meade, 1832-1907; styled Lord Gilford; sailor; Admiralty Lord 1874-80; 4th earl of Clanwilliam 1879.

[7] Richard William *Church, 1815-90; dean of St Paul's from 1871; active in the atrocities campaign. See 16, 22 Aug. 71.   [8] See 30 Mar. 77.

[9] Probably Francis Pym, 1849-1927, of Hasells Hall, Bedfordshire.

[10] Sir J. G. Wilkinson, *Dalmatia and Montenegro*, 2v. (1848).

[11] Questioned Bourke on Bulgaria Blue Book; *H* 232. 391.

[12] B. Brunswik, *La verité sur Midhat Pacha* (1877).   [13] See 22 Mar. 77.

Saw one [R]. H of C. 4¼-8 and 10¼-1. Spoke on the Treaties: & again in answer
to Chaplin: amid much enthusiasm but I might have done better.[1]

17. Sat.

Wrote to Mr Flanedy—Ld Stratford de Redcliffe—Sec. Cape & Natal Dinner[2]—
M. Gennadios (& draft)—Mr Middleton[3]—R.H. Elliot[4]—C.T. Roberts—W.J.
Godwin—M. Hynes—A. Strahan—Mr Wieler. Worked on Blue Books. Twelve
to dinner. Saw Ld Granville—Sir R. Phillimore—Dr W. Phillimore—Ld Carlingford & Lady W[aldegrave]—Dr A. Clarke.

18. 1 S. Lent.

Chapel Royal 10 A.M. (& H.C.). 5½ aftn. Wrote to Chancr of Exchequer—Hon
R. Bourke—Mr T. Fifoot—Rev. R.P. Douglas—Mr Askew—Mr E. Sturge—Ld
Granville. Read Mozley O.T. Lectures—Ch. Quart. on Stanley &c.—Mill, Otto-
mans in Europe.[5] Saw German Ambassador—Ld Granville (bis)—Mr E.
Hamilton. Dined with the Hardys.

19. M.

Wrote to Mr Herries—Mr Llewellyn—M. Gennadios—Rev. Mr Elkington[6]—Mrs
Th.—Mr Duckworth—Mr R. Greave. Saw Ld Granville—Mr Lefevre—Mr Hanb.
Tracy—Sir A. Panizzi—Mr Ouvry *cum* Mr Rickards, on the Newcastle distresses.
Finished the Blue Books. Read Wilkinson's Montenegro.

20. Tu.

Wrote to Mr Ellaby—Glasgow Deputies (suspended)[7]—Rev. C. Neville—Ed. D.
News[8]—Mr Herries (B.I.R.). Dined at Mr Bryce's. Saw Glasgow Deputies—M.
Gennadios 3-4—Mr Adam—Mr Wallace—Professor Stubbs—Mr Bourke—Dr
Sandwith—Mr Bryce—Mr Goldwin Smith.[9] H. of C. & H. of L. 4¼-7¼. Argyll
made a noble-hearted speech to a dead House.[10] Read N.A. Rev. on E. Ques-
tion—Speeches of Gk Foreign Minr.

---

[1] He introduced a debate on Derby's despatch to Elliot of 5 September 1876, defended his govt.'s
handling of the Gortchakov initiative on the Black Sea clauses in 1871, and replied to Henry
*Chaplin's charge that he had spoken at public meetings 'against his opponents, especially at times
when he knew they could not be there to repel them [the accusations]'; *H* 232. 470, 551.

[2] Untraced; probably declining to attend.

[3] Secretary of the Plumstead Common protection league; *T.T.*, 23 February 1877, 5f.

[4] Possibly Robert Henry Elliot, Mysore planter, wrote *Our Indian difficulties* (1874).

[5] John Mill, M.D., *The Ottomans in Europe; with the Secret Societies maps* (1876); notes on it in Add
MS 44792, f. 179.

[6] Joseph James Elkington, chaplain of the House of Mercy for rescue cases in Greek Street, Soho.

[7] See 10 Apr. 77.

[8] Not found published.

[9] Also John Richard *Green, 1837-83, historian and liberal; see Morley, ii. 561 for Green's
description.

[10] *H* 232. 637; Westminster and Bath also defended the campaign; Beaconsfield replied at length.

21. Wed.

Wrote to Hon C.L. Wood—Mr A.D. Shiroff[1]—Ed. Eton Coll Chron.[2]—Mr Grogan—Mr Askew—Mr Meek. Dined at Mr Milbanks. Saw Mr Tennyson—Sir G. Dasent—Mr Wortley—Mr Forster. Meeting at Granville's 12-2. Wrote out report of my short Speech at Surgeon's Hall. Read Bluntschli: & translated.[3] Also Pref. to Rambaud.[4] Began tidying.

22. Th.

Wrote to Ld Hartington—Mr Salisbury—Rev. W. Arthur—Mr M.J. Davies.[5] Saw Bp of Ely—Ld Wolverton—Mr Farrar (Clerk)—Mr Boord—Rev. T. Shore. H. of C. $4\frac{1}{2}$-$6\frac{1}{2}$.[6] Spent mg & aft chiefly in arranging letters, books & papers. This sounds dull: but it is always rather pleasant to see order arising out of Chaos. Read violent Tract on Priesthood &c.[7]—Wilkinson Dalm. Montenegro—Morris's Poems.[8] Dined at Ld Blantyre's. We had rather an animated conversation after dinner on Eastern matters. Sir H. Elliot & Lord B. about equally Turkish.

23. Fr.

Wrote to Mr Vickers—W.H. Mitchell—D.R. Pigott—T.H.S. Lycett—E.O. Masters—Rev. Mr Mossman—Rev. A.E. Brown[9]—Mr Kimber & Mr Middleton—R. Walker—G. Harris—A. Davidson—L. Morris—R.C. Healy—Ed. of Times.[10] H of C. 4-$5\frac{3}{4}$ P.M: & after dinner. Saw Mr Palgrave—Mr Boord—Duke of Argyll—Mr Cowen—Mr Courtney MP.—Dined at Sir W. James's: tea 5 PM with Lady Hardy. Saw Mrs Hume [R?]. Read Von Hammer[11]—Eton (by a Boy)[12]—Arthur on Vaticanism[13] and [blank.]

24. Sat. St Matth.

Wrote to Ed. Examiner[14]—Ed. Daily News[15]—G. Farquhar—E. Davis—Miss Cochrane—Mr Mackenzie—Rev. J. Macintosh[16]—Dr Wyckoff—Baron Tauchnitz

[1] An Indian; had asked for a spectator's seat in the Commons; Hawn P.

[2] Not published; probably commenting privately on its leader of 20 February criticizing his remarks at Marlborough (see 3 Feb. 77n.). Several later correspondents to the *Chronicle* complained at diarist's want of response to the leader.

[3] J. C. Bluntschli, 'Das Recht der Europäischen Intervention in der Türkei', *Die Gegenwart* (9 December 1876); quoted in 'Lessons in massacre'.   [4] A. N. Rambaud, *Français et Russes* (1877).

[5] Of Marlborough college, for an autograph; Hawn P.

[6] Put a question on Turkish consuls; *H* 232. 825.

[7] Perhaps *Human priesthood and clergy unknown to Christianity*, ed. by 'S.H.' (1860).

[8] Lewis Morris had sent his *Songs of two worlds* (1871); Add MS 44453, f. 128.

[9] Abner Edmund Brown, d. 1897; curate of Wooton 1871-82, of Wadenhoe 1882-91; Hawn P.

[10] Denying Beaconsfield's charge that he had described the failure of the conference at Constantinople to consider Christian subjects in Turkey as 'an accident'; *T.T.*, 24 February 1877, 8b, and Ramm II, i. 30.

[11] J. von Hammer-Purgstall, *Geschichte des Osmanischen Reiches*, 10v. (1827-35).

[12] [G. N. Bankes], *A day of my life ... By an Eton boy* (1877).

[13] W. Arthur, *The Pope, the Kings and the people*, 2v. (1877).

[14] Perhaps on its leader on his speech of 16 February; *Examiner*, 24 February 1877, 227.

[15] Sending an address 'from several Bulgarians' for publication; Add MS 44453, f. 132.

[16] Joseph Macintosh, rector of Llanerfyl, Welshpool.

—Mr E.J. Bryce B.P.[1]—Ld Granville—W.T. Rush—J. Hart—C. Napier—G.D. Ham[2]—B. of Customs—Mr Hibbert. Corrected the Press of my Lecture at Hawarden. 12 to dinner. Saw Ld E. Fitzmaurice—Gen. Cesnola. Tea at Lady Stanley's. Read Calvert on Educn Act[3]—A day at Eton—Mill!! on Ottomans.[4]

25. 2 S. Lent.

Ch. Royal mg & evg. Wrote to Mr Newton Smith.[5] Saw Ld Dudley—Sir W. Farquhar. Dined with the Wortleys. Read Mozley on O.T.—Rothe Leben und briefe[6]—Pamphlets of Wagner[7]—and divers others.

26. M.

Wrote to Chr of Exchr—Duke of Westmr—Ld Granville—Mr Langstredt—Rev. Mr Taylor—Rev. W.H. Child[8]—Mr Hammond—Mr Hamilton—Rev. Mr Collingwood[9]—Mr Schuyler[10]—Mr Lacey[11]—Mr Dawson—Mr Middleton—Sir H. Elliot & copy[12]—Rev. Withrow BP.[13] Luncheon at 15 G.S. Saw Ld Granville cum Ld Hn[14]—Mr Childers—Mr Lowe—Mr Goschen. Began, tentatively, "Who are the criminals?"[15] Read 'A day at Eton'—Hansard. H of C. $4\frac{1}{4}$-$6\frac{3}{4}$.[16]

27. Tu.

Wrote to Mrs Th.—Rob. Gladstone—Watsons—Mr Denbigh—Mr Edwards—Rev. M. M'Coll—Rev. W. Arthur—Sir H. Elliot—Mr Macquoid[17]—Hon R. Bourke. H. of C. $4\frac{1}{2}$-6 and in evg. Saw Mr Burt M.P. & Deputn[18]—Mr Hugessen—Scotts. Saw one [R]. Worked on Bulgarian Outrages. Read La Honte de l'Europe.[19] Went with H. to Exhibn of Old Masters.

[1] Name scrawled.
[2] George D. Ham, ed. Ham's Revenue and Mercantile Year-Book (1877).
[3] F. Calvert, Wrongs and remedies; or the wrongs of the elementary education acts (1877).
[4] See 18 Feb. 77.
[5] Rev. Joseph Newton Smith, curate in Ipswich; on disestablishment; draft at Add MS 44453, f. 137.
[6] See 11 Feb. 77.
[7] A. D. Wagner, Christ or Caesar?, 2v. (1874-7).
[8] William Humphry Child, curate in Barrow-in-Furness.
[9] Probably Charles Edward Stuart Collingwood, 1831-98; rector of Southwick from 1863; published on contagious diseases.
[10] Eugene Schuyler, American consul in Bulgaria, whose report was a determining factor in the development of the campaign in August-September 1876; see Shannon, 77-8 and 22 Jan. 77.
[11] Perhaps Thomas Alexander Lacey, curate in Wakefield.
[12] Acerbic exchanges on Turkey; this and letter of 28 February in T.T., 2 March 1877, 10b.
[13] A nonconformist.
[14] On whether to have a motion on Bulgaria; see Ramm II, i. 31.
[15] Published as 'Lessons in Massacre; or, the conduct of the Turkish government in and about Bulgaria since May, 1876, chiefly from the papers presented by command' (1877); Add MS 44696, f. 66. The pamphlet sold comparatively poorly, at about 7,000 copies.
[16] Questioned Bourke on Bulgaria; H 232. 1022.
[17] J. R. Macquoid of Chelsea wrote criticizing diarist's speech at Marlborough college; Hawn P.
[18] Thomas *Burt, 1837-1922; miner and liberal M.P. Morpeth 1874-1918; promoted Employers' Liability reforms; sec. to board of trade 1892-5.
[19] Untraced.

28. Wed.

Wrote to Mr [A.] Cohen—Rev. A. Bird—Rev. E.C. Lowe—Mary G.—Sir A. Slade[1]—Rev Dr Burgess—Dr Abrath[2]—Mr Puseley—Wms & Norgate—Mr Vickers BP.—Mr Woodfin BP.—Mr Hudson—Sir H. Elliot (& copy).[3] Attended Dr Sandwith's Lecture at G[rosvenor] House & spoke there.[4] Dined at the Speaker's. Saw Ld Hartington—Mr Forster—Persian Ambassr—Master of the Rolls—Mr P. Ralli MP—Sir W. Harcourt—Mrs Malcolm—Mr Knowles.[5] Worked on Bulgaria. Read a Day at Eton. Saw one—& a fire in Marg. Street as it began.

Thurs. March One. 1877.

Wrote to Baron Tauchnitz—Ed. Daily News—Ed. Times[6]—Mrs Mochler (2)—Hon C.L. Wood—Rev. B. Snow[7]—F.J. Dickinson—J. Latouche—Mr Paradise[8]—Mr Puseley—Mr Zerreh—Mr Pike—Mr Downes. Worked on Bulgaria: & chose my title.[9] Saw Mr Playfair—Sir Jas. Ramsay[10]—Sir Thos. Acland—Mr Mundella. Read Warburton's Poems[11]—Land Tenure in the Laws.[12]

2. Fr.

Wrote to Ld Granville—Made Novikoff—Mr Warburton—W.A. Prince[13]—J.P. Drake—Watsons (B.P.). H of C. 4½-5½.[14] Worked on Blue Books &c for Bulgaria. Saw Mr Mundella—Lord Hatherley—Baroness Lionel de R. Read 19th Cent. on Vatican Council.[15]

3. Sat.

Wrote to Mr Higham—Mr Lawrence—Mr Savill?—Mr Huggins. Saw Mr MacColl—D. of Argyll—M. Raffalovich.[16] Worked on Bulgaria. Tea at Lady Egerton's. Attended the morning performance at Surrey Theatre.[17] Twelve to dinner. Read Hugessen on Cromwell.[18]

[1] Sir Alfred Frederick Adolphus Slade, 1834-90; 3rd bart. 1863; soldier; receiver-general of inland revenue from 1875.

[2] Gustav Adolph Abrath, physician and author in Sunderland.

[3] See 26 Feb. 77n.

[4] No account found.

[5] Knowles had broken with Strahan after a rumbling row, Strahan attempting to hold his existing contributors, including Gladstone, for the *Contemporary*, Knowles to win them over for his new *Nineteenth Century*; see Add MS 44453, ff. 1-30 and P. Metcalf, *James Knowles* (1980), 270ff.

[6] Publication of exchange with Elliot; see 26 Mar. 77n.

[7] Benjamin Snow, rector of Burton-Pedwardine.

[8] Perhaps John Paradice, London bookbinder.

[9] See 26 Feb. 77n.

[10] Sir James Henry Ramsay, 1832-1925; 10th bart. 1871; a whig.

[11] R. E. E. Warburton, *Poems, epigrams and sonnets* (1877).

[12] *Systems of land tenure in various countries* (1876 ed.), by E. de Laveleye and others.

[13] William Alfred Prince of Jackson and Prince, London solicitors.

[14] Questions; *H* 232. 1250.

[15] By Manning in *Nineteenth Century* i. 122 (March 1877).

[16] Corresponded in French on Bulgaria; Hawn P.

[17] Presumably an extra performance of 'Jack and Jill', its Christmas pantomime.

[18] E. H. K. Hugessen, 'The life, times and character of Oliver Cromwell' (1877).

4. 3 S. Lent.

Chapel Royal 10 A.M. & 5½ P.M. Wrote to Mr A. Hayward—Mr Harrison—Mr Alexander—Mr De Lisle—Rev G. Williams. Saw Sir R. Phillimore—Lord Lyttelton. Read Mozley's Lectures[1]—Bernard, Bampton lect.[2]—Laveleye, Double Programme[3]—Keble on Court of Appeal[4]—and sundries. Dined with the Phillimores.

5. M.

Wrote to Editor of Times[5]—Mr Ellis (BP)—Mr Sandell[6] (BP)—Mr Chesson—Mr Bagge (BP)—Dr Abrath—Mr V. Fitzgerald. Worked much on Bulgaria. Saw Mrs Hetherington—Mr Alexander—Lord De Tabley—Rev. S.E.G. Read Life of Frampton[7]—Foreign Church Chronicle[8]—Day at Eton (finished).

6. Tu.

Wrote to Coates & Howys—Mr Raffalovich—L. Jackson—Col. Le Champion[9]—Mr G. Harris—Ld Granville—E. Talbot—T.C. Fyfe—E. Page—Mr Bourke. H of C. 4½-6.[10] Dined with Sir D. Marjoribanks. Worked much on Bulgaria. Saw Mr Murray[11]—Ld Hartington. Read Les Arméniens de Turquie.[12]

7. Wed.

Wrote to Messrs Clowes—The Ld Chamberlain—Rev. Dr Parker—Rev. Dr E.C. Lowe—Mr Sherlock—Mr Knowles—Mr Macmillan. Worked hard on Bulgaria, & fought against influenza. Read Dunn on Russia in Poland.[13] Dined at Mr Rathbone's: much conversation: Mr G. Smith, Mr H. Smith, Ld E. Fitzmaurice, Mr Stuart, Sir G. Young,[14] & others. Speaker's Levee afterwards. May Hardy[15] alas taken alarmingly ill.

---

[1] See 27 Jan. 77.

[2] T. D. Bernard, *The progress of doctrine in the New Testament* (1864).

[3] E. de Laveleye, 'The provincial and communal institutions of Belgium and Holland' in *Cobden Club Essays. Local government and taxation* (1875); on 'the double impress'.

[4] J. Keble, *Difficulties in the relations between Church and State* (1877).

[5] Dispute on Albanian affairs with Sir P. Colquhoun, judge in Corfu during diarist's commissionership (see 10 Jan. 59); *T.T.*, 5 and 6 March 1877, 6d, 8d and Ramm II, i. 33n.

[6] Perhaps R. B. Sandell, London paper merchant.

[7] *The life of R. Frampton, Bishop of Gloucester*, ed. T. S. Evans (1876).

[8] *Foreign Church Chronicle*, i (March 1877); perhaps 'The Pope and the Turks'.

[9] Lt. col. H. M. Le Champion of the Grove, Salop.

[10] Questions; details of Gordon's appt. to the Sudan; *H* 232. 1451.

[11] To arrange the advertisement next day of 'Lessons in Massacre'; see Ramm II, i. 33.

[12] Perhaps earlier version of *Les Arméniens en Turquie* (1880).

[13] Untraced work by Archibald J. Dunn. See 8 Mar. 77n.

[14] Sir George Young, 1837-1930; 3rd bart. 1848; author; served on commissions, including on Irish land.

[15] i.e. Lucy Marion Hardy; see 4 Mar. 76n.

8. Th.

Wrote to Ed. D. News[1]—General Tchernaieff.[2] Saw Mr Murray. Read [blank] on the Ottomans.[3] Worked much on Bulg. MS & correcting the press: influenza still presses.

9. Fr.

Wrote to Mr Middleton—Mr Castledyne[4]—Rev Dr Parker—Mr V. Fitzgerald—Messrs Clowes—Mr Simms—Mr Marvin[5]—Mr Raleigh—Mr Crake.[6] Worked much on Bulgaria: sent off the last copy to printer. Saw Mr Murray. Influenza mending, I dined with the Ths, Lds Bathurst & Redesdale: old fashioned talk: & Mrs Bishop,[7] with now a German name extra ably sang, & well. Read Dunn on Ottomans. H of C. $4\frac{1}{2}$-$5\frac{1}{2}$.[8] May thank God a little better.

10. Sat. [High Elms, Down, Kent]

Wrote to Rev. Mr Thirlwall[9]—Mr Murray—Mr Ouvry—Mr Holland—Mr Alexander—Mr Medlicot[10]—Mr Wellwood—Mrs Mochler. Finished correcting: & so closed a heavy job, which my influenza has made rather exhausting. We went off at 5 to Sir John Lubbocks: a notable party & much interesting conversation. I cannot help liking Mr J. Morley.[11] Read Tracts.

11. 4 S.L.

Ch mg & (part) aft. Called on & saw Mr Darwin,[12] whose appearance is pleasing and remarkable. Wrote to Mr Murray—and C.G. May better: thank God. Conversation with Mr Morley, Prof. [T. H.] Huxley & others. Read Tracts by [Thomas] Scott of Norwood—Mr Fowle[13]—Mr Coxhead[14]—and others.

12. M. [London]

At eight went out & cut an oak. We returned to town $11\frac{1}{4}$-$12\frac{1}{2}$. May again a little better. Saw Lady H.—Mr Murray—Sir A. Panizzi—Sir Jas Paget. Marlborough

[1] On his correspondence in 1876 with Selim Effendi; Add MS 44453, f. 178.

[2] Mikhail Gregorovich Tchernaiev, 1828-98; pan-Slavist; commanded the defeated Serbian army 1876; visited London as friend of Madame Novikov.

[3] A. J. Dunn, *The rise and decay of the rule of Islam* (1877).

[4] Probably Theodore Castledine of Regent's Park.   [5] See 31 Oct. 77?

[6] Augustine David *Crake, 1836-90; chaplain of Bloxham 1865-78; vicar of Havenstreet 1879-85; devotional writer.

[7] Lady Ann *Bishop, 1814-84, well-known soprano; she m. 1832 Sir H. R. *Bishop, 1858 M. Schultz.   [8] Questions; *H* 232. 1650.

[9] Thomas James Thirlwall, d. 1900; vicar of Nantmel from 1858.

[10] Perhaps Henry Edmonstone Medlicott, J.P., of Devizes.

[11] His first meeting with his biographer, John *Morley, 1838-1923; ed. positivistic *Fortnightly Review*, 1867-82, *Pall Mall Gazette*, 1880-3; liberal M.P. Newcastle 1883-95; chief secretary for Ireland 1886, 1892-5. Gladstone's letter to his wife next day (Bassett, 221) describes him as 'Mr Morley (Fortnightly Review)'.

[12] Charles Robert *Darwin, 1809-82; biologist. Morley's description of this weekend (Morley, ii. 562) curiously notes that Gladstone 'makes no mention of his afternoon call' on Darwin, though Morley coyly quotes the diary reference to himself without attributing a name.

[13] Probably T. W. Fowle, *An essay on the right translation of* αἰών (1877).

[14] J. J. Coxhead, 'Science the handmaid of religion' (1877).

House in evg. I saw Musurus Pacha: we had a few kind but awkward words. Saw Münster, *mum*: Sydney. At the Levee, the Queen smiled: but had not a word. Arriving at 2 instead of 3, I went round the pictures. Read Dunn on Ottomans— Sir G. Campbell[1]—D of Wn Correspce.[2] Wrote to Messrs Clowes—Mr Houndle—Dr Glover—Mr R. Cooke—Mrs Barrett.

13. Tuesday.

Wrote to Musurus Pacha—Rev. Mr Mossman—Rev. Mr Thirlwall—Ld Dudley— Mr Watherston—Mr Woodcock—Mr Birt [*sic*] M.P. Luncheon at 15 G.S. Saw Mr Hayward—Mr Knowles—Mr Bright.—H of C. $4\frac{1}{2}$-$6\frac{1}{2}$.[3] Read Miss Martineau Autobiogr.[4]—Geffken Ch & St.[5]—Campbell on the Eastern Question.

14. Wed.

Wrote to Mr Ouvry—Mr Lavin—Mr Rentoul—Col D.M. House[6]—Mr Shere—Mr Burnie—Mr Kennedy—Hon R. Stewart[7]—Mr Lewis—Mr Mullan—Mr Knight Watson. Saw Miss Irby[8]—Hon. F. Leveson—Ld De Tabley—Mr Kimber *cum* Mr Middleton—Ld Blachford—Mr Cooke (Murray)—Read Geffken—M. Rolins Jacquemin (Eastern Qu.)[9]—Shea on Hamilton.[10]

15. Th.

Wrote to Consul Schuyler (& B.P.)—Mr Shea (BP)—Mr T. Ogilvy—Mr Lambert, Reid, Macintosh, Bruce Stuart, Rev. Grundy,[11] Rev. Ince, Prof. Cav. L. Landi BP. Conversation on Tu. with H. & H. on causes of unbelief: today with S.E.G. on the position & prospects of the Church. Read Miss Irby on Bosnia[12]—Porter's Lecture—Gopdchevidch [*sic*] on Montenegro[13]—Dined at Ld Halifax's. Saw Ld OHagan—Sir C. Trevelyan. Wrote a proposed Preface for reprint of tract on Supremacy.[14] Saw Phillips: a character of some real interest as well as weakness [R].

[1] Sir G. Campbell, 'The races, religions, and institutions of Turkey', *Eastern Question Association Papers*, 4 (1877).

[2] *The Eastern Question. Extracted from the correspondence of... Wellington* (1877).

[3] Chamberlain's temperance deb.; *H* 232. 1861.

[4] *Harriet Martineau's Autobiography. With memorials by M. W. Chapman*, 3v. (1877).

[5] F. H. Geffcken, *Church and State; their relations historically developed*, 2v. (1876).

[6] Probably D. E. Hoste, colonel in Royal Artillery.

[7] Randolph Henry Stewart, 1836-1920; soldier; 11th earl of Galloway 1901.

[8] Adeline Irby, traveller and champion of Balkan Christians; her companion, Georgiana Mary Muir Mackenzie, wife of Sir C. Sebright, had d. 1874. See 7 Apr. 77.

[9] See 3 Nov. 76.

[10] G. Shea, *Alexander Hamilton; an historical study* (1877).

[11] Perhaps George Docker Grundy, vicar of Hey, Manchester.

[12] See 14 Dec. 76n.

[13] S. Gopčević, *Montenegro und die Montenegriner* (1877), of which Gladstone wrote a short anon. notice for the *Church Quarterly Review* (unpublished, Add MS 44696, f. 153) and which he used for his article, see 14 Apr. 77.

[14] Published as 'The Royal Supremacy; as it is defined by reason, history and the constitution. Being the substance of a letter published in 1850. . . . With a preface to the present edition' (1877); see 28 Apr. 50.

[In top right hand corner of inside back cover, which is ruled off:—]

Spectacles   .   Gen. Cesnola
               $\overline{36}$ Ilsington Villa
                                           Albion Road
May 11.2m.   S. Hampstead.

[*VOLUME XXXII.*]

[The inside front cover contains:—]

Private. No 32.

March 16. 1877–Dec. 31. 1878.

ὦ γῆς ὄχημα, κἀπὶ γῆς ἔχων ἕδραν,
ὅστις ποτ᾽ εἶ σύ, δυστόπαστος εἰδέναι,
Ζεὺς, εἴτ᾽ ἀνάγκη φείσεος, εἴτε νοῦς βροτῶν,
προσηυξάμην σε· πάντα γὰρ δι᾽ ἀψοφου
βαίνων κελεύθου κατὰ δίκην τὰ θνητ᾽ ἄγεις[1]
Eurip. Troades. 879
884.

[The Recto of the flyleaf has, in the middle of the page:]

Truth, crushed to Earth, will raise again,
Th'eternal years of God are hers;
But error, wounded, writhes in pain,
And dies amid her worshippers.

in Echo Au. 22. 78.[2]

[There is also some writing in pencil, much erased, the following being legible:—]

Mr Kenley 3 Y. Road

Miss M. Watson
13 Buckm Terrace
Glasgow

Stanley 168 Ont Road
Tondini   14 Ely Place

16 L sqre
West 28th dine

Ld N. 29th 4 PM
Murray 28th 5 PM

[1] 'Zeus, You, who sustain this earth, and have your seat upon it, whoever you are, knowledge hard to guess at, Zeus, whether you are face of nature or intelligence of man, I pray to you: for you, going on a noiseless path, conduct all human affairs in justice.'

[2] Improvement on the poem, 'Darwinism and dogma' in *The Echo*, 28 August 1878, 2f.

Fr. Mch 16.

Wrote to Mr Goschen—Mr Harris—Mr Reade—Mr Watt—Rev Mr Thomas—Mr Edwards. Kept my bed till one. Read Gopdchevidch, Montenegro—Bianconi on Turkey.[1] Saw Sir R. Phillimore—Mr Bright—Sir G. Campbell—Mr Palmer—Mr Randolph Stewart—Mr Cotes[2] MP. Dined with Lady L. Cotes.

17. Sat.

Wrote to Ld Granville—Mr Stillman—J.H. Bell—S. Long—Mr Mundella—Mr Cottingham—Mr Jacquemyns BP. Saw Mr Barker, & Mr Hignett, on the Aston Hall and other Mining Leases at Hawarden. Saw Mr R. Watt—W.H.G.—Mr Jas Wortley—Lord Bath—Mr C. Howard—Miss Irby—Lady Cork. Wrote a notice of Gopčovič for Ch. Quarterly.[3] Fourteen to dinner. Read Gopčovič and [blank] on Russia in Poland.

18. 5 S. Lent.

St Ann's mg and H.C. with Herbert before his voyage. Ch. Royal 5.30 PM. Wrote to Ld Hartington—Rev. T.W. Perry—Hon. C.L. Wood—Canon Ashwell—Mr Dodgson New Coll[4]—Mrs Bennett. Dined with the Godleys: much conversation on Eastern question. Saw Lennox. Read Mozley on O.T.—Many Tracts. Saw Mr Forster on Sir H. Elliot's return: & told him I must move if no one else did.[5]

19. M.

Wrote to Miss Mundella[6]—Mr Morson—T. Taylor[7]—A.T. Rees[8]—J.H.R. Todd[9]—C.M. Percy[10]—J. Morton—H.G. Heald—W. Lovell—W. Benning—Rev. Dr R. Palmer—Rev. R.M. Grier—Rev. W. Temple—Capt. Chapman[11]—M. Léon Jolivart[12]—Mr Templeton—Mrs Carlile—W. Bristow—Ed. Daily News.[13] 3-4¼. Conclave at Granville's on the Elliot matter. I held to my point. It was resolved to act if his return were announced. Saw Ld F. Cavendish—Mr Tennyson—Mr Bright—Mr Forster—Sir C. Lampson. Worked on papers: read divers Tracts.

[1] F. Bianconi, *La question d'Orient dévoilée, ou la verité sur la Turquie* (1876).

[2] Charles Cecil Cotes, d. 1898, s. of Lady L. Cotes (see 4 July 76); liberal M.P. Shrewsbury 1874-85; minor office 1880.

[3] See 15 Mar. 77n.

[4] Probably Edward Spencer Dodgson, undergraduate at New College, Oxford; business untraced; or Francis Vivian Dodgson, who matriculated there October 1877.

[5] Elliot was replaced at Constantinople, but by A. H. Layard, a liberal turkophil, on 31 March; see Ramm, i. 34n.

[6] M. T. Mundella, A.J.'s daughter and assistant.

[7] Of Burney reform club; *T.T.*, 23 March 1877, 6b.

[8] Perhaps Alan Rees, corresponded on Homer later in 1877; Hawn P.

[9] Perhaps John Miles Rogers Todd, solicitor.

[10] Probably Cornelius McLeod Percy, wrote on collieries.

[11] Probably J. C. Chapman, journalist; letters in 1878 in Add MS 44457, f. 198.

[12] French lawyer and novelist.

[13] On Elliot; see Add MS 44453, f. 213.

Also the supposed Ignatieff letters.[1] Eight to dinner. To Mr Tennyson's afterwards. He seems inclined to touch Montenegro.[2]

20. Tu.

Wrote to Sig. Mocenigo[3]—G. Young—Mr Bowser—Mr Brodhurst—Ld Coleridge. At 12.15 bid farewell to Stephy, who goes to the Cape for his health, and to Herbert who most lovingly accompanies him. H of C. $4\frac{1}{4}$-$5\frac{1}{2}$.[4] Saw Sir A. Panizzi—Mr Knowles—Ld Dudley—The French Ambassador—Sig. de Martino—Mr Murray—Mrs Meynell Ingram. Dined at Mr Beaumont's. Saw one. Read Von Hammer[5]—Chesson on Slavery[6]—The series of ambiguous letters.

21. Wed.

Wrote to S.E.G. & H.J.G.—Mr Drawbridge—Mr Mortlock—M. Zanckow—Rev. Dr Parker—Mr G. Wilson—Mr Ouvry—Mr Adam—Mr Murray—Pears & Logan BP. Dined at Ld Northbrooks. Dudley House concert after. Saw General Ignatieff at home 1-1.45 and again in evening. I cannot here record my impressions. Saw Count Schouvaloff—Lord Rosebery—Sir Thos Wade.[7] Read Paskewitch Campaign[8]—Palmerston's opinions.[9]

Memorandum written in anticipation of General Ignatieff, but not read to him.[10]

J'ai mes opinions et mes idées—des opinions sans valeur et des idées sans moyens d'exécution.

Il n-y-a rien de sécret—tout est pour la place.

Quant au peuple Anglais—je ne parle pas du Gouvernement, ni du Parlement, ni des riches, ni de l'armée, ni de la plupart de la presse metropolitaine—mais quant au peuple, je suis fermement d'avis qu'il s'est décidé, sur la question Orientale, dans le sens Chrétien. Son coeur et son esprit se sont également revoltés contre les crimes et la barbarie de la Porte et de ses Mahometains.

Mais, c'est seulement d'une façon tardive que la nation peut influer, dans une question de pareille nature, sur l'opinion et l'action du Parlement. C'est par le moyen des elections locales qui ont lieu de temps en temps. On peut dire avec certitude que les elections locales, depuis un sémestre, portent l'empreinte du sentiment ci-dessus avéré.

La plupart du parti Tory, je n'en doute, soutiendra même à l'outrance, la politique du Ministere, soit elle blanche, soit elle noire, soit elle de quelqu'autre teint. Je ne m'y fie

---

[1] Of Count Nikolai Pavlovich Ignatiev, 1832-1908, Russian minister at Constantinople 1864-78; on a mission to London; collaborated secretly with Derby; see Seton-Watson, 160ff.

[2] Tennyson's 'Montenegro', written in March, was published together with Gladstone's article (see 14 Apr. 77) in the *Nineteenth Century*, i. 539 (May 1877). His son recalled 'he always put [it] first among his sonnets'; see *Alfred Lord Tennyson . . . by his son* (1897), ii. 217.

[3] Perhaps Alvise Mocenigo, Venetian active in Philhellenic matters.

[4] Questions; *H* 233. 192.

[5] Quoted by diarist on 23 March.

[6] F. W. Chesson, *Turkey and the slave trade* (1877).

[7] Sir Thomas Francis *Wade, 1818-95; ambassador to China 1871-83.

[8] I. F. Paskevich, *La Russie dans l'Asie-Mineure, ou Campagne de Maréchal Paskewitch en 1828 et 1829* (1840).

[9] See 21 May 59.

[10] Holograph dated 21 March 1877; Add MS 44763, f. 85; Gladstone's spelling and accents retained.

nullement. Le parti Liberal, en énorme majorité (sauf les riches) souhaite une politique franche et ferme a faveur des Chrétiens, je dirais plus volontiers des races sujettes.

Il me semble qu', à l'époque de la Conférence, le Cabinet a permis la parole libre et vraie a Lord Salisbury, toujours en réservant l'action a soi-même. A l'heure qu'il est, je crois qu'il pense tres peu sur l'action Ministérielle. Jusqu'ici je parle de l'Angleterre, et des choses de dedans.

Quant à la situation générale, j'ignore la coutume du Protocol, j'ignore les conditions qui peuvent ou l'accompagner ou le suivre. Selon ce qu'on dit, il y a beaucoup a craindre, très peu d'espérer. Mais, les on-dits mis à part, je regarde la position actuelle, les resultats jusqu'à aujourdhui de la diplomatie troublée, de la politique douteuse, d'une quinzaine de mois passés.

Il me paraît que sur les bilan des comptes, nous avons perdu beaucoup de terrain, sans aucun gain considérable. Concert Européen, pas très solide. Diplomatie de l'Europe unie, premier organe de l'influence morale dans le monde, déchue, par le manque de succès de la Conférence de Constantinople, de sa haute position, jetée par terre, deconsiderée, blessée et affaiblie pour l'avenir aussi bien que pour le présent. La Porte justement fiere des coups qu'elle a portée a L'Europe, a la Russie, a l'Angleterre. La situation dans les Provinces aggravée de beaucoup: immunité de crimes, mépris de justice, la crainte et la misére des races sujetées, esprit des populations Turques et Mahometaines en même temps aigrie et exaltée. Voilà un compte-rendu assez triste.

22. Th.

Wrote to Dr Watts—Sir J. Sinclair BP.—Mr Ashbury MP & copy.[1] This was a mottled, busy day. 11-12. Mr Fawcett on E. question. also at H. of C. 1-3. City Temple Conference, & speech on preaching.[2] 3¼-4¾. Conference at H of C. on the very complex Plumstead Common Affair.[3] H. of C. to 6.[4] 8¼-10¼. Dr Schliemann's Lecture on Mycenae: & speech thereafter.[5] Saw the Master of Trinity. Then saw Phillips: but little progress X: & home. Read Freeman in Macmillan on Montenegro:[6] and. . . . Except Mr Sawyer[7] a Barrister, none of those who followed the Chairman at the Conference spoke to the question.

23. Frid.

Wrote to Mr Ashbury & copy—Rev. Mr Blakiston—Messrs Lefevre[8]—Mr Downes—Mr Kayll—Mr Markley—Mr Elsworth. Saw Ld Hartington & explained my proceedings with Fawcett: who never consulted him! Worked on Turkish question, documents. H. of C. 4-9 and 10-12¾. Spoke 1¼ hour on the

[1] James Lloyd Ashbury, 1834-95; tory M.P. Brighton 1874-80. Gladstone accused him of character assassination; *T.T.*, 4 April 1877, 8c.

[2] *T.T.*, 23 March 1877, 10c.

[3] The common at Woolwich; an action had been unsuccessfully brought against the Crown by its defenders, who had then been arrested for their inability to pay costs; *H* 235. 600. See 3 Aug. 76n.

[4] Prisons; *H* 233. 335.

[5] *T.T.*, 23 March 1877, 10f.

[6] E. A. Freeman, 'Montenegro', *Macmillan's Magazine*, xxxiii. 275 (January 1876).

[7] Unclear which; probably R. Sawyer, barrister on the Oxford circuit.

[8] Probably Henry Shaw Lefevre & Co., London merchants.

Eastern Question: carefully avoiding the *main* issue.[1] Read Campanella's Memoirs.[2] A short, disturbed night: for once. Much came home to me Ps. XXIII. 5.[3]

24. Sat.

Wrote to Canon [R.] Gregory—Mr Le Neve Foster—Mr Wilding—Mr Jeremiah[4]—F. Andrew, and Sir Drummond Wolff: after investigating papers & debate on Crete.[5] Saw Mr Murray. Dined with J. Wortley. Met the Chinese Embassy at early Tea, Mrs Malcolm's. Saw Mr Ryder. Read Campanella— Dionysiac Myth[6] and. . . .

25. Palm S.

All Souls 11 AM. Chapel Royal 5.30. Wrote to Mr Rylands. Saw Ld Dudley—Mr Balfour (who dined). Read Campanella—M. Conway on Xty. and Tracts.[7]

26. M.

Wrote to Ld Houghton—Sig. Campanella—Edmonston & Douglas—Sec. R. Academy—Mr Tennyson—Dr Wilson[8]—Mr Freeelands—Mr A. Austin—Mr Canning—A. Tylor[9]—A. Smellie—P.H. Hope—W. Severn—A. Cole—S. Mason— Sir D. Wolff. Saw Mr Tennyson.[10] Luncheon at 15 G.S.: Count Schouvaloff made a very outspoken declaration, which shows the situation to be indeed alarming. But only through storm can we arrive at calm. Saw Mr Hayward—Mr Kinnaird—A. Lyttelton. All Saints Ch. 5 P.M. Read Gattina, History[11]—Belleysan, Intrigues Moscovites.[12]

27. Tu.

Wrote to Messrs Braithwaite—Mr Forrest—Mr Crozier—Mr Wright—Mr Reeve—Mr Apre—Ld Clifton—Rev. A. Brodrick—Rev. F.O. Morris—Rev. R. Cornall[13]—Rev. T.B. Paget[14]—M. de Saint Mesmin.[15] Saw General Menabrea—

---

[1] Fawcett moved a resolution; Hartington and Gladstone, for different reasons, suggested its withdrawal; on the adjournment only 71 radicals supported Fawcett; *H* 233. 481.

[2] Giuseppe Maria Campanella had sent his *My life and what I learnt in it* (1874) and *Life in the cloister* (1877); Add MS 44453, f. 234.

[3] 'Thou shalt prepare a table before me against them that trouble me. . . .'

[4] Perhaps John Jeremiah, author of *Notes on Shakespeare* (1876).

[5] He had had an exchange with Wolff about Cretan massacres in 1867 in the previous night's debate. This letter, dated 23 March, in *T.T.*, 26 March 1877, 6d.

[6] R. Brown, *The Great Dionysiak Myth*, 2v. (1877-8).

[7] M. D. Conway, *Idols and ideals, with an essay on Christianity*, 2v. (1877).

[8] James Arthur Wilson, physician, had warned diarist of overwork in public speaking; Add MS 44453, f. 250.

[9] Alfred Tylor, 1824-84; geologist; Add MS 44453, f. 227.

[10] Who had asked for tickets for the Commons for 'the great debate'; Add MS 44453, f. 246.

[11] Petrucelli della Gattina, *Histoire diplomatique des Conclaves*, 4v. (1864-6).

[12] D. Bugistre-Belleysan, *Les Intrigues moscovites en Turquie* (1877).

[13] Richard Cornall, vicar in Bristol from 1862.

[14] Thomas Bradley Paget, d. 1893; vicar of Welton 1845-92.

[15] Probably Ernest Menu de St Mesmin, French scientist and writer.

Mr Boord. H of C. 2¼-6¾. Spoke in reply to Wolff, & on the Elliot Turkish Question.[1] Also saw Sir H.E. afterwards. Dined with the Jameses. Worked on Blue Books. Read H. Heine[2]—Stillman on Eastern Qu.[3]

28. Wed.

All Souls 8 AM. Wrote to Bp of Bath & Wells—Mr Leeman—Mr Brown jun.—P.A. Taylor MP—Rev. Canon Hole[4]—Mr Paterson—Mr Stead—D. White—Mr Reader—W. Fisher—Mr Malings—J.G. Talbot—Mrs Fawcett[5]—Rev. H. Escott[6]—Rev. E.D. Neill[7]—Mr Mackinnon—Ld C. Russell (& BP)—Mr J. Edmunds—Rev. Harvey (B.P.). Saw Sir A. Panizzi—Mr James (U.S.)[8]—Ld Zouch [sic]. Worked on books & papers. Began M'Coll on Eastern Quest.[9] Correcting proofs Pref. on Suprem.[10] After-dinner party chez Ld Houghton: to see Tennyson.

29. Th.

All Souls 8 AM. Visit of congratulation to J. Wortley. Wrote to Mr Collins—Mr Davis[11]—Mr Plumptre—B. Boyman—J. May—Mr Eastby (BP)—Mr Watkinson—Mr MacPhail—Sir J. Lubbock—Rev. Mr Sandilands—General Goodwyn[12]—Rev. F. Howorth[13]—Mr Flanagan—L.E. Griffiths—Mad Novikoff—C.G.—Mrs Th. Saw Mr Goulburn—M. de St Mesmin 1-2. Visited Mr Richmond's Studio: a treat. Portraits of Ln excellent. Also Mr [W.] Theed's. Saw Scotts—A. Tennyson—Mr Cooke (Murray). Read Abp Tait a. to Carter[14]—MacColl, Eastern Question—De Worms, do.[15]

30. G. Friday.

Chapel Royal at 12. All Souls, special Service 2-3¼. St Andr. W. St. 5-6½. Read Contemp. R. Renan on Spinoza—G. Smith on Falkland—Innes on Coming Conclave[16]—Notes on London—Teignmouth Shore on Some difficulties of

[1] H 233. 562; see 24 Mar. 77n.
[2] W. Stigand, The life and opinions of Heinrich Heine, 2v. (1875).
[3] See 7 Feb. 77.   [4] Samuel Reynolds Hole, prebendary of Lincoln cathedral.
[5] (Dame) Millicent *Fawcett, 1847-1929; educationalist and suffragist.
[6] Hay Sweet Escott, fa. of T.H.S.; rector of Kilve 1877; had sent a work; Hawn P.
[7] Edward Duffield Neill, 1823-93; American historian; presbyterian turned episcopalian.
[8] Henry *James, 1843-1916, whom he met at Houghton's soirée. James told his brother: '. . . Gladstone is very fascinating—his urbanity extreme—his eye that of a man of genius—and his apparent self-surrender to what he is talking of, without a flaw. He made a great impression on me—greater than any one I have seen here: though 'tis perhaps owing to my naïveté, and unfamiliarity with statesmen'; P. Lubbock, The letters of Henry James (1920), i. 53. James's subsequent published comment was much less favourable, complaining at Gladstone's 'almost squalid' view, expressed in a speech, that 'England had much more urgent duties than the occupation of Egypt'; Lippincott's Magazine, xx. 603 (November 1877), reprinted in English Hours (1905).
[9] M. MacColl, The Eastern question: its facts and fallacies (1877).
[10] See 15 Mar. 77.
[11] E. Davis, secretary of Greenwich liberals, on resolution; T.T., 4 April 1877, 5d.
[12] Henry Goodwyn, d. 1886; general 1871; wrote The Book of the Revelation of Jesus Christ (1877).
[13] A nonconformist.
[14] A. C. Tait, 'The Church and law. A letter in answer to . . . Canon Carter' (1877).
[15] H. de Worms, Baron Pirbright, England's policy in the East (1877).
[16] Renan, Goldwin Smith, A. T. Innes in Contemporary Review, xxix. 763, 846, 925 (April 1877).

Belief[1]—Ellis's Letter[2]—Merle d'Aubigné's Tract.[3] Saw Dean Stanley. Wrote to C.G.—Sir J. Stephen—Mr Rylett (Salford).[4]

31. Easter Eve.

Early Communion St Andrew's. Evg. All Saints 9-10½. Wrote to M. de St Mesmin—Dr Guttman—C.G. (Tel. and l.)—Mr O. Browning—Gen. Cesnola—Mrs Th.—Mr Ashbury. Saw D. of Argyll 5-6¼.—Mr Kinnaird—Mr Hayward—Mr Knowles. Luncheon at 15. G.S. Corrected Proofs & further corrected Preface on Supremacy. Read [blank.]

Easter Day Ap. 1. 1877

H.C. Trin Ch. 8-9. Chapel Royal 10. & 5.30. Wrote to Signor Gabba[5]—Rev. E. Talbot—HNG (BP.)—Rev. H.S. Byrth.[6] Read Mozley on O.T.[7]—Divers Tracts & Sermons.

2. M. [Holmbury, Surrey]

Trinity Ch. 8 A.M. Wrote to Ed. Echo—Sir Thos G.—Mr Hobson—Rev Mr Swayne—Mr M. Arnold—A.T. Innes—Ed. Charities Directory—Rev. R. Suffield—Mr Bebbington—L.M. Davies—T.D. Marshall—Mr Earwaker[8]—Rev. Mr Archibald[9]—Rev. Mr Marshall—Miss B. Vivian[10]—Mr Moorhouse (B.P.)—Wm Brook—Mr Standerwick.[11] Saw Mr Lefevre—Mr Russell—Ld Acton. Read Life of H. Heine—A newfashioned Tory.[12] Made a little attempt at acting on my Chaos. Off from Charing at 4.25 to Holmbury[13] at 6.45.

3. Wed. [sc. Tuesday]

Wrote to F. May & Co—Mr Hayes & Mr Williams—Mr Chamberlaine [sic]—Rev Mr Milner. Drove to Mr Thurlow's[14] & saw his portraits & objects: especially Queen Elisabeth. Walk with Mr Leveson. Read Herbert Spencer[15]—Newfashioned Tory—Sir J. Lubbock on Colonies[16]—Mr Gamon's Letter.[17] Conversation with Ld Acton—Mr Venables—our Host.

---

[1] By T. T. Shore (1877).

[2] Probably W. Ellis, *Three letters from a London merchant* (1866).   [3] See 17 June 43.

[4] Unable to accept Harold Rylett's invitation to the opening of Salford Liberal Club, but urging Salfordian activity on Bulgaria; the letter was published, undated, in *T.T.*, 18 April 1877, as if supporting J. Kay, the subsequently elected Home Rule candidate, and led to a row with Hicks-Beach; *H* 233. 1841 (24 April 1877).

[5] Perhaps Carlo Francesco Gabba, Italian legal author.

[6] Henry Stewart Byrth, vicar of Bardsley from 1862.   [7] See 27 Jan. 77.

[8] John Parsons Earwaker, 1847-95; historian of Cheshire.

[9] Probably John Archibald, episcopalian priest in Banffshire.

[10] Beatrice Vivian, a small girl in Camborne, had writen in admiration; Hawn P.

[11] Thomas Sanderwick had sent a relative's works on Homer; Hawn P.

[12] *A new-fashioned Tory. By 'West Somerset'* (1877).   [13] Seat of Lord E.F. Leveson-Gower.

[14] Thomas Lyon Thurlow, 1814-94, of Baynard's park, near Cranleigh.

[15] Spencer's *Principles*, i; see 20 Dec. 76.

[16] J. Lubbock, 'On the imperial policy of Great Britain', *Nineteenth Century*, i. 37 (March 1877).

[17] J. Gamon, 'The Consistory Court of Chester . . . with a letter of introduction to the Bishop of Chester by . . . Canon Espin' (1877).

4. *Wed.*

Wrote to Messrs Clowes—Dr Schliemann—Mr Godley—Dean of Westminster. Walk with our host mg. Went over to visit Mrs Grote afternoon. Whist evg. Conversation with Mr Standish—Mr Venables. Read H. Spencer—New Fashioned Tory—very new!—Discorso di Mancini.[1]

5. *Th.*

Wrote to Mr Murray—Sig. Mancini—J. Batey—J. Bond—Murray & Co—D. Burns—Mr Cookesley. Cut down three larches: but a *steel* axe failed me, with a very large chip. Conversation with Mr Venables—Mr Cheyney. Read New Fashioned Tory (finished)—Wallace's Russia on the Clergy.

6. *Fr.*

Wrote to Ed. Daily News[2]—Mr Knowles—Mr Forsyth[3] MP—M. Naudet[4]—Rev. Mr Thwaites[5]—Mr Mackie—Miss Irby (BP.)—Ld Hartington (Tel.) Read Miss Irby's Bosnian Chapters & made notes for her.[6] Read Miss Martineau.[7] Another beautiful drive & walk & much conversation.

7. *Sat.*

Wrote to Miss Irby—M. de S. Mesmin—Mr Kimber—Wrote Preface for Miss Irby's Book.[8] Granville came: conversation with him on the 'situation' & proposed motion.[9] Read Miss Martineau's Autobiogr. a strange but instructive book.

8. *1 S.E.*

Cranley Ch mg, very satisfactory: Ewhurst aft., empty otherwise. Wrote to Sir J. Lubbock—Mr Macmillan—Mr Godley—Mr J. Phillips (Spiritm).[10] A curious conversation on Ritualism & the P[ublic] W[orship] Act arose in the evg: Sir H. Cole much against it. Read B. Gould Lives of Saints[11]—Miss Martineau—Divers Tracts: incl. Milner on the Eucharist.[12]

[1] Sent by P. S. Mancini (see 8 Sept. 51); Add MS 44453, f. 265.

[2] 'Private'; suggesting it, being 'alone among the Morning Journals of London in sustaining the views which I think we both believe to be those of the nation', should 'appropriate a small space daily to printed extracts from the best provincial articles' on Turkey; Add MS 44454, f. 24.

[3] William Forsyth, 1812-99; scholar and tory M.P. Marylebone 1874-80.

[4] Joseph Naudet, French historian; in correspondence on the Institut de France; Add MS 44453, f. 166.

[5] Probably Edward Nembhard Thwaites, rector of Fisherton 1873.

[6] New chapters for the revised ed.; see 14 Dec. 76, 7 Apr. 77 and Add MS 44454, f. 22.

[7] See 13 Mar. 77.

[8] Dated 10 April 1877, to G. M. Mackenzie and A. P. Irby, *Travels in the Slavonic Provinces of Turkey-in-Europe* (2nd ed. 1877). See 14 Dec. 76.

[9] See 30 Apr. 77.

[10] To James Phillips of Holmbury: 'I know of no rule which forbids a Christian to examine into the preternatural agency in the system called spiritualism'; Add MS 44454, f. 30.

[11] S. B. Gould, *The lives of the Saints*, 17v. (1872-89).

[12] J. Milner, *Remarks on the new doctrine of the real objective Presence* (1874).

9. M. [London]

Off at 10½ with Granville: we discussed E[astern] matters. Meeting 12½-2½. H of C. 4¼-6.[1] Saw Sir A.P. Worked on a mass of letters & papers. Read Miss Martineau—and ⟨Irby's Montenegro⟩

10. Tu.

Wrote to Helen G.—Mr J. Mountford[2]—Rev. W.J. Starke—Rev. W.W. Harvey—Rev. S. Minton[3]—Rev. J. Beauchamp[4]—Major Lumley—Capt. Rogers—Mr G. Tallents BP.—Messrs Chatto & Windus[5]—Miss Irby—Mrs Beke—P. Lindley—W.H. Ellis—J. Sparkes—V. Oger—G. Howe—Goodman. Saw Dr Schliemann (2½-4)—Messrs Druce—Mr Strahan—Glasgow Univ. Deputn[6]—Sir R. Phillimore—Marylebone Inspector of Police, respecting Lunatics.[7] The Wortleys & Phillimore dined. Read Frilley on Montenegro[8]—Lady Strangford on Montenegro[9]—Br. Quart. Rev. on Turkish Quest.[10]—The Pope's Allocution.[11] Visited Christie's.

11. Wed.

Wrote to Mr Booth—Ld Hartington—Mr Ashbury M.P.—Dean of Westmr—Mr Mackenzie—Sig. de'Rinaldi—Rev. C. Tondini—Rev. J. Miller—Rev. H. Newton[12]—Mr Hayward—Mr Frisby[13]—Mr Kingsmill—Mr Harrison—Mr Middleton—Mr Waters. A seizure of diarrhoea, apparently due to the atmosphere (there was a thunderstorm) prevented me from going to the Schliemann meeting. Taken at once, it did not proceed. Read Miss Martineau—Frilley's Montenegro.

12. Th.

Rose at 11: sound. Wrote to Rev Mr Cookesley BP.—Rev Mr M'Coll—Messrs Daldy—Miss Kortright—Mr E.B. Webb[14]—Sec. Tower Liberal Club—Mrs Butler

[1] Questions and Supply; H 233. 817.
[2] Perhaps William Mountford, Unitarian minister; see 17 June 77.
[3] Samuel Minton; unbeneficed anglican priest living in Brighton.
[4] James Beauchamp, d. 1891; retired anglican priest.
[5] London publishers.
[6] Glasgow University Liberal Club proposed to nominate Gladstone for the rectorship, and was trying to reach agreement with the supporters of J. A. Froude, who withdrew; Gladstone agreed to be nominated; T.T., 6 March 1877, 8d, 13 April 1877, 5f. Letter from A. C. Mackenzie, president of the Glasgow University Liberal Association at Add MS 44454, f. 35. He defeated Northcote; see 15 Nov. 77n. and introduction above, section iv.
[7] Details untraced.
[8] G. Frilley and J. Wlahoviti, Le Monténégro Contemporain (1870), reviewed in diarist's article; see 14 Apr. 77.
[9] Lady Strangford, The Eastern shores of the Adriatic in 1863 (1864).
[10] British Quarterly Review, lxv. 476 (April 1877).
[11] See 19 Jan. 75.
[12] Henry Newton, 1838-1921; rector of Wryardisbury 1877-80, Horton 1880-96.
[13] Perhaps William S. Frisby, liberal in Leicester, later correspondence in Hawn P.
[14] Edward Brainerd Webb, engineer; wrote London Bridge (1877).

—Prof. Simon[1]—Mr J. Strachan—Mr Rolandi—Mr de Lisle. Saw Mr Dawson—Arthur Lyttelton; & it is edifying to see him.—Rev Mr Rodwell—Calls. Saw Mrs Macgregor. Read Life of Disraeli (*very* remarkable)[2]—Frilley on Montenegro—The Three *Documente*.[3]

13. Fr.

Wrote to Insp. Police Maryl[ebone]—Rev. Dr Benisch—Rev. J.B. Smith[4]—Ed. Monetary Gazette[5]—Mr Howard MP—Ed. Cosmopolitan Critic[6]—Sec. Mr Kay's Committee.[7] Saw Ld Granville—Scotland Yard Officer—Mr Russell Gurney—Murrays—Sir R. Phillimore—Mr Dodson. Dined at Sir C. Forster's. H of C. 4½-7 and 10½-12.[8] Read Life of Disraeli.

14. Sat.

Wrote to H.J.G. (l. & Tel)—Mr Matheson jun.—Canon Ashwell—Rev. Dr Badger—Mrs Th.—Murrays—C.S. Loch—A. Bourne. Read Life of Disraeli. Saw Ld De Tabley—The Wortleys—Mr H. Spencer—Mr M'Millan—D. of Argyll—Dr Schliemann. Began article on Montenegro.[9] Thirteen to dinner. I read Mr Newton's opportune letter aloud to the party.[10]

15. 2 S.E.

Chapel Royal 10 A.M. & H.C. Also 5½ PM. Read Bernard, B. Lectures[11]—Morris on Darwin[12]—and divers Tracts. Wrote on Montenegro: I feel it a holy work. In a walk of 3¾ miles between 9.45 and 12 I encountered passing through great thoroughfares 19 carriages in all. Wrote to Keble Coll—E. Lyttelton (a couplet).

16. M.

Wrote to Rev Mr [H. L.] Thompson—Mr Agnew—Mr Long—F. Jones. Saw Messrs Druce—Mr Hayward—Ld Granville—Mr Bright—Ld F. Cavendish—Mr

[1] David Worthington Simon of Spring Hill College, Birmingham; on the Strahan/Knowles row; Add MS 44454, f. 37.
[2] [T. P. O'Connor], *Benjamin Disraeli, Earl of Beaconsfield. A biography* (to 1846) ([1877]); well-informed but critical: 'The sublimity of the stakes cannot exalt the meanness of his passions.'
[3] Untraced.
[4] John Bainbridge Smith, d. 1904; rector of Sotby 1863-80; chaplain at Smyrna 1880-90.
[5] Not found published; perhaps in response to its leader of 11 April 1877 on Price's article 'One Per Cent'; its issue of 28 February had a cartoon of Gladstone entitled 'England's Best Chancellor', but with a leader claiming he 'miscalculated the late inflation'.
[6] Not found published; edited from Halifax, its contributions were unsigned, and its issues neither dated nor numbered.
[7] See 30 Mar. 77n.
[8] Hartington's motion for further Turkish papers; *H* 233. 1079.
[9] 'Montenegro, or Tsernagora: a sketch', *Nineteenth Century*, i. 360 (May 1877), reprinted in *Gleanings*, iv. 305; see 19 Mar. 77n. A Russian translation by Pobedonostsev was published in *Grazhdanin*, xxii.741 (22 November 1877); see R. F. Byrnes, *Pobedonostsev* (1968), 127, 433.
[10] On Schliemann; Add MS 44454, f. 8.
[11] See 4 Mar. 77.
[12] F. O. Morris, *All the articles of the Darwin faith* (1877 ed.).

Chamberlain. Worked a good while on Montenegro. H. of C. 4-6.[1] Dined with Lucy Cavendish. Read Disraeli. Luncheon 15 G.S. Two nuns.

17. Tu.

Wrote to Rev. W. Price—Dr Baxter Langley—Mr Knowles—Mr Loverdo[2]—F. Jones—H. Burdett.[3] Luncheon at Mrs Cav. Bentinck's. Breakfast with Mrs Burke. Saw Sir A.P.—Rev Mr Capel Cure.[4] Worked and wrote on Montenegro. Dined at Lord Selborne's. Saw one X. Conversation on Schliemann—Strzelecki &c.: many scholars. Also with Lady Russell on the Eastern Question. Read Disraeli.

18. Wed.

Wrote to Mr F. Jones—Mr Hodgson Pratt—Mr Middleton. Worked & wrote much on Montenegro. Read Life of Disraeli—Solomon on D. Deronda.[5] Dined at Ld Abercromby's. Saw Capt. Biddulph—Dowager Duchess of Somerset—Mr & Mrs Goschen. Saw Mrs Macgregor: who showed me letters of two persons the most extraordinary I have ever seen.[6]

19. Th.

Wrote to Hobar Pasha[7]—Mr Layard—Mr Poole—Messrs Spottiswoode. Finished, corrected & sent off my Article on Montenegro which from the intense interest of the subject has kept me warm, even hot, all the time I have been writing it. Eleven to breakfast. Saw Mr Bright—Mr Dodson—Mr De Lisle—Dr Allon—Mr Rodwell—Lord Acton—Consul White—Mr MacColl—Sir R. Phillimore. Walk with C. Read Disraeli. H of C. $4\frac{3}{4}$-$5\frac{1}{4}$.[8]

20. Fr.

Wrote to Mr Doherty—Mr Watherston—Mr Atkinson—J. Taylor—Sir G. Prevost—C.T. Newton—G. Mitchell—J. Griffiths—Mr Simonson. Saw Ld Granville—Mr Sawer jun.[9]—Mr Bright—Lord F. Cavendish—Dr Baxter Langley. $10\frac{1}{4}$-$12\frac{1}{4}$ Attended Court of Probate to give evidence in the Strzelecki will case.[10] H of C. 6-$8\frac{1}{4}$ and 10-$11\frac{1}{2}$. Spoke on official reporting.[11] Dined with the Jameses. Read MacColl, E. Question[12]—Frilley & Wladowiti—Life of Disraeli.

[1] Questioned Bourke on Bulgaria; *H* 233. 1216.
[2] J. Dionysius Loverdo, merchant, active in London liberalism.
[3] (Sir) Henry Charles Burdett, medical author; wrote *The Cottage Hospital* (1877).
[4] Edward Capel Cure, 1828-90; fellow of Merton, Oxford, 1852-64; rector of St George's, Hanover Square, from 1876.
[5] H. Solomon, *Daniel Deronda from a Jewish point of view* (1877).
[6] Rescue work; see 21 Apr. 77.
[7] Augustus Charles Hobart, 1822-86; naval adviser to the Sultan, organized manœuvres against Russia 1877.
[8] Questioned Northcote on cttee. on cattle plague; *H* 233. 1447.
[9] John Lamb Sawer, party in the Strzelecki case.
[10] Gladstone testified Strzelecki had made his will while in sound mind; *T.T.*, 21 April 1877, 13f.
[11] *H* 233. 1572.
[12] See 28 Mar. 77.

21. Sat

Wrote to Miss Cobb[e]—Mr Chamberlain—Mr Vickers—Bd of Admiralty—Mr E.T. Craig[1]—Canon Ashwell—M. Potocki[2]—Mr T.H. Highland.[3] Read the same works as yesterday. Saw Mr Sawer—Mrs Tyler—Lady Stanley (Gurton [*sic*][4] &c.). Missed Macgregor—6½ & 7 PM. [R]

22. 3 S.E.

Vere St Ch 11 AM. St Paul's 3.15-5.15: Canon Liddon: very notable. Saw the Dean—Mr M'Coll—Ld Acton. Wrote to Mr Loverdo. Read T. AKempis—Nosce Teipsum. Corrected proofs on Montenegro. Dined at Mr de Lisle's. Again missed M. at 1 & 11 PM. [R]

23. M.

Wrote to Mr Cyrus Field (Tel.)—Urban Club (do)[5]—Mad. Novikoff—Mrs Bellinger—Rev. E.A. Hardy[6]—Mr Gregory—Mr Skene—Mr Shorting—Mr Synge—Mr Champion—Mrs Th.—Ld Granville—E. Macgregor—Misses Macgregor—M. St Mesmin. Saw Mr Knowles—Bp of Ely *cum* Sir G. Prevost—Major Beaumont. H of C. 4½-7½: decided *not* to speak on Budget.[7] Read Disraeli's Life.

24. Tu.[8]

Wrote to Canon Ashwell—Sec. Guardian Off.—Messrs A.H. Browne—Rob. Gladstone—Whitaker & Co—Sec. Architectural Soc.[9]—Mr Sordina—Mr Ormerod[10]—Mr Toulmin—S. Higgins. Saw Mr Kinnaird—Mr Murray—Mr Goschen—Ld Hartington—Sir R.P.—Ld Hatherley—Mr Bright. H of C. 4½-7¼ and 11-2.[11] Dined with the Bp of Ely.

25. Wed.

Wrote to Solr of Treasury—Ld Granville—Made Akmatoff[12]—Treasurer Guy's—Rev Dr Benisch—Mr Druery[13]—Mr Holyoake—Mr Howard—Mr Botwood—C.W. Jones. Saw Seymour—Macgregor X: & decided. Saw Mr Forbes—Mr Kinnaird—Mr Stansfeld—Mr Gregory MP—Ld Carlingford. We dined at Ld

---

[1] Edward Thomas Craig, 1804-94; journalist, mainly in Manchester.

[2] Albert Potocki, on the atrocities; Hawn P.

[3] Of California; on the Mormons; Hawn P.

[4] Lady Stanley of Alderney; Girton college was then raising funds for building, and attempting amendment of the Oxford and Cambridge Act to allow women to receive degrees; see B. Stephen, *Emily Davies and Girton College* (1927), ch. xviiff.

[5] Business untraced.

[6] Perhaps Edward Ambrose Hardy, anglican chaplain in Cyprus 1878-81.

[7] Dispute about comparisons with the 1872-3 figures; *H* 233. 1674.

[8] Russia this day declared war on Turkey.

[9] See 30 Apr. 77.

[10] George Wareing Ormerod, 1810-91; geologist and antiquarian.

[11] Spoke on his letter, the Salford election, and on Irish parliament; *H* 233. 1841; see 30 Mar. 77n.

[12] *Sic*; probably a slip; Akatoff is a Russian name.

[13] Name blotted.

Carlingford's: much interesting conversation with Mr Millais[1] on Greek Art in relation to Mythology. Read Disraeli's Biography.

26. Th.

Wrote to Dr Acland—W. Agnew—Mr Hartshorn—Mr Farquharson—Canon Ashwell—Duke of Argyll—J. Smith—C.S. Roe—J. Millar—Mr Caldicott.[2] Read Life of Disraeli—Miss Martineau's Autobiogr.[3] Dined with the Wolvertons. Eleven to breakfast. Saw Mr Tennyson—Ld Granville *cum* Mr Bright—Dr Coghlan—And at the House on the E. Question Mr C. Howard, Mr Mundella, Mr Rylands *cum* Mr Waddy (who addressed me *ultro*), Mr Adam, Mr Forster, Mr Lefevre. I am within an ace of my decision. H of C. $4\frac{1}{2}$-6 and 10-11$\frac{1}{2}$.[4] Saw one: with hope [R].

27. Fr.

Diarrhoea in the night: kept my bed. Saw Dr Clark twice. Saw Mr Goschen—Ld Wolverton—Mr Bright[5]—Lord F. Cavendish. Wrote to Mr F. Hill—D. of Argyll. This day I took my decision: a severe one, in face of my not having a single approver in the *Upper* official circle. But had I in the first days of September asked the same body whether I ought to write my pamphlet I believe the unanimous answer would have been no. Arranged for the first (general) notice[6] to be given—in my absence.[7]

28. Sat.

Rose at one. Wrote to Mr Delane[8]—Mr Rylett—Editor of Dod's Peerage—Sig. Campanella. Read Comedy of Errors—King John. Saw Ouvry (Clerk)—Ld Granville *cum* Mr Foster [*sic*]—Mr Repington—Count Münster. Worked on my Resolutions: a little development. Two days letters & packets: near 100? Attended the Hunchback Performance at the Olympic.

29. 4 S.E.

All Souls mg. A sermon on the War: marvellous in its omissions. Mr Cadman's Ch evg. Sermon very long, so well-meant. Congregation excellent. Saw Duke of Argyll—do cum Ld Granville—Ld Wolverton—Mr G. Howard—Mr Repington. Read T. AKempis—Carter in 19th Cent[9]—also Rogers and other tracts. Early to bed. Wrote to Mr Hussey Vivian—Rev. Dr Benisch—Helen G.

---

[1] (Sir) John Everett *Millais, 1829-96; artist; cr. bart. 1885; first painted Gladstone in 1878, see 18 Mar. 78n.

[2] Perhaps John William Caldicott, headmaster of Bristol Grammar School.

[3] See 13 Mar. 77.

[4] Universities Bill; *H* 233. 1950.

[5] See Walling, *Diaries of John Bright*, 390.

[6] Of his Resolutions; see 7 May 77.

[7] See Morley, ii. 563.

[8] Gladstone unsuccessfully attempted to arrange a meeting, Delane being out of town; Add MS 44454, f. 75.

[9] T. T. Carter, 'The present crisis in the Church of England', *Nineteenth Century*, i. 417 (May 1877).

30. M.

Wrote to Mr Morley—Sec. Lib. Maryl. Assocn[1]—Ld Carlingford—Mr Eaton—Mr H. Howard—Mrs Mallet—Rev G. Campanella. Saw Sir T.G. and L.—W.H.G. on Eastern Question—Mr Forsyth MP—Mr Fawcett MP—Mr Lefevre MP—Ld Hartington—Ld Stratford de Redcliffe—Dr Schliemann—Dr Ph. Smith[2]—Mr [W. H.] James MP—Mr Ouvry—Mr C. Howard—Mr Mowbray. Finally determined the words of my Resolutions & announced them in the House.[3] With the conversations & incidents of the day the sky brightened a little. Read Olivia Raleigh[4] and [blank.] Attended Architect. Institute 8-10¼. Spoke on Schliemann's Lecture.[5] H of C. 4-6.

Tues. May 1. 77. SS. Ph. & J.

Wrote to Mrs Whitehead—Mr Macbryde—Rev. Mr Davey—Ll. Turner[6]—Mr Birt M.P.[7] Saw Ld Wolverton—Mr [E.]L. Stanley—Mr Harrison—Deputation of Nonconformists[8]—Count Schouvaloff (at Mr Goschen's)—Mrs Ralli—Mr Goschen—Sir A. Panizzi—Rev. E. Wickham—Ld Vernon & Lady James—Mr F. Leveson [Gower] MP—Mr Chamberlain MP—Mr Trevelyan MP. Dined at Mrs Ralli's. Mrs Goschen's party afterwards. Luncheon at 15 G.S. Read Sedley Taylor on E. question[9] and [blank]

2. Wed.

Wrote to Mr Barlow—Mr Bertram[10]—Mr Hawksley—J.R. Jolly[11]—Mr Fisher—Editor D. News[12]—Editor D. Express—G. Whale—Rev. Dr Lowe. 14 to dinner: & some in evg. Arranging letters & papers. Saw Mr Hayward—Mr Harrison—Ld Granville—and many others: chiefly on the Eastern Question. Read Jenkins's Janus[13]—and La Verité sur Midhat Pacha.[14]

3. Th.

Wrote to Rev. H. Parsons[15]—Warden of Keble—T.B. Potter—Mrs Wm (C.L.) Gladstone—Mr Linstott—Mr Buzacott—W.M. Hick—B. Puseley.[16] Eight to

---

[1] Probably the letter in *T.T.*, 3 May 1877, 11a.

[2] Philip *Smith, 1817-85, br. of Sir W.*; ancient historian.

[3] *H* 234. 101: 'I make this Motion on my own responsibility, and not as the organ of any Party or section of a Party.'

[4] Apparently a novel, author untraced.   [5] *T.T.*, 1 May 1877, 6e.

[6] Perhaps Sir Llewelyn Turner, 1823-1903; sailor; kt. 1870.

[7] *Sc.* Burt; letter in *D.T.*, 3 May 1877, 3d.

[8] Led by J. Chamberlain, from the Liberation Society's triennial conference; he accepted a resolution on Bulgaria; *D.N.*, 2 May 1877, 4f.

[9] S. Taylor, *The conduct of Her Majesty's Ministers on the Eastern Question* (1877).

[10] Perhaps Robert Aitkin Bertram, author of *A dictionary of poetical illustrations* (1877).

[11] On the Resolutions; *T.T.*, 4 May 1877, 11f.

[12] Denying a report in the *Morning Post* that the ex-cabinet had disavowed his position on Turkey: *D.N.*, 2 May 1877, 5e.

[13] J. E. Jenkins, *The Russo-Turkish War. Janus; or the double-faced ministry* (1877).

[14] See 15 Feb. 77.   [15] Probably Henry Parsons, minor canon of Llandaff.

[16] Berkeley Edward Puseley, s. of *D; journalist in Levant and Afghanistan.

breakfast. Saw Ld F. Cavendish—Mr G. Howard—Mr Knowles—Dr Benisch—Mr Morley—Count Münster—Mr F.L. Gower—Abp of York—Mr Holyoake—Mrs Wm Gladstone. Read Ld Palmerston's Life I[1]—Miss Hudson's letter.[2] Dined at Mr Pender's. H. of C. $4\frac{1}{2}$-$6\frac{3}{4}$.[3]

4. *Fr.*

Wrote to Ld Stratford de R.—D. of Argyll—Mr Laing MP—Rev. Dr Lowe—Mr H. Wilson—Mons. Douvet—Ld Granville. Saw Ld Wolverton (2)—Mr Bryce (2)—Dr Percy—Mr Lefevre—W.H.G. H of C. $4\frac{1}{2}$-$5\frac{1}{2}$: and down again at 11 to resume the subject of Monday's motion; when I found all over.[4] Lyceum Theatre for Mr Irving's Richard III: which I thought as a whole a great performance. [Royal Academy] Exhibition Private view, $12\frac{1}{2}$-$1\frac{3}{4}$. Read Olivia Raleigh—Rumbold on Montenegro.[5]

5. *Sat.*

Wrote to Mr H. Jones—Mr C. Parham. The 'post' brought me near 140 letters today which took some hours to examine: but they are most remarkable. Saw Ld F. Cavendish—Mr Taylor MP.—Mr G. Howard—Ld Granville *cum* Ld Wolverton. They opened the means of bridging over the chasm inadvertently made: and I readily went into the scheme.[6] It was carried through by G[ranville] at a meeting of his friends after the Academy Dinner: & he came to me at Wolverton's with H. to make known the result & consider some details of execution. What they ask of me is really, from my point of view, little more than nominal. They have in truth been awakened as from a slumber by the extraordinary demonstrations in the country. Read the new Blue Book[7]—Olivia Raleigh. 3-$4\frac{1}{2}$. Attended the Exhibition. $6\frac{1}{2}$-$10\frac{1}{4}$, At the [Royal Academy] Dinner: spoke for 'Literature!'[8] My *reception* surprised me, it was so good.

6. *5 S.E.*

Chapel Royal mg with H.C. All Saints evg. Wrote to Ld Wolverton—Ld Granville—Mr James MP—Ed. Daily News[9]—Sir C.A. Wood—Mr Oxenham—Dr Bennett. Saw Duke of Westminster—Mrs G. Howard—Mr West—Ld Wolverton. Read Dobney's Judas[10]—Thomas a Kempis—Neale's Mary Land[11]—and [blank.]

---

[1] See 17 Feb. 76.

[2] Untraced; perhaps by Elizabeth H. Hudson, whose publications included *Bertha, our first Christian queen* (1870).

[3] Universities Bill; *H* 234. 268.   [4] The House had been counted out; *H* 234. 353.

[5] (Sir) H. Rumbold's sketch of Montenegrin history 1858; see his *Recollections of a diplomatist* (1902), 300.

[6] Of the five resolutions, Gladstone agreed to modify the second and not move the third and fourth, in return for Granville's and Hartington's support; this provoked widespread radical dismay; Rossi, *T.A.P.S.*, lxviii, part 8, p. 54.

[7] Turkey n. 15, published 3 May; *PP* 1877 xci. 439.   [8] *T.T.*, 7 May 1877, 10c.

[9] 'I do not regard the matter [of the Resolutions] as so far gone (between the Front Bench & the friends of the Resolutions) as to be incapable of being materially bettered'; Add MS 44454, f. 110.

[10] H. H. Dobney, *Judas, or a brother's inquiry concerning the Betrayer. A dream* (1872).

[11] See 8 Apr. 75.

7. M.

This day came in about 100 [resolutions from] meetings, and say 200 letters or 250. Saw Mr James—W.H.G. Worked hard upon the Blue Book—& references & notes for Speech. House at 4½. For over two hours I was assaulted from every quarter, except the Opposition [Front] Bench which was virtually silent. Such a sense of solitary struggle I never remember. At last I rose on the main question; nearly in despair as to the result: but resolved at least not to fail through want of effort. I spoke 2¼ hours, voice lasting well: House gradually came round & at the last was more than good. It was over at 9.30. Never did I feel weaker and more wormlike.[1] Dinner at Sir W. James's: & H. of C. again 10¾-12¾. Read Olivia Raleigh—(Blue Book).

8.

I am the spoiled child of sleep: this night was an exception. Rose at 10.30. 11.30. Reg. Talbot's marriage.[2] Saw Ld Wolverton (2)—Ld F. Cavendish—Ld Hanmer—Ld Hartington—Mr Cheetham—Mr Chamberlain—Mr C. Howard—Ld F. Cavendish—Sir C. Forster. Wrote a lengthened letter on the procedure to Mr C. Howard[3]—also Mad. O. Novikoff—Ed. D. News.[4] H. of C. 4½-8 and 10-11¾: adjourned Debate.[5] The sky brighter. Read Neale on Maryland. Dined at Sir C. Forster's.

9. Wed.

Wrote to Mr Forster MP—J. Gray—G. Parker—G.T. Doo[6]—R. Harris—Barker & Hignett (Deed & dft)—S. Pearce—J. Latey[7]—Mr Mundella—Mr Macaulay[8]—J.P. Lundy[9]—T.W. Johnson—Supt Telegraphs. Went to work on the accumulated papers of the last few days, to arrange them. Saw Ld De Tabley—Dr Stainer[10]—Mr . . .—Sir A. Panizzi. Dined at the Grosvenor Gallery. I was much pleased with the pictures. The banquet was very well organised. Read Col. Baker on Turkey.[11]

[1] G. O. Trevelyan's notice of his agreed amendment to the second Resolution, and Northcote's motion to postpone Orders of the Day, led to prolonged procedural disputes; Gladstone then moved his first Resolution, but spoke as if all five would be before the House, thus regaining ground lost by the compromise of 5 May; *H* 234. 402, reprinted in Bassett, *Speeches*, 471. On 31 May 1878, Gladstone docketed his notes for this speech, remembered by Balfour as one of his most effective: 'Notes relating to my Resolutions of May 76 [*sc.* 77] but on that arduous evening when the time came I could make little use of them from having forgotten my eyeglass'; Add MS 44664, f. 99; see *D.L.F.C.* ii. 206. Chamberlain was the first liberal to support him. See Morley, ii. 565.

[2] Reginald Arthur James Talbot, 1841-1929, soldier, m. Margaret, da. of J. Stuart Wortley.

[3] In *D.T.*, 10 May 1877, 3f.

[4] Requesting publication of a letter; Add MS 44454, f. 112.

[5] On his Resolutions; *H* 234. 501.

[6] George Thomas Doo, 1800-86; engraver; on Peru; Add MS 44454, f. 98.

[7] John Latey, minor novelist and translator.

[8] George Campbell Macaulay (1852-1915, later professor of English at Aberystwyth) sent petition of fellows of Trinity, Cambridge, supporting the Resolutions; Add MS 44664, f. 118.

[9] John P. Lundy, American patristic scholar; Hawn P.

[10] (Sir) John *Stainer, 1840-1901; organist and composer; kt. 1888.

[11] J. Baker, *Turkey in Europe* (1877).

10. Th. Ascension Day

11 AM. All Souls and H.C. Eight to breakfast. Wrote to Sir J.T. Sinclair (B.P.)—Mrs Th.—Mr E. Hornby[1]—Rev. Mr Molesworth. H. of C. $4\frac{1}{2}$-8 and $9\frac{1}{2}$-$12\frac{1}{4}$: adjourned Debate.[2] Dined with the F.C.s. Saw Ld Wolverton—Mr Herbert RA.—Dr Percy—Mr M'C. Downing *cum* Mr OClery—Ld R. Montagu—Mr Whalley—Mr Cartwright—Mr James. Read Chatham's Life[3]—Layard's Speech Aug. 53[4]—Baker's Turkey.

11. Fr.

Wrote to Mr A.E. Brown—Ld Cardwell—Mr Ouvry—Messrs Pears—Dr Bennett—Mr Campbell Grace—Mr G. Potter—Rev. Dr Boyd[5]—Chancellor of the Exchequer. Finished Olivia Raleigh. Again worked on the accumulations of May 7 & 8 & in a manner got through. Also worked up the subjects of the Debate to be ready for the closing. Dined with the Jameses. H of C. $4\frac{1}{2}$-$8\frac{1}{4}$ and 10-$12\frac{3}{4}$.[6]

12. Sat.

Wrote to Miss Irby BP—Editor of Times[7]—Mr Delane (Priv)—D. Gilmour[8]—W.F. Mills[9]—Mr Marshall[10]—Mr Chevalier—G. Onslow—Ld Cowper. $5\frac{3}{4}$-$7\frac{3}{4}$. Cymrodorion Meeting on Pottery: Spoke.[11] Saw Dr Boyd—Count Vicheli—Mr Knowles. Luncheon at 15 G.S. Ten to dinner. Read Baker's Turkey—Finished Olivia Raleigh.

13. S. aft. Asc. "Expectation Sunday".[12]

St M. Munster Squ. mg—St Peter's V. Street evg. Wrote to Mr F.W. Chesson—Rev. Dr Lightfoot—Mr Bernard[13]—Mr Bristow—Ald. Reed. Saw Mr G. Howard—Duke of Argyll—Mr Knowles. Dined with the Leightons. Conversation with Lady L., Mr Leighton R.A., Mr Newton, Mr Prescott Hewitt. Read Bright on Papal Claims[14]—Judas (finished)—Lightfoot on St Clement[15]—Holland's *admirable* paper on Missions[16]—Home and Church.

[1] Perhaps Edmund Geoffrey Stanley Hornby, Westmorland tory and landowner.
[2] On his Resolutions; *H* 234. 623.
[3] See 5 Jan. 38.
[4] A. H. Layard, 'The Turkish question. Speeches delivered on August 16 1853 and February 17 1854' (1854).
[5] Probably Andrew Kennely Hutchison *Boyd, 1825-99; Church of Scotland minister and antiquarian.
[6] Penultimate day on his Resolutions; *H* 234. 732.
[7] Letter on Hobart Pasha; *T.T.*, 14 May 1877, 10b.
[8] David Gilmour, historian, of Paisley.   [9] Published on railways.
[10] George Marshall of Chislehurst sent cutting on Wolff; Add MS 44664, f. 129.
[11] Originally founded 1751, the society was refounded 1877 to promote interest in Welsh arts and literature. Speech in *T.T.*, 14 May 1877, 10a.
[12] Presumably anticipating next day's division.
[13] Thomas Dehany Bernard, anglican priest; Bampton lecturer 1864.
[14] W. Bright, 'The Roman claims tested by antiquity' (1877).
[15] J. B. Lightfoot, *The Apostolic Fathers: S. Clement of Rome* (1877).
[16] Probably one of H. Scott Holland's many articles.

14. M.

Wrote to Rev. W. Denton—Rev. T. Macdonogh[1]—Mr Harland—Mr Maunder—
Rev. Mr Dobney[2]—Mr Callan MP[3]—Mr Udell—Mr Waugh[4]—Earl Grey—Mr H.
Smith—Capt Bradley[5]—Prof. Blackie—Messrs May—Editor of Echo—Mr
Lucy[6]—Mr Chamberlain. Saw Ld Wolverton—Mr Goschen—Ld Hartington (in
Divn)—Sir A. Panizzi. H of C. $6\frac{3}{4}$-$8\frac{1}{4}$ and 10-$2\frac{1}{4}$. Spoke 1 h. 20 m. in closing the
debate. Voted in 223:354.[7] These numbers are not propitious: but much good
has been done, thank God. Read Col. Baker. Packing books. Worked on
Turkish papers.

15. Tu. [Hawarden]

Wrote to Mr Stallybrass[8]—Professor Church[9]—Sec. Cymrodorion—Ed. Malvern
Advr[10]—M. Neymarck[11]—Ld Winmarleigh—Mr C.R. Jones—Mr Ellis—J. Brock—
O. Wilde[12]—Mr Godley—Dr Grossmith. Off at 2.30. Dined in Chester at the
Palace. Rectory at 9.30. Read Baker's Turkey.

16. Wed.

Ch. $8\frac{1}{2}$ A.M. Wrote to Rev. Mr Williams—Mr Murray—Earl Grey—Mr [R. M.]
Theobald—Sir A. Gordon—Rev. Baring Gould. Attacked my Chaos: which is
worse than ever. Since taking bodily to the Eastern Question last September I
have not known order or peace: but my time has never I think been better
spent. Only would that God had instruments in plenty worthier of his purposes.
Worked on setting my writing table drawers to rights. Read Col. Baker—Genius
of Judaism[13]—Boyd Kinnear on Eastern Qu.[14]—Landa, I Slavi[15]—The Danger
Signal[16]—Parkinson, Oxford Theology.[17] Compline in evg as usual.

[1] Telford MacDonogh, curate of St Saviour's, Poplar, 1877.

[2] H. H. Dobney; see 6 May 77.

[3] Philip Callan, 1837-?; liberal M.P. Dundalk 1868-80, Co. Louth 1880-5.

[4] Francis Gledstanes Waugh, historian of the Athenaeum; Hawn P.

[5] Probably Capt. Herbert Bradley, retired from Royal Marines.

[6] (Sir) Henry William *Lucy, 1843-1924; parliamentary summarist for *D.N.* from 1872, for *Punch*
1881; ed. some of Gladstone's speeches (1885). Lucy had told him 'every moment beyond midnight
... [makes] impossible a full or verbatim report'; Add MS 44454, f. 130.

[7] *H* 234. 974.

[8] Perhaps James Steven Stallybrass, German translator.

[9] (Sir) Arthur Herbert Church, 1834-1915; professor of chemistry, Cirencester, 1863-79;
published on Greek porcelain.

[10] Perhaps sending a copy of his letter to Hereford liberal association, which it printed on 26 May
1877.

[11] Alfred Neymarck, French economist; published on rent.

[12] Oscar Fingal O'Flahertie Wills *Wilde, 1856-1900, dramatist; then an undergraduate at Mag-
dalen, Oxford, had sent his sonnet on the atrocities inspired by Gladstone's speeches, in the hope
Gladstone would get it published; Gladstone suggested *The Spectator*; Add MS 44454, ff. 124, 137;
Shannon, 187.

[13] By Disraeli's father; see 2 Apr. 58.

[14] J. B. Kinnear, *The mind of England on the Eastern Question* (1877).

[15] See 2 Feb. 77.   [16] Perhaps *The Danger of Democratic Re-action* (1864); on the franchise.

[17] J. Parkinson, perhaps *The fire's continued at Oxford; or the decrees of the Convocation . . . considered*
(1690).

17. Th.

Ch. 8½ A.M. & Compline. Wrote to Sir A. Gordon (B.P.)—Mayor of Birmingham[1]—Mr Chamberlain—Mr Broadhurst[2]—Mr Bennett—Mr Isbister—Ld Granville—Sec. E. Association—H.N.G.—Rev E. White—Dr H. Magnus[3]—Rev W. Davey—Mr C. Powell. Read Magnus, Farbensinn—Genius of Judaism—Rowell on Storms[4]—Baker's Turkey. Walk with C. surveying improvements &c.

18. Fr.

Ch. 8½ A.M. & Compline. Wrote to Mr G. Harris—Professor Turchi[5]—Mrs Th.—Professor Zumbini[6]—Mary G. Cutting at a great ash with Willy. Read Baker's Turkey—Magnus, Farbensinn—Wedgwood's Address 1783[7]—Heir to the Crown, Introdn.[8] Saw Mr Vickers. Worked on arranging books. Tea at Mary Glynne's.

19. Sat.

Ch. 8½ AM. Wrote to Mr R. Warburton—Ld Lymington—Mr H. Main—Ld Granville—Mr H. Voules—Lady Granville—Wms & W (dfts)—Messrs Chapman (B.P.)[9]—Sig. Petrucelli della Gattina—Sig. Senatore Gonzadini.[10] Worked on books: also on cutting the large ash. Read Zumbini on Bunyan[11]—Heir to the Crown—Les Effrontés de la Politique[12]—Baker's Turkey. Began the ever odious task of correcting my Speeches as made in the late Debate.

20. Whits.

Church 8 AM. H.C. 11 AM and 6½ P.M. Wrote to Sir Ch. Forster Bt—Ed. Daily News—Miss Irby—Sec. Eastern Association—Sec. Trinity House—Mr H. Bowie—Mr T.W. Reid.[13] Read M. Arnold's Last Essays[14]—Baring Gould on Suffering[15]—Stephen & Voysey on Authority[16]—Account of German Theology—

---

[1] George Baker; see 31 May 77 and Add MS 44454, f. 132.

[2] Henry *Broadhurst, 1840-1911; secretary of T.U.C. parliamentary cttee. 1872-90; liberal M.P. Stoke 1880-5, Bordesley 1885-6, W. Nottingham 1886-92, Leicester 1894-1906. This letter, on Turkey, in *T.T.*, 19 May 1877, 8d.

[3] Hugo Friedrich Magnus, German anatomist and classicist, had sent his *Die geschichtliche Entwickelung des Farbensinnes* (1877), reviewed by Gladstone; see 30 Aug. 77.

[4] G. A. Rowell, *Storm in the Isle of Wight* (1876).

[5] Marino Turchi, professor in Naples; see Add MS 44453, f. 101.

[6] Bonaventura Zumbini, Neapolitan professor; published *Gladstone nelle sue relazione con l'Italia, Nuova Antologia* (1910).

[7] J. Wedgwood, 'An address to the workmen in the pottery on the subject of entering into the service of foreign manufacturers' (1783).

[8] Drama by the duke of Medina-Pomar (1877); introduction on Don Carlos.

[9] London solicitors.   [10] Giovanni Gonzadini of Bologna; he d. 1887.

[11] B. Zumbini, *Saggi critici* (1876).   [12] Untraced.

[13] (Sir) Thomas Wemyss *Reid (1842-1905; liberal editor of *Leeds Mercury* 1870-87, *The Speaker* 1890-7; biographer of Houghton, W. E. Forster and Gladstone (1898); kt. 1894) had sent his *Charlotte Brontë* (1877); Add MS 44454, f. 142.

[14] M. Arnold, *Last essays on Church and religion* (1877).

[15] S. B. Gould, *Mystery of suffering: six lectures* (1877).

[16] Sir J. F. Stephen's reply (*Nineteenth Century*, i. 270 (April 1877)) to his article on Lewis; see 14 June 77. C. Voysey, 'Mr Gladstone on the course of religious thought' (1876).

Zumbini on Bunyan. Conversation with Mr Ottley,[1] a person of great charm—and Mr Bateman, who preached in evg, extremely well as I thought.

21. *Whitm.*

Ch. 8.45 A.M. & Compline. Wrote to Mr Chamberlain—Ld F. Cavendish—Rev. N. Hall—Sig. Benedetti—Sec. Eastern Assn B.P. Prosecuted the irksome task of correction. Read Baker's Turkey—D. di Pomar, Heir to the Crown—Magnus, Farbensinn. W. & I felled ash in Lodge Garden.

22. *Whit Tu.*

Ch. 8.45 A.M. and Compline. Finished my very irksome work of correction. Wrote to Sec. E. Assocn B.P.—Miss Watson—Mr Godley—Mr Randall B.P.—Rev Dr Gregg—Mr Budden—Mr Fergusson—Rev. Mr Cathen—Mr Callan MP. Read Baker's Turkey—Magnus, Farbensinn—finished D. di Pomar's Heir to the Crown. Tea with Miss Scott. Kibbled the large ash. Saw Mr Melly. Worked on arranging library.

23. *Wed.*

Ch. 8½ AM & Compline. Wrote to Mr Chamberlain—Miss Skene—Mons V. Oger—Bp Coxe—Ld Granville—Rev. Mr Mayow—J. Barnes—J. Murdoch. Worked five hours on searching & arranging letters. Visited the Potters and Mrs Swindley at their farms. Read Magnus, Farbensinn—Hutton, Essay on Clough.[2]

24. *Th.*

Ch. 8½ A.M. & Compline. Wrote to Baronne H. Behr[3]—Mr Ouvry BP.—Herr Döring[4]—Miss Skene—M. Saint Yves[5]—Sir R. Anstruther[6]—Mr Palgrave—Mr Martindale—Treasurer L. Inn—Mr J.M. Jones. Four more hours enabled me to make my personal selections &c. & give final order to my letters of 1871-6. This correspondence has more than doubled since I left office. Cut down an oak. Read Hutton on Goethe.[7] Finished Magnus on the Sense of Colour. Most interesting. Worked on arranging books.

25. *Fr.*

Ch. 8½ A.M. & Compline. Wrote to Mr Chamberlain—Mr Lattimer—Mr Buckley—Asa Lamb[8]—F.W. Chesson—Mr De Lisle—Ed. Daily News & Times[9]—Segr. Maddaloni Associazione[10]—Treasurer St Thomas Hosp.—F. Hill—John Ware.

---

[1] Edward Bickersteth Ottley, 1853-1910; Keble College, Oxford; curate of Hawarden 1876-80; principal of Salisbury theological college 1880-3. See *D.L.F.C.*, ii. 208.

[2] In R. H. Hutton, *Essays, theological and literary*, 2v. (1877 ed.).

[3] On Hellenism; Hawn P.   [4] Emile Döring, German Hellenist; Hawn P.

[5] Guillaume Alexandre Saint-Yves, wrote *Clefs de l'Orient* (1877).

[6] Sir Robert Anstruther, 1834-86; 5th bart. 1863; liberal M.P. Fife 1864-80, St Andrews Burghs 1885-6.

[7] See 23 May 77.   [8] Of Jefferson, Ohio, on American affairs; Hawn P.

[9] On Rajah Brooke, *T.T.*, 28 May 1877, 8c.

[10] Obscure; the family name of the Carafas and of the dukes of Andria.

Worked 3 h as Librarian. Read Chamerozow on the Borneo proceedings[1]—Hutton on Goethe—The Gladstone Ministry.[2] Cut down an Oak.

26. Sat.

Ch. 8½ AM & Compline. Wrote to Dr R.P. Keep, U.S.,[3] B.P.—U.S. Consul, Barranquilla 1 & BP[4]—President of Korthi Sullogos[5]—Professor Barrett[6]—Mr Thornton—Mons R.M. Veroga[7]—Rev. Mr Harding—Rev. Mr Leslie—Mr Montgomery. Kibbled a Sp. Chesnut with W. Two parties came: music, & discourse with them—220 and ab 15 respectively. Wrote exordium on Borneo affair.[8] Worked on Library. Read Parish Registers[9]—Macmahon on Engl. graduation[10]—Hutton on Goethe.

27. Trin. S.

Ch 11 AM & 6½ PM. Wrote to Mr Chamberlain—Ld Granville—Mr Van Elven[11]—Baron Loe[12]—Mr Ouvry—Mr Briggs B.P.—Mr Rees. Read M. Arnold Last Essays—Zumbini on Par. Lost—(finished) on Parish Registers—and [blank] Walk with C.

28. M.

Ch 8½ AM & Compline. Wrote to Professore Zumbini—P.F. Watson—Rev. Dr Irons—John Wood[13]—Mr Tywett (Grodno)[14]—D. Sellar BP—W. Dickson—G. Lindsay—M. Zankoff. Read Zumbini—Abbot on Religion[15]—Life of Fairbairn[16]—Letter to Southey on Wesley's Life.[17] Began an Oak with W. Homeric conversation with the Curates. We are more usually on Theology. What an excellent set! Ld Blantyre came; to view Leeswood.[18]

---

[1] L. A. Chamerovzow, *Borneo facts versus Borneo fallacies* (1851).

[2] Probably [W. C. M. Kent], *The Gladstone Government being Cabinet pictures, by a Templar* (1869).

[3] Robert Porter Keep, 1844-1904; American classicist.

[4] In Colombia; no consul there listed in *Congressional Directory* (1877).

[5] Untraced; Greek church affairs.

[6] (Sir) William Fletcher Barrett, 1844-1925; physics professor in Dublin 1873-1910; temperance worker; kt. 1912.

[7] Or 'Voroga'; neither found.

[8] Published as 'Piracy in Borneo and the operations of July, 1849', *Contemporary Review*, xxx. 181 (July 1877); Add MSS 44696, f. 157 and 44763, f. 119. His speech of 7 May 1877 discussed Sir James Brooke's actions in Borneo; subsequent disputes with Grey led to this article.

[9] *Parish registers: a plea for their preservation* (1867).

[10] Perhaps J. H. MacMahon, *Church and State in England, its origin and use* (1873).

[11] Not traced.

[12] Perhaps Baron Friedrich Carl Walther Degenhard von Loë, 1828-1908; Prussian general, later field marshal.

[13] Of Birkenhead; corresponded on religion and science; Hawn P.

[14] Obscure.

[15] F. E. Abbot, *The genius of Christianity and free religion* (1875).

[16] *The life of Sir William Fairbairn . . . partly written by himself* (1877).

[17] See 16 Aug. 76.

[18] See 9 Aug. 77.

29. Tu.

Ch. 8½ AM & Compline. Wrote to Lieut. Salusbury—Mr Gurdon—P. Grove—H. Binns—Miss Skene—Mr Spencer St John[1]—Mr Wratislaw L. & Tel.[2]—E.J. Collings—Rev. J. Davidson.[3] Read Warren on Holy Land[4]—Memoirs Emp. of Brazil[5]—Fairbairn's Memoirs—The Age of Science. Worked on my books. We felled an oak. Tea with the Miss Rigbys.

30. Wed.

Ch. 8¼ AM & Compline. Wrote to Sec. E. Assocn B.P.—Sir T. Fairbairn—S. De Wilde—E.D. Neill—C. Potter—J. Knowles. Read Fairbairn's Memoirs: an heroic record—Hutton on Matthew Arnold.[6] Arranging books & papers. We felled an oak. Saw Mr Vickers on last year's accounts. Corrected proofs of my Speech and Reply in the Eastern Debate.

31. Th. [Southbourne,[7] Birmingham]

Ch 8¼ A.M. Put together some notes on the Eastern Question. More clearing & putting by. Off before 11. Reached Birmingham at 3¼. A triumphal reception. Dinner at Mr Chamberlain's. Meeting 7–9½. Half occupied by my speech. A most intelligent orderly appreciative audience: but they were 25000 and the building I think of no acoustic merits so that the strain was excessive.[8] A supper followed. Read Ld Stratford de R. on Turkey.[9]

Friday June One 1877. [Hagley]

Wrote to Ld Granville—Messrs May—Ed Echo. Breakfast party 9.30. Much conversation with Mr M'Carthy[10] on the Birmm Board School system. Off at 10.45 to Enfield Factory: which consumed the forenoon in a most interesting survey with Col. Dickson[11] & his assistants. Then to the fine (qy over-fine?) Board School: where addresses were presented and I spoke half an hour? on politics. After luncheon to the Townhall. Address from the Corporation. Made a municipal Speech of say 20 min. A good deal of movement in the streets with us even today.[12] Thence to the Oratory: & sat with Dr Newman.[13] Saw Mr

---

[1] British minister in Peru; formerly secretary to Sir J. Brooke in Borneo, of which times he had sent memoranda; see 26 May 77 and *Contemporary Review*, xxx. 186, 191.

[2] Probably Albert Henry Wratislaw, Slavonic scholar.

[3] Probably James Davidson, curate in Chester. [4] C. Warren, *Underground Jerusalem* (1876).

[5] Perhaps A. Nowakowski, *Brasilien unter Dom Pedro II* (1877).

[6] See 23 May 77. [7] Joseph Chamberlain's house.

[8] The inaugural meeting of the National Liberal Federation in the Bingley Hall; Gladstone had hoped for the smaller Town Hall; see Garvin, i. 260; Ramm II, i. 43; *T.T.*, 1 June 1877, 10a. The resolution was seconded by Henry Hartley *Fowler, 1830-1911, liberal M.P. Wolverhampton 1880-1908; minor office 1885; president of board of trade 1892-4; Indian secretary 1894-5. See Morley, ii. 570 for this and later entries.

[9] S. Canning, Lord Stratford de Redcliffe, 'Turkey', *Nineteenth Century*, i. 707 (June 1877).

[10] Egerton Francis Mead McCarthy, 1838-1917; one of the anglicans on the school board.

[11] Major-general William Manley Hall Dixon, 1817-88; chairman of Birmingham Small Arms.

[12] Extensive report of the day's proceedings in *T.T.*, 2 June 1877, 11.

[13] An uneasy meeting, at which Chamberlain was present, see Morley, ii. 570; Gladstone resented Newman's refusal to support the agitation, see Shannon, 570.

Chamberlain's very pleasing children.[1] Then to the dinner: spoke again; conversation with Bright, & with Mr C.—To Hagley at 11.5. Read Zumbini's Saggi Critici.[2]

2. Sat.

Wrote to Capt. David—Rev. R.R. Suffield—Miss Skene—Mr Goschen MP.—Major Harvey—Elis. Tucker—Mr Thrupp[3]—Sec. Eastern Association. Saw Dr Wade—Mr Balfour. Read Zumbini—Houghton's Monographs[4]—Sir John Oldcastle.[5] The place is in great beauty and order.

3. 1 S. Trin.

Ch. 11 A.M. and H.C. The Rector[6] preached, excellent: his Curate Mr Bache in evg. is also a man of mark. Wrote a long letter in Italian to Bp Strossmayer. Saw the Rector—Ld F. Cavendish. Read Edw. Denison[7]—Sir John Oldcastle—and [blank.] Much interesting conversation in evg. An afternoon walk: place & weather lovely. Willy's birthday: blessings on him.

4. M. [London]

Sat to Photographer. Off at 10. Only reached H[arley] Street at four. H of C. 5½-8. Spoke and voted on Clerical Fellowships.[8] Dined with the F.C.s. Saw Thorn [R]. Saw Mr Anderson—Mr Delahunty. Read Rajah Brooke's Life[9]—Mr Froude on Becket.[10] I found awaiting me I think 400 to 500 letters and packets. Nothing but an office would give me real relief.

5. Tu.

Wrote to Mr MacColl—Mr Watts R.A.—Mr Gurdon—J. Croker[11]—W.S. Rogers[12]—C.L. Eastlake (B.P.)—Mr Wilkinson—Dr Smith—Mr Godley. Saw Dr Latham—Duke & Duchess of Argyll. Worked 9-7: chiefly on opening & sorting letters. In evg we went to the U.S. Minister's to see Gen. Grant.[13] He fulfils his ideal as a taciturn, self-possessed, not discourteous, substantial kind of man. Mrs Grant kind but alas 'dowdy'. Saw Mr Newman Hall—Mr Russell Gurney—and divers Americans. Read Macmillan on Brooke[14]—Burke's Memoirs Vol. II.—and worked on the subject. Corrected Speech made at Architectural Meeting.

[1] Including (Joseph) *Austen, 1863-1937 and (Arthur) *Neville, 1869-1940.
[2] See 19 May 77.
[3] Charles Joseph Thrupp, London barrister.
[4] See 24 June 73.   [5] See 25 June 54.
[6] i.e. W. H. Lyttelton; his curate was Kentish Bache, until 1876 a dissenting minister.
[7] Perhaps Letters and other writings of the late Edward Denison, ed. Sir B. Leighton (1872).
[8] H 234. 1260.
[9] G. L. Jacob, The Raja of Sarawak. An account of Sir J. Brooke, 2v. (1876); see 26 May 77n.
[10] J. A. Froude, 'Life and times of Thomas Becket', Nineteenth Century, i. 548 (June 1877).
[11] Presumably an untraced relative of the essayist.
[12] William Showell Rogers of Edgbaston; on poetry; Add MS 44454, f. 169.
[13] Ulysses Simpson Grant, 1822-85; at the end of his presidency Grant spent two years touring Europe with his wife Julia and a considerable though increasingly impoverished retinue.
[14] S. Evans, 'Rajah Brooke—the last of the Vikings', Macmillan's Magazine, xxxvi. 146 (June 1877).

6. Wed.

Wrote to Mr Sp. St John—M. de St Mesmin—Mr Simpson BP—T.G. Reynolds—
Rev. R.S. Morewood—Mr G. Grove—Mrs Mochler—Mrs Mawes—A. Xenos—J.
James. Saw Dr Schliemann—Mr Hodson (Caxton Celebr)[1]—Marquis of Bath—
Sir James Lacaita—Count Münster. Worked on Borneo Slaughter. Read
Debates of 1851—Commn Report of 1854[2]—Mocatta on Penins. Jews.[3] H of C.
4-6.[4] Dined with the Baths.

7. Th.

Wrote to Rev Dr Barry—Messrs Digby—Mr Chalmers B.P.—Mr Warburton
B.P.—Cashier Bank of Scotland—Mr Corfield Aut[ograph]—Thos Kent—Sp. St
John—T. Robertson—J. Foster—F. Lavis—Henry Todd.[5] Twelve to breakfast.
Saw Lord Wolverton—Canon Ashwell—Rev. N. Hall—Rev Mr Denton—Mr
Palgrave—Ld Granville *cum* Ld Hartington—Rev Mr Bagshaw[6]—Mr Lacaita.
Twelve to breakfast. Twelve to dinner. Worked on Borneo case. Read Holland
on Russo-Turkish Treaties,[7] and Tracts on Borneo Case.

8. Fr.

Wrote to Messrs Whitaker—Messrs Ivall—Rev W.W. Harvey—Mrs Bramwell—
Rev. Mr Macphail[8]—Hon. Mr Howard—Mrs Th—Mr Pease—Mr Gilby—Mr
Hodson—Mr Strahan. Read Parl. Paper on Ottoman Loans—A Recent Naval
Execution.[9] Saw Farrar & Ouvry (Cl.)—Irish Sunday Closing Promoters—Mr
Gurdon—Mr Behr[10]—Mr Childers—Mr Newdegate. Carried forward my Borneo
paper. Dined with Ld Wolverton—Devonshire House after. Saw one [R]. H of C.
$6\frac{1}{4}$-$7\frac{1}{2}$. Voted agt Mr Taylor's Sunday [Museum] opening.[11] But my mind is not
wholly undivided. Attended Mrs [*sic*] Schliemann's Lecture: and spoke.[12]

9. Sat. [*Dudbrook, Essex*]

Wrote to Mr Payne—M. de St Mesmin—Mr Godley—Mr Harington—Senior
Censor of Ch.Ch.[13] Read W.N., Borneo Pamphlet—Two months with General
Tchernaieff.[14] Attended Mr A. Grey's[15] marriage at St Georges. The breakfast at
Mr Holford's afterwards. The P. of W. gentlemanlike but as now usual shirked

---

[1] James Shirley Hodson, 1819-99; organized the Caxton celebration exhibition at S. Kensington;
see 30 June 77.
[2] Probably the select cttee. reports on the commissariat in *PP* 1854-5 ix.
[3] F. D. Mocatta, *The Jews of Spain and Portugal and the Inquisition* (1877).
[4] Women's disabilities; *H* 234. 1362.
[5] Of Co. Tyrone, wrote in gratitude; Hawn P.
[6] Perhaps Henry Salmon Bagshaw, d. 1913; vicar of Wood Newton 1875-1900.
[7] See 13 May 77.
[8] Perhaps Edmund W. St Maur MacPhail, rector of Plumpton from 1870.
[9] Untraced.   [10] i.e. Baron Behr.
[11] *H* 234. 1494.   [12] *T.T.*, 9 June 1877, 9e.
[13] T. Vere Bayne; probably on the long-overdue portrait by Watts.
[14] By P. H. B. Salusbury (1877).
[15] Albert Henry George Grey (1804-1917, s. of the Queen's secretary, liberal M.P. S. Northumberland 1880-6, 4th Earl Grey 1894) m. Alice, da. of R. S. Holford of Dorchester House (see 2 July 70).

saying a word: the Princess warm in manner as usual. Saw Sir A. Panizzi—Mr Duckworth—Ld Halifax. Off to Dudbrook[1] at 3. A large party. Conversation with Cardwell and Granville on past Annals: also Hayward, Ayrton, and others.

10. 2 S. Trin.

Navestock Ch mg and evg. Read Buchanan's Life[2]—Old Stones of New Church.[3] An interesting conversation with Lady W[aldegrave] at dinner on matters of religion & on Ld C[arlingford']s sister. We betook ourselves much to our rooms.

11. M. [London]

Reached H. St 12¾ PM. Wrote to Prof. Monier Williams—J.H. Parker—T. Turnerelli[4]—C.J. Plumptre—A. Strahan (Borneo MS.)—Ld Blachford—Mr Walton. Finished paper on Borneo Slaughter for the press. Luncheon 15 G.S. Dined with the F.C.s. 5¼-6¼. Attended conclave at H. of C. to advise on Irish Sunday Closing Bill. Read The New Republic[5]—Life of Charlotte Bronte.[6] Saw Ld Carlingford respecting his sister. Saw one. P.P.

12. Tu.

Wrote to Mr Macmillan—Sir W.S. Maxwell—Dr A. Clark—Mrs Mainwaring—Mr Moffatt—Rev. R.C. Jenkins—Mr W. Fry—Mr Somerville—Rev. W. Cox[7]—Mrs W. Bagehot[8]—Mr J. Cooper—Sir P.B. Maxwell—Mr D. Thomas. Worked on reducing books and papers to some order. Saw Mr Adams Acton—Mr Walpole. Saw Macgregor, bis X. Backgammon with Mrs M[acgregor?] Dined with the Benchers of Lincoln's Inn. Read Salusbury.

13. Wed.

Wrote to Mr Rodell—Rev. Mr Dowie BP[9]—Rev W.W. Harvey—Mr Hansard BP—Rev. J. Clarke—Rev. Sir H. Moncreiff—Mr Barran MP[10]—Mons. de Thoener—Mr Mountford—Sig. Mareschalchi[11]—Ed. Daily News—Mr Silverthorne[12]—Elis. Tucker. Saw Duke of Argyll—Mr Cuthbert[13]—Dr Günther[14]—Baron Romberg—Ly Ashburnham—Mrs Ponsonby—Mr Pickering. Saw one [R].

---

[1] House near Brentwood of Carlingford and Lady Waldegrave (now married).
[2] N. L. Walker, *Robert Buchanan* (1877). [3] Not found.
[4] [Edward] Tracy Turnerelli, anti-Russian propagandist; see 20 June 77; this post card is in *The autobiography of Tracy Turnerelli* (n.d., 1884?), 180.
[5] [W. H. Mallock], *The New Republic: or, culture, faith and philosophy in an English country house*, 2v. (1877).
[6] See 20 May 77n.
[7] Probably William Kipling Cox, secretary to the Church of England Temperance Society.
[8] Eliza Bagehot, whose husband died on 24 March 1877.
[9] John Alexander Downie, founder of the Christian Catholic Apostolic Church in Sydney, Australia; see Add MS 44453, f. 208.
[10] (Sir) John Barran, 1821-1905; liberal M.P. Leeds 1876-85, Otley 1886-95; cr. bart. 1895.
[11] Probably Alfonso Mareschalchi; b. 1851; deputy for Bologna 1895-1909.
[12] Perhaps Arthur Silverthorne, civil engineer.
[13] Perhaps A. A. Cuthbert of Glasgow, later corresponded on India; Hawn P.
[14] Perhaps Siegmund Günther, published on history and criticism, 1877.

Dined at Argyll Lodge. Read Stephen on Law of Evidence[1]—Salusbury's Two Months &c.

14. Th.

Wrote to Mrs G. Malcolm—Rev. J. Clarke—Mr W. Reynolds—City Comptroller—Mr J. Reed—Messrs Strahan BP.—H.J.G. BP.—Rev M. Woodward, & . . . . Dined at Ly Waldegrave's. Conversation with Duc d'Aumale. Saw Archim. Myriantheus—Lord Odo Russell—Dr Lightfoot—M. Gennadios—Mr MacColl—Mr Knowles—Mr Gurdon—Mrs Howe—Scotts—Sir W. Gregory—Mr Forster—Sir E. Watkin—Mr Russell Gurney—Mr Lefevre—Mr Kinnaird. The T.G.s respecting H.J.G. Seventeen to breakfast. Read Salusbury. Made a feeble beginning of Sequel Article on Authority.[2]

15. Fr.

Wrote to Mr Macbryde—Mr Gellan[3]—Dr Wilson—Dr Percy—Dr Graham—Mr de la Fleurière[4]—Mrs Th.—Prof. Petrovich[5]—Rev. T.T. Shore—Mrs Carter—Mr Dickinson—Thos Cobbe[6]—Mr Kenyon (autogr)—Mr Macintosh. Wrote on Authority. Saw Mr Lefevre—Mr J.S. Wortley. Saw Maitland [R]. Eleven to dinner. H of C. $10\frac{1}{2}$-$1\frac{1}{2}$: to vote on Irish Borough Franchise.[7] Read Life of Brontë.

16. Sat.

Wrote to Mr T.B. Potter—Bishop [Feild] of Newfoundland—Mr Simerberger[8]—E. Gurnell—Mr Knowles—Miss E. Tucker—Mr Murray—Mrs Th.—Mr Mankar[9]—Mr Peace. Wrote on Authority. Finished Russell on Martineau.[10] Read Salusbury. Saw ?

17. 3 S. Trin.

Ch. Royal mg & aft. Wrote on Authority. Wrote to the twin Miss Nevilles—Mrs Heywood—Ld Acton. Saw Ld Dudley—Mr Neville—Ld Wolverton. Dined with Sybella [Lyttelton]. Read Mountford[11]—Buchanan's Life.

18. M.

Wrote to Barker & Hignett—Rev. Mr Ashley—Rev. Mr M'Kenzie—Mr H.A. Hammond[12]—Dr Drysdale[13]—Mr Waugh—D. Dean—Miss Gurney—Mrs

---

[1] Sir J. F. Stephen, *A digest of the law of evidence* (1876).
[2] Published as 'Rejoinder on authority in matters of opinion', *Nineteenth Century*, i. 902 (July 1877), a reply to Stephen; see 8 Jan. 77.   [3] William Gellan of Great Percy Street, London.
[4] N. de la Fleurière, London liberal; corresponded on temperance; Hawn P.
[5] Perhaps Georges T. Petrovich, author of *Scanderbeg . . . essai de bibliographie* (1881); see 17 Oct. 76.   [6] Thomas Cobbe, author of *History of the Norman Kings of England* (1869).
[7] H 234. 1882.   [8] *Sic*; unidentified.
[9] G. S. Mankar of London; a supplicant; Hawn P.
[10] E. R. Russell, Baron Russell, *The autobiography and memorials of Mrs Harriet Martineau* (1877).
[11] W. Mountford, *Miracles, past and present* (1870).
[12] Henry Anthony Hammond, temperance advocate and versifier.
[13] Charles Robert Drysdale, London physician, asked his support for the defence of Bradlaugh and Besant in their trial for spreading birth control literature; reply untraced, but undoubtedly negative; Add MS 44454, f. 198.

Malcolm. Saw Ld Granville—Mr Kinnaird—Dr Percy:[1] with whom I visited the School of Mines. H of C. 4½–8.[2] Worked much on 'Authority' paper. Luncheon at 15 G.S. Saw Lady E. P[ringle]. Read Salusbury (finished).

19. Tu.

Wrote to Ld Granville—Mr Herries—E.L. Lawson—Sir W. Gregory—Dr Macartney[3]—Rev. Mr Bucknill—S. Sparkes[4]—F. Ouvry—J.D. Betts—J. Elsworth.[5] 11½. Attended the Vesey-Lawley marriage[6] at St George's Church: and at one the Breakfast. Saw Mr Leeman—Mr R. Lawley—Mr Adam—Capt. Maurice[7] *cum* Rev. T.T. Shore. Saw four X. Dined at Lord Cowpers. Read ? Worked on 'Authority'.

20. Wed.

Wrote to Lieut. Salusbury—Mr Cuthbert—Miss Cobden[8]—H. Wale—Mr Dawkins—Mr Upton.[9] Saw Lord Bath—Mr Knowles—Sir Thos Acland—Ld Granville. Dined with the F.C.s: Mrs Cav. Bentinck's party and Lady Cowper's Concert afterwards. Saw one X. Read Dods's Lectures[10]—The Russian Wolf[11]—The New Republic.[12] Finished MS. on Authority. H. of C. 4¼–5¾ (Irish Land).[13]

21. Th.

Wrote to Mr Knowles—Sig. Gallenga[14]—Mr E. Davis—Rev. G.D. Frost. Revised paper on Authority. Dined with Mr Cartwright. Saw Nubar Pasha[15]—Ld Granville (bis)—Mr Mundella—Sir E. Watkin—Mr Forster—Mr Bright—Ld Hartington—Mr Hardy. Most of these on the disquieting rumours respecting the

[1] John Percy, professor of metallurgy at the royal school of mines, Jermyn Street.

[2] Misc. business; *H* 234. 1934.

[3] Perhaps Samuel H. Macartney, physician in Edinburgh.

[4] Samuel Sparkes, of Binghampton, on Turkey; Hawn P.

[5] London auctioneer and agent.

[6] Eustace Vesey, 1851–86, s. of Lord De Vesci, m. Constance Mary, da. of Lord Wenlock.

[7] (Sir) John Frederick *Maurice, 1841–1912, soldier and reformer; s. of F. D. *Maurice, whose biography he was writing; he requested Gladstone to check his correspondence with Arthur Hallam; Hawn P.

[8] Ellen M. Cobden; Gladstone became involved in negotiations about her fa.'s biography; see 29 Jan. 78n.

[9] William Upton of Tower Hamlets Radical Association; on the liberal leadership; draft in Add MS 44454, f. 209.

[10] M. Dods, *Mohammed, Buddha and Christ. Four lectures* (1877).

[11] E. Tracy Turnerelli, *The 'Sacred Mission' of the Russian wolf among the Christian sheep of Turkey* (1877).

[12] See 11 June 77.

[13] Bill to extend Ulster tenant right clauses of 1870 Act; talked out; *H* 235. 65.

[14] Antonio Carlo Napoleone Gallenga, 1810–95; *Times* correspondent at Constantinople 1873–7, critical of Elliot; wrote *Two years of the Eastern Question*, 2v. (1877).

[15] Nubar Pasha, 1825–99; Armenian christian and Egyptian politician; minister in August 1877–8 following restoration of stability after the Goschen report (November 1876); again in office 1884–8, 1894–5.

intention of the Govt to ask for money with a view to military contingencies.[1]
Read C. Brontés Life—The New Republic. Seventeen to breakfast: The Chinese
Ambassador very pleasing: both intelligent and genial.

22. Th. [sc. Friday]

Wrote to Rev J. Clarke—Mr Ouvry—Mr Adams—A.C. Reed—Mr Fewtrell—
Vasili Ostroff[2]—Baxter Langley—Jas Orton—Mr Hodson—J. Spencer—Mr
Livingstone—F. Hill. Saw Mr F. Appleton—Sir S. Northcote—Mr Adam. Saw
one & advised [R]. Read D. Campbell on Turkey[3]—The New Republic—and
divers pamphlets. H of C. at 2½.[4] Midnight communication from Ed. D. News.[5]

23. Sat.

Wrote to Ld Granville—Mr Sec. Hardy—Rev. Dr Wilson—Mr Bellewes[6]—C.
Ewart—H. Cobb—Mr Tatham—Col. Laurie[7]—Hon R. Lawley—D. Campbell.
Mad. Goldsmid with great kindness came to sing to us in the forenoon. Saw
Rev. Dr Adams—Mr James MP.—Mr Mankar—Mr Kimber. Read The New
Republic—D. Campbell on Turkey—Rev. H. Formby on Rome & Monotheism.[8]

24. 4 S. Trin.

Chapel Royal mg and aft (St Joh. Bapt.) Saw Sir R. Phillimore[9]—Lord Carnarvon.[10] Corrected in part MS on Authority. Wrote to Helen J.G.—Ld Carnarvon—Rev. H. Formby. Read Buchanan's Life—Formby on Roman Monotheism—Goodwin on the Apocalypse: (it might almost as well be
Sanscrit.)[11]—Disruption Times by Beith.[12]

[1] The cabinet of 16 June considered requesting a £2m. vote-of-credit with an increase of the army
by 20,000 men, a careful copy of Gladstone's 1870 measure (see 30 July 70); Delane and F. Hill
spread a rumour the vote would be for £5m. (see Ramm II, i. 45 and Add MS 44454, f. 213). Faced
with giving the liberals 'an opportunity of raising fresh agitation' (Derby's Diary, 11 July 1877), the
cabinet abandoned the vote of credit on 11 July, falling back on moderate increases of the Mediterranean garrisons; see Millman, *Britain and the Eastern Question*, 299, 307; Buckle, vi. 146.
[2] Unidentified.
[3] Dudley Campbell (1833-1900, s. of 1st Baron Campbell; barrister) had sent his *Turks and Greeks*
(1877).
[4] Questions; *H* 235. 156.
[5] From F. H. Hill; details of expected vote of credit; Salisbury, Carnarvon and perhaps Cross
expected to resign; Add MS 44454, f. 213; Ramm II, i. 45n.
[6] George Bellewes, vicar of St Mark's, Marylebone.
[7] Probably Robert Peter Laurie, 1835-1905; active in volunteers; tory M.P. Canterbury 1879-80,
Bath 1886-92.
[8] H. Formby, *Monotheism . . . an historical investigation* (1877).
[9] 'G. called here twice. The first time I did not return till after he was gone. He stayed for some
time with Carnarvon in my room. I afterwards called on Carnarvon . . . G. had not been talking politics, but about Public Schools'; Phillimore's Diary.
[10] Carnarvon's diary for this day is mutilated; Add MS 60909.
[11] T. Goodwin, *The exposition . . . on the Book of Revelation* (ed. 1842-4).
[12] A. Beith, *Memories of disruption times* (1847).

25. M.

Wrote to Freshfields—H. Cobb—W.D. Adams—Mr Knowles—S. Cousins[1]—Rev. Mr Rawnsley[2]—Capt. Gardner[3]—Mrs Potter. Sat to Mr Theed[4] (jun?) for measurements. Finished correcting my Proofs on Authority. H. of C. 4-8: voted in a minority *with* the Govt.[5] Eight to dinner. Saw M. Bour—Lord Acton—D. of Argyll—Mr Bright—Dr Lancing—The Miss Cobdens—Mr Rylands—Mr Campbell—Mr Grant Duff.

26. Tu.

Wrote to Ed. Spectator—Rev. Mr Bowditch[6]—Rev. Mr Meyrick—W.H. Smith—Mr Purcell—Mr Vickers—Mr Hisborn—Sig. Zaga.[7] Read History of Printing.[8] Breakfasted with Sir J. Lacaita: Mr Irvine did not come. Saw Freshfields—Lord Acton—Ld Granville. 3-5. Conclave at Ld Granville's on E.Q. and sundries. Dined at Mr Palgrave's. He poured forth an uninterrupted stream of matter, mostly notable, some questionable; which fatigues a brain getting old, from its continuity. He is very sterling in goodness. 2-3. Mayall's for Statue.[9] Saw Phillips: and two. X.

27. Wed.

Wrote to Mr Bramwell—Mrs Elphinstone—E.H. Russell—Elliot Stock[10]—Mrs Josephine Butler—H.M. Westropp—Mrs Macgregor—Mrs Emerson—Mr Knowles—E. Burr—Mr Geach—Mr Dooley—J. Burnett—Dr F. Hirsch[11]—Mrs Th. Also draft of a long letter on the E.Q. relating to the possible Vote.[12] Saw Mrs Mochler—Mr Hodson (Caxton)—Mr Russell Gurney—Ld Hartn *cum* Mr Smyth—Mr Goschen *cum* Mr Stansfeld—Mr A. Peel—Mr Hayward—Ld Wolverton—Sir L. Mallet—Ld Camoys—Mr S. Booth. Dined at Sir E. May's. Palace Concert afterwards. The Emperor of Brazil most kind & mindful: asked for my last book on Homer. Princess of Wales as usual kind & free; P. of W. unchanged in manner, but not a word either to C. or me. Such is the Turkish fascination!

[1] Perhaps Samuel *Cousins, 1801-87, artist and engraver.
[2] Robert Drummond Burrell Rawnsley, 1818-82; rector of Halton Holgate from 1861; published sermons.
[3] Probably Herbert Coulstoun Gardner, 1846-1921, Carnarvon's s.-in-law; liberal M.P. N. Essex 1885-95; president, board of agriculture, 1892-5; cr. Baron Burghclere 1895.
[4] The sculptor; see 2 Aug. 60. This statue, dated 1879, is now in Manchester Town Hall.
[5] Govt. defeated on Indian officers' pay, despite support of some liberal front-benchers; *H* 235. 206; see *T.T.*, 26 June 1877, 9d.
[6] William Renwick Bowditch, d. 1884; vicar of Wakefield from 1845.
[7] M. Zaza, on Italian affairs; Hawn P.
[8] Probably Blades' *Caxton*; see 29 June 77n.
[9] Photographs for Theed's statue; see 25 June 77.
[10] London publisher.
[11] Franz Hirsch, German author; see Add MS 44454, f. 210.
[12] Published, dated 30 June, as a reply to an address from Worcestershire baptists, in *T.T.*, 3 July 1877, 11a; Ramm II, i. 46n.; Add MS 44454, f. 226.

28 Th.

H.J.Gs birthday: God help and bless her. Wrote to Rev. A.H. Mackonochie[1]—
Rev. J. Kirkham[2]—Mr J. Sparke—Miss M'Kenzie—Mr Hassoun.[3] Dined at Mr
Parkers. Read Hist. of Printing—Life of Bronte. Fourteen to breakfast. Saw Mr
Gallenga—Mr Jas Parker—Mr Purcell—Ld Blachford—Mrs Sidgwick—Dr
Birch—Warden of Keble—Sir H. Verney—Agnes (Wickham)—Lord E. Cecil—Mr
Boord—Mr Trevelyan—Mr Nash—Mr Childers—Mr Adam—Rev. Dr Butler—Ly
Ponsonby—Mr Murray—Lord Bath. Saw four, all singular, one or two hopeful
[R]. H of C. $4\frac{1}{2}$-$5\frac{1}{2}$.[4]

29. Fr.

Wrote to Macmillans—Mr Foljambe—T. Clerk Manchr—Mr Hodgetts—H. Hir-
lam—Mr Powell—Ld Granville—Mr Ouvry—A.C. Reed[5]—Mr Hodson—Mr Sin-
clair—Mr Blades[6]—Mr Clowes. Corrected my Draft on the rumoured Vote of
Credit. H. of C. $5\frac{1}{2}$-8 and 10-$1\frac{1}{4}$. Voted for Household Suffrage.[7] Read Life of
Caxton, Blades—Do C. Knight[8]—Life of Charlotte Bronté. Saw Mrs Brand—Mr
W.H. James.

30. Sat.

Wrote to Anonyma—Ld Granville—Mr Cuthbert—Mr Kinnaird—Messrs
Wedgwood. Read Caxton, Life—Charlotte Bronté, do. Saw Mr Stephens—Duke
of Argyll—Mr Blades—Sir A. Panizzi—Mr Hall—Mr Hutton—Mr D. Currie—Mr
Moffatt. 1-5. Caxton Celebration. Saw some of the books: presided at the
Banquet. Spoke on Caxton toast 30 or 35 min.[9] Twelve to dinner. The two did
not come to meet me at 11. It may be better [R].

5 S. Trin. Jul. One. 77.

Trin. Ch. 11 AM & H.C.—Chapel Royal evg. Saw Ld Wolverton—Miss Leslie—
Mr Lefevre. Conversation with E. & R. Lyttelton about my censures on Eton at
Marlborough.[10] Dined at Sybilla's. Read Bp of Gloucester on Ridsdale Judg-
ment:[11] I think perhaps the silliest and most unbecoming production I ever
knew. Wallace on Religious Upheaval in Scotland[12]—Rogers' Sermon[13]—
Formby on Monotheism.

---

[1] Alexander Heriot *Mackonochie, 1825-87; priest-in-charge of J. G. Hubbard's St Alban's clergy
house, Holborn; ritualist, several times prosecuted and suspended. Mackonochie was trying to
involve Gladstone in his Church League for the separation of Church and State; see Add MS 44623,
f. 77.
[2] John William Kirkham, rector of Llanbrynmair, Shrewsbury.
[3] Probably Rizk Allah Hassún, Arabic publisher and biblical translator.
[4] Indian judges; H 235. 416.   [5] On the Caxton cttee.
[6] William *Blades, 1824-90; printer; wrote Life... of W. Caxton, 2v. (1861-3); see 30 June 77.
[7] H 235. 588.
[8] C. Knight, William Caxton, the first English printer (1844).
[9] T.T., 2 July 1877, 7c.   [10] See 3 Feb. 77n.
[11] C. J. Ellicott, 'The Ridsdale Judgment', Nineteenth Century, i. 753 (July 1877).
[12] Robert Wallace, 'The study of ecclesiastical history in its relation to theology' (1873).
[13] W. Rogers, 'In perils of the sea. A sermon' (1877).

2. M.

Wrote to Mr M.E. West[1]—Ed. Daily News[2]—Mr M'Coll—Mr Freund—Sir R. Hill—Mr Bornford (Private).[3] Also my long letter on the rumoured vote which had first to run the Gauntlet of a meeting at Granville's 3-4¼.[4] Saw Mr Baxter— Ld Granville—Mr D. Currie—Mr Atkinson—Mr Kinnaird—Ld F. Cavendish—Ld Rosebery. H. of C. at 4.30.[5] Dined at Sir C. Forster's. Then to an ill acted play at the Aquarium Theatre: and afterwards saw (mostly without seeing) Zeozel's marvellous performances.[6] Saw Beaumont [R]. Sat to Mr Theed.

3. Tu.

Wrote to Messrs Wedgwood—Rev. Dr Sinclair—Prof. G. Smith—Prof. Gamgee[7]—M. Testard[8]—Rev. Dr Geikie[9]—Mrs Stevenson—Emperor of Brazil— Mr Frowde—Mr Baring—A. Grant—O. Blewitt—Mr Bellamy—E. Davis. Dined at Mr Moffat's. We were really shocked by his broken appearance. Saw Mr M. respecting Harry—Mr Russell Gurney—Mr Smyth & conclave—Mr Forster—Mr F. Hill—Sir C. Forster—Mr Newdigate. Saw Milbank [R]. H of C. 3½-7 and 10½-12¼. (to vote on Vaccination).[10] Read G. Smith in F.R. on the Liberal prospects[11]—Winter on S. Africa.[12]

4. Wed.

Wrote to Lord Selborne—Spottiswoodes—Mayor of Manchr—Miss Berry—Rev. Mr Stracey[13]—Prof. Plumptre—Mrs Th.—Mr Lymington—Mr Busbridge—Mr Towse—T. Lewis—Mrs Stevenson—Mrs Kinnaird—Sec. National Reform Union, with advice as to measures on return of the fleet to B[esika] Bay.[14] Saw Mr W. Baring[15]—Ld Granville—Mrs Th.—The Speaker—Lady Westmorland—Ld Leicester. Read G. Duff on The Debate[16]—Ld Stratford on Missions[17]— Englishman on Egypt.[18] Dined at The Speaker's: conversation with Lady Lindsay—Ly Skelmersdale's Concert afterwards. Neruda[19] wonderful: & so modest. Home at one.

---

[1] Moses Ebenezer West of Highbury.

[2] Sending his 'letter on the threatened or rumoured Vote of Credit' for publication; Add MS 44454, f. 233.   [3] Untraced.

[4] See 27 June 77.   [5] Plumstead Common; H 235. 600.

[6] The Royal Aquarium had a continuous variety programme, with 'Zazel' concluding the show.

[7] Arthur Gamgee, professor of forensic medicine, London university.

[8] Possibly Henri Testard, b. 1844; French editor and translator.

[9] John Cunningham *Geikie, 1824-1906; presbyterian, then curate in Dulwich 1876-9; rector in Paris 1879-81; published on the Old Testament.   [10] H 235. 750.

[11] G. Smith, 'The defeat of the Liberal party', Fortnightly Review, xxviii. 1 (July 1877).

[12] J. W. Winter, 'Gigantic inhumanity' ... note on woman slavery confederation (1877).

[13] William James Strachey, rector of Oxnead.

[14] The cabinet ordered the fleet to Besika Bay on 30 June; this letter untraced.

[15] Probably Walter Baring, 1844-1915; author of the Baring report on the atrocities; see Seton-Watson, 59.

[16] M. E. Grant Duff, 'The five nights' debate', Nineteenth Century, i. 857 (July 1877).

[17] Probably the second part of Stratford de Redcliffe's article, Nineteenth Century, i. 729 (July 1877).

[18] England in Egypt ... by an Englishman (1877).

[19] See 26 Mar. 70.

5. Th.

Wrote to M. Gennadios—Mr Whitford—Mr Strutt—Mr W.M. Clarke. Dined at Mr Cowper Temple's. Fifteen to breakfast. Saw Ld Hartington—Mr Wadding-ton—Mr Schuyler—Ld F. Cavendish—Mr Freeman—Mr Goldwin Smith—Rev. Mr Webb—Mr Hutton—Mr Bright—Saw friend of Anon [R]. Read Br Q.R. on Slavs—do on Ridsdale Judgment[1]—Harwood on National Ch[2]—Pamphlets on E.Q.

6. Fr.

Wrote to Rev. Mr Wilks[3]—Mr Alg. Turner[4]—Elliot & Fry—Mr Harwood—E. Davis—S. Chick[5]—Mr Knowles. Read The New Republic (finished)—Roving Englishman in Turkey[6]—Life of Bronte. Saw Mr Waddington—Sir W. Lawson—Mr James—The Speaker—Mr Adam—Mr Noel. H of C. 4½-5½.[7] Attended the Nonconforming conclave at Mr N. Halls from 8.30 to 11.30. We first discussed the E.Q. and then matters of religious interest.[8] Saw one [R].

7. Sat.

Wrote to Mr Murray—Messrs Unwin—Mr H. Taylor—Mr A. Atkinson. Worked on arranging books & pamphlets. 2½-4½. Radcliffe Trust Meeting. Dined at Ld Hatherley's. Saw Bp of Winchester—Mrs Cadman—Mr Toft. Saw Phillips: & two [R]. Read [Tennyson's] Idylls of the King—Cranmer & Wood Memoirs[9]—Harwood on Establishment.[10]

8. S. 6 Trin.

Chapel Royal mg. All Souls evg. Wrote to Mr Russell Gurney. Six to dinner. Read Formby on Monotheism—Harwood on National Ch.—Br. Q.R. on Libera-tion Soc.[11]—Harrison's Charge.[12] Saw Sir A. Panizzi—Count Pahlen—Ld Wolverton—do *cum* Ld Granville.

9. M.

Wrote to Sec. Ld Mayor—Rev. T. Mossman—Mr M'Lennan—Rev. Mr Comp-ston[13]—Mr Henderson—Mons. Gennadios—Mons.Boucher—Mr Brand—Mrs Mochler—Mr M'Coll BP.—J.S. Bogy—Mr Smith—Mr Pearson. Sat to Mr Theed.

---

[1] *British Quarterly Review*, lxvi. 111, 137 (July 1877).
[2] G. Harwood, *Disestablishment: or, a defence of the principle of National Church* (1876).
[3] William Wilks, 1843-1923; curate of Croydon 1866-79; vicar of Shirley 1879-1912; horti-culturalist.
[4] Algernon Turner, assistant clerk of the Commons, later financial secretary to the Post Office.
[5] Samuel Chick of the Marylebone liberal association.
[6] [E. C. Grenville Murray], *Turkey . . . by the roving Englishman* (1877).
[7] Misc. business; *H* 235. 891.   [8] See C. N. Hall, *Newman Hall* (1901), 273.
[9] R. F. Waters, *Genealogical memoirs of the kindred families of Thomas Cranmer . . . and Thomas Wood* (1877).
[10] See 5 July 77.
[11] *British Quarterly Review*, lxvi. 184 (July 1877).
[12] B. Harrison, 'The Church in its divine constitution' (1877).
[13] A nonconformist.

Took Helen to R. Academy: it pleased me less than on the first day. H of C. $4\frac{1}{2}$-$5\frac{3}{4}$.[1] Saw Mr Russell Gurney—Mr Slater [sic] Booth—Mr Holmes—Mr Lefevre. Read [blank] Saw Stanley—M'Konky [R]. We drove down to Richmond and dined with the Russells.[2] There are many remains of grandeur about him; but it is on the whole a piteous sight. He does not seem near death.

10. Tu. [On board Dublin Castle]

Wrote to Mr Ladell[3]—Mr Baxter—Jas Wilkie—C. Holland.[4] We set out at 10.20 for the Docks. Started in the Dublin Castle[5] at noon. Went over the Sunbeam[6] with Mr & Mrs Brassey: the most elaborate of all drawingrooms & all boudoirs. We spent the night at the Nore: good weather, kind reception, splendid fare. The Cape Deputies came with us as far as Gravesend.[7] In the evg Dr Hutchinson[8] lectured me on Spiritualism. Read Raoul Rochette on Greek Art:[9] Campanella's Autobiography Vol. II.[10]

11. Wed.

Sea bath early in the morning. The ship started at five and worked round the coast so as to pass Ventnor and St Catharine's Point—so striking—at sunset. The breeze was fresh, but the ship perfectly steady. A most prosperous day. Read Campanella(finished)—Raoul Rochette: Carey on Cape[11]—Mackoan on Egypt.[12] Backgammon with Herbert in evg. Music followed.

12. Th.

After the delightful salt bath, we steamed into Torbay and saw the spot at Torquay from which 45 years ago (minus 6 or 8 weeks)[13] I set out to commence my career of political effort and conflict at Newark. We then after breakfast went into the beautiful Dart. The Corporation and others came on board: some informal speaking. Then we landed & saw the very curious house of Charles I with its carvings & ceilings: the old Church with its beautiful 14th Century screen and other things observable. Next we went over the Britannia.[14] In aftn visited Mr Acland. Then to the proposed College site.[15] Next up the Dart to Totness. It

---

[1] South Africa Bill; reports of Consul Holmes on Bosnia; H 235. 974, 1010.

[2] At Pembroke Lodge.

[3] Perhaps Richard Ladell, London debt collector; involved in Mrs Thistlethwayte's affairs?

[4] Probably Charles Holland, rector of Petworth 1859; author.

[5] (Sir) Donald Currie's yacht.

[6] Thomas Brassey's yacht.

[7] Including, according to Morley, ii. 517, Paul Kruger (1825-1904, president of the Transvaal 1883-1900) in London for the South Africa Bill, permitting confederation. Currie patronized the delegates, see C. F. Goodfellow, Great Britain and South African Confederation (1966), 141.

[8] Perhaps Francis Hutchinson, London physician.

[9] D. Raoul-Rochette, probably Lectures on ancient art (1854).

[10] See 23 Mar. 77.

[11] Perhaps untraced work by M. A. Carey-Hobson.

[12] J. C. McCoan, Egypt as it is (1877).

[13] See 23 Sept. 32.

[14] The Royal Naval College, then on board H.M.S. Britannia.

[15] The plan to build a college ashore in 1874-7 came to nothing then, but was successfully resurrected 1896-1905.

is a gem. At Totness saw Church and Castle: and spoke a few minutes to the people. Back at seven. Mr Curry [*sic*] gave a feast to about sixty: with toasts & speeches in which I had a full share.[1] Read Raoul Rochette. Wrote to Ld Granville.

13. Fr. [*Exeter*]

Wrote to Mr J. Clarke—Mrs E. Hooper. Read MKoan on Egypt—Raoul Rochette. Went over Dr [H. W.] Acland's Yacht. 12-3. Steam to Plymouth. Then got into another Steamer & went *round*: landed, made a speech to the people, saw the Guildhall Council room and Church, & went off at 6.30 to Exeter. Arrived at night: a *weird* Procession of a mile with lime lights &c. to the Hotel: received an Address & spoke from the Inn to an assembly of many thousands, most patient under inhospitable rain.[2]

14. Sat. [*London*]

Wrote to Rev. S.E.G.—V. Fitzgerald—Bp Claughton—Mrs Howard—Sec. Relief Assocn (Woolwich)[3]—Rev. J. Thornton[4]—Mr Matthews[5]—F.W. Holland[6]—Mr Schoeffelin—A. Reed—J. Cross MP—A.J. Hughes—Mr Strahan—E. Ryley[7]—Dr Hirsfeld[8]—J. Nash—E. Davis. Our party breakfasted with the Bishop at the Palace. We then went over the Cathedral: & off at 10.30. The landlord (London Hotel) entirely declined to present a Bill. Reached London soon after 3. Worked till 8 on accumulated letters & papers, with good effect. Read History of Plymouth[9]—Q.R. on Ridsdale Judgment[10] and Revue Hist. on De Montfort.[11]

15. 7 S. Trin.

Chapel Royal (& H.C.) 10 A.M. Wrote to H.J.G.—Mr Knowles—Sir J. Sinclair. Read Barry's Sermon[12]—Harwood on Disestablishment—R. Montagu on E.Q.[13]—Formby on Monotheism—Clarke's Sermons.[14] Dined with the F.C.s. Saw Mrs Tylor.

16. M.

Wrote to Mr J.H. Parker—Mr Jenkins MP—Rev R. Warren[15]—W. Middleton—Mr M'Geagh[16]—D Currie—F. Hanbury. 12-1¼ Sat to Mr Theed: finally. 3-5.

[1] See *D.N.*, 13 July 1877, 3. Currie was liberal candidate there.
[2] *D.N.*, 14 July 1877, 5.   [3] Untraced.
[4] Probably John Thornton, vicar of Aston Abbotts, Aylesbury.
[5] Edward Walter Matthews, sailors' chaplain at Antwerp; Add MS 44454, f. 255.
[6] Frederick Whitmore Holland, 1838–81; vicar of Evesham 1872–81; archaeologist.
[7] London merchant.   [8] Perhaps Heinrich Otto Hirschfeld, German classicist.
[9] Possibly *The guildhalls of Plymouth. Their history, past and present* (1874).
[10] *Quarterly Review*, cxliii. 241 (July 1877).
[11] *Revue Historique*, iv. 241 (May–August 1877).
[12] A. Barry, 'Clergy and laity in the Church. A sermon' (1877).
[13] Lord R. Montagu, *Foreign policy; England and the Eastern Question* (1877).
[14] J.E. Clarke, *Common life sermons* (1872).
[15] Richard Peter Warren, vicar of Hyde from 1855.
[16] Possibly Robert MacGeagh, Belfast linen manufacturer; later a correspondent.

Bosnian Meeting—Spoke for half an hour.[1] 5-7. H of C. Voted in 156:152 on the Pigott appointment: the vote represented not the particular case so much as the overflowing of the cup, I think.[2] Dined at Miss Leslie's. Saw Mr Möhler—Mr Rearden—Mr Broughton—Mr . . .—Provost of Dundee & Deputn.[3] Looked up Bosnian papers. Saw two [R].

17. Tu.

Wrote to Mrs Stanley—Mr T.W. Brogden—Prof. Castelli—Prof. Mir Anked Ali[4]—Mr Taintor[5]—Mr Knowles—Rev. B.W. Savile—B.J. Roberts[6]—Mayor of Plymouth[7]—W. Hunt—Sir F. Sandford[8]—Mr Smythe BP—Mr Chick—Dr Dawson[9]—G. Rooslyn.[10] Worked on sorting books letters and papers. Saw Edw. Wickham—Mrs Currie—Ld Granville—Scotts—The Recorder—Mr M. Foster—Ld F. Cavendish—Sir A. Panizzi. Dined with the J. Talbots. Read Westmr Review on Macaulay's Hist.[11]—R. Rochette on Greek Art. Attended the House at 9 PM. & was counted out.[12]

18. Wed.

Diarrhoea. Kept my bed till 7½ PM. Wrote to Mr Westell—Mr Green—Mr Giffard[13]—H. Labouchere—Mr Roberts—Mr Burgess—Mr Luscombe.[14] Ten to dinner. Saw Macgregor [R]. Saw Ld Granville—Ld Wolverton—Sir Thos G. Read Raoul Rochette—Life of Charlotte Bronté—Ch. Qu. R. on Ch. & State[15]— Bear and Turkey.[16]

19. Th.

Rose at 10.45. Wrote to B. Williams—Professor Bryce—Rev. J. Clarke[17]—Rev. G. Campanella—Miss E. Scott—Robert Gladstone—Mr Whiddington—Mr Harrison Gale—Miss A. Jones—Rev. E. Wickham—Ed. Printing Times[18]—Mr Ouvry— J.J. Pakes[19]—Mr Gaylard[20]—M. Naudet—Mr Ladkin—Mr Banff—W. Setter—

[1] With Shaftesbury in the chair; report in *D.N.*, 17 July 1877, 3.
[2] Appt. of T. D. Pigott as controller of the Stationery Office voted down; *H* 235. 1330.
[3] No report found.   [4] Professor of Arabic at Trinity college, Dublin.
[5] Edward C. Tainter, Homeric scholar.
[6] A. B. Roberts of Aston, in correspondence on church affairs; Hawn P.
[7] Joseph Wills, mayor 1877-8.
[8] Sir Francis Richard John *Sandford, 1824-93; secretary to science and art department 1874; vice-chairman of the boundary commissioners 1885; cr. Baron Sandford 1891.
[9] R. Dawson, on Mrs Gladstone's convalescent home; see Add MS 44455, ff. 34, 37.
[10] *Sc.* Roslyn; see 21 Mar. 76.
[11] *Westminster Review*, li. 424 (April 1877).
[12] Resolution on 1854 Turkish loan; *H* 235. 1423.
[13] Probably John Walter de Longueville Giffard, 1817-88; br. of S. H. S. *Giffard (later Halsbury), also a barrister.
[14] Perhaps J. F. Luscombe, comptroller of accounts, customs house.
[15] *Church Quarterly Review*, iv. 464 (July 1877).
[16] Untraced tract.
[17] Perhaps John Erskine Clarke, vicar of Battersea 1872; published on social economy.
[18] Not found published; probably on the Caxton celebrations.
[19] John James Pakes, London rate collector.
[20] Thomas Gaylard, inspector of public health dust-bins in Kensington; see this day's speech.

G. Dyer—J. Bills—E. Tanner. Saw Stanley [R]. Saw Ld Granville—Rev. Mr Simpson—Mrs Th.—Mr Knowles. Also conversation with Ld Hartington, Mr [H.] Law, Sir W. Harcourt on the case of the Fenians.[1] H. of C. 4½-6.[2] Read Ch. Qu. R. on Indian Mutiny.[3]

20. Fr.

Wrote to Count Schouvaloff—Mr Kinnaird MP—H.N.G.—Archdn Denison—Mr G. Harris—Mrs Mockler—Mr Crook—Mr Cohen (Amsterdam)—Mr Chesson BP.—Mr Stead BP—Jos Cooper BP.[4]—Mr OConnor Power—Sir P.B. Maxwell BP.—Mr Spencer Stanhope B.P.[5]—Rev. Dr Deane—Rev. W. Sewell[6]—Rev. A. Bathe—Ld Hartington—Mr Fitzgerald O'Connor. Visited the fine Exhibition of Wedgwood at Phillips's. Saw Mr D. Currie—Ld Hartington. Worked without much seeming result on arrears of letters and chaos of papers. Read Nineteenth Century of June on Egypt.[7] H. of C. 9-12½. Spoke on the Irish prisoners—Had a little occasion for patience afterwards.[8]

21. Sat.

Wrote to Rev. W. Wilks—M. Gennadios (Gk Chargé)—M. Negropontes (Constantple)—M. Argurakis (Canea, Crete)[9]—Mons. Martin (St Peterb.)[10]—Mr G. Hazard BP—Dr Jex Blake[11]—Mr G.S. Smith BP.[12]—Messrs Wedgwood. Set to work in aftn at Mr K.s instance on an article for the N.C. about Egypt.[13] Saw Dean of Durham—Governor of the Bank—Mr Westell—Mr Knowles—M. Naudet: a most interesting gentleman of ninety one. In evg cooled my head with a walk. Over ½ hour at Metrop. Music Hall.[14] The show was certainly not Athenian. Read [blank.]

22. 8 S. Trin.

Ch. Royal 10 AM and 5.30 P.M. Saw Mr Butt M.P.—Lord Granville. Read some books of small account. Worked 7 or 8 hours on article under high pressure.

[1] See next day.   [2] Intervened on London's public health; H 235. 1534.
[3] Church Quarterly Review, iv. 387 (July 1877).
[4] Joseph Cooper of Walthamstow, published on Turkey and the slave trade.
[5] Probably (Sir) Walter Thomas William Spencer-Stanhope, 1827-1911; tory M.P. W. Yorkshire 1872-80; kt. 1904.
[6] Probably William Henry Sewell, 1836-96; vicar of Yaxley from 1861.
[7] See next day.
[8] Gladstone intended to abstain on the motion of John O'Connor Power (liberal M.P. Co. Mayo 1874-85) for the release of six Fenians, but effectively supported ending their term of imprisonment; Hartington, speaking later, sharply and explicitly differed from him; H 235. 1614, 1623.
[9] Christophoris K. Argurakis; draft, on the Turkish constitution, at Add MS 44454, f. 278.
[10] Thedor Thedorovich Martens, professor in St Petersburg; published on Anglo-Russian affairs; see 27 July 77.
[11] Sophia Louisa *Jex-Blake, 1840-1912; gained legal right to practise medicine 1877; a friend of Miss Irby.
[12] Probably George Sidney Smith, religious author.
[13] 'Aggression in Egypt and freedom in the East', Nineteenth Century, ii. 149 (August 1877), partly reprinted in Gleanings, iv. 341; an attack on E. Dicey.
[14] Near Edgware Road station; opened as a music hall 1862.

23. M.

Wrote to Capt. Suttaby[1]—Governor of Bank—Sir Thos G.—Transvaal Deputies[2]—Mrs Beke. H. of C. $4\frac{1}{4}$-$7\frac{1}{2}$.[3] Dined at Mr Hubbards. Saw Mrs Th.—Mr Adam—Ld Stratford de Redcliffe—Mr Cooke (Murray)—The Recorder—Mr Hubbard. Finished my paper on Egypt and the East.

24. Tu.

Wrote to Miss Powys—E.L. Lawson—W.S. Raleigh—C. Eastlake—Sir D.A. Lange—Mr Clapp—Mr Burrell—Mr Swanston[4]—M. Clarke[5]—Mrs Th.—Mrs F. Lawley.[6] Troubled with influenza. Saw Governor of the Bank—Rev. Mr W. Cadman—Mr Knowles—Ld De Tabley—Sir R. Phillimore—Saw Fitzroy—M'Conky [R]. Calls. Corrected proofs of my Article on Egypt. Read England in Egypt—Brodrick on Liberal Principles.[7]

25. St James. Wed.

Wrote to J. Lilley BP.—E.C. Waters—W.T. Rowe—Mr Tibbitts[8]—C.P. Stewart[9]— Mr Ouvry—Mr Groser—Mr Cunningham—Mrs Barrett—Dr Ph. Smith—Mr Mitchell Henry—Mrs Th.—Mr Austin—Mr Knowles. Dined with the Wests. Worked much on packing books & on clearing up my general chaos. Saw Mr Daniell—Mr West—Mr F. Leveson—Mr Ouvry (Clerk)—Bp Perry—Ld F.C.—Mr Mawdsley—Mr Peel. Attended Mr Brandram's[10] remarkable reading of the Merchant of Venice. Read Warren's Hist. of Bunker's Hill Assocn.[11]

26. Th.

Wrote to Sir Thos G.—Messrs Spottiswoode—M. Miatchewitch[12]—Mr G.W. Warren—Mr Raoul Jung[13]—Major De Hohsé[14]—Mr Middleton (Plumstead). 12-2. Conclave at Ld Granville's. We determined (Forster dissentient) *not* to support the foolish, mischievous motion about Parnell: but to help the Govt by a mild expedient for the remainder of the Session.[15] Read Parl. Papers on Turkey[16]—Alexander Hamilton[17]—and [blank.] Saw Cooper—Anson [R]. Dined

---

[1] *Sic*; possibly Francis G. Suttie, captain R.N.
[2] No copy found.
[3] Northcote's motion on business of the House—Parnellite obstruction; *H* 235. 1668; see 26 July 77.
[4] Perhaps George John Swanston, clerk in the Board of Trade.
[5] Marlande Clarke of London, on Shakespeare; Hawn P.
[6] Henrietta Lawley, wife of his former secretary.
[7] G. C. Brodrick, *Liberal principles* (1877).
[8] Thomas Abbot Tibbitts, solicitor.
[9] Charles Poyntz Stewart had sent his book; see 5 Aug. 77.
[10] Samuel Brandram, 1824-92; actor; well known for Shakespearean readings.
[11] George Washington Warren had sent his *History of the Bunker Hill Monument Association* (1877).
[12] Perhaps Father Antony Mackiewicz, a Polish revolutionary in 1863.
[13] Probably of the London merchant family.
[14] Not found; at 28 July as 'de Dohsé'.
[15] Northcote's Resolution on business of the House carried in 250:7 on 27 July; *H* 236. 82.
[16] Russian atrocities; *PP* 1877 xci. 821.
[17] See 18 Apr. 50.

with the F.C.s. H of C. $9\frac{1}{2}$-$10\frac{1}{2}$.[1] Saw The Speaker—Scotts—Lord Wolverton—Lord F.C. Worked on books & papers.

27. Fr.

Wrote to Lady Salomon[2]—Messrs Nelson—Vote Office—Mr King—Rev. J. Bell[3]—Mr A. Austin—Mons. P. Möller—Mr Vasey—Ed. Daily News[4]—Mrs Anson—Cav. L. Landa. Saw Fitzroy [R]. More packing & arranging. Dined with Ld Granville. H of C. $4\frac{1}{2}$-$8\frac{1}{4}$ & $9\frac{3}{4}$-1. Voted with Govt & said a few words.[5] Read Martens on Russian policy towards Turkey.[6] Calls & shopping.

28. Sat. [Hawarden]

Wrote to Mr Stormont—Mrs Helen G.—Mr S.J. Low—Major de Dohsé [sic]—Mr Ouvry. Started by the 12 train, after a busy morning in packing & putting by. Not yet in order, but less chaotic than at any time since coming to H[arley] Street. Reached Hawarden $6\frac{3}{4}$ PM. Read Alex. Hamilton (finished)[7]—Story of Elis. Canning[8]—Landa's Constantino[9]—Wills of their own[10]—Fatal days.[11] Worked on the accumulations found here.

29. 9. S. Trin.

Ch. 11 AM $6\frac{1}{4}$ PM. Read Bp of Worcester's Charge[12]—Archdn Harrison's Charge—Kaye on Justin Martyr[13]—Foreign Church Chronicle—and various Tracts.

30. M.

Ch. $8\frac{1}{2}$ A.M. Wrote to Sec. Distr. RR. BP.—Harry N.G. BP.—Mrs Giles—Messrs Murray—M.H. Hakim[14]—Ed. Maryleb. Merc.[15]—Sampson Low & Co[16]—Warden Trin. Coll. N.B.—Mr Snape—Mr Shawcross—E. Jones—E. Sturge—D. Puseley—Mr Henderson. Saw Mr Vickers. Read Fatal Days—Canon Jackson on Amy Robsart.[17] Worked three hours on my letter-sorting. Also worked on making up *set* of my printed works.

---

[1] Butt's Irish University Bill; *H* 235. 1863.
[2] Lady Cecilia, widow of Sir D. Salomons.
[3] Perhaps John Bell, d. 1883; rector of Brington from 1857.
[4] Correcting reported date of departure from London; *D.N.*, 28 July 1877, 5c.
[5] Supporting minor restrictions on freedom of debate in cttee.; *H* 236. 72.
[6] Probably T. T. Martens, *Das Consularwesen und die Consularjurisdiction im Orient* (1874); or an untraced article.
[7] See 26 July 77.
[8] H. Fielding, *A clear state of the case of Elizabeth Canning* (1753).
[9] Work given by Luigi Landa; see 15 Mar. 77n.
[10] By W. Tegg (1876).   [11] Untraced.
[12] By J. J. S. Perowne (1877).   [13] See 14 Sept. 65.
[14] M. H. Hakim of London, on Indian affairs; Hawn P.
[15] Denying he was in communication about becoming candidate for Marylebone; *Marylebone Mercury*, 4 August 1877, 2g.
[16] London publishers.
[17] Probably M.S., later published by J. E. Jackson in *Nineteenth Century*, xi. 414 (March 1882).

31. Tu.

Ch. 8½ A.M. Wrote to Messrs Reeves & Turner—Père Michaud—Hon A. Herbert & Mr Chesson—Jas Wilson—Mrs Kinnaird—E.C. Waters—Mr Woodman—H. Granby—A. Sellar—J. Hawke. Worked 3 hours on letters. Saw Mr Vickers. Read Fatal Days (finished)—Magnus, Farbensinn (II). Walk with E. Wickham.

Wed. Aug. One 1877.

Wrote to Miss Skene BP—Mr Pepper—Mr Drew—J. Hawke—Mr Latouche—E. Taylor—Rev. Mr Pares[1]—Messrs May. Church 8½ AM. Worked 3½ hours on letters. Cut away part of an Elm-stump to clear the walk. Read Magnus—Book I of Iliad: making notes on colour.

2. Th.

Ch. 8¼ A.M. Wrote to Earl of Derby (2)—The Speaker (offering to go up)—Mr Pakes B.P.—Mr J. Wilson—A.A. Toms B.P.[2]—Mrs Cox—Mr Parker—Mr Longmaid—Mr Jennings—Fox Butler—Cyrus Field. Worked on Letters 3½ h. Read Par Papers Turkey 25[3]—Magnus, Farbensinn—Iliad B. II & made notes.—A State Secret.[4] Walk with C.

3. Fr.

Ch. 8¼ AM. Wrote to Madam O. Novikoff—Ld F. Cavendish—Miss Skene—Mr T. Ogilvy—Mr Rusbridge—May & Williams—Mr Burnard—Chester Book Stall Manager. Worked 6½ hours on my letters: such converse with the dead! Read Tr. from Miss Skene of the letters of Abp Lycurgus[5]—A book of the Iliad—and [blank]

4. Sat.

Ch. 8¼ AM. Wrote to Mr Ouvry—Rev. Mr Grice[6]—Mr Watson B.P. Corrected MS text of speech at Antiquarian meeting. Six hours on my letters. A party of 1400 came from Bolton! We were nearly killed with kindness. I began with W. the cutting of a tree; and had to speak to them, but not on politics.[7] Read a book of the Iliad—and M. de Behr on Homer.[8]

---

[1] Perhaps John Pares, 1833-1915; social reformer; fa. of Sir Bernard*; not in orders.

[2] Alfred Augustus Toms, d. 1922; s. of Samuel *Rogers; curate in Whitechapel 1879-80, later in Devon.

[3] *PP* xcii. 1; issued on 30 July.

[4] Untraced tract.

[5] Letters from Lycurgus to Gladstone, 1870-5, were printed in F. M. F. Skene, *The life of Alexander Lycurgus* (1877) which is dedicated to Gladstone.

[6] Probably William Grice, perpetual curate of Sherborne 1848.

[7] *T.T.*, 6 August 1877, 7b, 8c: 'the very splinters which flew from this axe were picked up and treasured as relics'.

[8] Baron F. J. D. Behr, *Recherches sur l'histoire des temps héroïques de la Grèce* (1856).

5. 10 S. Trin.

Ch 11 AM. with H.C. and 6½ P.M. Wrote to Miss Skene B.P. Read Mountford on Miracle[1]—Hessey's Charge[2]—Vatican Influence (Stuart)[3]—E. Miller on Ridsdale Judgment[4]—Plumptre's Sermon[5]—and other Tracts.

6. M.

Ch. 8½ A.M. Wrote to Robn & Nicholson—Mr Picton—Mr Parker—J. Butt—Mr Hindley—C. Field—Wms & Norgate. Worked with W. on the big ash: when we were photographed. Tea party at 6. Worked 4 hours on my letters. Read Magnus (finished)—Dawson on Landscape[6]—Ackerman on Natal[7]—Iliad B.V. Mr Knox Little[8] came: he was to have been Stephy's guest. Worked upon the ash.

7. Tu.

Ch. 8½ A.M. Wrote to Ld Granville—Windsor Health Board Secy[9]—Rev T.T. Carter—T.T. Harman—G. Williams—Mr King BP—Mr Roberts. Read Parl. Papers on Turkey—Iliad B. VI—Odyssey B. I and B. II. We brought down the big ash. Worked 3½ hours on my letters & list. Mr Knox Little, as well as Mr Ottley, is excellent company, & shows well in all respects.

8. Wed.

Ch. 8½ A.M. Wrote to Mr J. Green—Baron Loe—Mr Harper—W.P. Adam—A.H. Smith[10]—F. Lomax.[11] Worked 3½ hours on my letters and list. I must now have extracted the letters of near five hundred correspondents. Working on another great ash. Saw Mr Vickers respecting a purchase of land. Conversation with W. Read Odyssey B. III B. IV.—and Baron Behr—Turkish Blue Book.[12] Worked 3½ h. on letters and list.

9. Th.

Ch. 8½ A.M. Wrote to Rev. M. M'Coll—Mr Mozley Stark[13]—Th. Ogilvy—W. Macdonald & B.P.—Ivall & Large—Treasurer of Guy's—The Speaker—[J.]A. Acton—J.C. Mellin—Mrs Wyatt. Letters and books 2 hours. We brought down a great ash. W. & G. went to Leeswood.[14] We much regret this partial migration. Read Odyss. V. VI.—Il. VII—Parl. Papers Turkey—Denton on Montenegro.[15]

---

[1] See 17 June 77.   [2] J. A. Hessey, 'Church and State questions in 1876' (1876).

[3] C. P. Stewart, *Vatican influence under Pius V and Gregory XIII* (1877).

[4] E. Miller, 'The future effects of the Folkestone Judgment' (1877).

[5] E. Plumptre, 'Perversions to Rome. A sermon' (1877).

[6] A. Dawson, *English landscape art in 1877* (1877).

[7] J. W. Akerman, 'Native government in Natal' (1877).   [8] See 17 Apr. 74.

[9] Business untraced; probably Clewer House of Mercy.

[10] Perhaps Algernon Howell Smith, 1845-1930; vicar of Tunbridge Wells 1875-85.

[11] Frederick Lomax, an organizer of the Bolton visit; see 4 Aug. 77.

[12] See 2 Aug. 77.

[13] John Mozley Stark, antiquarian bookseller, especially of theology, in Hull, from whom Gladstone bought; see 1 Feb. 58.

[14] Near Mold.

[15] W. Denton, *Montenegro. Its people and their history* (1877).

10. Fr.

Ch. 8½ AM. Wrote to Mr Knox Little BP—Messrs Farrar O—Mr Leflin[1]—Col. Somerset[2] O—Mr Harris—Mr Levy Lawson—Mr Anderton—Mr F.M. Roberts. 1½ hour on books & papers: so I shall go on till order is established. Read Odyssey VII. VIII.—Iliad B. VII—Girdlestone on Number[3]—Armit on New Guinea.[4]

11. Sat.

Having been a good deal troubled with neuralgia kept my bed till breakfast time & profited greatly. Wrote to Editor of D. News[5]—B. Puseley—A. Johnston—Rev. M. M'Coll—Rev. Dr Sinclair—Rev. F.B. Harvey.[6] Read Odyssey IX. X—Iliad IX. Theol. conversation with Mr Ottley, a person, I think, of very high promise. Were there hundreds like him! Kibbled the last felled ash. Drove with C. to see Mrs Swindley:[7] a patient sufferer. I read a little to her.

12. 11 S Trin.

Ch mg & aft. Wrote to Ld Granville. Read Life of M. Cochin[8]—The American Socialists[9]—Michaud's Ordinaire de la Messe.[10] Conversation with Mr Ottley.

13. M.

Ch. 8½ AM. Wrote to Supt Bookstall Chester—Aug. Craven—Mr Salisbury—W.E. Davies—D. Plimsoll—Spottiswoods. On Sat. and today I have actually resumed, with quivering hopes & small attempts my *Thesauros Homerikos* suspended for a twelvemonth. Read Odyssey XI. XII—Iliad X.—Denton on Montenegro. Felled some alders.

14. Tu.

Ch. 8½ AM. Ewloe School opening Service and Addresses 3½-5.[11] Preliminary luncheon at Mr Hancock's. Saw Bp of Grahamstown[12]—Mr Taylor. Wrote to Mr Errington MP[13]—Mr Appleton—Mr Freeman—Mr Dalton O—Mr Crandell O—Mr Carmichael—Mr Harrison—Mr Hadfield—Mr Cooper—Rev Mr Mirehouse.[14] Read Odyss. XIII. XIV.—Illiad XI.—Denton's Montenegro—My chapter on Colours. Worked on Thes. Hom.

---

[1] *Sc.* Laflin.   [2] Edward Arthur Somerset, 1817-86; formerly a tory M.P.

[3] C. Girdlestone, *Number: a link between divine intelligence and human* (1875).

[4] R. H. Armit, *The history of New Guinea* (1876).

[5] *Résumé* of the political situation; Add MS 44454, f. 321; Hill replied he had already made similar points; ibid., f. 328.

[6] Frederick Burn Harvey, rector of Chedington; historian of nonconformity.

[7] See 7 Sept. 77.

[8] Count F. A. P. Falloux, *Augustin Cochin*, tr. A. Craven (1877).   [9] Untraced.

[10] E. Michaud, 'Ordinaire de la Messe' (1877); draft for Swiss synod.

[11] *Chester Chronicle*, 18 August 1877, 6f.

[12] Nathaniel James *Merriman (1810-82; bp. of Grahamstown 1871; excommunicated his dean 1880) at the Ewloe school.

[13] (Sir) George Errington, 1839-1920; liberal M.P. Co. Longford 1874-85; a Roman catholic; cr. bart. 1885; in correspondence on Irish university quarrels; see Ramm II, i. 54.

[14] John Mirehouse, 1839-1911; rector of Colsterworth 1864-1909; antiquarian.

15. Wed.

Ch 8½ AM. Wrote to Mr Farrer O—Earl of Derby—Col. Jones (& BP)[1]—D. M'Gregor[2]—Mr MacPhail[3]—A.E. West—R. Pringle—J. Beddoes—J.J. Murphy.[4] Read Od. XV. XVI—Iliad XII.—Dutton's Hist. Crusades.[5] Worked on Thes. Hom. The young Hardys[6] came.

16. Th.

Ch. 8¼ A.M. Wrote to Mr W. Hamilton—Rev. J. Thomas—T. Williams—B. Leaves—W. Bryant. Worked on Thes. Hom. Read Od. XVII. XVIII (with Mr Merry—Buchholz &c.)—Leake—Nitzsch—Iliad XIII (part). Felled a small ash. Examined papers on my Tribute Loan & M[etropolitan and] D[istrict] RR securities. Attended the Hawarden Flower show. Worked on Thes. Hom.

17. Fr.

Ch. 8¼ AM. Wrote to Rev. H.B. Ottley[7]—Earl of Derby—Mr Hopwood O—Mr De Verdon[8]—Mons. Ballasteros[9]—Mr Knowles—Mr Briggs—Mr Mills. Worked on Thes. Hom. Read Odyss. XIX. XX.—Il. finished XIII began XIV. Saw Mr Williams (St Mark's) Conc. with C. on the Hampton & Moffatt affairs. Woodcutting with Herbert.

18. Sat.

Ch. 8½ A.M. Saw Mr Vickers—Mr Agnew—Mr Snape—Mr [blank] (Manchester)—Mr [blank] (Bamford Meml). Worked on Thes. Hom. Read Odyss. XXI. XXII: very awful, very grand—Iliad finished XIV: part of XV. Worked on cutting an alder. Wrote to Mr de la Fleurière—Rev. R.N. Grier[10]—Mr Nicholl— Lt Col. Neville—Mr Ridgway—Mr Marshall—Mr J.W. Wood[11]—Mr Geo. Grove. 4-6. Confronted the Salford & Darwin [sic] parties: had to speak for about a quarter of an hour.[12] There were near 3000: very well managed.

19. 12 S. Trin.

Ch 11 AM with H.C. and 6½ PM. Wrote to Mrs Th. & BP—Mr Hambleton BP— H.N.G. BP—Scotts. Read Mariner Newman[13]—Murphy Bases of Faith[14]— Hales's Works[15]—Pedigree of B.V.M.[16]—Michaud on the Mass.

[1] Perhaps Colonel Inigo William Jones of Kelston Park, Bath.
[2] Duncan MacGregor, principal of Baptist College, Dunoon, had sent his book, see 19 Aug. 77.
[3] William M. Macphail of Edinburgh; see Add MS 44453, f. 257.
[4] Joseph John Murphy, 1827-94; wrote on science and religion; Hawn P. See 19 Aug. 77.
[5] By W. E. Dutton (1877).   [6] Reginald and Marion Hardy; see 4 Mar. 76n.
[7] Henry Bickersteth Ottley, vicar of Newton-on-Trent 1876.
[8] Thomas K. De Verdon, religious author.   [9] Unidentified.
[10] Sc. R. M. Grier; see 2 Nov. 72.   [11] Possibly John W. Wood, minor poet.
[12] From Salford and Over Darwen liberal associations; he attacked the London press for warmongering, praised Birmingham for organizing; Chester Chronicle, 25 August 1877, 2a.
[13] By D. Macgregor (1877).
[14] J. J. Murphy, The scientific bases of faith (1873).
[15] J. Hales, Works, 3v. (1765).
[16] Perhaps M. Orsini, The history of the Blessed Virgin Mary (1872).

20. M.

Ch. 8½ AM. Wrote to Mr Winspear—Mr G. Berry[1]—Mr A. Turner—Messrs Robertson & Nichn—Mr H.A. Long.[2] Worked on Thes. Hom. Read Iliad: to part of B. XVI—Also Parl. Papers on Turkey—Hist. of Crusades. Addressed the 2000 who came today from Bacup and [blank]: for about 20 min. or more.[3] They were very hearty & enjoyed themselves much. It is the *reporting* that makes the difficulty in these things. Cut down the alder stump. Saw The Secretaries—Mrs Hampton.

21. Tu.

Ch. 8½ AM. Wrote to The Vicar of Leeds—Secy Spelling Reform Conf.[4]—C. Hindley—Mozley Stark—L. Stollwerck [*sic*]—Dr Macnamara[5]—Mr J.H. Greenhalgh[6]—Mr Leatham—J.W. Tate—A. Beale—W. Raleigh. Saw Mr Vickers. Worked on Ithacan &c. Geography for Macmillan.[7] With Herbert felled an Ash. Read Iliad—to middle of B. XVIII—Bowen's Ithaca[8]—Hist. of Crusades.

22. Wed.

Ch. 8½ AM. Wrote to Sec. Russian Emb.[9]—Dr Liddon—Mr H. Potter—Rev. Mr Fleming—J.C. King—Mr Aug. Frickenhaus[10]—Mr Errington MP. Read Iliad to end of XX.—History of Crusades. Worked on M'Millan article. Worked on Alders.

23. Th.

Ch. 8½ A.M. Wrote to Rev. G. Sutherland[11]—G. How[e]—F. Martin—Rev. A. Troup[12]—Mr J. Mackey—Messrs Chapman Solrs—Mr Lawson (& B.P.)—Rev. T. Michael—Rev. J.C. Hyatt[13]—Rev. M.W. Mayow—Mr Fraser. Read Il. XXI. XXII. part XXIII—Account of the Thames Docks. Mr Cyrus Field came. Eleven to dinner. A grand moon-eclipse. Worked on Domn of Odysseus.

24 St Barth.

Ch. 8.45 AM. And walk with Mr C. Field after it. Wrote to Mad. O. Novikoff—Ld Granville—Mr W. Moseley[14]—Mr Jas Howard—Mr A. Effendi Abkarius.[15]

[1] Graham Berry, of Melbourne; later correspondence in Hawn P.
[2] Harry Alfred Long, published on religion.
[3] *T.T.*, 21 August 1877, 4e.   [4] Papers at Add MS 44454, f. 340.
[5] Nottidge Charles Macnamara, published widely on diseases.
[6] J. S. Greenhalgh of Rochdale; sent a paperknife; Hawn P.
[7] 'The dominions of Odysseus, and the island group of the Odyssey', *Macmillan's Magazine*, xxxvi. 417 (October 1877); Add MS 44696, f. 262.
[8] Sir G. F. Bowen, *Ithaca* (1850). See 17 July 51.
[9] A. Davydow; business untraced.
[10] Augustus Frickenhaus, London insurance agent.
[11] George Sutherland, episcopalian incumbent in Wick.
[12] Episcopalian incumbent in Dollar.
[13] John Carter Hyatt, vicar of Queensbury 1859.
[14] William Moseley, district surveyor for Regent's Park area.
[15] Perhaps John Abcarius, English-Arabic lexicographer.

Finished Article for Macmillan. Finished the Iliad—and Account of Thames Docks.[1] Woodcutting with H.

25. Sat.

Ch. 8¼ A.M. Wrote to Mayor of Dewsbury—Sir H. Johnstone—J. Holdroyd—W. Calcott—R. Teasdale—Mr Cave O—S. Allen—H. Whiley—H. Graham. Corrected for press & put up my article for Macmillan. Ten to dinner: including Bp of Grahamstown. Conversation with Mr Ottley. Tree-work with W. Read Queen & Cardinal[2]—Nosce Teipsum.[3] Worked on books.

26. 14 S. Trin.

Ch. mg and Broughton Ch. evg. Walk with C. Wrote to Messrs Clay B.P.—Mr Lester—Mr Brown. Read Divers Tracts—Murphy, Bases of Faith, Hill, Continental Sunday[4]—Gother, Protestant Trial.[5] Wrote on Heb. Trad. in Homer.

27. M.

Ch. 8¼ A.M. Wrote to Canon Blomfield—Mr [T.] Newton (Inc. Tax Return)—Mr R. Moore (LNW)—Mr Lawson and Central News: Telegraphs.[6] Saw Mr Vickers—Mr Lester. Wrote on Hebrew Traditions in Homer. Worked on Books: my 4tos & upwards being in very bad arrangement. Cut small trees: walk with C: dismal weather, much threatening the cut corn. Read Hist. of Crusades—Martin on Ch. Revenues[7]—Hobart, Memoir & Essays.[8]

28. Tu.

Ch. 8¼ A.M. Wrote to Mr W. Saunders—Mrs Southey B.P.—A. Stearn—Mr W.A. Doby O—E. Stibbs—Mrs Merritt—J. Palmer—Mr J. Macnair[9]—Mons. de Lisle—Capt. Thomson—Sig. Carruti[10]—Mr Marshall—R. Hutchinson—E. Levy Lawson (& copy)—Mr Walcott—J.B. Wright—J.P. Betts. Cut down & kibbled a Spanish chestnut. Worked on Hebraic Traditions. Also had to open near 200 letters & packets: chiefly from London. Worked on book-arranging. Read History of Crusades—Martin on Church Revenues.

[1] A. Forrow, 'Thames and its docks: a lecture' (1877).

[2] An untraced earlier variant of Mrs C. Grant, *Queen and Cardinal: a memoir of Anne of Austria and of her relations with Cardinal Mazzarin* (1906).

[3] See 22 Apr. 77.

[4] C. Hill, *Continental Sunday labour* (1877).

[5] J. Gother, probably *Nubes Testium* (1686).

[6] Implying denial of authenticity of correspondence between himself and Negropontis on Greece and Turkey, reported in the *Telegraph*'s second ed. on 27 August; see *D.T.*, 28 August 1877, 5e and 19 Sept. 77n.

[7] F. Martin, *The property and revenues of the English establishment* (1877).

[8] V. H. Hobart, *Political essays. With short biographical sketch* (1877).

[9] J. R. MacNair of Glasgow, on church affairs; Hawn P.

[10] Domenico Carruti, Italian historian and biographer; Hawn P.

29. Wed.

Ch. 8½ AM. Wrote to Mr Levy Lawson—Most Rev. Migherdich Krimian[1]—Rev. W.W. Harvey—Mr Tschanschkoff[2]—Made Wassilieff BP[3]—Wms & Norgate— Rev. Dr Bartle[4]—M. Leon Seché[5]—Mr Doby O—Miss Giles BP—Mr Nelson—Mr Dunphy[6]—Mr Mitchell. Worked on arranging books. Worked on Thes. Hom. Read Hist. Crusades (finished)—Denton's Montenegro—Bartle's Jesus of Nazareth. Saw Mr Vickers—Mrs Stume, on her securities. Went over to see W. & G. at Leeswood where he & I felled a tree: a number of people were present. The place is pretty: but I regret their partial removal from Hawarden.[7] He bears it gently & well.

30. Th.

Ch. 8½ AM.Wrote to Mr H. Whitton Tel. & B.P.[8]—Jas Knowles—J. Ludlow O—W.H. Blanch[9]—Lord Bath BP.—Rev. Dr Miller—Mr Stibbs—Mr Bockett—Mr Padgham. Worked on the Colour Sense.[10] Worked on books a little. Began (with H.) the felling of a great Ash. Read Smellie's essay on King Arthur[11]—and divers other Tracts.

31. Fr.

Ch. 8½ AM. Wrote to Sir Arthur Gordon—Sir Geo. Bowen—Messrs Clay BP—Mr Macmillan—J. Lewis—W. Redfern—Mrs M'Coll. Corrected proofs for Macmillan. Worked on the Colour Sense. We brought down the Ash. Read Abbot on Bacon[12]—Dicey on Empire.[13]—Charles[14] came. I like his manful, simple, solid intelligence & character.

Sat. Sept. One 77.

Ch. 8½ A.M. Wrote to Rev. W.A. Brown—Rev. G. Macaulay—G. Vaughan—Rev. G. Grove[15]—A.F. Comper—A.F. Shipper—Lt W. Morris. A party stated at 600 came from Leigh & Rossendale. I submitted to the inevitable & turned the occasion to account by my references to Granville and by dealing pretty fully with

---

[1] To Migherdid Krimean, former patriarch of Armenia, on Turkish policy there; Add MS 44454, f. 361.

[2] Dragan Tsankov, Bulgarian nationalist leader; see Sumner, 253.

[3] Probably the wife of the orthodox priest; see 15 Feb. 65.

[4] George Bartle (Ph.D. Giessen; formerly head master of Walton college, Liverpool) had sent his *Jesus of Nazareth* (1877).

[5] Léon Séché, 1848–1914; French critic and historian.

[6] Henry Michael Dunphy, London barrister.

[7] See 9 Nov. 61, 9 Aug. 77.

[8] Henry Whitton, liberal in Newcastle, on Turkey; Hawn P.

[9] Perhaps of Blanch and sons, gunmakers.

[10] 'The colour sense', *Nineteenth Century*, ii. 366 (October 1877); on description of colour in Homer; see 17 May 77.

[11] A. Smellie, *The romance of King Arthur* (1877).   [12] See 5 June 76.

[13] E. Dicey, 'Mr Gladstone and our Empire', *Nineteenth Century*, ii. 292 (September 1877); a reply, see 21 July 77.

[14] C. C. Lacaita (see 31 Dec. 56); Hawarden Visitors Book.

[15] George Grove, vicar of Llanwenarth Ultra, Abergavenny.

the outrages now going on in a speech of perhaps 35 min.[1] Worked on Colour & Thes. Hom. Read Abbot on Bacon—Bunsen on the Egyptian Question, Ομηρική θεολογία.[2]—and [blank]

What is clear.
1. The Turkish Government is *not to be believed*.
2. That wholesale outrage is *committed* by large portion of its forces
3. That for these it has been *officially censured*—by Germany—alone?
4. That Capt. Wellesley acquits the Russian army generally
5. That the passions of war afford no palliation for cruelties to women & children
6. That these cruelties, detestable in any case, are yet more detestable if committed by *Christians*.
7. That there have been many of these cruelties committed by Christians: chiefly Bulgarians.

sanction of my name
joke—compliment—calumny.[3]

2. 14 S. Trin.

Ch. 11 A.M. and 6½ P.M. Wrote to Mr Macmillan—Count Schouvaloff, & copy[4]—Mr Gurdon—Mrs Winn. Walk with Charles [Lacaita]. Read Dr Bartle's queer Book—Vita del Card. Contarino[5]—Lewins on Vitalism.[6]

3. M.

Ch. 8¼ A.M. Wrote to M. Paul de Anino—Mr Murray (2)—Miss Jean Currie[7]—J. Woodhead—Rev W.E. Fleming[8]—Dr Lewins—Dr N. Hancock—Mr Summers—Mr Foxcroft[9] O—Mr Oakdew O—T. Cawnell. Worked on Colour—Thes. Hom. Read Nosce Teipsum—Abbot on Bacon.

4. Tu.

Ch. 8½ AM. Wrote to Mr W. Tattersall—Town Clerk of Nottingham—Messrs Farrer—Mr Thornton O—Mr Whibley—Mr Mugford—Mons. Borowski—Mr Fitzpatrick. Read Fortnightly Review—Paley on Q. Smyrnaeus.[10] Began the Posthomerica. Felled a sycamore. Ten to dinner. Worked on The Colour Sense.

[1] *Chester Chronicle*, 8 September 1877, 2c.
[2] See 26 Dec. 57.
[3] Holograph dated 1 September [1877], docketed 'Notes on Massacres. Granville's Speech'; Add MS 44763, f. 93. For Granville's Bradford speech, see *T.T.*, 29 August 1877, 9a.
[4] Denouncing as a forgery a supposed pro-Russian letter of 13 July to the Minister of War; Add MS 44455, f. 15.
[5] L. Beccadelli, *Vita del Cardinale Gasparo Contarini* (1746).
[6] R. Lewins, *Life and mind* (1877).
[7] Of Hendon; engaged in Bulgarian relief; Hawn P.
[8] William E. Fleming, anglican priest in Clogher; on the disestablished church in Ireland; Add MS 44455, f. 17.
[9] Sending Frank Foxcroft of U.S.A. an autograph; Hawn P.
[10] F. A. Paley, *On Quintus Smyrnaeus and the 'Homer' of the tragic poets* (1876).

5. Wed.

Ch. 8¼ A.M. Wrote to Govr Pope Hennessy—Gov. Sir A. Gordon—Ld Granville—Mr Levy Lawson BP—Mr Macmillan—Mr Woodruffe—C. Heseltine—Mr Pears Solr—Sir J. Watson—Col. Ross[1]—Mr Thomson. Worked on Colour-Sense. Corrected Revise[2] on Ithaca &c: & translated into heroics Il. II. 631-7. Worked on accounts. Woodcraft with Herbert. Read Quintus Smyrnaeus—Paley on do— Sir J. Watson's Statement.[3]

6. Th.

Ch. 8¼ A.M. Wrote to Ld Lymington[4]—Harry N.G.—Mr T. Murray BP—Rob. Gladstone—Mr M. Kerchan—Mr F. Hicks—Welland Vale Co.—Sir Jas Watson. Worked on the Colour Sense. Also woodcraft. Began to plan a republication of Essays &c. which Murray encourages.[5] Read Quintus Smyrnaeus—Schliemann, Proof Sheets on Mycenae & Tiryns.[6]

7. Fr.

Ch. 8¼ A.M. Wrote to Rev. W. Carus Wilson[7]—T.A. Welton[8]—F.A. Channing[9]— T.W. Russell—Jas Knowles—G. Webb—A.C. Yates.[10] Finished & dispatched my Paper on Colour-Sense. Went to Broughton for Mrs Swindley's funeral: but returned (after an hour) in consequence of its non arrival. Examined some cornfields. The wheat looked to my unskilled eye as if it had suffered: the oats better. Woodcraft. Read Quintus Smyrnaeus—Abbot on Bacon.

8. Sat.

Ch. 8½ A.M. Wrote to Robert Gladstone—Mr Lawson—G. Anderson—Messrs Watson—R. Dawson & copy—W.J. Raleigh—Dr Yeats[11]—T.W. Read—Mr Harrison—Welland Co. Worked on Thes. Hom. H. & I. felled a large elm. Worked on books. Read Quint. Smyrnaeus—Antiopium Address *from* China[12]— Abbot on Bacon: what a woful detail.

---

[1] Probably John Stephen Ross, retired soldier; a constituent.

[2] See 21 Aug. 77.

[3] A statement from his stock-broker, Sir James Watson.

[4] Newton Wallop, 1856-1917; styled Lord Lymington; liberal M.P. Barnstaple 1880-5, N. Devon 1885-91; 6th earl of Portsmouth 1891; had invited diarist to address the new Palmerston club at Oxford; Add MS 44455, f. 13; see 30 Jan. 78.

[5] Start of preparation of *Gleanings of past years, 1844-78* [*sic*], 7v. (1879); published by Murray; some articles from 1879 were included.

[6] Proofs of H. Schliemann, *Mycenae... preface by... W. E. Gladstone* (1878), with a fulsome dedication to diarist; see 20 Sept. 77.

[7] William Carus-Wilson, vicar of Maryland 1874.

[8] Thomas Abercrombie Welton, statistician; wrote on census inaccuracies.

[9] Francis Allston Channing, 1841-1926; barrister, fellow of University college, Oxford, and liberal M.P. E. Northamptonshire 1885-1910; cr. Baron 1912.

[10] Arthur C. Yates, journalist and author on politics.

[11] William Yeats, physician in Perth.

[12] Probably a tract from the Anglo-oriental society for the suppression of the opium trade.

9. 15 S. Trin.

Ch 11 AM 6½ PM Wrote to Mr W. Roskelly—Professor Milligan—Mr Jas Knowles. Read Milligan's 2 Articles[1]—Sanday on Gospel of St John[2]—Nott & Gliddon on Indigenous Races.[3] Walk with Walter James.

10. M.

Ch. 8¼ A.M. Wrote to Rev. T.M. Dickson[4]—R. Fleming—E. Windeatt[5]—A.J. Tilt[6]—Mrs Th. Worked on Books (manually) 1½ h. Worked on Thes Homerikos. Woodcraft with Herbert. Read Qu. Smyrnaeus—Windeatt on Totnes Records—Schliemann's Mycenian Vol. Classical conversation with Mr Godley & A. L[yttelton].

11. Tu.

Ch. 8¼ AM. Wrote to Mr Dawson Solr—Mr Pease MP.—W. Taylor—Mr Leeman MP—Mrs Jane Cross[7]—S.M. Glover. Mr Roden came, with his remarkable portrait of me.[8] He prosecuted his task while I worked peaceably at Thesauros Homerikos. (Connection with Hebrew traditions). Inquiries on the subject of the Dawson letter. Felled a cherry tree which is to be sold [blank] a foot over market price. Read Goldsmith on Owls—Quint. Smyrnaeus—Schl. on Mycenae. Conversation with [J. A.] Godley.

12. Wed.

Ch. 8¼ A.M. Wrote to Lord Salisbury—A. Wark—W. Delvalle[9]—Thorndike Rice (Tel.)[10]—Mr de la Fleuriere—A.J. Brereton—M. Chauffonier.[11] Mr Roden again watched, worked, & departed. We had however some conversation. Also conversation with Godley. Worked on Thes. Hom. Went to Buckley; saw Mr T. Read Quint. Smyrnaeus—Poems of . . .—Schliem. on Mycenae.

13. Th.

Ch. 8¼ A.M. Wrote to Mr Leeman MP. O—Rev. S. Gregory[12]—Ld Lymington—Mr Sedding—G.H. Briant—Robert Stuart—H.N.G.—E.F. Clarke[13]—T. Newton.

---

[1] W. Milligan on St John, *Contemporary Review*, xviii. 87, 212.

[2] W. Sanday, *The authorship and historical character of the Fourth Gospel considered* (1872).

[3] J. C. Nott and G. R. Gliddon, *Types of Mankind* (1854).

[4] Thomas Miller Dickson, d. 1897; formerly headmaster; presently without benefice; later a curate.

[5] E. Windeatt, had sent his *The parish church of St. Mary, Totnes, Devon* (1876).

[6] An artist, not traced with these initials; perhaps F. A. Tilt, known for engravings; see 13 Sept. 77.

[7] Probably involved in the Dawson affair.

[8] William Thomas *Roden, 1817-92; his rather poor portrait of Gladstone (now in Birmingham City Art Gallery) was for the Birmingham Council House, by subscription; Boase, *M.E.B.*, iii. 246.

[9] Walter Delvalle had written about electricity; Hawn P.

[10] Charles Allen Thorndike Rice, 1851-89; American journalist; Christ Church, Oxford; bought *North American Review* 1876 to which diarist contributed, see 21 June 78.

[11] Of the French Benevolent Society; Hawn P.

[12] Samuel Gregory, nonconformist minister in Leeds; Hawn P.

[13] Edward Francis Channing Clarke, barrister, sent a pamphlet; Hawn P.

Worked on Thesauros Homerikos. Saw Mr Tilt: who had a sitting from me such as Mr Roden's for his etching. Felled an ash with Herbert. He is such good company. Read Clarke's Three Dangers[1]—Hole's Ulysses[2]—Quintus Smyrnaeus—Schliemann's Mycenae. Twelve to dinner.

14. Fr.

Ch. 8½ A.M. Wrote to Mr Levy Lawson[3]—G. Errington—A. Macmillan—W. Tattersall—Mrs C. Goodall—W. Leach[4]—T.S. Baynes—A. Murdoch and B.P.[5] Saw Mr Vickers. Worked on Thes. Homerikos. Woodcraft with W. & H. Read Q. Smyrnaeus—Hole's Ulysses—Schreiber's *Versuch* on Ithaca[6]—Schliemann on Mycenae.

15. Sat.

Ch. 8½ A.M. Wrote to Mr C.N. Wilkinson—Mr B. Brooks BP—Dr Grosart—D. of St Alban's—Rev. H. Overy[7]—Mr Woodhouse O—Mr Greyson—Master of Charterhouse—Rev. Mr Falloon—Mr T. Dowson & BP[8]—Mr Ouvry Tel. Woodcraft. Worked on Thes. Hom. Read Qu. Smyrnaeus—L'Abbé Valin[9]—Schliemann on Mycenae.

16. 16 S. Trin.

Ch. 11 AM & H.C.—6¼ PM. Wrote to Wm Lyttelton—Duke of Argyll—Wms & Norgate—Mr A. M'Kenzie—Mr Leeman BP—L'Abbé Valin B.P.—Mr C. Hill. Arranged the remainder of my theol. 4toes, to prevent sleep after the ill-omened early dinner! Read The Survival[10]—Memoir of Rev. Mr Hawker[11]—La Réforme Catholique.[12]

17. M.

Ch. 8½ A.M. Wrote to Ld Wolverton Tel.—Mr Levy Lawson Tel.—Master of Charterhouse B.P.—Rev. J.T. Hodges—R.C. Jenkins—R. Berryman[13]—A. Macmillan—Grenville Murray[14]—J.H. Evans—J. Mackie—F. Thomas—J. Ericson. Three good hours on my quartoes and large books finished in the main the

---

[1] Not found.   [2] By R. Hole (1807).

[3] 'I have been very unwilling to come out, in a polemical way as it needs must be more or less, in relation to you and yours [in the Negropontis affair], but I am afraid that if I wait much longer the matter will become ridiculous'; Add MS 44455, f. 51; see 19 Sept. 77.

[4] Apparently declining to write on 'Episcopacy' for the *Encyclopedia Britannica*; Add MS 44455, f. 47.

[5] Alexander Murdoch of Glasgow, a 'Scottish working artisan', had sent verses; Add MS 44455, f. 41.

[6] By C. C. E. Schreiber (1829).

[7] Henry Overy, vicar of Lostwithiel; published tracts.

[8] Possibly Thomas Dowson, poet.

[9] Claude Marie Valin, author of *De l'Ultramontanisme et du Gallicanisme* (1877); see 30 Sept. 77.

[10] *The survival: With an apology for scepticism* (1877).

[11] F. G. Lee, *Memorials of. . . R. S. Hawker* (1876).   [12] Untraced; sent by Abbé Valin?

[13] Perhaps of Berryman and Turner, insurance brokers.

[14] Eustace Clare Grenville Murray (1824–81); diplomat in the Levant; fled to Paris after perjury charge 1869; journalist; published on Turkey (see 6 July 77); see 31 Dec. 77?

business of arranging my library wh is now in better order than for many years. Read Qu. Smyrnaeus—Schliemann on Mycenae. Woodcraft.

18. Tu.

Ch. 8½ AM. Wrote to Mr Thornton—Mr J. Murray—Mr . . .—Mr Levy Lawson Tel. l. & copy. Another 1½ hour on my library: odds & ends. Read Qu. Smyrnaeus—Schliemann's Mycenae—finished. The school feast was today. Dined at the Rectory. Conversation with Mr Ottley. Wolverton came—much conversation with him: he is hearty as ever, and refreshing in proportion.

19. Wed.

Ch. 8½ A.M. Wrote to Marquis of Salisbury—Lord Belper—Rob. Gladstone—Mr [E. M.] Barry (Pres. of Architects)—Mir Anked Ali—Mr Armstrong—Mr G. Smith—Mr Macmillan—Sec. G.W. Railway—Mr W. Middleton. Also wrote & read over to Wolverton a long letter to Ed. Telegraph, not a pleasant one to write or to receive.[1] Hawarden School Prize Day. I made the distribution: & an Address of perhaps ½ hour.[2] Walk with Wolverton, & much conversation. Read Qu. Smyrnaeus.

20. Th.

Ch. 8½ A.M. Wrote to Duke of St Albans—Mr E.A. Freeman—Rev. O. Shipley—Rev. P. Phelan[3]—Rev. Mr Macaulay—Mr Williams, Nottm,[4] Tel.—Mr Bailey, Wrxham, Tel.—Mr A.H. Johnstone—Mr Bate—Mr Ouvry—Mr Knowles—Mr M'Bean—Mr Agnew. Wolverton went off early. Corrected my proofs on the Colour-Sense. Began Preface for Schliemann.[5] Read Qu. Smyrnaeus—Newtons Report on Mycenae.[6] Cut an ash with Herbert. Saw the Mayor of Chester. Just made a taste of revision with a view to the republication of Essays &c.[7]

21. Fr. St Matth.

Ch. 8¾ A.M. A memorable day in 1847 D.G.[8] Wrote to Sec. G.W. Railway—Mr Williams Nottm (Tel.)—Mr Murray—Mr Buck—Mr Chesson—Mr Knowles—A. Ellis—Town Clerk of Nottingham—Mr Campbell—F. Redmond—W.A. Harrison—Mrs Pycock. Woodcraft with W. & H. Worked much on Preface to Schliemann and dispatched a portion to Murray. Read Quintus Smyrnaeus—Noel's House of Ravenspurg.[9]

---

[1] Published in the *D.T.*, 25 September 1877, 5g with the paper's qualified apology for charging that the Negropontis correspondence (see 9 Jan. 77n.) was an intrigue to stir up the Greeks against the Turks; see also S. Koss, *The rise and fall of the political press in Britain* (1981), i. 202 and 12 Mar. 78n.

[2] *Chester Chronicle*, 22 September 1877, 6f.

[3] Patrick Phelan, Roman catholic incumbent in Finsbury.

[4] See 27 Sept. 77.

[5] See 6 Sept. 77; preface of 35 pages, dated 'November 1877'.

[6] By C. T. Newton in *T.T.*, 20 April 1877, discussed in diarist's preface to Schliemann.

[7] Start of *Gleanings*; see 6 Sept. 77.

[8] Crisis of his daughter Agnes' erysipelas.

[9] By R. B. W. Noel (1877).

22. Sat.

Ch. 8½ A.M. Wrote to Duke of St Albans—Mr Williams Nottm 2 Telegr.—Mr Salisbury—Sir Thos G.—Welland Vale Co.—Mr G. Bellis—Mons. V. Oger—Rev Mr Noott & B.P.[1]—Mr S. St Emmans[2]—Lady Fox[3]—Mr Kirkman Hodgson. Woodcraft with Herbert. Worked much on Preface to Schliemann: and finished it late at night. Read Qu. Smyrnaeus.

23. 17 S. Trin.

Ch 11 AM and [blank] P.M.—We conceived a scheme for a monument to Henry Glynne, as a *pair* to that of S.[4] Wrote to Messrs Clowes B.P.—Mr Murray—Rev. C. Ivens[5]—Mr Ouvry—Mr Lawson—Ed. Echo[6]—A.M.A. (Bridgnorth)—Mr W.S. Raleigh—Mrs Winn—Reeves & Turner—Rev S. Simms[7]—Mr S.E. Thomas. Also copied out fair my long suspended letter to D. Telegraph. Read Life of Hawker—Simms on Oath of Allegiance—The Burials Bill.

24. M. [London]

Alarmed in the night by serious threatening of Diarrhoea, but it came round. Up at 7.15 and off at 8.45. Wrote to Mr Williams Nottm (Tel)—Rev. Mr Fleming—Rev. Mr O'Brien—Mr Castledale—Ed. Times—Ed. D. News—C.G.—Mr Hine—Mr Vickers—Ld Hartington—Mr Saunders O. On reaching Harley St at 3½ I found Mr [Levy] Lawson with an oral account of his correspondent's message such as I thought insufficient. So my letter went off with him.[8] Saw also Sir A. Panizzi—Phillips X—Dashwood &c.—Mr Green. Dined with Mr Macmillan at the Garrick Club: a literary party. Worked a little on my Chaos. Read Jebb, Primer of Greek Literature.[9]

25. Tu.

Wrote to Mr Gurney—Vicomte de Laon—Dr Zaimes[10]—Mr Williams (Nottm)—Mr Johnson (do)—Mr Palmer—Lady Robertson[11]—Mr Sneale—Marjoribanks (bis)—U. Sec. for India[12]—Mr J. Brock—Mr Knowles—Mr Agnew. Saw Mr Ouvry on Newcastle [Trust] affairs 1 h. Dr P. Smith & Mr [C. T.] Newton on the Schliemann Preface 2 h. Mr Murray on the republication of Essays[13]—London

---

[1] Edward Henry Lane Noott, d. 1905; vicar of Dudley from 1843.

[2] If St Eman intended, then pseudonym of Eman Martin *fils*, poet and novelist.

[3] Widow of Sir Charles Fox, 1810-74; engineer.

[4] Apparently never built.

[5] Coleman Ivens, curate of Whitton; published tracts.

[6] Sending a copy of his letter to the *Telegraph*; *Echo*, 25 September 1877, 3c.

[7] Samuel Simms had sent his *The oath of allegiance: what it imports* (1877), published in Belfast.

[8] See 19 Sept. 77.

[9] In the Macmillan series of *Literature Primers*, ed. J. R. *Green; Macmillan and Green persuaded Gladstone to contribute *Homer* (1878) to it; see Green to Gladstone, 18 September 1877, Add MS 44455, f. 60 and 20 Nov. 77.

[10] May read 'Zairnes'.   [11] Ellen, wife of Sir D. B. Robertson.

[12] Letter untraced; perhaps on Burma, on which he was in correspondence with Salisbury; Add MS 44455, f. 52.

[13] See 6 Sept. 77.

& Westmr Bank. Shopping. Dined with Mrs Th: went for an hour to the Alhambra where there was the prettiest & best ballet I ever saw.[1] Then read [Tennyson's] Guinevere aloud. Reduced my chaos to some kind of order.

26. *Wed.* [*Bestwood Lodge, Nottingham*]

Much packing & arranging. Wrote to Ed. Spectator—Ed. D. Telegraph—A.C. Mackenzie—Mr Ouvry—Mrs Th.—Mr Buckstone Tel. Saw Mr Knowles—Sir A. Panizzi—Scotts—Mr Ellis (Sub)—Mr Newton. 2.30-6.30 to Bestwood:[2] we were most kindly received. Saw Mr Lancaster—Mayor of Nottingham—Mr Ward—& others. Read Tracts on E. Question.

27. *Th.*

Wrote to Mr Noddall (Nk)[3]—Mr Sadler (Derby).[4] Read the College papers mg. At 11.20 drove down to Nottingham and spoke to a great concourse at the laying of the Foundation Stone of the new College.[5] At 2 came the *luncheon*, wh lasted till the evening: I went off at 5.30 after proposing prosperity in rather a long speech. In the interval I had visited the Castle & was much pleased. At 6 went to the Rink & addressed near 10000 for perhaps an *oretta*.[6] They were most patient & heard well. It was a hard day's work for the voice.[7] We wound up with $\frac{1}{2}$ hour at the Theatre: School for Scandal, very well done. Back to Bestwood for dinner at $9\frac{1}{4}$.

28. *Fr.*

Wrote to Mr Buckstone. Read Question d'Orient.[8] Visited the Church—The great Colliery[9]—Spent some hours at Newstead in viewing it. There are some most beautiful remains. Then on to Worksop & Sparken where I spent the evening on Trust matters with Mr Williams, Mr Ouvry, and Mr Wright. Saw Mr Lancaster.

29. *Sat. Michs.* [*Hawarden*]

Wrote to Mr Allsop.[10] At 9 we drove to Shirwalls & held a conclave there. The whole matter of the Church was cleared up with strong consent of Mr Blomfield, Mr Thompson, & Mr Lancaster: & matters put in train for a remedy. Then we saw an oak cut—and visited the Colliery. Off at 12 for Chester & Hawarden 6.30. Saw Mr C. Townshend—Mr R. Barker—Ld Lymington—and found a party at home. Read Bendan's Memoir[11]—Finished Question d'Orient &c.

---

[1] Alfred Thompson's 'Yolande'.
[2] Seat of the duke of St Albans, 6 miles north of Nottingham.
[3] Of W. T. and S. Noddall, Newark tailors.   [4] Not further identified.
[5] University college, later the University of Nottingham.
[6] 'A little hour'.   [7] *T.T.*, 28 September 1877, 8a; he appeared with Carnarvon.
[8] *La Question d'Orient comme conséquence inévitable du partage de la Pologne* (1877).
[9] Bestwood colliery, owned by the Bestwood Coal and Iron Co., well known for its poor labour relations; an early and radical branch of the Nottinghamshire Miners Association flourished there in the 1880s.
[10] Perhaps H. A. Allport, manager of the colliery.   [11] See 14 Mar. 76n.

30. 18 S. Trin.

Ch 11 AM and 6½ PM. Wrote to Ld Wolverton—Canon Ashwell—Scotts—Mr Barker. Wrote Notice of M. Valin.[1] Read Kenealy, Prayers[2]—Boissie:, Religion Romaine[3]—and [blank.]

Mond. Oct. One 1877.

Ch. 8½ AM. Wrote to Mrs Weldon—Mr R.H. Hutton (BP)—Mr Thomas—J.B. Wells—A. Sinclair—J. Middleton—J.F. Caskin—E.G. Salisbury—Rev. W. Nevins—Sir Harcourt Johnstone MP.—Mr Brough—Mr Cameron—G. Saunders[4]—T. Enley—Mr Ellis—Ld Mayor. Arranging letters. Finished Q. Curtius and wrote briefly upon him. Saw Mr Vickers—Mr Webb—Dr Dobie.[5] Thirteen to dinner. Read also 19th C. on The Empire.[6]

2. Tu.

Ch. 8½ A.M. Wrote to Sir H. Taylor—Rev. Dr Badger—Central News(Tel.)—Cav. Crespi [sic][7]—Mr Macmillan—M. Jenkinson—W.H. Reed—J.C. Walmsley[8]—J. Hitchman—A. Arnold. Read Badger on Islam[9]—Paton on Priesthood[10]—Prolegomena to Q. Curtius. Woodcraft with Herbert. Worked on Preface to Mycenean Volume.

3. Wed.

Ch. 8½ AM. Wrote to Messrs Clowes—Dr Ph. Smith—A. Simmons—Canon Ashwell—Hugh Owen—E. Davis. Worked on Preface to Schliemann. Wrote Notice of D'Eichthal's Pamphlet on Society for promotion of Greek studies.[11] Read D'Eichthal's pamphlet—R. Lowe on County Franchise. (The burnt child does *not* dread the fire!)[12]—Mrs Meer Hassan Ali on Indian Mahomedans.[13] Mr Dodson came: walk with him.

---

[1] Published in *Church Quarterly Review*, v. 253; see Add MS 44455, f. 138.

[2] E. V. H. Kenealy, *Poems and translations* (1864).

[3] By M. L. A. G. Boissier, 2v. (1874).

[4] George Saunders, 1859-1922; then at Balliol, later a journalist; on the Balkans (Churchill College, Cambridge, Saunders MSS).

[5] William Murray Dobie, physician at Chester general infirmary.

[6] See 31 Aug. 77n.

[7] Francesco Crispi, 1819-1901; Sicilian politician; once Garibaldi's secretary; prime minister 1887-91, 1893-6. See 6 Oct. 77.

[8] Perhaps James Vickers Walmsley of Old Brompton.

[9] G. P. Badger, *History of the Imams and seyyids of Oman* (1871).

[10] J. B. Paton, *The origin of the priesthood* (1877).

[11] Clearly the short notice in *Church Quarterly Review*, v. 545 (January 1878) of M. G. d'Eichthal, *Notice sur la fondation et le developpement de l'Association pour l'encouragement des études Greques en France* (1877).

[12] R. Lowe, 'A new Reform Bill', *Fortnightly Review*, xxviii. 437 (October 1877); see 9 Oct. 77.

[13] Mrs Mir Hasan Ali, *Observations on the Mussulmanns of India*, 2v. (1832).

4. Th.

Ch. 8½ A.M. Wrote to R. Thomson—J.J. Andrew[1]—Rev. H. Piggin[2]—Messrs Spottiswoode—W.W. Kerr[3]—T.W. Rawson[4]—Wilfrid Meynell[5]—Mr Helliwell—Rev. S.A. Barnett[6]—Jos. Green—L.B. Cowie—Mr Heaton—Mr Winsor—S. Mason—Jas Cowper. Worked on Primer (Ethnology).[7] Read Oenida Community(!)[8]—Mrs M.H.A. on Mahometans—Hutton on Bagehot.[9] Woodcraft alone.

5. Fr.

Ch. 8¼ AM. Wrote to Mr Gennadios—J. Latouche—Rev. Dr Sinclair—Rev. J.R. Humble[10]—Rev. R.E. Healey[11]—Editor of Times—A. Macdonald[12]—A.L. Lewis—R.G. Waters—W.T. Stead—T.H. Barker[13]—S. Tatton. Worked on Primer—Homeric Question. Saw W.H.G. (Estate &c.)—Mr Barker cum Mr Vickers. Walk with Sir R. Cunliffe & his party. Read Lewis on lost Tribes[14]—Other pamphlets—Mrs M. on Mahometans—Prolegom. to Q. Smyrnaeus.

6. Sat.

Ch. 8¼ AM. Wrote to Mr Godley BP.—Rev. E. Wickham—Rev. W. Durnford—Rev. D. MacColl[15]—Rev. N.W.G. Hunter—Hon. & Rev. O. Forester[16]—M. Gennadios BP—Mr Bryce—A. Forbes—J. Spence—W. Haughton. Worked on Primer—Preface to Schliemann. Saw Mr Vickers—Cav. Crespi [sc. Crispi] who came early & staid all day: he had not a great deal to say: a sound politician, no more. Read Mrs M. on Mahometans—Prolegom. to Q. Smyrnaeus.

7. 19 S. Trin.

Ch. 11 A.M. with H.C. & 6½ PM. Conversation with Herbert & Helen. Wrote to Mr Owen (Bristol)—Mr Knowles—Mr Foster—Mr Murray. Read Boissier, Rel. des Rom.—Secrets of Ritualism[17]—God & Society at variance[18]—Dr Hale's Innocent of Moscow[19]—Bp Eden's Charge[20]—Mr Piggin's Charge.[21]

[1] John James Andrew, religious author.   [2] Henry Piggin, see 7 Oct. 77n.

[3] William Williamson Kerr, barrister and author.

[4] Thomas William Rawson of Nottingham, on diarist's successful conversion of a tory during his visit; Add MS 44455, f. 116.

[5] Wilfrid Meynell, 1852-1948; author and ed. of poetry; see 15 Oct. 78n.

[6] Samuel Augustus *Barnett, 1844-1913; rector of St. Jude's, Whitechapel; social reformer and first Warden of Toynbee Hall 1884; canon of Bristol 1894.

[7] See 24 Sept. 77n.   [8] Untraced.

[9] R. H. Hutton, 'Walter Bagehot', *Fortnightly Review*, xxviii. 453 (October 1877).

[10] John Ralph Humble, curate of Tynemouth 1875.

[11] Randolph Eddowes Healey, 1847-1933; from Liverpool; rector of Crumpsall 1877-98.

[12] Perhaps Alexander Macdonald, d. 1881; miner and liberal M.P. Stafford 1874-81.

[13] Thomas Holliday Barker, 1818-89; sec. of U.K. Alliance 1853-83.

[14] Not found.

[15] Dugald MacColl, episcopalian incumbent of Salen, Mull.

[16] Orlando Watkin Weld Forester, 1813-94; rector of Gedling 1867-87; 4th Baron Forester 1886.

[17] Perhaps *The ritualistic conspiracy* (1877).   [18] Not found.

[19] C. R. Hale, *Innocent of Moscow* (1877).   [20] R. Eden, 'Charge ... August 28, 1877' (1877).

[21] H. Piggin, 'The Ministerial gift. An ordination charge' (1877).

8. M.

Ch. 8½ AM. Wrote to Mr Johnson—Mr Kernaghan[1]—G.R. Thomas—A. Macdonald—N.J. Newnham—Mr Rubenstein—Messrs Macmillan—Mr Salisbury—Messrs W. Hunt—Mrs Th.—Mr Balfour[2]—Mr Mudge—E.C.F.n. [*sic*]. Worked on Preface to Schliemann. Walk with Herbert to Dee Cottage &c. Saw The Rector. Col. Feilden[3] with Mr Ward & his party. Read on the Mahometans—Carpenter, Preventive Medicine.[4]

9. Tu.

Ch. 8½ A.M. Wrote to Mr Murray—Messrs Murray—Lord Monck—Mons. d'Eichthal—Dean of St Asaph—F. Battersby—W.H. Calcott—Dr A. Carpenter—R.K. Dent[5]—Mr Salisbury—Sir S. Scott & Co—H.J. Hardy[6]—Rev. W. Nevins. Worked much on Schliemann Preface. Also began reply to Lowe.[7] Felled an ash with WHG. Read Mrs M on Mahometans—Lowe on Suffrage (2°).

10. Wed.

Ch. 8½ AM. Wrote to Ld Granville—Messrs Clowes BP—E.H. Bayley[8]—C.A. Beckett—Sig. Malinverni[9]—Ld Eliot—Mr Strahan—C. Newton—Mr Lowater.[10] Four hours of work finished the Preface to Schliemann's Book. A long & pleasing walk with W. Lyttelton. My brain was rather tired as walk was work. Read Mrs M. on Mahometans—Le Moribond de l'Europe.[11]

11. Th.

Ch. 8½ A.M. Wrote to Made Novikoff—Ed. of Times 2[12]—Ed. K. Mercury—Messrs Macmillan—Mr J. Girdlestone[13]—Justice Lawson—Mr Earwaker—Mr Meyerstein[14]—Mr Bryce—J.C. King—S. Allin. Worked on The Suffrage, a reply

[1] Adam Kernaghan, London correspondent of the *Freeman's Journal*, had written to ask truth of rumours of diarist's Irish visit, so reporting could be arranged; draft confirming the visit at Add MS 44455, f. 164; see 17 Oct. 77.

[2] Inviting him to join the party visiting Ireland; Balfour replied (10 October 1877, Add MS 44455, f. 177): 'whether yr. estimate of my power of locomotion is or is not exaggerated it certainly is no difficulty of that sort which prevents me accepting your very kind invitation to accompany you to Ireland. Unfortunately I have fifteen good reasons for not going in the shape of guests at Whittinghame.'

[3] Randle Joseph Feilden, 1824-95; soldier, fought at Red River 1870; tory M.P. N. Lancashire 1880-5, Chorley 1885-95.

[4] A. Carpenter, *Preventive medicine* (1877).

[5] Robert Kirkup Dent of Birmingham, travel writer.

[6] Henry John Hardy, then a boy at Winchester; later a master there; corresponding on Homer; Hawn P.

[7] 'The county franchise, and Mr. Lowe thereon', *Nineteenth Century*, ii. 537 (November 1877), reprinted in *Gleanings*, i. 131. See 3 Oct. 77.

[8] Southwark radical; see 16 July 78.

[9] Perhaps Sisto Germano Malinverni, Italian surgeon and politician.

[10] L. Lowater of Nottingham, on divisions in the party there; Hawn P.

[11] [E. Gamber], *Le Moribund de l'Europe* (1865).

[12] On his supposed correspondence with Messrs. Geshoff; *T.T.*, 13 October 1877, 5f.

[13] James Girdlestone, London solicitor; on Greek ecclesiastical law; Hawn P.

[14] Probably Emil Meyerstein of London; had sent a book; Hawn P.

to Lowe. Cut & kibbled two trees in my clump: walk back. Read Mrs M. on Mahometans.

12. Fr.

Ch. 8¼ AM. Wrote to Prov. Trin. Coll. Dublin[1]—Abp of Dublin—Sig. Cristini—E.H. Bayley—J.C. King—Rev. R. Phillips—Mr Latham—J. Nash—J. Watt—Jas Knowles. Felled an ash with WHG. Worked on the Suffrage paper. Read Mem. on Bp Kettler[2]—Mrs M. on Indian Mahometans—Vol II.—Noels House of Ravenspurg. Diarrhoea came on in evg: I think from over head-work.

13. Sat.

Rose at 10.30. Wrote to Mrs Martindale—Rev. Mr Tomson[3]—Ld Waveney—Mr Shaw Lefevre—Rev. C.L.M. Jones—Mr Symonds[4]—M. Meyerstein—Mr Johnson—Rev. W.F.W. Torre. Walk with W.H.L. & Mr Ottley. Worked pretty well on the Suffrage paper. Read Mrs M. on Mahometans—House of Ravenspurg. Much conversation on archaic matters with my co-pedestrians.

14. 20 S. Trin.

Ch 11 A.M. (read the Lessons, *noble* ones) and 6¼ P.M. Wrote to Sig. Cristini—Mrs Barrett—Mr Bennett—Mr Keen—Mr W. Alexander—Mr Downing. Read Ch. Qu. on Dr Abbot—On Church of Ireland[5]—Puller's Letters[6]—Life of Hawker.[7] Worked an hour on Suffrage.

15. M.

Ch. 8¼ A.M. Wrote to Mr Lowe—Mr Knowles—Mr Ouvry—Mr Costelloe[8]—Mr Mundella—Mr MacCarthy—Helen G (BP). Finished, revised, and dispatched, MS on Suffrage. Woodcraft with WHG. Tea at the Cottage. Saw Mr Devey. Read Mrs M. on Mahometans of India. Dined at the Rectory: much conversation.

16. Tu.

Ch. 8½ A.M. Wrote to Made O. Novikoff—Edr of Echo—Ld Kenmare—Mr [H.] Law MP (2)[9]—Mr MacElvey—F.D. Finlay—Reeves & Turner—Rev. Dr Gregg—

---

[1] H. *Lloyd; see 19 June 67, 17 Oct. 77.
[2] 'A Latin bishop—Ketteler of Mainz', *Foreign Church Chronicle*, i. 137 (September 1877).
[3] Word scrawled; might read Jannon.
[4] Perhaps John Addington *Symonds, 1840–93; renaissance historian; see 8 Nov. 77.
[5] *Church Quarterly Review*, v. 178 (October 1877).
[6] F. W. Puller, 'The duties and rights of parish priests. A letter' (1877).
[7] See 16 Sept. 77.
[8] B. F. C. Costello, on the Glasgow rectorship; Hawn P.
[9] Irish law officer in the 1868 govt. (see 26 Feb. 69); regretfully declining to visit the north while in Ireland: 'It would have given me much pleasure to receive such a deputation as has been proposed, and while doing it to enter upon questions of public interest, were it not that I have felt it necessary to consider in what a position a visit paid to the North would place me with reference to other parts of Ireland. In those other parts, the differences that prevail with regard to prospective policy, and the present severance of so many Irish members on the popular side from the leaders

W. Bellhouse[1]—W.F. Kenny[2]—Supt Bookshop RR.—Mr Consul Pellet—Mr Aronsberg—Mr Downing BP—Herbert J.G.—Mr Hitchman—Mr Murray—C. Neale—Mr Godley—C.O. Shea [*sic*]—D.J. Ryan. Much sorting of letters & preparation for departure. Saw Mr Vickers. Read Mrs M.on Mahometans.

17. Wed.

Wrote to Mr Knowles—Mr Kingsmill—Scotts—Rev. S.E.G.

Irish Tour.[3]

Wed. Oct 17. 1877 [*Kilruddery, Bray*]

We set out at 10¾ with a boisterous sky: but, after a warm reception suddenly got up at Holyhead, we had an excellent passage with very kind treatment on board the Connaught. I was delighted with the grand appearance of the Wicklow Coast & we had a far stretching view (as I believe) along the line of Wexford, between four & five. At Kingstown it was dusk. A newsman called 'You're welcome to Ireland[']. A voice from behind 'No you're not[']. Mr O'Brien[4] from the F[reeman's] Journal interviewed me on the Quay. We drove off & reached Kilruddery[5] soon after 7: I need not say how we were received. A large party: long conversation with the Provost [H. Lloyd] of Trin. Coll. Read Rural Life in 18th Cent.[6]—Jasper More, Under the Balkans.[7]

and the party under and with whom I act, lead me to believe that no advantage would be gained were I to connect my visit in any degree or form with public affairs. On the other hand, though no such difficulties would meet me in the North, I think the selection of one part of the country to the exclusion of others would wound that kindly feeling which I find everywhere to prevail. It might also give rise to the belief that I was dissatisfied either with the reception or with the operation of the important laws relating to Ireland which form so large a part of the history of the last Administration. Such a belief would be the exact reverse of truth'; version in *T.T.*, 20 October 1877, 6e; draft at Add MS 44763, f. 95. For plans for an Ulster visit, see T. Macknight, *Ulster as it is* (1896), i. 342ff.

[1] William Bellhouse, an admirer in Leeds; Hawn P.

[2] W. T. Kenny of the Irish mercantile clerks' association; unable to give prizes to it; *Freeman's Journal*, 18 October 1877, 6a.

[3] Kept on separate 5 sheets of pale yellow paper, folded to form 20 edges, now bound at the back of Lambeth MS 1446. 'Bray £50. Builth 1' written in margin.

[4] William O'Brien, 1852-1928; journalist on *Freeman's Journal*; ed. *United Ireland* (imprisoned and journal suppressed 1881-2); home rule M.P. 1883-95; anti-Parnellite 1890; conciliator. For the interview, see *F.J.*, 18 October 1877, 5g: 'His arrival was something of a secret. Without actually shrouding his movements, he had sent no word to herald his coming, and made no sign to invite any popular intrusion on his privacy.... Not a single Irish Liberal politician, not one of Mr Gladstone's conspicuous political friends, was in sight. The secret had plainly been well kept.' Gladstone mentioned his letter to Law as explaining his limited travelling in Ireland, but emphasized 'really what I want is to see the people. I have this long time desired to do so.' The interview, a considerable scoop, was attacked as unfair, or a fabrication, by Irish tory papers; see *F.J.*, 22 October 1877, 7a.

[5] Seat, in Co. Wicklow (about 14 miles s. of Dublin at the foot of the Little Sugar Loaf mountain) of the 11th earl of Meath, a relative of Catherine Gladstone; see 23 July 38n.

[6] [W. Alexander], *Notes and sketches of northern rural life in the eighteenth century* (1877).

[7] R. J. More, *Under the Balkans* (1877).

18. Th.

St Luke & dear Agnes's birthday: *Benedictus benedicat*.

Wrote to Mr [W.] Sharman Crawford—Knight of Kerry[1]—Mr Bence Jones—Ld Emly—Mr Mitchell Henry. We went over the wick & beautiful pleasure grounds in the forenoon: afternoon walk over Bray Head with its noble prospects. Read Murray's Handbook of Ireland—Jasper More's Under the Balkans—MacCarthy's Plea for the Home Govt of Ireland.[2] Much perplexed with the number of kind invitations: the larger parts of my project gradually fade from view, & my movements must be in a small⟨er⟩ circle. Saw Corresp. Fr. Journal.[3] Even here, in the least Irish part of Ireland, there is much to observe & learn.

19. Fr.

Wrote to Rev. Mr Seymour (2)[4]—Mr Ouvry—Mr Fraser—Mr Richardson—Ld Bessborough—Ld Monck—Ld Kenmare—Mr Bussy.[5] Conversation with the Provost (Mus. Mycenae)—Mrs Lloyd[6]—on woman's Educn. Saw Saunders' Reporter[7]—Ld Brabazon. Gardens mg—a beautiful drive aftn. Read Jasper More's Under the Balkans—Capt. Burnaby's Ride through Asia Minor.[8] We drove by the Belle Vue pass—Walk with SL. Whist in evg. Conversation with Brabazon:[9] he seems full of mind & conscience: an invalid for the moment.

20. Sat.

Wrote twelve minutes for S.L. 2 or 2½ hours of *reading* the letters of the day. Corrected the proofs of article on the Franchise. 11-6¼. To Dublin: Christ Church, where were Mr Rowe[10] & Mr Vane. Went over Church, Crypt, & Synod Hall: most interesting: then to Viceregal Lodge for luncheon: walk aftn. Conversation with the Duke[11]—the Duchess—Canon Lee[12]—Lady Hodson[13]—Lady M[eath]—how good—& *still* how beautiful. Excellent music. But not enough of *Ireland*. However I have no choice. Saw Divers correspondents of papers. Read Acct of Busbrook Model Settlement.[14]

---

[1] Sir Peter George FitzGerald, 1808-80; known as the Knight of Kerry; agriculturalist; cr. bart. 1880. On 11 Oct. had invited diarist to visit Killarney; reply dated this day; Add MS 44455, f. 185.

[2] See 20 Jan. 72.

[3] See *F.J.*, 22 October 1877, 7b.

[4] Michael Hobart Seymour, wrote on the Irish church.

[5] G. M. Bussy; not further identified.

[6] Dorothea, wife of the provost.

[7] Of the Dublin tory daily *Saunders's News Letter*, which claimed on 20 October 1877, 3a, support for its complaint at O'Brien's interview (see 17 Oct. 77).

[8] F. G. Burnaby, *On horseback through Asia Minor*, 2v. (1877).

[9] Reginald, Lord Brabazon, 1841-1929; minor diplomat and author; 12th earl of Meath 1887.

[10] Henry Roe, assisting its restoration.

[11] The 7th duke of Marlborough, viceroy of Ireland 1876-80.

[12] William Lee, 1815-83; archdeacon of Dublin from 1864.

[13] Meriel Anne, wife of Sir George Frederick John Hodson, of Hollybrooke House, Bray, 1806-88; 3rd bart. 1831.   [14] Not found.

21. *21 S. Trin.*

Bray Ch mg (with H.S.) at 11—& 4 PM. A fine fabric. Aft. service intoned. Finished my (Proof-sheets) concluding words. Lengthened conversation on the state of Belief & other like matters with Lady Sherborne[1] & Ld Brabazon. Wrote to Mr Knowles B.P.—Mr Godley—Mr Potter. Read Mozley on Miracles—and [blank].

22. *M.*

Wrote to Lady Sherborne—Sir H. Bruce—Ld Castletown—Mr Knowles (Tel)— Mr Sharman Crawford—Ld Emly—Mr Gray MP.—Knight of Kerry. Off at 10½ to Dublin. We went over the College Halls & Library: luncheon with the Provost, whom I like more & more: and a short address to the Students, which they pressed hard for.[2] Then to the Bank.—The Museum, which was most interesting—& St Patrick's aft. service. At the close the Dean[3] conducted us over the Church. Home about six. Conversation with Dean of St P.—Ld Monck—Dr Lloyd, who described the Disestablishment as an "undoubted good". Read Barney Geoghegan[4]—Roberts on Mother Church.[5]

23. *Tu.*

Wrote eleven Minutes: & letters to Ld Spencer—Mr Darwin[6]—Ld Lifford—Ld O'Neill[7]—Miss Cusack[8]—Made Novikoff—Dr Adams—Mr Peake—Mr Lankester. In the forenoon, we went up the Sugar Loaf. Saw Central News Reporter—Mr Plunkett[9]—Bray Presbn Minister—Bp of Meath.[10] Read Burnaby, Ride through Asia Minor—Jasper More, Under the Balkans. Dinner party & music.

24. *Wed.*

Wrote 7 minutes: and letters to Ld O'Hagan—Rev. Mr Turner—Mrs Hampton—Mr J.B. Doyle[11]—Mr Lawrence—Croasdill—Beckhard—J. Murray—Mrs O'Brien—H.N. Gladstone—and. . . . Sat to Chancellor (Photogr.)[12] Went over Killiney Hill—& saw the old 6th Cent. Church. Saw Mr Deane—Judge Lawson—& Mr Sullivan, after his sad & grievous loss. A steamer was on the bay

---

[1] Elizabeth, 2nd wife of James Henry Legge, 1804-83, 3rd Baron Sherborne.

[2] *F.J.*, 23 October 1877, 7b.

[3] John West, 1806-90; dean of St Patrick's cathedral 1864-86.

[4] E. Jenkins, *Barney Geoghegan, M.P., and Home rule* (1877).

[5] W. Roberts, *Church memorials and characteristics* (1874).

[6] The biologist (see 11 Mar. 77); on colour in Homer; see Darwin's reply, Add MS 44455, f. 210.

[7] William O'Neill, *né* Chichester, anglican priest and composer; 1813-83; cr. Baron O'Neill 1868.

[8] Sister Mary Frances Cusack, 1830-99; convert from Anglicanism, known as the 'Nun of Kenmare'; founded convents and orders.

[9] Perhaps David Robert Plunket, 1838-1919; tory M.P. Dublin university 1870-95; Irish solicitor-general 1875-7; cr. Baron Rathmore 1895.

[10] William Conyngham, 1828-97; 4th Baron Plunket 1871; bp. of Meath 1876, abp. of Dublin 1884.

[11] Probably John Borbridge Doyle, Irish author.

[12] Widely advertised in the press, but no copy found.

with divers, still in search of his dead son.[1] Dinner party. Read Burnaby Ride throug[h] Asia.

25. *Th.* [*Royal Fitzwilliam Hotel, Rathdrum*]

Finished Burnaby Vol. 1. Read also [blank.] Planted a tree: and went off to Bray—Rathdrum[2]—Glendalough by Clara Valley—and back by Glenmalure to the Hotel. Glendalough[3] ought to have three hours. I have never seen anything equal to or like it. The harmony of the scenery with the remains is perfect. Tim Brough the Guide a great character. He will not allow that Ireland has improved. Saw some farms, cottages, & people: turning my small opportunities to account as well as I could.

26. *Fr.* [*Coolattin Park, Co. Wicklow*]

Wrote to Mr Stevenson. Saw Rev Mr Guinness (Temperance)[4]—Mr Mahaffy (Mycenian Remains.)[5]—Mr Foggarty (Aughrim)[6] a notable specimen, such as gives hope for R.C. Irishmen. We went by the Meeting of the Waters & Clash to Auchrim [*sic*] seeing small farms & cottages on our way with many conversations.[7] Reached Coollattin[8] at 5¾—most kindly & warmly received. A large family party. Read [blank.]

27. *Sat.*

Wrote Minutes (9) for S.L.—Also to Mr Dix Hutton[9]—Mr Dudgeon—Mr Weaver. Read Agamemnon, and Browning's Translation—Krauss on Magnus, in Kosmos.[10] A long drive over the property and visits to farms. Much conversation with Lord F[itzwilliam]—the Laurencesons[11]—Mr Ponsonby[12]—Mr Mahaffy.

[1] Robert Sullivan, drowned on 16 October.
[2] About 20 miles s. of Kilruddery; Parnell's house at Avondale is just s. of the town.
[3] The cathedral, round tower and monastic remains, 5 miles NW. of Rathdrum.
[4] Rector of Rathdrum, in favour of Sunday closing; report in *F.J.*, 27 October 1877, 5h.
[5] Lord Fitzwilliam brought in (Sir) John Pentland *Mahaffy (1839-1919; wit and classicist, provost of Trinity, Dublin, 1914) to entertain Gladstone, to which end Mahaffy brought Browning's translation of Aeschylus' *Agamemnon* (1877) (see next day); Gladstone deplored Browning's rendering 'in belly's strict necessity'; Mahaffy recalled: 'Fitzwilliam came to us and said, "I know your conversation must be most interesting but I am obliged to interrupt you for my lady is waiting." "Certainly," said Mr Gladstone, and then turning to me added, "This is indeed 'in belly's strict necessity'." I think it was the only joke, certainly the best I ever heard him make'; W. B. Stanford & R. B. McDowell, *Mahaffy* (1971), 97.
[6] Owned the large mills at Aughrim.
[7] He travelled third class for part of the journey to talk to artisans; *Bray Herald*, 27 October 1877, 1. One of the farms visited was on Parnell's estate; *F.J.*, 27 October 1877, 5h.
[8] Seat of 6th Earl Fitzwilliam (see 19 June 38), near Tinahely.
[9] Henry Dix Hutton, wrote on Positivism and land tenure in Ireland.
[10] Not traced.
[11] Michael Lawrenson, one of the largest farmers in Wicklow, and Fitzwilliam's under-steward.
[12] F. Ponsonby, lately Fitzwilliam's agent.

28. 22 S. Trin.

Shillelagh Ch at noon—only. Walk in aft. Wrote to Mr Knowles—Ed. Echo. Read Krauss—Magnus—Life of Kingsley[1]—Farrar's Life of Christ.[2] Conversation with Mr Ponsonby—Mr Mahaffy—& others.

29. M. [Powerscourt, Enniskerry]

Wrote to Miss Taaffe (B.P. & letter)[3]—Count Schouvaloff—8 Minutes—Lady Wilde[4]—Dr Kavanagh.[5] Conversation with Ld Fitzwilliam—Dr Kavanagh—Mr Mahaffy—Rev. Mr Galbraith.[6] Saw Cripples Institute (Miss Sullivan) at Bray. Off at 1. What a prize we leave behind in Lady A[lice Fitzwilliam]! The whole family is very satisfactory. Walked with Spencer [Lyttelton][7] to Powerscourt.[8] Here as elsewhere our reception was most kind. A sharp touch of diarrhoea assailed me—but a little care put all right. Read the Kottabos[9]—Trip of the Eva[10]—Under the Balkans.

30. Tu.

Wrote to Count Schouvaloff—Mr Godley—Mr J. Murray—Mr S. Grove—Mr Phillips Thompson. Read Sir J. Barrington, Personal Recollections[11]—Jasper More, Under the Balkans. In the morning we went to examine the Churchton ruin in the Park: altar window westwards: and through the grounds. In aft. we drove to Glencree Reformatory & went over the establishment. At the express desire of Father Dauchsen [sic][12] I made a short address to the boys. I did not expect the call! Then to the remarkable Hermitage,[13] so to call it of Sir John Crampton on Lough Bray. I thought it very captivating. Saw Mr Drought—Mr Lenorègne.

31. Wed.

Wrote Seven Minutes—and l. to Ld Granville—Madame O. Novikoff—Mr Marvin[14]—Mr Maurice Brooks.[15] Read Stoney on Univ. Reform[16]—Sir Jonah

---

[1] *Charles Kingsley: his letters and memories of his life, edited by his wife* (1877).

[2] F. W. Farrar, *The life of Christ*, 2v. (1874).

[3] Olivia Mary Taaffe, 1832-1918; prominent in Irish affairs.

[4] Lady Jane Francesca, wife of Sir W. R. Wills Wilde, and mother of Oscar* (see 15 May 77); business untraced—an unsuccessful invitation?

[5] President of St Patrick's College, Carlow; see 5 Apr. 75.

[6] Henry Galbraith, rector of Powerscourt.

[7] Who acted as secretary during this visit.

[8] Seat of Lord Powerscourt, with splendid gardens, on the Dargle river.

[9] *The Kottabos. A college miscellany* (n.d.).

[10] A. M. Kavanagh, *The cruise of the R.Y.S. Eva* (1865).

[11] Sir J. Barrington, *Personal sketches*, 3v. (1827-32).

[12] Father Gaughran of the Christian Brothers, who ran the Roman catholic reformatory; report in *F.J.*, 31 October 1877, 7a.

[13] Built by the duke of Northumberland for Sir Philip *Crampton, 1777-1858, surgeon; inherited by his son, Sir John Fiennes Twisleton *Crampton, 1805-86, diplomat.

[14] Of Glencree reformatory; in *F.J.*, 3 November 1877, 6b.

[15] Maurice Brooks, b. 1823; Dublin merchant and lord mayor 1873-4; liberal home-rule M.P. Dublin 1874-85.

[16] Untraced.

Barrington's notable book. Saw Mr Groves—Father Leahy[1]—Mrs Howard—Mr [H.] Law—Ld Talbot de M.—Mr Lefanu.[2] In the morning visited the *two* Churches—the *two* Schools—saw the Priest (Mr ODwyer)[3] & his house; farmers & others. In aft. we drove & walked to the Dargle Fall; in some respects without a rival in our islands. Large dinner party; as on each evening.

Thurs. Nov. One. 1877.

Wrote to Mr R. H. Hutton—Ed. Freeman's Journal (& covering l.)[4]—Dr Laffan (2)[5]—Mr [R.] Jasper More—Ld Hartington—Ld Mayor of Dublin—Eight Minutes—Mr Sh. Crawford (Tel.). Read Jasper More (finished)—Bryce's TransCaucasia[6]—Sir J. Barrington. Walked with Ld Monck & Sir W. Gregory[7] to Charleville. Dinner party. Conversation with Lady Monck (Ch)—Mr [P. J.] Keenan[8]—Mr Galbraith. Walk about the place.

2. Fr.

Wrote to Mr J. Murray—Supt LNWRR Dublin—Lady Anesley[9]—Capt. Blake Forster[10]—Nine minutes. Conversation with Ld M[onck]—to determine with his counsel many replies & proceedings. We drove to the Scalp; & walked up the noble approach by the Dargle. Large dinner party. Saw Mr Latouche—Mr West—Judge Lawson—Mr Lefanu. Read up the Schliemann letters & corrected & sent off for Press my Preface to his work on Mycenae.[11] In this House we find double prayers mg & aft: in all the others (thus far) single.

3. Sat. [Carton, Maynooth]

Wrote to W.H.G.—Mr Knowles—Mrs Lefroy (O)—and Eight Minutes. After planting a tree we went off to Bray & Dublin. Saw the National Gallery—Lord Mayor & Depn—College of Physicians Halls & Works of Art—Royal Dublin Soc—Leinster Lawn. Then drove off to Artaigne & went over the large & very interesting industrial School.[12] From there to Glasnevin, & the O'Connell Tomb & Tower.[13] Also the Chapel +. Noticing Statues & Buildings by the way. Reached Carton[14] at five. A large party. Saw Sir W. Gregory (Layard & D.

[1] Probably Thomas Leahy, priest at Sandyford.
[2] Probably William Richard Le Fanu, 1816-94; railway designer and commissioner of public works.
[3] For him, see W. R. Le Fanu, *Seventy years of Irish life* (1893), 197.
[4] Not found published; probably about the Dublin freedomship; see *F.J.*, 3 November 1877, 6b.
[5] Perhaps Thomas Laffan of Cashel who wrote supporting diarist's visit; *F.J.*, 20 October 1877, 7b.
[6] J. Bryce, *Transcaucasia and Ararat* (1877).
[7] See 14 Mar. 59. Charleville was Lord Monck's seat on the opposite side of the Dargle to Powerscourt.
[8] (Sir) Patrick Joseph Keenan, 1826-94; commissioner of Irish education 1871; kt. 1881.
[9] Mabel Wilhelmina Frances, *née* Markham, m. 1877 Hugh Annesley, 1831-1908; tory M.P. 1857-74; 5th Earl Annesley 1874; large landowner in Down and Cavan.
[10] Capt. Francis Blake Forster, J.P., Galway landowner.
[11] See 20 Sept. 77.
[12] Run by the Christian Brothers; report of speech in *F.J.*, 5 November 1877, 7a.
[13] i.e. in the national cemetery at Glasnevin.
[14] Seat of 4th duke of Leinster by Maynooth, 15 miles W. of Dublin.

Tel.)—Mr Hamilton—Mr Dennis Godley[1]—Ld Monck—Ld Anesley [*sic*]—D. of Leinster: much conversation with Duchess.[2] Read Sir J. Barrington on the Union—Sullivan's New Ireland.[3]

4. 23 S. Trin.[4]

Maynooth Ch mg with H.C.—& aftn. Prayers in evg: not daily. Read Dr Webster's singular Sermons[5]—Houston on the Pope as Antichrist[6]—the fine Dunraven-Stokes book largely[7]—Sullivan's New Ireland. Saw Rev Mr Wheelham[8]—Rev. Father O'Rourke[9]—two men of the people, with whom I had separate conversations. Wrote to Mr Knowles. Nothing can exceed the kindness here received. It is all redolent of the character & recollections of the dear Duchess Harriet.

5. M. [*Dublin*]

Wrote to Ld Meath (Tel.)—Ld Monck—Mr Mahaffy—Sir H. Moncreiff—Mr Justice [C. R.] Barry—Lady Esmonde[10]—Four Minutes—Mrs M. Sands. Read Sullivan's New Ireland—and Northern Rural Life.[11] Saw Dean Dickinson[12]—Mr O'Rourke—Dinner & evening party at the Archbishop's. Various conversations.

$11\frac{1}{2}$-$1\frac{1}{2}$. Visit to Maynooth College.[13] It produced upon the whole a saddening impression: what havock have we made of the vineyard of the Lord! Hard work, of its kind, & economy pervaded the whole: but they are honourably beginning a rich Chapel.

In aft. drove in the Park, through the curiously denudated valley: & our most kind hosts saw us off from the Station. In Dublin we walked to the Archbishops.[14] We were concerned to find this excellent man worse & still suffering: in an entourage I fear little worthy of him.

6. Tu.

Prayers in the Chapel at nine. Wrote to the Ld Mayor—Mr Doyle[15]—Mr Davies—& minutes. Party to breakfast. Then went to the really wonderful

---

[1] Denis Godley, 1823-90, br. of J.R.; secretary to commission on Irish church temporalities 1869-81, to Irish land commission 1881-8.

[2] Caroline, da. of Gladstone's old friend, Harriet, duchess of Sutherland, m. 1847 4th duke of Leinster and d. 1887.

[3] A. M. Sullivan, *New Ireland*, 2v. (1877).

[4] Entries for 4 and 5 November written in reverse order.

[5] By George Webster, chancellor of Cork.

[6] T. Houston, *The judgment of the Papacy and the reign of righteousness* (1851).

[7] E. R. W. Quin, Lord Dunraven, *Notes on Irish architecture*, ed. M. Stokes, 2v. (1875-7).

[8] Robert W. Whelan, Church of Ireland priest at Maynooth.

[9] John O'Rourke, Roman catholic priest at Maynooth; see 17 Nov. 77n.

[10] Louisa, *née* Grattan, widow of Sir John Esmonde, 1826-76.

[11] See 17 Oct. 77.

[12] Hercules Henry Dickinson, d. 1905; dean of the Chapel Royal, Dublin.

[13] The Roman catholic seminary whose endowment and grant-extension had been the occasion of Gladstone's resignation from the cabinet in 1845; see above, iii. xxxi.

[14] R. Chenevix *Trench, once apparently on diarist's prayer list; see 30 Sept. 41.

[15] Henry Edward *Doyle, 1827-92; director of the National Gallery, Dublin, from 1869.

operation at the Port: the lifting of 350 Tons by an Engine of 14 horse power; & all the attendant circs. Saw Graving Dock—Customhouse—then to St Michans. Here, with other things, I found a most curious record of Penance. From this I went to the Antiseptic Vaults and saw the open figures of the dead who lived before the Reformation, lying in their oak coffins. It was a wonderful, solemn, & most touching sight. In some cases I seemed to see an expression, & a painful one, on the Countenance. From thence to the Four Courts: sat for a while on the Bench of the Common Pleas. Then to the Record Tower where Sir B. Burke[1] was most kind. Next the Castle—Chapel—Guard Room. Then Chancellor's (the Photographer's). Then to Card. Cullen.[2] He delivered a mournful diatribe on the state of Ireland. At the close he asked kindly after Willy & said 'You know Mr Gladstone we could have given you a warmer reception, if it had not been for certain pamphlets which we in Ireland did not like very well.[']³ Then to the Marlborough Street Schools: singing, examinations, cookery. A notable organisation. The singing of the girls was the best I ever heard in a school. Then Deputation of Down Farmers.[4] Saw Mr Keenan—Ld Chief Baron—Ld Monck—Mr Mulholland—Provost of Trin. Coll.—Mr Pigott[5]—Judge Longfield[6]—& others. Large dinner party at the Provost's. Broke up at 12¼.—A long & laborious but most interesting day.—Read Irish Statistics.

7. Wed. [Abbeyleix, Queen's County]

Wrote to Mr Sharman Crawford.[7] Prayers at nine. Continued my puzzled meditations on the materials possible for today. Breakf. party.

Off at 11.40 for the City Hall. Saw the fine statues, especially Chantrey's noble Grattan. Received the freedom in the City Hall: & spoke say 50 min. treading upon eggs the whole time.[8] Dejeuner soon after two. Again spoke, say half the time: plenty more eggs! The Lord Mayor was most kind & made a very favourable impression.

Went through the rooms. Again saw the Abp with whom I have had only short conversations. Went off at 5 by the train to Abbeyleix,[9] after a very remarkable & affectionate reception. Groups gathered at every station. We arrived at 8.15, received in the most kind & gracious manner. A small party: & a charming evening. I cannot be too thankful for having got through today as I hope without trick & without offence. Read Mr Balfour in Fortnightly Rev.[10]

---

[1] Sir John Bernard *Burke, 1814-92; genealogist; keeper of Irish state papers 1855.

[2] See 29 July 45.

[3] See Morley, ii. 571. Cullen wrote in similar terms to the mayor of Dublin on 5 November; P. MacSuibhne, *Paul Cullen* (1977), v. 246.

[4] Organized by J. S. Crawford, offering gratitude for the 1870 Land Act; *F.J.*, 7 November 1877, 2e.

[5] Perhaps William Mulholland, and Philip R. Pigott, Dublin barristers.

[6] Mountifort *Longfield, 1802-84; regius professor of law from 1834; judge 1858-67.

[7] On the Down deputation (see 6 Nov. 77), in *F.J.*, 8 November 1877, 3d.

[8] *F.J.*, 8 November 1877, 2; only partly printed in *T.T.* as the telegraph broke down.

[9] Seat about 60 miles SW. of Dublin of John Robert William Vesey, 1844-1903; 4th Viscount De Vesci 1875; m. 1872 Evelyn, da. of 8th earl of Wemyss.

[10] On Indian civil service; *Fortnightly Review*, xxviii. 244 (August 1877).

8. Th.

Prayers at nine. Wrote to Mr Ph. Smith B.P.—Mr Donnell. Read Symonds on Renaissance[1]—Bryce on Mount Ararat.[2] Finally corrected, and sent off to Press, my Preface to Dr Schliemann's Volume. Walk with Ld de V[esci] mg in his woods. Drive with Lady de V. in aft.—These are rare people, whom it is difficult not to love. Conversation also with Mr [H. E.] Doyle whom I like much.

9. Fr.

Prayers at nine. Wrote to Dr Madden—Dr Joyce[3]—Mr Gill (O)—Mr O'Byrne Croke[4]—Mr Lloyd—Mr Davies MP.—Mr Macnamara—J.W. Madden—Jas Meyer—Mr Allwright. Read Symonds on Renaissance—Joyce on Irish Names. 10.30-4. Expedition by rail to Kilkenny: a place of great interest.[5] We saw St Canice—the Black Abbey—the R.C. Cathedral—the College—& the Castle. The two Bishops[6] were exceedingly kind: the R.C. Dr Moran really affectionate. St Canice is very notable: for the Bps seat, the tombstone Crosses, the old Cloaked figures, the structure in the Western triplet: *inter alia*. The Black Abbey remarkable for its tower, the beautiful *juncture* with the main fabric, & the history of the secularisation. The R.C. Cath. striking & effective. The position of the Castle is magnificent: but it has been recklessly modernised.[7] Walk with Lord de V.—Mr Nugent came.

10. Sat. [*Woodlands, Consilla*]

Prayers at nine. Wrote to Mr Isaac Butt—A.W. Wheeler[8]—L. Consell—A.L. Fearnley—J. Ragsbotham—G.B. Beater.[9] Visited the garden, farm, & stock, under guidance of the Scotch Bailiff. Off before three. Reached Woodlands[10] at 6.30. Our farewells were such as commonly belong to nearer ages & a closer intimacy. Conversation with Father T. Nolan[11]—Father J. Nolan (Kildare)[12]—Mr Dease MP.—Mr Doyle—Mr Hamilton—Sir B. Burke—Lady Burke.[13] Read Symonds on Renaissance—O'Mahony's Rome Semper Eadem.[14]

---

[1] J. A. Symonds, *The revival of learning* (1877), vol. ii of *The Renaissance in Italy*.
[2] See 1 Nov. 77.
[3] P. W. Joyce, wrote *The origin and history of Irish names of places*, 3v. (ed. 1875).
[4] Reading uncertain.
[5] About 20 miles south of Abbeyleix.
[6] Robert Samuel *Gregg, 1834-96, anglican bp. of Ossory 1875-8, of Cork 1878, abp. of Armagh 1893, and Patrick Francis *Moran, 1830-1911, Cullen's nephew, Roman catholic bp. of Ossory 1872; abp. of Sydney 1884, cardinal 1885.
[7] Originally Norman, remodelled in the early nineteenth century in the castellated style by the dukes of Ormonde.
[8] Of Abbeyliex; letter in Houghton library, Harvard.
[9] Perhaps George P. Beater, Dublin architect.
[10] Seat of Lord Annaly, on the far side of Phoenix Park from Dublin.
[11] Roman catholic parish priest at Abbeyleix for 50 years; 'a better representative of the Irish priest Gladstone could hardly . . . have met', *F.J.*, 12 November 1877, 7a.
[12] John Nolan, Roman catholic incumbent in Kildare.
[13] Barbara Frances, *née* MacEvoy, wife of Sir J. B. *Burke.
[14] See 29 Apr. 75.

11. 24 S. Trin.

Lucan Ch mg: Mr Benson:[1] the best Sermon I have heard in Ireland. In aft. we drove 6½ m to St Patrick's. Magnificent music: I thought the finest I had known in any Cathedral. A strawy Sermon. A great crowd: Viceregal Court present. Wrote to Ld Monck—Ed. Kilkenny Journal—Mr Chancellor—Mrs Th.—Ed. Echo. Long conversation with Mr Joynt[2] on the state of Irish matters. Read Notre Dame de Lourdes.[3] Large dinner party in evg. But the conversation I think was not alien to the day. The glass was reported as Stormy. But the wind had fallen. And I could not postpone without causing trouble & disappointment to many, especially to the people of Holyhead. So the plan stood.

12. M. [Hawarden]

An encouraging morning: but an evil glass. The party breakfasted early & we left a most hospitable house at 8.15. Innumerable greetings in Dublin especially as we neared the Port; & much enthusiasm when we embarked. In the interval after arriving I sat for a few minutes to the Artist of Zoz![4] The new Central Station is very noteworthy. I went on my back, to be if possible in condition! & narrowly escaped sickness, with discomposures only. The glass proved a true prophet: & the passage was very bad, lengthened also for an hour by deflection to visit a vessel in distress, whose crew however would not leave her. C., M., & the servants were all ill: so were almost all the passengers, & some sailors. We arrived at 4.30 (English): saw Mr Davies. A cup of tea made me speech-worthy enough. Closed eyes & lying on the back saved me from the worst.[5] I went to the Town Hall where despite the weather we had an enthusiastic meeting of say 800 or 900 & I spoke for a *mezzoretta*: throwing in what I thought requisite about the East; on all points they were most hearty.[6] Numbers greeted us here, & at nearly every station from Bangor to Rhyl especially. Set to work on my arrears of all kinds which looked most formidable & will chain me down for days. We got home before tea.

Let me thankfully conclude with recording that great mercy has attended both our going out & our coming in.

Tues. Nov. 13.[7]

Wrote to Messrs [blank] (Solrs)[8]—Mr Vickers—Jasper More—Rev. T. Lang (& B.P.)—Mad. Novikoff—Padre Tondini—Sir S. Scott & Co.—Rev.H. Martin[9]—

---

[1] Charles Maunsell Benson, anglican incumbent in Lucan.

[2] W. Lane Joynt, D.L., staying at Woodlands; described to Granville (Ramm II, i. 58) as 'our old agent'.

[3] Perhaps F. C. Husenbeth, *Our blessed Lady of Lourdes* (1870 ed.).

[4] 'He favoured "Spex", the talented artist of *Zoz*, with a sitting for a racy cartoon'; *F.J.*, 13 November 1877, 7a. *Zoz* sold the cartoon separately, price one shilling (*Zoz*, n.d. or pagination).

[5] This and previous sentence added at the bottom of the page.

[6] He answered Beaconsfield's recent speech on Turkey, and spoke on Ireland; *T.T.*, 13 November 1877, 6b.

[7] Usual diary text resumes here.

[8] Messrs Hughes, see 15 Nov. 77.

[9] Perhaps Henry Martin, curate in Sunderland.

Messrs Gill & Sons—J. Jones—C. Ernest (York Eclectic)[1]—Mr Murray—Mr Knowles—Mr de Lisle—W. Goolden[2]—A. Thorn—J. Walpole—R.D. Fraser— R. Baxter—E.G. Knapp. Unpacked & opened much: but more remains. Cut two trees in my clump near Bretton: & saw Mr Roberts & his beautiful cows. Saw Mr Roberts. Read Story of Irish Life[3]—Mr Forbes's remarkable article on the War.[4]

14. Wed.

A touch of lumbago obliged me to keep my bed till midday. Wrote to Mr Goldwin Smith—Sir T.E. May—Messrs Chapman—Rev Mr Molesworth— Messrs T. & B.—Rev. Mr Kingsmill—T. Edwards—Jas Knowles (Cambridge)— Mr Ouvry—Mr Doherty—Mr Denham—J.A. Browne—Mr Tilson. We drove over to Eaton & found many of the marriage party.[5] Conversation with the Duke of W[estminster] respecting Mr Forbes & the Eastern Question. Read May on Democracy[6]—Q.R. on (W.E.G.) E. Question—and on the New Republic (Hayward?).[7]

15.[8]

Fifty three letters & packets saluted me! Lumbago better but not gone. Wrote to Messrs Hughes (vice 13th)—Prof. Mahaffy BP—Prov. Trin. Coll. D. BP—Prof. at Maynooth BP—Prof. Molloy[9]—W. Colomb—T. Meacock—G.F. Ansell—Rev. Dr Gregg—Professor Armstrong[10]—H.N.G.—Ld De Tabley—Scotts—Watsons— [W.]T. Stead—A.F. Lee—F.W. Evans—Jas Burke. Read Pamphlet on 'Jamaica'— do on Liturgy for Methodists—Francis on Greek Independence.[11] Three clergy dined. Saw what is called a Lunar Rainbow: I believe for the first time. Its spectrum is curious. Saw Mr Vickers. Got to work on arrears of papers.

16. Fr.

Forenoon still in bed: but nearly right today. Wrote to E.A. Bridge (& BP.)— President of St Jarlaths[12]—T.B. Potter—A. Higginson—Rev. Knox Little—Mr

[1] Perhaps of the *Eclectic magazine of foreign literature*, published in New York.

[2] Walter Goolden had sent lectures; Hawn P.

[3] Perhaps *Tales of Irish life* [by M. J. Whitty], 2v. (1824).

[4] A. Forbes, 'The Russians, the Turks, and the Bulgarians at the theatre of war', *Nineteenth Century*, ii. 561 (November 1877); on Bulgarian reprisals against Turks; see 23 Nov. 77.

[5] Marriage (the previous day) of Lady Beatrice Constance Grosvenor, 2nd da. of the duke of Westminster, to Charles Compton Cavendish, 1850-1907; 3rd Baron Chesham 1882.

[6] T. E. May, *Democracy in Europe: a history*, 2v. (1877).

[7] [H. Craik] on Gladstone, [J. A. Hardcastle] on Mallock; *Quarterly Review*, cxciv. 555, 515 (October 1877).

[8] He this day defeated Northcote (1153:609) for the rectorship of Glasgow university.

[9] Perhaps Gerald Molloy, published on philosophy, geology, and Ireland.

[10] George Francis Armstrong, professor of history at Queen's college, Cork.

[11] F. Francis, *The diplomatic history of the Greek war* (n.d.).

[12] Canon Bourke; on Gaelic; in *T.T.*, 22 November 1877, 9f.

Maclehose[1]—Rev E.C. Lutley[2]—Ed. Hunt Monitor[3]—Mr Cheetham—Mr Tilley—C. Cox—J. Ritchie—W.H. Northy—A. Jervise—F. Francis—J. Gibson. Read 19th Cent. on Sun Spots—Sir E. Perry on Comte[4]—Matheson, Spirit of Xty[5]—Life & Times of Grant[6]—Goethe Bride of Corinth &c.[7] Continued the battle with my arrears. Felled a tree in aftn.

17. Sat.

Down at 11.30. Wrote to Mr Costello—Rev. N. Hall—Mr Parker—Rev. Dr Caird[8]—J.M. Miller—Father O'Rourke—Rev. J. Dawson—Rev. Jul. Lloyd[9]—E. Hughes—Mr Grierson—Mr Woollam—W.F. Potter.[10] Read [Commons'] Journals of 1834—O'Rourke's O'Connell[11]—Lectures by a Certain Professor.[12] Drive with C. & felled a fairish tree. Conversation on force with Mr Ottley & Mr Sanctuary.[13]

18. 25 S. Trin.

Ch 11 AM and (H.C.) and 6½ P.M. Wrote to Mr Herries BIR—Mr Ouvry—Mr Johnson—J. Ball—L.U. Shea—Edw Jones—J. Knowles—Sterndale Scarr—Mrs Wickham—Sir F.H. Doyle—Rev. F. Meyrick—Mr Forsyth MP—Mr Latouche—Miss Armitage (O). Read A. Knox on H. Eucharist[14]—Corresp. of Anglocath. Society—Adderley's Tract[15]—Johnson on Village Clubs[16]—De Vere's Introduction[17]—Bp Medley Sermon & Charge.[18]

19. M.

Ch. 8½ A.M. Wrote to Pres. Glasgow Lib. Club.[19]—Inner Circle Secy[20]—Messrs Davies—Lady Salisbury—Lady Gladstone—Mr Anderson MP—Mr Hamilton—E. Roberts (O)—Scotts—Mr Roundell—H.A. Bright—A. de Vere—Mr Buchanan—J.E. Thomas. Saw Mr Vickers—Mr J. Roberts. Felled a tree in the clump. Read Life of O'Connell—Bourke, Arian Origin of Irish[21]—Limerno Pitoceo[22]—&c.

---

[1] James J. Maclehose, of Glasgow, sent election figures; Add MS 44455, f. 255.

[2] Edward Chorley Lutley, curate of Bridgwater.

[3] Perhaps for the profile of A.P. Forbes in *The Monitor* (December 1877).

[4] *Nineteenth Century*, ii. 586, 621 (November 1877).

[5] G. Matheson, *Growth of the spirit of Christianity*, 2v. (1877).

[6] *General Grant, life and times* (1877).

[7] J. W. von Goethe, in *Favourite poems*, tr. W. E. Aytoun and T. Martin (1877).

[8] John *Caird, 1820-98, principal of Glasgow university, had sent official notice of the rectorial election; Add MS 44455, f. 252.   [9] Julius Lloyd, episcopal priest and author in Greenock.

[10] William Frederick Potter, architect.

[11] J. O'Rourke, *The centenary life of O'Connell* (1875); the third and subsequent editions (1877) contained Gladstone's long letter of this day to O'Rourke on O'Connell in the 1830s and Gladstone's mem. of 10 July 34.   [12] Untraced.

[13] Probably Thomas Sanctuary, 1822-89; archdeacon of Dorset from 1862.

[14] A. Knox, *The doctrine of the Sacraments* (1838).   [15] See 30 July 74.

[16] Not found.   [17] A. T. De Vere, preface to *Antar and Zara* (1877); on Irish history.

[18] J. Medley, 'A charge' (1877); 'A sermon' (1877).

[19] Thanking liberals for their support (see 15 Nov. 77); *T.T.*, 21 November 1877, 10c.

[20] Not found; possibly a club in Glasgow?

[21] U. J. Bourke, *The Aryan origin of the Gaelic race and language* (1875).

[22] P. Limerno [i.e. Teofilo Folengo], *Orlandino* (1526).

20. Tu.

Ch. 8½ AM. Wrote to Ld Tenterden (on the Layard Dispatch)[1]—Padre Lonardi[2]—Mr Knowles l. & Tel.—Mr Jasper More—Sir C. Adderley—Ld Granville—Mr Earp MP[3]—T. Williams—A.H. Sayce[4]—M. Marvin—F. Ouvry—W. Evans. Felled two trees. Read O'Connell's Life—Blackwood on The War—Do (Forsyth) on Montenegro.[5] Took to the [Homeric] Primer.[6]

21. Wed.

Ch. 8½ AM. Wrote to Rev. H.E. Fox[7]—W.P. Adam—Mr Whitfield—Bp of Fredericton—Rev. R. Suffield—Rev. J. Smith—Alex Hume—Alf. Ward—G.M. Bussy—A. Campbell. Read O'Connell's Life—Sinclair's Defence of Russia.[8] Conversation with Mrs Ffolliott.[9] Worked on Homeric Primer.

22. Th.

Ch. 8½ AM. Wrote to Ld Talbot de Malahide—J. Smith B.P.—W. Hartley B.P.—W. Wallace—G.W. Green—Mr Moylan—T. Briggs—F. Gale. Finished O'Rourke's O'Connell. Read Cusack's O'Connell[10] and [blank.] Ly Cowell Stepney[11] came: ten to dinner. Worked on Hom. Primer.

23. Fr.

Ch. 8½ AM. Wrote to Ld De Tabley—Earl Granville—Mr A. Fergusson—Made O. Novikoff—Dean of Durham. Read 'Ancien Diplomate' on Eastern Question[12]—St Patrick's Eve[13]—Freeman on Ottoman History.[14] Saw the Reporters[15]—Mr Dawson (Wesleyan)—Mr Evans (Elections—Bank for Hn)—Worked on Mr Forbes's Article for Lecture at 7 P.M. It lasted I am sorry to say 1½ hour.[16]

---

[1] Further moves in the Negropontis affair; see Ramm II, i. 58n. and Add MS 44455, f. 270.
[2] D. G. Lonardi.
[3] Thomas Earp, radical M.P. Newark 1874-85; see 1 Feb. 67.
[4] Archibald Henry *Sayce, 1845-1933; fellow of Queen's, Oxford, 1870-9; orientalist.
[5] *Blackwood's Edinburgh Magazine*, cxxii. 611, 553 (November 1877).
[6] See 24 Sept. 77n.
[7] Henry Elliot Fox, d. 1926; vicar of Christ Church, Westminster, 1873-82; later missionary in India.
[8] J. G. T. Sinclair, *A defence of Russia and the Christians of Turkey* (1877).
[9] Grace, wife of M. ffolliott, guests at the Castle.
[10] M. F. Cusack, *The Liberator; his life and times* (1877 ed.).
[11] Margaret, da. of 2nd Lord de Tabley, m. 1875 Sir Emile Algernon Arthur Keppell Cowell-Stepney, 1834-1909, liberal M.P. Carmarthen 1876-8, 1886-92; 2nd bart. 1877.
[12] *L'Empire Ottoman, 1839-1877... par un ancien Diplomate* (1877).
[13] By C. J. Lever (1871).
[14] E. A. Freeman, *The Ottoman Power in Europe* (1877).   [15] For the lecture.
[16] The speech, replying to Forbes' accusations in his article about Bulgarian atrocities (see 13 Nov. 77), was republished (copy at St Deiniol's, notes at Add MS 44664, f. 194) as a pamphlet with a preface apologizing for remarks on Midhat Pasha for which Gladstone could not give a source (in fact avoiding embarrassing R. Jasper More); see Ramm II, i. 60. Archibald Forbes, 1838-1900, war correspondent for the *D.N.* in the Russo-Turkish war, and others.

24. Sat.

Ch. 8½ AM. Wrote to E.S. Glanville[1]—Capt. Chapman—The Speaker—E. Phillips—Mr Keenan—Jas Wilson—Mr Ouvry—Mrs Th.—T. Wood—L. Dunne.[2] Off at 6 to Chester. Dined with the Bp: the party clerical: pleasant. Back at 11. Prayers. Conversation with Dean of Durham[3] on Univ. Extension—Dean of Chester. Read L'Empire Ottoman—St Patrick's Eve (finished)—Case of Railway Shareholders—and [blank.]

25. Preadvent S.

Ch. 11 AM and [blank.] Wrote to Rev. B. Haselwood[4]—Rev M.J. Evans[5]—Mrs Scott—Mr R. Johnson—Mr J. Prynne—Mr D.W. Freshfield.[6] Read Storr on Russia[7]—Symes on Future Punishment[8]—Evans's Zöckler on the Cross—Knox on H. Eucharist (finished)—Illingworth's Sermons.[9]

26. M.

Ch. 8½ AM. Wrote to Ld Hartington—Ld Granville BP—W. Downing—Prof. Kokkinos—S.E.G.—Rev. S.C. Foot—H.N.G. (BP)—Mr Fairfield—Mr Salmon. Conversation with C.G. respecting D[octo]r—with S.E.G. respecting 'Compulsion'. Saw Dean of Durham: & walk with him. Read Wilson on India[10]—L'Empire Ottoman—Joyce on Irish Names[11]—R. Brome, Plays.[12]

27. Tu.

Ch. 8½ AM. Wrote to Unwin Brothers (Tel.)[13]—Rev Mr Bateman—Rev. Mr Cheales[14]—Sec. Bennett Fund[15]—Mr Mundella—Mr Quilliam—Mr R.H. Elliot—Mr Adam—H.A. Greig[16]—E.W. Hooper—J. Knowles—Mr Manrick. Read L'Empire Ottoman—Brome's Mock Marriage—Wilde's Lough Corrib.[17] Worked a little on Homer. Cut two trees in clump. Saw Mr Vickers—Mr Evans & Mr Thompson.

28. Wed.

Ch. 8½ AM. Wrote to Mr Colin Lindsay—Mr Shekelton[18]—Dr Schliemann—Sir R. Phillimore—Mr A. Strahan—Messrs Hodder & S[toughton][19]—Mrs Th.—Mrs

---

[1] Of Dublin; on Irish industry; Hawn P.
[2] Perhaps L. Dunne, foreman of British stores at the Bosphorus and author of *A trip to Constantinople* (1862).   [3] W. C. Lake.
[4] Boulby Haslewood, 1829-97; vicar of Oswaldtwistle 1857-97; formerly chaplain at Arley.
[5] Maurice J. Evans had sent his tr. of O. Zoeckler, *The cross of Christ* (1877).
[6] Of the solicitors.
[7] Probably an untraced piece by John Stephens Storr, journalist.
[8] J. Symes, 'The Methodist Conference and eternal punishment' (1877).
[9] J. R. Illingworth, *Sermons preached in the chapel of Keble College* (1878).
[10] J. Wilson, *Government of India* (1877).   [11] See 9 Nov. 77.
[12] R. Brome, *Dramatic works*, 3v. (1873 ed.).   [13] Edward Unwin's publishing firm.
[14] Alan Benjamin Cheales, vicar of Brockham and author.
[15] Perhaps a fund for one of W. J. E. Bennett's ritualistic cases.
[16] Henry Alfred Greig, insurance broker.   [17] By W. R. W. Wilde (1867).
[18] *Sic.*   [19] London publishers.

Hughes—Mr Rawlins—T. Wood—Mr Naftel[1]—A. Abbot, & autographs. Read Mure—Nitzsch—Parker, Job's Comforters[2]—Brome, Mock Marriage—Empire Ottoman: finished. Carried a gift of books to Mr [C. H.] Bateman's District Library.

29. Th.

Ch. 8½ AM. Wrote to Archdeacon Ffoulkes—Mr Ll. Jones—Mrs Pheper?— Maccaroni Co—Rev. G. Grundy—Supt RR Bookstall (Chester)—Supt Parcel Office (Chester)—J. Morley—A. Hart—W. Jebb[3]—Mr Annandale. Worked on Primer. Saw Mr Vickers. Read Brome, Northern Lass—Lowe's Reply on the Suffrage.[4] Felled three Trees in clump.

30. Fr. St Andrew

Ch. 8.45 AM. Wrote to Lady Charlotte Clinton—Rev. Dr Parker—Mr Ouvry— Sig. G.B. Testa—Mr Raith—Mr J. O'Rourke—Mr J.W. North[5]—Mr Warburton BP.—Ld Granville BP.—Registrar of Charterhouse. Worked on Homeric Primer. Conversation with W. on his seat at Whitby.[6] Read Freeman on Forbes[7]— Russian Atrocities in Asia and Europe (Ottoman)[8]—Labour &c. in Jamaica[9]— Brome, Northern Lass[10]—Rent in a Cloud (Lever).[11]

Sat. Dec. One. 1877.

Ch. 8½ A.M. Wrote to Louey G.—E. Davis—Rev. F. Southgate[12]—Rev. Mr Grimley[13]—Redacteur du Valert—L. Barker—D. Sutherland[14]—R.P. Hindley—H.G. Sanders[15]—E.M. Southwell[16]—Rob. Gladstone. Woodcraft with W.H.G. Dinner party of 14. Read Bateman on Evolution[17]—Kossuth in C.R. on Magyarism.(!!)[18]

[1] Ernest L. Naftel, translator of German works.

[2] Joseph Parker, *Job's comforters: scientific sympathy* (1874).

[3] Perhaps W. F. Jebb of Kensington.

[4] R. Lowe, 'Mr Gladstone on manhood suffrage', *Fortnightly Review*, xxviii. 733 (December 1877); see 10 Dec. 77.

[5] Perhaps J. W. North, book illustrator.

[6] In 1880 Willy stood successfully for E. Worcestershire.

[7] Reply to Forbes (see 13 Nov. 77) probably in a newspaper; not in bibliography in Stephens, *Life of Freeman*, ii. 481.

[8] One of the many pamphlets on Forbes's accusations.

[9] Possibly *Jamaica enslaved and free* (1846).

[10] See 26 Nov. 77.

[11] See 23 Nov. 77n.

[12] Frederic Southgate, d. 1885; vicar of Northfleet from 1857.

[13] Horatio Nelson Grimley, professor of mathematics at Aberystwyth; had sent his *Tremadoc Sermons* (1876).

[14] David Sutherland, barrister; published on Indian law.

[15] Henry George Sanders, engineer in Notting Hill.

[16] Perhaps Edward James Southwell of Netherton House, Blackheath.

[17] One of C. H. Bateman's numerous articles; see 27 Nov. 77.

[18] L. Kossuth, 'Russian aggression as specifically affecting Austria-Hungary and Turkey', *Contemporary Review*, xxxi. 1 (December 1877).

2. *Adv. S.*

Ch. 11 A.M. & H.C. also 6½ P.M. Wrote to Rev. Dr Allon—Mr Taylor Innes—Ld Granville—J.P. Bourne—W.H. Morson—E.G. Swann[1]—Dr Ziemann—Rev. D. Jones—A. Turner—T. Dowson—A. Hume. Read Bateman on Darwin (finished)— Grimley's Sermons.

3. *M.* [*London*]

Wrote to Rev Mr Dampier—Mr Salmond—Mrs Spooner O—Dr Hugh Magnus. Off at 9¼. Harley St 3½. Got 4 or 5 hours of tearing open letters & packets. Saw Archdeacon Ffoulkes—Madame O. Novikoff—Mr Cartwright—Mr Stead—Saw Macgregor X. Dined at Sir R. Phillimore's. Much conversation with him.[2] Read Dowden's Shakespeare Primer[3]—Brackenbury's Art. on Forbes.[4]

4. *Tu.*

Wrote to Rev. Dr Allon—Master of the Charterhouse—Baillie Moncur—Mrs Schwabe—Rev. G. Whitehead[5]—Mr Scarr—Mr Middleton—M. Nublat—Mr Maurice—Mrs Reid BP—Mr Radclyffe. Saw Ld Granville—Ld Hartington—Do *cum* Ld G.—Mr West—Mr Mundella—Sir A. Panizzi (who does not sink)—Mrs Th. Dined with Mr Knowles at the Grosvenors. Conversation with Mr Forbes— Mr Ruskin[6]—Mr Knowles—Ld Houghton. Read Mr Forbes on 'Corresponding'.[7] Saw two [R].

5. *Wed.*

Wrote to Ed. Daily News[8]—Mr Hutchinson—Mr E. Adams—Mr Macqueen—Sir P. Colquhoun. 11½-3¼. Went to the opening service at Dr Allon's Independent Chapel. A notable Sermon from Dr Dale; & striking music. Deliberation with Ld De Tabley & Mr Ouvry on the whole question of our Newcastle Trust. Dined with Caroline Lyttelton. Saw Dr Schliemann—Mr Salmon, Greenwich. Saw one [R]. Read Pr. Consort Vol. III.[9]

6. *Th.*

Wrote to Mrs Eaton—H. Moritz[10]—W.H. Miller—P. Nicolson—Rev. J. Davis— R. Bulgarni—J.S. Welkins—Mrs Hutchinson—Mr Tschanskoff—Rev. R.W.

---

[1] Edward Gibbon Swann, minor poet.

[2] 'Mr & Mrs G. dined here. He in very high spirits full of his visit to Ireland. His opinion of the Irish Ch. worse than before his visit—and on the other hand of the tyranny exercised by the Cardinal (Cullen) over the Irish Priests. Cullen told G. his reception wd. have been much more enthusiastic but for the Vatican letter. He spoke with the deepest feeling of Northcote's opposing him for the Rectorship of Glasgow. He sd, wh was quite true, "You know I have never spoken agst. Northcote's 'political course'"'; Phillimore's diary, 3 December 1877.

[3] E. Dowden, *Shakespere; a critical study of his mind and art* (1875).

[4] Untraced article by C. B. *Brackenbury, who reported the 1877 war.

[5] Probably George Whitehead, curate of Atherington.

[6] See J. Evans and J. H. Whitehouse, *The diaries of John Ruskin* (1959), iii. 968.

[7] A. Forbes, ed. with others, *The War Correspondence of the Daily News* (1871).

[8] Private, on culpability of Disraeli; Add MS 44455, f. 299.

[9] i.e. T. Martin's *Life*; see 15 Dec. 77.   [10] Possibly Emanuel Moritz of Highbury.

Marston—Mr Pettifer[1]—Lady C. Pelham Clinton.[2] Saw Mr Knowles—Sir A. Panizzi—Mr Murray. S. Kens. Museum 12.45-2. Went over the Hissarlik objects, with very great interest.[3] Charterhouse Governors Board 2½-4¼. Dined with the Godleys: Mr Welby, Mr Brodrick. Much conversation. Read Magnanini, Armonia.[4]

7. Fr.

Wrote to Mr Winter Jones[5]—Mrs Bramwell—Mrs Nolan BP—Mr C.E. Lester— Sig. Palumbo[6]—Mr F.S. Williams—Mr Ouvry (O)—Gen. Cesnola—Mr C. Barry— Miss Hope. Saw Mr Godley—Mr Ouvry—Mr Knowles—Mrs Hope—Scotts—Ld Granville—Mr Jevons. Saw Phillips X. Dined at Pol. Economy Club. Mr Mundella made a most interesting statement & argument.[7] Worked on books, packing, &c.

8. Sat. [Hawarden]

Wrote to Rev. G.R.D. Cooke[8]—Mrs Phillips—Ed. Echo—Mr E. Hornby[9]— M. Pernolet[10]—Mr Darwin BP—Mr T.B. Potter—Professor Sanguinetti[11]—Mr Chynne.[12] Saw Mr Godley—Mr Macmillan—Mr Palgrave—Made Novikoff—Mrs Lawes. Luncheon at No 15. G.S. Read & noted on Colour Sense—Magnanini, Armonia. Left Euston 5.15. Reached Hawarden 11.15. Shopping.

9. 2 S. Adv.

Ch 11 AM 6¼ PM. Wrote to Duke of Argyll—Mrs Th. B.P. Read Magnanini— Minghetti, Stato e Chiesa[13]—Elogio Funebre di Monsig. Nardi[14]—Lindsay on Rome in Canada.[15]

10. M.

Ch. 8½ AM. Wrote to Prov. Trin Coll Dublin—Rev. Mr Burnett—T. Macknight— Bp [G. H.] Wilkinson—Mr Stopford—M. de St Mesmin—Jas Elliot—W. Clarke— J. Hewitt—Rev. J. Osler—Rev. T. Long—Sir Thos G.—Herbert JG. Read

---

[1] Replying to H. J. Pettifer of Birmingham, who, though a liberal, had sent a protectionist pamphlet; see Add MS 44455, f. 301.

[2] Charlotte, 2nd da. of 5th duke of Newcastle; d. 1886.

[3] Exhibition of Schliemann's discoveries.

[4] V. Magnanini, *Armonia della religione colle scienze e collo stato* (1877).

[5] John Winter *Jones, 1805-81; principal librarian of the British Museum 1866-78.

[6] Raffaele Palumbo, professor and author; tr. Gladstone's Homeric writings into Italian (1881?); diarist's proof in the Bodleian.

[7] On the conditions of Britain's manufacturing predominance, and dangers to it; *Political Economy Club* (1881), 61.

[8] George Probert Davies-Cooke, vicar of Shalbourne 1872.

[9] Probably (Sir) Edmund Grimani Hornby, 1825-96; jurist, published on Bulgaria.

[10] Arthur Pernolet, French engineer, later a deputy.

[11] Apollo Sanguinetti, Italian professor and author; see Add MS 44455, f. 293.

[12] Perhaps *sic*; word scrawled.

[13] By M. Minghetti (1878).

[14] G. P. Saccheri, *Elogio funebre di Mons. F. Nardi* (1877).

[15] C. Lindsay, *De Ecclesia et Cathedra*, 2v. (1877); on 'the Empire-Church'.

Minghetti—Cesnola on Cyprus[1]—Life of Prince Consort Vol. III. Worked on the Franchise.[2] Cutting trees with WHG in my Clump.

11. Tu.

Ch. 8½ AM. Wrote to Mr Jasper More—Mr Forsyth MP—Edm Hornby—W.P. Adam—Jas Knowles—Harry Day—Rev. Mr Robertson—Dr John Brown—R.H. Dunbar—R. Williams—W. Lister—Ld Kensington.[3] Read Life of Prince Consort—Mr Rathbone's Letter on Imports[4]—Mr Lowe (2°) on Suffrage in reply. Worked on Suffrage. Woodcraft with WHG.

12. Wed.

Ch. 8½ AM. Wrote to Mr Brentlinger[5]—Mr Ouvry—H. Clayton[6]—G.O. Jay—Dr Latham—Mr Richardson—J. Wood—Mrs Holland BP—J.C. Henderson—E.J. Watherston—M.J. Flockton[7]—Bishop Wilkinson—Sir Thos G.—Mr J.C. Nicholls. Saw S.E.G. on Parochialia—Herbert on Oxford affairs & life. Read Dawson, Origin of the World[8]—Life of Prince Consort.

13. Th.

Ch. 8½ AM. Wrote to Mr A. Peel BP—Messrs Baily BP—C. Tucker BP—Herr Magnus—Rev Mr Ashwell—Messrs Stephenson—Th. Martin—T.B. Green—J. Godkin—W.P. Adam—T.W. Russell. Woodcraft with W.H.G. Read Life of Prince Consort—My own Speeches of May & Aug. 1855.[9]

14. Fr.

Ch. 8½ AM. Wrote to C.G.—Mr Ouvry—Mr Knowles—G. Harris—Mr MacKee[10]—A. Browne—O. Blewitt. Felled trees with W.H.G. Worked upon, & began revision of, my short article in reply to Lowe on Franchise. Read Life of Prince Consort—Lord Bateman's Pamphlet(!)[11]—Sorristori on Montenegro.[12]

15. Sat.

Ch. 8½ A.M. Wrote to Mr Jasper More—T.M. Shannon—A.C. Ainger[13]—Mr Stratford—Mr Graham—Mr Edwards. Finished Paper on the Suffrage in reply

[1] Count L. Palma di Cesnola, *Cyprus* (1877).

[2] Published as 'Last words on the county franchise', *Nineteenth Century*, iii. 196 (January 1878), reprinted in *Gleanings*, i. 171.

[3] William Edwardes, 1835-96; 4th Baron Kensington (Irish) 1872; liberal M.P. Haverfordwest 1868-85; cr. a U.K. peer 1886.

[4] Not found.   [5] Of Clinton, Iowa, on Homer; Hawn P.

[6] Henry Clayton of Clay Cross; Add MS 44455, f. 297.

[7] Perhaps of Flocktons, the Sheffield manufacturers.

[8] Sir J. W. Dawson, *The origin of the world according to Revelation and Science* (1877).

[9] On the Crimean war; see 24 May, 3 Aug. 55.

[10] Perhaps Henry Sheil Mackee, professor of Greek at Magee college, Londonderry.

[11] W. B. B. Hanbury, Lord Bateman, 'Lord Bateman's plea for limited protection, or, for reciprocity in free trade' (1877).

[12] Untraced.

[13] Arthur Campbell Ainger, published on sport; Hawn P.

to Lowe's Reply: and revised it for Printer. Woodcraft with WHG. Read Life of Prince Consort: & made a beginning of a short article upon it[1]—Sorristori on Montenegro.

16. 3 S. Adv.

Ch 11 AM. and H.C.—[blank] P.M. Wrote to Spottiswoodes BP—Mrs A.L. Williams O—Mr Godley—J. Leith[2]—J. Patey—Messrs Baily. Read Ridsdale case[3]—C. Lindsay Eccl. et Cathedra—Bp Browne on The Understanding[4]—Origenes contra Celsum[5]—Wylie on Popish Hierarchy.[6]

17. M.

Ch. 8¼ AM. Wrote to Sir Bernard Burke—Ld Granville—Mr Bentley—Captain Cole—Mr Parker—Mr Richmond—Mr Barrat. Wrote & corrected a draft of 'Notice' for my republished Lecture, touching my error in the case of Midhat Pasha.[7] Worked on Martin Vol III.—Read Martin, finished—Düncker's History of Antiquity (Transl.)[8] Walk with the Rector, and calls.

18. Tu.

Wrote to Mr Jasper More—M. Waddington[9]—Sig. D. Carutti—Rev. W.T. Bullock—Rev. J.F. Smythe—Rev. R. Edwards—B. Shelburne[10]—A.R. Fairfield[11]—F. White—E. Jenkins—R. East—R.M. Brown—Mr Amsinck[12]—G.W. Vyse[13]—A. Bernard—C.C. Cox.[14] Woodcraft with Willy. Worked on Report of Lecture, correcting a bad Report with much vexation: nothing tries my temper more or more lavishly spends my time. Saw Mr Torr. Read Montenegro—Turchia e la Civiltà[15]—Duncker Hist. Antiquity.

19. Wed.

Ch. 8¼ A.M. and Sermon at 7½ P.M. Wrote to Pears Logan & Co—Messrs Spottiswoode BP.—Mr E.S. Pryce BP.[16]—Ld Granville—Rev. Mr Arthur—Rev. Chas Hill—Dr Mussalini[17]—J. Knowles—E.A. Bridge—G. Huntley. Woodcraft

---

[1] Review of volume iii of T. Martin, *Life of the Prince Consort*, published in *Church Quarterly Review*, v. 469 (January 1878), reprinted in *Gleanings*, i. 97.

[2] John Farley Leith, 1808-87; barrister and liberal M.P. Aberdeen 1872-80.

[3] The ritualist case, permitting the Eastward position; judgment given 12 May 1877.

[4] P. Browne, *The procedure, extent and limits of human understanding* (1728).

[5] *Origenis contra Celsum*, ed. W. Selwyn (1876).

[6] J. A. Wylie, *The papal hierarchy* (1878).   [7] See 23 Nov. 77n.

[8] M. W. Düncker, *The history of antiquity*, tr. E. Abbott (1877).

[9] William Henry Waddington, 1826-94; French minister for foreign affairs December 1877-9; at Berlin Congress 1878; prime minister 1879; ambassador in London 1883-93.

[10] Diarist's misreading of Bewicke Blackburn, who had written on 'Williams' who felled trees; Add MS 44455, f. 328.

[11] Arthur Rowen Fairfield of London, corresponded on Russia; Hawn P.

[12] George Stewart Amsinck of Ladbrooke Grove.

[13] Col. George Howard Vyse of the royal household.   [14] Charles C. Cox; Hawn P.

[15] Untraced.   [16] Edward Stisted Mostyn Pryce of Gunley Hall, Salop; a school inspector.

[17] *Sic*; perhaps Benedetto Musolini, d. 1885, Italian noble, deputy 1861 and senator 1881; published on Italian-British relations.

with WHG. Corrected & dispatched proofs of closing Article on Suffrage. Resumed that most penal task of correcting a Report in which I do not own two lines together. Read Moylan on Home Rule[1]—Turchia e la Civiltà—Montenegro—Miseria di Napoli.

20. Th.

Ch. 8½ AM. Wrote to Mr. de St Mesmin—D. of Argyll—Mr Mundella—E.S. Pryce—Rev R. Edwards—Mr H. Hamilton—Messrs Waterston—Mr Wait MP[2]— G. Halton—R. Leake—D.C. Moylan—Mrs D'Olier. Mr Jasper More came over. Much conversation with him on Midhat, Lady S[trangford?], &c. Woodcutting with WHG. Read Cesnola on Cyprus—Sorristori's Montenegro (finished).

21. St Thomas.

Ch. 8¾ AM. Wrote to Mr F. Schnadhorst[3]—Ld Granville—W.T. Stead—T.B. Potter—F.J. Hood—Messrs Freshfield BP.—Rev. M. MacColl—Rev. Dr Fanally[4]—Rev. W.F.W. Torre—W. Steele. Woodcutting at Bretton with Willy. Read Düncker—George Linton.[5] Worked at paper on Mr Martin's Vol. III.

22. Sat.

Ch. 8½ A.M. Wrote to Professor Blackie—Mr Bright—Mr Vickers—J.J. Gillan— Mrs Th.—Mr Forsyth MP—Rev. R. Yonge—Messrs Mullan. Woodcutting at the Bretton Clump with W.H.G. Read Tales from Homer[6]—Düncker's Hist. Antiquity. Worked more freely on Life of Prince Consort: history of Crimean War.

23. 4 S. Adv.

Ch. 11 A.M. and 6½ P.M. Corrected Proof (under Necessity) of Hawarden Lecture on the Forbes paper. Wrote to Ed. Daily News—also Edd. D.N., Times, D. Tel.[7]—Mr E.S. Pryce and. . . . Read Blackie on Pythagoras & Prefat. Epistle[8]— Charge of Bp Hughes[9]—do Bp Mackarness (Arg.)[10]—Report on Funeral Reform—Engl. Order of St Augustine[11]—Knox Little, Priest in Absolution[12]— and other Tracts.

24. M.

8¾-12. Went to Chester with W. & attended Mr Barker's[13] funeral at St Bride's. His son the Clergyman gave me a most happy account of his end. Shopping in

---

[1] Untraced work by Denis Creagh Moylan; see 29 Mar. 43, 20 Dec. 77.
[2] William Killigrew Wait, 1826-?; tory M.P. Bristol 1873-80.
[3] See Ramm II, i. 63.   [4] Not traced.
[5] J. Robinson, *George Linton; or, the first years of an English colony* (1876).
[6] A. J. Church, *Stories from Homer* (1877).
[7] Sending the 'Notice' on Midhat Pasha published prefatory to his lecture; *T.T.*, 25 December 1877, 6c.
[8] J. S. Blackie, *The wise men of Greece* (1877).
[9] J. Hughes, 'A charge . . . October 1877' (1877).   [10] G. R. Mackarness, 'A charge . . .' (1875).
[11] Not found.   [12] W. J. Knox Little, 'The priest in absolution' (1877).
[13] The solicitor; see 9 Mar. 40.

Chester. Worked on Art. for Church Quarterly. Wrote to Mr Wilson, Sheffield, (and copy)[1]–Rev. F. Lawrence–Rev. W. Griffiths[2]–Messrs Unwin–Sir R. Cunliffe–Mr Kennedy–Mr Crowther–Mr Streeter[3]–Rev. Dr Irons. Read Tales from Homer.

25. Tu. Xmas Day.

Church 11 A.M. with H.C. and 7 PM. Wrote to C.C. Cox–W. Wallace–Jasper More–Mrs Mockler–E. Beale–J.S. Burton. Worked on Martin Vol. III for a very short time. Read An Angel's Message[4]–The Christian Apologist:[5] with its odd assemblage & some singular paradoxes–Nineteenth Century on Midhat Pacha(!!)[6]–La Religion Romaine.

26. Wed. St Stephen.

Church 8¾ A.M. Worked pretty well on my Article, which is really on the Crimean War: and revised and dispatched it. Wrote to Rev. Canon Ashwell–Rev. Don. Fraser[7]–Rev. R. Yonge–Rev. A.J. Church–Mr Lowe MP–Mr Forsyth MP. Began the big beech 'washing away' roots with W. Read Düncker, Canaanites and Hebrews–Doran on Shakespeare in France.[8]

27. Th. St John.

Ch. 8¾ AM. Wrote to Rev. Mr [H. G.] Henderson–Canon Bourke–Rev. Mr Mayow–Mr A.G. Williams–Dr Haslett BP[9]–R. Hobart[10]–J.H. Parker–Mr Lowe–R. Wilson–W.M. Watson–V. Oger–W. Tallack. Woodcraft, on big beech &c. Read 19th Cent. on County Franchise[11]–Dr Bernhard, Atrocités Russes (a Penny-a-liner?)[12]–Cowan's Reminiscences[13]–Adkins re Hertford Farm. Conversation with Mr F. Leveson [Gower]–Ditto E. Wickham.

28. Fr. H. Innocents.

Kept bed till 1.30: lumbago. Wrote to Mr Thorold Rogers–C. Cowan–H.R. Irvine[14]–Messrs Robn & Nichn.–Mr Ouvry–W.B. Howes. Saw Mr F. Leveson.

[1] Henry Joseph Wilson, 1833-1914; Sheffield radical employer; sec. of Sheffield liberal association; campaigned against Contagious Diseases Acts; liberal M.P. Holmfirth 1885-1912. This letter, on early summoning of parliament, in *T.T.*, 29 December 1877, 6c.

[2] An occasional clerical correspondent; had sent sermons; Hawn P.

[3] E. W. Streeter of London; had sent books; Hawn P.

[4] *An angel's message... received by a lady* (1858).

[5] *Christian Apologist*, i. 129 (January 1878), on evolution, Jesuits, and Vaticanism.

[6] J. W. Gambier in *Nineteenth Century*, iii. 71 (January 1878).

[7] Donald Fraser, presbyterian minister of Marylebone church.

[8] J. Doran, 'Shakespeare in France', *Nineteenth Century*, iii. 115 (January 1878).

[9] Samuel Torrens Hasslett, physician in Donegal.

[10] (Sir) Robert Henry Hobart, 1836-1928; Hartington's secretary until 1885; later a liberal M.P.; cr. bart. 1914.

[11] Apparently reading his own article, see 10 Dec. 77n.

[12] Untraced.

[13] By C. Cowan (1878).

[14] May read 'Irwin'.

Read Cowan's Reminiscences—Cairn on Irvine[1]—La Roumanie et la Guerre actuelle.[2]

29. Sat.

Rose to breakfast: & assisted in finishing the felling of the condemned beech on the lawn. Wrote to Mr Cole (l. & B.P.)—Rev. W. Carnforth—R.S. Hawkins[3]—J.W. Wilson—Mr Bryce—Mr Beal—Mr Calcott.
Spent the morning in
1. Review of Hawarden Estate accounts
2. Arranging private papers of interest in relation to my own affairs.
Read Cowan.

30. S. aft Xmas.

Church 11 A.M. (E. W[ickham] excellent) and 6½ P.M. Wrote to Mr C.S. Parker—Mr Merriman—Mr Sievewright[4]—Col. Maude. Read Ruskin's Lecture (in 19th Century)—Dean Stanley on Absolution[5]—Life of Sir Titus Salt[6]—Matheson, Growth of Christian Spirit.[7]

31. M.

Ch. 8½ A.M. Wrote to C.G.—Marquis of Bath BP—Duke of Argyll BP—Jasper More l. & BP—Ld Wolverton—Messrs Blackwood—Editor of Princeton Review—Midhat Pasha B.P.—Mr Dunbar—Mr Joynt—Mr Spielmann[8]—Mr Merriman—Mr Cartwright. Mr Murray[9] Correspondent of Times & Scotsman came, fresh from Bulgaria; & spent the afternoon 1-6½. Wrote out Annual Account or Sketch of Property & Debts: and started a new Rel. & Char. Account Book. Read Cowan—Brassey on E. Question.[10]
And now let me close together the birthday year & the natural year. Great thankfulness should be the forefront of the record: for tho' I have not been busied as I could have wished and schemed, the part assigned to me in the Eastern Question has been a part great and good far beyond my measure.
But it has been a year of tumultuous life. And such life will not let my hard heart soften and break up as the soil after a frost, but keeps it stony, so that I am almost driven to ask whether God will finally have to break it by some more crushing stroke.
May he lead me and that promptly, it is my keenest prayer for myself through duty into rest. Thus only can I hope for a true penitence and purging.

[1] May read 'Caine'; if so, possibly T. H. Hall Caine, 'Richard III and Macbeth' (1877); on Irving.
[2] Untraced.   [3] Robert Samuel Hawkins of Thorburn Square, London.
[4] *Sic*; possibly Gustavus Adolphus Sieveking of Regent's Park.
[5] J. Ruskin, 'An Oxford lecture' and A. P. Stanley, 'Absolution', in *Nineteenth Century*, iii. 136, 183 (January 1878).
[6] [A. Holroyd], *A life of Sir Titus Salt* (1871).   [7] See 16 Nov. 77.
[8] Perhaps Marion Harry Alexander Spielmann, 1858-1948, art critic; letters extant for 1880s.
[9] Perhaps the notorious E. C. Grenville Murray (see 17 Sept. 77); Hawarden Visitor's Book not signed.
[10] T. Brassey, *The Eastern Question and the political situation at home* (1878).

Hawarden Jan. 1. 1878. Circumcision.

Church 8¾ A.M. Wrote to Mr Wilson (Tel.)—Prof. Blackie—J.E.T. Rogers—J.H. Parker—Lord R. Churchill[1]—Sir W.C. Trevelyan—C.G.—Sir G. Bowyer—Ld Acton. Felled an ash with W.H.G. Saw Mr [C. W. G.] Howard—who left us—Mr R. Burnett. Arranging papers & letters. Read Cowan: who falls off sadly in interest—Palumbo's Maria Carolina.[2]

2. Wed.

Ch. 8½ A.M. Wrote to Duke of Argyll—Mr Mundella—Mr J. Barlow (l. & BP)[3]—Consul of Greece at Rottm (B.P.)[4]—Mr Fairbrother—Rev. Mr Jones—Professor Blackie—C.G.—Ed. St Pancras Guardian.[5] Bretton Clump with W. We felled five Trees. Read Palumbo, Maria Carolina. Resumed Homeric Primer: & worked a little. Arranging letters.

3. Th.

Ch. 8½ AM. Wrote to Mr Chamberlain MP.—Mr Mundella MP.—Messrs Farrer (O)—Rev. Newman Hall—Rev. H.P. Goodrich—Rev. Mr Knox Little—A. Macdonald—Mr Bayley—Mr Harris—A. Sott—Mrs Gallenga. Woodcraft, with W.— They left us for Leeswood. The Duke & a party from Eaton came over to luncheon. Correcting proofs for The Church Quarterly. Read Palumbo's Maria Carolina—What a *Queen*!—Gen. Turr Tracts on Eastern Question[6]—The Queen, Lord B., & the War.

4. Fr.

Ch. 8½ AM. Wrote to Madame O. Novikoff—Marquis of Bath—C.G.—Rev M. MacColl—Mr Bateman B.P.—Walter James MP.—T. Fulton—Signor Palumbo—Messrs Spottiswoode. Finished & dispatched my Corrected Proof on Mr Martin's Vol. III. Walk with Stephy and visits. Saw Mr Vickers. Worked up & completed my (squib) verses on "Miss Flanigan".[7] Read [Byron's] Don Juan (to put me in trim for rhymes)—Account of the Lough Corrib District.[8]

5. Sat.

Ch. 8½ A.M. Wrote to Ld Granville—Lord Acton—Mary G.—H.J.G.—R.Y. Piper—Mr Kimber—W.A. East—J.C. Swan l. & B.P.—F.T. Grey. Woodcraft with

---

[1] Lord Randolph Henry *Spencer-Churchill, 1849-98; tory M.P. Woodstock 1874-85, Paddington 1885-98; Indian secretary 1885-6; chancellor 1886. Privately favoured a 'Home Rule' solution to the Balkan question, see W. S. Churchill, *Lord Randolph Churchill* (1906), i. 101.

[2] R. Palumbo, *Carteggio di Maria Carolina con Lady Emma Hamilton* (1877).

[3] Perhaps James William Barlow, 1826-1913; professor of history, Trinity, Dublin, 1861.

[4] Untraced.

[5] On Bulgaria; *St Pancras Guardian*, 5 January 1878, 4a.

[6] S. Türr, *Solution pacifique de la question d'Orient* (1877).

[7] Not found.

[8] See 27 Nov. 77.

Willy. Worked on Primer of Homer. Read Türr's Tract of 1867[1]—B. Brunswick on the Turkish Constitution[2]—Pope, Essay on Criticism.

6. Sun. Epiph.

Ch. 11 AM (with H.C.) and [blank.] Dearest C.s birthday. Wrote to C.G.—Lord Rosebery—Miss Collet—Mr J. Griffiths. Read the Brahmo Year Book[3]—Heathen England[4]—Davis, Annus Sanctus[5]—Cook & Birks on the Jews[6]—Duncker's History[7]—Bandinel's Letter on Convocn.[8]

7. M.

Ch. 8¼ A.M. Dear Herbert 24 today. Benedictus benedicat! Wrote to Ld Hartington—Rev. Mr Bandinel—Mr Grant Allen[9]—F. Houldsworth—A. Trendell[10]—Miss Hanson—Rev. Newman Parry[11]—Rev. E.C. Collard[12]—Rev. J.G. Rogers—Messrs Wilkins—Mr Dugdale[13]—J. Clark—G. Stewart—Mr Bryant—G. Ryan[14]—C.G.—Mr Deason—Mr Vickers. Read Düncker—Holtzmann's Lectures.[15]

8. Tu.

Ch. 8½ AM. Wrote to Bishop of Carlisle—Rev Dr Allon—Miss C. Marsh—Miss Hart—Mr Earwaker—Archdeacon Ffoulkes—Mr Knowles—J.T. Stead[16]—Mr Saberton[17]—E.S. Pugh.[18] Arranging papers. Worked on Homeric Primer. Walk with the gentlemen. Conversation with E.W. Read Düncker—Corneille, Cid: & Voltaire on do. Long conversation with Mr L. Barker.

9. Wed.

Ch. 8½ A.M. Wrote to Mr M'Kanny—Messrs Glyn—Mr P. Gilston—Miss Duggan—Mr A. Mackenzie—C.G.—Mrs Bramwell—Mr Earwaker—Mr Shelley—Mr C.S. Parker. Felled 7 trees from 12 to 20 in. diameter with Herbert. Wrote

[1] Untraced tract by Stephen Türr, see 3 Jan. 78.
[2] B. Brunswik, *La succession au trône de Turquie* (1872) or an untraced article.
[3] Sent by its compiler, S. D. Collet (1878); see Add MS 44456, f. 14.
[4] [G. S. Railton], *Heathen England and what to do for it* (1877).
[5] T. Davis, *Annus Sanctus* (1877).
[6] T. R. Birks, *The true prerogative and glory of the Jews* (1877).
[7] See 17 Dec. 77.
[8] James Bandinel, 1814-93, rector of Emly, sent his 'The Lay House' (1877).
[9] (Charles) Grant Blairfindie *Allen, 1848-99; scientist and man of letters; worked on Homer's colour sense 1878, see E. Clodd, *Grant Allen* (1900), 70.
[10] (Sir) Arthur James Richens Trendell, 1836-1909; organized international exhibitions at home and abroad; kt. 1900.
[11] Untraced; *sc.* Hall?
[12] Edwin Curwen Collard, vicar of Alton-Pancras, Salop.
[13] Perhaps William Stratford Dugdale, 1828-82; barrister and landowner.
[14] G. Ryan, London artisan, on artisans' housing; *T.T.*, 15 January 1878, 10f.
[15] H. J. Holtzmann, *Über Fortschritte und Rückschritte der Theologie unseres Jahrhunderts* (1878).
[16] Surname smudged.
[17] Perhaps Joseph Saberton, goldsmith.
[18] Edward Stuart Pugh, London merchant.

on the Peace to come.[1] Read M'Kanny's MS.—The Cid: finished—A most strange example, in my view, of a perfect or great drama.

10. Th.

Ch. 8.30 A.M. Wrote to Ld Tenterden (& copy)[2]—Bishop of Oxford—Mr Linklater—J.R. Morrison—Mr Farnal[3]—E. Clarke—Rev. Mr Tillotson—Rev. Mr Overy—J.R. Morell[4]—Mr Dobson—C.G.—J. Arnot[5]—W. Brough. Walk and calls at Farms with the Rector. Worked on the Peace to come & a little on Homer. Read Field's Journey[6]—Corneille Rhodogune [sc. Rodogune].

11. Frid.

Ch. 8½ AM. Wrote to Mr Arnot (Tel)—A.G. Williams—Rev. F.J. Parry[7]—Rev. J.A. Wylie[8]—Lord E. Cavendish—Messrs Glyn BP—Mr R. Williams (Carnarvon)—Messrs Ransom—Mr Vickers—Mr Adam MP—Mr Killick—C.G.—F. Mot. R. Dee Trust Meeting 12-1½. W., H., and I cut six trees at the Bretton Clump. Worked on The Peace to come. Read Finlay's History.[9]

12. Sat.

Ch. 8½ AM. Worked on The Peace. Saw Duke of Westmr[10]—Mr Vickers. Wrote to Marquis of Bath—Ld Lymington—Benj. Potter—Mr Geo. Rae—C.G.—Mr Knowles—W. Booth[11]—T.H. Webb—H.H. Heath. Woodcraft with Alfred L[yttelto]n. Mr Ruskin came: we had much conversation, interesting of course, as it must always be with him.[12] Mr Holland (Ch.Ch) also.[13] Read Field's Journey and Minghetti Chiesa e Stato.

13. 1 S. Epiph.

Ch 11 A.M. & 6½ PM. Wrote to Duchess of Leinster—Mr C.S. Parker—Mr E. Davis—Sir Thos G. Looked up some of Arthur Hallam's letters to find his

---

[1] Published as 'The Peace to come', *Nineteenth Century*, iii. 209 (February 1878); Add MS 44697, f. 97.

[2] Requesting information on unreleased documents; Add MS 44456, f. 36.

[3] Harry Farnal, foreign office clerk.

[4] John Reynell Morell, wrote on literature, history and diplomacy, and *Turkey, past and present* (1854).   [5] John Arnot of Greenock; on by-election there; Hawn P.

[6] Probably H. M. Field, *From Egypt to Japan* (1877).

[7] Perhaps F. W. Parry, vicar of Bickerton.

[8] James Allan Wylie, d. 1894; minister living in Edinburgh; had sent a pamphlet on Popery; Hawn P.   [9] See 10 July 54.

[10] A row with the duke of Sutherland; see Bassett, 221.

[11] Perhaps of Edinburgh; later corresponded on establishment; Hawn P.

[12] Diary extracts for Ruskin's visit quoted in *Letters to M.G. & H.G. by John Ruskin with preface by the Right Hon. G. Wyndham* (1903), which also includes [E. B. Ottley's] journal of the visit, and Scott Holland's recollections (see next note); see also Cook and Wedderburn, *Ruskin's Works*, xxxvi. lxxviii ff., J. Evans and J. H. Whitehouse, *The diaries of John Ruskin* (1959), iii.974, and L. March-Phillips and B. Christian, *Some Hawarden Letters 1878-1913* (1917), ch. i. The MS of Ottley's journal is in Add MS 46268. The house party also included Argyll, Acton and Alfred Lyttelton.

[13] i.e. Henry Scott Holland, who recalled his visit, dating it as 1881, in 'Gladstone and Ruskin', *The Commonwealth*, iii. 211 (July 1898).

testimonial to [F. D.] Maurice. They are astonishing. What a bulwark he would
have been, had it pleased the Most High to assign to him length of days. Read
the lessons in the morning Service. The LI [chapter of] Isaiah seemed as if
written for them in the East: and just after the Shipka pass.[1] Read Xtn
Apologist and [blank.] Much conversation & good.

14. M.

Ch. 8½ AM. Wrote to M. Paul de Anien[2]—C.G.—Mrs Th.—W. Brough—Dr
Firmeran[3]—Jas Stewart[4]—Cyrus Field—T.M. Dolan.[5] Walk with Ld Acton.
Worked on The Peace to come. Looking up passages & much conversation.
Also it was again a great day of conversation.

15. Tu.

Ch. 8¼ AM. Wrote to Mr H. Broadhurst—Mr Knowles B.P.—Rev. A. Grosart—
Rev. Dr Dale—E. Wilson—Scotts—C.G.—J. Wales. Finished, & revised, my
article on The Peace to come. Mr Ruskin went at 10¾. In some respects an
unrivalled guest, and those important respects too. Finished with Herbert the
work at the Bretton clump. There are 48 trees down. Walk with Ld Acton.

16. Wed. [London]

Wrote to ... [sic]. Off to London at 9.15 with Lord Acton. Arr. 3.30. Saw Ld
Granville—Sir A. Panizzi. Dined with Ld Hartington. Conversation with him—
with Bright—Childers. Attended Conclave at Granville's 11-12.40 & gave my
view, which was pretty general.[6] Read Freeman on the Party and Duke of
Argyll on Establishment.[7]

17. Th.

Wrote to Ld Tenterden—Sir P. Egerton—Mr J.A. Walker—Messrs Cassell—M.
Malamos—Mr Dearden[8]—Dr Pessalenti—Mr Stead—Mr Middleton—Mr T.G.
Bowles[9]—Ed. Echo. Saw Mr MacColl—Ld Wolverton—Sir R. Phillimore.[10]

[1] 'My righteousness is near; my salvation is gone forth, and mine arms shall judge the people':
the Russians had just captured the pass, the key to Roumelia, from the Turks.

[2] Or 'Arias'; neither traced.

[3] Perhaps Charles George Firman, physician in Gravesend.

[4] James Stewart, 1827-95; liberal M.P. Greenock January 1878-84.

[5] Thomas Michael Dolan, physician in Halifax, corresponded on hydrophobia in Homer; Hawn P.

[6] 'Queen's speech read and discussed: difference of opinion as to meaning of it'; Walling, *Diaries
of Bright*, 402.

[7] *Contemporary Review*, xxxi. 217, 365 (January 1878).

[8] Perhaps George Ferrand Dearden, curate in Swinton.

[9] Thomas Gibson *Bowles, 1842-1922, natural s. of Milner Gibson; clerk to I.R.B.; journalist; tory
M.P. King's Lynn 1892-1906; free-trader.

[10] 'G. came to dinner ... saying that in his whole political life he had never been so surprised as by
what he had just heard. "It is exactly as I wish (he said) but they ought to pay my railway fare back
to Hawarden." ... He was emphatic & decided in his opinion that if the Premier mentioned to the
Queen any of his colleagues who had opposed him in Cabinet, he was guilty of great ... perfidy. ...
G. said he had copies of 250 letters written by him to the Queen in none of wh. could a reference be
found to the opinion of his colleagues expressed in Cabinet'; Phillimore's Diary.

Worked on the mass of letters and papers accumulated: more than half the l. are Eastern. H. of C. 4½-8¾. Northcotes speech & many other signs show great & recent dissension in the Cabinet.[1] It is an immense gain, no less than surprise. The value of days at such a crisis is untold. Read [blank] on E. Question.

18. Fr. [Hawarden]

Wrote to Master of Charterhouse (l. & BP)—Sir Thos G.—H.J.G.—Mr W. Robertson—Mr W.J. Davy—Mr Abcarius—Messrs Spottiswoode. Saw Ld Wolverton—Scotts—Duke of Argyll—Mr Boydell—Ld Granville—W.H.G. Shopping. Luncheon in G. Square. Working off papers. Off at 4.50. Hawarden at 11.20. Worked on papers.

19. Saty.

Ch. 8½ A.M. Wrote to Sir Jas Watson—Watson & Smith—Mr Jas Stewart—Lady E. Pringle—Mr Jackins—Mr King. Saw the Rector. Hurried conversation with H. and H. Worked on [Homeric] Primer[2]—Also on Terms of Peace to come. Cut five trees with Herbert. Read the preposterous 'Revelations' from the Seat of War[3]—Norman on Armenia[4]—Mediation (Turkophile) Terms[5]—Catacazy on British Policy[6]—Westropp on the Round Towers.[7]

20. 2 S. Epiph.

Ch 11 A.M. with H.C.—and [blank.] Wrote to Mr Knowles—Mr Stead—Mr Ivory.[8] Corrected my article on 'The Peace to come' (proofs)—Read Eastern Pamphlets—Mr Arthur's clever History[9]—Foreign Ch. Chronicle.

21. M.

Ch. 8¼ A.M. Wrote to Capt. Maurice—Mr De Lisle—Mr S.F. Page[10]—Mr A. Maclauchlin—Mr E.R. Russell. Worked a good deal on Homeric Primer. Walk (River) with H, H, & M. Saw Mr Vickers (B[enjamin] Potter &c). Read Mr Catacazy, & Birkbeck, on E.Q.[11]—Norman's Armenia.

22. Tu.

Ch. 8½ AM. Wrote to Duke of Westminster—Dr Har⟨z⟩feldt—Mr Dillwyn—Jas Cleve—R. Hopwood—Sir Jas Watson—Mr Westropp—Mr Macpherson—A.C.

---

[1] Gladstone followed Northcote on 1870; *H* 237. 104.
[2] See 24 Sept. 77n.
[3] *Revelations from the seat of war. Russians, Turks, Bulgarians and Mr Gladstone* (1877).
[4] C. B. Norman, *Armenia and the campaign of 1877* (1878).
[5] Untraced.
[6] C. Katakazes, *Politique Anglaise en Orient* (1877).
[7] H. M. Westropp, *On the fanaux de cimitières in France, and the round towers in Ireland* (1863).
[8] Thomas Ivory, 1818-82; Wood and Forests counsel from 1862.
[9] See 23 Feb. 77.
[10] Perhaps Samuel Flood Page, wrote on military affairs.
[11] J. Birkbeck, 'The Eastern Question: an appeal to the British nation' (1878); dated 9 January 1878; he published a comment on Gladstone's 'Paths of Honour' later this year.

Reed—W.T. Stead—S. Chick. Cut two sizable trees with Herbert. Worked on Hom. Primer & at length got out of the knotty thorny 'Homeric Question'.[1] Counted 11 full grown buds, one or two partially blown, on the magnolia. Read Norman's Armenia—Ch. of E. Quart. on Culture abroad.[2]

23. Wed.

Ch. 8½ A.M. Wrote to Messrs Spottiswoode—W. Robertson[3]—C.S. Parker—Earl of Lincoln—Sir Ph. Egerton—Mrs Bramwell—Mr Knight Watson—Messrs Ransome—Jas Knowles—Mr Norman[4]—H. Brown—Rev. A. Brodrick. Woodcraft with Herbert. Corrected for press & dispatched Art. on 'The Peace to come'. Worked on Hom. Primer: but hampered with face-ache. Read Bright's Life—Norman's Armenia.

24. Th.

Ch. 8½ A.M. Wrote to Mr Mundella MP—J.H. Parker—Thos Ivory—J.S. Vickers—Williams & Co.—Geo. Mitchell—Don. Giov. Lonardi—Mr Adam MP—Mr Crum(?)—H.N.G. Woodcraft with W. & H. Finished my Primer on the Plots. But at six came a great disturbance: Northcote's engagement is gone, it seems, to the winds, & money is to be sought forthwith.[5] Such is the effect of five Telegrams that reached me. Read Munchausen[6]—Life & Times of Bright.

25. Fr. Conv. St Paul. [London]

Wrote to Mrs Wynn (Tel.)—H.N.G.—Rev. C.T. Wakeham[7]—Rev. Geo. Matheson[8]—H.N. Gladstone—Sir Jas Watson—Madame Novikoff. Much putting way of books pamphlets &c & off at 10¾. 73 Harley St at 6. Went to the House. Saw Ld Hartington—Mr Bright—Mr Childers—Sir W. Harcourt—Ld Kensington. A great agreement prevailed as to the mode of proceding. Dined with Mrs Thistlethwayte: and off soon after nine to the Phillimores. Saw Auberon Herbert: conversation about his brother [Carnarvon]. Read Onley's Tour.[9] Worked on letters & papers. I do not get rid of my face-ache. The times are enough for it. Would they did no worse.

26. Sat.

Wrote to Mr E. Davis[10]—Mr Macmillan—H. Edwards—T.W. Pearce—G. Marnitz—Ld Granville—H.J.G.—Mr Girvan—J. Clarke—J. Bishop—Mr King—P. Ralli.

---

[1] See 24 Sept. 77n.

[2] 'Continental culture', *Church Quarterly Review*, v. 347 (January 1878).

[3] William Robertson, author of *The life and times of... John Bright* (1877) and involved in undocumented negotiations with Bright, see 30 Aug. 78.

[4] Charles Boswell Norman; see 19 Jan. 78.

[5] On 23 January the fleet was ordered to sail to Constantinople, and notice given of a Vote of Credit; Carnarvon and Derby resigned, their letters reaching Beaconsfield on the 24th; Derby was persuaded to stay on; see Buckle, vi. 227-33.   [6] See 9 June 76.

[7] Edinburgh clergyman; Gladstone sent him 10/- for his book, though he does not record reading it; Hawn P.   [8] George Matheson, religious author; see 16 Nov. 77.

[9] M. Onley, *A woman to women on the Turkish horrors* (1876).

[10] On the eastern situation; *T.T.*, 28 January 1878, 10a.

Saw Rev. Mr MacColl (2)—Mr Knowles—Mr West—Mr Crossley—Duke of Argyll. 12–2. Meeting at Granville's. We determined to oppose the Vote about to be asked by the Govt & to make no secret of it. It will probably be by a motion before the Speaker leaves the Chair. Dined with the Phillimores. A long & interesting conversation with Carnarvon on Beaconsfield himself & on the policy.[1] Read the Crown & the Cabinet.[2]

27. 3 S. Epiph.

Kept my bed, & then the House, till aftn, soothing down my face-ache. Read mg service—Chapel Royal aft. Dined with Sybella Lyttelton: conversation with Albert Grey, a prime fellow. Wrote to Mrs Th. Read Eternal Punishment a reality (such the tract is not)[3]—Civilisation Hellenique[4]—Chatfields Tr. of Gk Hymns[5]—Ch of E. Quart. on Claims of Ch of E.—on Angl. Orders—& on Churchmen abroad.[6]

28. M.

Wrote to Ld Tenterden—Mr Rowntree[7]—Rev J. Clarke—Earl of Derby. Dined at Mr West's. H of C. $4\frac{1}{2}$–$7\frac{3}{4}$.[8] Saw Mr West—Ld Wolverton—Mr MacColl—Ld Granville—Mr Welby. Read Civilisation Hellenique. Worked on papers & letters.

29. Tu.

Wrote to Mr J.R. Jolly—J.E. T[horold] Rogers—G.J. Wylsor—Mr Maxtone Graham[9]—Mayor of Southport—Mr Gurdon—Messrs Ransome—Sir L. Mallet[10]—E. Banfield—W. Morley—Mrs Lloyd—Mr Kriens[11]—S.F. Page. 12–2. Meeting at Ld Granvilles on the proposal of the Government. To the astonishment of all Ld Hartington bolted & was with great difficulty brought up to the mark again. The resolution was finally taken for united opposition.[12] Luncheon at 15 G.S. Saw Scotts—Sir W. James—Mr Forster—Mr James—Ld Hartington—

---

[1] 'Carnarvon and the Gs separately invited themselves & came to dinner. G. in spite of some neuralgia roused himself & spoke with almost his usual vigour on a variety of topics—political chiefly. He originated nothing about the present prime minister—but answered Carnarvon's inquiries about his past career so far as he had come in contact with it. G. was careful to restrain the expression of his private feelings about Lord B. as he generally is. I was amused at hearing him defend plays & the Theatre—on no subject have his opinions undergone a more complete revolution. Great favour was shown to painting & music—why not to the drama?'; Phillimore's Diary.

[2] By 'Verax' (1878); on Martin's biography.

[3] Untraced tract.   [4] By K. Paparrhegopoulos (1878).

[5] A. W. Chatfield, *Songs and hymns of earliest Greek Christian poets* (1876).

[6] All in *Church Quarterly Review*, v. (January 1878).

[7] Probably Joseph Rowntree, 1836–1925; Quaker chocolate manufacturer and radical.

[8] Spoke briefly on Vote of Credit; *H* 237. 564.

[9] James Maxtone-Graham of Cultoquhey,1819–1901; active in Scottish liberal politics.

[10] Mallet had written to announce that Morley had agreed to write Cobden's biography, 'But before proceeding further I am anxious to know whether we have your authority & sanction to accept Mr Morley's offer'; Add MS 44456, f. 72; Gladstone's reply not found; he was a trustee of Cobden's MSS, with M. Chevalier.

[11] Edward Kriens, later Bismarck's biographer.

[12] 'Hartington hung back and almost resigned leadership. I back him'; Goschen's diary in Elliot, *Goschen*, i. 183. See 1 and 4 Feb. 78.

Mr Adam–Mr Mundella–Mr Rathbone–Sir W. James–Mr Godley. Dined with the Godleys. Read Civilisation Hellénique (Paparrigopoulos).

30. Wed. [Oxford]

Cleared my first post: off 9.40. Oxf. 11.45. Straight to the Corn Exchange meeting, very enthusiastic. Spoke say 50 m. Then an ovation through the streets to the house of Mr Thorold Rogers. Cathedral service at 5. Palmerston Club dinner 6¼–12¼! Spoke in proposing the prosperity of the Club: I said what was meant to do a little good.[1] Saw Ld Selborne–Ld Granville–Dr Pusey–Canon [W.] Bright. Read Norman's Armenia–Civ. Hellénique.

31. Th.

New Coll. Chapel 5 P.M. Survey at Ch.Ch.–The Meadows–Bot. Garden–New Coll–All Souls–Worcester–and above all Keble & the noble Chapel. Breakfast dinner & evening parties at the Dean's:[2] where they are so kind. Saw Provost of Worcester–Master of Univ.–Mr Sayce–Rector of Exeter–Mr B. Price–Mr Max Müller–Dr Acland–Prof. Rolleston–Dr Liddon–Bp of Oxford–Mr Kitchin–Professor Smith–Miss Smith.[3]

Friday Feb. One 1878. [London]

Wrote to my sister Helen–Sir Jas Fergusson–Ld Ripon–Principal Caird–Mr Davis (Greenwich). Breakfast party at the Dean's. Saw Master of Balliol–Professor Stubbs–Mr Clifton[4]–Mr Walford–and others. Walk & much interesting conversation with the Dean, especially about Ruskin. 12–2 To London. L[uncheo]n with Mrs Birks. Went to work on letters and papers. H of C. 4½–8½ and 9½–1½.[5] Dined with Meriel Talbot. Saw Mr Childers–Mr Dodson–Mr Mundella–Mr A. Balfour–Mrs Peddie.[6] Read Civilisation Hellénique.

---

[1] Meetings organized by J. Thorold Rogers and T. H. *Green; the Palmerston Club meeting, chaired by Lord Lymington, also honoured Cardwell, whose health was proposed by Alfred *Milner, then an undergraduate; *T.T.*, 31 January 1878, 10. These were perhaps Gladstone's most controversial Eastern Question speeches, especially the first. At the Corn Exchange: 'I think it is utterly vain to disguise or to keep in the shade that in regard to the Eastern Question when you speak of the Government you speak of Lord Beaconsfield ... it is Lord Beaconsfield's will that takes effect, fitfully and with fluctuations ... and that from time to time succeeds in bringing the country into danger ... for the last 18 months I may be said to have played the part of an agitator ... my purpose ... has been to the best of my power for the last 18 months, day and night, week by week, month by month, to counterwork as best I could what I believe to be the purpose of Lord Beaconsfield.' At the Palmerston Club on the £6m. vote of credit: 'It is not a proposal of peace; it is not a proposal of war.... That proposal is a proposal, I do not say to get us into war, but to get us near war.'

[2] Dean Liddell of Christ Church; attendance list in Add MS 44763, f. 125.

[3] Henry John Stephen *Smith (1826–83; Savilian professor of geometry 1860; close friend of Jowett; unsuccessfully contested Oxford University as a liberal in May 1878) and his sister, Eleanor Elizabeth, a leading Oxford philanthropist.

[4] Robert Bellamy Clifton, 1836–1921; professor of experimental philosophy at Oxford 1865–1915.

[5] Forster's amndt. (opposing the voting of 'unnecessary Supplies') to Northcote's Vote of Credit (technically to the motion that the Speaker leave the chair); *H* 237. 824.

[6] Probably Euphemia, wife of John Dick Peddie, 1824–85, Edinburgh architect and liberal M.P. Kilmarnock 1880–5.

2. Sat.

Wrote to Rev. H.R. Baker—Mr Turnerelli—Mr Ouvry—Baron Profumo[1]—Mrs Hadin—Mr Bandmann[2]—Mr Wolff—Mr Kilner.[3] Dined with the F. Cavendishes. Read Civilisation Hellenique. Saw Duke of Argyll—Mr Papasion[4]—W.H.G.—Ld Wolverton—Ld Granville—Ld F. Cavendish. 2-6¾. Went with W. to Ransome's Works and thence to the Rosefull Park Estate to see the remarkable operations of his Tree Cutter.[5] We then had tea at his house.

3. S. 4. Epiph.

All Souls mg and H.C. Chapel Royal evg. Wrote to Mr Ouvry. Dined at Mad. Rallis. Saw Ld F. Cavendish—Mr F. Leveson—Mr Gennadios—Mr R. Burke[6]—Mr Mavrocordato—W.H.G.—Ld E. Fitzmaurice.[7] Read Bandmann's Tale—St Thomas A Kempis—Civilisation Hellenique—Hughes on Mahometanism[8] and [blank.]

4. M.[9]

Wrote to Mr Shaw (O)—Mr Bunker (O). Saw Ld Hartington. Read Turkey Papers: worked on the subject & made notes. H of C. 4¼-8¼ and 10½-1. Spoke 1 h. 50 m. at my best: with little aid to the throat.[10] Dined at Sir C. Forster's. Read Lecture on Homer.

5. Tu.

Wrote to Mr Ouvry—Mr Purcell—W.T. Stead—Mr Bromley—J.R. Jolly—Mr Kirkham—G. Potter—W. Wallace—W. Lewis—Rev. Dr Barry—Rev. W. Denton—E.R. Johnstone—H.L. Brown—J.S. Latham—W.H. Combes[11]—W.T. Groom[12]—Mr Goschen. Luncheon with Mrs B. & a conversation on *the* breakfast. H. of C. 4½-8¼.[13] Dined at Sir R. Phillimore's.[14] Saw Hume [R]. Saw Mr [C.S.] Parker (Scots Ch. Patr.).

---

[1] Reading uncertain.

[2] Possibly Tony Bandmann, 1848-1907, published in German on music; had sent his 'Tale'.

[3] Probably *sic*, may just read 'Milner' (see 30 Jan. 78n.).

[4] S. Papazian, later one of the Armenian delegates to the Berlin Conference.

[5] A steam saw, praised by the diarist; see *T.T.*, 4 February 1878, 6c, *The Graphic*, 16 February 1878 and reproduction in this volume.

[6] Perhaps Ulick Ralph Burke, 1845-95; Dublin barrister and historian.

[7] Lord Edmond George Petty-Fitzmaurice, 1846-1935; liberal M.P. Colne 1868-85; under-sec. foreign affairs 1882-5; cr. Baron Fitzmaurice 1906; Granville's biographer.

[8] T. P. Hughes, *Notes on Muhammadanism* (1875, 2nd. ed. enlarged 1877).

[9] This day and the next written in the wrong order, corrected by diarist's arrows.

[10] On Forster's amndt.; *H* 237. 928; see 1 Feb. 78n. Gladstone repeated the burden of the charge made at Oxford (see 30 Jan. 78): 'it is a perfectly unreal Vote as it stands . . . if we are going to make war, or to make one step in the direction of war, that step should be a real one. Do not let us proceed by a mere flourish of trumpets.'   [11] Editor of the *Entre'acte*; see Add MS 44456, f. 83.

[12] William T. Groom, an admirer; Hawn P.   [13] Forster's amndt.; *H* 237. 1069.

[14] 'G . . . talked more unreservedly about his past career, Parlt. & the Queen than I have ever known him talk before. G's great oration last night much disappointed his foes & more than fulfilled the hopes of his friends. Nevertheless the proceedings at Oxford were a mistake in point of judgement & taste. But for them the Govt. wd have been now in a great difficulty'; Phillimore's Diary.

6. Wed.

Rose as usual but had to return to bed with tight chest. By strong measures was able to dine with Ld Ripon, which I was very anxious to accomplish.[1] Saw Ld Granville—W.H.G. Read Paparrigopoulos—Greece and Turkey[2]—Lackeys of the Turk.[3]

7. Th.

Wrote to Ld Tenterden—Ed. Daily News—Three Editors (identical).[4] Great stir & dismay, from the rumours put about by Govt & the War-press. Saw Ld F. Cavendish—Do *cum* Ld Granville—W.H.G. Got up to go to Ld G.s at 3.30. H of C. till 6¾. A bewildered scene.[5] Returned home to bed. Read Civilisation Hellénique—Fortnightly on E. Question (Laveleye)—Do on Ld Melbourne (Houghton).[6]

8. Fr.

Rose at 2. Wrote to Dr Carpenter—E.R. Johnson—E. Bushell—O. Rose—E. Walsh—T. Shea—Miss Doyle. H of C. 4½-8¼ and 10-1. Spoke over an hour & voted in 125:329 against the Six Millions.[7] Saw Mr M'Coll—Mr W.H. James— W.H.G.—Mr Childers—Mr Bright—Ld F. Cavendish—Sir R. Phillimore. Dined at Sir C. Forster's. Returned home, as was to be expected with a relapse. Read Paparrigopoulos—Fortnightly Review.

9. Sat.

Spent the day in bed, boiling myself down. Saw W.H.G. Wrote to Ed. Daily News[8]—Mr [blank] (per WHG.) Read Paparrigopoulos—Princeton Review[9]— Æneid Book II.

10. S.

Again kept my bed until Dusk—Then came down to the Drawingroom. Read Thomas A Kempis—Paparrigopoulos—Hughes on Mahometanism—Princeton Rev. on Evolution.[10] It was a noble subject of reflection for the day in solitude, to contemplate the great sabbath dawning in the East.

---

[1] i.e. mending fences after the rift over Ripon's conversion; see 21 Aug. 74.

[2] *Greece and Turkey. The indisputable rights of Greece* (1878).

[3] *The Lackeys of the Turk; an indictment, a protest and a warning* (1878).

[4] Sending for publication copy of his letter to Negropontis of 21 July 1877; *D.N.*, 8 February 1878, 5a.

[5] Rumours of a Russian attack on Constantinople (armistice signed on 31 January), were confirmed, then denied, by Northcote, leading eventually to withdrawal of Forster's amndt.; H 237. 1211.

[6] *Fortnightly Review*, xxix. 153, 207 (February 1878).

[7] H 237. 1360; fleet this day ordered to Constantinople to protect 'British life and property'.

[8] Note on his health appeared in *D.N.*, 11 February 1878, 5b.

[9] *Princeton Review*, liv (January 1878); perhaps D. S. Gregory, 'The Eastern Problem'.

[10] *Princeton Review*, liv. 150 (January 1878).

11. M.

Better. Rose at midday. Wrote to Me Novikoff—Mrs H. White—H. Abel[1]—Mr Allsopp[2]—Mr Duncan—Mr Walker—Mr Elliott—W. Wallace—H. Roberts—C.G. Nuttall.[3] H. of C. 4½-6¾. Spoke briefly. The temper of the majority is a thing hardly credible.[4] Saw Ld Granville—Sir H. James—Dr A. Clark—Mr Mundella. Read Civilisation Hellenique—La Grèce et l'Italie.

12. Tu.

Rose at 11 AM. Wrote to Sir Thos Acland—J.H. Parker—Mr Colebrook (O)—Mr Ruault (O)[5]—Rev. R.W. Rowan[6]—Rev. J.C. Gill[7]—D.J. Curry—Jas Anderson—Ed. S.E. Gazette—Mr Hirlam—Mr Duncan—Mr Allen—Mr Woolard—Mr Bayley—Lee Smith[8]—Mr Leonard. Saw Scotts—Ld Granville—Mr Bright—Mr Murray—Sir W. Harcourt—Ld Monck—Mr E. Ashley—Sir H. James. H of C. 4½-6½.[9] Dined at J. Wortley's. Read Paparrigopoulos.

13. Wed.

Rose at 12: better. Wrote to Mr A.G. Symonds[10]—Mr Stevens—J. Lupton—Rev. Dr Parker—J.W. Kirkham—R. Berry—J. Wise—J. Ackland—F. Ouvry. H. of C. 3½-5.[11] Saw Mr Lefevre—Mr Earp—Mr Chamberlain—Mr Bright—Mr Stansfeld—Ld Hartington *cum* Sir W. Harcourt—Sir C. Forster—Mr Potter—Mr MacColl—and others. Dined at The Speakers. Evening party afr. Read Civilisation Hellenique—Lenormant 'Monnaie'.[12]

14. Th.

Rose at 11. Wrote to Mr Turnbull—Mr Broadhurst—Mr Scrimgeour—Mr Strickland—J.H. Bateman—Ed. Irish Monthly[13]—Mr Fox Bourne—Rev. H. Martin—Captain Maurice—Ld R. Montagu—Mr Gomme—Mr Ellis—Mr Norman—Mr Bayliss—Mr Eyles—W. Bench—Rev. Mr Callaway.[14] Luncheon 15 G.S. Saw Mr T[histlethwayte] who held forth on prophesy and politics. Calls. At 3.30 had a conference with Ld Carnarvon at Sir R. Phillimores.[15] He treated me

[1] C. Abel of Berlin; Egyptologist; later correspondence in Hawn P.

[2] Probably (Sir) Henry Allsopp, 1811-87; brewer and tory M.P. E. Worcestershire 1874-87; cr. bart. 1880, Baron Hindlip 1886.

[3] Perhaps the constituent; see letter in *T.T.*, 14 February 1878, 6f.

[4] *H* 237. 1446.

[5] Word badly smudged.

[6] Robert W. Rowan, 'a clergyman and landed proprietor' at Ballymena, wrote to express support on the Eastern Question; Hawn P.

[7] Jeremiah Cresswell Gill, curate at Lee, Kent.

[8] Perhaps Ferdinando Dudley Lea Smith of Hales Owen, Birmingham.

[9] Misc. business; *H* 237. 1503.

[10] Arthur G. Symonds, secretary to the National Reform Union, Manchester.

[11] Misc. business; *H* 237. 1568.   [12] F. Lenormant, *La Monnaie dans l'antiquité*, 3v. (1878-9).

[13] Not found published; possibly on hymn translation; see *Irish Monthly*, vi. 232 (1878).

[14] Probably Henry Callaway, 1817-90; bp. of Kaffraria 1873-86.

[15] 'Carnarvon met G. at my house at 3.30 today by appointment made thro' me. He thought there were certain matters wh. he could without any breach of faith communicate to him & wh. G. ought to know. I was not present at their conference'; Phillimore's Diary.

very confidentially & declared we were at one. His impressions as to the Cabinet are very dark. H. of C. $4\frac{1}{2}$-7. Spoke briefly E.Q.[1] Twelve to dinner. Saw Mr Norman—Mr Bright—Mr C. Howard—Ld Ripon—Mr Morley—Sir R. Peel—Mr Bayley. Read Rangabé Litt. Neo-hellenique.[2]

15. Fr.

Wrote to Mr Bryce—Mr Pope—Mr Ouvry—C. Forjelt—H.A. Schulz[3]—General Bowie—Mr Herington—Mr Kriens (O)—Mr Gatty[4]—Mr Hartog[5]—Mr Oastler—Bishop Kip.[6] Dined at Ld Carlingford's. H of C. $4\frac{1}{2}$-$5\frac{3}{4}$ and $10\frac{1}{2}$-1. Voted in 227:242 on [O. Morgan's] Burials Resoln.[7] Saw Trades Societies &c. Deputation—Mr Adam—Capt. Norman—Mr A. West—Capt. Beaumont—Sir H. Johnstone *cum* Count Schouvaloff. Read Dr Doran's London;[8] Civ. Hellenique.

16. Sat. [Brighton]

Worked upon arranging papers. Off at 1 to Brighton. Saw Captain Maurice—Mr Price—Scotts. We took at once to the Pier and inhaled fresh life from our old friend the sea. Most kindly received at Mrs Warner's:[9] much conversation on Eastern matters with Lord C. Paget. Read Brown's Dionysiak Myth[10]—Verifier's Scepticism in Geology[11]—Princeton Review on E. Questions—Lindenschmit on Schliemann.[12]

17. Septa S.

Ch mg & evg. Much walking. Tea at Mr T. Warner's. Read Scepticism in Geology—Minton on Future State[13]—A few words on Prayer—Selborne on the Rubrics[14]—and [blank.]

18. M. [London]

Wrote to Mr Broadhurst: with drafted Resolutions.[15] 11-$12\frac{1}{2}$. A delightful visit to the Aquarium. Off at 1.15 to London. Trustees B.M. Meeting at 4. H. of C. $4\frac{1}{2}$-$7\frac{3}{4}$.[16] Dined at Grillion's: a most pleasant party. Saw Mr Broadhurst & the other promoters $5\frac{1}{2}$-$6\frac{1}{2}$. Saw Mr Samuelson—Mundella—F. Leveson—F.C.—

[1] *H* 237. 1632.

[2] A. I. Rizos Rankabes, *Précis d'une Histoire de la littérature néo-hellénique*, 2v. (1877).

[3] Perhaps Hermann Schultz of Sherrington Gardens, London.

[4] Probably *sc.* Gattie.

[5] Marcus Manuel Hartog, 1851-1924; taught zoology at Manchester 1878-82; professor at Cork 1882-1909.

[6] Apparently *sic*; unidentified.   [7] *H* 237. 1836.

[8] J. Doran, *London in the Jacobite times*, 2v. (1877).

[9] His hostess on an earlier visit; see 14 May 64.

[10] See 24 Mar. 77.

[11] Verifier [J. Murray, *fils*], *Scepticism in geology and the reasons for it* (1877).

[12] H. Lindenschmit, *Schliemann's Ausgrabungen in Troja und Mykenae* (1878).

[13] S. Minton, *Letters to the Christian World* (1877).

[14] R. Palmer, Lord Selborne, *Notes on some passages in the liturgical history of the reformed English Church* (1878).

[15] See next day.   [16] County Government Bill; *H* 237. 1853.

W.H.G.—Lefevre—Stansfeld—Rylands—W.H. James—on the meeting. Saw Ld Acton—Mr Knowles. Read Scepticism in Geology—Nicholson's A. to Manning[1]—Wyke Bayliss, Witness of Art.[2]

19. Tu.

Wrote to Master of Charterhouse B.P.—Mr Foster (O)—Mr Macgregor—Mr Dacosta[3]—Mr Brockbank—Mr Mundella—Mr Finlason—Ld Granville—Rev A. Hume—Mr Meves[4]—Mr Avery—Mr Hines (O)—E. Davis. Carried to [26] Villiers Street[5] in the morning an amended draft of the Resolutions. Dined at Mr Cartwright's. Read Green's Elisabeth[6]—Prothero's Simon de Montfort.[7] H. of C. $4\frac{1}{2}$-$7\frac{1}{2}$.[8] Saw [blank.] At the House I learned the abandonment of the Meeting.[9] Saw Duke of Westminster—Mr Mundella—Ld Hartington—Mr Chesson—Mr Pender—Sir H. Maine. At Mr C.s a deputation called me from dinner & discussed in much dismay but without any murmuring or ill temper the business of the withdrawal. I am to write a letter.

20. Wed.

Wrote to Mr Broadhurst (& draft)[10]—Messrs Boldero & Foster[11]—Mr Knowles—Ed. Daily News (2)[12]—Mr Huidekoper[13]—Mr Planché—Mr Fox Bourne—Mr J. Watt—Mr Wradieff—Mr Abel—Messrs Trübner—Miss de Lisle[14]—Sir Thomas G. Thirteen to dinner. Began a new paper on the E. Question.[15] Saw Messrs Broadhurst, Howell, and Guile:[16] & agreed to write as above. Saw Mr Murray—Sir A. Panizzi—Lord Acton—Lady Waldegrave. Read Southall on the Origin of Man.[17]

21. Th.

Wrote to Solr Treasury (O)—Messrs Ransome (O)—Mr Knowles—Mr J. Hawden—Messrs Spottiswoode B.P. H. of C. $4\frac{1}{2}$-5.[18] Read Civilisation Hellenique.

[1] J. A. Nicholson, *A reply to Cardinal Manning's Essay* (1878).
[2] Sir W. Bayliss, *The witness of art or the legend of beauty* (1876).
[3] Several London merchants of this name.
[4] Perhaps Augustus Meves (*père* or *fils*), who wrote on Louis XVII; see 17 June 60.
[5] Offices of Broadhurst's Labour Representation Committee.
[6] In J. R. Green, *History of the English people*, 4v. (1877-80).
[7] G. W. Prothero, *Life of . . . de Montfort* (1877); see 12 Mar. 72.
[8] Irish franchise; *H* 237. 1929.
[9] He had agreed to speak to Broadhurst's Workmen's Neutrality Committee at the Agricultural Hall, Islington; reports of an attack by medical students, organized by Ashmead Bartlett, caused its cancellation; see Ramm II, i. 69 and H. Cunningham, 'Jingoism in 1877-78', *Victorian Studies*, xiv. 438 (1971). Correspondence in Broadhurst MSS, London School of Economics.
[10] In *T.T.*, 21 February 1878, 10d.   [11] London printers.
[12] Public thanks for resolutions sent; *D.N.*, 21 February 1878, 3c.
[13] Frederic Huidekoper, American author; see 28 Apr. 78.
[14] Margaret, d. 1895, 15th child of Ambrose Phillipps de Lisle; until Gordon's death she carried an axe to symbolize her admiration for Gladstone; see Purcell, *De Lisle*, ii. 317.
[15] Published as 'The paths of honour and shame', *Nineteenth Century*, iii. 591 (March 1878), and as a pamphlet with preface of 9 March.
[16] Daniel Guile, d. 1883; secretary of the friendly society of ironfounders 1863-81.
[17] J. C. Southall, *The recent origin of Man* (1875).   [18] Factories Bill; *H* 238. 63.

Saw Ld Wolverton—Ld Granville—Mr Godley—Mr Childers—Mr Knowles—
Mr Kimber. Opera Comique at 9 PM to see the Sorcerer:[1] very well got up &
most amusing. Worked on a short article for Mr Knowles's next number.

22. Fr.

Wrote to Sol. Treasury—Mr Bayley—Mr Roberts—Messrs Spottiswoode—Mr
Nicholl—Mr Henderson. Dined with the F.C.s. H of C. $10\frac{1}{2}$-$1\frac{1}{4}$ (County Suffrage).[2]
Kept the House for some remains of cold; worked steadily on my paper and
finished it. But had in the evg much nausea, & slight diarrhoea, as the result.
Read Wordsworth on Univv.[3] Saw Mr Bright—Mr Errington—Sir Thos Acland.

23. Sat.

Wrote to Ld E. Cavendish—E. Lintott BP[4]—Mr Fox Bourne (O)—Rev. A. Stonehouse—Rev. Newman Hall—F. Hill—J.B. Hay—A.M. Reid—H. Abel—Mr A.
Blackwood—F. Johnson. Read F. Hill on Suffrage[5]—Q.R. (Hayward) on Ld Melbourne[6]—Les Roumains du Sud.[7] Saw Maronite Quêteurs—W.H.G.—Ld Kinnaird—and F. Cavendish—Duke of Argyll (E.Q.) Tea at Argyll Lodge.

24. Sexa S.

Chap. Royal mg & evg. Read Roumains du Sud (finished)—Entre Clerc et
Laique[8]—Conder, Bases of Faith[9]—Philochristus.[10]
Between four & six three parties of the populace arrived here the first with
cheers, the two others hostile. Windows were broken & much hooting. The last
detachment was only kept away by mounted police in line across the street
both ways. Saw the Inspector in evg. This is not very sabbatical. There is
strange work behind the curtain if one could but get at it. The instigators are
those really guilty: no one can wonder at the tools.[11]

25. M.

Wrote to R. Strange BP—Treasurer of Guy's Hospital & dft.[12]—W. Middleton—
W.H. Ablett—A. Goodson—Mr Pope—Mr Watson (O). Corrected proofs of

[1] By Gilbert and Sullivan.   [2] Voted in 219:271 for Trevelyan's motion; H 238. 255.
[3] C. Wordsworth, *Scholae Academicae* (1877).
[4] Edward Lintott of Mile End Road, London.
[5] F. Hill, *The county franchise difficulty, how removable* (1878).
[6] *Quarterly Review*, cxlv. 188 (January 1878).   [7] Untraced.
[8] Ibid.   [9] E. R. Conder, *The basis of faith* (1875).
[10] [E. A. Abbott], *Philochristus. Memoirs of a disciple of the Lord* (1878).
[11] The *D.N.*, 26 February 1878, 5c, noted 'there were ugly symptoms of the worst sort of social
decadence in the disturbances of Sunday' and denounced 'organized ruffianism'. T. P. O'Connor
claimed Parnell and his sister Anna were in the crowd (*Memoirs of an Old Parliamentarian* (1929), i. 8).
[12] Asking him (as a governor) officially if it was true that, as a letter in the *D.N.* reported, a notice
posted in the hospital read: 'On Thursday at eight o'clock, the traitor Gladstone will (or thinks he
will) hold a meeting in favour of Russia at the Agricultural Hall. Shall this be? No! Come early and
get front seats, and treat him as his treachery deserves'; E. D. Lushington, the Treasurer, replied
rather evasively and Cardwell, the President, joined with Gladstone in requesting his public denial;
letters published in H. L. Eason, 'Students and politics', *Guy's Hospital Gazette*, 547 (1936); see Add
MS 44456, f. 113.

N.C. Article & made additions: sent off. Saw Mr Homan—Mr Knowles—Mr Bright. H of C. $4\frac{1}{4}$-$5\frac{1}{2}$.[1] Read Remains of Drake[2]—Green's Hist. England—Civilis. Hellenique (finished)—E.Q. Tracts.

26 Tu.

Wrote to Mrs J.H. Giles—A.C. Shelley[3]—Mr Broadhurst—E. Davis—E.A. Budge[4]—R. Hall—E. Feather. Luncheon at 15 G.S. where Mrs Th. gave me a touching account of the noble Christian death of old Lord Bathurst. Read Hunter's Indian Mahomedans[5]—Borthwick's Address.[6] Saw Miss Leslie— W.H.G.—D. of Argyll—Ly Russell. Saw Harris, & another X. H. of C. $4\frac{1}{2}$-5.[7] Dined at Ld Selborne's.

27. Wed.

Wrote to Rev. J.L. Blake[8]—Mrs Mockler—Made Novikoff—Earl Spencer—Rev. Dr Belcher—Mr Ouvry—J. Lacey—A. Yeaman[9]—Mr Lane Fox[10]—Dr Magnus. Saw Mrs Giles—Mr Budge (a very remarkable youth)[11]—Sir T. Acland—The Speaker—Mr Knowles—Mr Burt—Sir A. Panizzi. Read 'Mind' on Colour Sense[12]—19th Cent I. II, on The Situation[13]—Hunters Indian Mahomedans. Ten to dinner.

28. Th.

Wrote to Mr Baker (O)—J. Elliot—Rev. A.C. Wilson—Princess Ben Ali[14]—Sec. Science & Art Dept.—S. Smith—H. Harbour—Mr Middleton—A. Surgeon— W. Roxburgh—A. Laurenson.[15] Attended the Tennyson Marriage at the Abbey:[16] a beautiful sight & remarkable assemblage. Saw Ld Carnarvon—Mr Bryce—Sir C. Lampson. Dined with the Wortleys. Read G. Smith on the Liberal party[17]—Hunter's Ind. Mahomedans—Brownlow Maitland on Prophecy.[18]

[1] Factories Bill; *H* 238. 302.

[2] C. F. T. Drake, *The literary remains* (1877), ed. W. Besant.

[3] Actor and impresario; see 16 June 79n.

[4] (Sir) Ernest Alfred Thompson Wallis *Budge, 1857-1934; Egyptologist; keeper at British Museum from 1893. Gladstone paid part of his fees as a non-collegiate student at Cambridge (see his *D.N.B.* entry).

[5] W. W. Hunter, *Indian Mussulmans* (1872-6).

[6] A. Borthwick, Baron Glenesk, 'An address on the Eastern Question' (1878).

[7] Income tax; *H* 238. 379.

[8] Presbyterian minister in Berwickshire; dialect poet; Hawn P.

[9] Perhaps James Yeaman, 1816-86; Dundee merchant and M.P. 1873-80.

[10] George Lane Fox of Bramham Park, 1816-96.

[11] See previous day.

[12] Note by Grant Allen on Gladstone's article on 'colour-sense', *Mind*, iii. 129 (January 1878).

[13] *Nineteenth Century*, iii. 567, 571 (March 1878).

[14] Unidentified.

[15] Arthur Laurenson, 1832-90, of Lerwick, Shetland; staunch liberal; translated the sagas; on Homer's colour sense; Hawn P.

[16] Lionel Tennyson, 1854-86, the poet's 2nd s., m. Eleanor Locker. She later m. Augustine Birrell.

[17] G. Smith, 'Whigs and Liberals', *Fortnightly Review*, xxix. 404 (March 1878).

[18] B. Maitland, *The argument from prophecy* (1877).

Frid. March One 1878.

Wrote to Ld Hartington—Divers autographs—Dr Magnus BP—E. Bennett (O)—
Major Harvey[1]—Messrs Houghton—H. Pycroft[2]—Mr Harbour (Tel.)—F. Gale—
G. Whale—F. Ridley—J. Gregory—A. Whittall. Read Roman Russe[3]—Hunter's
Mahommedans (finished)—The Witness of Art.[4] Saw Mr Flanedy—Ld Gran-
ville cum F. Cavendish—Mr Phillips [sc. Philips] MP.—Mr Talbot M.P.—Ld
Hartington. H of C. $5\frac{1}{4}$-$7\frac{1}{4}$.[5] Seven to dinner.

2. Sat.

Wrote to Bp Strossmayer—Sig. Matteucci[6]—Mr Ouvry—Mr Rushbrooke (&
BP)—Mr Vickers. Attended Mr [R.] Bosworth Smith's Lecture on Carthage.
Saw Mr Bosworth Smith—Ld Granville—and [blank.] Dined with Ld Lorne &
Princess Louise. Her deportment is very notable. Saw Mrs Pirie [R]. Calls.
Arranging papers. Read Witness of Art—Borthwick's Address.

3. Quinqua S.

Chapel Royal mg & aft. Dined with Sybella. Read Farrar's Eternal Hope[7]—
Brownlow Maitland on Theism[8]—Contemp. Review.

4. M.

Wrote to Rev. Mr Holman—Monsignor Krimian—Mr Oraghimian (cov.)[9]—Mr
Longueville[10]—Mr Menzies—Chev. Yrigoyti[11]—Mrs Fenwick Miller—Ld Sel-
borne—F. Hardy—Mr Stokes[12]—Miss Moon—Miss de Lisle. H of C. 5-7.[13] Saw
Mr Godley—Mr (Colonial Bprics) [sic]—Mr Agnew—Mr Adam—Mr Bennett[14]—
Sir D. Marjoribanks—Sir W. Gregory—Greenwich Teachers Deputn. Read
Pepys's Diary[15]—Our bodily Life. Twelve to dinner.

The news of the Peace arrived.[16] It seems scarcely to leave openings for
future quarrel. With the fearful feelings that have been entertained by some it is
hard to feel any security. Instinctively I feel a weight taken off my shoulders:
but with this, I suppose on the removal of tension, an increased sense of mental
exhaustion.

[1] Perhaps George Sheppard Harvey, major in Royal Artillery.
[2] Henry T. Pycroft, schoolmaster in Auckland, New Zealand; Add MS 44456, f. 16.
[3] Possibly La société russe. Par un Russe, 2v. (1877).
[4] See 18 Feb. 78.   [5] Poor law; H 238. 541.
[6] A common Italian name.
[7] F. W. Farrar, Eternal hope (1878), an important text in the 'eternal punishment' debate.
[8] B. Maitland, Theism or agnosticism: an essay on the grounds of belief in God (1878).
[9] Probably, like Krimian, an Armenian representative.
[10] Thomas Longueville, 1844-1922; journalist.
[11] Probably Charles E. Yriarte, journalist and art historian; wrote Montenegro (1877).
[12] C. W. Stokes (see 8 Aug. 66) by now probably in the pay of the tories for anti-Russian agitation;
see H. Cunningham, 'Jingoism in 1877-78', Victorian studies, xiv. 440 (1971).
[13] Army affairs; H 238. 638.
[14] i.e. W. C. Bennett of Greenwich who was organizing a motion supporting Gladstone's conduct;
T.T., 5 March 1878, 10a.
[15] Probably in the Braybrooke ed. revised by M. Bright, 6v. (1875-9).
[16] Treaty signed at San Stephano on 3 March.

5. Tu.

Wrote to Messrs Houghton—Mr C. Stokes—Mr De Wilde[1]—P. Kenny—H. Ladd (BP)—"H.K.G."—Dr Patterson BP—A.S. Canning—Mr Sec. Evarts[2]—Dr N. Porter. Read Paterson's Tracts—Pepys's Diary—Shakesp. Henry VIII. H. of C. 4½-6½.[3] Saw Sir Thos Acland. Saw Hume [R]. Attended the Lyons Mail: a notable melodrama, well got up & acted.[4]

6. Ash Wed.

All Souls Ch 11 A.M. Wrote to Miss Cobden BP—Mr Cowper Temple—Mrs Waddington—Miss de Lisle—Mr F.S. Mills—Messrs Murray—Mr G. Offer—Mr H. Goodrich. H. of C. 4-5½.[5] Saw Dr Bennett—Scotts—Mr Adam. Read Jenkins's Lutchmee & Dilloo[6]—Wilson's Resources of Modern countries.[7]

7. Th.

Wrote to Rev. Mr Campbell Connell[8]—Mr J.R. Jolly (2—the decisive letter & one covering it)[9]—A.J. Wilson—R. Roberts—W.B. Freeman—Mr Frettingham (O)—Mr Plimsoll MP—Mr Strip—A. Kitson[10]—Mr Jones. Read Booth on Meat Supply[11]—Wilson Resources &c.—Jenkins Dilloo & Lutchmee—Cobden on the Russian War 1857.[12] Dined at Sir H. Verney's. Saw Sir A. Panizzi—Mrs Ralli—Sir Joseph Hooker.

8. Fr.

Wrote to Rob. Gladstone—Sir Jas Hogg—F. Ormonde—W.G. Black[13]—Mr Blennerhassett MP.—E.A. Budge—A. Strahan—Pres.Civ. Engin.—Philipson & G. H. of C. 4½-6¼. Saw Sir W. & Lady M. Farquharson—W.H.G. Read Pepys's Diary—Wilson, Resources &c.—Jenkins, Lutchmee & Dilloo.

9. Sat.

Wrote to Mr Granville Vernon—Mrs Brookfield—Mr Rosenberg[14]—H. Broad-hurst—Mr Lefevre (O)—Sir L. Mallet—J. Gregory—Treasurer of Guy's—Editor of

---

[1] Corresponded on bronze; Hawn P.
[2] See 17 July 63; he was secretary of state 1877-81.
[3] Misc. business; H 238. 770.　　　　　　　　[4] With Irving, at the Lyceum.
[5] Irish franchise; H 238. 796.　　　　　　　[6] E. Jenkins, Lutchmee and Dilloo (1877).
[7] A. J. Wilson, The resources of modern countries, 2v. (1878).
[8] Alexander Campbell Connell, curate of Monk's Eleigh, Suffolk (Crockford gives different Christian names); on Lord Lincoln's education; Hawn P.
[9] Announcing decision not to stand again for Greenwich: 'although I ought not by any act of my own to subject the borough to the inconvenience of a by-election, yet neither should I cause to it a serious risk of remaining unprovided with fit candidates in the Liberal interest in the event of a dissolution which might be summary'; T.T., 11 March 1878, 10a and Add MS 44456, f. 122. The letter did not exclude his standing elsewhere.
[10] Perhaps Arthur Kitson of Philadelphia; later letter at Add MS 44498, f. 70. Or James Kitson, see 13 Mar. 78n.　　　　　　　　　　　　　　　　[11] T. C. Booth, Our meat supply (1878).
[12] On 18 March 1857, in J. Bright and J. E. T. Rogers, Speeches... by Richard Cobden, ii. 57 (1870).
[13] William George Black of Glasgow; Hawn P.
[14] Perhaps William George Rosenberg, artist.

'The Theatre'[1]—Geo Harris—Mr Budge BP—Mr Kibbin—Rev. Mr Wood—Dr V.E. Stais—G. Whale. Seven to dinner. Read Lutchmee & Dilloo—Pepys's Diary—Wilson's 'Resources' &c. Saw E. Wickham—Mr Stuart Wortley. Calls. Wrote Preface to my last N.C. Article for republication.[2]

10. 1 S. Lent

Chapel Royal 10 & 5. To Wells St also for H.C. I felt so painfully anxious about Ruskin.[3] Read Brownlow Maitland on Theism (finished)—Farrar's Eternal Hope (finished)—Virchow's Discourse.[4] Wrote to Mr Farrar—Mrs Browne—Mr Salkeld. In aft. another gathering of people was held off by the Police. I walked down with C. & as a large crowd gathered, though in the main friendly, we went into Dr Clark's & then in a Hansom off the ground.[5] Saw Dr A. Clark—Rev. E. Wickham.

11. M.

Wrote to Mr Hall BP—Mr Whiting Leeds (Tel.)[6]—Vestry Clerk of Plumstead— Mr Chadwick—Mr Shelley—M. Colombies—Rev. W.F. James—Sir E. Hornby— Jas Watkinson[7]—Rev. T.H. Pattison BP[8]—Mr Mundella MP—Mr Kenney—F. Rule—Miss Goalen—J.P. Caesar[9]—E. Léger (O)—Mr James MP. Saw Ld Napier—Ld F. Cavendish—Mr Cross—M. Gennadios—Count Münster—Sir Jas Paget—Sir M.H. Beach[10]—Lord J. Manners—Mr Mundella—Sir K. Shuttle-worth—and others. H of C. 4½-6.[11] Went to the Levee. The Prince, for the first time, received me drily: the Duke of Cambridge, black as thunder, did not even hold out his hand. *Prince* Xtn could not but follow suit. This is not very hard to bear. Read Lutchmee & Dilloo—Trollope's Rome[12]—Eastern Q. Pamphlets. Dined at Grillion's.

---

[1] Influential letter on proposed National Theatre: 'the drama requires ... some great centre of attraction and of elevation', as with art and the Royal Academy; briefly quoted in *The Theatre*, iii. 103 (13 March 1878).

[2] See 20 Feb. 78n.

[3] The first of Ruskin's breakdowns, widely publicized in the press.

[4] R. L. C. Virchow, *The freedom of science in the modern state. A discourse* (1878).

[5] According to *The Guardian*, 13 March 1878, 365: 'By the time the corner of Cavendish Square was reached the conduct of the mob had become so threatening that Mr and Mrs Gladstone sought a temporary refuge in the house of Dr. Andrew Clarke, which they left a little later in a cab, attended by an escort of four mounted constables.'

[6] J. E. Whiting wired saying Leeds Liberals 'unanimously invited' Gladstone to stand there—'this enquiry unofficial'; Gladstone replied he intended 'to defer for some time making any arrangements for a seat in Parliament'; *T.T.*, 12 March 1878, 9f and Hawn P.

[7] An 'aged labourer' in Chester, wrote on Bulgaria; *T.T.*, 13 March 1878, 11c.

[8] Thomas Harwood Pattison, religious author.

[9] Julius P. Caesar, wrote on missions.

[10] Sir Michael Edward *Hicks Beach, 1837-1916; 9th bart 1854; tory M.P. E. Gloucestershire 1864-85, W. Bristol 1885-1903; colonial secretary 1878-80; chancellor 1885-6, 1895-1902; Irish secretary 1886-7; president of board of trade 1888-92; strong free trader.

[11] Ship designs; *H* 238. 1057.

[12] T. A. Trollope, *A peep behind the scenes at Rome* (1877).

12. Tu.

Wrote to Mrs Simpson—Mr Ouvry—Mr Caine[1]—W. Hall—J.H. Ellis—J. Knowles (Carmarthen)—Mrs Robertson—Mr Dickinson—Rev. W. Scott[2]—Mr Clegg. Dined at F.C.s. H of C. 4¼-8½ and 9½-12.[3] Arranging papers. Luncheon at 15 G.S. Saw Mr West—Mr Ashley—Mr Bright—Sir H. James—Mr Lowe—Ld F. Cavendish—on the Layard matter. Read Prothero on Simon de Montfort. What a giant! and what a noble giant! What has survival of the fittest done towards beating, or towards reaching him?[4] Read also Green's Hist.—Lutchmee & Dilloo—Case of the Armenians. Spent the evg in H of C. Library.

13. Wed.

Wrote to Miss De Lisle—Rev. S.E.G.—Mr E. Johnson—Mr Jas Kitson jun.[5]— Padre Tondini—Mr Hayward (O)—Mr Ouvry—Mr Johnstone Wallace—Sir C. Forster—Mr Strahan. Dined at Ld Shaftesbury's. Saw Ld Granville—Mr Knowles—Mr Balfour—Sir A. Panizzi—Ld Shaftesbury—Sir Thomas Wade—Mr Burn[6]—Duke of Argyll (on the Sutherland scandal)[7]—Mr E.Ashley. Saw two X. Saw Church of St John the Evangelist.

14. Th.

Wrote to Messrs Townshend & Barker—Mirza Peer Buksh[8]—F. Harris—T. Shea—D. Nicoll—T. Cutborn—Mr Burckhardt (O)[9]—Mr Kimber. Read Headlam on Plays &c.[10]—Lutchmee & Dilloo (finished). Saw Sir T. Bazley & others from Manchester.[11] 12-1. Deputation to Charity Commrs on Plumstead Common.[12] Saw E. Macgregor & promised the price of a sewing-machine [R]. Dinner, & party to the Globe Theatre. Toole excellent: company good.[13]

15. Fr.

Wrote to Rev. B.W. Savile—Mr Bashin—Mr Symonds—T. Brown—J.K. Aston— Mr Ouvry—F. Johnson—Rt Hon H. Law—Rev. S.E.G.—Mrs Th.—Robn & Nichn.

[1] William Sproston *Caine, 1842-1903; baptist; liberal (unionist) M.P. Scarborough 1880-5, Barrow 1886-90; liberal unionist chief whip 1886-90; left unionists 1890; liberal M.P. Bradford 1892-5; had written to offer Gladstone Scarborough; Add MS 44456, f. 145.

[2] Perhaps Walter Scott, curate of Freckleton 1874.

[3] E. Ashley moved a resolution (defeated in 132:206) regretting Layard's part in the Negropontis letters affair; Gladstone did not speak though many of his letters were read to the House; H 238. 1156.

[4] See 19 Feb. 78, 12 Mar. 72n.

[5] (Sir) James *Kitson (1835-1911; Leeds manufacturer, cr. bart. 1886; liberal M.P. Colne valley 1892-1907) had asked Gladstone to stand for Leeds; letter, declining immediate decision in T.T., 15 March 1878, 11a. Despite this, the Leeds liberal committee resolved to adopt him as a candidate; T.T., 16 March 1878, 9f. See also 11 Mar. 78n. Gladstone stood for Leeds as well as Midlothian in 1880.

[6] See 18 Mar. 78.   [7] See Bassett, 221.

[8] Unidentified; sent a volume, see 27 July 78.

[9] Not further identified; no link with the historian traced.

[10] C. E. S. Headlam, *The Iphigeneia of Euripides with notes* (1875).

[11] He declined an invitation to speak; T.T., 15 March 1878, 11a.

[12] Supporting the Plumstead vestry (see 22 Mar. 77); ibid.

[13] 'Ici on parle français' with John Lawrence *Toole, 1830-1906; see also Add MS 44475, f. 135.

H of C. $4\frac{1}{2}$-5.[1] Corrected reprint of N.C. Article & Preface. W. James & the Godleys dined. Saw Mr Bowman—Mr Godley—Mr Adam—Mr Baxter—Lady Stanley. Worked on Iris.[2] Read Bell's Telephone[3]—Fors Clavigera[4]—Pepys's Diary.

16. Sat

Wrote to Rev. S.E.G.—A. Criely—T. Dowson—J.A. Bright—S. Duncan—J. Bryce—A.R. Damen[5]—Rev. J. Burden[6]—Messrs Baily—W.C. Russell[7]—F.W. Chesson. Worked on Iris: made progress in the paper: it is a charming little subject. Read Pepys. Dined at Lady Marion Alford's. Saw Ld Granville—Scotts—Ld Bath. Visited Christie's.

17. 2 S. Lent

Chapel Royal 10 AM (with H.C.)—$5\frac{1}{2}$ PM. Wrote to Ld R. Gower. Read Philochristus—Birks on Physical Fatalism[8]—Divers theolog. Tracts. Saw Dr Clark.

18. M.

Wrote to Mr Millais RA[9]—E. Eyton MP—E. Mavrocordato—Miss Savile—Mr Macrae—R. Lindsay—G. Heaton—Mrs Grote. Finished Iris: & am for once a little pleased with my work. Saw Duke of Argyll—Lord Lyons—Sir Thos G.—Mr Dodson—Ld Cork. Saw Prince Hassan[10]—Ibrahim Bey. Luncheon at 15 G.S. Attended at Mr Burns's the very interesting exhibition & explanation of the Telephone & the Phonograph. 9-11 PM.[11] Read Fornelli on Curci.[12] H. of C. $4\frac{1}{4}$-$5\frac{1}{4}$.[13]

19. Tu.

Wrote to Mr Hargreaves (O)—Mr Mowbray (O)—R.B. Spooner—A. Macdougal[14]—Freshfields—Theodore Reumert—C. Enwright—Sir W.C. James—

---

[1] Navy estimates; *H* 238. 1404.

[2] Published as 'The Iris of Homer: and her relation to Genesis ix. 11-17', *Contemporary Review*, xxxii. 11 (April 1878).

[3] A. G. Bell, *The voice by wire and postcard* (1878).

[4] Ruskin's monthly letters to labouring men.

[5] Perhaps Arnold Damen, author of 'The Catholic Church' (1875?).

[6] Probably John Burdon, rector of English Bicknor 1844.

[7] William Clark Russell, 1844-1911; novelist; see Add MS 44458, f. 279.

[8] T. R. Birks, *Modern physical fatalism and the doctrine of evolution* (1876).

[9] Millais wrote on 16 March (Add MS 44456, f. 170): 'I have often wished to paint your portrait. From our last meeting the drive has become so strong that I do not hesitate to ask the favour of a sitting . . . one hour at a time is all I would wish'; see 26 June 78.

[10] Prince Hassan, 1854-88, third s. of the Khedive of Egypt; at Christ Church, Oxford 1869; served in Egyptian force in 1876-8 Balkan war.

[11] In 1878 several demonstrations of the telephone were held, Bell's Telephone Co. being floated in June; see F. G. C. Baldwin, *The history of the telephone in the United Kingdom* (1925), i.

[12] N. Fornelli, *Il libro del Padre Curci e i partiti politici in Italia* (1878).

[13] Misc. business; *H* 238. 1495.

[14] Alexander MacDougal, Glasgow liberal; Hawn P.

Mr Cowper Temple—A. Strahan—A. Allchin—Mr Devine—A. Xenos—E. Wilson—M.H. Hakim. H of C. 3¾-4¼.[1] Dined with the Ellices. Corrected and dispatched my MS. on Iris. Saw Lady Harcourt—Sir W.H.—Mr Ellice—and others. Saw Four: possibly a little good for three [R]. But what a poor wretch I am. Read Virgil Æn. V.—Moraitinis on Greece.[2]

20. Wed.

Wrote to Ld E. Clinton—J.R. Herbert—Mr [W.] Clark Russell—H. Williams—C.S. Jerram[3]—Mr Collingwood—Mr Herbert Finck—Dr Bennett—Rev. J.G. Wood[4]—Mr Ouvry—J.L. Toole—Rev. S.E.G.—T. Lewis—A.J. Bolton[5]—A. Orton[6]—J. Russell—J. Mathews—W. Brook. Saw Father Tondini—Mr Mavrocordato and Mr . . .—Mr Boydell & Mr Surr(?).[7] Tea with the T.G.s. Eight to dinner: conversation on E. Question. Read Pepys—Macmillan on Heligoland—On Reform in Russia[8]—Parl. Papers on Turkey.

21. Th.

Wrote to Mons. Lefevre—Ld J. Manners—Mr Brotherton (O)—J. Glyn—W. Ryan—Mr Porter—Mr Chant—Mr Scollock (O)—Sir [T.]E. Perry—A.F. Morgan[9]—Dr Blaikie. Read Sir E. Perry's Minute[10]—Reeve's Petrarch[11]—Pepys. Saw Mr Barran MP.—Mr Adam MP.—Mr Bright MP.—Mr Norman—Sir W. James—Mrs Grote—Ld J. Manners. Dined at Mrs Grote's. H of C. 4½-5½ & 10¼-11¼.[12]

22. Fr.

Wrote to Mr [R. T.] Clarke (Leeds)[13]—A. Strahan—E.A. Budge—Mr Adams—Mr Vickers. H of C. 4½-5.[14] Visited Messrs Doulton's very remarkable exhibition.[15] Corrected & sent to press Essay on Iris. Saw Sir Jas Watson—Mr Arthur—Mrs Moscheles[16]—Mr C. Howard MP. Spent the forenoon at a breakfast of Nonconformists round Mrs Birks's table: much interesting conversation. 8-10. Attended the service of the very beautiful Passion Music of Bach at St Anne's. Dined with the F.C.s. Read Irving's Address[17]—Memoirs of the Strangfords.[18]

---

[1] Misc. business; H 238. 1590.   [2] P.A. Moräitines, La Grèce telle qu'elle est (1877).
[3] C. S. Jerram, in correspondence on Homer; Hawn P.
[4] John George Wood, 1827-89; unbeneficed priest in Upper Norwood; natural historian.
[5] Albert John Bolton, architect.
[6] Possibly Arthur Orton, 1834-98, the Tichborne claimant, then in gaol; but letter not traced.
[7] Sic; obscure.   [8] Macmillan's Magazine, xxxvii. 171, 161 (March 1878).
[9] Alfred Fairfax Morgan, wrote Triplicate paper on Triunities (1877).
[10] On 14 March Sir T. E. Perry (see 12 July 53) sent 'a long note on an Indian topic which is not without importance'; Add MS 44456, f. 160. Very probably this was Perry's 'Note [of 8 March] on the occupation of Quetta', unsuccessfully dissenting from the occupation; I.O. C/140 f. 194. Perry often leaked India Council information to the Liberal leadership.
[11] H. Reeve, Petrarch (1877).   [12] Questions; Scottish roads; H 238. 1759.
[13] Arranging the deputation's visit; see 28 Mar. 78.
[14] Declaration of Paris; H 238. 1842.
[15] Exhibition of their wares in Lambeth; T.T., 22 March 1878, 3e.
[16] Lived in Sloane Street.   [17] J. H. B. Irving, 'The stage' (1878).
[18] P. E. F. W. Smythe, Lord Strangford, Original letters and papers, ed. Lady Strangford (1878).

23. Sat. [Latimer]

Wrote to Mr Henry Irving—J.B. Murray—H. Cunningham—G.H. Vernon—Rev W.T. Barry[1]—J. Marks—A.J. Stean—G. Mitchell. Received Greenwich Deputn and addressed them.[2] Saw Baron Tauchnitz—Mr E.A. Budge—Mr Barran MP.— Mr Adam. Off at 4.15 to Latimer:[3] a pleasant party. Conversation with F. Leveson—Mr Eddis.[4] Read Memoirs of the Strangfords.

24. 3 S. Lent.

Ch mg & evg. Read Mem. of Strangfords—Physical Fatalism[5]—Philochristus. Conversation with C. Howard & F.L.—Mr Balfour—Mr Eddis.

25. M. Annuncn. [London]

Wrote to Earl of Leicester—Ld Lyons—Dr Hooker—Mr Tabor—J.B. Hopton— Mr Campbell—Rev. A. Southey—Rev. W.P. Duff[6]—Scotts. Back to London 11.30-1.30. H of C. $4\frac{1}{2}$-7.[7] Dined with the Phillimores. Saw Ld Carnarvon—Mr Richard MP—Mr Mundella MP—Mr Forster MP—Mr Barran MP—Mr Courtenay MP[8]—Dr Liddon. Saw Tatchell [R]. Read Pepys—Memoirs of the Strangfords (finished)—Notice of the Bust of Thucydides.[9]

26. Tu.

Wrote to Prof. Sbarbaro—Lady Cardwell—Messrs Brown—Mr Brown Murray— Mr Huidekoper—H.G. Rich—J.S. Vickers—Mr Brock B.P.[10]—Mr Rath—F. Harris—Mr Watts. Dined with the F.C.s. Saw Mr Knowles—Consul White— Neville Ln & E.L. Talbot: (conversation on India at much length)—Dr Liddon— F. Cavendish. Read Pepys's Diary—Radcliffe's Proteus[11]—Pamphlets. Saw two [R].

27. Wed.

Wrote to Scotts—HNG (B.P.)—Mrs Brassey—Mr Hanson—Mr Olding—Gover-nor of Cold Bath Fields—W. Nevins—Mr Vickers—W.D. Adams[12]—Mr Ash-burnham—Mr Poulson. Saw Mr Martineau—Scotts—Mr Barran—Inspector of

[1] William Thomas Barry, d. 1908; vicar of Holm from 1874.

[2] Declining their request to reconsider his decision not to stand there again; *T.T.*, 25 March 1878, 10d.

[3] Chesham's place; see 25 Feb. 65.

[4] Arthur Shelley Eddis, 1817-93; London barrister; authority on bankruptcy.

[5] See 17 Mar. 78.

[6] W. Pine Duff, minister in Edinburgh, requested diarist's recollection of his fa. Alexander *Duff, missionary; see 16 May 79n. [7]Mutiny Bill; *H* 238. 1977.

[8] Lionel Henry *Courtney, 1832-1918; liberal (unionist) M.P. Liskeard 1876-85, Bodmin 1885-1900; under-sec. home office 1880-1, colonies 1881-2; financial sec. 1882-4; proportional representationalist.

[9] Probably W. L. Collins, *Thucydides* (1878).

[10] Probably William Brock, *père*, Baptist minister. [11] C. B. Radcliffe, *Proteus* (1878).

[12] William Henry Davenport Adams, 1828-91; author of *English party leaders*, 2v. (1878), which described Gladstone's resignation in 1845 as 'the action of an unnecessarily fastidious conscience' (ii. 465).

Police—Mr Fawcett—Mr Bright—Mr Mundella—Ld Sydney—Sir A. Panizzi—Mr Trevelyan—Ld Dudley—Lady Marjoribanks—Mr Trevelyan. Saw Linwood [R]. H of C. 4¼-5½.[1] Dined at Ld Dudley's. Read Radcliffe—Lettre Roumaine[2]—Pepys.

28. Th.

Wrote to Mr Baxton—Mr Knowles—Mr Bloom (O)—Mr Deidor (O)—Mrs Gregory—E.A. Budge—Col. Laurie. Arranging Papers. Dined at Lady Lyttelton's. H of C. 5-6¼.[3] Saw Sir R. Phillimore[4]—Count Münster—Mr Bryce—Ld Penzance—Mr Knowles—Sir W. Harcourt—Mr Bright—Mr Gaskell. Received the Leeds Depn at 3.15 & spoke at some length.[5]

29. Fr.

Wrote to Rev. S. Hall—Rev. T. Crawley[6]—M. de St Mesmin—Mr Ritchie—Mr Penna[7]—Mr Earley—Mr Schäfle (O)[8]—Mr Senior—H.G. Reid[9]—Mr Knowles— Geo Potter—Chatto & Windus—T. Wilson. Meeting at Ld Granville's 3-4½. Our 'Cabinet' would have been 19 but for Halifax's gout. H of C. 2-3, 4¾-5¾ and 9-10¼.[10] Read Pepys—Positivism on an Island.[11] Saw Ld Wolverton—Ld Granville—Mr D. Grant[12]—Mr Sandford MP[13]—Mr F. Boydell[14]—Mr Mundella MP— Mr Bright—Mr Chamberlain MP—Mr Fawcett—Ly Lothian—Ld Hartington.

30. Sat.

Wrote to Count Münster—Rev. Boldero (O)[15]—A. Alpiar—Ralph Harrison— G.J.P. Eyre[16]—Lady Marion Alford—Ld E. Clinton—Mr Ouvry—J. Todd—Mr Kiernan—Mr Ritchie. Luncheon at 15 G.S. Saw Pall Mall Exhibition—Conduit Street ditto. Dined at A. Tennyson's. Saw Ld Granville—Mr Browning—Dr A. Clark—Duke of Argyll—Sir Jas Paget—Ly Lothian. Read Pepys—Chesney on Russia & India.[17]

---

[1] Irish poor law; H 239. 67. [2] Untraced.

[3] Mutiny bill and its obstruction; H 239. 122.

[4] 'At 7 p.m. G. dashed into Arlington St. with the news that Ld. Derby had resigned & that the Govt. were going to call out the military reservists. He came to ask me to look into the International Law on the conduct of affairs in a Congress—the preliminaries etc. & he had conversed at length with Count Munster, who thought Russia to blame on the point of determining not to allow certain things to be discussed. G. & I thought Russia right in this, wrong about Bessarabia'; Phillimore's Diary.

[5] Lead by Barran and Baines, it offered support, reporting the meeting (see 13 Mar. 78n), but apparently made no formal offer of the seat; Gladstone 'seemed much affected'; T.T., 29 March 1878, 8b.

[6] Probably Thomas William Crawley, rector of Heyford, Weedon, from 1851.

[7] Frederic Penna, authority on voice production; see Add MS 44456, f. 202.

[8] Possibly Albert Eberhard Friedrich Schaeffle, critic of socialism; much tr. into English.

[9] (Sir) Hugh Gilzean Reid, 1836-1911; owned newspapers in Scotland; advanced liberal M.P. Aston 1885-6; kt. 1893. [10] Irish universities, Turkey; H 239. 229.

[11] W. H. Mallock, 'Positivism on an island', Contemporary Review, xxxii. 1 (April 1878).

[12] Daniel Grant of Greenwich; liberal candidate Marylebone 1868, 1874, M.P. there 1880-5.

[13] George Montagu Warren Sandford, d. 1879; tory M.P. Maldon 1854-7, 1859-68, 1874-8.

[14] Probably Francis Boydell, younger br. of the former Hawarden agent.

[15] Probably Henry Kearney Boldero, d.1900; rector of Grittleton from 1860.

[16] Charles James Phipps Eyre, 1813-99; rector of Marylebone 1857-82. See 20 July 79.

[17] Nineteenth Century, iii. 227 (February 1878).

31. 4 S.L.

Chapel Royal 10 AM—All Saints 4 PM. Saw D. of Argyll—Dr A. Clark—Sir R. Phillimore. Tea at A[rgyll] Lodge. The P.s dined with us. Read Clifford in 19th Cent.—Elam in Do[1]—And many theological tracts.

Monday Ap 1. 78.

Wrote to Mr Toole—Mr Raleigh—Mr Irons—Jas Hutton—H. Ogden—C.F. Dobell—Rev. J. Oakley—Sir Thos G.—Made Novikoff—Writer of unsigned letter. Read (part) A. Arnold on Disestabl.[2]—Bowrings Autobiogr.[3] Saw Phillips X. Sat (shortly) to Mr Theed.[4] Saw Ld F. Cavendish—Ld Granville—Mr Bright—Sir C. Dilke—Miss Scott—Ld Hartington *cum* Mr Stansfeld. H of C. $4\frac{1}{2}$-6 and $11\frac{1}{4}$-$5\frac{1}{2}$: sat thus late on the Irish Sunday Closing Bill which is met by an obstruction really scandalous.[5] Walked home in a morning of diamond light.

2. Tu.

Wrote to Dr A. Clark—Scotts—Sir Thos G.—L. Hemer—W. Parsons—Mr Bateman U.S.[6]—Sig. Barabino[7]—Rev. H. Formby[8]—Rev. R.A. Davies—J. Dashwood—J.S. Exell[9]—H.M. Murray—Mr Blackhorn. Saw Mrs Watkins—Ld Granville—D. of Argyll—Ld F. Cavendish—Mr Hankey—Ld Hartington—Mr Fawcett. Read Pepys's Memoirs. Twelve to dinner. H of C. $4\frac{1}{2}$-$7\frac{1}{4}$ and $10\frac{1}{4}$-$11\frac{1}{2}$. (Indian Finance).[10]

3. Wed.

Wrote to Rev. T. Lowe[11]—Miss L. Nate—Miss Kortright—W. Freeman—F. Wolverson—Home Secy (O)—Mr Pettifer—Mr Warren—J. Brode. H of C. 12-6 on the Vaccination Bill.[12] $7\frac{3}{4}$-$12\frac{1}{2}$. Devonshire Club dinner. A short speech was wrung out of me.[13] G. & H. did their work well. Read Hansard 1854 & 1870.

4. Th.

Wrote to Ld Hartington—G.L. Clark—Lady M. Alford—J. Ogle—Rev S.E.G.—Mr Freeman. Thirteen to breakfast: a really notable one. Read Flassan on Congress of Vienna[14]—Bowring's Autobiography. H of C. 4-$7\frac{1}{4}$ and 1-$3\frac{1}{4}$ (Irish Sunday Closing).[15] Saw Ld F. Cavendish—Rev M. M'Coll—Mr Toole—Mr Browning—Sir Thos G.—Mr Bright.

[1] Ibid., iii. 712, 687 (April 1878).
[2] A. Arnold, 'The business aspect of disestablishment', ibid., iii. 733 (April 1878).
[3] *Autobiographical recollections of Sir John Bowring* (1877).
[4] See 25 June 77.   [5] Intervened at the end of the debate; *H* 239. 369.
[6] Perhaps J. B. Bateman, wrote earlier on 'national sin'; Hawn P.
[7] Georgio Barabino, Italian journalist; see Add MS 44453, f. 271.
[8] A nonconformist; see 23 June 77.
[9] Ed. the *Homiletic Quarterly*; unsuccessfully requested a contribution; Hawn P.
[10] *H* 239. 417.   [11] Thomas Lowe, d. 1898; vicar of Sabden from 1877.
[12] Spoke supporting Pease's bill; *H* 239. 501.
[13] No report found; Granville and Hartington earlier received a huge deputation.
[14] G. de R. de Flassan, *History of the Congress of Vienna*, 3v. (1829).
[15] And answered Northcote on the budget; *H* 239. 557.

5. Fr.

Wrote to Mrs Grote—J. Wall (O)—H. Hughes—Miss Cobby—H. Harborne—A.G. Symonds—A.M.C. Weir—G. Harborne. H of C. $4\frac{1}{4}$-$7\frac{1}{2}$ and 9-$11\frac{1}{2}$. Spoke on the Congress: Northcote answered me in a manner totally at variance with his private language.[1] Saw Ld F. Cavendish—Ld Granville—do *cum* Ld Hartington—Sir W. James—Mr Stansfeld—Mr Bright—Mr Mundella—Mr Lowe—Sir S. Northcote—Mr Childers—Mr Agnew. Visited the Novar Pictures.[2] Meeting at Ld G.s 2-3.[3] Read Pepys.

6. Sat.

Wrote to Mr Beal—Mr Vickers O—Mr Knowles O—Dr Newaly MP[4]—Mr Charrington—R. Aird[5]—W. Colam—Mr Burnstone O—A. Hyams—Mr Newdegate O—Messrs Murray—F.J. Norman—H. Hughes. Dined with the Civil Engineers. About half of them roared for War upon Adderley's very improper speech. I spoke for H. of C. & tried to give him (he is an excellent man) just a gentle tap. Read Birkbeck, Path of duty[6]—Willis, Calvin & Serverus[7]—Pepys.[8] Saw Mr Peel—Lord Lindsay—Sir A. Gordon. 5-6. Tea at Sir W. Harcourt's.

7. 5 S. Trin.

Chapel Royal 10 A.M. St Pauls (Dr Liddon) 3.15-5.15. Saw Dean of St Paul's—Ld Blachford—Ly Lothian & Lady Brownlow. Two Lytteltons dined. Wrote to Mrs Th. Read Calvin & Servetus—Bagot on Inspiration[9]—Finished Arnold on Disestablishment.

8. M.

Wrote to Ed. Daily News—A. Xenos—R. Hudson—A. Pryor—S. Evans—Professor Jebb BP—Professor Blackie BP—Dean of Windsor BP—F. Collings. Worked much on Turkish papers. Read Pepys—D of W.s Memm of 1829.[10] Saw Ld Wolverton—Ld Hartington—Mrs Vaughan. Dined with Sir C. Forster. H of C. (& H of L.) $4\frac{1}{4}$-$8\frac{1}{4}$ and 11-$12\frac{1}{2}$. Spoke 1 h. 40 m. on Message.[11]

9. Tu.

Wrote to Mr Whalley MP—A.J. Evans[12]—W. Catlin—Miss Cobby—Mr Stead—Mr Miller—Mr Ouvry. Attended Coffeehouse Company Meeting in Seven Dials

---

[1] Question put on basis of his talk with Phillimore (see 28 Mar. 78n.); *H* 239. 733.

[2] Munro of Novar's collection about to be sold at Christie's; see *T.T.*, 11 March 1878, 7f.

[3] See Walling, *Diaries of Bright*, 407.

[4] Reading uncertain; 'B.P.' may be intended; no M.P. of this name.

[5] Robert Aird, 'a working man in Wislaw'; letter on jingoism in *T.T.*, 11 April 1878, 11a.

[6] See 21 Jan. 78.   [7] By R. Willis (1877).   [8] See 25 June 49.

[9] D. Bagot, *The inspiration of the Holy Scriptures* (1878).

[10] On the Eastern question, in Wellington's *Despatches, correspondence, and memoranda 1819-1832*, vi. 142-5, 212-9 (1877).

[11] On the Queen's message calling out the reserves; he sharply attacked Salisbury's despatch of 1 April for 'misstatements'; *H* 239. 869.

[12] (Sir) Arthur John *Evans, 1851-1941; archaeologist; published on Balkan affairs; Keeper of the Ashmolean, Oxford, 1884; m. 1878 E. A. *Freeman's da., Margaret.

and spoke. The workmen below cheered as we came out, but some were markedly silent & obtuse as I thought.[1] Saw Sir A. Panizzi—Ld Hartington—Mrs Th.—Ld F. Cavendish—Mr Bright—Mr Crake.[2] Presided at Metaphysical Soc.s dinner & discussion.[3] H of C. 10-1. Voted in the small minority of 64.[4] Read Pepys—Moncure Conway on the War question.[5]

10. Wed.

Wrote to Sig. Malinverni—J. Norwood—L.J. Nicolson—C.Hill—J. Russell—Mr White (O)—Mrs Th. Attended meeting of working men's Delegates, near 500 & spoke ½ hour.[6] A very interesting occasion. Also we had a notable dinner with the Abercrombies. Conversation with Lady A—Ld Derby—Lady Derby—Ld Carnarvon—Lady Lansdowne—Ld Shaftesbury. Read Pepys—and divers Tracts. Saw Mrs Grote—Ld Granville. H of C. 4½-6.[7]

11. Th.

Wrote to Dr Schliemann l. & B.P.—Rev. Mr Crawley—H.D. Nourse[8]—Rev. A.A. Jenkins—Mr Jas Cartwright[9]—Mrs Fleming—Mr Dammeyer (O)—Mr Ouvry—W. Bude—Mr Deverell—J. Hughes—Dr Norton.[10] Saw Mr Allwright—Scotts—Mr . . .—Mr Hayward (re Th. &c.) H. of C. 4½-7.[11] The Newcastle boys came. Read Calvin & Servetus—Pepys's Diary—Divers Tracts.

12. Fr.

Wrote to Bp. [C.J.] Abraham—Ld R. Grosvenor—Ld Granville—Mrs Th.—Mr Gurdon—Sec. Academy—Treasurer of Guy's—Miss de Lisle—Rev. J.G. Rogers—Rev. J. Young—Mrs C.B. Dodge—Rev. G.T. Barret—Mons. Carapanos (l. & B.P.)[12]—Rev. W. Selwyn—Mr Pender—O. Taylor—J. Hunns—Mr Hilton—J.D. Hall—G.L. Howe.[13] Saw Ld Granville—Sir A. Panizzi. H of C. 9-12¾: with the banishment of strangers and the hooting incident: Capt. Denzil Onslow, as is his manner, playing a conspicuous part.[14] Read Pepys—Brooks (Pure faith) on the Croydon Congress—Dodone et ses Ruines.

---

[1] No report found.

[2] William Hamilton Crake, commissioner for the lieutenancy of London.

[3] M. P. W. Boulton read a paper, 'Has a metaphysical society any *Raison d'être*'; Brown, *Metaphysical Society*, 94.

[4] On the reserves; Hartington abstained; *H* 239. 1038.

[5] Untraced letter or article sent by M. D. Conway (see 15 June 76).

[6] *D.N.*, 11 April 1878, 3a.

[7] Employers' liability; *H* 239. 1042.

[8] Henry Dalzell Nourse, barrister.

[9] James Joel Cartwright of the public record office.

[10] Perhaps Arthur Treherne Norton, physician; nearly a neighbour, in Wimpole Street.

[11] Budget deb.; *H* 239. 1105.

[12] Constantine Carapanos, historian, wrote in French to arrange a meeting and sent his *Dondone et ses ruines* (1878); see 22 Apr.78.

[13] Perhaps Granville L. Howe; see Add MS 44526, f. 59.

[14] Gladstone voted in 12:57 against the withdrawal of Strangers when Irish M.P.s tried to discuss govt. reaction to Leitrim's murder; the deb. was not reported; *H* 239. 1262. Denzil Roberts Onslow, tory M.P. Guildford 1874-85.

13. Sat. [Windsor]

Wrote to D. of Argyll (B.P.)—Mr Moncure Conway—Mr Whalley MP—Rev. J.G. Rogers—Rev. D. Macgregor—Rev. H. Allon D.D.—Rev. H. Martin—Rev. Geo. Brooks—Mr Blennerhassett MP—J. Russell—Mrs Th.—C. Cowan—T.W. Russell—T. Mackie[1]—D. M'Kenzie. Arranging papers &c. Dined with Mr Knowles at the Grosvenor. Saw Mr Smith Harrison[2]—Ld Hartington—W.H.G.—Jas Wortley—Mr Chinnery.[3] Off to Windsor by the 11 PM train. Read Selwyn Eyre on Russian Life[4]—and [blank.]

14. Palm S.

St George's 11 A.M. and 4½ P.M. Walk with C. Wrote to Sir C. Forster. Read Clericus Cantab. on the Ancient Liturgies[5]—Br. Quart. on F. Harrison—On Disestablishment[6]—Princeton Rev. on the Bible & the Public School—on Preaching to the Dead[7]—Formby, Philos. Ancient History.[8] Much conversation with the Dean. Saw Mrs Ponsonby & her remarkable daughter.[9]

15. M.

St George's 10.30 AM and 4.30 P.M. Visited the Chapter Buildings. Walk about Eton. Saw Ld W. Russell—Mrs Ponsonby. Wrote to Mrs Hampton—Rev W. Selwyn—Supt G.W.R. Read Br. Quart on Mycenae—The War—The E. Question[10]—Fortnightly on Disraeli[11]—Princeton Rev. on the Synod of Dort. I find my old friend the Dean quite unchanged & as true & satisfactory as ever.

16. Tu. [Lysways, Lichfield]

Wrote to C.G. Off at 7.15 to London: & arrived at Lichfield at 12.30. The funeral[12] at one was most striking from the numbers character & feeling of those present. I liked particularly the repetition of the processional hymn, to cover the whole distance. He was laid in the rock: 12 feet from the surface. Alone; but not alone. His name must live: he is one of the band of great Bishops.

Saw Archdeacon Allen—Bp Abraham—Ld Selborne—Mrs Selwyn—Rev. W. Selwyn—Sir C. Forster—Mr Lonsdale. Attended the Memorial meeting in the Hall, and spoke a few words on the Dean's invitation. Bp Abraham took me

[1] Thomas Mackie of Edinburgh; see Add MS 44454, f. 6.

[2] Gentleman; lived at Elmhurst, Woodford.

[3] Sic; Thomas *Chenery, 1826-84; ed. The Times 1878-84; moderately sympathetic to liberalism; see History of The Times, ii. 521. See 17 Apr. 78.

[4] S. Eyre, Sketches of Russian life and customs (1878).

[5] Clericus Cantabrigiensis, The primitive doctrine of the Eucharistic sacrifice as exhibited in early Liturgies (1876).

[6] British Quarterly Review, lxvii. 379, 462 (April 1878).

[7] Princeton Review, liv. 361, 451 (March 1878).

[8] See 23 June 77.

[9] Mary Elizabeth, wife of (Sir) H. F. *Ponsonby, 1825-95, Victoria's secretary, had two children: Alberta, m. 1891 Col. W. Montgomery, and Magdalen.

[10] British Quarterly Review, lxvii. 321, 482, 506 (January-April 1878).

[11] F. H. Hill in Fortnightly Review, xxix. 477 (April 1878).

[12] Of G. A. Selwyn; see The Guardian, 17 April 1878, 544.

over the Cathedral; & showed me the Gospel (7th Cent) & Chaucer MSS. Spent aft. & night at Lysways.[1] Read Evans, Illyrian Letters[2]—Eyre, Russian Life.

17. Wed. [London]

Wrote to Editor of Times[3]—Mr Chenery (Priv.)—J. Nicolson—Ed. Guardian—Mr Bowyer—Mr Deverell[4]—Mr Whittle. Read Selwyn Eyre—Lecky's Fall of Walpole (in V. I)[5]—Pepys's Memoirs. All Souls Church 8 P.M. Conversation with D. of Argyll. The Duchess shows a brave spirit. Drove to see Churches: Longdon, & St Michael's Lichfield. Reached Harley St at 3.30 P.M. Found a great mass of letters, & set to as a galley slave should.

18. Th.

All Souls Ch. 11 A.M. Wrote to Principal Librarian—Gen. Bainbrigge—Mr Hubbard BP—W. Morris—R. Heming—C.J. Guthrie[6]—Mr Barnard—L. Jewitt—Mr Bevan (O)—Rev. T.G. Forrest[7]—Rev. W.C. Walters.[8]

Even on this solemn day I could not manage evening Church. Indeed the circumstances of this Lent have been singularly adverse to that recollection which is the very first condition of a due & profitable observance. Even a material reduction of food I find now to tell upon strength in a way that I knew nothing of 30 years back. 2.30-5. To the Memorial Hall for the remarkable meeting of Nonconforming Ministers, when I spoke for an hour. The preparation was very small: perhaps all the better.[9] Never did I address a better audience. Read Qu. Rev.—divers Articles—Ch. Quart. Rev. on Arnold & Clough[10]—Divers Tracts—Selwyn Eyre on Russia.

19. Good Friday.

Trinity (Parish) Ch. 11-1 with H.C. St Anne's 4-6 (Bach Music: most beautiful: yet not what I like for *today*). Visited Dowager Dss of Somerset. Read Deverell, The Pilgrims[11]—Ch. Quart. on Future Punishment—Hewitt, Elem. Catechism[12]—Quart. Rev. on Lecky (finished)—Rhodes on Unity Sect. I.[13]

20. Easter Eve.

All Souls 11 AM and All Saints 9 PM. The beautiful and touching service of former times has alas! lost every characteristic feature.

[1] Seat of Sir Charles Forster; see 18 Mar. 58.
[2] A. J. Evans, *Illyrian Letters* (1878).
[3] On Selwyn's acceptance of the bpric. of New Zealand; copy also in *The Guardian*, 24 April 1878, 585.   [4] William Trapnell Deverell; historian and liberal.
[5] In his *History of England in the eighteenth century*, i (1878).
[6] Perhaps Charles John Guthrie, 1849-1920; advocate, historian and free-churchman.
[7] Thomas Guest Forrest, d. 1903; vicar of Upton from 1877.
[8] W. Carey Walters, nonconformist; Hawn P.
[9] On the eastern question; *T.T.*, 19 April 1878, 6a.
[10] *Church Quarterly Review*, vi. 117 (April 1878).
[11] W. T. Deverell, *The pilgrims and the Anglican Church* (1871).
[12] Tract by J. W. Hewett.   [13] M. J. Rhodes, *The visible unity of the Catholic Church*, 2v. (1870).

Wrote to Mr Entwistle l. & BP—Mons. Carapanos—Dr Granville[1]—H.A. Schulz—W.T. Deverell—Mr Rosenblatt (O)—Editor (Unitn paper)—Rev. Willis Nevins—Rev. W. Higman—Canon Ashwell—Rev. A. Albright—Professor Holmgren BP[2]—Mr James MP—F.L. Price—Ld Norton—Mr Mitchell—J. Hodges—T.J. Hughes[3]—Mr Howell—Mrs Th. 3¾-8. We drove down to Pembroke Lodge. Saw Ly Russell & the family[4] with M. & Me Detthegoyen(?). Then for a few minutes to see Lord Russell at his desire: a noble wreck.[5] He recognised us, & overflowed with feeling. Read Quart. Rev.—Pepyss Mem. (finished Vol.)

21. Easter Day.

St Andrew's Wells St 11.15 A.M. & H.C. Much *most* beautiful music: but some defect in the vocal Executive power. Chapel Royal 5.30 P.M. Wrote to E. Talbot. Read Calvin & Servetus (finished)—Bateman's Lecture[6]—Gill on Ritualism[7]—Lee on P.W. Act[8]—and other Theolog. Tracts.

22. M.

All Souls Ch. 11 A.M. Wrote to Supt Bookstall Chester—Mr Ouvry—Mr Allbright—Mr Lascelles—Dr MacOscar[9]—Mr Corn. Brown[10]—Treasurer Kent Blind—Mr Hugh Hodgson[11]—Ed. Daily News. Saw Sir A. Panizzi—Mons. Const. Carapanos—and Mr W.F. Larkins. Five hours work in *moving* things to my new sittingroom on the first floor, & in packing books &c. for Hn. Read Eyre on Russia (finished)—MacColl's Three Years of E.Q.[12]

23. Tu. [Keble College, Oxford]

Wrote to T.J. Hughes—M. Taylor—Dr Bendan—Mr Salmon (O)—Supt G.W.R. Station—Mrs Williams—Rev. M. M'Coll—E.H. Watson[13]—A. Macdonald. Saw Scotts. Off at 2.15 to Oxford: the Lodge at Keble. Dinner party, & much conversation. Read Evans on Illyria—Diplomatie et l'Orient.[14]

---

[1] Joseph Mortimer Granville, 1833-1900; London physician specializing in neuralgia.

[2] Probably Frithiof Holmgren, Swedish medical writer on colour-blindness; doubtless on Homer.

[3] T. J. Hughes, wrote as 'Adfyfr' on landlordism in Wales.

[4] Presumably including Bertrand *Russell, 1872-1970, brought up by his grandparents; he recalled Madame D'Etchegoyen as 'an old French lady living in Richmond . . . a niece of Talleyrand, who used to give me large boxes of the most delicious chocolates'; B. Russell, *Autobiography* (1967), 27.

[5] He d. 28 May 1878.

[6] Perhaps J. Bateman, 'Two lectures on the final and universal triumph of the Gospel' (1848).

[7] T. H. Gill, 'A letter . . . touching "Ritualism"' (1878).

[8] See 4 Apr. 75.

[9] John MacOscar, London physician, sent his br. William's *Poetical Works* (1878); Hawn P.

[10] Cornelius Brown, preparing his *Annals of Newark-on-Trent* (1879) which recorded the diarist's career in his first constituency. See 13 Aug. 78.

[11] Of Oakley Square, London.

[12] M. MacColl, *Three years of the Eastern Question* (1878).

[13] Of Boston; had sent a book on spelling; Hawn P.

[14] *La Diplomatie et la question d'Orient 1877-1878* (1878).

24. Wed.

Magdalen Chapel at 10. Visited Corpus Library with Mr Laing[1]—Mr Ruskin's rooms[2] & all their objects, a most notable abode: Taylor Gallery, Turner Drawings, Pictures, & Lecture Room. Saw the Aclands & many more. Mr Copeland—Bp of Oxford. Dinner of ninety in Hall followed by evening party. Wrote to Central Press (Tel.) Read Evans's Illyria—Wordsworth, University Life.[3]

25. St Mark's.

8-10: H.C.—a congregation of communicants: very striking. At $12\frac{1}{2}$ the opening service in the Library. At $1\frac{1}{2}$ to near five, luncheon and speeches in the Hall: mine a long one, in proposing Prosperity to Keble College.[4] Then service $5\frac{1}{4}$-7 & sermon from Dr King: in part seraphic. Then presentation of the Warden's picture—& interesting speech from him. Then dinner & evening party again: a day close packed with functions. Read Keble Charter[5] & other papers—Wordsworth's Univ. Life. Conversation with the Warden—Bp of Cape Town[6]—Bp of Oxford—U.S. Minister[7]—Lavinia—Mr Balfour—The Chinese Professor.[8] Read Evans's Illyria—Wordsworth's Univ. Life. Wrote to Professor Clifton—Dr Hayman.

26. Fr. [Hawarden]

Keble Chapel 8 A.M. Wrote to Mr Allbright. Read Evans's Illyria—Rawlinson, Origin of Nations[9]—Natal Woman Slavery.[10] Saw Bp of Salisbury—Herbert J.G.—Dr Jowett—Dean of ChCh—Mr Greswell—R. of Exeter—Dr Dobie. Off at 11.40. Hn at $5\frac{1}{2}$. Mr Ottley's case grave, but hopeful.[11] Opening a mass of letters & papers, as usual.

27. Sat.

Ch. $8\frac{1}{2}$ A.M. Wrote to Mr Webster—J.J. Jones—Mr Marsden—E. Sturge—Mr Wrigley—A.W. Tuer[12]—Mr Davies—Mr Marland Clarke—Mrs Weldon—Traffic Manager, Chester—Supt. Bookstall, Chester—Sir S. Scott & Co—Rev. E. Wilberforce—Rev. G.C. Hutton—Rev. R.T. Blake—Rev. Dr Caird—Ven. Archd.

---

[1] Robert Laing; taught modern history; published on university reform.

[2] Ruskin had rooms there as Slade professor; he was then at Brantwood recovering from his breakdown; see E. T. Cook, *Life of Ruskin* (1911), ii. 406.

[3] See 22 Feb. 78.

[4] Official opening of Keble College; Gladstone was 'greeted with loud, long, and enthusiastic cheering, and waving of hats and caps', and controversially praised Newman 'as an academical name ... greater than either of those [Keble and Pusey]'; full account in *The Guardian*, 1 May 1878, 613.

[5] His govt. superintended its approval; see 17 Apr., 14, 21 May 70.

[6] William West Jones, d. 1908; bp. of Cape Town from 1874.

[7] John Welsh; American ambassador 1877-9.

[8] James Legge, 1815-97; professor of Chinese from 1876.

[9] G. Rawlinson, *The origin of nations* (1877).

[10] See 3 July 77.

[11] An illness; see 5 May 78.

[12] Andrew White Tuer, 1838-1900; publisher and author.

Harrison—Rev T.W. Mossman—C.E. Gladstone[1]—A.E. Mathews. I had a long and very satisfactory conversation with Helen, before her departure, on the unsettled state of belief at her college.[2] Also conversation with W. & walk with the Rector, paying divers visits to parishioners. Arranging my tracts as published & preparing for a little Homer, please God. Read Evans's Illyria—Rawlinson Origin of Nations.

28. Low Sunday.

Ch. 11 AM and [blank], reading the Lessons. Wrote to Very Rev Dr Newman l. and B.P.[3]—Rev. E. Coleridge—Mr A. Allbright—Mr R. Leake.[4] Read Formby, Philos. of Hist. (poor)[5]—Huidekoper, Christ's Mission to the Underworld[6]—Rawlinson, Origin of Nations—Thirner, Church & State.[7]

29. M.

Ch. $8\frac{1}{2}$ AM. Wrote to Messrs Macmillans—Mr A. Allbright—Messrs D. Sherratt & Co—Mr Julian (Lpool).[8] Worked $6\frac{1}{4}$ hours on Homeric Primer. What a treat! Cut an oak with W. Conversation with W., & with C.,on place & parish affairs. Read Evans's Illyria—Rawlinson, Origin of Nations.

30. Tu.

Ch. $8\frac{1}{2}$ A.M. Wrote to Mr A.C. M'Kenzie—Messrs Ransome—Ed. Daily News—With signature (masses of incl.)—G. Onslow—W.J. Williams—Mr Duffield[9]—Mr Jefferys—Mrs Good. Felled an oak with W. Saw Mr Vickers on place arrangements. Today I got about five hours at the Primer. Read Evans's Illyria—Williams, Armenian Campaign.[10]

Wed. May One. SS. Ph. & J.

Church $8\frac{3}{4}$ AM. Wrote to Messrs Clay B.P.—Earl of Portsmouth—Rev. J.G. Jones[11]—Rev. R.C. Owen—Mr C. Stevenson. Six hours today on Homer. Felling two oaks with Willy. In evg attended Miss Vincent's[12] Cookery practice &

---

[1] Charles Elsden, b. 1855, 5th s. of Robert Gladstone; later a naval captain.

[2] Newnham college, Cambridge.

[3] Sending his article 'The Iris of Homer' in response to Newman's letter on his speech at Keble; *Newman*, xxviii. 351.

[4] Robert Leake, 1824-1901; president of Salford liberal association 1870; M.P. S.E. Lancashire 1880-5, Radcliffe 1880-95. See 8 May 78.

[5] See 14 Apr. 78.

[6] F. Huidekoper, *The belief of the first three centuries concerning Christ's mission to the underworld* (1854).

[7] *Sic*; perhaps one of the publications of Augustin Theiner who wrote much on this subject.

[8] J. W. Julian; see 2 May 78.

[9] Alexander James Duffield, 1821-90; engineer and author; see Add MS 44456, f. 256.

[10] Charles Williams, *The Armenian campaign* (1878).

[11] Perhaps John G. Jones, rector of Somerby from 1861.

[12] May Vincent of the S. Kensington cookery school; diarist's remarks on English cooking in *T.T.*, 2 May 1878, 8a; see also that day's leader: 'Mr Gladstone may be congratulated on having, in the midst of his indefatigable labours for the popular welfare, at last found a subject on which most persons will agree with him'—an overoptimistic view, see 26 Feb. 79n.

instruction, & contributed a little speech. Read Evans (finished)—Williams on Arm. Campaign.

2. Th.

Ch. 8½ AM. Wrote to Rev Mr Williams & others—Mr J.W. Julian (E. question)—d[itt]o private—Rev. Mr Hepple[1]—R.H. Williams—S.B. Jopson—J.E. Teale[2]—R. Leake. After three fair Homeric days, I was sorely cut up today by the E. Question, writing a lengthened letter to Liverpool,[3] and reading Bright's fine speech & the Manchester proceedings.[4] Attended the cookery practice at Pentre: *cottage* practice. Read E. Burritt on Russia[5]—Hepple on Anglo-Judaism—Rawlinson, Origin of Nations. My letter to Liverpool took me two hours to write, and gave me more fatigue than six hours of Homeric work.[6] Of that a very little modicum today.

3. Fr.

Ch. 8½ A.M. Wrote to Archdeacon Palmer[7]—Reporter of Manchr Examr—W.J. Williams—Mr Allbright—Mr Trendell—Mr Lancaster—Mrs Dale—L. Morris—Mr Corbett. Worked on Homer from five to six hours: say *six*. Cut an oak with W.H.G. Read Congregational Chaos[8]—Rawlinson, Origin of Nations.

4. Sat.

Ch. 8½ AM. Wrote to Mr Hartley[9]—W.J. Pillow—J.F. Hunt[10]—A.M. Reid—Rev. E. Chambers—Rev. S.H. Booth[11]—Miss Bell—R. Leake. Another six hours on Homer. Got through 'The Olympian system'. Felled an oak, W. another. Tea with the Miss Rigbys. Saw Mr Vickers. Read Rawlinson Or. of Nations—Jebb, Greek Primer.[12]

5. 2 S.E.

Ch 11 AM with H.C. & 6½ P.M. Read all the Lessons. Worked 2 h. on the Olympian scheme, revising MS. & Wrote to Messrs Clay. Saw Mr Ottley for the first time & conversation. He recovers well. Read Christie's Reply[13]—New Englander on Future Punt.[14]

---

[1] Untraced correspondent, had sent his book.
[2] James Eastoe Teall of Upper Holloway, see Add MS 44456, f. 281.
[3] Long letter to J. W. Julian, read to the working men's conference in Liverpool on 3 May; *T.T.*, 4 May 1878, 12e.
[4] See *T.T.*, 1 May 1878, 12c.
[5] E. Burritt, chapter two of *Chips from many blocks* (1878).
[6] The Homeric primer; see 24 Sept. 77n.
[7] Arthur Palmer; archdeacon of Toronto 1869-75; latterly living in Bristol.
[8] Untraced tract.
[9] Congratulating John Hartley of Accrington on liberal successes in local elections; *T.T.*, 8 May 1878 7f.
[10] John Francis Hunt, spiritualist; see Add MS 44456, f. 289.
[11] Samuel Harris Booth, secretary of the Baptist Union.
[12] See 24 Sept. 77.
[13] See 2 May 75.
[14] Not found.

6. M.

Ch. 8½ AM. Wrote to Duchess of St Albans—Jos Arch[1]—Miss Cobden—Miss Hort[2]—E.A. Budge—Professor [F. W.] Newman—G.H. Kemp[3]—G.N. Curzon[4]— Bp Abraham—Rev. W. Edwards. Worked on an Oak with W. Read Rawlinson. Conversation with S.E.G. on his return: also with Mr O[ttley] who continues to improve.

7. Tu.

Ch. 8½ AM. Wrote to Prof. Rolleston B.P.—Ld Wolverton—Mr Douglas—Mr Williams (Carnarvon)[5]—Rev. S.H. Booth—M.D. Macleod—Messrs Clay B.P. Six to seven hours on Homer today—I think my best day's work on the Primer. Woodcutting with W. Read Helen's babies[6]—Rawlinson O. of Nations.

8. Wed.

Ch. 8½ A.M. Wrote to Mr T.M. Forrest—Rev. W. Dodge[7]—Lord Shand[8]—Marquis of Hartington. Saw Sir R. Cunliffe—Mr Leake—Mr Hughes. A Deputation of 130 came from Manchester & the towns, and some 20 from Wales, about the Addresses. I spoke (under an hour) in reply.[9] The whole was 2 h. Reading for it in the morning. Worked on Homer, but only 2 or 2½ hours. Read A. Arnold on Byzantine Institutions.[10] Conversation with S.E.G. on Future punishment. His mind does indeed grow in strength & wisdom.

9. Th.

Ch. 8½ A.M. Wrote to Mr W.J. Williams—Mr R. Brown jun—Rev. Dr Allon—Rev. G.R. Roberts[11]—Miss Bird—Mr Bloor. Near seven hours I think of work on Homer. Read Hayward's Goethe[12]—Rawlinson O. of Nations. Woodcutting with W.

[1] Joseph *Arch, 1826-1919; organized Agricultural Labourers Union 1872; liberal M.P. N.W. Norfolk 1885-6, 1892-1902.

[2] Perhaps Margaret, sister of F. J. A. *Hort.

[3] Had written for advice on ordination; Hawn P.

[4] George Nathaniel *Curzon, 1859-1925, invited diarist to lecture at Eton, which he was about to leave; see 30 May, 20 June, 6 July 78; letter in Ronaldshay, Life of Curzon (1928), i. 29 and Add MS 44456, f. 248.

[5] W. J. Williams, secretary of the North Wales quarrymen's union, organizing next day's Resolutions.

[6] Helen's babies, with some account of their ways . . . By their latest victim [J. Habberton] (ed. 1878).

[7] William Dodge, d. 1930; curate in Lambeth 1872-80, in Deptford 1882; vicar of Southwark 1884-1910.

[8] Alexander Burns Shand, 1828-1904; judge of the court of session 1872-90; Scottish educational commissioner.

[9] Deputation representing 135 towns and 203 organizations of the Northern Counties Liberal Associations, led by R. Leake (see 2 May 78n.) on the eastern question; T.T., 9 May 1878, 10c.

[10] Perhaps R. A. Arnold, From the Levant, 2v. (1868).

[11] George Robert Roberts, d. 1898; unbeneficed; rector of Fulmodeston 1887.

[12] See 18 Jan. 36.

10. Fr.

Ch. 8½ A.M. Wrote to Lord Hartington—Mr Green—Mrs Th.—J. Bateman[1]—E. Pearson.[2] Walk with S. and woodcutting with W. Good six hours on Homer. Saw Lady Frost[3]—Mr Ottley. Read Rawlinson—Hayward's Goethe.

11. Sat.

Ch. 8½ A.M. Wrote to Mr Childers (Tel)—Mrs G.D. Pennant—Mrs A. Besant— Prof. Rolleston—T.J. Prior—Miss Baddiley—J. Leach—C.H. Lake—G. Harris—J. Tonkyn. Saw Mr Vickers on the year's accounts. Finished the text of my Primer for Homer. Worked on Proofs. I got altogether good 7½ hours. Read Mrs Bezant [sic] on E.Q.—A vigorous & just invective.[4]

12. 3 S.E.

Ch. 11 AM and 6½ P.M. Read all the Lessons. S. preached admirably. Wrote to Ld Hartington—Mr Childers—Mr Godley—Ed. Echo—W. Hyam. Conversation with Mr Ottley: with S.E.G. in evg. Walk with C. Saw Hurst.[5] Read Meth. Mag. on Future Punishment—R. Gladstone on the Baptists[6]—Roberts on Apost. Succession[7]—Origen agt Celsus.

13. M.

Ch. 8½ A.M. Wrote to Mr J.E. Fielden—Messrs Clay B.P.—Rev. W. Hutt[8]—Mr W. Mather. Willy & I felled a good oak for the Rector. 6½ hours on revising MS of the Primer & on proofs. I have just contrived to squeeze the business into the Vacation. Preparations alas! for departure.

14. Tu. [London]

Ch. 8½ A.M. Off at 9. Harley St 3½. Wrote to Mr Cordingley—Dr Campbell—Mr Raleigh—Archdn Palmer—Mr Northey[9]—Mr Creighton.[10] Dined at Lady Morley's. Saw Sir H. James—Ld Granville—Sir W. Harcourt—Mr Childers—Mr Mundella—The Speaker—Ld J. Collier. H of C. 4½-7½.[11] Saw V. Bennett X. Read Hayward's Goethe.

15. Wed.

Wrote to Mr J. Bloomfield—Sec. B. & F. Schools—J.W. Dickson—W. Crawford— O. Talleman—Professor Pritchard—Messrs Clay—J. Hughes—W.H.G.—

[1] J. R. Bateman of Paternoster Square, London; Hawn P.
[2] Perhaps Edwin Pearson, London publisher and illustrator.
[3] Mary, wife of Sir T. G. Frost (see 12 Oct. 71).
[4] Sc. Besant; probably in a newspaper; not in T. Besterman's bibliography of her.
[5] James Hurst, 1808-88, Hawarden gamekeeper for 44 years.
[6] Untraced piece by Robert Gladstone.   [7] By G. B. B. J. Roberts (1877).
[8] William Wayman Hutt, 1822-94; fellow of Caius 1845-61; rector of Hockwold from 1861.
[9] Perhaps Edward Richard Northey, J.P. in Epsom.
[10] Perhaps Mandell *Creighton, 1843-1901; historian; ed. E.H.R. 1886-91; bp. of Peterborough 1891, of London 1897.
[11] Land reform; H 239. 1886.

C.F. Booth—Ld Acton—Dr Lawrence.[1] H. of C. 3¼-5¼. Irish B. Franchise. Saw Mr Newdigate—Sec. to Armenian ExPatriarch—Mr Allbright—Mr Godley—Mr West—Mr A. Peel—Mr Smith's Committee man—Mr Hankey. Read Bosworth Smith on Carthage.[2] I grappled partially today with an accumulation of about 500 letters & packets. Dined at Guy's Hospital, & proposed a toast.[3]

16. Th.

Wrote to Freshfields BP—Mr Ladner BP—Miss Battersby do—Mr Macenter[4] do—Mr Duvergne O—Miss Keith O—Mrs Hardy—Rev. W. Stephenson[5]—Rev. R.E. Sanderson—Sub Editor (Fleet St)—Mr Williams (Carnarvon)—Mr Trevelyan MP—C. Sharp—E. Garrick—W. Yates—F. Pellatt[6]—E. Glasser—D. Morne—J. Rowcliffe. H. of C. 4¾-8 and 1-1½.[7] Nine to breakfast. Saw Expatriarch Arm. & Sec.—Mr Godley—Mr Knowles—Mr Morley and Rev. Mr Brereton[8]—Ld Granville—do *cum* D. of Argyll—Mr Rollo Russell—Mr Salusbury—Lord Rosebery *cum* Mr Adam[9]—Ld Hartington—Mr C. Howard—N. Lyttelton. Read Lady Chatterton's Diaries.[10] Dined at F.C.s.

17. Fr.

Wrote to Lord Glasgow—A. Strahan—Jas Watts—W.H. Jones—A. Burnett—Sec. E.L. Children's Hospital—H. Pitman[11]—R. Burnett—A. Macewan—C.J. Parham BP—Messrs Clay (2) l. & B.P.—Capt. Freeman—Mr G. Calvert—Mr Bright—Mr R. Maine. Corrected proofs of Ch VI Primer. H. of C. 4¼-6½.[12] Dined with the James's. Consultation with him on the Midlothian case. Saw Gray—& another. X Read Bosworth Smith on Carthage.

18. Sat.

10-11¾. An interesting breakfast, about ten people, *chez* Mrs Birks. Wrote to J. Barratt—P. Clark—W. Davies—W.B. Potter—Mrs Field—Rev. J. Petrie[13]—Rev. M. Amphlett[14]—J. Turquand BP[15]—B.W. Weaver—L.H. Wight—W.R. Dennis—W.T. Deverell. Worked on proofs of Hom. Primer. Nine to dinner. Saw Sir A. Panizzi—Mr Wortley—Mrs Th. Read Hayward's Goethe—Fortnightly No II on Lord Beaconsfield.[16]

---

[1] Probably Henry Cripps Lawrence, physician at St Bartholomew's.
[2] R. B. Smith, *Carthage and the Carthaginians* (1878).
[3] No account found.
[4] Probably *sic*.
[5] Perhaps William Stephenson, curate of Goosnargh, Preston.
[6] Fortunatus Pellat & co., London brokers.
[7] Supply; Irish Sunday closing; *H* 240. 95.
[8] Perhaps Shovell Brereton, d. 1881; vicar of Briningham from 1861.
[9] First step towards Midlothian; see next day.
[10] E. H. Dering, *Memoirs of Georgiana, Lady Chatterton* (1878).
[11] Perhaps Henry Pitman of the short-hand family.
[12] Misc. business; *H* 240. 157.
[13] James Petrie, episcopalian incumbent in Wick.
[14] Martin Amphlett, 1815-86; rector of Church Lench from 1844.
[15] Perhaps Paul James Turquand, independent minister in London.
[16] *Fortnightly Review*, xxix. 691 (May 1878); articles by F. H. Hill.

19. 4 S.E.

Chapel Royal & H.C. 10 A.M. Portland St Ch 7 PM. Dined at Lady Lytteltons. Saw Lord Bath—Lord Lyttelton. Read Origen & Celsus in Fraser[1]—Gubernatis Zoolog. Mythology[2]—Rainy on Ch. & State[3]—Dupanloup, Voltaire Centenary: I agree with him, but he is not *fair*.[4]—N.A. Rev. on Human Depravity.[5]

20. M.

Wrote to Rev. Mr Spurgeon—Mr Jenkins MP.—N.T. Foster[6]—Mr Hodgson Pratt—Rev. Sir G.W. Cox—Messrs Clay—Mrs Baxter—Mrs Butler—B. Haughton[7]—Messrs Townshend & Barker—Mrs Weldon—Dr A. Clark—H.G. Reid— Mr Budge—W.C. Russell—J.N. Park—S. Smiles—Mr Surr BP.—J.T. Taylor—Ed. Daily News. Worked on proof-sheets of Homeric Primer. Read E.Q. Pamphlets. Dined at Sir C. Forster's. Saw Mr Joseph. H of C. $4\frac{1}{2}$-$8\frac{1}{4}$ and $10\frac{1}{4}$-$12\frac{3}{4}$ (Indian Troops debate).[8]

21. Tu.

Wrote to Mr Henderson—Mr Thompson—E. Oxenford[9]—Wid Milanovich Voivoda[10]—Mr Mundella—Mr Campbell—M. Hickie—W.A. Hunter. Worked up some of the case for the Debate. Dined at Sir Ch. Forster's. H of C. $4\frac{1}{4}$-$8\frac{1}{4}$ & after dinner. Spoke $1\frac{1}{4}$ hour in answer to the Attorney General: with some satisfaction, but imperfectly.[11] Read Hayward's Goethe—Sharp's Poems.[12]

22. Wed.

Wrote to Mr G. Largie—Mr J.H. Addison[13]—Messrs Clay—Dean of ChCh—Mr Stedingle—Mr J.C. Trench. Corrected remaining proofs of my Homeric Primer. H. of C. 3-5.[14] Saw Mr Knowles—Scotts—Sir H. Johnstone—Dr Andrew Clark—& others. $5\frac{3}{4}$-$11\frac{1}{4}$. To Shadwell: presided at the Children's Hospital dinner, after going through the Wards: & spoke at some length for the institution.[15] Read Bosworth Smith.

---

[1] *Fraser's Magazine*, xcvii. 548 (May 1878); 'Three letters by F. W. Newman, J. A. Froude, and F. W. Newman'.

[2] Count A. de Gubernatis, *Zoological mythology; or the legends of animals*, 2v. (1872).

[3] R. Rainy, *Church and state, chiefly in relation to Scotland* (1878).

[4] F. A. P. Dupanloup, *Premières lettres . . . sur la centenaire de Voltaire*, 3v. (1878).

[5] *North American Review*, cxxvi. 466 (May 1878).

[6] Of Birmingham; had written on Homer; Hawn P.

[7] Perhaps Benjamin Haughton, of Lawford and Haughton, civil engineers.

[8] Hartington's resolution; *H* 240. 264.

[9] Misremembering of E. Oxenbridge of St John's Wood; versifier; Hawn P.

[10] Or Mid Wilanovich Voivodas, governor of Moldavia; business untraced.

[11] On the Bill of Rights and the govt.'s unconstitutional and illegal use of Indian troops; *H* 240. 387.

[12] W. Sharpe, *The Conqueror's dream. Poems* (1878).

[13] John H. Addison of the *Liverpool Daily Post*; on starting a weekly edition; Hawn P.

[14] Contagious diseases; *H* 240. 474.

[15] *D.N.*, 23 May 1878, 6f.

23. Th.

Wrote to Mrs Abraham (O)—Rev. R. Simpson—P.J. Sheldon (O)[1]—Col. L. Fremantle[2]—Rev. J.G. Rogers—Manager Nat. & Prov. Bank—Dr Macdonald—A.E. Jones—E.B. Michel—A. MacEwen—Mr Counsel. 3-4¼. Scotch meeting at W. Palace Hotel. Spoke on E.Q. at some length.[3] Seventeen to breakfast: including the Scottish Deputation; who made themselves very acceptable. Read Hayward's Goethe. Examining Acts &c. Saw General Barlow.[4] H of C. 4¼-8¼ and 10-3. Voted for law & Constitution against a majority of 121.[5]

24. Fr.

Wrote to A.C. M'Kenzie—W. Forbes—R. Forder—Warden of Keble—Mr Sec. Cross—Rev. J. Bond[6]—H. Miller. Made some hard work & progress on an Art. for N.C.[7] Saw Mr Godley on Homeric Primer and proofs—Ld Granville—Col. Lyon Fremantle—Mr J.G. Rogers. H. of C. 4¼-7 and 10¾-2½.[8] Read Acts & references.

We dined with the F. Cavendishes. As we sat down the Duchess of Argyll by whom I sat had a seizure. Removing into the next room with aid she rapidly grew worse & was soon unconscious. Doctors were called from all quarters: I brought Clark. Nothing could be done. The family came in, & we cleared the ground. There came some in diamonds & garters from the Concert at Marlborough House. She sank into a gentle repose & breathed her last about 3 A.M. Requiescat.

25. Sat.

Wrote to J. Hermann—A. Duffield—Messrs Freshfield—Messrs Spottiswoode—Prof. [F. W.] Newman—Mr Macmillan. Worked much & long upon my article. Saw Mr Knowles twice: we fixed the title. Radcliffe Trust Meeting 2-3. Conversation with Carnarvon: see Mema. Saw the F.C.s—And went to see the Duchess as she lay, lifeless: less than 20 hours before I sat by her at dinner. C. went to Wellington. M. & I dined with the Sherbornes. Saw Lady C. Neville—Madame Bylandt[9]—Sir C. Trevelyan—Ld Leitrim.[10]

26. 5 S.E.

Chapel Royal 10 A.M. Marylebone Old Ch at 3.30. Then went to Argyll Lodge, & saw the Duke & the family. Saw Jas Wortley—Col. Clive—Mr M. Bernard—Dr A. Clark—Ld Lyttelton. Read Birmm Old & New[11]—Life of Moore[12]—Spurgeon

---

[1] Perhaps J. P. Sheldon, earlier a correspondent on Vaticanism; Hawn P.

[2] Arthur James Lyon Fremantle, colonel of the Coldstream guards.

[3] Deputation of Scottish nonconformists; *D.N.*, 24 May 1878, 2a.

[4] Not found; perhaps Major General Joseph Lyon Barrow, retired Indian army, is intended.

[5] *H* 240. 610.   [6] Probably John Bond, chaplain at the royal military academy, Woolwich.

[7] 'Liberty in the East and West', *Nineteenth Century*, iii. 189 (June 1878).

[8] Misc. business: *H* 240. 627.   [9] The wife of Charles Bylandt, the Dutch minister.

[10] Robert Bermingham Clements, 1847-92; 4th earl of Leitrim on murder of his father on 2 April 1878.

[11] R. K. Dent, *Old and new Birmingham*, published in parts (1878), and as a book (1879).

[12] S. Smiles, *George Moore* (1878).

Hist of Tabernacle[1]—Hoare on pre-Xtn Hospitals.[2] Wrote to Rev. C.N. Hoare—Sir J. Lacaita—C.G.

Secret.
Yesterday I saw Carnarvon, whose conversation was remarkable. He said significantly he had lost most of his faith in the words of many men. We had been talking of his (old) colleagues—and he pointed to Cross. But what I wish particularly to record are two statements given in the strictest confidence, which show how little at present within the royal precinct liberty is safe
1. It has happened repeatedly not only that Cabinet ministers have been sent for to receive 'wiggings' from the Queen—which as he said it is their affair & fault if they allow to impair their independence—but communications have from time to time been made to the Cabinet warning it off from certain subjects and saying she could not agree to this and could not agree to that
2. The Prince of Wales has said to Carrington, who is his friend, that when he comes to the Throne he intends to be his own foreign minister. (Why not learn the business first?)
    On the first of these I said it recalled James II and the Bill of Rights to which he assented. It is at any rate a position much more advanced than that of George III who I apprehend limited himself to a case of conscience like the Coronation Oath. But that controversy was decided once for all when Geo. IV after a terrible struggle agreed to the Roman Catholic Emancipation Bill.
    I said that such an outrage as this was wholly new, totally unknown in every Cabinet in which I had served; and that the corruption must be regarded as due to Lord Beaconsfield, which he entirely felt.
    As to the second point I said that if it were realised the Prince made King would not only be his own Foreign Minister, but would probably find that he would have his Foreign Office in foreign parts.[3]

27. M.

Wrote to J. Watson & Smith (Tel.)—Mr Spottiswoode—Marquis of Lorne. A laborious day. Finished my article for the Nineteenth Century. H. of C. 4¾-8 and 10¼-11¾. Looked up Acts, and spoke on the law &c. of the case of the Indian troops.[4] Late at night, worked on proofs of Homeric Primer. Saw Lord Hartington—Sir W. Harcourt—Lord Bath—Sir H. James—Ld F.C.—W. Lyttelton—C. Howard—Mr Childers. Dined with the F.C.s.

28. Tu.

Wrote to Messrs Spottiswoode 2—Mr W. Austin—Messrs J. Watson & Smith—Mr Knowles—A.J. Canning—H. Miller—H. Martin—C.G.—Scotts—Dr Dysdale—A. Pryor[5]—C.E. Another pretty hard day. Corrected and dispatched all the proofs of my article for N.C. Worked on proofs of Primer. Saw Mr Ouvry. Dined at 'the Club'. Saw Macgregor X.

---

[1] C. H. Spurgeon, *The Metropolitan Tabernacle* (1876).
[2] Untraced; probably by C. N. Hoare.
[3] Initialled and dated 26 May 1878, Add MS 44763, f. 130.
[4] *H* 240. 767.
[5] Perhaps Arthur Pryor, landowner in Essex.

29. Wed.

Wrote to Rev. Mr Woodward—J. Rees—E.A. Budge—Joseph Arch—Mr Weisen-feld—Mr Godfrey—Mr Fewster[1]—Mr Freeze—Mr Palmer. H. of C. 5-6. Saw Mr N. Hall. Worked on proofs of Primer. 3-5. At the Univ. Club. The vote about Keble was passed *nem. con.* We happily got rid of the question about the un-attached: whom a majority I think would have excluded.[2] 6¼-12¼. Dined at Dr Allons. A most hospitable reception & interesting conversation which in the evening became semi-public.

30. Th. Ascension Day.

Wrote to Mr Quinlan (O)[3]—Mr Atkin (O)—Mr Tallack—Mr Ouvry—Mr Dursley—Messrs Clay BP—G. Whitfield—J. Wingfield[4]—W.T. Stead. St James's at Noon: and H.C.—Thirteen to breakfast—much pleased with Miss Swanwick.[5] Saw Mr [C. A.] Thorndike Rice—Mr Curzon—E. Macgregor—Sir A. Panizzi—Mr Knowles—Sir J. Lacaita. Finished & dispatched the proofs of my Primer. Read Hayward's Goethe.

31. Frid.

Wrote to General Bowie—E.P. Pearson—F.J. Aldress—R. Southcombe—S. Morley MP—W.J. Williams—H.W. Seal[6]—W.T. Stead—T.T. Waterman—Treasr Mid. Temple—J. Latey—G. Harris—Mr Godley. Dined at Mr Wests. Worked much on arranging papers: but much remains. Calls. Saw Ld Northbrook—Mrs Grote—Ld Allington [*sc.* Alington]—Mrs Th.—Sir W. Harcourt—Mr West—Mr F. Hill.

Sat. June One 1878.

Wrote to Rev. Mr Whittington[7]—Lt Col. Clive—Mr Simmons—Mr Taylor—Mr Thomas—Messrs Barker & Co—Mr Gardner—Messrs B.H. & C.—Mr Living-ston[8]—Ed. Mayfair—Rev. Mr Horton[9]—Dr Dale—Mr Harris. Breakf. at Grillions. Dined at Coll. Physicians. Saw Duke of Argyll—Ld Winmarleigh—The Speaker—Mr Aveling[10]—Mr G. Harris. At the dinner Huxley's discourse on Harvey was remarkable: but he could not forbear a small touch at Belief.[11] Sat

[1] C. E. Fewster of Hull, on the liberal party's history; Hawn P.

[2] Gladstone spoke supporting the extension of membership of the Oxford and Cambridge club to non-collegiate graduates, and moved the previous question to avoid a hostile vote; United University Club Minutes Book, 128. Gladstone was put up to speak by E. Talbot; Add MS 44456, f. 340.

[3] Possibly Thomas Quinlan of the war office's clothing dept.

[4] Possibly John Harry Lee Wingfield of Tickencote, Stamford; a tory.

[5] Anna *Swanwick, 1813-99; novelist and promoter of women's education.

[6] Perhaps William Henry Seal, poet.

[7] Perhaps Richard Whittington, of Merchant Taylor's school, London.

[8] Perhaps J. L. Livingston of Liverpool; earlier a correspondent; Hawn P.

[9] Perhaps Francis Horton, curate of Bickerton.

[10] Thomas William Baxter Aveling, 1815-84; a leading congregational minister.

[11] Harvey's tercentenary; *T.T.*, 3 June 1878, 13b; Gladstone spoke briefly.

to Watts from 12 to 4.[1] He would but for courtesy willingly have had more. This length of time is really a national vice in English artists.

2. S. aft. Asc.

Chapel Royal 10 A.M. and 5.30 P.M.—At 6½ (to 8½) I attended Mr Newman Hall's remarkable service. He preached a Sermon some part of which would at Oxford 35 years back have brought him into the clutches of Vice Chancellor Winter. It was very brave. Wrote to Messrs Murray—Mr Ouvry—Rev. Dr Hornby—Ed. Echo—Mr Macmillan—Mr Godley—Rev. Mr Simpson—Mr Rathbone—Rev. Dr Dale—Mr H. Miller—Mr C. Montagu—Mr Kitson. Charles L[yttelto]n, & Edward dined. Read MacNaught Coena Domini[2]—St Raphael's Bristol[3]—Nineteenth C. on Voltaire—do Newton Gr. Relig. & Inscr.[4]—Contemp R. on Future Punishment.[5]

3. M. [On train]

Began with nausea and diarrhoea. It went off in aftn. Saw Dr Clark. Wrote to Duke of Bedford—Forfar Incumbent—Mr Marsh—Dr A. Clark—Mr Millais—Mr Irving (O)—C.G.—W.H.G. Saw W.H.G. (2)—Mr Ouvry—Roumanian Envoy—Ld Granville—Ld Lansdowne cum Deputn[6]—Mr Carrington. Read C.R. on Indian Fasts—Hayward's Goethe. Off at 8¾: joined the family party at St Pancras & travelled all night in a Pullmann bed with rest but no (continuous sleep). Conversation with the Duke [of Argyll].

4. Tu. [Roseneath, Dumbartonshire]

Wrote to C.G. We reached Roseneath[7] at 10 by Helensburgh. My nausea returned & the liver was a little deranged. Walk over this beautiful place with Lorne & others. He has been beyond anything attentive & kind. The party increased to about 30 in all. Saw the Duke in the evening. He asked my prayers. He will have better. Also Dr Macgregor.[8] Read Longfellow's Christus[9]—B. Smith's Carthaginians[10]—D. of A. (proof) on E. Question.[11]

[1] The portrait for Christ Church begun 19 May 74, shown at the Gaudy 1878 and found unacceptable; see 16 May 76n.
[2] By J. MacNaught (1878).
[3] The House of Charity at St. Raphael's, Bristol (1878).
[4] Nineteenth Century, iii. 1052, 1033 (June 1878).
[5] Contemporary Review, xxxii. 364 (June 1878); three articles.
[6] No account found.
[7] One of Argyll's seats, near Helensburgh, used as his chief Scottish home during the rebuilding of Inveraray after the fire of 1877.
[8] James *MacGregor, 1832-1910; minister of St Cuthbert's, Edinburgh, 1873-1910; well known for fervent preaching.
[9] By H. W. Longfellow (1873).
[10] See 15 May 78.
[11] G. D. Campbell, duke of Argyll, The eastern question from 1856, 2v. (1879); the preface is dated January 1879, but sections of the work circulated earlier; see 14 Oct. 78.

5. Wed. [Sheffield]

Rose better than yesty & packed for departure. After breakfast Dr Story[1] read a service, chiefly from Scripture, in the Library. We then set out in the Steamer for Kilmun. Many people were gathered: but the actual services were audible only to those within the building, a kind of vault above ground. Mr De Bunsen[2] read part of the Burial Service: Dr Macgregor made a prayer in the nature of an impressive & eloquent Sermon: and Dr Story delivered the blessing. This was an odd hash. Everything besides was beautiful and soothing. The Duke gave way on parting from the coffin of the beloved.[3] I bade farewell to him his daughters and all his family: their bearing, I mean especially the Duke & his daughters was admirable. The natural investiture of the burial place at Kilmun is noble in the highest degree: shaded by the mountains, kissed by the sea, sheltered from the storms, it is a figure of the gracious rest into which she has surely entered.

A portion of us went over straight to Greenock & thence to Glasgow. Here I visited Mr Smith[4] in St V. Place, and saw divers gentlemen: also I went to the Exhibition of Pictures which was highly interesting. Left Glasgow at 5. Reached Sheffield 12½. Went to Victoria. Read Bosworth Smith's Carthaginians.

6. Th. [Clumber]

Wrote to Mr Richmond—Sheffield Station Master—Mr Hayward—Mr Blackwell—Jas Lister—Mr Ouvry—S.E.G.—C.G. Off at 9.15 to Worksop. Excellent breakfast & good appetite after my derangement at the Lion. Then Mr Morris drove me over to Clumber. Arrived 11½. Went with Mrs Comber to see the unhealthy pictures, also surveyed the porcelain. Worked hard 4 or 5 hours upon the letters.[5] Mr Williams came in aftn. We walked to the waterworks & woods: then dined. Read Bosworth Smith.

7. Frid.

Wrote to W.H.G.—Mr Pennington—Bp Abraham—Prof. Cosciar[6]—Mr Newman—Mr Charles—Mr Adams—Mr M.H. Hakim. Today I worked on the papers with very short intervals from 8 A.M. to 7 P.M. & had assistance very pleasantly given from young Mr Richmond. Short and pensive walk—how could any walk here be other than pensive? Yesterday I walked with Mr Williams, saw the Turbine, & the young planting: also the Oak of 27 feet, which I had never known to exist. In evg read Bosworth Smith—D'Ohmann on Ottoman Empire[7]—Trial of Queen Caroline.[8]

---

[1] Robert Herbert *Story, 1835-1907; minister of Roseneath 1860-87; church reformer; professor of ecclesiastical history at Glasgow 1886-98.
[2] Henry George de Bunsen, chaplain to the duke of Sutherland.
[3] i.e. the duchess; see 24 May 78.
[4] Of Watson and Smith, his stockbrokers, at 40 St Vincent Place.
[5] Newcastle trust business.
[6] See 28 Mar. 76?
[7] Untraced.
[8] Probably *The Hour of Trial. A few stanzas [on the trial of Queen Caroline]* (1820).

8. Sat [Hawarden]

Worked on the papers from 7 to 2 P.M. and in a manner finished this stage of a very heavy business. Every one ought to arrange his papers on receipt; as far as the main points are concerned. Saw Mr Williams—Mr Dyer—Visited the garden. Off at 3. Visited Sparken:[1] magnificent cows. Reached Chester at 8.15 and Hawarden at 9.15. Read Bosworth Smith—Eurip. Andromachè.

9. Whits.

Ch. 11 A.M. (H.C.) and 6½ P.M. Wrote to Mr [J. R.] Green & made the corrections he suggested in the Homeric Revise. Read Huidekoper, Judaism in Rome[2]—Prenshore on Fasting Communion.[3] Much conversation with hearty & cheery Mr Gregory.[4]

10. Whitm.

Church 8.45 AM. And again at 10½, when Stephy delivered a very able and admirable sermon on the Clubs. Wrote to R.W. Hanbury[5]—Capt. Verney[6]—Mayor of Nottingham—Rev. D.B. Hooke[7]—Mr Miller—Mr Collins—H. Walford[8]—Mr Hibbert—J. Walker—E.A. Freeman—E.F. Bateman—U. Froude.[9] Read I Danneggiati Politici[10]—Athenaeus B.I.—Huidekoper—Smith's Dict. Antiquities—Bosworth Smith, Carthaginians—Eurip. Androm. We *walked* at the Festival of the Shepherds.

11. Whit Tu. & St Barnabas.

Ch. 8¾ AM. Mr Wright—Mr Dawson—C. Laflin—F. Clater—A. Evans—S.D. Waddy—Rev. Dr. Butler—Duke of Argyll—The Speaker—Mr Standish—Mrs Wemyss—Mr Holyoake. Finished Bosworth. Read Eurip. Androm. Read Report on Friendly Societies and Books of the Order of Shepherds. Saw Deputies of the Order—Mr Evans. 7-8¾. Took the Chair at the Shepherd's Meeting: and addressed them at some length.[11]

12. Wed. [London]

Ch. 8½ AM. Wrote to Mr Taylor Innes—Geo. Harris—C. Hull—Mr Gowan—E.F. Gray[12]—Mr Boothroyd—J. Gill. By the desire of the Shepherds I was formally

---

[1] By Worksop.   [2] F. Huidekoper, *Judaism at Rome B.C. 76 to A.D. 140* (1876).
[3] Untraced; reading uncertain.   [4] John Bates Gregory, managed Hawarden colliery.
[5] Robert William Hanbury, 1845-1903; tory M.P. Tamworth 1872-8, N. Staffs. 1878-80, Preston from 1885. See 17 June 78.
[6] (Sir) Edward Hope Verney, 1838-1910; captain R.N. 1877, contested several seats as a liberal; 3rd bart. 1894.
[7] Probably David Hooke, vicar of Beckingham, Notts., 1873-98.
[8] Henry Walford, master at Haileybury; later rector of Ewelme.
[9] *Sic*; not a relative of the historian.   [10] Not found.
[11] On thrift, the poor law and the duties of enfranchised working men; *T.T.*, 12 June 1878, 11b. The Loyal Order of Ancient Shepherds was one of the largest Friendly Societies; see P. Gosden, *Self-Help* (1973), 40.
[12] Probably Edmund Dwyer Gray, 1845-88; s. of Sir J. Gray; owned the *Freeman's Journal*; home rule M.P. 1877-88.

admitted a member of the Order. Great part of the Addresses read to me was really noteworthy for sound practical excellence. Read Longfellow's new Volume[1]—Eurip. Androm. (finished)—Fortnightly on Ld Beaconsfield—Vaccin.[2]

13. Th.

Wrote to Mr Dalrymple—Mr Solway. Saw Mr Knowles—The Speaker—Sir H. James—Mr A.T. Rice—Mr Newm. Hall—Mr Freeman—Mr Palgrave—Mr Rylands. Six to breakfast. H of C. $4\frac{1}{4}$-$7\frac{1}{2}$. Spoke on Mr Rylands's motion.[3] Read N.C. Symposium[4]—Chatham's Speeches.[5]

14. Fr.

Wrote to Dr Hornby—Messrs Routledge—Miss Swanwick—Mr Blackmore—Mr Macklehose—Mr Hallam—Messrs Murray—W.J. Williams—Blanchard Jerrold—Mr Bryce—Rev. A.T. Rice—Rev. Mr Bussell[6]—Rev. Serjeant[7]—Mrs Stephen[8]—Ld E. Clinton—Sir J. Watson—G.W. Vyse. Saw Mr Ouvry—The Speaker—Mr Dumaresq—Mr Adam—Mr Goschen—Mrs Morrison. Dined with the R. Neville's. Saw Russell: & another [R]. Read N.C. Symposium finished—The Conqueror's Dream.[9] H. of C. at $6\frac{1}{2}$.[10]

15. Sat.

Wrote to E.M. Richards—J.S. Randell[11]—Mons. S. Alpiny[12]—Rev. Mr Rorison—Rev. Dr Hannay[13]—Rev. W. Denton—Registrar, Aberystwyth—G.F. Watts—W.H. Mills[14]—E. Feather—D. Hay[15]—J.D. Hilton[16]—J.E. Page.[17] Fifteen to dinner: a pleasant party. Saw Sir A. Panizzi—Mr Millais—Ld Shaftesbury—Ld Halifax—Mr Hayward. Arranging books & papers. Began a Morceau on the Popular judgment in Politics for Mr Knowles.[18] Read Tracts—Mr Endean on Canon Farrar.[19] Arranging books & papers.

---

[1] H. W. Longfellow, *Kéramos and other poems* (April 1878).

[2] *Fortnightly Review*, xxix. 867 (June 1878).

[3] On treaties of 1856 and 1871; *H* 240. 1408.

[4] 'A Modern "Symposium"', *Nineteenth Century*, iii (May 1878); see 15 June 78.

[5] Perhaps *The speeches of the earl of Chatham with a biographical memoir* (1848).

[6] Frederick Vernon Bussell, chaplain of the Worksop workhouse.

[7] Perhaps Oswald Pattison Serjeant, rector of Syresham.

[8] Margaret E. Stephens, sent her late husband Thomas's* *Literature of the Kymry* (2nd ed. 1876).

[9] See 21 May 78.

[10] End of deb. on property valuation; *H* 240. 1527.

[11] Perhaps James S. Randell, wrote on education for the poor.

[12] Apparently involved in Turkish affairs; see 31 Dec. 78 fly leaf.

[13] Perhaps Alexander Hannay, Congregationalist minister and temperance reformer.

[14] William Hathorn Mills, wrote *Ballads of Hellas* (1878).

[15] Perhaps Dalrymple Hay; see 18 Feb. 64.

[16] Perhaps J. Deane Hilton, temperance writer.

[17] John E. Page, of Wolverhampton; journalist, on Greek lexicography; Hawn P.

[18] 'A Modern "Symposium". Is the popular judgment in politics more than just that of the higher orders?', *Nineteenth Century*, iv. 184 (July 1878), reprinted in *Gleanings*, i. 193.

[19] J. R. Endean, *What is the eternal hope of Canon Farrar?* (1878).

16. *Trin S.*

Chapel Royal 10 A.M. Old Marylebone 3.30 P.M. Saw J.S. Wortley—The T.G. daughters—Mr Albert Grey. Read Endean (finished)—Farrar's Reply in C.R.[1]— Catholic World on Future Punt[2]—Tulloch's Address[3]—Macnaught Coena Domini[4]—Various Tracts.

17. *M.*

Wrote to Rev. Dr Hutton—Mr Ouvry—Mr Sherrard—Mrs Hope—Mr Sec. Cross—Mr E.A. Budge—Messrs Spottiswoode B.P. H. of C. 4-7¼: and at 10.30. Spoke a few sentences on Mr Hanbury's shabby retreat.[5] Saw Mr Adam MP— Mr Mills MP.—Mr Hankey—Mr Godley—Mr Barry. Saw Harris & another [R]. Wrote my short paper for Mr Knowles's Symposium. Visited the Guards Chapel.

18. *Tu.*

Wrote to Ld Portsmouth—D. Slocombe[6]—Mr Millais—Mr Jesse White—H. Edwards—Watson & Smith—Ld De Tabley—Mr Hornsby Wright—Mr Freder- ick[7]—Scotts—G. Whale—B. Owen—Dr Hornby—Dr Hutton—Mr Knowles—R. Burnet. Saw Lady Portsmouth—Mr Baxter—Dr [G. C.] Hutton—Scotts. Dined at Mr Godleys. H of C. 2-3: again at six. And 10½-1½. Three visits in a day *now* form a rare event for me. Spoke on the Scottish Established Church: which, in that character has not I think another decade of years to live.[8] Saw M. Russell 3¼-5¼: with interest & uncertainty [R]. Read Memm of the Greek Sullogoi of Con- stantinople: with displeasure.[9]

19. *Wed.*

Wrote to Rev. M. MacColl—L. Blackwell—G. Whitehouse—Spottiswoodes (BP.)—Watsons (BP)—Mr Macfarlane—Mons. Jean D'Aristocles (Gk Memm)[10]—Captain Sidebotham[11]—Earl of Shaftesbury—Rev. S.E.G.—W.H.G.— Dr Marcus[12]—G. Ward—Mrs Grote—Mr Budge—Mrs Thompson. H. of C. 4-6.[13]

---

[1] F. W. Farrar, 'Eternal hope. A reply', *Contemporary Review*, xxxii. 569 (June 1878).

[2] Untraced.

[3] J. Tulloch, 'Position and prospects of the Church of Scotland' (1878).

[4] See 2 June 78.

[5] R. W. Hanbury withdrew his notice of a motion criticizing Gladstone's article (see 24 May 78); *H* 240. 1616.

[6] David Slocombe of Swansea, on joining the Shepherds; see 11 June 78; quoted in *T.T.*, 22 June 1878, 12f.

[7] Possibly J. J. Frederick, war office clerk.

[8] 'I do not see what arguments there are in favour of the Established Church, and I will reserve to myself any arguments that I may have to raise on the general question, until I hear on what grounds the Establishment is supported'; *H* 240. 1789.

[9] Presumably sent by D'Aristocles; quoted in [Baron Malortie], *Diplomatic sketches* (1879), iii. 187.

[10] See previous day.

[11] Probably William Sidebottom, 1841-1933; active in Cheshire politics and the volunteers; tory M.P. High Peak 1885-1900.

[12] Lewis Marcus, d. 1879; professor of latin at City of London college for ladies.

[13] Courtney's Women's Disabilities Removal Bill; *H* 240. 1800.

Saw Mr Bristow—Lancashire Congl Deputn—Mr Macmillan—Mr Muspratt (2)[1]—Mr Adam—Mr Leeman—W.H.G.—Ld R. Grosvenor (who conveyed our conclusion about the Flint Boroughs)[2]—Ld Just. Thesiger[3]—Mr Graham—Mrs Cowper Temple. Corrected proofs for Symposium. Dined at Mr Graham's. Chinese Minister's afr.[4] Saw Watts [R]. Read Llewellyn on Vivisection.[5]

20. Th.

Wrote to Mr R. Hunter—Mr J. West—Ld Granville—W.H.G.—H.J.G. H. of C. 4-5½ and 10-11.[6] Read De Lolme on the Constitn.[7] Thirteen to breakfast. Saw Mr Bryce—Mr MacColl—Mr Curzon—Mr Holyoake—Mr Errington—Sir G. Campbell—Ld Hanover *cum* Sir E. Cunliffe[8]—Mr Denton—Mr Leeman—Dr Haine—F. Leveson—Mr Childers—Mr Adam—Mr Samuelson. Saw Watts: also Bennett & another. A singular & sad opening of human life [R].

21. Fr.

Wrote to S. Peters—H.N.G. (l. & B.P.)—Dr Hornby—Mr Cooper—Rev. Mr Ogle[9]—J. Jones—Prof. Pritchard—Rev. Mr Rogers—Mr [J. E.] Hilary Skinner—Sig. L. Velli[10]—Mr Pincott—Rev. A.B. Vivian[11]—Mr Shepheard. Saw Dr Waters—Ld Hanmer—Sir E. Perry—Sir A. Panizzi—Sir C. Trevelyan—Duchess of Cleveland. Saw Linwood X. Dined at Sir C. Trevelyan's. Lord Houghton's afterwards. Began paper for North American Review.[12]

22. Sat.

Wrote to H. Walford—S. Bailey (l. & B.P.)[13]—Mr Adam (2)—Sir J. Lacaita—Rev Mr Baker—Mr Bryce—Miss K. Field—Mrs Francis—Rev. R. Scott—Mr Millais—Ld Granville. Dined at Mr Waddy's: to meet a large Wesleyan party. Saw Mr Thompson (3)—Scotts—Dr Moulton[14]—W.H.G.—Mr Jenkins—Mrs Th.—Lady Westmr. Read Geddes's Homer[15]—Hayward's Goethe: Pamphlets—The Turks Tract.

---

[1] Edmund Knowles Muspratt, 1833-1923; Liverpool chemical manufacturer; president of the Financial Reform Association; possible candidate for Flint boroughs (*T.T.*, 22 June 1878, 12f.).

[2] i.e. not to stand there.

[3] Alfred Henry Thesiger, 1838-80; lord justice of appeal from 1877.

[4] First grand reception by Kuo-Ta-Jen, recently arrived first accredited Chinese envoy.

[5] By W. H. Llewelyn (1876).

[6] Scottish roads; *H* 240. 1888.

[7] J. L. de Lolme, *Constitution de l'Angleterre* (1771).

[8] *Sic*; *sc*. R. H. Cunliffe.

[9] Probably John Lockhart Ogle, d. 1924; taught at Merchant Taylor's 1878-80.

[10] Luigi Velli, of Rome; wrote on Newman; Hawn P; see 23 June 78.

[11] London nonconformist; had sent verses; Hawn P.

[12] Signed article, 'Kin beyond Sea', *North American Review*, cxxvii. 179 (September 1878), reprinted in *Gleanings*, i. 203: published in New York, ed. A. Thorndike Rice.

[13] Of Bath; Hawn P.

[14] William Fiddian *Moulton, 1835-98; Wesleyan biblical scholar; headmaster of the Leys, Cambridge, from 1874.

[15] W. D. Geddes, *The problem of the Homeric poems* (1878); discussed in Gladstone's 'The slicing of Hector', see 11 Sept. 78.

23. 1 S. Trin.

Chapel Royal 10 A.M. Charlotte St 7 PM. Saw Ld Clanwilliam—Ld Lyttelton—Mr Thompson. Wrote to Mrs Morrison—Mr Thompson. Read Morris's Life[1]—Parousia[2]—Physiologist on The Devil[3]—Velli, Ente Supremo.

24. M. St John B.

Wrote to Mrs Oliver of Thornwood[4]—Professor Geddes—Rev. Mr Bailey—Dean of Manchester—Rev E.C. Wickham—Messrs Macmillan—C.J. Chesshyre—Mr Budge—Mr Hodge—Mr Warren. Dined at Lord F.C.s. Saw Mr Adam *cum* Ld Rosebery & Mr Reid on the Midlothian seat—Ld F. Cavendish—Mr Baxter—Mr & Mrs Dumaresq (who breakfasted). Read Mrs Oliver's interesting Memoirs of the Gledstanes—Hayward's Goethe (finished)—Sir S. Romilly's Speeches.[5] Saw Gray [R]. H of C. $3\frac{3}{4}$-8.[6]

25. Tu.

Wrote to J. Wood BP.—J. Hoffgaard—J. Douglas—Mr Fairbrother[7]—Mr Panchaud—J. Richards—Mr Knowles—Mr Lowne[8]—E. Stanhope. Distribution of copies of my Primer.[9] Saw Ld Granville—Mr Barclay MP.—Ld E. Clinton—Sir H. Johnstone—Mr Ouvry. H of C. 5-$6\frac{1}{2}$.[10] Read Delolme—Fortnightly on Science & the dislike to it. *NB*.[11] Seven to dinner: Newcastle Trust. Saw Linwood: *cui bono?* [R]

26. Wed.

Mary returned. Wrote to H.J.G. BP.—T. Warne[12]—J. Evans—Prince L.L. Bonaparte—T. Turner—J. Haswell—Rev. Mr Mahaffy—Ld Blantyre. Sat to Mr Millais $11\frac{1}{2}$-$1\frac{1}{2}$.[13] Luncheon at Prince Bonaparte's & much interesting conversation of his $1\frac{3}{4}$-$4\frac{1}{2}$!![14] Eight to dinner. Saw Sir R. Phillimore—Mr Cartwright—Sir H. Johnstone. Read India Vernacular Press Papers[15]—Jenkins on Disestablishment[16]—De Lolme on Constn.

---

[1] Probably W. B. Morris, *The life of St Patrick* (1878).
[2] *The Parousia: a critical inquiry into the New Testament* (1878).
[3] *The Devil demonstrated. By a Physiologist* (1878).
[4] Mrs Oliver of Thornwood, Hawick, had sent her *The Gledstanes and the siege of Coklaw* (1878), its conclusion adulatory about the diarist.
[5] *The speeches of Sir S. Romilly in the House of Commons*, 2v. (1820).
[6] Cattle plague; *H* 241. 133.
[7] Samuel Fairbrother of Hawarden.
[8] Edward Yates Lowne of Camberwell on state sponsorship of the theatre; Add MS 44457, f. 72.
[9] See 24 Sept. 77n.   [10] Cattle plague; *H* 241. 211.
[11] G. H. Lewes in *Fortnightly Review*, xxix. 805 (June 1878).
[12] Perhaps of Frederick Warne, publishers.
[13] Reproduced in this volume. The first of Millais' three portraits—three-quarters length standing—dated 1879, commissioned by the duke of Westminster, though the initiative apparently taken by Millais (see 18 Mar. 78n.); sold after the home rule crisis to Sir Charles Tennant and now in the National Portrait Gallery; a popular engraving, a pair with Millais' Disraeli, was sold from 1881. See 6 Aug. 78 and J. E. Millais, *Life and letters of Sir J. E. Millais* (1899), ii. 110, where this sitting is dated 1879.   [14] See 12 Nov. 73.
[15] See Ramm II, i. 71.   [16] E. Jenkins, *Church and the law* (1878).

27. Th.

Wrote to Chairman Flint Lib. Com.—W.J. Williams—E.D. Wright—Mrs Dunbar—Mr Jesse Hart—Mr Huntriss[1]—Mr W. Evans—Helen J.G.—Rev. W. Hirst[2]—W. Kelly—Rev. F. Bony.[3] Twelve to breakfast: Mrs Ponsonby & Mrs Webb make excellent company. Saw Mr Grove—Mr Froude—Mr Adam—Ld F. Cavendish—Ld R. Grosvenor—Sir H. James—W.H.G. Ld Granville's (on Indian Press) 2½-4. Dined at Lady Cowper's. Read India Papers (finished)—Contessa E. Allori[4]—T. Hughes on the 'Old Church'.[5]

28. Fr.

Helen's (Mrs H.G.'s) birthday. All blessings be with her. Wrote to Ld R. Grosvenor—Mr Kavanagh—Rev. Mr Capes—Mrs Dempsey—Mr Saddler—Mr Laing MP—Mr Harris. Saw Harris X. Day: who goes home D.G. Saw Mr Stillman—Mr Fawcett—Mr Stoughton—Mrs Stoughton—Ld Huntley. Dined with Mr Childers. Mr Cunliffe Brooks after. Made a beginning for N.A.R.[6] Read Contessa D'Alloro—De Lolme—F.H..X

29. Sat. St Peter's.

Wrote to Miss M'Kenzie BP.—W. Lyttelton B.P.—J. Watson & Smith—J. Macbain—Manager N. & S.W. Bank Rhyl—Rev. J.H. Morgan[7]—Macmillans—Rt Rev. Dr Döllinger—Editors Internat. Review[8]—A. Hyams—Mrs Weldon—Mrs Bonsil—Mrs Ramsay—E. Vitali[9]—Mr Stothard. Wrote "some" for NRA. Review. Read De Lolme—Ram on War[10]—Verax, ans. to Quarterly[11]—Contessa E. d'Alloro. Dined at Miss Leslie's.[12] Conversation with her—with Mr Russell—Sir A. Panizzi.

30. 2 S. Trin.

St Paul's mg. St M.M., Munster Squ. evg. Saw Sir Walter James—Ld Wenlock—Edw. Lyttelton. Dined at Sybella's. Read Ram on War (finished)—Macnaught, *Coena Domini*[13]—Baldwin Brown's Address.[14]

Mond. July One 78.

Wrote to Ld C. Russell BP.—Mr Ruskin BP—Mrs Collins (O)—Mr Elliot[15]—Mr Barnard—Sir Geo. Bowen—Dean of Windsor (BP.)—Rev R. Scott—J. Ram—Mr

---

[1] Reading uncertain.   [2] William Hirst, incumbent of Cumberworth.
[3] Apparently a nonconformist.
[4] *Notti insomni. Memorie della contessa Elisa d'Alloro raccolte da Roberto Stuart* (1878).
[5] T. Hughes, *Old Church, What shall we do with it?* (1878).
[6] See 21 June 78.
[7] Probably John Holdsworth Morgan, d. 1908?; vicar of Forest Hill 1872-88, of Anstey 1888-92.
[8] Not published.
[9] Egidio Vitali, London wine shipper.
[10] J. Ram, *The philosophy of war* (1878).
[11] [H. Dunckley], *The Crown and the Constitution. Reply of 'Verax' to the Quarterly Review* (1878).
[12] The Misses Leslie lived at Bourdon House, Davies Street.   [13] See 2 June 78.
[14] J. B. Brown, 'Our theology in relation to the intellectual movement of our times' (1878).
[15] Robert Elliot, Northumbrian miner, had sent verses; Add MS 44457, f. 85.

Clarkson—M. Leyden—Rev S.E.G. Further distribution of Primers. Arranging papers & letters. Dined with Sir W. James. H of C. 10¼-1¼ (Cattle Bill).[1] Read De Lolme. Wrote for B.N.A. Review. Saw Mr Thorndike Rice[2]—Mrs Grote—Mr Laing—Mr Fawcett—Mr Stanhope—Ld Hartington—Mr Boord—Sir G. Campbell—Sir W. James—Mr Edwards—Mr Goschen.

2. Tu.

Wrote to Messrs T. & B.—Messrs Watson—Made Novikoff—Mrs Conder[3]—Mr Ouvry—Mr Thorne—Mr Planché—R. Elliot. Saw Mr Saunders (Dentist) 11½ AM.—Ld Granville—Ly M. Farquhar—Mr Stanhope—Mr Adam—Sir Thos G.—Mr Agnew. Dined at Sir Thos G.s. Saw Beaumont—& Gray who D.G. is to [go] to friends tomorrow [R]. Read Verax: reply (finished)—De Lolme—Tracts.

3. Wed.

Wrote to Sir E. Perry—Pres. Hull Institution[4]—Mr H. Laurence[5]—Watson & Smith (Tel)—Rev. R. Brydom—Rev. A. Westcombe—Mr Tennyson B.P.—Mr Ruskin B.P. Dined with the Cardwells. Saw Beaumont, & two more, with some hope at least for one. Sat to Millais 12-1¾. Luncheon party afterwards. Saw Ld Cardwell. Wrote for N.A. Review. Read Delolme, & divers.

4. Th.

Wrote to Mrs Simon—W.T. Stead—Mr Du Ranci—Mrs Heywood—Sir W.C. James—Mrs Birks—N. Pocock—A.T. Rice—E. Jenkins MP—Rev. Dr Hornby—Mr Winnerz[6]—Watson & Smith. Fourteen to breakfast. Saw (specially) Prof. [W. G.] Geddes—Mr Thorndike Rice. Saw Mr Fawcett—Mr Farley *cum* Gen. Despotovich[7]—Sir T.E. May, an invalid—Mr Palgrave—Mr Green—Ld Hatherley—Mr Festing.[8] Dined at Mr Palgrave's. Wrote for N.A. Review. Read Fortnightly on Ireland.[9]

5. Fr.

Wrote to Mrs Morrison—Mr S.E. Thomas[10]—Rev. Mr Leigh—Sig. Domenighini[11]—Watson & S.—Mr Bramwell—Mr Adam—Mr H. Hennessy.[12] Dined at Lady Ashburton's. Read Virg. Æn. VI. Saw Bp of Bath & Wells—Ld Rosebery—Ld Fortescue—Sir A. Panizzi—Mrs Th.—Mr Cowper Temple. H of C. 11-12.[13] Wrote for N.A.R.

---

[1] *H* 241. 500.   [2] i.e. about the *North American Review* article; see 12 Sept. 77.
[3] Probably the wife of Dr E. R. Conder of Leeds, correspondent later in the year; Hawn P.
[4] Business untraced.   [5] Perhaps Herbert Laurence, London dentist.
[6] Name scrawled.
[7] Mileta Despotović, a Serb who had long served in the Russian army, acted as one of two Bosnian representatives at the Berlin conference; Sumner, 531.
[8] Probably Major E. R. Festing of the cttee. on education, science and art.
[9] *Fortnightly Review*, xxx. 26 (July 1878).
[10] Probably the journalist, who ed. *Celebrities of the day* (1881).
[11] See also 9 July 78, presumably the same family.
[12] Henry Hennessy of the Royal college of science, Dublin; had written on Irish education, supporting the 1873 Bill; Hawn P.   [13] Probably the last deb., on Irish land; *H* 241. 944.

6. Sat. [Eton]

Wrote to Mr Williams—Mr Poulton—Mr Jasper More—Mr Ouvry—Mr Taylor[1]—Mr Tweedie[2]—Sir R. Blennerhassett. Read Hutton's Scott[3]—Geddes's Homer.

At 11 we went to the Herbert Lonsdale marriage.[4] May God avert its evil omens & turn it to honour & good. We remained near the West End of the Church & left the Church forthwith at the close of the service. We had already declined the breakfast. Saw Mr Thorndike Rice—Ld Granville. At 4.40 we started for Eton: & were most kindly received by Dr & Mrs Hornby. The Lecture was 8-9½: very kindly received.[5] This was an employment as congenial as that of the forenoon was jarring. Indeed our children remonstrated against our going to the marriage at all.

7. 3 S. Trin.

Eton Chapel 10½-1. A deeply interesting scene: Holy Communion, & (probably) 150 boys communicants. St George's in the afternoon. Some guests to dinner. Visited Curzon's room: & the room of the Debating Society to show the old books. Conversation with Dr Hornby—Miss Evans[6]—Mr Maldon—Mr Lux-moore—The Dean. Read Algers on Future Life[7]—Memoir of Mr De Lisle & Sermons[8]—Bp of Winchester's Charges.

8. M. [London]

Wrote to Mr Williams—Mr Townshend—Mr Clement (O)—H. Sandbach—Mr Vickers—Mr Puseley—Mr Hervon—Mr Steare. St George's 10½ AM. Off at 11.35 to London. Dined at Ld Granville's. Saw Hawtrey Monument. Saw Sir T. Biddulph—Gen. Ponsonby—Dr Hornby—Ld Hartington—V.C. Wrench—Ld Granville—Mrs Tyler—Mr Adam MP.—King Pepple![9]—& Mr Blydon.[10] Saw Gray. X. I give by way of specimen the requests which the Post brought me today.
1.A. for a picnic at Clumber.
2.B. to visit a sculptor & judge the bust of a man I have not seen 3 times in the last 30 years.
3. Autograph (Canada)

[1] John Taylor of Liverpool; on Seaforth church; Add MS 44457, f. 107.
[2] James Tweedie of Biggar; declining to lay foundation stone; Hawn P.
[3] R. H. Hutton, *Sir Walter Scott* (1878).
[4] Constance Gladys, 3rd da. of Sidney Herbert, m. St George Henry Lowther, 1855-82, 4th earl of Lonsdale; in 1885 she m. earl De Grey, 4th marquis of Ripon. Educated a Roman catholic, she is described in *The Complete Peerage*, viii. 137 as 'a very handsome woman, fond of music, a friend of Edward VII'.
[5] Organized by the young G. N. *Curzon; see 6 May 78n., *T.T.*, 8 July 1878, 11e, and *Eton Chronicle*, 18 July 1878, 1126. Curzon arranged the questions in advance, believing his contemporaries would be 'too shy'; Add MS 44457, f. 81. See also R. W. Pfaff, *Montague Rhodes James* (1980), 30.
[6] Jane Evans, H. N. Gladstone's Dame.
[7] See 5 Aug. 71.
[8] C. Tondini, 'Two sermons preached on the death of A. L. M. Phillipps de Lisle' (1878).
[9] Obscure.
[10] E. W. Blyden (see 16 June 60), entertained by diarist at the Commons; see H. R. Lynch, *E. W. Blyden* (1970), 180.

4. Do (U.S.)
5. E. Return of papers.
6.F. To visit a public celebration already twice refused.
7.F. to acquaint him when I am to speak on Indian Press Act, & arrange for his admission.
8.G. To subscribe a second time towards a Sewing machine for a person whom I do not know.
9.H. To find a situation for a Civil Engineer
10.J. To make an appointment & hear the case between two Liberal Marylebone Institutions.
11.K. Blind College at Munster. Request to attend Anniversary.
12.L. Canadian requests a letter on the Eastern Question, in which he is interested.
13.M. To attend Anniversary of the Belfast Clerks Association, for a subscription.
14.N. To attend a Conversazione at King's College on Friday.
With these were three or four letters on public & private affairs which really pertained to the substantial business of the day. It was an easy post & did not in all I think bring more than 30 to 35 letters & packets.
H. of C. 4¼-8. An astounding announcement of the new Asiatic Empire: hard to take in at once.[1] Read Hutton's Scott.

9. Tu.

Wrote to Col. Romilly—Mr J. Langford—Capt. Verney—Rev. M. M'Coll—C.W. Jones—Miss Domenighini—Mrs Grote—Mr Ouvry—G. Smith—Mr Nicholls—B. Parry—Dr Stainer. Sat long under the hands of Mr Saunders. Saw Mr E. Talbot—Ld Selborne—Sir W. Harcourt—Mr Forster—Mr Stansfeld—Sir J. Stephen—Ld Cottesloe. H. of C. 2¼-4.[2] Dined at Mr Verney's. Read Hutton's Scott.

10. Wed.

Wrote to Mr Livingstone. 11-2. Sat to Mr Millais. 2-2½. H. of C.[3] Saw Mr Fawcett—Mr Adam—Lady Stanley—Mr Walpole. 2½-5. Meeting at Granville's. The leaders obtained postponement till the Protocols appear. 12 to dinner. Conversation with Prince L. Napoleon who pleased every one. Read Hutton's Scott. Wrote for N.A.R.

11. Th.

Wrote to Rev. Mr Hodgson—Rev. Mr Wakeham—F. Dickinson—D. Robertson—Mr Richardson BP—Certain Bulgarians (Bourgas)[4]—Editor of Echo—Mr Orlebar[5]—Mr Serpell—Mr Millais—Mr Ashworth—H. Pitman—W. Thomas.

[1] Questioned J. A. Cross on his revelation of the Anglo-Turkish convention of 4 June, by which Britain obtained Cyprus and undertook to defend 'the Asiatic territories of the Sultan' against Russia in exchange for internal reform; *H* 241. 966.
[2] Highways; *H* 241. 1071.   [3] Real Estate Intestacy Bill; *H* 241. 1163.
[4] On tolerance of Moslems in the new provinces; copy in *T.T.*, 15 July 1878, 10f.
[5] Augustus Scobell Orlebar, a schoolboy at Eton, had written on diarist's lecture there; Hawn P.

Fifteen to breakfast. Saw Sir [T. G.] Briggs—Mr Planché—Bp Coplestone—Mr Green—Mr Luttrell—Prof. Seeley—Mr Leeman—Mr Chamberlain—Mr C. Howard—Mr F. Leveson. H. of C. 4¼-6¼ & 11½-3. (Irish Sunday Closing Bill.)[1] Attended Meeting of Charity Voting [Reform] Assocn and spoke at it.[2] Read De Lolme. Wrote for N.A.R.

12. Fr.

Breakfast in bed: & rose at 11. Wrote to Ld Halifax—Mr Millais—Mr Sykes Whalley—Warden of Trin. Coll. NB.—Mr Libbey[3]—Mr Stanley Clarke[4]—Mr Westropp BP—Mr Bayley—J. Howard—Dr Roberts. To Mr Saunders at 3.30. Royal Academy 4¼-5½. Dined with Mr Bryce: & conversation with Bp of Manchester—Dr Abbot—Mr Bryce jun.[5]—Mr Robertson Smith.[6] Saw two [R]. Read Hutton's Scott—Poole's Turkey (Preface).[7]

13. Sat.

Wrote to Dean of Winchester—Rev. Mr Lendrum—Mr Scott Fraser[8]—Mr Connell—S. Peters—Mr Macmillan—R.H. Hutton—N.J. Smith—R. Bruce—Mr Stack. 3-5. Radcliffe Trust Meeting. 5-7. Marlborough House Garden Party. The Princess greeted us most kindly. Saw Ld Bath: & various diplomatists: Musurus very genial but sad: the Belgian sad about the Treaty with Turkey. Dined with the Dean of St Pauls: conversation with Ld Blachford, Bp of Colorado, Mrs Church.[9] Wrote for N.A.R. Read Hutton's Scott.

14. 4 S. Trin.

St Pauls mg (H.C.) 10½-1½. Munster Squ. evg. Saw Ld Granville *cum* Ld Wolverton. Conversation with Helen on her studies. Read London Divines.[10]—Bonwick's Egyptian Religion[11]—Parousia:[12] & divers.

15. M.

Wrote to Mr Stearns (O)—R. Hamilton—J. Tweedie—Ld Granville—Mr Stack—M. Stark—S. Walk—Ly Spencer. H. of C. 4-8 (Spoke on Irish Intermediate

---

[1] H 241. 1248.

[2] T.T., 12 July 1878, 10d.

[3] Jonas M. Libbey, editor of the *Princeton Review*.

[4] Perhaps of Accrington Liberal Club; this day's letter to its chairman on proposed visit to Hawarden printed in a cutting from the *Daily News*, mounted in the journal.

[5] Unclear; James Bryce, his host, d.s.p.

[6] William Robertson *Smith, 1846-94; semitic scholar; as free church professor at Aberdeen, centre of controversy in late 1870s, lost his chair 1881 for indiscreetly 'advanced' articles in *Encyclopaedia Britannica*, which he ed.; professor of Arabic at Cambridge 1883.

[7] *The people of Turkey. By a Consul's daughter and wife*, ed. S. L. Poole, 2v. (1878).

[8] J. Scott Fraser of Liverpool had sought advice; Hawn P.

[9] Helen Frances, wife of R. W. Church.

[10] Anon. work sent by the author, Malcolm Stark, journalist; Gladstone sent a note of encouragement, Add MS 44456, f. 116; see 20 Nov. 78n.

[11] J. Bonwick, *Egyptian belief and modern thought* (1878).

[12] See 23 June 78.

Education)[1] and 10½-11½. Dined with the F. Cavendishes. Another visit to Mr Saunders. Wrote for N.A.R: finished the MS. Read Hutton's Scott—Berlin Treaty[2]—& sundries.

16. Tu.

Wrote to G. Harris—E.A. Budge—Watson & Smith—Mr Thorndike Rice—Miss Humphreys—Mr Richardson B.P.—Mr Ouvry—T. Cooper—E. Robinson—Ld Halifax (BP)—Archdn Denison B.P.—M. Gennadios. Finished MS for N.A.R. Saw Ld Provost of Glasgow—Ld Granville—Mr Adam—Mr Bayley[3]—Ld Spencer—Ld Bath. Saw two [R]. Dined at Spencer House. H of C. 5½-7¼ and 11-11¼. Spoke on Cattle Bill v[ersus] Treaties.[4] Sir R. Wallaces party 4½-5½.

17. Wed.

Wrote to C. Layton BP[5]—Mr Macunslane[6]—Mr Gardiner—Mr Morley—Mr Hodson. Dined at Lord Hatherley's. Sat to Millais 1-3¼. Nat. Portr. Gall. meeting 3¼-4½. H of C. 12-1 and at 4¾.[7] Worked on revision for N.A.R. Saw Scotts—Ld Hatherley (Hook Letters)[8]—Sir C. Dilke. Finished Hutton's Scott.

18. Th.

Wrote to Mr Higman—C. Layton (B.P.)—R. M'Donnell—Rev. W. Cadman—Rev. W. Todd Martin[9]—Mrs Charter—Mr Warren—Mr Leake. Read Q.R. on Crown & Army.[10] Fourteen to breakfast. Saw Abp of Dublin—Mr Hutton—Dr Abbot—M. Delganni[11] cum M. Gennadios—Sig. Tuccillo—Mr Macdonald—Southwark Deputation—Sig. Pantaleone—Bp of Ely—Sir A. Panizzi. Saw Hamilton (friend), Linwood [R]. H of C. 6½-8¼: & H. of L.[12] Finished revision of MS.

19. Fr.

Wrote to Prof. Rolleston—A. Macdonald—J.H. Irving—Mr Daly (O)—Ld Hartington—F. Pattison[13]—Mrs Pettigrew—Mr Childers. H. of C. 3¾-6.[14] Read Wilkinson[15]—C.Q.R.—Beaconsfield's Speech[16]—Encyclop. Brit. Saw Ld Wolverton

---

[1] Supporting Lowther's Bill; H 241. 1497.
[2] Signed on 13 July 1878; official version in PP lxxxiii. 675.
[3] Edric H. Bayley, secretary of the Southwark liberal association; see 20 July 78.
[4] H 241. 1667.
[5] Charley Layton, London printer and publisher.
[6] Apparently sic.
[7] Contagious diseases; H 241. 1688.
[8] Probably on the quite extensive use of Gladstone's letters in W. R. W. Stephens, Life of W. F. Hook, 2v. (1878); correspondence on the use of these in Add MS 44457.
[9] William Todd Martin, Ulster presbyterian minister and anti-Darwinist.
[10] Quarterly Review, cxlvi. 232 (July 1878).
[11] Greek minister for public worship.
[12] In the Lords, Beaconsfield's statement on the Congress of Berlin, with Granville, Derby, and Salisbury, and the dispute about Derby's 'veracity'; H 241. 1753.
[13] Perhaps Frank (1834-1922), Mark Pattison's br.
[14] Contagious diseases; H 241. 1974.
[15] G. H. Wilkinson, 'The broken covenant' (1878).
[16] Probably T.T. report; see 18 July 78n.

—Do *cum* Ld Halifax—Bp Doane (Albany)[1]—Ld Hartington—Mr Phillips—Ld F. Cavendish—Mr Childers—Bps of N. Scotia, Rupert's Land, and.... Saw Russell [R].

20. Sat.

Wrote to Rev W. Webb—Princ. Librarian (O)—Ld Granville—Mr Bellamy[2]—Mr Hankey. Saw Mr Leake—Mr Bayley—& others. Off at 3 to Bermondsey (Southwark): & spoke 1 h. 20 m (in very strong heat) to a crowded room.[3] Court Theatre: Olivia:[4] a family party.

21. 5 S. Trin.

St Mich. Ch. Square mg. Munster Square evg. Saw the T.G.s & discussed Helen's[5] case. Wrote to H.J.G.—Mrs Watkins. Read Parousia—Helie, Loi unique[6]—Manning, Unity of the Church.[7]

22. M.

Wrote to S.E. de Vere—Hon G. Onslow—Mr Sherlock Hare[8]—Rev. W.T. Martin—Rev. Dr. Webster—Rev. A. Macintyre—Mr Vickers—Mr Grove—Mr Knowles—Mr Adair—Mr Sampy. H. of C. $4\frac{3}{4}$-$6\frac{1}{4}$. Read Gray's China[9]—Dacosta on India.[10] Last visit (pr.) to Mr Saunders. Corrected revises for N.A.R. Dined at Lady Taunton's. Saw Mrs Th.—Dean Stanley—Mr Adam—Adm. Egerton—Sir H. James—Sir W. Harcourt.

23. Tu.

Wrote to Mr A. Smith—Mr Thorndike Rice—Mr G.K. Martin—Bp of Fredericton—Mr C. Layton BP (2)—Lady Westbury. Read up Indian Press Papers. Finished correcting proofs NAR. Dined with the F.C.s. H. of C. 4-$8\frac{1}{4}$ and $9\frac{3}{4}$-$1\frac{3}{4}$. Spoke (1 h) on Indian Press Act: & replied.[11] Good was certainly done by the debate. Read Protocols.[12]

24. Wed.

Wrote to Rev. Stopford Brooke—Mr Cyrus Field—Sec. Poplar Young Mens Assocn—Rev. Mr Fleming—Rev. Dr Nevin[13]—Rev. H. W. Phillot[14]—Mr Stead—

---

[1] William Croswell Doane, 1832-1913; bp. of Albany, U.S.A. 1869; a friend of Pusey; see Add MS 44457, f. 146.

[2] Perhaps Henry Thomas Bellamy of the Audit department.

[3] Praising 'what is commonly called the Birmingham organization for the Liberal party'; *T.T.*, 22 July 1878, 10c.

[4] With Ellen Terry; *T.T.*, 20 July 1878, 10f.   [5] i.e. his sister.

[6] Perhaps A. Hélie, *La Rome des Papes* (1861).   [7] See 27 Feb. 42.

[8] London barrister.   [9] J. H. Gray, *China*, 2v. (1878).

[10] J. Dacosta, *Facts and fallacies regarding irrigation as a prevention of famine in India* (1878).

[11] Moved a motion for an Address, attacked the Act and defended the Indian press from charges of disloyalty; defeated in 152:208; *H* 242. 48.

[12] Of the Congress of Berlin; *PP* 1878 lxxxiii. 391.

[13] Robert Jenkins Nevin, American clergyman; see Add MS 44461, f. 164.

[14] Henry Wright Phillott, rector of Staunton-on-Wye, sent Latin verses; Add MS 44457, f. 150.

Mr Dean—[J. E.] H. Skinner—Mr Slocombe—E. Percival—Mr Elridge.[1] Sat to Millais 12-1½. Fifth & *last* sitting. H. of C. at 1¾.[2] Dined with the Phillimores. Saw Marquis Vitelleschi—Lady Gilford[3]—Sir R. Phillimore. Read Protocols: Hansard—Hill on Dr Johnson[4]—Roth on Russian Peasantry.[5]

25. Th. St James.

Marriage day & T.G.s birthday. Not of the calm its memories require.
Wrote to Mr Laporte[6]—Mr Howarth—Mr Thornley[7]—Mr Wilson—Mr Thomas—Sir Thos G.—F.S. Buckey—G. Spencer—F. Ouvry—H.L. Roth—Dr Elam—Mrs Th.—Mr [blank]. Eleven to dinner. Saw Ld Granville—Bp [Medley] of Fredericton—Mr Lowe. H of C. 4¼-7½: and after dinner.[8] Read Protocols—Denison's Notes of his Life.[9]

26. Fr.

Wrote to J. Watson & Smith—Capt. Burnaby (& draft)[10]—Sec. Metrop. Dist. Co BP—Mr Clark cum Mr Sim—Messrs Walford—Rev. M. M'Coll—Made H. Loyson—Mr Jos Moore—Mr Fyffe[11]—Mr Barrett—Mr Lang. Finished correction of revises for N.A. Review. Dined with the F.C.s. Read Protocols—Cyprus. Saw the O'Conor Don—Ld F. Cavendish—Mr Saunders—Dr Acland—Miss Hosmer, & her Statue.[12] Suffered all day from depressing & sharp pain of a gumboil.

27 Sat.

Was better in the morning but with my face completely distorted. Rose at 11.30. Wrote to Messrs Williams & Co—Mr Vickers—Mr Fitzharry—Mr Hawkins—J. Hall—Miss Mitchell. Walk in Regent's Park: now perhaps as well wooded as Hyde Park. Retired early. Read Protocols—Q.R. on Mad. Du Deffand[13]—Mirza Peer Buksh—Revue Internationale.

28. 6 S. Trin.

St James's Mg Charlotte St evg. Saw Ld Granville—Bp [Mylne] of Bombay—Père Hyacinthe & Mad. Loyson.[14] These three came to luncheon. Much

---

[1] Perhaps G. J. Eldridge, British consul in Beirut.   [2] Probably for questions; H 242. 135.
[3] Elizabeth Henrietta Meade, Lady Gilford, later Lady Clanwilliam.
[4] By G. B. Hill (1878).
[5] Henry Ling Roth, anthropologist, had sent his *Agriculture and peasantry of Eastern Russia* (1878).
[6] Perhaps Kroll Charles Laporte of Southport, correspondent in 1880; Hawn P.
[7] Perhaps James Thornely of Southport, an admirer; Hawn P.
[8] Questioned Bourke and Northcote on Anglo-Russian agreement; H 242. 219, 230.
[9] G. A. Denison, *Notes of my life, 1805-1878* (1878); much material on diarist.
[10] Frederick Augustus Burnaby, 1842-85; journalist and mercenary; agent of Stafford House cttee. in Turkish war 1877-8; commanded a Turkish brigade 1877; contested Birmingham as a tory 1880. See Add MS 44457, ff. 138, 188.
[11] Charles Allan Fyffe, London barrister.
[12] See 5 Dec. 66; perhaps the fountain given to Lady M. Alford; see C. Carr, *Harriet Hosmer* (1913), 227, 318.
[13] *Quarterly Review*, cxlvi. 141 (July 1878).
[14] Gladstone referred to his case in his speech on 30 July.

interesting conversation. Otherwise a restful day. Read Parousia—Ch. Quart. R. on Cathedrals[1]—Bp Dupanloup on Voltaire[2]—Massari, Vitt. Emmanuele (his last days)[3]—Alger on Future State[4]—& sundries.

29. M.

Up as usual: nearly right again. Wrote to Ld Selborne—Mirza Peer Buksh—Mrs Marriner—Mr Layton—Miss Swanwick—Mr Merell (O)—Rev. Mr Sanderson—Mr Haseldine[5]—Miss Talbot (O)—Rev. Mr Mountain.[6] H of C. $4\frac{1}{4}$-8 and 10-$12\frac{1}{2}$.[7] Worked much upon the Protocol folio & nearly finished. Also read The People of Turkey.[8] Saw divers: Mr Cross. Dined at Sir C. Forsters.

30.

Wrote to Watsons—Ld Beaconsfield—& draft[9]—Ld Granville—Mr Waterman—Bp of Winchester—Mrs Shears. Finished the Protocols: & worked up the whole subject. It loomed very large & disturbed my sleep unusually. So much the better for humility & casting all care on Him who careth. Saw M. Gennadios—Mr Bryce—Mr Rathbone MP.—Sir C. Dilke—Mr Home Fitzwilliam.[10] H of C. $4\frac{1}{2}$-$8\frac{1}{4}$ and $10\frac{1}{2}$-$12\frac{3}{4}$. Spoke $2\frac{1}{2}$ hours. I was in body much below par but put on the steam perforce. It ought to have been *far* better.[11] Read The People of Turkey.

31. Wed.

Wrote to Capt. Burnaby—Mr Busbridge[12]—Sir Jas Watson—Sig. Massari—Mr Ouvry—Scotts—Mr Chesson—Mr Perkes—Prof. Wilkins—Mrs Baxter—M.H. Hakim—Miss Swanwick—Mrs Abraham—Lord Selborne—Mr Scott—Mr Foster—Mr Wright. Dined at Mr MacColl's. 5 o clock tea at Holland House. Lady H. very kind. Read divers. Saw Sir A. Panizzi—Scotts—Mr Gibson—Ly Holland—Lord Bath—Sir R. Phillimore—Mr Gallenga. Rose late: the speech exhausted me a good deal as I was & am below *par*.

London Aug One 1878.

Wrote to Rev. Wilberforce BP.—F.W. Chesson—A. Connell[13]—G.B. Smith—Mr Stewart—Dr Stainer—Mr Jefferson—Messrs Bickers—Mrs Th. H of C. $4\frac{1}{2}$-$6\frac{1}{2}$.[14]

---

[1] *Church Quarterly Review*, vi. 503 (July 1878).   [2] See 19 May 78.
[3] G. Massari, *La vita ed il regno di Vittorio Emanuele II di Savoia*, 2v. (1878).
[4] See 5 Aug. 71.
[5] John Thomas Hazeldine, London solicitor.
[6] Probably Armine Wale Mountain, vicar of Stony-Stratford, a Radcliffe trust advowson.
[7] Hartington moved his resolution on the Protocols; *H* 242. 527.
[8] See 12 July 78.
[9] Asking for substantiation of Beaconsfield's charges that diarist had maligned him; Gladstone read this letter (reply not yet received) to the Commons this evening. See Add MS 44456, f. 166, with reply giving examples.
[10] Charles Home Lloyd Fitzwilliams, Cardigan J.P.
[11] *H* 242. 672; in Bassett, *Speeches*, 505; printed as a pamphlet, see 3 Aug. 78.
[12] Of G. F. Busbridge, London papermakers.
[13] Alexander A. Connell, of Ipswich wrote in support; Hawn P.
[14] Eastern affairs; *H* 242. 872.

Saw Mr Taylor Innes—Mr Howard Evans[1]—Mr Childers—Ld Carnarvon—Mr Howard—Marquis of Lorne. Dined at Sir R. Phillimore's. Read Fortnightly on Earl B.[2]—The Turkish People. Saw Mrs Th. in evg. I wish to help but know not how.

2. Fr.

Wrote to Mr Kelly—A.J. Symonds—W. Steele—Hugh Reed[3]—Thos Ness—Deffett Francis BP.[4]—Lord Geo. Hamilton[5]—Rev. W.J. Heaton[6]—Rev. Morton Shaw—Mrs Baxter BP—Rev. Mr Reade—Mr Layton. H of C. $9\frac{3}{4}$-$2\frac{3}{4}$. Voted with H[artingto]n in minority of 141.[7] Eleven to breakfast. Saw Mr Gennadios—Count Zohrab[8]—Mr MacColl—Miss Swanwick—Mr Knowles—Mr Rathbone—Mr Childers—Mr Boord MP. Spent four or more hours on papers, readings, & reducing to order. Read Routledge on India[9]—X. Greeks before Congress.[10]

3. Sat.

Wrote to Prof. Palumbo BP—Messrs Smith Chester—W. Miller—Mr Pearson BP. Spent some hours on packing books & arranging papers. Dictated my speech of Tuesday to the shorthand writer from the very *bad* report in the Times. It took four hours, of stiff work: instead of probably twelve. Saw Mr Smith. Went with C. to examine the Millais portrait:[11] surely a very fine work. Read Routledge: under much remaining exhaustion.

4. 7 S. Trin.

Charlotte St mg Chapel Royal aftn. Saw Miss Leslie. Read Aiger on Future State[12]—Abbé Martin on Ritualists[13]—Tyrrwhitt on Pantheism[14]—Coxe on Pope Pius IX[15]—Murphy Scientific Bases of Faith[16]—Adler's Reply to Gold. Smith[17]—V. of Wakefield Ch.

[1] Howard Evans, 1839-1915; congregationalist; journalist, sometime ed. *The Echo.*
[2] *Fortnightly Review*, xxx. 250 (August 1878).
[3] Perhaps Hugh Reid of Pimlico.
[4] J. Deffett Francis of Swansea; see Add MS 44445, f. 5.
[5] Lord George Francis *Hamilton, 1845-1927; tory M.P. Middlesex 1868-84, Ealing 1885-1906; Indian under-secretary 1874-80; at Admiralty 1885-6, 1886-92.
[6] Probably William Cartledge Heaton, vicar of Holy Trinity, London.
[7] H 242. 1121.
[8] Possibly James Zohrab, British consul at Erzerum.
[9] J. Routledge, *English rule and native opinion in India* (1878).
[10] By G. J. Shaw-Lefevre, *Fortnightly Review*, xxx. 271 (August 1878).
[11] See 26 June 78.
[12] See 5 Aug. 71.
[13] Abbé Martin, 'What hinders the ritualists from becoming Roman Catholics?', *Contemporary Review*, xxxiii. 113 (August 1878); for diarist's reply, see 23 Aug. 78.
[14] R. St J. Tyrwhitt, 'On evolution and pantheism', *Contemporary Review*, xxxiii. 81 (August 1878).
[15] A. C. Coxe, 'The Vatican Council. A letter to Pius the Ninth' (1870).
[16] See 19 Aug. 77.
[17] H. Adler, 'Jews and Judaism. A reply', *Nineteenth Century*, iv. 133 (July 1878).

5. M.

Wrote to Duke of Argyll—Mr Westell—Author of The Parousia[1]—Herr Von Gerbel[2]—G.B. Smith—A.C. Shelley—T.P. O'Connor[3]—Colonel Irwin[4]—Scotts—J. Henry[5]—Mr Stearn—Mr Ouvry—Mr Harris—Mr Millais. Worked on packing &c. H. of C. $5\frac{1}{2}$–$7\frac{3}{4}$ & $10\frac{1}{4}$–$12\frac{1}{4}$. Spoke on Education Vote.[6] Dined at Willy's. Read Transvaal case:[7] & Plowden. Saw Watts. Saw Sir A. Panizzi & had some conversation of interest, though its hue was still rather sad: he believes, however. Saw Mr Adam—Ld Hartington—Mr Childers.

6. Tu.

Wrote to Miss Smith—Rev. [A.]B. Wilberforce—Rev. Mr Phillott—Mr Thomas—Ld Hatherley—Receiver of Police[8]—E. James—E. Everitt[9]—Ed. Echo. Sat once more to Millais: whose ardour & energy about his picture inspire a strong sympathy. Luncheon at 15 G.S. & evening visit, by special request. Meeting at Devonshire House $2\frac{1}{2}$–$3\frac{3}{4}$.[10] H. of C. 4–7: spoke on Northcote's truly ignoble finance.[11] Further preparations for departure: the daily hurry & almost tempest of the last seven months leave such a confusion. Read Routledge on India. Saw Mr Gurdon—Mr Knowles.

7. Wed. [Hawarden]

Wrote to Watsons BP—Mr Dalgleish—Mr Bickers—D. Bates—H.M. Blair[12]—W. Hyam—Mrs Watt. Shopping. Worked all the morning on arranging books & papers and packing. This confusion, this *move* from London for the year, is the only one not irksome to me. Off at 2.30. Hawarden (late) at 9.15. Set to open my letters & papers. Read Col. Ouvry on Stein[13]—Frohschammer on Vaticanism.[14]

8. Th.

Ch. $8\frac{1}{2}$ AM. Wrote to Mayor of Birmingham[15]—Watson & Smith—Dr Macdonald[16]—Mr Wilkinson—J.S. Hodson—D. Smith—L. Berg[17]—Mr Finney.

[1] Not further identified; see 23 June 78.   [2] C. N. von Gerbel of Dresden, poet; Hawn P.
[3] Thomas Power O'Connor, 1848–1929; London journalist from 1870; home rule M.P. Galway 1880–5, Liverpool 1885–1906; wrote widely on Gladstone, especially *Gladstone's House of Commons* (1885).
[4] Perhaps William Irwin, 1810–89, col. of 34th foot, but also a general.
[5] Edinburgh liberal; later correspondence in Hawn P.
[6] H 242. 1245.   [7] Perhaps A. Aylward, *Transvaal of today* (1878).
[8] Business untraced.   [9] Perhaps Francis William Everitt Everitt, London barrister.
[10] See 9 Aug. 78n.
[11] Northcote had proposed a loan of up to £2 million, and referred to Crimean precedents; H 242. 1319.
[12] Henry Martin Blair, F.R.G.S.   [13] H. A. Ouvry, *Stein and his reforms in Prussia* (1873).
[14] J. Frohschammer, *The romance of Romanism* (1878).
[15] Thanking the city for an advance copy of T. Bunce, *History of Birmingham corporation*; *T.T.*, 10 August 1878, 9f.
[16] Thanking D. G. F. Macdonald for his pamphlet on crofters; *T.T.*, 14 August 1878, 7f.
[17] Louis Berg of Liverpool; on diarist's comments on Beaconsfield and Jewish disabilities, *T.T.*, 12 August 1878, 6e and Hawn P.

Worked much on books & papers. Finished Col. Ouvry on Stein—Finished Frohschammer. Read Past & Present of Morrow[1]—Two decades & a Lustrum.[2]

9. Fr.

Ch. 8½ A.M. Wrote to Farrar Ouvry & Co (B.P. the deeds demitting my Newcastle Trusteeship)—Mr Leecraft—Mr Unsell[3]—Mr Hopwood—Mr Hitchman—Mr Williams (Bookseller)—Sir A. Gordon—Rev. Mr Tracy[4]—Mr Etheridge—Mr Mott. Began to write England's Mission for Mr Knowles.[5] Worked upon arranging letters books & papers which here too will take much time. Read Hodson's Claudian[6]—Shuldham, Clergyman's Sore Throat[7]—Ld Beaconsfield, Mock—Heroic Poem.[8]

10.

Ch. 8½ A.M. Wrote to Sig. Massari—C. Tuttle—H. Mason—Mr Waras?—Mr Linet?—The O'Connor Don—Mr Macmillan—Miss Spencer (O)—Mr Wm Carr.[9] Wrote 'England's Mission'. Worked on Books & papers. Saw Mr Vickers. Read Claudian Raptus Proserpinae[10]—Holyoake, Rochdale Coopern[11]—Dowden on Shakespeare.[12]

11. 8 S. Trin.

Hawarden Ch. mg & evg. Attacked with another lowering gumboil. Wrote to the Duke of Argyll. Read Kettlewell on the Authorship of the Imitatio[13]—Cecil's Memoirs of J. Bacon and J. Newton (part).[14]

12. M.

Long sleep: rose at nine. Wrote to Mr Chester l. & BP.—Mr Knowles—Mr Mackie—Mr E. Noble—Miss Bagot (O). Corrected Revise of Speech for Press & put headings. Worked on England's Mission. Visit to St John's. Read Mr Dowden on Shakespeare—finished Hodgkin on Claudian.

[1] Perhaps [G. Seton], *The Past and Present* (1878).
[2] By 'C.W.G.' (1875?).
[3] James W. Unsell or Unisell, on diarist's Latin version of 'Rock of Ages'; Hawn P.
[4] Frederick Francis Tracy, 1829–88; rector of Beccles 1872–81; vicar of Kirk Christ, Isle of Man 1881–5.
[5] 'England's Mission', *Nineteenth Century*, iv. 560 (September 1878); on the Berlin treaty and Britain's world role. He told Granville (Ramm II, i. 76): 'I endeavoured to conform to the spirit of a conversation held at D[evonshire] House [on 6 Aug. 78] . . ., in which it was agreed to leave the Govt. alone, as far as might be, in regard to their Asiatic Protectorate.'
[6] T. Hodgkin, 'Claudian: the last of the Roman poets' (1875).
[7] Edward Barton Shuldham, London physician, had sent his *Clergyman's sore throat, or, follicular disease of the pharynx* (1878).
[8] *Beaconsfield: a mock-heroic poem and political satire* (1878).
[9] Perhaps William Carr of Leeds; see Add MS 44461, f. 101.
[10] C. Claudianus, *De Raptu Proserpinae* (perhaps 1874 ed.).
[11] G. A. Holyoake, *Self-help by the people. History of co-operation in Rochdale* (1858).
[12] See 3 Dec. 77.
[13] S. Kettlewell, *The authorship of the De Imitatione Christi* (1877).
[14] R. Cecil, *Memoirs of John Bacon* (1801); *Memoirs of John Newton* (1808).

13. Tu.

Ch. 8½ AM. Wrote to Mr Spencer (Hn)—Mr E.A. Freeman—Mr J. Turner—Mr Lehmann. Worked much on England's Mission: but not with great satisfaction. Walk & calls—saw Mr Bowman—Mr Taylor—Missed Mr Hurlbutt. Read The Two Noble Kinsmen[1]—Shuldham on Cl. Sore Throat (finished). Revised & annotated Mr Cornelius Brown on WEG & Newark.[2]

14. Wed.

Ch. 8¼ AM. Wrote to Mr Cornelius Brown 1. & B.P.—Rev. Principal [Caird] of Glasgow Univ.—Dr Shuldham—Mr Macleod—Mr Layton BP—Mr Marston—Mr Monahan[3]—Mr Knowles Tel. Corrected for a future reprint my 'Kin beyond Sea'. Worked on 'England's Mission'. Worked on Library wh will require many hours. Saw Mr Webb—Mr Taylor.

15. Th.

Overslept. Wrote to Mr Macmillan—Mons. P. Douvet—Miss [Emily] Faithful—Mr Priestman[4]—Mr Leecraft—Mr O'Sullivan—Pres. Harvard University[5]—Rev. Mr Richard—Mrs Grant—Mr Ord—Mr Leach—Capt Whibley—Mr Graf (O).[6] Worked four hours on books. Saw Mr Johnson—Mr [T.] Quellin Roberts—Dr Birmingham:[7] a new and great arrival. Much conversation respecting his matters. Attended the Flowershow (in the Castle grounds): and addressed the Assembly at some length.[8] Read Dowden's Shakespeare, and. . . .

16. Fr.

Ch. 8¼ AM. Wrote to Mrs H. Mackenzie—Mr Livingston—J.H. Burbier—S.L. Stratton[9]—A. Strahan—J. Cole—C. Brown—Co. H. Gay.[10] Conversation with S.E.G. (Jurisdiction)—Mr [J. A.] Godley. Worked again 3½ hours on books & papers. Wrote on England's Mission: which I must largely *re*-write. Read China Famine[11]—Dowden's Shakespeare. The Godley party came.

17. Sat.

Ch. 8¼ AM. Wrote to Mr King (Bookseller)—Rev. J.P. Morgan—Rev. C.W. Holson (O)—J. Williams—J.G. Williams—Captain Whibley—Mr Harwood—

---

[1] Sometimes attributed to Shakespeare (1634 ed.).

[2] See 22 Apr. 78.

[3] James Henry Monahan, 1804-78; retired Irish chief justice; wrote *The method of law* (1878).

[4] John Priestman of College Gardens, London.

[5] Declining the invitation of President Charles William Eliot, 1834-1926, to give ten lectures on political economy at Harvard; Add MS 44457, f. 156. Subscribers had set up a fund for the lectures, Gladstone's name emerging from a list including Marshall, Fawcett, Jevons and Cliffe Leslie; Harvard Corporation minutes, 29 January 1877, 13 May, 24 June 1878.

[6] Perhaps S.J. Graff of the Admiralty, India branch.

[7] *Sic*; D. C. Burlingham, physician at Hawarden from 1878.

[8] On duties of electors, and on gardening; *T.T.*, 16 August 1878, 6a.

[9] Stephen Stratton of Birmingham had sent music of a song on Gladstone; Hawn P.

[10] Col. Henri Gay of Paris had sent his *Observations sur les instincts de l'homme* (1878); Hawn P.

[11] *China Famine. Illustrations* (1878).

H. White—J. Hall. Reduced my work on my Library to half an hour or so. Worked on England's Mission. Conversation with Mr Godley—Mr [A.] Macmillan—Rev. Mr Thompson—Mr Bicknell.[1] Attended the Sandycroft Festival. Ten to dinner. Read Russell on Trevelyan's Macaulay[2]—Dowden's Shakespeare.

18. 9 S. Trin.

Ch. 11 AM. & H.C.—6½ PM. Wrote to Mr Hopwood. Read Kettlewell on Thos A Kempis—Harrison, Spirit People[3]—Jewish Reply to Colenso.[4] Walk with Mr M. & Mr G.

19. M.

Ch. 8¼ AM. Wrote to Mr O'Sullivan—Sir Thos G.—Mr Ouvry—Mr Jolly—E.J. Reynolds—Rev. H. Solly—Rev. J.D. Thomas.[5] Worked long on England's Mission. Worked on books. Read Wilson on the Friends of the Foreigner[6]—Lais Philosophe[7]—Dowden's Shakespeare—En Hollande.[8]

20. Tu.

Ch. 8¼ AM. Wrote to Spottiswoodes BP.—G. Hopwood—F. Merrifield[9]—J. Colquhoun—F.W. Chesson—Mrs Th.—T.J. Smith—Mr Green. Began on a dead sycamore with W.H.G. Worked on books 2 h. Worked on England's Mission—Read En Hollande—Dowden on Shakespeare.

21. Wed.

Ch. 8½ A.M. Wrote to Mr Knowles BP. Worked on England's Mission: the subject is difficult & has required some rewriting. Woodmans work. Read Dowden—En Hollande—Wilson, Resources of Mod. Countries[10]—Ld Stratford de R. on Greek Negotiations.[11]

22. Th.

Ch. 8¼ AM. Wrote to Made O. Novikoff BP—Rev. F. Meyrick—Sir A. Layard—Mr Knowles—Paul Gill—Mr Howood. Finished MS of 'England's Mission'. Worked on books. Worked with W. at a dead sycamore. Read Parl. Papers Turkey No 45[12]—Ewing's Collapsed Programme[13]—Puseyism Prostrated[14]—Dowden—En Hollande.

---

[1] Walter Lionel Bicknell, author of *Sunday Snowdrops* (1879); Hawn P.
[2] Probably a review by E. R. Russell.
[3] W. H. Harrison, *Spirits before our eyes* (1879).
[4] Probably A. Benisch, *Bishop Colenso's objections . . . critically examined* (1863).
[5] John Davies Thomas, curate in Deptford.
[6] E. D. J. Wilson, 'The friends of the foreigner', *Nineteenth Century*, iv. 327 (August 1878).
[7] *La Lais Philosophe, ou Mémoires de Madame D.* (1761).
[8] Untraced.   [9] Of the local government board.
[10] See 6 Mar. 78.
[11] *Nineteenth Century*, iv. 377 (August 1878).
[12] On treatment of Moslems; *PP* 1878 lxxxi. 895.
[13] T. J. Ewing, *A collapsed programme* (1878); satirical verses on Gladstone.
[14] Untraced tract.

23. Fr.

Ch. 8½ A.M. Wrote to Watson & Smith—Rev. Dr Grosart—Mr Raleigh—Mr Anderson MP—Scotts—Editor of Echo[1]—Rev. Dr Caird[2]—Mr H.H. Ormond—Mr G. Fogge—Mr A. Macdougall[3]—Mr W. Robertson—Rev. J.C. Gill (BP). Worked on books. I think I have 700 Vols of English Poetry. Read La Lais Philosophe—Reign of Geo. VI (curious)[4]—Casti (parts)[5]—Dowden's Shakespeare—En Hollande—Kingsley's Australian Tale.[6] Made an *exordium* for a reply to Abbé Martin.[7]

24. Sat. St Bartholomew.

Church 8¾ A.M. Wrote to Mr Raleigh Tel.—Ed. National Press. Tel.—Rev. J. Rowlands—Sir Thos G.—Mr Hopwood—Mr Yates—Mr Vickers. Worked on books. Corrected half the proofs of 'England's Mission'. We brought down the dead sycamore near W.s pond. Read Dowden's Shakesp.—Faas Schonk[8]—Voltaire, Poems—La Lais Philosophe (finished).

25. 10 S. Trin.

Ch. 11 A.M. & 6½ PM (read Lessons). Corrected remainder of proofs, as it was urgent. Wrote to Earl Granville—Bp of B. & Wells—Mr Vickers—Mr Knowles. Read Bugg's Pilgrim's Progress[9]—Newman Gram. of Assent[10]—Persecutions of French Protestants 1815, 6[11]—Pascal Private Thoughts[12]—Christian Apologist— and other Tracts.

26. M.

Ch. 8½ AM. Wrote to Mr V. de Tivoli[13]—Mr Bicknell—Mr Bullock—M. Gennadios BP—F. Taylor—C. Herbert—Rev. C. Higgins—Miss de Lisle—Mrs Ralli BP—J.H. Edge[14]—J.A. Craw. Worked 3½ hours on arranging books. Kibbled the sycamore. Tea in Park with Mrs Hn & Co. Read Notice of St Simon[15]—Thorold Rogers on Laud: rather poor[16]—Faas Schonk. Prettily written, but the end disappoints. Ten to dinner. Wrote a little on Abbé Martin.

[1] Denying he will be visiting Glasgow in November, *The Echo*, 24 August 1878, 2.
[2] Announcing gift of £50 prize for essay at Glasgow university; *T.T.*, 26 August 1878, 7f.
[3] Alexander Macdougall, Glasgow liberal; Hawn P.
[4] *The reign of George VI* (1763); imaginary history of the 20th century.
[5] See 18 Sept. 61.
[6] Henry Kingsley, *The recollections of Geoffry Hamlyn*, 3v. (1859), or his *The Hillyars and the Burtons* (1865).
[7] Published as 'The sixteenth century arraigned before the nineteenth: a study on the Reformation', *Contemporary Review*, xxxiii. 425 (October 1878), reprinted in *Gleanings*, iii. 217; for Martin, see 4 Aug. 78.
[8] A tale, apparently anonymous.
[9] F. Bugg, *The Pilgrim's Progress, from Quakerism to Christianity* (1698).
[10] See 27 Mar. 70.
[11] C. Perrot, *Report on the persecutions of the French protestants* (1816); on the 'terror' of 1815.
[12] See 18 July 30.   [13] Italian translator living in London.
[14] John Henry Edge, Irish author, wrote on land.
[15] Probably P. A. R. Janet, *Saint-Simon et la Saint-Simonisme* (1878).
[16] J. E. T. Rogers, *Historical gleanings*, 2v. (1869-70), includes sketches of Laud, Wilkes, Tooke.

27. Tu.

Ch. 8½ A.M. Wrote to Duke of Argyll—Rev. Mr West—E.J. Collings—Messrs Cole—Jasper Moore—Mr Fenton (O)—Mr Salmond—W.R. Green.[1] Woodcraft with W. & H. in the paddock. Worked on books. Worked on Abbé Martin. Read Ancien Diplomate on 'Succession'[2]—Thorold Rogers on Wilkes—Hinder Gentleman on Swedenborg.[3]

28. Wed.

Ch. 8½ A.M. Wrote to Mr J. de Morgan—Messrs Watson—Dr Shuldham—Rev. S.T. Rand[4]—Alderman Wigglesworth—S.A. Parasurakis[5]—Mr Knowles—Mr Brough—Mr Edwards. Dear Helen's birthday. Benedictus benedicat. Walk with the Rector. Worked on arranging books. Worked on Abbé Martin. Read Dr Brown's Essays[6]—Thorold Rogers on Horne Tooke.

29. Thurs.

Ch. 8¼ A.M. Wrote to C.G. (tel.)—Mr Forster MP.—D. Currie l. & BP—Mad. Novikoff—Wms & Norgate—J.R. Martin—T. Macdonald—Messrs Dain[7] & Leeman—W.H.G. (BP)—Scotts—Mr Howell—T. Ramsay—Mr Robertson. Worked on arranging books: after (I guess) 30 hours my library is now in a passable state and I enjoy, in Ruskin's words "the complacency of possession, & the pleasantness of order". Read E. India Journal—Ingram on Polit. Economy[8]—Memoirs of Automathes.[9] Eleven to dinner. Walk with Bp of Bath & Wells.

30. Fr.

Ch. 8¼ A.M. Wrote to Duke of Argyll—Mr Ellice MP—Messrs Glyn—Bp of Carlisle—H. Jephson[10]—S. Wilks—W. Hastie—W. Robertson (J. Bright) BP.—Mrs Th. Wrote Mema respecting Mr Bright.[11] Wrote on Abbé Martin. Saw Mr Geo. Melly, & party from Newcastle. Woodcraft, and walk with the Bishop. Read Hist. of Automathes—Th. Rogers on Tooke.

31. Sat.

Ch. 8½ AM. Wrote to Mrs Stuart Wortley—Mr Macmillan—Mr G. Grove—Mr J.T. Knowles—Mr Vickers—Surveyors of Taxes BP—Mr H.C. Knight (O)—Scotts—Herr Wallerstein.[12] Wrote on Abbé Martin. Woodcraft with Willy. Tea

---

[1] Perhaps William Robert Green, ed. *Green's Norwich monthly* (1868).
[2] Possibly *Le Congrès en miniature, par un Diplomate* (1878).
[3] Perhaps *E. Swedenborg, the spiritual Columbus, by U.S.E.* (1876).
[4] Silas Tertius Rand, tr. Bible for Canadian Indians.
[5] Socrates A. Parasurakes, ed. *Pan-hellenic Annual* (1879).
[6] Probably J. B. Brown, *Our morals and manners* (1878).
[7] Horatio Dain, London solicitor.
[8] J. K. Ingram, *Essays in political economy* (1878).
[9] Automathes [R. Griffith], *Something new. Miscellaneous essays*, 2v. (1772).
[10] Henry L. Jephson, one of the clerks at Dublin Castle; assisted in Irish legislation 1882.
[11] Not found.
[12] Declining to assist Henry L. Wallerstein of Frankfurt in starting a monthly review; Hawn P.

party here. Read Rogers on Tooke—& on Wiclif—Life of Automathes—Nineteenth Cent. on Nubar Pasha & Armenia[1]—Greg's Foreign Policy.[2]

Sept. One. S. Trin 11.

Church 8¼ A.M. (with H.C.) and 6½ P.M. Wrote to Lord Lyttelton—Marquis of Ripon. Wrote on Abbé Martin. Read Bp Forbes Cons. Mod.[3]—Möhler Symbolik[4]—Macmillan, Two sides to a Saint[5]—Hist. of Automathes—Huss on the Church[6]—Winn on Materialism.[7] Walk with Agnes & E. Wickham. Worked on Abbé Martin.

2. M.

Ch. 8½ AM. Wrote to Messrs Sotheran—M. Robertson—J.C. Chapman—H. d'Avigdor[8]—J. Macrea—R.R. Dares—D. Puseley—Rev. W. Bathgate[9]—Mrs Harwood—T. Walker—G.H. Cook. Worked on Abbé Martin. Worked in the plantation. Read Dowden—Dante Hérétique &c.[10]—finished Thorold Rogers.

3. Tu.

Ch. 8¼ AM. Wrote to Robn & Nicholson—R.R. Davies[11]—Mr Lambert—F. Lampard—G. Melly—J. Gurney—A. Steare—Writer of Art on Hom. Primer. Worked much on Abbé Martin. Felled a fir with W. Conversation with him on his plans as to Residence. Read Sketches of Wild Wales—Abbé Martin in Contemp.—Freeman on Froude's Becket in do.[12]

4. Wed.

Ch. 8¼ AM. Wrote to Mr Benson Maxwell—Mrs Ainsworth[13]—Mr Hitchman—G. Hopwood—F.W. Hawkins[14]—Mr Thorndike Rice—Mr Knowles—Mr Brough—F. Rule—Watsons BP. Sorting letters & papers. Wrote much on Abbé Martin. Read Malay Conquests[15]—What stops the way[16]—Contemp. on Indian Thought. Walk with Mr Greer.[17]

[1] By E. Dicey, *Nineteenth Century*, iv. 548 (September 1878).
[2] W. R. Greg, 'Foreign policy of Great Britain', ibid., iv. 393 (September 1878).
[3] See 29 Mar. 50; this and Möhler discussed in *Gleanings*, iii. 234.
[4] See 18 Oct. 45.
[5] *Macmillan's Magazine*, xxxviii. 385 (August 1878).
[6] Perhaps Jan Hus, *Liber egregrius de imitate Ecclesiae* (1520).
[7] See 3 Sept. 76.
[8] Elim Henry D'Avignor, 1841-95, gentleman.
[9] William Bathgate, minister and theologian in Kilmarnock.
[10] E. Aroux, *Dante hérétique, révolutionnaire et socialiste* (1854).
[11] R. Rice Davies had sent his *Cambrian sketch book... legends of Wild Wales* (1875).
[12] *Contemporary Review*, xxxiii. 113, 213 (August, September 1878).
[13] Perhaps Sophia Ainsworth, *née* Hanmer, d. 1882; a nun; see A. J. Hanmer, *Mrs Sophia Ainsworth* (1894).
[14] Of the London Office of *The Theatre*, on theatrical subsidies; Hawn P.
[15] Sir P. B. Maxwell, *Malay conquests* (1878).
[16] Untraced.
[17] See 3 July 75?

5. Th.

Ch. 8½ AM. Wrote to Earl Granville—Mr W.H. Thompson[1]—Mr C.H. Davey.[2] Finished paper on Abbé Martin. A little woodcraft. Read Malay Conquests—Life of Sir K. Digby[3]—Fortnightly on Heyer, Ausbildung der Priesterherrschaft.[4]

6. Fr.

Ch. 8½ AM. Wrote to Mr Negamells[5]—Mr Rich. Baxter—A.E. West—Mr Marris (O)—R. Wright—Mr M'Kenzie. Correcting my paper on Abbé Martin. Filled up a broad gap: & laboured to devise a title, not the easiest part. Saw Mr Greer: & other clergy. Walk by the River. Tea at Mr Hurlbutt's, & went over his house & place: saw the gas machinery. Read [blank.] Read Fortnightly on Indian Thought.[6]

7. Sat.

Ch. 8½ AM. Wrote to Rev Dr J.O.A. Clark—Dr A. Clark BP.—Mr Knowles—Ld Selborne B.P.—Sir F. Doyle—Sir S. Scott & Co—Mr Archer—Mr C. Hill—Mr Fennell—Mr Hankey MP. Finished correction of MS. which has extended to too great length. Tea party in aft. Saw Rev. Mr Hodgson—Mr Vickers—Mr Ward. Woodcraft. Read Doyle's Ode[7]—Trollope on Iceland in F.R.[8]

8. S. 12 Trin.

Ch. 11 A.M. (Mr Hodgson[9] preached, forcibly) & 6½. Wrote to Sir R. Phillimore l. & BP.—Mr A. Strahan l. & B.P. Read Bp Pilkington's Remains—*non* mi piacciono[10]—Dodd's Church History[11]—Collin[12]—Butler's Memoirs[13]—Wilkinson on Materialism[14]—Foreign Church Chronicle—and [blank.]

9. M.

Ch. 8½ AM. Wrote to Mr Macmillan—Mr Adam MP—Rev. Mr Suffield—Duke of Argyll—Miss M'Kenzie—M. Ivanovich[15]—Messrs Sotheran—D.F. Murphy—W.A. Findlay—Mr Langley—Mr Falshaw—H. Waddy—G. Fogge—A.T. Jay[16]—

---

[1] Perhaps William Hepworth *Thompson, 1810-86; master of Trinity, Cambridge, from 1866.

[2] Of the savings department of the G.P.O.

[3] *Private memoirs of Sir Kenelm Digby, written by himself* (1827).

[4] 'Fortnightly' written (wrongly) over original periodical's name, obscuring it.

[5] Word scrawled.

[6] *Fortnightly Review*, xxx. 387 (September 1878).

[7] Sir F. H. C. Doyle, *Robin Hood's Bay, an ode* (1878).

[8] *Fortnightly Review*, xxx. 175 (August 1878).

[9] Robert Hodgson, 1844-1917; contemporary of Stephen Gladstone at Oxford; vicar of W. Bromwich 1872-83, of Walsall 1883-92; rector of Handsworth 1892-1904.

[10] James Pilkington in his *Works*, ed. J. Scholefield (1842); 'they don't please me'.

[11] C. Dodd [H. Tootell], *The Church history of England* (1737).

[12] Probably the works of H. J. von Collin, German poet.

[13] Perhaps C. Butler, *An account of the life and writings of Alban Butler* (1799).

[14] W. F. Wilkinson, *Modern materialism* (1878).

[15] Probably the Serbian war minister.

[16] Of Russell Square, London; had requested a pamphlet; Hawn P.

T. Slatten—G. Ryan—S. Steer—Sir S. Scott & Co. Woodcraft with Herbert. The Sidgwicks[1] came: conversation with them—& with Mr Ottley. Read Brassey on Colonial Force[2]—Dante Hérétique &c.—Fairbairn, Churches & Colleges[3]— Frohschammer on Romanism.[4]

10. Tu.

Ch. 8½ A.M. Wrote to Sir D. Marjoribanks—Mr Westropp—Messrs Sotheran— Mr Mortimer—Mr Anderson—Mr Redfern[5]—J.D. Hay—Rev. Mr Brown. Read Grant Duff's Address[6]—Geddes, Homeric Question. Long walk & much conversation with Mr Sidgwick—Mr Holland[7] came. Worked on Hom. Question.

11. Wed.

Ch. 8½ AM. Wrote to Miss V. Blackwood—Mr Peacock—W. Murray—F.C. Blackburn—F. Johnston—Mr Knowles—S. Foy.[8] Worked much on a possible character of Hector in reply to Prof. Geddes.[9] Woodcraft with Herbert. Tea *sub Dio* in a lovely spot. Read Grant Duff. Conversation with Mr Sidgwick.

12. Th. [Bettisfield Park, Whitchurch]

Ch. 8½ AM. Wrote to my son Harry—Mr Barry—Mr Knowles—Mr C. Jolly.[10] Corrected proofs of my long article for Contemporary.[11] Read Dowden's Primer of Homer. 3.20-5.50 By Chester to Bettisfield: most hospitable reception.[12]

13. Fr.

Wrote to Dr Döllinger l. & BP.—Mr Knowles—Mr Forster MP—Mr Thorold Rogers—Mr A. Strahan B.P. Worked on Hector. Read Iliad—Dowden, Shakespeare Primer. Drove in aft. to a circuit of three churches. Examined trees: an oak near 28 f. Conversation with Sir R. Cunliffe—Ld Hanmer—& others.

14. Sat. [Hawarden]

Read Iliad—Dowden's Shakespeare. Again out among the trees. We were sorry to leave our old & sterling friend. Spent the afternoon at Cloverley[13] which flourishes amazingly. Left it at 5¼: Hawarden at 8¼. Worked on material for Hector. 2 hours opening letters.

[1] Henry *Sidgwick, 1838-1900, philosopher and liberal reformer, and his wife Eleanor (see 10 Aug. 75).

[2] T. Brassey, 'A colonial naval volunteer force' (1878).

[3] A. M. Fairbairn, 'The Churches and the Colleges' (1878).

[4] See 7 Aug. 78.   [5] Perhaps William Redfern, commission agent.

[6] Perhaps his 'Echoes of the late debate', *Nineteenth Century*, iv. 478 (September 1878).

[7] H. Scott Holland; Emily Faithfull, journalist (see 18 July 68), was also a visitor; Hawarden Visitors Book.

[8] Samuel W. Foy of the Bank's bill office.

[9] Published as 'The slicing of Hector', *Nineteenth Century*, iv. 752 (October 1878); a criticism of Geddes, see 22 June 78.

[10] Probably of the Greenwich liberal family.

[11] See 23 Aug. 78.   [12] Lord Hanmer's place.

[13] Mrs Heywood's seat, 2 miles SE of Whitchurch, Salop.

15. 13 S. Trin.

Hn Ch. 11 AM & H.C. There was Mr E.B.[1] who lately believed nothing: a very interesting person, as are all of that family. God be praised. Church also in evg. Wrote to Mr Willis Nevins—Rev Mr Bateman—H.N.G. (B.P.)—Jas Knowles B.P. Read The Divine Order[2]—Jewish Reply to Colenso (finished)[3]—Priestley on Revealed Religion.[4]

16. M.

Ch. 8½ AM. Wrote to Rev. J. Bullock—Ld Hanmer—W. Downing—J. Bagshaw— Jas Sholl—Ld Robartes—Sir Thos G.—J. Sands[5]—C.T. Gatty.[6] Walk with the Rector: and visits. Worked on Hector for N.C. Read N.C. on Voltaire & Du Chatelet: (rather a loathsome article to be written by a woman.)[7]—Ugo Foscolo on Boccaccio.[8]

17. Tu.

Ch. 8½ A.M. Wrote to Earl of Rosebery—Earl Granville—Ld Tenterden—Sir A. Layard—Rev. R. Whitling[9]—H. Irving—F.P. Fenner—Mrs Th.—S. Foy—S. Pope[10]—E. Holt—Miss Irby—Mr Knowles. Conversation with Mr [Eustace] Balfour. Also with WHG (Whitby &c).[11] Correcting Revise for Contemporary. Woodcraft with WHG. Read U. Foscolo on Boccaccio—Lewis on Irish Education Act.[12]

18. Wed.

Ch. 8¼ AM. Wrote to Mr A.E. West (2)—Messrs Spottiswoode B.P.—Sir R. Phillimore B.P.—Mr Redfern BP—Mr Sketchley BP—W.H. Northy—Mr Downing—J. Sievewright—Mr Steed—H. Penn—W. Wren[13]—Mrs Wynn. Finished 'The Slicing of Hector'—Worked on Hector Art. for Thes. Hom. Walk with C.G. Read Ugo Foscolo and Brown's Burlington Oration.[14]

---

[1] Eustace Balfour (see 5 Oct. 72), A.J.*'s brother; Hawarden Visitors Book.
[2] Perhaps *The Divine Office* (1878).
[3] See 18 Aug. 78.
[4] J. Priestley, *Discourses on the evidence of revealed religion* (1794).
[5] John Sands of Tranent, Midlothian, wrote on St Kilda; Add MS 44457, f. 274; see 21 Sept. 78.
[6] Charles Tindal Gatty, Liverpool antiquarian; wrote on china.
[7] Eliza Clarke, 'Voltaire and Madame du Chatelet at Cirey', *Nineteenth Century*, iii. 1052 (June 1878).
[8] By N. U. Foscolo (1825).
[9] Robert Charles Storrs Whitling, vicar of Otterford.
[10] Samuel Pope, barrister.
[11] He did not again contest it, but stood successfully for E. Worcestershire 1880.
[12] By C. E. Lewis, M.P.; perhaps his 'To the electors of . . . Londonderry' (1878).
[13] Walter Wren, 1834-98; liberal financial reformer; elected for Wallingford 1880, declared void on petition; contested Wigan 1882, N. Lambeth 1885-6.
[14] Probably J. Baldwin Brown, 'Our theology in relation to the intellectual movement of our times. An add-ess' (May 1878); refers to Gladstone as 'our great Christian patriot and statesman'.

19. Th.

Ch. 8½ AM. Wrote to Mr A.S. Wilkins—Warden of St Columba's[1]—Mr Hayward—Mr Jas Graham—W. Dunlop (& BP)—D. Currie—Mr Carter (O)—Mr Steed—R.C. Young[2]—Mr Taylor. The Duke of Bedford[3] came. Showed him the Park & Castle: he was *most* worthy. Conversation respecting his brother's Peerage.[4] Worked on Thesauros Homerikos (Hector). Read Tennyson, Princess—Examen du Gouv. d'Angleterre comparé aux Const. des Etats Unis: Livingstone & others.[5]

20. Fr.

Ch. 8½ AM. Wrote to Pears Logan & Co—Manager N.A. Review—Mr Pennington—Rev. L. Dowdall[6]—Rev. Mr Gallaway[7]—Mr Strahan B.P.—Cyrus Field BP—Mr Hitchen BP.—Central press (Tel.)—Mr Knowles—Scotts—E.T. Smith—T.C. Scott—Mr Woolat BP. Duchess of Bedford & ladies came 1½-4. Showed her the Park & Old Castle. Conversation respecting Ld Odo. Woodcraft with WHG. Read Gouv. d'Angleterre &c.—Rice on Irish Educn Act.[8]

21. Sat. St Matth.

Ch. 8¾ AM.—Never let me forget the turn on this day 31 years back, in dear Agnes's awful illness.
Wrote to Rev Mr Henderson—Herr Fleischer[9]—Editor of Echo—W. Tallack—W.R. Milner—W.T. Vincent—Rev. W.W. Merry—Mrs G.—Miss Irby—Mrs Th.—Mr Strahan—Mr Cameron—G. Walker U.S.[10] Saw Dr Burlingham—Photogr. Societies. Herbert in bed with Asthma. Read Verses of Marini II[11]—Sands, Life in St Kilda[12]—Smith's Dict.—Kenrick's Phoen.[13] Worked on Thes. Hom.

22. [14] S. Trin.

Ch. 11 AM. and 6½ PM. S.s Sermon this morning wd have done honour as I thought to the ripest Christian & pastoral experience. Wrote to Earl of

---

[1] Probably John Vodin Walters, vicar of St Columba's, Haggerstone.

[2] R. Calder Young of Ulverston, on church affairs; Hawn P.

[3] Francis Charles Hastings Russell, 1819-91; 9th duke of Bedford 1872; m. 1844 Lady Elizabeth Sackville West, mistress of the robes 1880-3; she d. 1897.

[4] Lord Odo Russell accepted with the duke's support a peerage for his services at Berlin, but afterwards declined it, writing to Gladstone on 8 October (Add MS 44457, f. 23): 'Great was therefore my surprise when the Duke told me that in your opinion by accepting this peerage I was virtually repudiating the political principles of my family and of my party, and that you held that I should defer the acceptance of the Queen's offer until our party was once again in power.'

[5] [W. Livingston], *Examen du gouvernement d'Angleterre comparé aux constitutions des Etats-Unis* (1789).

[6] Lancelot John George Downing Dowdall, curate in Bristol; his s. (Sir) Laurence Dowdall (1851-1936) was secretary to Balfour and Morley while Irish secretary.

[7] Perhaps William Brown Galloway, anglican theologian.

[8] R. Rice, 'Irish Intermediate Education Act: suggestions for the practical working of it' (1878).

[9] Richard Fleischer, German historian and editor of the *Deutsche Revue*; Hawn P.

[10] Perhaps for an autograph.

[11] G. B. Marino, *Adone*, quoted at 23 July 80 f.l.

[12] J. Sands, *Out of the world; or, life in St. Kilda* (1876).

[13] See 16 June 63.

Rosebery—Sir D. Marjoribanks—Ld Acton—Mr Crapp—Mr Leyden. Read Milman Hist. Jews[1]—Also Kenrick & Rawlinson[2]—Dr Hutton on Disestablt[3]—Bp of Gibraltar's Sermons[4]—Working Man on Cath. Revival.[5]

23. M.

Ch. 8¼ AM. Wrote to Rev. Dr Hutton—Mr Knowles BP.—Ed. of Echo and draft[6]—Earl Powis—W.S. Ogilvy[7]—G. Mitchell—G. Haycraft—Mr Adam—R. Rees[8]—A. Strahan—Mr Binney—Mr Bullock—J.A. Cave. Read Editions of Decameron to verify my statement in Art. for Contemp Rev.[9] Read St Kilda—Internat. Review on W.E.G.[10] Corrected (& added to) proofs of Art. on Hector in Homer.

24. Tu.

Ch. 8½ A.M. Wrote to Bp of Adelaide—Sir Dudley Marjoribanks—Rev. Mr Mossman—Rt Hon Mr Adam—Mr Shannon (O)—G.R. Smith—Rev. F. Pacificus[11]—Mr Harris—Mr Roslyn—Mr Waugh—Mr Hayward—Mr Godfrey. Saw Mr Vickers—Mr Whiteing U.S.[12] Woodcraft with W. & H. Worked on Homer. Read Life of Wyllie[13]—Sands on St Kilda—Bismarck: le Vrai et le Bien (poor).[14] 'Company' arrived.[15]

25. Wed.

Ch. 8¼ AM. Wrote to Smith Elder & Co—H. Sotheran & Co—Rev. Ray Palmer[16]—Rev. J.P. Mahaffy—Prof. Leone Levi—Mr Mallinsdy—Mr Peckham—Mr Simpson—J. Hodge. Read Wyllie on Foreign Policy of Ld Lawrence—Cooper's New Theory[17]—Sands on St Kilda (finished). Saw Mr Pritchard. Much conversation with Sir A. Gordon. We (three) felled a large ash.

[1] See 13 May 30.
[2] See 26 Apr. 78.
[3] Probably one of Vernon Wollaston Hutton's pamphlets.
[4] By C. W. Sanford (1878).
[5] *The Catholic Revival. By a working man* (1877?).
[6] Denying an accusation in *T.T.* that he had misquoted bp. Heber; Add MS 44457, f. 304.
[7] Perhaps Walter Tulliedeph Ogilvy of the British Museum.
[8] Arguing that by-elections have 'returned in large majority those who disapprove the conduct of the Ministry'; *T.T.*, 26 September 1878, 8f; the origin of 'Electoral facts', see 29 Sept. 78n. and 9 Oct. 78.
[9] See 23 Aug. 78.
[10] 'Ex-Premier Gladstone. By an American', *International Review*, v. 588 (1878); adulatory: 'Not now in office, he is, nevertheless, still in power.'
[11] Provincial of the Capuchins in Chester.
[12] Perhaps Charles Goodrich Whiting, 1842-1922; literary ed. of the *Springfield Republican*.
[13] J. W. S. Wyllie, *Essays on the external policy of India, edited with a brief life, by W. W. Hunter* (1875); on 'masterly inactivity' etc., defending non-intervention in India's frontier states.
[14] Untraced tract.
[15] Arthur Gordon, bps. of Capetown (W. W. Jones) and Adelaide (A. Short), Miss A. P. Irby and Arthur Lyttelton.
[16] Of Newark, New Jersey, U.S.A.; on the *International Review*; Hawn P.
[17] Probably T. Cooper, *Evolution* (1878).

26. Th.

Ch. 8½ A.M: and 3½-5 P.M. at Confirmation (Bp [Jones] of Cape Town). Wrote to Mr Pennington—Mr J. Talbot—Mr Dickson U.S.[1]—Mr Gillman—Bp of Adelaide—Mr Dunington (Rev)—Earl of Kintore (O)—Mr O'Hart—Mr Humphrey—Mr Leedle. Walk with Sir A. Gordon. Dinner party. Read Wyllie on Masterly inactivity—Gouvernement des Etats Unis comparé &c. Worked a little on Homer. Conversation with Miss Irby.

27. Fr.

Ch. 8½ AM. Wrote to Ld Hartington—Prof. L. Levi—Rev. J.E. Walker[2]—Rev. A.E. Lord[3]—Miss Williams—Miss M. Burton[4]—Rev. Mr Mahaffy—Mr Peckham—Mr Peacock—Mr Crosland—Mr Mitchell. Saw Bp of Cape Town—Bp of Adelaide—Sir A. Gordon—Miss Irby. Worked on Hom. Thesauros. Woodcraft with W. & H. Read Wyllie, Mischievous Activity—Wassilowitch, Memoir on Bosnia & Herzegovina.[5]

28. Sat.

Ch. (late) 8½ AM. Wrote to Earl of Rosebery—Mr W.P. Adam—Mrs Tearle[6]—Mr Entwistle (O)—Rev W. Blake—Sir D. Marjoribanks—Sir W.C. James BP.—Mr Wickham. Saw Miss Irby—Sir A. Gordon; long conversation on his plans for the future—Mr [blank]—Mr [J. P.] Mahaffy (who dined here) on Homer—Irish Divinity School—&c. Read Wyllie on E. Turkistan &c.—Mahaffy on Greek Manners.[7]

29. 15 S. Trin & St Mich.

Ch. 11 AM & 6½ P.M. Wrote to Earl Granville—Ld C. Hamilton[8]—Capt Knox (O)[9]—Editor of Echo—Mr Buttress[10]—Mr Worthington—Mr Marling—Mr Mostyn Williams—Sec. Sund School Assocn—Mr C.R. Fagan—Mr Lawton—Mr R. Buchanan[11]—Mr O'Byrne—Rev. Dr Irons. Read Herford's Religion in England[12]—Lord's Sermon on Mrs Scott[13]—Irons, 1st Cent. of Xty[14]—Xtn Apologist

---

[1] Probably for an autograph.

[2] James Edward Walker of Corpus Christi College, Oxford, religious author.

[3] Nonconformist minister in Walton-on-Thames; Hawn P.

[4] Of Edinburgh; had written in admiration; Hawn P.

[5] Perhaps by P. St Vassiliou who published his *Guerre d'Orient, 1876-1878* (1880).

[6] Probably the wife of Edwin Tearle, vicar in London.

[7] Probably J. P. Mahaffy's comments on Gladstone's Homeric primer, *Macmillan's Magazine*, xxxviii. 405 (August 1878).

[8] Hamilton disputed diarist's argument on by-elections (see 23 Sept. 78n.); Gladstone promised 'a complete dealing' with the subject, which became 'Electoral facts'; *T.T.*, 4 October 1878, 6b and 9 Oct. 78.

[9] Commander Henry Knox, R.N., on Homer; Add MS 44459, f. 209.

[10] Perhaps Allan Buttress, unbeneficed anglican priest.

[11] Perhaps Robert William Buchanan, 1841-1901; poet and novelist; later a correspondent.

[12] B. Herford, *The story of religion in England* (1878).

[13] A. E. Lord, 'The shock of corn. A sermon on the death of Mrs Mary Scott' (1878).

[14] W. J. Irons, 'The first hundred years of Christianity' (1877).

No X—Papers for the Times[1]—Heygate, What Chmen shd do[2]—and Divers Tracts. Saw Rev S.E.G.

30. M.

Ch. 8¼ A.M. We gave up our journey for the day on account of storm. Wrote to Mr R. Weymouth—Bishop Jenner[3]—Rev. M. M'Coll—Rev. Dr Irons—Rev. Mr Torr—Messrs Cassell—Mr Jas Tweedie l. & BP.—Sir Thos G.—Mr Morley (2)—Mr Buchanan—Mr Salisbury. Woodcraft with Herbert. Our company departed. Worked on Thes. Hom. Read Sergeant on Greece[4]—M. Arnold Sohrab & Rustum—Weymouth on Obrinus &c.[5]

Tues. Oct. One 78. [Peveril Hotel, Douglas, Isle of Man]

Ch. 8¼ A.M. Wrote to Duke of Argyll BP—Mr O.B. Cole BP—Mr Knowles—Lt Govr I. of Man[6]—Mr Stead—C.G. Packing. Off at 10¾ to Liverpool and Isle of Man. Reached Douglas at 6¼ after a good passage. Acquaintance made on the way with the Att. General,[7] Mr [blank] (House of Keys) & others. We were exceeding well accommodated at the Peveril. But all secrecy was blown to the winds by an outstripping Telegram: a crowd followed up the Pier: & the evening was a series of calls messages cards & what not, from reporters, Governor's Messengers, & volunteers. Read Leslie Stephen's Johnson.[8] Stephy & I had evening prayers, which will be renewed daily.

2. Wed. ['Falcon's Nest', Port Erin, Isle of Man]

Evg prayers at Port Erin.

In the morning we walked up to Kirk Bradden:[9] saw the seven(?) ancient crosses & much that was characteristic in & about the buildings & in the pretty vale. We then saw the Governor & laid out plans. Off at 10 for Castle Town. There we saw the College,[10] a vigorous & flourishing establishment. I was put on to address the boys. Then to the old Edward III Castle with its clock: now a gaol: but there is probably no ancient building in the 'adjacent islands' with such a mass of its work unchanged. Then we went to Port St Mary by Rail: & on foot visited the very curious rock 'Chasms'. From thence down to Port Erin,[11] the 'Falcon's Nest', very homelike & comfortable. Read Vehse on Shakespeare[12]—

[1] *Papers for the Times* [ed. W. Lewin], nos. 1, 2 (1879).
[2] W. E. Heygate, 'What churchmen should do at this time' (1878).
[3] Henry Lascelles Jenner, 1820-98; bp. of Dunedin, 1866-71; rector of Preston, Kent; bp. in Paris 1882-93.
[4] L. Sergeant, *New Greece* (1878).   [5] Untraced work by R. F. Weymouth.
[6] H. B. *Loch (see 11 Oct. 71); known as the governor, but technically only a lieutenant-governor; referred to by Gladstone on this visit by both titles. Correspondence on the visit in Add MS 44457.
[7] Sir James Gell, 1823-1905; attorney general of Man 1866-98; later governor. Gladstone was accompanied on this visit by Stephen Gladstone.
[8] L. Stephen, *Samuel Johnson* (1878).   [9] A mile NE. of Douglas.
[10] King William's College. Report of the day's proceedings in *Mona's Herald*, and *T.T.*, 3 October 1878, 7f.   [11] On the S.W. tip of the island.
[12] C. E. Vehse, *Shakspeare als Protestant, Politiker, Psycholog und Dichter* (1851).

L.Stephen's Johnson—The Attorney General's Minute on Island Hist. & Law.[1]
He the A.G. entertained us most kindly at luncheon. Tel. to H. Bailiff of Peel.

3. Th. [Government House, Douglas, Isle of Man]

Prayers with S. in evg. Wrote to Ld Granville—Ld Rosebery—C.G.

We started about nine: a four hours & a half walk besides $\frac{1}{2}$ hour for luncheon, brought us to Peel.[2] Saw something more of the life & occupations of the people. Also saw Scotland & Ireland very well. At Peel went over the Castle & Ecclesiastical ruins. It is a noble & a touching sight, all taken together and the wild rushing sea (as it often is) around. Conversation with High Bailiff[3]— Ramsay [sic] Deputation—and others. Off by train to Douglas. Here two speeches had to be made; one in answer to an Address, one to the crowd outside.[4] Then we settled our affairs & went up to Government House where a warm hospitality persuaded us to prolong our stay till Monday. Much conversation with Govr today as well as yesterday. Read L. Stephen's Johnson— Washington Irving's Life of Goldsmith.[5]

4. Fr. [Laxey, Isle of Man]

Evening Prayers. Wrote to Bp of Sodor & Man[6]—Mr Summers (2 Tel)—C.G.— High Bailiff of Castleton[7]—Mr Counsell (O)—Mr Cowen (O)—Mr Goldsmith. Rain kept us until after luncheon. The Lt Govr then drove us to Laxey where we saw the Lead Works & wheel: afterwards we walked on to Ramsay & were met & taken up at some distance off by Mr Cayll.[8] Went to the Mitre, a comfortable Inn; and after tea to a large & crowded meeting where I received an Address & spoke at some length. Various visitors here as at Douglas. Read L. Stephen's Johnson (finished) and Irving's Goldsmith.

5. Sat. [Government House, Douglas, Isle of Man]

Evg prayers as usual.

Before (regular) breakfast we went up to St Maryhall & saw the very interesting & rather numerous old crosses: also some stone work in the Church. Mr Cayll drove us by the beautiful road to Sulby and up the Sulby Glen to the Chapel House. We then walked over the shoulder of Snaefell to Government House refreshing in a Cottage by the way. In the evening there was a dinner party of some principal official men & residents. Read Goldsmith—Vehse's Shakespeare.

[1] Gell supervised and annotated a revised ed. of the Manx Statutes, 1417-1895.
[2] Nearly 20 miles N. of Port Erin, on the W. side of the island.
[3] Robert J. Moore, high bailiff of Peel; see Mona's Herald, 4 October 1878, 4.
[4] Gladstone insisted the occasion be non-political, thus to an extent defusing an acrimonious dispute on the island over the nature of the welcome; Mona's Herald, 9 October 1878, 3.
[5] W. Irving, The life of Oliver Goldsmith, 2v. (1844).
[6] Rowley *Hill, 1836-87; bp. of Sodor and Man from 1877.
[7] J. M. Jeffcott.
[8] A. Kayll, of the Island.

Millais' first portrait of Gladstone, painted 1878–9.
See 26 June 78

Gladstone by Franz von Lenbach, painted in Munich.
See 13 Oct 79

'Tree felling by machinery—Mr Gladstone watching a trial of the New Patent Steam Feller near Tulse Hill'. *The Graphic*, 16 February

Gladstone at Hawarden, 1877. 'The very splinters which fell from this axe were picked up and treasured as relics' (*The Times*,

The Midlothian Campaign, 1880.
Facsimile of 4–6 April 1880

Notes for the opening of the first Midlothian Speech,
25 November 1879. *Add MS 44666, f. 63*

Sketch by George Howard, M.P.
See 5 June 79

The house party at Dalmeny during th[e]
first Midlothian Campaign.
See 28 Nov 79

6. S.

St Thomas's Douglas 11 AM. with H.C. and Onchan Ch in evg: rather a notable man there Mr Howard: but said to be a little mad.[1] Read Peel Cathedral Plans—Row Bampton Lecture I—and Appendices.[2] 8 miles walk with the Governor to Douglas Head & in a ring round the tower.

7. M. [Hawarden]

Wrote to Mrs Watts—Lt Governor I.M. from Lpool.—Sir Thos G. (B.P.)—Mr A. Jennings.

We were accompanied by our kind host to the Pier: we both left the Island, & arrived at Liverpool, amidst an ovation. The people even pursued me through the streets: & in galloping cabs I twice could not fully escape. I had to wind up with two short speeches, on the Landing stage, & at Messrs Heywoods where Mr H. constrained me as he thought the crowd in front of a Bank would in these times be misunderstood.[3] Saw Ed. Manx Times & others on the way. The Att. General, High Bailiff & others came down to take leave. In Liverpool saw my nephews R. & W.—Mr [E. R.] Russell of the Daily Post—Mr Holt (Liberal Association)[4] and others. Reached Hawarden at half past six.

I look back with amazement at the notice given me during this little excursion, which was to be so private, & which has drawn out eight (longer & shorter) speeches. I am the first to recognise the cause: the deep hold taken by the Eastern Question & the prominence, into which I have been forced, in relation to that question. It will yet, I hope, all work well.

8. Tu.

Ch. 8¼ A.M. Wrote to Pears & Logan BP.—Publisher of Mona's Herald—Publisher of Manx Times[5]—Rev. D.J. Davies[6]—L. Sergeant[7]—W. Summers[8]—H.H. Hanmer[9]—Mr Silverthorne—Rev. E.R. Wilberforce—C.G.—Mr Tupper—Mr Parsloe—Mr Muirhead. Wrote paper on ὄβριμος & its compounds in Homer.[10] Cut down a Beech with Willy. Walk & conversation with him on Estate matters, & on his residence. Read W. Irving's Life of Goldsmith: & what a life!

---

[1] John Howard, d. 1892; vicar of Onchan from 1847; a well-known eccentric, periodically confined in an asylum; A. W. Moore, *Manx worthies* (1901), 42.

[2] By C. A. Row (1877).

[3] *T.T.*, 8 October 1878, 4e; the City of Glasgow bank failed on 2 October.

[4] Robert Durning Holt, cotton broker and president of the Liverpool liberal association.

[5] Thanking the inhabitants of Man for their welcome, and regretting their loss of deposits in the bankrupt Glasgow bank; printed in *Isle of Man Times*, 12 October 1878, not in *Mona's Herald*.

[6] David Jones Davies, d. 1910; taught at Merchant Taylor's 1870-8; rector of N. Benfleet from 1878.

[7] Lewis Sergeant, d. 1902; Hellenist and author.

[8] William Summers, d. 1893; iron merchant and liberal M.P. Stalybridge 1880-5, Huddersfield 1886-93.

[9] Henry H. Hanmer, Liverpool cotton broker.

[10] Part of 'On Epithets of Movement in Homer', *Nineteenth Century*, v. 463 (March 1879).

9. Wed.

Ch. 8½ AM. Wrote to Mr R.F. Weymouth[1]—W. Nevins BP—O.B. Cole BP—Sir G. Prevost BP—Dean of Durham BP—R. Hardwick—P. Mostyn Williams[2]—Thorndike Rice—A. Macmillan—Capt. Drury[3]—W. Pennack[4]—Rev. C.R.N. Lyne[5]—Rev. Rowland Ellis[6]—Mrs Th.—Lt Govr Isle of Man—J. Bryce—J.F. Cook—E. Baring—F. Wyllie—Jas Knowles—H.C. Webb—J.W. Evans—Jas Power—Dr Hogg[7]—C. Hill. Began Art. on Electoral Statistics for N.C.[8] Woodcraft with Herbert. Read Davies on Jesus Coll.[9]—Life of Goldsmith—Lowe on Imperialism.[10]

10. Th.[11]

Ch. 8½ AM. Wrote to Ld Wolverton—Mr A.E. West—Ld O. Russell—Rev. T.G. Horton[12]—Rev. R.M. Gaunt—Serjeant Pulling[13]—W.H. White[14]—G. Wills[15]—F. Hibbert[16]—C.E. Lester—R.W. Lewis—E.A. Budge—T.T. Hayes. Drew forms & Queries for Electoral Statistics. Walk with C. Howard & much conversation. Saw Rev. Mr Owen. The Argylls came: he, with Colin,[17] & 3 daughters. Much conversation. Read Life of Goldsmith—Early Life of Grattan.[18]

11. Fr.

Ch. 8½ AM. Wrote to Farrer Ouvry & Co BP.—Geo Potter—G.B. Smith—Sir D. Marjoribanks—Wilfrid Meynell—P. Mostyn Williams—Mr Schnadhorst—E. Herford—Mr Zicaliotti[19]—Dean of Bangor—Earl of Rosebery—Mr Knowles Tel.—Mr Johnstone (O)—Rev. Mr Lister l! & B.P.[20]—Mr Stead—A.B. Munro. Read Lester on Mexico[21]—Munro on Liberal Policy[22]—Hibbert on Comml

[1] Richard Francis Weymouth, headmaster of Mill Hill school.

[2] Peter Mostyn Williams (known as Pedr Mostyn) of Rhyl, prominent in Eisteddfods and in nonconformist campaigns.

[3] Perhaps Edward Drury Drury, district surveyor in London.   [4] London wine merchant.

[5] Charles Richard Nunez Lyne, unbeneficed anglican priest in Exeter.

[6] Rowland Ellis, vicar of Mold.

[7] Perhaps Henry Lee Hogg, physician in Shropshire.

[8] 'Electoral Facts', *Nineteenth Century*, iv. 955 (November 1878); lists of calculations at Add MS 44763, f. 139. For this article's origins, see 23, 29 Sept. 78n.

[9] Untraced.

[10] *Fortnightly Review*, xxx. 453 (October 1878).

[11] One of this day's correspondents, 'A Coventry working man', sent Gladstone's reply on trade depression to *T.T.*, 14 October 1878, 10c.

[12] Thomas Galland Horton, religious author.

[13] Alexander Pulling, barrister on the Welsh circuit.

[14] Perhaps William Hale *White, 'Mark Rutherford', 1831-1913; novelist and director of admiralty contracts 1879-91.

[15] Perhaps (Sir) George Alfred Wills (1854-1928) of the tobacco family; the 1878 budget altered Gladstone's 1863 provisions and the family organized protests; see B. W. E. Alford, *W. D. & H. O. Wills* (1973), 131.

[16] See 11 Oct. 78n.

[17] Lord Colin Campbell, 1853-95, Argyll's 5th s.; barrister and liberal M.P. Argyll 1878-85.

[18] G. N. P[lunkett], *The early life of Grattan* (1878).

[19] Alexander Zicaliotti, Liverpool tobacco manufacturer.

[20] Probably Edward Charles Lister, d. 1895?; rector of Stanningley 1876-94.

[21] C. E. Lester, *The Mexican republic. An historic study* (1878).

[22] A. B. Munro had sent his untraced work.

Distress[1]—The People & the Politicians[2]—Jeffcott on Manx Names[3]—Life of Goldsmith. Walk with the Duke & conversation. Also with C. Howard. Saw Rev. Mr Ellis. 14 dined.

12. Sat.

Ch. 8½ A.M. Wrote to Miss Manning l. & B.P.—Dr Acland—Miss Cox (O)—Mr Strahan—Mr Godley—J.A. Cream—Miss Alison (O)—Farrer Ouvry & Co B.P.— Mr Gillespie—J.H. Russell—Rev. Mr Rawson—Rev. Mr England.[4] Saw W.H.G. (affairs)—Dean of Chester. Walk with the Duke. Woodcraft with W.H.G. Read M'Coll on Layard[5]—Lester's Mexico (finished)—Irving's Goldsmith (finished). Mr Ruskin came: health better & no diminution of charm. 12 to dinner.

13. 17 S. Trin.

Ch. 11 AM and 6½ PM. Wrote to Mr Wills—Mr Knowles—Mr West—Rev. Mr M'Coll—Mrs Th.—Mr Sands—Mr Mott—Messrs Chatto & Windus—Sir G. Prevost. Walk with the Duke, Mr Ruskin, & party. Read Mrs Butler's Saint Catherine[6]—Archd. Harrison's Charge.[7]

14. M.

Ch. 8½ A.M. Wrote to Mr R.J. Lindsay—Rev. Mr Torre—Mr Thomas—Mr Lewis—Mr Hardy—J. Morley—A.W. Peel—Rev. Dr Butler—Herr C. Abel— Dowager Lady Cowper—Mr Adam MP.—Sir Thos G.—Ed. of Echo—Mr Strangway—Miss Binns (o)—Miss Adams BP.[8]—Rev. Mr Stephens—Rev. Mr Wilberforce—Sir R. Phillimore. Walk with Mr Ruskin. Read Chap I of the Duke's able book on E.Q.[9] & discussed points with him. They all went off at 2. Mr Ruskin at dinner developed his political opinions. They aim at the restoration of the Judaic system, & exhibit a mixture of virtuous absolutism & Christian socialism. All in his charming & modest manner. Read Elsdale on Tennyson.[10] Worked on Electoral Statistics.

15. Tu. [London]

Wrote to Mr Elmore[11]—Mr Mostyn Williams—Mr Allington Hughes—Ed. Whitehall Review[12]—Rev. Mr Delavingne—Mr G. Wheeler[13]—Mr M'Coll—

---

[1] F. Hibbert, *Bad trade and how to avoid it. By a cotton spinner* (1878).
[2] Not found.   [3] J. M. Jeffcott, *Mann, its names and their origins* (1878).
[4] Perhaps James England, professor at Queen's college, Liverpool and workhouse chaplain there.
[5] Probably M. MacColl's comments in 'Turks, Bulgarians, and Russians', *Nineteenth Century*, ii. 838 (December 1877).
[6] Josephine E. Butler, *Catherine of Siena. A biography* (1878), sent by her husband; Add MS 44457, f. 51. The third ed. (1894) contained Gladstone's letter of 14 October 1878 to Canon Butler expressing appreciation: 'It is interesting to divine the veins of sympathy which may have guided Mrs. Butler in the choice of her subject.'
[7] B. Harrison, 'The more excellent way of unity in the church of Christ' (1878).
[8] Probably Elinor Lily Davenport Adams of Edinburgh, who earlier sent verses; Add MS 44443, f. 53.   [9] See 4 June 78.
[10] H. Elsdale, *Studies in the Idylls. An essay* (1878).   [11] Perhaps Alfred *Elmore, 1815-81; painter.
[12] W. Meynell, acting for the editor, had sent an issue with lists of converts to Rome; Add MS 44457, f. 27.   [13] Perhaps George Domville Wheeler, vicar of Wolford.

Ld Wolverton—Mr Flynn. Goodbye to Mr Ruskin, & off for London at 9.5. Arrived at 3.30. Saw Mr Wills—Mr Rice—Hon N. Lyttelton. Dined at 9 B. Square. Set to work on the usual chaotic mass of letters & papers. Read Cook on Cyprus[1]—Caird on Agriculture[2]—Contemp. Rev. on American competition.[3]

16. Wed.

Breakf. & dinner with Mrs Birks. Luncheon 15 G. Square. Wrote to Lady Alice Peel—Arundel Socy[4]—Mr Markley[5]—Mr Black—Secy R. Acad.—Mrs Watts[6]—Mrs Joyner[7]—Mr E. Pearson—Lt Kavanaugh[8]—Mr F. Knollys[9]—Gov. Jamaica[10]—Mr J. Knowles—Mr King—Mr Bodkin.[11] Saw Mr Stead—Mr MacColl—Sir A. Panizzi—Madame Novikoff—Mr Hayward—Scotts—Dr Weymouth—Mr Jackson[12]—10-11½ on El. (Statistics)—Mr Stead, on E.Q. papers—Miss Duvray. Saw Monty—Witney [R].

17. Th.

Breakf. Mrs B. Dinner Ld F.C.s. Wrote to Mr Mathias U.S.[13]—Mr W.R. King[14]—Mr Geo. Leeman MP—Jas Aston—A. Dunn. Saw Mrs Tyler & the Walkers—Mr F. Lawley—Mr Murray & Mr Cooke—Ld Odo Russell—Edw. Lyttelton. Worked on Kin beyond Sea.[15] Worked on Electoral Facts. A hard day. Saw one [R]. No reading!

18. Fr.

Breakf. Mrs Birks. Dinner at 15 G.S. Saw S.E.G.—Agnes Wickham—Ld Wolverton—Mr Cave—Mr Wills—Mr Colet[16]—Mr Bramwell—Mr Fludye—Sir A. Panizzi—Messrs Scott. Dined at 15 G.S. Much conversation with Mlle Domray.[17] Finished the statistics & the paper on Election Facts: a hard day. No reading: saw one. Bookpacking & shopping.

[1] Probably W. S. Cooke, *The Ottoman Empire and its tributary states* (1876).

[2] J. Caird, *The landed interest and the supply of food* (1878).

[3] *Contemporary Review*, xxxi. 458 (October 1878).

[4] Founded 1848 for the publication of facsimiles etc.; business untraced.

[5] J. T. Markley sent a work on spiritualism (Hawn P); Gladstone replied: 'I do not share the temper of simple contempt [for spiritualism] . . . I remain in what may be called contented reserve'; *T.T.*, 18 October 1878, 8f.

[6] Possibly (Alice) Ellen *Terry 1847-1928, recently divorced from G. F. *Watts.

[7] M. A. Joyner; see 9 Nov. 78.

[8] Lieut. James Caveneaugh, R.N., Greenwich liberal; changing date of Greenwich meeting from 31 October; *T.T.*, 21 October 1878, 9f; see 30 Nov. 78.

[9] Francis *Knollys (see 4 Oct. 63), secretary to the Prince of Wales from 1870; a well-known liberal.

[10] (Sir) Edward Newton, 1832-97; governed Jamaica 1877-83; business untraced.

[11] Of Dublin; probably Christopher Bodkin; sent a pamphlet; Hawn P.

[12] Perhaps M. S. Jackson; see 26 Oct. 78.

[13] F. W. Mathias of St Louis, U.S.A., sent his tr., *The conquest of the world by the Jews*; Hawn P.

[14] Declining invitation of William R. King to visit the Luton liberal association; Hawn P.

[15] For a pamphlet edition; see 28 June 78.

[16] Perhaps Mark Wilks Collet, a director of the Bank of England.

[17] i.e. a friend of Laura Thistlethwayte's, probably the same as 'Duvray' at 16 October.

19. Sat. [Latimer, Buckinghamshire]

Wrote to Rev. D.B. Hooke—Mr F. Dawson—Lieut. Kavaneagh—Mr C.T. Newton—Mr Ellis—Mr Weir—Mr Glover—Mr Wright—Dr Parker—Mrs Staite. Read Catholic Barrister on R.C. Education.[1] Breakf. with Mrs Birks: & off before 9 with a large party to the happy marriage at Latimer.[2] The service was at 11.45. The banquet at one: when I (the oldest person present) was set up to propose the bride and bridegroom. How[ever?][3] if the speech was bad the marriage was good. Walk in aftn. Wrote to Ed. D. News—Mr Mitchell. Saw Ld Carrington & many guests.

20. 18 S. Trin.

Ch 11 AM. Baptism afr Ch evg. Wrote to S.E.G.—Bp Abraham—Mr Peachey.[4] Read C.Q.R. on Irvingism—The conquest of the world by the Jews—Q.R. on Protestantism of Ch. of E.[5] Walk with C.

21. M. [Woburn Abbey]

Wrote to Mr W.F. Wilson[6]—Mr Cowper Temple—Mr Bosomerville—A. Peel— Mr Caird. Read R.H. Lang's Cyprus[7]—Q.R. on Revival of Turkey. Off at 3. Reached Woburn[8] at six: about 16 m rail & sixteen road. We were most kindly received & found a pleasant party. Conversation especially with M. d'Harcourt[9] and H. Cowper on Renaissance.

22. Tu.

Wrote to Ed. Echo[10]—Mrs Wynne—Mrs Roberts—Mr Barker—E.C. Robins[11]— Press Association (Tel)—Mr Potter[12]—Mr E. Franklin[13]—Mr Theobald—Mr Downing. Out with the Duke mg & aft. seeing School—Trees—town of Woburn &c. Also I cut down a Deodara [sic] assisted by the Duke. Deputation came from Bedford: but I steadily declined to go. Conversation with Mr Howard. Read QR. on Petrarch—Ld Lawrence on Malta[14]—Lang on Cyprus. Mary's playing is much appreciated.

[1] Not further identified.
[2] Mary Susan Caroline, da. of 2nd Baron Chesham, m. 8th Viscount Cobham, Catherine Gladstone's nephew.
[3] Two small triangular wedges affecting pages 136-45 have been cut out of the text, apparently to remove blots at the edge of the page.
[4] Perhaps Alfred Peachey, clerk to the Feltmakers' company.
[5] *Quarterly Review*, cxlvi. 519 (October 1878).
[6] Walter F. Wilson of Kentish Town; on Homer; Hawn P.
[7] R. H. Lang, *Cyprus: its history, its present resources and future prospects* (1878).
[8] Seat in Bedfordshire of the 9th duke of Bedford.
[9] Marquis D'Harcourt, d. 1883; French ambassador in London 1875-9.
[10] Not visiting Bedford; *The Echo*, 23 October 1898, 1.
[11] Edward Cook Robins, London architect.
[12] George Walpole Potter, curate in Abingdon; on future retribution, in Lathbury, ii. 105 and Hawn P.
[13] Perhaps Ellis Abraham Franklin, City banker.
[14] Not found published; probably a letter to the press.

23. *Wed.*

Wrote to Mr Combes—Dr Von Döllinger. Corrected proofs of 'Electoral Facts' for 19th Cent. Long walk round the Park with Ld Tavistock:[1] it seems almost unique for extent & variety. Read Lang's Cyprus—Q.R. on Cyprus—Q.R. on Thiers.[2] Conversation with M. d'Harcourt—Lady Tavistock who has much mixed—& others.

24. *Th.* [*Wrest Park, Bedfordshire*]

Wrote to Spottiswoodes—Mr Adam MP—J. Murray—Hon Sir A. Gordon—Sec. Clerk's Union—Mrs Wynne—Rev. S.E.G. After seeing the Duke's Chapel of Ease, F.L. & I started for the beautiful park of Ampthill. What a situation for a house! then we walked on to Wrest,[3] stateliest of great places. Lady Cowper's kindness overflows as freely as her intelligence shines. A small very pleasant party remained after the Bedfords who came over bid goodbye. Read Morley's Diderot[4]—Lang's Cyprus.

25. *Fr.*

Wrote to Messrs Pears & Logan BP (2). . . . Read P. Aretino:[5] who has more force & point as a writer than I had supposed—Dr Johnson & his friends[6]—Lang's Cyprus. We enjoyed this conversible circle of kind people. Walked out, as also yesterday, to examine the very curious wreck wrought by the *tornado* of Thurs. morning along a very narrow & short line: also to observe the noble oaks reaching above 25 feet in circumference.

26. *Sat.* [*Cambridge*][7]

Wrote to Treasurer Mid. Temple—Prince Louis L. Bonaparte—Rev. R. Bushell—Mr W. Clarke—Mr A.S. Murray—Mr M.S. Jackson. Off at 2.45 to Cambridge: where I met at dinner Prof. Westcott,[8] Mr Stuart[9] & an interesting party as well as Helen with her Principal Miss Clough.[10] Read Trelawney on Byron & Shelley[11]—P. Aretino—Lang's Cyprus—Schwickert, de l'Allemagne.[12] Much

---

[1] George William Francis Sackville Russell, 1852-93; styled Lord Tavistock; liberal M.P. Bedfordshire 1875-85; 10th duke of Bedford 1891; m. 1876 Lady Adeline Marie Somers-Cocks.

[2] *Quarterly Review*, cxlvi. 443 (October 1878).

[3] Seat of 7th Earl Cowper; see 22 Apr. 66. His wife Anne was Ripon's cousin.

[4] J. Morley, *Diderot and the Encyclopaedists*, 2v. (1878).

[5] See 27 Dec. 43.

[6] See 24 July 78.

[7] He and Catherine Gladstone stayed with Henry and Eleanor Sidgwick.

[8] Brooke Foss *Westcott, 1825-1901; Broadchurch biblical scholar; regius professor of divinity at Cambridge 1870-90; social reforming bp. of Durham from 1890.

[9] James Stuart, 1843-1913; professor of mechanism at Cambridge 1875-89; contested Cambridge University 1882; liberal M.P. Hackney 1884-5, Hoxton 1885-1900; promoted university extension; friendly with Mary Gladstone.

[10] Anne Jemima Clough, 1820-95; principal of Newnham hall 1875, of Newnham college from 1880. Helen Gladstone studied at Newnham 1877-80 without sitting the tripos; she was secretary to Miss Clough 1880-2, and to Mrs Sidgwick, and was vice-principal of North hall 1882-96.

[11] E. J. Trelawney, *Records of Shelley, Byron and the Author*, 2v. (1878).

[12] J. J. Schwickert, *De l'Allemagne littéraire et philologique* (1879).

morning conversation at Wrest where Lady C. has been most kind. Much to see here in China pictures & books.

27. 19 S. Trin.

Trinity Chapel at 10.30. Univ. Sermon (Bp of Ely) at 2 P.M. King's College at 3½. Tea with Alfred Lyttelton.[1] Saw Lady Lothian—Mr Stewart [sc. Stuart] & his workrooms—Mr A. Legh[2]—Mr [Oscar] Browning—Mr Clark—& others. Dined in Trinity Hall: which I did also 47 years ago.[3] Wrote to Spottiswoodes. Read Holland's Sermon[4]—Ch. Q.R. on Development—M. Queen of Scots—& divers.[5]

28. M. SS. S & J.

Wrote to Mr Adam Tel. & L.—Spottiswoode's—Tel. & L.—Curate of Hawarden Tel.—Mr J.W. Cooper[6]—Mr Budge. At 11 AM. to see the noble Olympian Casts at the F[itzwilliam] Museum—also the Library. Then to Corpus—Mr Lewis's Collection[7]—over the College—& saw the valuable MSS of the Library. Being somewhat deranged I lay down in the aftn & was able to join the dinner party when the meal had concluded. Saw Dr Lightfoot—Mr S. Taylor[8]—Mr Hamrad[9]—Mr Fawcett—Mr Hall[10]—Master of St Johns—& much conversation with our host. Read Lang's Cyprus—Q.R. on Dryden (part).[11]

29. Tu.

King's Chapel Service at 5 PM. Wrote to Mr Engleheart—Sir A. Gordon—Mr G. Potter—Rev. Canon Lowe—Mr H. Paull[12]—Dean Nicolson—Mrs Wortley—Mr Mostyn Williams—Rev. A.H. Burton[13]—Mr Tozer (O)—Mr Laurence (& Sec. Gr. Lib. Assn)[14]—W.H.G. Saw Master of Trinity—Master of St Johns—Master of Downing—Provost of King's—St Johns Chapel & Coll.—Magd. Coll. & Library. Saw Mr Gurney—Mr Budge—Mr Jackson—& others. Finished Q.R. on Dryden. Went over Nuneham [sic] College: much pleased with the structure & all I saw. Dined with Mr Balfour.

---

[1] Then an undergraduate at Trinity.

[2] Sic; none of this name then at Cambridge; if 'Leigh', then several possible, including Augustus *Austen Leigh, 1840-1905; fellow of King's 1862; Provost from 1889.

[3] i.e. in the hall of Trinity College; see 15-19 Dec. 31.

[4] F. J. Holland, 'The constraint of Christ' (1878).

[5] Church Quarterly Review, vii. 123 (October 1878).

[6] John William Cooper, d. 1906; Cambridge barrister and J.P.

[7] Samuel Strange Lewis, d. 1891, fellow of Corpus; had a collection of classical antiquities in a gallery next his rooms.

[8] Sedley Taylor, 1834-1920; fellow of Trinity, Cambridge, 1861; scientist and musician; published on Bulgarian atrocities.

[9] Apparently sic.

[10] Henry Hall, d. 1897; vicar of St Paul's, Cambridge 1862-90.

[11] Quarterly Review, cxlvi. 289 (October 1878).

[12] See 16 May 62?

[13] Alfred Henry Burton, ca. 1850-1934; revivalist preacher and writer.

[14] (Sir) Percival Maitland Laurence, 1854-1930; tutor of Cavendish college, Cambridge, 1876; later a barrister and judge in South Africa; see Add MS 44458, f. 97 for his request for a ticket to the Greenwich meeting.

30. Wed. [Hawarden]

Wrote to Mr Adam MP—Mr Daniels—Mr Bourne—Mr Harrald[1]—Ld R. Grosvenor. Saw Mr Staunton[2] & others. Much conversation with my kind & noteworthy host. Off at 11. Hawarden at 6.30: with the Bp of BloemFontein.[3] Read Q.R. on Rise of the British Empire[4]—Lang's Cyprus (finished)—Oetker on Heligoland.[5]

31. Th.

Ch. 8½ AM. Wrote to Mr Knowles—Mr Thomas—Mr Wilberforce. Read Dunckley's powerful paper.[6] Worked on letters &c. Worked also on Affghan & other points of the political case. 2.30–10.30. To Rhyl: presided at a luncheon extremely well served & at a great & warm meeting of 5000 which with some effort in the great Rink Building I addressed for 1½ hour; acting also as Chairman. There was some very good speaking: & a feeling towards me by which I was much embarrassed.[7] Saw D. of Westminster—Ld R. Grosvenor—Mr Watkin Williams—Mr Roberts (MP)—and others. Conversation with Bishop of B[loemfontein].

Friday. All Saints N. 1.

Wrote to Ld Cardwell—Mr G. Hopwood—Scotts—Made Novikoff—Sir Thos G.—Rev. Mr M'Lean[8]—Mr Cossham—Mr Stapelton—Mr W. Severn—Mr Pendebury[9]—Secs Open Ch. Assocn[10]—Rev. Canon Oakeley. Much conversation with Willy on his plan for building a new House.[11] Also we visited the site. It has a magnificent view but I suspect a bad soil. Walk with Mr [E. R.] Wilberforce. Long conversation with him on the case of Seaforth Church now vacant.[12] Read Ld Stratford de Redcliffe in 19th Cent.[13]

---

[1] Joseph W. Harrald of Upper Norwood, on *Spurgeon; Hawn P.

[2] Perhaps John Staunton, 1800-79; Caius college; presented his library to Birmingham 1875.

[3] Allan Becher *Webb, 1839-1907; bp. of Bloemfontein 1870-83, of Grahamstown 1883-98. Stayed at Hawarden Castle.

[4] Quarterly Review, cxlvi. 331 (October 1878).

[5] F. Oetker, Helgoland Schilderungen und Erörterungen (2nd ed. 1878).

[6] H. Dunkley, 'The progress of personal rule', Nineteenth Century, iv. 785 (November 1878); as 'Verax', published sundry expositions of royal influence; see 29 June 78.

[7] Spoke on Afghanistan; T.T., 1 November 1878, 8a.

[8] Perhaps Hippisley Maclean, d. 1895; vicar of Caistor 1844-86.

[9] W. H. Pendlebury of Bolton, on Homer; Hawn P.

[10] John Kirk, secretary of the Open-Air Mission.

[11] Built 1883 as Hawarden House (later the Red House) SW. of the village; later occupied by Lady F. Cavendish and, briefly, by Morley.

[12] Wilberforce became canon of Winchester, being briefly succeeded in Gladstone's living of Seaforth by John Lyndhurst Winslow, vicar of Seaforth 1878-9. See 20 Nov. 78n., 7 Dec. 78, 17 Feb. 79.

[13] Nineteenth Century, iv. 932 (November 1878).

2. *Sat.*

Ch. 8¼ A.M. Wrote to Bp of Winchester—Mr Taylor Innes[1]—Ld Granville—Ld Northbrook—Ld Fortescue—Canon Ashwell—Mr Horsley R.A.[2]—Rev. Mr Knapton BP[3]—Rev. Mr W.R.W. Stephens[4]—Miss Cartwright—Mr Macarthy[5]— J.H. Clayton—J. Petherick[6]—Mr Crosby Lockwood[7]—T.J. Heywood—Herr Abel B.P.—Mrs Hughes—Mr Stead—W. Pole—Mr Stearn—Mr Higgins—J. Lee—W.S. Lee—Mr Stephen—J. Usher—P. Parry. Further conversation with Willy & Gertrude: & examined sites nearer us & the Church. Also full conversation with Mr Wilberforce on the Seaforth vacancy & the Church. I see more of Neville [Lyttelton]; & like him in proportion. Read Herr [blank, *sc.* Oetker] on Heligoland (finished)—Rhodopè Commission Papers[8]—Lowe on Pol. Economy 19th C.[9]

3. *20 S. Trin.*

Ch. 11 AM & H.C.—Also [blank.] Wrote to Duke of Argyll—Bishop of Chester— Rev. Mr Suffield. Walk with N. Lyttelton. Read Mr Knapton's Sermon—Dr Littledale's remarkable answer to Abbé Martin.[10]

4. *M.*

Ch. 8¼ AM. Wrote to Mr W.C. Jenkinson—J.H. Wright—Rev. T. Russell—Rev. J. Myers[11]—Miss Cusack—S.G. Rathbone—Rev. Mr Gardiner[12]—Rev. Dr Littledale—Messrs Pears & Logan—Sec. Acad. Hongroise[13]—Chairman Lib. Assoc. Greenock[14]—Editor of Lynn News[15]—Dr Wilde[16]—Mr Thomas—Mr Infield—G. Harris—C.H. Lake—C. Hindley. Woodcraft with N. Lyttelton. Read Trees in

[1] This letter, dated 1 November 1878, is in A. Taylor Innes, *Chapters of reminiscence* (1913), 129-30; it prepares the way for Gladstone's noncommittal statement to Rainy on Scottish disestablishment (see 23 May 79) by arguing: 'In the Scotch case, which is alone alive, it is a serious matter to throw overboard the whole of those who will refuse to adopt the abstract doctrine of Disestablishment, but who do not desire to urge the maintenance of an Establishment for the minority', Gladstone supporting numbers as well as principle as a criterion for disestablishment.

[2] John Callcott Horsley, 1817-1903; exhibited at R.A. from 1836.

[3] W. J. Knapton had sent his Address; see 3 Nov. 78.

[4] William Richard Wood Stephens (1839-1902; rector of Woolbeding 1876-94; dean of Winchester from 1894) working on his life of W. F. Hook, using letters lent by Gladstone.

[5] Probably *sc.* M'Carthy; see 14 Nov. 55.

[6] His newsagent.

[7] London publisher of almanacs and handbooks.

[8] International commission on supposed Russian atrocities at Rhodopé; see 16 Dec. 78.

[9] *Nineteenth Century*, iv. 858 (November 1878).

[10] R. F. Littledale, 'Why Ritualists do not become Roman Catholics', *Contemporary Review*, xxxiii. 792 (November 1878).

[11] Perhaps Alfred Joseph Myers, vicar of St Simon, Chelsea.

[12] Perhaps William B. Gardiner of Glasgow; see Add MS 44464, f. 99.

[13] Perhaps on Beust's departure from London; see *T.T.*, 23 November 1878, 5e.

[14] i.e. J. R. Jolly.

[15] Not found published.

[16] Frederick George Stanley Wilde, physician in Taunton, had sent his *Brainfag from mental worry and overwork* (1877); Hawn P.

Towns[1]—Wilde on Brainfag—Speech of Sir H. Parkes[2]—Wormstall's Hesperien[3]—Davies on Slate[4]—Institutions Comparées.[5]

5. *Tu.*

Ch. 8½ A.M. Wrote to Duke of Argyll—Ed. Daily News—Rev. Mr Beaven[6]—Rev. Mr Henderson—Bishop of Peterborough BP—Mr Allen—Mr [S. A.] Hart F.S.A.—Mr Mogford—Mrs Grote—Rev. M. M'Coll—Rev. E. Wickham B.P.—Mr Knowles—Mr Findlay—T. Williams—Mr Gadsby[7]—F.R. Lawley. Woodcraft with N. Lyttelton. Read Davies, Slate Quarries—Friend of India on Affghan Q.[8]—Campbell Scarlett on do[9]—Institutions Comparées. Eight to dinner.

6. *Wed.*

Ch. 8½ AM. Wrote to Mr Mostyn Williams—Earl Fortescue—Ld De Tabley—Sir Ar. Gordon—Rev. J. Kallaway—Rev. Dr Irons—R. Leake[10]—Mr Adam MP—J. Watt—A. Keen—J.S. Lewis. N. L[yttelton] went: a fine fellow. Woodcraft near the Mill. Read Institutions Comparées. Worked for 5 hours on perusing & correcting Essays for the Reprint: rather a daring measure.[11] Saw Mr Green.[12] Worked on books & papers.

7. *Th.*

Ch. 8½ A.M. Wrote to Lord Tenterden—J.S. Gladstone—Mr Murray—Mr Dillwyn MP—C. Hindley—Mr Hose l. & BP.[13]—Rector of Sephton[14]—De La Fleurière—Mrs Hedley—C. Foster—E. Robson—Jas Knowles—A.C. Ellis. Worked on a large ash. Saw Mr Torr, on Buckley Institute. 5 more hours on revising for reprint. I dispatched to Mr Murray nearly the whole material for the first Volume. It will be published on something like the Tauchnitz scale and plan. Read Mrs Grote on Political Events[15]—Godwin on a Central Theatre.[16]

8. *Fr.*

Ch. 8½ A.M. Wrote to Mr Bayley Potter—Mr W. Wren—Messrs Hinde (O)—Mr J.E. Brown—Mr Leeman MP—Mrs Th.—Mr J.R. Haig[17]—Dean of Manchester—

---

[1] Untraced.
[2] Sir H. Parkes, *Speeches on various occasions connected with the public affairs of New South Wales* (1876).
[3] J. Wormstall, *Hesperien. Zur Lösung des religiös-geschichtlichen Problems der alten Welt* (1878).
[4] D. C. Davies, *Slate quarrying* (1878).   [5] See 19 Sept. 78.
[6] Alfred Beaven Beaven, headmaster of Preston grammar school.
[7] John Gadsby, London publisher.
[8] By one of F. Lawley's collaborators on the *Telegraph*; sent by Lawley, Add MS 44458, f. 104.
[9] Untraced paper by Peter Campbell Scarlett, 1804-88, diplomat.
[10] On the political situation; *T.T.*, 8 November 1878, 8e.
[11] i.e. the start of sustained work on preparing *Gleanings*; see 6 Sept. 77.
[12] Secretary of the Manchester liberals; *T.T.*, 8 November 1878, 8e.
[13] J. W. E. Hose (see 3 Dec. 78); business untraced.
[14] Englebert Horley, rector of Sefton 1871, involved in the appt. at Seaforth.
[15] H. G[rote], *A brief retrospect of the Political Events of 1831-32* (1878).
[16] G. Godwin, *On the desirability of obtaining a National Theatre not wholly controlled by the prevailing popular taste* (1878).
[17] James Richard Haig, 1831-96, of Blairhill, Perthshire; F.S.A.

Mr Williams. Woodcraft: the ash came down, with a split, under wind. Worked on Essays—Blanco White—G. Leopardi. Read Institutions Comparées (notes), and. . . .

9. Sat.

Ch. 8½ A.M. Wrote to Lieut. Cavenaugh—Sir E. Perry—Père Hyacinthe—Mr Murray (2)—Mr Pughe Jones[1]—Spottiswoodes—Mr H. Phillips—Scotts—Mr Wilson—Mr Coombs—Mr Atwell—Mr Ellison. Woodcraft in aftn. Saw Mr Vickers. Worked on Essays for Reprint: G. Leopardi—Suffrage (from Symposium). Read Miss? Joyner's Cyprus[2]—Instit. Comparées (Notes)—began Mozley on Blanco White.[3]

10. 21 S. Trin.

Ch. 11 AM. & 6½ P.M. Admirable Sermon by S. & singing practice afterwards. Wrote to Mrs Wortley—Publisher of Manchr Examiner l. & B.P.[4] Read Mozley on Blanco White (finished)—Père Hyacinthe, Réforme Catholique[5]—Hopps in the Truthseekers.[6]

11. M.

Ch. 8½ AM. Wrote to Sir Henry Layard—Mr Wallis—Mr H. Moore—Mr Morison—W.H.G.—M. Jovanovitch—Ld Fortescue—Prof. Geddes—Mons. Sigalis[7]—Miss Joyner—Mr Libbey (Princeton Rev.) Woodcraft, a little: weather wild. Read Wild's Thalassa[8]—Stewart on the Martyrs.[9] Read a few things for the evg work. 6-9. To tea at Mr Torr's: then to the Meeting for the Institute where I spoke to an attentive man-audience over ¾ hour.[10] Saw Mr Cook. Saw Mr Vickers.

12. Tu.

Ch. 8½ AM. Wrote to Ld Tenterden—H.N.G.—Mr Riach—Mr Kelly BP—Ed. of Echo—Mr Coombs—Mr Bright—Bedford Liberal Association[11]—Mr Bright MP—A. Ward[12]—J.G. Dodson—W. Phillips—Mr Mostyn Williams—Lieut. Cavenaugh—Louey G. (Fasque)—Mr Kilburn—J.R. Jolly. Read Wedderburn on Protected Princes of India[13]—Stewart on the Martyrs—Thom on Peter the Great's Will.[14] Saw Mr Townshend. Worked on the Reprint.

[1] Robert Pughe Jones, barrister on the N. Wales circuit.
[2] Mrs M. A. Joyner, *Cyprus, historical and descriptive* (1878).
[3] J. B. Mozley in *Christian Remembrancer*, reprinted in his *Essays*, 2v. (1878); see *Gleanings*, ii. 63 for a tribute.   [4] Not published.
[5] C. J. M. Loyson, *Les Principes de la réforme catholique* (1878).
[6] J. P. Hopps, *The truth seeker* (1878).
[7] Possibly Jean Sigaux, published *Souvenirs d'Orient* (1876).   [8] By J. J. Wild (1878).
[9] A. Stewart, *History vindicated in the case of the Wigton martyrs* (n.d.); see *Gleanings*, iii. 225n.
[10] Organized by Rev. W. F. W. Torre to raise funds for the Buckley institute; *T.T.*, 13 November 1878, 4d.   [11] Replying to its address; *T.T.*, 14 November 1878, 8a.
[12] Perhaps (Sir) Adolphus *Ward, 1837-1924; historian.
[13] D. Wedderburn, 'Protected princes of India', *Nineteenth Century*, iv. 151 (July 1878).
[14] W. J. Thoms, 'The will of Peter the Great', ibid., iv. 88 (July 1878).

13. Wed.

Ch. 8½ AM. Wrote to Lord Northbrook—Mrs Burnett l. & BP.—Rev. Mr Merry BP—D.B. Monro BP[1]—O. Browning BP—Rev. Dr Bartle—F. Leslie (U.S.)[2]—C. Macgregor—Scotts—Mr Murray—Mr Allen—Mr Morris—G. Moore—Dr Temple—Mr [blank.] Woodcraft. The Wests came: conversation with him. Worked on the Reprint (Erastus &c.) Putting books & papers in order.

14. Th.

Ch. 8¼ AM. Wrote to Madam Novikoff—Ld Cranbrook—Mr Findlay—Rev. Mr Williams—Mr Kilbourn (O)—C. Harris (O)—G. Phillips—R. Somerville[3]—J.W. Edwards[4]—Sir F. Doyle—Mr A. Dunn[5]—Sig. L. Feriji[6]—Mr Plant[7]—Mr Manning—J.L. Conn—J.B. Hay[8]—Rev. J. Ellis.[9] Much conversation & walk with West. Woodcraft. Worked on articles for reprint. Reperusal of Patteson moves even me to tears.[10] What an eyrie height he reached! What he did, for God & for the Church. Praise to the Highest in the height! Read Stewart on the Wigton Martyrdoms. It is a very curious case. Conversation with West.

15.

Ch. 8¼ AM. Wrote to French Ambassador—Ld Granville—Sec. Affghan Committee[11]—Sir E. Perry—Mr Baker—Mr Allnutt—Mr Edwards—Mr Llewellyn Lewis[12]—Mr Bright—Mrs Lockhart—Mr Spalding—Mr Westell—Mrs Arding. Woodcraft. Read Lockhart on Saving.[13] Worked on Vol. II. of reprints. The Baths came.[14] Conversation in evening, & late.

16. Sat.

Ch. 8½ AM. Wrote to Mr E.H. Bayley—Ld Granville—Prof. Knight[15]—Mr Coghlan—Mr Craighead—Rear Adm. Maxse[16]—Mrs Stuart Wortley—J. Box—F. Pope—Mr Briant—Mr Jackson. Walk with Ld Bath and Mr West. Worked on Reprints: much. 11 to dinner: Duchess of Westmr & the Locks came.

[1] David Binning Monro, 1836-1905; fellow of Oriel, provost there from 1882; Homerist.
[2] Frank Leslie of New York unsuccessfully requested an article for the *Popular Monthly*; Hawn P.
[3] Perhaps R. G. Somerville of Glasgow; later wrote on Gladstone genealogy; Hawn P.
[4] Perhaps John William Edwards, barrister to the education cttee.
[5] Unsuccessful liberal candidate in Southwark.
[6] Name scrawled.
[7] Probably William Plant, London auctioneer.
[8] John Baldwin Hay of Southport; Hawn P.
[9] Possibly John Clough Williams Ellis, 1833-1913; fellow of Sidney Sussex, Cambridge, 1856-77; rector of Gayton 1876-89.
[10] C. M. Yonge's biography of J. C. Patteson; see 2 July 74n.
[11] Needing 'a day to consider'; see Bodley MS Eng. lett. e. 118, f. 135 and 18 Nov. 78n.
[12] Walter Llewellyn Lewis, London barrister; Hawn P.
[13] Mary Jane Lockhart sent her 'Something about saving' (1878).
[14] The tory peer, active in support of the Bulgarian atrocities campaign.
[15] William Angus Knight, 1836-1916; professor of moral philosophy at St Andrews 1876-1902; Wordsworthian editor and critic.
[16] Frederick Augustus *Maxse, 1833-1900; retired sailor; wrote on social issues; radical, but opposed home rule.

17. 22 S. Trin.

Ch 11 AM (and H.C.) also [blank.] Wrote to Mr Hayward—Mr Sheldon Amos—Mr A.G. Puller. I read through Mrs Bennetts account of Dora Tyrrell in 'Passing away'.[1] And with very sad feelings. The picture is beautiful and holy: the narrative very touching. But I cannot think it normal: and part I think mythical. It reads like a case of childhood projected against nature into youth. Why were those fine powers & that promise which we recalled in the child thus without a sign of progress or development? Most surely these are not the normal results which our Lord died to achieve. And a lot of vices or faults are here laid upon her early years to make up a case of moral as well as ecclesiastical conversion, about which we heard nothing when the child, at that time remarkable, used to come over here. Walk with the party, and much conversation.

18. M.

Ch. 8½ AM. Wrote to Dean of Chester—Mr Edwards—F.W. Potter[2]—Mr Reachman—Mr Fitzpatrick—Messrs Longman—Sec. Affghan Association[3]—Ld Granville—Mr Read BP—Mr Strahan—Priv. Sec. Ld Cranbrook—Mr Gallenga. Woodcraft. Worked on Reprints. Read Institutions Comparées. The Clergy helped out our party.

19. Tu.

Ch. 8½ AM. Wrote to Sir Ar. Gordon BP—Messrs Leeman BP—Mr Samuelson—Scotts—Ld Carnarvon—Mr J. Heys—Mr Schnadhorst—Mr Bendall[4]—Hon F. Lawley. Walk with C. The Baths went, much regretted: & Mr Murray. Worked on reprints. The Lochs[5] came. Read Jennings on the U.S. Government.[6]

20. Wed.

Ch. 8½ AM. Wrote to Col. Mure & draft[7]—Mr Malcolm Stark—J.E.T. Rogers—Mr Andrews—Mr G. Harris—Mr Luke—Mr Agnew—Mrs Bailey. Read Col. Mure's Speech—Luke's [*sc.* Stark's] Biography of W.E.G. (& corrected it).[8] Worked on

---

[1] His cousin, Mrs A. R. Bennett, sent 'a little book called *Passing away*', about her da. who d. aged 20; see Add MS 44108.

[2] *Sc.* G. W. Potter; Hawn P.

[3] Wrote this day to the Afghan committee (Bodley MS Eng. lett. e. 118, f. 136 and *T.T.*, 23 November 1878, 5e): unable to join the cttee., but 'The Government mean . . . if there is to be war, to begin it without taking any steps to ascertain the views of Parliament . . . the war will be made with Indian money and Indian troops, and the Act of 1858 again, as I consider, broken and trodden underfoot.' Recall of Parliament announced on 22 November.

[4] Perhaps J. L. Bendall, clerk in the board of trade.

[5] H. B. *Loch, lieut. governor of Man, and his wife Elizabeth.

[6] Untraced correspondent.

[7] Colonel William Mure, 1830-80; liberal M.P. Renfrewshire from 1874; had sent his speech on imperial policy (*T.T.*, 30 October 1878, 6e) which Gladstone's draft opposed; Add MS 44458, f. 159.

[8] Stark sent his 'penny life' of Gladstone 'by a London journalist' (copy at Add MS 44458, f. 173) for correction; an enlarged hardback was published January 1879, see also M. Stark, *The pulse of the world* (1915), 62, 74.

reprints. Walk in much fog with the Lochs. Conversation on the Seaforth Candidates.[1] The Frosts dined.

21. Th.

Ch. 8¼ AM. Wrote to Bp of Chester—Mr Macfie—Mr Chesson—J. Murray—G. Leeman—La Derazione del Dovere[2]—Mr E.R. Russell (2)—M. Brunswik[3]—W. Hodges—Rev. Mr Morgan—W. Main—Mr Maccullagh BP—Rev. Mr Mossman B.P.—Mrs Th. Woodcraft. This morning the *rime* on the trees was wonderful & lovely to a degree. When it fell, under the limes, in the afternoon, it was like snow or small icicle an inch deep. Worked on reprints. Read Maud[4]—Smiles's Life of Dick[5]—The Naturalist.[6]

22. Fr.

Ch. 8¼ AM. Wrote to Sir E. Perry BP—Principal Caird BP—Mr Redish l. & BP[7]—Mrs Lockhart BP—Rev. Mr M'Coll—Rev. Mr Bellairs—Rev. Mr W. Webb—Mr Samuelson—Mr Jolly—Mr Saunders—Mrs Bailey—F. Verney.[8] Woodcraft. Worked largely on reprint: for which my preparations advance with expedition. Read Maud (finished)—Life of Rob. Dick.

23. Sat.

Ch. 8¼ AM. Wrote to Central Press (Tel)—Ld Northbrook—J.A. Godley—J. Murray—J.H. Bailey—Mr Jennings BP—Sir R. Phillimore—W.H.G.—F. Proctor[9]—Mr Hüttel[10]—J.H. Carse. Woodcraft. Worked on reprint. Saw S.E.G. on W.s plans. The Gordons came. Much conversation with Sir Arthur. Read Smiles's Dick—Mrs Gill on Ascension I.[11]

24. Preadv. S.

Ch 11 AM (admirable Sermon from Mr Ottley on Ecclesiastes) and [blank.] Wrote to Miss Chambres—Mr Murray—Dr Conder—Mr Childers 2—Me Novikoff—Rev. W. Denton BP—Rev. Dr Plumptre. Read Plumptre's Sermon[12]—

---

[1] See 1 Nov. 78; De Tabley recommended W. Harris ('he is a High Churchman (as it is called)—but devoid of nonsense and is perfectly *sound*'), E. R. Russell, and R. B. Bacon; Add MS 44457, ff. 56, 100.

[2] Obscure.

[3] Benoît Brunswik, French politician and authority on the Eastern Question; wrote *Le Traité de Berlin* (1878).

[4] i.e. his review of *Maud*, for *Gleanings*. See 25 Nov. 78.

[5] S. Smiles, *Robert Dick, baker, of Thurso, geologist and botanist* (1878).

[6] *The Naturalist*, ed. C. P. Hobkirk and G. T. Porritt, 10v. (1875-85).

[7] Probably Samuel Reddish of Derby, a liberal; Hawn P.

[8] Frederick William Verney, 1846-1913; once a curate, relinquished orders 1873; barrister and councillor to Siamese legation; liberal M.P. Bucks 1906; sent verses, Add MS 44458, f. 163.

[9] Frederick Proctor of Alton; see Add MS 44458, f. 181.

[10] Perhaps John Edmund Hüttel, merchant in the City.

[11] I. Gill, *Six months in Ascension* (1878).

[12] E. H. Plumptre, 'Peace or war? A sermon' (1878).

Pullyblank, S. on the Mount[1]—Walker, Titles of Psalms[2]—Webb on Ch. Establishment[3]—*Cathedra Petri*[4]—Borlase on Cornish Saints.[5]

25. M.

Ch. 8½ AM. Wrote to Mr Wilfrid Oates—Sir Geo. Bowen—Ld Halifax—Rev. Dr Rowsell—Mr G. Harris—Mr K. Snowball[6]—Mr W. Thomson—Mr Waddy MP. Read Maud once more: &, aided by Doyle's criticism, wrote my Note of Apology & partial retractation.[7] The fact is I am wanting in that higher poetical sense, which distinguishes the true artist. Also prepared article on Farini for the press. Woodcraft. Read Smiles's Dick—Richard the First.[8] Conversation with A.G. on his future course.

26. Tu.

Kept my bed till 2 with slight menace from within, & physic. Wrote to Mr Hussey Vivian—Mr J.L. Thomas[9]—Mr Leeman MP—Miss Poulton BP—Editor of Echo—Newsman (Thomas)—Mr J. Murray—Mr Godley—Miss Higgs—Mr Richards—Mr Samuelson MP.—Rev. Mr Pullyblank—Rev. Mr Wilberforce—Sir F.H. Doyle—Sig. Premi[10]—Mr Mundella Tel.—Mr Childers Tel. Read Richard the First—Life of Dick—Hussey Vivian's Tour.[11] Saw Mr Vickers.

27. Wed. [London]

Ch. 8½ AM. Wrote to Mr Fitzgerald—Messrs Pears—Mr Ede[12]—Mr Macvittie[13]—Mr Wigley—Ld Northbrook—Rev. Mr M'Coll. Dined at 15 G. Square. Saw Miss Ponsonby—Mr Hayward—Mr Herbert. Saw Macgregor [R]. Worked 2½ hours on Chaos. 10¾-6. Hn to Harley St. Read Northbrook's Memorandum[14]—Horace Seymour on U.S. Govt[15]—Indian Bluebook.[16]

28. Th.

Wrote to Dr Leary—Mr Murray—Capt Maurice BP—Lt Cavenaugh BP—Rev. Mr Simpson—Rev. Mr Dempsey—Mrs Hilton—Mr Barber—H. Pratt—

---

[1] Joseph Pulliblank, 1843-1912, curate of Walton, Liverpool, sent his *Lectures on the Sermon on the Mount* (1877).

[2] By J. E. Walker (1879).   [3] W. Webb, *England's inheritance in her Church* (1878).

[4] See 25 Sept. 58.

[5] W. C. Borlase, *The age of the Saints: a monograph of early Christianity in Cornwall* (1878).

[6] *Sic*; R. K. Snowdon, who proposed himself for Seaforth; Hawn P.

[7] *Gleanings*, ii. 146n.: the Crimean war 'dislocated my frame of mind, and disabled me from dealing even tolerably with the work as a work of imagination'.

[8] [Sir J. B. Burges], *Richard the First: a poem* (1800).   [9] Apparently a newspaper reporter.

[10] Perhaps Cornelio Benedetto Premi, author of *L'Italia politica-economica* (1868?).

[11] H. H. Vivian, *Notes of a tour in America* (1878).

[12] George Ede, to whom Gladstone sent advice; Hawn P.

[13] Possibly Charles Edwin M'Vittie, d. 1916; surgeon in Afghan campaign 1880; later HM's surgeon.

[14] 'Memorandum by the earl of Northbrook, on Viscount Cranbrook's Despatch to Lord Lytton of Nov. 18th 1878' (1878).

[15] Horatio Seymour, 'The government of the United States', *North American Review*, xii. 359 (1878).

[16] Central Asia, number 1, with an appendix on 1870-3 correspondence; *PP* 1878 lxxx. 443.

Mr Edwards. Saw Mr Murray—Mr Forster—Lady Phillimore—Mr Godley—Ld Northbrook—Col Brackenbury[1] with Mr M'Coll. Dined with the Wests—an Affghan evening. Saw Witney X. Read Indian Bluebook—Kebbel on personal Govt.[2]

29. Fr.

Wrote to Ld Hartington—Ld Cranbrook (& draft)[3]—Ed. Edinb. Daily Review[4]— Lt Cavenaugh—Mrs Pugin—Mr Maclaren—Mr West. Dined with the Godleys. Worked long on Indian papers. Saw Sir F. Doyle—Mr Godley (2)—Mr Good- yer—Lord Monck—F. Lawley—Sir A. Panizzi—Dr Jack[5]—Mr Macmillan. Read I. Papers: also Birmm Organisation papers & plan[6]—Chronicle of Budgepore.[7]

30. Sat.

Wrote to Mr Munday[8]—Ld Granville—Dr Littledale. Read Chronicle of Budge- pore—Affghan on England.[9] Saw Ld Granville—Ld Wolverton—Mr Godley. Worked on Parl. papers. 1½-11. To Greenwich festival. Spoke ½ hour on Liberal organisation. Went on at 5 to Woolwich & rested one hour. Then to the Rink Meeting & spoke near two hours.[10] Great crowd, perfect attention, much enthusiasm. The two words 'never failest' from the Collect[11] were as it were given me at prayers for a pillar to lean on. We had a little party on return.

Adv. Sunday D. 1. 78.

9¼-2¼. Expedition to Southfield Ch Wandsworth to hear Mr J. Winslow: a truly holy man I thought.[12] Saw Ld Granville & Ld Wolverton. St Andrew's Wells St 4 PM. Dined at Sir R. Phillimore's & much conversation.[13] He judi- cially thinks the war most guilty. Read Bp Goodwin on the Pentateuch[14]

---

[1] (Sir) Henry *Brackenbury, 1837-1914; served in India; one of Wolseley's group; Ripon's secre- tary 1880; in Ireland 1882; used Indian and Irish experience to found British military intelligence 1886-91.

[2] T. E. Kebbel in *Nineteenth Century*, iv. 1137 (December 1878).

[3] Sending corrections to the Afghan blue book; Add MS 44458, f. 190.   [4] Not published.

[5] William Jack, 1834-1924; school inspector; with Macmillan's 1876-9; professor of mathematics at Glasgow 1879-1909.

[6] Not found; presumably details of caucus organization.

[7] I. T. Prichard, *The chronicles of Budgepore, or, sketches of life in upper India*, 2v. (1870).

[8] Charles F. Munday, comptroller of the navy dept. at the Admiralty.   [9] Not found.

[10] On Bulgaria, Cranbrook's dispatch of 18 November, and Afghanistan; in *T.T.*, 2 December 1878, 7a.

[11] 'O Lord, who never failest to help and govern them whom thou dost bring up in thy steadfast fear and love; keep us, we beseech thee, under the protection of thy good providence, and make us to have a perpetual fear and love of thy holy Name'; collect for second Sunday after Trinity, pre- sumably being used as a 'general' prayer.

[12] i.e. talent-spotting for Seaforth church, for which Winslow was chosen; see 1 Nov. 78.

[13] 'Gladstone dined here—he content [?] & happy after his noble oration yesterday. We had much conversation of a very interesting nature upon the whole political state of affairs. . . . He receives often letters complaining of the civilities wh. he utters on the Queen & the Royal Family especially Prince of Wales'; Phillimore's Diary.

[14] By H. Goodwin (1867).

–Mr Hoare on Religion of Egypt[1]–R. Williams & Mr Desprez on the Book of Daniel.[2]

2. M.

Wrote to Mr Murray–Rev. E. Wilberforce–Mr Thorndike Rice–and. ... 3-4½. Meeting at Ld Granville's.[3] No great result but feeling on the whole good. Dined at Mr Mundellas. Conversation with him–Ld Lawrence–Mr Childers– Mr Massey. Saw Mr Murray–Mr Godley. Read Chronicle of Budgepore.

3. Tu.

Wrote to Mr Easterly[4]–Mr J.W.E. Hose–Mr Norman–Duke of Argyll– W.H.G.–Mr Chattaway[5]–Mr Ryley[6]–Ed. Plymouth Mercury.[7] Meeting at Granville's 3-5. Decided to do something.[8] Dined at Ld Rosebery's. Conversation with him–Ld Northbrook–Mr Adam. Saw Mad. Novikoff–Sir C. Trevelyan–Mr Kinglake. Saw Southwark Depn (Mr [E. H.] Bailey & others)[9]–Mr Godley–Mr G. Harris–Mr Murray–Mr Forster MP. Read Chron. of Budgepore–M'Kenzie on Cost of Affghan War.[10]

4. Wed.

Wrote to Me Novikoff–Baron Fölkerschamb–Mr Taylor Innes–Mr Costelloe–H.L. Jephson–Mr Whittingham–Mr Coffingwell–C. Carthew–Professor Palumbo–Mr Horatio Seymour[11]–Mr Toynbee[12]–Rev. J.L. Winslow–Mr Farley–Rev. R. Yonge–D. Puseley–J. Crews–R. Oliver[13]–J. Hoyle–Miss Crighton[14]–Mr Linnington[15]–Mr Ryan. Saw Sir A. Panizzi–Scotts. Shopping. Dined with the Ripon's: political conclave there until late. Saw two [R]. Read Farley's Egypt &c.[16]–Chronicle of Budgepore.

5. Th.

Wrote to Dr Bennett–Mr Planché–Mr Barret–Mr Coffingwell–Mrs Watts. Read Central Asia Papers[17]–Farley on Syria &c.–Chron of Budgepore Vol II.

[1] J. N. Hoare, 'The religion of the ancient Egyptians', *Nineteenth Century*, iv. 1105 (December 1878).   [2] P. C. S. Desprez, *Daniel... with an introduction by R Williams* (1865).
[3] On the India blue book and recall of Parliament; Ramm II, i. 90.
[4] Dr. Easterly, one of the speakers on 30 Nov. 78.
[5] Perhaps Charles Chattaway, commission merchant.
[6] E. Ryley of Manchester, corresponding on religion; Hawn P.
[7] Presumably *Western Daily Mercury*, published in Plymouth; no letter published.
[8] See 6 Dec. 78.
[9] Southwark liberal association inviting him to stand there at the next election; Gladstone's letter declining in *T.T.*, 9 December 1878, 9f.
[10] J. T. Mackenzie, 'The best means of defraying the expenses of the Afghan war' (1878).
[11] Horatio Seymour, 1810-86; U.S. Democratic politician and anti-Tweed reformer; see 27 Nov. 78.
[12] Probably William Toynbee, London barrister, who sent verses on liberalism 1880; Hawn P.
[13] Roderic Oliver, London solicitor.
[14] *Sic*; perhaps one of Mandell Creighton's four daughters.
[15] Perhaps Adolphus Henry Linnington, merchant in the City.
[16] J. L. Farley, *Egypt, Cyprus and Asiatic Turkey* (1878).
[17] See 27 Nov. 78 and *PP* 1878-9 lvii. 369, the latter especially used for his speech on 10 December.

Saw Ld F. Cavendish—Mr Knowles—Mr Godley—Mr Lowe (H of C.) H. of C. 4¼-8. Spoke briefly: in part with a view of checking debate.[1]

6. Fr.

Wrote to Ld Blantyre—Bp of Chester—Rev. Mr Morison—Lt Govr I of Man—Rev. E.R. Wilberforce—Miss de Lisle—J. White BP—R. Elliot BP—Mr Barton—A. Strahan—L. Berg—Mr Norman. Saw Mr Adam (seat)—Do *cum* Ld Wolverton—Professor Fawcett—Mr Murray—Sir W. James—Mr Bryce. Luncheon at 15 G.S. Saw . . . & another [R]. Dined with the Godleys. Saw Mr Winslow who accepts the Vicarage of Seaforth. Read Central Asian papers—Chronicle of Budgepore. Meeting at Ld Hartington's. The motion was fixed: not in my form: but it is effectual.[2]

7. Sat.

Wrote to Guy Roslyn—Mr Leeman MP—Rev. Mr Howell—Rev. E.G. Potter—Rev. B.W. Savile—Mr Parker—Mrs L.G. Faussett[3]—Mr Williamson—J. Miller—H. Frances—C. Adin[4]—T. Falvey—W. Dougall—C. Bolam—Mr Hole. Sat to Mr Adams 3-3¾.[5] Saw Mr Winslow: full conversation on Seaforth. I was greatly pleased with him. Called for Terry (gone) and others [R]. Saw Ld Northbrook—Sir T.F. Elliot[t]—Mr Mivart. Dined at Ld A. Russell's. Read Central As. papers (finished)—Chronicles of Budgepore.

8. 1 S. Adv. [sic]

Ch. Royal 10 A.M. St James's 7 PM. Saw Mrs Hamilton—Sir A. Panizzi—Ld F. Cavendish. Read Desprez St John & Daniel[6]—Chief Baron Kelly's Tract[7]—Bp Goodwin on the Pentateuch[8]—Randall on Judicial Committee[9]—Abbé Martin's Reply.[10]

9. M.

Wrote to Mr Powell—Mr Govier.[11] Worked hard & long on the Parl. Papers. Read Chron. of Budgepore. H. of C. 6¼-8¼ and 10¼-12½.[12] Saw Mr West—Mr Waddy—W.H.G.—Ld Carlingford—& others. Dined at Sir C. Forster's.

[1] Reserving his position, but requesting information; *H* 243. 111.
[2] A compromise: a motion, moved this evening by Whitbread, disapproving of the govt.'s conduct of Afghan policy, but stopping short of an amndt. to the Address; Rossi, *T.A.P.S.*, xlviii. 8. 87; spoke on it this evg.; *H* 243. 179.
[3] Perhaps the wife of R. G. Faussett, Student of Christ Church and vicar of Cassington.
[4] Charles Adin of Manchester sent photographs; Hawn P.
[5] Probably a sitting for J. Adams Acton who made several busts, undated, of Gladstone, in addition to his statue (see 18 Oct. 66).
[6] P. C. S. Desprez, *Daniel and John* (1878).
[7] Sir F. Kelly, 'A letter to the Lord High Chancellor upon the late Order in Council' (1878).
[8] See 1 Dec. 78.
[9] J. Randall, *The Judicial Committee of the Privy Council* (1878).
[10] J. P. P. Martin on ritualism in *Contemporary Review*, xxxiv. 77 (December 1878).
[11] Reading uncertain.
[12] Queen's speech deb.; *H* 243. 310.

10. Tu.

Wrote to Mr Bryant.[1] Read Chron. of Budgepore. Dined at Sir C. Forster's. Again worked on the Papers until 3½. H. of C. 4¼-8¼ and 10¾-12. Spoke 2¼ hours.[2] An accusatory task, not congenial. But I, knowingly, over-stated nothing & set down nought in malice.[3] Saw Sir W. Harcourt—Ld Kinnaird—Ld Carlingford.

11. Wed.

Wrote to Miss Swanwick—J.D. Rogers[4]—Rev. J. Christie—Dr E. Biscamp—Mr Sanderson—Mr Budd—Mr Powell—Mr Williams. Dined at Lady Stanleys. An interesting party: & much historical conversation after dinner. Read H. on India:[5] Guthrie on Trade[6]—Chronicles of Budgepore. Saw Mr White (Père Hyac.)[7]—Ld Wolverton—Sir Alex. Gordon—Mr Godley—Mr Stuart Wortley. Worked on sheets for Reprint Vol I & wrote detailed Contents.

12. Th.

Wrote to Major Primrose[8]—Mr Murray—Mad. Novikoff—Miss Jervis—Lady Derby—Mr F. Birch—Sir Al. Gordon—Mr Bright—Lt Gov. Isle of Man l. & BP. Attended Charterhouse Board. Dined with the Ripons: a pleasant quiet party. Saw Mr Godley (on inscriptions for Guards' Chapel)—Sir A. Panizzi—Sir T. Acland—Mr Rathbone—Ld Granville—Mr Adam—Mr Agnew (Manager)—Mr L. Stanley—Mr Knowles. Read Chron. of Budgepore (finished)—Beaconsfield's (supposed) Address.[9] H of C. 4½-8.[10]

---

[1] Of Bryant and May, arranging for statue of Gladstone by Joy to be sculpted for Bow Vestry; *T.T.*, 3 Feb. 1880, 6d.

[2] A detailed critique of the despatch of 10 May 1877 and Sir L. Pelly's statement to the Amir's envoy in November 1877 (*PP* lvii. 535, 573); *H* 243. 541.　　　　　　　　　[3] *Othello*, v. ii. 341.

[4] Perhaps John Davenport Rogers, historian of the British Colonies.　　　　　[5] Untraced.

[6] Perhaps G. Guthrie, *Bank monopoly the cause of commercial crises* (1864).

[7] Frederick Anthony White of Kinross House, S. Kensington; White's mem. of the meeting is at Lambeth MS 1472, f. 25: 'Called by appointment on the Rt. Honble. W. E. Gladstone, who recd. me most kindly on Mr Meyrick's introduction. My object was to get his cooperation at a meeting for Père Hyacinthe. He said he cd. not enter actively into any new combination. His age & lack of time obliged him to make that rule. He had some doubt abt. the movement fearing it wd. become exotic. I assured him the object of all concerned in it was to make it indigenous & selfsupporting, wh. he was glad to hear. He said he might perhaps subscribe again, but could not move actively. But I might use his name. . . . He apologised for not having seen me yesterday when I called; but he was deep in preparing his intricate speech and could not be disturbed. He was as calm as possible in spite of his excitement last night and when I went in I found him discussing the the [*sic*] merits of some lines of Virgil. Whether Hi fletes or hic fletes & whether in superos referred to the gods. I cd not quite make out the meaning, but it seemed to be choosing mottoes for great warriors—Wellington, Marlborough &c. [see next day's n.]—& his friend was evidently a learned Theban [?] who soon departed & left me alone. Mr Gladstone is a perfect gentleman, & when I said good bye I said "I am sure I may ask you to remember the matter before God" he replied: you could ask me nothing better Mr White: I am perfectly content that the Alpha & Omega of it be with him.' For Hyacinthe, see Matthew, 'Vaticanism', 439.

[8] Everard Henry Primrose, 1848-85, Rosebery's br.; in fact lieutenant-colonel (see *recte* next day) in Grenadier Guards; organized inscription for the Guards' Chapel to which Gladstone contributed; see 25 May 79. See Add MS 44458, ff. 214, 223.

[9] Probably Disraeli's Queen's speech, regarded by liberals as inadequate (*H* 243. 3) or an untraced squib.　　　　　　　　　　　　　　[10] Queen's speech deb.; *H* 243. 639.

13. Fr.

Wrote to Me Novikoff (O)—Mr Leeman—S. Ross—Rev. Mr Jenkins—Mayor of Clonmel—Lady Sandhurst—Messrs Clowes—Mr Constable—Mr Macdonnell—Archdn Allen. Read Christie on Russia.[1] Saw Col. Primrose—Mr Bowman—Lord Dufferin—Mr Childers—Mr Grant Duff—Mr Law—Mr Adam—Mr Leeman—Mr Lowe MP. Boggled over an exordium to an article for N.C.[2] H of C. 7-8 and $9\frac{1}{2}$-$2\frac{1}{2}$. Voted in 227:328; an actual & considerable improvement.[3] Excellent speaking on our side.

14. Sat.

Wrote to Ld Blantyre—C. Bradlaugh!—E.R. Mullins[4]—Mr Kernaghan—Lt Gov. I. of Man—Rev. W. Hughes—A. Baker—C. Geddes—J. Lewis—Mr Coupland[5]—Mr Nuttall. Dined with the Wests. Worked on paper for Nineteenth Century. Read Pamphlets: and new Central Asian Papers.[6] Saw Mr Trevelyan—Serjeant Simon[7]—Mr Knowles.

15. 3 S. Adv.

Chapel Royal 10 AM (with H.C.) and $5\frac{1}{2}$ P.M. Saw Sir R. Phillimore—Sir W. & Lady M. Farquhar—Ld Wolverton. Revised & paragraphed Ecce Homo.[8] Read Mr Oxenham's Introduction to his new Vol.[9] Wrote to Mr G. Shaw Lefevre[10]—Mr Weaver.

16. M.

Wrote to Messrs Hinde[11]—The Prince of Wales—Lt Govr Isle of Man. Dined with the F.C.s. H. of C. $4\frac{1}{4}$-$8\frac{3}{4}$ and $10\frac{1}{2}$-$11\frac{1}{2}$. Spoke on Rhodopè and on charging India.[12] Saw Sir Arthur Gordon—Mr Prince—Mr Mullins (Sculptor)—Mr Goschen—Mr Childers—Mr Weaver—W.H.G.—Mr Adam—Sir T. Acland. Read The Serpent of Cos.[13]

---

[1] J. Christie, *Men and things Russian: or holiday travels in the lands of the Czar* (1879).

[2] 'The friends and foes of Russia', *Nineteenth Century*, v. 168 (January 1879).

[3] *H* 243. 847; i.e. an 'improvement' on the opposition's votes on the Eastern question.

[4] Edwin Roscoe Mullins, 1848-1907, sculptor; see 11 Feb. 79.

[5] Perhaps Charles Coupland, London solicitor.

[6] Central Asia, number 2; *PP* 1878-9 lxxvii. 63.

[7] (Sir) John Simon, 1818-97; serjeant-at-law 1864; liberal M.P. Dewsbury 1868-88; kt. 1886. Spoke on 16 December on Rhodopé commission.

[8] For *Gleanings*.

[9] H. N. Oxenham, preface to *Catholic eschatology and universalism* (2nd ed. 1878).

[10] George *Shaw-Lefevre, 1831-1928; barrister; liberal M.P. Reading 1863-85, Bradford 1886-95; minor office 1868-74; commissioner of works November 1880-3, 1892-4; P.M.G. 1883-5; president of local govt. board 1894-5.

[11] Grenadine manufacturer.

[12] Spoke on Rhodopé commission, and seconded Fawcett's amndt. on govt. proposal to charge India for the Afghan campaign; *H* 243. 870, 895.

[13] By [Charles Hartley] (1878).

17. Tu.

Wrote to Rev. Mr Law[1]—Lord Blantyre[2]—W.H.G.—Rev. Mr Suffield—Mr But-ler—Mr Agnew. Worked much on 'The Foes and friends of Russia'. H of C. 4¾-6 and 10-12½. Voted agt charging India: majority for charging 110.[3] Read Serpent of Cos (finished). Saw Mr Adam—Sir Alex. Gordon—Mr Escott.[4] Dined at Sir R. Phillimore's.

18. Wed.

Wrote to Mr Knowles—Ld Blantyre—Chairman Indian Press Meeting—Mr Sol-tan[5]—Mr Colbart—Mr Josh. Cox—Rev. W. Sewell—Mr Forster MP—Ed. Daily News. Read the Burns trip to Iceland.[6] Saw Ld Granville—Mr Buxton—Mr Piper to H.G. Saw M'Gregor X. Worked hard on Russia's Friends and Foes. The F. Cavendishes dined here. Mr Law spent an hour & a half with me: of much interest.

19. Th.

Wrote to Messrs Parry & Gramon[7]—Ed. Daily News[8]—Keeper of Vote Office[9]—General Ponsonby—Miss Lewin[10]—Sig. Vitali—Mr Kinnaird—Mr Sturge—Spot-tiswoodes—Mr Rae. Saw Mr Godley (2)—Mr Stuart Wortley & Mrs S.W.—Sir A. Panizzi. The Godleys dined with us. Finished my paper for the 19th Century and revised a part. Worked also on preparing Tracts for the Reprint.

20. Fr. [Hawarden]

Wrote to Messrs Spottiswoode BP—Lady Sandhurst l. & BP—Mr W. Saunders—Mr [J.] Passmore Edwards—Mr Escott—J. Williams—L. Stanley BP. Finished the revision of my paper & sent it off. Also worked hard on various papers & packed for departure. Saw Mr Murray. Off, in a thick fog, but with glee, at 4.45 PM. Did not reach Hawarden until 12.30. Set to work on the chaos there: & to bed between 2 & 3 AM.

21. Sat.

Rose at nine: and saw the sun! Such a treat for a cockney at this season! Wrote to M. Zafiropulo[11]—Rev. Carr J. Glyn—C. Buckden—T.G. Crippin—Mr Stead—

[1] Thomas Graves Law, 1836-1904, convert to Rome and back 1855-78; historian; Gladstone helped him become custodian of the Signet Library, Edinburgh; see *Collected essays of T. G. Law*, ed. P. Hume Brown (1904), xi.

[2] On the Rhodopé grant; sent next day with Blantyre's reply for publication in *D.N.*, 19 December 1878, 5d.   [3] *H* 243. 1035.

[4] Thomas Hay Sweet Escott, d. 1924; taught at King's college, London, 1866-73; journalist and author. 'G., Liddon, Augustus [Phillimore], Mr Escott (the World) dined here'; Phillimore's Diary.

[5] William Edward Soltan of the Liverpool branch of the Bank of England.

[6] Described by A. Trollope in 'Iceland', *Fortnightly Review*, xxiv. 175 (July 1878).

[7] Perhaps Parry and Garnham, London chemists.

[8] On possible Manchester candidacy; see *D.N.*, 20 December 1878, 6d.

[9] James Collins, Deliverer of Votes.

[10] Jessie Lewin, Mrs Grote's niece; on her aunt's illness; Hawn P.

[11] Stephanos Zafiropulo of Marseilles on Homeric geography; Add MS 44458, f. 201.

Mr Packard—W. Grove—Mr Cookny—Mr Ewans[1]—Miss Learoyd[2]—Mr Swanston—Mr Thales Lindsay—Editor of Leeds Mercury. Read Arnold on Landowners[3]—Bp Ellicott on Anglocath. Movement[4]—The Book of Benjamin[5]—Sketch of Ld Beaconsfield.[6]

22. 4 S. Adv.

Hn Church mg & evg. Wrote to Spottiswoodes BP—Mr Knowles—Mr Murray. By special desire of Mr K. corrected, abridged, & dispatched my article for Nineteenth Cent.[7] Read Hook's Life[8]—Dixon's History.[9]

23. M.

Wrote to J. Elsworth—Mr Goldwin Smith—Messrs Hinde & Sons—Mr Gansden jun.—Editor Scots Banking Mag.[10]—Treas. Visiting & Relief Assocn—J. Hand BP—Mr Rose—Mr Wrick. Worked on Papers for Reprint. Read Dean Hook's Life—Dixon's Hist Ch. of Engl.—Life of Dick.[11]

24. Tu.

Ch. 8½ A.M: & thoughts of my dear eldest sister's birthday. Assuredly she is in the rest of God.

Wrote to Spottiswoodes (Tel)—Messrs Agnew—Dean of Chester—Ed. of Daily News—Ld Moncreiff—Ld Granville—Mr de Hichstrasse—Manager Cambr. Warehouse—Rev. Mr Law—Mr Bickford—Mr Henderson. Great cold: I could not chop wood. Worked on Reprint: paragraphing, Contents, &c. Read Life of Dean Hook—Life & Times of Stair[12]—Dixon's Hist Church of Engl. Thermom. 5% or 3% before morning.[13]

25. Xm D: Wed.

Ch. 11 AM with H.C. & 7 PM. Wrote to H.J.G.—Mrs Th.—J.H. Parker—Mr Halliday—Mr St Clair. Read Life of Hook—Extra Physics.[14] We worked on clearing the pond of snow for skaters.

---

[1] Word smudged.
[2] Da. of Nehemiah Learoyd of Finsbury Park.
[3] A. Arnold, 'Cost of landed gentry', *Princeton Review*, liv. 578 (1878).
[4] C. J. Ellicott, *Some present dangers of the Church of England* (1878).
[5] *The Book of Benjamin. Appointed to be read in households* (n.d.).
[6] J. C., *Earl Beaconsfield; a political sketch* (1878).
[7] See 13 Dec. 78.
[8] W. R. W. Stephens, *The life and letters of W. F. Hook*, 2v. (1878). See 10 Feb. 79.
[9] R. W. Dixon, *History of the Church of England* (1877).
[10] Declining to write an article on the financial situation for the first number of *Scottish Banking and Insurance Magazine*; *T.T.*, 28 December 1878, 3e.
[11] See 21 Nov. 78.
[12] Perhaps *Some passages in the life of John, second earl of Stair* (1835).
[13] i.e. 29° of frost, Fahrenheit.
[14] *Extra physics and the mystery of creation* (1878).

26. Th. St Stephen.

Ch. 8.45 AM. Wrote to F.H. Hill—Mr Lambert—Mr Shelley—C.J. Marsh[1]—Rev. W.R.W. Stephens—Mr Lichtenberg[2]—Messrs Boyce—Mr Puseley. Worked for Reprint. Read Hook's Life—Dixon's History. Worked for the skaters at the pond. Granville came in evg. Political conversation. I may be wrong but I do not think his water-drinking[3] has been favourable to his general mental force and especially his initiative. His nice tact and judgment remain.

27. Frid.

Ch. 8¾ AM. Wrote to Messrs Clay BP—A.G. Williams—T.H. Worrall—Sir Jul. Benedict—Mrs Wynne—Mrs Prentice—Rev Mr Zincke. Worked on proofs for reprint. Conversation with Granville: who went off after luncheon. Read Hook's Life—Dixon's History—Zincke on the Limagne.[4]

28. Sat. Holy Innocents.

Church 8¾ AM. Wrote to Mr Passmore Edwards[5]—Ld Moncreiff—Mr Feldwick[6]—Mr Saunders—Mr De Rimon—J.O. Jackson[7]—Messrs Clowes & Sons— W.E. Coles—G. Harris—H.H. Jones—C. Ashby. Worked for Reprint. Read Dixon's Hist.—F.R. on Limagne—Laveleye in Ditto on Berlin Treaty.[8]

29. S. after Xm.

Church 11 AM. and [blank.] Wrote to Duke of Argyll—Mrs Warner—Ed of Echo[9]—Mr Corcoran—Mr Lambert—Mr Watson Hanmer.[10] Read Life of Dean Hook II—Bp of Rochester's Pastoral Letter.[11]

Sixty nine years of age! One year only from the limit of ordinary life prolonged to its natural goal! And now these three years last past, instead of unbinding and detaching me, have fetched me back from the larger room which I had laboriously reached and have immersed me almost more than at any former time in cares which are certainly cares of this life.

And this retroactive motion has appeared & yet appears to me to carry the marks of the will of God. For when have I seen so strongly the relation between my public duties and the primary purposes for which God made and Christ redeemed the world? Seen it to be not real only but so close and immediate that the lines of the holy and the unholy were drawn as in fire before my eyes. And

---

[1] Of the court of bankruptcy; an enquiry for Mrs Thistlethwayte?

[2] George Philip Lichtenberg, London surgeon.

[3] i.e. at a spa.

[4] F. B. Zincke, *Fortnightly Review*, xxx. 821 (December 1878).

[5] Presentation of a silver axe; letter and later verses in Latin and Greek in *The Guardian* (1879), 5, 118.

[6] William Edmund Feldwick of Sevenoaks; on Homer; Hawn P.

[7] John Oswald Jackson, biographer of Princess Alice (1879).

[8] *Fortnightly Review*, xxx. 616 (November 1878).

[9] Thanks for birthday greetings; *The Echo*, 30 December 1878, 2.

[10] Liberal in Bowden; sent £50 for charity; Hawn P.

[11] By A. W. Thorold (1878).

why has my health, my strength, been so peculiarly sustained? All this year and more—I think—I have not been confined to bed for a single day. In the great physical and mental effort of speaking, often to large auditories, I have been as it were upheld in an unusual manner and the free effectiveness of voice has been given me to my own astonishment. Was not all this for a purpose: & has it not all come in connection with a process to which I have given myself under clear but most reluctant associations. Most reluctant: for God knoweth how true it is that my heart's desire has been for that rest from conflict & from turmoil which seems almost a necessity for a soul that would be prepared in time to meet its God for eternity.

I am aware that language such as (this is often) I have here used is often prompted by fanaticism. But not always. It is to be tried by tests.[1] I have striven to apply them with all the sobriety I can: and with a full recollection that God sometimes sees fit to employ as his instruments for particular purposes of good those with whom notwithstanding He has yet a sore account to settle.

I am still under the painful sense that my public life is and has the best of me: that it draws off and exhausts from my personal life almost all moral resolution, all capacity for Christian discipline in the personal and private sphere. This it is which makes me anxious for a lawful escape from an honourable struggle, & which but for the clearness of the evidence that it is honourable & is pleasing to God, would make me wretched while it lasts.

If I am to be spared for another birthday God grant that by that time there may have been a great shifting of events and parts & that I may have entered into that period of recollection and penitence which my life much needs before its close.[2]

30. M.

Ch. 8½ A.M. Wrote to Lord Ronald Gower—D. of Argyll BP.—Mr E. Bull—Mr Tillett BP—Mr G. Millar—Rev. H.G. Henderson—Bp of Rochester—Mayor of Chester—Editor of Mayfair[3]—Rev. R. Winterbottom[4]—Mr M'Mordie[5]—Miss de Lisle. Read Dixon's History—Winterbottom on Genesis—MacMordie's Lecture—Life of Dean Hook—Mr Lefevre's Address.[6] Cut down a beech with WHG.

31. Tu.

Ch. 8½ AM. Wrote to Mr Vickers—Sir Thos G.—Mrs Macray BP—Mr Bickford—Mr Bradshaw—Mr Stillman—Mr Raleigh—Mr Spencer—Messrs Leeman—R. Gordon BP—Mr Lefevre BP—Mrs Bewick—Dr Bennett—Mr Wootton—W. Milne. Worked on papers & wrote out my Annual Estimate. In the midst of

[1] Probably *sic*; might read 'texts'.
[2] Extracts in Hammond, 83-4.
[3] W. C. Russell who unsuccessfully solicited an article; Add MS 44458, f. 279.
[4] *Sic*; Rayner Winterbotham, 1843-1926; episcopalian incumbent in Fraserburgh 1878-86, in Edinburgh 1886-99; had sent his *On the real character of the early records of Genesis* (1878).
[5] Hans MacMordie had sent his 'The Queen's university in Ireland . . . An address' (1878).
[6] G. J. Shaw-Lefevre, 'A decade of inflation and depression' (1878).

distress, I have thriven. Indeed hard work with the pen has done something: an unexpected incident of my old age. Read Dixon's History—Hook's Life.

Farewell to a dying year is ever a thing of interest; much of that interest painful but not all. Looking back I see scarcely a glimmering of improvement in the kinds of self-command that I most need, and I have still to fear lest in a darkened conscience I tamper with the law and judgment of my God. It is surely surely time, when "three score years & ten" begin to sound in mine ears, that penitence should at length make an effectual work so that I mock not my Saviour.

But also in looking forward this coming year stirs my innermost desire that it may by God's favour wind up or at the least effectually contract and close in the exterior activities of my life, and enable me to shape it for recollection, for worship, for peace, and for holy labour.

It will indeed, if this be so, be a year of flowering hope to me from which to date as I trust a kind of new and better life.

AMEN.

[The inside back cover contains:—]

Hagley June 2.77. Weighed 11 st. 11 lbs.

—

Athen. Deipnos. XIII.81.

—

Mons. W. Alpine
      Chemin de fer de H. Pacha Ismior—
           Hardar Pacha. Constple.

Mr E.A. Budge 54 Hill's Road Cambr.

Fontmell Shaftesbury

           Mornington Cres.
Watts case of Hislop Albert Villas Mirtley

                    [End of Volume XXXII]

[VOLUME XXXIII]¹

£5

Books 25/

Private.

No 33.

January 1. 1879 to July 23. 80.

All dedicated
To closeness and the bettering of my mind
Tempest I. 2.

Tells fibs too with such pretty air
You scarce would wish the truth were there[2]

Bister Ch £5   Alms Ap. 18. 24/6
St Johns £2. Ap 4   TynddywSch £2 2 0
Rev. West £10. Ap. 13?
Leven £2

How Wordsworth lived
   'Doing nothing but what it was a delight for him to do, and doing this only when he was disposed to labour.
B. Cornwall p. 143.[3]

To Browning
Into their cellar-homes seek thou thy way
And lift their dark romances into day.
Ibid. 102

Judith, the daughter of Merari, weakened him with the beauty of her countenance.
Judith Chap. XVI.

---

[1] Lambeth MS 1447.

[2] These two lines are in pencil; the other three mottoes are on a scrap of paper fastened to the foot of the first page.

[3] In B. W. Proctor (Barry Cornwall), *An autobiographical fragment and biographical notes* (1877).

Hawarden. Jan. 1. 1879. Wedn. Circumcision.

Church for H.C. at 8 A.M. Wrote to Messrs Williams—Ld Blantyre—Miss Lewin—Mr Fairbrother—S. Gould[1]—Mr Lovell[2]—Messrs Pears—Mr Adam—Mr Coles—Mr Kells.[3] Saw Mayor of Chester—Mr Vickers. Walk and parish calls with the Rector. Wrote and subscribed a Testamentary Memorandum containing the upshot of my thoughts about the disposal of my property. Read Hook's Life—Life & Times of Stein[4]—Hawley on Free Trade (U.S.)[5]

Testamentary Memm. Left for perusal
Prefatory.

As it is not, and may not be for some time in my power, from the incessant pressure of public affairs, to give the time necessary for the consideration of a formal Will, I have reviewed and modified this informal paper, in view of the uncertainty of life. And I know so well the perfect and blessed union which, through no desert of mine, prevails in my family, that I consign to my beloved Wife and children this paper, as the true impression of my desires touching my worldly goods, with the prayer that they will act upon it irrespective of my legal Will[6] which I intend God willing to bring into conformity with it.

In the third right hand drawer of my letter-writing table at Hawarden will be found papers which as I trust will give all or nearly all the needful indications either as to my property itself, or as to the persons having custody of deeds and documents, and from whom further information may be had.

So may it please God. W.E. Gladstone. Hawarden. April 25. 1881.

In reviewing and disposing of this subject, I leave this paper for perusal as it may be useful, but its particular provisions are of course to be overruled by the Will I am now drawing. WEG. Sept. 28. 1885.

Testamentary Memorandum

Twenty eight years and upwards having now elapsed since the date of my Will, & many changes having occurred over and above those due to mere lapse of time, I think it wise to record, in this holograph paper, an outline of the provisions which I desire to be carried into effect after my death, and which I mean for the basis of a new Will, to be executed when I find it convenient; together with certain explanations.

Under the last Codicil to my Will, dated Dec. 26. 1861, my wife and sons are now my Executors.

My wife being now provided for life with a residence sufficiently stocked, namely Hawarden Castle, and with a sum of nine hundred pounds a year for the maintenance and charges thereof, I wish to leave to her a jointure of two thousand pounds;[7] but this to be *inclusive* of the monies due to her, if any, under Marriage Settlement, and Deed thereto appertaining.

Of Furniture, and all other moveables belonging to me, and not specially appropriated before my death, I desire her to select for herself whatever she shall think fit: I leave to her, however, all Jewels and Ornaments.

---

[1] Sabine *Baring-Gould, 1834-1924; rector of East Mersea, of Lew Trenchard (his own living) 1881; novelist and historian.

[2] C. H. Lovell, involved in the Church Association; Hawn P.

[3] J. A. Kells; not further identified.   [4] By J. R. Seeley, 3v. (1878).

[5] R. Hawley, *An essay on free trade* (1878).

[6] See 21 Nov., 11 Dec. 49.

[7] '(Since provided by way of Annuity WEG S. 28 1885).'

She, with consent of my Sons, to present to friends such tokens, and to servants such gifts in money, as she may deem proper and becoming.

I desire that there shall be kept as heirlooms (1) Patents of Offices (2) Prints and Books presented to me by the grace and favour of Her Majesty (3) All family Pictures and Drawings; with Sculptures of like character.[1] (4) MS Papers of special interest: including any of family history. (5) Generally such articles as have come into my possession from persons, or for causes, of note; unless the Executors shall see fit to do otherwise for special reason in particular cases.

I leave my papers to the care and controul of my Executors: also my Copyrights, should any of them have any value.

Subject as above, I leave my moveables, not specially appropriated at my death, to my eldest Son: and subject also as follows.

The Executors to allot, in Plate and other Articles, to each younger Son to the value of two hundred pounds; and to each Daughter to the value of one hundred pounds.

I desire that the portion of each of my three younger sons, out of my personal Estate, shall be fifteen thousand pounds.[2] No part of this has yet been allotted to them: but it is my hope or intention to make a partial allotment, should I be spared, a twelve month hence.

I desire that the portion of each of my daughters be nine thousand pounds. Of this I already charge seven thousand as paid to my daughter Agnes: six and upwards for her fortune and the remainder for the charges appertaining to her marriage.[3] Two thousand, therefore, will remain to be paid, and placed under the provisions of her Settlement, or to be held in trust for her and her children, as my Executors shall deem most convenient.

My Executors are also to provide for the payment to my unmarried Daughters, until marriage, of Four hundred a year, in equal shares, if two: of three hundred a year, if one only.

And to my wife, as soon as may be after my decease, of a sum of Five hundred Pounds, independently of the Jointure hereby provided.

I leave to my eldest son, now free of any charge,[4] all my landed property. Nearly the whole of this is in the Parish of Hawarden, and I take the value of it to be about £155,000. There is also a small residue of the Seaforth Estate as yet unsold, value about £5000. This however it is my intention to sell, except probably some trifling part. It will be remembered that, in acceding to the ownership of Hawarden, my eldest son has already received a considerable amount from my Estate.

Apart from moveables, I take my personal Estate at this date to be (probably) in value from £100,000 to £105,000 after paying charges of succession (see my Rough Book B, p. 23); or, deducting debts, from £92,000 to £97,000.

Taking from this three sums of 15000£ = £45,000
two   "   "   9000£ =   18000
one   "   "   2000£ =   2000
Total   65,000

There remains a free residue of £30,000, more or less: ⟨this is charged with the Jointure and partial annuity to daughters which might together be roughly taken at one half of it⟩[5] But I desire my Executors not to rely on this residue; as, if I am spared, I hope to use it in

[1] 'No 3 has regard to keeping not all together but only in the family at large, and with any exceptions that may seem desirable WEG Ap. 25. 1881.'

[2] 'Herbert having chosen a profession which cannot support him is to have twenty thousand pounds WEG June 19. 84.'

[3] Two words added on 24 April 1881.

[4] 'except in favour of his wife (WEG Jan 1. 1879)'.   [5] 'Struck out WEG Ap. 25. 81.'

my life-time for a purpose of good not yet fully matured. To such a purpose my Library may also be devoted; nor do I fix the sum of £15,000[1] as my absolute limit in this respect.

I may here observe that I take the fortune inherited by me from my Father at £120,000, and my wife's fortunes at about £12,000, besides a sum nearly equal, which was lost in the Oak Farm. My *gross* earnings in the Public service have been about £80,000. And my literary earnings may I think by this time have reached the *gross* sum of £10,000. In the acquisition of the Hawarden Reversion, I sustained a charge of about £83,000; made up of £57,000 principal money, and interest at 5 per Cent (compound) from Jan 1. 1866 until the reversion accrued.

On the other hand, I in no way restrain my Executors from realising the value of such parts of my moveable personalty (as to other personalty I likewise leave them free) as they may think fit to part with: especially for example Ivories and Italian *Cinque Cento* Jewels. There is also a sum of £10,000[2] to accrue on the demise of my Sister Helen for their benefit, or as I may specially direct.

I wish to leave my Advowson of Saint Thomas Seaforth to my son William Henry, and my Advowson of Saint Thomas Toxteth (which I hope on the first avoidance to place on a proper footing) to my son Stephen Edward, the Rector of Hawarden.

The provision of my Will charging the eldest son and chief representative to aid the rest I desire to stand as it was in 1850.

Also the bye-provision in Codicil No 2 regarding the Estate of Lacovia[3] in Jamaica.

All the above-named pecuniary dispositions are to be inclusive of any provisions of my marriage settlement in relation to younger children: which provisions accordingly will take no separate effect.

In reckoning above sums inherited and received, I have omitted, I perceive, our share of Sir Stephen Glynne's Residue; which may be considered as raising my wife's fortune from about £12000 to between £15000 and £16000.

In the large proportion of my total property which I leave to my eldest son, I have had particularly in view the very peculiar circumstances of the Hawarden Estate and have desired to place him in such a position that he may act with greater energy and effect in the reduction, and as I hope even the extinction of the debt on the Estate. I feel confident that he will apply with due diligence to this operation, no less than that he will ever bear in mind the duties which will appertain to Him as Head of his House.

This I think, with formal clauses, will suffice for my general purpose. *Quod faxit Deus* W E Gladstone Jan. 1. 1879.

P.S. I have omitted to specify in this paper, that I desire my Residue to be divided among my four sons in equal shares. But I think it may not be large. WEG Jan 4. 1879.

Since this paper was written, I have paid £5000 on account of my son Harry to the House in which he is now a partner: the balance due to him will therefore be £10,000.

I have corrected in the body of the paper[4] a provision about the residue, which was put down without sufficient consideration: I have also struck out in p. 6 another provision affecting it. On reflection, and as I have now been able to make over at once to my eldest son some portion of my income, I desire that my wife's jointure, and the partial annuity to unmarried daughters, be a charge upon my landed Estate; of course not in addition to, but in lieu *pro tanto* of any provision under my marriage settlement. W E Gladstone Hawarden April 25. 1881.

[1] 'Or any other sum WEG Ap. 25. 81.'
[2] 'Now accrued. That will be 1 m[ille] to 2 m more WEG Ap 25. 1881.'
[3] Left by Sir John to Helen Gladstone; Checkland, 373.
[4] 'or rather in the P.S. WEG Ap 25. 1881.'

2. Th.

Ch. 8¼ A.M. Wrote to Dean of Windsor 1 & BP—Messrs Clowes BP—Ld F. Cavendish—Mr Ashton Warner[1]—Mr Custance[2]—Mr Ireland—Mr Bentley[3]—Jas Ram—Rev. Mr Law—J.C. Wakefield[4]—Rev. Canon Curteis—Mrs M. Wood. Worked for Reprint. Felled a Wych Elm with W. Read Hook's Life—Minto on Affghan Question[5]—Ld S. de R. on Eastern Question (a sad dilapidation of a strong mind?)[6]—Fortn. Rev. on [blank.]

3. Fr.

Ch. 8½ AM. Wrote to Messrs Clowes BP.—Dr Hack Tuke[7]—Mr Williamson—Mr Jenkyn Ingram—J.G. Ronald—Mr Murray—Mr Lattimer—J.C. Cox—F. Blood. Worked for Reprint. The Frost party came to luncheon. Conversation on Chester politics. Read Hook's Life—Brugsch Hist. of Egypt[8]—Dixon's Hist. Ch. of E.[9]

4. Sat.

Ch. 8½ A.M. Wrote to Duke of Westminster—W.L. Gladstone—Mr Fairfield[10]—Mr Copland[11]—D. Grant—G. Harris BP.—F. Boydell. Examined the Estate a/cs with Willy—& arranged with him for the year. Conversation with Mr Parker. C. read my Testamentary Memorandum of Thursday and approved of the family arrangements. Worked for the Reprint. Read Life of Dean Hook—Dixon's Hist. of Ch. of E.—F. Kemble, Girlhood.[12]

5. 2 S. Xmas.

Ch. 11 A.M. and 6.30 P.M. Prepared Bp P[atteson] for the reprint. Wrote (i.e. sent) to Messrs Clowes. Read Dean Hook's Life—Copland's Publications.[13]

6. M. Epiph.

Diarrhoea in the night prevented my rising for H.C. on dearest C.s birthday. All blessings on her. Wrote to Messrs Clowes—Mr C. Brown—Mr Murray—Mr Vickers. Read M'Carthy's History[14]—Mrs Butler's Girlhood—Finished Dean Hook—what a man, what a husband!

---

[1] Of the E. London hospital for children.
[2] Henry Neville Custance, secretary of the Metropolitan Hospital Sunday Fund.
[3] George *Bentley, 1828-95; published Stephens' *Hook* and Gladstone's lecture on it (see 10 Feb. 79).
[4] Perhaps Joseph C. Wakefield, London printer.
[5] W. Minto, 'Saddling the right horse', *Nineteenth Century*, v. 132 (January 1879).
[6] Lord Stratford de Redcliffe, 'Passing events in Turkey', *Nineteenth Century*, v. 2 (January 1879).
[7] Daniel Hack Tuke, 1827-95; London physician specializing in insanity.
[8] H. Brugsch, *A history of Egypt*, 2v. (1879).
[9] See 22 Dec. 78.
[10] Arthur Rowen Fairfield, of Waterloo Place, London; corresponded on Russia; Hawn P.
[11] James Copland; see next day.
[12] F. A. Kemble, later Butler, *Record of a girlhood* (1878).
[13] J. Copland, *Reasons why we believe the Bible* (1878).
[14] J. M'Carthy, *A history of our own times*, 4v. (1879-80).

7. Tu.

Annoyed during the night with diarrhoea: took the usual decided remedy, and kept my bed, especially viewing the extreme cold, until dusk. Wrote to Mr F.W. Chesson (2)—Rev. Mr Palmer—Mr M. Stark—Mr MacColl (BP)—Messrs Clowes & Son. Saw Mr Carrington—Mr Barker. Sent my excuse to the Rent Dinner. Read J. M'Carthy's Hist.—Dixon's Hist. Church of E.[1]—F.A. Kemble's Records.

8. Wed.[2]

Better, & rose at one. Wrote to Mr J. M'Carthy—Messrs Clowes BP—Messrs Rees—Rev. Mr Hopgood[3]—J.H. Chamberlain—C. Meynell[4]—Mr Bentley—J.R. Jolly. Worked for reprint: completing & dispatching Vol. III. Worked on Vol. IV. Read F.A. Kemble's Records—McCarthy's History—Dixon's History.

9. Th.

Rose at 10½. Weather still very cold: but good walk with E. Wickham & much conversation on Oxford &c. Wrote to Master of the Rolls—H. Williams—W. Downing—Messrs A. Brown—Ld Hatherley—Rev. Mr [W. W.] Malet—Mr McCarthy—Rev. Mr Law—Mr Ludlow (O)—J. Leach[5]—Mr Gilston.[6] Worked for reprint of Vol. IV. Read Justin McCarthy—Dixon's (Henry VIII) Ch of E.—Lady C. Elliot's Poems.[7]

10. Fr.

Ch. 8¼ A.M: resuming normal movements—the cold notwithstanding. Wrote to Messrs Clowes & Sons—Sir Wilfrid Lawson[8]—M. Gennadios—Rev. Mr Crosbie[9]—M. Wylie—Mr Murray—C. Dunn—Mr Vickers. Worked for Reprint: & finished & sent off the copy for Vol. IV. Woodcraft. Read Dixon's History—McCarthy's History—Lady C. Elliot's Poems.

11. Sat.

Ch. 8¼ A.M. Wrote to Mr Adam MP. (2)—Ld Granville—Mr O'Sullivan—H. Hurlbutt—Mr Thornborough—Secs Metrop. Vis. Association—Rev. Mr Suffield—Helen J.G.—Scotts—Mr Astley—F.B. Elliot.[10] Read Dixon (finished Vol. I.)—Walkerston on Female Employment[11]—Various Tracts—Lady C. Elliot's Poems—McCarthy's History. Worked for Reprint.

[1] See 22 Dec. 78.
[2] Meeting in Edinburgh this day, Rosebery presiding, formally agreed to invite diarist to contest Midlothian; *T.T.*, 9 January 1879, 9f. See 30 Jan. 79.
[3] Joseph Bartholomew Davey Hopgood, vicar of Lannarth 1872.
[4] Charles Meynell, 1828-82; Roman catholic apologist; had sent a letter of C. J. Fox; Hawn P.
[5] John Leach, liberal in Yarmouth.
[6] Perhaps Peter Gilston, Leeds liberal.
[7] Lady C. Elliot, *Medusa and other poems* (1878); see Add MS 44459, f. 18.
[8] Sir Wilfred *Lawson, 1829-1906; liberal M.P. Carlisle 1859-65, 1868-85; temperance reformer and anti-imperialist.
[9] Howard August Crosbie, 1844-1918; vicar of Milnrow 1878-83.
[10] Frederick Boileau Elliot, d. 1880; husband of Lady Charlotte Elliot (see 9 Jan. 79).
[11] Probably a pamphlet, though untraced, by Mr Walkenshaw; see 14 Feb. 79.

12. 1 S. Epiph.

Hn Church 11 A.M. & 6½ P.M. Wrote to Ed. Yarmouth Indept[1]—Mr Adam MP—Mr Edmonds—Lieut. Meldrum. Read Rifts in the Veil[2]—Martineau 'Endeavours'[3]—The Congregationalist—Lee on Prereformation Scotland.[4] Worked a little on my [W. G.] Ward Article with a view to Reprint.[5]

13. M.

Ch. 8¼ AM. Wrote to Mr Neil (Sydney) dft.[6]—Mr Clark (Adelaide) do[7]— Manager Central Press Assn—Sir Jas Watson—Mr King—Mr M. Bailey—Rev. Dr J.G. Rogers. Worked hard on Ward, & reincorporated the principal excised parts. Woodcraft with Herbert. Read Memoir of Balzac.[8] A strange but touching picture.

14. Tu.

Ch. 8¼ A.M. Wrote out letters to Mr Neill (Sydney)—Mr Clark (Adelaide) —copies to Central Press. Wrote also to W. Richmond—Mr Taylor (O)—Scotts. Worked for Reprint: I am now preparing Copy for Volumes V and VI. Off at 5¼ to Chester. Back at 11½. Saw the Bishop—on St Thomas Toxteth—The Dean— Mr Dodson—Duke of Westminster—The Mayor. Attended the Mayors very sumptuous banquet & proposed his health.[9] Read Curwen's History of Booksellers.[10]

15. Wed.

Ch. 8¼ A.M. Wrote to Rev. Mr Burnaby[11]—Mrs Geo Mayhew (O)[12]—Mr Walkerston—Mr Hardcastle—W. Buchanan—N. Furner—C.L. Smith[13]—Mr Morley—Mr Barnes—E.M. Damala[14]—Arthur Hill—H. Taylor—Mr Lawson—Mr Colson—H.C. Hines—G.B. Smith. Worked for Reprint. Walk with the Rector visited Ewloe School and made divers calls: 3-5½. Worked for Reprint. Read Curwen's History of Booksellers: Speech of Parkes.

---

[1] On N. Norfolk election; see *Yarmouth Independent*, 18 January 1879, 4.

[2] *Rifts in the veil; a collection of inspirational poems and essays*, ed. W. H. Harrison (1878).

[3] J. Martineau, *Endeavours after the Christian life*, 2v. (1843-7).

[4] R. Lee, *The reform of the Church of Scotland* (1864).

[5] i.e. for *Gleanings*, v, which restored sections omitted at Lockhart's request in the original *Quarterly* article; see 22 Sept., 4 Dec. 44.

[6] W. Neill of the City bank, Sydney, N.S.W., and A. S. Clark, of the City bank, Adelaide, had forwarded resolutions supporting Gladstone, whose replies are in *T.T.*, 16 January 1879, 8a.

[7] See previous note.

[8] Probably H. H. Walker, *The Comédie Humaine and its author* (1879).

[9] *T.T.*, 16 January 1879, 6c.

[10] H. Curwen, *A history of booksellers* (1873).

[11] Perhaps Henry Fowke Burnaby, 1834-1917; taught at Eton; rector of Buckland 1872-94.

[12] Wife of George Jeremiah Mayhew of Epsom.

[13] Declining invitation of Clement L. Smith, secretary of the literary cttee. of Phi Beta Kappa at Harvard, to give its annual oration in June 1879; Hawn P.

[14] Had sent papers on the Greek church; Hawn P.

16. Th.

Ch. 8¼ A.M. Wrote to Hon. P. Stanhope—Sir Henry Parkes—G. Lefevre—N. Catherall—F.W. Hunt[1]—L. Hemer—Mr Murray—Mr Danrey—Jas Hill. Worked for Reprint. Read McCarthy's History—The Constitution Violated[2]—Dick's Life[3]—Curwen's Hist. Booksellers. Woodcutting with Herbert. Saw Mr Jones— Mr Vickers. Mr Illingworth[4] came.

17. Fr.

Ch. 8¼ A.M. But the cold (18 degrees of frost) affected my bowels & obliged me to keep the House. Wrote to Messrs Clowes BP.—Mr Adam MP.—Mr Yerbury[5]—D. Knight—J.E. Page—Scotts—Mr Keogh[6]—Mr Lovell. Worked much for Reprint. Saw Mr Vickers—Mr [James] Stuart—Mr Geo. Butler. Read Dick's Life—Curwen's Booksellers—Q.R. on Party Governt.[7]

18. Sat.

Ch. 8¼ AM (the frost gone). Wrote to Mr Bayley Potter MP—Ld Granville—Mr Lefevre MP.—Mr Plender jun.—T. Fenwick—A. Smythe[8]—Rev. T.G. Law BP.— Mr Redpath—Mr Knowles—Mr Lawn. Walk with Mr Stuart, Mr Illingworth & Mr Ottley. Worked for Reprint. Read Dick—Curwen.

19. 2 S. Epiph.

Ch 11 AM (with H.C.) & 6½ PM. Wrote to Messrs Clowes—Mr Coles l. & B.P. Read Muir's Mahomet (SPCK)[9]—Mr Coles MS.[10]—Forms of marriage[11]—and [blank.] Worked on Proofs of [*Gleanings,*] Vol. III (Ecce H[omo]) Walk with Mr [James] Stuart & the party. Much conversation with him & Mr Illingworth.

20. M.

Ch. 8½ AM: in great cold, without damage DG. Wrote to Lord Rosebery—Sir Wm Muir[12]—Mr Goschen—Mr Nuttal—W. Fogg—C. Cowan—Mr Murray—Mr Field. Worked much for Reprint. Cut down a sycamore. Mr Stuart went: fare-well conversation after breakfast. Read Dick: finished. A remarkable, an *heroic* man. Curwen's Booksellers.

[1] Frederick William Hunt, London architect.
[2] Tract on Disraeli's iniquities.
[3] See 21 Nov. 78.
[4] John Richardson Illingworth, d. 1915; fellow of Jesus, Oxford, 1872-83; rector of Longworth from 1883; contributor to *Lux Mundi* (1890); Hawarden Visitors Book.
[5] Frank Yerbury of London, on religion; Hawn P.
[6] Probably William Keogh, Irish lawyer; s. of the judge.
[7] *Quarterly Review*, cxlvii. 277 (January 1879); see Ramm II, i. 91.
[8] Alfred Smythe, poet; see Add MS 44459, f. 138.
[9] (Sir) W. Muir, *The life of Mahomet and history of Islam*, 4v. (1858-61).
[10] Perhaps A. Coles, 'Wine in the Word. An inquiry concerning the wine Christ made' (1878).
[11] Untraced.
[12] Sir William *Muir, 1819-1905; Indian finance minister 1874; on India council 1876-85; principal of Edinburgh university 1885-1902.

21. Tu.

Ch. 8½ A.M. Wrote to Dean of Rochester—Lord Cottesloe—R. Brown jun.[1]— Herr Harfeldst[2]—Rev. Dr Hayman—Lt Govr [H. B.] Loch—Mr Cheetham—Mr Yerbury—A. Hume—Mr Stevenson. Worked for Reprint—some hours. Felling trees with WHG. Read B. Brunswic, Traité[3]—Stein and his Times[4]—Curwen's Booksellers—Aul[us] Gellius on Colour.[5]

22. Wed.

Ch. 8½ A.M. Wrote to Messrs Clowes & Sons B.P.—Dr Magnus l. & BP—Mr Lowe MP.—Lt Salusbury—Rev. Mr Pryce—Mr Dechman—Mr Vickers—Mr Collings—Mr Rodell—W.H.G. Sent off the copy of Vols V. & VI of my Tracts. Little now remains beyond a very slight survey of the Proofs. Saw Dean of Chester— Mr Vickers—Valentine.[6] Read Brunswic Tr. de Berlin—Stein's Life and Times— Curwen's Booksellers. At 11 P.M. we found the Chimney on fire & the disturbance lasted for some time—No damage D.G. Woodcraft.

23. Th.

Ch. 8½ A.M. Wrote to Williams & Norgate—R. Knight—W. Johnson—J. Anderson—J. Murray—W.J. Dowser—H.N.G.—Mr Vickers—Mrs Th.—A. Lang—Mr Wise. Woodcraft. Read Life & Times of Stein—Brunswic, Traité de Berlin—Lang & Butcher's Odyssey[7]—Imperial Ben.[8]—Curwen's Booksellers. Made just a beginning for my 'Epithets of movement['].[9]

24. Fr.

Ch. 8½ A.M. Wrote to Ld Granville—*Draft* to Mr J. Cowan[10]—Ld Lyttelton—Rev. Mr M'Coll—C. Townshend—Messrs Clowes & Son—Mr Adam—A.M. Reid—Mr Johnson. Woodcraft with H. Worked on Epithets of movement. Read B. Brunswick—R. Brown on Solar Worship[11]—Colley to Brackenbury[12]—Bret Harte, the Roaring Camp[13]—Seeley's Hist. of Stein.

25. Sat. St Paul.

Ch. 8.45 AM. Wrote to Lt Govr I. of Man—Edr of Guardian[14]—Rev. Mr Phillot— Mr Ashworth—Ld Cottesloe—Sir Thos G.—Mr Brewster—Mr Owens—Rev. G.

---

[1] Robert Brown, b. 1844; classicist. [2] Reading uncertain.
[3] Benoît Brunswik, *Le traité de Berlin annoté et commenté* (1878).
[4] See 1 Jan. 79. [5] A. Gellius, *The Attic Nights* (1795), ch. xxvi.
[6] A servant? See 27 Jan. 79.
[7] A. Lang and S. H. Butcher, *The Odyssey* (1879).
[8] J. G. Ashworth, *Imperial Ben. A Jew d'esprit* (1879).
[9] 'On Epithets of movement in Homer', *Nineteenth Century*, v. 463 (March 1879).
[10] See 30 Jan. 79. [11] See 24 Mar. 77.
[12] Letter from (Sir) George Pomeroy Colley (1835-81; Lytton's secretary 1879-80, governed Natal 1880-1; commanded troops in Transvaal 1881) to C. B. Brackenbury on Afghanistan; see Add MS 44459, f. 41 and Ramm II, i. 92.
[13] F. B. Harte, *The luck of Roaring Camp and other sketches* (1870).
[14] Sending details about the *Biograph* (see 28 Jan. 79n.).

Morgan.[1] Woodcraft with W. Worked on Epithets of movement in Homer. Read Seeley's Hist. of Stein—Curwen's Booksellers.

26. 3 S. Epiph.

Ch. 11 A.M. and [blank] P.M. Wrote to Miss Nightingale[2]—Messrs Clowes—Mr Rabbula (O) [sic]—Mr Murray. Read Bp Binney's Letter[3]—Wilkinson on Theism[4]—Papers for the Times[5]—Divers Tracts—QR on Aggressive Nonconf:[6]— Pryce on British Church.[7]

27. M.

Ch. 8½ A.M. Death of young Valentine. Requiescat in Domino.

Wrote to Ed. Northern Whig[8]—Mr Godley—Mr Hook O—Mr Fish O—Mr Berth—W.P. Murray[9]—Mr Dickinson—Mr Jackson—Mr Gilfillan BP—W. Wells[10]—Mr Hillyard—Mr Trimmer—C. Burnett—C. Spick—A. Cooke. Woodcraft. Attended C.s Tea party. Worked on Homeric Epithets of Movement. Read Brunsvic, Traité de B.—Life & Times of Stein—Moore's Poems—Curwen's Booksellers.

28. Tu.

Ch. 8½ AM. Wrote to M. de la Fleurière—Miss Collet—Miss M. Hyslop[11]—J. Treherne—R. Steventon—Ed. of Biograph[12]—G.B. Smith—W. Wood—Mr Harris. Saw Scott's Fire Escape worked. Walk with the Rector: and divers calls. Read Traité de Berlin—Life & Times of Stein—Curwen's Booksellers—Buttmann on θοός.[13] Worked on the Epithets of movement.

29. Wed.

Ch. 8½ AM. Wrote to Ld Hartington—R. Leake—Mr Linnell—H. Wilson—E. Barton—M.R. Sharp—Rev. C. Bowen—Scotts—Sir A. Gordon. Walk with F. C[avendish]. Conversation on Midlothian: saw the stock &c. at Roberts's.

[1] Godfrey Morgan had sent his 'British church service' (1878).
[2] On India, in Cook, *Life of Florence Nightingale*, ii. 292.
[3] H. Binney, 'A letter to the Lord Archbishop of Canterbury' (1878).
[4] W. F. Wilkinson, *Modern materialism* (1879); on proof of God.
[5] *Papers for the times*, ed. W. Lewin. No 1, 2 (1879).
[6] *Quarterly Review*, cxlvii. 49 (January 1879).
[7] J. Pryce, *The Ancient British Church* (1878).
[8] See 28 Jan. 79n.
[9] William Powell Murray, barrister, of the London bankruptcy court; probably on Mrs Thistlethwayte's affairs.
[10] William Wells asked permission to quote from diarist's speeches; not found published; Hawn P.
[11] Lived in Regent's Park.
[12] Not identified by name; *The Biograph*, i. 78 (February 1879) contained a well-researched biographical sketch of Gladstone, concluding with his answer—mainly a reference to his Oxford speech of 30 Jan. 78—to six questions on his move from conservatism to liberalism; Gladstone complained to the *Northern Whig* (see 27 Jan. 79 and *The Guardian*, 29 January 1879, 135) that this statement had been made privately; *The Biograph* denied this in 'An explanation', i. 194 (March 1879).
[13] In one of the many grammatical works of P. C. Buttmann.

Worked on Epithets of movement. Read Stein Life & Times—Curwen's Booksellers. Evening spent in conversation especially with Bright on India.[1]

30. Th.

Only rose to breakfast on account of an internal insecurity. Finished my public letter to Midlothian: after reading it to Bright & the ladies. Dispatched it. Also wrote to Mr Cowan (Priv)—Messrs Clowes BP—Mr Wilkinson—R. Leake—W. Brown—A. Cooke. Saw Mr Vickers—Mr Green Manchester.[2] Much conversation & long walk with Bright. We talked much on politics. On a crisis he said the entire Liberal party will require you to come forward: I gave him, besides the coward's reason, three strong reasons against it.[3] Worked on proofs & Contents for Reprint Vol. III. Read Life & Time of Stein. Evening chiefly with J. B[right].

To John COWAN, 30 January 1879.[4]   *The Times*, 3 February 1879, 10c.

I have had the very high honour to receive the invitation signed by you on behalf of the Executive Committee of the Midlothian Liberal Association, and as the chairman of these meetings, in which I am requested to become a candidate for the county at the next election.

You have also been kind enough to supply me with evidence which entirely satisfies my mind that the invitation expresses the desire of the majority of the constituency.

I do not hesitate to accede to this flattering request.

Under anything like ordinary circumstances my choice would have been, after having served already in 11 Parliaments, either retirement or, at any rate, the least conspicuous and most tranquil seat which it might be within my option to obtain; but the circumstances of the present juncture are far from ordinary. At no period of my public life have the issues awaiting the judgment of the nation been of such profound importance. The management of finance, the scale of expenditure, the constantly growing arrears of legislation, serious as they are, only lead up to still greater questions. I hold before you, as I have held in the House of Commons, that the faith and honour of the country have been gravely compromised in the foreign policy of the Ministry; that by the disturbances of confidence, and lately of peace, which they have brought, they prolonged and aggravated the public distress; that they have augmented the power and influence of the Russian Empire, even while estranging the feelings of its population; that they have embarked the Crown and people in an unjust war, full of mischief, if not of positive danger to India; and that by their use of the treaty-making and war-making powers of the Crown they have abridged the just rights of Parliament and have presented that prerogative to the nation under an unconstitutional aspect which tends to make it insecure.

Thus the particular subjects before us, which separately are grave enough, all resolve themselves into one comprehensive question—the question whether this is or is not the way in which the country wishes to be governed. I hope that when the time arrives the constituencies will decide this issue, in whatever sense it may be, at any rate in a manner perfectly plain and definitive. I think that in the invitation before me the Liberals of Midlothian

[1] Bright stayed from 29 January to 1 February.

[2] Benjamin L. Green, secretary of Manchester liberal association.

[3] Bright noted: 'Much talk . . . on possibility of change of Govt. and on difficulty of new Govt. in connexion with old colleagues and with elements of trouble in the non-official portion of the Liberal Party'; Walling, *Diaries of Bright*, 416.

[4] (Sir) John Cowan, 1814–1900; paper manufacturer at Penicuik; chairman of Midlothian liberal association from 1879; cr. bart. 1894. The text above is taken from *The Times*; there is a draft at Add MS 44763, f. 142, from which the paragraphing is taken.

have sought to do what they could towards thus presenting the question intelligibly as a public and not a personal question. It is with a similar view that I loyally and gratefully accept the offer and will co-operate in giving it effect.   I have in this letter addressed you only on national affairs, which at present more than usually outweigh for every district and every interest its own particular and local questions; but I am aware that there are special subjects in which the skilled agriculturists of Midlothian feel a special concern, and I need hardly assure you that if I receive the honour of their confidence these subjects will have my careful and unbiased attention.

31. Fr.

Ch. 8½ A.M. (Another of these curious seizures from insufficient covering on walking in aftn with Mr B. & Mr [C. H.] Bateman[1]) Mr B. delighted in him. Wrote to Messrs Glyn & Co—Rev. E.R. Wilberforce—Rev. Mr Winslow—Rev. Mr MacColl—Mr Coldstream—A. Gardner—Messrs Clowes BP.—Vicar of St Thomas Leeds—Dr Roth—Mr Knight—Mr Bentley—Mr Raleigh—Mr Vickers. Worked some time for Reprint. Read Freeman on Geddes—Do on study of Greek[2]—Life & Times of Stein. Walk with Bright.

Sat. Feb. One 1879.

Wrote to Dean of Rochester—Messrs Wyman—B.L. Green—Mr Trebuch—Mr Adam—Mayor of Chester—Prof. S. Colvin—Messrs Clowes Bp—Mr Enoch[3]—Mr Blair—Mr Stark. Bright went: leaving golden opinions. Conversation in mg. Walk with F. C[avendish]. Worked for reprint. Worked on Adjectives of Movement. Read Life & Times of Stein—Ashton on Reciprocity[4]—Dr Roth on Health.[5]

2. 3 S. Epiph.

Ch 11 AM (and H.C.) also 6.30 PM. Wrote to Duke of Argyll. Read Ryder's A. to Littledale[6]—Ch Q.R. reply to old Q.R.[7]—Presbyter on Comprehension (a noodle!)[8]—Christopher, Introd. & Sermons[9]—Osgood on Bryant.[10]

3. M.

Ch. 8½ AM. Wrote to Messrs Clowes & Sons BP.—Ld Granville—Mr Forster MP.—Rev. Mr Constable—Rev. Mr Stephens—Bp of Chester—Mr O'Flanagan[11]—Messrs Spottiswoode—M. Saunders—T. Moore—J. Wright—W. Raleigh—B.D.

---

[1] The curate at Mold.

[2] E. A. Freeman in *Contemporary Review*, xxxiv. 442 (February 1879) and *Fortnightly Review*, xxxi. 290 (February 1879).

[3] Frederick Enoch sent verses; Hawn P.

[4] S. E. Ashton, *Commercial depression. A plea for reciprocity* (1879).

[5] M. Roth, *The fever-dens in the West-Central and North-Western districts of London* (1879).

[6] H. I. D. Ryder, in *Contemporary Review*, xxxiv. 458 (February 1879).

[7] On Protestantism; *Church Quarterly Review*, vii. 261 (January 1879).

[8] Untraced tract.

[9] A. M. W. Christopher, perhaps *A few thoughts on the best means of fortifying the minds of educated young men against . . . Popery* (1868).

[10] S. Osgood, *Bryant among his countrymen; the poet, the patriot, the man* (1879).

[11] Perhaps Rev. J. R. O'Flanagan, an occasional correspondent; Hawn P.

Isaacs. Woodcraft with W. Worked for Reprint. Worked on Adjectives of Motion. Read Stein Life & Times—Curwen's Booksellers—Angus on Virgil.[1]

4. Tu.

Ch. $8\frac{1}{2}$ A.M. Wrote to Mr E.R. Russell—Mr Leeman MP (2)—G. Bramwell—Mr Mackee O—Mr Donaldson—Mr Murray—Mr Douglas—Mr Hancock—Messrs Houghton & Co[2]—Messrs de la Tremouille[3]—Mr Piggott. Cut two trees with WHG: in relief of cottages. Finished my paper on Homer's Epithets of movement. Read Stein's Life & Times—Mystery of Isis[4]—Which Infirmity.

5. Wed.

Ch. $8\frac{1}{2}$ A.M. Wrote to Mr A. Taylor Innes—Mr Anderson MP.—Mr Bate (Raleigh)—Mons. de Lechoville—Mr A. Davidson—Messrs Clowes BP—Rev. P. Collier—Mr A. Boyle[5]—Rev. G. Allom—Rev. T. Long—Mr J.H. Davidson. Wood cutting with WHG. Worked for Reprint. Read Hume's Essays[6]—Stein's Life & Times—MacCarthy on Revised Code[7]—Boyle on E. Question.

6. Th.

Ch. $8\frac{1}{2}$ AM. Wrote to Mr Smitton—Rev. Mr Stone[8]—A.J. Wilson[9]—G.F. Maguire—J. Seward—Mr Froude—T. Jack[10]—Mr Orange[11]—W. Booth. Cut two trees with WHG. Revised (in part) paper on Epithets of movement. Read Hume's Essays (Pol.)—Life & Times of Stein—J. Simon, Appendix—Curwen's Booksellers.

7. Fr.

Ch. $8\frac{1}{2}$ AM. Wrote to Messrs Clowes & Son BP.—R. Neville[12]—J.W. Russell[13]—E. Prior—Miss Ruskin[14]—Rev. Dr Sexton[15]—N. Kirran—Mr Hipwell—A. Restney—Mr Evans—Mr Cunningham Graham[16]—Lieut Luscombe[17]—Rev. Mr Wilber-

---

[1] J. Angus, *Four lectures on the advantages of a classical education* (1846).

[2] London stationers.

[3] *Sic*; untraced.

[4] Perhaps H. P. Blavatsky, *Isis unveiled*, 2v. (1877).

[5] A. Boyle had sent his 'The sympathy and action of England in the late Eastern crisis' (1878).

[6] D. Hume, *Essays and treatises on several subjects* (1758).

[7] E. F. M. MacCarthy, 'The Government Code; its injurious effect upon national education' (1879).

[8] Henry Edward Stone, Baptist minister in London.

[9] Ambrose John Wilson, 1853-1929; priest in South Africa and Australia; headmaster of Lancing 1895.

[10] Thomas C. Jack, secretary of Edinburgh Chamber of Commerce.

[11] James Edward Dakin Orange, publisher.

[12] Ralph Neville, barrister.

[13] James Ward Russell; not further identified.

[14] 'Do you know anything of a woman named Ruskin who seems to have attended my mother on her deathbed?', now destitute; to Sir T. Gladstone, 9 February 1880, Hawn P.

[15] George Sexton, divine and historian, had sent his *Scientific materialism calmly considered* (1874).

[16] On hiring fairs, in *T.T.*, 10 February 1879, 6c, to 'R. C. Cunninghame Graham', i.e. Lieut. Robert Cunninghame Cunninghame Graham, or, more likely, Robert Bontine Cunninghame Graham, 1852-1936; author, laird and radical M.P. N. Lanarkshire 1886-92.

[17] A. M. Luscombe sent classical verses; Hawn P.

force—Sir Thos G. Worked for reprint. Finished revisal of paper on Epithets of Movement. Walk with C. and visits in the village. Read Stein's Life & Times—Rumer, Causes of Distress[1]—Experience in Lunatic Asylum[2]—Curwen's Booksellers.

8. Sat.

Ch 8¼ AM. Wrote to D. McC. Carr—Sir F. Leighton—Mr Mansell BP—Mr McColl BP—Mr Meynell BP—Mr Colborne—Mr Hawkins—C. Crawley[3]—Sir Thos G.—Mrs Staley—C. Silk—A.M. Lang[4]—E.H. Wolf[5]—W.T. Stead. Felled & kibbled a tree with Willy. Busy in arranging papers. Read divers Tracts—Life and Times of Stein—Exper. in Lunatic Asylum—Looked a little into Hook.[6]

9. Septa S.

Ch 11 AM 6½ PM. Wrote to Clowes & Sons. Worked on proof. Walk with F.C. Read St Paul at Athens[7]—Sexton on Materialism—Christopher on Confessional[8]—And some of Hook's Life.

10. M.

Ch. 8½ AM. Wrote to Messrs Clowes BP—Mr Hutcheson—F. Durham—Messrs Seton & Mackenzie. Worked on proof. Worked nearly all day on the Life of Dr Hook & made notes for my Lecture. 7–8¼. Made my Address in the Schoolroom much crowded by a very attentive audience.[9] A little party of guests afterwards. Read Stein's Life & Times—Experience in a Lun. Asylum.

11. Tu.

Ch. 8½ AM. Wrote to M. André Hidromeus l. & BP.—Mr Knowles—Mr Bontflower (O)[10]—Mr G. Stewart—Mr Kennedy—Mr E.R. Mullins[11]—Ld Kensington—Capt. Atherstone. Felled trees with W.H.G. Worked on Thes. Homerikos[12]—the first day since when? Read Stein's Life & Times—Experience in a Lunatic Asylum.—Lord Beaconsfield's (supposed) Address: a clever parody.[13]

12. Wed.

Ch. 8½ A.M. Wrote to Messrs Clowes BP—Mr J. Knowles BP—Ed. Daily News—Hon. Sir A. Gordon—R. Brown jun.—Mr Kynaston[14]—H.C. Merivale—Mr

[1] A. Rumer, *Political causes of commercial depression and distress* (1879).
[2] *My experiences in a Lunatic Asylum. By a sane patient* (1879); sent by the author, Herman Charles Merivale, 1839-1906; Add MS 44459, f. 98.
[3] Of 131 Piccadilly.   [4] Perhaps Arthur Moffatt Lang, authority on engineering in India.
[5] Of Coventry; had sent a volume; Hawn P.   [6] See 10 Feb. 79.
[7] C. Shakspeare, *St Paul at Athens* (1878).   [8] See 2 Feb. 79.
[9] On Stephens' *Life of Hook*, for which Gladstone had lent his letters; *T.T.*, 11 February 1879, 10a; reprinted in full as a pamphlet.
[10] Probably a merchant in Leith; see *T.T.*, 15 February 1879, 5f.
[11] The sculptor; see 22 Feb. 79.
[12] Begun in the 1860s, worked on spasmodically; never published.
[13] *The Premier's defence of his Administration. An appeal to the justice of the British nation* (1879).
[14] Herbert Kynaston, 1835-1910; principal of Cheltenham 1874-88; classicist.

Richardson—Messrs Pears—Colonial Institute[1]—Mr Lovell—Mr Havard—Mr Dalton—V. Bauer[2]—T. Downs—E. Slater—Messrs Fogg. Dee Trust Meeting 12–1. Saw Mr Carrington—WHG—to charge him with messages for London. Worked for reprint. Also for Thesauros Homerikos. But at what a snail's pace it advances! Began Mozley's Strafford[3]—Read Stein's Life & Times—and [blank.] Axe work in aftn.

13. Th.

Ch. 8½ AM. Wrote to Ld Kensington Tel.—Mr Vickers—W. Smith—Mr Frowde[4]—D. Holmes—Mr Thorndike Rice—L. Stebbing—E. Cox—J. Knowles. Cut in part a large sycamore. Worked on Thes. Homer. Read Stein—Mozley's Strafford—Cox on the Teeth[5]—Constable on Science &c.[6]

14 Fr.

Ch. 8½ AM. Wrote to Mons Gurshoff [sc. Geshoff]—Mr Mummery—W.H.G.—Dr Anthony[7]—R. Ellis—Mr Walkenshaw[8]—Mr Godley—Mr R. Snowball—Messrs Wms & Norgate. Saw Mr Vickers. Finished felling a large sycamore. Worked on Thes. Hom. (Iris). Read Stein—Mozley's Strafford (finished)—Morgan's Poems[9]—Curwen's Booksellers.

15. Sat.

Ch. 8½ AM. Wrote to Mr Stoughton (U.S. Minr St Petersburgh)[10]—Mr R.A. Macfie—Mr Thomas—Rev. J. Morgan—Mr W. King. Worked rather long on Thes. Hom. 'Night' rewritten *pluries*.[11] Saw Mr Rogers (Lpool). Made Farm calls. Tea with Miss Scott. Read Life & Times of Stein.

16. Sexa S.

Ch. 11 AM and H.C.—Also 6½ PM. Wrote to Messrs Clowes BP—Mr Davidson—Mrs Th.—Q[ueen's] F[erry] Station Master. Worked on proofs Vol V. Read Shakespeare's Vol. on St Paul[12]—Huxley Addresses in US.[13]—Radcliffe on Unity & Variety[14]—Headlam on Progress[15]—Sexton on Materialism.[16]

---

[1] See 17 Mar. 79.

[2] Probably Vasily Vasil'evich Bauer, Slav author.

[3] In J. B. Mozley, *Essays, historical and theological*, 2v. (1878).

[4] Henry *Frowde, 1841–1927; managed London office (at Macmillan's) of Oxford University Press 1874–1913; published diarist's ed. of Bp. Butler. This letter, on the new Lectionary, in *T.T.*, 20 February 1879, 10a.

[5] Untraced.

[6] H. S. Constable, *Fashions of the day in medicine and science* (1879).

[7] Probably John Anthony, physician in Birmingham.   [8] See 11 Jan. 79?

[9] Perhaps J. A. Morgan, *Macaronic poetry* (1872).

[10] Edwin Wallace Stoughton, 1818–82; lawyer and friend of Grant; American ambassador to Russia 1877–9; probably a note of introduction for Dufferin, the new British ambassador there.

[11] 'several times'.

[12] See 9 Feb. 79.

[13] T. H. Huxley, *American addresses* (1877).   [14] See 26 Mar. 78.

[15] S. D. Headlam, *Priestcraft and progress* (1878).   [16] See 7 Feb. 79.

17. M.

Ch. 8½ AM. Wrote to Messrs Spottiswoode—Sir Jas Watson—W.H.G.—S. Morley MP—Mrs Wynne—Mr P.W. Campbell[1]—Mr Radcliffe—Bishop Strossmayer. Worked a little on Thes. Hom. Much on arranging papers and books and on selecting and packing for London. I hope to work a little on Thesauros there, as I am not under the same honourable obligation to go into the front on the subject now coming up as that which lay upon me in the Eastern matter. We shall see. Finished kibbling the sycamore of Saturday. Saw Mr Vickers—S.E.G. Dined at the Rectory. Read Stein, Life & Times. Finished Curwen's Booksellers. Conversation with S.E.G. & Mr Gambier on the rumours about Mr Leeman.[2]

18. Tu. [London]

Church 8½ AM Wrote to Rev. Mr Kennedy—Mr Culshaw—Sec. Univ. Club—Mr Mackenzie—Lieut Bacon[3]—Mr Knowles—Mr Thorne. Saw Mr Vickers. Visited Bryant. Saw S.E.G.—Mr Macewan—[Mlle.] F. Bianca[4]—Mr Birkbeck—Mr Skinner—Mr Ensell—Rev. Mr Pratt. 12¾–6.35. To London from Q.F. and by Irish Mail. Worked upon the usual chaotic mass: riddled a little by Willy & J.A. Godley's kindness. Worked on proofsheets Epithets of movement. Finished Seeley Vol. II. Read divers Tracts.

19. Wed.

Wrote O!!! But a very busy day. Saw Ld Hartington—Ld Granville—Mr Goschen—Sir C. Forster—Mr Byrom[5]—Mr Morley—Mr Knowles—Mr Cowper Temple—Scotts—W.H.G. Mansion House Meeting on Extension of Univ. Teaching: signs of an altered feeling towards me.[6] Moved the First Resolution. 7½–11½. Hamlet at the Lyceum. What food for thought. Read The City Clerks[7]—Cape Correspondence.[8]

20. Th.

Wrote to Spottiswoodes BP—Herr Jul. Gertig—Messrs Mortimer—Sir Thos G.—R.W. Maude—B.W. Carter—R.C. Edwards[9]—Miss Von Grimlach—Stephen Mussett—Mrs Twiss—Mr Targett[10]—Mr Murphy—Jas Wright—Mr Lawson—F.W. Smith—Thos Hale.[11] Read Duke of Argyll.[12] Finished proofsheets of Article for

[1] Patrick William Campbell, election agent for Midlothian; letters in Add MS 44116.

[2] On 5 February Gladstone offered his living of St Thomas, Seaforth, to William Luther Leeman, d. 1905, s. of the M.P. (see 25 Jan. 53), previously chaplain to Lord Halifax; rumours about Leeman's drunkenness circulated; the offer was partly withdrawn, but eventually confirmed; Hawn P.

[3] (Sir) Nicholas Henry Bacon, 1857–1947; served in Egypt 1882; a tory; 12th bart. 1945.

[4] Possibly a rescue case; several letters noted in 1879.

[5] Probably Edward Byrom, deputy lieutenant of Devon.

[6] *T.T.*, 20 February 1879, 11a.

[7] From Glasgow? See 22 Feb. 79n.

[8] Blue Book of February 1879 on events of November–December 1878; *P.P.* 1878-9 lii. 427.

[9] Perhaps Robert Clarke Edwards, architect.

[10] Perhaps Targett and Barrett, lithographers.

[11] Of St Stephen's Square, London.

[12] Now published; see 4 June 78.

N.C. H. of C. 6¼-8¼ and again after dinner.[1] Worked on parcels. Saw Ld Hartington—Sir A. Panizzi—Mr Ludovic.

21. Fr.

Wrote to Messrs Leeman—Mr Leeman MP—Mr [T. P.] O'Connor—E. Williams—Mr Cockshutt—P.F. Bhandane—R. Darling[2]—Rev. S.E.G. (2)—J. Rogers—W.B. Holmes—Mr Reynolds—Mr Hamblin—Rev. Harris. Saw Mr Godley—Mr Whitwell—Mr Knowles—Sir W.C. James—Mr Forster—Sir W. Harcourt—Mr Goschen—Ld Granville—Mr West. Dined with the F.C.s—Lady Granville's afterwards. Read Cape Papers—Argyll, Chap. I.

22. Sat.

Wrote to Dean of Windsor—Messrs Spottiswoode BP—Messrs Clowes & Sons BP—Rev. J.M. King—Miss Tucker Bp—Mr Plender BP—Mr Pratt BP—Mr Mackenzie—Mr Rossiter—D. Kennedy[3]—D.A. Campbell[4]—Mr Halliwell Phillips—C. Kent—Mr Lloyd—Mr Squires—Mr Newton—Mr Collins—Mr Deacon—Mr Blair—Mr Thornton. Worked on Revises for N.C. Proofs for Reprint. Mr Mullins, Sculptor, came to make what he could of me 11-1.[5] Read Argyll E.Q.—Eastwick Affghan Wars.[6] Calls. Saw Mr Dumaresq—Miss Talbot.—Witney X.

23. Quinqua S.

Chapel Royal 10 AM 5½ P.M. Wrote to Miss Hope—Miss Ponsonby—Mr Russell. Saw Mr Ouvry—Mrs Th. Read Nevins Ireland & the Popes[7]—19th C. on Dupanloup—Mallock in do on Reason & Dogma[8]—And Tracts.

24. M.

Wrote to Mr Whitton—Mr Allnutt—Mr Henly—Sir S. Scott & Co—Bishop of Chester—Rev. Mr Leeman—Dr Liddon BP—Mr Cowan BP—Mr Emery—J.S. Mills—Mr Agnew. Shopping. Saw Mr E. Russell (Lpool)—Scotts—Mr Adam—Mr Childers—Sir W. James. Read Duke of Argyll's Work. Dined at Sir W. James's. H of C. 5¾-8.[9]

25. Tu.

Wrote to Mr G. Mitchell—Mr Thorold Rogers—C.T. Townshend—Rev. C. Leeman Tel.—P.M. Lawrence—Mr Byng Hall—F. Ouvry—R. Roper—J. Fletcher—Mr

---

[1] Business of the House; *H* 243. 1524.   [2] Edinburgh businessman.
[3] Duncan Kennedy, secretary of the Glasgow United Trades Council; this letter, on free trade, in *T.T.*, 27 February 1879, 5e.
[4] Donald A. Campbell, wrote on insurance.
[5] E. R. Mullins (see 14 Dec. 78); this bust's whereabouts unknown.
[6] W. J. Eastwick, *Lord Lytton and the Afghan war* (1879).
[7] W. P. Nevins, *Ireland and the Holy See in the Middle Ages* (1879).
[8] W. H. Mallock, 'The logic of toleration', *Nineteenth Century*, v. 64 (January 1879).
[9] Misc. business; *H* 243. 1658.

Luke—Mr Howell—C. Cowan. Saw Mr Murray—Agnews—Dowr Dss of Somerset. Worked on papers, for order. Read D of Argyll—Eastwick on Afghan War—Winter's Becket[1]—Whom to Follow.[2]

26. Ash Wed.

Ch. 11 AM & 12 AM. Wrote to Bp of Chester—Rev. Mr Leeman—Rev. J. Bickford—Rev. S.E.G.—Mr Cheeswright[3]—Mr Benedict N.Y. Histor. Soc.[4]—Dr F. Winslow—Dr A. Robertson—Messrs Paterson & James—G.L. Gomme[5]—Mr Dorking—Mr Pratt—Mrs Murphy—Mr Furness. Saw Sir E. Perry—Mr Bentley—Miss Lewin. Read Duke of Argyll—Fawcett on Indian Finance[6]—Mr G. Smith's 'Whom to Follow'.

27. Th.

Wrote to Ld Hartington—Mr W. Byrom—Rev. Leeman (Tel)—Rev. G. Butler—Rev. T.G. Law—Mr Widlake—W.L. Gladstone BP—Messrs Clowes BP—Messrs Leeman—G. Smith—Sir W. James—A.L. Hardy.[7] Saw Ld Hartington—Mr Hayward—Mrs Th.—Prof. Fawcett. Worked on proofs for reprint. Read D. of A. Eastern Question—Hyndman Poverty of India.[8] Dined at Miss Ponsonby's: Mrs Th. gave me intelligence which touched & moved me.

28. Fr.

Wrote to Rev. Mr Leeman Tel.—Bp of Chester—Mr Pratt—Hon Rev. Mr Stuart[9]—Mr J. Spencer—Mr H.S. Candell[10]—Rev. S.E.G.—Mr Eastwick[11]—Mrs Th.—Mr Ouvry. Dined with the Jameses. H of C. $4\frac{1}{2}$-8 and $9\frac{3}{4}$-$11\frac{1}{4}$ on Indian Finance.[12] Read Osborne's Reply to Wilson[13]—Affghan Minutes (Ld Canning)[14]—Divers Tracts—Duke of Argyll's Book.

Sat March One 1879.

Wrote to Messrs Clowes BP.—Sir A. Gordon—Mrs Th.—Bp of Chester—Mr Innes—Duke of Argyll. Twelve to dinner. Saw Mr Ouvry—Mr C.L. Leeman with

[1] C. T. Winter, *Becket* (1879).
[2] By G. Smith; not further traced.
[3] Probably James William Cheeswright, framemaker.
[4] The New York Historical Society's journal, *A Magazine of American History*, iii. 53 (January 1879) contained 'Gladstone on American Ox Tail' by 'Advocate', an attack on Gladstone's ignorance of America, illustrated by his remark to the Kensington School of Cookery (see 1 May 78) that Americans throw away oxtails unused.
[5] Folklorist in Barnes; Hawn P.
[6] H. Fawcett, 'The financial condition of India', *Nineteenth Century*, v. 193 (January 1879).
[7] Perhaps Alfred Lloyd Hardy, genealogist.
[8] H. M. Hyndman, 'The bankruptcy of India', *Nineteenth Century*, v. 443 (March 1879).
[9] Andrew Godfrey Stuart, 1812-89, s. of 2nd earl of Castle Stewart; rector of Cottesmore 1844.
[10] Correspondence on Miss Stuart's Roman catholicism in Add MS 44459, f. 133ff.
[11] William Joseph Eastwick, 1808-89; Cobdenist; member of India council 1858-68; see 22 Feb. 79n.
[12] Fawcett's motion for a select cttee.; *H* 243. 1975.
[13] One of S. G. Osborne's many letters to the press?
[14] Presumably minutes by Canning while Governor General, but not found published.

his brother Mr J. Leeman: a long & rather harrowing but satisfactory conversation.[1] Saw Sir A. Panizzi. Read Wood on Lunacy Law[2]—Duke of Argyll (finished I.)

2. 1 S. Lent

Charlotte St Ch. 11 A.M and H.C.—St George's aftn. Wrote to D. of Argyll BP.—Mr Ouvry. Saw Ld E. Clinton—Mrs Hope—Sir C.A. Wood. Read Stoughton on State of Religion in Cent XVIII[3]—Nevins Ireland & the Pope—Beckford, Rel. in Australasia.[4]

3. M.

Wrote to Mayor of Southport—Mr Gurdon—G. Spencer—R.C. Stone—J.M. Peake—W.H. Morson—Hon & Rev. Mr Stuart—Capt. Verney—Rev. Dr Vaughan—Rev. C.P. Butler—Rev. J. Haughton—W.P. Christie—Rev. C.G. M'Crie[5]—Rev. Willis Nevins—Major de Dohsé—Rev. A.W. Coghlan[6]—Rev. J. Ferguson—Mr Holyoake. Saw J.S. Wortley. Arranging papers &c. Read Haughton on Free Trade[7]—Duke of Argyll Vol II—Reports on Cyprus Harbours—Donaldson on Women in Greece.[8]

4. Tu.

Wrote to Professor Jebb—Messrs Clowes—Col. Starke[9]—Mr Peppercorn.[10] Saw Ld Granville—Mr Gurdon—Mr MacColl—Mr Kinnaird—Mr Leveson—Mr Bright—Rev. Mr Stuart: & conversed for 1¼ hour with his daughter[11] on the Roman Controversy. It was apparently fighting against a foregone conclusion. But her resistance was faint: she was reserved, and avoided all admissions: as if *instructed*. Worked on my room, now in tolerable order. But how rebellious is the ὕλη:[12] as in the old theories of creation. Eight to dinner. Read Duke of Argyll—Mem. on Cyprus[13]—Jebb on Progress of Greece.[14] H of C. 10½-1¾: voted in 226:291 for Trevelyan.[15]

5. Wed.

Wrote to Bp of Chester—Rev. S.E.G.—Rev. W. Nevins—Major M'Kenzie—Mr Sutton—Bp of Melanesia[16]—Mr Heptonsball—Mr Scollock—Mr Mullins—Mr

---

[1] See 17 Feb. 79n.   [2] W. Wood, *Insanity and the Lunacy Law* (1879).
[3] J. Stoughton, *Religion in England under Queen Anne and the Georges 1702-1800*, 2v. (1878).
[4] By J. Bickford (1878).   [5] Free church minister in Ayr; Hawn P.
[6] Of Dublin, on the Irish church; Hawn P.
[7] Ch. viii of J. Haughton, *The depression of agriculture with a proposal for its remedy* (1879).
[8] J. Donaldson, in *Contemporary Review*, xxxiv. 700 (March 1879).
[9] William Starke, lieut. colonel in 15th foot.
[10] F. Peppercorn of the Strand asked nomination to the Charterhouse; Hawn P.
[11] A. G. Stuart had two living daughters, Mary and Janet. See 28 Feb. 79n.
[12] 'raw material'.
[13] Anon. papers on Cyprus forwarded to F. Hill of the *Daily News*; Add MS 44459, f. 162.
[14] R. C. Jebb in *Macmillan's Magazine*, xxxix. 419 (March 1879).
[15] Household suffrage in the counties; *H* 244. 137.
[16] John Richardson Selwyn, 1844-98; bp. of Melanesia 1877.

Mayson—J. Nisbet—S. Lucas—Mrs Th.—Rev. Mr Stuart—Miss Stuart. Saw Rev. Mr Leeman—Ld Dunmore—Prof. Tyndale—Mr Cooke (Murray's)—Anon: 2. Dined at Mr Lefevres: Ld Hartington's afterwards. Worked on arranging papers &c. Read Duke of Argyll—Poems of the Future.[1]

6. Th.

Wrote to Bp of Chester BP.—Messrs Clowes BP—Mr Dunne BP—Mr M'Coll BP—Mr Vita—Mr James Anderson[2]—Herr Richter[3]—Ed. Daily News—Me F. Bianca. Dined at Ld Northbrook's: Lady Granville's afr. Saw Mr Macmillan—Archim. Myriantheus—Lord Northbrook—Ld Granville—Mr Bylandt—Sir E. Perry—Sir C. Trevelyan—Mr Childers. Saw Panizzi. I worked up my courage and asked him to let me say the Lord's Prayer which he at once did; and he preferred having it in Latin which I think showed that he assented with a real meaning. Read D. of Argyll—Rambaud's Russia.[4]

7. Fr.

Wrote to Mrs Tate—Mrs Bedell—Mr Woods—Mr Crosbie—Rev. Leeman (Tel)—Marquis of Lorne—Mr Spencer BP—Mr Ohlmann—Rev. Mr Mackey[5]—Mr Finlayson[6]—Mr Wizbroo[7]—Canon Hillyard. Saw Dr Bosworth Smith—Mr Lowe—Mr W. Cowper—Sir C. Forster—Sir C. Trevelyan—Mr Froude—Mr Dumaresque [sic]—Mrs Watts—Mr Hankey—Mrs Groves. Read D. of Argyll (Affghanistan)—M'Millan, Haberd. Hall[8]—Soury, Jésus et les Evangiles.[9] H. of C. 5¼-7.[10] Dined at Sir C. Trevelyans.

When wakeful in the dark I lie
Then show me Jesus throned on high
And angel choirs in order bright
And fill my soul with beams of light

Then let my silent hymn arise
Like incense curling to the skies:
'Praise to the Father, Spirit, Son;
Thy kingdom come: Thy will be done'[11]

[1] V. M. Vita had sent his *Poems of the future* (1879).
[2] Former colonial servant in Canada, petitioned Charterhouse governors for assistance; Hawn P.
[3] Possibly the German conductor who was in London later this year, but no link traced.
[4] A. N. Rambaud, *The history of Russia*, tr. L. B. Lang, 2v. (1879).
[5] Donald George Mackey, d. 1888; in India; canon of St Ninian's, Perth, 1878-85; vicar of Cleeton from 1886.
[6] Edinburgh merchant.
[7] *Sic*; obscure.
[8] *Macmillan's Magazine*, xxxix. 390 (March 1879).
[9] By J. Soury (1878).
[10] Attended, but did not vote on Courtney's motion on women's electoral disabilities; *H* 244. 505.
[11] Holograph dated 7 March 1879, Add MS 44763, f. 144.

8. Sat.

Wrote to Hon & Rev. Mr Stuart—Mr Ouvry—Mr Leith—Mr Stead—Rev. W.L. Leeman—Rev. B. Wilberforce—Rev. M. MacColl—Mr Bainbrigge. Dined at Mrs Ralli's. Saw Mr Hayward—Mr Newton—Scotts—Rev. Mr Oxenham—Mrs Murphy: satisfactory [R?]. Pottering, or meditating, on further progress with the Thesauros. Read Duke of Argyll—Wiesener, Jeunesse D'Elisabeth.[1]

9. 2 S. Lent.

Chapel Royal 10 AM and 5.30 PM. Wrote to Mr Murray—Lady Selborne. Worked on MS of 1845.[2] Read Stoughton, Anne & Georges—Soury, Jesus et les Evangiles—Jenny's Room[3]—Colenso (Letters).[4]

10. M.

Wrote to Sir R. Phillimore—Ld Granville—Mr Murray—Dean Warburton—R.G. Sarviad[5]—Messrs Rimell—Mr Fordyce[6]—Wms & Norgate—Paterson & James. Worked on my Butlerian paper—Presumptuously so called. At 11 went to see Ld Granville, and saw his fine house now ruined for the time by the burning of the upper portion. He was still in the first confusion, so to speak, of the event but "thankful" for much" [sic] and his serene temper not in the least disturbed. Saw Mr F.L. Gower—Mr Gore—& examined the house a little. H. of C. at 4½.[7] Saw Mr Groves—Bp of Ely. Eleven to dinner. Read D. of Argyll—Sieg des Judenthums.[8]

11. Tu.

Wrote to Mrs Groves BP—Sir Arthur Gordon—Rev. Jackson Goulby—Mr Nicholson—G.R. Humphrey—Hon. R. Denman—Ph. Smith—J. Lyon—J. Knowles—Mr Griffin BP. Worked on Law of Probable Evidence: finished Revision. 12-1¼. At Bow St with C.G. about the very wicked impostor Mackie.[9] Saw Sir A. Panizzi—Mr Byrom—Sir H. James—Mr Bright—Mr Leeman MP. H of C. 5-7½. As I could not give a satisfactory vote & did not wish to be misunderstood, I came away.[10] Saw Phillips: a strange imbroglio [R]. Read Duke of Argyll—Sieg des Judenthums—Ld Teignmouth's Journals.[11]

---

[1] L. Wiesener, *La jeunesse d'Elisabeth d'Angleterre 1533-1558* (1878).

[2] i.e. 'The law of probable evidence and its relation to conduct', also known as 'Probability as the guide of conduct', written in 1845 (see 26 June 45), published in *Nineteenth Century* (May 1879), reprinted in *Gleanings*, vii. 153 and in *Studies subsidiary to the works of Bishop Butler* (1896), 334.

[3] *Jenny's room; a religious story* (1877).

[4] J. W. Colenso, *The Zulu War* (1879); correspondence with Frere.   [5] Name smudged.

[6] James Dingwall Fordyce, Edinburgh lawyer.   [7] Navy business; H 244. 529.

[8] By Wilhelm Marr (1879); a central text of anti-semitism.

[9] Mrs Gladstone gave evidence against Skirving Thompson, *alias* J. A. Mackie, a deaf and dumb trickster, who had defrauded her charitable home at Woodford, amongst others; he was committed for trial; *T.T.*, 12 March 1879, 13f.

[10] Sir W. Lawson's resolution on drink defeated in 164:252, Hartington voting against Lawson; H 244. 632.

[11] C. J. Shore, Lord Teignmouth, *Reminiscences of many years*, 2v. (1878).

12. Wed.

Wrote to Mr Raph. Roche BP—Mrs Lavis—Mr A. Morley[1]—Sir R. Phillimore—J. Macdonell—E. Foster (Yorksh. Indept Leeds)[2]—Mr Knowles—Rev. Mr Atty—R. Wright—Mr Goldie—Mr Yates—Mr Mahaffy—Mr Tomms MP. Visited Royal Academy. Dined at the Speakers. Saw C. Lyttelton—Mr Lowe—Sir Arthur Gordon—Mrs Th.—Ld R. Grosvenor—Mrs Ralli—Edw. Hamilton. Read D. of Argyll—Newman, Grammar of Assent[3]—Sieg des Judenthums. Attended Lady Cowper's concert.

13.

Wrote to Messrs Clowes BP—Hon & Rev. Mr Stuart—Hon & Rev. Mr Byng[4]— E. Stanford—Mr Rendell[5]—G.A. Scott. H. of C. $4\frac{1}{2}$-$5\frac{1}{2}$.[6] Saw Mr Godley—Mr Bentley (Clerk)[7]—Mr T. Hughes—Mr Mahaffy—Mr . . .—Ld Ripon. Dined at Ld Ripons. Read Duke of Argyll (finished)—Jeunesse d'Elisabeth. Royal Academy with C. & M.

14. Fr.

Wrote to D. of Argyll—Dr Dunbar[8]—Miss Thomas—Mr Smith (G.B.)—Mr Tagart—Mr Wall—Mr Miller—Mr Ibeson—Rev. T.H. Lloyd[9]—Ed. Machiny Market[10]—Miss Asplet[11]—Mr Frankland—Mr Smythe—Mr Elwin—Rev. S.E.G.—C.C. Young. Fought against a cold & went to dine at Mr Penders. Conversation with Ld Granville—Mr Bright—Mr Berry. Read Jeunesse d'Elisabeth—Judenthum & Germanenthum.

15. Sat.

Kept my bed through the day but came down to a dinner of sixteen persons. Talking did me harm. Read Tudor Characters[12]—Jeunesse d'Elisabeth. Saw Ld Granville.

16. 3 S. Lent.

Church Prayers &c. in bed. Made some verses in the night. Read Contemp. Rev. on Confession[13]—Soury, Jésus et les Evangiles (finished)—Winter's Becket

[1] Arnold Morley, 1849-1916; barrister and liberal M.P. Nottingham 1880-95; liberal chief whip 1886-92; P.M.G. 1892-5.

[2] Correspondence with E. Foster on Gladstone's possible candidature in Leeds, in *Yorkshire Independent*, 14 March 1879, 1.

[3] See 27 Mar. 70.

[4] Francis Edmund Cecil Byng, 1835-1918; chaplain to the Speaker 1874-89; 5th earl of Strafford 1899.

[5] William Rendell, sec. to St John's school for children of poor clergy.

[6] Egyptian finance; *H* 244. 830.

[7] The clerk of G. Bentley, publishing his lecture on Hook; Add MS 44459, f. 180.

[8] Henry Dunbar; d. 1883; physician and classicist; published a Homeric concordance (1880).

[9] Thomas Henry Lloyd, vicar of Nerquis, Mold, 1878.

[10] Declining to comment on cheap patents, *Machinery Market*, 5 April 1879, 16.

[11] Maida Asplit of Frome, on a French child; Hawn P.

[12] First volume of S. H. Burke, *Historical portraits of the Tudor dynasty*, 4v. (1879-83).

[13] *Contemporary Review*, xxxiv. 717 (March 1879).

(finished)—Stoughton, Religion under Anne & the Georges—Burke's Tudor Characters. Kept my bed except for an hour or two. Saw Dr Clark.

17. M.

Bed all day. Wrote to Sir A. Gordon—Sec. Colonial Institute[1]—Mr Godley—Mrs Th. Also draft letter to Mr Hayward on the sceptical argument against a future life. This I will keep for review before sending it off.[2] Read Jeunesse d'Elisabeth—Tudor Characters—Sir Arthur Gordon's Proof-Address on Fiji.[3]—Saw Dr C.

18. Tu.

Conversation with W.H.G. & instructions respecting Childers's proposed question for a Commission on Indian Finance. With M.G. for a letter to Ld Granville which she executed (as I found next day) extremely well.[4] Saw Sir R. Phillimore on the Bp of Oxford's Appeal.[5] Read Ronayne on Irish Univ. question[6]—Jeunesse d'Elisabeth—Tudor Characters. Saw Dr Clark.

19.

Saw Dr C. But I am now better D.G. and rose between two and three. C. better also, went to her concert which is to produce £300 for the Orphanage. Read Tudor Characters—Jeunesse d'Elisabeth. Saw H.M. King of the Belgians who called when nearly all were gone to C.s Concert. Wrote to Rev. Mr Baron[7]—Mr Shrimpton[8]—Miss Lambert—Mr Thompson—Mr Childers—Mr Kelvie—Mr Knowles—Messrs Spottiswoode B.P. Corrected with labour my old & disinterred paper on the Law of Probable Evidence.

20. Th.

Rose at noon: much better. Wrote to Mr M'Conchie—Mr Knowles—Mr Cooper BP—Mr Greve—Mr Dreyfuss[9]—Bp Abraham—Mr Vaughan Jenkins[10]—Mr Victor Oger—Rev. Mr Suffield—Mr Nicholls—Mr Ronayne—Mr Rendle—W.S. Cooper[11]—T. Hayes jun.—Mr Bicknell. Saw Ld Granville—Mr Bayley Potter—Mr Newton—Ld Lansdowne. Dined at Ld Bath's: Conversation with Lady B. Read Jeunesse d'Elisabeth—Tudor Portraits.

[1] Illness preventing attendance at its dinner; letter, praising Sir A. Gordon, read out; *Royal Colonial Institute Proceedings*, 172.

[2] Sent on 6 April; Add MS 44207, f. 172.

[3] A. Gordon, 'Fiji . . . Address before the . . . Highland Philosophical Society' (1878).

[4] Not in Ramm II.

[5] Dispute between bp. of Oxford and the Church Association; see *The Guardian*, 22 January 1879, 108.

[6] Sent by the author, Charles Ronayne of Youghall; Hawn P.

[7] Robert Benjamin Baron; secretary of Church of England temperance society 1876-9; vicar of St Cleophas, Toxteth 1879.

[8] Henry Shrimpton, vicar of Newington 1872.

[9] Probably of Dreyfuss and Teweles, London merchants.

[10] Of Monkton Combe, Bath.

[11] Possibly William Samuel Cooper, wrote on Scottish soldiers.

21. Fr.

Rose at 12. Wrote to Miss Phillimore—Mr Murray—Messrs Spottiswoode—Mr Harding—Mr Sudlem—Mr Munday[1]—Mr Beverley—Mr Emmott[2]—Mr Goodman—Mr Rendle—W. Morris[3]—Rev. Mr Tucker—Rev. M. MacColl—Ld R. Grosvenor—Peter Duff.[4] Wrote P.S. (ἐλαφρὸς) on Homeric Epithets of movement. Saw Miss Lambert (A)—Mr West—Mr Knowles: we discussed & arranged matters belonging to the paper on Probable Evidence.[5] Read Tracts—Burke's Tudor Characters—Wiesener, Jeunesse d'Elis.

22. Sat.

Wrote to Scribners Sons—Ld Granville—Mr F.A. Morgan—Mr ?Ostelmann[6]— Mr Cunningham—Mr Bartholomew—Rev. S.E. Gladstone—Mr Lloyd—Mr Brierley—Mr Da Costa[7]—Mr Laflin—Mr Carr—Mr Vickers—Mr Hart. Saw Messengers. Saw W.H.G.—Mr Walter James—Sir Harcourt Johnstone. Read Wiesener—Tudor Portraits (finished)—Tracts—Life of Bp Selwyn.[8]

23. 4 S. Lent.

Morning prayers at home with C.—Aftn St Geo. H. Square. Wrote to Sir C. Forster. Read Life of Bp Selwyn—Stoughton, Religion 18th Cent.—Foreign Church Chron.[9]—Tracts. Saw Sir A. Panizzi.

24. M.

Rose at 10.30. Worked on Report of Hook Address. Wrote to Sig. Cav. Gentili[10]—F. Knollys—A.E. West—W. Pratt—Mr Burnett—J.F. Rolph—W.R. Trench[11]—Mr Morton—S. Massett—Messrs W. Clay and Sons—G. Fernandez— J. Norwood—Miss Evans—Sig. Vitali—Mr Stoneham—Geo. Smith—Treas. M[iddle] Temple. Rose about seven [p.m.]: but ventured on going to Mr Irving's box for fear of causing disappointment; and was the worse for it. His performance of this inexhaustible part seemed to me to show growth.[12] The Ghost was much improved. Ophelia excellent. Visited Mr I. in his room. Read Hamlet— Jeunesse d'Elisabeth—Political Catechism.[13]

[1] Thomas Munday of Greenwich, a constituent.

[2] Christopher Frederic Emmott, solicitor.

[3] William *Morris, 1834-96; socialist, artist and poet; writing as secretary of the Protection of Ancient Buildings Society requesting diarist's opposition to 'restoration' of St Germain's Church, Isle of Man; Add MS 44459, f. 197. Gladstone apparently required details of the Society's principles; see N. Kelvin, *The collected letters of William Morris* (1984), i. 507, 512.

[4] Edinburgh manufacturer.

[5] See 9 Mar. 79.

[6] Perhaps *sc.* Ohlmann.

[7] John Dacosta, published on Indian affairs.

[8] H. W. Tucker, *Memoir of the life of George Augustus Selwyn*, 2v. (1879).

[9] *Foreign Church Chronicle*, iii (March 1879); on Loyson.

[10] Pietro Gentile had written from Rome on his forthcoming book on Vatican tapestries, to which Gladstone subscribed; Hawn P.

[11] William Richard Trench, wrote *Realities of Irish life* (1868).

[12] Gladstone's second visit to the production at the Lyceum; see 19 Feb. 79.

[13] *Political Catechism; a treatise in four parts, on organic reform* (1858).

25. Tu.

Kept my bed till dusk. Wrote to Hon Sir A. Gordon—Mr Devonshire[1]—Rev. Mr Law. Saw Mr Bryce. Read Lecky's Hist. England[2]—Rambaud Hist. Russia[3]—Jeunesse d'Elisabeth (finished)—Paulicians &c.[4]—Hamlet.

26. Wed.

Rose at noon. In early morning Mr Ouvry informed me that Clumber was burning.[5] Further letters & information show the event to be serious. Loss I hope there will scarcely be, & most will be saved. Saw [blank.] Wrote to Messrs Holloway—Miss F. Robertson—Rev. M.C. Browne[6]—Rev. W.H. Winn[7]—Rev. R.R. Suffield—Messrs Bentley—Mr Donaldson—Mr Ouvry—G. Harris—R. Russell—J. Leach—Mr Killich—J.A. Kells. Saw Dr A. Clark—Dr Ginsberg: a noteworthy man[8]—Mr Morier. Finished proofs of Hook Addr. Dined with the Cowper Temples. Read Lecky's Hist.

27. Th.

Rose at 11.30. Wrote to Duke of Newcastle—The Speaker—Chev. Norchi[9]—Ed. Daily News—Dr Mackenzie—Mr R. Brown jun.—Canon Williams—Rev. W.L. Leeman—Mr Ouvry—Lieut. Holmes—Mr Coney—Mr Willott—F.A. Eaton[10]—H.H. Jones—Mr Roberts. Visited W. Dumaresq & Mrs Tyler. Saw Ld Wolverton—Ld C. Campbell: he has stuff in him—Rev. T.G. Law. I intreated him not to part company with his old habits & aims: he was very kind & our conversation was in the main satisfactory. Read Rambaud—Lecky—Hamlet—Wilson on Currency.[11]

28. Fr.

Rose at 10.30. Wrote to Ld Wolverton (for P. of W.)—Ld Aberdeen—Mrs Ellice—Rev. Mr Conners—Mr Ouvry—Mr Stead—W. Reid—Mr Fernandez—Dr Carpenter—Rev. Mr Mackay—Messrs Dyer—Rev. Dr Allon—Mr Gurdon. Read Lecky—Rambaud—The Liberal on Gleanings.[12] Saw Mrs Tennyson—Mr Tennyson—Ld C. Campbell *NB.*—Lord De Tabley—Ld Granville—Ld F. Cavendish—Ld Hartington. To these three last I gave my reasons for desiring to avoid taking part in the Zulu debate: especially that of enabling me at the proper time to make clear my position when the proper time came. H. of C. $5\frac{3}{4}$-8.[13] Lowes

---

[1] Probably Thomas Harris Devonshire, solicitor.
[2] See 17 Apr. 78.   [3] See 6 Mar. 79.
[4] Tracts on the Paulician Church of Armenia.
[5] Duke of Newcastle's house in Nottinghamshire; Gladstone was a trustee of the estate.
[6] Probably Michael Charles Brown, curate at Chudleigh 1879-80, rector of High Hampton 1880.
[7] Perhaps William Nelson Winn, curate to chapel of ease, Islington 1875.
[8] Christian David Ginsburg, 1831-1914; Hebraic scholar; revised the Old Testament.
[9] Perhaps of Norchi and Co., marble importers in Wigmore Street.
[10] Frederic Alexis Eaton, 1838-1913; ed. Murray's Handbooks 1870-80; secretary of the Royal Academy.
[11] A.J. Wilson, *Banking reform* (1879).
[12] G.W. Foote in *The Liberal*, i. 145 (April 1879).
[13] Dilke's motion on the Zulu war; *H* 244. 1991. Lowe stopped his speech in mid-sentence.

speech ended with an entire physical incapacity to proceed: I hope there may
be no serious cause. But these things are always uneasy in the cases of men
whose course of health has as a rule been absolutely unbroken.[1] Dined at kind
Sir C. Forsters.

29. Sat.

Once more came down D.G. to prayers and breakfast. Wrote to Editor of the
Liberal—Mr Bentley—Mr Knowles—Mr Lawson—Mr Cooke—Rev. S.E.G.—Mr
Kinnaird—Mr Hazzledine.[2] Dined at Lady Waldegrave's. Conversation with Ly
W. & Lady Airlie. Read Lecky: Lords Report—Corrected Revise &c. of Hook.
Saw Ld F. Cavendish—Mr Ouvry—Mrs Th.—Ld Halifax—Mr & Mrs Lowe—Mr
Greville—Lady Lothian.

30. 5 S. Lent.

Chapel Royal 10 AM. & St James's Evg. Wrote to Rev. Mr Jenkins—Rev. Mr
Ottley BP.—Capt Knox—Ld Granville—Mr Ouvry. Saw Sir R. Phillimore[3]—
W.H.G. Dined with the Jameses. Read Life of Selwyn—Prayers of Conv. Com-
mittee[4]—Monotheismus des Israeliten[5]—Parson Brown, his Talk.[6] Saw Sir A.
Panizzi. Eheu!

31. M.

Wrote to Duke of Portland—A.G. Williams—Mrs Hyam BP—G. Mitchell—Capt.
Maitland[7]—Mr Parker C.B.—Mr Ouvry—Mr Millais—Mr Russell—Mr Waugh.
Saw Ld De Tabley—Mr Ouvry—Mr Childers MP—Mr Anderson MP—Bishop
Selwyn—Mr Waddy MP—Mr Leeman MP—W.H.G. Attended Elliotts Photogr.[8]
Attended Bp Selwyn's Lecture. It is most interesting to see his heroic father so
strongly & variously reproduced in him. Dined at S[elina,] Lady Lyttelton's. H of
C. 10½: 3¼. Voted in 246:306 agt Cape War.[9] Read Lecky's Hist.—Lord, Idleness
v. Ignorance.[10]

---

[1] Lowe's biographer stated 'the effect was altogether temporary', but the incident may have given
Gladstone the excuse to offer Lowe a peerage without office in 1880; Patchett Martin, *Life of Sher-*
brooke, ii. 448.

[2] Of the London grocers.

[3] 'I thought him aged & grave. We had a long & very interesting conversation about politics, &
especially his future career. He gave me I think 5 reasons, in regular sequence, why he should not be
Premier again. Three of them were 1) his age 2) the immense work of cleansing & repairing there
wd. be to do 3) his pledge to Granville & Hartington—not exactly stated what—but I inferred that
except they joined in the request, it was a matter of honour not to take it.' Phillimore's diary.

[4] *The Book of Private Prayer. Presented to the Convocation . . . by a Committee of the Lower House* (1879).

[5] By W. Hecker (1879).

[6] Possibly in one of the 'Brown Papers' series by Arthur Sketchley [George Rose].

[7] Horatio Laurence Arthur Lennox Maitland, captain R.N.

[8] Elliot and Fry, London photographers.

[9] *H* 245. 124.

[10] H. W. Lord had sent his pamphlet.

Tues. Ap. One. 79.

Wrote to Messrs Eardley Solrs & dft[1]—Mr Summers—Mr Graham Berry—Mr Weymouth—Ed. Tinsley's Magazine[2]—Rev. Mr Wood—Mr R.H. Elliot—Mr Roberts—Mr Gilbey—Mr Gausden. Dined at Lord Bath's. Saw Messrs Eardley's Clerk—Mr Wickham—Mr Knowles—Mrs Blunt. With Mr Knowles I discussed largely the paper on Probable Evidence.[3] Read Lecky—Wellington Coll. Correspondence.[4] H. of C. $4\frac{1}{2}$-$7\frac{1}{4}$. Spoke on Wellington College.[5]

2. Wed.

Wrote to Mr Shelley—Mr Elijah Ford[6]—Mr Duncan (& draft)[7]—Mr Noldwatt?— Mr Grissell—H.W. Lord—Sir J.M. Hogg—J. Hord—Mr Phillips. Read Lecky— Rambaud—Lord's Report on Intemperance. Saw Mr Berry *cum* Mr Pearson—Mr Chamberlain—Mr Forster—Sir H. Johnstone—Mr Baxter—Ld Barrington—Mr Goschen—Ld G. Hamilton—Mr Adam. Dined at Mr Cartwrights. Conversation with Mr Feuerbury on Wine Duties.[8] H of C. $3\frac{1}{2}$-6: voted in 167:172 on Mun. Council Qualific.[9]

3. Th.

Wrote to Mr Morris—Prof. M. Williams—Mr G. Macmillan[10]—Mr Clapp. Sat to Mr Millais 12-1.[11] Chelsea Coffee Tavern Opening 1-2. Spoke at this meeting.[12] Mr Milbank's luncheon. Saw Phillips X. Dined at Sir C. Forster's. H. of C. for Budget $4\frac{1}{4}$-$7\frac{1}{4}$. Spoke briefly, to deprecate speaking.[13] Returned to the House with Childers $10\frac{3}{4}$-$12\frac{1}{4}$. We referred to 1839 and drew some Resolutions for consideration.[14]

4. Fr. [Althorp]

Wrote to Ld Hartington—Pres. Architects—Mr Wallerstein—Lord A. Compton[15]—Messrs Bentley—Ed. Daily News—Mr Strut—Mrs Th.—Mr Th.—

[1] Eardley Holt & Co., London solicitors, this day served a subpoena on Gladstone to appear in Padwick v. Thistlethwayte (a debt action) before the Master of the Rolls on 7 April; the case did not come to court; Lambeth MSS 2768, f. 86. See Introduction above, section viii.

[2] Not found published; several articles reflected protectionist opinion in Birmingham.

[3] See 9 Mar. 79. [4] *Wellington college and the Horse Guards: a correspondence* (1878).

[5] In part, defending his son-in-law's record as headmaster on J. R. Yorke's resolution for an inquiry into the college's affairs; *H* 245. 149. 'Mr Gladstone saved us': see D. Newsome, *A history of Wellington college* (1959), 198.

[6] Perhaps the letter on salaries in *T.T.*, 4 April 1879, 106.

[7] Of the Liberal Association of Portobello, Edinburgh; Add MS 44459, f. 219.

[8] *Sc.* Feuerheerd; see 9 Apr. 79.

[9] Supporting a Mundella-Chamberlain bill to abolish property qualification for municipal corporations; *H* 245. 193.

[10] George A. Macmillan, 1855-1936; of the publishers; secretary of Hellenic society 1879, of British School in Athens 1886; Hawn P. [11] See 18 Mar. 78n.

[12] On self-control and drink; *T.T.*, 5 April 1879, 12a.

[13] i.e. to allow time to study the figures; *H* 245. 295.

[14] Not moved or traced; Gladstone missed the ex-Cabinet meeting which discussed the budget and decided to take no action; see Gladstone to Hartington, 4 April 1879, Chatsworth MSS. See 28 Apr. 79.

[15] Lord Alwyne Frederick Compton, 1855-1911; s. of 2nd marquis of Northampton; Ripon's A.D.C. 1882; liberal unionist M.P. Biggleswade 1895-1906.

Mr Evans—T. Baker—J. Taylor.[1] Saw Sir A. Panizzi: it was sad but not without some consolation: and his helplessness increases attachment. After much preparation, left by 3 PM. train & reached Althorp at 5.30. All was kindness itself. Saw Ld O'Hagan (Irish prospects)—Sir Geo. Dasent—Ld Granville. Read Lecky's Hist.—Religious parallelisms.[2]

5. Sat.

Wrote to Mr Thistlethwayte (& draft)—part of draft to Mrs Thistlethwayte[3]— E. Russell. Read Lecky—Ravestein, Classifications Prehistoriques[4]—Russell, Heroines of Shakespeare[5]—Edwards on Libraries.[6] The hounds met here. Saw Sir R. Knightly and others. Conversation with Ld Granville—Mr Earle—H. Langham[7]—Ld O'Hagan. Walk with Mr E. Ashley & Mr Earle.

6. Palm S.

Great Brinckton Ch mg (saw the interesting Tomb Chapel)—Little B. aftn. Saw Ld Spencer—Sir W. Harcourt—Ld Granville—Mr Spencer who interested me much about his desire to read Dante. Conversation with Helen respecting Sir W.H. Read Life of Selwyn—Stoughton Relig. Hist.[8]—Hecker, Israeliten u. Monotheismus—Uniformity of Nature.[9] Sundaylike conversation all luncheon. Wrote out my draft to Hayward on the Sceptical argument agt a future State—& sent it through Mr Knowles.[10] Also to Mr Knowles—Mrs Scott— Station Masters Weedon & Broughton Hall. In the night a little bowel-attack: due I think to a check on the action of the skin from linen sheets. I put flannel round me which seemed to bring me round.

7. M.

Kept my bed till two. Wrote to Mr Wylie—Mary G.—Colnaghis—H.N. Earp.[11] 3-6½. Drove 9 m to Sir C. Isham's,[12] and saw his old English books, most interesting to the Bibliographer. Also the Welsh Dict. of 1547 which is of *historic* interest. Sir C.I. touched on Spiritualism with me, and with Mr Dasent on his favourite belief in Fairies. *Most curious* are the little low benches and stumps placed under his trees by the drive up (on the left) said to be for their accommodation. He is pleasing and gentlemanlike & the buildings are interesting. Lady I. is Prof. [H. H.] Vaughan's sister. We fell in with the Miss Robertsons,

---

[1] Text from here to 7 April written on a separate sheet, tipped in; the second time the diary was left behind on a visit to Althorp, Spencer's seat near Northampton, see 5 Nov. 73.

[2] Untraced tract.

[3] Her financial difficulties; see 1 Apr. 79n.

[4] E. de Meester De Ravestein, *À propos de certaines classifications préhistoriques* (1875).

[5] W. R. Russell, *Representative Actors* (1872).

[6] E. Edwards, probably *Free Town Libraries* (1869).

[7] Herbert Hay Langham of Cottesbrooke Park, Northampton.

[8] See 2 Mar. 79.

[9] L. Stephen, 'The uniformity of nature. A paper read before the Metaphysical Society' (1879).

[10] See 17 Mar. 79.   [11] Of the Newark family; see 20 Nov. 77.

[12] Sir Charles Edmund Isham, 1819-1903; 10th bart. 1846; m. 1847 Emily Vaughan; antiquarian; constructed huge rock garden at his house, Lamport Hall.

who sang. Read Lecky—Israeliten u. Monotheismus.—Conversation with Ld
S[pencer] on Hawarden Mines &c. "Lady A."[1] came: & our party rose again in
the evening to 16.[2] Saw Ld Wolverton—Sir A. Panizzi: whose speech was *I*
thought affected. His faithful attendant[3] thinks him very low. I said to him, as I
have done of late: Shall I say our little prayer now before I go? He looked at me
and said 'What the devil do you mean?' I said: I mean our prayer, the Lord's
prayer: that is right, is it not? He said 'Yes'. (He had asked it shd be in Latin.)

8. *Tu.* [*Hawarden*]

Off at 8.30 to Weedon. Hawarden at 3¼. Saw the Parish Church at Rugby on the
way. Set to work on my papers. Wrote to Editor of Scotsman—Hon C.R.
Spencer[4]—Mr Canburoff—Mr Cameron—Mr Crosbie—Mary Gladstone—Mr
Denver—Mrs Th.—Mr Dickson—Mr Hughes—Mr Hobbs—Mr Ouvry. Church 7
P.M. Read Lecky—The Spirit World[5]—Acct of Phil[adelphia] & Reading Rail-
way[6]—Isr. & Monotheismus. So well housed at the Rectory.

9. *Wed.*

Ch 8½ AM. Wrote to Agnes Wickham—A.G. Williams—Mr Corn. Brown—Mr
Ouvry—Mr Dalton—G.W. Dumbell[7]—Mr Feuerheerd[8]—Jos Ashworth—Mr
Fadella[9]—C.T. Winter—Mr Bellis—Mr Nelson—Mr Healey—C.H. Hart[10]—
Archd. Harrison. Examined Phil[adelphia] & Reading RR papers, and the parti-
culars of my purchases. Saw Mrs Burnett—W.H.G.—Read Lecky. Worked on
Probability Revises.

10. *Th.*

Holy Communion at 7.15: and M. Prayers 8.30. Wrote to Mr Leake—Dean of
Christ Church—Mrs Th. (2, & copy 1)—Bishop of Derry—Mr Knowles—E.L.
Turner—W.W. Jones—H. Macarthur—Messrs Jarrold[11]—Landlord at Worksop.
Finished Revises of Probability: some hours of work. Read Lecky—Il. I. (half)—
Life beyond the Grave.[12] W.H.G. & I felled two Alders.

11. *Good Friday.*

Church 10.30 A.M. and 7 o'clock P.M. Wrote to Mary Gladstone—Mr Ellice
MP—Mr Macanliffe—Cav. P. Gentili—Mr Wimborn—Mr Fadella. Walk with

---

[1] i.e. Lady Ailesbury, regarded with amusement and affection by Gladstone.
[2] Text in diary proper resumed here.
[3] Louis Alexander Fagan, Panizzi's friend and biographer; worked in British Museum prints
department.
[4] Charles Robert Spencer, 1857-1922; liberal M.P. Northamptonshire 1880-95, 1900-5; household office 1886, 1892-5, cr. Lord Althorp 1905; 6th Earl Spencer 1910; known as 'Bobbie'.
[5] *The Spirit World, No. 1* (1853).
[6] In which he was a shareholder.
[7] Banker on the Isle of Man.
[8] London wine merchant. [9] Had sent a book; Hawn P.
[10] Perhaps Charles Henry Hart, prolific American biographer and art historian.
[11] London publishers.
[12] *Life beyond the grave, described by a spirit through a writing medium* (1876).

W. and H. Read Life beyond the Grave (finished)—Bp Selwyn's Life (finished Vol I)—Stoughton, State of Religion, finished Vol. I.—Bp of Derry on the Psalms, Lectures II and V.[1]

12. Easter Eve. [Worksop]

Ch. 8½ AM. Wrote to Mr Cartwright MP—Sir W. Lawson MP—Archd. Harrison—Rev. Morton Shaw—Mr Duncan (amended)—Mr Adam MP—Mr Groves—Rev. J. Page Hopps[2]—Mr L. Fagan—Mr Cornelius Brown. Packing & preparing for journey. Off at one. Reached Worksop at 7. Courteously treated in Manchr & conversation on RR. facts with Stationmaster. Saw Mr Williams. Read Lecky's Hist.

13. Easter Day.

Off at 9¾ to Shirwalls Ch with Mr Williams. After service & H.C. examined the fabric. Saw Mr Brown. Luncheon at Mr Tylden Wrights. Back by Worksop. Visited cottage. Worksop Ch evg. Congregn, service, Sermon, excellent. Strange![3] Wrote to M.G.—Mrs Th.—Ld Wolvn. Read Thos A Kempis—Dr Stoughton—Emotional Religion.[4]

14. M.

Wrote to "Earl of Mar"[5]—Lord Salisbury—C.G.—Capt. Phipps RN[6]—Mr S. Peters—Mr Honeyman.[7] At 10¼ moved from the Lion (good) to Mr Williams's.[8] Mr Ouvry M & I made a 30 miles circuit. First to Welbeck: saw the storerooms & other buildings—without nourishment. Then by Thoresby to Tuxford. Saw the Church, & had luncheon. Then to Clumber at 3.15. Examined the ruin & many of the objects injured or saved.[9] Saw Housekeeper & Gardener & inspected a good deal. Back at six. Read Lecky—Morton Shaw Burials.[10] Much conversation with Mr O[uvry] on the Trent, & Mr W[illiams] on the Estate.

15. Tu.

Wrote to Mary G.—Mrs Atkinson—Treasurer Guy's—Rev. G. Dunnett—C.G.— and Mr Cartwright. Again to Clumber, & thence to Osberton, partly to form an idea of the Architect Mr Anderson's taste, & to consult Mr Bovill.[11] We *three* spent some time on the papers: rescued a few of much importance: & *felt* the

---

[1] W. Alexander, *The witness of the Psalms to Christ and Christianity* (1877).

[2] Unitarian minister; on Blanco White, in *T.T.*, 6 May 1879, 9f.

[3] 'Excellent Sermon from a drinking Vicar who has *delirium tremens*'; Bassett, 224, with other letters on the visit.

[4] H. S. Escott, *Papers on emotion in religion* (1876).

[5] John Francis Erskine Goodeve Erskine, 1836-1930; claimed earldom of Mar, eventually successfully by Act of 1885.

[6] William Hugh Phipps, retired captain, R.N.; business untraced.

[7] Thomas Honeyman of Lasswade, sent tory literature circulating in Midlothian; Add MS 44459, f. 230.

[8] One of the Newcastle trustees.   [9] See 26 Mar. 79.

[10] M. Shaw, *The burial question* (1879).

[11] Osberton Hall, seat of F. J. S. Foljambe, also a Newcastle trustee.

utter chaos of the mass. Saw Mr Cookson—saw Miller & witnessed the garden operations. Also Mr Nattali, Mr Windle, Mr Taylor, on their several duties: & Mr Sweeting.[1] Read Lecky—Stoughton.

16. Wed. [Clinton Arms, Newark]

Wrote to C.G.—Mr Cartwright—Mary G.—Mr J. Wootton—Mr Earp M.P.—Rev. T. Buxton[2]—D. of Portland. Off at 11 to Newark: arr. 12¾. Saw the Vicar—the Handleys[3]—Mr Tallents—Mr Perfect[4]—Mr Burnaby. Considered a variety of questions for the improvement of the Estate. Went again over the noble Church & to the School where I had to address the boys for a few minutes. We left off at 5. Here I am in the Clinton Arms, the scene of the Election toils and revels of 47 years ago.[5] Read Lecky—Stoughton.

17. Th. [Mentmore, Leighton Buzzard]

Newark Ch. morning. Prayers at 8 A.M. Wrote to Mr Redish B.P.—Sig. Vitali—Mr C.C.P. Clark[6]—C.C. Fitzroy[7]—E.S. Fairman[8]—R.G. Smith—Mr Richardson—Mr Tammage—Lady F. Cavendish—Scotts—Mr Trant[9]—Mr Conant—Mr Childs. Off to London at 9: worked on papers. Saw Mr Branston—Mr Ouvry—Mr Adam—Mr Bentley—Scotts. H of C. 4¼-8. Spoke on Greek border.[10] Off to Mentmore.[11] Arr. 11¼. Read Lecky's Hist.

18. Fr.

Wrote to Dr Weisse[12]—Mr Ramsay—Mr C.W. Green—Mr St G. Mivart—R. Midgley—R. Hughes—Mr Ludlow. Walk to Wing Church with Lord R[osebery] & Ld Carlingford. Saw some of the curiosities of this extraordinary house. Read Hesiod—Lecky—Divers Tracts.

19. Sat.

Wrote to Dean of Bristol—Mr Turner of Aylesbury[13]—F. Fuller—J.J. Wilson—Rev. Mr Anderson—Rev Mr Linklater.[14] Saw Mr Bassett—Walk with Ld R. & much conversation: *inter alia* on the Padwick Thistlethwayte suit. Read Lecky—Anderson on Scots Kirk[15]—Döllinger on British India.[16]

---

[1] All of the estate.
[2] Thomas Buxton, d. *ca* 1892; unbeneficed anglican priest.   [3] See 31 Oct. 25.
[4] James Perfect, stationer in Newark.   [5] See 24 Sept. 32.
[6] Charles Cotesworth Pinkney Clark, American; wrote *The Commonwealth reconstructed* (1878).
[7] Major Cavendish C. Fitzroy of Cranley Place, London.
[8] E. S. J. Fairman, long resident in Cairo; later letter in Hawn P on Egyptian finances.
[9] William Trant, on Dean Hook; Add MS 44459, f. 244.
[10] H 245. 540.
[11] Occupied by Rosebery since his marriage in 1878 to Hannah Rothschild; see 19 Mar. 64.
[12] Z. A. Weisse, physician in New York, sent his *Origin . . . of the English language* (Hawn P).
[13] See 21 Apr. 79.
[14] Robert Linklater, curate of St Peter's, London docks 1869-80; later in Cowley, Oxford.
[15] R. Anderson, *History of Scotland* (1874).
[16] Translated as J. J. I. von Döllinger, 'The British Empire in India', *Contemporary Review*, xxxv. 385 (June 1879).

20. 1 S.E.

Ch. 10½ AM & 6 P.M. Wrote to Mrs Hampton. Read Ch. Q.R. on Eccles. Commissioners—Plymouth Brethren—Elisabethan Martyrs[1]—Stoughton Religion in 18th Cent.—Thomas a Kempis—Tracts. Drive in aft: saw the beautiful house.

21. M. [London]

Wrote to Mr Lister (F.O.)[2]——Miss Yates (O)—Miss Bagster (O)—Sir F. Leighton—Rev. D.V. O'Hare[3]—Mr Hardcastle—Messrs Freshfield—Mr Atkenson—Mr Mitchmier—Miss Drummond (O)—Ld F. Cavendish—Rev. M. MacColl—Rev. W. M'Farlane[4]—Mr Bradshaw—Mr Platton—E.A. Clough—C.P. Melly[5]—R. Brown—F.L. Price—S.J. Reid[6]—Mr Sambrook[7]—Capt. Jackson.[8] At 10.30 planted a tree: & at 11 met the Aylesbury Deputation; whom I addressed for some 25 minutes.[9] Saw Rev. Mr Grubb[10]—Mr Rylands—Mr Hart—Ld Rosebery. Off at 12 & Home at 2.45. Worked on papers &c. H of C. 5¾-7¾.[11] Read Lecky—Q.R. on African War.[12]

22. Tu.

Wrote to Very Rev. F. Oakeley—Rev Mr Johnstone—Sec. State War[13]—A.G. Symonds[14]—T.E. Symonds[15]—Duke of Portland—Mr Bathgate—R. Cameron—Mrs Condon—T. Hill—Mr Robinson—Mr Wright—Spottiswoodes—Mr Giffen.[16] Saw Mr Bentley—R. Brown jun.—Mr Ouvry—Do *cum* Mr Rickards—Mr Forster—Sir Harcourt Johnstone. Saw two X Corrected 2d Revises of Paper on Probable Evidence. H. of C. 4¼-7¾.[17] Dined at "The Club". Read Northcote on Finance[18]—Boucherville Govt.[19]

23. Wed.

Wrote to Mr La Thangue[20]—Mr Longmead—Rev. Mr Roberts—Edr Touchstone—C.J. Kennedy—Messrs Barker—Mr Ouvry—Mr Devine—T.F. Laws—

---

[1] *Church Quarterly Review*, viii. 217 (April 1879).

[2] (Sir) Thomas Villiers Lister, 1832-1902; assistant undersecretary at foreign office 1873-94; kt. 1885; business untraced.

[3] Teacher at St Cuthbert's, Durham; on Virgil; Hawn P.

[4] Probably William Charles Macfarlane, vicar of Dorchester, Oxon. from 1856.

[5] Charles Pierre Melly of Liverpool.

[6] Stuart Johnson Reid, d. 1927; biographer and publisher.

[7] *Sic*; possibly Samborne S. Palmer-Samborne of Gloucestershire.

[8] Captain Christison S. Jackson of Victoria Road, London.

[9] *T.T.*, 23 April 1879, 6b.

[10] Charles Septimus Grubbe, d. 1910; vicar of Mentmore 1869-99.

[11] Civil service estimates; *H* 245. 721.

[12] *Quarterly Review*, cxlvii. 552 (April 1879).

[13] Business untraced.

[14] Unable to attend National Reform Union meeting in Manchester; *T.T.*, 26 April 1879, 6d.

[15] Perhaps Thomas Edward Symonds, naval architect.

[16] (Sir) Robert *Giffen, 1837-1910; chief of statistical department of board of trade 1876-97; free-trader and liberal unionist; K.C.B. 1895.

[17] Sugar bounties; *H* 245. 860.   [18] See 2 Aug. 62.

[19] Not found.   [20] Henry Herbert La Thangue, art historian.

R. Harley[1]—E. Hughes—Rev. Mr Healy. Saw Canon [R. C.] Jenkins—Messrs Cocks & Biddulph—Mr Nicholson—Mr Giffen—Mad. Bianca—Mr Bickers—Ld Lyttelton. H of C. $3\frac{1}{2}$-$4\frac{1}{2}$.[2] Dined with Mr M[aurice] Brooks. Read Lecky's History. Worked on financial figures.

24. Th.

Wrote to Mr S. Beaumont—Rev. Mr James—Rev. Mr Serjeant—Mr Herb. Griffith[3]—Mr Woodall—M.J. Dick—Mr Smith BP—Mme Sutton (O)—Mr Westlake. H. of C. $4\frac{1}{2}$-8 and 10-12.[4] Dined with the F.C.s. Seven to breakfast 10-11$\frac{3}{4}$. Saw Duke of Argyll—Dr [R. F.] Weymouth—Mr McColl—Dr Allon—Lord F. Cavendish—Mr Westlake cum Mr Bumpus.[5] Read Serjeant on Ritualism.[6]

25. Frid.

Wrote to Miss M. Watson—Perth Librarian—Messrs Barker—V. Rev. Mr Oakeley—Rev. Mr Halliwell—E.O. Farrell—Dean of St Paul's—Rev. Mr Thornhill[7]—Rev. T.S. Bacon[8]—Messrs Mudie[9]—Spottiswoodes—Dr Fleming—Mr Barker—Mr Housden—Mr Sherlock—G. Harris—Mr Morrison—Messrs Bedford—Mr Woodall—Mrs Th. Saw Mr Bowie—Mr Cook (Murray)—Mr Agnew—Duke of Argyll. Dined at Sir H. Verney's. H of C. $10\frac{1}{2}$-12$\frac{3}{4}$. Spoke briefly on Charities.[10] Read Lecky—Thornhills Passion of Dido.[11]

26. Sat.

Wrote to Lord Malortie[12]—Rev. Sir W. Cope[13]—Rev. H. Simkinson[14]—J.A. Symonds—Ed. Penny Illustr.—Rev. Dr Bagot—Mr David Grant[15]—C. Law—A. White—J. Annand—T. Barlow—A.W. Baker—W.E. Yeats—W. Atkins. Saw Sir Jas Watson—Rev. E. Wickham—Mr L. Fagan—Scotts—Ld Winmarleigh—The Speaker. Attended Sir Jas Hogg's (public) dinner at Willis's Rooms.[16] Saw Payen—Collerade [R]. Read Leckie [sic].

[1] Robert Harley of Mill Hill sent a paper on Stanhope; Hawn P.
[2] Ulster tenant right bill; H 245. 946.
[3] C. Herbert Griffith of London; Hawn P.
[4] P. Rylands' resolution deploring growth in national expenditure; H 245. 987.
[5] Probably John Westlake, London barrister, and John Bumpus; perhaps on the Padwick case.
[6] Untraced; perhaps by J. F. Serjeant, vicar of St Mary, Fulham.
[7] William Thornhill, canon of Rathcoole, had sent a book; Hawn P.
[8] Thomas Scott Bacon, anglican priest in Baltimore, U.S.A. had sent his *The reign of God not the 'Reign of law'*, an attack on Argyll; Hawn P.
[9] Lending library founded by Charles Edward *Mudie, 1818-90.
[10] As in 1863, on need to tax charities; H 245. 1206.
[11] W. J. Thornhill, *'The passion of Dido'*, tr. (1878).
[12] See 14 July 66; requested an interview about his book on diarist; Add MS 44459, f. 252. See 21 July 79.
[13] Sir William Henry Cope, 1811-92; 12th bart. 1851; rector of Easton.
[14] Probably Charles Hare Simkinson, vicar of Blackheath; a constituent.
[15] Probably the Glasgow merchant.
[16] Board of Works dinner; D.N., 28 April 1879, 2e.

27. 2 S.E.

St Pauls Ch. St. 11 AM and Chapel Royal 5.30 PM. Wrote to Mr Ouvry—Mr Murray. Read Randle's 'For ever'[1]—Stoughton 'Religion in England—Wright, Irish Div. School[2]—Colenso, Serm. on the War[3]—Les Traditions Papistes—Hist. of Union Chapel—Allon Lect. on Disestablishment.[4] Wrote on 'For ever'.[5]

28. M.

Wrote to Prof. Stuart—Publisher Daily Review—Dr Allon BP—Mr Hitchman—Mr Robinson—A. Dixey.[6] Arranging papers & separating the Thistlethwayte presents for return.[7] Went over my financial figures for speech this evg. H of C. $4\frac{3}{4}$-$8\frac{1}{4}$ and $10\frac{1}{4}$-2. Spoke $1\frac{1}{2}$ hour for Mr Rylands Resolution & voted in 230:303.[8] Saw Mr Donaldson (Asst)—Mr D. Grant—Mr Dumaresq.—Arranged my Ivories in case. Dined at Sir C. Forster's. Read Leckie—Stoughton.

29. Tu.

Wrote to Mr Housden—S.H. Cutter—E. Grenthorpe—F.A. Laing.[9] H. of C. $4\frac{1}{4}$-$5\frac{1}{4}$.[10] Dined at Mr Dundas's. Read Lecky—Th. Martin IV.[11]—Saw Duke of Westminster—MM Geshoff & Yancoloff[12]—Mr Anning—Mr Childers—Ld Granville—Mr Goschen—Rev. Mr Holland—Mr Wortley—Lord Grey—Ld Cardwell—Mr Elliot.

30. Wed.

Wrote to Dr Stewart—Mr Churchill Babington—W. Mawer[13]—Rev. Mr Hellier[14]—Mr Collingwood—F. Wright—Mr Catesby—Mr Lake. Dined at the Temple: where they unexpectedly put us up to speak:[15] Royal Society afterwards. Saw Baron Malortie—Mr Annand—Mr Agnew—Professor Huxley—Mr Ouvry—Lord Young—Mrs Birks—Sir Coutts Lindsay. Visited the Grosvenor Gallery: some most delightful works:[16] Christie's (do): and went to hear the loud Telephone in R. Society's rooms.[17] Read Cookson on Party![18]

---

[1] By M. Randles (1871); on future retribution.
[2] C. H. H. Wright, *The Divinity School of Trinity College, Dublin and its proposed re-construction* (1879).
[3] J. W. Colenso, 'What doth the Lord require of us?' (1879).
[4] Both by H. Allon (1878).
[5] Not found.
[6] Probably Albert Dixey of Islington.
[7] To assist her assets in the Padwick case. See Introduction above, section viii.
[8] A general attack on Northcote's 'financial revolution'; *H* 245. 1294.
[9] Frederick A. Laing, author of *A history of English literature* (1873).
[10] Misc. business; *H* 245. 1404.
[11] Just published (see 21 Dec. 74); Gladstone did not review this volume, though he had the previous three.
[12] Ivan Dimitrov Geshov, Bulgarian merchant, nationalist and lobbyist, and his colleague.
[13] Walter Mawer of the Strand, on bp. Butler; Hawn P.
[14] John Shaw Hellier, vicar of Bromley 1865.
[15] No report found.
[16] 'The B[urne]-Jones's are splendid'; L. Masterman, *Mary Gladstone* (1930), 154.
[17] Demonstration by Frederick Allen Gower of his improved Bell model.
[18] M. Cookson, 'The nation before party', *Nineteenth Century*, v. 755 (May 1879).

Thurs May One 1879. SS. Philip & James

Thirteen to breakfast. Wrote to Professor Park[1]—J. Macgregor—J.A. Corkhill[2]—Rev. W. Lucas[3]—Rev. M. MacColl—Rev. E. Summers[4]—Ed. Athenaeum[5]—Mr Catlow—Miss De Lisle—Dr Cash Reid. Dined at Argyll Lodge. Saw Ld Colin Campbell—Ld Houghton—Sir John Lefevre—Dean of St Pauls—Mrs Th.—who made a kind of scene about the presents—Mr Agnew—Mr Oakeley—Ld Moncreiff. Read Th. Martin Vol. IV. Worked on correcting & preparing Edinb. Address of 1860 for reprint in Gleanings [VII]. Thirteen to breakfast.

2. Fr.

Wrote to Mr Ouvry—Mr Bromley—H. Job—W.P. Duff—Rev M. M'Coll—C.J. Walker—R.W. Locke—Mr Geo. Wilson. Saw Mr MacColl—Mr *John* Murray. Corrected Edinburgh Address of 1865 for Gleanings [VII]. Read Lady Strangford in N.C.[6]—Th. Martin Vol IV. Private view of R. Academy Pictures 1-2½. H of C. 6-8. Spoke shortly on Lefevre's motion.[7] Saw one [R].

3. Sat.

Wrote to Mrs Th (& draft)—J.M. Cox—H.F. Bussey[8]—A. Burton[9]—Mr Satrondattis—Major M'Kenzie[10]—R. Gladstone—A. Dacosta—A. White—W.G. Leveson[11]—Lady Salisbury. Saw Mr Millar—Ld Carnarvon—Mr Hayward—Mr Lowe—Bp of London—Sir Jas Paget—Pr. of Wales—Italian Secy of Leg.?[12] Attended the Princes Levée. 5¾-11. At the Royal Academy. Dinner lasted four hours. Much of stilted or prosaic speech. Lord B. *not* warmly received by the general Company. The P. of W. was just as of old: & the Royalties generally free and gracious.[13] Read Mrs Bishop on the La Ferronaye's in NC[14]—Theodore Martin Vol IV.

4. 3. S. Easter.

Trinity Ch. & H.C. 11 AM—and Ch. Royal aft. Saw Ld Granville—Sir C.A. Wood—Dr A. Clark. Wrote to Mrs Th—Ld Granville—Mr Hubbard—Mr B.

[1] John Park, d. 1913; professor of logic at Queen's college, Belfast from 1868.

[2] Perhaps John Corkhill, picture restorer.

[3] William Lucas, d. 1901; principal of proprietary college in Hull 1866-81; vicar of Ottringham 1881-93.

[4] Edgar Summers, d. 1907; headmaster in Abingdon 1870-83; vicar of Brading 1884-96.

[5] On France and the move to prevent declaration of infallibility in 1869; *The Athenaeum*, 10 May 1879, 602.

[6] E. A. Smythe, Lady Strangford, 'East Roumelia', *Nineteenth Century*, v. 822 (May 1879).

[7] On Irish land; *H* 245. 1622.

[8] Harry Findlater Bussey, a journalist; ed. *The Newspaper Reader* (1879).

[9] Perhaps Alexander Bradly Burton, d. 1888; rector of W. Meon from 1872.

[10] James Dixon Mackenzie of Dingwall; major late 79th foot; perhaps a distant relative.

[11] Granville William Gresham Leveson-Gower, 1838-?; liberal M.P. Reigate 1863-6.

[12] T. Catalani.

[13] *T.T.*, 5 May 1879, 5a; Millais' portrait of Gladstone formed the centre-piece, see ibid., 3 May 1879, 5a.

[14] M. C. Bishop, 'Mrs Craven and her work', *Nineteenth Century*, v. 849 (May 1879).

Morice—Ld Glasgow. Read A Victim of the Falk Laws[1]—Philosophy of the Plan of Salvn[2]—Plumptre on Religious Thought.[3]

5. M.

Wrote to Hon? Mrs Cavendish—C. Edwards—Sir Thos Frost—Mr Thompson—Mr Dacosta—Mr Hubbard—E. Hewson—Mrs Elder—Mr Molony—Mr Tipping. Worked on digging out the figures of 1860. And on arranging books and papers. Breakf. with Mrs Birks. Nine to dinner. H of C. $4\frac{1}{4}$-$7\frac{1}{4}$. Spoke in Ways and Means.[4] Saw Mr Howard—Mr Patton—Duke of Argyll—Mr N. Hall—Rev. Mr Winn & his friend—and. . . . Saw Gerald: no good [R].

6. Tu.

Wrote to Messrs Pears O—Mr Knowles—J. Green—Ed. Daily News—Rev. C. Wood[5]—A.E. West—Mr O'Flanagan—W.P. Duff—J.S. Hudson—Mr Ouvry (2)—Sir C. Forster—E. Newton—W. Trant—A.F. Rouse. Read Theod. Martin IV—Ld Coleridge's Poems[6]—Nicolaides on the Patriarch Cyril.[7] Saw Lord Kinnaird. Saw Payne [R]. Arranging books &c.

7. Wed.

Wrote to Mr Bryce—Bishop of Derry[8]—Rev. Dr Smith—Rev. H.E. Mathew[9]—Rev. E. Wilkinson[10]—C. Mackenzie—M. Sheridan[11]—Gen Sir J. Adye—Mr Hutchison O—Mr George—G.J. Reed—Mr Dunphie[12]—H. Matthews[13]—Mr Magoun[14]—J. Leach. Twelve to dinner. Went to R. Acad. with C. Read 'New Englander' on Maryland Toleration—on Spinoza[15]—Th. Martin Vol. IV. Saw Mr Cooke (Murray)—Lady Russell—Mr Palgrave—Mr Mivart.

8. Th.

Wrote to Arthur Gladstone—Rev. Mr Clinton[16]—E. Saunders—Bishop Antkin—Mr Atkinson—Mr Naftel—Mr Wadham[17]—Mr Ouvry—Messrs May—

---

[1] *A victim of the Falk Laws; the adventures of a German priest in prison and in exile, told by the victim* (1879). [2] By [J. B. Walker] (1845).

[3] E. H. Plumptre, *Movements in religious thought. Three sermons* (1879).

[4] Dispute with Northcote about the 1860 budget and his use of it in the deb. on 28 Apr.; *H* 245. 1729.

[5] Perhaps Charles Robert Wood; curate in Ramsey 1879-80; rector of Bredfield 1880.

[6] J. D. Coleridge, *Memorials of Oxford* (1844).

[7] Probably by Demetrius Nicolaides of Constantinople

[8] William Alexander, 1824-1911; bp. of Derry from 1867.

[9] Perhaps Henry Staverton Mathews, rector of Bentworth from 1847.

[10] Edward Wilkinson, rector of Snargate 1870-81, of Christ Church, Leamington 1881.

[11] Perhaps Mathew Sheridan, Dublin merchant.

[12] Charles J. Dunphie had sent a book, probably his *Sweet Sleep* (1879); Hawn P.

[13] Probably Henry *Matthews, 1826-1913; Roman catholic; tory M.P. Dungarvan 1868-74, E. Birmingham 1886-95; home secretary 1886-92; cr. Baron Llandaff 1895.

[14] George F. Magoun of Iowa college; congregationalist; several letters in Hawn P.

[15] *New Englander*, xxxviii (1879), also with a review of *Gleanings*.

[16] Perhaps William Osbert Clinton, d. 1921; curate of Panteg 1879-80, rector of Scaldwell 1880-5.

[17] Perhaps John Charles Wadham, solicitor.

Mr Fratelk—Dr Sayer[1]—Mr Webb. Read Martineau on the Jews[2]—Th. Martin Vol. IV—Dor, Sens des Couleurs[3]—Ligue contre les Vivisections. Dined at Ld Airlie's. Saw Lady M. Alford—Dean of Westminster—Miss Broughton—Mr Knowles—Ld Blachford—Prof. [W.] Robertson Smith. Fourteen to breakfast.

9. Frid.

Wrote to C.P. Melly—Mr Trenchard—Rev. J. Penistan[4]—Rev. J. De Soyres[5]—Dr Garstang—Mr Spence—Mr Cronin. Ten to dinner. A beginning of a cold. Read Th. Martin Vol IV—and Stoughton Vol II. Saw Ld Hartington—Mr Hutchison[6]—Mr Adam—Mr Stansfeld—Mr . . . . H. of C. $5\frac{1}{4}$-7.[7]

10. Sat.

Rose at noon. Wrote to Col. A.J. Rogers[8]—Mr Austin—Mr Cheetham—Scotts—Mr Fagan—Rev. Mr Thom—Rev. Dr Rigg—& two more. Devonshire House Meeting on Indian Finance 1-3. It was rather wished that I should make the motion but on my objecting this was not pressed.[9] At 3 we went to pass judgment on the position for the Russell Statue in the Central Hall. Then called on Lord Egerton—& others. Saw Rev. C. Wood. Dined at Ld Kimberley's. Read Th. Martin IV.—Ld Kimberley on the Cape.[10]

11. 4 S.E.

Kept my bed all day. Read Morning Prayers &c. Read Life of Dr Duff[11]—Stoughton Vol II (finished)—One generation of a Norfolk House[12]—began.

12. M.

My cold gave way, & the weather changed. Let us hope it is the end of winter! Rose at 1.30. Wrote to Miss de Lisle—P. Russell—Rev. H. Testard[13]—H.A. Allison—Mr Marriage[14]—Earl Spencer—Mrs Th.—Th. Martin. Attended the Argyll Marriage in the Presb. Church.[15] The service was a mingle-mangle. We went to Argyll Lodge afterwards. Saw Lord R. Gower—Duchess of Westminster.

[1] Perhaps Thomas Sayer, physician in Kirby Stephen.
[2] R. Martineau, *Mythology among the Hebrews* (1877).
[3] H. Dor, *De l'Évolution historique du sens des couleurs; réfutation des théories de Gladstone et de Magnus* (1879).
[4] Joseph Penistan, 1819-93; vicar of St Blazey from 1870.
[5] John De Soyres, 1847-1905; barrister; priest 1878; curate in London 1877-9; professor of history, Queen's college, London 1881-6.
[6] Probably John Dyson Hutchinson, 1822-82; liberal M.P. Halifax from 1877.
[7] Blennerhassett's resolution on distress; *H* 246. 20.
[8] Retired officer; business untraced.
[9] Hartington asked a procedural question and Dillwyn moved a motion on 13 May; Gladstone presented a petition on 12 June; *H* 246. 237, 1723.
[10] Perhaps Kimberley's speech of 25 March; *H* 244. 1670.
[11] See 16 May 79n.
[12] A. Jessopp, *One generation of a Norfolk house* (1878).
[13] A nonconformist.
[14] Perhaps Edmund Marriage of Hereford Gardens, London.
[15] Frances, da. of 8th duke of Argyll, m. E. J. A. Balfour (see 5 Oct. 72), A.J.'s br.

Rose at 1.30: cold quite subdued. Read Lecky's Hist 18th Cent.—Jessop, Norfolk House—Th. Martin Vol IV. finished.

13. Tu.

Rose at ten. Wrote to Under Sec. India—Rev. Dr Dale—Rev. Ch. Wood—W.[H.]D. Adams—J.J. Bellis—W.J. Ball—Mr Blagrove—E. Kaiser—L. Serjeant—Baron Malortie—Mr Hannis Taylor[1]—H. Harbour—J. Taylor—Messrs Murray—Rev. Mr Lovell.[2] Dined at the Bp of Ely's. Finished revising my 'Law of Probable Evidence' for Vol. VII. of Gleanings. Saw Mr Molesworth[3]—Mr Fawcett—Mr Lowe—Mr Forster—Ld Hartington—Bp of Ely—Mr Adam—Mr Salusbury. H of C. 4¼-8. Spoke briefly on Mr Dillwyn's altered motion.[4] Read Lecky's Hist.

14. Wed.

Wrote to Scotts—Mr Mavrocordato—J. Leach—Rev. Mr Robertson—A. Johnston—Mr Cheetham—W. Owen—Mr Corcoran. Read Lecky—Washbourn on Bulgaria[5]—Oakley [sic] on Catholic Prospects. Worked on 'the Evangelical Movement' for Br. Qu. R.[6] Saw Mr Duff—Mr Godley—Miss Nightingale (a lengthened conversation)[7]—Mr Molesworth—Mr Millais—D. of Westmr. Fourteen to dinner.

15. Th.

Wrote to Duke of Argyll—Mr Th. Martin—Ly A. Russell (O)[8]—Miss E. Hewitt—Rev. Sir H. Moncreiff—Lalmohun Ghose[9]—Baron Malortie—F. Wilding—E. Wickham—W. Bernard[10]—Mr Ouvry—Mr Sayer. Twelve to breakfast. Saw Mr Paton[11]—Ly Lothian—Ld Granville & D. of Argyll—Mr & Mrs Warburton—Lady Alice Gaisford—Mr Playfair—Mr Burn Jones.[12] Dined at Lady Lothians. Read Dr Jessop—Fernon's No Dynasty[13]—&c.

[1] Hannis Taylor, 1851-1922; American lawyer and historian; ambassador to Spain 1893-7.

[2] George Francis Lovell, fellow of St Edmund hall, Oxford.

[3] St Aubyn Walter Molesworth (later Molesworth-St Aubyn), barrister and tory M.P. Helston 1880-5. [4] A rowdy discussion of the royal prerogative and India; H 246. 265.

[5] G. Washburn, Contemporary Review, xxxv. 503 (June 1879).

[6] Published as 'The evangelical movement, its parentage, progress, and issue', in H. Allon's congregationalist British Quarterly Review (July 1879), reprinted in Gleanings, vii. 201. The result of his reading of Lecky, who replied in Nineteenth Century; see Memoir of W. E. H. Lecky by his wife (1909), 133.

[7] Discussing India; see Cook, Life of Nightingale, ii. 293.

[8] Lady Agatha Russell, 1853-1933, Lord John's da.; keen historian and reformer; mentally ill from 1884.

[9] Barrister and delegate of the Indian Association; liberal candidate in Deptford 1885-6; replied to diarist's letter with exposition of Indian complaints: 'the unrepresented millions of India look to the leaders of the Liberal Party, and in particular to yourself Sir, for the redress of these grievances'; Hawn P.

[10] William Bernard; liberal in Hull; Hawn P.

[11] Rev. J. B. Paton of Nottingham, on Bulgarian affairs; Hawn P.

[12] Sic. Sir Edward Coley *Burne-Jones, 1833-98; pre-Raphaelite artist; friend of Mary Gladstone; cr. bart. 1894. See 30 Apr. 79n. His window in Hawarden church, celebrating the Gladstones' marriage, was designed 1897, installed after Gladstone's death.

[13] Untraced.

16. Fr.

Wrote to Mr Plunket MP—Harry N.G.—Messrs Kempster—J.P. Godfrey—A.R. Gladstone—Mr Kimber—C. Hoare—H.H. Jones—Mrs Th. Continued work on Evangel. Movement. Saw Mr Lefevre—Mrs Malcolm—Dr Smith—Sir W. Muir—Mr Duff—and others. Saw Phillips X & two more. Dined with Mr Duff & proposed The Memory of his Father.[1] Read Life of Dr Duff.

17. Sat. [York House, Twickenham]

Wrote to Mr Knowles—Miss de Lisle—W.H.G. (O)—Mrs Macleod—Mr Duncan—Mr Rochussen[2]—Mr Cyrus Field—Rev. Mr Jellett[3]—Rev. J.C. Robinson[4]—Dr Rabbinavitz?[5] Off at 4 to York House Twickenham: Mr Grant Duff's.[6] Read Speech of D of Argyll—Indian Budget—Jessop on the Norfolk House—Stephen, Evang. Succession.[7] Conversation with Mr J. Morley—Mr Bryce—Mr Grant Duff.

18. 5. S.E.

Twickenham Ch 11 AM and HC: also 7 PM (part). Saw Lady Alice Peel—Mr Morier—Mr Hildebrand—Mr J. Morley. Read Stephen Ev. Succession—Jessopp, Norfolk House (finished)—Rigg, Wesley's Churchmanship.[8]

19. M. [London]

Wrote to Mr Gunn—Mr Iatrondakes—Mr Norris—Mr Machin. Back at 12¾. Attended crowded attentive meeting of Addl Curates Society and spoke there.[9] Calls with C.G. Saw Mr Knowles. Visited Christie's—Josephs.[10] Sir W. James & 2 Phillimore's dined. Read Indian Budget—Stephen Ev. Succ. finished—Wesley's Churchmanship—Addl Curates Sermon & Papers.

20. Tu.

Wrote to Master Beach [sic]—J.H. Parker—J.R. Welsh[11]—Mr Wilfrid Oates—A. Townshend—Rev. Mr Mahaffy—Rev. S.E.G.—W.H.G.—Mr Wahat—Mr Fairhurst—E. Legge[12]—Mrs Macleod—Rev. Dr Lee. Meeting at Ld Hartington's 12-1¾ on Irish Univ. Bill. Saw Mr Edwards—Lady Russell—Mr Adam—Ld

---

[1] Alexander *Duff, 1806-78, Scottish missionary in India; Gladstone was reading vol. i of his *Life* (1879) by G. Smith; vol. ii, published late 1879, concludes with a panegyric by Gladstone, presumably the speech given this evening.

[2] Perhaps Charles Rochussen, Dutch art historian.

[3] Morgan Woodward Jellett, incumbent of St Peter's, Dublin, arranging the depn.; see 21 May 79.

[4] John Carleton Robinson, rector of St Margaret, York 1877.

[5] Israel Jehiel Michael Rabbinowicz, physician and scholar; published on Judaism in French and German.

[6] See M. Grant Duff, *Notes from a diary, 1873-81* (1898) ii. 138.

[7] Sir J. Stephen, *Essays in ecclesiastical biography* (1849) ii. 65.

[8] J. H. Rigg, *The churchmanship of John Wesley* (1879).

[9] Report in *T.T.*, 20 May 1879, 12b.

[10] Edward Joseph, art importer.

[11] Printer.

[12] Edward Henry Legge, 1834-1900; soldier and assistant serjeant-at-arms in the Commons.

Dufferin—Sir [blank] Rose—Count Karolyi,[1] who I must say was very gentle-manlike—Lord Derby. Dined with the Wests. Duchess of Bedford's afterwards: the German Empress looked worn & sad, & her talk was similar. Saw Mrs Lucas? aft [R]. Read Wesley's Churchmanship (finished)—Began Article on Greece for Nineteenth Century.[2]

21. Wed.

Wrote to Mr Newman—Lalmohun Ghoze—Dr Jessopp[3]—Duke of Buccleuch. Saw two [R]. Dined with Lord Aberdeen. Much conversation with Mrs Cowper Temple—with Sir A. Gordon—& with Mr Fowler, afterwards. Read [blank] Went by invitation to afternoon tea with Lady Derby. Found myself face to face with Lord Beaconsfield; & this put all right socially between us, to my great satisfaction. Then Lady D. entered on the sore subject of the relations with Ld Salisbury: & I was encouraged to offer some suggestions. H. of C. $4\frac{1}{2}$-$5\frac{1}{2}$: Irish Univ. Bill.[4] Wrote on Greek frontier for N.C. Saw Irish Church (Minor Incumbents & Curates) Depn.[5] Saw Duke of Argyll—Sir C.A. Wood.

22. Th. Ascension Day.

Church for H.C. at 8 A.M. Wells Street. Eight to breakfast. Saw Bp of Winchester—Bp of Ely—Mr Hillebrand—Sir E. Perry—Sir A. Gordon. H of C. $4\frac{3}{4}$-$7\frac{1}{2}$ and $10\frac{3}{4}$-$12\frac{1}{2}$. Conclave behind the Chair on Fawcett's amendment. By concert, I proposed in the H. its withdrawal.[6] Dined with Sir F. Doyle. Curious statement from Lady Emery[7] on long hair. Worked hard on my Greek art: finished, revised, & dispatched it to Messrs S[trahan].

23. Fr.

Wrote to Lady Derby—Miss D. Doyle—Mr Howard—Mr Morgan—H.S. Volken BP—Mrs Armstrong—Rev. Mr Blaikie—Mr Bachdder—Mr Anderson—Mr Crilly—Mr Harris—Mr Carment—Mr Watts R.A.—Sig. Farinelli[8]—Rev. R. Yonge—P. Margetson[9]—Rev. Dr Rainy.[10] Saw Lalmohun Ghoze—Mr Grant

---

[1] Count Aloys Karolyi, 1825-89; Austrian ambassador in London 1879-88. See 4 May 80.

[2] 'Greece and the treaty of Berlin', *Nineteenth Century*, v. 1121 (June 1879).

[3] Augustus Jessopp, 1823-1914; historian; headmaster in Norwich 1859-79; rector of Scarning 1879-1911; see 11 May 79.

[4] *H* 246. 930.

[5] On their condition; Add MS 44460, f. 50.

[6] On Indian finance; *H* 246. 1089.

[7] *Sic*; sc. Lady Emly, or possibly Diana Emily, Doyle's sister?

[8] Possibly Antonio Farinelli, published in Florence on Dante.

[9] London merchant.

[10] On Scottish disestablishment, dated 24 May, published in *Edinburgh Daily News, The Guardian*, 25 June 1879, 868, and in *Life of Principal Rainy*, ii. 6: 'I certainly desire that this question, which has been recognised as pre-eminently one for the Scottish people to consider, should not be raised by the [Liberal] party until the Scottish people shall have pronounced upon it in a manner which is intelligible and distinct.... It is no part, however, of my duty either to urge the question forward or to keep it backward.' 'It seems to have given satisfaction to men of all the parties concerned in the discussion', *T.T.*, 28 June 1879, 5f. See also the letter to A. T. Innes, 2 Nov. 78n.

Duff MP—Mr Waddy MP—Mr James MP. Read up Indian matter incl. Dr Döllinger[1] to be ready for the Debate. Also read Stephen, Clapham Sect.[2] Dined with the Jameses. H of C. $5\frac{3}{4}$-8 and $10\frac{1}{4}$-$12\frac{3}{4}$.[3]

24. Sat.

Wrote to Rev. Dr Jessopp—Rev. C.A. Salmond[4]—Rev. T.T. Shore—Rev. W.J. Stobart[5]—J.D. Loverdo—J. Butler—Mr Hugh Watt[6]—M. Gennadios—Sig. Serena[7]—A. Cooke—Sir Ch. Reed—Mr Trenchard[8]—Mr Knowles—Mr Devine— G. Sauer[9]—N. Parry—W. Rudd—H. Job. Dined at Sir Thos G.s—gathered a little military opinion. Corrected proofs of article on the Greek frontier. Read Wassa Effendi on Albania.[10] Saw Sir A. Gordon—Ld & Lady Howard (at great length)— Lady Stanley—Sir Thomas G.

25. S. aft Ascension.

Duke St Ch mg. Guards' Chapel reopening aftn. Saw my inscription, set up in paper.[11] The singing was very animated: the fabric a good transformation. Read J.H. Thom[12]—Stephen's Clapham Sect—French Govt MS on Epiros.[13] Saw M. Gennadios. Wrote to Ld Howard—Rev. J.H. Thom. First day of putting away winter trousers.

26. M.

Wrote to J.H. Parker—Mr Threlfall[14]—A.P. Porter—Professor Young[15]—Rev. Mr Boyton[16]—Hon. Miss Canning[17]—Mr Vickers—Mr Thurling?—E. Lane—Mr Knott—Mr Plant—Spottiswoode's. Saw Mr Newdigate—Bp of Winchester—Mr Adam—Ld Granville. Sat $2\frac{3}{4}$ h. to Mr Watts, who did *much* good.[18] H. of C. 4-$5\frac{1}{2}$.[19] Completed art. on Greek frontier for Nineteenth C. Dined at Bp of Winchesters. Duchess of Edinburgh's afterwards. She has got over her shyness.

---

[1] See 19 Apr. 79.
[2] See 17 May 79; ii. 287.
[3] Interjected on Indian finance; *H* 246. 1197.
[4] Charles Adamson Salmond, Scottish presbyterian with contacts with Princeton; Hawn P.
[5] William James Stobart, 1840-1919; vicar of St Augustine's, Bermondsey 1878-1902.
[6] On Scottish church affairs; Hawn P.
[7] Augusto Serena, Italian man of letters; wrote on Dante.
[8] Edward Penny Trenchard, Greenwich merchant.
[9] George Sauer, translator and author of *Handbook of European Commerce* (1876).
[10] Wassa Effendi, *The truth on Albania and the Albanians*, tr. E. St J. Fairman (1879).
[11] See 12 Dec. 78.
[12] His *Blanco White*; see 6 May 45 for Gladstone's review of it.
[13] Doubtless given by Gennadios.
[14] Thomas Threlfall, barrister.
[15] John Young, 1835-1902; professor of natural history, Glasgow, 1866-1901.
[16] Charles Boyton, canon of Derry; see Add MS 44460, f. 53.
[17] Louise Canning, d. of Stratford de Redcliffe; she d. 1908; see 7 June 79.
[18] See 16 May 76n.
[19] Estimates; *H* 246. 1244.

27. Tu.

Wrote to Rev. Dr Allon—Rev. Dr Rainy—Mr Prior—Mr Hanbury. H. of C. 2¼-4½. Spoke briefly on Cape affairs, with a purpose of good.[1] Saw Mrs Hope—Lady Gladstone—Ld Carnarvon—Mr Goschen. Finished Stephen on Wilberforce. Dined at Mr Goschens. Wrote a good deal on the Evangelical movement.

28. Wed.

Wrote to Rev. T.G. Law BP—Rev. R.R. Suffield—Ven. Sir G. Prevost—Messrs Townshend & Barker—Messrs Barkers—Mr M'Kinoch—H. Samuelson MP—Ld Howard of Glossop—Rev. H. Algar[2]—Rev. C.A. Salmond—Mr J. M'Lean—Mr Gurkin—T.E. Lawson—Mr Reddish—W.J. Upton—C.P. Austin—Dr Dunbar—Sir Thos Frost—P.W. Campbell—G.M. Towle—H.L. Pratt—Hon. Miss Canning—Dr Weymouth—Mr Macleod—Mr Johnson—Mrs Link—Mr Surtees. Ten to dinner: a very pleasant company. Saw Mr Jolly. Saw Phillips X. A long day on letters & papers. Read Lecky.

29. Th.

Wrote to Kegan Paul & Co[3]—Rev. Dr Hornby—L. Serjeant—Mr Chrysoveloni—Mrs Wickham—Mrs Th. Nine to breakfast. Worked well on paper for Dr Allon. Attended meeting of London Library & its Committee. Went to S.P.C.K.s Office and hunted up the Sikes Tracts.[4] Also reperused. Saw Mr Macmillan—Mr Morley—Mr Knowles—Sir A. Gordon—Mr P. Stanhope—Dr Birch—Mr Murray. Saw Ricardo—West—both with interest [R]. Dined at Mr Murray's.

30. Fr.

Wrote to Rev. J.E. Scull—C. Phillimore[5]—A. Shelley—Mr Cheetham—Mr Chapman. Worked hard on paper for Dr Allon: finished it, and revised the whole. Dined at Mr Beaumonts. Took C & M to the Academy. Saw Ld Morley—Lord R. Gower.

31. Sat. [Eton College]

Wrote to Messrs Glyn—Rev. Dr Allon—Rev. Mr Henderson—Rev. T.V. Bayne—Mr Nanson—J. Perfect—Mr Maddison—J. Charles Cox—Prof. Calderwood[6]—Dr Jabez Hogg[7]—Dr Burlingham—Rev. Dr Lee—A.S.G. Canning—Mr Vincent—R. Allen—J.B. Lane[8]—Mr Upton (O)—Mr Mongan (O)—Mr Goodman.[9] Much

---

[1] Defending Bartle Frere's personality, as opposed to his policies; *H* 246. 1374.

[2] Henry Algar, curate of Willoughby; on Homer; Hawn P.

[3] Publishers of the *Nineteenth Century*.

[4] Thomas Sykes, 'Dialogues between a minister of the church and his parishioner', discussed in *Gleanings*, vii. 216; Gladstone used the 1823 ed.

[5] Charles Bagot Phillimore, d. 1894, br. of Sir R.J.

[6] Henry Calderwood, 1830-97; professor of moral philosophy, Edinburgh from 1867; chairman of Edinburgh school board 1874.   [7] Jabez *Hogg, 1817-99; ophthalmic surgeon.

[8] Possibly Col. J.H.B. Lane, d. 1886, of King's Bromley.

[9] Edward John Goodman of the Savage club, wrote on the meeting; see Add MS 44460, f. 127 and 14 June 79.

conflict with chaos in papers & letters: off by 4 PM. train to the Deanery. Saw Dr Hornby at Eton on the question of a Tutor for the Duke of Newcastle—and walk & long conversation with the Dean on the Derby-Salisbury case.[1] Read Eloge on Mrs Grote[2]—and Ld Grey on Colonies.[3]

Whits. June One. 1879.

St George's mg with H.C. and aft. Walk & conversation with the Dean. Saw Canon Pearson.[4] Read Shadows of the Cross[5]—Christ the Revealer (finished)— and [blank].

2. M. [Holmbury, Surrey]

Wrote to Lady Derby. St George's Chapel 10½. Off to town at 12.5 and to Holmbury at 2. Reached it at 5 in pouring rain. A pleasant party here as usual.[6] Saw Mr Murchison. Read Tennyson Loves Tale[7]—Opinion Anglaise sur le Projet de Loi de M. Jules Ferry[8]—Bagehot on Gibbon.[9]

3. Tu.

Wrote to Mr Campbell—Dean Dickinson—Mr Baker—Ld Mayor's Sec.—Sec. Mariner Soc.[10] Read [H. H.] Dickinson's Address—Bp Alexander's Ishmael[11]— Paul Courrier[12]—finished Bagehot's Gibbon. Drive & walk. Conversation with Mr White—Lady Airlie—Mr Leveson—Ld Hinchinbrook.[13] W.H.G.s birthday. Benedictus benedicat.

4. Wed.

Wrote to Ld Howard—Mr Butterwick[14]—Mary G.—Mrs Th. Drove to the Deep- dene:[15] a villa inferior I think only to Cliveden. Read Paul Courrier[16]—Contemp. Rev. on Russia[17]—Green's Hist of England[18]—Tennyson Loves Tale (finished). Much conversation.

[1] Row springing from the deb. of 18 July 1878; Add MS 44460, f. 72.
[2] Perhaps J. Fournet, *Madame Henriette Grote. Notice biographique* (1879).
[3] H. G. Grey in *Nineteenth Century*, v. 935 (June 1879).
[4] George Charles Pearson, canon of Canterbury and rector of St Margaret, Canterbury.
[5] *Shadows from the Cross* (1879).
[6] Lord E. F. Leveson-Gower's place.
[7] Probably the 1879 reprint.
[8] Untraced tract on Ferry's educational proposals.
[9] W. Bagehot, *Literary studies* (1879), ii. 1.
[10] Alfred Watton, sec. of Mariners' benevolent society; business untraced.
[11] By W. Alexander.
[12] P. L. Courier de Méré, perhaps *Pamphlets politiques et littéraires*, 2v. (1832).
[13] Edward George Henry Montagu, Lord Hinchinbrook, 1839-1916; tory M.P. Huntingdon 1876-84; 8th earl of Sandwich 1884.
[14] William Thomas Butterwick, commission agent.
[15] Thomas Hope's neoclassical extravaganza near Dorking, demolished 1969. Disraeli wrote much of *Coningsby* there.
[16] See 3 June 79.
[17] *Contemporary Review*, xxxv. 422 (June 1879).
[18] See 19 Feb. 78.

5. Th.

Wrote to Rev. Dr Hornby—Mrs Hope—Miss Canning—L. Serjeant—O. Brauer—Mr Shelley. G. Howard[1] made a most clever sketch of me in the forenoon. Read Green's Hist. Engl.—Fortnightly Rev. on Music[2]—Dr Winn on Mind & Particles[3]—Coleridge's Poems. Saw E. Wickham (on D. of N[ewcastle])—Mrs Havard—Mr Sheehan—Mr Howard (Dillwyn's m. &c.). Worked on proofs of Vol VII.

6. Fr.

Wrote to Ld Coleridge—Messrs Clowes BP—Mr Murray—Mr Richmond BP—Dr Winn—Rev. Mr Henderson. Read Contemp. Rev. (Mrs Proctor) on The Week[4]—Coleridge's Poems—Courrier, Letter to the Academy. ++ Worked on proofs & MS for Gleanings Vol. VII. Much conversation: & charming drive.

7. Sat. [Frant Court, Tunbridge Wells]

Wrote to Ly G. Fullerton—Rev. Dr Rainy—Mr Rogers—Lady Stepney—C.G. After much forenoon conversation off at 12.45 and reached Frant Court at 4.[5] I spent much of the afternoon & evg with my host whose freshness at his great age is truly wonderful. Read Fisher, Beginnings of Christianity, seemingly a noteworthy book.[6] And Zumbini's Studii su Petrarca.[7]

8. Trin. S.

Frant Church mg (with H.C.) and Evg. Drove with Lady S. in afternoon to the beautiful ruins at Bayham Abbey: sad, sad, sad. Wrote to Mrs Hampton. Much conversation with Ld S. Also with Mr Newton. Read 'For Ever' (Mr Randles)[8]—and Dr Fisher's remarkable book.

9. M. [London]

Wrote to C.G.—Rev. S.E.G.—Mr W. Taylor—Messrs Townshend & Barker—Mr Wilkinson—Mr Shore—Miss Stoddart—Mr Boyd. Saw Ld Stratford before leaving for ½ hour and reached H. St at 1¼. Spent near 4 hours in opening & reading letters. Saw Mr Galton[9]—Sir P. Egerton—Rev. Mr Taylor—& others. Read 'For Ever'. Dined at Grillions. Mr Macmillan's afterwards. Saw J. Hill (Evans) [R].

---

[1] George James Howard, 1843-1911; liberal M.P. April 1879-80, 1881-5; 9th earl of Carlisle 1889; well known as an artist. This sketch is now at Castle Howard, and is reproduced in this volume.

[2] *Fortnightly Review*, xxxi. 894 (June 1879).

[3] J. M. Winn, *Mind and living particles*, 2v. (1878).

[4] *Contemporary Review*, xxxv. 404 (June 1879).

[5] Stratford de Redcliffe's seat; for the visit, see Bassett, 226; see also 29 Dec. 96.

[6] G. P. Fisher, *The beginnings of Christianity* (1877).

[7] By B. Zumbini (1878).

[8] See 27 Apr. 79.

[9] Perhaps the eugenist; see 19 May 32n.

10. Tu.

Wrote to Dr Weymouth—Rev. W. Durnford—W.D. Adams—J.W. Hall—Mr Chrysoveloni—Lalmohun Ghoze—R. Brown jun.—L. Thompson—Sir Thos Frost—Dr B. Kösk—Mr Lethaby—Mr Russell—Miss Lowe—Mrs Jones—Mr Gomme. Attended Soc. Bibl. Archaeol. $8\frac{1}{2}$-$10\frac{1}{2}$.[1] Saw Mr Boscawen. Saw Messrs Murray. Saw Ricardo: failure [R]. M. & C.G. came in evg. Worked on Proofs. Harrison on Spirits:[2] Dr Weymouth's Address: read.

11. Wed. St Barnabas.

Wrote to Mr Gray (Bank of E)[3]—Dr A. Clark—Rev. Mr Robinson—Mr Adam MP.—Mr Blake. 4-$8\frac{1}{4}$. To Mill Hill. Went over the buildings & delivered an Address of perhaps $\frac{3}{4}$ hour after distributing the prizes. An institution strikingly *alive*.[4] Read Mill Hill Magazine: & worked on papers about the School. Dined at Sir Thomas Aclands. Conversation with him—Mr Bernard—Mr Hutton—Mr Acland.[5] Read Wilson in Fraser on Indian Finance.[6]

12. Th.

Wrote to Mr H. Westropp—Rev. Dr Allon BP—Mr Reid—Miss Hewitt—Mr Denham—Mr Goodman—Mr Waggett (O).[7] H. of C. $5\frac{1}{2}$-$8\frac{3}{4}$. Spoke (1 h) on Indian Finance.[8] Ten to breakfast. Saw Mr Cyrus Field—Mr Knowles—Mr Goschen—Sir C. Dilke and Deputation on Greece.[9] Saw Chesterfield [R]. Read Mr Stanhope's Speech—Morley on Ch. & State in France.[10] Well tired.

13. Frid.

Wrote to W.H.G.—Mr Pearson—Mr Shelley—H. Wilson—Mr Norman—Mr Pitcairn[11]—Capt Verney—Dr Haig Brown—E.A. Budge—Accountant B of E.—Dr Parker—Mr Southgate (O)—Mr Higham (O)—Ld Stratford de Redcliffe—Ld Granville—Ld Leicester—Rev. J. Marnham[12]—Ld Norton—Mr Macfie—Mr Rogers (O). Discussed the Rent & Farm question for $1\frac{1}{2}$ hour with Mr Barker of Chester. Saw Mrs Th.—Saw Percy [R]. Dined at Ld Selbornes: Conversation

---

[1] Papers by M. G. Maspero and W. St C. Boscawen; *Proceedings of the Society of Biblical Archaeology* (1879), 44.

[2] See 18 Aug. 78.

[3] Samuel O. Gray, deputy cashier of Bank of England; letter not extant in Add MS or Bank archives.

[4] Weymouth's nonconformist school in Finchley; *T.T.*, 12 June 1879, 9e.

[5] (Sir) Arthur Herbert Dyke *Acland, 1847-1926, s. of Sir T. D.; tutor at Keble college 1872; resigned orders 1879; steward of Christ Church 1880, bursar of Balliol 1884; liberal M.P. Rotherham 1885-95; social reformer and vice-president of cttee. on education in Cabinet 1892-5; 13th bart. 1919.

[6] 'Indian budgets and Indian deficits', anon. article, presumably by H. Wilson, in *Fraser's Magazine*, xcix. 667 (June 1879).

[7] Probably John Francis Waggett, barrister.   [8] *H* 246. 1739

[9] Attempting to persuade Gladstone to use his senior position to get time for a debate on Greece; Gladstone agreed about the need, but was reluctant to be the mover; Ramm II, i. 97.

[10] *Fortnightly Review*, xxxi. 647 (May 1879).

[11] J. J. Pitcairn, of St John's Wood, on Homer; Hawn P.

[12] A nonconformist.

with Sir A. Gordon. Read Fortnightly on Clifford—do on Philip II (Ld Ducie)[1]—Harrison on Spirits.

14. Sat.

Wrote to Mr J.R. Jolly—A. Wilson—R. Knight[2]—R. Spencer—W. Booth—Mr Jas Bird—Mr Vanderweyde.[3] 2-5¼. Went to the Criterion Theatre for Mr Vandenhoff: terrible atmosphere: very good acting: empty house.[4] Spent 2 h on arranging papers. Saw Ld Granville—Ld Wolverton—M. About.[5] Read Harrison—Fisher.

6-11. Attended the dinner of the Savage Club. Too long and the clouds of tobacco were fearful. In other respects most interesting. It was impossible to speak ill to so quick & sympathetic an audience. I returned thanks for Literature & was (like the *ensemble*) too long: but nothing could exhaust their patience. The Chairman had a special faculty for his work.[6]

15. 1 S. Trin.

Laid up with deranged liver & bowels. Dr Clark came: lays the blame on eight hours of heat & on preserved peas. Read the Litany—I was poor & exhausted. Read T. A Kempis—Duff's Life—Harrison on Spirits—Fisher (a little) on St John.

16. M.

Two doses of Castor Oil had set me right, when Dr C. came in evg. Wrote to Mr A.C. Shelley—Ld Dunraven—Mr Ralli MP—Sir C. Forster MP—J.H. Levy[7]—Rev. Dr Lowe—W.H.G.—H. Wilson—Mr Markley—Mr Whitten—Mr Morgan—Mr Sergeant—H.J. Allen—Mr Sayer—W. Miller. Rose in evg. Read Harrison on Spirits—Duff's Life—Bale on Brain Exhaustion.[8]

17. Tu.

Rose at 10.30. Wrote to Mr Berkeley BP.—Mrs A. Jones—W.S. Gladstone—T. Edmonston—Mr Morrison—Mr Marsden—Mr Ferreira[9]—Mr Fanshawe—Hon. R. Bourke—Rev. Dr Allon—Rev. Geo. Butler—J. Kirkwood—Rev. T. Walters[10]—Rev. A. Wrightson[11]—Mr Davis—Mr Kelly—Mr Powell—G. Kennedy—W.P. Duff.

---

[1] *Fortnightly Review*, xxxi. 667, 718 (May 1879).

[2] Robert Knight of Calcutta, d. 1890; in England to establish *The Statesman*; see Walling, *Diaries of Bright*, 424.

[3] Probably A. Vandervelde of the Belgian legation.

[4] Benefit performance for Henry J. Vandenhoff organized by A. C. Shelley, who thanked diarist for attending and reported a loss of £12; Hawn P.

[5] Edmond François Valentin About, 1828-85; French novelist, journalist and anticlerical. At the dinner.   [6] Dunraven presided; *T.T.*, 16 June 1879, 6b.

[7] Joseph Hiam Levy, published on vaccination and political economy; wrote *Wealthy and wise* (1879).

[8] G. G. P. Bale, *The elements of the anatomy and physiology of Man* (1879).

[9] Probably Manuel Ferreira of Islington.

[10] Perhaps Thomas Walters, priest living in Bangor.

[11] Arthur Bland Wrightson, rector of Hemsworth.

Worked on Revises Art. on Evangel. Movement. Worked on Homeric Scepticism & MS of Mr Westropp.[1] Seven to dinner. Saw Ld Granville—Scotts.—Ly Lothian & Ly Brownlow—Mr Knight—Mr A. Peel—Ld Halifax—Mr Balfour. Saw Morris: & do cum Percy [R]. Read Life of Duff.

18. Wed.

Another night of ailment & physic: kept my bed all day. Saw Mr Th. Martin at great length—on divers matters. Wrote a few lines to Helen. Read much of Duff—and Harrison.

19. Th.

Wrote to Mr Ouvry—Mr Shelley—Bp Abraham—Messrs Dawson—Rev. Canon Trench—J. Scarth[2]—Mr Hardy—Mr Billingham BP—E. Fisher[3]—Archdn Palmer—Mr Broadhurst—E.A. Freeman—Mr Molony—Mr Macdougall—Mr Kavanagh—S. Smith—Ld Wolverton. Saw Miss Swanwick—Mr Newton—Dr Birch—Mr Welby—Mr West—Dr Haig Brown—Mr Bright. Read Life of Duff. H. of C. $4\frac{1}{4}$-$6\frac{1}{4}$.[4] Went to see the Lady of Lyons: acting very good, drama has I fear a central fault.[5]

20. Frid.

Wrote to Dr Allon—Mr Bourke—Mr Spence—Mr Stillman—Direttore Tipogr. Romana[6]—Mr Selford—Mr Westropp—Mr Murchison—Rev. J.C. Watts[7]—Sec. Ld Mayor—Sir Jas Watson—Ld Wolverton. Finished correcting Revises of 'the Evangelical Movement' & dispatched it. H of C. at $3\frac{1}{2}$. Attended Meeting of Welsh Members on aid to Education in Wales.[8] Saw Ld J. Manners—Mr Richard—Sir C. Dilke—Mr Bright—Ld Hartington. Dined at Mr Palgrave's. Read Life of Duff—Tracts. H of C. $10\frac{1}{2}$-$12\frac{3}{4}$. Spoke on Cyprus. A sickening case.[9]

21. Sat.

Wrote to Rev. Dr Allon—Rev. Mr Wilson—Rev. T.S. Bailey[10]—Sir H. Holland—Mr. Lindsay—A. Wark[11]—Fred. Hill—Mr Balfour—E.B. Davies—Mr Creasy—Mr Barton—Mr Flanedy—Mr Fisher. Saw Mr Stillman—Ld Hartington—Mr Hayward—Mr Dumaresq. Saw Mrs Chesterfield—promised conditionally £10. Also saw another [R]. Read 'Lord Beaconsfield' & tracts.[12] Dined at Spencer House.

[1] Paper on 'Homeric Doubts' sent by H. M. Westropp; Add MS 44460, f. 146.
[2] John Scarth, vicar of Holy Trinity, Gravesend; social reformer.
[3] Perhaps Edward Robert Fisher, anglican priest living in Nice.
[4] Flogging in the army; H 246. 183.
[5] Irving's production at the Lyceum.
[6] Business untraced.
[7] Methodist minister and author.
[8] See 1 July 79.
[9] Impassioned plea to avoid another Ionia; H 247. 374.
[10] Perhaps Thomas John Bailey, d. ca 1890; curate in London; historian.
[11] London stockbroker.
[12] Probably T. T. Hayes, Lord Beaconsfield (1878).

22. 2 S. Trin.

St James's mg. Vere St (Mr [W.] Page Roberts *NB*) evg. Wrote to Sir Jas Watson—Mr Walker—Mrs Chesterfield—Mr Rolando[1]—Mr Ogilvy—Mr Gaisford. Saw Ld Wolverton—Rev. E. Wickham—W.H.G.—Mr Geo. Howard—Arthur G.—John G. (Bowden). Read 'For Ever'—Duff Life finished Vol. I.

23. M.

Wrote to Dr Weymouth—Messrs Clowes B.P.—R. Elliot (O)—Mr Jas Milne (O)[2]—P. Lavery (O)—Sir Lewis Pelly—Mr Gibson—Mr Percy Cliff—Mrs Carter—A.G. Murray[3]—Rev. Dr Allon—Dr Caird (O)—Duc de Bassano[4]—Lord J. Manners—Dr Hornby—Mr Ouvry—Mr Miller—G.B. Smith—W.E. Benn[5]—Mr Harris—T. Wheen.[6] H. of C. $4\frac{1}{2}$-$5\frac{3}{4}$.[7] Saw Ld Hartington—Mr Forster—Mr F. Leveson—Mr Bright—Mr Rylands. Read Miss Swanwick's Egmont[8]—Harrison on Spirits. Attended the French acting at Mrs Rallis. Admirable. S. Bernhardt beyond my expectations.[9] Read Chinese in Australia: with shame.[10]

24. Tu. St John Bapt.

Wrote to Messrs Unwin—S. Langley—Mr Creasy—F. Verney—Miss Hickson—Messrs T. & B. BP—Dean of ChCh—Dean of Rochr—Dean of Ely—Prof. Blackie—G. Butler—G.D. Pennant—Rev. Dr Allon—Rev. R.C. Hales[11]—Rev. L. Berkeley—Rev. Kearney[12]—J. Pringle—Mr Clark—A. Dale—Miss Smith—Messrs Burke—Mr Marey—Sec. Lib. Assocn.[13] Saw Ld Dunraven—Ld Bateman—Mr Wortley—Mr ... MP. Saw Harris X: & another. Sat to Photographer: *in casa*. Dined at Sybella Lyttelton's. Read Harrison (finished Vol I)—Miss Swanwick's Egmont—Flori's L. to Beaconsfield[14]—Epiro.[15]

25. Wed.

Wrote to Mr Cowper Temple—Sir E. Wilmot BP—Mr Elliot Stock BP—Messrs Barker—Rev. Can. J. Glyn—Miss Swanwick—Dean of Chester—Bishop of

---

[1] Possibly A. Rolando, ginger beer manufacturer.

[2] Perhaps J. Milne, education cttee. clerk.

[3] A. Graham Murray, Edinburgh advocate.

[4] Napoléon Hugues Joseph Maret, 1803-98; 2nd duc de Bassano; one of Napoleon III's courtiers.

[5] Probably of the congregationalist family.

[6] Thomas Wheen, nonconformist in Castleford; on Irish universities; Add MS 44460, ff. 165, 185.

[7] Flogging in the army; *H* 247. 476.

[8] By A. Swanwick (1846).

[9] Private performance by Sarah Bernhardt, 1845-1923; this was her first season in London, in *Phèdre* with the Comédie Française; Gladstone also attended her art exhibition; see *Memoirs of Sarah Bernhardt* (1907), 314.

[10] L. Kong Meng, ed., *The Chinese question in Australia 1878-9* (1879).

[11] Richard Cox Hales, d. 1906; rector of Woodmancote 1860-88; surrogate bp. of Chichester from 1875.

[12] Perhaps Arthur Henry Kearney, vicar of Ixworth 1878.

[13] i.e. S. Chick.

[14] A. Flori, Marquis de Serramezzana, 'A le premier ministre d'Angleterre. Observations sur la politique anglaise en Orient' (1879).

[15] Not found.

Moray—Mr M'Millan—Mr Planché—G. Wilson—Dr Villari—Dr Lewins—Dr A. Cacha—Capt. Greville[1]—Rev. H. Algar. Saw Irish Presb. Deputn[2]—Ld Granville—Lady Derby—Mr Bright—Cocks & B. Dined at Ld Blantyres. All the Leinsters were exceeding kind. Conversation with Lady M.[3] on aid by Private Secretaries, which she greatly urged. Saw Chesterfield: *touching* facts [R]. Finished Miss Swanwick's Egmont. H of C. $3\frac{3}{4}$-$5\frac{1}{2}$.[4]

26. Th.

Wrote to Ed. D. Chronicle—Canon Farrar—Dr Weymouth—R.R. Simpson— Hon. Mr Hincks—Rev. Dr Allon—Mr Watts R.A.—Mr Murray—Mr Bassett—Mr Dawson—Mr Barker—Mr Vincent—Mr Robinson. Eleven to breakfast. Saw W.H.G.—Mrs Sidgwick—Ly Brownlow—Mr Holland—Ly Stepney—Mr Leveson Gower. Dined with the F.C.s—saw two [R]. Read Lecky's Hist—E. Bowring's tr. Goethe's Wayward Lover.[5]

27. Fr.

Wrote to Harry—Mr Balley—Mr Graham—Wm Smith—Mr Sam Parry—B. Wilson—C.T. Newton—H.J.G.—Mr Wright—Mr Twining—Mr Alex. Tod[6]—Mrs Th. Saw Ld Wolverton—F. Cavendish—J. Ogilvy—Mr Childers—Miss Chesterfield— Mr Cowper Temple. Twelve to dinner. Worked on arranging letters papers & books. Read Lecky's Hist. Engl.—Report on Ultramontane Bills. Devonshire House Meeting $12\frac{1}{4}$-$1\frac{3}{4}$.

28. Sat.

May the Almighty bless my expatriated sister. Wrote to Sig. Alemani—Mr Salkeld—R. Brown jun.—L. Stanley—Major Scott Phillips[7]—Mr Lecky—Mr Tanner—Mr Monteith. Saw Mr MacColl—Count . . .—Lady Colebrook[8]—Lady L. Grant—Ld Carnarvon. Saw Chesterfield—also Evans [R]. Dined at the Dean of Westminsters. Continued work on arranging books & papers. Read Dean Church Lect. I.[9]—Lecky's Hist. of England[10]—and E. Roumelia Ordinance.[11]

29. 3 S. Trin.

Little St Paul's mg. Chapel Royal evg. Tea at Sir W. Farquhar's. Saw Ld Granville—Sir R. Phillimore—Archdeacon Denison. Read Dean Church Lect II.—

[1] Captain Algernon William Bellingham Greville of Granard House, Longford.
[2] No account found; probably on the O'Connor Don's Universities Bill.
[3] Mabel, da. of 4th duke of Leinster.
[4] Irish universities; *H* 247. 596.
[5] E. A. Bowring, *The poems of Goethe* (1853).
[6] Of Walmer lodge, Deal.
[7] J. Scott Phillips of Kensington, corresponding on evangelicalism; Hawn P.
[8] Elizabeth, wife of Sir T. E. Colebrook (see 16 Feb. 64).
[9] R. W. Church, *On some influences of Christianity upon national character. Three lectures* (1873).
[10] See 17 Apr. 78.
[11] *Statut organique de la Roumélie orientale* (1879).

Foreign Church Chronicle–De Soyres, Montanism[1]–Waller, Apocalypse[2]–Aubrey de Vere, Legends[3]–Philosophy of Xty.[4]

30. M.

Wrote to Rev. Dr Allon–Messrs T. & B.–Rev. Mr Edwards–W.F. Mayor–W. Riddell–Sec. State H.D.[5]–R. Knight–A. de Vere–J.T. Ogilvy–Mr Cuthbert–Mr Mansell–Mr Goodhue[6]–A. Taylor–Mr Mayor–Mr Burke–Ellis & White.[7] Dined at Mr Milbank's. Saw Sir C. Dilke–G. Howard–Mr Mundella–Mr MacColl–Ld Granville–Mr Wade–W.H.G. on Estate affairs. Conclave at Devonshire House 2.30-4 on Chaplin's motion & the Amt.[8] Worked on Greek Frontier Papers. Began preparing Art. on Evangelical Movement for Vol. VII of Gleanings.[9]

Tues. July One. 1879.

Wrote to Robertson & Nicholson–Messrs Murray–Messrs Clowes–Messrs Watson & S.–Sir Jas Watson–Mr Hodges. Saw Sec. S.P.C.K.[10]–Mr Vivian–Ld Houghton–Mrs Thornhill[11]–Ld Clanwilliam. Dined at Ld Crewes. Attended the beautiful Rhododendron show.[12] Finished & dispatched Article for Gleanings. H. of C. at $5\frac{3}{4}$: and $10\frac{1}{2}$-$1\frac{1}{2}$. Spoke on the Higher Education in Wales.[13] Read Lecky.

2. Wed.

Wrote to H.N.G.–Bp of Moray–M. Lalande[14]–D. Whibley–Mr Donnelly–Mr Benjamin–Mr Macmillan–P.A. Major–Mr Macnare–Mr Puseley–Mr Cromer[15]–J. Smith–Mr Wellman[16]–Hon R. Meade. Dined at Ld Sydney's: Mrs Brancy's (Com. Française) after. Examining Homeric books at London Library. Saw W.H.G.–Lady James–Ld Granville–Capt. Clark–Duke of Edinburgh–Count Schouvaloff–Lord Chief Justice. Read Samuelson Sp. & Appx.[17]

---

[1] J. De Soyres, *Montanism and the Primitive Church* (1878).
[2] C. B. Waller, *The Apocalypse viewed under the light of the doctrines of the unfolding ages* (1878).
[3] A. T. de Vere, *Legends of the Saxon saints* (1879).
[4] [W. D. Pirie], *The philosophy of Christianity* (1872).
[5] R. A. *Cross; business untraced; no letter in Cross MSS.
[6] William Stephen Goodhew of Gothic House, Canonbury Park.
[7] London booksellers.
[8] See 4 July 79.
[9] See 14 May 79.
[10] William Henry Grove, d. 1915; secretary of S.P.C.K. 1878-90.
[11] Probably the wife of Albert Frederick Thornhill, mission priest in Holloway.
[12] Probably part of the Royal Agricultural Society's show at Kilburn.
[13] Giving a generalized support, doubtless recalling his own govt.'s refusal of funds (see above, vii. lxiv); *H* 247. 1157.
[14] Perhaps A. Lalande, London shipper.
[15] See next day.
[16] George Welland, engraver.
[17] B. Samuelson, 'The Agricultural Holdings Act 1875. Speech ... March 25th 1879' (1879).

3. Th.

Wrote to Mr F. Leveson—Mr Lecky[1]—Mr Rogers—E.P. Hill[2]—A. Davis—Mr Vickers—Sir Jas Watson—M. Ernest Nys[3]—H.L. Price—E. Fisher—Mrs Th. Dined at Lady M. Alford's. Read 'Three to One'.[4] Eleven to breakfast. Saw Mr & Mrs Halliday[5]—Ld Odo Russell—Mr Brown jun.—Lady Lothian—Mr Balfour— Mr Burt *cum* Mr Cromer—Lord Fortescue—Lady Stanley—Lord A. Compton. Saw Evans [R].

4. Fr.

Westmr Abbey service: H.C. and Sermon from Dean Stanley, for Sir A. Gordon's departure tomorrow. Wrote to Mr Donaldson (NB)[6]—Rev. Jas Owen[7]—S. Forster—J. Arkell—Rev. J. Ingram—J. Francis—J. Jos Fisher. 12½-1¾. Meeting at Devonshire House. Dined with the F. Cavendishes. H of C. 4½-8 and 10-1½. Hartington's speech capital: but he should have let Macduff go on with his motion & divide.[8] Read Stonehouse's Tom Keld's Hole.[9]

5. Sat. [Eton College]

Wrote to Sir F. Doyle—Rev. Dr Hayman—Mr Chaytor[10]—Mr Roberts—Mr Farmer—Mr Stonehouse—Mr Redmond—Prof. Reynolds—Mrs Th.—Mr Clode—Mr Whibley—Mr Geldart—Mr Grant—Mr Wright—Rev. W.H. Lowe.[11] Kept my bed after an indifferent night from neuralgia. Rose to go to Ld Lawrence's funeral in the great Abbey (pulcritudo tam antiqua et tam sacra)[12] at noon. A vast attendance: well deserved! Saw Adm. Hamilton. Off at 4½ to Eton. First the U. shooting fields match: then to dinner and my Lecture on Homer 8¼-9½.[13] A party to meet us.

6. 4 S. Trin.

Eton Chapel mg & St George's aftn. Saw Dean of Windsor—Mr Warre[14]—Mr Durnford—D. of Newcastle. Read Ch. Quarterly[15]—Dr Rigg's Address[16]—Leckie on Convocation.

[1] See 14 May 79n.
[2] Of Crompton, Cheshire; on Homer; Hawn P.
[3] Belgian professor and international jurist.
[4] [J. L. Elliott], *Three to One; a comedy in two acts* (1850).
[5] Probably William Halliday Halliday, barrister and Devon J.P., and his wife Maria.
[6] Probably (Sir) James *Donaldson, 1831-1915; rector of the High School, Edinburgh 1866; professor in Aberdeen 1881-6; principal there 1886; patristic scholar; kt. 1907.
[7] James Owen, vicar of Lechryd.
[8] Chaplin's motion for a royal commission on agricultural distress; Macduff spoke but did not move his amndt.; Hartington accepted the motion, with free-trade reservations; *H* 247. 1425. See Rossi, *T.A.P.S.*, lxviii, 8. 98.
[9] William Stonehouse of Whitby sent his *Tom Keld's hole* (1879?).
[10] His coalman.
[11] William Henry Lowe, 1848-1917; lecturer in Hebrew at Christ's, Cambridge 1875-91.
[12] 'Such ancient and sacred beauty.'
[13] Short report in *T.T.*, 7 July 1879, 12c.
[14] Edmond *Warre, 1837-1920; taught at Eton from 1860; headmaster there 1884-1905.
[15] *Church Quarterly Review*, viii. 273 (July 1879).
[16] See 18 May 79.

7. M. [London]

Wrote to Canon Ashwell—Mr Livingstone—A. Bennett—Mr Trenchard—Mr Wilberforce—Mr Hooper—Mr Fottrell[1]—W. Miller—Mr Ouvry—Mr Trengrouse.[2] Saw Count Münster—Sir Thos Acland—Sir C. Dilke—Ld Tenterden—Mr Knowles—Mr Childers. Devonshire Ho. Meeting $2\frac{1}{2}$-4. Dined at Sir J. Lefevre's. Read Cooke on Boswell—Temple Bar on T. des Reaux.[3] H of C. $4\frac{1}{4}$-$5\frac{3}{4}$.[4] Mr Knowles asked whether I approved his inviting one article by Mr Guinness Rogers which was to recommend replacing me in the Leadership of the Liberals. I replied decidedly not. I thought too that the appearance of such an Article in his Review might raise a suspicion that I was concerned in it. He agreed to exclude the whole argument.[5] Came up from Eton at $11\frac{1}{2}$.

8. Tu.

Wrote to Messrs Clowes BP—J.W. Russell—W.H. Cooke—Rev. J.G. Rogers—G. Mitchell—J.F. Cobb—Mr Manning—Mr Sampson—Rev. N. Hall—Mr Cowper Temple—Ld Granville. Saw Dr Hayman—Mr Sarjeant. Read Greek papers—Glennie's Europe & Asia.[6] Finished Corrections, and thus I hope all printer's work for my seven! Volumettes of Gleanings. H of C. $3\frac{1}{2}$-$5\frac{1}{2}$.[7] Saw Sir C. Dilke, Mr Campbell, Mr Stansfeld, Sir W. St Aubyn, & others, on the very unfortunate affair of Saturday night.[8] S.E.G. came in evg. Tea at Lady Derby's. Saw Chesterfield [R]. Visited the Dumaresqs.

9. Wed.

Wrote to Mr Stanley King—W.B. Pearson—Rev. H.R. Baker—Williams & Co—Rev. Mr Archibald—Rev. Mr Meredith[9]—Dr Carter Blake[10]—G. Unwin—Mr Vickers—Mr Downes—O.B. Cole—Mr Peacock—M. Smith—Rev. Mr Roberts. Began to work a little for a political article in N.C.[11] H. of C. $4\frac{3}{4}$-$5\frac{3}{4}$.[12] Saw Mr Bright, Mr W.H. James, Mr Adam, M. Gennadios. Dined at Ld Cardwells. Dss of Westminster's afterwards. Read Catholic Presbyterian[13]—... on San Marino.

---

[1] (Sir) George Fottrell, 1849-1925; later clerk to the city of Dublin; see Add MS 44460, ff. 221, 276.

[2] R. Trengrouse, liberal organizer in Putney.

[3] William Henry Cooke, 1843-1921, barrister, sent his 'James Boswell', *Temple Bar*, lvi. 314 (July 1879); the same number included J. E. T. Rogers on Tallemant des Réaux.

[4] Army flogging; Irish filibuster; *H* 247. 1784.

[5] i.e. from J. G. Rogers, 'The union of the liberal party', *Nineteenth Century*, vi. 361 (August 1879).

[6] John Stuart Stuart Glennie, Hellenist, sent his *Europe and Asia* (1879); Hawn P.

[7] Misc. business; *H* 247. 1887.

[8] Chamberlain attacked Hartington's position on flogging in the army, extending his censure on 7 July; *H* 247. 1551, 1806.

[9] William Macdonald Meredith, episcopalian priest in Edinburgh; on church affairs; Hawn P.

[10] Charles Carter Blake, anthropologist.

[11] 'The country and the government', *Nineteenth Century*, vi. 201 (August 1879).

[12] Sunday drinking; *H* 247. 1970.

[13] *Catholic Presbyterian*, ii. 1 (July 1879).

10. Th.

Wrote to O.B. Cole B.P.—Mr M'Naughton[1] (O)—Rev. W. Denton—Rev. A. Craib[2]—Herr R. Fleischer—Clerk of St Bartholomew's—E. Hering—H. Mence—W.H. Cooke. Dined at Mr West's. Lady Brownlow's afterwards. H. of C. 4¼-5½.[3] Eighteen to breakfast. I now feel this a fatigue. Saw Ld Granville—Ld Dunraven—Mr Herbert—Mr Grant Duff—Sir J. Lambert—Rev. Mr Rogers—Mr Mahaffy—Mr Welby—Mr Waddy. Read Stuart Glennie.

11. Fr.[4]

Wrote to Mr Th. Hankey MP—Mr Stuart Glennie—Mr E.W. Stapley—Messrs T. & B.—Hon R. Lawley. Dined with Sir D. Marjoribanks. Mr Thistlethwayte's afr. Worked on paper for N.C. Read Nemesis[5]—Stuart Glennie. Saw W.H.G.—Mr Forster—Mr Bright—Ld Granville—Sir T. Acland—Mr Hayward—Mr B. Hope.

12. Sat.

Wrote to Mr Aundre[?]—Duke of Marlborough—Mr Scharf—Mr Holyoake—G. Mitchell—T.A. Bamford—'Nemesis'—Mr Sampson—Mrs Mays. Dined at Mr Parkers. Read Stuart Glennie. 1½-2¾. To luncheon with the [W.] Page Robertses. Radcliffe Trust Meeting till 4.45. Saw Ludovic—a woful tale [R]—Ld Carnarvon—Lady Selborne. Worked on paper for 19th Cent.

13. 5 S. Trin.

Chapel Royal mg & evg. Saw W. Dumaresq. Read Beginnings of Christianity—For Ever—C.Q.R. on Petrine Claims & on Wisdom[6]—N.C. on Doubt in C. of E.[7]

14. M.

Wrote to Sir S. Scott & Co—Rev. Mr Franklin—Mr Serridge—M Gennadios BP—Miss E. Paul (O)[8]—Mr Willick—Mr G. Burns. Saw Ld Granville—Mr Dodson—Mr Price—Mr Bright—Mr Burke—Crown Prince of Sweden[9]—Gr. Duke of Baden[10]—Mrs Brand—Mr Lefevre. Worked on paper for N.C. Dined at Ld Reay's. Read A.G. on Indian Troops.[11] H of C. 4¼-7.[12]

[1] Probably Samuel MacNaughton, evangelical author in Edinburgh.
[2] *Sic*; not found.
[3] Army estimates; *H* 248. 56.
[4] And spoke in the Commons on reporting; *H* 248. 188.
[5] Nemesis [A. F. Robbins], *Five years of Tory Rule* (1879).
[6] *Church Quarterly Review*, viii. 1 (April 1879).
[7] *Nineteenth Century*, vi. 66 (July 1879).
[8] Perhaps Ellen, da. of Sir R. J. Paul, bart.
[9] Gustavus V, 1858-1950; king 1907. See 9 Aug. 79.
[10] Frederick William Louis, grand duke of Baden 1852; his da. Victoria m. Gustavus of Sweden 1881.
[11] Speech by the Attorney General on legality of use of Indian troops, discussed in 'The country and the government', 213.
[12] Army flogging; *H* 248. 344.

15. Tu.

Wrote to Mr Ryland[1]—Rev. Dr Hayman—Rev. Mr Gulick—W. White—Mr Turner—Mr Weeden—Mr Robbins. Dined with the Meaths. Worked on paper for N.C. H of C. 3¾-7 on Flogging in the Army.[2] Saw Gen. J.J. Wilson[3]—Mr Samuelson—Mr Burke—Messrs Murray—F. Cavendish—Mr Baillie Cochrane. Read Stuart Glennie—Letters on Bosnia.[4]

16. Wed.

Wrote to Rev. J.B. Farler[5]—Lady M. Alford—Spottiswoodes BP—Rev. J. Morgan—Mr Carslake—C. Tucker—Nemesis—Mr Knowles. Worked on 19th Century Paper. B. Palace Concert 10½-1½. Calls: Saw Phillips X. Saw Mr Warwick Brookes—Mr Nevins—Ld Hartington. Read Q.R. on Scotch Politics—on Irish Univ. Bill.[6]

17. Th.

Wrote to B. Jerrold—Mr Mansfield—M.F. Tupper—J.B. Jones—J.W. Foster—J.W. Werth—Dean of Chester—Sir Jas Watson—Herr Von Gerbel[7]—J. Hodges. Ten to breakfast. Twelve to dinner. H of C. 5¼-7¼ and 10¾-1¼. Spoke & voted agt flogging.[8] Saw Gen. Ponsonby—Mr Holyoake—Mr Knowles—Lady M. Alford. Worked on 19th Cent. Paper. Read Q.R. on P. Consort.[9]

18. Fr.

Wrote to Rev. Newman Hall—Ed. Leisure Hour—Mr Fletcher Park—Mr Campbell Hanwell—Spottiswoodes—Messrs Debenham[10]—Dr Clark—Mr Hitchen—Mr Mullins—Miss J. Hill—Miss J. Morris. Patriotic Fund Commission 12-2¼:[11] & H of C. till 3. Dined with Duke of Leeds. Saw Montesquieu [R]. Saw Sir W. James—Lady Harcourt. Worked on N.C. paper. Read Greek Papers—Bluntschli on the Congress of Berlin.[12]

19. Sat.

Wrote to Rev. Mr George[13]—Spottiswoodes—Mr Mackenzie—Messs. Duncan—Abp of Canterbury—Mr H. Irving—Mr Bryce—Mrs Corke—Rev. Mr Robinson—Mr Forbes Watson.[14] Saw Mr Linklater—Ld F. Cavendish—Chesterfield. X—

---

[1] *Sc.* Rylands.   [2] Spoke briefly; *H* 248. 480.

[3] *Sic*; none with these initials traced.

[4] Perhaps *The new crisis in Bosnia* (1879), reprinted from the *Manchester Guardian*.

[5] Perhaps John Prediger Farler, d. 1908?; archdeacon of Magila, Central Africa 1879-89.

[6] *Quarterly Review*, cxlviii. 255, 289 (July 1879).

[7] C. N. von Gerbel of Dresden sent poems; Hawn P.

[8] *H* 248. 652.   [9] *Quarterly Review*, cxlviii. 1 (July 1879).

[10] Debenham and Freebody, London retailers.

[11] He was a commissioner of the Royal Commission of the Patriotic Fund.

[12] J. C. Bluntschli, probably 'Die Organisation des europäischen Staatenvereines', *Die Gegenwart* (1878); see his *Kleine Schriften*, ii. 279.

[13] Probably John George, curate in Conway 1878-81, in Flint 1881.

[14] Perhaps a relative of Forbes Watson, 1840-69, botanist.

Alice Gladstone: at W. Dumaresq's. He lies seemingly in the jaws of death: a sad scene but not without the mercy of every Christian consolation.[1] Finished & dispatched with rather hard work my N.C. paper.

20. 5 S. Trin.

St Michael's Ch mg. Mr Fleming[2] is a striking preacher: but I was shocked at the prayer for Time of War. Abate the pride, assuage the malice—yes! but of whom? In evg I went to the desolate Marylebone Ch: about 15 men and 150 women & girls, with some 50 schoolgirls who *sat* with their back to the Altar through the prayers, formed the congregation in a Church built I think to hold over 2000: while the Rector,[3] perfectly complacent, delivered a sermon which I can only call pious chatter, perfectly effete, on a grand text (Nathan & David) which he did nothing to open. In the evening I read Spurgeon's vivid & noble Sermon of last Sunday[4] on the Crisis & the Wars: what a contrast!

Saw Sir Thomas G.—Mr Gore—Dr A. Clark—Miss E. Hill: good prospects DG [R]. Called at W. Dumaresq's: The cloud slightly thinner. C. is unremitting in her visits there. Read Judgments in Mackonochie case[5]—Ld C.J.s Letter to Lord Penzance[6]—Spurgeon's Sermon—Trinity House Sermon.

21. M.

Wrote to J.H. White—Ld C.J. Cockburn—Mr Fothergill[7]—Sec. Admty (O)—Mrs Cowe—Mr Higgs—Ld Hatherley—Ld Hartington. Saw E. Macgregor: mixed results X. Sat to Watts 4-5¼. Mr Mullins the sculptor worked on my head through the forenoon.[8] Saw M. Gennadios—Mr Bright—Sir R. Phillimore. Read B.Q.R. on Greece[9]—Five Years Tory Rule finished[10]—Mr Rose's Letters[11]—Mr G. & the Greek Question.[12] Dined with the F.C.s.

22. Tu.

Wrote to Mrs Maurice—Mr Herbert Spencer—Mr Whitfield—Messrs Spottis-woode—Mr Grant Duff—Rev. Dr Irons—Mr Toeg—Capt Brown[13]—Mr Gor-don—Mr Henry. Dined at Sir C. Forster's. H of C. 9½-2. Spoke near 1 h on Greek

---

[1] See 28 May 80 for his death.

[2] James *Fleming, 1832–1908; vicar of St Michael's, Chester Square 1873–1908; hon. chaplain to the Queen; well-known preacher and protestant.

[3] C. J. P. Eyre; see 30 Mar. 78.

[4] Commended in his article; see 9 July 79n.

[5] *Judgment of . . . Lord Penzance in which the proceedings in the case of Martin v. Mackonochie are considered* (1878).

[6] A. J. E. Cockburn, 'A letter . . . to Lord Penzance . . . on his judgment in the case of Coombe v. Edwards' (1878).

[7] Probably Ernest Henry Fothergill, curate in Islington.

[8] See 11 Feb. 79.

[9] *British Quarterly Review*, lxx. 177 (July 1879).

[10] See 11 July 79.

[11] See 2 Aug. 45.

[12] [Baron C. von Malortie], *Diplomatic sketches* (1878-9), vol. iii: *Mr Gladstone and the Greek question*, a well-researched survey and defence.

[13] Capt. John Brown of Harrow and Rose Hall, Derbyshire.

Frontier.[1] Mr Mullins came as yesterday. Devonshire House Meeting 12¾. Saw Mr Rose—The O'Conor Don—Mr Adam—Messrs Murray—Mr Home Fitz-william[s]—Sir C. Dilke. Read Irons on Faith & Reason[2]—Macmillan on Jannina[3]—WEG & the Greek Question—Fraser on the Government[4]—L'Epire et la Quest. Grecque.[5]

23. Wed.

Wrote to Mr Knowles l. & Tel.—Dean of Westmr—E.C. Whitehurst—E. Beb-bington—Principal [Caird] of Glasgow U. BP—E. Macgregor—M. Stark—J.H. Parker—Mr Elliot BP. The day was warm with little sun: the first that could be called a day of summer. Saw Mrs Th. Packing & arranging. Worked on paper for N.C. Read Lenormant on Ld Brougham.[6]

24. Th. St J. Bapt.

Wrote to Earl Granville—Mrs Th.—Spottiswoodes BP—Mr Beales—Rev. J. Comper—Mr Redhouse—Mr Kenworthy—Mr Darwin. H of C. 4¼-6¾ and 10¾-1. Spoke briefly on Irish Univ. Edn.[7] Haymarket Theatre to see Miss Neilson[8] in Romeo & Juliet. We paid her a short visit. Finished with some difficulty my work on the proofs, & in the abbreviation of Art for N.C. to 26 pages: an ample length. Packing & arranging. Saw Campbell [R].

25. St James. Fr.

Wrote to Mr R. Brown jun.—Sir Thos G.—Rev. J. Fowler[9]—Mr Austin—Cheva-lier Ott[10]—Mr H. Shaw—Mr Cornelius Brown—Mrs Ginsberg—Messrs Wyman.[11] Several hours of packing and arranging books & papers. Saw Mr Maurice Brooks—W. Dumaresq—whose vital struggle still continues with multi-plied & strange vicissitude—Mr Fawcett—Mr Adam—Mr Childers. H of C. 3½- 7 on India Loan.[12] Dined with Mr Maurice Brooks:[13] to discuss Irish Education. It seems they will make up a plan of some kind.

26. Sat. [Hawarden]

Wrote to Mr Salkeld—Mr Hitchman—Spottiswoodes B.P.—P.W. Campbell—Miss Nightingale—Ed. Echo—Mr Knowles—Mr Wainhouse—G. Dyer—Mrs Burton. Hard work packing & putting away till start at 2.15. Saw Mrs

[1] H 248. 1061.
[2] W. J. Irons, probably *An examination of Mr Mill's three Essays on religion* (1875).
[3] *Macmillan's Magazine*, xl. 1 (July 1879).
[4] *Fraser's Magazine*, c. 1 (July 1879).
[5] Untraced; on Epirus and Albania.
[6] Reading of 'Lenormant' uncertain.
[7] H 248. 1253.
[8] Lilian Adelaide *Neilson, 1848-80; the best-known Juliet of her epoch.
[9] Joseph Thomas Fowler, 1833-1924; historian; vice-principal of Hatfield's Hall, Durham 1870-1917.
[10] Asking diarist's help in erecting a statue to Rabelais; Add MS 44460, f. 280.
[11] London printers.   [12] H 248. 1331.
[13] See 31 Oct. 77.

Mathews—Miss Dixon. Reached Hawarden at 9.30: spending an hour at Chester, where we visited the Palace & had tea. Read Booth, Problem of the World &c.[1]—Saunders on America.[2]

27. Th. [sc. Sunday] 7 S. Trin.

Ch. mg & evg. Wrote to C.G.—Ld Acton—Rev. J. Fowler—M.G.—Rev. H.J. Coleridge. Examined Oxford Journals to gather particulars about Mr Sibthorp.[3] Read Notices of Rabelais—"Month" on Probabilism—Do on Cobbett[4]—&c.— Foreign Church Chronicle—Booth's Problem—Ultimate Triumph of Xty[5]— Reign of God. v. Reign of Law.[6]

28. M.

Ch. 8½ AM. Wrote to Mr T.M. Brigg—John Hilton[7]—John Booth—Mary G.— C.G.—W.H.G. Read Saunders on U.S.—Moeran on Ritualism[8]—Johnston on Educn in India[9]—Booth's Problem—and [blank.]

29. Tu.

Wrote to Waterston & Co—Mr Dobson—Mr Hitchman[10]—Bp of Exeter—Mrs Ellis—Mr Mayor—J.C. Burleigh[11]—Mr Macfarlane—Mr Fairchild[12]—H. Benjamin[13]—Mrs Russell. Worked on books & papers. Read Dryden's Tempest— The Bishop (qy Gloucester?)[14]—the Commercial Traveller[15]—Saunders on U.S.—Wilson, the Missing Link.[16]

30. Wed.

Ch. 8¼ AM. Wrote to Mr W. Saunders—H.N.G. BP—Mr Roberts—Mr Hamel— Mr Brindley—Mr Bickley—Mr Cottingham. A laborious morning on unpacking & arranging books. Read Saunders on America—Dryden's Tempest, & Shakespeares—Statement on 'P. & O. Contract[17]—Wilson, The Missing Link.

[1] J. Booth, ed., *The problem of the world and the Church* (1879).
[2] W. Saunders, *Through the light continent* (1879).
[3] Checking this diary at 10 and 17 May 29, 30 May 30 for reminiscences of R. W. Sibthorp (see 10 May 29), convert to Rome and back, for J. Fowler, his biographer; Gladstone's letter was much used by Fowler, see 20 Apr. 80.
[4] *The Month*, xvii. 374, 396 (June 1879).
[5] By H. Field (1879).
[6] See 25 Apr. 79n.
[7] Of the United Kingdom Alliance office in London.
[8] By E. B. Moeran (1879).
[9] J. Johnston, *Our educational policy in India* (1879).
[10] J. Hitchman; of Hawarden?
[11] John C. Burleigh of Walthamstow who had sent a pamphlet; Hawn P.
[12] Perhaps William Fairchild, London veterinary surgeon.
[13] Horace Bernton Benjamin, antiquarian and geologist.
[14] Obscure.
[15] *The Commercial Traveller in light and shade* (1856).
[16] D. Wilson, *Caliban: the missing link* (1873).
[17] Not found.

31. Th.

Ch. 8¼ A.M. Wrote to J. Watson & Smith—The Lords of the Treasury[1]—Mr Kimber—W.H.G.—Miss Milne (O)—Mr Dobson—Mad. Manginelli—Mr Fagan—Rev. Morton Shaw—Mr Ouvry. Worked much on books & papers. Read Saunders on U.S.—Booth, Problem of the World and the Church—Tempest (Shakespeare)—M. Shaw, Athann Creed[2]—Caliban, the Missing Link.

Hawarden Fr. Aug 1. 1879.

Wrote to E.G. Salisbury—M. Laurie—J.D. Merton—Dr J.H. Gladstone—Keeper of the Vote Office—Mr Armitage—Mr Johnson—Mr Adam—W.H.G. Read Booth—Adye on the Army (finished)[3]—Rogers on the Liberal Party.[4] Spent 5 or 6 hours on arranging papers.

2. Sat.

Ch. 8¼ AM. Wrote to R.P. Wright[5]—Mr Childers—Mr Barnett—Rev. Mr Leeman—Rev. Mr Gairdner—Mr Bell—Mr Wayland. Spent some hours in a beginning for my collection of *Mites*.[6] Worked on arranging Library. C. very busy with her plans for the Bazaar. Read Robertson on the Const & Laws of Scotland.[7]

3. 8 S. Trin.

Ch mg with HC and Evg at 6.30. Wrote to Messrs Watson & Smith—Ld Wolverton. Read Bacon, Reign of God—Schulte, Religion in Germany—Drew on Dr Rushwell[8]—Overton's Apology[9]—Zeal without Innovation.[10]

4. M.

Ch. 8¼ AM. Wrote to E.G. Salisbury—Rev.J. Harvey—Dr Weisse—Th. Barlow[11]—Wm Lyle[12]—Miss E.H. Smith—Sir Jas Paget—Mrs Wm Gladstone (Charlotte). Read Tempest (finished)—Knowles on Synth. & Analysis[13]—Booth, Problem of the World—Robertson on Scotch Law &c. Fourteen to dinner. Saw Sir Thos Frost—Mr Willmer[14]—Mr Mott. Worked on arranging Library. The weather cleared in the forenoon for the Bazaar. I piloted the Birkenhead Excursionists about & gave them a most conversational Address.[15]

---

[1] Correspondence untraced.   [2] See 14 Apr. 79.
[3] J. M. Adye, 'The British army', *Nineteenth Century*, vi. 344 (August 1879).
[4] By J. G. Rogers; see 7 July 79n.
[5] (Sir) Robert Patrick Wright, 1857-1938; Scottish agriculturalist.
[6] i.e. of small coins.
[7] Probably E. W. Robertson, *Scotland under her early kings*, 2v. (1862).
[8] J. F. von Schulte and G. S. Drew in *Contemporary Review*, xxxv. 773, 815 (August 1879).
[9] See 29 Oct. 54.   [10] See 27 Oct. 54.
[11] Thomas Barlow, Indian merchant.
[12] Of Rochester, U.S.A., had sent a poem; Hawn P.
[13] Perhaps J. Sheridan Knowles, *Lectures on dramatic poetry* (1873); delivered 1820-5 on classical drama.
[14] Charles Willmer, 1819-97; owned *Birkenhead News* from 1877; mayor there 1891-2.
[15] No report found.

5. Tu.

Ch. 8¼ A.M. Wrote to Sir Erskine Perry—Mrs Hope (Tel)—Dr H. Dunbar—H. Wilson (O)—E. Armitage[1]—P. Kenny—Mr Bryce. Worked 3 to 4 h. on arranging books. Read Grosart's Introduction to Eliot[2]—Letters of an Armenian on Ireland[3]—Booth's Problem of Ch. & World (finished). Incessant rain drowned the Bazaar: the last Bazaar I hope that we shall hear of at this place. I love them not. Sixteen to dinner.

6. Wed.

Ch. 8¼ AM. Wrote to Mr R. Wilberforce—Ld Granville—Mr Reynolds—[W. J.] O'Neill Daunt—G.B. Smith—Duke of Westmr—Mr Scarr—Mr Vine—Mr Fraser. Saw Mr Vickers—Dean of Chester. The Newcastle[4] boys came. Read the Hampden Chapter in Canon Ashwell's Biography.[5] A wirr-warr! Read also Robertson's Scotland—finished reading the "Armenian's" letters.

7.

Unwell from a chill: rose late. Wrote to Mr Cowper Temple—Mr Warburton—Ed. Daily News—F. Goos[6]—Mr Adam—T. Potts. Worked on books. Worked on reviewing old verses qy Poems: and on Translation of a bit of Dante. Read Wilson on Tempest—Robertson Constn Scotland.

8. Fr.

Ch. 8½ A.M. Wrote to Mr Hutchinson—C. Bradlaugh—Mrs Hope. Young Newcastle & his brother went in the evening. We hope they will renew the visit. Worked on Dante—Lady Mary[7]—& a Latin Hymn. Worked on arranging Tracts. Read Robertson—Prendergast on Irish Estates.[8]

9. Sat.

Ch. 8¼ AM. Wrote to Sir Jas Watson—Chamberlain of C.P. of Sweden—W. Graham—Mr Adam—Ld Wolverton. Worked much on Tracts: am now approaching a state of order. 3¼-5¼. The Crown Prince of Sweden paid his visit; & was very gracious. We showed, & fed, him all we could! Read Carey & others on Copyright[9]—Broadhouse on Violins[10]—Robertson on Scot & Constn. Twelve to dinner.

[1] Of Liverpool; see 23 Aug. 79.
[2] Sir J. Eliot, *The Monarchie of Man*, ed. A. B. Grosart (1879).
[3] [R. Hellen?], *Letters from an Armenian in Ireland to his friends at Trebisond* (1757).
[4] i.e. the duke of Newcastle and his brother.
[5] The MS of A. R. Ashwell, *Life of Samuel Wilberforce* (1880) i, ch. xi on the Hampden affair in 1848, sent for approval; Add MS 44460, f. 305.
[6] Of New Jersey, U.S.A., on religion; Hawn P.
[7] See 13 Aug. 79.
[8] See 11 July 67.
[9] H. C. Carey, *The International Copyright question* (1872).
[10] J. Broadhouse, *Facts about fiddles* (1879).

10. 9 S. Trin.

Ch 11 AM 6½ PM. Wrote to Mr Adam MP—Mr Samuels—Rev. T.G. Law. Read Law's Introd. to Challoner[1]—Preface to Douay Bible of 1877—Nicholson on The Living Voice[2]—Linklater's Sermon[3]—Mallock, Is Life worth Living.[4] Walk with Mr Burn Jones, who is still half an invalid.[5]

11. M.

Ch. 8¼ AM. Wrote to Duke of Argyll—Rev. Mr Fowler—Dr Acland—Mr Wilberforce BP—H.N.G. (BP)—Mr Paterson 1. & BP—E. Evans—Mr Alex. Balfour[6]—Miss Jackson. Worked on putting together "Molecules". Also a little on Dante's Gate: what a snail's pace is alone possible! Saw Mr Vickers—Mr Cottingham—Archdn of Chester—Sir Thomas Frost. 5¾-11. Went to Chester to open the Exhibition. Spoke to the company for 30 or 35 min.[7] Dined with the Dean afterwards. The very faintest tinge of yellowing is just beginning to appear on some of the crops. Read Robertson.

12. Tu.

Ch. 8½ AM. Wrote to Baron Malortie—G.B. Smith—T. Sinclair[8]—J.H. Rawlins—Sir F.H. Doyle—Mr Jas Howard—Mr Ouvry—Mr Shelley—Mr King—J. Moore. Read Horsley's Speeches[9]—Isham Diaries[10]—Sinclair's 'Mount'—Morley's Burke.[11] Prolonged conversation with Mr Burn Jones & Mr Ottley on Gen. I and on Judaism. I was too keen and rough. A little axe-work. *Our first pure summer's day for the year.* Last evening we drove home through the sweet smell of hay freshly cut.

13. Wed.

Ch. 8½ AM. Wrote to Watson & Smith—Rev. Dr Lowe—Mr Macintosh—Mr Jas Lawton—T.S. Gladstone—Mr Murray—G. Noble—Archdn Hincks—Mr Saunders. Faced a heavy arrival from London. Read my chapter on Judaism in the 'Studies'[12] & inflicted it on Mr Burne Jones. Read Bagehot on Scott[13]—Robertson on Scotland—Morley's Burke. Saw Mr J. Griffiths—B. Potter—C. Lyttelton. Worked on Transl. from Dante: & gave up with a sigh the hope of rendering 'Lady Mary' into decent German verse.

[1] R. Challoner, *Martyrs to the Catholic Faith* (1878); preface by T. G. Law.
[2] By J. A. Nicholson (1877).
[3] R. Linklater, 'A sermon ... preached before the boys of Wellington College' (1879).
[4] W. H. Mallock, *Is life worth living?* (1879); reprinted articles.
[5] See *Memorials of E. Burne-Jones* (1904) ii. 91.
[6] Alexander Balfour, 1824-86, of Liverpool and Mount Alyn, Denbigh.
[7] On beauty in manufactures; *T.T.*, 12 August 1879, 10e.
[8] Thomas Sinclair had sent his *The Mount* (1878).
[9] See 11 Aug. 42.
[10] T. Isham, *The Journals* (1875).
[11] See 29 Feb. 68.
[12] *Studies on Homer*, ii, section x.
[13] W. Bagehot, *Literary studies*, ii. 146.

14. Th.

Ch. 8¼ AM. Wrote to Professor O'Connor—J.C. Ady—J.R. Jolly—Dr A. Clark—H.N.G.—F. Pulling—Mr Thornton—G. Crowe—Mr Jas Caird. Worked some hours on my Library. Read Bluntschli on Jews in Roumania[1]—Robertson on Scotland. Also re-read my Chapter (1858) on the Jews & gave it to Mr Burne Jones who approved. Cut a very tough sycamore with Herbert.

15. Fr.

Ch. 8½ AM. Wrote to Miss Fitzgerald—Mr Ouvry—Mr Murray—C. Hindley—Rev. J.F. Higgins—Mr Macrae Moir—Mrs Th. Did kibbling work with Herbert. Began an Introduction to Homeric Mythology.[2] Read Robertson (finished)—The Parl. Drama of 1874.[3] Worked on my Library. Mr Burne Jones went: & left good memories behind him.

16. Sat.

Ch. 8¼ AM. Wrote to Mr Robertson—Mr Gairdner—G.H. Powell—W.P. Christie—Messrs Paulson & Wheeler[4]—Rev. Dr Rigg—Rev. T. Webber[5]—H. Lee. Worked on my Library. Read Morley on Burke—Bolingbroke, Patriot King[6]—Renan, Part des Peuples Semitiques.[7]

17. 10 S. Trin.

Ch 11 AM and 6½ P.M.—H.C. at noon. Wrote to Rev. Mr Leeman—Mr Gairdner. Read Secession to Rome[8]—Life of Mr Clegg[9]—Mallock on Life—Moral State of England.[10] Walk & conversation with [F. H.] Doyle.

18. M.

Ch. 8¼ AM. Wrote to Mr J. Hitchman—R. Cust[11]—C. Acland[12]—Jas Caird—J. Ellis—A.L. Gladstone[13]—D. Slocombe. Worked on Introd to Hom. Mythol. Read Bolingbroke, P. King—M. Müller on the Science of Religion[14]—Morley's Burke.

19. Tu.

Ch. 8½ AM. Wrote to Mr Ganderton—Mr Vickers—C. Mann—Mrs Th.—Mr Tillotson—C. Williams—H. Skoines[15]—W. Wren—Sir S. Scott & Co.—W.P. Adam.

---

[1] J. C. Bluntschli, *Der Staat Rumänien und das Rechsverhältniss der Juden in Rumänien* (1879).
[2] 'The Olympian system *versus* the solar theory', *Nineteenth Century*, vi. 746 (October 1879).
[3] Untraced article.   [4] Agents association; Hawn P.
[5] Probably William Thomas Thornhill Webber, vicar of St John's, Holborn 1865.
[6] H. St John, Lord Bolingbroke, *Letters on the spirit of patriotism; on the idea of a Patriot King* (1749).
[7] E. Renan, *Nouvelles considérations sur le caractère général des peuples sémitiques* (1859).
[8] [W. E. Jelf], *Secession to Rome* (1873).
[9] Possibly an earlier version of *The Diary and Autobiography of the Rev. James Clegg*, ed. H. Kirke (1899).   [10] By [R. Graham, Lord Preston] (1693).
[11] Robert Needham *Cust, 1821-1909; in India 1843-67; poet and translator; Hawn P.
[12] (Sir) Charles Thomas Dyke Acland, 1842-1919; liberal M.P. Cornwall 1882-92; 12th bart. 1898.
[13] *Sic*; a conflation of A. R. and W. L., Robertson Gladstone's sons?
[14] F. M. Müller, *Lectures on the origin and growth of religion* (1878).
[15] Henry Skoines, St Pancras poor law guardian, organizing the meeting; see 21 Aug. 79.

Read the Patriot King. Worked on Library some hours. Walk with [F. H.] Doyle. Read also Macmillan on Horticulture.[1] $4\frac{3}{4}$-$10\frac{3}{4}$. To Chester. Dined with Sir T. Frost. Then attended an enthusiastic meeting of 3000 to start B[eilby] Lawley on his Candidature: spoke 50 m.[2] Saw S.E.G. on Mr Gamlin's tenure.

Can it be that the decline of mind along with body—which reaches by analogy into the vegetable creation—signifies a rest of the powers as in a fallow—with a refreshed revival to follow?[3]

20. Wed. [London]

Wrote to Mr Adam—Mr Wilberforce—Euston Statn Mr—W. Lattimer—Capt. J. Spark—Major Pond[4]—Mr Gairdner—E. Dumaresq—Mr Knowles—Mr Brambley—Mr Pink—T. Ford—Mr Haddon—Mr Hopwood—C.G. Started before 8 (to accompany F. Doyle): worked my correspondence on the rail: Harley Street at 2.35. Saw Dr A. Clark. Dined with Mrs Dumaresq: he was finally unable to see me. Saw Maitland & another [R]. Read Branicki, Nationalités Slaves:[5] & to bed at midnight, well tired.

21. Th.

Wrote to Mr Goschen—Mr Horder[6]—Mr Constantinides (Cyprus)[7]—Mr Gurdon, & Arthur R. G[ladstone]—Mr Hayward—Ld Rosebery[8]—C.G. Read Hayward on Cavour[9]—The Cure of Souls[10]—Nationalités Slaves—Dacosta on Finances of India[11]—and other Tracts. Saw W. & E. Dumaresq—Mr Knowles. Saw divers [R]. Attended the very interesting festival in St Pancras Workhouse: & spoke to the old folks for some 20 or 25 min.[12] Then went about the place. Saw Chesterfield [R].

[1] 'A new vocation for women', *Macmillan's Magazine*, xl. 341 (August 1879); commended in his speech on 28 August as a solution to the depression.

[2] Adumbrating Midlothian themes; *T.T.*, 19 August 1879, 11.

[3] Holograph, dated 19 August 1879, Add MS 44763, f. 152.

[4] James Burton Pond, 1838-1903; American journalist and traveller. Pond tried to attract Gladstone to America, eventually offering £4000 for twenty lectures there; see his *Eccentricities of genius* (1901), 348.

[5] K. Branicki, *Les Nationalités slaves. Lettres au révérend P. Gagarin* (1879).

[6] Rev. W. G. Horder, on coffee taverns; *T.T.*, 28 August 1879, 4f.

[7] Probably Georgios Konstantinides; see 3 Sept. 79.

[8] Plans for Midlothian accommodation; unable always to use Dalmeny as a base; NLS, Rosebery MSS.

[9] [A. Hayward] in *Quarterly Review*, cxlviii. 99 (July 1879).

[10] J. M. Cobbam, *Cure of souls* (1879).

[11] J. Dacosta, *The Indian Budget for 1877-1878* (1877).

[12] 'It is necessary that the independent labourer of this country should not be solicited and tempted to forego his duty to his wife, his children, and the community by thinking that he could do better for himself by making himself a charge upon that community. There is no more subtle poison that could be infused into the nation at large than a system of that kind. We were in danger of it some 50 or 60 years ago, but the spirit and courage of the Parliament of 1834 and of the Government of that day introduced a sounder and a wiser system'; *T.T.*, 22 August 1879, 8d.

22. Fr.

Wrote to Mr W. Barry—Mr Hayter M.P.[1]—Mr Callander—Sig. A. Brunialti[2]—Mrs Th.—Librarian St Luke's Club[3]—La Marquise de Saffray[4]—Mr Lefevre MP—C.G.—Messrs Macmillan—Mr Knowles—Mr Weeks—Ed. D. Chronicle. Saw Mr Pond (U.S.)—Mr S. Gladstone—Mrs D. No 17. Shopping & calls. Packing books. Dined & passed evg at the U.U. Club. Read for some hours.

23. Sat. [Courthey, Liverpool]

Off at 10.10. Saw Mr Armitage & Mr Rogers in Lpool. Courthey at 5. A singular but an interesting ménage. Read La Russie et l'Angleterre[5]—Life of S. de Montfort.[6] ⟨Wrote⟩ Surveyed the place: well kept.

24. 11 S. Trin.

In the morning Arthur [Gladstone] drove me to the dismal Church in Warwick Street:[7] congregation about 60 all told. It weighs upon me—what can I do? Hymns in evg. Wrote to C.G.—and M.G. Read Driven to Rome[8]—Confucius.

25. M. [Hawarden]

Off soon after ten. Saw Mr Barker. Hawarden at 1. Found the Nevilles: & faced a terrific mass of letters. Read La Nuova Grecia[9]—finished Driven to Rome. Read Simon de Montfort.

26. Tu.[10]

Kept my bed with cold. Read Doyle's Lectures[11]—S. de Montfort.

27. Wed.

Rose in evg. Read Doyle—De Montfort—Morley's Burke.

28. Thurs.

Rose at one: having I hope got the enemy under. I had I think near 200 letters & packets to grapple with! Wrote to Baron de Ferriéres[12]—J. Fraser—J. Redfern—J. Simpson—A.C. Yates—G.B. Smith—A. Elliot—J.W. Hall—Th Burkitt—W.J.

---

[1] i.e. Sir A. D. Hayter; see 27 June 67.
[2] Attilio Brunialti, Italian professor; published on politics.
[3] St Luke's Central Club and Institute, London.
[4] Of d'Engranville and Rue de Clichy, Paris; business untraced.
[5] Untraced tract.
[6] By G. W. Prothero (1877); see 12 Mar. 72, 12 Mar. 78.
[7] i.e. St Thomas's, of which he owned the advowson.
[8] Driven to Rome. By an ex-Anglican clergyman (1877).
[9] See 7 Oct. 79?
[10] On opposite page is written: 'Tues 26 Aug. Kept my bed. Wrote to Herbert and Read Doyle & de Montfort.'
[11] F. H. C. Doyle, Lectures on poetry (1877).
[12] Baron Charles Conrad Adolphus du Bois De Ferrières, 1823-1908; liberal M.P. Cheltenham 1880-5.

Bond—W.J. Pool—J.A. Forrest—W.G. Burroughs[1]—J.H. Deansfield[2]—R.S. Ashton[3]—S.H. Crosbie—J. Brinton—W. Pierce—Mr Trendell—Mr Westell. Got out for the flowershow, & spoke $\frac{1}{2}$ hour on Garden cultivation which seems a subject for the times.[4] Finished Morley's Burke—read Bolingbroke—Life of Wordsworth.[5] Saw Mr Johnson—Mr Ottley: long & interesting conversation.

29. Fr.

Rose at eleven: and worked much on arranging letters and papers. Wrote to Sir F.H. Doyle—Messrs Glyn—Messrs Scott—Messrs Watson—Mr Flint—Mr Seddon (O)—Mr Cadell[6]—Mr Russell—Mr Saunders—Mr Field—Mr Barratt—Mr Bulgin—J. Read—Mayor of Southport—Rev. Mr Walters—Rt Hon Mr Adam—Mrs Barker—Mr OSullivan—Mrs Maurice—Mr Cuthbert—Mr Wildman—Mr Langford—T.C. Horsfall—Mr Huggas—Rev. Mr Goalen—Rev. Mr Calvert.[7] Saw Mr Vickers on Estate & Estate accounts. Read Simon de Montfort—Lenormant on The First Sin.[8]

30. Sat.

Ch. 8$\frac{1}{2}$ AM. Wrote to S.E. Stationmaster—Mr Williams—J. Cowan—J. Morley—R. Denman—Mr Routledge—Mr Brambley—Mr Jas Thornely—Mr Widdicombe—Mr Wyndham—Mr Allingham—Rev. P.P. Agnew[9]—Miss Goalen—Lord R. Gower—J.J. Ridge[10]—A. Davids—W. Wesley[11]—Ch. Cowan—J. Cowan—H.A. Bright—J.M. Howell—J.B. Pond. Worked on books. Dined at the Rectory. Began with W. the examination of places for the journey to Venice which all things considered it seems right to undertake. Read De Montfort—Annuaire Bureau des Longitudes.

31. 12 S. Trin.

Ch. 11 AM 6$\frac{1}{2}$ PM. Wrote to Ld Coleridge—Rev. Mr Sarson[12]—Mr Hinell—Mr Jas Bates. Read 'Midnight Thoughts'[13]—Ld Coleridge's Judgment[14]—Sarson's Sermon—Foreign Church Chronicle—Bagshawe, Credentials of the Church.[15]

Monday Sept One 1879.

Ch. 8$\frac{1}{2}$ AM. Wrote to Rev. J.B. Bagshawe—Sir F.H. Doyle—J. Morgan—R.B. Spark—A. Blane—Rev. Mr Robertson Smith—A. Williams—Mr Vivian

---

[1] W. Gore Burroughs, anglican priest in Mullinavat, wrote attacking Newman; Hawn P.
[2] Of Huddersfield; on his St Pancras speech; Hawn P.
[3] Robert Stone Ashton, religious author.   [4] *T.T.*, 29 August 1879, 8d.
[5] Probably *The poetical works of William Wordsworth. With a life of the author* (1865).
[6] Francis Cadell of Cockenzie.
[7] Perhaps Charles George Calvert, anglican chaplain at Heidelberg 1877.
[8] C. Lenormant, perhaps *De la divinité du Christianisme dans ses rapports avec l'histoire* (1869).
[9] Philip Peters Agnew; missionary in Australia 1878-9; latterly in Wolverhampton.
[10] John James Ridge, temperance reformer.   [11] Of Birkenhead; sent verses; Hawn P.
[12] George Sarson, rector of Orlestone 1878; had sent his 'Sermon'.
[13] *Mid-night thoughts* (1682).
[14] B. Coleridge, *Judgment of the Court of Appeal* (1878).
[15] John B. Bagshawe sent his *The credentials of the catholic church* (1879).

Webber[1]—O. Williams. Read Mivart, Anim. & Plants[2]—Proctor on the Pyramid[3]—Whewell, Bridgw. Treatise[4]—Nagelsbach, Hom. Theol.[5]—Bagshawe, Credentials of the Catholic Church. Worked on Homeric paper a little.

2.

Ch. 8½ AM. Wrote to Lady Lothian—Sir R. Phillimore—Ld Rosebery—Spottiswoodes—Mr Roach Smith—A.P. Smith—Mr Appleton—F. Hill[6]—J. Holden—Watsons BP—Mr Wadham—Mr Hickson. Saw Rev. Mr Woodward—Rev. S.E.G. respecting Mr Bellairs: walk to Wepre: he told me much. Studying Journey Books. Worked on Library. Do on Homeric paper, a *wee*. Began Philip II.[7]

3. Wed.

Ch. 8½ AM. Wrote to Sec. P.M. General—Dr Döllinger—Sir F.H. Doyle—Mr [G.] Barnett Smith—Mrs Th.—Canon Ashwell—Jos Bates—Mr Pennington—J. Rench—Archdn Allen—Watsons—Mr A. Macdonald. Reviewed letters to Bp Wilberforce sent for my permission to publish.[8] They are curiously illustrative of a peculiar and second-rate nature. Worked on Library. And on Homeric paper. Felled a poplar with W. Read Bagshawe on the Credentials of the Church—Max Müller, Lectures[9]—Philip II—Constantinides, Homerikè Theologia.[10]

4. Th.

Ch. 8¼ AM. Wrote to Central Press (Tel)—Mr Westell—Mr Godley—Mr R. Gladstone (O)—Rev. J. Jones—Rev. Mr Sanderson—Mr C.E. Austin.[11] Worked on Homeric paper. Visitors to luncheon & tea. Felled trees with Willy. Read M. Müller, Lectures: finished his Introduction—Homerikè Theologia—Cotton [Smith] on WEG's Homer.[12]

5. Fr.

Ch. 8¼ AM: also at 7 P.M. service of humiliation for the weather.[13] Wrote to Mr Atkinson (O)—Watsons—Ld Granville—Mr Hankey—Mr Alexander—Mr

---

[1] Vivian A. Webber, published on emigration and travel.
[2] St G. J. Mivart, *Contemporary Review*, xxxvi. 13 (September 1879).
[3] R. A. Proctor, *Contemporary Review*, xxxvi. 93 (September 1879).
[4] W. Whewell, *Astronomy and general physics considered with reference to natural theology* (1833), the first Bridgwater Treatise; see 13 Nov. 34.
[5] C. F. von Naegelsbach, *Die homerische Theologie* (1840).
[6] Frederick Hill, on death of his brother, Sir Rowland Hill; in *The Guardian*, 10 September 1879, 1265.
[7] See 19 Mar. 56.
[8] In the biography; see 6 Aug. 79, 22 Nov. 80.
[9] See 18 Aug. 79.
[10] By Georgios Konstantinides (1876).
[11] Charles Edward Austin, author of *Undeveloped resources of Turkey in Asia* (1878).
[12] See 21 Feb. 76.
[13] Apparently locally ordered, though the weather nationally was disastrous; over six inches of rain fell in two days in North Wales on 21-2 August, and the harvest was largely lost; see *The Guardian*, 27 August 1879, 1202.

Knowles—Mr Matheson—Dr Jack—Mr Donald Nicoll[1]—Mrs Royce. Worked on my Homeric paper. Read Cazalet on the Double Standard[2]—Philip II—Max Müller. Tree felling with W. & H.

6. Sat.

Ch. 8½ AM. Wrote to Mad. Novikoff—C. Hindley—Mr Livingstone—Rev. Mr Barnett—Rev. W.L. Leeman—Mrs M. O'Connell—G. Mitchell—H.H. Gibbs[3]— Messrs T. & B. Tree work with WHG. Worked on Homeric paper. Worked on Library. Party to dinner. Farming conversation with Mr Johnson. Read Philip II.

7. S.

Ch 11 AM & HC. Wrote to Spottiswoodes—S. Osborne BP—Rev. A. Scott[4]— Rev. Mr Crawley—Mr Macgregor—Mr Atkinson (O)—Sir R. Phillimore—Mrs Roberts—Mr Horton—J. Jones—Mr Greenough—Messrs [Thomas] Cook. Read Philip II (finished)—Nevins's Autobiogr. (trashy?)[5]—Cotton White [sic] on Evo-lution[6]—Scott, Evidences of Xty.[7] Nursed for a cold in aft & evg.

8. M. [Arley, Northwich]

Wrote to Ed. Daily News—Author of Philip II—Mr Sanderson—Mr Godley—Mr J. Grant. 8-10½ AM. To Arley. 11-1. Dedication service, and H.C. Walk with [R. Egerton-]Warburton. Interesting conversations in the evg with Mr Yates—also Mr Tugwell. Read Doyle's Lectures (to RW)[8]—In Memoriam—Hamlet Travestied.[9]

9. Tu. [The Coppice, Henley]

Chapel Service 9 AM. Off at 11. Reached the Coppice[10] before 7: a perfect nest. Unbounded kindness. Wrote to Lord Acton—my sister Helen—W. Hyam—Mr Thomas. Read In Memoriam—A Day's Ride[11]—Vocabulary—M. Theresa & M. Antoinette.[12] Harvest very various: an unusual proportion bad. Hay still out, even in one case south of Oxford. Also floods again.

10. Wed.

Wrote to Mrs Th.—Bp Strossmayer—C.G.—Mr Field. Walk with Sir R.P. Visited Miss P[hillimore']s Cookery School. Drive to the beautiful Gray's Court and

---

[1] Donald Ninian Nicol of Ardmarnoch, barrister and landowner; a tory.
[2] E. Cazalet, *Bimetallism and its connection with commerce* (1879).
[3] Henry Hucks Gibbs, 1819-1907; director of Bank of England 1853-1901; tory M.P. City of London 1891-2; cr. Baron Aldenham 1896; tractarian.
[4] Alfred Scott, curate in Campden 1877-80.
[5] W. P. Nevins, *Why I left the Church of Rome* (1870).
[6] J. Cotton Smith, *Evolution and a personal creator* (1874).
[7] Abraham Scott, 'Three sermons on the evidences of the scriptures' (1832, new ed. 1879).
[8] Who was blind.
[9] Perhaps *Prinz Hamlet von Dännemark [Travestied from Shakspere by J. F. Schink]* (1799).
[10] Sir R. Phillimore's.
[11] C. J. Lever, *A day's ride* (1878 ed.).
[12] *Maria Theresa und Marie Antoinette. Ihr Briefwechsel während der Jahre 1770-1780* (1865).

Henley. Read M. Therése et M. Antoinette—Lever, A Days Ride. Long study of the Dolomite District in evening, with the W. Phillimores.

11. Th. [London]

Wrote to Herbert J.G.—Mr F. Ouvry—Mr E. Hamilton—Mrs Maurice (O)—Rev. Sec. S.P.G.—Mrs M. Simons (O)—Mr J. Flaherty—Mr Clements (O)—Mons. Gopcevich.[1] Saw Ld Granville—Mr Paget—Rev. Mr Suffield—Dowr Duchess of Somerset—Mrs Dumaresq—Mrs Th. (what shall I say?)—Miss Phillimore. 10½-12¾. From the Coppice to Harley St. Encountered about 100 letters & packets. Corrected in part Proof Sheets of Article for N.C.[2] Read 'Grain Stores'.[3]

12. Fr.

Wrote to Rev W. Awdry—Mr Salisbury—W. Souter—E.C. Ward—Messrs Bagster[4]—Messrs Cook—Lord Acton—W.H.G.—Mrs Th.—Mr Upton—F. Draper[5]—N.J. Louis. Saw Mr Bredall (Cook)—Mr Farley—Mr King—Sir J. Lacaita—Scotts—Ld Granville—Ld Rosebery. Read divers. Saw Lawrence—Atkins [R]. Dined at Ld Rosebery's. Shopping & preparations for departure.

13 Sat.

Wrote to H.J.G.—Messrs Cook—Miss Thomas—Rev. H.B. Hill—Mr Hartley—J. Elliot—J. Gillespie[6]—R.N. Hall—H.H. Howell—Rev. R. Linklater—Ed. Daily News—Ed. D. Chronicle—Ed. D. Telegraph—Mons F. Salomon[7]—Ed. Iron-monger—Dr Schliemann—Mr Errington. Breakfasted with Mrs Birks. 10½-12. Attended Southwark Police Court re Morgan.[8] Saw Mr Cook—Mrs Th. (luncheon)—Mr Donaldson—W. Dumaresq: a long conversation. I leave him with little eventual hope: but whatever comes to him will & must be well. Much packing & preparation.

14. 14 S. Trin. [On ship]

St Pauls (All S.) at 11 AM. Old Marylebone 3.30. Saw W. Dumaresq & bade fare-well—Dr Hood[9]—Col. Garden.[10] Wrote to Mr Knowles l. & BP—Ld Rosebery—Messrs Cook—Ly M. Alford—Miss de Lisle—Mr Bowden Green. Dispatched revises. Read.... Dined with Mrs Birks and left town by the Night Train to Flushing. The passage was smooth and the route is one which may be

[1] Spiridon Gopčević, Montenegrin diplomatist; see 15 Mar. 77.
[2] See 15 Aug. 79.
[3] Untraced.
[4] Samuel Bagster, publishers.
[5] Perhaps Francis Draper, gilder and painter.
[6] Perhaps James Gillespie, Edinburgh surgeon.
[7] Perhaps Ferencz Salamon, of Budapest.
[8] Cross-examined in case of Edward Morgan of St Saviour's workhouse who claimed Gladstone agreed to finance his purchases at the Public Supply Stores; remanded, later found insane by Dr Bianchi, his chief hallucination was 'that one of the Misses Gladstone was in love with him'; *The Guardian*, 17 and 24 September 1879, 1303, 1335.
[9] Peter Hood, 1808-90; society physician and sportsman; attending Dumaresq.
[10] William Alexander Garden, retired Indian army lieut. colonel.

recommended for the avoidance of fatigue. Attendance & provision on board the steamer good.

SEPT 15-OCT. 24. *See separate Journal; within.*[1]

[*15. Monday*] [*Cologne*]

After a quiet friendly dinner with our kind neighbour Mrs Birks, Mr Patton[2] being the only guest, we went to Victoria and off by L[ondon] C[hatham and] D[over railway] to Queenborough and Flushing. 15 m. A good passage brought us in 8 hours to our landing: and after an interval of an hour 7 h of rail took us to Cologne (Disch)[3] and Helen with whom we spent the rest of the day. I noted the harvest better & more advanced than ours: also the rapid turning to the plough. In the Cathedral I am still disappointed. It does not live. Saw Mr Schmidt:[4] much pleased with him. I can only hope & fear about dear H.s return home. Read Bädeker: Dante Par[adiso]: St Ronan's W[ell].[5]

16. Tu. [*Hotel Belle Vue, Munich*]

15 hours from 6 P.M. brought us to Munich (Belle Vue). Read Bädeker: Dante Par.—St Ronans Well. We found ourselves plunged into a summer following autumn. We found our friend Ld Acton waiting us at the Station.

17. W. [*Tegernsee*][6]

Saw Ld Acton—Count d'Arco:[7] Mad. Novikoff:[8] Herr Lehnbach,[9] and the wonderful, unearthly picture of Bismarck. Visited National Museum—Schatz-kammer—Reiche Kapelle. The Directors infinitely kind. Off at 2.30 and at 6 were welcomed by Mad. D'Arco, Dr Döllinger, & the party at the Tegernsee. Read Dante Par.—St Ronan's Well.

18. Th.

This was a luxurious day: the whole forenoon in conversation with Dr D. & in the afternoon a drive to Kreuth in the same carriage. We dine at 1½. It does not well suit me physically but the moral & social atmosphere are delightful. Read Dante Parad—St Ronan's Well—Life of Titian.[10] Worked on our route for the Dolomites (No this was Friday).

[1] This travel diary is a booklet of 28 pages inserted into the diary text. Catherine, Mary and Herbert Gladstone made up the party. Mary Gladstone's diary, Add MS 46259, has much detail on this holiday.

[2] Probably Frederick Joseph Patton, barrister.

[3] The hotel where his sister Helen had resided for many years as 'Mrs Gladstone'.

[4] Physician attending his sister.

[5] See 3 Apr. 57.

[6] For this visit, see W. O. Chadwick, 'Acton and Gladstone' (1976).

[7] Emmerich, Count Arco-Valley, 1852-1909; Bavarian diplomat; his sister Maria Anna (1841-1923) was Acton's wife.

[8] In Munich by 'a singular coincidence'; Stead, *M.P. for Russia*, ii. 37.

[9] *Sic*; the portrait painter; see 11 Sept. 74, 11 Oct. 79. Lenbach painted 80 portraits of Bismarck.

[10] Perhaps that by R. F. Heath (1879).

19. Fr.

Wrote to Padrone at Grand Hotel Venice—Lady M. Alford—C[onstance,] Lady Lothian. We drove round the lake in aft. to the Duke's Farm[1] & saw some of his stock—5 m of walk back with Dr D. Likewise most of the forenoon with him. He is slightly deaf: slightly less easy with his English: at 80 not diminished in musculature:[2] the mind as heretofore free comprehensive and profound. Read Dante Parad—and St Ronan's Well. The days fly past!

20. Sat.

Wrote to Sir Jas Paget[3]—Mr Wilberforce—W.H. Gladstone—Ld Rosebery. Morning in open air garden walk with Dr D., Mr [H. N.] Oxenham joining us towards the close. Afternoon walk with them & Ld Acton. Some most lovely spots. Read Dante Par.—Murray's Handbook—Wives & Daughters[4]—Rev. des Deux Mondes on Merimée.[5]

21. St Matt. & 15 S. Trin.

Went to the Parish Church to hear (imperfectly) the Sermon: some things in the service new to me: good congregation, fair share of men; few young. Walk with Dr D. & Mr O.—Conversation on Dante's papal & antipapal views. St Thomas respecting Papal Infall. (for the Greek Church) and Absolution (for the Bps & Leaders)—on Church & State in England, & the condition of the English Church. We had our Morning Service together at 10.30 AM. Read Dante—Wittgenstein on Buddhism & Xty[6]—C. . . .

22. M.

Morning again chiefly with Dr D. & Mr O.—Afternoon much of Dr D. We were seduced into putting off our departure; though this maims our trip to the Dolomites. It is difficult to leave a place & society like this. In evening much with Ld Acton. Read Dante—Mrs Gaskell Wives & Daughters—Kebbel on the Beaconsfield Novels.[7]

23. Tu.

Further rich draughts of conversation with Dr D.—Also with Lord A. Walk & drive to Der Bauer in der Aus. Read Dante Paradiso—Mrs Gaskell—Rev. 2 Mondes on Merimée—On Horace Walpole.

24. Wed. [Innsbruck]

At last the time of departure arrived in dread reality. Ever overflowing in kindness Lord Acton and Madlle F. Arco came with us all the way to Achensee.

---

[1] Charles Theodore Wittelsbach, 1839-88; duke of Bavaria.
[2] Though see Chadwick, op. cit., 12.   [3] On meeting in the Dolomites; Add MS 44460, f. 295.
[4] By E. C. Gaskell (1865).   [5] *Revue des Deux Mondes*, xxxiv. 721 (August 1879).
[6] E. zu Sayn-Wittgenstein, *Der Schutz der Christen im Orient* (1860).
[7] T. E. Kebbel, 'Political novels of Lord Beaconsfield', *Nineteenth Century*, vi. 504 (September 1879).

A lovely drive. Then we met the Wittgenstein ladies[1] & went upon the ink-blue lake. On at 4 PM. by the incomparably beautiful descent upon Jenbach. Joined the rail. Innspruck at 8.30. Tirolese Hof. Read Dante Parad.

25. Th. [Landro]

Up early to see the Cathedral monuments (a fair congregation there & a few women communicants. Then Bank & Luggage business. Off at 9.46 AM. The Brenner pass more than satisfied my old road recollections of June or July 1832.[2] Reached Toblach before 6.30.—The first Dolomite, seen soon after passing Bruneck, is glorious. I was not very well. Splendid drive to Langro[3] by moonlight: arrived before 8. It is a short hour's drive (a miscarriage caused us some delay). Italian is here freely spoken though not as the mother tongue. Most kind hostess, & the cleanest of hotels. The walling in of the place very remarkable. Read Dante: the Vulture Maiden.[4]

26. Friday.

An excellent night: but I was not right, took castor oil & remained on my back. On account of rain the party could only take a walk. Read Dante—Life of Titian—the Vulture Maiden. I finished this remarkable tale, open to criticism but well deserving to be read. The party walked out but the weather was bad & comparatively little could be seen even in this remarkable place.

27. Sat. [Cortina]

We went down to Cortina[5] in the forenoon. Both the Langro Inn & the Aquila d'Oro at C. are excellent. In the afternoon we went up to the Tre Croci 6000 feet nearly. The tops could not be extensively seen. Read Dante—At Odds—Life of Titian.

28. 16 S. Trin.

Went to the principal Church to hear the Sermon. A very large congregation & signs of much parochial care. Then we had our Morning Church prayers together. Read Dante (four Cantos) and 'The Legacy' Life of R. Martin.[6]

29. M. [Pieve di Cadore]

After breakfasting, paying, & seeing Mr Stillman[7] who has been exceedingly kind to us, we started at 9.15. H. & I walking, C. and M. in legno.[8] A glorious

[1] The Countesses Elenore Casimire Ludovic and Caroline Louise Leontine, daughters of Gustave and Harriet (née Pigott) Sayn-Wittgenstein; lived at Tegernsee; Caroline was a friend of Liszt and Wagner. Mary Gladstone's diary mentions 'L. Wittgenstein'; Add MS 46259, f. 31.

[2] See 2 July 32.   [3] About 6 miles from Toblach on the road to Cortina.

[4] By W. von Hillern, tr. E. F. Poynter (1876).

[5] In the valley of the Boite, a tributary of the Piave.

[6] Dinah Mulock, A legacy. Being the life of... John Martin, 2v. (1878); see Add MS 46259, f. 33.

[7] W. J. Stillman; see 15 Mar. 75 and Hawn P. For this meeting, see W. J. Stillman, Autobiography of a journalist (1901), ii. 211.

[8] 'by coach'.

journey on foot to Auronzo.[1] 6¾ hours: ¾ hour we rested & had luncheon. Left Auronzo 4.30—A breakdown, none thank God hurt, C. shaken. An hour's delay. Reached Pieve di Cadoro[2] at 8¼: indifferent road, a good deal of hill. The moon helped us a little, after sunset. The mischief was that the Auronzo landlord refused us horses, evidently to make us stay for the night—& that we did not know we could telegraph to Pieve. Good Inn: Progresso. My whole walk was I think 26 miles. Read One Canto at night. Wrote to Carodogana—Mr Stillman.[3]

On the 29th I took the opportunity of the hill-walk with Herbert to open as fully as I could the question of his future career. I did not press him to reply. He took it all kindly but in what he said there was evidently some leaning towards the line of politics.

30. [Grand Hotel, Venice][4]

Up early to see the view—the pictures in the Church—the *casa* di Tiziano (out-side only). Off at 9.15. 20 miles by Perarolo & Longarone to the charming Vittorio: Then we issued from this Serravalle, as it was most appropriately called, at once into the plain country, having descended from Tre Croci 3000 feet each day. A splendid drive: but the dolomite character became gradually less marked. There were however very fine views of great hills—Marmarolo and I believe Autolao, until nearly the last. Bad Railway to Venice passing under Conegliano. The entry by moonlight in the gondola was nothing less than deli-cious. Grand Hotel: we were very well lodged—mosquito & other troubles a little damaged the night for others. Read full four Cantoes.

Wed. October One. 1879.

Wrote to Caportazione. Much troubled at non-arrival of baggage. Saw Lady M[arian] Alford[5]—Mrs Story—Mr Poynter[6]—Mr Story—Mr Browning[7]—Mr Grenville Berkeley—Herr Blumenthal.[8] Went to St Mark's for a general survey:[9] Lady M.A. gave us the most delightful drive so to call it along the Grand Canal from end to end as well as the Giudecca. Noted especially the Ca-doro, Giusti-niani and Foscaro Palaces. But in Venice more than anywhere the whole dominates and absorbs the parts. The moon full, the weather delightful, the site of the hotel excellent, and accommodation good. Band played in the Piazza at night: we all sat & *iced* before Florians.[10] Read Dante Inf—Abridged history of Venice.

---

[1] East across a pass to the valley of the Anziei.
[2] On the Piave.
[3] Rest of entry written at foot of p. 12 of the travel diary.
[4] At the end of the Grand Canal, opposite S. Maria della Salute.
[5] 'Drawn at that end by the strong attraction of Lady Marian Alford'; Ramm II, i. 101.
[6] (Sir) Edward John *Poynter, 1836-1919; artist; appt. director of National Gallery by Gladstone 1894; kt. 1896. See M. Lago, *Burne-Jones talking* (1982), 9.
[7] Robert *Browning, in Venice for the autumn; *D.N.B.*
[8] Banker and agent.
[9] The west front was being 'restored'; Gladstone signed Burne Jones's petition of protest; see *Memorials of Burne-Jones*, ii. 96 and C. Dellheim, *The face of the past* (1982), 79-80.
[10] The café in St Mark's Square.

2. Th.

A good day. Went to the Academia (Lady M. & Mr Poynter) 12-2. S. Maria del Orto at 5. Rich treats. Saw Casa del camelo. Mr Blumenthal sent his manager, & soon after the baggage arrived. Luncheon at a really good yet modest Restaurant ([blank]). Visited Clerle's. There has been I think a great drain upon the 'oggetti' since I was here 20½ years ago:[1] but I made some pleasant purchases: for use, some: some ivories for the Cabinet. Dined again at the *Table d'hôte*: middling yesterday, better today. Read Dante, good progress: Abridged Hist of Venice: finished Life of Titian. We feel now a little settled: & with the company here and coming it is most pleasant.[2]

3. Fr.

Wrote to the Editor of the Tempo: Morandini (written yesterday,—card):[3] Sig. Crespi:[4] Sig. Caburlotti.[5] Read Dante—Padre Curci[6]—Abridged History of Venice. Another hour at Clerle's, and one at Favanti's. I had a luncheon party at the San Moisé: we were 7 including Contessa Marcello so beautiful in 1859[7] and still very handsome. The whole bill was under 14 fr. Conversation with Contessa M.—Mr Poynter—Lady M.A.—Prof. Lorenzi.[8] We went over the Doge's Palace. The historical grandeur of the paintings is astonishing: as is indeed part of the ornamentation.

4. Sat.

Wrote to Sir Jas Lacaita—Mrs Thistlethwayte. Saw Sig. Velluti—Sig. Minghetti (twice, & long)—Sig. Bonghi[9]—Sig. Le Segre (pover'uomo—). Went with Lady M. to examine the objects of Art at Rietti's and Richetti's.[10] Our principal work among lions today was an examination of the famous Grimani Breviary.[11] A very great work in extent: smaller ones may perhaps be seen of more uniformly high beauty.

5. S.

Ch 11½ AM and H.C. Went much among the Churches: but with all my inquiries could not get to a Sermon. Two hours with Minghetti and Bonghi. We saw the Crown Princess[12] at 6¾: very genial, much depressed. Tea & much conversation with Ld Acton. Read Dante, & Church on d[itt]o.[13]

[1] See 23-6 Feb. 59.
[2] Written in a separate box, probably *re* this day: 'Tea with Lady M.A. & her party. Saw the Priest Camillo Franzi: an anti-Vaticanist.'
[3] Giovanni Morandini, 1811-88.
[4] Probably Paolo Crespi, d. 1900; Florentine risorgimentist; or F. Crispi, see 2 Oct. 77.
[5] Unidentified.
[6] C. M. Curci, probably *Italien und die Kirche* (1879).
[7] See 25 Feb. 59.
[8] Probably Giovanni Lorenzi, Italian classicist.
[9] Ruggiero Bonghi, 1826-95; wrote on Gladstone, see 27 Feb. 80.
[10] Diamond dealers.   [11] In the Marciana library.
[12] Of Germany.
[13] R. W. Church, *Dante. An essay* (1878).

6. M.

Wrote to Sig. Guglielmo—Archdn Denison—Messrs Cook. Read Dante—Dal-medico[1]—Ruskin. Saw much—at St Mark's (how they robbed Constanti-nople!)—S. Zacharia—the beautiful Bellini especially)—S. Giov. in Bragola (Cima da C[onegliano] a most holy altarpiece)—S. [Giorgio degli Schiavoni] the extraordinary series of Carpaccios, which go so far to justify Ruskin's ardour.[2]

7. Tu.

Wrote to Ed. D. News[3]—Landlord of Belle Vue Munich—Mr Robert Stuart—Landlord Aquila Nera Cortina. Dined with Lady M. Alford in the fine palatial suite which seems to exist in all these Palace Hotels. The day was spent 11-5½ in a very interesting expedition to Torcello and Burano.[4] We saw the old Churches[5] at T. the lace manufactory, the Church &c. at Burano. All full of interesting remains and symbols of the old history and tending to modify the received views. Most important is that line of Martial

Aemula Baianis Altini litora villis.[6]

Lovely day. The malaria is deplorable. Read Dante—Memoir of Tipaldi—Stato di Grecia[7]—Hist. of Torcello. Saw Clerle. Saw Dean of Westmr—Ld A. Compton—Countess Marcello—the young Count & Countess both noteworthy—Mrs Story—Lady Acton—Sig. Minghetti—Sig. Bonghi.

8. Wed.

Saw Count Macingo[8]—Dr [E. C.] Kokkinos *cum* Cav. Tipaldo the Greek Consul—Mr Cook—Sig. Minghetti—Lord Acton—Dean of Westmr. Read Dante—Zanelli.[9] Worked on accounts in preparation for departure—shopping, and packing. Saw St Mark's in the forenoon with Mr & Mrs Rooke. Visited the Armenian Convent in the afternoon: conversation *inter alia* on the English Administration & Armenian opinion about—on Russo-Armenia—on their eccl. position. Tea at Lady M.A.s rooms. Saw Count Narat. Wrote to Sig. Zervòs.

9. Th. [On train]

Wrote to Mr Daily—Sig. Ricciardi—Sig. Favanti. Read Dante—Memoirs of Cairoli family.[10] At twelve went to the Morosini Palace and saw the historical collections of very extraordinary interest.[11] Then to St Stephen's Church. To

---

[1] A. Dalmedico, *Prose e versi* (1870).

[2] Described by Ruskin in the supplement to *St Mark's Rest*.

[3] Details of movements; *D.N.*, 11 October 1879, 5c.

[4] Islands in the lagoon, north of Venice.

[5] Basilica of St Maria, with a huge campanile, and the Byzantine St Fosca, both then in poor condition.

[6] 'The shores of Altini rival the villas of Baiae'; Martial, iv. 25. 1.

[7] Probably P. Tipaldo-Foresti, *Biografia di G. K. Tipaldo . . . con aggiunta: La Grecia negli ultimi 45 anni* (1878).

[8] Apparently *sic*; unidentified.   [9] Perhaps D. Zanelli, *Roma e S. Pietro* (1867).

[10] *La famiglia Cairoli*, tr. from English by F. Torraca (1879).

[11] On the Campo Morosini; arms and picture collection partly sold off in 1894.

Serano's with Lady M. A[lford]. To S. Elena in afternoon. A charming spot;
beautiful cloister pillars. Visit from one of the Armenian Padri to get a new
autograph. On the plea that the one I gave had been stolen. It afterwards
appeared nearly certain that this was a falsehood, for which no motive other
than a mercenary one of the meanest rank could be assigned. Saw Ld Acton to
whom & Lady A. we gave a luncheon at San Moisé. We dined with Lady M.A.
and her party and in heavy mood came off at 10¼. Travelled all night: changing
carriages at 4 & 7 AM.

10. [Belle Vue Hotel, Munich]

A splendid day's journey until towards dusk we engaged into the plain of
Munich: the whole 380 m? We sent off Herbert direct and our mutilated party
went to the Belle Vue Hotel. Much aid from Count d'Arco's extreme kindness.
Read Dante—passing into the third great division—and Cairoli Memoirs (Ital.
Tr.) The Dolomite top is to be seen once before entering Botzen from S. &
once, very fine, through an opening on the road from it to Brixen. To the E., of
course.

11. Sat.

Read Dante—Cairoli Memoirs. Sat to Lehnbach.[1] Saw the Exhibition (all
nations): many fine things: a wonderful head of Herkomer's.[2] Went to Dr D. in
the forenoon: & had a long walk with him in the afternoon. Conversation on
Dante & on various matters of Theology. Most instructive, most harmonious.
Hof Theater in evening. I could not hear. What I could see was good. Wrote to
M. Got[3]—M. Hyacinthe Loyson.

12. 18 S. Trin.

Engl. Church. mg & aft. Went to the Gasteich at 10: but the Sermon was over.
Congregation devout, building (very small) very full, service in German. Saw
Countess [de Leyden][4] & Lady Blennerhassett: General Stanton.[5] Again with
Dr Döllinger at 2: at 4 he entertained us most genially to dinner, and we sat till
8. The change to chill, & some standing, overset me, but the night put me right
again. Read Dante: got more learning from Dr D. about the old commentaries.

13. M. [On train]

Read hardly any Dante: all was busy. Sat to Lehnbach & his Photographer.
Went over the Pinakothek (with the courteous Director Professor Rehber) the
Glypothek & the Library, where among many curious objects I saw that

---

[1] Sc. Lenbach; see 11 Sept. 74. This portrait is in the Scottish National Portrait Gallery in Edinburgh; another version at Hawarden. The photograph taken at the sitting on 13 Oct. 79 forms the
frontispiece to this volume, and the rather poor portrait is also reproduced above.

[2] Sir Hubert von *Herkomer, 1849-1914; Bavarian artist and Slade professor at Oxford 1885-94.

[3] Edmond-Francois-Jules Got, 1822-1901, doyen of the Comédie-Française; probably arranging
tickets, see 17, 20 Oct. 79.

[4] Countess de Leyden, mother of Charlotte, Lady Blennerhassett.

[5] George Staunton, 1809-80; general 1877.

wonderful Greek Ivory bas relief of the 11th Century, as it is affirmed to be. Also Makart's Picture called the Triumphal Entry: full of talent, but very gross.[1] Dined at 3 with Countess [de Leyden] & her daughter Lady Blennerhassett. Dr Döllinger came to our tea and I had a final conversation and affectionate Adieu. God be with him in all his thoughts & words & works. The faithful Count D'Arco accompanied us to the station & the ladies also came thither. We started at 7.12 & travelled all night. In happy solitude as far as Stuttgardt.

14. Tu. [Hotel Bedford, Paris]

Read much Dante—Murray's Paris Handbook. Rapid journey, carriage never crowded so that C. & M. always had 4 places. The last 100 miles before Paris were travelled through pleasant country full of the marks of industry and thrift. Some patches of harvest were still in the field. Reached Hotel Bedford[2] soon after 5.30. It is beautifully clean and comfortable with the best cuisine, as we found at six, that we have seen on the whole journey: we have a charming sittingroom & two good bedrooms with a hole for me to dress in. Wrote to Directeur des Postes.

15. Wed.

Wrote H.J.G.—Lady M. Alford—Lord Acton. Saw Mad. Novikoff—Mr Kinglake—Lady Huntingtower[3] (with whom we had tea). Drove round to make a series of calls: and went to the Bibliothèque where the Director spent two hours in showing us the most choice of the wonderful treasures there. Read Dante—Socrate et l'Amour Grec[4]—Nouvelle Revue, Introduction and Türr's Article.[5]

16. Th.

Wrote to Mr A. Strahan—Mons. E. Perrin[6]—M.E. de Girardin[7]—Mrs Th—Ed of Guardian[8]—M. Borel.[9] Saw Mr Kinglake—M. Benoit Brunswik—Mr Brown—Mr Connor. Spent some 3 hours in the Louvre. It is indeed a marvel. No picture more lovely than Sandro Botticelli's B.V.M. and child. The ivory *figures* work is much behind Munich, for the renaissance. The Palissy collection very comprehensive. It is vain to describe without hours, and quires. Book & curiosity shops. Read Dante—Jeunesse de Lord Beaconsfield.[10]

[1] 'The entry of Charles V into Antwerp', painted in 1878 by Hans Makart, 1840-84; *The Oxford Companion to Art* describes his pictures as 'feverishly composed . . . in turgid colour schemes'.
[2] In the Rue de l'Arcade, behind the Madeleine. Salisbury also used this hotel.
[3] Katharine Elizabeth Camilla, widow of Lord Huntingtower.
[4] J. M. Gesner, *Socrate et l'amour grec* (1877).
[5] *Nouvelle Revue*, i. 5, 56 (1879); its first number.
[6] Emile Perrin, 1814-85; general administrator of the Comédie-Française from 1871.
[7] See 28 Jan. 67; he supported Thiers and de Broglie; deputy for Paris from 1877.
[8] *The Guardian*, 22 October 1879, 1486, reported the interview of 20 October but without a gloss; this letter may have been announcing his movements.
[9] Probably Jean-Louis Borel, 1819-84; minister of war 1877-9.
[10] By Victor Valmont (1878).

17. Fr.

Wrote to Mad. Novikoff. Made calls: walked in old Paris: noticing curiosity shops. Saw The Conte [*sic*] du Paris[1]—Rev. Dr Nevins—General Kiréeff[2]—Mr M. Herbert.[3] Saw Notre Dame—Madeleine—St Germain des Prés—& two other Churches. The effect of Notre Dame is not at all equal to that of the Abbey; but the doorways and rose windows are splendid and many other things noteworthy. The effect of size in the Madeleine is destroyed by a wrong principle of distribution into spaces and by recess. The Churches here are even worse darkened than any of ours: & the fewness (as well as apparent indifference) of persons in them—these few almost wholly women—is very remarkable. In the evening we went to the Théatre Français, M. Perrin kindly giving us his box. The style of acting has altered since my earliest recollections being more vehement and demonstrative. The play was Hernani.[4] M. Maubant[5] (Duc de Silva) was nearest (I thought) to the older school. Mlle Bernhard's articulation when not too rapid (for me?) is incomparable & she is a most finished actress. Mounet-Sully[6] is first-rate in his kind: but I liked most the old kind. Read Dante—Hernani. (The piece however remarkable is full of wild incongruities: very un-Shakespearian ?)

18. Sat.

Read Dante—Socrate et l'Amour Grec. We went to the Louvre, chiefly for the statues: one could never weary in looking at the Venus of Milo. We also went to some of the pictures especially the S. Botticelli, marvellous in loveliness. And to the Tanagra figures and the three emplatremens of gold. I then went among the book and curiosity shops. Ivories are very rare here, and very dear. At five we had a tea—Mad. Novikoff, Ly Huntingtower, Mr Kinglake, Mr Dana (U.S.). We dined with M. Emile de Girardin.[7] Much conversation with M. Scherer—Mr Girardin—M. Lebey—Mr Bardoux (Minister of Instruction) and others. Also Mad. Addam & Vicsse Brimont Brissac. We only learned afterwards that to both these it was a scandal to invite ladies. It is said A. was the mistress of Gambetta. Scherer struck me very much. Agnes's birthday: God bless her. Also poor Mrs Ths.

[1] Louis-Philippe, 1838-94, comte de Paris; the French pretender.

[2] Alexander Kiréev, Olga Novikov's brother.

[3] Michael Henry Herbert, 4th s. of Sidney*, 1857-1903; diplomat.

[4] The leading play of romantic theatre, by Victor Hugo. Its first performance in 1830 caused a riot; the revival of 1877, the production which Gladstone saw, was the first to use the full text.

[5] Fleury Polydore Maubant, a leading exponent of the classical style.

[6] Jean Mounet-Sully, 1841-1916; with the company from 1872.

[7] Olga Novikov arranged the party, which had a marked republican tone, for Girardin, proprietor of *La France* (see 28 Jan. 67); Stead, *M.P. for Russia*, ii. 39. Henri Adolphe Edmond Scherer, 1815-89, theologian and critic, was senator 1875-89; Edouard G. Lebey, journalist (wrote in November 1879 on help for Spanish flood victims; Hawn P); Benjamin Joseph Agenor Bardoux, 1829-97, was minister of public instruction 1877-9. Juliette Adam, novelist and hostess, was confidante of Gambetta (and wife of his friend Edmond Adam), but not his mistress, who was Léonie Léon.

19. 19 S. Trin.

Rue d'Aguesseau Ch at 11 and H.C.—Père Hyacinthe's at 4 to 6. He delivered a noteworthy sermon, the end quite noble, on the scene of the Transfiguration. The Church was crowded. Saw Dr Nevins—Dean Stanley—Madame Novikoff. Read Dante—Le Divorce.[1] Dined with Mr Waddington (in force, our whole party).[2] He did not open on the Eastern question and I thought it would be bad taste in me. Conversation with Mrs W. on Père H. and M. Bercier. With Leon Say[3]—the Minr of Justice—and the head of the Consular Dept.—So went the evening. After the Sermon I had a pretty full conversation with Père Hyacinthe: & recommended organisation.

20. M.

Wrote to M. Peyronnet (Soleil)[4]—Rev. Mr Newton—Mr Grogan—Surveyor of Customs (Victa)—M. Langel[5] (Duc d'Aumale)—M. Larocque—The Russian Ambassador.[6] Long morning calls, & Catechism, from M. Guerault of the Telegraphe, and M. Savouillon of the Gaulois.[7] Also Rev. Mr Wood. Shopping & settling at Bank & chambers. In the evening our Huntingtower friends, who had taken Catherine greatly into their confidence, took us to the Théatre Français where we fortunately saw Les Fourberies de Scapin and Le Gendre de M. Poirier[8] with Got (incomparable) Coquelin, Croisette & other excellent actors. Home late to pay & pack. We entertained Miss Stanley & Miss Wyn at dinner. Saw Mr [M. H.] Herbert who recalls his father's charm.

21. Tu. [Bettishanger, Kent]

Up at 5¾. Off at 7.35 from the Nord Station. A luxurious journey through the fostering arrangements of Messrs Cook. We reached Dover at half past three, and at five Bettishanger[9] the delightful nest of our old kind and dear friends. We could not on landing renew more happily our acquaintance with our country than in this pure and happy home. Read Dante—Le Gendre de M. Poirier—and [blank.]

22. Wed.

Wrote to W.H.G. and to Mr Childers. Began the forenoon with a long farming conversation & view of accounts, and in afternoon drove to Mr Long's farm. He

---

[1] Perhaps Le Divorce, par le meilleur ami des femmes (1790).

[2] Waddington (see 18 Dec. 77), appointed by the new republican president, Grévy, led a centre left and republican left government, which fell in December. He m. Mary King, who d. 1923; description of this party in her My first years as a Frenchwoman (1914), 92.

[3] Jean Baptiste Léon Say, 1826-96; minister of finance 1872-3, 1875-9, 1882; ambassador in London 1880.

[4] A journalist.   [5] Of the Orleanist family; Aumale's secretary.

[6] Prince Orlov, Russian ambassador in Paris since 1872.

[7] Spoke quite extensively and controversially on foreign affairs, and working-class progress; English report in T.T., 22 October 1879, 5a; see 22-3 Oct. 79 and Fitzmaurice, ii. 182.

[8] By Molière (1671) and E. Augier (1854) respectively.

[9] Sir Walter James's.

has established thirty acres of garden or fruit ground. Read Dante—Scherer on Dante.[1]—Q.R. of 1846 on French Agriculture and Land Tenure.[2] The Granvilles came over to luncheon: much conversation with him. Also with Godley & Sir W. J[ames] on the [*Gaulois*] 'Interview' reports about which G. is uneasy.

23. Th.

Wrote to Ed. Daily News—Lady Derby—Mr Field. Finished my Dante. It was almost more than I had hoped to accomplish during my tour. Read Scherer. We drove over to Walmer for luncheon and saw the improvements. Conversation with Granville on the Interviewers' reports: sent up my paragraph with his approval.[3]

24. Fr.

Wrote to.... Read Scherer—Q.R. on Scherer's Milton—Do on his Goethe.[4] Walked with Godley and the junior Walter [James] to see the machine called the American Devil executing a cutting on the new L[ondon] C[hatham and] D[over] line from Dover to Deal. With 11 men it does the work of 60. The contractor says the money saving is not great—but Query. Saw the Farm Yard. Planted two trees. A cold in the larynx took hold of me.

25. Sat. [*London*]

Cold notwithstanding, we were up at eight and off soon after nine to Shepherd's well:[5] accepting with reluctance the close of a most hearty and delightful visit to our dear old friends.
And here I repass to my regular book.

Saturday Oct. 25. 1879.

Wrote to Sir Wilfrid Lawson—Mr Dessilla—A. Billson—Geo. Potter—G. Macdonald[6]—W.S. Moir[7]—Mr Brady—Mrs S.H. Vaux—Rev. Jas Fraser[8]—Rev. Canon Scott—R.W. Thrupp—Mr Jas Knowles—Mr Bussy. Dined with Ld Rosebery: saw Mr Hayward—Mr Bushell (Liverpool)—Mr Bayard (U.S. Senator).[9] Read Scherer. My cold became bad. $9\frac{1}{4}$-$1\frac{3}{4}$. Bettishanger to London. Several hours given to the opening of letters.

---

[1] In E. H. A. Scherer's *Études critiques*, 10v. (1865ff.), from which subsequent reading came.
[2] [By J. W. Croker], *Quarterly Review*, lxxix. 202 (December 1846); notes at Add MS 44763, f. 153.
[3] Announcing the interview had a want of 'full harmony with Mr. Gladstone's intention' (no details given): *D.N.*, 25 October 1879, 5b.
[4] M. Arnold in *Quarterly Review*, cxliv. 143 (January 1878).
[5] The station for Bettishanger.
[6] Probably George *Macdonald, 1824-1905; novelist.
[7] Perhaps William Young Moir, episcopal incumbent at Old Meldrum.
[8] James Chalmers Dean Fraser, poet and episcopalian incumbent at Banchory.
[9] Thomas Francis Bayard, 1828-98; Democratic senator for Delaware 1869-85; secretary of state 1885-93; ambassador in London 1893-7; threatened with impeachment 1895 for opposing protection.

26. 20 S. Trin.

Kept my bed. Saw Dr A. Clark. Read Ch. Qu. R. on Grosseteste and on Rome[1]—'Catherine & Crawford Tait'—she deserved a Memorial.[2]

27. M.

Wrote to Mrs H. Gladstone—Lady M. Alford—Madam Jung[3]—Miss Archer—J. Burt[4]—Mr Yorston[5]—T.E. Allen—Mr Guisoult—H. Hughes—Mr Ouvry. Rose at two: the enemy, I hope, beaten. Read 'Love Blinded' a *good* Italian one volume Novel: in translation. Resumed my work on the mass of letters awaiting me: and finished opening & sorting. Read Marie Antoinette[6]—Louis XIV et la F. Royale.[7] Dined with Mrs Birks.

28. Tu.

Wrote to Mr S. Morley (2)—Mr Waddy MP—Mr Billson—P. Harman—F. Allnutt—W. Morgan—Mr Taylor Innes—City Remembrancer—C.H. Williams[8]—Mr Adam MP—L. Joyce—R. Knight—Rev. J. Kay—Rev. W.H. Grove—Mr Stone—C. Laud—Rev. R.C. Jenkins—Rev. S. Baring Gould—J.A. Godley—Ch. Ewart—E. Arnold. Saw Mr Scott (Central N.)—Mr Adam MP.—Mr Waddy MP.—Scotts. Dined with our hospitable next door neighbour [Mrs Birks]. Read Marie Antoinette &c. Found Mr Waddy under a tenacious conviction that I am the coming man.

29. Wed.

Wrote to Mr Little—W. Goodman—Sec. Treasury—Mrs J. Stuart Wortley—C. Maguire—F. Ouvry—W. Grogan. Read Miss Bevington on Mallock.[9] Saw Mr Kearsley[10]—Lord Hartington—Mrs West—Mr Murray—Mrs Th. Dined with Edith Dumaresq and had 1½ hours conversation with the invalid, now certainly advanced in strength. Packing books, and arranging effects.

30. Th.

Wrote to Ld Norton—Earl of Rosebery—Mr Roberts MP[11]—Rev. W. Cuff[12]—J. Johnstone—Mr Donaldson—Maitre d'Hotel (Bedford)—Mr Sec. [W. M.] Evarts—Mr Knight—Scotts—Mr Stearn—F.A. White—Mr Shelley—J. Latey—

---

[1] *Church Quarterly Review*, ix. 31 (October 1879).

[2] W. Benham *Catherine and Crawford Tait. A memoir* (1879); many of her children died of scarlet fever.

[3] Probably the wife of Gustavus Jung, London merchant.

[4] Regretting he cannot accept Glasgow Liberal Association's address; *T.T.*, 29 October 1879, 6b; a decision later changed.

[5] C. H. Yorston of Edinburgh United Trades Council; on the campaign; Hawn P.

[6] See 9 Sept. 79.   [7] Probably in Tallemant or Bachaumont, see 6, 8 Nov. 79.

[8] Charles H. Williams of Clifton; earlier corresponded on Vaticanism; Hawn P.

[9] L. S. Bevington, 'Modern atheism and Mr Mallock', part i, *Nineteenth Century*, vi. 585 (October 1879).

[10] Thomas Harvey Kearsley of Green Street, Grosvenor Square.

[11] John Roberts, 1835-94; liberal M.P. Flintshire 1878-92.

[12] William Cuff, Baptist minister in Shoreditch.

C. Holland—Mr Westell—Mr Carr. Saw Dr Hood—Sir W. Harcourt—Mrs Th.— Mr McColl—Mr Knowles—Mr Grogan—Sir Jas Paget. Working on Parl. papers. Shopping. Dined with Mrs Birks. Read N.A. Review on the Slidell Correspondence.[1]

31. Fr. [Wellington College]

Wrote to Earl of Rosebery—Lady Huntingtower—Lady Portsmouth[2]—S. Parkhouse[3]—Sir Jas Watson—J.G.C. Hamilton—Herr Fleischer—Messrs Duncan—H. Wallis[4]—G. Willis—Mr Thomas—H.N.G. Saw W.H.G. 1¾–5. To Wellington College: a journey of 60 to cover 30. Everything is good & wholesome in this household: the children delightful, and full of health and beauty. Read Marie Antoinette &c.—Contemp. Rev. (Lit.) on W.E.G.[5] Much packing & sorting in A.M.

Sat. Novr One. 1879.

Wrote to Mrs Wynne—Sir C. Wood—Rev. Dr Nevins. Read Contemp. Rev. on the Ancien Regime—Marie Antoinette &c. Chapel 10 AM. Mr Fearon[6] preached extremely well. Saw Mr Fearon—Mr Randall—E. Wickham—Dr Orange.[7] Walked over to luncheon at Mr Raikes Currie's pleasant place: saw the beautiful Chapel. Small party to dinner.

2. S. 21 Trin.

Church 9. A.M. Midday—and 8 P.M. Hearty and edifying services. Read Contemp. Rev. on The Deluge—Moret, La Grande Devôte.[8] Wrote to M. de Lille— E.R. Russell—Mr Suffield. Walk with E. W[ickham]. A party of Masters in evg.

3. M. [Hawarden]

Chapel at 8.15 AM. Wrote to Mrs Mockler—H.J.G.—Mr Donaldson. Read Moret, La Grande Devôte. After thinking over the matter went to receive the School Address: & addressed the boys for ab. 40 min.[9] Then cut down three small birches. Off at 3 to Hawarden after packing & play with the very dear children. Arrived before eleven. A warm popular greeting at Saltney. All well & glad at our return of which my coming is an earnest. Saw Mr Griffin—Saw Rev. Mr [R. R.] Suffield—Bp of Oxford—Principal of Jesus.

[1] O. F. Aldis, 'Louis Napoleon and the Southern conspiracy', North American Review, cxxix. 342 (October 1879); see Ramm II, i. 105.

[2] Eveline, wife of 5th earl of Portsmouth and Carnarvon's sister; she d. 1906.

[3] Samuel Henry Parkhouse, poor-rate collector for Kensington.

[4] Henry Wallis, 1805–90; owned the French Gallery in Pall Mall; asked Gladstone, unsuccessfully, to sit for a portrait set in Westall's bookshop; Hawn P.

[5] Reviews of Gleanings by 'a liberal' and 'a conservative', Contemporary Review, xxxvi. 398 (November 1879).

[6] William Andrewes Fearon, 1841–1924; master at Winchester; headmaster of Durham 1882–4, of Winchester 1884–1901.

[7] James Leslie Randall, d. 1922; rector of Sandhurst 1878–80, archdeacon of Buckingham 1880–95 and William Orange, physician at Wokingham.

[8] By Eugène Moret (1879), on Madame de Maintenon.   [9] T.T., 4 November 1879, 9b.

4. Tu.

Ch. 8½ AM. Wrote to Rev. Mr Bateman—G.W. Smalley—Mr Hunter Blair[1]—J. Littleboy—R. Christian—Rev. J.B. Rowlands—Earl Granville—Mr Scudamore—C.B. Norman—J. Simmons—Mr J. Cowan—C.G.—M. Lewis—R. Nisbett—C.A. Reiss[2]—S. Samuel—J. Elford[3]—W.H. Watson. Dr Nevins[4] came: much conversation. The Rectory party dined. Axe-work with WHG. Read Moret, Grande Devôte—Case of Abbé Laurens.[5] Unpacking & dealing with the mass of papers.

5. Wed.

Ch 8¼ AM. Wrote to Mr Williams—Ld Cardwell—Rev. Mr Griffiths—Rev. S. Wilkinson[6]—J.J. Murphy—C.G.—Mr Slaughter[7]—Mr Lockyer[8]—N.J. Louis—Mr Thornton—Agnes. Finished felling a good sized sycamore. Dined at the Rectory. Walk & much conversation with Dr N., eccles. & secular, on U.S. War, trade, & Constitution. 12½-2. We saw Messrs T. & B. and settled with them the grave question of the deduction to be allowed from the rents. It is to be 15% and as a rule in kind. Read Moret—Louis XIV Biographies[9]—Abbé Laurens (finished).

6. Th.

Ch. 8¼ AM. Wrote to Messrs Watson—Mr Burne Jones—Rev. Mr Hobson—Sig. C. Ricchetti—Mr Gaffihin[10]—Mr Fairweather—Rev. R.A. Phenix[11]—M.F. Tupper—Mr Reed—C.G.—Mr Searle—Mr Lavin—Mr Balck—S. Owens. Dr Nevin went. Felled an alder with W. Read Moret, Grande Dévôte—Marie Antoinette &c.—Biographies of the Court of Louis XIV—Waddy on Finance[12]—Tallemant des Reaux.[13] Axe work with Willy. Prosecuted work on papers.

7. Fr.

Ch. 8¼ A.M. Wrote to W.A. Dumaresq—Rev. M. MacColl—Messrs Myers—Mr Salisbury—A. Seymour BP[14]—Mr MacQuoid—Mr Whittaker—R. Gladstone—C.G.—Dr Acland—Mr Davy—Mr Dorrien—Mr Ramsay[15]—Mr Robinson. Axe

[1] Forbes Cromartie Hunter Blair, undergraduate at Trinity, Cambridge, inviting Gladstone, presumably unsuccessfully, to join the 'Claypipe' debating society there; Hawn P.

[2] Charles A. Reiss of Princes Gate, London.

[3] John Elford of Homerton; on Philip II; Hawn P.

[4] R. J. Nevin of the U.S.A.; see 24 July 78.

[5] Abbé Laurens, *Le Cas d'un Curé Gallican, ou explication de l'infaillibilité du Pape et de l'Église Ultramontaine* (1875?).

[6] Samuel Wilkinson, d. 1907; vicar of Warrington 1872-90.

[7] Probably (Sir) William Capel Slaughter, 1857-1917; of Slaughter and May, solicitors.

[8] (Sir) (Joseph) Norman *Lockyer, 1836-1920; scientist; see 5 Mar. 73.

[9] Probably in Tallemant; see next day.

[10] *Sic*; unidentified.   [11] Nonconformist minister.

[12] S. D. Waddy, *Liberal and Conservative finance* (1879).

[13] G. Tallemant, Sieur des Réaux, *Les Historiettes . . . Mémoires pour servir à l'histoire du XVII siecle*, 2v. (1834-5).

[14] Albert Eden Seymour, vicar of Barnstable 1877.

[15] George Gilbert Ramsay, 1839-1921; professor of humanity at Glasgow 1863-1906; supplied the figures on students' careers used in diarist's Glasgow Rectorial on 5 December.

work, in solitude. Prosecuted my work on the chaos of papers. Read Moret, Grande Dévote—Marie Antoinette &c.—Whittaker on Free Trade[1]—Escott's 'England'.[2] The Rector came to tea & talk on parish and family.

8. Sat.

Ch. 8½ AM. Wrote to Bp of Down & Connor—Sir W.C. James—Mr M'Carthy MP—Professor Baynes—Major Manderson[3]—Miss Archer—Rev. Canon Moore[4]—Mr Brodrick—A.C. Yates—W. Morris—R. Pringle—Mr Shelley. Walk with the Rector. Saw Mr Vickers—Thom—Dr Burlingham—called on the Hursts. Read Marie Antoinette &c.—from Bachaumont (finished)[5]—La Grande Dévote (finished). C. came in evg.

9. 22 S. Trin.

Ch. morng and evg. Wrote to Mr Murphy—Messrs Watson & Smith—and Rev. Dr Hayman. Read Mozley's Sermons (New Vol)[6]—The tendre Dévote—Four Chapters of Mr Murphy's remarkable work.[7]

10. M.

Ch. 8¼ AM. Wrote to Sec. Metr. Distr. R.R. Co.—Earl of Pembroke—Dr Acland—Made Novikoff—E. Blair[8]—Archdn Blomfield—A. Balfour—Edgar Vincent[9]—Miss Anderson—Messrs Cassell—Mr Macdonald—Rev. Mr Cruttwell.[10] Felled an alder. Read the tendre Dévote—Rawlinson on Affghan War[11]—Adye on the Army.[12] Worked on arranging letters.

11. Tu.

Ch. 8¼-9½ AM with Holy Communion, for the coming Mission in the Parish. Wrote to Gen. Sir John Adye—Lord Cardwell—Lt Col. Barnett[13]—Mr Warburton—Capt. Vincent—Prof Blackie—Mr Macintosh—W.H.G.—Mr Knowles—Mr Escott—Mr Devoto[14]—H. George[15]—Mrs Wynne. Read the Tendre Dévote—

---

[1] (Sir) Thomas Palmer Whittaker, 1850-1919; manufacturer and newspaper owner; liberal M.P. Spen Valley 1892-1919; had sent his 'Free trade, reciprocity and foreign competition' (1879).

[2] T. H. S. Escott, *England; its people, polity and pursuits*, 2v. (1879).

[3] Thomas Claridge Manderson, major in Royal Engineers 1877; business untraced.

[4] Edward Moore, canon of Canterbury from 1867.

[5] Bachaumont [i.e. J. B. R. J. Lemer], *Scènes de la vie parisienne* (1878).

[6] J. B. Mozley, *Oxford university sermons* (1879).

[7] Joseph John Murphy, 1827-94; Quaker mill owner and author in Belfast; had sent the 2nd ed. (1879) of his *Habit and intelligence*.

[8] Probably Edward Stopford-Blair, d. 1885, landowner in Wigtownshire. Or see 4 Nov. 79.

[9] Edgar Vincent Vincent, 1857-1941; in the Guards 1877; in E. Roumelia 1880; worked on Turkish debt; financial adviser to Egypt 1883-9; governed Ottoman Bank 1889-97.

[10] Charles Thomas Cruttwell, 1847-1911; fellow of Merton 1870; headmaster of Bradfield 1878, of Malvern 1880-5; rector of Denton 1885-91.

[11] H. C. Rawlinson, 'The results of the Afghan War', *Nineteenth Century*, vi. 377 (August 1879).

[12] See above, vii. xcv and 1 Aug. 79.

[13] Henry Crosby Barry Barnett, lieut. colonel 1877 in Madras staff corps; business untraced.

[14] *Sic*; unidentified.

[15] Note of thanks to Henry George (1839-97; American land reformer and 'single taxer') for

George (U.S.) on Progress—Scherer on Louis Blanc's Engl. & on Louis XV. Axe work. Walk with C.

Queries on the Army.

1. Is the system of short service applicable as a general rule to India? (i.e. service of three years)
2. Is it applicable to the minor e.g. Colonial Emergencies: and could the Marines be made on a small scale available for these?
3. Is the system of reserves inapplicable to India?
4. To the officers, at least of certain grades?
5. Might it not now be applied to the Cavalry and Artillery?
6. With an abundance of recruits, might the minimum age of enlistment be raised to 19?
7. Is the British Army overweighted with Staff, & costly appointments at the head?
8. Is there no way of economising upon numbers except by reducing the number of men in each battalion?
9. Can the Cost of material be reduced by manufacturing less & using Contract & purchase more?
10. Can the Reserves be partially called out with propriety, except as to Volunteers?[1]

12. Wed.

Ch. 8½ AM. Wrote to Sec. State for Colonies—Mr Macmillan—Rev. Mr Suffield (2)[2]—Watson & Smith—R.B. Ladley BP—W. Thomson—T. Mitchell—F. Ouvry—Mr Giffen—Mr Hayward—G. Hyde[3]—W. Tolley.[4] Read Baker's Cyprus[5]—Dangers &c. of Engl. Protestm[6]—Une tendre Dévote—Case of Logiealmond.[7] Kibbled a Sycamore.

13. Th.

Ch. 8¼ A.M. Wrote to Lady Breadalbane—Mr Jos Arch—Mr Knowles—Mr Speller—Mr Stead—Mr Kelso—J. Fyfe—Rev. M. M'Coll—W.H.G.—Mr Godley—Mr Infield.[8] Axe work in aftn. Worked on the comparative effect of free trade legislation & Railways on our Exports.[9] Read Une Tendre Dévote—Randall's Tract[10]—Baker's Cyprus. Made an exordium for a possible Glasgow Address. Nine to dinner.

sending his *Progress and poverty* (privately printed 1879, published 1880); see H. George, *Life of Henry George* (1900), 323.

[1] Initialled and dated 11 November 1879, Add MS 44763, f. 156. Gladstone apparently sent these queries to Adye, who sent figures extracted from the Estimates, a table (drawn up with Campbell Bannerman) on the policy changes of the past two years and a mem. on the Afghan war; Add MS 44461, ff. 139-52.
[2] On foundation of Reading Junior Liberal Club; *T.T.*, 19 November 1879, 10f.
[3] His tailor in Oxford Street.
[4] Perhaps the London cabinet maker.
[5] S. W. Baker, *Cyprus as I saw it in 1879* (1879).
[6] Untraced tract.
[7] Glenalmond College affairs.
[8] Probably H. J. Infield, active liberal in Brighton.
[9] See 16 Dec. 79.
[10] J. Randall, probably *The Judicial Committee of the Privy Council* (1878).

14. Fr.

Ch. 8½ A.M. Wrote to Lord Rosebery—Sir A.H. Elton BP—Watson & Smith—J. Whittaker—Reeves & Turner—Rev. Mr Randall—Sir S. Scott & Co—W.H.G.—Mr Adam—L.J. Fish[1]—Mr Dawson—C. Groom. Worked on a big beech. Worked on an outline of my scheme of work for Midlothian. Read Une Tendre Dévote—Baker's Cyprus.

15. Sat.

Ch. 8½ AM. Wrote to Sig. Ricchetti—Sig. Blumenthal—Messrs Barker—A. Mitchell[2]—Mr Paley BP[3]—J. Hatfield—Mrs Wynne—Reeves & Turner—Scotts—J. Bailey—Mr Hayward—Mr Hoadley O—J. Wilson—G. Skinner.[4] Felled the Beech. Tea with Miss Scott: & conversation on her affairs. Also Mrs Stume on hers. Worked on a possible Glasgow Address. Read Une Tendre Dévote (finished)—Baker's Cyprus.

16. 23 S. Trin.

Ch mg & evg (H.C. at noon). Wrote to Mrs Wynne—Reeves and Turner. Read Dr Lee's trumpery Life of Mr Hawker[5]—Stevens's Poem.[6]

17. M.

Ch. 8½ A.M. Wrote to Mr Maclagan MP—Ld Rosebery—Mr Creighton Tel. (2)—J. Nixon[7]—Mr Binney—Rev. J. Morgan—Rev. R.H. Smith[8]—Mrs Stuart Wortley—J. Cowan—J. Taylor—Mr Waters—J. Henry—Mr Simpson. Saw J. Bailey and settled for a new extension of bookshelves. Kibbling the beech of Saturday. Read Baker's Cyprus. Worked on materials for Midlothian. And a little on attempt at a Rectorial Address.

18. Tu.

Ch. 8½ A.M. Wrote to Messrs MacCracken—Mr Giffen—Mr Grolley—Mr Stevens—Mr Crawford—W. Bayliss—C. Rossetti[9]—Reeves & Turner—H. Gallimore—Rev. Mr M'Govern[10]—Rev. J.R. Jenkins—Rev. G.W. Brameld. Worked on papers for Midlothian. And on Glasgow Address. Small dinner party. Saw Mr R. Frost. Read Baker's Cyprus—and several Tracts.

---

[1] Of Accrington, on church and state; *T.T.*, 18 November 1879, 6d.

[2] (Sir) Arthur *Mitchell, 1826-1909; professor of ancient history at Royal Scottish Academy from 1878; sat on sundry commissions; K.C.B. 1887.

[3] Probably Frederick Apthorp Paley, classical scholar; see Add MS 44240, f. 216.

[4] Deptford auctioneer and constituent.

[5] See 16 Sept. 77.

[6] W. Stevens, *Truce of God and other poems* (1879).

[7] Christopher J. Nixon, Dublin physician and professor at the Catholic university, had sent an inaugural address; Hawn P.

[8] Robert Harvey Smith, minister in Helensburgh; on the Campaign; Hawn P.

[9] Perhaps the poet, though no letter traced.

[10] J. B. McGovern, minister in Manchester; on Dante; Hawn P.

19. Wed.

Ch. 8½ A.M. Wrote to Duke of Argyll—Rev. Mr MacColl—O.B. Cole BP—MacCrackens—Mr Rignold—Mr Pilkington[1]—Reeves & Turner—Ed. Scots Banking Mag.—Mr Tennant[2]—The Lord Mayor. Conversation with S.E.G. on the idea of making him Diocesan Proctor. Began upon a large Ash. Worked on Glasgow Address, which I now think will take form. Also upon political papers. Read Hist. 19th Century—Boswellianea—Sir J. Suckling, Poems & Tract.[3]

20. Th.

Ch. 8½ A.M. Wrote to Principal of Glasgow [University]—J. Hamilton—W. Latimer—W.P. Adam—Rev. J.M. Capes—Col. Brackenbury—Mr Trevithick[4]—Robn Gladstone—Messrs Carpenter & Westley[5]—Mr Johnes O[6]—Sir J. Watson—R. Frost—G. Wright—A. Billson—M. Lebey—Ed. D. News—Ed. Scotsman. Read Swift—Sheridan—Pope's Dunciad. & Worked on an Address for Glasgow University. Also on the big ash. Read the Lancashire Chap's Lament[7] aloud in the School in evg for the amusement of the Hawardeners.

21. Fr.

Ch. 8½ AM. Wrote to Ed. Border Advertiser—Ed. Ben Brierley's Journal[8]—Miss E. Church BP—Miss Cockcroft O—Reeves & Turner—MacCrackens—Sig. Giacchetti[9]—Rev. Mr Leeman—Rev. Mr Jarvie[10]—Mr Johnstone Wallace—Mr Bowie—Mr Ground—Mr Nicol—Mr Johnstone—Mr Sellar—Mr Godley—Mr Barnes BP.[11] Again worked on the big ash; wh is obstinate. Read Johnson. Worked on political tracts & documents for my Northern Campaign. Saw St[ephen] respecting the Proctorate: wh I conditionally encouraged.

22. Sat. [Courthey, Liverpool]

Ch. 8½ A.M. Wrote to Duke of Argyll—E.C. Petgrave[12]—Mr Paterson—A. Creeson—W. Barnes BP—C. Bolton—G. Hopwood—Mr Cafflisch—E.A. Edwards—Mr Pumphrey—Mr Morris Wood—Town Clerk of Edinburgh[13]—G.E. Troup[14]—Mr Wahab [sic]—C. Ross—A.L. Bruce.[15] Preparing for departure &

---

[1] Perhaps Frederick P. Pilkington, Edinburgh architect.

[2] (Sir) Charles *Tennant, 1823-1906; chemical manufacturer; liberal M.P. Glasgow 1879-80, Peebles 1880-6; cr. bart. 1885.

[3] Perhaps the 1874 ed. with introduction by W. C. Hazlitt.

[4] Probably F. H. Trevithick of Paignton, vice-president of E. Devon liberal association.

[5] Opticians in Regent Street.

[6] Herbert Owen Johnes of Garthmyl, Montgomeryshire.

[7] Probably 'Hard times; or, the weyvur to his wife by a "Lancashire Lad" (James Bowker)', in J. Harland, *Lancashire Lyrics* (1866), 304; on the cotton famine.

[8] Neither published.

[9] Francesco Giacchetti, transport official in Turin; on George Stephenson's virtues; Hawn P.

[10] Alexander Jarvie, 'evangelist' in Glasgow.

[11] W. Barnes; not further identified.

[12] Ezekiel Charles Petgrave, solicitor and author.   [13] William Skinner.

[14] George Elmslie Troup, Scottish free-churchman and author.

[15] Alexander L. Bruce of Edinburgh.

working on materials for campaign. S. & I brought down the great ash, nearly dispatched last evg. 3½-6. To Courthey. Saw Rev. S.E.G.—Mr Billson—& Mr Russell. The tradition of hospitality flourishes as ever here. Read Scherer—Beavis on U.S.[1]

23. *Preadv. Sunday.*

Seaforth Ch 11 A.M: an interesting occasion for me. Long drive each way in rain & cold. Childwall Ch. aftn. Wrote to Principal Caird—Sir Jas Watson—Mrs Hampton—Mr T. Roberts—Rev. Mr Leeman. Read Ecce Christianus[2]—Scherer Etudes.

24. *M.* [*Dalmeny House, Edinburgh*][3]

Set out at 8¾: the journey from Liverpool was really more like a triumphal procession. I had to make short speeches at Carlisle Hawick & Galashiels: very large numbers were assembled & at Edinburgh where we only arrived at a quarter past five, the scene even to the West end of the City was extraordinary, both from the numbers and the enthusiasm, here and there a solitary groan or howl. We drove off to Dalmeny with Ld Rosebery and were received with fireworks & torches. I have never gone through a more extraordinary day. Read Scherer.

25. *Tu.*

Wrote to Mr Clapperton[4]—Mr Piper[5]—Mr Waterston[6]—Mr Ferguson.[7] Worked through the early day on the great mass of matter offering for discussion: Mr Böhme[8] at the same time working on his bust of me. Off at 2.15. Much enthusiasm on the road. Spoke in the Music Hall 1½ hour.[9] Then to the Liberal rooms to see Sir Jas Watson & Mr Adam. Then to the Council Rooms where I received an Address & spoke in reply. Returned to Dalmeny before seven. Read Scherer. Wrote late at night, against my rules, for Gl. Address. Conversation with Mr Böhme—Ld R.—Ld Dalrymple.[10]

26. *Wed.*

Wrote to Mr Brock—Mr [H. E.] Crum Ewing—Mr Forbes Mackenzie.[11] Read Scherer. Walk with Ld Rosebery. Saw Mr Adam—Mr Douglas.[12] 2.30-8.30. To

---

[1] Perhaps L. U. Beavis, 'The nation's capital is moveable' (1871); on Washington.

[2] By [W. D. Ground] (1879).

[3] Rosebery's house, in the country 7 miles W. of Edinburgh (see 23 Nov. 39). Reports of most of the speeches of the campaign, corrected from *The Scotsman's* reports, are in W. E. Gladstone, *Political speeches in Scotland, November and December 1879*, ed. J. J. Reid (1879, reprinted, with introduction by M. R. D. Foot 1971).

[4] See 24 Dec. 79.   [5] Frederick Piper of the Press Association; Hawn P.

[6] Probably the Edinburgh stationer.   [7] See 10 Dec. 79.

[8] (Sir) Joseph Edgar *Boehm, 1834-90; sculptor; cr. bart. 1889; this bust was commissioned by Rosebery and is at Dalmeny.

[9] Also printed in Bassett, *Speeches*, 553.

[10] John Hew Dalrymple, 1848-1914; 11th earl of Stair 1903; on the platform at Dalkeith.

[11] Probably Colin James (Forbes) Mackenzie, 1835-96, of Portmore, Peebles.

[12] Probably John Douglas, Edinburgh correspondent of the *Glasgow Herald*.

Dalkeith. Addressed 3000 people $1\frac{1}{2}$ hour. Then (after tea at provost Mitchell's[1] and scores of introductions) to a 'Ladies" meeting, with Committees also, where presents were given to C. & I spoke again.

27. Th.

Wrote to Ld Granville—Made O. Novikoff—Mr J. Moore—Rev. R.H. Smith—Mr J. Inglis[2]—Sir [T.] E. Colebrooke MP—Ld Provost of Perth Tel.—Ld Mayor of London. Read Scherer. Saw Mr Tennant. Mr Böhme worked as before. Off at $1\frac{1}{2}$ to West Calder where I spoke I fear $1\frac{3}{4}$ h. which they say was the time at Edinburgh. The enthusiasm, great along the road, was at the centre positively overwhelming. Returned to a dinner of forty covers: spoke on toast.

28. Fr.

Wrote to Mr Mayerowicz[3]—Ld Provost Perth—Mr Stuart Glennie—Mr Anderson—Mr Pryer[4]—Mr Rollo—Mr Bright—A. Allan—W.S. Moir. Sat to a photographer. Drove to Hopetoun[5] with Ld R. by the beautiful shore road: a great home with a soupçon of Vanbrugh. Conversation with Ld R. on the leadership.[6] Received Leith Address & spoke my thanks. A luncheon of 300: made the circuit of the company. Saw Mr Adam (& agreed on the affair of E. Aberdeenshire)[7]—Mr Jenkins respecting Dundee[8]—Mr Richardson (Lib. Address)—Mr [blank] (Edinb. Scot). Read Scherer. Saw Mr Adam—Mr Ward U.S.[9]—W.H.G. (on Secretary)—Ly Grant[10] and others. Read Scherer—19th Cent. Irish Land.[11]

[1] Alexander Mitchell.

[2] Many of this name in Edinburgh.

[3] Perhaps Brachiah Mayerovitz, Hebrew scholar.

[4] Perhaps Thomas Pryor, Greenwich factory owner.

[5] Seat near Linlithgow of John Adrian Louis Hope, 1860-1908; 6th earl of Hopetoun; cr. marquis of Linlithgow 1902; a tory.

[6] Rosebery noted in his diary (Dalmeny MSS); 'I drove with Mr G to Hopetoun.... He encouraged me to speak very frankly to him as to his position & said that Bright was the repository of his views on that subject & that he would write to him that afternoon. He shewed me his letter afterwards in which he recalled to him the five reasons which he had given Bright at Hawarden agst. his resumption of the leadership. 1. That his physical strength was not equal to it 2. that the work to be done was great and ungrateful 3. that he would encounter a more personal & bitter opposition than anyone else 4. that he was perfectly loyal to Granville as the leader of the party 5. The personal opposition of the Queen to him'; the letter to Bright (Morley, ii. 599) mentions Hartington as well as Granville.

[7] Sir A. H. Gordon (see 22 July 55) won E. Aberdeenshire as a tory 1875, was unopposed as a liberal 1880.

[8] E. Jenkins, a liberal M.P. (see 26 Apr. 75), withdrew from the Dundee contest 1880, contesting Edinburgh as an independent imperialist 1881. Gladstone declined the freedom of Dundee, because of shortage of time, accepting it in 1890; Dundee Advertiser, 2 December 1879.

[9] Samuel Ward, 1814-84; American author and financier; a friend of Rosebery; later letters in Add MS 44484.

[10] Susan, née Ferrier, wife of Sir A. *Grant, principal of Edinburgh university.

[11] Nineteenth Century, vi. 953 (December 1879).

29. Sat.

Wrote to Mr Crossley B.P.—T.W. Snagge[1]—Mr Bartholomew[2]—Mr Mac-dougall—Mr Brodie—Mr Godley—Mr Potts—Mr Minchin[3]—Mr Nicolson. 2¼-7¼. To Edinburgh: spoke 1¼ hour on Finance to 5000 people or more: then for some 20 or 25 minutes to a wonderful meeting of 20000 at the Waverley market. People were continually handed out over the heads who had fainted and were as if dead.

30. Adv. S.

10-5. To Edinb. Cathedral mg & St Giles aft.[4]—Saw the restorations—Luncheon at Royal Hotel—Tel. to Principal Caird with List of Doctors[5]—conversation with Dr Wallace—Ld Aberdeen. Much conversation with Rosebery. Read Scherer—Cath. Presb. on Religion in Holland.[6]

Dec One 1879. [Taymouth Castle, Perthshire][7]

Wrote to Mr Taverner Knott[8]—Mr Ouvry—Mr Findlay—R. Corrie (O)[9]—R. Knight—Mr Hirsch[10]—Mrs Montgomery—A.H. Greaves—Dean Stanley—S. Grogan—Sir Jas Watson l. and Tel. After planting five trees, & arranging papers, & setting aside gifts & addresses—both very numerous—for separate packing, off at 11¼. Reached Taymouth at 6½. Short speeches at Inverkeithing & Dunfermline—Two speeches & two drives at Perth: finally a speech at Aberfeldy. The enthusiasm everywhere marvellous seemed to culminate in this warm-hearted little town. We were greeted at T. with the utmost kindness. More gifts, more addresses. Read Hodgson's Turgot.[11]

2. Tu.

Wrote to Sir J. Watson. Worked six hours on my Glasgow Address. Saw Mr Corrie—Mr Ramsay—Lady B—Lady Airlie—Ld C. Campbell—Principal Tulloch [of St Andrews]. Read Scherer—Osborn on India.[12] Drive & walk on Drummond Hill. Killin deputation & Address in morning: spoke in reply.

---

[1] (Sir) Thomas William Snagge, 1837-1914; barrister; see Add MS 44666, f. 145.
[2] Probably John George *Bartholomew, 1860-1920; Edinburgh cartographer.
[3] J. George Minchin, London banker and active liberal.
[4] i.e. Scott's episcopalian masterpiece in Palmerston Place in the morning, the presbyterian 'cathedral' in the afternoon.
[5] Arrangements for 5 Dec. 79.
[6] The Catholic Presbyterian, ii. 401 (December 1879).
[7] Seat of Lord Breadalbane, see 15 May 76.
[8] Portrait painter in Edinburgh; portrait displayed at the Edinburgh Corn Exchange during the Midlothian campaign in April 1880; see Knott to Gladstone, 4 April 1880, Hawn P.
[9] Of Corrie and Hanson, Edinburgh Baltic traders.
[10] H. Hirsch, on difficulties of Jews in Roumania; T.T., 20 December 1879, 116.
[11] W. B. Hodgson, Turgot; his life, times and opinions. Two lectures (1870).
[12] R. D. Osborn, 'India under Lord Lytton', Contemporary Review, xxxvi. 553 (December 1879).

3. *Wed.*

Wrote to Miss Rose—Sir J. Watson—Eytinge (Tel.)[1] Worked hard on my Glasgow Address: perhaps 6 hours or more. Walk after luncheon: fine bright frost all this time. Mr Campbell sang incomparable comic songs in evg. Conversation with Pr. Tulloch—& others.

4. *Th.* [*Glasgow*]

Wrote to T., Johnstone—Mr Underhill[2]—C.J. Thomson[3]—Mrs Buchanan—J. Morton—Mr Gowland—D. Pringle[4]—Mrs Th. Walked to (near) Aberfeldy. Farewell in a few sentences to the crowd there: & off with many of our party to Glasgow. Fervid crowds at every station. The torchlight procession at Glasgow was a subject for Turner. Large dinner and evening party at good, kind, Sir J. Watson's.[5]

5. *Frid.*

An overpowering day. After a breakfast party, I put my notes in order for the afternoon. At 12, delivered the inaugural Address to 5000.[6] The blue caps as well as the red cheered fervently at the close. Then went to the Academical luncheon, where I spoke. Away at 4. At 5.15 off to St Andrew's Hall. Spoke 1½ hour to 6500 or 7000. Finally at 9 to the City Hall: spoke again to 3000. Did not God of His mercy wonderfully bear me through?

6. [*Dalzell, Motherwell*]

Wrote to Mr Mitchell[7]—Mr Craig—and Mr Adam. Saw Mr Adam: chiefly on the Liverpool banquet. Off at 11¾ to Dalzell:[8] so pretty. Addresses & speech at Motherwell on the way. The departure from Glasgow was *royal*. Saw Hamilton Palace in aft. How deeply mournful! Then received the Freedom from Hamilton, & spoke. Large party in aft of Lanarkshire Liberals: & some 24 at dinner. Much interesting conversation with Mr Fraser[9] on family history. Read Scherer. A most friendly & pleasant party here.

7. *2 S. Adv.*

We drove to Hamilton mg: for prayers & Holy C.—Motherwell Presb. Church in evg. I rather like the older Presb. way. Wrote to six of my correspondents: & got some reading.

---

[1] *Sic*; unidentified.   [2] Charles Underhill, Edinburgh surgeon.
[3] Active in Edinburgh and Musselburgh liberal politics, wrote establishing a distant relationship; Hawn P.   [4] David Pringle of Leith; sent respects; Hawn P.
[5] His stockbroker, with whom he stayed; Watson's 'goodness' was rather suspect, see above, vii. cix.
[6] His Glasgow rectorial was published in his *Political Speeches* (1879).
[7] John Mitchell of Mossley on diarist's supposed faggot vote in 1846; *T.T.*, 11 December 1879, 9f.
[8] Staying with J. C. Carter-Hamilton of Dalzell; liberal M.P.; see 23 Jan. 71.
[9] See 3 Nov. 57; 'I was fortunate enough to meet Mr Frazer . . . and learned much from him about the family; though he has not quite established the descent yet'; to Sir T. Gladstone, 13 December 1879, Hawn P.

8. [Hawarden]

Off after breakfast. Great stir all the way. Inevitable speeches at Preston Wigan Warrington Chester besides words elsewhere. At Chester we were met by a torchlight procession of working men, some thousands, with bands: probably 20000 men in the streets. No police visible. Reached Hawarden, amid demonstrations, for dinner.

9. Tu.

Rose between 10 & 11: nursing my throat. But in aftn I joined Willy in felling a sycamore. Revised my Rectorial Address: made some notes: & sent it off to Mr Murray for publication, with a letter of instructions. Worked further on the revision of my Speeches, & dispatched a portion of the corrected proof to Mr Reid.[1] Wrote also to the Editor of the Scotsman a letter respecting the ends of various threads.[2] Continued my unpacking and work on accumulations. Conversation with W. Read Scherer.

10. Wed.

Wrote to Mr Reid (2)—Made Novikoff—Mr Ferguson Dft[3]—Mrs J. Stuart Wortley. Church 8½ AM. Axe work with WHG. Worked hard upon the proofs of my speeches & sent them off with two letters to Mr Reid. Read Scherer. F. Cavendish came: conversation with him. C. laid up: overdone I think with the interests of our journey.

11. Th.

Ch. 8½ A.M. Wrote to Mayor of Chester—J.J. Reid BP—Mr Crawford BP—Mr Corstorphine BP[4]—Jas Rorrison—J. Ferguson—Rev. C.H. Brooke[5]—Rev. J. Brown—Sec. Midland R.R.—Rev. Mr Collett[6]—Mr Harrison MP.[7]—Mr Wickham Inskip—R. Butcher—Mr Beilby (O)—Mr Hunter—Mr Lindsay—Mr Carrel—T. Orrock[8]—M. Hudson—P. Clarkson—Mr Ticcolson—Mr Murdock—Mr Crilly— Dr Haslett. Finished correction of the Speeches in Scotland. We brought down a sycamore: with labour and damage. Read Scherer. Saw the Rector (Mr Ward)—F. Cavendish.

[1] John James Reid, 1844-89; Edinburgh advocate and secretary of E. and N. of Scotland liberal association, which sponsored publication; he ed. and wrote a preface to *Political speeches*, and was one of the chief organizers of the campaign.

[2] Published as 'Mr Gladstone on some Objections to his Speeches', *The Scotsman*, 11 December 1879, 5a.

[3] J. Ferguson, president of Glasgow Home Rule Association; declining to support proposal for parliamentary inquiry into home rule; *T.T.*, 24 December 1879, 6e.

[4] William Corstorphine of Glasgow, had written in admiration; Hawn P.

[5] Charles Hyde Brooke, translator of French religious works.

[6] Perhaps Edward Collett, curate, then vicar, of Bower Chalke.

[7] James Fortescue Harrison, 1819-?; liberal M.P. Kilmarnock 1874-80.

[8] Probably Thomas Orrock, Edinburgh boot-maker.

1879.

Mon. Nov. 24	1. Carlisle	500
	2. Hawick	4,000
	3. Galashiels	8,000
Tues. 25	4. Edinb. Music Hall	2,500
	5. Edinb. City Hall	250
Wed. 26	6. Dalkeith Corn Exch.	3,500
	7. Dalkeith Ladies & Committee	750
Thursd. 27	8. West Calder Assembly	3,500
	9. Dalmeny, after dinner	50
Friday 28	10. Dalmeny, Leith Address	50
Sat. 29	11. Edinb. Corn Exchange	5,000
	12. Edinb. Waverley Market	20,000
Mon. Dec. 1	13. Inverkeithing Address	500
	14. Dunfermline ditto	3,000
	15. Perth, Freedom	1,500
	16. Perth, Open Air, Addresses	4,000
	17. Aberfeldie, Address	500
Tues. Dec. 2	18. Killin Address, Taymouth	50
Thurs. Dec. 4	19. Sir J. Watson's, after dinner	30
Fri. Dec. 5	20. Inaugural Address Glasg.	5,000
	21. University Luncheon	150
	22. St. Andrew's Hall	6,500
	23. City Hall	2,500
Sat. Dec. 6	24. Motherwell, Addresses	2,000
	25. Hamilton Freedom (Dalziel)	100
Mon. Dec. 8	26. Carlisle, Station	1,000
	27. Preston, Station	2,000
	28. Wigan, outside ditto	6,000
	29. Warrington, Station	1,000
	30. Chester, Procession	3,000
		86,930

There were speeches running from six or eight minutes up to an hour & three quarters. There were some shorter addresses to crowds at stations, and acknowledgments of votes of thanks.

Those above given occupied about $15\frac{1}{2}$ hours.[1]

12. Fr.

Ch. $8\frac{1}{2}$ AM. The Post which brought 73 letters & packets yesterday fell today to 57! It is a terrible oppression. Yet the creation of an office would probably be worse. Wrote to Mr Kibble White[2]—Mr MacPhilpin (Tuam News)[3]—A.L. Gladstone—Mr Duncan, Abn—Rev. Mr Sandilands[4]—Makhom Lal Day[5]—Rev W.J.

[1] Initialled and dated 11 December 1879, Add MS 444763, f. 164. Figures in holograph listed in two columns.

[2] Sc. Kibblewhite; of the Morden Arms, Greenwich?

[3] No copies of this paper found extant.

[4] Percival Richard Renorden Sandilands, 1826-90; vicar of Chudleigh 1875-90.

[5] Lal Behari Day, 1824-94; Indian educationalist; author of Recollections of Alexander Duff (1879) who ordained him into the Scottish Free Church, which strongly opposed the Vernacular Press Act.

Gordon[1]–Sig. Lesciotti BP–Mr J. Newlands–Rev. Sir G.W. Cox–Rev. T.W. Mossman–Mr Glendinning–Rev. B.W. Savile–E.L. Stanley–Mrs Rothery[2]– Dss of Leinster–Chancr of Exchr–J. Coleshill–F.W. Newman–H.B. Dutton– C. Cumming–Mr Ouvry–G. Paton–Mr Loudon (O)–E.C. Ward–Mr Ramsay (O)–Dr Baker–Mr Sherlock–R.R. Davies–A.J. Lloyd–G. Onslow–D. Bryce– R. Wilson–Mr Furse jun.[3]–Mr Barber (O)–J.J. Reid–J.G. Bally–J.T. Knowles– Mr Marples: 40 in all. Wolverton came. Much conversation. Twelve to dinner. Read Scherer. Walk with F.C.

13. Sat.

Ch. 8½ AM. Wrote to Sir Thos Gladstone–Miss Graham–Lord H. Scott MP– M. Gennadios–Mr Murray–Watsons–Scotts–Sir Jas Watson–Rev Mr M'Coll–Mr Rathbone MP–Sig. Loverdo–G. Harrison jun.–Messrs Riving- ton–Rev. Canon Hose[4]–Rev. Dr Hebert–M.C. Sadlier[5]–Mr Paumpakes[6]–T.B. Potter MP–T.A. Antony–Mr M'Laren–Mr Laing MP–Mr Britten–F. Lucas– Mr Isard[7]–Mr O'Byrne–J. Field–Mr Ingham[8]–Mr Perkins–Mr Evans (O)–J. Ranken[9]–C.T. Davis. Walk with Ld Wolverton, and conversation with him on the Leadership. C. better. Twelve to dinner. Afternoon party of neighbours to see the presents. Read Loring on Indian Finances[10]–Macmillan on Colour Sense.[11]

14. 3. S. Adv.

Ch 11 AM and 6½ P.M. Wrote to Rev. J. Gordon-Milne–Sir Thos G.–Mrs Collet–W. Barnes. Read Armstrong[12]–Mossman & St Cath. of Genoa on Purgatory[13]–Thos a Kempis–Longman on religion.[14]

15. M.

Ch. 8½ AM. Wrote to Watson & Smith–Mr Lawson–Mr Agnew–Mr Shiells[15]– D. Lyon–F. Ouvry–Chr Bushell–J. Howell–R. Irvine–Miss A. Wilson. Placed a few books in the new bookcases. Walk with W. & a party. Spent the forenoon

---

[1] Perhaps William Ireland Gordon, minister in Walkerburn.

[2] Probably the wife of H. C. Rothery; see 1 July 62.

[3] Perhaps Charles Wellington Furse, 1821-1900; vicar of Cuddesdon 1873, archdeacon of West-minster 1894.

[4] George Frederick Hose, 1838-1922; archdeacon of Singapore 1874, bp. there 1881-1908.

[5] (Sir) Michael Ernest *Sadler (1861-1943, educationalist), then a boy at Rugby; sent pro-liberal result of school debate; Hawn P.

[6] Name scrawled.

[7] Joseph Isard of Holland Road, London.

[8] Robert Wood Ingham, 1846-1928; barrister; judge 1892.

[9] Probably James Rankin of Edinburgh; corresponded on church affairs 1880; Hawn P.

[10] Apparently *sic*; not found.

[11] *Macmillan's Magazine*, xli. 125 (December 1879).

[12] E. J. Armstrong, *Poetical works* (1877).

[13] The 'Treatise on purgatory' from *Vita e dottrina* by St Catherine of Genoa, 1447-1510, the mystic about whom F. von Hügel wrote.

[14] Possibly W. Longman and F. B. Harvey, 'Church Rate Legislation' (1868).

[15] Probably Ross Shiells, Edinburgh merchant.

in discussing my notes on comparative fruits of Railways and Free Trade. Read Scherer—and [blank.]

16. Tu.

No Morning Prayer. Saw the Mission Priests. Wrote to Mr Dannatt jun.[1]—Rev. D.D. Stewart[2]—D.W. Lowe—C. Tennant MP—Mr Johnson—Mr Williams—Mr Armitage—Dr Mackenzie—Mr Somerville—Rev. Mr Theodosius[3]—Rev. M. MacColl—A.M. Fairbairn[4]—Mr Lesty[5]—Mr Burnet—Mr Purcell—Mr Shapcoll— Mr Palmer—Mr Morley—L. Lewis[6]—Mr Wilson—Mrs Page (O)—Rev. Mr Capes. Made a sort of beginning at 6 P.M. to a paper in prosecution of yesterday's conversation.[7] But I am not equal, at that time of the evening, to the effort of composition. Read Scherer—finished Hodgson's Turgot. Walk with Mr Sidgwick[8] & much interesting conversation then and aliter.

17. Wed.

Ch. 8½ AM. Wrote to Earl of Rosebery (2)—Mrs D. Gladstone—Lord H. Scott MP—Ed. Daily Review—Mrs J.S. Wortley—Rev. Dr Hebert—Mrs Chamier—E.H. Brodie—R. Leake[9]—S.D. Waddy—W. Breck—Mr Harrold—T. Lea MP[10]—C.C. Hall[11]—Symons. Axe work with WHG. Conversation with Mr Sidgwick. Read Luckock's After Death[12]—Sir G. Cox's Reply.[13]

18. Th.

Ch. 8½ AM. Wrote to Manager Press Assn (Tel)—Abbé Laurens[14]—Rev. Mr Carsclaw (O)—Ld Wolverton—Sir J. Watson—J. Field—F. Ouvry—Mr Murray— Mr Collins—Mr Armitage—Messrs Stewart—Rev. S.S. Lewis—Rev. W. Mottram—Mr Artley—Ed. Falkirk Herald[15]—Mr A.E. West—Mr Lang—T. Angus—Mr Lithgow—Mr Ransom—A. Brook. Wrote on Mythology:[16] and on Economics: together, rather too much. I am not very fit for composition after 5

---

[1] Thomas William Dannatt, Greenwich auctioneer.

[2] David Dale Stewart, rector of Coulsdon; published 'Evangelical opinion in the nineteenth century' (1879), a development of Gladstone's article.

[3] James Henry Theodosius, 1824-93; chaplain of Coton Hall asylum from 1873.

[4] Andrew Martin *Fairbairn, 1838-1912; congregationalist; principal of Airedale college 1877, of Mansfield college, Oxford 1886-1909.

[5] Written over another name.

[6] Probably Lewis Lewis; curate of Chirk 1872-80; rector of Melverley 1881.

[7] Published as 'Freetrade, railways, and the growth of commerce', Nineteenth Century, vii. 367 (February 1880).

[8] Henry Sidgwick and his wife, Eleanor, were staying at the Castle.

[9] On difficulties of Jews in Roumania; T.T., 20 December 1879, 11b.

[10] (Sir) Thomas Lea, 1841-1902; liberal (unionist) M.P. Kidderminster 1868-74, Donegal 1879-85, S. Londonderry 1886-1900; cr. bart. 1892.

[11] Charles Cuthbert Hall, wrote on religious subjects, especially India.

[12] H. M. Luckock, After death (1879).

[13] One of the many controversial pamphlets of Rev. Sir G. W. *Cox.

[14] Abbé Joseph Laurens, published on Vaticanism (1879); Hawn P; see 4 Nov. 79.

[15] On his controversial quotation of Lady Nairne's 'Land o'the leal'; Falkirk Herald, 20 December 1879.

[16] Start of 'Religion, Achaian and Semitic', Nineteenth Century, vii. 710 (April 1880).

PM. The Sidgwicks went. He is very noteworthy, as is she, though rather taciturn in company. Felled a sycamore with W. Read Scherer—Abbé Laurens.

19. Fr.

Ch. 8¼ A.M. Wrote to Duchess of Marlborough—Countess Russell—Editor of Scotsman[1]—ditto Private—Lord F. Cavendish—Mr G. Harrison jun.—Professor Robertson—Rev. T. Rogers—Mr Imrie—Mr Waddy—Mr Marcy—J.J. Reid—W.E. Best[2]—J.L. Rice[3]—Mr Roberts. Axe work with W.H.G. Read F. Russell on Election Expenses[4]—Ames, Hist. of Printing[5]—Scherer, on Biran.[6] Wrote on Economics.

20. Sat.

Ch 8¼ AM. Wrote to Mr Jas Robertson—J.B. Newman[7]—Messrs Watson—Messrs Dutton—Rev. E.S. Cooper—Mr Rathbone MP—J.J. Reid—A.E. West—J. Murray—Mr Cameron—Mr Burnet. Again revised Speeches. They reach 255 pages! Worked on a large Sp. Chestnut with W. Wrote a little on Economics. Read [blank.]

21. 4 S. Adv.

Ch mg & evg. Wrote to Ld Granville—Bp of Ely—Rev. Mr Ffoulkes. Read Life of Wilberforce[8]—Ffoulkes's Sermon[9]—Jenkins on Modern Atheism[10]—Sermons and Tracts.

22. M.

Ch. 8¼ A.M. Wrote to Lord Wolverton—Mr Cumming—Mr Jesse Taylor—Sir J. Fergusson—Mrs Buchanan—Mr Anderson—Mr Maitland—J. Cunningham—H.B. Dutton—Mr Connell—P. Kenny—D. Allan—J. Adam—J. Walker—R. Knight—D. of Argyll. W. & I felled a tall chestnut. Worked on Economic paper. Read Catullus—Jenkins on Atheism—Life of Bp Wilberforce. Saw WHG. respecting the Colliery and wrote draft.

23. Tu.

Ch. 8¼ AM. Wrote to Earl Granville—Ed. Scotsman[11]—Do private—Do BP—Mr Sutherland—Ld H. Scott MP—F.H. Turner[12]—J.P. Devine—Messrs Watson &

---

[1] Replying to criticism; *The Scotsman*, 22 December 1879, 4.
[2] William Edward Best, d. 1906; chaplain of Oxford poor law union 1872-95.
[3] Isaac L. Rice of New York; sent a pamphlet on music; Hawn P.
[4] Untraced.
[5] J. Ames, *Typographical antiquities* (1749).
[6] On M. de Biran; see 22 Oct. 79n.
[7] Possibly John B. Newman, American physician and author.
[8] First volume of S. Wilberforce's *Life*; see 6 Aug., 3 Sept. 79.
[9] E. S. Ffoulkes, 'Dogma distinguished from doctrine. A sermon' (1879).
[10] Probably one of R. C. Jenkins' many tracts.
[11] On faggot votes; *The Scotsman*, 25 December 1879, 5.
[12] Frederick Holden Turner, London solicitor.

Smith—Mr Ouvry—E.F. Davis—R. Wilson—A. Ramsden—D. Rutter—J. Cruess. Walk with the Rector: & three Parish calls. Read Northcotes Financial Speech: with satisfaction![1]—Bunbury's Geography[2]—Wilberforce's Life—Catullus. Worked on the materials & figures for my Economic paper. Also on my Annual Sketch of property.

24. Wed.

Ch. 8½ AM. Wrote to Messrs Cranston—Messrs Stewart & Clapperton—Mr Bourke MP—Mr Adam MP—Mr Newmarch—W.T. Stead—Mr Grahame—Mr Hosking—Mr Marcy—Mr Webb. Worked on Economic Paper. Felled a tree with W. & H.—Read Catullus—Bunbury, Geography—Life of Wilberforce.

25. Th. Xmas Day.

Ch 11 AM and H.C. 7 P.M. Wrote to Mr Murray—Bp of Durham BP. Read Westcott on St John[3]—Brahmo Year Book[4]—Wilberforce's Life. Would fain have written a short record but could not find time.

26. Fr. St Steph.

Ch. 8½ AM. Wrote to Dr Döllinger 1. & BP.—Duke of Argyll—Mrs Mockler—Mr Ferguson—J.H. Parker—A.J. Wilson—Miss Robb (O)—H.N.G. BP—A. Leon—R. Knight—H.S. Luard? Read Wilberforces Life—Preface &c. Spanish Gk Test—Bunbury's Geography. Walk with C. & axe-work. Worked on arr. books. Worked on Economics.

27. Sat. St John.

Ch 8½ AM. Wrote to Dss of Marlborough—Miss De Lisle—Rev. Mr Henderson—E.M. Fraser—R. Winton[5]—Principal Tulloch—Mr Broadhurst—Mr Sutherland—Mr Corstorphine—Prof. G.B. Arnaudo[6]—J. Lovell—Mr Crawford. Worked on Economics. Arranging books. Walk with C. Read Nihilismo—Tondini's proselyting Tract[7]—Life of Bp Wilberforce.

28. 1 S. aft Xmas.[8]

Ch 11 AM & 6½ P.M. Wrote to Father O'Malley.[9] Walk with E. Wickham. Read Bp Wilberforce's Life—Fairbairn[10]—Dr Westcott on St John—Answer to Miss [blank].

And now I am writing in the last minutes of the seventh decade of my life.

[1] S. H. Northcote, 'Probate . . . duties. Speech' (1879).
[2] E. H. Bunbury, *A history of ancient geography among the Greeks and Romans*, 2v. (1879).
[3] B. F. Westcott, *An introduction to the study of the gospels* (1860).
[4] *The Brahmo Year-Book for 1879*; on Indian theism.
[5] Robert Winston of Chelsea radical association, on municipal reform; *T.T.*, 1 January 1880, 8a.
[6] Giovanni Battista Arnaudo had sent his *Il Nihilismo* (1879); on Herzen.
[7] C. Tondini, *The primacy of S. Peter demonstrated from the liturgy of the Greco-Russian Church* (1879).
[8] Extracts from 28 to 31 December conflated in Morley, ii. 597.
[9] Joseph O'Malley, on his sermons and on Rome; see Add MS 44461, f. 291.
[10] See 9 Sept. 78.

This closing is a great event. The days of our life are three score years and ten. It is hardly possible that I should complete another decade. How much, or how little, of this will God give me for the purposes dear to my heart? Ah what need have I of what I may term spiritual leisure: to be out of the dust and heat and blast and strain, before I pass into the unseen world.

But perhaps this is a form of selflove. For the last 3½ years I have been passing through a political experience which is I believe without example in our Parliamentary history. I profess it [*sic*] to believe it has been an occasion, when the battle to be fought was a battle of justice humanity freedom law, all in their first elements from the very root, and all on a gigantic scale. The word spoken was a word for millions, and for millions who themselves cannot speak. If I really believe this then I should regard my having been morally forced into this work as a great and high election of God. And certainly I cannot but believe that He has given me special gifts of strength, on the late occasion especially in Scotland. But alas the poor little garden of my own soul remains uncultivated, unweeded, and defaced. So then while I am bound to accept this election for the time, may I not be permitted to pray that the time shall be short? Three things I would ask of God over and above all the bounty which surrounds me. This first that I may escape into retirement. This second that I may speedily be enabled to divest myself of everything resembling wealth. And the third—if I may—that when God calls me He may call me speedily. To die in Church appears to be a great *euthanasia*: but not a time to disturb worshippers. Such are some of the old man's thoughts, in whom there is still something that consents not to be old. Though I am well aware that my wonderful health is contingent on the freedom of my actual position, and that I could not bear the strain of anxiety. All this I ought to have written on my knees: from which indeed were I never to rise.

> Last among the last
>   Least among the least
> Can there be a place for me
>   At the marriage feast?

29. M.

Ch. 8½ AM. Wrote to Duke of Sutherland—Ed. Daily News, & draft[1]—J.R. Jolly—M. Gennadios—Mr Maclaren (O)—J.B. Mantrop—J. Sharman—Burslem Liberals (Tel.)—Mr Ouvry—Sir Thos G.—Dr Blair (O)[2]—D. Allen—E.A. Wood. Read Bp Wilberforce—Arnaudo, Nihilismo. Worked on my room to bring it into order, which was tranquillising. Otherwise this was the most protracted of birthdays. Ninety letters by post, followed by 27 Telegrams coming in from hour to hour. The Liverpool Deputation was here for three hours and I had to make a speech of some length to them, not wholly an easy one.[3] Conversation with Mr Billson—Mr Rathbone—Mr Johnson—& C.G. respecting Herbert.

---

[1] Sending copy of his letter of 27 December to Broadhurst; *D.N.*, 30 December 1879, 5f.

[2] Probably William Blair, physician in Jedburgh.

[3] *D.N.*, 30 December 1879, 3a; Gladstone felt impelled by the wording of the address to comment on party politics, and to give an interesting account of his involvement in public affairs since 1875. Burslem liberals, *inter alia*, also sent an address.

So I was far indeed from my centre this day. I return to it at night for a moment only. The one thing needed for me, as far as I can see is the withdrawal of this load, always far too heavy for a weak soul like mine, and a free time for penitence and prayer: with study too if God will for that would help steadiness and not impair it. O that the time may come, & may come quickly.

30. Tu.

Ch. 8½ AM. Wrote to Mayor of Chester—Rev. Mr M'Coll—Rev. J. Irving[1]—Rev. Newman Hall—Miss de Lisle—Miss Cusack—P.E. Roberts—Mr Calderwood—Mr Bosemworth—R. Richardson—S. Langley—Hon R. Bourke—W. Woodall[2]—T.J. Brogden[3]—Watsons—Scotts—Mr Thom—Mr Dutton—Mr Dobson—L. Berg—Mr Walker—Mr Watson—W.E. Brown—J. Knowles—Mr Collins. The Lytteltons came. Axe work with W. Read Bp Wilberforce—Bunbury's Geogr.

31. Wed.

Ch. 8½ AM. Wrote to J.E. Thompson O—Mr Dodson MP—Mr Leeman MP—Baroness Burdett Coutts—Rev. Geo Butler—Rev. Osborne Browne—M.F. Tupper—G. Morley—Mr Ouvry—Miss Paull[4]—Miss Pfeiffer[5]—Mr Barton. Long conversation with Charles, & arrangement as to liquidation of mortgage. Walk with C. Worked on Economics. Worked on Books. Worked on annual statement of property. Read the Life of Bishop Wilberforce. It is indeed an edifying book. I knew him, admired him, loved him living. But the laying out of his full character from early days onwards tells me much I did not know, and lifts upward my conception of him both in greatness and in goodness.[6] To speak of the distance between him & myself in the eye of God would be futile: it is an immeasurable distance. I would fain hope it has not been enlarged during the year that will die in a few minutes. But alack alack my years flow on and still find me, as they leave me, a man spiritually too weak for his place, a man all whose energies are drawn into the outer life, who has none remaining for moral guidance, nothing but dregs to offer to his God and Saviour. How long, O God? Thou only knowest. But it looks as if 1880 would find some solution for the question, and either give me my long wooed retirement or at worst place me on the ledge from whence I shall D.V. be carried into it by a single spring. Yet, before I close, I must here record my peculiar sense of the divine support both physical and moral granted to me in Scotland. It could not have been without a purpose. To that purpose in its essence may I answer faithfully: yet as to the form I am permitted to hope *that* which seems to me most healthful, most urgently needful, for the soul.

Good bye, old year.

[1] James Irving, minister in Tunbridge Wells, on disestablishment; *T.T.*, 1 January 1880, 11b.
[2] Perhaps William Woodall, London dentist.
[3] Perhaps Thomas W. Brogden, barrister.
[4] Mary Anna Paull of Plymouth; corresponded on drink; Hawn P.
[5] Emily Jane Pfeiffer, 1827-90; poet; see Add MS 44456, f. 196.
[6] Morley's extract ends here.

1. Th. Circumcision [January 1880]

Ch. 8½ A.M.—Also for Baptism of Agnes's baby at 3 P.M.[1] Wrote to Solr to Treasury—Mr Kennedy—C. Cooper—T.G. Shaw—Mr Jackson (O)—Mr Connell—J. Jones—Mrs Th.—Messrs Lewis—Messrs Burns & Co—Rev. J. O'Hanlon[2]—Mrs Crossley—C.W. Hawkins—Mr Corstorphine BP—C.W. Thomas. Walk to Aston. Saw C. Lyttelton—E. Wickham. Worked on paper of Economics. Read—& fell asleep. Sixteen to dinner.

2. Fr.

Ch. 8½ AM. Wrote to Mr J. Baker Greene[3]—Kate Gladstone BP—Miss de Lisle BP—Mr Hedley Jones—Messrs Williams—Mr Womersley[4]—J.W. Browne—J.B. Day—Rev. Mr Mayow—Mr Ouvry—Mr Whittegg—Mr Brough—Mr Elder—W. Dunlop—D.M. Meal—T. Cragg. Felled tree with W. Worked on paper of Economics. Read Wilberforce (finished I)—Baker Greene on Hebrew Migration from Egypt.

3. Sat.

Ch. 8½ AM. Wrote to Messrs Wagstaff—Mr Fairbrother—T.H. Bryant—Rev. Dr Plumptre—Messrs Currie—T.S. Pindar—Mr Freeman—E.M. Fraser—Mr Millward—J. Snow. Remitted somewhat of my work today having upon me a low face-ache: the reaction after heavy pressures under which I received from the mercy of God such remarkable support. Arranging books, 2 hours: a mere nothing in effect. Worked on paper of Economics. Read Baker Greene—Modern Review on Reviewing—do on St Thomas Aquinas.[5] Axe work with W.

4. S aft Circumc.

Ch 11 AM and H.C.—Kept the house in evening with face ache. Sent off to Mr Knowles the bulk of my article, which I got into trim yesterday. Read Life of Sumner—Westcott on St John—The case of Bp Wessenberg[6]—Newman on the Irenicon.[7]

5. M.

Kept my bed till 11: rose greatly relieved. Wrote to Lord Hartington—Ld F. Cavendish—Mr Jas Knowles BP—E.A. Freeman BP—Mr Watherston—General

---

[1] Lucy Christian Wickham, his grand-daughter.

[2] John O'Hanlon of Dublin, later a canon, had sent books; Hawn P.

[3] John Baker Greene sent his anonymously published *Hebrew migration from Egypt* (1879).

[4] Perhaps Robert Womersley, London chemical manufacturer.

[5] First number of the *Modern Review* (January 1880); its editor was R. A. Armstrong.

[6] Perhaps W. Hales, *Abridgement of a correspondence between the courts of Rome and Baden respecting the appointment of Baron Wessenberg vicar capitular of the diocese of Constance* (1819).

[7] See 4 Feb. 66; also J. H. Newman, 'Certain difficulties felt by Anglicans in Catholic teaching' (1876); a reply to Pusey's Eirenicon.

Hutchinson[1]—Rev. A.C. Ramsay[2]—Mr Crelly—J. Marks—T. Hopper—Mr Benjamin. Finished residue of Art. & dispatched it. Walk with E.W. & S.E.G. Read The Foam of the Sea Vol I[3]—Lenormant on Eleusis.[4] Worked on books.

6. Tu. Epiph.

Dearest C.s birthday. With her to Church (and H.C.) $8\frac{1}{2}$-$9\frac{3}{4}$ A.M. Wrote to Made Novikoff—Mr Venables—Mr Leecraft—Mr Newmarch—J. Ferguson—Rev. Mr Crosthwaite—Ld Lyttelton—Sir S. Scott & Co—Prof. Sbarbaro—Mr Waddy MP. The forenoon was given to Estate matters with Willy, Mr Barker; and then C.G. I today finally decided on a plan which I can now afford, & which will secure a gradual improvement of his position, which I think is too much crippled for the *owner* by law of this Estate & for the position it confers. It is the upshot of some thought, and is an *onward* step for me. $4\frac{1}{4}$-$6\frac{1}{4}$. Attended the after dinner proceedings of the Audit, & spoke at some length. Willy & the Rector both spoke well. Mr Ottley dined—for his last day. Read Contemp. Rev.—Hillebrand on Engl. in 18th Cent.[5]—and Foam of the Sea.

7. Wed.

Ch. $8\frac{1}{2}$ A.M.—A reluctant good bye to Mr Ottley.[6] Wrote to Mr R.B. O'Brien[7]—Mr Adam MP—Mr Dodson MP—Mr Richard MP—Mr Chester—Mr Birdsall—Mr Mounsey—J.J. Reid—T. Macknight—Rev. M. M'Coll—Mr Delapryme—R. Hutchison—R. Martyr.[8] Wrote Pref. to my Financial Speech,[9] in reply to Northcote. Axe work with W.H.G. Also in walking explained to him my new plan on his behalf from July 1 Next. Read From the Sea Foam (finished)—Nihilismo.

8. Th.

Ch. $8\frac{1}{2}$ AM. Wrote to J. Watson & Smith—H. Holiday[10]—W. Brough—Mr Yorston BP—R. Knight (O)—Ld Lyttelton—Mr Wilkinson—L.C. Alexander—A.M. Geldart[11]—A.J. Dadson[12]—W. Romsen[?]—Mr Landreth—Mr Simpson—Mr Bryant. Axe work with Willy. Worked on the Olympian System.[13] Read Hebrew Migration and [blank.]

[1] William Nelson Hutchinson, 1803-95; general 1873; inventor.
[2] Andrew Chrysostom Ramsay, vicar of St Botolph, Lincoln.
[3] *From the foam of the Sea*, by 'Marcellina' (1880).
[4] F. Lenormant, *Monographie de la Voie Sacrée Éleusinienne*, i (1864).
[5] In the *Contemporary Review*, xxxvii. 1 (January 1880).
[6] The curate (see 20 May 77), to be curate in Hoxton.
[7] Richard Barry O'Brien, 1847-1918; Irish barrister and author; see 5 Nov. 80.
[8] Perhaps R. E. Martyr, clerk in the board of trade.
[9] i.e. preface, with comments on Northcote, to *Political speeches*, dated 'January 1880'.
[10] Henry *Holiday, 1839-1927; pre-Raphaelite artist.
[11] Edmund Martin Geldart, unitarian minister, on theology in universities; Add MS 44462, f. 27.
[12] Perhaps Alfred William Dadson, London barrister.
[13] See 18 Dec. 79.

9. Fr.

Ch. 8¼ AM. Wrote to my Sister Helen—Ed. Scotsman (2)—J. Buchanan[1]—T. McClure—E. Mounsey—Messrs Farrer—Messrs Harper, N.Y.—Rev. Mr Beeby[2]—Mr Dawson (O)—Mr Tagart—A. Hill—L. Booth[3]—Mr Heatley—T. Moore. Read letters of Marie Antoinette[4]—Nineteenth C. on Essex & Queen Elisabeth—& on Canning.[5] Mr Godley came. Axe work with Willy. Worked much on paper arranging. And a little on The Olympian system.

10. Sat.

Ch. 8½ A.M. Wrote to Sir Thos G. (Tel)—Dr Schmidt (Tel)—Ld Granville—Rev. Mr T. Hughes—Rev. Mr Dyneley—Mr Dodson MP—J. Benjamin—Mr Mundella MP—R.W. Wilson[6]—Mr Bleeck[7]—J.J. Reed—J. Burns[8]—Mr Bassett—R. May[9]—Mr Scott—Mr Binns—Mr Sowrey. Soon after noon, we had alarming accounts of my dear Sister Helen, still alas! at Cologne. I am perplexed as to moving. Tom & Louisa at once go to London. Walk with Godley & N. Lyttelton. Arranged corrections of Preface & for new Edn of Speeches. Discussed Economics with Godley: Affghanistan with N. Lyttelton. Eleven to dinner. Read Giffen's Essays.[10]

11. 1 S. Epiph. [London]

Wrote to Walter L.G.—Dr Stainer—Mr Knowles—Leeds Churchwarden—Chester Office Tel.—T.G. Tel—Mr Wayland[11]—Made Adam[12]—Daily News Tel—Mr Newmarch—Mr Brookway—Mrs Wynne Tel—Mrs Th—Mr Baynes—Mr W. Brough—Mr Rule (O)—and from the rail, to Ld Lyttelton—C.G. (2)—Sir J.K. James—Mr Knowles—Mr Salusbury—Miss Arden.[13] Made ready & left Hawarden at 10.15 AM. London 4.35. Saw T.G.—worked on letters: preparations for journey. Off at 8.25 for a night journey and passage with T.G. and Louisa.[14]

12. M. [Cologne]

We reached Cologne at 11.15 English time. Saw Dr Schmidt: Mrs Watkin.[15] Later we saw Helen: thin & weak with little strength to speak, but whereas it

---

[1] James Buchanan of the *Gloucester Standard*: was diarist ever resident in Gloucester? Hawn P.

[2] Robert Beeby, rector of Uldale, Carlisle.

[3] Perhaps Lionel Booth, a near neighbour in London.   [4] See 9 Sept. 79.

[5] *Nineteenth Century*, vii. 27, 107 (January 1880).

[6] Robert William Rankine Wilson, barrister in New Court, London.

[7] Perhaps Henry Bleck, importer of antiques; or Du Bled (see 12 Jan. 80), involved in Helen J. Gladstone's affairs.

[8] (Sir) John Burns, 1829-1901; heir to shipping fortune, with Midlothian connections; 2nd bart. 1890; cr. Baron Inverclyde 1897.

[9] Perhaps of the match factory; diarist in touch with Bryant at this time about his statue; see 10 Dec. 78n.

[10] First series of R. Giffen, *Essays in finance* (1880).

[11] H. L. Wayland of Philadelphia had sent a hat; Hawn P.   [12] See 18 Oct. 79?

[13] Possibly Henley I. Arden, pseudonym of Henrietta Knight, novelist.

[14] i.e. his brother Sir Thomas and his wife; Catherine Gladstone remained at Hawarden.

[15] Or Watkins (see 10 June 51), his sister's Roman catholic maid.

was a case of despair on Saturday evening there is now a little hope. The medical & nursing care close and excellent. But indeed the scene is sad. Wrote to C.G.—Mr Du Bled—Mr Langmead—Rev. Mr Walters. Read T. A.Kempis—Psalms—Lessons &c. We walked in the town: & saw Dr S[chmidt] repeatedly: down to 11 P.M. By that time there had been slight action in the two ways but he thought the weakness still formidable. Read Evans on India[1]—Adm. Martin on Cyprus (yest)[2]—Walters, L. to Electors.[3]—Huidekoper, Judaism in Rome[4]—Barry Cornwall, Life.[5] Saw H. again, evg. My purpose is to be wholly passive here. Further conversation with Watkins on the curious matter of the Priests: I may say the sad matter. We three visitors of course converse much: I am much struck with L[ouisa].

13. Tu.

The day opened with good accounts confirmed at 11 A.M. by Dr S. It was a day of promise. We spoke much of the arrangements for the future: Dr S. cheerful in his tone, though not positive. I saw Helen twice: but not for long. Walk with T. & L. Wrote to C.G.—Rev. Dr Talmadge[6]—Mr Ouvry. Read Huidekoper—Barry Cornwall (Proctor)s Life: a very interesting Volume.

14. Wed.

Wrote to C.G. Walk with T.G. Saw much of the old town & its mazes. A touch of bowel complaint led me to forbear from dining & keep on my back. I only saw Helen once. Her kindness & thoughtfulness are very remarkable. In the morning we saw Dr Leichenstein as well as Dr Schmidt. Nothing positive could be said for three or four days: danger was not absolutely gone, but *viel geringer*:[7] hope evidently predominated. The vomiting was only stomach vomiting. But in the course of the day it resumed its formidable (antiperistaltic or stercorarious) character. Remedies were applied towards evening, in hope. Saw Mr Hamel.[8] Read as yesterday.

15. Thurs.

Wrote to Watsons—C.G.—WHG—Scotts—Dodson—J.J. Reid. The morning rose gloomily upon us, the remedies of yesterday not having acted. More was tried today especially electricity. With no effect up to the time when I write this at 5.30: while the strength is ebbing away. Louisa is with her a good deal & very good. When I went in today she kept me long. Asking her first, I said the Pater Noster, with the verse Asperges me. She said many things, & also told me she had more to say if her strength sufficed. There was more light in the room:

---

[1] A. B. Evans, *India. Two discourses delivered in the Church of St. Andrew, Wells Street* (1857).

[2] Probably an untraced letter to the press.

[3] J. T. Walters, 'Tory of Liberal? for which shall I vote? A letter to the middle class and operative electors' (1880).

[4] See 9 June 78.   [5] See 1 Jan. 79f.l.

[6] John Mayow Talmadge, rector of Fifield, Oxford.

[7] 'much less'.

[8] A protestant businessman who assisted Helen Gladstone.

I saw more emaciation and was more troubled at her aspect. Her spirit however is truly on high in warm devotion.

I saw the Priest Föcker[1] at his own desire after he had been with her for a few minutes & offered a prayer. He had not been sent for, but had seen her some months back, recommended by Dr Schmidt. The evening was for the most part distressing from her piteous cravings. There was one most bright interval. L. named me & I went up to the bed & repeated verses from Ps. 121 which she took up most devoutly: & she then spoke most lovingly & said twice 'I think' or 'I hope' 'we shall meet again['']. She has been led into a great error: I cannot say whether it may not have been a great sin: yet I can dismiss her fearlessly to the great account, mine is a sadder & a darker tale. Read Barry Cornwall (finished)—Huidekoper—Lady Lytton's Shells, rather trashy:[2] Miss Webster's verses:[3] Dickens's Letters.[4]

16. Fr.

Wrote to C.G.—Mr M. Lavin. Read Webster. Saw Professor L[eichenstein] twice, Dr S. at many intervals. Seven hours in the Chamber of sickness, & as it proved of death. At $7\frac{1}{2}$ the rapid decline began. At 10.10 all was over. The latest period was peace blessed peace. There was much that was beautiful before. She fervently answered Amen to the Pater Noster. Almost her last words, if not the very last were to be assured about 'her poor birds'. She had already spoken for the dog. She also uttered words of the deepest humility. But she was quite un-equal to continuing thought or effort. *Requiem aeternam dona ei Domine*.

Immediately upon the death followed a rush of thoughts & cares. Got to bed by midnight.

17. Sat.

Wrote to C.G.—Dr Döllinger—Mrs Wynne—Ld Granville.

The day was spent in matters relating to the decease. We saw repeatedly Dr Schmidt, Mrs Watkins and also Mr Henkel. Walked awhile after dusk. Until then, and again after dinner to near midnight worked on the large mass of effects, especially the books, of which I arranged I think about 1200.

18. 2 S. Epiph.

Attended the quiet soothing service. What Psalms: what a First Lesson. Wrote to C.G. (fully)— Messrs Freshfield—A.L. Gladstone—Herr Henckel—Mrs Wynne. Made an examination of all the books of devotion: it was very inter-esting & important & set forth the whole history of her mental transition since 1870. I packed all these Volumes apart. They show she died at one with us as before.[5] We had also most curious conversation with that devoted woman

---

[1] Described by Mrs Watkins as 'an Old Catholic but who would not be recognised as an Old Catholic among the clergy of Cologne'; *Autobiographica*, iv. 39.

[2] Lady Bulwer Lytton, *Shells from the sands of time*, 2v. (1876-7).

[3] A. Webster, perhaps *Disguises. A drama* (1879); a verse drama.

[4] *The Letters of Charles Dickens*, ed. G. Hogarth and M. Dickens, 3v. (1879-81).

[5] Gladstone noticed that his sister's Roman catholic devotional works were all pre-1870, save a few unused or unopened; *Autobiographica*, iv. 41.

Watkins, about these books, and especially about the history of her parting with her money, the 10 m[ille] given her by her Father years before he died. The 'Church' got hold of it all. See my letter to C.G.[1] Read Money & the Soul.[2]

19. M.

Wrote to Mr Knowles—Père Focker—Mr Bosworth—Messrs Cornish—Redaction Indepce Belge—do Rue Mad. Bruxelles—W.H. Gladstone. Saw Mr Henkel—bis. A walk after dusk. Corrected a portion of proofs. Revised WHGs letter to Vickers. Read through the uncut Vol. on Morphia-Craving. Copied my letter to M. Henkel for record:[3] & resumed work on Books & effects (which are a huge chaos) as also upon papers. Sat up late.

20. Tu.

Wrote to C.G.—Messrs Freshfield—Mrs Wynne—Ld Lyttelton (2)—Mr Knowles (T. & BP)—Sir J. Watson—Ld Granville—Mr Grenville Berkeley. Busy with arrangements for transmission of these sad & dear remains: also so devastated. And with the other plans, & packing. Very hard frost. Walk to St Geryon's. Sold many of the books. Read The Cure of Souls[4]—Der Englische Land Squire.[5] Finished corr. proofs of Article.

21. Wed.

Wrote to Mr Westell—Sir R. Phillimore—Officer of Customs Victoria. Read Luise Hensel[6]—The Cure of Souls. We had a painful difference with Dr Schmidt as to his charge of 9300 odd marks, including 5000 for the operation (without visits). More selling of books, counting of money, packing &c. We were incessantly busy until we started at half past ten and travelled all night.

22. Thurs. [London]

Wrote to C.G.—Ld Granville Tel. Reached London a little before six. Saw West—Mrs Birks—found C.G. here. Dined with the Wests. Interview with Ld Granville at Dover. Saw Bp Coplestone[7] in the Boat. Read Cure of Souls. Worked on letters and papers. It is matter for much thankfulness to have been permitted the accomplishment of this journey.

---

[1] 'The priests through Wiseman it seems got every penny of it. All this & the pressure upon her to get it (says W[atkins]) she afterwards looked back upon with much displeasure'; Hawn P.
[2] Perhaps J. Gotthelf (i.e. A. Bitzius), *Geld und Geist* (1843), tr. as *The Soul and Money* (1872); Ruskin promoted Bitzius's novels and ideas.
[3] Asking him to confirm in writing his statement that Helen told him 'I am Alt-Catholik'; Hawn P.
[4] J. M. Cobban, *Cure of souls* (1879).
[5] Untraced; one of his sister's books?
[6] J. H. Reinkens, *Louise Hensel und ihre Lieder* (1877).
[7] Reginald Stephen Copleston, 1845-1925; bp. of Colombo 1875-1902.

23. Frid.

Wrote to W.H.G.—Rev. Mr Brydom—Ed. Daily News—Mr Geo. Potter—Mr Rich M'Ghee[1]—Provost of Hamilton—Mad. Novikoff—Lady M. Alford—Rev. Dr Hutton—M. Gennadios—Mr Irwin—Mr Knowles—Mr Hartley—Mr Collins—Mr Joseph—Mr Bryce. Saw Mr Read—Mr Westell: H.J.G.'s Estate. Saw Sir Thos G. (3)—Scotts—Mr Knowles (19th C. Art.)—Mr Wortley—Mrs Wortley—Sir R. Phillimore—Mr Ouvry—Lord Edw. Clinton—Also these two together—W. Dumaresq, alas gone back in health. Dined at Sir R. Phillimore's.[2] More work on letters & papers: a full & hard day.

24. Sat. [Fasque]

Off at 10 A.M. with the T.G.s to Fasque. Breakfast with Mrs Birks. Made a stage of the journey with Ld Hartington, alone, & conversed on the situation. Reached Perth before 10: remained over 2 hours. Wrote to Arthur R.G. Read Fitzpatrick's Whately.[3]

25. Septua S.

Ch 11 AM & 3 PM in the Chapel here so full of dear memories. Saw Mrs Jolly & some old friends. Walk with T.G. Read Fitzpatrick's Whately—Luise Hensel, by Bishop Reinkens. Funeral arrangements considered. The coffin rests in the Hall. We arrived about 3 A.M. & rose to breakfast at 9.30.

26. M.

Wrote to Mr C.L. Booth—Lord Acton—Dr Percy—Miss Conway—O.B. Cole—Ld F. Cavendish—Mr Scott—Mr Westell. Examining some of Helen's papers—many matters stand for discussion. Our duty as Administrators will be complicated enough. Walk and calls. The nieces are excellent. Read Luise Hensel—Fitzpatrick's Whately.

27. Tu.

Wrote to C.G.—Mr Rathbone MP.—Mrs Wynne—(Memo. on the Leith Hospital case, at T.G.s desire)[4]—Mr Fitzpatrick[5]—Mr A. Mirams.[6] Read Luise Hensel—Fitzpatrick's Whately. Further conversation with T.G. on Leith Hospital & H.J.G.s matters. Walk with Louey. How good these girls are. The funeral was at

[1] Of Glasgow, on the campaign; Hawn P.

[2] 'We talked a good deal of politics. His relations with Ld Hartington are uneasy. He feels that the Midlothian affair has practically affected his intention not to take office (that really is to be Premier) again. He undertook Midlothian at Granville's request, after he had pointed out the difficulties wh. might arise in consequence. He does not mean to be in his place in the H. of C. until a month after it has met'; Phillimore's Diary.

[3] W. J. Fitzpatrick, *Memoirs of R. Whately, archbishop of Dublin*, 2v. (1864).

[4] Founded by Sir John Gladstone, and under-endowed; Hawn P.

[5] William John Fitzpatrick, 1830-95; Roman catholic author of *Whately*; see 24 Jan. 80 and Add MS 44462, f. 40.

[6] Augustus Mirams, barrister.

12. Watkins was consoled & pleased. Mr B.[1] however had not the sympathetic spirit of Mr Harris: nor was the commendatory blessing given. However we ought to be most thankful that as if in answer to our prayer our dear sister has been freely restored to the unity of the Spirit and the bond of peace. I miss sorely the funeral communion.

28. Wed. [Courthey]

9 AM to 9¾ P.M. Journey to Courthey, with Arthur [Gladstone]. Explained to him as well as I could the whole case of his Aunt's temporal affairs. Read Luise Hensel—The Cure of Souls (finished)—Fitzpatrick's Whately.

29. Th. [Hawarden]

Wrote to Mr Ouvry—Lord Granville—Louey G (BP)—Mr Suffield. Visited Ld & Lady Ramsay. Saw Mr Rathbone—Mr Billson—in Liverpool: then home, arriving at one P.M. Attended the Mission Service 7-8½: remarkable Address from Mr Cole. Began to work on the accumulated disorder. Read Kirkpatrick's [sic] Whately—Case of the Ceylon Ch. Establt.[2]

30. Fr.

Ch. for Holy Commn at 8 A.M. This came in the place of Funeral Communion.—Church again 7-8½ PM. Wrote to Walter L. Gladstone—Mr Roberts MP—Mr Giffen (BP.)—Messrs Elphinstone—Mrs Wolffsohn—Rev. Dr Pusey—Rev. J. Barclay[3]—Captain Wells—Rev. V. Rorison[4]—Rev. Jas Thompson—Rev. J.V. Loot[5]—Mr Richardson—S. Broughton—F.G. Longman—Creswicks—Mr Morris—Mr Poulton (O)—A. Austin—Mr Sawyer—L. Berg—Jas Grant—Jas Gordon—A.P. Keep—J.W. Shaw—Mr Shearer—J.J. Elder. Worked with WHG on the accumulated mass. Finished Fitzpatrick's Whately. Read Contemp. Rev. on Turkey[6]—F. Harrison on Cabul.[7] Felled an alder with WHG.

31. Sat.

Ch. 7-8½ P.M. Wrote to Mr T.H. Jackson B.P.—Dean of St Paul's—Rev. F. Ferguson[8]—Rev. R.T. Lewis—Mr Robertson—Mr Braidwood—J.B. Mantrop—Hunt & Rochell—C.J. Booth[9]—Mr Webster—J. Geary BP—J. Aitken—W. Simons—W. Sargeant[10]—M. Lissach—S. Cowan—W.E. Brown—C. Tagart. Read Contemp. Review—Q.R. on Duke of Somerset[11]—Rice on Music.[12]

---

[1] Andrew H. Belcher, episcopalian priest at Fasque.

[2] Probably *Three letters on the necessity of a Church Establishment in Ceylon. Reprinted from the Examiner* (*ca.* 1850); signed 'M'.

[3] John Barclay, canon of Chester and rector of Runcorn.

[4] Vincent Lewis Rorison, episcopalian incumbent at Forfar.   [5] *Sic*: unidentified.

[6] *Contemporary Review*, xxxvii. 601 (December 1879).

[7] In the *Fortnightly Review*, xxxii. 767 (December 1879).

[8] Fergus Ferguson of Glasgow, on a cutting; Hawn P.

[9] Perhaps of the Liverpool family, but not the C. J. Booth, father of the sociologist, who d. 1860.

[10] Perhaps William Sergeant, liberal in Bayswater.

[11] *Quarterly Review*, cxlix. 230 (January 1880).   [12] Untraced.

Feb. One. 1880. Sexa S.

Holy Commn 8 AM. Church 11 A.M. to 1 & 6½ PM. to 9. Wrote to Rev. Mr Hutchinson—Mr Ebenezer Palmer[1]—and.... Read Fitzpatrick's Whately (finished)—The Gospel for the 19th Cent.[2]—Hutchinson's Tracts[3]—Hyacinthe, Northcote, and Capel in N.C.[4]—Mr E. Palmer's Poems.

Mon. Feb. 2. Purificn.

Wrote to Mr Rathbone MP[5]—Mr J.C. Farley—Scotts—Mr G. Povall[6]—Sir Thos G. Church 7 P.M. (Mr Kelly). Read Wilson on Reciprocity &c.[7]—Cowper's Task[8]—Rawlinson on Afghanistan—Dicey on Egyptian Protectorate.[9] Saw Mr Vickers—Ld R. Grosvenor *cum* WHG—Mr Bromley. Felled an ash with WHG.

3. Tu.

Ch. 7 P.M.-8¼. Wrote to Sir Herbert Oakeley[10]—D. of Argyll—Mr James MP.— Dean of St Paul's—Mr E. Joseph—R.W. Wilson—W. Simons—D. Bodington— Rev. Jos. Cochrane[11]—Ld Nelson—Miss Hogg.[12] Read Q.R. on Hellenism[13]—Cowper's Task—Wilson on the Land Quest.—and tracts.

4. Wed.

Ch. 7 PM-8¾. Wrote to Herbert (on his offer)[14]—Rev. Sir H. Moncreiff—R.A. Wood BP—Mr Rathbone MP. BP—Rev. Mr Rodwell—J. Stuart—J.R. Grant—Mr Alderson. Troubled with my early & kind monitor of excess, the toothache. Walk with C.—At Aston. Read Case of the Armenians[15]—Shelden Amos on the Constn[16]—Wilson on the Land—Cowper's Task—Letters of Ld Althorp.[17]

---

[1] Had sent the 3rd ed. of his *Tendrils in verse* (1880).

[2] *The Gospel for the nineteenth century; (an enquiry suggested by ... passages in J. S. Mill's 'Essays on religion')* (1880).

[3] Untraced; sent by a correspondent.

[4] *Nineteenth Century*, vii. 256, 318, 361 (February 1880).

[5] On the Liverpool by-election; printed in the press; Add MS 44462, f. 64.

[6] *Sic*; perhaps 'Povah' intended.

[7] A. J. Wilson, *Reciprocity, Bi-Metallism, and Land Tenure Reform* (1880).

[8] First published in 1785.

[9] By H. C. Rawlinson and E. Dicey respectively, *Nineteenth Century*, vii. 197, 333 (February 1880).

[10] Sir Herbert Stanley *Oakeley, 1830-1903; professor of music at Edinburgh from 1865; kt. 1876.

[11] Probably James Henry Dickson Cochrane, unbeneficed priest in Liverpool.

[12] Probably Annie Claudina Hogg, sister of 1st Lord Magheramorne.

[13] *Quarterly Review*, cxlix. 125 (January 1880).

[14] To act as his father's secretary; see 16 Mar. 80.

[15] Possibly J. Creagh, *Armenians, Koords, and Turks*, 2v. (1880), or one of the many tracts on the Armenian question.

[16] S. Amos, *A primer of the English Constitution and government* (1873).

[17] Possibly *A copy of the correspondence between the Chancellor of the Exchequer [Lord Althorp] and the Bank of England* (1833).

5. Th.[1]

Called at 3.30. We went to the closing Communion Service at 4, a solemn scene. There must have been near 200 in the Church. I had very special subjects, in an eminent degree, today for the Holy Sacrifice which we then not exclusively but peculiarly offer. Home and to bed again before 6. Wrote to Cogan & MacLardy—Mr J.H. Burton—Mrs Th.—Mr W. Brownsea—Messrs Kerby & Endean.[2] Mr Coles dined with us. Read Wilson on Land—Pallavicino on Pontificate[3]—Mongredien on Free Trade[4]—Indian River Basins[5]—Bagehot Economic Studies.[6] Visited Mr Roberts.

6. Fr.

Ch. 8¼ A.M. The old order is now resumed. Wrote to Rev. Mr Crosthwaite—Ld F. Cavendish[7]—Mr Newmarch—Mr Rathbone—Mr Fawcett—Ld Derby—Mr Giffen—S.R. Lawley—Mrs W. Bagehot—Sir T.D. Acland MP—Dr Badenoch—D. Davies—W. Douglas—Col. Laurie—A. Beer—W.H.G.—Mr Longley—S. Lloyd MP.[8] Walk with S. & calls. Read Foreign Ch. Chronicle[9]—Crosthwaite Correspondence—Church & State (futile)—S. Australian Univ. Addresses[10]—Escape of Prince Charles.[11] In the evening face or tooth ache seized me severely.

7. Sat.

I did not face the morning air. My poor head, which is my tool, requires me to soothe and spare it. Wrote to Townshend & Barker—Messrs Harper—Messrs Brown—Mr Macmillan—Rev. Mr Wyndham[12]—Rev. Mr Goulden[13]—Mr Henderson—Messrs Ellison—Mr Bartley—J. Wood—J. Lowe[14]—Mr Chapman—Mr Corthson—Mr Hitchman—J.B. Pond. Read Amos on the Constitution—Cowper's Task—Are we to pay? (Natal).[15] Worked on my accounts.

8. Quinqua S.

Ch. 10.30 & 6½ PM. Wrote to Mr Macmillan BP.—D. of Argyll—W.H.G.—Rev. R. Linklater—Mr Gomdell—Mr La Fleurière—Mr Ladmore—Rev. Mr Pieritz[16]—

---

[1] Parliament met this day.
[2] Publishers and booksellers in Oxford Street.
[3] S. Pallavicino, *Istoria del Concilio di Trento*, 2v. (1656).
[4] A. Mongredien, *Free trade and English commerce* (1879).
[5] Not found.
[6] W. Bagehot, *Economic studies*, ed. R. H. Hutton (1880).
[7] This and next six names marked 'B.P.', i.e. sent off-prints of free trade article; see 16 Dec. 79.
[8] Sampson Samuel Lloyd, 1820–89; banker and tory M.P. Plymouth 1874–80, S. Warwicks. 1880–5.
[9] *Foreign Church Chronicle*, iv (1880).
[10] Not found.
[11] Perhaps [G. W. Dodd], *Boscobel. A Narrative of the adventures of Charles the Second after the Battle of Worcester* (1859).
[12] Probably Thomas Heathcote Wyndham, retired priest in Salisbury.
[13] Alfred Benjamin Bernard Goulden, curate in Southwark.
[14] Of Stockport, on dissolutions; *T.T.*, 10 February 1880, 10a.
[15] Untraced; no copy found in Natal university library.
[16] George Wildon Pieritz, d. 1884; missionary, retired in Oxford.

Author of Gospel for 19th Cent. Church *very* full at night. Walk with C. Read Miss Toosey's Mission[1]—Gospel for the 19th Century.[2] Wrote a long memorandum of the evidence in regard to Dear Helen's religious profession.[3]

9. M.

Ch. 8½ AM. Wrote to Lady Stapleton[4]—Earl of Kintore—Mr J. Usher—Mr J.B. Manthrop—Sir Thos G.—Miss de Lisle—Mr R.B. Smith—Prof. Sbarbari—Mr Stead—Mr R. Brown, jun.—Mr L.P. Crawfurd (Eton).[5] Began work on a large chesnut. Attended the farewell Gamlin Teaparty. Saw Miss Scott on her affairs—Mrs Stume on the question of religious communion. Read Waring on U. States.[6] Read Cowper's Task—Waring on America—The Runaway[7]—Scott on Centralisation.[8]

Tu. 10.

Ch. 8⅛ AM. Wrote to Sir T. Acland 1. & BP—Ld Granville—Prof Fawcett MP—J.E. Gladstone—Mr Sheldon Amos—Mr Parkinson—R. Leake—Mr Fithian[9]—A.G. Smith—W. Curry. Read Il Nihilismo—The Bystander[10]—G. Smith?—Nouvelle Revue—Political Art.—do M. Paulia[t] on Homer[11]—The Runaway—Cowper's Task. Worked on the Sp. Chestnut.

11. Wed. (Ash).

Ch. 8½-10¼, with Holy Communion. Wrote to Williams & Norgate—Professor E. Wiebe[12]—M. Pauliat 1. & BP[13]—Mr Holmes M.P.[14]—Mr Mac Cobha[15]—Rev. Mr Knox Little—Messrs Middlehurst—Mr Lentry—A. Brown—J. Graham—A. Mynott—H.W. Lee. Brought the Sp. Chestnut down: 4¼ hours in all. Read Pauliat (finished)—The Runaway (finished)—Il Nihilismo—Cowper's Task—The Fifth Book is very noble in its moral strain.

---

[1] *Miss Toosey's Mission. By the author of 'Laddie'* [E. Whitaker] (1878).

[2] See 1 Feb. 80.

[3] In *Autobiographica*, iv. 37.

[4] Mary Catherine, da. of Adam S. Gladstone, m. 1878 Sir Francis George Stapleton, 1831-99, 8th bart.

[5] Lionel Payne Crawfurd, 1864-1934; at Eton, had written on Homer; later priest and author.

[6] C. Waring, *Some things in America set forth in thirteen letters* (1880).

[7] [E. A. Hart], *The Runaway* (1872).

[8] Not found.

[9] (Sir) Edward William Fithian, 1845-1936; barrister; secretary of the Commons Preservation Society; kt. 1905.

[10] First number of the periodical published in Toronto.

[11] L. Pauliat, 'La Société au temps d'Homer', *Nouvelle Revue*, ii. 350 (1880).

[12] Perhaps Edward Wiebe, published on children's education.

[13] Louis Pauliat, French colonial historian and Homerist, who had presumably sent his article.

[14] Hugh Holmes, 1840-1916; tory M.P. Dublin university 1885-7 (law officer 1885); judge 1887.

[15] Charles J. MacColla; on his *Breach of promise* (1879); *T.T.*, 14 February 1880, 5e.

12. Th.

Ch. 8½ A.M. Wrote to Messrs Pears Logan & Co—Mr A. Forbes 1 & BP—Mr Downing BP—Mr Josiah Leaver—Rev. H.F. Clinton[1]—E. Purcell[2]—Lord Crewe[3]—Mr Ouvry—W.H.G.—H.N.G.—Mrs Th. BP—H.W. Lee. Saw Mr Bowman—L. Waters. Walk with the Rector. Worked on books. Worked on Homeric Paper, tardily resumed. Read Melbourne Review on Marriage Laws[4]—finished Cowper's Task. Read Fairbairn.[5]

13. Fr.

Ch. 8½ AM. Wrote to WHG & Messrs [blank]—Miss de Lisle—Mad. Novikoff—R. Richardson—Councr Mandley—J. M'Donald (O)—A. M'Donald MP.—Mr Leslie Hunter[6]—B. Brunswic—Mrs Macfarlane—Mrs Wynne—R. Knight—Mr Claydon—Mr Gillow—Mr Barnes—Mr Paterson—Mr Gurdon. Read Fairbairn—Chiara's Albania[7]—E. Lyttelton in 19th Cent.[8]—Nicols on Hist. of the Earth.[9] Kibbling the Chestnut. Worked on Coxe & Olympian system.

14. Sat.

Wrote to Sir Thos G.—J. Bartley 1 & BP—Sig. Mangozzi[10]—J.G. Wilson US.[11]—Mr [F.] Vivian Dodgson—Mr Thompson—W.F. Gandell[12]—Sec. to Ld Mayor—Miss Ruskin—Mr Piper—Mr Hellen—Mr Farley—Mr Walford—Ld Rosebery. Saw the Rector (Church Seats)—Miss Fitzmaurice. Worked on Mad. N.s book.[13] Read Mad. N.s book—History of the Earth. Kibbling the chestnut: awkward work.

15. 1 S. Lent.

Ch. 11 AM & 6½ PM. Wrote to Messrs Farrer Ouvry & Co—Sir Thos G.—Mr Knowles—Mr Ouvry. Read the Biography of the noble Dora Pattison.[14] How, by reflex action, it stings. Never did I more feel what a wretch I am. And yet even to her (like Bp Butler) death was terrible. The Vol. took all my time.

---

[1] Henry Fiennes-Clinton, rector of Cromwell, Newark.
[2] Edmund Sheridan Purcell (d. 1899; biographer of Manning and de Lisle) had requested help in getting a post on *Daily News*; Add MS 44494, f. 206 (misplaced).
[3] Hungerford Milnes, 1812–94; 3rd Baron Crewe 1835; a liberal.
[4] St John Topp, 'The marriage and divorce laws', *Melbourne Review*, iv. 429 (1879).
[5] A. M. Fairbairn, *Studies in the life of Christ* (1880).
[6] (George) Leslie Hunter, Scottish artist, then living in London.
[7] Piero Chiara sent his *L'Albania* (Palermo, 1869).
[8] E. Lyttelton, 'Athletics in public schools', *Nineteenth Century*, vii. 43 (January 1880).
[9] A. Nichols, *Chapters from the physical history of the earth* (1880).
[10] Possibly Antonio Mangoni of Naples, published on Italian finances.
[11] James Grant Wilson, 1832–1914; American author, had sent 'a copy of a privately printed volume just issued', apparently one of his many works on President Grant; Hawn P.
[12] Liberal organizer in Hackney.
[13] O. Novikov, *Russia and England from 1876 to 1880*, with a preface by J. A. Froude; reviewed by Gladstone in *Nineteenth Century*, vii. 538 (March 1880).
[14] M. Lonsdale, *Sister Dora* (1880), Mark Pattison's sister, famous for nursing the poor.

16. M.

Ch. 8½ AM. Wrote to Duke of Argyll—Miss Burnett—Messrs T. & B.—Hon Mrs Pennant—Earl of Rosebery—Mr Hitchman—E. Saunders—Madame Novikoff—Master of Charterhouse—Mr Haughton—W.H.G.—J. Wood—Mr Downing—Mr Williams—Mrs Th.—Ly M. Alford. Worked on a projected paper on Made Novikoff's book. Worked on my Library. Saw the Rector (Dined at R.)—Mrs Burnett. Read Mad. Novikoff—History of the Earth. Haunted with the recollections of Sister Dora.

17. Tu.

Ch. 8½ AM. Wrote to J. Watson & Smith—Mr Griffiths—Mr Knowles—S. Langley—C. Cowan—Miss King—Chairman Sunderland Lib. Club—Prof. Thurston[1]—Pericles Tzikco[2]—J.T. Stephen[3]—W.H. Thomas. Walk with the Rector. Worked on paper respecting the Novikoff book. Read the Book—also Le Droit Social.[4]

18. Wed.

Ch. 8½ AM. Wrote to Ld Crewe, & copy—Earl Granville—Ed. Daily News—Madame Novikoff—E.D. White—W.H.G.—Scotts—Mr Lane—Mr Lillie—Mr Agnew. Worked on Article. Also on arranging Library. Also on kibbling chestnut. Read Madame Novikoff—Le Droit Social—Murdoch's Rhymes & Lyrics.[5]

19. Th.

Ch. 8½ AM. Wrote to Dr Carpenter—Miss Lonsdale[6]—Mr Illingworth—Sig. Chiara—Mr Thomas—Rev. R. Owen—Rev. Knox Little—Mr Nicols—J. Kay. Worked on Article. Worked much on Library. Finished 'Russia & England'. Read Theory and Practice.[7] Saw L. Waters—Mr Lawley—Mr Dodson—and others. Dined at Mr (Sheriff) Johnson's. Finished kibbling Chestnut.

20. Fr.

Ch. 8½ AM. Wrote to Ld Granville—Spottiswoodes—Mrs Th.—D. Munro[8]—D. Rhys—Prof. Hanyon—W. Barnes—A.J. Wilson. Worked on article. Worked on Library. Planting on the round landmark hill in Hawarden where we hope to make a little spot of public rest if not recreation. Saw Mr Woodward. Read Il Nihilismo—Old England[9]—and [blank.]

---

[1] Robert Henry Thurston, 1839-1903; American engineer and educationalist; requested a copy of diarist's Glasgow rectorial; Hawn P.

[2] Author of *Paolo Gianini*, 3v. (1879); a novel.

[3] Probably the London commission agent; not of the literary family.

[4] Not found.

[5] A. G. Murdoch, *Lilts on the Doric Lyre* (1873).

[6] Margaret Lonsdale, author; see 15 Feb. 80n.

[7] Untraced.

[8] Probably Lewis Munro of Dingwall; sent cutting on 2 Jan.; Hawn P.

[9] [H. Gandy], *Old England; or the government of England prov'd to be monarchical and hereditary* (1705).

21. Sat

Ch. 8½ AM. Wrote to Messrs Townshend & B.—Regr of Charterhouse B.P.—Mr Pascoe BP—W. Barnes BP—Mr Furnival—Rev. T.C. Russell[1]—A.D. Shaw—R. Smith—Mr Fordham—A. North—Mr And. Tod—Rev. Dr Hillier.[2] Worked on Library. Finished article. Read Il Nihilismo—and examined a number of books and tracts chiefly Theol. Saw Rowlands—Miss Burnett—and others.

22. 2 S.L.

Ch 11 AM & 6½ PM. Wrote to Makkan Lal Day—Messrs Spottiswoode BP.— Made Novikoff—W.T. Webb—W.L. Kiloh—A.R. Cooke. Read The Gospel for the Nineteenth Century: & skimmed many theological books.

23. M. [London]

Left Hawarden at 9.15 with a heavy heart. Harley St at 3.30. H. of C. 4.30-7¼.[3] Ten to dinner. Wrote to Mr Thielmann[4]—Mr Cherrett—Mr Pryse. Saw Ld Chesham—Archdeacon Allen—Mr Gurdon—Sir W. Harcourt—Ld Harting- ton—& others. Finished Il Nihilismo. Read England under Lord Beaconsfield.[5] Touched the mere fringe of the Chaos that awaited me in H St.

24.[6] Tu.

Wrote to Ld Rosebery—Mrs Hampton—Mrs Wallace—Miss Lonsdale—Rev. Mr Champy[7]—Made Novikoff—Mr Ouvry—Mr Morgan—Mr Clapp—Mr Flaxman— Mr Knowles. Corrected Proofs of 19th Century. H. of C. 4½-7¼.[8] Dined at Ld Granville's. Saw Mr Newdigate—Ld Granville—Mr Hayward—Lady Rosebery— Mr Adam—Rev. Mr MacColl—Mr Knowles—Count Bylandt—Count Monte- bello and others.

25. Wed. St Matth.

Wrote to Ed. of Examiner—Mrs Bennett—Messrs Trübner—(Mr Hedley Jones)—Mr Sp. St John—Mr Beechbrooke—Sig. Lisciotti—Mr Chick—Mr Lee B.P.—Mr Bates—Mr Colman—Miss Bowie—Mr Bates—Mr Oates[9]—Col. Laurie. Saw Ld R. Grosvenor—Mad. Novikoff—Mrs Watkins—Mr Ouvry—Sir W. Har- court—Mr Loser[?]—Mr Adam—W.H.G. Visited R. Academy. Dined with the Speaker. Worked on my Chaos. Read Engl. under Lord B.

---

[1] Thomas Cusack Russell, a nonconformist.
[2] Edward John Hillier, d. 1908; fellow of Trinity, Cambridge 1848-58; vicar of Cardington 1856.
[3] Irish newspapers; H 250. 1214.
[4] Perhaps Adolf Wilhelm von Thielmann, published Pro-Caesare. Social-conservative Betrachtungen (Berlin, 1878).
[5] Sent by the author, P. W. Clayden (1880); a well researched liberal indictment, used by Glad- stone in preparing the 1880 Midlothian Campaign.
[6] This and next day dated '25' and '26' respectively.
[7] Joseph Chamney, anglican priest at Dromiskin, on Latin hymns; Hawn P.
[8] Spoke on privilege; H 250. 1315.
[9] Austin Oates, involved with Helen J. Gladstone's affairs, returned one of her books; Hawn P.

26. Th.

Wrote to Spottiswoodes (2)—Mr Foljambe MP—Rev. Mr Blakiston[1]—Rev. A. Coghlan—J.G. Bennett—Mr Hedley Jones—Mr Burnley—Rev. S.G. Hatherley—Rev. Chancellor Whitaker[2]—A. Way[3]—F. Adams—Mr Fordham—Mr Herford—Mr Parkes—Mr Carbutt[4]—R.H. Blades.[5] Dined at Mr West's. Saw Marquis of Bath—Mr Thorndike Rice—Mr Cyrus Field—Mr Bright—Mr F. Leveson—Lord Selborne. Read Hubbard on Rev. & Debt[6]—England under Lord B. More fight with Chaos. H of C. $4\frac{1}{2}$-$7\frac{1}{4}$ & $10\frac{3}{4}$-12.[7]

27. Fr.

Wrote to Made Novikoff—Sir Thos G.—Mr Dinnin—Mr Ouvry—Mr Barclay—Mr Richardson—Rev. H. Duncan—Capt Gorringe[8]—Mr Maneile—R.H. Thomas. Saw Mr Chick—Mr Storey—Mrs Th. Read Bonghi on W.E.G.[9]—England under Lord B. Spoke at H of C. on Obstruction. Dined with the Jameses. Then spoke $\frac{3}{4}$ hour at St Pancras Meeting in fearful heat. Much tired. H of C. $4\frac{1}{2}$-7. Spoke on the Obstruction-Resolutions.[10] Dined at Sir W. James's. Went to Marylebone Political Meeting & spoke $\frac{3}{4}$ hour.[11]

28. Sat.

Wrote to Watson & S.—G.S. Leecraft—T.H. Muir BP—Herr Hangen—Herr Weilmann[12]—J. Barr—E. Purcell—Mr Fordham—Mr Myles and. . . .
Merchant of Venice 2-5. Irvine's best, I think. Saw Ld Granville—Mr West—Mr MacColl—Mr Ottley. Dined with Ly Cowell Stepney. Read Speech of Loyd Lindsay—Cowan [sic] on E. Question[13]—Macfarlane on Ireland[14]—Cassels on Duration of Parlts[15]—England under Ld Beaconsfield.

29. 3 S.L.

Chapel Royal mg & aft. Saw Miss Irby cum Me Novikoff—Dr Clark (who dined with us)—Ld Granville. Read Capes on Our Knowledge of God[16]—Milton's ans. to Parker[17]—Dale Stewart on Evang. Opinion[18]—& other tracts.

---

[1] Perhaps Charles Dendy Blakiston, curate of Haywards Heath.
[2] George Herbert Whitaker, 1847-1930; principal of Truro theological college 1878-85; Hawn P.
[3] Of Bath, on Homer; Hawn P.
[4] E. N. Carbutt, wrote from Biarritz about printing speeches; Hawn P.
[5] Rowland Hill Blades, 1826-98; printer and bibliographer.
[6] J. G. Hubbard, 'National finance. Two letters, reprinted from *The Times*' (1880).
[7] Northcote's Resolution on business of the House; *H* 250. 1450.
[8] Perhaps Hugh Gorringe of Kingston, Brighton.
[9] Ruggiero Bonghi (see 4 Oct. 79) published two essays on Gladstone at this time, on Church and state, and on finance, see his *Opere*, iv (1935).
[10] Supporting Northcote's proposals; *H* 250. 1594.
[11] Supporting Chambers and Grant, the liberal candidates; *T.T.*, 28 February 1880, 10b.
[12] Frederick L. Weinmann sent his work on Pompeii; Add MS 44462, f. 132.
[13] 'The memorable speech of Joseph Cowen, M.P., delivered at Newcastle . . . January 31st, 1880.'
[14] D. H. Macfarlane, *Ireland versus England* (1880).
[15] In *Contemporary Review*, xxxvii. 392 (March 1880).
[16] J. M. Capes, *What can be certainly known of God and of Jesus of Nazareth?* (1880).
[17] W. Milton, 'Mr Parker's fallacies refuted; a letter' (1880).
[18] D. D. Stewart, *Evangelical opinion in the nineteenth century* (1879).

Mond. Mch One 80.

Wrote to B.T. Barnes—Helen G.—Mr Aldis—A. Nixon—Mr Babbage[1]—Mr Richards—Mrs Hampton—Mr Blades—Rev. Mr Tugwell[2]—Miss A. de Crecy—C.J. Thynne[3]—Mr Melhuish—Rev. J.M. Capes—J. Morgan &c.—Scotts. Saw Mr Panchaud[4]—Mr Bagot Molesworth[5]—E. Macgregor. Shopping, & working on my Chaos. Read Mr Capes (finished)—England under Lord B.—19th Cent. on The Navy, on Home Rule.[6]

2. Tu.

Wrote to Dean of Windsor BP—Rev. G. Cook—Rev. H. Derrig[7]—Rev. C.D. Duport[8]—Mr Labilliere[9]—H.H. Howorth[10]—Govr Pope Hennessy—Sec. Sullogos (Lephosia)[11]—Mr Fagan—Mr Vitali—Sir H. Moncreiff—J. Davies—C. King—F. Hinde—A.W. Adams—Sig. E. Stai[12]—Rev. Mr Tucker. Saw Mrs Mathews—Lord Bath—W.H.G.—Scotts—Mr Bright. Attended conclave on 'local option' and reluctantly agreed to speak. H of C. $5\frac{1}{2}$-$7\frac{1}{2}$.[13] Read Life of Dr E. Darwin[14]—Tourgueneff Pères et Enfans[15]—Fawcett on Indian Finance.[16] Worked on papers.

3. Wed.

Wrote to Ld Lyttelton—W.H.G.—Mr Reavis[17]—C.E. Mace—Mr Marshall—Dr Hatzfeld—Govr of Brentwood Asyl. B.P.—J. Watson & Smith BP—W.D. Scott—W. Paterson—E. Moffatt—Mr M'Guiness—H.S. Griffiths—Arnold [W.] White—Sir Thos G. Worked vigourously for hours on reducing to order books papers & letters. Saw Mr MacColl—W.H.G.—Ld R. Grosvenor *cum* W.H.G.—Lady Derby—Count Arco—Lord Bath—Mr Hayward. Read Vict. Review on Protection[18]—Fraser on the Elections.[19] Severe neuralgia pain at night. My share of bodily pain in life has been small. It is a great instrument of assimilation, hard to dispense with.

[1] Perhaps Henry Prevost Babbage, 1824-1918, s. of C.*; general in India, retired 1874.
[2] George Tugwell, geologist and rector of Bathwick 1871.
[3] Probably John Charles Thynne, 1838-1918, barrister.
[4] Robert Augustus Panchaud, London china dealer.
[5] George Bagot Gossett Molesworth, 1853-1917; barrister; ordained 1915.
[6] Spencer Robinson and the Knight of Kerry in *Nineteenth Century*, vii. 389, 493 (March 1880).
[7] Hugh Carey Derrig, curate of Mugrisdale.
[8] Charles Durell Duport, H.M. school inspector.
[9] Francis Peter Labillière, London barrister; on colonial union; Hawn P.
[10] (Sir) Henry Hoyle Howarth sent his *Irish monks and the Norsemen* (1880); Add MS 44462, f. 94.
[11] The Syllogues were guardians of the Greek language; see [Baron Malortie], *Diplomatic Sketches*, volume iii: *Mr Gladstone and the Greek question* (1879), 175n.
[12] Emmanuel Stai of Birmingham; Hawn P.
[13] Game laws; *H* 251. 158.
[14] E. Krause, *Erasmus Darwin* (1880).
[15] Reading Turgenev's novel in French (1863), though E. Schuyler's English tr. was available (1867).
[16] H. Fawcett, 'Indian finance. Three essays' (1880); republished articles.
[17] Logan Uriah Reavis, 1831-89; American author writing on christianity and commerce; visited London late in 1879.
[18] See 13 Nov. 80.
[19] *Fraser's Magazine*, ci. 421 (March 1880).

4. *Th.*

Wrote to F. Berkeley—Rev. Mr Baker—Rev. Lendrum—J. Elford[1]—Mr Darley—J. Clare—Mr Wylrow—P. Kenny—Mr Smeeton—Geo. Ware[2]—P.W. Clayden—C. Dibdin[3]—Mr Marshall—T. Jones—Mr Kavanagh[4]—Mr Challenger[5]—C.E.P. Rhodes[6]—Lt Luscombe—Dr Jex Blake—Dr A. Heine—W.H. Harper. A quiet day: rose at 10. Dined with the Wests. Saw Mr Welly—Mrs Th. Read Elfrida[7]— Carpenter on the Sea.[8]

5. *Fr.*

Wrote to Capt. de C. Bisson[9]—G. Brandis[10]—Mr Moreton—Mr Clouston—S. Higgins—P. Shorter—Jas Fell—Mr Hatson—Mr Ketcham—R. Knight—Rev. Mr Suffield—Ed. Scotsman[11]—Gustav Sarnow—C. Delmath—Herr Appelstadt— W.S. Aldis—R.W. Kenyon—R.C. Field—Mons. E. Nys—Sir Thos G. Saw Mr Lyulph Stanley—W.H.G.—Ld Hartington—Mr Bright. H of C. $4\frac{1}{2}$-$7\frac{1}{2}$. Spoke on Sir Wilfrid Lawson's Resolution.[12] Read Elfrida—England under Lord B. Still working for *order*.

6. *Sat.*

Wrote to Lady Gladstone—Mr Nettleton[13]—Count? Mocenigo—W.E. Darwin[14]—Robert Gladstone—Miss Simpson—Mr Bulgarnic—Mr Stodewell— Mr Cohen QC—H. Lee—L.E. Neal—Mr Porley—Thos Cook—Ld Rosebery—Mr Stanton.[15] Worked a little on the Homeric Mythology. Saw Lady Rosebery. Read England under Lord B.—Elfrida—Water Supply of London.[16]

---

[1] Of Homerton; Hawn P.

[2] George Ware (1829-95; music-hall artiste) sent his song, 'The Three Jolly Britons', asking permission to dedicate it to Gladstone; unclear if permission was granted; Hawn P.

[3] Charles Dibdin, 1849-1910, savings bank clerk; on banks, Hawn P.

[4] Probably Arthur MacMurrough Kavanagh, 1831-89; tory M.P. Wexford 1866-8, Carlow 1868-80; on Irish Land Commission 1880, see 17 July 80n.

[5] Samuel Christopher Challenger, Methodist minister in Bromley.

[6] Not a relative of the imperialist; perhaps Charles Rhodes, china dealer.

[7] [W. Mason], *Elfrida: a dramatic poem* (1772).

[8] W. B. Carpenter, 'The temperature and life of the deep sea' (1871).

[9] Captain Frederick Shirley de Carteret Bisson, F.R.G.S., wrote from the Beaconsfield Club asking for Gladstone's comments on his work on education; Hawn P.

[10] Georg Morris Cohen Brandes, 1842-1927; Danish literary critic and historian; wrote widely on British affairs, including Disraeli (see 17-29 May 80).

[11] Denying nine fabrications; *T.T.*, 9 March 1880, 9f.

[12] Unable to support Lawson on local option; *H* 251. 465.

[13] John Oldfield Nettleton, stockbroker.

[14] William Erasmus Darwin, 1839-1909; first son of C.R.*; horticulturalist; see 2 Mar. 80.

[15] Walter John Stanton, 1828-?; liberal M.P. Stroud 1874, 1880-5.

[16] F. R. Conder, 'The water supply of London', *Fraser's Magazine*, cii. 185 (August 1880).

7. 4 S.L.

Charlotte St Ch mg & Vere Street evg. Saw Mr Tennyson. Wrote to Lord Acton. Read Catholic Presbyterian, various Article[1]—The Divine Afflatus[2]— Sermon on Simpson Evans[3]—Colebrooke on Indian Faiths.[4]

8. M.

Wrote to Miss Burnett—Mr Grinfield[5]—D. Grant—E.C. Robins[6]—W. Miller—A. Miall[7]—Mr Simmonds—E.L. Stanley—Ld Wolverton—Dr Herzfeld—Rev. R.C. Jenkins—Dr Döllinger BP—Mr Hanns—Rev. R. Sewell[8]—Mr Barlow—Mr Macrae Moir—Mr Beveridge.[9] Saw Sir Thos G. on H.s affairs—Ld Granville—Mr Childers—Ld Kensington—Mr Bright—Lady Rosebery (2): & dined—Ld Rosebery (2). Wrote a little on Homer. Read England under Lord B.
Dissolution announced.

9. Tu.

Wrote to Mr Quail—Mr De Morgan—Rev. D. Griffiths—Mr C.B. Norman—Rev. J.M. Evans[10]—Mr Sadlier[11]—J.A. Smith—Lord Hanmer—Miss Minot—Mr Irwin— Prof. Nixon. Eight to dinner. $3\frac{1}{2}$ Conclave on the ganglion of seats Flintshire W. Chesh. & E. Worcestershire. Most difficult affair to meet all.[12] Saw Mr Wilkie, Mr Saunders (Deputn) Mr Fyfer—for the press. Saw Jas Wortley—W.H.G. (on the Colliery, too)—Mr MacColl. Nine to dinner. Conclave in evg on first draft of my Address.[13] Wrote a little, perforce, on Homer.

10. Wed.

Wrote to Mr Hayward—Ld Wolverton—Ld Granville—Ld Rosebery Tel.—Mr Ouvry—Mr Smitche—Mr Mould—Mr Grinfield—Mr Whitfield—Mr Bayley Potter—R. Richardson—W. Goalen—Mr Atkins—Mr Corcoran—Mrs Th.—Mr Lynch. Saw the *Press* gentlemen. Conclave at Devonshire H. $12\frac{1}{2}$-$1\frac{1}{2}$. Attended the Levée: the Queen with her usual high manners put on a kindly smile. Saw Ld Wolverton (2)—Ld Granville—Mr Childers—Sir H. Ponsonby—Ld Ripon— Sir C. Forster—W.H.G.—D. of Bedford—Mr Hughes—Ld Kensington—Ld R.

---

[1] *Catholic Presbyterian*, iii (March 1880); perhaps article by D. MacColl on the early British Church.
[2] See 15 Aug. 75.
[3] Perhaps R. Emerson, 'An address to the Clergy and Parishioners of St. Leonards, Shoreditch . . . containing an enquiry What has the Vicar [T. S. Evans] done?' (1843).
[4] H. T. Colebrook, *Essays on the religion and philosophy of the Hindus* (1858).
[5] C. J. Grinfield of Weston-super-Mare; an admirer; Hawn P.
[6] Edward Cookworthy Robins, F.S.A.
[7] Arthur, son and biographer of Edward *Miall.
[8] Robert Sewell, minister in Londonderry; Hawn P.
[9] James Beveridge of Glasgow; on Scottish poetry; Hawn P.
[10] John Michael Evans, priest in Buckley.
[11] Perhaps F. Sadlier, chaplain at the Curragh.
[12] Lord R. Grosvenor was unopposed in Flintshire, W. C. West and C. Crompton were defeated in W. Cheshire, W. H. Gladstone and G. W. Hastings gained their seats from tories in E. Worcs.
[13] Final version in *Political speeches* (1880), 357.

Grosvenor—Mr Cowper Temple—Mr Cross. H. of C. at 1¾.[1] Read Engl. under
Lord B. Partly recast my Address.

11. Th.

Wrote to Mr Chrysovoloni—Mr Ward—Mr Chick—Mr Hine—Mrs Hope—Mr
Infield—Mr Jolly—Mr Beatts—Mr Groves—Herr Karolyi—Mrs Heywood—Mr
Nuttall 1 & BP—Mrs Macdonnell—Mr Richardson 1. & Tel.—J. Maclaren—Lord
Edw. Clinton—Mr Davidson—Mr Saunders. Finally corrected & dispatched my
Address. Saw Mr Whitfield—Mr Ouvry—Mr Wheeler—Mr West (2)—Earl
Granville—Ld F.C. *cum* Mr Foljambe—Sir Thos G.—Mr Childers—Mr A. Peel—
Sir C. Forster—Mr Lowell—Ld R. Grosvenor—Miss Thompson—Mr Wheeler—
Count [blank.] Saw Bertram [R]. H of C. 4½-7½: spoke briefly on Budget.[2]

12. Fr.

Wrote to Lt Kavanaugh—Lord Hanmer—Mr Dairn (Leeds)[3]—Mr Ashworth—
J.B. Gibson[4]—G.M. Towle—A.G. Williams—R. Richardson—Mr Hyndman[5]—Mr
Ouvry—Ld Clifton—Mrs Wright—Mr Dowe—Dr Rogge[6]—Ld Crewe—Mr
Hughes—Mr Crawford and. . . . Read England under Lord B. Saw Ld R. Gros-
venor—Mr Whitfield Photogr (sat to him)—Mr MacColl—Mr Bryce—Sir W.H.
James—W.H.G.—Mr Kitson (Leeds)—Mr Fawcett—Mr Childers—Mr Adam—
Lady Rosebery. H of C. 2½-5½. Spoke on Indian & Afgh. Expences.[7] 9¼-10¾. Went
to the remarkable meeting in Newman Street: spoke 40 m indoors, & for some
6 or 8 min to 10000 in the open air from a window.[8]

13. Sat.

Wrote to Mr Ouvry (2)—Mrs Heywood—Rev. Mr Pearson—Rev. Mr Husband[9]
—Lord R. Grosvenor—J. Kavanagh[10]—S. Cartmell[11]—Bp of Edinburgh[12]—
Mr Richardson (Tel.)—Mr Bertram[13]—C.G.—Ed. D. News—Mr Lewis—Mr

---

[1] The House met at 1.50 p.m.
[2] Establishing time-table for its discussion, and raising points about the £8m. deficit; *H* 251. 834.
[3] Gladstone was returned for Leeds as well as Midlothian, H. J. Gladstone being unopposed at the
subsequent by-election; see 7 Apr. 80 etc.
[4] Dr J. Burns Gibson, liberal in Willesden; Hawn P.
[5] Letter untraced; Hyndman's letter to Gladstone was quoted in this day's speech. Henry Mayers
*Hyndman, 1842-1921; imperialist in 1870s, becoming a revolutionary about this time; attempted to
stand as an independent for Marylebone 1880, withdrew after his candidacy was denounced by
Gladstone (at this day's meeting) for letting in the tories; see C. Tsuzuki, *H. M. Hyndman and British
socialism* (1961), 28-30.
[6] Friedrich Wilhelm Rogge, 1808-89; German author; Hawn P.
[7] Supporting Fawcett's resolution that all expenditure of the Afghan war should not be borne by
India; *H* 251. 930.
[8] The occasion splendidly described by W. L. Watson, quoted in Kilbracken, *Reminiscences* (1931),
109-12: 'I had been Gladstonized.' Report in *D.N.*, 13 March 1880, 5g, which refers throughout to
'Hindman'.
[9] Probably George Radclyffe Husband, vicar of Laneham.
[10] Probably James Kavanagh of Portarlington; later letter in Hawn P.
[11] Studholme Cartmell, on proposed visit to Carlisle; Hawn P.
[12] H. Cotterill.   [13] William Bertram, liberal activist in Edinburgh.

Channing—Mr Crawford—Mr Holiday—D. Lewis. Worked on Achaian Mythology. Saw Lord F. Cavendish—Mr West—Ld Ripon—Prince Louis Napoleon— Mr Cartwright—Mr Morley—Mr Tennyson—Ld Bath. Eleven to dinner. Tennyson & his son came in later. Read Engl. under Lord B.

14. 5 S. Lent.

St George's H. Squ. mg—and St James's evg. Wrote to Mr A.G. Murdoch—Rev. Mr Ashley—Ld Acton—Ld Chesham—Sig Bonghi—Mr Knowles—M. Gennadios—Sir W. Farquhar. Saw W.H.G.—Bertram—W. Dumaresq—Lady Rosebery—Mr Cunningham—Sir W. James—Mr Ellice. Finished & sent off my MS on Religion Achaian & Semitic.[1] Read Princeton Review[2]—Jesus et la Religion Naturelle.[3] Dined with the Jameses.

15. M.

Wrote to Bp of Exeter—Scotts—Ld Edw. Clinton—Mr Lambault (O)—Squire Judson[4]—S.D.G. Russell—Mr Tanenberg—Sir B. Phillips[5]—Mr Jardine Craig—Mr Boodle—Mr Newsome—W. Paine—M. Uranga BP—J. Miller jun.—Dr A. Clark— Sir C. Wood. Saw Mr Chick—Mr Hamilton—Mr West—Mr Godley—Mr Adam— Ld Rosebery—Lord Wolverton—Ld Cork—Mr Robinson—Dr B. Gibson—Mr Dodson—Mr Childers. Dined at Sir C. Forster's. H of C. $4\frac{1}{4}$-8. Spoke on the Probate Duty Bill.[6]

16. Tu. [Dalmeny House, Edinburgh]

Wrote to Mr Newton—Mr . . .—Scotts. Saw Herbert G. & instructed him as Private Sec. Packing & off at 9.30. Was obliged to address the people at every point (5) before Edinburgh—At York there were I think 6000: very quiet. At Edinburgh the wonderful scene of Nov. was exactly renewed.[7] Reached Dalmeny 8.30 PM. Read Tracts on Mr Cowan[8]—Pr. Consort Vol. V[9]—Tourgenieff Terres Vierges.[10] Evening with Mr Reid & Mr Richardson[11] on the arrangements to be made.

17. Wed.

Wrote to Mr Madan[12]—Mr Toynbee—Mr Murray—Messrs C. Scribner & Sons[13]—Mr Adam l. & 2 Tell. Drove to Edinburgh. Great & most enthusiastic

[1] See 18 Dec. 79. [2] *Princeton Review*, lv. 177 (March 1880).
[3] Nemesio Uranga, Spanish writer on religion, had sent his *Jésus et la religion naturelle* (1880).
[4] Of Sowerby, sent verses; Add MS 44462, f. 189.
[5] Sir Benjamin Samuel Phillips, 1811-89; liberal London merchant and alderman; lord mayor 1865-6. [6] In fact, a general reply to Northcote's budget; *H* 251. 1022.
[7] Reports in *T.T.*, 17 March 1880, 13e.
[8] J. Cowen's speeches on the Eastern Question produced a series of tracts in reply.
[9] The fifth volume of T. Martin's *Life*. [10] By I. S. Turgenev (1877).
[11] J. J. Reid and Ralph Richardson, W.S., secretary of the Midlothian Liberal Association, who handled the details of the campaign.
[12] Perhaps Falconer Madan, 1851-1935; fellow of Brasenose, Oxford 1876-80; librarian and bibliographer.
[13] New York publishers; had sent £67/18/2 as royalties on the American edition of *Gleanings*; Hawn P.

meeting in the Music Hall. Spoke 1½ hour: questions &c. followed.[1] Worked up
Probate Duty figures. Quiet evg at Dalmeny. Read England under Lord B.
Began Pr. Consort Vol. V.

18. Th.

Wrote to Mr Hinde Palmer[2]—Rev. Mr Enraght[3]—Lord Dalrymple—Herbert
John G.—Mr MacCulloch—Mr Tennant MP—T. Reeves[4]—J. Rankin—Mr
Knowles Tel.—Mr Myers WE. Meeting at Corstorphine in Free Kirk. Sp. 1¼
hour. And at Ratho in School: ¾ hour. All signs good. And dear dear Herbert is
out for Middlesex.[5] God be with him! Read Lefevre on Game Laws[6]—Life of
Prince Consort.

19. Fr.

Wrote to Mr Macewen[7]—J.W. Burns—Rev. Mr Guthrie[8]—Spottiswoodes—
Scotts—Mr Knowles (Tel)—Ld Granville. At 12½ to Cramond Meeting. Free
Kirk full. Spoke some 20 .. 25 min. At 3¼ to Dalkeith. Great & enthusiastic
meeting. Spoke 1 h. 20 or 25 min. Tea at Provost Mitchell's and back to D. at
7.15 *special*. Saw Ld Young—Rev. Mr White—Mr Nicolson *cum* Mr.... Read
Th. Martin Vol V.—Corrected and dispatched proofs of Religion Achaian and
Semitic.

20. Sat.

Wrote to Mr Rippin (Tel)[9]—Mr Atkinson—R.W. Wallace—Rev. Mr Hutchin-
son—A.E. West[10]—Mr Jas Barr—Mr Davies—Mr Mitchison.[11] Travelled 40 miles
& delivered three speeches of 45 or 50 min. each at Juniper Green, Colinton
(Balerno) and Mid Calder. Tea at Rev. Mr Scotts U.P.[12]—Enthusiasm unabated.
Read Pr. Consort. Large party at Dalmeny. Saw Mr Clow (Glasgow U.)[13]—Dr
Donaldson[14]—Mr Pillan(?)—Lady Hopetoun—Dr Wallace—and others.

---

[1] This and subsequent speeches are in *Political speeches in Scotland, March and April 1880* (1880).
[2] Sending letter of support to John Hinde Palmer, 1808-84, liberal M.P. Lincoln 1868-74, 1880-4.
[3] Richard William Enraght, vicar of Bordesley; on highchurchmen's liberal voting; Hawn P.
[4] Thomas Reeves, sculptor, sent a design for Gladstone/Disraeli medallions; Add MS 44462, f. 207.
[5] H. J. Gladstone was defeated in Middlesex, the only liberal against two tories for the two seats. See 9 Apr. 80.
[6] G. J. Shaw-Lefevre, *The game laws* (1874).
[7] Perhaps William C. MacEwen, Edinburgh advocate.
[8] David K. Guthrie, Free Church minister in Liberton.
[9] H. W. Rippin, on the S. Essex campaign; Hawn P.
[10] Helping H. J. Gladstone in Middlesex; West, *Recollections*, ii. 97.
[11] W. G. Mitchelson of Newcastle, on foreign policy; Hawn P.
[12] William Scott, minister in Balerno.
[13] William MacCallum Clow, theology student at Glasgow; later a Free Church minister.
[14] James Donaldson; Dalmeny Visitors Book.

21. Palm S.

Down to Edinb. Cathedral. Service with H.C. 11-1½. Free St George's in aft.—
Walked out 7 m with Lord Rosebery, & much conversation. Wrote to Mr Mac-
dowall—Mr P. Stanhope—Mr S. Morley. Large party at Dalmeny. Saw Dr
[James] Donaldson—Mr Hogg[1]—Mr Reid—Mr Playfair and Lady R. on the Jews.
Read Wylie on Religion[2]—Thos a Kempis.

22. M.

Wrote to Mr West (further)—Mr Jerningham—Mr Macinnes[3]—Herbert J.G.—
D. Brown—Mr M'Kenzie. To Edinb. (after working as usual on my papers) at
1.15. & short complimentary Address at the Liberal Club.[4] Then to George St
& on to the City Election Committee: short Speech. Then by train to Gilmerton: spoke 45 or 50 min: then, after tea, to Loanhead, & after more tea, spoke
again for some time on Russian aggrandisement. Everywhere the greatest
enthusiasm. Mr . . . gave me interesting details about Magyar and Bohemian
Students. Back to Dalmeny at 7.20. Saw Dr Walter Smith[5]—Prof. [H.] Maine—
Col. Gillon.[6] Read Engl. under Lord B.—Life of Prince Consort.

23. Tu.

Wrote to Mr Bryce (2)—Rev. Sharman (Plymouth) Tel.—Mr Vyvyan (Bridgnorth)[7]—Mr Acton (Nottm) Tel.[8]—T.T. Hayes—R.J. Lindsay[9]—J.M. Wright—Dr
Moxey[10]—W.H.G.—Mr Officer[11]—Miss Bird—Mr Adam—G. Brown. Off at 2.10
for Gilmerton: spoke there for 50 min. Then to Loanhead. Spoke over an
hour.[12] Tea at Free Manse & drive 10 m. to Rosebery. Enthusiasm everywhere
the same. Saw Rev. Mr Goalen—so fresh!—Lord Reay—Mr Mackie—Mr Macfie—& others. Evening with Lord R. & much conversation. Read War of Independence—Life of Prince Consort.

24. Wed. [Edinburgh]

Wrote to Herbert J.G.—Mr Adam MP—Mr Macgeagh—Mr Atkinson—Sir J. Sin-
clair—Ed. Daily News—Mr Cohen QC—Mr Little (O)—J. Lang—W. Graham—
Mr Brogden—O. Morgan—Mr Wylie—Mr Williams—Mr Hardy Coulson—J.W.
Maclaren.[13] Saw Mr Inglis. Worked hard till 4.30. Off at 5 to Penycuick. At 7

---

[1] Thomas Alexander Hog, 1835-1908, of Newliston, Midlothian; staying at Dalmeny with his
wife Harriet; Dalmeny Visitors Book.
[2] J. A. Wylie, probably The history of Protestantism, 3v. (1874-7).
[3] Mason MacInnes, Edinburgh manufacturer.
[4] Not in Political Speeches; see T.T., 23 March 1880, 10f.
[5] Walter Chalmers Smith, 1824-1908; minister of High Free Church, Edinburgh.
[6] Andrew Gillon of Wallhouse, Deputy Lieutenant of Midlothian.
[7] Support for Edward R. Vyvyan, unsuccessful liberal candidate at Bridgnorth; Hawn P.
[8] Frederick Acton, liberal organizer in Nottingham.
[9] Robert John Lindsay, Edinburgh lawyer; correspondence on finance in Add MS 44462.
[10] D. A. Moxey of Edinburgh, on pronunciation; Hawn P.
[11] Agent of the convention of royal burghs; see T.T., 26 March 1880, 7e.
[12] Misremembering; this day's speeches were at Gorebridge and Pathhead.
[13] Of Edinburgh; sent a poem; Hawn P.

spoke for a few minutes outside (reluctantly, but to recommend a fair hearing for all) and 1¼ hour in the P[enicuik] Kirk. Tea at the Manse. Got out of train in Edinburgh at ten. Found my stomach had struck work & passed an uneasy night. Read Northcote on Afghanistan[1]—Life of P. Consort—and Tracts.

25. Th.

Rose for service at the Cathedral & H.C. 11-12¾: but went to bed afterwards. Wrote to Dr Wilton[2]—J. Kavanaugh—and. . . . Tel. Read Life of Pr. Consort— War of Independence[3]—Thomas a Kempis. Saw Ld Rosebery.

26. Good Friday.

Not able to go out: but doing well. Read my books in bed. Also produced a few verses. Read Life of P. Consort—War of Independence—Lowe on the late Parlt.[4] Saw Ld Rosebery. Wrote to Duke of Argyll—Lord Granville—Master W. Brown[5]—Mr Cawston—Mr Bristowe—Mr Tanenhay?—Mr Donaldson—Mr Bathgate—Mr Commissioner Kerr[6]—E. Allen—W.A. Stevens[7]—S. Chick (2)—Mr Godley—W.E. Bruce[8]—S. Jones—Mr Foster.

27. Sat.

Wrote to Mr Barker—Mr Kitson Tel.—Mr Eldred Tel.[9]—A.L. M'Clure—Jos. Newton—Lock & Whitfield[10]—A.E. West—Dowager Dss Somerset Tel.—Mr Jamieson—Sir Th. Martin (draft)—Mr Miller—Jas Allan—Rich. Lees[11]—J.H. Drake—Mr Cox—J. Craig. Saw Ld Young—Ld Shand—Ld Rosebery—Mr Richardson—Mr Stilly—Rev. Mr Sandford. Finished Vol. V of P. Consort. Much disgusted with p. 148.[12] Read also 'A Church Dignitary'. Service at Cathedral 11 A.M. and St John's 5. P.M.

28. Easter Sunday [Dalmeny]

H. Commn 9 AM. Cathedral. Morning service St Johns 11 AM. Attended West Kirk aftn. Wrote to Walter L. Gladstone—C.W. Bayley—Mr Sturrock (O)[13]—J.A. Godley—B. Taylor. Saw Ld Moncreiff—Ld Young—Mr Rollo. Much conversation

[1] Probably Northcote's public letter to Dalkeith, chiefly on finance; Gladstone attacked the letter's contents on 25 March and in subsequent Midlothian speeches.

[2] Perhaps John Wilton, physician in Sunderland.

[3] Perhaps H. P. Johnson, *The campaign of 1776* (1878).

[4] R. Lowe, 'The docility of an "imperial" parliament', *Nineteenth Century*, vii. 557 (April 1880).

[5] Probably an autograph.

[6] Robert Malcolm Kerr, commissioner of lieutenancy for London.

[7] William A. Stevens of London had accused him of popery; Hawn P.

[8] Of Kirkliston.

[9] J. W. Eldred, on the campaign at Sidcup; Hawn P.

[10] Photographers in Regent Street.

[11] Of Galashiels, on the campaign; Hawn P.

[12] Rude comments in letters by Prince Albert and Palmerston on Gladstone's tactics on the Fortifications Bill in 1860, see Morley, ii. 47 and Walling, *Diaries of Bright*, 438, diarist's draft reply at Add MS 44462, f. 300.

[13] Perhaps John Sturrock, short-hand writer in Edinburgh.

with Ld R. on Dr Macgregor's[1] Sermon, which was remarkable but covered I thought too wide a field. Read St Hilaire Bouddhisme[2]—Roman Cathm & America—Thos a Kempis. Much could I have wished a time of more tranquillity and recollection.—Back to D[almen]y.

29. Easter M.

Wrote to Solicitor General—Messrs Bacon (O)—Rev Mr MacColl—Mrs Lee—Ed. Scotsman—D. Grant—Mr Halliburton.[3] Presided at a luncheon banquet of 40 or 50 conveners: & spoke. Read many political Tracts—Ld Bath on Bulgaria[4]—Cromb's Essay[5]—How Ben behaved himself[6]—T. a Kempis. Saw Mr Macfie[7]—Mr Glendinning[8]—Mr Brown (Newhall)—Mr Richardson—Mr Melvin[9]—and others. Helen came.

30. Tu. [Laidlawstiel, Galashiels]

Wrote to Miss Lambert (O)—Mr MacCartney—Mr Ogilvy—Ld Rosebery (Tel.)—Mr Palmer—Mr Burton—Mr Puseley—B. Taylor Tel.[10] Read English Fragments—Ld Reay on French Land Law.[11] Off at 12½ by carriage & train. Spoke at Peebles—Innerleithen, reached Stow by Laidlaw Stiel at 4. Spoke 1 h. 20 m. to near 4000. High tide of enthusiasm. Slept at Laidlaw Stiel.[12] Saw Sir D. Wedderburn[13]—Mr Tennant—Ld Reay—Rev. Mr Robertson.

The beginning of the Elections. May God from heaven guide every one of them: and prosper or abase and baffle us for His glory: lift us up, or trample us down, according as we are promoting or opposing what *He* knows to be the cause of Truth, Liberty, and Justice.

31. Wed. [Edinburgh]

Wrote to Mr H. Evans (Tel)—Mr E.R. Evans[14]—Sir Theodore Martin K.C.B.—Mr W.H. James—Mr Geo Hens[15]—Draft letter to the Electors[16]—M. Gennadios. Off about 11 for Thornilee and Edinburgh after further conversation with Lord Reay. At Edinburgh went through the Corn Exchange: first escaping from a tail through the purlieus of the Scotsman Office. Then to the Committee Meeting

---

[1] i.e. James *MacGregor; see 4 June 78.
[2] J. Barthelémy-Saint-Hilaire, *Le Christianisme et le Bouddhisme. Trois lettres* (1880).
[3] W. W. Halliburton of Edinburgh G.P.O.
[4] J. A. Thynne, Lord Bath, *Observations on Bulgarian affairs* (1880).
[5] Untraced; name unclear.
[6] F. W. Drew, *How Ben behaved himself* (1880).
[7] Of Borthwickhall; chaired next day's meeting at Stow.
[8] Peter Glendinning of Leuchold, Dalmeny.
[9] James Melvin of Ratho; Hawn P.
[10] Of Peterborough, on the campaign; Hawn P.
[11] D. J. Mackay, Lord Reay; apparently an untraced MS.
[12] Reay's seat near Galashiels.
[13] Sir David Wedderburn, 1835-82; 3rd bart. 1862; liberal M.P. Ayrshire 1868-74, Haddington 1879-82.
[14] E. Rose Evans of Cheshire, on civil servants; *T.T.*, 24 April 1880, 7f.
[15] Of the Metropolitan Police.
[16] Published, dated 5 April, in *T.T.*, 6 April 1880, 5e.

at Lib. Club, where I spoke on the Election & on Lord Grey. Then worked in George St until dinner time. Public dinner in the Music Hall. Good speaking. Spoke twice. But the Polls proved the greatest interest. By 11 P.M. the doom of the Govt came in view & I alluded cautiously to it.[1] Slept in Ed[inburgh].

Thursd. Ap. One 1880. [Dalmeny]

Wrote to Herbert J.G.—Sir W.R. Farquhar—Mr J. M'Lean—Mr B.A. Heywood[2]—Dr Bowie—Electors of Midlothian (Circ)—Marquess of Bath—Mr Gill Tel.—Viscount Bury[3]—Mr Gowan[4]—Mr W. Armstrong[5]—Mr West—Dean of Windsor—Liberals of Leeds (Tel.) Read Monmouth.[6] Drove by Eskdale & Dalkeith Gate to Bonnyrigg, where I spoke near an hour, amidst the usual manifestations. We drove past the Buccleuch Gate which I last saw as a guest at Dalkeith thirty years ago. Such changes!

2. Fr.

Wrote to Walter Gladstone—Sir W.R. Farquhar—Mr J. Morley—Mr Buchanan—Dr Bowie—Sir D. Marjoribanks—Rev. Mr Smith—Mr W.W. Hunter—Ld Halifax. Went by carriage & rail to West Calder. Spoke 1 h. 25 m, amidst the old enthusiasm.[7] Great hospitality of the U.P. Manse.[8] Home about seven. Read England under Lord B. And so ends the second series of the speeches in which I have hammered with all my little might at the fabric of the present Tory power.[9]

3. Sat.

Wrote to Sir Thos G.—Solicitor General—Ld Wolverton—A.W. Gordon[10]—Mr Wilkinson—Sec. Hampstead Lib. Committee—Mrs Russell—Prof. Hodgson[11]—Mr Marshall—Dr Kirk[12]—Mr Havelock[13]—J. Latey—Mr Keeling—Mr Taylor (O)—M. Victor Oger. Cut down a Spanish chestnut in the Dalmeny Park: by order. Party at Dalmeny in evg. The day was quiet: but my papers & letters, & the incoming news made it busy. It seemed as if the arm of the Lord had bared itself for a work He has made His own.

---

[1] *T.T.*, 1 April 1880, 7b.

[2] Of Beckenham, on religion; Hawn P.

[3] Start of a row about Vaticanism; letters published in *The Echo*; see Bodley MS Eng. lett. b. 4.

[4] Of Hamilton, on finance; Hawn P.

[5] Probably of the *Greenwich Observer*, on the election; Hawn P.

[6] *Monmouth; a drama* (1880).

[7] Eighteenth and last Midlothian speech; *Political Speeches, March and April 1880* (1880), 326.

[8] James Wardrop, U.P. minister there.

[9] Beaconsfield this day told the Queen, who was in Baden, that the govt.'s defeat was certain; he told her on 7 April she need not leave Baden until the 15th, which advice she followed; *L.Q.V.*, 2nd series, iii. 73-6.

[10] Of Edinburgh; on the campaign; Hawn P.

[11] William Ballantyne Hodgson, liberal and economist; on contagious diseases, Add MS 44463, f. 27.

[12] Robert Kirk of Glasgow, on Playfair's campaign; Hawn P.

[13] John Havelock of Newcastle sent cuttings; Add MS 44463, f. 25.

4. 1 S. East

St John's Edinb. and H.C. mg. Free St George's aft. Wrote to Editor Northern Advr—Ed. Scotsman—Walter L.G.—Mr Laporte BP.—Mr Jenkins—Mr Jas Thomson—Mr Barclay. Saw Mr Cooper—Ld Young—Ld Rosebery. Read Lee's Liturgical Offices—Thos a Kempis. Sir D. Macnee[1] told more of his stories. A lull in Election news: but the reflections on what has past are overpowering.

5. M.

Wrote to Mr Gool Tel.[2]—W.L. Gladstone Tel.—Accrington Committee Tel.— Mayor of Leeds—Mrs May, or Ankey[3]—W. Lawrence—W.H. Gladstone—Lord Wolverton—Mr Howard—Mr Guild—Mr Creyke MP[4]—Mr Barran MP—F. Söhns[5]—J.R. Godley—Mons. A. Gigot[6]—Mr Fawcett MP—Rev. [J.]E. Gladstone—F. Bremner—T. Knott[7]—C. Russell—J.C. Swan[8]—Mr Woolsey—Mr Macewan (O). Drove into Edinburgh about four. Saw Mrs Russell—Mr Butti— Mr Bremner—Mr Reid—Youngs—Breadalbanes. At 7.20 Mr Reid brought the figures of the poll G[ladstone] 1579, D[alkeith] 1368: quite satisfactory. Soon after, 15000 people being gathered in George St I spoke very shortly from the windows & Rosebery followed, excellently well. Home about ten. Wonderful, & nothing less, has been the disposing guiding hand of God in all this matter. Finished England under Lord B. Wrote my address of thanks.[9]

6. Tu. [In train][10]

Wrote to Mr Cremer Tel.[11]—Mr Chipham (Tel) Leicester[12]—Herbert J.G.—Miss Hilson (O)—Ed. Scotsman—Mr Neale (O)—S. Cartmell—Mr Dicks (O)—Mr Kitson Tel.—Mr Schutz—Lib. Comm. Droitwich Tel.—Mr Gibson Carmichael[13]— Mr Childers. A heavy day with post, incessant Telegrams, and preparations for departure. We drove however to Linlithgow, saw the beautiful Church & fine old castle; & I made a short non-polemical speech to the people. Saw Mr Thomson—(a distant cousin). Careful concealment of the plans of departure, until well on in the evening. Left this most hospitable of all houses at 8.30 and got into the 9.25 escaping by secrecy all demonstration except from some 200 who seemed to gather on the instant. Travelled all night & had time to ruminate on the great hand of God so evidently displayed.

---

[1] Sir Daniel *Macnee, 1806-82; portrait painter.
[2] Sic; unidentified.
[3] Obscure.
[4] Ralph Creyke, 1849-1908; liberal M.P. York 1880-5.
[5] Of Edinburgh; sent a painting; Hawn P.
[6] Translating Gladstone's articles into French; see 16 Oct. 80.
[7] The artist (see 1 Dec. 79), requesting a sitting to finish his portrait; Hawn P.
[8] John Cameron Swan of the Newcastle Liberal Association, on the campaign; Hawn P.
[9] This phrase added in the margin.
[10] Extracts until 20 April in Morley, ii. 616.
[11] W. R. Cremer, liberal organizer in Marylebone.   [12] Ibid. in Leicester.
[13] (Sir) Thomas David Gibson-Carmichael, 1859-1926; friend of Rosebery; succeeded Gladstone in the Midlothian seat 1895-1900; governed colonies; 11th bart. 1891; 1st Baron Carmichael 1912.

7. Wed. [Hawarden]

After 3 hours of successful sleep amidst frightful unearthly noises at Warrington we went off to Chester and Hawarden, saluted enthusiastically but escaping all crowds. Hawarden was preparing to decorate and make a festival but we got it postponed for Herbert's entry tomorrow. Set to work at once on a mass of letters & papers. Wrote to Electors of Leeds[1]—Mr Jas Kitson and draft[2]—Mr E. Hussy—Viscount Bury (2)—Editor of Echo—Mr O.R. Griffiths—Messrs Paterson—Mr Geo. Howard—Messrs Bickers—Sec. Glasgow Univ Lib. Club—Mr D. Sutherland—Ld Granville—Rev. D. Macgregor. The day occupied with papers, letters, and Telegrams: and reading my Vatican Tracts.

8. Th.

Ch. $8\frac{1}{4}$ AM. Wrote to Mr Reed Edinb. Tel.—Mr Johnson (Devon) Tel.[3]—Mr Beal Tel.—Ld Wolverton—Mr Jas. Kitson—Rev. J.J. Goadby[4]—W.M. Murray—W. Rathbone—Ed. Exeter Gazette—Sir T. Acland MP—Mr Ralph Richardson—Mr Earp Tel.—Lord Bury—Mr Erldwick[5]—Mr Whitworth—Mr Keeling—Rev. J. Hopkins[6]—Mr Townshend—G. Harrison.

About one Herbert entered in triumph.[7] We were there and could not but be much moved. He made a capital speech to the people. I followed him. We considered the difficult case of Leeds; and I was much perplexed with the question of the London entry.[8] The triumph grows & grows: to God be the praise.

9. Fr.

(Ch. $8\frac{1}{2}$ A.M.) Wrote, after full consultation to Mr Kitson proposing a plan for Leeds.[9] Wrote also to Mrs Th—Mr Schidrani Tel.—P. Stanhope—Prov. of Dingwall—Herr A. Karolyi—Mr Macgitting (O)—Mr Henderson—J. Bennock[10]—R. Richardson—F.G. Wickham—F.D.F. O'Connell—Mr Crum Ewing—Messrs Behanna—Lord Reay—Lord Bury—Mr Brand—D. Forbes BP—E.G. Hardy—Messrs Rose—J. Baxter—Mr Nesbitt[11]—Ed. of Echo—Rev. S. Minton—Mr Wilkinson. Letters &c. passed 100. Read Guy Mannering:[12] what a treat! Helped by E. Lyttelton: capital fellow. Mr Plimsoll came & staid the evg. *ex professo*[13] about

[1] Confirming he would sit for Midlothian rather than Leeds; *D.N.*, 10 April 1880, 3c. He vacated both seats on taking office, thus technically not having to choose between them; see to Baines, 10 May 80.

[2] Sending his Address, and discussing Herbert's possible candidacy at Leeds; Add MS 46044, f. 8.

[3] Election business there.

[4] Joseph Jackson Goadby, 1828-98; Baptist minister and author in Leicester.

[5] May read 'Erlstrick'.

[6] John Hopkins, rector of Rhoscolyn, Holyhead.

[7] Though defeated in Middlesex, he made a strong impression; Mallet, 75.

[8] Great demonstration in favour of Gladstone (and hence of his premiership) planned by S. Plimsoll and others; see next d. and T. A. Jenkins, 'Gladstone, the Whigs and the leadership of the liberal party', *Historical Journal*, xxvii. 355 and Morley, ii. 620.

[9] On invitation by the Leeds Four Hundred to Herbert Gladstone to speak there, and raising questions of cost and procedure about his adoption as a candidate; Add MS 46044, f. 9. He was elected unopposed on 10 May.   [10] Of London, sent congratulations; Hawn P.

[11] Possibly John Nesbitt, artist living in Edinburgh.

[12] By Scott; see 5 Dec. 48.   [13] 'Avowedly'.

the reception, but overflowing with his own subject the Mercantile Marine. He is however an original & childlike man, full of reality & enthusiasm. I told him of my objections to the reception.

10. Sat.

Ch. 8½ AM. Wrote to Watson & Smith BP—T.Nichols (O)[1]—Earl Granville—Mr Hardy—R. Tuck—Earl of Rosebery—Mr Calderwood—W.H. Stone—Ed. Exr Gazette—W.H. Gladstone—Mr Bennett—Mr Bradbury—A. Harris—E. Hewson—Sir W. Farquhar. Walk with Herbert and E.L. Postal arrivals 140! Horrible!

Wolverton arrived to dinner and I spent the evening in full conversation with him. He threatens a request from Granville and Hartington. Again I am stunned: but God will provide. Read N.C. on Deep Sea—& on Home Rule (2).[2]

11. 2 S.E.

Ch 8 AM. Holy Communion. 11 AM and [blank.] Wrote to Duke of Westminster—Mr Plimsoll MP[3]—Jas Kitson jun. (& draft)—Mr [G. S.] Baden Powell—Editor of Echo—A.E. West—Dr Craig[4]—Ld Reay—Ld Bury—Helen G.—J. Wall. Read Gospel for the 19th Century.[5] Examined Liturgical books. Read Prota Giurleo to Leo XIII.[6] Saw two gentlemen from Mid Cheshire. Further conversation with Wolverton on the London reception: on Leeds—& on the great matter of all.

12. M.

Ch. 8½ AM. Wrote to Duke of Argyll—Mr Adam MP—Ld Wolverton—W.R. Cremer—Mr Agnew MP—Rev. J.C. Rogers—Prof. Hennessy—Mr Bright—Dr Dunbar—Mr Dow, U.S.[7]—Mr Sands—Mr Powell—Mr Hall Blyth[8]—Sir Dan. Lange—Mr Dickson—J. Cowan. Wolverton went off in the morning: and is to see G. and H. today. Read Brugsch Hist Egypt[9]—B. Powell on Protection[10]—Guy Mannering. Wrote some Mema of names, applicable to this occasion.[11] Hard day. But all are pretty hard, in this my 'retirement'.

13. Tu.

Ch. 8½ AM. Wrote to Ld Wolverton—Ld Powerscourt—Solicitor General—Mr P. O'Connor (O)[12]—Prof. P. Sbarbaro—Mr Costelloe—Mr Dawson—Mr Richardson—Mr Fearn—Ld Bury—Ld Bath—Ld Reay—J. Bates—Mr Farmer—W. Baker—W. Logan—Mr Craig. Read Guy Mannering: *dear* Guy Mannering—Sir

---

[1] Thomas Nichols, treasurer of the Cambridge Reform Club.

[2] *Nineteenth Century*, vii. 593, 567, 583 (April 1880).

[3] Declining the London reception; *T.T.*, 13 April 1880, 9f.

[4] James Craig of Dalkeith, on poor relief; Hawn P.   [5] See 1 Feb. 80.

[6] L. Prota-Giurleo, *Leone XIII e S. Tommaso d'Aquino. Osservazioni critiche sull'Enciclica del 4 agosto 1879* (1880).

[7] Perhaps Neal Dow, 1804-97; American temperance reformer; ran for president 1880.

[8] Benjamin Hall Blyth, 1849-1917; railway engineer based in Edinburgh.

[9] See 3 Jan. 79.

[10] G. S. Baden Powell, *Protection and bad times, with special reference to the political economy of English colonisation* (1880); see Add MS 44463, f. 76.

[11] Jottings for a cabinet, not separately identifiable.   [12] Perhaps T. P. O'Connor.

John Adye on E.I.N. Army.[1] Walk with N. Lyttelton: a real fine fellow. Began tentatively an anonymous letter on the Conservative Collapse.[2]

To LORD WOLVERTON, 13 April 1880.[3]   Add MS 44349, f. 132.

The letter herewith was written last night. This morning an answer from Plimsoll much relieves my mind as either the London movement is at an end, or at any rate, I am wholly out of it.

The enclosed letter from S. Turnill[4] whom I do not know should be from Turn*well*, for he states his case excellently, and there is in my opinion great force in it. The claim so to speak of G. and H. or rather I should say of G. with H. against me or rather as compared *with* me is complete. My labours as an Individual cannot set me up as a Pretender.

Moreover if they should on surveying their position see fit to apply to me, there is only one form and ground of application, so far as I see, which could be seriously entertained by me, namely their conviction, that on the ground of public policy, all things considered it was best in the actual position of affairs that I should come out. It cannot be made a matter of ceremonial as by gentlemen waiving a precedence or a matter of feeling, as by men of high and delicate honour determined to throw their bias against themselves. They have no right to throw their bias against themselves—they have no right to look at anything but public policy: and this I am sure will be their conviction. Nothing else can possibly absolve them from their presumptive obligation as standing at the head of the party: which for the time represents the Country.

We have had no envoy from Leeds but an encouraging telegram which stated that none would be needed. Herbert has just set out for Oxford.

14. Wed.

Ch. 8½ AM. Wrote to Mr Cowper Temple—W.J. Mayor (O)—Mr Schnadhorst— Geo. Melly Tel.—W.S. Alhurst—Mr Bright MP—Ld Wolverton—Sec. R. Academy—Mr Macknight—Mr Greenwood—Mr Thompson—Mr Kitson—Mr Knowles—J. Hill—J. Owens—Mr Pender—Mr Rudall[5]—Mr Whicker—Mr Groser—Mr Meadows—W. Thomson. Worked on Anon. Letter: really drawn forth by the letter of Lord Bath. Willy made his triumphal entry at four o'clock & delivered a very good speech. Nevy, too, spoke well, from the carriage. Read Guy Mannering: and that most heavenly man George Herbert.

15. Th.

Ch. 8½ AM. Wrote to Mr Kitson jun. (Tel)—Mrs Heywood—Marquis of Hunt-ley—Mrs Fitzgerald—Rev. G. Hunsworth[6]—Mr Wilcockson (O)[7]—G. Martineau[8]

---

[1] J. M. Adye, 'Native armies of India', *Nineteenth Century*, vii. 685 (April 1880).

[2] Published anon. as 'The Conservative collapse; considered in a letter from a Liberal to an old Conservative [i.e. Lord Bath]', signed 'Index', *Fortnightly Review*, xxxiii. 607 (May 1880), of which Morley was just ceasing to be editor; see Hirst, *Early life of Morley*, ii. 91.

[3] Copied by Catherine Gladstone; her perhaps eccentric punctuation retained. Partly quoted in Morley ii. 620.

[4] Not found.   [5] Francis A. Rudall, secretary of Epsom liberal association.

[6] Congregationalist minister in Kidderminster; on Worcestershire nonconformist support for W. H. Gladstone; *T.T.*, 19 April 1880, 10b.

[7] Henry Wilcockson of Hungerford Road, London.

[8] Gustave Martineau, brandy merchant in London.

—A. Mitchell—Mr MacConville—Ed. of the Echo—Herbert J.G.—Rev. J. Maclaren—Secretaries Exhn Merthyr—Mr Ord (O)—Mr Dawson—Mr Dickson—Mr Thomas—Mr Puseley—Mr Thomson—Mrs Scobie—Rev. R. Yonge—Mr Crymlan—J.W. Bell. Walk with Neville L. Read Monmouth[1]—Guy Mannering. The Post is still over 100 each morning.

16. Fr.

Ch. 8½ AM. The post below 80. This cheered my eye. Wrote to Mr Jas Kitson jun.—Messrs G. and Co—F.Schnadhorst—Mr Whitehurst—Signor Volti—Rev? Mr Rees—Rev. Mr Williamson—Mr Jas Knowles—F. Lowe—Mr Woolley—Mr Leisk[2]—Mr Atkins—J. Newman[3]—W.N. Japp—Ld Granville. Worked on my "Letter". 1½-5½. Mr Bright came over from Llandudno & we spent nearly all the time in conversing on the situation. He is most kind and satisfactory.[4] Also saw Mrs Hamilton. Read Guy Mannering.

17. Sat.

Ch. 8½ AM. Wrote to Author of "Monmouth"—Mr Clemensha (O)[5]—Mr Chadwick—R.P. Williams—Rev. Sir Geo. Cox—Rev. S.F. Fitzroy—Sig. Mareschalchi—Mr Bow (O)—Jas Hill—F.L. Price—Mr Duckett—Mr Knowles—W.G. Blackie.[6] Finished my 'letter' & revision of it. Cut down a sycamore with WHG. Read Guy Mannering.

18. 4 S.E.

Holy Commn 8 AM Mg service 11 & evg 6½ PM. Wrote to Rev. Mr Christie BP—Earl Granville—Ed. Daily News—Ed. Exeter Gazette—Ed. Spectator—Rev. T. Richardson—H.W. Holland[7]—B.W. Savile—J.K. Philip—J. Thompson—Mr Knowles BP—Sir S. Scott & Co—Mr Rathbone—N. Marks—G. Harris—Mr Williams—Sir J. Lambert. Saw Mr (Sheriff) Johnson.[8] Read Gospel for 19th Cent.— Divine Veracity v. Divine Justice[9]—Caird on the Philosophy of Religion.[10]

19. M. [London]

Ch. 8½ AM. Wrote to Lady Augusta Noel[11]—Dr J. Brown BP—Herr Schidrowitz[12]—Rev. J. Davies—Principal Caird—J. Wood—J. Leeman—A. Wood—

---

[1] See 1 Apr. 80.
[2] John Drever Leisk, London broker.
[3] Joseph Newton, liberal journalist; Hawn P.
[4] 'It is not likely he will take office in a Govt. of which he is not the head'; Walling, *Diaries of Bright*, 437.
[5] Alfred and Barclay Clemensha were the principal grocers in Preston.
[6] Walter Graham Blackie, publisher and author.
[7] Perhaps Henry William Holland of Kensington.
[8] William Johnson of Broughton Hall, Flintshire.
[9] Untraced.
[10] J. Caird, *An introduction to the philosophy of religion* (1880).
[11] Da. of 6th earl of Albemarle, she m. Ernest Noel, liberal M.P. Dumfries 1874-86.
[12] To the London correspondent of *Neue Freie Presse*, on Austrian policy; *T.T.*, 21 April 1880, 11f.

Mr S. Laing—Mr Penna—Mr Dowding—J. Kay—Mr Husband—Mr Wallerstein—
Mr Reavis—Mr Robinson. Saw Mr Gallimore—Lord Granville—Lord Wolverton. A reluctant goodbye before one. London at 6.30. A secret journey but
people gathered at Chester station and Euston. I vaguely feel that this journey
is a plunge, out of an atmosphere of peace into an element of disturbance. May
He who has of late so wonderfully guided, guide me still in the critical days
about to come.

20. Tu.

Wrote to Mr Morley—Miss Thompson—Mr Ibbotson (O)[1]—W. Murray—Mr
Jeffery. Read Life of Sibthorp.[2] This blank day is I think probably due to the
Queen's hesitation or reluctance, which the Ministers have to find means of
covering. Saw Ld Hartington—Ld Wolverton—Ld Granville—Ld F. Cavendish—
Rev. D. Melvill—Mr West (2)—Mr Knowles—Mr Hayward—Mr Lefevre—Scotts.
Nine to dinner. Visited the dentist: who operated a good deal. Saw Mr & Mrs
Lowe—Madame Ralli—Ld Hammond.

21. Wed.

Wrote to Mr Rudge Rootes—Mrs Cornwallis West[3]—M. Nikolaides[4]—M. Apos-
tolides[5]—Messrs Edmonston—Mr Barran MP—Mr Jameson—J. Watts—Mr
Stearn—Mr Towle—G. Potter—Ed. Daily News. Read Barber on Bradlaugh[6]—
Life & letters of Sibthorp: a holy man. Saw Ld Wolverton (2)—Ld Granville—
Mr Forster—D. of Argyll—Mr Childers—Mr Wallerstein—Rev. Mr M'Coll—Mr
J. Morley—Ld Halifax—Mr West.

22. Th.

Wrote to Miss Rudd (O)—Rev. J. Christie BP—Rev. Mr O'Flanagan—F. John-
son—Serj. Sherlock—Dr F.W. Rogge—Rev. Mr Ash[7]—Mr Philips—S. Evans—Mr
Blakey[8]—J.L. Bates—Mr Thos Lewis.[9] Corrected proofs of 'The Conservative
Collapse'. Saw Mr Scott (C. News)—Mr Ouvry—Mr West—Mr Morley—Mr
Adam—Ld Wolverton—Ld F. Cavendish—Russian Ambr—Portuguese Minr—
Dutch Minr & others, at Lady Reay's crowded evening party. Dined at Lord
Reay's. Read Sibthorp's Life & Letters. Ld Hartington at 7 PM related to me
what took place at Windsor.

---

[1] Walter Ibbotson, campaigner for jury reform; see Add MS 44462, f. 222.
[2] J. Fowler, *R. W. Sibthorp: a biography, told chiefly in his own correspondence* (1880); the book
concludes with a quotation from Gladstone: 'I can never think of him but as a simple, rare, truly
elect soul', which is also the epigram at the beginning. See 25 Apr. 80.
[3] Mary, *née* Fitzpatrick, wife of W. C. Cornwallis West (see 3 May 72).
[4] G. Nikolaides, scholar in Athens; Hawn P.
[5] Greek scholar in London, sent the Lord's Prayer in 100 languages; Hawn P.
[6] Untraced.
[7] Perhaps Richard Robert Drummond Ash, vicar of Midhurst.
[8] Perhaps James Blakey of the national debt office; see Add MS 44484, f. 238.
[9] Perhaps Thomas Lewis, d. 1892; independent minister and principal of Bangor college.

Secret.

April 22. 1880. At 7 PM Hartington came to see me at Wolverton's house and reported on his journey to Windsor.

The Queen stood with her back to the window—which *used* not to be her custom. On the whole I gathered that her manner was more or less embarrassed but towards him not otherwise than gracious & confiding.

She told him that she desired him to form an Administration and pressed upon him strongly his duty to assist her as a responsible leader of the party now in a large majority. I could not find that she expressed clearly her reason for appealing to him as a responsible leader of the party, and yet going past *the* leader of the party, namely Granville, whom no one except himself has a title to displace. She however indicated to him her confidence in his moderation, the phrase under which he is daily commended in the D. Telegraph, at this moment I think Beaconsfield's personal organ & the recipient of his inspirations. By this moderation the Queen intimated that Hartington was distinguished from Granville as well as from me.

Hartington in reply to H.M. made becoming acknowledgments and proceeded to say that he did not think a Government could be satisfactorily formed without me: he had not had any direct communication with me: but he had reason to believe that I would not take any office or post in the Government except that of First Minister. Under these circumstances he advised H.M. to place the matter in my hands.[1] The Queen continued to urge upon him the obligations arising out of his position and desired him to ascertain whether he was right in his belief that I would not act in a ministry unless as First Minister. This he said is a question which I should not have put to you except when desired by the Queen.

I said H.M. was quite justified I thought in requiring positive information & he therefore in putting the question to me. Of my action he was already in substantial possession as it had been read to him (he had told me) by Wolverton. I am not asked I said for reasons but only for Aye or No and consequently I have only to say that I adhere to my reply as you have already conveyed it to the Queen.

In making such a reply, it was my duty to add that in case a Government should be formed by him, or by Granville with him, whom the Queen seemed to me wrongly to have passed by—it was to Granville that I had resigned my trust, and he H[artingto]n was subsequently elected by the party to the leadership in the House of Commons—my duty would be plain. It would be to give them all the support in my power, both negatively, as by absence (and) or non-interference, and positively. Promises of this kind I said stood on slippery ground and must always be understood with the limits which might be prescribed by conviction. I referred to the extreme caution, almost costiveness, of Peel's replies to Lord Russell when he was endeavouring to form a Government in December 1845 for the purpose of carrying the repeal of the Corn Law. In this case however I felt a tolerable degree of confidence because I was not aware of any substantive divergence of ideas between us, and I had observed with great satisfaction, when his address to N.E. Lancashire came into my hands after the writing but before the publication of mine to Midlothian that they were in marked accordance as to opinions if not as to form and tone, and I did not alter a word. In the case of the first Palmerston Government I had certainly been thrown into rather sharp opposition after I quitted it but this was mainly due to finance—I had not approved of the finance of Sir Geo. Lewis, highly as I estimated his judgment in general politics: & it was in some ways a relief to me, when we had become colleagues in the second Palmerston Government, to find that he did not approve of mine. However I could only make such a declaration as the nature of the case allowed.

[1] Hartington prepared for this audience by writing three memoranda; two are in Holland, *Devonshire*, i. 273ff; the third is in Chatsworth MSS 340.

He received all this without comment, and said his conversation with H.M. had ended as it began each party adhering to the ground originally taken up. He had not altered his advice but had come under H.M.s command to learn my intentions, which he was to make known to H.M. returning to Windsor *this* day at one.

He asked me what I thought of the doctrine of obligation so much pressed upon him by the Queen.

I said that in my opinion the case was clear enough. H.M. had not always acted on the rule of sending for the leader of the Opposition. Palmerston was the known and recognised leader of the Opposition in 1859; but the Queen sent for Granville. The leader if sent for was in my opinion bound either to serve himself or to point out some other course to H.M. which he might deem to be more for the public advantage. And if that course should fail in consequence of the refusal of the person pointed out, the leader of the party could not leave H.M. unprovided with a Government but would be bound in loyalty to undertake the task.

I did not indicate nor did he ask what I should do if sent for. He did not indicate nor did I ask what he should do if the Queen continued to press him to go on in spite of his advice to her to move in another direction.[1]

23. Fr.

Wrote to Ld Ailesbury—Spencer Lyttelton—Ld Selborne—Ld Derby[2]—F. W. Smith[3]—H. Frowde—Mr Childers. Lords G. & H. came at 3.40 & brought me the Queen's command to go to Windsor and see her at 6.30 PM. Wrote Memm of Audience (pt). Wrote Memm of yesty with Lord H. Saw Ld Wolverton—Mr West—Mr Godley—Mr Hagopian & Mr Baronian[4]—Dean of Windsor—Prince Leopold—Mr Hayward—Mr Law—Gen. Ponsonby. Returned from Windsor at 9.20 and spent the evening till past 12 on the arrangements for the new Adminn with Granville—Hartington—Adam—Wolverton—chiefly: saw also Rosebery—F. Cavendish—Mr Hayward—Mr Law—Mr F. Leveson—variously. Read Q.R.

Soon after half past three today Lord Granville & Lord Hartington arrived ⟨at⟩ from Windsor ⟨from⟩ at my house, and signified to me the Queen's command that I should repair to Windsor where she would see me at half past six.

The purport of Lord H[artington']s conversation with me yesterday had been signified. They had jointly advised hereupon that I should be sent for with a view to the formation of a Government, and H.M. desired Lord Granville would convey to me the message. I did not understand that there had been any lengthened audience, or any reference to details.

Receiving this intimation I read to them an extract (herewith)[5] from an article in the *Daily News* of yesterday descriptive of their position relatively to me, and of mine to them, and then said that, letting drop the epithets, so I understood the matter. I presumed therefore that under the circumstances as they were established before their

---

[1] Marked '*Secret*'; initialled and dated 23 April 1880, Add MS 44764, f. 43. See Morley, ii. 621 and *Autobiographica*, iv. 48.

[2] Asking Derby to take 'some office of weight in the Cabinet'; Add MS 56445, f. 45; Derby declined.

[3] Frederick W. Smith, liberal organizer in Tufnell Park.

[4] Armenian representatives.

[5] No longer attached to the MS, but quoted in Morley, ii. 625n.

audience they had unitedly advised the Sovereign that it was most for the public advantage to send for me. To this they assented. I expressed, a little later, my sense of the high honour & patriotism with which they had acted: said that I had endeavoured to fulfil my own duty but was aware I might be subject to severe criticism for my resignation of the Leadership five years ago, which I had forced upon them: but I did it believing in good faith that we were to have quiet times and for the first years 1875 and 1876 to the end of the Session I had acted in a manner conformable to that resignation and had only been driven from my course my [*sc.* by] compulsion. They made no reply but Granville had previously told me he was perfectly satisfied as to my communications with him.

I at once asked whether I might reckon, as I hoped, on their cooperation in the Government. (Resumed Ap. 25.) Both assented. Granville agreed to take the Foreign Office, but modestly & not as of right. I proposed the Indian Office as next, or as very near, in weight, and perhaps the most difficult of all at this time, to Hartington, which he desired time to consider. I named Childers as the most proper person for the War Office. As I had to prepare for Windsor our interview was not very long: and they agreed to come again after dinner.

We spoke of the Governor Generalship—at least I spoke to Granville who staid a little after H[artington] and I said Goschen's position as to the franchise would prevent his being in the Cabinet now: but he should be in great employ. Granville had had the lead in the conversation: and said the Queen requested *him* to carry the message to me.[1]

April 23. 1880. At 6.50 I went to the Queen who received me with perfect courtesy from which she never deviates. H.M. presumed I was in possession of the purport of her communications with Lord Granville & with Lord Hartington; and wished to know, as the Administration of Lord Beaconsfield had been 'turned out' whether I was prepared to form a Government. She thought she had acted constitutionally in sending for the recognised leaders of the party and referring the matter to them in the first instance.

I said that if I might presume to speak, nothing could in my view be more correct than H.M.s view that the application should be so made (I did not refer to the case as *between* Lord Granville & Lord Hartington) and that it would have been an error to pass them by and refer to me.

They had stood I said between me and the position of a Candidate for office, and it was only their advising H.M. to lay her commands upon me which could warrant my thinking of it after all that had occurred. But since they had given this advice it was not consistent with my duty to shrink from any responsibility which I had incurred, & I was aware that I had incurred a very great responsibility. I therefore humbly accepted H.M.s commission.

H.M. wished to know, in order that she might acquaint Lord Beaconsfield, whether I could undertake to form a Government or whether I only meant that I would make the attempt.

I said I had obtained the cooperation of Lord Granville & Lord Hartington, and that my knowledge and belief as to prevailing dispositions would I think warrant me in undertaking to form a Government; it being H.M.s pleasure. I had ascertained that Lord Granville would be willing to accept the Foreign Office; and I had also to say that the same considerations which made it my duty to accept office seemed also to make it my duty to submit myself to H.M.s pleasure for the office of Chancellor of the Exchequer together with that of First Lord of the Treasury.

She asked if I had thought of any one for the War Office which was very important. The Report of the Commission would show that Lord Cardwell's system of short service

[1] Initialled and dated 25 April 1880, Add MS 44764, f. 48; see Morley, ii. 624 and *Autobiographica*, iv. 51.

had entirely broken down, & that a change must be made at any rate as regarded the Non-Commissioned officers. Lord Hartington had assured her that no one was committed to the system except Lord Cardwell and he was very unwell and hardly able to act. Lord H[artingto]n knew the War Office and she thought would make a good War Minister.

I said that it seemed to me in the present state of the country the first object was to provide for the difficulties of Statesmanship & then to deal with those of administration. The greatest of all these difficulties I thought centered in the Indian Office and I was very much inclined to think Lord Hartington would be eminently qualified to deal with them & would thereby take a place in the Government suitable to his position & his probable future.

She asked to whom then did I think of entrusting the War Office? (Resumed here April 24.) I said Mr. Childers occurred to me as an administrator of eminent capacity and conciliatory in his modes of action—his mind would be open on the grave subjects treated by the Commission which did not appear to me to be even for Lord Cardwell matters of committal, but simply of public policy to be determined by public advantage. She thought that Mr. Childers had not been popular at the Admiralty and that it was desirable the Secretary for War should be liked by the army. I said that there was an occurrence towards the close of his term which placed him in a difficult position[1] but relied on his care and discretion. (She did not press the point but is evidently under strong professional bias.)

She spoke of the Chancellorship and I named Lord Selborne.

She referred to general action and hoped it would be conciliatory. I said that every one who had served the Crown for even a much smaller term of years than I had the good or ill fortune to reckon would know well that an incoming Government must recognise existing engagements and must take up irrespective of its preferences whatever was required by the character and honour of the country. I referred to the case of Scinde and Sir R. Peel's Cabinet in 1843;[2] which she recognised as if it had been recently before her.[3]

She said I must be frank with you Mr Gladstone and must fairly say that there have been some expressions, I think she said some little things, which had caused her concern or pain. I said that Her Majesty's frankness so well known was a main ground of the entire reliance of her ministers upon her. That I was conscious of having incurred a great responsibility and felt the difficulty which arises when great issues are raised and a man can only act and speak upon the best lights he possesses, aware all the time that he may be in error. That I had undoubtedly used a mode of speech and language different in some degree from what I should have employed had I been the leader of a party or a candidate for office. Then as regarded conciliation, in my opinion the occasion for what I had described had wholly passed away and that so far as I was concerned it was my hope that H.M. would not find anything to disapprove in my general tone: that my desire and effort would be to diminish her cares, in any case not to aggravate them: that, however, considering my years, I could only look to a short term of active exertion and a personal retirement comparatively early.

With regard to the freedom of language I had admitted she said, with some good-natured archness, 'But you will have to bear the consequences' to which I entirely assented.

She seemed to me, if I may so say 'natural under effort'. All things considered I was much pleased.

I ended by kissing H.M.s hand.[4]

[1] The Spencer Robinson row; see 18 June 70.　　　　　　　　　[2] See 27 May-3 Aug. 43.
[3] As it had been, as Gladstone had discussed the case at length in his speech of 17 March; *Political speeches... March and April 1880*, 23.
[4] Written on Windsor Castle notepaper; initialled and dated 24 April 1880, Add MS 44764, f. 50.

24. Sat.

A long day of incessant work. Wrote Mema of yesterday. Wrote to Duke of Argyll—Mr Hayward—Sir W. Harcourt—D. of Marlborough—Sir S. Northcote—Lord Kimberley—Mr Forster—Mr Bright (2)—Mr Lowe—The Queen—at 2.30. reporting progress. Conclave most of the day: Granville—Hartington—Wolverton—Adam, and in part Forster. Saw Mr Childers—Ld Northbrooke—Ld F. Cavendish—Ld Selborne—Ld Rosebery, also Lady R.—D. of Argyll—Lord Ripon—Mr M'Coll—Mr Godley—Mr West—Mr Goschen—Mr Forster—Ld Halifax. Dined with the Ripons.[1] At 7 P.M. the Prince of Wales came & was in the main satisfactory. He staid ¾ of an hour.

To LORD KIMBERLEY, 24 April 1880, 'Secret'. Add MS 44225, f. 158.

The arduous task I have undertaken is rendered especially difficult by the fact that more than one of the appointments beyond sea are, at this critical juncture invested with an importance exceeding that even of the large majority of offices in the Cabinet.

One of these, the Governor Generalship or Viceroyalty of India, I place in importance beyond all except perhaps two of the offices for which I have to recommend at home: and to determine upon a satisfactory appointment is a vital part of the new arrangements at their first stage.

The great value of your services at home & in the House of Lords, and no other cause, has made it a matter of difficulty to decide upon asking you to consent to be named for this great office, which offers at the present moment such labours and such opportunities.

I desire however very earnestly to press it upon you. As Secretary for India Hartington will give it his unqualified support with you if needful, and Granville's approval is only mingled with concern at losing your aid in the Lords. To mere ambition I do not desire to appeal, but I feel that at no period of its existence has the office offered brighter promise of reward in the highest forms of which it is susceptible.

My quarters are here until 2 p.m. tomorrow but at 2.30 I am to be at Granville's house & to remain there for some time.[2]

25. 4 S.E.

Chapel Royal 10 AM.—and nothing more. Wrote to The Queen (2)—Duchess of Bedford—Ld Kimberley—Mr Stansfeld—Mr Whitbread—Ld Cardwell—Ld Granville. Dined at Sir R. Phillimore's.[3] Read Sibthorp's Life & Letters: singularly adapted, I find, to my very peculiar condition.[4] Saw Ld Granville—Ld Hartington—Mr Harcourt—Mr Childers—Ld Kimberley—Ld Ripon—Ld Wolverton—Mr Adam. Worked at Granvilles from 2½-7. But I was only able to *rescue* a small portion of the day.

---

[1] Gladstone mentioned the possibility of India to Ripon, apparently offered it unsuccessfully next day to Goschen, and then formally to Ripon; see Wolf, *Ripon*, i. 318.

[2] Kimberley arranged to come to Granville's on 25 April, when he declined verbally; Add MS 44255, f. 160.

[3] 'He [Gladstone] told me all his official arrangements—was not at all reticent & very amicable. I urged upon him the necessity of leaving the H. of C. at 10 every night & having [?] a Lieutenant take his place at that hour. He said this would be done. Probably Ld Hartington wd not object'; Phillimore's Diary.

[4] Sibthorp (see 20 Apr. 80), an evangelical, joined Rome 1841, left it 1843, reverted to Rome 1865. Gladstone probably refers to the process of the change, not its direction.

To LORD KIMBERLEY, 25 April 1880.   Add MS 44225, f. 161.

You left me, as you would see, rather stunned by the effect of an answer against which pray understand I make no complaint, for I ought to believe, and I *do* firmly believe, in the reasons which have governed your judgment. However having now in a manner recovered my breath, I must act for the best: and I now propose for the advantage of the Government and the public, that you should allow me to submit your name to Her Majesty for the office of Secretary of State for the Colonies.[1]

26. M.

Wrote to Mr Arnold—Earl Sydney—Earl Strafford—O Conor Don—Rev. Mr Spurgeon—Ld Northbrook—Gen Ponsonby (Tel)—Ld Carlingford—Adm. Egerton—Mr Hayward—Mr Saunders—Mr Bryce—Mr Lefevre—Sir H. James: Welby, Gurdon, Hamilton, West & others: a Treasury dinner & inception of financial conspectus 8-12. Conclave at Granville's. Granville, Hartington, Adam, Wolverton; with Forster and Childers at times. Work unintermitted. Saw Ld Ripon—Spencer Lyttelton jun—Duke of Argyll—Lord Tenterden—Sir C. Dilke[2]—The Speaker—Sir H. Ponsonby—and others.

27. Tu.

Wrote to Mr Cowper Temple—The Queen 1.2.3.4.—Mr Stansfeld (repeated)[3]—Sir H. Ponsonby—Mr Mundella—E. Macgregor[4]—Mr G. Duff—Mr Playfair—The Speaker—Telegrams to & from Windsor. Conclave at Ld Granville's. Ld Hn—Ld G—Ld W—Mr Adam—Mr Forster. Saw D. of Argyll—Mr Childers. Dined at Sir E. Perry's & met the Russian Ambassador who inadvertently appropriated my hat, & was only detected after a long search. Our conversation was friendly but non-political. As Harley St is so inconvenient my midday batch of work say 12-7 is done at Ld Granville's.

To J. CHAMBERLAIN, 27 April 1880, '*Secret*'.   Chamberlain MSS 5/34/1.

I have made progress since yesterday afternoon; and I may add that there is a small addition to my liberty of choice beyond what I had expected. Accordingly, looking as I seek to do all along to the selection of the fittest, I have real pleasure in proposing to you that you should allow me to submit your name to Her Majesty as President of the Board of Trade in the new Administration, with a seat in the Cabinet; to which you will be glad to know that your friend and colleague Mr. Bright already belongs.

Your political opinions may on some points go rather beyond what I may call the general measure of the Government; but I hope and believe there can be no practical impediment on this score to your acceptance of my proposal.

I will however pray you specially to observe the word inscribed at the head of this note: for I see with dismay that the scope of my intercepted conversation with Sir Charles Dilke yesterday is in the papers of this morning.

[1] Letter accepting at Add MS 44225, f. 163.
[2] The interview at which Dilke declined office unless Chamberlain was in the Cabinet; Gwynn and Tuckwell, i. 309.
[3] Second offer of deputy-speakership, rather than the cabinet; J. L. and B. Hammond, *James Stansfeld* (1932), 218.
[4] (Sir) Evan Macgregor, 1842-1926; principal clerk in the admiralty; permanent secretary 1884-1907; kt. 1893.

The rule is to observe the strictest secrecy until Her Majesty's pleasure has been taken.

If you desire to see me, I shall be at Lord Granville's house at and after twelve.[1]

To A.J. MUNDELLA, 27 April 1880.   Add MS 44258, f. 163.

I have the pleasure of proposing to you that I should submit your name to the Queen as Vice President of the Committee of Council on Education. I *expect* that Earl Spencer will be President.[2] It is not necessary to speak of the vast importance of the work of this office, and of the great distinction attaching to the post.

One thing I will venture to say. The charge for Education is enormous. When the object in view is of such value, it is apt to be assumed, taken for granted, that the money is all necessary and well laid out. I hope you will think that it is the duty of the official man representing the department to make vigilant inquiry not only into any augmentation, but into wasteful charges which may have crept in, and into charges also which having been originally necessary may have become needless and therefore wasteful.[3]

28. Wed.

Wrote to Lady Annaly—Mr Watkin Williams[4]—Mr Richardson—Mr Herschel[5]—The Queen—Mr Caird—Mr Brassey—A.W. Peel—Ld Annaly.[6] Conclave 5-8 PM. Saw Mr Fawcett—Ld Wolverton—Ld F. Cavendish—Bp of Colombo—Mr Mundella—Ld Granville—Ld R. Grosvenor—Sir W. Harcourt—Sir H. Ponsonby—Mr Herries—Mr Primrose[7]—Mr Dodson (2)—Ld Selborne—Ld Hartington—Ld Ripon.

$12\frac{3}{4}$-5. To Windsor where we were sworn in at a Council. Much popular feeling at all points of arrival and departure. Audience of H.M. 3-$3\frac{1}{2}$. I think H.M. was completely satisfied and relieved. No reading!

To A.W. PEEL, M.P., 28 April 1880, 'Secret.'   Add MS 44270, f. 325.

I am very desirous, if it can be contrived, to associate your name with the new administration. The Home Office, which will be under Sir W. Harcourt in the House of Commons, will supply plenty of work for more than one hand, and if you would consent to follow Ibbetson and Ridley in the office of Under Secretary, I would gladly adopt this arrangement and submit it to the Queen, while I know it would be agreeable to Sir W. Harcourt.

I should have been very glad to offer you a higher office, while I recollected that you were last in an office which naturally enough was not wholly according to your tastes.

---

[1] Version in Garvin, i. 301.

[2] Spencer was hurrying home from the Continent; communication with him became muddled; see Add MS 44308.

[3] Mundella accepted, 27 April 1880, Add MS 44258, f. 163, observing: 'I recognise the force and justice of your observations. . . . I should deem it my duty to exercise the utmost care and vigilance to secure the highest educational results at the lowest possible charge to the country.'

[4] Watkin Williams, barrister and liberal M.P. 1868-80; judge 1880.

[5] (Sir) Farrer *Herschell, 1837-99; barrister and liberal M.P. Durham 1874-85; solicitor general 1880; lord chancellor 1886, 1892-5.

[6] Luke White, 1829-88; former liberal M.P.; Irish landowner; m. 1853 Emily Stuart; 2nd Baron Annaly 1873.

[7] (Sir) Henry William Primrose, 1846-1923; one of Gladstone's secretaries April-June 1880, 1884-6; Ripon's secretary 1880-4; chaired customs and B.I.R. 1895.

But the varied and urgent pressure of considerations which affect the formation of a Government prevent me giving scope to my inclinations: and I am sure you will accept this proposal as the measure not of my will but of my power.[1]

29. Th.

Wrote to Pres. Royal Acad.—Duke of Bedford—Mr Stansfeld—Marchss of Lothian—Ld Cowper—Marquis of Bath—Sir J. Adye—Mr Leeman MP.—Mr Hibbert—Mr Watkin Williams M.P.—The Queen 1.2.3.—The Electors of Midlothian—Mr Richardson—C.G.—Mr Courtney MP—Mr Maclaren—Mr Balfour— Earl of Kenmare—Sir Thos G.—Mr Baxter—Ld C. Bruce[2]—Ld Granville. Dined at Mr Pender's[3] to meet R.A.s: also evening party. Saw Herbert J.G.—Mr Greville—Mr Hibbert—Ld R. Grosvenor—Lord F. Cavendish—Ld Granville—Ld Wolverton—Mr Greenwood[4]—Mr Barran MP—Sir A. Hayter—Mr West— A. Peel—Mr Herbert RA—Sir F. Leighton—Mr Knowles. Read Fortnightly on the State of affairs.[5]

Ld G[ranville].
What do you say about Lowe?
Would he mind?
Viewing his services I do not think HM is right?
WEG Ap 29. 80 Midnight
(Changed my mind & wrote to H.M. at 7 am.[6]

30. Frid.

Wrote to Mr Law—Lord O'Hagan—The Speaker—Att. General—Ld Ailesbury— The Queen 1.2.—Mons. E. Girardin—Ld R. Montagu. The progress made will now allow me to begin work in D St. Read Sibthorp. Saw Lord Cowper—Lord Kenmare—Ld Lansdowne—Ld Granville—Mr Maclaren—Ld Kensington—Lucy Cavendish—Ld Morley—Sir J. Adye—Mr Holmes—Ld A. [sc. C.] Bruce. Stole 20 m. for Grosv. Gallery.[7] Granville gave the first Cabinet dinner in C.H. Terrace. We decided that Layard could not retain his post.[8] In the evening I had a pleasant conversation with Count Karolyi who gave me satisfactory assurances respecting the Treaty of Berlin.[9]

[1] Peel accepted.
[2] Lord Charles William Brudenell-Bruce, 1834-97; liberal M.P. N. Wilts. 1865-74, Marlborough 1878-85; household office 1880-5.
[3] See 27 Feb. 65; a keen collector.
[4] Frederick Greenwood, d. 1909, just ousted as tory editor of *Pall Mall Gazette*, founded instead *St. James's Gazette*; see 1 May 80.
[5] His own article, and Morley on home and foreign affairs; *Fortnightly Review*, xxx. 726 (May 1880).
[6] Holograph, Add MS 44764, f. 72. Gladstone's tenacity gained a viscountcy rather than a barony for Lowe.
[7] The Pre-Raphaelite gallery.
[8] On 6 May Layard was recalled from Constantinople on leave, replaced temporarily by Goschen (after Carlingford declined it) as ambassador extraordinary; but he never returned, being officially relieved in March 1881.
[9] See 4 May 80.

Saturday May 1. 1880.

Wrote to The Queen 1.2.—Earl of Cork—Mr Greenwood—Ld Kenmare—Mr Waddy QC.—Sir D. Marjoribanks—Ld Ailesbury—Ld R. Montagu—Mons. Girardin. Stole 50 m for Royal Acad. under Mr [J. C.] Hook's guidance. Saw Mr Osborne Morgan—Mr Molesworth—Mr Trevelyan—Mr C. Bannerman[1]—Ld F. Cavendish—The Speaker—Sir H. Ponsonby—Sir S. Northcote—Ld Morley— W.H.G.—Ld Coleridge—Mr Horsley—E. Macgregor—Mr Gibson. Attended Academy Dinner & spoke for the Ministers.[2]

To F. GREENWOOD, 1 May 1880.   Add MS 44544, f. 2.

Thank you very much for your note,[3] & I was glad to have the privilege of making your acquaintance.

It would ill become me to use any language which might appear to imply a prospective disparagement of the Pall Mall Gazette: but as to the past, I can assure you that the expressions to which I am glad to see you[?] can refer with satisfaction were sincere, & that I fully abide by their purport.

I cannot doubt that you will find a suitable field for the exercise of your remarkable powers.

To S. D. WADDY, 1 May 1880.   Add MS 44544, f. 2.

I thank you for your letter,[4] but my reply must commence with an expression of my regret at your exclusion from Parliament: only as I trust for a time, & the shorter time the better. It is an ill return for your two gallant fights.

I am not able to distinguish between sections, but I apprehend that the number of persons not belonging to the established churches is larger in the present Parliament, & probably in the administration just formed (as I may now call it) than in any former one.

If among them there is no member of the Wesleyans I sincerely regret it. I need not assure you that the circumstance is not due to any prejudice against them in any quarter. Appointments to Civil Office cannot be substantively governed by religious profession, yet I should be glad, for better knowledge, if you could confidentially supply me with a list of the Wesleyans now in the House of Commons.

2. S 5 Easter.

Chapel Royal at noon, and H.C: also at 5.30 P.M. Wrote to Duke of St Albans— Ld Breadalbane—Ld Fife—Ld F. Cavendish[5]—Mr E. Ashley—Ld Granville—The Queen—Count Karolyi (draft) & note. Saw Mr Hamilton—Ld Granville—Ld

[1] (Sir) Henry *Campbell-Bannerman, 1836-1908; liberal M.P. Stirling burghs from 1868; secretary to war office 1871-4, 1880-2, to admiralty 1882-4, to Ireland 1884-5; war secretary 1886, 1892-5; led the liberal party 1899; prime minister 1905-8.

[2] T.T., 3 May 1880, 9d; see 4 May 80.

[3] See 29 Apr. 80 and Greenwood's letter of that day in J. W. Robertson Scott, *The story of the Pall Mall Gazette* (1950), 241, on his meeting with Gladstone and on the sale of the *P.M.G.* to 'a thorough-going party-man of advanced Liberal views [H. Yates Thompson]'. Morley succeeded Greenwood as editor.

[4] Of 30 April, Add MS 44463, f. 305; Waddy was defeated at Sheffield; see 4 Feb. 74. No reply to this letter found.

[5] Asking him to move for a select cttee. on Bradlaugh; by Walpole's casting vote, the cttee. prevented Bradlaugh affirming; Arnstein, 37.

Sydney—Ld Wolverton—Mr Adam. Dined at Sir R. Phillimore's. Read Sibthorp—Cath. Presb. on Presbn History[1]—Stanley on Roman Variations.[2]

3. M.

Wrote to Sir G. Bowyer—Mr Chamberlain—R. Richardson—Lord Torrington—Ld Carington—Ld Wrottesley—Ld Spencer—The Queen—Ld Dunraven—Ld Monson—Mr Trollope.[3] To Windsor at 11¾: had an audience, graciously given: then Council. Back at 3.30. Saw Mr Ashley—Ld Aberdare—Mr Chamberlain[4]—Ld Granville—Mrs Birks—Sir H. Ponsonby. Cabinet 4-6¾. Dined at Grillion's. Conversation on House matters with C. Read Sibthorp Life & Letters.

Audience. May 3. 80.

Sir C. Dilke: Apology,
1. Republicanism,
2. Unbecoming language,
3. Opposition to Dowry course proposed.

Submissions for office. Composition of Govt. Day for meeting 20th. H M to go 21st.[5]

Cabinet. May 3. 1880[6]
LD. HARTINGTON.

Ripon—whether to go out [to India] on the 14th. Ld. Lytton wishes to remain to the end of June. Decided not to interfere with Lord Ripon's plan for the 14th.
Last dispatches from India Jan. 7.
Sir D. Stewart to have chief political command as well as military.
Ld. Granville. What language to hold to Russia about Central Asia? He is to draw him [Lobanov] out as he complains of not having got a *answer* from Lord B[eaconsfield] and Lord S[alisbury] . ∴. an answer [?][7] to *something.*[8]
Indian Finance—Ld. N[orthbrook?] estimates
80-1 War Expenditure 7½ m vice 2100m[ille].
Kimberley. Galeclaa land
  Tambouclu &c. land } To be annexed to
             Cape Colony.
  and . . .
Promise of the late Govt. to hold good.[9]
Shall Frere continue at the Cape? No.[10] (Chambn. argued for it: Harcourt partially.)

---

[1] *Catholic Presbyterian*, iii. 321 (May 1880).

[2] Not found under this title; perhaps one of A. P. Stanley's many pamphlets.

[3] Anthony Trollope, 1815-82; novelist; thought Gladstone had merely forgotten him, but now believes himself shunned on purpose; Gladstone docketed that his rudeness was unintentional, due to 'the *absorption* of the present time & I pray him to forgive it'; see Add MS 44464, f. 34.

[4] Discussing Pitt, and Chamberlain's likeness to him; Garvin, i. 309.

[5] Holograph, Add MS 44764, f. 76. Dilke's explanation of his handling of a question on republicanism during the campaign was accepted; Gwynn and Tuckwell, i. 308.

[6] Add MS 44642, f. 2.   [7] Ink blot obscures this word.

[8] See Granville's mem. on conversation with Prince Alexis Lobanov-Rostovsky (1824-96, Russian ambassador 1879-82) PRO 30/29/143; Ramm II, i. 125.

[9] After some delay, the Cape was allowed to annex Gcalekaland, Tembuland and Bomvanaland, as promised by Hicks Beach; see Goodfellow, 190.

[10] Must be understood as 'No recall', for Frere was not immediately recalled, and Chamberlain noted: 'I stood alone in urging a complete reversal of the general policy of Lord Beaconsfield. . . .

Herat agreement read.

Mr. Forster. Irish Legislation. To prepare Bill for No. 2 Cabinet. Wed. 2.30. Inculcation of Secrecy.

4. Tu.

Wrote to Ld Ilchester—Lord Sudely—Mr Anderson MP.—Lord Methuen—Mad. Novikoff—Ld Ribblesdale—Sir A. Gordon MP.—Ld Granville (3)—Mr Leveson MP. Conclave 3-5 on conversion of Malt Duty into Beer Duty. Saw Mr Hamilton—Ld F. Cavendish—Lord Leigh—Lord Spencer—Ld Monson—W. Dumaresq (much better)—Lady Stanley. Dined with Mrs Birks. Read F.O. papers.—Letters of Sibthorp.

To Count A. KAROLYI, Austrian ambassador, 4 May 1880.[1]

[First letter:] I thank your Excellency for your letter; which, uniting frankness with kindness, renders my task an easy one.

Without discussing the accuracy of certain expressions in the report you have forwarded, I proceed at once to the subject. At the moment when I accepted from the Queen the duty of forming an Administration, I forthwith resolved that I would not, as a Minister, either repeat or even defend in argument polemical language, in regard to more than one foreign Power, which I had used individually when in a position of greater freedom and less responsibility.

Two points have been raised by your Excellency. I will dispose of the first by expressing my regret that I should even have seemed to impute to His Imperial Majesty language which he did not use.

Your Excellency says that His Imperial Majesty expressed, in conversation with Sir H. Elliot, 'his deep regret at my hostile disposition towards Austria.' Permit me to say I have no such disposition towards any country whatever, and that I at all times have particularly and heartily wished well to Austria. In the performance of the arduous task of consolidating the Empire, I feel a cordial respect for the efforts of the Emperor, and I trust that their complete success may honourably and nobly mark his reign.

With respect to my animadversions on the foreign policy of Austria in times when it was active beyond the border, I will not conceal from your Excellency that grave apprehensions had been excited in my mind lest Austria should play a part in the Balkan peninsula hostile to the freedom of the emancipated populations, and to the reasonable and warranted hopes of the subjects of the Sultan. These apprehensions were founded, it is true, upon secondary evidence; but it was not the evidence of hostile witnesses, and it was the best at my command.

Your Excellency is now good enough to assure me that your Government has no desire whatever to extend or add to the rights it has acquired under the Treaty of Berlin, and that any such extension would be actually prejudicial to Austria-Hungary.

I wanted to recall at once Sir Bartle Frere, to reconsider the annexation of the Transvaal and to recall Sir Henry Elliot'; Chamberlain, *Political Memoir*, 4 and Schreuder, 67.

---

[1] Letter printed in *Political speeches, March and April 1880*, 364, forwarded by Granville on 6 May; Gladstone's speech of 17 March 1880, ibid., 41, attacked Sir H. Elliot and Austria's policy generally, hinting at possible Austrian Balkan expansion; Karolyi's letter of 1 May requesting 'some friendly words' in that day's speech and both diarist's replies in Gooch and Temperley, *British documents*, ix, App. I; see also Ramm II, i. 121n. The letter was debated in the Lords on 21 May, *H* 252. 170.

Permit me at once to state to your Excellency that had I been in possession of such an assurance as I have now been able to receive, I never would have uttered any one of the words which your Excellency justly describes as of a painful and wounding character. Whether it was my misfortune or my fault that I was not so supplied, I will not now attempt to determine; but will at once express my serious concern that I should, in default of it, have been led to refer to transactions of an earlier period, or to use terms of censure which I can now wholly banish from my mind.

I think that the explanation I now tender should be made not less public than the speech which has supplied the occasion for it; and as to the form of such publicity, I desire to accede to whatever may be your Excellency's wish. I have only to thank your Excellency alike for the matter and the manner both of your oral and of your written communications.

Add MS 44544, f. 2.

[Second letter:] I add a line with regard to your closing suggestion. The very limited field accorded to me on the night of the 1st, and the strict exclusion of even defensive politics, prevented my acting upon it. Had I mentioned foreign powers it would I think have been going beyond the precedents, & my allusion must have been in such very general terms as perhaps to draw attention more to what it did not contain than to what it did.

To Madame O. NOVIKOV, 4 May 1880.   Add MS 44544, f. 3.

I thank you for your kind letter.[1] A great change, & a strange one, has passed upon me. In respect to speech I pass under new conditions. For the time, I hope the short time, during which I personally may continue in office, I shall have very heavy labour for I have felt obliged to be Finance Minister as well as head of the Government. All private & personal communications will I fear as a rule be beyond my reach. Indeed I should be ashamed to confess to you how rare have been even heretofore my communications with my own children. But in regard to our foreign policy I would say we shall have no prejudices & no preferences, no plots & above all no resentments. In a few weeks the state of affairs will probably have required us to make trial by practical discussions of the dispositions of all the Chief Governments. But the dispositions with which we shall approach these discussions will be such as I have described.

I am truly concerned to hear of your son's illness, but I gather with satisfaction from your letter that his state no longer causes you anxiety.

5. *Wed.*

Wrote to Miss Burnett[2]—The Queen 1.2.—Mr ... MP.—Mr Maclaren (Ld Adv.) Cabinet 2½-6. At one time it roved a good deal: but progress was made. Read Life of Metternich[3]—finished Timoleon.[4] Saw Ld Granville (2)—Mr Goschen— Ld Ripon—Sir C. Dilke—W.A. Smith [*sic*]—Sir A. Galt—Mr Bright. We dined at Marlborough House. Much conversation with Prince & Princess: both very kind, & very free, not stiff. Preparations for moving.

---

[1] Of 20 April, from Moscow, Add MS 44268, f. 212; her letters were processed by the secretaries.
[2] Daughter of his deceased agent.
[3] *Memoirs of Prince Metternich, edited by Prince R. Metternich*, 5v. (1880-2).
[4] Probably J. F. J. Arnoldt, *Timoleon, eine biographische Darstellung* (1850).

Cabinet. May 5. 80, 2.30 PM.[1]

2. Irish Land Purchase Clauses. Bright, Ld. Spencer, Law, Lefevre: to prepare the heads of a plan.

1. WEG recounted certain subjects for the legislation and other Parl. work of the Session.[2]

3. Burials Bill. Basic[?] option between 1. Silent Burial. 2. Xtn and orderly religious observance. Ld. Chan[cello]r to communicate with archbishop and state[?][3] Govt. is disposed to legislate—without specification—and learn what he will support. Also to ascertain how far Morgan's Bill goes beyond the plan carried in the Lords.

4. Game—discussed at large. Q[uer]y extend Maclagan's Act to England and grant inalienable common[?] right as to ground game.

5. Tenants Compensation. Can hardly be dealt with.

6. Committee on East India Govt. Act. Favour the appointment but whether this year or next will be considered.

7. Harcourt. Q[uer]y get provision from the Water Companies rather than pass a Suspensory Bill.

8. Bill for a Royal Commission to ascertain the property of the London Companies.

9. Bankruptcy Bill—perhaps to be proceeded with.

10. Late Chancellor's Bill on Land. Chancr. to prepare a minute.[4]

Next Cabinet Wed. May 12. 2.30.

May 5. 1880 [Legislation].[5] 1. Irish Borough Franchise. 2. Commee. on India Govt. Bill. 3. Burials Bill. Lords. 4. Fiscal measures. 5. and 6. Game. Tenants' Improvements. 7. Corrupt Practices.

General: Probate, Inventory and Succession Duties; Corrupt Practices; Savings Banks; Transfer of Land; Devolution of Land; Tenants Improvements; Game; Burials' Bill.

Ireland: Grand Jury Laws; Peasant Proprietors; Electoral franchise in boroughs; University.

Scotland: Game; Tenants' Improvements. *sup.*

6. Th. Ascension Day.

Chapel Royal 1-2¼ & H.C. Wrote to Mr Watkin Williams—Earl of Zetland—Ld Listowel—Ld Clarendon—Mr Johnson MP—Ld Hartington—E. Macgregor—J. Morley—Scotts—Rev. SEG—Miss Gibson—Sir Thos G. Eight to dinner. Saw Mr W.A. Smith—Dr A. Clark—Mr Godley—Sir C. Ducane[6]—Mr F. Hill—Ld Spencer—W.H.G.—M. Jovanovich—Mrs Th. Preparations for moving,[7] wh cross most inconveniently the stream or rather torrent of business. Three hours of official reading 9-12.

To LORD HARTINGTON, Indian secretary, 6 May 1880.   Add MS 44544, f. 4.

I would note hastily on your letter[8]

1. That the situation is peculiar. Parliament meets on the 20th—it is necessary to have determined on our principal measures before that date. The Cabinet has met early but

---

[1] Add MS 44642, f. 5.   [2] See list below.   [3] Word smudged.
[4] See 29 May 80.   [5] Add MS 44642, f. 6.
[6] Sir Charles Ducane, 1825-89; chairman of customs board 1878-89; much correspondence on wine duties in Add MS 44544.
[7] To 10 Downing Street, see 12 May 80.
[8] Of 6 May, Add MS 44145, f. 29, on procedure in Cabinet, suggesting members should circulate memoranda on proposed legislation.

under the exceptional circumstances I think it was best to examine tentatively certain subjects & appoint a day for the further consideration of such subjects as required time & elucidation.

2. I am not aware of any rule in the Cabinets in which I have served that Bills should as matter of course or generally be introduced by circulated Memoranda. In by far the larger number of instances within my experience I think it has been the other way.

3. Still I quite admit the disadvantage at which we approached certain subjects yesterday but I trust the very proper postponement of decision till a future day will remove it.

7. *Fr.* [*Mentmore*]

Wrote to Lord Bath—Mr Prescott—The Queen—Address to Midlothian—Mr Herries. Off to Mentmore at 5.40. Heavy work for moving. Saw Mr Ouvry—Ld Edm. Fitzmaurice—Ld Hartington—Ld Granville—Ld Rosebery—Count Menabrea—Mr Goschen. Read Lewes on Actors[1]—Eastwick on Afghan War.[2]

To C. J. HERRIES, 7 May 1880.   Add MS 44544, f. 4.

I hope to receive, not later than Monday or Tuesday morning, the heads of the project to be considered by the Government for the repeal & commutation of the malt tax. We made I thought good progress the other day; & when we have the heads on paper, we may do more.

I shall be very glad also of any information in figures or otherwise which your experience may enable you to prepare as illustrative of the case.

8. *Sat.*

Wrote to Mr Goschen—Ld Stratford de Redcliffe—Sir H. Taylor—Mrs Hampton—Mr Richardson—Ld Hartington—Ld Granville—Mr Forster—Mr Freeman. Long walk. Conversation with Lord Northbrook—Rev. Mr Bird[3]—Ld Rosebery. Worked on papers & minutes. Read Life of Sibthorp—Memoirs of Metternich.

To LORD HARTINGTON, Indian secretary, 8 May 1880.   Chatsworth MSS 340.960
'*Private*'

I have been over the list of the H. of Commons. Playfair has occurred to me as possible but I am far from having arrived at any positive notion. We shall I think have to go back upon very drastic measures of retrenchment in India & I hope you will carefully examine into the sufficiency of the measures for inquiry taken by the late Government last year. They did not seem to me to be sufficiently impressed with the gravity of the case even as it then stood.

In point of ability Playfair would be very good but I do not know whether he has ever turned his mind to retrenchment.

Would it not be well to consult Freddy [Cavendish], who has had much experience in the Public Accounts Committee: also Wolverton: & perhaps Sir W. Anderson who was *admirable* in all these questions but I fear may now be a little past his work.

There is another subject calling for your consideration graver than some that we have touched in the Cabinet—and next I think in its claims on you to Afghan policy. *Can* Indian finance bear the existing strain or can it not—must we consider whether we

---

[1] C. L. Lewes, *Memoirs . . . containing anecdotes of the English and Scottish stages*, 4v. (1805).
[2] W. J. Eastwick, *Lord Lytton and the Afghan War* (1879).
[3] Probably Robert James Bird, vicar of St Bartholomew's, London.

should take serious steps for relieving it sensibly in the war expenditure. Which of course means immediate further taxation in England.

As far as present evidence goes Northcote's estimates will not be borne out by receipt, and the anticipations of some of the newspapers are wholly unwarranted.

To W. E. FORSTER, Irish secretary, 8 May 1880.   Add MS 44544, f. 5.

I think Childers has inadvertently led you to an incorrect impression.[1]

Bright introduced the subject of his Purchase clauses, a few remarks explanatory of his meaning were made, & it was agreed that he should get the heads on paper which he thinks might be dealt with during the year.

There is not, & I think there cannot be any formal rule about the mention of business in Cabinet, & this year from circumstances we are less than ever in form: but there was not the slightest movement *towards* any decision. You know I daresay that the matter is a specialty with Bright. Indeed he looked upon the occupiers' clauses of the [1870] Land Act as of comparatively small interest.

Let me take this opportunity of saying another word on a subject of real importance.

Ireland has been illegitimately paid for unjust inequalities by an unjust preference in much lavish public expenditure.

The Lord Lieutenant is not the real Parliamentary officer for Ireland.

I am afraid you may find in the Secretary's office a bad tradition. I do not recollect ever, during nearly 10 years for which I have been Finance Minister, to have received from a Secretary for Ireland (though some of them have been Treasury men) a *single suggestion* for the reduction of any expense whatever.

I hope that with many other honours you will take to yourself the honour of breaking this bad tradition.

9. S. aft. Asc.

Ch. 11 A.M. and 6 P.M. Wrote to Mr C.C. Sibthorp[2]—Ld Lyons—Mr Dodson. Conversation with Ld Aberdeen. Read Sibthorp—much. Read Uranga, Religion Naturelle—a contrast.[3]

To J. G. DODSON, president of the local government board,   Add MS 44544, f. 5.
9 May 1880.

We shall have a difficult work of selection to perform with a crowd of competing subjects & a very scanty stock of time.[4] I should say the claim of each may be stated thus in mathematical phrase; it will vary directly as the importance & inversely as the detail. i.e. the controvertible detail. But I think the case you put forward should be well considered & you would promote this if you could undertake to ascertain with precision for our information the stage which the question has reached, & the prospect of accord upon it.

---

[1] Forster to Gladstone, 7 May 1880, Add MS 44157, f. 127: 'Childers writes that [?] you discussed last Wednesday a Bill for extending the Bright Clauses. Had I supposed this was likely I should have put off coming here [Dublin].' See Hammond, 168.

[2] Thanking Coningsby Charles Sibthorp of Canwick Hall for the book (see 20 Apr. 80): 'I have found the perusal of it most soothing as well as most enchaining'; Add MS 44544, f. 6.

[3] See 14 Mar. 80.

[4] Dodson wrote on 8 May, Add MS 44252, f. 74, pressing an Employer's Liabilities Bill: 'many classes of working men are most anxious about it'.

Scotland, Ireland, nonconformists, farmers, workmen, all have some amount of special demand upon us & one would like to meet them all as far as may be practicable.[1]

I rejoice in your good expectations from Chester.

10. M.

Wrote to Ld Spencer—Sir H. Ponsonby—The Queen—Ld Selborne—Mr Baines—Col. Carington[2]—Sir F. Doyle. Read Sibthorp—Lewes on Actors. Walk with Ld Rosebery & confidential conversation. Much work done with Godley: who is *perfect* in his difficult *métier*.[3]

To E. BAINES, 10 May 1880.   Add MS 44544, f. 6.

The critical moment at which your letter was written[4] & the continuing strain which followed have caused a seemingly strange delay in my reply, & will I hope excuse that delay in your indulgent judgment.

It was to me a matter of lively satisfaction that I was never called upon to redeem the pledge given as to a preference of Midlothian over Leeds. Both were vacated at once by my acceptance of office.

I hope for an opportunity, though it must be some time hence, of expressing what I think & feel on the whole of the Leeds procedure; most of all on those parts of it which were only beginning at the date of your letter.

In the meantime I thank you for your important personal share in bringing about results as remarkable as they are gratifying, & I thank you yet more particularly for your closing words.

To Sir F. H. C. DOYLE, 10 May 1880.   Add MS 44150, f. 219.

I thank you for a most interesting letter, the letter in every line of a true friend.[5] And one part of the reply at any rate is easy. Let me say at the outset with how much pleasure I receive your good report of your health. Numbering two more years than you, I will not accept your argument about breaking up, and I hope it may be falsified by the facts.

As regards the *pièce de resistance* of your letter, it is only too interesting to my Egotism and could hardly have a reply except in an autobiography. I like you have my own pessimism and my own fears, but they lie in another region. I have no fears in this country from the progress of popular liberties. My fears are excited by the manner in which a large proportion of the educated community is wheedling itself out of the greatest and brightest of all its possessions, the 'jewel of great price'. That great divorce between the actual Christian religion and the trained human reason, which has long marked most countries of the continent, has during the last twenty-five years been too perceptible in this country, and is producing its natural fruit in the declining morality of the upper portion of society. You, with your fears, are to me like a man, who, when his house is

---

[1] Dodson reported on 15 May, ibid. f. 76, that the Cabinet committee to which the Bill was referred (see 12 May 80) had decided to adopt Brassey's Bill.

[2] William Henry Peregrine Carrington, 1845-1914; liberal M.P. Wycombe 1868-83; household office 1880-2; on Egyptian campaign 1882.

[3] J. A. Godley (see 26 Aug. 72); Gladstone's principal private secretary 1880-2.   [4] Not found.

[5] Of 28 April, from Madeira, Add MS 44150, f. 217, mentioned in his *Reminiscences* (1886), 405; Doyle discussed Gladstone's shift from 'High Toryism to Radicalism', recalling: 'Some forty-five years ago you thus spoke to me of the Scotch political temper: "A Scotch Tory is worse than an English Whig; a Scotch Whig is worse than an English Radical, and a Scotch Radical is worse than the Devil himself" '.

threatening to take fire, spends all his alarms on his haystack. I was born with smaller natural endowments than you, & I had also a narrower early training. But my life has certainly been remarkable for the mass of continuous and searching experience it has brought me. Ever since I began to pass out of boyhood, I have been feeling my way; owing little to living teachers, but enormously to dead ones (over and above the four gospels). It has been experience which has altered my politics. My Toryism was accepted by me on authority and in good faith. I did my best to fight for it. But if you choose to examine my Parliamentary life you will find that on every subject as I came to deal with it practically, I had to deal with it as a Liberal elected in 1832. I began with slavery in 1833 & was commended by the Liberal Minister Mr Stanley. I took to Colonial subjects principally, and in 1837 was commended for treating them liberally by Lord Russell. Then Sir R. Peel carried me into Trade, & before I had been six months in office I wanted to resign because I thought his Corn Law Reform insufficient. In ecclesiastical policy I had been a spectator; but if you choose to refer to a speech of Sheil's in 1844 on the Dissenters Chapels Bill you will find him describe me as predestined to be a champion of religious equality.[1] All this seems to show that I have changed under the teaching of experience.

With regard to my description of Scotch politicians, one branch of it surprises me because Scotch Tories are, I incline to think, more inclined to extremes than English ones: but the main part does not seem wholly strange, for certainly there was 45 years ago a great deal of violence in Scotch feeling, & this simply because the people had not been trained to liberty, of which they had no taste till after the Reform Bill.

As respects the kind of change wrought in me, so far as I can be a witness to it, I am not less disposed than in my youth to recognise authority or to revere antiquity: but I have learned to set a great value on liberty which unhappily neither Eton nor Oxford ever taught me to appreciate, & I have learned also that the upper classes of the community are as classes wretchedly ill-qualified to be its guides; for though they have great advantage from their opportunities, they have still greater disadvantage from their temptations and they rarely do right until they become afraid of the consequences of doing wrong. On the other hand, I do not idolise the masses, & I am as far as possible from being an optimist in politics. In like manner, I feel more shame than pride at our present state; but I compare it favourably with the legislation of half a century ago, which I think was in a number of points, now amended, disgraceful to us as rational beings, not to say as Christians.

With respect to the Monarchy, I think it much stronger now than when William IV could not drive in the City of London; it has little to fear except from the possibility that there may at some period be unworthy wearers of the crown.

With respect to the late elections, I am ready to contend that we the Liberals have been fighting, as to the main issue, a consecutive battle against ideas & practices neither Liberal nor Conservative. The new Parliament will be tested by its acts. It will not draw its inspiration from me. No doubt it will make changes which will be denounced as revolutionary & then recognised as innocent, or even good. But I expect it to act in the main on welltried & established lines, & do much for the people and little to disquiet my growing years or even yours.

To LORD SELBORNE, lord chancellor, 10 May 1880.   Selborne MS 1867, f. 102.

I return your enclosures with many thanks: Lord Radstock seems to be a man above the standard common in what I may call his line.[2] A particular interest attaches also to

---

[1] *H* 75. 377 (6 June 1844); see above, iii. xxxi.
[2] Selborne sent an untraced paper by Radstock on Indian affairs; Add MS 44297, f. 41.

the Chandu Sen movement[1] in India, & to testimony proceeding from that quarter. I am confident that the Missions have nothing to fear from Ripon.

A word about the Burials question which for the moment is in your hands & cannot be anywhere so well. I can see plainly enough that we have a nice operation to perform in making out our Bill of Fare for the Session. Its brevity will absolutely forbid legislative work of the toughest kind. It is but the wrecked fragment of a year: yet it is our duty to turn it to account. There is something in Lowe's doctrine of the 'golden moments' though not perhaps so much as he may have thought. If the Burials question is introduced in the House of Commons I have little doubt that it will seriously curtail our available time, & will be used advisedly for that purpose.

I do not believe the Dissenters will be fastidious about it, & they would not expect the extrusion of the religious element from the proceedings. I have no doubt you will clearly ascertain for us whether there is any idea of this kind involved in what has already taken place. I also hope you will consider, & consult with Granville, as to the choice between 'religious' & 'Christian'.[2] I should be very sorry if the difference between the two words became the occasion of throwing the question into the House of Commons at the outset. For my own part I lay no stress on the distinction & can hardly think that any considerable part of the Peers would: least of all the Archbishops or Lord Harrowby.

Charles Wood, son of Halifax, is I believe very desirous to have his say about the Burials Bill. Perhaps you will communicate with him. I am not apprised of his views, but his spirit would I think be conciliatory.

11. Tu.

Wrote to The Queen—Lord Granville—Ld Aberdare—Rev. Mr Fowler—Sir C. Dilke—Mr West. Worked on the Malt and Wine questions. Walk with Rosebery. Examination of Books. Read Lewes on Actors—finished Sibthorp. Saw Mr J. Morley.

To Sir C. W. DILKE, foreign under-secretary, 11 May 1880.   Add MS 43875, f. 7.

With regard to the Wine Duties,
1. I shall be happy to see M. Leon Say, but I think the detailed negotiation will have to be carried on by the F.O. or the B. of T. with a careful reservation of course of binding opinion & of the discretion of the Treasury on all points where revenue is sensibly concerned.
2. For 1880-1, I consider the door absolutely closed against any reduction entailing loss to the Exchequer, and for 81-82 also & what lies beyond we should remain free.
3. I do not think the idea of a duty *ad valorem* on wine can in any shape be entertained.
4. Until Revenues & Charge are in a more normal state it is hard to compare the claims of wine with those of any other article.
5. When we reach that happy condition, plans such as are described by Mr Herries Dec. 10 77, or a modification of the Spanish proposal (Mem. p. 2) might probably be entertained.

[1] *Sic.* Keshab Chandra Sen, 1838-84; a leader of the non-racial, non-sectarian Brahmo Samaj in which Gladstone showed interest, reading its *Year Book* in the December of most years in the later 1870s. For Sen, see N. Sinha, *Freedom movement in Bengal, 1818-1904, Who's Who* (1968), 248ff.
[2] The Burials Bill (permitting non-Anglican services in parish churchyards) referred to 'Christian services'; Derby and Dunraven were unhappy about the vagueness of the term; *H* 252. 1049, 1051.

6. To maintain the high rate for some six degrees or thereabouts below 42%, or even after due notice to increase it, would be a positive reform.
7. The principle of a separate & higher rate on wine in bottles seems also sound.
8. The present double rate was adopted at a time when it was thought by the Customs a great object to simplify their operations. We seem now to be less restrained on this head.
9. I do not desire to shut the door against 'negotiation' but I have little faith in it; I do not admit that the Treaty of 1860 was a precedent for it & I fear that if we now adopt the principle that our revenue is to be handled on any but fixed grounds, we shall practically find ourselves buying in a dear market & selling in a very cheap one.[1]

12. Wed. [London]

Wrote to Ld Morley—Ld Ailesbury—Mr H. Mason MP.—Duke of Edinburgh—Mr Albert Grey—The Queen—Ld Granville—Mr Lowe—Ld Suffolk: & minutes. Left Mentmore before ten. Survey at No 73. In D St before twelve. A wilderness & a chaos. Saw Freshfields—Scotts—Ld Lyons 1-2. The Queen at 3.30. Very gracious. Cabinet 4-6¾. Good progress. Wells St Service at 8.15. Evg at home: struggling vainly with confusion. Read Hist. of Taxes.[2]

Cabinet. May 12. 1880.[3]
South Africa. To promote Confederation.
  Transvaal—retain sovereignty. Grant free institutions. Telegram agreed on.
  Natal.
  Frere and territorial extension: to avoid.
  Disarmament of Basutos. To go forward on the responsibility of the Cape.
Game Laws. Ld. Advocate attended—indefeasible right as to ground game promised by Scotch members. Lord Advocate to draw his Bill.
Commission on [London Livery] Companies—not to be in [Queen's] speech.
Peace Preservation in Ireland—next Cabinet.
Burials' Bill. Archbishop's suggestions for Clergy Relief considered. Provide against disturbance. Observances to be Christian and orderly. Cemetries wd. be Church yards for the purpose of the Act. [Start the Bill] In the Lords.
Liability of Employers for Injuries to Workmen. Committee of Cabinet appointed to frame a Bill.

To LORD HARTINGTON, Indian secretary, 12 May 1880.   Add MS 44145, f. 35.

Are you ready, or shall you be ready before the next Cabinet, to throw light, or give an opinion, on the question whether Indian Finance is likely this year to require serious aid from England? Any such aid will involve fresh taxation.[4]

[1] No reply found; report of meeting with Say, dated 28 May, is at Add MS 44149, f. 10.
[2] S. Dowell, *A sketch of the history of taxes in England* (1876), the first part of his *History of taxation*, complete ed., 4v. (1884).
[3] Add MS 44642, f. 8. Undated holograph note reads 'Do you continue to approve appointing Lowe to be the head of the Civil Service Commission without pay?' 'Very much. G[ranville].' Lowe declined the offer; Add MS 44302, f. 198.
[4] Hartington's reply of 14 May 1880 (returned to him and now Chatsworth MS 340.961) stated: 'even if we admit that we ought to contribute a portion of the cost of the war, the amount & mode of the contribution need not necessarily be decided on now; but might be postponed until we know what the whole cost of the war is' and that, concerning the ability of Indian finance to bear the burden, 'at present there is nothing to show that it cannot'.

13. Th.

Wrote to Ld Shaftesbury—Mr Cowper Temple—Ld Cowper—Sir H. Havelock Allan[1]—Bp of Bath & Wells—and minutes. Dined with the Wests. Read Peel on Malt Duties,[2] & many Pol. papers. Saw Mr Goschen *cum* Ld Granville—M. Gennadios—Ld Spencer—M. Leon Say—Mr Ouvry—Mr West. Saw E. Macgregor. Attended the Queen's drawingroom—$2\frac{1}{2}$-$4\frac{1}{4}$.

14. Fr.

Wrote to Ld Hartington—Mr West—Mr Lowe—The Speaker—The Queen 1.2.3.—& minutes. Dined at Mr Ths. Chinese Ambrs[3] party afterwards. Saw Musurus Pasha, & made minute of conversation—Mr Walpole—Saw Mr Goschen—Mr Godley. Conclave B.I.R. on Malt Duty at 3.30. Cabinet 4-$6\frac{3}{4}$. Read Ld Wentworth on Settled Estates Bill.

Cabinet. May 14. 80. 4. PM[4]

Peace Preservation Ireland Act. Opinions of O'Hagan, Law, Barry, and pr. Sullivan. Continuance Act for a year drafted for the late Govt. but dropped. Act not to be renewed; but general duty to be recognised.

Minute on the Irish Land Act and proceedings of the Agric. Commission[5] wh. will not drop the Irish inquiry. Spencer to retire [from the Commission]. Some new members to be chosen.

Amendment by extension of the Bright Clauses [of the 1870 Land Act]. Too complex for this year.

Flogging in the Army. Childers to prepare for the *abolition*.

Companies Commission. Offer to Companies of a Royal Commission to be made.

Committee on Ships foundered in bulk & Maritime Insurance.[6]

Bankruptcy. Chancellor to consider what to do as to the *Bill* or *subject*

Census Bill. Religious Census in Ireland only.[7]

Ballot Bill—to be reviewed.

Cabinet—Monday 2.30.

Musurus Pasha called on me. He entered into Turkish history, pitched very high the practical progress and improvements made since the Hattisherif of Gul-Knaneh in 1839;

---

[1] Sir Henry Marsham *Havelock-Allan, 1830-97; soldier and liberal (unionist) M.P. Sunderland 1874-81, S.E. Durham 1885-92; Gladstone regretted there was no office for him; Add MS 44544, f. 8.

[2] Sir R. Peel, 'Speech . . . March 10, 1835, on the motion of the Marquis of Chandos relating to the Repeal of the Malt Tax' (1835).

[3] Marquis Tseng Chilse, 1839-90; Chinese representative 1878-86.

[4] Add MS 44642, f. 11. Undated holograph list at f. 13 reads: 'O Irish Peace Preservation; and Borough Franchise Ireland; + Game; + Burials; O Ireland—Purchase Clauses; O Tenants Compensation; + Liabilities of Employers; + Renewal of Ballot Act. Indian Finances. South Africa.' Undated holograph note [to Hartington?], f. 14, reads: 'Under the circs. and with the news of your letter, I do not see any *necessity* for opening Indian Finance today'; another holograph note, f. 16, reads: 'Queen very desirous to settle Burials say[s] it is a scandal.'

[5] i.e. the Richmond Royal Commission on agricultural depression; *PP* 1881 xv; see 19 June 80.

[6] Select cttee. on merchant ships laden in bulk reported on 9 March 1880, *PP* 1880 xi. 545. Another cttee., on ships missing and foundered since 1873, ordered 1 June, chaired by Chamberlain, reported 23 July 1880; *PP* 1880 xi. 1.

[7] The 1881 census for Ireland included questions on religious affiliation (that of 1851 for England had been based on the clergy's calculations); *PP* 1881 xcvii.

cited Lord Palmerston's statement that Turkey had made more progress than any other country in the same time: said that since 1839 England had been thought to have a special interest in the maintenance of the Ottoman Empire: said they could not move too fast but had within themselves great means of improvement: that *autonomies* were *anatomies*, i.e. vivisections of the Empire: that the provinces ought to receive institutions, and that the governors might be appointed for five years; looked forward to a Turkish Parliament and the representation in it of all the provinces not politically emancipated: feared the influence of Russia but still more the plans of Austria: could not recognise the occupation of Bosnia Herzegovina as an annexation or as other than a temporary arrangement: referred to my having during the former Govt. warned them against contracting loans, & wished they had taken that advice, which he wrote home at the time.

I told him that my union of opinion on Foreign Affairs with Lord Granville was such that whatever Lord G. said might be considered as coming from me—that if in my conversations there was anything not in accord with him, it would probably be due to some accidental error on my part.

That I did not feel aware of the existence of a separate and vital English interest in the maintenance of Turkey, but only the interest we had in good order: that I thought Turkey had been, unhappily for herself, led to rely upon the notion that the British nation recognised such an interest & might be depended upon to support her in the last resort.

Yes he said Lord Beaconsfield had encouraged that idea and had at the same time done nothing whatever for them—he was glad that our policy was to be substituted for his.

Musurus having referred to the Crimean War as made to sustain this English interest, I said I rather viewed it according to the picture exhibited in the life of the Prince Consort as a war made in support of European legality, which the Czar was endeavouring to infringe in the case of Turkey.

He approved of the idea that the local liberties of the inhabitants of the Balkan Peninsula should not be overshadowed by any foreign influence whatever, and of what I had said about Austria.

I said the Treaty of Berlin was the legal and natural base of our policy—(and he declared Turkey was anxious to give it complete effect): that we did not wish to see separate & special influence exercised in Turkey by other powers, nor by ourselves: that we entertained a sincere good will towards the Empire and desired the supremacy of the Sultan to be maintained; but conditionally upon effective measures for the security and prosperity of the populations, for which the means ought to be efficacious, and the best means would be what we call administrative not political autonomy. With this view the actual tie (lien) ought to be light.

He said that these ideas would give perfect satisfaction to the Porte. The exclusion of foreign influence seemed to be the notion on which he had been instructed to work. He said that Austria had unquestionably entertained the idea of going forward to Salonica.

I said as to the Parlt. that it ought not to interfere with international arrangements, & that the system of representation ought to be carefully adjusted.[1]

To LORD HARTINGTON, Indian Secretary, 14 May 1880.   Chatsworth MSS 340. 962.

I think your letter[2] states the case extremely well and I follow your argument generally. Even however if it be adopted in full I suppose it is a question whether we ought to remit the Loan of two millions. There is an objection to doing it this year, that it would derange our finances, & for a small [?] object.

---

[1] Signed and dated 14 May 1880, Add MS 56445, f. 95; forwarded to Granville; *Autobiographica*, iv. 55.   [2] See 12 May 80n.

15. Sat. [*Windsor Castle*]

Wrote to Sir G. Balfour—Prince of Wales—Miss Marsh—Ld Granville—Scotts—
Mr West—Mr Maurice Brooks. Read Lubbock's Essays[1]—Macdonell on French
Empire.[2] To Windsor at five. Dined with H.M: who, apparently much at her
ease conversed for more than an hour in the Corridor. Saw Ld Wolverton—Mr
Godley—Ld Granville—Mrs Tyler—E. Macgregor—Mr Welby—Mr Goschen—
Prince L. of Hesse—Princess Beatrice—Pss [blank] of Hesse.

16. Whits.

Palace Chapel at 10 & 12 with H.C.—St George's aftn. Walk with the Dean: &
divers long conversations. Young Ld R. Cecil dined: took the opportunity for
inquiries & messages.[3] Read Fairbairn on Religion[4]—St Hilaire on Buddhism.[5]

17. M. [*London*]

Further conversation with the Dean. Off at 10½ to London. Cabinet 2½-5½. Saw
M. Leon Say—Mr Goschen—Mr Childers—Ld R. Grosvenor—Mr Godley—
Wrote to The Queen—Armenian Patriarch (Comb)—Mr Ashley. Worked on
the [Queen's] Speech. Twelve to dinner. There can be no doubt that Cardwell
has undergone a severe shock & has but partially recovered. Read Macdonell
on the Empire in France—Sketch of Ld Beaconsfield by Brandis [*sic*].[6]

Cabinet. May 17. 80. 2.30 PM.[7]
Queen's Speech in draft—read—considered Para by Para—corrected—approved.
Proposed commun[icatio]n with Russia on Central Asia considered: without final result.[8]

18. Tu.

Wrote to Sir H. Ponsonby—Ld Spencer—Mr Chadwick—The Queen: &
minutes. Saw Mr Albert Grey—Do *cum* Mr Hugh Mason[9]—Sir W. Harcourt—
Mr Godley—Mr West—Ld R. Grosvenor—Mr Welby (2)—Ld F. Cavendish—Sir
T. May—Ld Granville. Dined at Ld Aberdeen's. Saw E. Murphy [R]. Read Macdonell—Brandis on Beaconsfield.

19. Wed.

Wrote to Ld Selborne—Mrs Bernal Osborne—Mr Furness[10]—Mr Childers—Ld
Hartington—Mr Thorold Rogers—and minutes. Read Brandis—Macdonell on

---

[1] J. Lubbock, *Addresses, political and educational* (1879).
[2] J. Macdonell, *France since the First Empire* (1879).
[3] i.e. to Lord Salisbury; Lord Robert Gascoyne-*Cecil, 1864-1958, Salisbury's 3rd son; conservative free trader and internationalist.
[4] See 12 Feb. 80.   [5] See 28 Mar. 80.
[6] G. M. C. Brandes, *Beaconsfield. A study*, tr. Mrs G. Sturge (1880); first published in German in
1879. See 29 May 80.   [7] Add MS 44642, f. 17.
[8] Diarist's holograph note, f. 18, reads: 'I meant to have said a word to *you* [Granville] about
Merv before it came on here.' 'Can you give me a hint in what number [?] G[ranville].'
[9] Grey and Mason moved the Address on the Queen's speech.
[10] Horace Howard Furness, American author; see Add MS 44464, f. 135.

the French Empire. Saw Mr Godley—Mr A. Grey—Ld Spencer—Mr West—Mr Dalton—Ld Enfield—Musurus Pacha—The Speaker. $11\frac{3}{4}$-$3\frac{1}{2}$. To Windsor for Speech Council. Audience: H.M. gracious & quite unconstrained. Speech dinner, about forty: and evening party. Afterwards till half past twelve. Tired enough.

20. Th.

Wrote to Mr Russell—Earl Granville—The Queen. Nine to breakfast. Read Macdonell. Saw Archim. Myriantheus—Ld Enfield—Mr Godley—Ld Granville—Ld R. Grosvenor. Conclave on Savings Banks—Lord F.C.—Mr Repington—Mr Welby. Conclave on P.O. Money Orders Bill.

At 4.15 I went down to the House with Herbert. There was a great & fervent crowd in Palace Yard: & much feeling in the House. It almost overpowered me as I thought by what deep & hidden agencies I have been brought back into the midst of the vortex of political action and contention. It has not been in my power during these last six months to make notes as I could have wished of my own thoughts & observations from time to time: of the new access of strength which in some important respects has been administered to me in my old age: and of the remarkable manner in which Holy Scripture has been inwardly applied to me for admonition & for comfort. Looking calmly over this course of experience I do believe that the Almighty has employed me for His purposes in a manner larger or more special than before, and has strengthened me & led me on accordingly, though I must not forget the admirable saying of Hooker that evil ministers of good things are like torches, a light to others, waste & destruction to themselves.[1] In all things, at all times, by all instruments & persons, may His will be done. H. of C. $4\frac{1}{2}$-$8\frac{1}{2}$ and $9\frac{1}{2}$-$11\frac{1}{2}$. Spoke 1 hour on the Address.[2]

21. Fr.

Wrote to Mr Chamberlain—Marq. of Bath—Sir C. Dilke—The Queen—& minutes. H. of C. 4 P.M.-$8\frac{1}{2}$ P.M. Spoke on Bradlaugh & on report of Address.[3] Went late to the interesting dinner at Ld E. Clinton's. Saw M. Gennadios—Ld Granville—Aristarchi Bey—Do *cum* M. Bylandt—Mr Godley—Ld Acton—Duchess of Connaught: who is really above the common order[4]—Ld F. Cavendish—Lady E. Clinton—Ld E. Clinton—Ld R. Grosvenor—Mr Knowles. Conclave at the Speaker's room on the Bradlaugh case at 3 P.M.[5] Lady Granville's in evg.

Aristarchi Bey[6] called on me today introduced by M. Bylandt.
He said some notable things.
His account of the Sultan agreed in all points with that of Sir H. Layard. His account of

---

[1] Version of this para. in Morley, iii. 1.　　　　　　　　　　　　[2] *H* 252. 132.
[3] The 'conclave' hastily decided to meet opposition to Bradlaugh's taking the oath (having been prevented from affirming, see 2 May 80) by a second select cttee.; Wolff's motion raised the issue; Gladstone also clashed with Balfour on Turkey; *H* 252. 191, 242.
[4] Princess Louise Margaret of Prussia, m. 1879 Prince Arthur, duke of Connaught; she d. 1917.
[5] Extracts from Brand's diary in Add MS 56453, f. 40.
[6] See 29 Mar. 64 (Turkish attaché in Paris).

the Ministers was still worse. He hoped the advent of the new Government might avail to check and mitigate the descent of Turkey in the scale—arrested it could not be—it was the march of history & doom. He did not found any serious hopes upon a Parliament. The crying wants of Justice, Education, Finance, could not be supplied by the Government. He saw nothing for it but an International Commission, assuming the virtual direction of the Empire in these vital matters.

He admitted that the Treaty of Berlin did not go beyond Europe and Armenia: but it would be very much to deal satisfactorily with Europe. (He is a Greek.)

He had seen M. Freycinet and found him most cordial towards England.

He (A.B.) thought the renewal of the *entente cordiale* would most effectively promote the settlement of the Turkish question. Germany would favour its plans, at least sentimentally, Russia would not oppose, and the interest of Austria would be to have tranquillity & content upon her borders.

As long as Fuad & Ali were alive he had hopes from them for Turkey—but they had no successors.[1]

To J. CHAMBERLAIN, president of the board of trade,   Add MS 44544, f. 10.
21 May 1880.

Before answering the inclosed letter,[2] I think it well to refer it to you.

I am not favourable to organic changes in the relative positions of Cabinet offices, & other high administrative posts, but it appears to me that this is a case for vindicating on behalf of the Board of Trade its fair prerogative.

If you were to look back to the records of your department 35 & 40 years ago, you would find how much of the public trade business was transacted in it.

Revenue was then largely involved; & hence, I imagine, it came about that this business was taken over in a great degree by the Treasury. I myself have drawn up New Tariffs in both; at the Board of Trade in 1842 & 1844-5; & at the Treasury in 1853[3] & 1860.

Why & how the old Board of Trade functions also passed in part to the Foreign Office I do not so well know.

But at any rate it seems to me that this somewhat interesting question of the Sugar Bounties affords a good opportunity for our considering whether the Board of Trade might not in this case again play its old part, acting as responsible adviser to the Foreign Office & consulting the Treasury before recommending any thing which touched revenue. But the fiscal question is secondary & the trade question primary.

Of course we should have to consult Lord Granville.

22. Sat.

Wrote to Ld Granville—Sir H. Ponsonby—Mr Stansfeld—The Queen—Ld Hartington—Mr Bayley Potter—Mr Forster—and minutes. Dined at the Duke of Argyll's: interesting conversation. Saw Mr Godley—Ld R. Grosvenor—Mr Chamberlain—Mr Gallimore. Cabinet 2½-5½. Read Macdonell—Brandis on Lord B.

[1] Initialled and dated 21 May 1880, Add MS 56445, f. 99.
[2] Not found; on the sugar bounty; Chamberlain suggested a meeting; Add MS 44125, f. 26.
[3] Hamilton's copy reads '1833', but Gladstone clearly intended '1853'.

Cabinet. May 22. 2½ PM.[1]
Parl. Paper for the week considered.
Conversation on Land Question & Cairns Bills.[2]
Bradlaugh Committee—approved.[3]
a) Retention of Sir Bartle Frere b) Disarmament of Basutos, a measure of the Cape Govt.
    a) Nature of answer to be given considered.
    b) answer considered.
Constitution of Committees of 15. We shall claim 8, leaving 1 for Home Rulers, 6 for Conservatives.
The Frere Interregnum.
Navy flogging. Ask Taylor to put off motion. If not, put it in the rear of Army.

To M. T. BASS, M.P., 22 May 1880.   Add MS 44544, f. 11.

I am desirous to know whether there is any likelihood of your being in town next week.

If there is, I should much like to see you; & the question, on which I wish to have the advantage of speaking to you, includes the old & sore subject of the Licenses. I am sincerely desirous to consider whether by any & what means they may be got rid of & this in a confidential conversation with yourself.[4]

It is rather bold, bearing in mind that my Exchequer is not in the flourishing condition of Exchequers at Burton upon Trent.

So, if you can come, I hope to see you: but not to the prejudice of your health, for you may remember that when you were good enough to invite me to Rangemore, I appointed myself as your Physician Extraordinary & scolded you for being without a great coat in an open carriage on a raw October afternoon.

To W. E. FORSTER, Irish secretary, 22 May 1880.   Add MS 44544, f. 11.

Dr Washburn's letter is most interesting.[5] But I agree with Granville that the time for the Union is not come, & I agree in the following words which he uses: 'I hope Forster will ask his correspondent to use his influence to keep the Bulgarians & Roumelians quiet.' If any facts of undue obstructive interference by the Turks can be shewn, those I suppose might be made the subject of just remonstrance by us.

Otherwise I think their present duty is the establishment of good & equal laws for all classes of their populations. This will be the best preparation for the future.

23. *Trin S.*

Chapel Royal mg: and H.C. Guards Chapel 3.30. (Dr Liddon). Read Caird's Sermons[6]—Ewald's Geschichte[7]—Sibthorp's Office of H.C.[8] Wrote to Mr Bright —and minutes. Saw Mr Hamilton. Dined at Mrs Heywoods.

---

[1] Add MS 44642, f. 20; added at top of sheet in pencil: 'Ouvry, Otway, Entracts, Cabinet Sat.'.
[2] See 29 May 80.
[3] See 24 May 80, and Arnstein, 52n.
[4] See 26 May 80; letter agreeing to come at Add MS 44464, f. 155.
[5] Letter to Forster from George Washburn, 1833-1915, of Robert College, Constantinople, proposing union between Bulgaria and E. Roumelia; Add MS 44158, f. 8 and Ramm II, i. 128.
[6] J. Caird, *Sermons* (1858).
[7] G. H. A. von Ewald, *Geschichte des Volkes Israel bis Christus*, 3v. (1843-52).
[8] See 20 Apr. 80.

24. M.

Wrote to Ld Kimberley—Rev. Mr Fowler—The Speaker—Ld Granville—The
Queen—Sir R. Phillimore. H. of C. $4\frac{1}{2}$-$8\frac{1}{4}$ and $8\frac{3}{4}$-$1\frac{1}{2}$. Bradlaugh debate. My share
of business miscellaneous.[1] Read Brandis on Lord B. Shopping. Saw Liverpool
Deputation[2]—Mr Ouvry—Mr Godley—Ld R. Grosvenor—Mr Welby—M. Brati-
ano—Ld F. Cavendish.

To H. B. W. BRAND, the Speaker, 24 May 1880.   Brand MSS.

I confess that I had no idea before the discussion on Friday to what an extent there
would be a disposition in the House to make capital out of Bradlaugh's loathsome &
revolting opinions by a deviation from judicial impartiality.

Our reference to the Committee was not well drawn and to amend it is awkward: still I
assume that we shall carry the Committee.

It seems to me that the matter principally hangs on the preliminary question whether
the House shall interfere, in the matter of the oath, with the course of law.

Can the following propositions be made good:

a. The analogy with courts of justice fails in essential particulars e.g.

There is no party in the case here, who holds a position like that of adverse counsel
who challenges the oath of a witness—and we have no powers of investigation to enable
us clearly to establish the case but are dependent upon fragmentary information which
we cannot sift and verify.

b. Bradlaugh is not yet a member *of our assembly*. It is Statute law which brings him there.
When he is there, he is under our jurisdiction like others. But the House never has done
any act in regard to one not yet qualified to sit among us, except helping him to sit.

c. The Statute leaves it to the servant of the House to administer the oath, and this servant is necessarily under the authority of the House and of nobody else. It may therefore
be difficult to deny very broadly the competence of the House.

d. But the *capacity* of the House to make an inquisition may be questioned, and its *practice* of abstention is clear.

e. I hope therefore that when the Committee sits the effect of its proceedings may be to
dispose it to keep on the line of its old practice. It will not be possible, I think, to deny
that other cases of inquisition may arise, if we open this one.

f. If the Inquisition is one fit to be made I do not yet see how to defend Mr Bradlaugh
whom we do not permit to affirm, and who now proposes to take the Oath in the sense
and with the effect of an affirmation. I do not see, therefore, how to avoid a most inconvenient judgment, if once we admit that we are judges at all and will undertake the office
of determining whether or not a member desirous to comply with the forms is or is not
complying with the substance.

To LORD KIMBERLEY, colonial secretary, 24 May 1880.   Add MS 44544, f. 11.

1. Over and above the question of confederation, have we not, unless my memory
deceives me, understood that Sir B. Frere has in hand the question of Colonial Contribution to War Expenses, & can do more, in regard to present & future charges, for us, than
any other man? In fact that the plea for keeping him is double?

2. Would it be well also to say that in regard to any questions of policy, on which Sir
B. Frere's known opinions might suggest to him a course at variance with our views, pre-
cautions have been taken to obviate any such contingency.

[1] Second select cttee. on Bradlaugh; *H* 252. 407; Arnstein, 51.
[2] No report found.

25. Tu.

Wrote to Ld Salisbury—Sir W. Harcourt (2)—Mr Dillwyn—Bp of St Albans—The Queen—and minutes. H. of C. 4½-8 and 10¾-12½. Spoke on S. Africa and Sir Bartle Frere.[1] Dined at Spencer House. Read Brandis. Saw Herbert G.—Ld R. Grosvenor—Mr Godley—Ld Wolverton—Ld Kimberley. Conclave on Savings Banks.

26. Wed.

Wrote to The Queen—Count Menabrea—Sir P. Braila—Prince of Wales—Sir C. Ducane—and minutes. The Derby afternoon was chiefly spent in reducing drawers of papers &c. to order.[2] Saw Freshfields—Mr. Godley—Mr Bass & Mr [M.]A. Bass—M. Contostaulos[3]—Ld F. Cavendish & Mr Welby—Sir G. Colley—Mr Chitty—Mr Childers—M. Leon Say. Dined at Ld Chancellor's. Read Brandis.

27. Th.

Ten to breakfast. Wrote to Sir W. Harcourt—Lord Cowper—Mr Ouvry—Abp of Cyprus[4]—Mrs Th.—The Queen. H. of C. 4½-9¼ and 10-12¾. Spoke on Privy Seal.[5] Read Brandis—Fitzgerald on Croker.[6] Saw Ld Wolverton—Ld R. Grosvenor—Mr Godley—Mr Bright—Ld Granville—Count Menabrea—Lord Bath—Dr Eckenbrecher—Mr Vivian—Herbert G.—Sir G. Campbell—Mr Forster—Sir C. Dilke.

To C. J. HERRIES, chairman of the board of inland revenue,   Add MS 44544, f. 13.
27 May 1880.

Having received several fragmentary papers on the subject of the Malt drawback I am rather uncertain as to the upshot, but I am afraid I am to gather from your memorandum of yesterday[7] that your estimate of the actual deficit for the year is raised, after recent enquiries, by 286 m[ille]? It is a heavy blow if so.

28. Fr.

Wrote to Ld Granville—Sir C. Dilke—Mr Murray—Mr Herries (2)—The Queen 1.2. & minutes. H. of C. 4¼-8¼ and 8¾-12½. Nasty work of Northcote's on the Bradlaugh Committee.[8] Read Brandis. Saw Mr Godley—Lord R. Grosvenor—Ld F. Cavendish—Mr Welby—Mr Childers. Received late at night the sad news of W. Dumaresq's death.[9] May the Divine mercies to his young widow be in ample proportion to the unusual weight of sad vicissitudes which she has been called to bear.

[1] Defusing immediate pressure for Frere's recall; H 252. 462.
[2] Cf. 1 June 70, 24 May 71.
[3] Alexander Contoslaulos, Greek ambassador.
[4] Sofronius, abp. of Cyprus.
[5] H 252. 561.
[6] P. H. Fitzgerald, Croker's Boswell and Boswell Studies in the 'Life of Johnson' (1880).
[7] Not found.
[8] Northcote gave the names of tories recommended privately but not placed on the cttee.; Gladstone also spoke in deb. raised by Irish M.P.s on use of secret service monies in Ireland; H 252. 655, 674. See 1 June 80.
[9] His nephew by marriage; see 20 May 50n.

29. Sat.

Wrote to Mr Pease MP–The Queen 1.2.–... MP.–Mr W. Williams MP.–Mr Fowler MP.–Ld Granville–Ld Leicester–and minutes. Cabinet $2\frac{1}{2}$-$5\frac{1}{2}$. Tea at Lady Derby's. I gave two large dinners, F.C. kindly presiding at the C. of E[x-chequer's] Table. The Prince of Wales was very kind, & very conversible. Finished Brandis [*sic*]. His description of Beaconsfield's mind as metallic & mine as fluid, has merit.[1]

Cabinet. Sat. May 29. 1880.[2]

1. Water Bills Agreements. Committee on, to be moved by Sir W. Harcourt–to inquire whether desirable for the Metropolis to acquire.
2. Bradlaugh Committee. Adhere to the printed list.
3. Question as to the composition of Committees generally. Determined to raise it on the appointment of the Grain Cargoes Committee.
4. What line shall the members of the Govt. take in the Committee? They will consult together. Childers, Bright: against the jurisdiction.[3]
5. Determined to oppose Committee on the Education Bill.
6. Harcourt raised the recall of Frere. G. regretted the advice we had given not to recall: but it was thought now impossible. So others. Chamberlain agreed. Hoped an excuse wd soon be given.[4]
7. Chamberlain raised the question whether the Afghanistan Dispatch could be published. (Gran.) proposed an omission about Candahar. On the whole impossible: but the fact of a Dispatch to be announced.[5]
8. Cairns Bills to be let pass without opposition through the H. of Lords.[6]

That in the choice of members to serve on Select Committees regard should be had among other points to the numbers by which the various forms of political opinion are represented in the House and in ordinary cases the composition of the Committees should correspond as far as may be in this respect with the composition of the House.[7]

---

[1] The passage in Brandes (see 17 May 80) at p. 305 reads: 'Gladstone is a character, a man capable of development and always developing, and of extraordinary gifts, especially of great practical understanding ... but he is uninteresting and wanting in originality. The character of Lord Beaconsfield, on the contrary, is absolutely original; there is something daemonic in him. His mind is of the metallic order, while Gladstone's is of the fluid sort. Disraeli became what he is all at once, and could scarcely change....'

[2] Add MS 44642, f. 21. Undated note by Hartington, perhaps referring to an earlier circulation of the Afghan dispatch, reads: 'The Cabinet all saw it, & nobody made any observation except Northbrook. I made a few not very important, alterations in consequence. The Queen gave a general approval.' Undated note by Granville reads: 'Farrer says that Chamberlain is the best & quickest chief he has had since Milner Gibson.'

[3] This sentence may have been intended to refer to point 6.

[4] This and previous sentence written under point 4, but transferred to here by an arrow.

[5] Hartington's dispatch of 21 May 1880 which recognized the dangers of a 'too hasty withdrawal', adumbrated the arguments for a 'subdivision of the Afghan kingdom' but preferred the 'reconstruction of ... Afghanistan as a whole', but avoided defining 'a fixed policy which would admit of no modification'. The dispatch presumably came before the Cabinet for notice, as there is no indication that its dispatch had been delayed after 21 May. Gladstone's letters to the Queen (CAB 41/14/7) seem to confirm that the dispatch was not discussed prior to its sending.

[6] Tory land bills announced before the dissolution; see H. Perkin, *The structured crowd* (1981), 120.

[7] Undated holograph at Add MS 44642, f. 23.

30. 1 S. Trin.

Chapel Royal at noon, & St Margaret's 6½ PM. Saw Sydney. Visited our niece Edith [Dumaresq] & saw her dead husband, now at peace. She is wonderfully sustained. Read Rigg's Addresses &c.[1]—Miller on Church & State[2]—Six Sermons & Tracts by G. Whitfield.[3]

The guidance appointed for the Church is Providential, general, and indeterminate; not mechanical, or logical, or statutory.

The Church is a society provided with the best human means of permanence in an authoritative constitution. But the best human means are fallible. Nevertheless there are certain limitations upon fallibility observable in the government of the world, as for example in this that there has been everywhere in the common judgment a recognition in some degree of a natural or moral law: there has been what may be termed a margin of error. But error is kept within this margin by means of latent adaptations which we can neither reduce to rule nor be sure to observe. It seems to be in the same manner, by a method of latent adaptations, that the Church at large has been marvellously preserved, amidst so many divisions and so much of all kinds of sin in the central unity and verity of the Faith.[4]

31. M.

Wrote to Dr Prothero Smith—Mr Freeman—Mr Childers—Mr Bryce—Mr Samuelson—Ld Granville—Ld Northbrook—Duke of Connaught—The Queen and minutes. Attended the Levee 2-3. Saw Ld Granville—Mr Godley—French Ambr—Count Karolyi—Dean of St Paul's—Ld F. Cavendish—Ld R. Grosvenor—Mr Earp—Mr Cooper—Sir C. Dilke. Finished Macdonell. H. of Commons 4¼-8¼ and 9¼-12½. Northcote shuffled, without profit.[5]

To J. BRYCE, M.P., 31 May 1880.   Bryce MSS 10, f. 28.

I am very glad to know Mr Evans's view; but his letter does not cause me any qualms of conscience.[6]

To rake up as I have done repeatedly all the past misdeeds of an allied Power is a course that could only be warranted in me, even when acting in a purely personal capacity, by grave and well founded suspicions that that Power was about to break in upon the legally established rights & prospects of the subject races in Turkey.

I had no option in honour & propriety but to accept Karolyi's explicit declaration on that subject.

When I had accepted it, I should have deviated from all my ideas of right action had I not—at the least—'banished' from my mind what I certainly cannot in any other sense withdraw.

What Austria's *conduct* in Bosnia & Herzegovina may be I have had no *adequate* opportunities of knowing: but her position there was conferred by the united authority of Europe, & no one had, under the circumstances, anything better to suggest.

[1] J. H. Rigg, *Discourses and addresses on leading truths of Religion and Philosophy* (1880).
[2] E. Miller, *Church in relation to the State* (1880).
[3] G. Whitefield, *Six sermons* (1750).
[4] Holograph dated 30 May 1880, Add MS 44764, f. 91.
[5] On late govt.'s estimates; *H* 252. 808.
[6] Arthur Evans, letter (untraced) sent by Bryce; see Bryce MSS 11, f. 32.

To H. C. E. CHILDERS, war secretary, 31 May 1880.   Add MS 44544, f. 14.

With reference to the subject I named to you the other day, & to other matters, I am desirous now to get a fair survey of the financial position for the year, and with this view I write to ask whether you think it will be in your power to make any, and if any what amount of favourable impression upon the estimates for your Department as handed over to you by our predecessors in office.[1]

Tues. June One 1880.

Wrote to Ld Chancellor—Ld Hartington—Rev. Mr Paget—Sir H. Ponsonby—Sir C. Dilke—Principal Tulloch—The Queen—The Speaker—and minutes. H. of C. $4\frac{1}{4}$–$12\frac{1}{2}$ except two half hours at house. $12\frac{3}{4}$–3. To the Bank for the Biddings. Saw Govr of the Bank—Ld R. Grosvenor—Mr Welby—Ld F. Cavendish—Mr Godley—Count Corti—D. of Argyll—Lady Ripon. The House was persuaded to throw out the foolish Bill on the *congé d'élire*: more easily than I had expected.[2]

To H. B. W. BRAND, the Speaker, 1 June 1880.   Brand MSS.

Although it is only an opinion & of no consequence I wish to qualify a statement in a former letter[3] to you on the Bradlaugh case. When I wrote that letter I had not consulted the Parl. Oaths Act. On consulting it I found that the law imposed upon the person elected the duty of taking the Oath, that it appointed no Administrator, and that its statutory power was confined to making Regulations which seem to have been meant to be of a subsidiary character and not to grant any jurisdiction over the member in regard to his conduct as taker of the oath. I own therefore that without presuming to deny I am very much disposed to doubt, and wholly unprepared to affirm the jurisdiction which so many take for granted as belonging to the House.

To the Rev. F. E. PAGET, 1 June 1880.   Add MS 44544, f. 15.

I have communicated with the Lord Chancellor on the subject of your letter.[4] In his view, which I am not able to dispute, it would be inconsistent with the principle of the Bill to limit the liberty of the Nonconformist to ground distinct from the churchyard. Of course they might limit themselves to it of their own free will.

My impression is that burials with non-conformist services in Churchyards will not be numerous. Yet I do not deny that there are some inequalities, adverse to the Church, in the settlement proposed. It was so in the Church Rate settlement. These inequalities are in the nature of set offs against the great real or supposed inequality the other way in the national endowments & position of the Church.

You will have seen, if you read *The Times* of yesterday, that plans are in preparation for striking out the compensatory parts of the Bill, & for widening in favour of agnostics & others the clauses which grant the right.

I feel much the kindness of your reference to our early days at Christ Church: & of the undeserved credit which you give me. The time of life which we have reached makes me

---

[1] Childers replied (4 June, Add MS 44129, f. 41): 'I cannot hold out to you any hope of a substantial saving.'

[2] Monk's bill to abolish the *congé d'élire* election of bps; *H* 252. 944.

[3] See 24 May 80. Brand replied (3 June 1880, Add MS 44194, f. 202) that it was at the discretion of the House either to receive or not to receive Bradlaugh without infringing the Oaths Act.

[4] Add MS 44464, f. 196, on the Burials Bill.

long greatly for such quiet as we then enjoyed. Certainly, it has not been a disposition to meddle in questions of Church & Dissent that has brought me back to office.

Are you ever in London on a Thursday morning? If you are pray announce yourself on some of these occasions to breakfast here at 10 o'clock. Your kindly complying would give particular pleasure to my wife & me.

To Sir H. F. PONSONBY, the Queen's secretary, 1 June 1880.   Add MS 44544, f. 15.

1. The case of the committees stands thus. In the late Parliament, out of a Committee of 15, the rule was that the Government had 8, the opposition including the Home Rulers, who together were 6/13 of the House, had 7.

We now mean to ask for 8, & leave 7 to the opposition & the Home Rulers, they together being 6/13 of the House. The essential point is that they shall be satisfied with six, as we were in the late Parliament.

2. The subject of the Secret Service was only mentioned by me as matter of fact.[1] One of its incidents is, its being so secret that I have grown old without ever having an opportunity of forming a practical judgment upon it. I do not doubt however that something of the kind is necessary.

2. W.

Wrote to Ld Chamberlain—Sir C. Dilke—Mr D. Grant—and minutes. 3½-5. Saw Law Officers with Mr Dodson: & received a large Deputation on the Employers Liability Bill.[2] 6½-7½. To meeting at the Opera House in honour of Herbert. Spoke ½ hour.[3] Heard him close: carefully & well. Dined at Lady Stanley's. Saw Woods & another [R]. Saw Mr Somers MP—Mr Russell MP—Mr Cheetham MP—Ld R. Grosvenor—Mr Herries *cum* Mr Young—Ld Hartington *cum* Ld Northbrook—H. Hunt—Mr Knowles—Mr Godley. Read Kenealy, New Pantomime.[4]

3. Th.

Wrote to Duke of Argyll—Sir F.H. Doyle—The Queen—Patriarch of Alexandria *per* Archim. Myriantheus—and minutes. H. of C. 4¼-8½ and 9½-1¼. A party row.[5] 3-4. Workmen's Depn.[6] Thirteen to breakfast. Saw Sir W. Gregory—Rev. Mr Rawlinson—Mr Oakley—Mr Welby *cum* Ld F.C.—Ld R. Grosvenor—Mr [J.] Ramsay *cum* Dr Cameron[7]—Mr Fowler MP. Conclave on Employers Bill.

4. Fr.

Wrote to Mr Howard MP—Sir T. Chambers MP—The Queen—Mr Fowler MP—Sir C. Dilke—Bp of Manchester—Lady Rosebery and minutes. Dined at Sir C. Forsters and saw Miss Lonsdale.[8] Saw Mr Godley—Herbert G—Lord R. Grosvenor—Ld F. Cavendish *cum* Mr Welby—Mr Hayward *cum* Mr Blowitz[9]—

---

[1] See 28 June 80n.   [2] *D.N.*, 3 June 1880, 6e.
[3] Ibid., 2d.   [4] E. V. H. Kenealy, *Goethe; a New Pantomime. Poems* (1850).
[5] Employers' liability; *H* 252. 1085.   [6] No report found.
[7] Charles Cameron, 1841-1924, physician and liberal M.P. Glasgow 1874-95; see 7 June 80n.
[8] The author; see 19 Feb. 80.
[9] Henri Georges S. A. Opper de Blowitz, 1832-1903; foreign correspondent of *The Times*; business untraced.

Mr Wade *cum* Mr Seebohm. H. of C. 4¼-8 and 10½-3. No less than three touch & go affairs: opium especially.[1] Sir C. Ducane *cum* Mr Seldon[2]—Lady Foster (respecting D.D. & H.J.G.).[3]

To W. FOWLER, M.P., 4 June 1880.   Add MS 44544, f. 17.

I see you have given notice, before the Second Reading, of a motion to refer the Savings Banks Bill after the Second Reading to a Select Committee. I therefore ought to say to you, after our conversation of yesterday, that I am aware of no case in which a Bill principally financial has been so referred, & that from my point of view the motion is equivalent to one for the rejection of the Bill.[4]

I need hardly say that I am at least equally opposed to your new notice: indeed I must own I have read it with a little surprise after the conversation we had had.

5. Sat.

Wrote to Bp of Hereford—Ld Hartington—The Queen—Hon. L. Stanley MP. (cancelled)[5]—and minutes. Conclave on Finance at 2.[6] Cabinet 2½-5¾. Dined at M. Leon Say's. Read Nouvelle Revue. Saw Mr Godley—Ld Granville—The Lord Mayor—Ld F. Cavendish—Mr Welby—Ld R.G. *cum* Ld Wolverton—The French Ambassador.

Cabinet. June 10 [sc. 5] *1880. 2.30 p.m*[7]
1. Finance. To add 1d to Income Tax. Repeal the Malt tax. Impose Beer Tax. Hold fund for reducing Wine Duty & promoting Foreign Treaties. License Tax if necessary.
2. Irish Land Bill. To appoint Tues. fortnight morning sitting for the Bill. That on or before that time we will declare our intent.
3. Bartle Frere Memorial. W.E.G. to prepare an answer & submit to two or three colleagues.[8]
4. Volunteer Review in Hyde Park. Not to be there: without inclosures.

6. 2 S. Trin.

Chapel Royal mg (with H.C.) and aft. The King of the Hellenes called and sat an hour. Some interesting conversation. Dined at Marlborough House. All very kind: the Princess almost affectionate: but I love not this kind of Sunday evening. Saw divers [R]. Read Fowler's Tracts[9]—Scotch Sermons[10]—Mason on Vestiges of Creation &c.[11]

[1] Ordnance survey, Irish poor law, and J. W. Pease's observations on opium trade; *H* 252. 1227.
[2] Samuel Seldon, principal of statistical dept., customs house.
[3] Perhaps a proposed engagement with a relative of Lady Foster (*née* Day); H. J. Gladstone did not marry until 1901.
[4] Fowler instead moved an amndt. deploring extension of limits on deposits; *H* 253. 333.
[5] On a canonry; Add MS 44544, f. 17.
[6] Granville, Childers and Dodson summoned; Add MS 44642, f. 29.
[7] Add MS 44642, f. 30; dated '10', but clearly the cabinet of 5 June (see letter to the Queen this day, CAB 41/14/12); there was no cabinet on 10 June.
[8] Memorial for Frere's recall signed by 91 liberal MPs; Add MS 44624, f. 105.
[9] Perhaps the various pamphlets on land by W. Fowler, M.P.
[10] *Scotch sermons* (1880).
[11] T. M. Mason, *Creation by the immanent agency of God* (1845); a refutation of Chambers' *Vestiges*.

7. M.

Wrote to Mr Dillwyn—Sir C. Ducane—Mr Knollys—Mr Forster—Mr Bass—The Queen: & minutes. H. of C. 4¼-8 and 9¼-12¾.[1] Read Contemp. Rev. on [blank.] Conclave on Malt 10½-11½. Saw the French Ambassador—Ld F.C.—Ld R.G.—Mr Godley—Att. Gen.—Mr Childers—Sir C. Dilke—and others.

To W. E. FORSTER, Irish secretary, 7 June 1880.   Add MS 44544, f. 17.

I am afraid there are some difficulties in your way but we will do what we can.[2]

1. Savings Banks have been announced & therefore must come on; but I will try to have a short statement & short debate.

2. The House will be rather startled if we ask for Fridays *and* Tuesdays, to begin on Friday next. Possibly it can be justified by stating it to be urgent that the Irish question so seriously raised on Friday evening should be rapidly disposed of? I see no other way.

3. I do not quite see your objection to saying that the Irish Franchise Bill must for the moment be displaced to let the others go on. So much for procedure.

4. *On the main question.* Reflecting on the discussion of Saturday, I am inclined to think that if we propose a Bill such as you contemplate there would be advantage in founding it on Section 18 of the Land Act, & making it an extension of the *latter part* of that section such as to include the temporary emergency.

8. Tu.

Wrote to The Queen 1.2.—Sir C. Du Cane 1.2.—Lord Hartington—and minutes. 10½-1½. Conclave on Licence Duties & Malt Tax. Read Hist. of Cyprus[3]—Vambery in 19th Century—a prig.[4] 12 to dinner. Evening party afterwards. Saw Mr Godley—Lord RG—Lord F.C.—Mr Welby—Mr Knowles—& others.

9. Wed.

Wrote to Mr Knollys—Sir C. Ducane (2)—Mr West—Ld Hartington—Ld Granville—Sir W. Harcourt. Went to see Sarah Bernhardt in Phèdre at the Gaiety: ⅔ full. My opinion remains as it was.[5] Saw Mr West—Mr T. Russell—Mr Godley—Ld RG—Ld FC—Mr Primrose—Mr Welby. Worked on my papers about Malt and Wine. Read 19th Cent.

To LORD HARTINGTON, Indian secretary, 9 June 1880.   Chatsworth MSS 340. 969.

In thinking over the statement I have to make tomorrow, India naturally crosses my mind—and these are the ideas which seem to me just, for the actual situation:

1. If we were *now* in a condition to determine finally what courses England ought to take with respect to the cost of the Afghan War, there would be an immense advantage in getting rid of the question at the present time.

2. If at any given date during the Session we could be *sure* of being in such a condition, it would have been worth while to postpone our financial operations accordingly.

[1] Cameron's motion for select cttee. on navy stores; navy estimates; *H* 252. 1353.
[2] Forster to Gladstone, 6 June 1880, Add MS 44157, f. 132, asking for time-tabling changes.
[3] Perhaps [F. T. Gammon], *Cyprus: its history and prospects* (1878).
[4] A. Vambéry, 'England and Russia in Asia', *Nineteenth Century*, vii. 917 (June 1880).
[5] See 23 June 79.

3. But neither of these I think is the case and it is even *likely* that we cannot judge of our position and duty definitively, until you have got the troops out of Afghanistan.

4. In this state of circumstances, while it is clear that we cannot come to any new negative conclusion, we should by making any proposal to aid India before we have full knowledge only be opening a door without closing it, and we could assign no well-defined ground for our proceeding.

5. At the same time I think that viewing the actual state of Indian balances there is enough of uncertainty hanging over the question of your prospective command of cash to constitute a reason against our going on without any margin whatever, and therefore in favour of our demand for a moderate surplus, without prejudging the matter.[1]

I hope you may approve these views.

[P.S.] Mr Welby, our righthand man, is disposed to think well of the suggestion which I made to you and Northbrook.

10. Th.

Wrote to The Queen—Lord Granville—Mr West—Sir W. Harcourt—Sir C. Ducane—and minutes. Saw Mr West—Mr Godley—Mr Primrose—Ld R.G.—Ld F.C.—Mr Myers. Worked on Malt Wine &c. H of C. $4\frac{1}{4}$-$8\frac{1}{2}$ and 9-$1\frac{1}{4}$. Spoke 2 h. in Financial Statement.[2] The reception excellent. Read 19th Cent on 'Collapse'.

To W. E. FORSTER, Irish secretary, 10 June 1880.   Add MS 44544, f. 19.

The inclosed letter[3] states strongly the view of the Duke of Argyll on the land question in Ireland, which is *based* upon the two propositions I have scored on the side.

There is no doubt of the stringency of my general pledges in 1870.

Can you inform us before Saturday by figures not only of the graduated increase of evictions but of the counties or districts in which such increase has taken place? And will not this confirm or confute the Duke's statement that they are evictions of men unwilling, not of men unable, to pay their rent?

11. Fr.

Wrote to Lord Sydney—Sir C. Ducane—The Queen—French Ambassador—Duke of Westminster—Mr Herries—& minutes. H of C. $2\frac{1}{4}$-$5\frac{3}{4}$ and $10\frac{1}{2}$-$1\frac{1}{4}$. Financial plan prospers.[4] Saw Mr West—Mr Young—Sir R. Lingen—Ld R.G.—Mr Godley—Mr Childers—Mrs Th.—Sir C. Dilke—Mr Bass. Dined at Lady Huntingtower's. A disagreeable intimation from Mr Herries of an error of over 400 m[ille] in stating the balance of the year.[5] I think he is to blame. Meditated on the means of repairing: at the cost of sleep. Read 'Eastern Statesman' in C.R.[6]

[1] Hartington replied (10 June, Add MS 44145, f. 55): 'I concur generally in your views about the financial position in regard to India.'

[2] *H* 252. 1622; see 5 June 80.

[3] Untraced.

[4] *H* 252. 1761.

[5] The copy of Gladstone's letter to Herries this day, Add MS 44544, f. 20, unfortunately omits figures. See also 27 May 80.

[6] 'An Eastern statesman' [G. Washburn], 'What can a liberal government do for Turkey', *Contemporary Review*, xxxvii. 893 (June 1880).

12. Sat.

Wrote to Sir C. Ducane—Bohemians [*sic*][1]—Ld Kimberley—Bp of Lincoln—The Queen 1.2.—and minutes. Dined at Mr Hubbard's: a Bank party. Saw Ld Wolverton—Mr Godley—Mr West—Lord R.G.—Lord Granville—Herbert G. on Church prfert—Mr Primrose on C.L. Pensions. Saw Roscoe [R]. Read Contemp. Rev.

Cabinet. Sat. June 12. 80. 2½ p.m.[2]
Parl. business
1. Richard: for disarmament. Meet by a conciliatory speech.
2. Local option. Question open.
3. Law's draft Bill on Ejectment for nonpayment of rent in Ireland. Terms of the draft discussed and determined. Discussion of the policy, Chamberlain v. Argyll. W.E.G. produced statistics, & suggested words. Bill agreed to (after 2 hours in all) in this form. Argyll reserved his freedom (*to me.*)
4. Granville mentioned the case of Tunis. No jealousy of France: no jurisdiction in the case.
5. Persia wants to know whether she is still to withhold supplies from the Russians. No—but maintain their independence.

1870.[3] A great settlement. Ejectment not disturbance. Casus Causens. Seconder's [?] argument. Is the non-payment due to *distress or to conspiracy*? Our Bill will only touch the first? Statistics of ejectment. Safer to extend the Ulster Tenant right to Ireland than [blank]

To LORD KIMBERLEY, colonial secretary, 12 June 1880. Add MS 44544, f. 21.

[First letter:] It would be well if we could settle the Col. Defence question out of the Cabinet for *the present* for it has stiff business today.[4] Could not you, Childers, & I do it.[5] I think Camperdown excellent.

[Second letter:] The Commission was issued & put in motion by our predecessors. We are not called upon to approve or condemn.

I think it a very nice question whether we ought to identify ourselves with it by making an appointment to it.

I fear we can hardly so appoint without approving & identifying.

The objections to stopping the enquiry seem conclusive. I think it worth *considering* whether we should give the Commission its tether, let it take its time, & perhaps make itself harmless.

Viewing the anxiety of members of the Cabinet, I quite agree the subject should be mentioned.

---

[1] Armenian address of thanks; see *T.T.*, 11 June 1880, 10e.
[2] Add MS 44642, f. 35. Undated holograph note [to Law?] reads 'Have you any information to show whether the increase of ejectment is mainly in the distressed districts? W.E.G.'
[3] Add MS 44642, f. 36.
[4] Kimberley to Gladstone, 12 June 1880, Add MS 44225, f. 182: 'Carnarvon keeps pressing me for our answer about the Col. Defence Commission. . . . I should be glad to be able to raise it at the Cabinet to-day.' The Royal Commission 'for the defence of British possessions and commerce abroad' was appointed in 1878 with Carnarvon as chairman; it reported in September 1881, May and July 1882, its reports never being published; see Carnarvon's statement on 4 May 1883, *H* 278. 1831 and Schreuder, 9-10.   [5] See 15 June 80.

13. 3 S. Trin.

Whitehall mg, Chapel Royal aftn. Dined at Ld Rosebery's. Saw Ld R—Sir C. Dilke. Saw Mr Forster—Lord Hanmer. Read Miller (finished)[1]—Leathes[2]—What Church[3]—Hubbard—O. Shipley.[4]

14. M.

Wrote to D. of Argyll 1.2.—Ld Leicester—Ld Portman—The Queen—and minutes. Saw Duke of Argyll—Ld Granville (2)—Mr Forster (2). Long & anxious conversation with the Duke of Argyll on his letter of resignation.[5] In Harley St to obtain books & H.J.G.s effects. H of C. 4½-1½ on The O Donnell business, except half an hour. A grave affair ended well.[6]

To the DUKE OF ARGYLL, lord privy seal, 14 June 1880.   Add MS 44104, f. 175.
'Secret'.

While I do not presume to measure beforehand the effect on your mind of any considerations I can offer, I think I may fairly ask you not at this moment to give to your letter the rigidity of a final announcement.[7]

I ask you also to consider them in the spirit of candour, which you would undoubtedly exhibit on almost every political subject.

Would it be quite equitable to press against the Cabinet the proposition—

'it is notorious that we had determined not to deal with the subject during the present session.'

I aver that the only subject we had determined was *not* to deal with the purchase clauses of the Irish land Act.

We never considered the question of ejectments connected with the present distress in Ireland.

For myself, I can most strictly say the proposal of O'Connor Power has had no other effect than to draw my *attention* to a question which, like many other questions with strong claims, I had not considered, & had had no time to consider.

I must also say of that question, that the Evidence in regard to it grows & varies from day to day.

I *was* under the impression that ejectments were diminishing, but I now find from figures first seen on Saturday that they seem rather to increase.

I find also that they are attempted wholesale; & that 40 Constables fail to give the strength necessary to sustain the law.

This state of facts entails on me—& I think many colleagues might be disposed to say the same thing—the duty of enquiring, where I had not previously known there was urgent cause to inquire.

[1] See 30 May 80.

[2] S. Leathes, *Old Testament prophecy* (1880).

[3] Perhaps *Which is the true church?* By C. F. B. Allnatt (1879).

[4] O. Shipley, 'A specimen of recent Anglican controversy with Rome. A letter to Dr Pusey' (1880).

[5] Compromise agreed on; Argyll not to resign, the Bill to be limited to 1880-1 and to scheduled districts, and 'Gladstone to reserve our entire freedom for the future' and 'to deprecate unreasonable expectations'; see Argyll to Sir J. MacNeill this day in Lady F. Balfour, *Ne Oblïviscaris* (n.d.), i. 285.

[6] Long series of points of order following F. H. O'C. O'Donnell's attack on the role of Challemel-Lacour, new French ambassador, in 1870; *H* 252. 1904.

[7] Precis of Argyll's letter of this day, stating his inability to accept any share of responsibility for decision of last Saturday's Cabinet, Add MS 44104, f. 173; letter in Argyll, ii. 349.

On inquiry, I find reason to believe that many ejectments are on account of an inability to pay rent caused wholly by destitution, & that destitution due to the circumstances of the last harvest.

Hereupon I have to ask myself a twofold question 1. In a country where we have numbers of occupiers living strictly from hand to mouth, and where the harvest has in certain districts been so destroyed as to cause frequently an absolute though temporary destitution, is it quite just that on an ejectment served for not paying that which the man could not pay, he should forfeit entirely the little estate or interest in the land, which was created for him by us under the Land Act of 1870, under the name of compensation for disturbance?

2. Is the adoption of such an extreme proposition consistent in spirit on the part of those who, in 1870, admitted that for tenancies under £15 then existing the fact of 'exorbitant' rent—*without any distinct condition of inability to pay*—should operate to prevent the destruction of the principle of disturbance in cases of ejectment for non payment?

My answer to question 1 is 'No, it is not just'. To question 2 'No, it is not consistent.'

Now I put question 3—am I to shrink from doing what is just & consistent because (as I admit) I shall be told that I am doing it at the bidding of O'Connor Power?

It is a sound and just rule that we should discard the fear of being thought afraid.

It may perhaps be said that is a *casus omissus* in the Land Act. I seriously think it is less in disparagement of the ordinary rules of property than what we did in the Land Act.

I have lost no time in writing—pray let me see you, to ascertain the exact amount & breadth of any difference between us—at any time except between 4.15 & 5.30 when I shall be fast on the Bench.[1]

15. *Tu.*

Wrote to D. of Argyll—Sir H. Ponsonby—Ld Selborne—Mr T.B. Potter MP.—Mr Ouvry—Messrs Krüger & Joubert—Rev. Mr Shipley—The Queen—and minutes. Saw Mr Forster—Ld Granville—& both these with the Duke of Argyll who at length agreed, with great pain, & much affection, to the locally restricted Irish plan. Conclave on Colonial Defence Commn at 3.[2] Saw Ld Spencer—Sir C. Dilke—Mr Godley—Ld R.G.—Ld Rosebery—Sir H. Layard—Mr Knowles. Ten to dinner: & evening party.

To the DUKE OF ARGYLL, lord privy seal, 15 June 1880.   Add MS 44104, f. 181.
'Secret'.

I ought to have given you the enclosed yesterday.

To it, after our conversation, I would only add the plea I then made; that in a state of things which requires the legislative interference of Parliament to keep the people from starvation (which has just, and only just, been effected) it is impossible to apply, without qualification of any kind, the ordinary rules of property. Where a portion of the community has had to cast itself on public funds with a view to the maintenance of life, the State has to consult for the general good upon rules larger than those that apply to ordinary circumstances.

---

[1] Docketed by Gladstone: 'Proposed answer—or shall I simply ask to see him? If it is go let it come here to be copied. WEG June 14. 80. 12½ PM'; by Granville: 'An excellent answer but he is so fond of argument that I think it would be safer to see him. If he goes, is it quite certain that others will think it right to stay.' Letter sent, for Argyll replied this day (Add MS 44104, f. 177) with further complaints at lack of notice of discussion. This letter is in Argyll, ii. 351.

[2] See 12 June 80.

At the same time, and in perfect consonance with this view of the matter, I view without jealousy, indeed with sympathy, whatever tends to tie up and inclose as it were this intervention so as to fasten it upon the peculiar & exceptional circumstances of the case.

I by no means admit to myself that we are going to establish by implication any general rule for Ireland that inability to pay rent shall be held compatible with the claim for disturbance compensation.

Believe me there is not any need for your assurances as to your feelings in this critical affair: they speak for themselves: no one who knows you can mistake or undervalue them, true though it may be, as to myself, that under the ruthless pressure of hourly business I may seem to force my way through it all with a stony indifference. Nothing can alter my feeling of gratitude.[1]

To S. J. P. KRUGER and P. J. JOUBERT, 15 June 1880.   Add MS 44464, f. 219.

Gentlemen, I have received your letter of the 10th of May;[2] and I observe that it must have been written before the announcement of the policy of Her Majesty's Government with respect to the Transvaal, made on the 20th of that month in the Speech from the Throne, could have reached you. I will not, however, on that account content myself with a simple acknowledgment.

It is undoubtedly matter for much regret that it should since the annexation have appeared that so large a number of the population of Dutch origin in the Transvaal are opposed to the annexation of that territory; but it is impossible now to consider that question as if it were presented for the first time. We have to deal with a state of things which has existed for a considerable period, during which obligations have been contracted, especially, though not exclusively, towards the native population, which cannot be set aside.

Looking to all the circumstances both of the Transvaal and the rest of South Africa, and to the necessity of preventing a renewal of disorders which might lead to disastrous consequences not only to the Transvaal but to the whole of South Africa, our judgment is that the Queen cannot be advised to relinquish her sovereignty over the Transvaal; but, consistently with the maintenance of that sovereignty, we desire that the white inhabitants of the Transvaal should without prejudice to the rest of the population enjoy the fullest liberty[3] to manage their local affairs; we believe that this liberty may be most easily and promptly conceded to the Transvaal as a member of a South African confederation.

16. Wed.

Wrote to D. of Argyll—M. of the Rolls—Ld Hartington—Duke of Richmond—and minutes. Attended the City Celebration & spoke for Govt. 6 to 8 minutes.[4] Sat to photographers. Saw Ld R.G.—Mr Godley—D. of Cleveland—D of Westminster—D. of Cambridge (Afghanistan)—Sir Thos G. (H.J.G.s Estate)—Sir T. Acland—and others. 4-5. Farmer's Alliance Depn: rather remarkable.[5] Dined at D. of Cambridge's. Saw Legard, Woods, & another [R].

---

[1] This para. in Argyll, ii. 353, from which the last sentence is taken.
[2] Add MS 44464, f. 97. The reply, dated on the secretary's copy 8 June but sent on 16 June, was largely based on Kimberley's mem. of 6 June; see Schreuder, 58-9 and Add MS 44225, f. 180.
[3] Kimberley's draft read 'enjoy full liberty'.
[4] Dinner for King of the Hellenes; *T.T.*, 17 June 1880, 10c.
[5] A liberal tenant farmers' organization, which played a considerable part in the 1880 election, addressed by Gladstone on the govt.'s agricultural policy; *D.N.*, 17 June 1880, 2d. Later papers at Add MS 44625, f. 80.

To LORD HARTINGTON, Indian secretary, 16 June 1880. Add MS 44544, f. 22.

(1) I do not think there is a case for pressing Stansfeld further.[1] I hope he is pleased; & if so I am glad for he has always shown himself loyal.

(2) Judging from testimony I am quite willing that you should go on with Evelyn Baring. You would learn all about his present appointment from the Foreign Office.

(3) I see no reason to doubt that you have acted wisely in the appointment of Mr Aitchison.

(4) Even amidst your most urgent calls, I hope the really urgent case of the Press Act has not been lost sight of & that the strange proceedings of Salisbury & Lytton will be reviewed. The case of the Arms Act I believe also deserves consideration.

17. Th.

Wrote to Ld Granville (3)—Ld Chancellor—Sir C. Ducane—D. of Connaught—The Queen—Sir H. Ponsonby—& minutes. H. of C. 4¼-7 and 9½-12½.[2] Saw Mr Godley—Mr E. Russell—Mr Oliphant[3]—Prof. Ramsay—Mr Newton—Père Hyacinthe—Ld F.C. Saw Roscoe [R]. Sixteen to breakfast. Read Cymbeline.

18. Fr.

Wrote to D. of Argyll—Ld Kenmare—Sir C. Dilke—Rev. R. West—Mr A.E. West—Mr Fowler MP—The Queen—and minutes. Saw H.N.G. on his affairs—Mr Monk MP—Ld Wolverton—Mr Godley—Ld R.G.—and others. House of Commons 2¼-7 and 9¼-1.[4] Dined with the Jameses. Read Cymbeline.

To the DUKE OF ARGYLL, lord privy seal, 18 June 1880. Add MS 44544, f. 23.

Harcourt tells me the matter in dispute about Heriot's Hospital is now left open for review.

You will not be pleased with the change of form as to the provision for cases of ejectment, which Forster was obliged to adopt last night. But there was no choice: he had got into an exceptional position under the rules of the House and did not get the support from the Speaker, which through May he had expected, so that under the circumstances we should have had obstruction covered with a plausible plea, from the landlord side. We shall lose no time in proceeding to full and clear explanation.

To Sir C. W. DILKE, foreign under-secretary, 18 June 1880. Add MS 43875, f. 23.

On this draft I have to say

1. Viewing the great disadvantage of prolonged unsettlement of trade & revenue, I took the date 15 Aug. as giving the shortest sufficient time for the negotiation of a treaty with France, & without any idea of reducing our duties upon an *expectation*.

[1] To become Financial Minister in India; Hartington recommended Baring, who accepted; Add MS 44145, f. 61.

[2] The opposition moved the adjournment on the Relief of Distress (Ireland) Act (1880) Bill after Forster announced he would move a new clause in cttee., the Speaker ruling that discussion of the clause was allowed; *H* 253. 213.

[3] Laurence *Oliphant, 1829-88; novelist, traveller and journalist; liberal M.P. Stirling burghs 1865-8; proposed 1878-80 British protectorate in Palestine with Jewish settlement, see A. Taylor, *Laurence Oliphant* (1982), 190, 199.

[4] Spoke on treaty of Berlin, Ireland, savings banks, and drink, voting against Lawson's Local Option Resolution; *H* 253, 297, 302, 325, 361.

2. We might a little prolong the time if we could thereby get the Treaty.
3. The Bill will not be in Committee before June 30th & need not quit the H of C. till some time later.
4. By that time, France ought to know her mind & we could either finally fix a date, if necessary, a little, but not much, after Aug. 15, or if there were no prospect of results during the autumn we could postpone the affair till the opening of next Session.

19. Sat. [*Littleburys, Mill Hill*]

Wrote to Sir T.E. May—Ld Granville 1.2.—The Queen 1.2.—D of Richmond—Ld Blachford—Mr Ashton—Mr Welby—and minutes. Cabinet 2½-5. Saw Ld Granville—Mr Godley—Mr H. Seymer[1]—Ld R.G.—Mr West. Off at 5.15 with Ld Aberdeen to Littleburys his temporary but historical abode: the house of Nell Gwynne, at least in part. Read Cymbeline—Memoir of F.R. Havergall.[2]

Cabinet. Sat. Ju. 19. 80. 2½ p.m.[3]
1. Case of Mr. Bradlaugh. Decided simply to support Labouchere's motion.
2. Address voted last night in H of L. Examine precedents.
3. Ground game Bill. As to interference with existing leases. To ask for their plan as to Moorlands. Proposal for limited time.
4. Sarcastic questions—not to be answered.
5. Commissions in Ireland. Two at once? Not to interfere.[4]
6. Desultory conversation on the proposal as to Irish Land.
7. Telegrams from Ripon. Liberate Ripon from any *obligation* to find a sovereign for Afghanistan.[5]
8. Prince Napoleon Monument at Woolwich. No objection.
9. Understanding with Russia.
10. Abp. of C[anterbury]'s desire for postponing the operation of the Burials Bill.[6]
11. English Sunday Closing. To be an open question.

To Sir T. ERSKINE MAY, 19 June 1880.   Add MS 44154, f. 70.

It is with fear and trembling that I withhold assent from any conclusion of yours on the Law of Parliament, but I find my own scruples and objections stubborn, and I am (what I understand to be) a Hot Kerite[7] on this affair of Bradlaugh.
I will not now state my grounds but will only mention the course of proceeding which would best have pleased me as most tending to keep the House out of the fray. Namely
1. If Mr B with a letter first written to the Speaker to say that he deemed this the most respectful course, were, on the ground of the Report of the Committee, to tender himself to *affirm* at the table.
2. If then Sir D. Wolff or Sir H. Giffard or anyone else were to put his objection forward by a motion—

---

[1] Horace Alfred Damer Seymour, 1843-1902, starting work as private secretary *vice* H. Primrose, staying throughout this govt.; later a customs commissioner and at board of works.
[2] M. V. G. Havergal, *Memorials of F. R. Havergal* (1880).   [3] Add MS 44642, f. 38.
[4] The Richmond Commission (see 14 May 80n.) was already dealing with Ireland; the Bessborough Commission examined the 1870 Land Act; see 26 June 80.
[5] Despite this, Ripon continued to seek a settlement with Abdur Rahman, Lytton's nominee, recognizing him, but not appointing or proclaiming him, as Amir; see S. Gopal, *British policy in India 1858-1905* (1965), 132 and Gopal, *Ripon*, ch. ii.
[6] The Queen was advised that delay would be unwise; CAB 41/14/14.
[7] 'A kind of artificial caoutchouc for coating telegraph wires' (*O.E.D.*).

3. If we were simply to divide upon, and as I hope negative, the objection.
The House would then be committed to no doctrine and no novelty whatever on the
subject.

20. 4 S. Trin. [London]

Mill Hill Ch. mg—Saw Dr Weymouth afterwards. Read Row's Bampton L.[1]—
Memoirs of Miss Havergall—Leathes on Prophecy. Back to Lond. evg & dined
in B. Square: but Ld W. had not been able to come up. Wrote to Mr Murray.

21. M.

Wrote to Miss Lonsdale—Ld Leicester—Sir C. Dilke—The Queen—Ld Cardwell—D. of Argyll—Mr Forster—Mr Grogan—Mr Jas. Bright—Mr Leeman MP—
Mr Parker MP—A.E. West—The Queen [sic] and minutes. Saw Mr Godley—Mr
Hamilton—Ld R.G.—Mr Welby—Ld Wolverton—Sir Thos G.—Ld Tenterden. H
of C. 4½-8¼ and 9¼-1¼: Bradlaugh case.[2] Read Andrew on N.W. Frontier.[3]

To Jacob BRIGHT, M.P., 21 June 1880.   Add MS 44544, f. 24.

The way for a full & comprehensive consideration of the points which the Brewers
desire to raise is that they should state them in the first instance to the Board of Inland
Revenue. The Board will then communicate with me; & if the Brewers are dissatisfied
with the conclusions at which I may arrive upon conference with the Board, I will take
care that there shall be sufficient time before the Committee on the Bill for further communication & for meeting together if necessary; but I am afraid I cannot undertake to
receive separate Deputations from the separate portions of the country & subdivisions of
the trade.

I think it will be for their general convenience that, if you think fit, this note should be
published.[4]

To W. E. FORSTER, Irish secretary, 21 June 1880.   Add MS 44544, f. 24.

Please to consider this letter.[5] My impression is that the Duke's amendment is already
involved—a man hopelessly involved as he describes could not be in a legal sense willing
to continue in the holding on fair terms: but everything is due to the Duke which can be
conceded without mischief.

22. Tu.

Wrote to Sir C. Ducane—Bp of Exeter—D. of Connaught—Abp of York—Sir H.
Ponsonby—The Queen, and minutes. 12 to dinner. Read Cymbeline—May's
Hist.[6] Saw Mrs Ralli—Mr Godley—Ld R.G.—Ld Powerscourt—Ld Granville—
Herbert J.G. H of C. 4¼-7¾ and 10-1¼. Spoke 1 h on the Bradlaugh case.[7]

---

[1] See 6 Oct. 78.
[2] Labouchere's motion to allow Bradlaugh to affirm; H 253. 443; see 19 June 80.
[3] W. P. Andrew, Our scientific frontier (1880).
[4] Not found published.
[5] From Argyll, not traced.
[6] Probably T. E. May; see 26 Jan. 61.
[7] Opposing the suggestion of a general act to deal with the case, and opposing Giffard's amndt. to
prevent Bradlaugh affirming or swearing, which was then surprisingly carried in 275:230;
H 253. 624.

To Sir H. F. PONSONBY, the Queen's secretary, 22 June 1880.   Add MS 44544, f. 25.

As Her Majesty is so good as to have regard to my engagements in commanding my attendance at Windsor, I take leave to say that Saturday in the afternoon is almost of necessity devoted to the Cabinet & that the trains are not suitable for an audience at one, but if an audience at 12 could be arranged, there is a train arriving at 11.55 & I could get back for the Cabinet about two.

If not I think I had better run a little risk in the House & ask for Friday at 3 P.M.

Please answer by telegraph.

P.S. I had forgotten that there is a Council on Friday which I find is fixed for one. I could readily arrange to be at the Council if it would suit Her Majesty to see me before or after it.

23. Wed.

The Queen—Ld F. Cavendish—Mr Godley—Sir H. Ponsonby Tel. Saw The Speaker—Mr Hopwood[1]—Mr West—Mr Bass jun.—Mr Godley—Lord R.G.—Mr Forster. Sixteen to dinner. H of C. 12¼-3½ on the Bradlaugh affair. He is a consummate speaker.[2] Saw Ld Portman & Ld Leicester on the Prince of Wales's affairs. Much conversation at dinner & after on the Bradlaugh business. Walk in evg. Saw Simpson [R].

24. Th.

Wrote to Sir H. Ponsonby Tel 1.2.—Ld Halifax—Sir S. Northcote—Mr Forster—Sir C. Dilke—The Queen—& minutes. H of C. 4¼-8¼ and 9-1. Severe day: my own revenue Bill & all sorts of communications on the Bradlaugh case running parallel through the evening.[3] 12-3½. With the B.I.R. Conclave on Malt & Beer: & then seeing the Burton Brewers.[4] Saw Mr Godley—Ld R.G.—Sir J. Lacaita. Sixteen to breakfast. Read Cymbeline.   •

To EARL FITZWILLIAM, 24 June 1880.   Add MS 44544, f. 25.

I thank you much for your kind & temperate note.[5] I cannot wonder that you should be startled at the title & *reputed* character of our Bill; nor do I lightly estimate your title to speak upon the subject in respect of your efforts & conduct as well as of your interest & station. I think however that when we come to explain both the motives & the exact scope of the measure you will perhaps find reason to take a more favourable view of it. Forster will tomorrow, on proposing the second Reading, state the object & nature of the Bill, & I shall probably have to join in the debate at a later time. If there should be any point in which you think I can hereafter give you information, you will I daresay kindly afford me the opportunity.

[1] Charles Henry Hopwood, 1829-1904; barrister and liberal M.P. Stockport 1874-85.
[2] Bradlaugh spoke from the bar of the House, then declined to withdraw; this led to his arrest, on Northcote's motion, by the serjeant at arms, and imprisonment in the Clock Tower; *H* 253. 629; Arnstein, 74ff.
[3] *H* 253. 719, 727.
[4] No account found.
[5] Not traced; on the Compensation for Disturbance Bill.

To W. E. FORSTER, Irish secretary, 24 June 1880.   Add MS 44544, f. 25.

Will you be so kind as to have drawn out for me, or if you think fit for the Cabinet, a memorandum shewing the successive forms under which there appeared in the Irish Land Bill of 1870 words & provisions of exception to the rule that Ejectment for non payment of rent should not be disturbance, until the measure became an Act.

25. Fr.

Wrote to Ld Hartington—Hon. Rev. S. Lawley—Mr Fowler—Mr Whitbread—Mr Forster—Mr Herries (2)—The Queen (2)—Abp of Canterbury—Sir W. Harcourt—and minutes. H. of C. $2\frac{1}{4}$-$6\frac{3}{4}$.[1] Read Cymbeline—Voysey's Prayer book.[2] Saw The Speaker—Conrad Zohrab[3]—Mr Chamberlain—Ld Granville—Mr Godley—Ld R.G.

To W. E. FORSTER, Irish secretary, 25 June 1880.   Add MS 44157, f. 142.

1. Do you see any insurmountable objection to *allowing* Parnell's Bill to be blocked so as to secure a real discussion on the principle, which it really seems to require? Flesh and blood can hardly stand a repetition of last night, such as not I but others suffered it.
2. I must fear say a few words to you about the Duke of Devonshire before I can quite see my way—to write to him with no hope of his accepting would be hardly advantageous?[4]
3. I hope you will be large and free to-day in showing the necessity of *doing something* and this you can effect far better than any other man.

The other great point which I hope we may make clear in debate—for otherwise great misfortune may impend—is the strictly *bounded* character of what we do. We have only kept Argyll by showing him how carefully our measure is framed to bar all inferences, all prejudices touching anything that lies beyond its own four corners. The Irish Land Act is a sort of Land Charter: and I think it is vital to our chances of steering through the rough waters to show that every question arising under it will be held over until the Commission shall have reported.
4. Will you try to have a list of good names for the Cabinet to-morrow.

To LORD HARTINGTON, Indian secretary, 25 June 1880.   Add MS 44544, f. 26.

If Bradlaugh comes we shall I think be tolerably prepared for the probable course of events.[5] But it will be far better that he should not come and that to enable him to forbear some one should give notice at once of a motion to rescind. I have further to observe
(1). It would be a great advantage, and would perhaps be agreeable to both sides, if this notice could be decided without prolonged debate.
(2). Do not you think it would be a still greater advantage if *Whitbread* would make it—and could you promote this or, failing you, could I?[6]

---

[1] Questions, Ireland, drink; *H* 253. 834.
[2] C. Voysey, *The Revised Prayerbook* (1871).
[3] Entering Gladstone's employment as valet.
[4] Forster on 24 June 1880, Add MS 44157, f. 141, proposed Devonshire as chairman of the Irish land commission.
[5] Hartington reported talks with Labouchere and Grosvenor on the Bradlaugh affair; Add MS 44145, f. 65.
[6] See 1 July 80. Hartington this day wrote to Whitbread; ibid., f. 71.

26. Sat.

Wrote to Mr Vickers—Watson & Smith—Mrs Th.—Mr Vivian MP—Mrs Birks—
M. Leon Say—Mr Herries—Mr D. Currie MP—Sir C. Dilke—The Speaker—The
Queen—and minutes. Cabinet 2-5¼. Dined at the Duke of Bedford's. Saw two
[R]. Saw Mr Chamberlain—Ld Granville—Ld R.G.—Ld Wolverton—Mr God-
ley—Mr Leveson—Duke of Leinster.

Cabinet. June 26. 80. 2 p.m[1]

1. Bradlaugh case. Two hours. WEG to propose a Resolution drawn by [Lord] Chanr. &
   amended.[2]
2. Parnell's Bill for Public Alms. Commee. of Cabinet to meet next Monday & consider if
   some relaxation of terms to Guardians.
3. Irish Land Commission. Bessborough[3]—Kavanagh—M[aster] of Rolls—Lefevre—
   ⟨Ridley⟩ and one, or two, more.[4]
4. Lord Spencer to introduce his Education Bill in the H. of Lords.

To Mrs BIRKS, 26 June 1880.   Add MS 44544, f. 27.

I am so sorry to learn[5] that you have been disquieted with apprehensions of coming
loss in connection with the approaching conversion of the Malt Duty into a Beer Duty.
And I do not suppose that my unskilled observations can have much effect in reassuring
you. Nevertheless I would beg you at any rate not to take any practical step in haste
because of these apprehensions. Were this the first time I had been engaged in measures
which modify the position of a great trade I should not venture to say this. But having
seen all our trades, or nearly all, handled by legislation, I have become so to speak inured
to these alarms and have known from experience that in every case (for I am not certain
that there is a real exception) they have been unfounded, and the very changes so sincerely and strongly deprecated have been the means of increased transactions and
increased profits.

Details are still under consideration: but in the meantime I have thought you would
not dislike, and at any rate would assign to a good motive, my placing these general considerations before you.

To H. B. W. BRAND, the Speaker, 26 June 1880. '*Private*'.   Brand MSS.

The Cabinet have long and very carefully considered their duties in relation to the
position which the House of Commons has unfortunately been tempted to assume. They
felt the reluctance to undertaking a Bill which I had anticipated, on the ground of the
immense sacrifice it would entail. On the other hand they are desirous to challenge as
little as possible the decision of the House. And they have determined that I shall on
Monday give notice of a Resolution (for Wednesday or Thursday as may seem most convenient), copy of which I inclose. It leaves untouched the whole proceeding as to *Oaths*.[6]

---

[1] Add MS 44642, f. 41.
[2] Drafts at ibid., f. 42. See 1 July 80.
[3] One name here illegible.
[4] See 17 July 80.
[5] His Harley Street neighbour's letter untraced.
[6] Brand sent drafting amndts., and hoped the Resolution would pass; Add MS 44194, f. 212.

27. 5 S. Trin.

Savoy Chapel 11½ AM (to hear Ld Mulgrave) and St James's evg. Saw Ld Northbrook–Duke of Argyll–Ld Halifax–Ld De Tabley. Wrote to Mr Hussey Vivian–Ld Chancellor–The Speaker–Mr Herries. Read Life of H. de Losinga[1]–Knox Little[2]–Leathes on Prophecy and [blank.] Much rest & new life today. Tea at Argyll Lodge.

To H. HUSSEY VIVIAN, M.P., 27 June 1880.　　　　　　　　　Add MS 44544, f. 28.

We carefully considered at the Cabinet the method of proceeding by Bill in the case of Bradlaugh.[3] There is one of the objections to it which I think you will not fail to appreciate. It is this: that there is no reasonable hope of Bradlaugh's abstaining during the lengthened time over which the proceedings must extend, from entering the House, so that the whole difficulty of *police*, which is the main difficulty would remain untouched.

Lord Northbrook tells me he understood you to say to him that you thought questions ought not to have been put to him when he tendered himself at the Table to affirm.

That putting of questions has I am afraid been the root of all our trouble.

But I have some hope that we might found upon this idea a motion sufficiently conciliatory to help us out of our difficulties, which are otherwise likely to be serious enough. It seems now that Bradlaugh did *not* volunteer a confession of his unbelief but that it was drawn from him by inquiries.

28. M.

Wrote to Mr Lock–Duke of Westmr–The Queen–Rev. D. Robertson–and minutes. Saw Siamese Ambassador and suite.[4] NB. interpreter. Saw Ld F.C.–Ld R.G.–Mr Godley–Mr West–Ld Granville–Ld Spencer–Sir C. Dilke–Sir H. Layard–M. Leon Say–Miss Frere[5]–Mr Biddell. 11¾-3½. To Windsor for Council–Audience of the Queen: so blooming! H of C. 4½-8¼ and 10-1.[6] But away to Tea. Dined at J. Talbot's. Read Cymbeline (finished)–Walpole's Hist. Vol. III.[7]

29. Tu. St P[eter]

Wrote to Ld Northbrook–The Queen–Ld Kimberley–Ld Granville–and minutes. Twelve to dinner. Evening party afterwards. Read Fraser on the Govt.[8]–Life of Elihu Burritt[9]–King Lear. Saw Ld R.G.–Mr Godley–Ld Halifax–Mr Forster–Mr Earp. H of C. 2½-7.[10]

[1] E. M. Goulburn and H. Symonds, *The life, letters and sermons of Bishop Herbert de Losinga*, 2v. (1878).
[2] W. J. K. Little, *Sermons* (1880).
[3] Letter of 26 June supporting abolition of oath; Add MS 44465, f. 26.
[4] Chao Phya, who presented the Order of the White Elephant to the Queen on 2 July.
[5] One of Frere's four unmarried daughters.
[6] Navy estimates; *H* 253. 975.
[7] H. Walpole, Lord Orford, *Memoirs of the reign of George II*, 3v. (2nd ed., 1847).
[8] *Fraser's Magazine*, ci. 857 (June 1880).
[9] *Elihu Burritt; a memorial volume containing a sketch of his life and labours* (1879).
[10] Spoke on adjournment of Irish deb.; *H* 253. 1165.

To LORD KIMBERLEY, colonial secretary, 29 June 1880.   Add MS 44544, f. 29.

I agree that the Frere question enters a new phase, and of course is one for the Cabinet. But ought we to proceed in it before receiving by post his statement of the situation *in extenso*?[1]

30. Wed.

Wrote to Dr Lyons[2]–Ld Granville–Mr Duchhayn[3]–Watson & Smith–Williams & Co–Archdeacon Jones–and minutes. Attended the Levee. Conclave at Foreign Office on the means of coercing Turkey[4] $3\frac{1}{4}$-$4\frac{3}{4}$. Saw Ld F.C.–Ld RG–Mr Godley–Herbert G. (on his subject for a fine speech)–Lady Derby–Ld Egerton–Mr Carl Bock–Ly Ripon–Ld Sydney. Dined at Ld Tweeddale's. Read King Lear. Saw Sumpter [R].

Thurs. July One 1880.

Wrote to The Queen 1.2.–Prince of Wales–Mr Bright–Ld Chancellor–Mrs Ralli–Ld Granville–& minutes. H of C. $4\frac{1}{4}$-$8\frac{1}{2}$ and $9\frac{3}{4}$-$3\frac{3}{4}$. Proposed the Bradlaugh Resolution: which we carried.[5] Thirteen to breakfast. Saw Mr Godley–Herbert G–Lord R.G.–Mr Welby–Ld Kenmare–M. Tachard–Mr Herbert Spencer–Mr Law–Dr Phillimore. A severe day: 18 hours with but one or $1\frac{1}{2}$ of interval.

To John BRIGHT, chancellor of the duchy, 1 July 1880.   Add MS 43385, f. 280.

Do you not think that, with the tact which you would bring to bear, you could write a note to the members of your Society at Bewdley (who I believe are persons of considerable influence), to move them in favour of Sir John Adye, whose whole influence and ability–and they are great–have been directed for a series of years–towards promoting moderation in establishments, and a policy of peace and justice?

There are soldiers and soldiers: an analysis of the Parliament shows that we have near one hundred of them in the House of Commons already: and this is one better than any now there.

They would I am sure have voted for Colonel Thompson–and if they do not wish the present Government to yield its place to some other they will I am sure recollect that no Government can properly discharge its duties without some military aid, and that no military aid is so safe as that of men who sitting in the House of Commons are placed under the good and popular influences which act there, instead of sitting in their offices *as Sir John Adye now does*, liable only to the direct action of the influences which are exclusively professional.[6]

[1] Replying to Kimberley's letter of this day, Add MS 44225, f. 184: 'Carnarvon's policy has completely broken down . . . there is no longer any good reason for not recalling him [Frere].'
[2] Robert Dyer Lyons, 1826–86; physician and liberal M.P. Dublin 1880–5.
[3] Apparently *sic*; no copy found.
[4] Over Smyrna; Childers, Northbrook and Granville attending; see Ramm II, i. 140.
[5] In 303:249, resolving every person returned as M.P. be permitted to affirm, 'subject to any liability by statute'; *H* 253. 1261.
[6] By-election following a petition; Adye was not nominated, E. Baldwin, relative of the Prime Minister, winning the seat as a liberal. No reply found.

2. Fr.

Up at 10. Wrote to Ld Granville 1.2.3.—Mr Forster 1.2.—Sir C. Ducane—Ld Lansdowne—The Queen—Messrs T. & B.—and minutes. H. of C. 2¼-7.[1] Dined at Ld Wolvertons. Read Mad. de Remusat.[2] Saw Mr Hortin[3]—Mr Welby *cum* Lord F.C.—Mr Godley—Lord RG—Ld Wolverton—Mr Currie—Mr Ashburnham— Dowager Lady Ashburnham.

3. Sat. [*Littleburys, Mill Hill*]

Wrote to Mr Vickers—The Queen—Sir Thos G.—& minutes. Inl. Rev. Conclave on Malt Duty 12¼-2. Cabinet 2¼-4¼. Saw Mr Godley—Lord R. Grosvenor—Ld Spencer. Off to Littleburys at 5¾. Read King Lear—Shakesp. The Man & the Book.[4]

Cabinet. Sat. Jul. 3. 80. 2 p.m.[5]
1. Charge of Burials Bill [in the Commons]. Mr. Osborne Morgan. Yes.
2. Employers' Liability. Committee. Refuse Select Committee time notwithstanding.
3. Recall Sir Bartle Frere. Refuse to act on *Telegram*.
4. Compensation for Disturbance. Make no change of front during the Debate on the Second Reading.[6]
5. Census Bill—introducing in the Lords.
6. Goschens's Telegram with the offer of Porte.[7] Answer him that we decline to entertain a new proposal: & to use his own discretion as to communicating the matter ⟨with⟩ to other Ambassadors.
7. Tel. to Cape agreed on.
8. Tel. on Russo-Chinese questions not involving immediate action. Good offices have been offered.
9. Trevelyan's motion: do nothing now: form = the cons[ideratio]n of a new arrangement.[8]

Cape. Q[uer]y Answer: Have received with much concern the account from the Cape, which shows that the proposal of the Ministry for a Conference with a view to Confederation has been frustrated, and we are aware that this intelligence bears materially upon the announcement formerly made in the House of Commons; but we cannot, from the succinct Telegraphic notices which have arrived, form a comprehensive judgement on the occurrence, and when the dispatches arrive we shall lose no time in proceeding to consider them.[9]

[1] Bradlaugh affirmed; *H* 253. 1386.
[2] C. E. J. de Remusat, *Mémoires, 1802-8*, 3v. (1880-1).
[3] Probably H. G. Horton of the Inland Revenue.
[4] C. M. Ingleby, *Shakespeare. The Man and the Book* (1877).
[5] Add MS 44642, f. 44.
[6] See 5 July 80.
[7] For exclusive Anglo-Turkish negotiation on the Greek frontier; CAB 41/14/16. The Berlin conference on the frontier had just ended; F.O.C.P. 4255, p. 53.
[8] See 6 July 80.
[9] Add MS 44642, f. 47. Gladstone thus secured some delay in Frere's recall, which was effected by Kimberley on 1 August; J. Martineau, *Life of Frere* (1895), ii. 395.

4. 6 S. Trin.

Ch. mg & evg. Saw Dr [F. H. A.] Scrivener. Saw Ld F. Cavendish: who came down for the day with Ld Ab[erdee]n Lucy & WHG. Walk in this beautiful district. Read Leathes—B St Hilaire on Buddhism—on Methodism—Maine[1]—Good on Vest. of Creation.[2]

5. M. [London]

Back to London at 10¾. Wrote to The Knight of Kerry—The Queen—Ld Listowel—Mr Forster—Ld Granville—and minutes. Worked on Irish Land. H of C. 4¼-8½ and 9¾-2. Spoke 1¼ h. on Irish Disturbance Compensation. A good division.[3] Read King Lear. Saw Mr Godley—Ld R.G.—& others.

To LORD LISTOWEL, lord-in-waiting, 5 July 1880.   Add MS 44544, f. 31.

I have just received your very considerate letter.[4] There is I think much exaggeration, and misapprehension about Mr. Forster's Bill; on which I have to speak to-night. On the other hand however I believe much may be done by amending and additional provisions in Committee, to mitigate alarm and meet the objections of reasonable men.

6. Tu.

Wrote to The Queen—Duke of St Albans—Baron Dowse—Mr Richard MP—D. of Argyll—Mr . . . & minutes. Bye-Cabinet at H of C. 2½-4.[5] Saw Ld R.G.—Mr Godley—Mr Fawcett—Ld Chancellor—Sir Thos G.—Mr Morier. B.I.R. Conclave 12-1½ on Malt Duty & Licences. H of C. 12¼-5, 5¾-7, 10½-12½.[6] Saw Graham, Roscoe, & another [R]. Read King Lear. Twelve to dinner.

To the DUKE OF ARGYLL, lord privy seal, 6 July 1880.   Add MS 44544, f. 31.

1. I return Mr Hussey & his inclosure. Your answer to him was I think excellent.[7]
2. Of the two points raised in your letter today; on the *first*,[8] the difference between us is verbal only. My account of the Bill was, so to speak, structural only. I treated the exception as part of the essence of the arrangement & the present modification as only having reference only to an unforeseen & extra-legal state of things.
3. The second point[9] is I think of less moment. But I do *not* agree upon it. I think these exceptional remedies were filched, so to speak. Nevertheless I acknowledge them; *factum valet*. But their origin & their moral effect on the people must always be borne in mind,

---

[1] Sir H. J. S. Maine, perhaps *Ancient law* (1861) and many subsequent editions.
[2] See 6 June 80.
[3] 2°R carried in 295:217; *H* 253. 1725.
[4] Not found.
[5] Informed cabinet about the Compensation Bill; note summoning members at Add MS 44642, f. 51.
[6] Trevelyan's motion on army officers; *H* 253. 1788; see 3 July 80.
[7] Defending Forster's Bill; Add MS 44104, f. 180.
[8] Stating Gladstone's view as: 'the main principle of the Land Act of 1870 was to create an Estate in the Tenant: and that the payment of Rent as a necessary condition of that Estate, was "an exception"—and not a fundamental principle. To this view I demur. I hold that both in fact, and in all equity, the payment of Rent was an essential and inseparable condition . . .'; ibid., f. 191.
[9] 'it is illusory to represent the Irish landowner as possessing all the rights possessed by an English or Scotch Landowner . . .'; ibid.

when we come to estimate that side of the case which is connected with popular feeling & the practical work of administration.

4. An analysis of the division will doubtless be made, but my present impression is that the Parnell votes would be 30 or 35. One Home Ruler of the Shaw Section told me my speech converted him to the Bill! Mr Maurice Brooks.

I am glad you think that on the whole I kept faith.

7. Wed.

Wrote to Ld Granville 1.2.—and minutes. H. of C. 4-6.[1] Dined with the Sudeleys. A great Welsh ovation. Saw Count Karolyi—Mr Godley—Ld R.G.—Ld F.C.—Mr Roundell (on his motion)[2]—Ld Aberdare—Ld Hartington—Saw Graham—Beaumont. Finished King Lear.

8. Th.

Wrote to Ld Granville—Ld Lansdowne—Sir H. Ponsonby—Ld Wrottesley—Ld Chancellor—D. of Sutherland—The Queen—& minutes. H of C. $4\frac{1}{4}$-$6\frac{1}{2}$, $7\frac{1}{2}$-$8\frac{3}{4}$, & $9\frac{3}{4}$-$1\frac{1}{4}$. More disturbances in our Disturbance Bill.[3] Saw Ld R.G.—Mr Godley—Mr Forster—Ld Lansdowne—Ld Hartington. Read Measure for Measure—O. Browning's France.[4]

To the DUKE OF SUTHERLAND, lord privy seal,   Add MS 44544, f. 32.
8 July 1880. 'Private'.

Lord Wrottesley resigns the Lord Lieutenancy of Staffordshire. If it would be agreeable to you to succeed him, I should be very glad, & I could undertake on your then resigning what is still more properly your county, to offer the Lord Lieutenancy of Sutherland to your son. Or, if you are disposed to remain as you are, I would propose to recommend him to the Queen for Staffordshire.[5]

9. Frid.

Wrote to Mr Jenkins—The Queen 1.2.3.—Sir W. Heathcote—Rev. S.E.G.—Rev. D. Robertson—& minutes. H of C. $2\frac{1}{4}$-7 and 9-1. Spoke on Irish Disturb. & Univv. Clerical Restrictions.[6] A troubled day. Saw Mr G—Ld R.G.—Ld F.C.—Mr Whitbread—& others. Saw Fitzgerald X. Read Measure for Measure.

To Sir W. HEATHCOTE, 9 July 1880.   Add MS 44544, f. 33.

I am glad to have an occasion for writing to you as I trust it may bring me an assurance from yourself that you are well.

The Radcliffe Trust is my subject. Do you propose to remain a Trustee—in which case

[1] Irish fisheries; H 253. 1819.

[2] See 9 July 80.

[3] Pell's amndt. to limit the bill to evictions since November 1879; H 253. 1921.

[4] O. Browning, *Modern France 1814-79* (1880).

[5] No reply found; Sutherland declined, for Wrottesley, whose resignation was open to postponement (see Ramm II, i. 143), remained Lord Lieutenant; see also 13 July 80.

[6] Roundell's resolution to abolish any clerical restriction for fellows or heads of Oxford and Cambridge colleges, save the deanery of Christ Church, withdrawn following Gladstone's request; H 254. 110. Mem. in support of the resolution signed by many liberals at Add MS 44624, f. 114.

all your Colleagues will indeed be happy—or does the natural desire of rest lead you to renounce the meetings for the future?

I have undertaken to put this question to you as the Trust is in difficulty about gathering a *quorum* and under present circumstances I am myself unable to attend.[1]

How much we should have to say could we but meet. The world moves round & round at an ever accelerated pace & its inhabitants, some of them at least, are more & more dizzy. But you are not among *these*.

10. Sat.

Wrote to Ld Rosebery—The Queen 1.2.—Mr Forster—Mr Williams MP—Mr West—Mr Chambers. Cabinet 2-4½. Saw Phillips X. Saw Mr Godley—Ld R.G.—Ld F.C.—Mr Forster—Mr Bright—Ld Granville—Lady G. Read Lettere a Panizzi[2]—Measure for Measure.

Cabinet. Sat. Jul. 10. 80. 2 p.m.[3]
1. Motion for taking Wednesdays: Compensation for Disturbance (Tues)—Employers' Liability (Wed)—Customs & Inland Revenue (Thurs.)—Hares and Rabbits—Irish Relief of distress—Burials' Bill,
   Irish Borough Franchise | simple continuance.
   Review of Ballot Act |
2. Prince Louis Napoleon Monument. Aug. 7.79, July 24.79, Hansard 248.1176. Matter closed. No political significance. Should it have been foreseen that this wd. attach it might have been more prudent &c.[4]
3. Metropol. Govt. Bill. 2R on Tuesday. Get rid of it—sense of necessity of dealing with the question.
4. Irish Disturbance Compensation. Attorney General's Clause. Adhere to the Clause. (WEG afterwards suggested to strike out of Condition 3 the word 'unreasonably' & add without (offering a) the proposal of any reasonable alternative[)].[5]

To the DUKE OF ARGYLL, lord privy seal, 10 July 1880.   Add MS 44544, f. 34. *'Private'*.

After the Cabinet broke up, being a good deal oppressed with a sense of the difficulties into which we had slid unawares in connection with the Law Clause, it occurred to me that a simpler & better mode of proceeding would be merely to propose words for clearing what we have declared to be the original meaning of the Bill i.e., in Condition (3) to strike out 'unreasonably' before 'refused' and let it run thus:

That such terms have been refused by the Landlord *without the proposal of any reasonable alternative*.

These words raise *neither* of the difficulties that beset the new clause.

Forster seems to like them and will consult with Law.[6]

Monday at noon I go to Windsor for an audience. But I invite your attention to this suggestion. *What we meant* is what I seek to stick to.

---

[1] Heathcote wrote resigning; Add MS 44209, f. 216.
[2] L. Fagan, *Lettere ad Antonio Panizzi* (1880); he sent it to the Queen; Guedalla, *Q*, ii. 106.
[3] Add MS 44642, f. 53.
[4] See 16 July 80.
[5] Amndt. to clause 1, section 3, on temporary provision for compensation, successfully moved by Gladstone on 16 July; *H* 254. 736.
[6] Argyll's reply (12 July 1880, Add MS 44104, f. 195) objected to 'reasonable alternative' as too vague.

To W. E. FORSTER, Irish secretary, 10 July 1880. Add MS 44544, f. 33.

We have I suppose these two points at least to consider to-day upon the Attorney General's Clause.

(1) When the rent is not extravagant, and the landlord gives permission to sell, but the tenant does not find a buyer, is the landlord still to be liable in damages?
If he is, then

a. The tenant may take care not to find a buyer.

b. We go beyond the Ulster custom.

c. We can hardly say that in the original Bill was contained anything which could have led a Judge to mulct[?] the landlord when he had bonâ fide given the permission to sell.

(2). The case of extravagant rents properly so called we may & must treat as new matter? A necessity for dealing with it has perhaps hardly yet been shown? But I do not suppose we are in principle prevented from dealing with it if sufficient ground can be shown.

The first of the two points appears to be the stiffest? Do not reply.[1]

To LORD ROSEBERY, 10 July 1880. Rosebery MSS.

You will have seen that Lansdowne has—unfortunately I think for all parties—resigned his office[2] on account of the Irish Disturbance Compensation Bill. No limitation of the Bill would satisfy him; only its withdrawal.

Do you not think you may now reconsider your 'selfdenying ordinance'? You are I hope profiting much by your visit to Homburg; & Hartington with Granville has arrived at the conclusion that if now—when the *reek* of the election is no longer on you—you will accept this office, there is no sort of occasion for you to hurry back. I wish indeed that we had a prospect of an immediate decision about Afghanistan. But the probability is (though I do not say the certainty) that it may be delayed for some weeks. What we all feel to be a kind of necessity I think is, to cut out when the season for moving comes.

The Bradlaugh affair & the Irish matters, making unexpected demands upon our time, together with the shabby feebleness of Northcote, who dare not speak against the will of his tail, have much retarded business & the Prorogation must be late. It will I hope come—at some time or other. With kind regards to Lady R.

11. 7 S. Trin.

Mr Eyton's[3] Ch. in the forenoon: but he did not preach. Chapel Royal aft. Saw Ld Kenmare—Ld Wolverton—Mr & Mrs Thistlethwayte—Gen. Cunningham. Two conversations, with Walter Phillimore, & Sir W. James respectively, on the case of the Oxford Fellowships. Read Leathes—Mason Good[4]—Neale's Patriarchate of Antioch[5]—Abbé Martin, & Mallock, in Nineteenth Cent.[6]

[1] Forster's reply (11 July 1880, Add MS 44157, f. 143) suggested using the Consolidated Fund or the Church Surplus to lend to landlords rents not recoverable 'from reasonable Tenants unable to pay by reason of the special distress'.

[2] As under-secretary for India; Rosebery declined (having already refused it at the formation of the govt.); Crewe, *Rosebery*, i. 136. Hartington wrote, n.d., 'I think you might try Rosebery again; but it is generally supposed that he wanted the Cabinet, and that this was the real reason of his refusal'; Add MS 44145, f. 75.

[3] Robert Eyton, 1845-1908; curate of St Mary, Graham Street; later rector of St Margaret's, Westminster.

[4] See 6 June 80.

[5] J. M. Neale, *A history of the Holy Eastern Church . . . memoirs of the Patriarchs of Antioch*, 5v. (1850).

[6] *Nineteenth Century*, viii. 119, 19 (July 1880).

12. M.

Wrote to Ld Granville—Mr Forster—The Queen 1.2.—Lord Leigh—Gen. Fox Rivers[1]—and minutes. H of C. 4¼-8 and 10½-1.[2] Off to Windsor at 11.45 & back at 3.45. I had an audience of the Queen. She is, as ever, perfect in her courtesy: but as to confidence, she holds me now at arm's length. Saw Mr Godley—Lord R.G.—& others. Read Measure for Measure.

To W. E. FORSTER, Irish secretary, 12 July 1880.   Add MS 44544, f. 34.

I own myself a good deal startled about the plan of lending the rent-money but I am in these circumstances disposed to defer if we can at all see our way. It seems to me so like a notice not to pay, & I have the fear that there could be no real examination into inability when supply from a public fund was in view.

I sent my suggestion of Saturday to Argyll; but have not had an answer. On reflection I think favourably of it.

No answer from Dowse.

If you hold to your plan about loan, you had better I think ask Godley to send round to the Cabinet to meet at 6 in my room behind the House, when supply will probably have begun.

I hope you have profited by your short outing.

13. Tu.

Wrote to Ld Hatherton—Rev. Mr Mayow—Sir G. Bowyer—D. of Argyll—The Queen—and minutes. H of C. 2¼-7: Irish Disturbance, & a row.[3] Fourteen to dinner: & evg party. Saw Mr Godley—Ld R.G.—Ld Kenmare—Mr Blunt—Mr Hayward—Count Karolyi—and others. Read Much Ado about Nothing—Madame Rémusat.

To LORD HATHERTON, 13 July 1880.   Add MS 44544, f. 35.

The Lord Lieutenancy of Staffordshire is vacant through the resignation of Lord Wrottesley: and I have to propose that you should allow me to submit your name to the Queen as his successor in the office; an arrangement which I feel confident will be generally and justly approved.[4]

14. Wed.

Wrote to Mr Forster—M. Zapropoulos—The Queen—Mr Leveson Gower—Ld Granville—Sir H. Ponsonby—& minutes. Licensed Victuallers & City Restaurant Depn 12-1.[5] Saw Mr Godley—Ld R.G.—Ld F.C.—Mr Forster—Mr Vivian. Saw three [R]. Read Much Ado about Nothing. H of C. 1-6.[6] Dined with the Goldsmiths' Co & returned thanks for the Ministry.[7] The staircase is very fine.

[1] Augustus Henry Lane Fox *Pitt-Rivers, 1827-1900; soldier and anthropologist; see Add MS 44465, f. 98.

[2] Order of govt. business, budget, Irish distress; *H* 254. 180.

[3] Clash with Churchill, who immediately moved to report progress on the Compensation for Disturbance Bill; *H* 254. 322.

[4] He declined; see 8 July 80.   [5] No report found.

[6] Compensation for Disturbance Bill; declared the govt. would not be defeated 'by the kind of opposition which has been adopted'; *H* 254. 463.

[7] No report found.

To W. E. FORSTER, Irish secretary, 14 July 1880.   Add MS 44544, f. 35.

I cannot well be in the House before one.

If Parnell & Co are to move to report progress I suppose our line should be to get a division upon the question as soon as possible. The concession, repelled by one section as worthless from its smallness, is held by the other to destroy by its greatness the value of the Bill.

It is hard to steer through a sea of passions and prejudices like this. What is in my mind more serious is our want of particular information on the point raised by George Hamilton.[1] Surely we ought to be able to do for other Counties that which some one on his behalf has done for Donegal.

He has divided the evictions into (1). Expulsions. (2). Care takings. (3) Persons replaced in their tenancies on giving an acknowledgment of the debt—This class by much the largest.

What appears to me is that if this replacing in tenancy has been in the other Counties what it has been in Donegal, then our statements are seriously hit. In such a case I should say the compilers of one of the returns, who took notice of care-taking, ought certainly to have taken some notice of what was so much more important.

But *is it so?* This I think it is quite vital to ascertain. And I assume it can be done before the Report on the Bill, which probably ought to be postponed for a few days.

If it is only a question of more or fewer 'care-takers', I do not think the substance of the figures is seriously touched.

I see the Licensed Victuallers at twelve.

To F. LEVESON GOWER, M.P., 14 July 1880.   Add MS 44544, f. 35.

The few words which passed between us last night[2] were insufficient, on my part, for the subject to which they related. As I said, I regard the 'care-taking' cases as only one degree better than the actual expulsion.

The important question is whether there is any large number of *replacements in tenancy* among the class of the evicted.

If there has been anything of this kind it is a heavy blow to our figures, and to the compilers of them, who maintained that these were cases of care-taking, & ought *a fortiori* to have mentioned a fact so greatly more important.

But as yet I do not see reason to believe it—we must certainly in justice to all parties get to the bottom of the facts.

15. Th.

Wrote to Ld Shaftesbury—Mr Forster—Sir W. Harcourt—The Queen—& minutes. H. of C. $4\frac{1}{4}$-$8\frac{1}{4}$ and $8\frac{3}{4}$-$1\frac{1}{2}$. Ten to breakfast. Saw Mr Godley—Ld R.G.—Ld F.C.—Ld Granville—Mr Vivian—Mr Welby. House made progress today after a little storm which cleared the air.[3] Finished Much Ado & began L.L. Lost.

To W. E. FORSTER, Irish secretary, 15 July 1880.   Add MS 44544, f. 36.

Granville quite agrees as to our persistent method of proceeding on the Disturbance Bill.

---

[1] Details of evictions in Donegal given by Hamilton on 13 July; *H* 254. 333.
[2] Apparently privately.
[3] Dispute over value of holding affected by the bill; *H* 254. 492.

What do you think of the following mode of action—provided it be orderly.

1. To proceed with the amendments down to line 32. (Parnell) (or possibly down to the end of the *additions* to the Clause, which however would take more time.)

2. Then to move that the Chairman report the Bill with amendments to the House.

3. Announcing at the same time with reference to the right of redemption, and any thing else that may be right to consider, that we will take it on the Report.

4. And declaring that we do this for the purpose of obtaining the judgment of the House upon the Bill—as a whole.

I write this that you may think the matter over before the House meets.[1]

16. Fr.

Wrote to Dean of Westmr—D. of Portland—Sir G. Young—Mr Tennyson—Ld Granville—The Queen 1.2.—& minutes. H of C. 2¼-7 and 9-2½: a weary day. Our defeat however on the Monument was on the whole a public good.[2] Saw Mr Godley—Mr Hamilton—Ld RG—Ld F.C.—Mr Ouvry. Read Mad. de Remusat— Love's Labour Lost.

17. Sat. [Littleburys]

Wrote to The Queen—Ld Fitzwilliam—Scotts—Lady Dudley—Watsons—Bp of Tasmania—Rev. H. Wood[3]—Rev. Mr Childers[4]—& minutes. Cabinet 2-4½. Saw Ld RG—Mr Godley—Ld F.C.—Ld Spencer. Saw Howard [R]. Read Love's Labour Lost. Conversation with Harry on his arrangements. Fourteen to dinner. Conversation with Count Münster. Off to Littleburys at 11: a delightful drive.

Cabinet. July 17. 1880. 2.p.m.[5]

1. Montenegrin Frontier. All Powers have agreed to give the Porte 3 weeks for the Corti plan: then Dulcigno.[6] All agree to send a ship: France finally; but stipulating that this shd. be laid down in principle for the Greek Frontier also. We are to ask concurrence from the ⟨English⟩ other Powers.

2. Queen's writing to Sultan on behalf of acquiescence. Cabinet gratified, advise & accept.

3. Arrival of German Officers at Constantinople mentioned. Information awaited.

4. Irish Disturbance Bill. a) go forward; b) limit of £30: to be 'valuation'.

5. Land Commission: Ld. Bessborough, Mr. Shaw, O'Connor Don, Baron Dowse, Kavanagh. Its terms agreed on.[7]

6. Theological Degrees at Presbyterian Colleges.[8]

[1] No reply found.

[2] Gladstone voted against Briggs' motion opposing the erection in Westminster Abbey of a monument to Louis Napoleon, killed in the Zulu war; some ministers avoided voting, the Queen being powerfully opposed to Briggs' motion; *H* 254. 727, 730.

[3] Perhaps Henry Hayton Wood, d. 1882; fellow of Queen's, Oxford 1851; wrote on geology.

[4] Charles Childers, 1830-96, uncle of H.C.E.; anglican chaplain at Nice 1843-84.

[5] Add MS 44642, f. 54.

[6] i.e. assistance to Prince of Montenegro to take Dulcigno; Ramm II, i. 144.

[7] Names given by Forster on 19 July; *H* 254. 784; its report of 4 January 1881 effectively conceded the 'three F.s', save for Kavanagh whose dissenting report accepted arbitration, and a peasant proprietorship with compensation to landlords; *PP* 1881 xviii. Gladstone was alarmed by its radical proposals, see letters in Dec. 80 *passim*. William Shaw, 1823-95; Home Rule M.P. Cork 1874-85; replaced as Home Rule leader early in the 1880 session by Parnell.

[8] Irish presbyterians requested a charter; matter raised by Forster, see Add MS 44642, f. 55.

7. Ld Spencer mentioned that he had authorised Art Students to visit S. Kens[ington] Museum privately, without additional attendances, on Sundays. He will receive a Deputation.

To EARL FITZWILLIAM, 17 July 1880.　　　　　　　　　　　　Add MS 44465, f. 116.

Let me repeat the assurance I have already given of the weight I attach to any representation of yours concerning Irish Land, and the concern with which I learn your strongly adverse view.[1]

But I would ask whether you think it to be morally within the limits of our power to withdraw the Irish Disturbance Compensation Bill.

It is resisted by a *kind* of opposition to which no Government can give way without discredit to itself, or without weakening the power of the House of Commons for the discharge of its functions.

Every consideration of duty which binds me to hear reason, & to gather evidence, binds me to show a firm front to opposition of this nature, the aim of which is to overrule the majority by the minority.

Setting aside frantic declarations, such as were made yesterday by Mr. Chaplin, the opponents of the Bill have systematically scoffed at its careful and strict limitations, have announced & denounced it as a Bill to arrest for two years the payment of rents, & have then described the excitement and alarm caused by their misrepresentations as the fruits of the Bill itself.

Pray understand that by the opponents I mean the opponents sitting opposite. Nearly all who object on our side of the House have been most moderate and cautious.

Had the Debates been of the ordinary length & course, the Bill would have passed for the small measure that it is, and a few ordinarily rational decisions of the Judges would speedily have established its limited and strictly practical character.

But the intermediate discussions, as well as the heated language, have tended to cause the Irish people to regard it as a measure of vast magnitude, which is of itself a very dangerous misconception.

In the meantime, while every explanation we offer to the Tories is received by them (I except the late *Cabinet*) as fresh food for obstruction, and any concession we offer them is repelled as worthless, a large majority of Irish members support the Bill, and in a testing division yesterday their numbers were *for* 55 *against* 14.

Under these circumstances I would on my side request you also to consider the situation, & what is best to be done; for I am sure your candour will perceive that from any point of view the objections to the withdrawal of the Bill are, to say the very least, neither few nor small.[2]

18. 8 S. Trin.

Mill Hill Ch mg & evg. Walk with C. Read Leathes on Prophecy—Knox Little's Sermons[3]—Church's Socrates[4]—Chaucer.

[1] Expressed on 16 July; Add MS 44465, f. 116.
[2] Fitzwilliam replied (19 July, Add MS 44465, f. 133) that he hoped the form of deb. would allow the bill's withdrawal 'with dignity'.
[3] See 27 June 80.
[4] F. J. Church, *The trial and death of Socrates* (1880).

19. M. [*London*]

Returned to D. St at 11½. Saw Mr Hamilton—Sir T.G.—Ld R.G.—Ld Granville—Ld F. Cavendish. Wrote to Mr Dodson—Ld Shaftesbury—Mr Lodge¹—Ld Granville—Mr Westell—Ld Listowel—Sir C. Dilke—The Queen—& minutes. Read Q.R. on Ministry—Ed. Rev. on Ministry—Do on the Divorce.² H of C. 4¼-8¼ & 8¾-3 AM: much exhausted.³

To J. G. DODSON, president of the local government board,   Add MS 44544, f. 37.
19 July 1880. 'Private'.

There is a pleasure in receiving your very prompt and handsome letter,⁴ but it does not outweigh the pain of learning the unfortunate result at Chester.

In no case can I think it right that you should at present resign your office. I hope that some early opportunity of replacing you in Parliament may arise. I will not abandon at once even the hope that Waddy's point of law may be found to have something in it. You will be much missed in all proceedings on the Employers' Liability Bill during your exclusion, if excluded you are: but your help even from without will be of great value. And let us see what a little time may bring forth.

To LORD LISTOWEL, lord-in-waiting, 19 July 1880.   Add MS 44544, f. 37.
'*Private*'.

I have received your letter⁵ with much concern. But as your responsibility with regard to the Disturbance Bill will not begin, at soonest, before its arrival in the House of Lords, and as the time at least of that arrival is as yet uncertain, I hope I may at any rate interpret your letter as only a notice of what you intend to do.

I should like if you will allow me to send for your perusal, when I recover it, a letter, now in circulation among my colleagues, from Fitzwilliam;⁶ with my reply, which does not argue the matter at length, but rather describes the present 'situation'.
I send the letters which have come in.

20. Tu.

Wrote to Ld Hardinge—Mr Richard MP—The Queen—Sir C. Dilke Bt.—Ld Granville—Lady Fitzgerald—and minutes. Twelve to dinner. H. of C. 2¼-7 and 9¼-1. Working the Revenue Bill.⁷ Saw Dr A. Clark. Saw Mr Godley—Lord RG—Lord F.C.—Ld Wolverton—Dean of Westminster-& others.

21. Wed.

Wrote to Ld Granville—Bp of Chester—Mr Summer [*sc.* Summers]—Mr Robartes MP—Mrs Molyn—The Queen—& minutes. Saw Mr Godley—Ld RG—

¹ Probably John W. Lodge of Sowerby Bridge; corresponded earlier in 1880; Hawn P.
² *Edinburgh Review*, clii. 281, 258 (July 1880).
³ Compensation for Disturbance Bill; *H* 254. 787.
⁴ Of 18 July, Add MS 44252, f. 78; election found void on petition and the writ suspended; Dodson was elected at Scarborough on 31 July on the resignation of Sir H. V. B. Johnstone.
⁵ Resigning as unable to support the 'Irish Land Bill' in the Lords; Add MS 44465, f. 135. Resignation successfully delayed, see 16 Aug. 80.
⁶ See 17 July 80.
⁷ And questions; *H* 254. 901.

Ld F.C.—Sir H. Ponsonby—Mr Morley—& others. H of C. 12¼-5¾.[1] Finished Love's Labour Lost: poor. Dined at Ld Airlie's.

22. Th.

Wrote to D. of Argyll—Ld Hardinge—Ld Kimberley 1.2.—Ld Granville—Ld Houghton—The Queen 1.2.—Mr Fremantle—Ld Chancellor—Mr D'Arley[2]—Mr Forster—Rev. Mr Eyre—& minutes. Saw Mr Godley—Ld RG—Ld F.C.—Mr Forster *cum* Mr Law—Mr Dodson—Sir E. May—The Speaker—The Law Officers—Mr West. H of C. 4¼-12½: ½ h. tea, ¾ h dinner at home.[3]

23. Fr.

Wrote to Mr Broadhurst MP.—Ld Granville 1.2.—The Queen 1.2.3 (Tel) 4 (Tel)—Sir C. Ducane—& minutes. Read Henry VIII. Saw Mr Godley—Ld R.G.—Ld F.C.—Marquise du .... H. of C. 2¼-7 and 9½-2.[4] Dined at B. Alfred de Rothschild's. A severe week: rather overdone.

[The inside back cover contains:—]
　　　　　　　　　　3 Euston Grove NW
Rev T.G. Law Sidney Cottage Bushy Heath Herts
A. Thorndike Rice 551 Broadway New York
Rev. R.R. Suffield 60 South Street Reading
Mr G. Harris 94 Highbury New Park. N.
J. Cowan, Beeslade, Edinb.
　　　44 Denbigh Street

Hyacinthe 7 Rue Rochechouart
J. Hill. 7 Bridport St Blandford Square[5]

---

[1] Revenue Bill; *H* 254. 1058.
[2] George Steel Darley of Rotherham; see Add MS 44462, f. 56.
[3] Spoke on Post Office Bill; *H* 254. 1162.
[4] Working the Revenue Bill; *H* 254. 1208.
[5] Also some deleted and illegible writing in pencil.

[Volume XXXIV][1]

[The inside front cover contains:—]

Semino in onda, e fabrico in arena
Persuado lo scoglio, e prego il vento
Adone XIII. 26.[2]

Private.

No 34.

JULY 24. 1880–AP. 9. 82.

O, 'tis a burden, Cromwell, 'tis a burden
Too heavy for a man that hopes for heaven
Henry VIII. iii. 2

For my part, my sole concern is to manage the third & last act of my life with
decency, & to make a handsome exit from off the stage. Provided this point is
secured, I am not solicitous about the rest. *I am already, by nature, condemned to
death. No man can give me a pardon from this sentence: nor so much as procure me a
reprieve.*

Bp Gardeyner (Burke, Portrait II, 272)[3]

Er that das gute und rechte, meist ohne sich um die gewinnende form zu
bekümmern.

Stahr's Tiberius p. 73.[4]

τι ταῦτα; ενεβης, ἐπλεύοτις [*sc.* ἐπλευσας], κατήχθης. Ἔκβηθι.
M. Aur. Ant. III. 4[5]

227 O St.
The Cottage The Green N. Hampstead.

[1] Lambeth MS 1448.
[2] G. B. Marino, *Adone*, canto xiii, stanza 26, lines 1-2.
[3] See 28 July 80n.
[4] Adolf Stahr, *Tiberius* (1863), 73: 'He does what is good and right, usually without bothering
himself about the profitable form.'
[5] Marcus Aurelius, *Meditations*, iii. 3: 'What of this? You have embarked [on life], you have set sail,
you have come to port: now go ashore'; cf. C. Bonner, *Harvard Theological Review*, xxxiv. 49 (1941).

Sat. Jul. 24. 1880. [Littleburys]

Wrote to Dep. Master Trin House[1]—Mr R. Bourke MP—Sir Thos G.—Baron Ferrieres[2]—Mr Tillet MP—The Queen—Mr C.S. Read—and minutes. Read Shakesp.—Nouvelle Revue. Saw Mr Godley—Ld R.G.—Ld Kimberley. Saw Howard [R]. Abandoned, through fatigue the Trinity House Dinner: & went off at 6 to Littleburys. Cabinet 2-4½.

Cabinet. Jul. 24. 80. 2 p.m.[3]

✓ 1. Employers Liability. Insurance Clauses. Not to be accepted.

✓ 2. Parl. business. Thursday. Ind[ian] Financial statement: *hoped* for Aug. 5.

✓ 3. Ld. Waveney. Candahar to be a free City. To be got rid of: premature & injurious.[4]

✓ 4. Irish Land Commission. Rate of progress: leave it to its course.

✓ 5. Irish Land Commissn. (Bessb[orough], Dowse, O'Connor Don, Kavanagh, Shaw) add to? Stop as you are.

✓ 6. Merchant Shipping Bill in conformity with Report of the Committee. Bring in: & *alors comme alors*.

✓ 7. Goschen's Tel. of Jul. 23. Does it lead up to a place of liberty for cutting out of Anglo-Turkish Convention. To be done by conversation, not a note, as to the reproach on breach of Treaty.

✓ 8. Census in Armenia: to be approximate & very rapid.

✓ 9. Rotumah or Granville [*sc.* Grenville] Island: add to Fiji Group.[5]

9.[*sic*] Sir B. Frere. Conversation.

Jul. 24 [1880]. That the only hope for the Ottoman Power is to be found in the model offered by the best examples of local autonomy: the Lebanon, Samos, Crete. That the Turkish Govt. if it decline the decision of the Mediators is hurrying on to the ruin of the Empire. That a moral conflict, much more than a material collision, with the Powers will probably distort the peace throughout the Empire & that wherever it is disturbed the Sultan's authority may & in some cases certainly will never be restored.[6]

To R. BOURKE, M.P., 24 July 1880.   Add MS 44544, f. 39.

In your temperate speech of last night,[7] you appeared to believe that I had never before admitted the serious responsibility which I had incurred by persistently and strongly questioning much of the Foreign policy of the late Government. My recollection is that I had done this even with wearisome iteration. It would be difficult to ransack matter which in one form and another is enough to fill volumes; but two references can at once be given to passages which, though not the fullest that might be found, completely admit

[1] Declining the dinner.

[2] Baron Charles Conrad Adolphus De Ferrières, 1823-1908; liberal M.P. Cheltenham 1880-5.

[3] Add MS 44642, f. 57. Items of business printed as re-ordered by Gladstone.

[4] Waveney withdrew his motion on 28 July; *H* 254. 1660.

[5] Annexed to Fiji in May 1881; see W. P. Morrell, *Britain in the Pacific Islands* (1960), 169. Kimberley to Gladstone, 20 July 1880, Add MS 44225, f. 192: 'I want to make a tiny annexation, namely the island of Rotumah.'

[6] Add MS 44642, f. 60; holograph note.

[7] With a brief exchange on this point; *H* 254. 1293. Bourke replied: 'I am glad to learn that you approve the doctrine of *unofficial* responsibility'; Add MS 44465, f. 169.

the principle, which you are quite right in jealously asserting. I send the extracts (Hansard. Vol. 232 (1877) p. 554 & 242 (1878) 672.d.) herewith.

25. 9 S. Trin.

Mill Hill Ch mg & aft. A. Lyttelton & others from London. Walk with him. A fine fellow in deed & truth. Read Church's Socrates—Grinfield Hist of Preaching (poor)[1]—... on Newmans Apologia—Jenkins on The Western Schism.[2]

26. M. [London]

Wrote to Ld Granville—The Queen 1.2.—and minutes. 10-11¼ Back to London, much renovated. Dined at Sir E. May's. H. of C. 4½-8¼ and 9¾-2. Spoke ¾ hours on 3 R. Disturbance Bill.[3] Worked on the papers. Saw Mr G[odley]—Ld RG—Herbert J.G.—Sir C. Dilke—Mr Law. Read Henry VIII.

27. Tu.

Wrote to Mr Caine (Tel.)—Ld Kimberley—The Queen—Mr Forster—and minutes. Read Henry VIII. Saw Mr G—Ld R.G.—Ld F.C. cum Mr Welby—Ld F.C.—Mr Fawcett—The Attorney General—Mr Herries. H of C 3½-7: and 10¾-11¾.[4] Saw Mrs St Maur: also ... [R]. 14 to dinner. Conversation with Abp of C. on the Clerical Univ. question.

28. Wed.

Wrote to Mr Herries—Ld Hartington—The Queen—and minutes. Dined at Sir W. Harcourts. Saw Mr G—Ld R.G.—Ld F.C.—Mr Monro—Ly Harcourt, and Mrs [blank.] Saw Gibson—Grantry [R]. H. of C 12½-6: working the Customs & I.R. Bill. The Opposition blundered sadly![5] Read Henry VIII—Burke on Tudor period.[6]

29. Th.

Wrote to The Queen 1.2.—Ld Granville—Ld Kimberley—Ld Advocate—Mr Jolly—Mr Maclaren M.P.—Lord Provost of Edinburgh[7] and minutes. H. of C. 4½-7¾ and 10½-2.[8] Saw Mr G.—Ld R.G.—Ld F.C.—Mr Waddington (bis)—Dean of St Pauls—Sir A. Paget. Read Henry VIII. Q.R. on M. Antoinette.[9] Twelve to breakfast.

---

[1] T. Grinfield, *The History of Preaching* (1880).
[2] R. C. Jenkins, *Privilege of Peter and the claims of the Roman church* (1874).
[3] It was then 3°R; *H* 254. 1436.
[4] Questioned on Dodson's vacation of seat; *H* 254. 1529.
[5] Lord G. Hamilton's motion to prevend 1*d*. increase in income tax defeated in 230:94; *H* 254. 1628.
[6] S. H. Burke, *Historical portraits of the Tudor dynasty and the reformation period*, 4v. (1879-83); see fly-leaf quotation at 24 July 80.
[7] On Scottish land reform; *T.T.*, 3 August 1880, 5f.
[8] Spoke on Hares and Rabbits Bill; *H* 254. 1756.
[9] *Quarterly Review*, cl. 141 (July 1880).

30. Fr.

Wrote to Mr Hardcastle—Mr Pease ... and minutes. H. of C. 2½-7. (1 hour at home).[1] Seized with chill & nausea. Better when warmed.

To LORD KIMBERLEY, colonial secretary, 30 July 1880.　　　　　Add MS 44544, f. 41.

Here is the Queen's reply; & a telegram which I will send immediately, for I think there is no doubt what it should be. I have put off Lawson until Monday. To be hurried in the choice of a successor is an astonishing return for our long-suffering in keeping Frere in office.[2]

By hook or by crook we ought to be able to give an answer on Monday.

31. Sat.

Wrote to[3]—The Queen 1.2 & (Tel) 4.

Such was the state of my nerves and muscular system on Saturday the 31st, as it is exhibited by the lines written above. I was mercifully spared having to return to the House last night at nine. I slept ten hours: saw Mr G. Harris on Seaforth affairs and got up at 11 seemingly well. I went into the cold room, saw Mr G., Ld R.G., & Lord Kimberley on Frere's case: got all ready for the Cabinet at 2. Meantime I had been for ¾ of an hour not shivering but shaking as a house is shaken by an earthquake. I had a fire lighted, & put on a thick coat, & proceeded with my work. But C. got sight of me & wisely went off to Dr Clark who peremptorily forbad the Cabinet & all business whatever & sent me into bed about 2. PM.[4]

Jul 31 Aug 3. 1880.

Close confinement to bed, strong & prolonged perspirations, poulticing, hot drinks & medicines. Temp. fell from 103 to 101 at night, & to 100 Sunday morning, but rose again to 103 by the evening. No reading writing or business; only thoughts. I did not suffer. On Sunday I thought of the end—in case the movement had continued—coming nearer to it by a little than I had done before: but not as in expectation of it. C. read me the service. Monday the temperature had fallen I think to 101-2 but it was thought well to call in Sir W. Jenner whom I greatly liked in his *clinical* character. He was very strict about the economies, e.g. of speech and effort. On Tues. however I saw Godley & dictated a letter[5] respecting tomorrow's Cabinet. In the evg the temperature had gone down—& Dr C. was delighted: thought the battle won.

[1] Questions, Hares and Rabbits Bill; *H* 254. 1784.

[2] Kimberley replied (31 July, Add MS 44225, f. 213): 'we ... must make the best of it' and proposed Hercules Robinson as Frere's successor; see 24 Dec. 80.

[3] Illegible name; handwriting deteriorates markedly from 29 July, to virtual illegibility at this point.

[4] Draft notes in Hamilton's hand for cabinet read: 'Cabinet. Jul 31. 80. 2 PM. Afghanistan. Obstruction. Frere'; Add MS 48607, bundle 1. Following the British defeat at Maiwand, Ripon was given full discretion to reconsider the question of Kandahar; Sher Ali was persuaded to leave; Gopal, *Ripon*, 23. See also 12 Nov. 80.

[5] To Granville, in Ramm II, i. 155. Compensation for Disturbance Bill overwhelmingly defeated in Lords on 3 August.

Wed Aug 4- Fr. Aug 6.

Another phase—When Sir W. J[enner] came in the morning the temperature was declared at 99 and the lung congestion to be gone: reading permitted. During these days I saw my sons & daughters—Ld R.G.—Ld F.C. (S.B. Bill)—Ld Chancellor (Burial's Bill)—Ld Hartington—Sir R.P.[1] Dr C[lark] incessant in visits, and unbounded in kindness. Read Shakespeare—Burke, Tudor Portraits—Fortnightly, Religious Liberty and French Land[2]—Madame de Remusat, Preface by her son.[3] The permission to read took effect on Wed, & was a great boon. Each day was a day of progress. Physic soon gone by. The only annoyance remaining was irritation of the back from poultices: but this became milder each night, & each day. I slept nine hours each night: & came to look more 'well' than on Thursday before the chill when I felt like a piece of wood. C. was incessantly with me: an incomparable nurse, in all the higher aspects. Under her Mrs Hampton was installed. I had no serious care except on the Convocation Clause of the Burials Bill: & this was removed by the determination of the Cabinet to hold to the Bill in its original framework.

To C. J. HERRIES, Chairman of the Board of Inland Revenue,   Add MS 44544, f. 42.
6 August 1880.

I avail myself of one of the earliest moments of returning capacity for business to write to you.

Let me first thank you for the great ability, and no less conspicuous patience, and kindness with which you have assisted me in the rather arduous matter of our Inland Revenue legislation.

And, bearing in mind that this is now the 6th of August, let me beg that you will proceed to make your arrangements for vacations in your Departments, with no let or hindrance, unless such as the limited demands of the measure in the House of Lords may entail.

Will you also perform for me the very pleasing duty of conveying my thanks to those who have assisted you and me from the day when we first opened the subject until now.

I can only say that I have always been accustomed to look back on the business transacted with the Inland Revenue Department in former years as coming nearest among all my experience to what I should consider a model, on their side, of good public service, and that that experience of former years has been completely revived in the transactions of the last three months.

7. Sat.

Wrote to Mr Reed MP. Read Fortnightly Rev. on Spn of American Colonies[4]—Mad. du Remusat, Intr. & Vol. I.—What a character of Napoleon!—Burke's Tudor Portraits: finished Vol. II.—He too is a partisan. Saw Mr Godley—Ld L. Gr.—Ld Granville—Dr Clark found me advancing: it is a new stage: I dressed fully & left my room. To bed at 10½ PM.

[1] 'Had an interview with G. wh. lasted nearly ½ an hour. He looked & was better than I had expected to find him. He talked most of the time—not about politics, but on Shakespeare's Henry VIII & the decay of theological study at Oxford. This distresses him, but he saw no effectual remedy. He never intended his [1854] Reform measure to produce this result'; Phillimore's Diary.

[2] *Fortnightly Review*, xxxiv. 1, 8 (July 1880).   [3] See 2 July 80.

[4] *Fortnightly Review*, xxxiv. 147 (August 1880).

8. *11 S. Trin.*

Good daily progress, appetite returning, moisture of atmosphere prevented my going out. Dr C. only came once. Mg & evg prayers, *solus*. Saw Ld Granville—Lady Herbert—Mr Godley—W.H.G. (Worcester Canonry &c.).[1] Read Ewald, Gesch. des Volk's Israel[2]—Voysey, Sermon[3]—Morgan, Hymn Transl.[4]—Quarter Sessions of Eliz[?] XVII[5]—Sir W. Palmer, English Reformation.[6]

9. *M.* [*Windsor*]

Wrote to Arthur Lyttelton—Mr Macmillan—and minutes. I rose for luncheon: started at 4½ for Windsor. Received at the Deanery with infinite kindness: & much enjoyed the evening's conversation. Saw Mr Godley—Ld R.G.—Ld F.C.—Mr West—Ld Granville. Read Madame de Remusat—Ewald, Geschichte—Contemp. Review.

10. *Tu.*

St Georges 3 P.M. Saw Ronald Gower—Lady Cowell Stepney—Dr Clark—E. Hamilton. Much conversation with the Dean. Long & beautiful drive in the noble Park. What an abode for Majesty this is! It is all Majesty. Saw the new Monuments. Read 19th Century—Manning (trash) & Justin MacCarthy[7]—Mad. de Remusat—Ewald Geschichte.

11. *Wed.*

Wrote to Mr Welby—Ld Granville (2)—and minutes. Also dictated a Memm on the case of Convocation with ref. to the Burials' Bill.[8] Drive to St Leonards. Walk on the Terrace, ¾ hour, a great advance. Much conversation with the Dean. Saw Mr E. Hamilton—Mrs Hamilton—Mr Anson. Read Mad. de Remusat—La Conference de Berlin—Tuke's Irish Pamphlet.[9]

To R. E. WELBY, 11 August 1880.   Add MS 44544, f. 42.

Unless it can be shewn that there is some particular virtue on behalf of India in the proposal to let drop into her lap £550,000 at the particular times when the quarterly payments ought to be made, I am unfavourable to giving piece-meal relief in this form. Were I favourable to it, individually, I should not consider it to lie within my discretion but should consult the Cabinet. If the Indian Department attaches a particular value to the concession, they ought to present us with the best sketch they can of their prospective cash account.

[1] Successfully offered to W. J. Butler of Wantage on 17 Aug.; see 8 June 57.

[2] See 23 May 80.

[3] C. Voysey, probably a sermon in *The mystery of pain, death and sin* (1878); see 2 July 76.

[4] D. T. Morgan, *Hymns and other poetry of the Latin church* (1880).

[5] Perhaps ch. i of A. H. A. Hamilton, *Quarter sessions from Queen Elizabeth to Queen Anne* (1878).

[6] W. Palmer, *Compendious ecclesiastic history* (new ed. 1880), though Palmer was not a knight.

[7] H. E. Manning, 'An Englishman's protest'; J. McCarthy, 'The landowners' panic', *Nineteenth Century*, viii. 177, 305 (August 1880).

[8] Add MS 44625, f. 51; on the 14th clause, dispensing clergy from penalties and referring to convocation's resolutions; see *Life of Tait*, ii. 404 and Ramm II, i. 158.

[9] J. H. Tuke, *Irish distress and its remedies. The land question* (1880).

Have you heard anything as to the idea of a large economy by the reduction of balances in India, or is the information, which will be necessary in order to [make?] a judgment on this important matter, in a tolerably forward state of preparation?
[P.S.] I take into view with respect to the £550,000 that the time is very unfortunate & inconvenient for us. At the same time, this of course is not a vital matter. It would be a great advantage to consider the whole subject together; & this there is still much reason to hope we can do in the Recess.

12. Th.

St George's 3 P.M. Wrote minutes. Drive with C. Much conversation with the Dean; and further advance in convalescence. Read Tuke on Ireland—Mad. de Remusat—and [blank.]

13. Fr.

St Georges 3 P.M. Wrote to Ld Granville (2)—Ld F. Cavendish—Mr Kitson jun.—and minutes. Finished Mem. on Convocation. Drive with the Dean &c. Walk & much conversation with him. Visited the Garden & the very remarkable Mausoleum.[1] Read Mad. de Remusat—Tuke on Ireland finished—Tuke on do in 19th Cent.[2]

To J. KITSON, 13 August 1880.   Add MS 44544, f. 43.

I have not yet resumed on any large scale the transaction of business, but I think the time has come when I ought to write to you on the subject of my intended visit to Leeds.

I have no doubt that I ought to avoid during the coming autumn any addition to my necessary duties, which can properly be dispensed with, and I am therefore desirous to be permitted to postpone for the year that visit to which I have looked forward with the greatest interest.

That this is a postponement only I need hardly give you my assurance; for until I shall have personally appeared in Leeds to acknowledge the unbounded kindness of your great community both to myself and specially to my son Herbert, I shall feel with uneasiness that I have one clear and definite duty palpably unfulfilled.

I feel sure you will be sensible of the weight of the prudential motives which lead me to make this request.[3]

14. Sat. [Holmbury][4]

Back to London at 11½. Wrote to Ld Hartington—Messrs Townshend & Barker—Mr Talbot M.P.—Mrs Th.—The Queen 1.2.—Scotts (2) and minutes. Read Mad. de Remusat. Saw Ld Hartington—Ld Granville (2)—Mr Forster—Mr Childers—Ld F.C.—Mr Hamilton—Dr A. Clark—Mr Gabbitas. After four hours of business (a great step onwards) I went with a party to Holmbury: following orders I only appeared in the evening.

[1] The royal mausoleum at Frogmore.
[2] On peasant proprietors; *Nineteenth Century*, viii. 182 (August 1880).
[3] See 7 Oct. 81 for Gladstone's visit to Leeds.
[4] Lord E. F. Leveson-Gower's place in Surrey. See F. Leveson-Gower, *Bygone years* (1905), 299.

To LORD HARTINGTON, Indian secretary, 14 August 1880.　　　Add MS 44544, f. 43.

I am not, I think, disposed to give too much weight to the parsimonious tendencies of a Chancellor of the Exchequer in the matter of Indian Finance & our contribution to the War.

But there seem to me to be two conclusive reasons against the amendment of a plan at present.

1. That it must be highly disadvantageous to *announce* the basis of a plan without getting the assent of Parliament to it; but it is too soon to ask the assent of Parliament for we cannot give it sufficient information.

2. That the question raised about Indian Treasury balances forms so considerable an element in the case that it cannot be put out of view & should if possible be decided before we make up our own minds.

The *hope* of winding up the affair this autumn is a hope only but it seems a solid one, & the ground in this case is so arid that it is most desirable that our proposal when it appears should be complete.

15. 12 S. Trin.

Ch with Holy C mg. Garden walk with Granville—D. of Argyll. Read Ewald, Volk Israel—Green, Hist. Henry VIII[1]—Catholic Presbyterian[2]—Knox Little, Sermons[3]—Bp Milman on Convalescence.[4]

16. M.

Wrote to Ld Listowel—Ld Chancellor—Ld Zetland—Lady M. Alford—Miss Canning—The Queen—Mr Hamilton. Read Me de Remusat—Green's History—Hamilton Speech & Mem.[5] Saw Ld Granville—Duke of Argyll—Mr Bright, on the recital about Convocation which makes me anxious. Drive with our kind host. Walk with C.

To LORD LISTOWEL, lord-in-waiting, 16 August 1880.　　　Add MS 44544, f. 44.

I am beginning to resume business, & I take an early opportunity of assuring you of the great regret with which I submit to Her Majesty your resignation of office in the Household.

Whatever my own belief as to the necessity, & the innocence, of the measure rejected by the House of Lords, & however inconvenient the consequences *may* prove, I freely own that many sound & attached Liberals shared your scruples, & I sincerely trust the incident may in no way affect your general relations to the party or the Government.

[P.S.] Forgive my limiting the sense of the word 'many' by saying that it is used in comparison with other more or less similar occasions.

To LORD ZETLAND, lord-in-waiting, 16 August 1880.　　　Add MS 44544, f. 44.

Illness interfered sadly with the regularity of my business, & it is only now that I find time to assure you directly of what you know through other channels, the great regret with which I received the intimation of your views respecting the Disturbance Bill, & with which I submit to the Queen your resignation of Office.[6]

---

[1] In J. R. Green, *History of the English people*, 4v. (1877-80).
[2] *Catholic Presbyterian*, iv (August 1880).
[3] See 27 June 80.　　　　　　　　　　　　　　　　　[4] R. Milman, *Convalescence* (1865).
[5] Probably by J. G. C. Hamilton, the liberal M.P. (see 23 Jan. 71), but neither letter nor mem. traced.
[6] Zetland's letter of resignation of 19 July 1880, Add MS 44465, f. 150.

With full reserve of my own convictions, I do no more than justice in admitting that as a matter of fact you had not a few companions, especially in the House of Lords, who shared your leanings on this occasion, & whose zealous liberalism could not be questioned. I earnestly hope therefore that what has occurred may stand as an isolated fact, & may not in any way be found to affect your future & general relation towards the party.

To LORD SELBORNE, lord chancellor, 16 August 1880.   Selborne MS 1867, f. 108.

I have asked Bright (who has been here) and he has kindly undertaken for me to find out if he can whether there is likely to be any serious movement against the recital in the Burials Bill about the action of Convocation.[1]

It is so much an established practice to make recitals of this kind in the case of Ecclesiastical Legislation undertaken by the Government—though the cases have been mostly those of Commissions, because Commissions have been more frequently employed—and it is in every way so reasonable and appropriate, that I cannot regard the omission as anything less than a deliberate slight or, in other words an insult.

This is a step with regard to which I cannot compromise: it is contrary to my personal honour to have anything to do with such a proceeding. I consider myself to have been pledged to the Clergy, by a long course of conduct, to oppose them without fear when civil right requires it, but in all cases to treat them with respect. In this way I have tried to maintain some harmony between the orders of the state, and to bring the Clergy not to look upon Liberals as necessarily enemies. About Establishment I care less than many, and about the other amendment in the B. Bill I care little (*except* so far as good faith to the Archbishop requires) but on this matter I am very stiff. I assume that the University members who are a kind of representatives of the Clergy will not throw them over. If they did, *that* might make a difference.

17. Tu.

Wrote to The Queen—Abp of Canterbury—Rev. Mr Butler—J.G. Talbot—Bp of Jerusalem—Ld Granville—Dean of Worcester & minutes. Drive to Gomshall & walk. Read Made de R.—Daudet's Jack.[2] Saw Ld R. Grosvenor.

To A. C. TAIT, Archbishop of Canterbury, 17 August 1880.   Add MS 44331, f. 139.

I received on Saturday your Grace's letter respecting a change in the composition of the Lower House of the Convocation of Canterbury.[3] And I shall be happy to bring the matter under the consideration of my Colleagues.

This can be done, if your Grace desires it, before the Government separates for the recess but I should advise if there be no urgent reason to the contrary that the matter should stand over until the Cabinet meet in the Autumn, when, as I think, there would be a better opportunity of giving it consideration.

I consider your Grace to convey and concur in a desire that the Licences of the Crown should be given for the framing of a Canon to effect the proposed change.

I return herewith the two inclosures of which I keep copies.[4]

[P.S.] I feel very much the kindness of your Grace's separate note[5] and I have much reason to be thankful for the excellent progress I have made.

---

[1] Copy of the Bill with copious emendations by Selborne at Add MS 44297, f. 69.
[2] A. Daudet, *Jack. Moeurs contemporaines*, 2v. (1876).
[3] Sent on 14 August, Add MS 44331, f. 134.
[4] Ibid., f. 141.
[5] On his illness.

18. Wed.

Down to breakfast. Wrote to Ld Hartington (2)—Ld Chancellor—Helen G.—
J.G. Talbot M.P.—Mr Godley—Mr Cowan M.P.—A. Austin—Ld Granville Tel.
and L.—and minutes. Drive to Shere[1] & walk with my host. Saw Ld F.C. in evg.
Whist in evg. Read 'Jack'—Mad. de Remusat.

To LORD SELBORNE, lord chancellor, 18 August 1880.   Add MS 44544, f. 45.

Many thanks for your letter.[2] The only qualification I feel inclined to apply to it is that
I attach a greater importance than you appear to do to the position & action of the University Members. I hardly see how the Government can support its dealings with the
Archbishop in the face of their hostile action; to so great an extent do I view them, &
they have always been viewed, as representatives of the clergy. Walpole was always as
weak as water, and he seems now to be weaker. One would almost say a new gender is
required for him, bearing the same ratio to feminine that feminine does to masculine.
This is rather illnatured about so good a man.
[P.S.] See W's speech on Bouverie's motion in 1870.

19. Th.

Wrote to Mr Godley—Ld Ed. Granville—Sir H. Verney—Mr Bright—The
Queen—Mr Childers and minutes. Read Me de Remusat—Miot Melito's Mem.
(began)[3]—Daudet's Jack. Harry came. Drove to Abinger & Wotton. Walk with
F.L.G[ower].

To John BRIGHT, chancellor of the duchy, 19 August 1880.   Add MS 43385, f. 282.

Many thanks for your letter.[4] You have done, kindly & handsomely, all that was possible
from your point of view.
As regards myself, my position is as follows. I think it irrational, and illiberal, to object
to the recital of the action of Convocation in a matter, in which they were specially empowered to act by the Crown i.e. the Ministry. If this was wrong, the objection lay against
the conduct of the Ministry in so empowering them. When thus empowered, they
become to all practical intents and purposes a Commission acting under the Crown.
Had they been a Commission, no one would have objected to the recital, which is I
may say in these cases a matter of course. But a slight is to be passed upon them because
they are the Clergy; although they acted like a Commission, under the responsible minister of the day.
I think this argument is rather hard to answer.
However the Clergy have certain virtual representatives of their own, the members,
namely, for Oxford and Cambridge Universities.
If these representatives hold by the Clause as it is, i.e. with its recital, then I feel myself
bound to make an effort to come up to town before the Clause comes on, to see Richard
and his friends if they will come to see me, and to attend the House if necessary.
But if these representatives of the Clergy take a different view, or are so divided as to

[1] Visiting Lord Arthur Russell at The Ridgeway, Shere.
[2] Of 17 August, Add MS 44297, f. 71, on 'very great ... sensitiveness of the Liberal clergy of the
higher school'.
[3] *Mémoires du Comte de Mélito*, 3v. (3rd ed. 1880).
[4] Of 17 August, Add MS 44113, f. 130, on the word 'Christian' in the Burials Bill, and the Convocation 'recital'. No reply found.

have collectively no view at all, then I do not know that I should be called upon to take, or justified in taking, this forward position. I should then rather incline to stand by, and let the Clause take its chance with the other amendments, although I have already stated what I think of this amendment in itself. In *this* case probably it would be as well that I should be out of the way when the Bill goes into & through Committee?

Meanwhile I have taken means to ascertain *what* is the sense, or no sense, of these University members; and I hope to be in possession of it some time today.

There is another idea on foot about adjourning the House, which might for the *present* dispense with all these discussions: but on this I need not enter—you may be more advanced when this reaches you, in your knowledge of it than I am. I will send a copy of what I have written to Hartington.

20. Fr.

Wrote to Mr Bright—Ld Granville 1.2.—Mr Wylie—Mr Godley 2 & Tel. Stationmaster Gomshall—The Lord Advocate and minutes. Read as yesterday. Drive & walk with Mrs L. C. went to London to attend in Harley St. Whist in evg.

To John BRIGHT, chancellor of the duchy, 20 August 1880.   Add MS 43385, f. 286.

I find that the University members, representatives of the Clergy, have no united or decided opinion about the Convocation Clause, but want to bargain with the Govt. to let the Mt. Edgecombe Clause stand—in which I presume they will fail. Under these circumstances, I shall not feel myself bound to take any very special or personal part as to the Convocation Clause but shall stand content with the general intention of the Govt. to hold to its terms with the Archbishop if it can.

Looking at the two questions (a) of the recital (b) of the enacting part, my impression is that the Clergy will be a good deal divided on b. but not on a. I think Mr Fowler[1] will very likely burn his fingers with *his* clause of relief—so far as I can judge without knowing its precise terms. What the Nonconformists ought seriously to consider (on your advice) is I think this: *whether they are wise in provoking a risk of postponing the Bill?* For it should be borne in mind that the House of Lords will be strong in replacing anything *which has been supported in both Houses by the Government*. I may perhaps come to the House when the Bill is on, & if so I may state the reasons for Clause 14 *quoad* the recital, which appear to me not less simple than on historical grounds conclusive.

21. Sat. [London: Holmbury]

Off at 8½ to London for the Cabinet 12-2¼. Back to Holmbury at 6¾. Worked in London. Wrote to The Queen 1.2.3.—Ld Lyttelton—Ld Cardwell—Ld Dalhousie—and minutes. Saw Ld Granville—Mr Godley—Ld R.G. Read Daudet's Jack—Me de Remusat. Party enlarged: much conversation; and Whist.

Cabinet. Aug. 21. 80. Noon.[2]
1. H. of L. business. To persevere with the Bills. Press Constabulary vote.
2. Telegrams about Dulcigno approved—without the annex.
3. Ld. G. to converse with Labanoff [*sic*] on the Kauffmann correspondence.[3]

[1] Proposed amndt. by H. H. Fowler, see Bright to Gladstone, 17 August 1880, Add MS 44113, f. 130.   [2] Add MS 44642, f. 62.
[3] Correspondence on Central Asia and Kauffmann's supposed 'hostility and duplicity' since 1878, which Gladstone believed not proven; Ramm II, i. 163.

22. 15 Trin.

Ch. mg & evg. Saw Mr Bowman—Sir L. Pelly—Mr Street. Wrote to C.G.—Rev. Mr Savile. Read The Great Secret[1]—Bp Milman's Convalescence—Miss Strickland, the beheaded Queens.[2] Much conversation in evg: but wholly unedifying.

23. M.

Wrote to C.G.—Mr Godley Tel—Ld Spencer—Miss Nimmo[3] and minutes. Walk with F.L. G[ower]—explaining freely to him my views as to the relations between his brother [Granville], Hartington, & myself. He gave his opinion that I ought to remain as long as my health enabled me. Finished Me de Remusat—Read 'Jack'. Whist in evg.

24. Tu. [London]

Back to D. St 1.30. Conversation with General Claremont—& General Morris.[4] Good accounts from Harley St. Saw Ld Granville—Ld Spencer—Ld R. Grosvenor—Mr D. Currie—Mr Forster. Wrote to Ld Hartington—Mr Childers—Ld Lyttelton—Ld Enfield—Ld Waveney—Dr Magnus—Bp of Ceylon—and minutes. Read 'Jack'—Jebb's Greece.[5]

25. Wed.

Wrote to Catherall—Sir W. Harcourt—The Queen 1.2.3.—Ld Carnarvon—Ld Clanricarde—Ld Hartington—Ld Kinnaird—and minutes. Saw Mr Godley—Ld Granville—Mr Westell—Mr Forster—Mr Bright—Mrs Th. Saw Howard. Read Jack (finished) a really notable book in divers points. Read Jebb's Greece.

To LORD HARTINGTON, Indian secretary, 25 August 1880.   Add MS 44544, f. 48.

1. I sent Enfield's note to Granville & you early today.[6]
2. As to Adam I presume you are satisfied that the Governorship in question[7] need under no circumstances be abolished.
3. If this is so, & if he understands the Councils may have to take their chance, I think you are quite ready to proceed.
4. In the regular course, I think it is for you to submit his name to Her Majesty.
4.[sic] I apprehend that no arrangements will be made as to Adam's present office, until we come near the time of his quitting it. I quite agree with you that Courtney should be kept in view; it may be a question whether he stands first on the list.
5. I have passed on without comment the papers about the communication to Abdurrahman; but it appears to me probable that we shall have to see our way about Candahar before we can do much good in that matter.

---

[1] By B. W. Savile (1855).
[2] In vol. iv of Agnes Strickland, Lives of the Queens of England, 12v. (1840-8).
[3] Miss E. Nimmo (distant relative), on Pius IX; Add MS 44544, f. 47.
[4] Edward Stopford Claremont, 1819-90; soldier, military attaché in Paris 1858-71, and courtier; Charles Henry Morris, 1824-87; military attaché in Vienna 1874-5; lieut.-general 1880, retired 1881.   [5] R. C. Jebb, 'Modern Greece; two lectures' (1880).
[6] Responding to Hartington's note of inquiry; Add MS 44145, f. 88.
[7] Of Madras, which W. P. Adam accepted, vacating the first commissionership of works; see 25 Nov. 80.

26. Th. [On ship][1]

Wrote to Miss Canning[2]—Sir A. Gordon M.P.—Ldy M. Alford—Mr Henderson MP.[3]—Rev. Mr Eyre—Ld Ribblesdale—and minutes. Saw Ld Granville—Ld Chancellor—Ld R. Grosvenor—Mr Godley—Mr Hamilton—Mrs Bennett. Preparations for the trip. Off at 2 to Gravesend: address & warm reception. The pauper trust was really interesting. Began D. Copperfield.[4] At night in the Channel.

27. Friday. [On ship: Dartmouth]

Saw (again) Plymouth Harbour, Portland, & spent much of the day in Dartmouth, arrayed in its best by lovely weather & for the regatta. Saw Mr L[acaita]—Mr Gibson. Read D. Copperfield.

28. Sat. [On ship: Falmouth]

Wrote to The Queen—Ld Granville (L. & ciph. Tel)—Ld Lyttelton—Mr Loch— Ly Sandhurst—D. of Bedford and minutes. Read Delphine (began)[5]—David Copperfield: with increasing admiration. Saw Falmouth Harbour & town. Lacaita prudently left us here. Passed the Land's End: then a roll from the Atlantic: well, but on my back.

To the DUKE OF BEDFORD, 28 August 1880.   Add MS 44544, f. 49.

A Garter has fallen vacant by the death of Lord Stratford de Redcliffe, & I have to propose to you with the sanction of the Queen,[6] that you should be added to the Order.

I do not forget your former reply on a like occasion but some men get younger as they live on, & you have drawn closer through the Duchess your relations with the Sovereign.

One word on another subject. You may remember that two years ago we conversed on the subject of the Peerage offered to your brother at Berlin.[7] I then said that,without doubt, in the event of the accession of a Liberal Government to power, there would be no difficulty in his receiving this honour. What was then from me an opinion has become by the force of circumstances a pledge. Yet, in your brother's interest, it seems to me that circumstances also dictate a short delay. He has been called, since we came in, to take a leading part in an important transaction at Berlin. But that transaction, relating to the Greek Frontier, remains as yet of necessity incomplete. What I should like is to wait awhile; & if in a few months the will of Europe shall have taken substantial effect, the Peerage might then be given with *emphasis* & taken with an amount of satisfaction beyond the common.

29. [On ship: Dublin]

Reached Dublin in time to land suddenly & go to Christ Church. The congregation all agog. Out of doors an enthusiastic extempore reception. Off before

[1] Cruising with Donald Currie on his steamship the *Grantully Castle*; daily reports in *T.T.*
[2] Arranging £500 civil list pension for Lady Stratford de Redcliffe; Add MS 44544, f. 49.
[3] Frank Henderson, 1836-89; liberal M.P. Dundee 1880-5.
[4] By *Dickens (1850).   [5] By Mme. de Staël (1802).
[6] The Queen had refused to allow it to be offered to Derby; Bedford accepted, having declined it during the 1868-74 govt.; Bahlman, *Hamilton*, i. 40.
[7] See 19 Sept. 78.

five. Read Row's B. Lecture[1]—The Armenian Church.[2] Quiet waters again today & bright sun. Evening service on board—hymn singing till ten.

30. M. [On ship: Colonsay]

Wrote to Ld Aberdeen—Dean of Windsor—Ld OHagan—Duke of Leinster and minutes. Went over the Hercules.[3] Deputations from Greenock & a short reply. Reached Greenock early after a rapid run. Off before 10 to the South of Bute & outside the Mull. Weather propitious: very little swell. We anchored off Colonsay. Read D. Copperfield—Delphine—Jebb.

31. Tu. [On ship, near Tobermory, Mull]

On to Oban—and from thence to Skye: we landed and went up to Loch Corusk. The Cucullin mountains have more grandeur as far as I know than anything in the Islands. A stiff pull back to the ship. We returned to a point beyond Tobermory for the night. The chief people sent their cards on board. Read as yesterday. Conversation with Dr Clark. Wrote to Granville—l. & two Tels. On the way back from Skye wrote a draft for the Queen's speech.[4] My head was muddled after it.

Wed. Sept. One 1880.

Starting about five in rain (the only rain for 24 days) we had pitching & rolling from the Atlantic off the point of Ardnamurchan for an hour or two but all the rest was prosperous. We saw the grand coasts East & West. The Harris hills are really grand (not like the Cucullins) and Cape Wrath satisfied all expectations. Especially facing the range from the light-house to Garoh. We ran on with great rapidity, saw the Orkneys in the dark, passed Thurso—the abode of Dick[5]—cleared the formidable Pentland [Firth] before eleven & steamed across the Moray firth. Read D.C. Vol II—Delphine—Progress of the World.[6]

2. Th. [On ship: Leith]

Wrote to Granville & supplied an omission in the draft: also Tels: also letter to the Queen. At 5.30 saw the Aberdeenshire land quite close then Aberdeen (dim) Stonehaven, Dunottar, Montrose and the other points. The ship anchored in the Forth. Municipal authorities & liberal associations came on board with addresses. I spoke briefly in reply.[7] We then landed: drove in Leith & Edinburgh. Paid a representative visit to the Lord Provost. Sailed for the South between six & seven: still greatly favoured in our weather. Read D.C.— Delphine—Jebb's Greece.

[1] See 6 Oct. 78.
[2] Perhaps S. C. Malan, *A short summary of the Armenian Church and people* (1868).
[3] A guardship; *T.T.*, 31 August 1880, 6d.
[4] See Ramm II, i. 165.
[5] i.e. of Robert Dick, scientist, whose biography he had read; see 21 Nov. 78.
[6] Perhaps M. G. Mulhall, *World progress since 1800* (1880).
[7] *T.T.*, 3 September 1880, 8b.

3. Frid. [On ship: Yarmouth]

Wrote further for the Queen's Speech. Wrote to. . . . We worked rapidly to the South: anchored in Yarmouth roads. Parties came off: address & reply. On in the evg. Read Delphine—David Copperfield—Progress of the World.

4. Sat. [London]

Early arrival at Gravesend between eight & nine: festal landing after a muster on board and one address of thanks to the Ship's company. Other thanks are indeed due both to God & man for the singularly prosperous circumstances of this voyage. Reached London at 10.30. Saw Granville—Forster with Granville—Sir C. Dilke. Cabinet 12-2. House of C. 2-6½. Received with great warmth. Made rather a long speech on the Eastern question, in great heat; & was much fatigued.[1] Twelve to dinner. Retired early. Read D. Copperfield: to the end. A most noteworthy book—It alters my estimate of Dickens. Wrote to The Queen 1.2. Revised the first part of the speech & dispatched it.

Cabinet. Sept. 4. 80. Noon.[2]
1. Draft Speech for the Prorogation, as printed:[3] further considered & settled.
2. Ld. Granville mentioned form of instruction to Admiral required by the proceeding of the French Govt.[4]

> *Sketch.* Forster did not give or profess to give the opinion of the Govt.—or even his own opinions. He did not refer to any case which had arisen but only a case which might arise on a frequent repetition of certain proceedings. It is therefore easy to say that the Govt. do not entertain the opinion that by the rejection of the Reg[istratio]n Bill or otherwise any occasion has arisen for considering changes in the constit[utio]n of the House of Lords.[5]

5. 15. S. Trin.

Chapel Royal mg. & aft. (H.C.). Wrote to Sir C. Dilke—Ld Granville—Mr Cowan and minutes. Read N.C. on Villon—on Burials Bill[6]—Delphine, what I may call the religious episode—Row, B. Lectures.

To Sir C. W. DILKE, foreign under-secretary, 5 September   Add MS 43875, f. 30.
1880.

I was glad to receive a pretty favourable account of you at your door this afternoon—and I heartily wish you as favourable a recovery as my own.

I should be inclined to tell the Spaniards that for us, as we are governed by fiscal considerations only, the business of negotiation is slight; the only question being whether they & other Powers especially Portugal are disposed to take such steps as would make it

[1] *H* 256. 1318.
[2] Add MS 44642, f. 64.   [3] Add MS 44625, f. 71.
[4] French reluctance over Montenegro; Bahlman, *Hamilton*, i. 44.
[5] Rest, mostly deleted and only partially legible, expresses concern about 'various proceedings' recently in the Lords; Forster's speech on 3 September (*H* 256. 1210) strongly criticized the Lords' actions.
[6] *Nineteenth Century*, viii. 481, 501 (September 1880).

worth our while to include wines above 20% in our financial arrange.nents of next year, disturbing thereby our present wine scale which is generally satisfactory in its most important part. But that as we must have regard to Portugal not less than Spain we think confusion would arise from proceeding in detail as to the same subject matter at more centres than one. On this account we desired London but would not refuse Madrid if the Spanish Government can arrange with the Government of Portugal to be a party to the arrangement.

6. M.

Wrote to The Queen 1.2.3.—Ld Granville—Baroness B. Coutts and minutes. Cabinet 2½-5. Saw Mr Childers—Ld Granville—Ld F.C.—Ld R.G.—Mr Hamilton—Ld Rosebery—Sir W. Harcourt. Saw Grant—& another [R]. Dined at Ld Rosebery's. Read Delphine.

Cabinet. Monday Sept. 6. 80. 2½ p.m.[1]
1. WEG stated he had made certain *verbal* changes in the Speech to avoid tautology. Also he had substituted 'judgement' (of the Powers) for 'opinion';[2] approved.
2. Ld. Granville explained the conduct of the French as bearing upon concert. They want their instructions substituted. Decided to hold our ground if the other Powers agree.
3. Russia to be incited to adhere to the concession of 'Dinosi'.[3]
4. Much conversation on future contingencies of the Greek Frontier question—without any decision. (General inclination not to condemn *voies de fait* in the case of unity[?] & supported by concert).
5. Retain Candahar? Telegram to Ripon agreed on.[4]

Would it be well to let the Queen see Adye's able paper about Candahar? [W.E.G.]
Yes, & there were others: Col. East. It was stated that Wolsey [*sic*] agreed. [Granville].

To BARONESS BURDETT COUTTS, 6 September 1880.   Add MS 44544, f. 51.

I have received your letter[5] at a moment when I may seem to answer it less clearly & more abruptly than I could wish amidst the arrears caused by my rather long absence & the preparations for the final breaking up.

I hope however that nothing I may say will appear to betoken either unmindfulness of many kindnesses received at your hands, or regret for my having at a former period submitted your name to Her Majesty for an honour on the amply sufficient grounds which these suggested, & which so well warranted the act.

I am not quite certain as to the interpretation of your letter, & I can hardly think that you find cause to ask counsel from me in any matter of whatever kind. If however I am wrong in this, I place myself at your command on Wednesday or Thursday next at any

[1] Add MS 44642, f. 67.
[2] 'The Governments ... have communicated to the Sultan their judgment' on the Montenegrin and Greek frontiers; *H* 256. 1336.
[3] i.e. Dinosi plus 30 square kilometres to be ceded to Turkey; see Ramm II, i. 166.
[4] Roberts' victory at Kandahar over Ayub, Abdul Rahman's recalcitrant brother, was on 1-3 September; it was eventually evacuated in 1881; Wolf, *Ripon*, ii. 42 ff. and Gopal, *British Policy in India*, 133-4.
[5] On her marriage with W. L. Ashmead Bartlett; Gladstone agreed with James Knowles in hoping 'the thing may go to ground' but the marriage took place in 1881, after a series of meetings.

hour, though I am afraid I should be obliged through stint of time to ask you to come into London for the purpose of seeing me.

If on the other hand, your purpose is not consultation on any matter of business or otherwise, but only explanation, then, exercising the best judgment that I can, I think I must ask you to excuse me. I have no title to expect from you any account of matters involving your duty interest & happiness, on which it is for you alone to judge. If I however erroneously put questions, I should be in a false & something of an inquisitorial position. If I were able thoroughly to understand & concur, my concurrence would be of little value. If it happened on the other hand that I was not able [to] declare a similarity of judgment, the issue of the conversation might give us both unnecessary pain, without any prospect of compensating advantage. It is better I think to avoid an interview with a purpose of *this* class, & I will ask you to rest satisfied with the assurance of my hearty desire that you may be guided aright in all your judgments, & that none of them may cast the slightest shadow on a name which by your good deeds you yourself have raised to such distinction.

7. *Tu.*

Wrote minutes: & to Ld Dalhousie—Ld Thurlow—Mr Childers—Ld Enfield—Lady M. Alford—Messrs Murray—The Queen & Tel. House & quasi Cabinet $1\frac{3}{4}$-3. Prorogation. Saw Mr West—Sir F. Doyle—Mr Childers—do cum Lord Hartington—Mr Carrington—E. Hughes—Sir J. Lacaita—Gen Kirieff—Ld Rosebery—Sir R. Wilson. Dined at Ld Rosebery's. Read Delphine.

Present members of the Cabinet. Sept. 7. 1880 (At H. of C.).[1]
Ld. Hartington, Ld. Kimberley, Mr. Childers, Mr. Bright, Mr. Gladstone, Ld. Chancellor, Mr. Dodson, Mr. Forster. Agreed on terms of Tel. to the Queen respecting Kandahar and of preliminary Tel. to Viceroy in anticipation of the definitive one.[2]

8. *Wed.*

Wrote to Rev. S.E.G.—Ld Advocate—Sir A. Gordon—Ld Hartington—Mr West 1.2. & Tel.—Ld Granville and minutes. Visit to Harley St. where the great fight is hopefully maintained.[3] Saw Mr Welby—Sir R. Lingen. Saw ... & Scarsdale [R]. Read Delphine. Dined at the Russian Embassy. Much conversation with the Grand Duke Constantine. Long conversation with Mr Knowles who came from Baroness B. Coutts.

To LORD HARTINGTON, Indian secretary, 8 September   Add MS 44544, f. 53. 1880.

1. Having heard no more ($1\frac{1}{2}$ PM) of the C[andahar] Telegram[4] I hope no news is good news.
2. It would I think be very advantageous if you could appoint before you leave Town the Commission to examine whether a large economy can be effected in your local balances by some such means as I have suggested. Mr Welby is in full readiness to confer with

---

[1] Add MS 44642, f. 70.
[2] Evacuation of Kandahar once tranquillity established; the Queen objected, but gave way on 11 September; *L.Q.V.* 2nd series, iii. 138 and Holland, i. 304-6.
[3] May Hardy's illness.
[4] On the evacuation of Kandahar; *L.Q.V.*, 2nd series, iii. 137.

your functionaries on the composition of this body. (Yesterday I mentioned the matter to Childers, of whose opinion on practical finance I think very highly. His first view was warmly favourable.[)]

3. It seems probable that when detailed explanation of the 'miscarriage' comes before the House of Commons there will be desire among members to sift it to the bottom. This may connect itself with the question whether it would be well, in conformity with the precedents, to have a Committee next year on the Indian Government Act.

9 Th

Wrote to Mr Cowan[1]—Mr Tennyson—Mrs Th.—Abp. of Cantab.—The Queen Tel.—Ld Granville—Mr Furnival—Ld Hartington and minutes. Packing books. Saw Phillips X. Read Delphine and [blank.]

To LORD HARTINGTON, Indian secretary,   Chatsworth MSS 340. 1009.
9 September 1880.

I sincerely wish you may be right in your easier view. But I cannot feel able to rely on it. It is not that I think Ripon *must* be missing opportunities; but he *may*.[2] No doubt he must make arrangements for Candahar before leaving it; but how can he make them— what for instance can he say to Abdur Rahman, before he gets our Telegram? As regards Abdur Rahman's own opportunity to establish himself it is not improbable that every day may be impairing the facilities which this great victory opens to him; And I suspect it is a just sense of the importance of time for our view of the matter which has led to the interposition of these delays; the real desire being as we know that we should not quit Candahar at all.

To A. C. TAIT, archbishop of Canterbury, 9 September 1880.   Add MS 44544, f. 54.

I wish to trouble Your Grace with a short explanation respecting the Convocation Clause of the Burials Bill; for although I have not heard of your making any complaint with regard to the course taken by the Government I am desirous that you should know by what influences it was determined—& in particular that you should also know the grounds of my own conduct.

The Cabinet have felt a great anxiety to fulfil, in letter & in spirit, the arrangement entered into between Your Grace & the Lord Chancellor, & consequently they wished to maintain the 14th clause.

Individually I went one point further; for, though not caring about the clause greatly in itself I think the rejection of a proposal of that nature, regularly arrived at with the sanction of the Crown, & the substitution of another by private action in the House of Commons is a bad & dangerous or at least inconvenient precedent. I was therefore prepared to see the leading Non-Conformists, & to use the best means in my power to induce them to support the clause; as well as to go to the House for that specific purpose.

But this was necessarily dependent on the adoption of a similar course by the members for the Universities, whose position in the House of Commons is in a very special sense that of representatives of the Clergy.

In this state of the facts & expectations, I found that Mr Hope had made a speech which was understood to be adverse to the Clause, & that Mr Walpole openly declared his disapproval of it. I satisfied myself further by private communications that there was

---

[1] Thanks for support during his illness; *T.T.*, 11 September 1880, 8a.
[2] Hartington to Gladstone, 9 September 1880, Add MS 44145, f. 92: Ripon 'is not likely to take any step which may make the retirement from Kandahar more difficult'.

no chance of effective support from the University members; & therefore I abandoned all intention of taking a special & personal part.

It had now become evident not only that the Government could not carry the Clause but even that they could not make any decent way[?] in support of it; & I could not but agree with Mr Bright when he represented to me that, however desirous my colleagues might be to keep faith with Your Grace, there could be no advantage in their marching into the Lobby with a minority ridiculously small.

Pray do not take the trouble to acknowledge this letter,[1] though I have thought an explanation due to Your Grace after the manner in which [I] had entered into a free & friendly concert for the settlement of the question of burials.

10. Fr. [Mentmore]

Wrote to Ld Ripon—Ld Granville Tel. . . . & minutes. More packing & setting in order. Visit in Harley St. Read Delphine. Off to Mentmore 3.45. Conversation with Ld Rosebery. Sir J. Lacaita (on the more than deplorable B. Coutts marriage).

To LORD RIPON, viceroy of India, 10 September 1880.   Add MS 43515, f. 1.
'Secret'.

Lady Ripon quitted London before I had on recovery from my illness settled down into my normal place; and I am afraid it is uncertain whether I may have an opportunity of bidding her a personal farewell, as our recess now begins and my visits to town, which I fear cannot be avoided, will be of uncertain date. May all joy and all good go with her.

I cannot take my departure without writing you a few lines to say how entirely satisfactory to my own mind, and I believe to the whole Cabinet, is the manner in which you have borne yourself amidst the extraordinary difficulties of your position. I do not see that you have done anything which I could wish undone, or that you have omitted anything which I could wish you to have dealt with. In this letter, which I mark secret, I must say a word on your recent telegram, inquiring as to your liberty to direct the evacuation of Kandahar. The Cabinet considered this Telegram on Monday the 6th: and they cordially assented to your evident wish. Indeed we were anxiously waiting the time when you could feel that circumstances were ripe for your inquiry. I for one felt strongly that time might now be of extreme importance to you in this matter, and the Telegram was one which it was most desirable to send at once. Still a reference of it appeared to be required: and resistance has been offered under the name of requests for information and delay. I suggested that an intermediate telegram should be sent to you, to make known that the Cabinet were perfectly decided, and to enable you to augur the result. I do not know that more could be done. I sincerely hope, yet not without anxiety, that you have not been hampered: feeling that the moment may have been a golden one for you to propose, and (say possibly) for Abdur Rahman to accept, what might become less and less easy with the lapse of each twenty four hours.[2]

I am sorry to say this is not the first case of obstruction, nor will it be the last. Since the time of our last Government there has been a serious and unhappy change. To what influence it is due, we may readily conjecture. What strikes me is the decline of practical

---

[1] Tait sent thanks, also expressing concern at developing differences between the upper and lower classes; Add MS 44331, f. 150.
[2] Ripon replied (2 October 1880, Add MS 44286, f. 223) that the delay 'has not been of any consequence'—immediate withdrawal would have been opposed by the India Council.

understanding with which it is attended. The high manners and the love of truth remain I am sure unimpaired: and these are what we have to rely on.

The results of the 3½ months Session have been excellent: and in the Eastern Question we have made some progress, though we have a new obstacle to contend with in the 'personal Government' of the Sultan, greatest of all the liars upon earth.

[P.S.] You stole from me a valuable man in Primrose:[1] but I am thoroughly & admirably well served.

11. Sat.

Wrote to Ld Granville—Also Telegrams: and to Mr Seymour. Put on heavy pressure and finished Delphine, a very clever, very silly book, of sentiment run mad. Much & pleasant conversation.

12. S. 16 Trin.

Parish Ch mg with H.C. and evg. Drive with Ld Rosebery. Wrote to The Queen—Mr Childers—C.G. and minutes. Read Fortn. Rev. on Orthodox Critics—on the Visible Church (slippery & insufficient).[2] Duke of Argyll, (Conversation with Dr Donaldson on). Conversation with R. on H.M.

13. M. [Hawarden]

Wrote to Ld Granville—Ld Hartington—Mrs Ellice—Mrs Th. and minutes. Read N.C. on the horse[3]—Fortnightly on the Deccan[4]—Stages of Hindoo religion[5]—Goldsmith's Poems[6]—M. Napier's Corresp.[7] Walk with Ld R. left these most kind friends about 3: Hn at nine seeing Bp of Chester on the way.

14. Tu.

Neuralgia: I think from the soft air, though there was a turn to cold. Used quinine & a trick of G.G.s in the ear. Wrote to Rev. Mr Henderson—Mr Fraser—Mr Knowles—Ld R. Grosvenor—Mr Hamilton—and minutes. Read Quaker Cousins and Cromwell Family.[8] Began unpacking. Relieved in evg: but made a sorry day's work. Conversation with H. in evg on his affairs.

To J. T. KNOWLES, editor of the *Nineteenth Century*,   Add MS 44544, f. 57.
14 September 1880.

I have read the interesting paper on the horse in the Nineteenth Century for September and if it be not impertinent I should be glad if you could obtain for me from Mr. Blunt

---

[1] See 28 Apr. 80.

[2] Grant Allen on critics, J. D. Lewis on the church; *Fortnightly Review*, xxxiv. 273, 347 (September 1880).

[3] W. S. *Blunt, 'The thoroughbred horse: English and Arabian', *Nineteenth Century*, viii. 411 (September 1880); see next day.

[4] Sir D. Wedderburn in *Fortnightly Review*, xxxiv. 210 (August 1880).

[5] H. T. Colebrooke, *Essays on the religion and philosophy of the Hindus* (1858).

[6] First collected ed. (1786).

[7] *Selections from the correspondence of . . . Macvey Napier, Esq. Edited by his son* (1879).

[8] Agnes Macdonell, *Quaker cousins*, 3v. (1879); the reference to Cromwell is obscure.

any indication of sources or authorities tending to show that Arabia was like northern Africa an original seat of the horse.[1]

In his postscript he speaks of it as having been there 'probably for many thousands of years'—I have not been able thus far to find much evidence of its existence before Mahomet, or of its abundance in his time.

Mr. Blunt's description of Arabia & its tribes does not of itself suggest that the horse was indigenous.

The whole physical history of the horse is most interesting: &, of all the keys to the primitive classical mythology, strange to say is the most effective.

I do not write this from a disposition to disparage the Arab. In my youth I rode an Arab second-cross mare who had few rivals in her paces among hacks; but she would bear on no condition either curb whip or spur—I loved her right well; Lord Jersey and two other puisne judges wished for her to breed from.

[P.S.] The interview [with Lady Coutts] took place but came if possible to less than nothing. So we are in face of a Private downfall almost beyond example & amounting also to a public calamity.

15. Wed.

Wrote to Mr Strong—Duke of Bedford—Ld Portman—Mr Newmarch—Sir G. Bowen—Sig. Campanella—Capt. Fitzgerald (Tel.)[2]—and minutes. Began the work of repacking & setting in order. Walk with W.H.G. Also conversation on Estate debts. Read Quaker Cousins—Pusey on Eternal Punisht[3]—Justin M'Carthy Vol. IV.[4]

16. Th.

Ch. 8½ A.M. Wrote to Abp of Canterbury—Ld Hartington—Ld Reay—Ld Granville—Ld Rosebery—Mr Conningsby Sibthorpe—Rev. S. Smith and minutes. Walk with W.H.G. Read Munster Circuit[5]—Quaker Cousins—Pusey on Eternal Punishment—Nouv. Revue on Love in Australia[6]—J. McCarthy Vol IV.

To LORD REAY, 16 September 1880.   Add MS 44544, f. 59.

I think that by looking at your paper[7] I should run a risk of spoiling it through interference with the freedom of its thought.

Our ideas are not recondite, nor are they developed except in proportion to what is immediate or at least not remote.

We are for the concert of Europe: we hope it will continue to subsist; we think that then it will prevail: for surely Europe will not run away from the Turk with its tail between its legs.

But it would be too bold to say positively it will be so maintained as to prevail: for we must remember that it united in 1853 and 1854, but not in 1855. Should it be broken up

[1] On 28 September Knowles sent Gladstone a long paper by W. S. Blunt; Add MS 44231, ff. 326-33. Gladstone was much interested in the Homeric horse.

[2] Maurice Fitzgerald, equerry to the duke of Connaught.

[3] E. B. Pusey, *What is of faith as to everlasting punishment* (1880), a reply to F. W. Farrar.

[4] J. MacCarthy, *A history of our own time from the accession of Queen Victoria to the Berlin Congress*, 4v. (1879-80).

[5] J. R. O'Flanagan, *Munster Circuit* (1879).

[6] 'Tasma', 'L'Amour aux antipodes', *Nouvelle Revue*, v. 848 (1880).

[7] Not found.

in its entirety, two duties will remain, one to let it be known who has broken it, the other to see whether enough remains to be sufficient for the aim in view.

What I have said in these last lines is the part of our creed which has as yet been least opened out, and which might perhaps be developed with great utility from time to time.

Pray remember us kindly to Lady Reay—and to your healthful, bracing breezes.

To A. C. TAIT, archbishop of Canterbury, 16 September   Add MS 44544, f. 59.
1880.

The second subject opened in your letter[1] is one of the greatest interest.

It is certainly the business and duty of the politician, by his measures, to labour towards the union of classes.

But I am afraid that portion of the work, which depends upon teaching, is beyond his province, mainly from the absorbing nature of his cares, especially under present conditions: and also in a degree because the stream of his thought would be thought to be made muddy by an infusion of narrow notions and ends belonging to his sectional position.

I would however suggest that it might be very interesting if a beginning were made by setting out, through one of the reviews or otherwise, a carefully digested statement of the actual nature of the supplies of literature now afforded to the several classes of society.

17. Fr.

Ch. 8½ am Wrote to Mr Hamilton—Ld Chichester—S.R. Lawley—Mr McCarthy—Mrs Th. and minutes. Drive & walk with C. Saw Bennion [R]. Worked on arranging personal Tracts &c. Read McCarthy's Hist—Munster Circuit—Quaker Cousins—Pusey on Et. Punishment.

18. Sat.

Ch 8½ a.m. Wrote to Capt. Verney—Ld Granville 1.2.3. & Tel.—Mr Cowan [sc. Cowen] M.P.—Mr OShea M.P.[2]—Mr Childers—Sir Thos G—Dr A. Clark—Mr Reid—Sir F. Doyle and minutes. Drive and walk with C. Visits. Some work on papers &c. Read Pusey—Munster Circuit—Quaker Cousins—McCarthy's Hist.

To H. C. E. CHILDERS, war secretary, 18 September 1880.   Add MS 44544, f. 60.

1. With regard to yours of the 14th,[3] I do not think it to be any part of Her Majesty's duty to point out to us whom we should consult. To ask Lord Napier would imply that we thought his opinion of serious value. I for one have a most cordial respect for his character but a mean estimate of his opinion on a question of this kind, when he has neither official responsibility, nor recent information, & when military men charge their so called professional opinions with political elements, & thus give authority to very worthless doctrine.

2. You are at a most interesting centre for the Irish Land Question. (Read Courtney's

---

[1] See 9 Sept. 80n.

[2] Captain William Henry O'Shea, 1840-1905; m. 1867 Katharine Page Wood (relative of Lord Hatherley) from whom he was divorced 1890, Parnell being the co-respondent; as home rule M.P. Co. Clare 1880-5 negotiated between Parnell and the govt. 1882-4.

[3] Sent from Donegal, Add MS 44129, f. 88: the Queen wants various soldiers' opinions before decision made on Kandahar.

rather appalling speech at Liverpool.) The differences between Donegal and Galway with Mayo, with the resemblances & the probable causes of these differences, seem to lie at the root of the whole matter.

The shortsighted vote of the House of Lords has given the question an aspect of Parliamentary urgency, which it did not possess before.

To Captain W. H. O'SHEA, M.P., 18 September 1880.   Add MS 44544, f. 60.

I thank you for your kind letter[1] & I am greatly touched by the remarkable signs which you are good enough to report, & which I take as proof of the warmth of Irish feeling far exceeding the measure of my own desert.

It is likewise with great satisfaction that I have read your account of the important local proceedings with respect to the land question in Ireland. They are all the more gratifying (as taken so soon after the recent short-sighted action of the House of Lords, &) as exhibiting the union of the people & their pastors in opposition to extreme & subversive schemes.

19. 17 S. Trin.

Ch. mg & evg. Walk with C. Wrote to Marchioness of Lothian—Ld Granville—Lord Acton—Mrs Hawker—Sir Thos G. and minutes. Read Pusey on Et. Punt.—Lee, More Glimpses[2]—Via Crucis.

To LORD ACTON, 19 September 1880.   Cambridge University Library.

Though probably Dr. Magnus is not a correspondent of yours you are sure to know better than I do whether there is any way in which I can serve him.[3]

I have corresponded with him about the Colour sense & he has written ably upon it, on what rather seems to me to be the right side.

I inclose his last letter on his personal position.

The note is addressed to you at Tegernsee, partly in a calculation of chances on good faith, partly also perhaps of the multitude of pleasant recollections which are stirred by the name, of the kindest among hostesses and of all around her. And I hope that if you reply to this note you will be able to report to me that our venerated friend 'the Professor' [Döllinger] can still with impunity walk his three hours at a time hatless in the sun.

He must have wondered I think at my evolutions and transmigrations, since those quiet hours at Tegernsee and in Munich.

You will also I hope tell me of the approaching close of your banishment from England. Even you I suppose cannot fully perform your work without certain material conditions fulfilled.

I have made thank God an excellent recovery but am not quite sure of my capacity for a long & hard day's head work. It was head-weariness which first told me I was not well. Think of our making a voyage of 2000 miles round the island, & of 200 hours in those stormy seas we had not above six of disagreeable or sensible motion.

Granville is going to Balmoral. He has had hard and some vexatious work: & I hope that grand climate, for such it is, will do him good.

I need not tell you how heartily & how anxiously we pull together on the Eastern

---

[1] Not found.

[2] F. G. Lee, *More glimpses of the world unseen* (1878).

[3] Acton replied (25 September 1880, Add MS 44093, f. 230): 'the thing a competent German may easily obtain in England is the Taylor lectureship'. 'Teachers' of languages were appointed at the Taylor Institute at Oxford; A. Hamann resigned in July 1880, A. A. Macdonell later replaced him.

Question in its various phases. We are now looking almost daily for the close or crisis of the first by the delivery of Dulcigno and its district: but the mind of the Sultan, who *is* the Turkish Government, is a bottomless pit of fraud and falsehood, and he will fulfil *nothing* except under force or the proximate fear of force.

His delays & shufflings give scope, in the meantime, for Slav agitation and the Balkan countries cannot be relied on to keep the peace if he lifts his hand or causes other hands to be lifted.

We have had a strange incident of private life presented to us in the Burdett Coutts engagement, which I fear will be a marriage. It will be I think a grievous scandal but she is obviously blind and rushes to her destruction. To marry her, Mr. Bartlett breaks faith with a young lady of the Shirley family.

20. M.

Ch 8½ a.m. Wrote to Ld Hartington Tel.–Ld Granville 1 & Tel.–Ld Chancellor 1.2.–Mr Murray–Mr Salkeld–Rev. Mr Mason–Hitchman–Sir R. Lingen–E. Hamilton and minutes. Saw Mr Vickers–Mr Carrington (Mortgages)[1]–Drive & walk with C. Read Quaker Cousins–Pusey on Eternal Punt.–Conversione di Carlo II.[2] 14 to dinner. Conversation with Mr Oakley, also with Mrs Oakley.[3] Worked on books.

21. Tu. St. Matthew

Ch 8½ a.m. Wrote to Ld Hartington Tel.–Ld Chancellor–A.E. West–Ld Coleridge–Ld Spencer–Sir C. Dilke–Mr Vickers–Murrays and minutes. Saw Mr Taylor. Worked on books. Read Quaker Cousins–Conv. di Carlo II–Munster Circuit–Pusey on Et. Punishment. Went over my Mem. on the religious profession of my deceased sister: I think it is accurate.[4] Read Nouv. Revue on Theology.[5]

22. Wed.

Ch 8¼ a.m. Wrote to Ld Granville–Mrs Bellairs–Mr Welby–Rev. Mr Butler–Mr Beale [*sc.* Beal]–Sir Thos G and minutes. Walk with Harry & conversation on his affairs. Granville came to a late dinner: conversation with him on public affairs. Read Quaker Cousins–Conv. di Carlo II finished–Pusey on Et. Punishment finished.

23. Th.

Ch 8½ a.m. Wrote to Messrs Williams–Messrs Roberts–Mr J. Ogilvy–Mr Lefevre–Mr Jas Watson–Bp of Hereford–and minutes. Early part of the day spent mainly in conversation with Granville who went at 1.30. We spoke

---

[1] Alfred Carrington, Chester solicitor.
[2] G. Boero, *Istoria della conversione alla Chiesa Cattolica di Carlo II, Rè d'Inghilterra* (1863).
[3] John Oakley of St Saviour's Hoxton, the visiting preacher and his wife.
[4] See 8 Feb. 80.
[5] Dr Clavel, 'Grandeur et Décadence de la Théologie', *Nouvelle Revue*, vi. 266 (1880).

especially on H.Ms attitude—the E.Q.[1]—and Legislation for next year. Read Quaker Cousins—McCarthy's History—Ret. Review on Belief & on Edn.[2]

24. Fr.

Ch 8½ a.m. Wrote to Ld Granville 1 & Tel.—Ld Chancellor 1.2.—Duke of Bedford—Mr Spurgeon—Sir R. Cunliffe and minutes. Saw Dean of Chester—Mr Vickers 12-2. with whom I went over the accounts of my property 1875-9. I then drew up a Memorandum of my plan for easing W.s position & gradually reducing the debt by giving up £2000 *per ann.*[3] This Memorandum I gave to him for careful perusal. Read Quaker Cousins: finished a pleasant because good book. Read Hahn Albanesische Studien.[4]

To LORD SELBORNE, lord chancellor, 24 September 1880. Selborne MS 1867, f. 122.

I do not for a moment question your decision to resign your seat in the Oxford Commission.[5]

On general grounds I should think it rather late to appoint a new member.

But I am tempted to ask your opinion of an idea which occurs to me. It is, to appoint the Master of University, whose Academical position is high, but who also has taken so deep an interest in the Clergy question.

I do not conceal that I am most uneasy about that question. I doubt whether the House of Commons will accept the *shreds* of clerical restraint which, as I understand, the Commission will leave. I am most anxious 1. as to a large clerical infusion in the teaching body, 2. as to the place of Theology in the studies of the University, for which I have not learned that the Commission have seen their way to easy provision, and 3. I am doubtful about being able to make any sufficient argument for the clerical restrictions as such. All this is very obviously stated, or rather hinted: but it led to the suggestion that Mr. Bradley might be useful in the Commission on this special matter.

Pray understand I have not a word to say against Mr. Richards: but he stands I suppose on grounds which are general.

25. Sat.

Ch 8½ a.m. Wrote to Ld Hartington—Mad. Novikoff. . . . Worked on Library. Saw W.H.G. on Mem. & on Colliery. Tea party in aftn. Saw Mr Oakley on Law of Patronage. Read McCarthy's Hist—Collectanea Antiqua & . . . .

To Madame O. NOVIKOV, 25 September 1880.   Add MS 44544, f. 65.

I sympathise with your alarms,[6] & I will at once convey to the Foreign Office the statement out of which they grow.

[1] For this, see Ramm II, i. 181.
[2] Apparently consulting the *Retrospective Review* (1820-8); perhaps its review of *Areopagitica* in vol. ix (1824).
[3] Hawn P.
[4] See 29 Dec. 76.
[5] Selborne was succeeded as chairman by M. Bernard; Liddell was approached before Bradley, see 7 Oct. 80.
[6] Of 23 September, Add MS 44268, f. 214: 'We learn, alas, on very good authority, that Hartmann & Co. are determined to blow up the new ship, Liradia, which, as you know, is going to make a sea voyage with the Grand Duke C.'

I can venture to assure you that the best means at our command would be used for following up to its sources any evidence bearing upon such a subject & for the prevention of a detestable crime.

You will however perceive that you have conveyed the matter to me only in the form of rumour. I cannot doubt that if you are correctly informed particulars will be given as on which we can act.

The Grand Duke Constantine was extremely gracious & I was struck with his intelligent & active mind.

Well I date my letter on a critical day; for I have just been reading over Telegrams of Thursday night from Cettinjë & I suppose that today the action may begin, which now seems inevitable.

The shifts & falsehoods of the Sultan in the Montenegrin question since we have been in office have beaten everything I had ever before known or heard of. God defend the right; & send us a speedy issue.

The Government will not meet in London till early in November: events might draw me up for a day or two at any time.

26. 18 S. Trin.

Ch mg & evg. Wrote to Ld Chancellor—Ld Granville . . . and minutes. Read Roberts on the Bible[1]—Littledale Reasons agt Rome[2]—Capes on Knowledge of God[3]—Macdonald 'Day to Day'[4]—Redman Aspect of the Times.[5]

27. M.

Ch 8½ a.m. Wrote to Ld Granville 1.2.3. Tel.—Mr Hamilton Tel. 1.2. & l.—Mr S. Lawley—Mrs Th.—Ld Hartington's Private Sec. Tel. and minutes. Ed. Daily News—Ld Granville Tel. 2.—Mr Hamilton Tel 3. Saw W.H.G. on Mem. & Colliery. Worked on Library. Bush clearing about old Castle. Read McCarthy—Munster Circuit. A day of stir: but not of doubt.

In concert

1. To acquaint the Sultan that if a Turkish soldier crosses the Montenegrin frontier [or acts against the Montenegrins in their occupying of Dulcigno & its district?][6] it will be a *casus belli* with [this country and . . .].
2. To summon all British subjects to quit the service of the Sultan.
3. To offer Albania as far as the Kalamas its independence.
4. To reinforce the fleet: and to propose to the Powers to use the ship force for the occupation of the Dulcigno district.
5. To hold regiments at Malta in readiness for the same purpose.[7]

---

[1] A. Roberts, *The Bible of Christ and his Apostles* (1879).
[2] R. F. Littledale, *Plain reasons against joining the Church of Rome* (1880).
[3] J. M. Capes, *What can be certainly known of God and Jesus of Nazareth? An enquiry* (1880).
[4] R. Macdonald, *From day to day* (1878).
[5] M. Redman, *The aspect of the times to the end of this age* (1876).
[6] Gladstone's square brackets. See also Ramm II, i. 186.
[7] Holograph, docketed 'S. 27. Telegram & Mema.'; Add MS 44764, f. 103.

To F. H. HILL, editor of *Daily News*, 27 September 1880.[1]   Add MS 44466, f. 114.
'Private'.

I expect to reach Downing Street on Wednesday by 4.30. In the meantime I write to say that the Sultan seems to have overshot his mark in declaring that if Montenegro moves to fulfil the Treaty of Berlin by occupying the Dulcigno district, it is a *casus belli*. Please not to declare this expressly as known, unless you know it from some other source.

The course which I conceive that policy and principle alike recommend is to fasten the whole responsibility *on the Sultan*, as distinct from the Porte. This is probably the only chance of bringing him to reason while there is yet time. I think it worth while to offer you this suggestion.

28. Tu.

Ch 8¼ a.m. Wrote to Ld Northbrook Tel.—Mr Hamilton—.Tel. 1.—Ld Granville 1 & Tel.—Mr Macdougal[2]—Mrs West—Ld Lieut. of Ireland—Ld Tenterden—Duke of Argyll Tel.—Ld E. Fitzmaurice—Ed. Pall Mall Gazette[3]—Ld Chancellor & minutes. Read Hahn Alban. Studien—Marbeau's Bosnie[4]—Donisthorpe on Labour.[5]

To A. E. WEST, commissioner of inland revenue,   Add MS 44544, f. 66.
28 September 1880.

I am to be in London tomorrow evening at latest.
1. Your memorandum shewing 31 & 69 %, or 28m̄ & 62m̄ respectively for real and personal property is taken from an income tax at how many pence?
2. It will be yet more interesting & valuable if again taken for 1880; viewing the new burden on Probate.
3. Moreover, to make it just, we must I think exhibit the amount of local grants in the three kingdoms given in relief of realty, which can be supplied by the Treasury. I suppose this should be a separate account.

29. Wed. St Mich. [London]

Ch 8¼ a.m. Off at 10.50. Reached London at 4. Saw May Hardy, after her heavy trying illness, most gentle and cheerful: Mr Hamilton—Ld Tenterden—Ld Lyons—Mr Herbert. Saw three: with some very little advantage [R]. Dined at Mrs Th.s Villa. W. Hampstead.[6] Read Speech of Mr Dodds—Ld Tenterden's Mem.[7]—Mr Donisthorpe. Wrote to C.G.

---

[1] Holograph; Hill was sent a copy. Hill replied he had done his 'best to give effect to it'; Add MS 44466, f. 118. The first leader concluded: 'to leave things to settle themselves would simply be to open an indefinite period of anarchy and unsettlement'; *D.N.*, 28 September 1880, 4f.

[2] William MacDougall of Glasgow junior liberal association; *T.T.*, 1 October 1880, 9f.

[3] i.e. J. Morley; for leaks to the *Pall Mall Gazette* shortly after this, see Medlicott, 163.

[4] E. Marbeau, *La Bosnie depuis l'Occupation Austro-Hongroise* (1880).

[5] W. Donisthorpe, *The claims of Labour* (1880).

[6] See 24 July 80 f.l.? A temporarily rented villa, not recorded in the P.O. Directory.

[7] Mem. on 'negotiations and proceedings respecting the Montenegrin frontier', F.O.C.P. 4139A.

30. Th.

Wrote to C.G.—Ld Hartington—The Queen—Ld Granville & minutes. Cabinet 12-4. Saw Ld Granville—Mr Welby—Mr Godley. Read Frost's Memoirs: poor.[1] Saw Dashwood & another [R]. Wrote minutes on the situation.[2] Dined with Mrs Birks: saw C[harles?] Gladstone.

Cabinet. Noon. Sept. 30. 80.[3]
1. Cabinet called to consider the situation created by the refusal of the Porte to execute its engagements as to the Montenegrin frontier. The general disposition was a) to accompany the concert of Europe as far as it will go. b) to stimulate it. c) to mark as clearly as possible the responsibility of breaking it up.[4]
2. State of Ireland[:] represented the condition of certain parts of Ireland. Mr. Forster is to proclaim illegal and to prevent any meetings held to prevent men from taking farms cleared by eviction—and to try the question of the Land League, probably in the person of Mr. Parnell, if the Law Officers arrive at the conclusion that it is an illegal association. English L.O. to be consulted.[5]
3. Ld. Kimberley submitted a Telegram on Basutoland: approved with amendment.
4. Fleet to collect at Malta.

Frid. Oct. 1. 1880.

Wrote to C.G. & minutes. Wrote draft on E.Q. for consideration. Saw Ld E. Fitzmaurice—Ld Granville 2.—Count Münster—Mr Forster—Mr Morley—Mr Bright—Sir J. Lacaita—Mr Hoare (Scotts)—Mr Gurdon. Read Cowper's Hist. of Cambridge[6]—G. Eliot's Jubal.[7] Went in evg to see Mr C. Warner[8] in Othello at the New Sadler's Wells. I was greatly struck with his powers & especially his *power*.

Count Münster called on me, unofficially, to ask after my health.
   However, we talked on the Eastern Question.
   He stated very freely that we had all a common interest in maintaining the Concert, and settling the question.
   And that it 'seemed impossible' for the six Powers to recede before the Turks.
   We were alike sensible of the dangers of a general shock to Turkey by making an appearance in the Dardanelles or Bosporus. I said it seemed to me not impossible to arrange for a milder and safer measure of material pressure upon Turkey. He did not give any opinion.[9]

[1] T. Frost, *Forty years' recollections* (1880).
[2] In Ramm II, i. 189.
[3] Add MS 44642, f. 71. See Medlicott, 158.
[4] Holograph draft proposals for local action at Add MS 44764, f. 105.
[5] For the prosecutions, see Introduction above, section vi.
[6] Probably C. H. Cooper, *Memorials of Cambridge*, 3v. (1880).
[7] G. Eliot, *The legend of Jubal and other poems* (1874).
[8] Charles *Warner, 1846-1909; actor known for melodramatic interpretations.
[9] Holograph, dated 1 October 1880; Add MS 56445, f. 95; Gladstone had been unable to dine with Münster on 30 Sept.; Add MS 44544, f. 67. In *Autobiographica*, iv. 58.

2. Sat [Holmbury]

Wrote to C.G.—Mrs Th.—The Queen tel.—Ld Spencer—Ld Granville—Murrays and minutes. Saw Ld Granville: much—Mr West: for whom I framed the outline of a measure on the death duties. Off at 3.55 to Holmbury: an evening of conversation. Read Newman, Characteristics.[1]—G. Eliot, Agatha &c.[2] Scull, Greek Mythology.[3] Much concretion of method of procedure in the Eastern question.

1. Unification of duties.
2. Abolition of intestacy rate.
3. Simplification of consanguinity scale:
   One rate for children (& widows)—children to include lineal descendants;
   One rate to include lineals upwards & collaterals (descended from the grandfather?);
   One rate for any other relation or stranger in blood.
4. Abolish exemption on *legacies*—raise limit of exemption on Estates.
5. Put leaseholds as they were before 1853?
6. Consider the possibility of extinguishing or mitigating the evil of reversionary bequests without an undue charge upon residuary legatees.
7. Preliminary instead of posterior deduction of debts.[4]

To LORD SPENCER, lord president, 2 October 1880.[5]   Add MS 44544, f. 67.

The main subject of discussion on Thursday was the Eastern Question, as affected by the Montenegrin decision not to face the Albanians *plus* the Turks.

The Sultan had so far receded by implication as to promise a satisfactory plan by Sunday October 3 at latest. In this delay we acquiesced. As to the substance there is no disposition to recede. Even should there be another Cabinet I would not advise you to come at the slightest risk or at any grave inconvenience, not because we estimate your presence lightly, but because the Cabinet are so united in a tendency of mind which seems to be exactly yours!

The best thing I can do is to send you (herewith) a copy of my report on the Cabinet of Thursday to the Queen. She is pleased with it.

The Chancellor has given his mind to the Irish question and encourages us to go against the League i.e. probably Parnell. He has written an excellent minute and the next thing is to see whether the Irish Law Officers can take the same view of the law.

3. 19 S. Trin.

Felday Church 11. a.m. and H.C.—3 P.M. Conversation with G. Leveson—with Granville—with Mr Shearm.[6] Read Newman, Charact. What fascinations, what illusions! Wrote to Marquis of Bath—Librarian of Maynooth—Mr Goschen.

---

[1] *Characteristics from the writings of... J. H. Newman, arranged by W. S. Lilly* (5th ed. 1880).
[2] G. Eliot, *Agatha, A poem* (1869).
[3] S. A. Scull, *Greek mythology systematized* (1880).
[4] Undated holograph, docketed by West: 'Mr Gladstone's Seven Questions. Unification Scheme'; Add MS 44764, f. 157.
[5] At Aix-les-bains; Add MS 44308, f. 42.
[6] Probably Edward Shearme, of Malin's Court.

To G. J. GOSCHEN, ambassador at Constantinople,   Add MS 44544, f. 67.
3 October 1880.

You have no time to read a long letter, or even a short one. Every fresh envelope addressed to you must be a fresh shock to your nerves. Yet I cannot help inflicting upon you an earnest, but I believe impartial word of encouragement if I may so speak, and at any rate of acknowledgement. You are something of a pillar; something that a man can lean on: you have shown, in circumstances of great difficulty, a combination of acuteness, uprightness of mind, courage, and assiduity, such as it does one good to see.

I wish I could think you have got through the roughest of the work; but I feel confident that the qualities, which have carried you thus far, will carry you to the end.

I write on the day which is to produce the Sultan's satisfactory arrangement. And a true day of rest it will prove to have been, if he is now at length at the end of his dodges. If he is not, what I should hope, what I should always advise, would be that we should make him speak plainly instead of mumbling. What I mean is that when, from himself or any of his creatures, he says if he will give up something which he cannot stand, & which is quite definite, he will give up something else quite as good, which is perfectly indefinite. When he comes to substituting, we should treat his words as mere wind, until we get the what, the where, the how, and the when.

We do not bate any jot of heart, hope, or intention: & I could say much of Granville & the Cabinet, none of it but what is good, only I must not exceed my sheet.[1]

4. M. [London]

Left Holmbury at 8¾. Drove to Dorking & got a slight chill. Luncheon at 15 G.S. but kept the house in evg. Wrote to the Queen—Mr Herries—C.G.[2]—Mr West— D. of A. Tel. and minutes. Read Newman, Characteristics—Contemp. 'Why keep India'.[3] At 3.30 seven Ministers met in my room. The Sultan's communication had not as was expected arrived. But we further discussed & prepared for the contingencies. Successive interviews with Granville. About 5 the pith of the answer arrived. We determined to propose the occupation of Smyrna: and framed & sent Telegram accy.[4] Saw M. Challemel Lacour—Baron Hengen Müller.[5] Saw Me Novikoff—Mrs Th.

5. Tu.

Wrote to C.G.—Ed. Daily News—Lord Sudley and minutes. Saw Dr Clark—bis: kept the house & my sofa. Saw Ld F. Cavendish—Ld Granville 1.l. Read Newman, Char.—Fortnightly, Irish Land—Century of English Poetry—Are we Englishmen?[6]—Obstruction or Clôture[7]—Dem. Possession in India.[8]

---

[1] In Elliot, Goschen, i. 201.

[2] Letters until 11 October in Bassett, 229ff.; for this crisis, see Medlicott, ch. vi.

[3] Contemporary Review, xxxviii. 544 (October 1880).

[4] i.e. that the allied fleets should proceed from the Adriatic to Smyrna, and that that port should be held as a material guarantee; circular telegram to five capitals sent, see Ramm II, i. 193 and Medlicott, 158.

[5] Baron Hengelmüller de Hengervar, Austrian chargé d'affaires in London 1879-88; see Ramm II, i. 192.

[6] In Fortnightly Review, xxxiv. 409, 422, 472 (October 1880).

[7] Nineteenth Century, viii. 513 (October 1880); by R. Lowe.

[8] Ibid., 646.

6. *Wed.*

Rose at 11. Wrote to Lord Chancellor—Ld Granville 1.2.—Mrs Agar—C.G.—Ed Daily News and minutes. Saw Ld Granville 1.2.3.—Dr Clark—Mr H. & Mr G. Dined at 15 G.S. but not well. Read Blackies Introduction[1]—Newman, Characteristics—Whitehead, Market Gardening[2]—Russell, on Moral Judgement.[3]

7. *Th.*

Kept my bed. Wrote to Mr E.R. Russell—Dr Clark (2)—Ld Rosebery—Mr Forster—Dean of Ch.Ch.—C.G.—Ld Granville and minutes. Saw Ld Chancellor—Ld Granville 1.2.—Dr Clark. Read Blackie's Faust—Newman's Characteristics: a book to be much complained of.

To W. E. FORSTER, Irish secretary, 7 October 1880.   Add MS 44544, f. 68.

Granville and I have our minds pretty full as you may conceive of absorbing matter. We have the assents of R[ussia] and I[taly] but we still wait anxiously the answers of G[ermany] A[ustria] and F[rance]. The indications rather tend to show that non-participation is the *most* we have to expect; no chance of disapproval.

I cannot however shut out the anxieties which belong to the state of Ireland and which reach me audibly from without as the name of that country is in the mouths of all. I certainly had hoped, with or without reason, that by this time we should know the view of the law taken by your Law Officers. And I think the members of the Cabinet generally will fail to understand the delay. If they cannot of themselves take the responsibility of coming up to the Chancellor's mark, has not the time arrived when they should put themselves into the train and come to London to meet him and the English Law Officers for a final decision?[4] Sending of course the earliest notice by Telegraph in order that the A.G. and S.G. may be summoned, of whom the A.G. is or was lately at a considerable distance.

I am afraid you have nothing good to report of the state of the country but I would not ask you, oppressed as you must be, to answer me beyond a word on that subject.

To H. G. LIDDELL, Dean of Christ Church, 7 October 1880.   Add MS 44544, f. 69.

It has been a misfortune, to say the least, from the first, that your name has not been on the list of the Oxford Commission.

There is now a vacancy; Selborne has thought it his duty to retire; & after consulting him I propose to you that you should allow me to name you to the Queen, to fill up his place. I very earnestly hope that you will agree to this proposal; & I am sure that your acceptance will give much satisfaction in the several quarters where a judgment would be passed upon it.

The subject has come upon me at very short notice, & the Commission recommences its sittings on the 9th. This must be my excuse for asking that, if you should be prepared to do so, you will kindly for the sake of saving a day telegraph to me your reply.[5]

---

[1] J. S. Blackie's introduction to his tr. of *Faust* (1834, 2nd ed. 1880).

[2] Sir C. Whitehead, *Market gardening for farmers* (1880).

[3] Untraced piece by E. R. Russell (see next d.).

[4] Forster replied, 8 October 1880, Add MS 44157, f. 152, promising a decision on prosecution of the Land League shortly, and reviewing the Irish situation.

[5] Liddell declined to serve, explaining he had twice turned down tory invitations; Add MS 44236, f. 361. Bradley, Master of University college, then accepted, markedly strengthening the liberal tone of the commission; see Ward, *Victorian Oxford*, 312 and 24 Sept., 5 Dec. 80.

8. Fr.

Rose at 11. a.m. restored I think by "the oil". Wrote to Marquis of Bath—Master of Univ. Coll.—Ld Granville 1.2.—Mr Justice Lawson—Mr Duffield[1]—C.G.—and minutes. Dined at Ld Northbrooks, with Granville. Saw Mr Godley—Ld Granville—Sir J. Lacaita—Ld Spencer—Dr A. Clark. Conclave with Sir Cooper Key at 3 P.M.[2] Saw Dashwood [R]. Read Newman—Blackie's Faust—Reisebriefe eines Diplomaten.[3]

9. Sat.

A bad day in Turkish matters. Austrian negative came, which carries the German.[4] Wrote to Ld Granville 1.2.—Ld Chancellor—Hon. R. Lawley—D. of Argyll—Ld Portsmouth—Prof. Blackie—Mr Forster—The Speaker—C.G. and minutes. Saw Italian Ambassador—Mr Morley—Mr Evans—Mr G. & Mr H. Went in evg. with Herbert to see Marie Stuart.[5] Finished Blackie's Faust.

To the DUKE OF ARGYLL, lord privy seal, 9 October 1880.   Add MS 44544, f. 71.

We have reluctantly summoned the Cabinet for Monday. The Austrians have sent in a shabby answer. The Turkish note is unacceptable—there can be no negotiation upon it, and they 'admit the proposed demonstration' at Smyrna; they advise that part of the Customs duties be given to the Prince of Montenegro but they will take no part. Behind this is Germany probably in the same sense; & France perhaps is a little worse.

Under these circumstances Granville will ask Austria whether she proposes that those powers who may be willing to *execute* should be the mandatories of Europe—as France & England were in the case of the Lebanon in 1860. In this way the moral concert might be maintained.

If Austria (having Germany behind her) declines this, the concert will be broken up, for the practical purpose. If she answers affirmatively, then the question will have to be considered whether we shall encourage a limited combination to go forward. The other alternative seems to be non-action, & the triumph, at any rate for the time, of the Turkish *non-possumus*; which is something like the establishment of their right to decline the execution of their engagements. I write these few lines as the only aid I can give you on receiving your disagreeable summons. The Irish Law officers have not yet given their opinion but we shall probably have it on Monday.

To W. E. FORSTER, Irish secretary, 9 October 1880.   Add MS 44544, f. 71.

I send you copy of a note which I addressed this morning to the Lord Chancellor & sent down to him by messenger together with your letter. It contains I think pretty nearly all I could say to you; if his answer arrives before post time I will send it you herewith.

I do not see why legislation should necessarily mean only suspension of *Habeas Corpus*. We are now I believe inquiring whether the law allows under certain circumstances of

---

[1] Divie Bethune Duffield of Michigan; on Don Quixote; Add MS 44544, f. 70.
[2] First Sea Lord, with earlier experience of Smyrna waters; P. H. Colomb, *Memoirs of Sir A. Cooper Key* (1898), 214.
[3] Reading of title uncertain.
[4] Italy and Russia accepted the Smyrna initiative, Austria, Germany and France did not; Medlicott, 158-9.
[5] At the Court theatre.

combinations to prevent the performance of certain duties, & the enjoyment of certain rights. If it does, as I understand the matter, we prosecute. If it does not, why may not the law be brought up to the proper point by an Amending Act.[1]

The other matter is grave. Austria sends a shabby answer. It admits the proposed demonstration but will not cooperate. Granville sends to know whether they mean responsibly to constitute the operating powers mandatories of Europe. The Cabinet will have to decide what is to be done.

To LORD SELBORNE, lord chancellor, 9 October 1880.   Add MS 44297, f. 90.

I send you a very full letter from Forster[2] in answer to my representation about the delay.

What I am disposed to write to him is very much a repetition of what I have already said, viz. that *unless* the Irish Government, Law Officers of course included, determines to prosecute, the needful course is for the Irish Law Officers at once to come over summoning their English brethren to London to consider the matter under your Presidency.

My opinion to which Forster proposes to submit the matter in the first instance is really of no account, the only question is whether we are competently advised that the Land League is illegal. If we are, I say go on. If we are not, a most grave question arises as to the state of the law, though I cannot think that question to be solely or primarily whether we should suspend the *Habeas Corpus* Act.

If you are in the country, this will go to you by messenger, & I need not press the need for dispatch in your reply.

P.S. Dean of Christ Church declines.[3] I have written to Master of Univ. Failing him shall I try Richards?

10. 20 S. Trin.

Graham St Ch mg, Vere St evg. Saw Ld Granville—Ld Spencer—Mr Godley. Dined at Mr Godley's. Wrote to C.G. Read Newman—Lewis, Introduction to Sander[4]—Faithful unto Death.[5] The news came that the Sultan gave in. A day of joy & thankfulness: with a faint tinge of doubt.

11. M.

Wrote to Ld Granville—The Queen 1 & Tel—Mr Bethune Duffield—Mr Barran MP.—C.G.—Sir W. James & minutes. Dined at the Admiralty: conclave with G.H. & Northbrook. Saw French Ambassador—Ld Hartington—Mrs Birks—Ld Granville 1.2.3.—R. Lawley—Mrs Foley—May Hardy. Read Newman, Charac.

Today the non-arrival of the note made us anxious: knowing the half heartedness of three[6] among the Powers, we could not but fear the Sultan had come to know it also & thereupon had once more broken his word. Evening Tel. was bad.

---

[1] Version of this paragraph in Reid, *F*, ii. 258. Forster wrote next day, Add MS 44157, f. 162, announcing Law Officers' recommendation to prosecute the Land League.

[2] See 7 Oct. 80n.

[3] To join the Oxford Commission, *vice* Selborne; see 7 Oct. 80; Selborne jotted a reply—'I entirely agreed with your view as to Ireland'—on the back of Gladstone's letter and returned it.

[4] D. Lewis's long introduction in his ed. of Nicolas Sander, *The rise of the Anglican schism* (1877).

[5] *Faithful unto death. By Zandile* [F. E. Colenso] (1872).

[6] i.e. Austria, Germany, and France; the Sultan did know of their caution, *via* Paris, but there was also a counter-rumour; see Medlicott, 164.

12. Tu. [Hawarden]

In the forenoon Gr. & I had a very sombre conversation preparing for the worst. I was under the circumstances prepared to proceed *en trois*[1] without mandate but he & H. rather differed & it was not a measure I could properly attempt to force. Between 11 & 12 G. came in with the news that the note had arrived 'all right'. Thanks be to God. We discussed the next coming steps, in a much altered frame. Though nothing is sure until done, in a case like this.

Conversation with Herbert J.G. Packed my books & clothes. Off at 2.15: and reached Hawarden 8.30 a small simmering sensation on the way. Read Talbot on the Greeks[2]–Lymington in 19th Cent.[3] Wrote to Ld Granville 1.2.–The Speaker–Ld Bath–Mr Morley–Ld Spencer–Sir H. Ponsonby–The Queen & minutes.

13. Wed.

Ch 8½ a.m.: so peaceful. Wrote to Ld Granville–Mr Hitchman–Scotts and minutes. Walk with Harry & Alfred Lyttelton–C.G. & Mary still more invalids. Read Lewis, Introduction to Sander–Hutton Biography & account of the Birmingham Riots[4]–Guy Mannering (resumed).[5] Worked on unpacking books &c.

14. Th.

Ch 8½ a.m. Wrote to Ld Mount Temple–Ld Granville–Sir G. Bowyer–D. of Argyll–Sir G. Cunliffe–Messrs Townsend & Barker–Mr Ashley M.P.–Rev. Sir G. Cox–Sir W. Harcourt–Mr [A. D.] Wagner–Lady Ossington–Mr Young & minutes. Saw Mr Palgrave. Walk with Stephen: Very interesting conversation on his future. His mind is deeply thoughtful, hoping before and after. Conversation with Alfred [Lyttelton] on professions. Read Hutton, a most interesting work–Lewis Introd. to Sander–Guy Mannering.

To the DUKE OF ARGYLL, lord privy seal, 14 October 1880.　　Add MS 44544, f. 73.

The object of my note was to save you the journey if possible. After we stopped the Cabinet on Sunday there came through Monday and on Tuesday morning a period of doubt and difficulty.

Austria refused us three things in succession.
1. To man the Montenegrin frontier.
2. To go to Smyrna.
3. To empower those who were willing to go.

The French contrived to get her into the van & say as she had declined they must.

---

[1] i.e. Britain, Russia, and Italy.
[2] T. Talbot, *Greece and the Greeks* (1880).
[3] On tenant right, *Nineteenth Century*, viii. 672 (October 1880).
[4] *The life of William Hutton: including a particular account of the riots at Birmingham in 1791* (1816).
[5] See 9 Apr. 80.

Germany was already pinned to her tail. So she has to bear the burden of the whole of the chicken-hearted policy.

Her conduct however has been straightforward.

It is likely there will be great difficulties in starting and putting forward the Greek frontier question.

Looking farther ahead I fear they [*sc.* there] may be some risk of a reconstitution of the alliance between the Three Emperors, and of squaring the questions to arise in the Balkan Peninsula. I wonder what Her Majesty thinks of this.

I have not written a line to Her Majesty on the dénouement.[1] I cannot say what would please and I do not wish to say what would annoy.

To Sir George BOWYER, 14 October 1880.   Add MS 44544, f. 74.

I thank you sincerely for your free speech[2] but I am not able to agree with you.

For many long years I have been agreeably surprised that the English occupier has raised no inferences in his own favour from the case of Ireland. I do not believe he is so unreasonable as to do it at the present juncture when all the Irish facts are so peculiar & distinct. Yours is the first intimation that has ever reached me of the kind.

Neither can I agree as to the Disturbance Bill, the rejection of which has done so much harm.

But having had my say in public on this question, I will not reopen it.

15. Fr.

Ch 8½ a.m. Wrote to Ld Granville 1 & Tel—The Queen 1 & Tel—Ld Monck—Ld Spencer Tel—Mr Ross—Mr Godley Tel—Talbot—Dean of Windsor—Scotts—Ld Chancellor—Mr Cowan and minutes. Rearranged my history department in Library. Read The Mirror—Guy Mannering—Pope. Prologue—Lewis Introd. (finished).

16. Sat.

Ch 8½ a.m. Wrote to M. Albert Gigot—The Queen—Bp of Moray—Me Novikoff—Mr Westropp and minutes. Walk with Ld Spencer & conversation on Ireland again in evg.[3] Worked on Library. Read Q.R. on the Govt—Guy Mannering—Gigot, Introductory Essay.

To A. GIGOT, 16 October 1880.   Add MS 44544, f. 75.

Only to-day I have been able to read, with the attention it deserved, the Introduction which you have prefixed to your Translation of certain Tracts of mine relating to Politics.

Offering you my best thanks for the flattering terms in which you are pleased to speak of me, I must assure you of the extreme interest and the very general concurrence with which I have perused your very able Introduction.[4]

A very broad and even fundamental distinction is I think established between the

---

[1] Argyll's reply (19 October 1880, Add MS 44104, f. 220) urged the Queen be told.

[2] Letter this day deploring government's land policy, especially in its effect on England; Add MS 44466, f. 166.

[3] See P. Gordon, ed., *The Red Earl* (1981), 162.

[4] Albert Gigot, 1835-1913, liberal catholic prefect and author, tr. Gladstone's articles on the cabinet, the crown and the Prince Consort as *Questions constitutionelles*, with an introduction (1880).

cases of France and of America (may both prosper under their respective institutions) by the fact that the one State is Federal and the other not.

I certainly would, were it in my power or province, recommend the adoption of a different system for appointments to the Civil Service from that which now prevails in the United States. Indeed I do not understand why so shrewd a people continues to endure what is at once a nuisance and a blot.

To Madame O. NOVIKOV, 16 October 1880.   Add MS 44268, f. 223.

Good work has been done in the Dulcigno business; but the Turk has not acted yet.[1]
I have had the misfortune to differ from Sir H. Elliot on Eastern politics, but I am bound to say that I place entire reliance upon his honour, and I am satisfied he does not knowingly fall short in the discharge of any of his important duties as the agent of the British Government at Vienna.

17. S. 21. Trin.

Ch mg & evg. Wrote to Ld Granville—Ld Monck—& minutes. Walk with Ld Spencer. Read Ecce Christianus[2]—Tabor's What is Truth[3]—Gregory on Apocalypse[4]—Acct of Fund Clergy & Zealots.[5]

18. M. St Luke

Church 8½ a.m. and H.C. Ld Spencer went. Wrote to Mr Grenville Berkeley—The Queen—Rev. Mr Mason—Sir Thos. G.—Ld Granville—Ld Bath—Miss K. Gladstone and minutes. Read Ecce Christianus—Alsop on Home Rule[6]—Grattan's Speeches & Irish History.[7] Guy Mannering. Walk with Harry & Alfred L. Saw old Bennion—very near his end. Went to work on a Sketch for devolution.

19. Tu.

Ch 8¼ a.m. Wrote to Mr Godley l. & Tel.—Sir H. Ponsonby—Sir W. Harcourt 1.2.—Sir Arthur Gordon—Mr Herries—The Queen and minutes. Walk, with Harry & A. also conversation with Harry on his affairs, so satisfactory in all but the contemplated absence from us in our declining years. Read Pitt's[8] & Grattan's Speeches & Union History—Mr Wood on Science in H.S.[9]—Guy Mannering. Again wrote on Devolution.

20. Wed.

Ch 8½ a.m. Wrote to Ld Granville—Mr Wood—Ld Advocate—Mr Vickers—Rev. T.G. Law—Mr Litton M.P.[10]—Mr Hayward and minutes. Dean Church & party

---

[1] Novikov had sent congratulations, but asked, 'are you really sure that Sir H. Elliot is not playing a double game at Vienna?'; Add MS 44268, f. 221.   [2] [W. D. Ground], *Ecce Christianus* (1879).
[3] J. A. Tabor, *The Supreme Law illustrated, in answer to the question What is Truth?* (1879).
[4] A. Gregory, *Discourses on the Book of Revelation* (1875).   [5] Untraced.
[6] J. W. Alsop, 'Home Rule. An address' (1880).
[7] H. Grattan, *Speeches . . . comprising a brief review of the most important political events in the history of Ireland* (1811).
[8] W. S. Hathaway, *The speeches of William Pitt*, 4v. (1806).   [9] One of J. G. Wood's many tracts.
[10] Edward Falconer Litton, 1827–90; Dublin barrister; liberal M.P. Co. Tyrone 1880–1; land commissioner 1881.

came. Walked in morn. Conversation at night on the persons most fit to receive preferment. Read Panizzi's Life[1]—Guy Mannering (finished).

21. Th.

Ch 8½ a.m. Wrote to Ld Granville 1 & Tel—Ld Kimberley—Mr Knollys—Ld Cavendish—Ld Cowper—Ld R. Grosvenor—Ld Portman—Dean of Windsor— Herbert J.G. and minutes. Saw Dean of St Paul's. Read Warren on Book Plates[2]—Panizzi's Life—Lonsdale on Sister Dora.[3] Farm visit with C.

To LORD KIMBERLEY, 21 October 1880.   Add MS 44544, f. 78.

I thoroughly sympathise with the spirit in which you write[4] about Ireland, while I think you will agree with me that the next thing we have to do is to watch the effect of the blow that is to be struck on Nov. 2.[5] & that we are not yet ripe for the consideration of anything that is to follow. I am not without *hope* that the effect may be considerable. In return for your inclosure I send you a very good letter I have had from Cowper for your perusal.[6] One thing only I will say as to what lies beyond the trials. Does the law, or does it not, stamp with illegality any combination for the purpose of dissuading people from the fulfilment of their contracts, even by means that carry no suspicion of violence? If it does, this ought to enable us to deal with a public body like the Land League. If it does not, I cannot but think that it ought; & that until we know the effect of such a law we are hardly in a position to raise a question as to the suspension of the *Habeas Corpus*.

22. Fr.

Ch 8½ a.m. Wrote to Mr Godley Tel.—Ld Granville—l. & Tel.—Ld Kimberley— Ld Advocate—Ld Cowper—Mr Fagan—Ld Monck—Ld Portman—Miss Montmorency and minutes. Finished & revised my paper on Devolution. Read Life of Panizzi and [blank.]

To LORD COWPER, Irish viceroy, 22 October 1880.   Add MS 44544, f. 79.

The inclosed Paragraph from our faithful and able ally the Pall Mall Gazette drew my attention this morning.[7] It seems to me not to proceed upon a clear order of ideas. I hope we have nothing to do with the doctrine here attributed to Mr Justice Burton. I further hope that we are not upon the lines of the O'Connell trial—which Peel used to describe as his attempt to get a verdict against one who was endeavouring to show the enormous amount of physical force he had at his command, to curb, or (therefore) to unloose. But it would have been an unjust charge against O'Connell that he was indifferent to the Maintenance of Law and Order or gave countenance to the intimidation of individuals.

On the other hand I conceive that we do not see anything obsolete or abominable in

---

[1] By L. A. Fagan, 2v. (1880); see 22 Oct. 80.

[2] J. L. Warren, *Guide to the study of book plates* (1880).

[3] See 15 Feb. 80.

[4] On 19 October, Add MS 44225, f. 227, supporting prosecution but expecting suspension 'at last'.

[5] The date of the serving of indictments on Parnell, Dillon, three other Home Rule M.Ps. and sundry others.

[6] See Add MS 44466, f. 196.

[7] Paragraph printed with this letter in Cowper, 414: Burton argued that 'the mere massing of men together to demand legislate changes . . . justifies a criminal charge. . . . What becomes of Mr Gladstone's Midlothian campaign?'

a law which makes combination to further breach of contract an offence, and that we think such a law ought eminently to be put in action when the means are as dangerous as the end is unwarrantable, when they directly interfere with the rights, free choice and personal security of individuals, and impart actual and even proximate peril to the public peace. If this is in aim and substance tolerably right I need not trouble you to answer, but if I am seriously wrong I should like to be corrected.[1]

To L. A. FAGAN, 22 October 1880.   Add MS 44544, f. 80.

I received the kind gift of your work[2] the day before yesterday and I have since that time perforce read the first volume and begun the second.

I will not longer delay answering your appeal, and the fact I have already mentioned involves the principal part of what I shall now say, namely that you have in my opinion so executed your task as to produce a work of even greater interest than I had expected.

Panizzi had long acquired a strong hold upon my feelings, and the way in which he has dwelt upon my mind since his death shows me that it was even stronger than I knew of during his life-time.

I was therefore jealous for his honour and not without apprehension as to a Biography undertaken immediately after his decease and executed with great dispatch.

I must however pay you the tribute of saying that I do not find in this instance that speed has indicated carelessness, it has rather meant(?)[3] caution, nor has that jealousy in anticipation been revised, on the contrary it has been disarmed by the perusal I have accomplished. In exhibiting him with justice as a very remarkable personality, you have had at once a difficulty and an advantage in happily combining with your picture of the individual a history of two great subjects, the Museum, and the Italian movement.

Had I leisure, I could say much about Panizzi, but I must close by offering you my early and hearty congratulations on your success as a Biographer.[4]

23. Sat.

Ch 8½ a.m. More work on Devolution. Wrote to Bp of London—Ld Granville—Rev. Mr Law and minutes. Walk with the Rector, and much serious conversation on his future and plans of parochial ministry. Read Life of Panizzi. Saw Monck on Ireland—also Hayward & Ld Reay.

Obstruction and Devolution

Obstruction. 1. The question of obstruction in the proceedings of the House of Commons has grown to such a magnitude that it seems to require the consideration of the Government during the present recess.

2. We have subjects more or less in prospect, some of which may present increased inducements to this practice. On these it seems likely that obstruction may present a further aggravation of character.

---

[1] Cowper replied on 24 October, Add MS 44466, f. 221: 'I don't think Justice Burton's doctrine will come in.'

[2] Sent with a letter, Add MS 44466, f. 175. Gladstone had lent his Panizzi letters in March; ibid. 44462, f. 142.

[3] Copyist's insertion.

[4] Letter partly quoted in the second ed. of Fagan's *Panizzi* (1880), i. ii.

3. Even without taking obstruction into account, while legislation has fallen into great arrear, the labours of Parliament have become unduly and almost intolerably severe.

4. It is the extreme pressure of business, which is the secret of the strength of the obstructor proper, and which makes it pay him so well to pursue his vocation at all costs. Were the time at the disposal of the House equal to the calls upon it, it would be in respect to him, a fund virtually unlimited, and it would no longer be so well worth his while to draw upon it.

5. The work of encountering him by repression is extremely difficult, and, as matters now stand, of doubtful issue. In the case of the Irish obstructor, this repression might answer his purpose by supplying him with a new national grievance: and as his extremest resistance would probably be popular with his constituents, the House might find that it had more than a merely personal conflict to handle.

6. It will also be admitted that any serious changes in the role of the House of Commons, if repressive of the liberty of debate, would be grave public evils, even should we be able to avert, by their means, evils graver still.

7. It is worth while to inquire whether there may not be a way, different from that of repression, but in case of need auxiliary and preparatory to it, by which we may neutralize or reduce within more moderate bounds the scandalous evil of obstruction, and the heavy inconvenience of prolonged and manifold legislative disorder.

Devolution 8. This way of proceeding I shall call devolution. By devolving upon other bodies a portion of its overwhelming tasks, the House of Commons may at once economise its time, reduce its arrears, and bring down to a minimum the inducement to obstruct; for obstruction will then be only the infliction of suffering, whereas now it is the frustration of purpose, the defeat of duty.

9. At the same time, whatever repression can do for us will still remain, not less than before, at our command.

10. Of this Devolution, part may be to subordinate and separate authorities. On this portion of the subject I will not now touch. But part may also be to subformations out of the body of the House itself; on something like the same principle, though not in the same form, as those on which the French Chamber divides work among its Bureaux. I shall here rudely sketch some portion at least of what I think may helpfully be undertaken in this direction.

Local Government 11. But I must add that besides the defeat of obstruction, and the improvement of our attitude for dealing with arrear, I conceive that Devolution may supply the means of partially meeting and satisfying, at least so far as it is legitimate, another call. I refer to the call for what is called (*in bonam partem*) Local Government and (*in malam*) Home Rule.

12. One word must be added to these introductory sentences. During a Parliamentary recess since Mr. Brand became Speaker, and when we were last in office, there was a small meeting in Palace Yard, at which Sir T. Erskine May attended. He then gave a general opinion in favour of the devolution of a portion of the duties of the House to Grand Committees. The suggestion was generally approved. It evidently meant something beyond, and distinct from, what is intended in a mere extension of the practice of referring Bills to Select Committees. But the idea was not at the time pursued into much detail. It forms, I need hardly say, the groundwork of the suggestions here appended.

13. They might be extended, in scope as well as in particulars, beyond the present sketch; but this will perhaps suffice at least for raising a very important and rather many-sided question.[1]

[1] Taken from revised draft, signed and dated 23 October 1880; Add MS 44764, f. 1, another draft at f. 110. Details of Grand Cttees. follow, printed in Hammond, 198ff. Paper circulated to 'some Ministers' and later printed; Add MS 44764, f. 152 and PRO CAB 37/4. See 11 Nov. 80.

To LORD HARTINGTON, Indian secretary, 23 October   Add MS 44145, f. 134.
1880.

1. You have I think stated the case most fully and clearly about Fawcett; and, if you can be sure beforehand that he will not take it as a slight, I think you will do well to offer him the Council for India.[1] He ought not to take it otherwise than well, but one never knows in these cases.

I am not however aware that he has been given to understand that the door of the Cabinet is permanently closed against him. If I remember right, in replying to a sort of challenge-letter from him on this subject I was careful to avoid any general declaration.
2. You will kindly think over the question, which you deemed it premature to discuss at the opening of the last Session, whether in conformity with the old practice there might not advantageously be appointed next Session a committee on the Indian Government Act.

The havock effected by the late Government in the provisions of the Act against unconstitutional abuse of the military power of the Executive, and the approval of their proceedings by the late Parliament, seem to supply, besides some other topics, rather strong reasons for a Parliamentary reconsideration of that part of the question.
3. You observed to me, some time back, that you did not quite see the connection between the question of the Indian Balances and that of the subvention we shall have to propose in aid of the war charge. It is not strange that there should be a little difference between your idea of the question and mine, due to our different points of view respectively. Were this a question of a perfectly defined obligation, like a bet or a ground rent, I should not see the connection nor admit its existence. But the duty, which we both acknowledge, is eminently of that class which moralists call duties of indeterminate obligation. Motives of justice, policy and relative ability, are mixed, both as to the proposition, and especially as to the amount. A general relation subsists, as Sir R. Peel wisely said in 1842, between the finance of India and ours, and when we make our proposal for a contribution we cannot wash our hands of the general subject. Nor could I for one form a just idea of the sum we ought to give, unless I were able to answer affirmatively or negatively the question whether, through sheer neglect and gross crudity of financial arrangements, a sum of several millions, available towards the charge of the war, could or could not be had without burden or impoverishment to any body, but on the contrary with some permanent saving as well as great immediate relief to India.

The truth is, I cannot separate my ideas on this particular question from other ideas, as to the general rules of finance and the needful conditions for their existence, which a prolonged experience has brought for me into the body of elementary truths.
P.S. I believe you will find that Halifax when Sec: of State for India used to grouse a good deal over the heavy balances. And it conveys a strange idea of Indian finance when we find that the very simple information we have asked for, is not to be had in Calcutta.

24. 22 S. Trin.

Ch mg & evg. Walk with Ld Monck & Ld Reay—also with the whole party. Wrote to Mr Godley—Ld Hartington—Sir R. Ponsonby—Att. General & minutes. Read C.Q.R. on Julian—Aquinas—Future Punishment.[2]

[1] Proposed in Hartington's letter of 22 October, Add MS 44145, f. 130.
[2] *Church Quarterly Review*, xi. 24, 59, 206 (October 1880).

25. *M.*

Ch 8½ a.m. Wrote to Mr Forster—Ld Northbrook—Mr Brett[1]—Ld Granville—Dr Irons—Mr Godley—Mr Vickers and minutes. Company went and came. Conversation with Hayward. Walk & lengthened conversation with Stephen. Saw White—Lawrie—J. Roberts. Read Life of Panizzi—Coleridge on his Eclogue[2]—Life of Charles.[3]

To W. E. FORSTER, Irish secretary, 25 October 1880.   Add MS 44157, f. 186.

I sympathise deeply in all your troubles:[4] more deeply than perhaps could readily be inferred from the small weight of any remarks or suggestions I can offer.

The first *normal* Cabinet I think will be on the 10th or 11th November. Of course it might be necessary for us to meet before. The Turk is not yet at the end of a store of frauds & falsehoods, which may prove inexhaustible.

Apart from foreign policy and from Ireland there will be the regular work of the November meetings namely to determine the main outlines of legislation for next session; & it is almost a matter of course to continue together for a good while. So there will be ample means of appreciating the moral effect of the prosecutions on the League. You have been compelled to purchase the advantage of a superior method of proceeding at a heavy price in the postponement of the first stroke. Having done this I should rather advise making much of this first stroke, & giving it a character as marked & pointed as possible. I do not know whom you are to prosecute, but I hope not too few, if they are bad men, & at the same time men of mark.

With[5] regard to the suspension of the Habeas Corpus Act, I look to it with feelings not only of aversion on general grounds, but of doubt and much misgiving as to the likelihood of its proving efficacious in the particular case. The crimes which at present threaten to give a case for interference, grow out of certain incitements made by speech. What we want is to enforce silence, abstention from guilty speech. I do not see how this is to be done by *Habeas Corpus* IF it cannot be done by prosecution. Legal prosecutions can be multiplied if necessary far more easily than apprehensions necessarily arbitrary under the suspension of the Habeas Corpus Act. When we were going to pass the Westmeath Act, we knew beforehand pretty exactly who were the handful of people it would be necessary to apprehend as ringleaders in crime. But it would be quite a different matter, & I am afraid a novelty in politics, to apprehend Parnell Biggar & Co., who not only are not suspected of intending to commit crime, but who we know have no idea of committing it, & who only think of intimidating landlords with a possible crime now & then to back the intimidation. I know it is commonly admitted even by those who dislike the suspension of Habeas Corpus, that it would be effectual. I have not yet heard *how* it is to be effectual: & there arises the odious question whether we are to impound a knot of obscure tools, while the real instigators go free.

It will be a very great misfortune if, departing from the precedents of 1833 & 1870, we

---

[1] To Reginald Baliol *Brett (1852-1930; Hartington's secretary 1878-85; liberal M.P. Penrhyn 1880-5; courtier and imperialist; 2nd Viscount Esher 1899) approving the Kandahar dispatch; Add MS 44544, f. 81.

[2] No obvious title found; perhaps S. T. Coleridge's later comments in *Biographica Literaria* (1817) on *Lyrical Ballads* (1798), which Gladstone might have regarded as Eclogues.

[3] Perhaps O. Frederick, *Life of Charles XII* (tr. 1879) or possibly *Life of Charles Roussel; or Industry and honesty* (1880).

[4] Forster's letter this day, Add MS 44157, f. 178, describing spread of disorder and urging need for suspension of Habeas Corpus.

[5] Part of this para. in Hammond, 194.

have to propose any measure of coercion without at the same time declaring our intentions in the matter of remedial legislation. Giving the Land Commission credit for all possible dispatch, it must I suppose be impossible for us to know before Christmas what we are to propose in the matter of Land. I incline to believe with you, that the subject has become urgent in point of time; the rejection of the Disturbance Bill has at once made it so. But I do not abandon the double hope as to the stroke on the 2nd November.[1] 1. that it may do much to paralyse the Land League & arrest mischief. 2. that the landlords will not tempt fortune by a sudden recourse to wholesale evictions.

One of the forms of remedial proceeding will be giving greater facilities to the transaction of local & sectional, and therefore for Irish, subjects. I have prepared a paper dealing at least rudimentally with this matter, which I am going to send to Granville, & which I hope may reach you before the Cabinet meets. Do not suppose I dream of reviving the Irish Parliament; but I have been reading Union speeches & debates, & I am surprised at the narrowness of the case, upon which that Parliament was condemned. I think the unavowed motives must have been the main ones.

You speak of an approaching *disette*[2] of police as possible. At any rate you had a good margin to begin with. When I was visiting Ireland in 1878 [*sic*], I was astonished at their *then* superfluous numbers. Forty or fifty years ago (I know they have since undertaken some new secondary duties) when the people were eight millions, and far less *loyal* than now, there were 8000 police: there are now I believe near 12000 for $\frac{2}{3}$ of that population. It was a great, nay gross, mistake of Sir R. Peel's to take the whole charge on the Consolidated Fund.

Nothing I think can be better than the Memorandum you sent to Godley.

Monck, who has been here, is inclined to look with favour upon Judge Longfield's plan for dealing with the land. I incline to think that if the House of Lords had not in its wisdom struck out of our Land Bill, the power to assign, we might not at this moment have had a Land question before us. But this is a bye-gone.

P.S. I am delighted with the returns you sent me, so far as agricultural distress is concerned. As to the other questions, it is difficult for me to appreciate the answers without *some* idea of the personal ability & impartiality of the answerers.

To LORD NORTHBROOK, 25 October 1880.　　　　　　　　　Add MS 44544, f. 82.

1. I have just received your letter and as you are to be in Birmingham on Friday I hope you will come on to us Chester 7 miles. Broughton Hall [is] a small station at $2\frac{1}{4}$ where we would meet you. You would meet the Baths & Rosebery.

2. Happening to have a batch of rather interesting matter from Forster & Cowper at hand I send it for your perusal should you be so inclined.

There is not a great deal to be said about Ireland; but anything you are likely to say would do good rather than harm in defence of my general line of action.

3. Hartington may generally be depended upon for holding his ground and probably, you will have seen, before this reaches you, his draft dispatch on Candahar. I should be sorry indeed if I thought there was in him, or anywhere in the Government, a disposition to recede from the line we have hitherto taken on this question.

4. I have not yet seen your paper on Pishin and therefore I can only speak generally about the Prince of Wales. But my opinion is that if you impress upon him personally the obligation of secrecy he will *not* disregard it: and, especially considering his age, it is

---

[1] See 21 Oct. 80n.　　　　[2] 'Scarcity'.

desirable to encourage, where it can be safely done, his friendly interest in public questions.[1]

26. Tu.

Ch 8½ a.m. Wrote to Sir W. Harcourt—Central Press and Press Assocn Tel.—H. Seymour 1 & Tel. Ld Sherbrook [*sic*]—Duke of Argyll—Ld Granville—Ld Kimberley—Archbp. of Canterbury—Justice Lush—Mr Forster & minutes. Long sederunt with F.C. also walk with him. The T.G.s came—much conversation on our sister Helen's affairs. Read Panizzi (finished)—Smart on Ruskin.[2]

To the DUKE OF ARGYLL, lord privy seal, 26 October 1880.   Add MS 44544, f. 83.

I am very sorry you continue suffering or apprehensive about your gout.

My idea for the first normal Cabinet is the 10th, or 11th. This I will arrange with Granville. But in any case I think you may reckon on good notice, setting aside exceptional cases.

The Turk,[3] that is the Sultan, is a bottomless pit of iniquity and fraud. He is not only a liar, but seems as though he might compete with Satan for the honour of being the Father of it, and stand a fair chance of winning. However, Her Majesty thinks we ought to endeavour to regain his 'confidence'.

No one can at this moment say whether he means or does not mean to fulfil his last pledge as to Dulcigno.

To W. E. FORSTER, Irish secretary, 26 October 1880.   Add MS 44544, f. 82.

I wrote at some length yesterday but I forgot to answer your question about Lyons & the Nuncio.[4]

In O'Connell's time application was made by Peel's Government to the Pope and a missive was got from him in the sense desired.

The case is different now, and the Protestants would view it differently. Nothing could be done without the Cabinet. I am not sure the Cabinet would like it. It was not very effective before: and it would be less so now.

Your kind message is gone to Herbert.

27. Wed.

Ch 8½ a.m. Wrote to Ld Granville 1. & Tel.—Goschen—Herbert G.—Rev. Dr Dale—Mr Morley—Mr Godley & minutes. Again revised my paper on Devolution. Walk with T.G. in floods of rain: & more conversation on Helen's affairs. Read Dale's sermon[5]—Dionysiak Myth.[6] Ten to dinner.

---

[1] Northbrook wrote on 24 October, Add MS 44266, f. 78, on his speech about to be given in Birmingham, telling Gladstone not to hesitate about Kandahar, mentioning a Cabinet paper on Pishin and Kandahar requested to be seen by the Prince of Wales, and doubting the Prince's reticence. Northbrook's reply of 27 October, ibid., f. 82, regretted his inability to come to Hawarden; he sent the mem. to the Prince.

[2] An earlier version of W. Smart, *A disciple of Plato. A critical study of John Ruskin* (1883).

[3] Argyll to Gladstone, 25 October 1880, Add MS 44104, f. 222: 'The Turks seem to be behaving with their usual unprincipled cunning....'

[4] Asking for Lyons to ask the Nuncio in Paris to get the Pope to 'do real good' with Irish bps. visiting Rome; Add MS 44157, f. 180.

[5] R. W. Dale, *The Evangelical Revival and other sermons* (1880).

[6] See 24 Mar. 77.

To G. J. GOSCHEN, ambassador at Constantinople,   Add MS 44544, f. 84.
27 October 1880.

Many thanks for your letter.[1] Granville has sent me your personal Telegram of Sunday especially (but every Telegram you send comes to me at once and of course).

You cannot I think have a more entire sympathy than from him and from me. You will have seen from his reply, that you cannot too strongly contradict once for all our being 'art and part' with the Times. These foreigners are so slow in learning the seriously altered position of that newspaper: how the provincial press has gained ground on the metropolitan: how the other metropolitans of the penny press have gained ground on the Times. There does not now exist for this country 'a leading Journal'; but this the Continent does not understand.

As to the question whether there is to be a halt after Dulcigno, or after the Montenegrin frontier, that is a question on which as far as I recollect nobody is finally committed. Probably the French are most committed against it: and of them we now know that they mean, for the present at least, to back out. I do not see how any definitive judgment can be formed, until we know when and how we are to get out of the first and simplest of the questions.

I believe you and we are completely at one as to intentions, desires, and propositions. But mood is acted upon by *entourage*, and our, let me rather say Granville's entourage is different from yours. He is in closer communication with the Foreign Governments, you with the Constantinople ambassadors, and these, upon the whole, and notably in one if not more instances, are better than the Governments. He is in the best position of all for judging how great a weight we can safely hang upon what ought to be a cable but sometimes seems a thread, the European concert. He has got to pursue a most difficult aim, by means as difficult and in doing this he has very properly renounced the big drum, and never uses a word except what, as far as England is concerned, he means to act upon within the limits of course of the other two conditions. A task not only of Hercules but of Sisyphus.

I feel the question that will arise after we get quit of Dulcigno, and say of Montenegro, to be a most grave one. Sole action might be Quixotic, and would also require a new start. But what form combination may take, and when, can I fear only be judged at the last moment; most certainly if there is to be a halt, it will not be, so far as I am concerned, a case of 'rest and be thankful' but rather of *reculer pour mieux sauter*.

I write this on the instant from Hawarden for tomorrow's messenger and of course without its passing under any ministerial eye before it leaves. Yet I write boldly in proportion as I believe that *our* concert, at any rate, holds, and will hold.[2]

To J. MORLEY, 27 October 1880.   Add MS 44544, f. 83.

I read with particular satisfaction your article of yesterday:[3] for I have not as yet obtained any sufficient answer to the question I have sometimes put: '*how* is the suspension of the *Habeas Corpus* to frustrate a conspiracy against property & bring about a payment of rents?' Even if it became necessary hereafter, which God forbid, for the protection of life & the repression of violence, this, taken alone, will not meet the specific form of social disease which is now afflicting Ireland. As I am writing, let me say that I also read with great interest a few days back the PMG's article on the High Church Party[4]

[1] Of 15 October, replying to that of 3 Oct. 80; Add MS 44161, f. 269.

[2] Part in Elliot, *Goschen*, i. 203; described to Granville as 'an anodyne letter', Ramm II, i. 210.

[3] Leader in the *Pall Mall Gazette*, distinguishing between effects of Habeas Corpus suspension and prosecution of Parnell.

[4] *Pall Mall Gazette*, 25 October 1880, 1581.

in the Church of England; agreeing, I think, with what it said until I came, near the end, to a statement that they were wrong in not leaving the Church. This, I think, from the writer's point of view, would have been just, if he had said they ought not to leave but to disestablish & disendow (if they could). As it is, the allegation requires of the High Church man that he should contravene a fundamental article of his belief, namely that our Saviour through the Apostles founded an institution called in the Creed the Holy Catholic Church, to be locally distributed throughout the earth, that it is [a] matter of duty to abide in this church, & that for England this church is found in the Church of England. I do not well see how with this belief he is to go out of it. Do not think of answering this note.[1]

28. *Th. S.S. Simon & Jude.*

Church 8½ (with H.C.) Wrote to Duke of Leinster—Mr Leeman M.P.—Sir Thos. G.—Mr Tennyson—Mr H. Doyle—Major Baring[2]—Dr Dale B.P. and minutes. Walk with Mrs T.G.—party in woods & park. Read Dale's Address—Spedding on Tennyson Turner—Tennyson Turner, Poems[3]—Kay on Austria Hungary[4]— Dionysiak Myth.

To J. J. LEEMAN, M.P., 28 October 1880.   Add MS 44544, f. 86.

I thank you on my own behalf for your considerate letter.[5] I am afraid I must leave my youngest son to exercise his own discretion. He has a good deal of speaking to do for his constituents: and it would be dangerous for him, at the outset of a Parliamentary career, to go much beyond his own immediate province in addressing further assemblies. At the same time I shall not volunteer to him my opinion which would prevent his acceding to your wish.

To Alfred TENNYSON, 28 October 1880.   Tennyson Research Centre, MS 5958.[6]

Believing that I owe the gift of your Brother's Sonnets to your kindness, I must not, although I am not yet fully saturated with them, any longer delay my thanks for a book so beautiful, and so delightful.

That I was ignorant of them (though I had heard of their rare merit) during his life-time may seem both strange and damnatory to you, for you do not and cannot know by what a wall of adamant my profession shuts me out from most of what is worth knowing in this world.

His deep, tender, fascinating imagination hardly impresses me more than does, all along, the singularly ethical character of the book. Few volumes of poetry, as I conjecture, form such a piece of portrait-painting: few as I feel, and fewer still, inspire so deep a regret, and sense of loss, for not having known the person who produced it.

Most touching and penetrating is your tribute.[7] I compare it for contrast with the

[1] Morley replied (30 October, Add MS 44255, f. 23) on difficulties of 'making public opinion about Ireland more generous, candid, and impartial', and arguing that High Churchmen should perhaps leave the Church of England if they believed it deprived of Catholicity by Parliament or the courts.
[2] Evelyn *Baring, 1841-1917; in Egypt 1877-80; finance minister on viceroy's council 1880-3; British agent in Egypt 1883-1907; cr. Baron Cromer 1892. See Add MS 44466, f. 231.
[3] C. Tennyson Turner, *Collected sonnets. With an introductory essay by J. Spedding* (1880).
[4] D. Kay, *Austro-Hungary* (1880).
[5] Not found; Joseph Johnson, s. of George Leeman; liberal M.P. York 1880-3.
[6] By permission of the Lincolnshire Library Service.
[7] Alfred Tennyson's poem, 'At Midnight', which prefaced the volume.

verses of Catullus to his dead brother, of which however neither you nor any one can surpass the beauty.[1]

I remember your kindness in coming here: nothing but the extravagance of the proposal checks me from praying you to come again where at all times you would be welcome.

Let me before I close revert to a subject on which you corresponded before with me, and also with my successor. I rely on your kindness to let me know if now, or at any time during this my last and I hope shorter tenure of office, it would be agreeable to you that that subject should be raised. Having said this I shall trouble you no more about it.[2]

[P.S.] Mary wishes to express her agreement in what I have said of the introductory verses—and the Book.

29. Fr.

Ch 8½ a.m. Tom & his party went. Wrote to Ld Northbrook—Ld Clifton—Ld Kimberley—Bp of Manchester—Mr Godley tel. & minutes and minutes. Ld Rosebery came. Drive & farm call with C. Read Chain of Geological Firm[3]—Tennyson Turner Sonnets—Brown, Dionysiak Myth and Hillebrand, Germ. Thought.[4]

30. Sat.

Ch 8½ a.m. Wrote to Mr Godley Tel. 1.2.—Sir H. Ponsonby l and Tel.—Press Assocn Tel.—Ld Granville—Mr Otway—Mr Hertslet[5]—Mr Newton—Sir W. Harcourt—The Queen (Duplicates) and minutes. Saw Ld F. Cavendish—Ld R. Grosvenor—Ld Rosebery—Mr McColl. A hard day of business with small intermission. Read Shaker's Theology[6]—Dionysiak Myth. Walk with the party.

31. 23. S. Trin.

Ch 11. a.m. 6½ P.M. Wrote to Ld Kimberley—Ld Granville—The Queen—Mr Errington M.P. and minutes. Read Fuller's Commentary[7]—Wilkin's on Future Punisht.[8] Walk & conversation with Ld Bath.

Mond. Nov. 1. 1880 All S.

Wrote to Mr Villiers Stuart—Mad. Novikoff—Ld Granville l. & Tel—Ld Kimberley—Scotts—Duke of Argyll—Mr Fawcett. Walk with Ld Bath, & much

---

[1] Catullus's 'Ave atque Vale', poem ci. Gladstone's observation might have upset Tennyson who had written 'Frater Ave atque Vale' in June 1880 (published in *Nineteenth Century* (March 1883)) but Tennyson's reply agreed with Gladstone's comment; see *Tennyson, a memoir*, ii. 239.

[2] i.e. an honour, here unspecified, eventually accepted in the form of a peerage in 1883 (Gladstone had offered a baronetcy in March 1873); the last para. of Tennyson's reply (omitted by Hallam Tennyson in *Tennyson, a memoir*, ii. 239) again declined a baronetcy, adding: 'in declining a Baronetcy for myself, I feel still more than I did that I would fain see it bestowed on my son Hallam *during my lifetime* . . .'; Add MS 44466, f. 251.　　　　　[3] Untraced.

[4] C. Hillebrand, *Six lectures on the history of German thought from the Seven Years' War to Goethe's death* (1880).

[5] Sir Edward *Hertslet, 1824-1902; librarian of the foreign office; had sent Hahn (see 24 Sept. 80); Add MS 44544, f. 87.

[6] *A brief exposition of the established principles and regulations of the . . . Shakers* (1851).

[7] T. Fuller, probably *A comment on the eleven first verses of the fourth chapter of S. Matthew's Gospel* (1652).

[8] Perhaps J. Wilkins, *Notes on the Church catechism* (1877).

conversation. Also with [blank.] Read Wilkin's finished.—Dionysiak Myth. Odo Russell came. Church 8½ a.m.

To the DUKE OF ARGYLL, lord privy seal, 1 November   Add MS 44104, f. 230.
1880.

Through a mistake of mine your letter of the 28th[1] has only come to me to-day, and I write simply for the purpose of expressing my agreement with you as against the words imputed to Chamberlain. We were under no pledge whatever with regard to Irish Land. Moreover, in my judgment, there was no urgency attaching to the subject, apart from the circumstance of famine and further still I believe that urgency would have been met by the Disturbance Bill had the Lords chosen to pass it.

The rejection of that measure I fear greatly altered the situation for the worse. As to pledge, our only deviation from the old position has lain in the appointment of the Commission: but as to urgency it is another matter.

[P.S.] Cabinet for the 10th. You perceive the difficulties which baffle calculation as to our times of proceeding: but unless Ireland throw us off the rails I should certainly hope we may be back at our homes say in the beginning of December.

2. Tu.

Ch 8¼ a.m. Wrote to The Queen Tel 1.2.—Mr Forster Tel—Herbert G. Tel— H.N.G.—Mr C.S. Palmer—Mr Brassey M.P.—Mr Cowan—Dr Birdwood[2] and minutes. Walk & much conversation with Ld Bath—Also much conversation with Odo Russell. Read account Waldeck—Account of Mad. de Boissy[3]—Scribner's Mag on Bordenstown.[4] Dufferin came. It is a most agreeable party.

To T. BRASSEY, M.P., 2 November 1880.   Add MS 44544, f. 89.

I thank you for your letter[5] & return the inclosure. We are doing or trying to do the best we can. It is annoying to see with what facility many minds run to the suspension of the *Habeas Corpus*. And as a thing to be done *at once*! Has your brother reckoned what time it would take, even with a fuller case than we now have, to pass an act for this purpose? And how many have thought out, or shown, in what way this suspension is to secure the payment of rents? We shall probably know a good deal more a fortnight hence than we do now.

3. Wed.

Ch 8½ a.m. Wrote to Mr Godley l & Tel—The Queen l & Tel—Mrs Th—Ld Kimberley—Sir Thos G.—Ld Advocate—Ld Clifton and minutes. Saw Mr

---

[1] Add MS 44104, f. 224, complaining about Chamberlain's speech at Birmingham: the Govt. not pledged to deal with Irish Land.
[2] Thanking (Sir) George Christopher Molesworth Birdwood (1832-1917, physician and author) for his *Industrial arts of India* (1880); Add MS 44544, f. 89.
[3] M. R. D. Smith, *Recollections of two distinguished persons. La Marquise de Boissy and the Count de Waldeck* (1878).
[4] 'Bordenstown and the Bonapartes', *Scribner's Monthly Magazine*, xxi. 28 (November 1880); the issue also contains an appraisal of Gladstone.
[5] Not found.

Leveson (H.J.G.)—Odo Russell—Ld Bath—Ld Dufferin. Read Dionysiak Myth. Long walk with the party.

4. Th.

Ch 8¼ a.m. Wrote to Sir H. Ponsonby—Ld Granville—Mr Forster—Sir C. Herries—Mr West—Mr Sclater Booth—Sir Thos. G.—Mr E.L. Pierce—Mr Bryce and minutes. Conversation with Ld O. Russell—Ld Dufferin—Mr MacColl—Walk & conversation with W.H.G. Read Irish Constab. Reports—Contempy on Irish Land[1]—OBrien on Irish Land—Dionysiak Myth.

To W. E. FORSTER, Irish secretary, 4 November 1880.　　　　　Add MS 44544, f. 89.

I have received this morning the Constabulary Reports,[2] up to the 27th (I suppose) and have read them without any fresh access of discouragement. I telegraphed to you about the Cabinet on the 10th. I also sent you the Queen's request for direct reports from Ireland which probably Cowper would send. Anything I might say on the 9th about Ireland would be short, and I think I see the rocks to be avoided. I daresay you will kindly let me have any suggestion which you may desire to make. I have not yet read the Longfield Land plans but am much struck by its ingenuity as reported to me. Also I am struck with Villiers Stuart's proposal for converting tenancies, as now understood, into fees. Perhaps in the case of the dead hand there might be given a conditional right to claim such conversion. It is really at first view a more workable scheme than peasant purchases, & far better for the Government to assist in. I am told the Duke of Abercorn has been recommending it. An article in the new Contemporary for Nationalizing the Land does not strike me as affording any daylight whatever.

Pray let the Queen see the last reports of the Constabulary. Could you direct a short memorandum on the Tithe agitation 1831-2 (I think) to be prepared for the Cabinet? It would be important to know its relation to crime & to the Coercion Act of 1833.

5. Fr.

Ch 8¼ a.m. Wrote to Hon. Rev. Mr Freemantle—Messrs Pears—Mr Godley—Mr Graham[3]—Mr R. OBrien—Mr Forster—Earl Nelson—Miss de Lisle—Mr Parker MP. & minutes. Saw Rev. Mr M'Coll—Mr Welby. Walk with M.H.G. Read O'Brien (finished)—Poole on the Ten Tribes[4]—Dionysiak Myth.

To Rev. W. H. FREMANTLE, 5 November 1880.　　　　　Add MS 44544, f. 90.

I am sorry that an accidental delay on the part of a friend whom I consulted has put off till this date my reply to your letter of the 18th ult.[5]

And I am further concerned to have arrived at the conclusion that I ought not to take part in the subscription for the Père Hyacinthe's undertaking. In my official position I intend as far as I can to keep aloof from the region of controverted matter, and knowing how these affairs mix themselves up with diplomacy I think it right to abstain in this instance.

---

[1] *Contemporary Review*, xxxviii. 716 (November 1880).
[2] Printed for the Cabinet; Harcourt MSS dep. 106.
[3] James Graham, accountant, on railway nationalization; Add MS 44544, f. 91.
[4] W. H. Poole, *Anglo-Israel, or the Saxon race proved to be the lost tribes of Israel* (1879).
[5] Add MS 44465, f. 191, sending an untraced statement on Père Hyacinthe.

I have in no degree changed my opinion of his personal character or my disposition to pay him whether by subscription or otherwise any mark of respect in his personal capacity.

To R. Barry O'BRIEN, 5 November 1880.[1]   Add MS 44544, f. 91.

I thank you for kindly sending me your work and I hope that the sad and discreditable story you have told so well in your narrative of the Irish Land question may be useful at a period when we have more than ever of reason to desire that it should be thoroughly understood.

I venture on the single remark that your account of the Bill of 1870 would I think be more exact if it mentioned distinctly the compensation for disturbance which the authors of the Bill considered to be by much its most important feature.

6. Sat.

Ch 8½ a.m. Wrote to Ld Hartington—Ld Granville—Made Novikoff—Sir C. Gavan Duffy and minutes. Mr Welby: 3½ hours, or 4 h, on Treasury matters. Long walk. Read Duffy's Young Ireland.[2]

7. 24. S. Trin.

Ch 11 a.m. with H.C. & 6½ P.M. Saw Mr Welby—Mr M'Coll. Wrote to Mr Forster—Ld Granville—Ld Powerscourt and minutes. Much anxious reading from Ireland absorbed a large part of my Sunday. Read Longfield on Irish land[3]—Presbn Review:—Taylor Innes on Presbytm—Dewitt on Revision.[4]

To W. E. FORSTER, Irish secretary, 7 November 1880.   Add MS 44157, f. 211.

I have received your letters of the 5th & 6th; a mighty budget.[5] On the subject of a Land Bill I will not enter as I presume we cannot practically approach it until we know something of the recommendations of our Commission. I confine myself to other matters.

The objection to my announcing a strong Land Bill conditional on quiet (and vice versâ, no quiet no Land Bill) I am afraid is this, that it would not be true. We could not withhold from the country a Land Bill required by its wants on account of crimes committed by a limited portion of the population? and it is also lamentably true that at almost every juncture of Irish History disturbance and fear have propelled not retarded remedial legislation. *Hopes* might be expressed in the sense you sketch, but hardly announcements?

From the apparent state of your mind we are near a serious discussion on the question of suspending the Habeas Corpus Act.

I quite agree that if it is to be done, when the facts [are?] now before us, no time ought to be lost in calling Parliament together for the purpose: and probably also that, if the proposal is made, it should be carried with the strong hand.

I own that for my own part, I have as yet neither seen any justifying statement of facts,

---

[1] O'Brien (see 7 Jan. 80) had sent his *The parliamentary history of the Irish land question* (1880).

[2] The first volume of Sir C. G. Duffy, *Young Ireland. A fragment of Irish history 1840–50*, 2v. (1880–3).

[3] M. Longfield, 'Land tenure in Ireland', *Fortnightly Review*, xxxiv. 137 (August 1880); an important influence, see 14 Dec. 80 and Bahlman, *Hamilton*, i. 83.

[4] *Presbyterian Review*, i. 480, 499 (1880).

[5] Letters, with enclosure from E. W. O'Brien, at Add MS 44157, ff. 191-206.

nor any argument to describe to me for what exact purpose the suspension is intended.

There is in these cases a great and just weight due to precedent; though when the question is an Irish one, precedent chiefly defines to us lines which we should not go *beyond* in the repressive sense.

We shall have to compare the purposes of our suspension with the purpose of former suspensions; & the justifying facts with former justifying facts. The Cabinet will require to be prepared for a great battle in Parliament: and if they are wise they will have an entire case in their hands before deciding.

Ought the Habeas Corpus Act to be suspended except on account of danger to life? Has it heretofore been suspended except mainly on this ground? Is the danger to life such as to require it? What is that danger as measured by actual outrages, in comparison with the outrages of former times? Is it possible to ask Parliament for an arbitrary power to imprison suspected misdemeanants? If we are to have a stronger Act than the Westmeath Act, have we broader facts to base it on? Shall we submit our facts as we then did to a Committee of Parliament? How shall we stand as to the ratio of mischief & remedy, in comparison with the case of 1833?

There may be very good reasons against that which would certainly occur to my mind as the first & most reasonable thing to be done; namely to put down the Land League itself, if need be, by prohibiting any combination of men formed for the purpose even apart from violence—of inciting others to disobey the law & to break their contracts.

It appears to me a contingency not to be treated as impossible that by invading the Constitution we might check outrages so as to reduce them within ordinary limits, & yet that the League if permitted to exist, might continue what I take to be the deepest and widest part of the mischief, namely the conspiracy against property. I have suggested many troublesome questions; but in truth we cannot sift & cross examine ourselves too much in the face of so wretched a necessity as that we may have to discuss. An aggravation of the evil will be, the separation between our measure of coercion & what we may propose as relief.

I send you a good letter from Powerscourt. Having now read Judge Longfield I am not sure whether his plan will thoroughly hold water.[1]

[P.S.] I should much like to have in London by Tuesday morning some statement or sketch of the comparative facts of crime & evictions.

8. M. [*London*]

Wrote to Ld Granville (2)—Made Novikoff—Ld Spencer—Ld R. Grosvenor and minutes. Off at 10.30—D. St 4.30. Dined at Ld F.C.s. Saw the P. Secs. Ld Granville $5\frac{1}{2}$-$6\frac{1}{4}$ and again in evg. Do cum Ld Hartington—We discussed Ireland & India for tomorrow. Read Sir C. Duffy. Church $8\frac{1}{2}$ a.m.

9. Tu.

Wrote to Ld Rosebery—Mr Forster Tel.—The Queen and minutes. The Prince of Wales. Saw Priv. Secs.—Lady Ripon—Ld Granville (on the line tonight)— Ld Wolvn. Ruminated much on what I should say: felt myself more than ever a poor creature. "But I will give you a mouth and wisdom". $6\frac{1}{2}$-$11\frac{1}{2}$ Lord Mayor's dinner. Made my speech without any gross offence that I know of. It was not (I hope) quite half an hour.[2] Read Young Ireland.

---

[1] Details of outrages in October sent on 8 November; Add MS 44157, f. 213.

[2] *T.T.*, 10 November 1880, 6c. Hamilton noted 'There seems to be a consensus of opinion that

10.

Wrote to The Queen—Lord Spencer and minutes. Cabinet 2-6. Dined with the Benchers.[1] Saw Ld Kenmare—Sir J. Lacaita—Mr Murray—Private Secs. Read Young Ireland.

Cabinet. Nov. 10. 1880. 2. p.m. Lord Granville's.[2]
1. Ld. Granville recited the facts since last meeting as to Monten[egrin] frontier. Terms of Ld. Granville's answer to Count Menabrea agreed on after a full conversation on the general subject.[3]
2. State of Ireland. Hopes Cabinet will decide Monday or Tuesday. Expects trial *may* be in 2d w[eek] Decr. If D[efendant]s desire postponement to Jany it prob[abl]y wd not be refused. Venue in Dublin.
3. No offer of [Army] officers to be made to Cape for Basuto War.

Project[4]
1) Prohibit by law all combinations or associations for the purpose of inducing persons to break contracts or refuse the payment of legal debts. Membership thereof or participation in their proceedings to be punished as a misdemeanour.
2) When in the judgment of (H.M. or of) the Viceroy of Ireland the action of such associations shall endanger the public security in the whole or any part of the country, their meetings and all other proceedings whether under their existing or any other name may be prohibited by proclamation, and after such proclamation any person attending such meeting or taking part in or endeavouring by whatever means to give effect to such proceeding ⟨shall⟩ may be arrested and unless a member of one of the Houses of Parliament shall not be bailable.
3) The Land League of Ireland to be prohibited by act under the conditions of 2).
4) Provisions 2) and 3) to remain in force for ([blank]) years.[5]

11.

Wrote to Ld Granville—Ld Halifax—Mr Forster and minutes. Dined at Mr West's. Worked on Devolution. Saw Ld Kimberley—Mr Bulkeley Hughes—Ld R. Grosvenor—Mr West—Ld F. Cavendish—Mrs Th.—Ld Granville—Priv. Secs. Saw Drew [R]. Read Young Ireland—Palmer on Belief in Vict. Review.[6]

Having had the advantage of reading the Minutes of some Ministers to whom I sent the first draft of the Paper on 'Devolution and Obstruction'[7] I now send it to be printed for the Cabinet with these remarks.
1. I admit that the survival for practical purposes of Grand Committees would revive the name more than the thing and would be in the main new though holding on to the old.

Mr. G. spoke in a statesmanlike way'; Bahlman, *Hamilton*, i. 74. Gladstone used the speech as a basis for delaying coercion; see 19 Nov. 80.

[1] *T.T.*, 11 November 1880, 6d.
[2] Add MS 44642, f. 73. Granville was ill.
[3] Delivered orally, urging continued use of the concert in the Greek frontier question; Ramm II, i. 219.
[4] On a separate sheet, Add MS 44642, f. 74.
[5] 'Sullivan's plan?' added in pencil at foot of page.
[6] See 13 Nov. 80n.
[7] See 23 Oct. 80; comments printed for Cabinet together with this note; Add MS 44625, f. 4.

2. It seems essential that if any plan of this kind be adopted there should be a simple method of appointment, and one as far as may be self-working: & the body once appointed should not be open to easy change.

3. It may be question whether the House has yet attained a sufficient consciousness of the existing & impending evils to be willing to face a drastic remedy: but unless it has arrived at this willingness I believe it will have still to draw upon its stock, if any, of unexhausted patience before getting rid of obstruction or reducing arrear.[1]

To W. E. FORSTER, Irish secretary, 11 November 1880.   Add MS 44544, f. 93.

Parnell's speech of yesterday seems to me curious, perhaps hopeful.[2] To test his allegation, as well as for other reasons, you will I daresay give directions that we may on Monday have the *latest* accounts of crime & outrage.

I should like also to know (if you have not provided them already) what number of persons on each suspension of the Habeas Corpus Act, have been imprisoned under the arbitrary power.

The Standard has a noteworthy article today on the Cabinet & Ireland.

12. Fr.

Wrote to Ld Portarlington—Ld Hartington—Mr Forster—Mr E.R. Russell—The Queen and minutes. Cabinet 3-6¼. C. of Exchequer 2-3 P.M. Saw Mr Rathbone (en route). Dined at home. Read Young Ireland—Hor. Seymour on Amn & European Agriculture.[3]

Cabinet. Nov. 12. 80. 3. p.m[4]

1. Dover Harbour: Notices should be given for the Private Bill. If after examination of the convict labour question any larger plan at Dover should be found desirable for the employment of convicts, it can be substituted for the private plan.

2. Convict labour. Harcourt to give a mem. of the *modus operandi* when the present system was adopted.[5]

3. Wali [Sher Ali] to retire from Candahar. Abduo [*sic*] Rahman to be asked whether he can take over Candahar from us. Some papers to be published.[6]

4. Subjects of Govt. measures for next Session considered—explained in my Mem.— Dodson's Mem.—Harcourt's Water Bill—Chancellor mentioned Patent Laws—Ld. N[orthbrook] Navy Corporal Punishment. Bankruptcy? Bill to be prepared. Committee on Corrupt Practices and Ballot: Ld. Northbrook, Sir W. Harcourt, Mr. Bright, Mr. Chamberlain, Attorney General, Sir C. Dilke, Hibbert.

5. Candahar dispatch. Cabinet approved Ld. Hartington's change of phrase substituting disapprobation of for inability to consent to permanent retention. Did not agree to insert 'under existing circs'.

6. Monday Cabinet on Devolution. Wedy on Ireland.

[1] Holograph, initialled and dated 11 November 1880; Add MS 44764, f. 152.
[2] At Enniskillen, *T.T.*, 11 November 1880, 6c: the Land League 'to work by the simple, legal, and constitutional method of combination'; it has saved tenants from eviction and 'also saved the lives of many landlords and many agents'.
[3] H. Seymour, 'Address ... before the New York State Agricultural Society' (1880).
[4] Add MS 44642, f. 75.
[5] See Harcourt's mem. on use of convicts for public works; PRO CAB 37/4/78.
[6] On 18 January 1881; *PP* 1881 lxx. 35.

Mem. Nov. 12

As before: 1. Suffrage etc. 2. London Govt., 3. Local Govt. generally. 4. Land Laws.

As now: 1. Forms and business of Parliament. 2. Irish Land. 3. Ballot Act. Corrupt Practices. 4. Death Duties (Mortgage Duty). 5. Bankruptcy. 6. Criminal (Code) Procedure. 7. Irish Electoral Franchise.

To LORD HARTINGTON, 12 November 1880.   Chatsworth MSS 340. 1033.

Of the language of Trevelyan's note[1] I will say nothing for his conduct in Parliament has I think been a model. As to the substance of the note I wish he would ask himself which of the men in the House of Commons now in office could have been passed by in order to give him a higher office than the one, unequal I admit to his claims, which I actually offered him.

He cannot I am sure fail to observe that other men, his seniors, some of them higher in official rank, some of them like himself marked by Parliamentary service, were left out of the list of the present Government.

With regard to Adam's vacancy, I propose that you and Granville should meet soon with R. Grosvenor early next week.—

I have spoken to your brother—'Your man', if I may so call him, in F.s office would raise a rebellion in the H. of Commons. But all this will keep.

13. Sat.

Wrote to Ld Leigh—The Queen and minutes. Dined with Mrs Birks & heard more of the Beer trade.[2] Saw Scotts—Cooper—DeBorne.[3] Saw Mr Evelyn Baring—Mr Bright—Mr Forster—Ld Granville—Priv. Secs. Read Vict. Rev. on Belief[4]—Young Ireland—Life of Bp Doyle.[5]

14. 25. S. Trin.

Chapel Royal mg & aft. Saw Mr West—Ld Halifax. Wrote to Mr Childers—Earl Cowper. Read Vict. Rev. on The Stage.—Dean M'Cartney & H.S.,[6]—Abp. of Cantab. Charge[7]—Dr Barry Boyle Lectures.[8]

To LORD COWPER, Irish viceroy, 14 November 1880.   Add MS 44544, f. 93.

I have not yet reached the point indicated by your letter,[9] for this reason among others, that I am not at all clear as to the means offered by a Suspension Act for reaching

[1] G. O. Trevelyan to Hartington, 9 November 1880, Chatsworth MSS 340. 1032 (forwarded to Gladstone by Hartington and returned), protesting that 'last April these claims were ignored, and I was treated in a manner as wounding to my feelings as it has been fatal to my political future'; no specific post requested.

[2] His neighbour in Harley Street, apparently of a brewing family; see 26 June 80.

[3] A rescue case; see next d.

[4] Presumably the *Victoria Magazine*, which was edited until June 1880 by Emily Faithfull who visited Hawarden (see 10 Sept. 78n.). No copy found, the British Library one being missing.

[5] W. J. Fitzpatrick, *The Life, times and correspondence of . . . Dr Doyle* (1880).

[6] H. B. Macartney, *The experiment of three hundred years. A statement of the efforts made by the English government to make known the Gospel to the Irish Nation* (1847).

[7] Tait's charge (1880) referred to the Burials Bill; see *Life of Tait*, ii. 409ff.

[8] A. Barry, *The Manifold witness for Christ* (1880); the Boyle lectures 1877–8.

[9] Of 13 November 1880, Add MS 44466, f. 320 and Cowper, 427. Docketed 'circulated', strongly supporting suspension of Habeas Corpus.

the root of the mischief. However the matter requires the most searching consideration. For this, the explanation of your views is a needful element & I will at once circulate your letter among the ministers.

I am very glad that you are so much impressed with the necessity of close secrecy.

In a Memorandum lately prepared about the Anti-Tithe agitation[1] the totals of offences are given for 1831 & 1832. There is no distinction of agrarian offences from others. Some light however will be thrown upon the case if you will kindly send me by Telegraph or return 1. The totals of *all* offences for say 1829-31, and 1834-6. 2. The totals of all offences other than those reported as agrarian from 1870 to the present time.

If you have returns specifying the different classes of offences please to send them. In any case I should like to know the number of homicides for each of the years I have named.

15. M.

Wrote to W.H.G.—Mrs Th.—Sir Thos. G.—Viceroy Tel—Scotts—The Queen l & Tel and minutes. Saw Priv. Secs—Mr Forster—Sir H. Parkes—Ld R. Grosvenor. Dined at Mrs Ralli's. Read Vict. Rev. on Irish Land[2]—Tcherkess & his victim.[3] Cabinet 2-5.

Cabinet. Nov. 15. 80. 2 p.m[4]

1. Conversation on the article of Saturday in the Standard[5] betraying knowledge of what took place in the Cabinet on Friday.
2. Devolution and obstruction. Lengthened conversation. Granville to obtain the account of the American system clôture. Dodson [of] French clôture—Bureaux.[6] May's plan of committees.[7]

16. Tu.

Wrote to Mr Forster (2)—D. of Cambridge—Mr Rathbone—Mr Chadwick—Ld Hartington and minutes. Ten to dinner. Saw De Borne [R]. Saw Priv. Secs.—Ld R. Grosvenor—Mr Forster—Ld Granville—Ld Nelson—do cum Ld Hartington—Ld F. Cavendish—W. Lyttelton. Read Young Ireland.

To W. E. FORSTER, Irish secretary, 16 November 1880.   Add MS 44157, f. 222.

[First letter] What you said to me last evening before leaving the Cabinet Room much impressed my mind.

Looking more closely at your returns of offences (which appear excellent), I took out

[1] Printed for the Cabinet, Harcourt MSS, dep. 106.

[2] See 13 Nov. 80.

[3] *The Tcherkess and his victim: sketches illustrative of the moral, social and political aspects of life in Constantinople* (1880).

[4] Add MS 44642, f. 78.

[5] Leading article in *The Standard*, 13 November 1880, with details of planning of timing of the Session, and listing proposed bills (Irish Land, water, ballot, bankruptcy) and stating: 'the Cabinet in the course of next week will definitely abandon the notion of coercion'; copy at Add MS 44642, f. 80; almost certainly leaked by Chamberlain, see Garvin, i. 328.

[6] Reports printed at Add MS 44625, ff. 106ff.

[7] See 23 Oct. 80; Gladstone's proposal was supported by Bright and Chamberlain, otherwise opposed or not thought worth proceeding with; Chamberlain, *Memoir*, 9. See 23 Oct. 80.

the figures copied clearly on the paper within. You said most judiciously on a former day that if we are to ask for the suspension of *Habeas Corpus* it ought to be on a case of great strength and clearness. But do these figures, after all the allowances to be made for 'protection', indicate *such* a case? As far as I can judge, there is a tendency in Ireland, upon a series of years, to a decline in the *total* number of homicides.

The immense increase in *property* offences (agrarian) for 1880 seems to me to mark the true character of the crisis, and the true source of the mischief viz. the Land League. But I incline to assume that any suspension of *H.C.* must be founded on danger of life.[1]

Add MS 44544, f. 94.

[Second letter] I send you a copy of a scrap (the fruit perhaps of perplexity) which impresses roughly the leaning of my mind as to a possible form of proceeding by legislation for the defence of property against improper combinations.[2]

17. Wed.

Wrote to Mr Forster—Mr Heneage M.P.—Mr Chamberlain—The Queen l & Tel and minutes. Saw Mr Bright—Ld Kimberley—Ld Spencer—D. of Argyll—Lady M. Beaumont. Dined at the Admiralty—an anxious Cabinet on Irish affairs. 2–6. Read Ld Rosebery's Address[3]—Young Ireland.

Cabinet. Nov. 17. 80. 2 p.m.[4]

1. Ireland. WEG proposed that Ministers shd. state their views upon Forster's paper & proposal.[5] D. of A[rgyll] could not conceive a doubt or difficulty. (J. C., Ld. S., WEG, Ld. K) Land was also talked of. General discussion *without prejudice*.

   The currents of opinion were most curious. Every Peer, except Kimberley, was in favour of Forster's proposal: they will have no battle to fight. Of the Commoners Hartington gave F. a *nearly* thorough support; Childers—silent; Dodson, a few words, not of favourable aspect; Chamberlain, Bright, Harcourt: against; W.E.G. full of difficulties.

   1.[6] When was the H[abeas] C[orpus] Act last suspended?—Recommended by SIMPLICITY.
2. We have no information as to the comparative state of things at times when the H.C. Act has been suspended.
3. This extends over the whole of Ireland.
4. The root of the mischief is in the Land League which incites and orders breach of contract in nonpayment of rents beyond a standard they indicate.
5. The *criminals* are really agents of the Land League.
6. Can we punish agents and let principals go free?
7. At the time of former suspensions, there were no such *principals*. (O'Connell & the *law*).
8. What does the Master of the Rolls advise.

[1] Forster replied, 16 November 1880, Add MS 44157, f. 223, agreeing that suspension should depend 'on danger to the person rather than property, but I think we must take into account terrorism[?] by means of personal outrage'.

[2] Not found; presumably lost with the Forster MSS.

[3] A. P. Primrose, 5th Lord Rosebery, 'A Rectorial Address' (1880), as Rector of Aberdeen University.

[4] Add MS 44642, f. 81. Extracts from Chamberlain's resignation letter (see Chamberlain, *Memoir*, 10) at ibid. f. 84.

[5] Details of eviction returns and request for coercion, repeated in Forster's letter of 18 November; Reid, *F*, ii. 269 and Add MS 44625, f. 94. See also Bahlman, *Hamilton*, i. 77.

[6] These points listed on separate, undated sheet; Add MS 44642, f. 82.

The reign of terror which prevails is terror lest danger should be incurred by venturing on the exercise of certain undoubted civil rights.

H. C. Act for crimes against the State. Swing riots [of 1830]; no *Habeas Corpus*.

We have chosen our line—to try the existing law—how, unless upon a great outburst of crime, can we fundamentally alter that line? But dist. a) *new* powers b) powers beyond the constitn.

Westmeath. [Select] Committee appointed Mch. 9. 71; met 13th (Documents). 20⁻ 30th: Evidence—Six days; 31st: Report. 1860-8: Homicides 8, 9 years; [18]69, 3; [18]70. 5. [18]67, *nine* murders & attempts to murder in 12 mo. Fb. 70–Jan. 71, acc. to Ld. Hn.

Can we not *watch* those whom we should *take up*?[1]

1. Agt. a large majority of Irish members.
2. Without a Bill of redress.
3. Touches only the instruments.
4. Pledge to exhaust the ordinary Law.
5. Uncertainty as to individuals to be arrested.
6. A great extension of the *purpose* of Habeas Corpus Acts.
7. Want of precedents. Westmeath: against agents of secret societies.
8. The evil is distinctly done by a PUBLIC society: *whose leaders we shall have no power to take up*.[2]

Observe the curious difference between the Peer Ministers—who have not the battle to fight—& the Commons Ministers, who have. [WEG]

I quite admit this—but then is it not a little the secondary difficulty of the debate, which prevents some of the House of Commons reflecting upon what is really the right thing for the country. I hear of liberal members exceedingly strong for immediate coercion—not only Courtenay who is probably not a good foolometer, but men like Sam Morley & Fry. Mundella[?] says the feeling at the Reform Club is strong [Granville].[3]

To J. CHAMBERLAIN, president of the board of trade,   Chamberlain MSS 5/34/3. 17 November 1880. '*Private*'.

I have received your letter[4] and have read it I need hardly say with much anxiety.

Today we shall have the advantage of a fuller and more general expression of views than has yet been afforded.

Should they appear, at first sight, to be irreconcileable, I hope that we shall come to no decision, but take at least a day to consider the matter, which in any case is one of very great gravity.

To W. E. FORSTER, Irish secretary, 17 November 1880.   Add MS 44544, f. 94.

Let me remind you that we have not yet received any figures on eviction and they are a very material part of the case. I mean any figures since those for the *quarter* ending with September which do not avail.

[1] Undated holograph; Add MS 44642, f. 86.
[2] Undated holograph; Add MS 44642, f. 88.
[3] Undated exchange of notes; Add MS 44642, f. 90.
[4] Threatening resignation if Forster's policy adopted; Garvin, i. 328. No reply found to Gladstone's letter. A minute by Chamberlain dated 18 November [1880] on the futility of coercion is at Add MS 44125, f. 48.

[P.S.] Please to consider before the Cabinet a point not touched in your Memorandum, whether you are prepared to go before a Committee, as was done in the Westmeath case.

18. Th.

Wrote to Ld Kinnaird—Ld Granville 1.2.—Mr Forster 1.2.—Mr Dodson—Ld Nelson and minutes. Read & worked much on the question of Irish coercion. Saw Ld F. Cavendish—Mrs Heywood—Mr Godley—Mr Bright—do cum Ld Granville. Dined with Ld F.C.s. Read Trevelyan's Fox[1]—Young Ireland.

I beg my colleagues to consider a point which only occurred to me late last night, and which I do not quite know how to deal with.

Can the case be argued in Parliament for the suspension of the *Habeas Corpus* Act without reference to the conduct of Parnell and the other thirteen men now under trial? And can this conduct be discussed in Parliament *while* they are under trial? On Feb. 27. 1833, Lord Althorp was proceeding to quote Mr Steele, when O'Connell said across the Table that Mr Steele was under prosecution. Lord Althorp then used the words 'Very well: it is of no consequence, and I will not use it.' Hansard Vol 15. 1225.[2]

19. Fr.

Wrote to Ld Carlingford—The Queen Tel & l—Ld Spencer and minutes. Saw Mr Forster—Mr Bright—Lord Granville—Mr F. cum Lord G. The Cabinet appointed for two only went to business at 3 and separated at four. It was an anxious morning with storms overhanging: but the time taken is likely to ⟨supply⟩ give an opening. Saw Mr Godley respecting Mr Hill—Ld Rosebery—Mr Bryce—Dr Butler. Saw Macgregor: & two others [R]. Dined at Mr Godley's. Read Young Ireland.

Cabinet. Friday Nov. 19. 1880. 2 p.m.[3]
Conversation beforehand.
Conversation on Irish question began at 3.
Parliament to be prorogued until the 2nd.
F[orster] thought that if he could announce the three F.s probably the agitation wd cease. 1. Latest & best information as to outrages. 2. Proceedings of Commission to be accelerated.
Mr. F. will look after both these subjects in Ireland.
Cabinet Thursday 2 p.m.

1.[4] The course I recommend and prefer is 1) postponement of all legislative action until after the trials, and 2) the assembling of Parliament at the earliest convenient date after their conclusion (assuming that this is *before* the *usual* period for opening the session) with 3) a free and unsparing use of military and police to protect the

[1] Sir G. O. Trevelyan, *The early history of Charles James Fox* (1880).
[2] Holograph, initialled and dated 18 November 1880, Add MS 44764, f. 153. See Introduction above, section vi.
[3] Add MS 44642, f. 92.
[4] Undated holograph (dated by Morley, 'Nov. 19. 1880'); Add MS 44642, f. 93; notes by secretaries on Committees on Ireland since 1688 follow.

innocent, and to watch probable offenders as well as to apprehend those who actually offend. Of course the Govt. would continue by every means in their power to expedite the trials. We should thus have the great advantage of considering both subjects together and, were coercion still necessary, of passing our measure more easily and rapidly than we could now do it.

2. Should the Cabinet disapprove of this, I then have to face 1) a difficulty from my Guildhall Speech: 2) a great difficulty in calling Parliament to legislate during the trials, after we have engaged to try first the existing law, 3) a greater difficulty still in passing by remedies of the milder sort such as *some*[?] of those contained in the Peace Preservation Act, and 4) a perfect stultification of myself, which I have not seen to be compatible with honour, if after the speech I made in 1871 on the Committee before the Westmeath Act I were now with a case decidedly weaker to propose a proposal to the House of Commons for a suspension of the Habeas Corpus Act without the pre-liminary testing and confirming process before a Committee. The Westmeath Com-mittee took its evidence in six days of work and made its report on a seventh sitting. I do not see why a Committee now need take a longer time, as it might suffice to lay the facts for two Counties (the worst) in the first instance.

To what do you propose to adjourn the Cabinet? [W. E. Forster].
What do *you* say? [W. E. G.]
Next Wednesday or at latest Thursday. This would give time to meet for despatch of business the following Thursday [W. E. Forster].[1]

We are to quarrel on a question of five? weeks.
Every one should consider what he can do to prevent this.
    If it will secure union I am willing—in the teeth of many objections—to call Parlt.—refer the case to a Committee (a question of honour?) and if it stand examn. there to go on with a Suspension Bill.
    If it will not I am for the delay till after the trials.[2]

To Sir C. J. HERRIES, chairman of board of inland revenue,   Add MS 44544, f. 95.
19 November 1880.

1. I agree with you that the public and Parliamentary feeling would be a powerful ob-stacle to the abolition of the consanguinity scale.
2. It would be very difficult to act upon the Succession Duties until Parliament has deter-mined what to do with limited ownership. They could hardly therefore be included in any measure for next year.
3. If there is a temporary advantage from overlapping so much the better but I should not be content with any diminution of the *permanent* revenue from these Death Duties.
4. The percentage in respect of (reformed) Probate Duty might still be taken from the Corpus and the Legacy Duty from the bequest. If this can be done once for all so much the better.
5. Mr. West has a rough memorandum of heads for a measure, given him by me.

20. Sat [*Sandringham, Norfolk*]

Wrote to Mr Popic[3]—Sir Ch. Dilke—Scotts—Mr Ogilvy—Sir Thos. G.—Sir W. Harcourt—Mr Robert Gladstone and minutes. Saw Ld Wolverton—Ld R.

[1] Undated exchange of notes; Add MS 44642, f. 103.
[2] Holograph dated 19 November 1880, Add MS 44764, f. 156.
[3] Probably Eugène Popovic, Italian journalist; see Add MS 44465, f. 71.

Grosvenor—Mr Forster—Ld Granville—Sir R. Wilson—Dr Acland—Maj. Baring. Off at 1¾ to Sandringham where we were most kindly received: as always. Read The Tcherkess & his Victim.

21. PreAdv. Sunday

Church mg and evg. Farm & garden walk in the afternoon: a weight upon me, but I do not like to dissent. A noisy evening, no mark of Sunday. Renewed conversation with Dr Acland on Oxford—Conversation with Major Baring—Duke of Edinburgh—Sir D. Probyn,[1] on the Prince's affairs. Mrs Stonor[2] respecting Ld B. & her Father. Read Abps Charge—Dr Acland's Address.[3] Weighed 11 stone 11 lbs. The Princess said last night "You will have your favourite hymn Rock of Ages". This was indeed what is well called in Scotland 'mindful'.

22. M. [London]

Left Sandringham at 10.30. Wrote to Mr Reg. Wilberforce—Ld Selborne—Sir H. Verney—Ld Spencer—Rev. Mr Nevins—Sir W. Harcourt—Mr Litton MP.—Mrs Th. & minutes. Saw Sec. of Armenian Patriarch—Sir W. James—Mr Godley—Ld Granville—Scotts. Read the Tcherkess and his victim—Young Ireland. Dined with the Godley's. Saw one [R].

To R. G. WILBERFORCE, 22 November 1880.   Bodley MS Eng. lett. e. 159, f. 9.

With respect to my letters, there are two and only two which I should wish to be withdrawn. They are those relating not to your Father but to your Uncle the Archdeacon and they are dated Sept. 4. 1854 and Oct. 17. 1854.[4]

I am afraid that I must from real incapacity ask you to excuse me from undertaking in any shape the task of criticism, which, while I heartily wish well to your Biography, requires a mind more free than mine.

23. Tu.

Wrote to Ld Lyttelton—D. of Argyll—Att. General—Ld Kimberley—Ld E. Clinton—Sir W. Harcourt—Mr Budge—The Queen l & Tel and minutes. Evg. at home. Saw Herbert J.G.—Sir A. Gordon—Mr Ouvry—Mrs Th—Mr Herbert R.A. and inspected his Susannah & other works. Read The New Era[5]—Young Ireland.—Life of Sir R. Hill[6]—Peasant Life in England.[7]

---

[1] Sir Dighton Macnaghten Probyn, 1833–1924; treasurer to the Prince, who was hoping to visit South Africa; Magnus, *Edward VII*, 157.

[2] She was Peel's daughter; see 18 Mar. 52.

[3] H. W. Acland, 'The public health. An address' (1880).

[4] R. G. Wilberforce sent for acceptance proofs of vol. ii of the *Life* of his father, further instalment on 2 December; Add MS 44467, ff. 94, 97. Gladstone excluded from use two letters on Robert Wilberforce's apostasy, one of them remarkable, quoted above, vii. cxii.

[5] By Virginia Vaughan (1880); sent by H. *Holiday, Add MS 44544, f. 111.

[6] G. B. N. Hill, *The Life of Sir Rowland Hill*, 2v. (1880).

[7] F. G. Heath, *Peasant life in the west of England* (1880).

To the DUKE OF ARGYLL, lord privy seal, 23 November   Add MS 44544, f. 96.
1880.

I am glad to hear of the limited improvement you report. It is however but limited, especially in conjunction with the symptoms about the Eye.

I agree entirely in what you have said as to the freedom of our position in regard to Irish Land.[1] We approach the question as other men can, & should. But I am struck with the state of opinion in Ireland among Conservative men & classes (Monck, Emly, Powerscourt, Errington, & so forth) especially if it be true that Kavanagh, the hardest headed Irish Tory I have known in Parliament, has made up his mind to some considerable measure.

24. Wed.

Wrote to Mr Forster—Viceroy of Ireland—Ld Nelson—Ld Coleridge—Scotts—The Queen 1.2. & Tel.—H.N. Gladstone and minutes. Drive with Mr Childers. Saw Ld Clonmel[2]—Ld F. Cavendish—Ld Granville. (Saw DeBorne & another [R])—Sir G. Wolseley—Sir F. Roberts—Duke of Cambridge. Read Young Ireland.

To LORD COWPER, Irish viceroy, 24 November 1880.   Add MS 56453, f. 6.

I am persuaded after reading your letter of yesterday,[3] that in a very difficult case you have arrived at a wise conclusion.

For my own part, I incline to the belief that an outbreak of secessions from the Government, either way, at this particular moment, when the double question of order and of land reform is at issue, would render it impracticable for us to effect any good solution of that question in its two branches.

It is with regret, and perhaps with mortification, that I see the question of land reform again assuming or having assumed, its larger proportions. My desire certainly would have been to remain on the lines of the Act of 1870, if not exactly as it passed, yet much as (I speak of the occupation Clauses) it left the House of Commons. It is needless to inquire in what proportions the scarcity, or the agitation, or the Disturbance Bill, or (last not least) the rejection of that Bill, may have brought about the result; for there it is.

I think that, on this side the channel, we feel not less really, if less acutely, than you in Dublin, the pain, embarrassment, and discredit, of the present condition of Ireland. Acquiescence in its indefinite continuance I think quite out of the question: and acquiescence in its continuance for even a few weeks seems to me dependent on these conditions;

1. That the disturbance so largely affecting property, and causing terror, should not assume the form of a great increase of crime affecting life.

2. That by means of this delay we put ourselves in a position to propose with authority as an united Government a remedy applicable to the whole of the mischief.

The paralysis of very important rights affecting the tenure of land is the special characteristic of the present mischief in Ireland; and it may be right to apply a thorough remedy a little later, rather than a partial (indeed as I think a very doubtful) remedy a little, and only a little, sooner. What I personally think a very doubtful remedy is a suspension of the Habeas Corpus Act proposed alone, carried after much delay, in the teeth of

[1] Lack of public commitment to legislate, asserted in Argyll to Gladstone, 22 November 1880, Add MS 44104, f. 237.

[2] John Henry Reginald Scott, 1839–91; 4th earl of Clonmell 1866; a tory.

[3] Suspension of Habeas Corpus 'the only remedy', but he will not resign; in Cowper, 434.

two-thirds of the representatives of Ireland (without taking British allies into account), and used in order to cope with a wide-spreading conspiracy embracing in certain districts large fractions of the population, and largely armed with means other than material for its action.

You may rely upon it that, when the time you indicate arrives, the Cabinet will look at the duty of defending proprietary rights without any mawkish susceptibilities, and the Suspension, should you and Forster then still see cause to desire it, will be more impartially entertained. For my own part, what I lean to expecting is that, if requisite it will not be sufficient, and that we may have to legislate directly against the Land League: not against its name only, but against the purpose of all combinations aiming at the non-payment of debts and non-fulfilment of contracts at the very least, when these illegal aims are so pursued as to endanger the public security.

Let me say in conclusion that our practical accord at this time in particular gives me, as I am sure it will give our colleagues, the liveliest satisfaction.

To W. E. FORSTER, Irish secretary, 24 November 1880.   Add MS 44544, f. 98.

Your letter has gone into circulation.[1] As I said on Saturday that no candid man could ascribe your previous conduct to obstinacy, so I am sure all will admit that in most difficult circumstances you have now, as you did then, acted in the best light of your judgment & conscience. I am afraid we must expect some extension of the paralysis before we are ready to act; but in my view this will be a much less evil than the proposal of a truncated remedy by a divided authority. God grant, for all reasons, that matters may grow no worse, & indeed may grow better as to life offences, in the interval before us. Of *this* I do not despair.

25. Th.

Wrote to The Speaker—The Queen—Ld Coleridge—Master of St John's Camb.—Ld Northbrook & minutes. Cabinet 2-5. Conclave on succession to Adam & consequent changes.[2] Saw Ld Granville—Mr Adam—Lady M. Beaumont. Dined at Lady M. Beaumont's. Read Young Ireland.

Cabinet. Nov. 25. 1880. 2. p.m[3]
1. Mr. Forster referred to his letter[4]—announcing that he would defer to the wish in the Cabinet for delay. Resolutions of Commission will be considered after evidence is closed next week. (F. submits because he cannot get the suspension without it). Resolutions expected week after next at latest.
   F. suspects that coercion will be necessary in January: and cannot undertake to go on without it, whether we are ready with our Land Plan or not.
   W.E.G. said that if we had the two plans of Land and coercion, coercion would take precedence.

[1] To the cabinet, of 23 November 1880, Add MS 44157, f. 234, with details of the prosecutions and asking for summons of parliament 'without delay'; in Reid, *F*, ii. 270.
[2] W. P. Adam went to govern Madras, replaced as commissioner for works by Shaw Lefevre; see Bahlman, *Hamilton*, i. 75, 81. Adam was much put out by not being elevated to the peerage; see letters to Loch and others in Blair Adam MSS.
[3] Add MS 44642, f. 104; undated accompanying notes read: [Granville:] 'Have you told Hartington you wish him to stay after the Cabinet'; [Childers:] 'It is proposed to transfer to County authorities a considerable amount of work now devolving on Parliament, and to consolidate central County authorities with subordinate local authorities; and if it is also intended to pass a County [blank'].   [4] See 24 Nov. 80n.

Trials begin on 17th or 20th.
Prorogue Parlt. to 6th Jan. 'for dispatch of business[']
Cabinet to meet about 15th or 16 Decr. Council Sat. 27th (3 p.m.?).
Discussion on Bills to be introduced.
Importation of arms into Ireland increases. Forster reserves any proposal till next
Cabinet.
Intestacy Bill to be brought in if found convenient.

To H. B. W. BRAND, the Speaker, 25 November 1880.   Brand MSS.

The question you have referred to me though small is somewhat complex[1]—in the
examination it involves and I must refer to the Treasury for a report on what is in my view
the principal argument on behalf of a change, namely the allegation as to what has taken
(place) in the Whitehall or Downing Street Departments since 1849. As regards the augmentation of the Salary of Mr. Raikes to £2500, I confess that I did not approve of it; nor
do I attach much weight to the proceedings of the House of Lords, which is under no
controul by either the House of Commons or the Government. When I am more fully
informed, I hope to communicate with you further. I had always been under the impression that to obtain a Clerkship of the House of Commons, remunerated as it now is, was
an object of much & wide-spread desire on the part of young men, some of them highly
qualified.

The sad question of Ireland is, in the view of a portion of mankind, quite simple: they
conceive that order and freedom would for the present be certainly restored by clapping
two or three scores of men into prison without any necessity for bringing them to trial.

Such is not my view. During more than 37 years since I first entered a Cabinet I have
hardly known so difficult a question of administration, as that of the *immediate* duty of the
Government in the present state of Ireland. The multitude of circumstances to be taken
into account must strike every observer. Among these stand the *novelty* of the Suspension
of Habeas Corpus in a case of Agrarian crime stimulated by a *public* Society, and the
rather serious difficulty of obtaining it: but more important than these is the grave doubt
whether it would really reach the great characteristic evil of the time, namely the paralysis of most important civil and proprietary rights, and whether the immediate proposal of
a remedy, probably ineffective and even in a coercive sense partial, would not seriously
damage the prospects of that arduous and comprehensive task which without doubt we
must undertake when Parliament is summoned:[2] probably at a time earlier than is usual.
The Cabinet have worked hard to understand the question but they are not infallible
while they have sought only to act for the best.

Perhaps it may surprise, it will certainly not displease, you to learn that outrage affecting *life* is somewhat lower than in 1879.

I have not forgotten your kind invitation to Glynde which floats before me as a
pleasant vision. We shall leave town on Saturday: but I would fain hope the winter may
not pass without our visiting you. Meantime I will ask you to continue yet for a little the
wise reserve with which you contemplate the Irish problem.

26. Fr.

Wrote to The Queen—Mr Spottiswoode—Mr West—Lord Chancellor—D. of
Argyll—Sir C. Herries—Sir H. Ponsonby Tel.—Att. Gen. for Ireland and minutes.

[1] Brand (24 November 1880, Add MS 44194, f. 216) forwarded May's mem. on Commons' establishment, and hoped for Habeas Corpus suspension.
[2] Thus far, of this para., in Morley, iii. 51.

Wrote Mem. on Death Duties. Saw Ld R. Grosvenor—Mr Godley—Mr Forster—Ld Granville—Ld Spencer. Read Young Ireland.

Change in Probate and Legacy Duty.

1. Value of the Estate to be sworn forthwith as now.
2. But debts to be deducted.
3. Subject to a future ratification of account when they have been ascertained and paid.
4. Duties to be charged and levied forthwith.
5. (1) Upon the Estate, at 2½ on the rate amount, or at such other percentage as shall represent the average incidence of the present Probate Duty.
6. Upon the bequests and upon the residue in the case of Wills.
7. And upon the heirs at law in the case of intestacies.
8. The rates of duty in lieu of the present legacy duty to be as follows:
   a. on widows and children one per cent
   b. on parents brothers and sisters and their descendants three per cent
   c. on more distant relations and on strangers in blood ten per cent.
9. Line of exemption from Probate or Estate Duty to be raised but no Legacy to be exempt from duty in any Estate over the exemption line.
10. Where any bequest is subject to one or more reversions the highest rate attaching to any of them is to be charged.
11. When the 10% rate thus becomes chargeable, one half of it to be taken from the residue.
12. Provision as to reversionary bequests not to take effect before Jan. 1. 1882.
13. Six months (?) from date of proof or administration to be allowed for payment of Legacy Duty.
14. Law of domicile to be reconsidered with reference to Probate Duty.[1]

To H. LAW, Irish attorney general, 26 November 1880.   Add MS 44544, f. 99.

I write one line to back a letter Forster has written to you, & to place you at liberty, so far as I am concerned, to refer to the Government speaking as I do on their responsibility, with reference to the postponement of the trials. We think it most important for the cause of justice & of peace in Ireland that there should not be a day's delay, & we are at a loss to conceive how, in the state of things which exists, either the convenience of persons, or even the regular course of ordinary justice, can properly be made a cause of delaying them. I do not know how far you can make use of this but at any rate I wish that you should be able to do it so far as we can enable you.
   Referring you to Forster's letter.

27. Sat. [*Hawarden*]

Wrote to Lord Herries—Duke of Cambridge—Mr Lefevre—Miss Phillimore—The Queen—Mr Bulkeley Hughes—Mrs Th. and minutes. Read Tennyson Ballads[2]—Greece & the Times[3]—Wordsworth Ch & Univv.[4] Council at Windsor at 1 P.M. Audience afterwards for ½ an hour. The Q. was really most gracious.

---

[1] Holograph initialled and dated 26 November 1880, Add MS 44764, f. 159. These duties were readjusted in the 1881 budget; see S. Buxton, *Finance and politics* (1888), ii. 292ff.
[2] A. Tennyson, *Ballads and other poems* (1880).
[3] *Fortnightly Review*, xxxiv. 556 (November 1880); by W. J. Stillman.
[4] Probably C. Wordsworth, 'A letter to the members of Lincoln College, Oxford, on certain proposed changes in their College' (1880).

Saw the Dean of Windsor—Arthur Lyttelton—Ld Spencer. 4.10-10. To Hawarden, stopping in Saltney. Found the Telephone established: most unearthly.[1]

28. Advent S.

Ch 11 a.m. and 6½ P.M. Wrote to The Queen Tel.—Prince of Montenegro Tel[2]—Sir H. Ponsonby—Mr Godley—Mad. Novikoff—Mr Trevelyan M.P.—Mr Macfarlane M.P.—Ld Northbrook—Mr Lefevre Tel. Read Hillebrand[3]—Macfarlane Irish Land—Bp of Manchester's Charge.[4]

To D. H. MACFARLANE, M.P., 28 November 1880.   Add MS 44544, f. 101.

Allow me to thank you for your kindness in sending me your interesting pamphlet on the case of Ireland.

I do not trouble you with any remarks on matters of argument set forth in it, with which I may differ or agree: but I feel it my duty to refer, and I hope it may be for the last time, to an error of fact, which I notice, not because it affects myself, but because it bears upon the important political question, whether the Acts of 1869 and 1870, and the attempt of 1873, were 'the outcome of Fenian disturbances', and were so described by me.

I am not aware of having ever so described them, or of having stated that the Fenian outrages in Manchester and Clerkenwell 'ripened public opinion'.

What I have said and still say is that, amidst the multitude of competing subjects, and all our legislative arrears, they drew to the case of Ireland attention which would not otherwise have been given; and this brought it under the impartial action of the national judgment and conscience. The outrages were in my opinion the cause of the measures no otherwise than as hearing a bell at a given time on a given day is the cause of a man's going to church.

Hence it was that, in 1865, I believed the Irish Church question to lie outside the domain of practical politics and of my own probable participation, and that in the end of 1866 I declared publicly my opinion that the time had come when religious equality might forthwith be established in Ireland.

You will I am sure believe that in dealing with what I think an inadvertance I do not make the slightest imputation upon your sincerity and candour.[5]

To Madame O. NOVIKOV, 28 November 1880.   Add MS 44544, f. 100.

I am very sorry to have been obliged to leave town without acceding to your kind request:[6] for I should have been glad to convey to you personally the expression of my

[1] Probably used in its Glynnese sense, 'proceeding from some gnome or fiend: or again something nasty and revolting', [G. W. Lyttelton], *Contributions towards a glossary of the Glynne language* (1851).
[2] Prince Nicolas of Montenegro, 1841-1921; Nicholas I 1910; see Add MS 44467, 69 and Bahlman, *Hamilton*, i. 82.
[3] See 29 Oct. 80.
[4] J. Fraser, 'A charge . . . 1880' (1880).
[5] (Sir) Donald Horne Macfarlane (1830-1904; liberal M.P. Carlow 1880-5, Argyll 1885-6, 1892-5; kt. 1894) had sent his 'Ireland *versus* England' (1880) which stated *re* disestablishment: 'Mr Gladstone has explained but a few weeks ago that it was not so, but the outcome of Fenian disturbances.' Macfarlane thought the motive 'purer'; his reply accepted Gladstone's explanation; Add MS 44467, f. 96.
[6] For 'a chat'; Add MS 44268, f. 235.

concurrence in your feeling about the treatment to which you have been subjected by a portion of the Tory or Jingo Press. I say a *portion* of it only, and indeed it is bad enough that there should be such a portion—but I know of its existence from experience—I and those like me are fair game: but you ought on every ground to have been exempt.

I shall always consider, without knowing anything below the surface, that your temperate, highly clear and acute, and above all open and fearless statement of Russian views and Slav ideas in the midst of us during an angry and excited time has been a real service to the cause of peace and national goodwill: and moreover I am ashamed of any fellow-countryman who is so purblind as not to see this obvious truth.

We must meet again in Cabinet about the 15th.

A happy journey be yours.

The thought of Montenegrin presence in Dulcigno & its district, though the subject be small, is in principle one for great thankfulness. Again I must say that so far as I have seen & known we have had from your Government nothing but loyal and effective help. I have little doubt but that had not the stroke acted without being struck three of us at least would have gone to Smyrna.

29.

Ch 8½ a.m. Wrote to Mr A. Arnold MP—Spiridion Gopćević—Att. General for Ireland—Earl Nelson—Sir R. Wilson—Mr Forster—Sir G. Wolseley—D. of Argyll—Ld Granville—Sir C. Herries—Mr Hamilton Tel. and minutes. Worked on Irish Land. Tree work with W.H.G. Dined at the Rectory. Read Hillebrand on German Thought.—The New Era.

To the DUKE OF ARGYLL, lord privy seal, 29 November   Add MS 56446, f. 3.
1880.

1. What objections are there to free sale, by Irish tenants, of their interest in their occupations?
2. Can we not, by some plan based on Longfield's idea, give to the Irish occupier an increased security of tenure and yet avoid the mischief of a recurrent State interference for the determination of rents?
3. Must we not again get a fixed starting point by an interference once for all; & may we not build this interference upon a renewal and some extension of the clause in the Land Act about exorbitant rents.

The state of Ireland is so serious that I do not know what form our deliberations may take; but for my own part I am very desirous to keep if possible on the lines & basis of the Land Act.

It was I think originally Carlingford's idea to check the arbitrary exercise of power by fixing it. It is now Longfield's idea. I always liked it from the first: and I should like *now* to make it our basis, as the mildest form in which we can have a modicum of sufficient strength.

From my point of view I do not see much difficulty in drawing preliminary Resolutions; and they may be very useful in giving us time, which cannot fail to be greatly needed.

One of my chief alarms is a seriously divided Commission; I did not think Forster dreaded it as much as I do.

Be this as it may, land is my great anxiety; the disturbances are temporary, but in this we ought at least to aim in good faith at permanence.[1]

[P.S.] I sent you a copy of a mem. respecting Mayo.

[1] This letter, and Argyll's reply, in Argyll, ii. 356ff.

To W. E. FORSTER, Irish secretary, 29 November 1880.   Add MS 44544, f. 101.

(1) I send you copy of a memorandum from Mr Clive, of Mayo County.

(2). The subject of land weighs greatly upon my mind and I am working upon it to the best of my ability.

(3). I have a dream that the figures you showed us at the last Cabinet, when compared with those you had previously given us for the *twelve* first days of November, shewed a slight though a very slight improvement in the totals of agrarian outrage?

[P.S.] We must I think carefully *consider* the question of a new valuation for Ireland.[1]

30. St Andrews.

Ch 8½ a.m. with H.C. Wrote to Ld Northbrook—Ld Granville—Miss De Lisle—Sir C. Dilke—Ld O. Russell and minutes. Read The New Era—Abbé Martin on Ritualism[2]—Hillebrand, German Thought—Macmillan on Ireland—do Copyright. Worked on Irish Land. Dined at the Rectory.

Wed. Dec. One 80.

Ch 8½ a.m. Wrote to Ld Granville 1.2.—Sir C. Herries—The Queen—Ld Chancellor—Miss de Lisle—Mr Scudamore—and minutes. Worked on Irish Land[3] and on Death Duties. Walk with W. & C. Parker—Dined at the Rectory. Read on Irish Land—Justin MacCarthy[4]—Mr Mahoney[5]—Prof. Webb[6] and Prof. Hillebrand.

To LORD SELBORNE, lord chancellor, 1 December 1880.   Tait MSS 100, f. 169.

In answer to the Archbishop's question I can only give an opinion, which you can correct or confirm. I think it unlikely that the Govt. will undertake to legislate upon 'the traffic in Church livings', nor could I advise it, although personally I should give a cordial assent to the prohibition of sales of next presentations.

I should think it also most desirable that congregations should be protected against the arbitrary acts of those patrons who use their power of presentation in order to enforce sudden and violent changes of usage upon congregations. But this would require the attainment of a great *desideratum* which we have not yet reached, namely something in the nature of a congregational organization.[7]

[P.S.] Thanks for the *main* announcement of your note.

2. Th.

Ch 8½ a.m. Wrote to Mr Godley Tel—Sir R. Lingen—Mr Leeman—Mr R.D. Williams and minutes. Worked on Irish Land. Read Hillebrand—

---

[1] i.e. to replace the Griffith valuation of 1852-68, regarded by landlords as an unfair basis as a standard for fair rent in 1880; see Bew, 25.

[2] J. P. P. Martin, *Anglican Ritualism* (1880); sent by Margaret de Lisle.

[3] Early draft of the Resolutions; see 14 Dec. 80.

[4] In the *Nineteenth Century*, viii. 861 (December 1880).

[5] R. J. Mahoney, '"Credo Experto". A short statement concerning the confiscation of improvements in Ireland. Addressed to ... W. E. Forster' (1880).

[6] Untraced pamphlet or article by Thomas E. Webb, professor in Dublin.

[7] Forwarded by Selborne to Tait; Tait MSS 100. See 22 Dec. 80.

Lifford ⎫
T.P. OConnor ⎪
Bence Jones ⎬   on Irish Land[1]
Miss OBrien ⎭

also, reply to Russell;[2] and the New Era. Saw Mayor of Chester: rather perturbed. Worked on new path with W. & Harry.

3. Fr.

Ch 8½ a.m. Wrote to Ld Granville—D. of Argyll—Mr Forster—Sir C. Dilke—H.J.G.—Sir C. Herries—Sir H. Ponsonby and minutes. Tea at Mr Hurlbutts. Read Memoirs of Mr Herries: long.[3]

To the DUKE OF ARGYLL, lord privy seal, 3 December   Add MS 44544, f. 104.
1880.

I agree very much in your objections to free sale,[4] as you understand it. But by free sale may be understood sale not subject to *veto*. Therefore my question referred to 'free sale, or sale'. The question to be solved is can there be a free i.e. non-permissive sale, such as shall not encroach on the property of the landlord? I am inclined to think there can, and to find the means of it in the Longfield idea.

I am working constantly on this subject: and unfortunately there is a great deal to read besides the Evidence before the Commission.

What we really want is to get below generalities, and to touch the testing points and forms of the question. For this purpose I put *challenging* propositions.

For example I am disposed to hold the following proposition, to which we made approaches in the Land Act and in the debates on it.

'In a country like Ireland, in most parts of which employments are so little diversified as not to leave a real freedom of choice, the occupation of land upon living terms is itself money's worth, and is also money's worth of a kind that ought not to be represented in the rent.'

Pray turn this over in your mind.

To W. E. FORSTER, Irish secretary, 3 December 1880.   Add MS 44158, f. 15.

1. I cannot shut my eyes to the fact that the conspiracy against property in Ireland widens and takes root.
2. How will Ulster and its custom come out in the return of outrages.
3. Can you *depute* somebody to give me, or direct me to, information on this specific question. What happens under the Ulster custom if when a tenant offers his interest for sale, the landlord announces an increase of the rent? Is the landlord's power in this respect unlimited, or how far does it extend?
4. I dread exceedingly the idea of a Report seriously divided, i.e. of two against three and

---

[1] Charlotte O'Brien and Lifford in *Nineteenth Century*, viii. 876, 880 (December 1880); T. P. O'Connor in *Contemporary Review*, xxxviii. 981 (December 1880); W. Bence Jones in *Macmillan's Magazine*, xliii. 125 (December 1880).
[2] Probably H. Tennyson, on Russell and the Crimean War, *Nineteenth Century*, viii. 995 (December 1880).
[3] E. Herries, *Memoir of... J. C. Herries... with an introduction by Sir C. Herries*, 2v. (1880); see Bahlman, *Hamilton*, i. 87.
[4] In letter of 1 December 1880, Add MS 44104, f. 245. For Longfield, see 14 Dec. 80n.

think it may make our Commission nearly useless to us so far as authority is concerned; and authority in the present circumstances is, if not the main matter yet a powerful element in the case.

5. The three Fs may be liable to a variety of constructions: but in their popular meaning they will I fear break the Cabinet without conciliating the Leaguers. This law however I take to be quite impossible.[1]

6. We seem unfortunate in this respect. We adopted two measures both most reasonable 1) to try the existing laws 2) to inquire, and yet it is upon the cards that both these may have increased our difficulties.

7. Turning more to outrages; it would be most interesting if your people could find any authentic information as to the reasons which induced Lord Grey's government, a strong and wise one, to prefer the military Law Clauses in 1833 to the suspension of *Habeas Corpus.*

4. Sat.

Ch 8½ a.m. Wrote to Sir C.J. Herries—Mr Forster—Sir A. Gordon—Mr Vickers—Sir W. Williams and minutes (prob. 100?). Walk with S.E.G. & much conversation. Saw Harrison. Saw Mr Dunne[2] on Irish Land. Began the Irish Land Evidence.[3] Read Herries Memoirs.

To W. E. FORSTER, Irish secretary, 4 December 1880.   Add MS 44158, f. 17.

I thank you for the important communications received today.[4] Dowse's able paper, if it does not convey any perfect reassurance to the mind, is full of interest, and is a fact of weight in itself.

I must also own that evidence comes in, rather more than I should have expected, of a desire for a measure such as the brewers would I suppose call treble X.

At the same time I feel a considerable apprehension that the effect of his measure would be in the main to convert landlords into incumbrances. I do not doubt their security in that position; but the change is radical and is among
'Things unattempted yet in prose or rhyme.'
There is another point of great importance as to the practical bearings of the scheme. What is the evidence as to the general condition, and progress or no-progress of the small men who hold under long leases, 99 years or upwards? This is most important as throwing light upon fixity of tenure.

With Dowse's paper in our hands, we can now in some degree mark out the lines which constitute our limits of deviation, & bound our choice on the one side & on the other.

The vital principle of the Land Act was to restrain by smart fines all arbitrary exercise of power on the part of the landlord, and thus to give security to the tenant. This principle may be carried much further by some plan which would be an expansion of the

---

[1] This sentence *sic* in the copyist's hand; this use of 'law', however, seems unGladstonian.

[2] Finlay Dun, br. of James Dun, curate of Hawarden; author of articles in *The Times*, reprinted as *Landlords and Tenants in Ireland* (1881); 'the successful working of the [1869] Church act affords a good basis for any new land scheme': the 1869 Commissioners disposed of glebe lands to owner-occupiers.

[3] The Bessborough Commission's, with two volumes of evidence; *PP* 1881 xviii; see 26 June 80.

[4] Land proposals by Dowse, one of the Commissioners, and resolutions from Ulster M.P.s on Irish Land; Add MS 44158, ff. 7-14.

little memorandum I gave you. It seems also clear that there must be a public interference for a *first* adjustment of rents to constitute a starting point.

I have seen today a Mr. Dunn, brother to a curate here, who stated the three F.'s extremely well and argued for them stoutly. He has I believe done some work as Times Commissioner in Ireland. He seemed to admit that they would convert the landlord into a rent charger, if every thing for all time was to be settled between landlord & tenant with a Court in the background.

I should like much to know the opinion of my old and able coadjutors, Carlingford & the Master of the Rolls.

I will not worry you with general remarks, but if I can lick my ideas into definite shape I will send them.

5. 2. S. Adv.

Ch 11 a.m. with H.C. and 6½ P.M. Wrote to Lord F. Cavendish—Mr E. Baines— Mr Bright—Dean of Ch.Ch.—Ld Cowper and minutes. Saw Mr [Edgar] Vincent[1] on The Porte and Greece. Read Dean Liddell's Sermon,[2] and others—Foreign Church Chronicle—Ward on Free Will.[3]

To John BRIGHT, chancellor of the duchy, 5 December 1880.   Add MS 43385, f. 288.

I do not clearly perceive what honour is desired for Mr. Ashworth?[4] For further understanding I return, temporarily, your inclosure.

In the matter of Irish land, the soup is thickening. I am very glad your mind is alive upon it. I think the question will come very seriously before us, whether we shall acting on the principles of the Land Act limit the exercise of proprietary rights for the safety of the country, or whether we shall set out upon a new principle, convert the landlord virtually into an incumbrancer or rent-charger, and give over in the main to the present occupiers the proprietary character.

I hope you will read as much as you can of the evidence.[5]

To H. G. LIDDELL, Dean of Christ Church, 5 December   Add MS 44544, f. 105.
1880.

I thank you very much for your interesting and let me add delightful Sermon. You will not I hope think it a bad compliment if I associate it with Dean Stanley's in the Abbey at the commemoration of Edward the Confessor. The only fault I can find with it is that it is not opened to the world by publication.

Though I am much absorbed at this time by yet more pressing calls, I am troubled and anxious about the matters connected with the handling of clerical Fellowships in Oxford. I had arrived at the conclusion that upon the whole the best course would be for many reasons to have a liberal appropriation of Fellowships to Theology as a study, and to trust, for the presence of Clergy in the Governing body (to which I attach the highest value &

---

[1] Hawarden Visitors Book.

[2] H. G. Liddell, 'A commemoration sermon' (privately published, 1880).

[3] Perhaps [W. G. Ward], 'Mr Mill's denial of freewill', *Dublin Review*, xxii. 326 (January 1874).

[4] 'Ashton' written in on the letter by Bright who suggested him for an unspecified 'honour or title' on 4 December, Add MS 44113, f. 136; Bright's reply on 7 December, ibid., f. 138, suggested a knighthood or baronetcy.

[5] Bright's reply stated: 'It is evident that Parnell & Co. only want to provoke a revolt, & that their purpose is more revolution than a mere reform, however broad, of their land system.'

importance) to this appropriation. The Commission,[1] with far larger opportunities of judgment, have proceeded upon other lines; and I should be very sorry to do any thing to mar their work, which however I cannot guarantee against attacks possibly destructive. The weakness of their proceeding seems to be that they have endeavoured to meet an objection of principle by large concessions of degree. Please to consider what I have said as not intended for general circulation.

I send herewith an Address delivered at Glasgow; only on account of the analytical statistics of employment among the undergraduates there. Do not take the trouble to acknowledge it.[2]

6. M.

Ch 8½ a.m. Wrote to Sir W. Harcourt—Mr Childers—Mr Welby—Sir H. Ponsonby and minutes. Read Herries Memoirs—Irish Land Evidence—Madame de Mauves.[3] Worked on the new walk: and [blank.]

To Sir W. V. HARCOURT, home secretary, 6 December   Add MS 44544, f. 106.
1880.

With reference to Sir E. Du Cane's paper would you kindly cause me to be informed as to
1. Total number of convicts employed on public acct. for each of [blank] last years to 1880, specifying the places.
2. Number for whom employment will be supplied by existing undertakings in each of the years 1881-4.
3. Perhaps it can also be stated whether there are any works of structure, reclamation, or otherwise, which can be recommended & which are so situated that they might be carried on from the subsisting establishments for convicts.

With & upon the answers as to these questions will come the serious enquiry as to new works, which would probably be referred to a Cabinet or administrative Committee.

I am sorry to say that an invitation or command to Windsor deprives me of the pleasure of dining with you & Lady Harcourt on the 15.

7. Tu.

Ch 8¼ a.m. Wrote to Mr Forster 1.2.—Ld Hartington, Circular—Ld Granville—Mr Gopcevic—Ld R. Grosvenor—D. of St Albans—Ld F. Cavendish—Sir C. Herries 1.2.—Sir H. Ponsonby—The O'Connor Don—Sir W. Harcourt & minutes. Saw Mr Carrington. Worked with W. on the walk. Read Irish Land Evidence—Lpool Directory 1780—Madame de Mauves—Herries Memoirs. Working & walk with W. Worked on Death Duties.

To W. E. FORSTER, Irish secretary, 7 December 1880.   Add MS 44158, f. 34.

Many thanks for your communications received this morning.[4]
The general outlook becomes alarming, when our own [Bessborough] Commissioners

---

[1] i.e. the Selborne commission of 1877 which left the matter of clerical fellowships to the free choice of the colleges; see Ward, *Victorian Oxford*, 310. See 7 Oct. 80.
[2] Liddell replied with thanks on 23 December, Add MS 44236, f. 363, delaying writing until 'I knew that you were safe in your retirement at Hawarden'.
[3] Not found; a novel?
[4] Copies of letter by Bessborough, and Dowse, and memoranda from the O'Connor Don, Kavanagh and Shaw, sent on 6 December; Add MS 44158, ff. 20-32.

seem to mean (or some of them) that the State i.e. the people of the country are to compensate the Irish landowners for certain rights, i.e. for a portion of their property, now to be taken away from them.

Are not the Commissioners going rather far in the use of their powers and taking the real initiative out of our hands and into theirs?

I have received and read the O'Connor Don's plan. On a first perusal it seems to me utterly wild. What will be the effect on the public mind of the promulgation of such schemes with quasi-authority?

The present prospect before us is that our Commission, taken as a whole, will, instead of composing, uniting, and helping towards settlement, mainly serve to distract and to inflame?

Would it not be better that on these burning questions they should simply, if so it must be, record their differences in a few general terms of motion and amendment, rather than produce Essays some of which may act as firebrands?

I have now before me Mr Dowse's and the O'Connor Don's papers—Bessborough's note—and the general description of Shaw's views. It is on these *data* that I speak.

I do not think either the Cabinet or the Parliament will agree either to confiscate rights of property, to charge the English [*.ic*] Exchequer in whatever disguise with a very large, perhaps a huge, liability, as the price of a Land Act founded on a set of principles altogether new both to our own legislation and to the policy of 1870.

You have a very anxious task on your hands. It is well that the Cabinet meet next week. [P.S.] I entirely agree as to secrecy. Under that seal I send the O'Connor Don's papers to Lord R. Grosvenor as a Parliamentary opinion. (Does he mean the Duke of D[evonshire] to sell us Lismore Castle, Duke of L[einster] Carton, and so forth—if they choose?)[1]

To Sir W. V. HARCOURT, home secretary, 7 December 1880.   Harcourt MSS dep. 8.

I am afraid we have our hands much too full at this moment, with the very menacing Irish Land question and other matters only less grave before us, to entertain just now the question of any new arrangement for Scotch business which should include an addition (always a very serious affair) to the official staff in the House of Commons.[2]

Of course it would not meet the *national* part of the desire but as you have your Under Sec. in the House of Commons, which is not always the case, you can perhaps give some facilities to Scotch business which you could not give single-handed: and as we may *hope* to have both Law Officers in Parliament, there is here also a little ray of light. Generally I am afraid Scotch prospects for the coming Session are not bright. The sister that sits by 'the melancholy ocean' will carry every thing against the 'land of brown heath and shaggy wood'. [P.S.] For the said Irish Land Question I hope you, and all, will brace all your spare energies.

To Sir C. HERRIES, chairman of the Board of Inland   Add MS 44544, f. 107.
Revenue, 7 December 1880.

I have now nearly read the whole & I must say always with increasing interest.

This is no merit upon my part; I knew your Father long though not intimately, & received kindness from him.

[1] Forster's reply, 7 December 1880, ibid., f. 35 (circulated to Granville, Hartington and Bright) argued: 'I do not see how we can avoid admitting in our bill the fact which is the main cause of the discontent and also of the bad working of the present landlord system, viz. the contest between law and equity.'
[2] Harcourt's proposal of 6 December, Add MS 44196, f. 107, for a Scottish Department with its own minister was inspired by Rosebery; Crewe, *Rosebery*, i. 139.

Hardly any one else now alive is in the same position, unless it be Ld. Beaconsfield.

I have a great curiosity, never likely to be satisfied, to know why he did not get the Chancellorship of the Exchequer (1) in 1828 and (2) in 1852.

Goulburn was good; but I think Mr Herries was better. Both were real economists, of a type almost unknown in the present day.[1]

8. Wed.

Ch 8¼ a.m. Wrote to Mr Godley 1 & Tel.—Sir W. Harcourt—Mr Childers—Duke of Argyll—Mr Brodrick—Mr Jas. Wilson and minutes. Saw W.H.G. on Mortgage business—& walk with him. Saw Mr Tomkinson. Worked on Irish Land. Read Land Evidence—Herries—Madame de Mauves (finished)—Duffield's Don Quixote[2]—Brodrick on English Land—Irish Land Laws.

To G. C. BRODRICK, 8 December 1880   Add MS 44544, f. 108.

I thank you very much for your work on land, which at any time would be valuable and at this time will have increased value and importance.

Mr Bateman p. 185[3] has exhibited me, and me alone, to the public gaze. Unfortunately his statement is most inaccurate. I am not in his class of great landowners at all, having I think nearer 2500 than 3000 acres. Besides, the Hawarden Estate, under 5000 acres, and heavily encumbered, is vested in my son. I regret this especially as his Tables are useful and must have cost him much pains. I should however have had one class of yeoman, and carried the squires at the least down to the line of 500 if not 400 acres.

9. Th.

Ch 8½ a.m. Wrote to Mr Forster 1.2.3. & Tel.—The Queen—Sir C. Herries—Mr Hick Tel.—Mr Welby & minutes. Wrote on the case of the Irish Land Law. Read a large mass of sad reports from Ireland & perplexing land minutes. Herries Memoirs—Smith's Raban[4]—and Sterne's Life.[5] Wood cutting with W.

SECRET. Case of Irish Land Law.[6]

The principles of the Land Act of 1870, taken generally, were:—

I. As to occupiers—(1.) To confirm the Ulster custom and any other custom which assured to the tenant the sale of his interest in his occupation. (2.) To obtain for agricultural tenants in Ireland certainty of compensation for their improvements. (3.) To restrain effectually capricious evictions, by imposing upon the landlord a necessity of paying heavily for them, in the shape of compensation for disturbance. (4.) To improve

---

[1] Herries replied (8 December, Add MS 44467, f. 116) stating that Huskisson and Palmerston in 1828 made Herries' 'exclusion from the Exchequer a sine quâ non of their joining', and recalling his father's 'deep disappointment' in 1852: 'Mr D[israeli] had positively refused to join unless as Chancellor of the Exchequer'.

[2] A. J. Duffield, *Don Quixote, his critics and commentators* (1881).

[3] i.e. p. 185 of Brodrick's *English land and English landlords* (1881), which includes Gladstone as a 'Great Landowner' in Flintshire, uniquely identifying him in a footnote: Brodrick's tables were based on J. Bateman, *The great landowners of Great Britain* (1878), 167, whose entry on Gladstone pointed out that two-thirds of his Flintshire property 'are returned as the late Sir S. Glynne's'.

[4] W. C. Smith, *Raban; or, Life splinters* (1880).

[5] In the 1872 ed. of L. Sterne's *Works*.

[6] Printed for the Cabinet, PRO CAB 37/4/81; holograph version at Add MS 44625, f. 207 is docketed 'Print this forthwith at the F.O. 20 copies. WEG D9.'

the landlord's security for his rent by a forfeiture, subject to exceptions, of the tenant's title to compensation for disturbance, in the event of non-payment of his rent. (5.) To encourage the granting of leases, by exempting them from the operation of the Act.

Also II—(6.) To encourage, by pecuniary advances, the formation of a peasant proprietary.

It is necessary to observe that the Land Act was settled by compromise with the House of Lords; and to consider the form of the Bill as it left the House of Commons, expressing, as it then did, the views of the House and of the Government.

It differed from the Act in one, indeed, I believe, in two, particulars of great importance. (1.) The Bill allowed eviction for non-payment of rent to be treated as disturbance at the discretion of the Judge, under special circumstances. The Act only gave this discretion—(a.) In holdings under 15l. a-year. (b.) In such holdings, only when the rent was exorbitant. (2.) I believe that the Bill recognized the tenant's power to assign his interest.

Besides these changes, forced upon us by the controlling and obstructing power of the House of Lords, there was certainly at least one lack in the Bill, in that it placed no other restraint upon augmentations of rent than the compensation for disturbance.

The tenant had no defence against any augmentation, except one so great as to make it worth his while to abandon his home and livelihood rather than submit to it. Leaving untouched the question, whether the protection against great augmentations was sufficient against small augmentations, which by repetition might become great, there was hardly any defence at all.

Notwithstanding this weakness in the Bill, and the greater weaknesses in the Act, it was passed with the general approval of the Irish members; it was received with unequivocal satisfaction by the people of Ireland; it greatly promoted the prosperity of the country, and it laid the Land question in Ireland generally to sleep. The demands for further change were very practical, generally temperate, and by no means such as to disturb the more widely-prevalent sentiment of satisfaction.

Upon this (for Ireland) happy state of things, there supervened a series of bad seasons, 1877-79, the last of which, in parts of a few counties, brought the people near to famine. While they were in this state there took place, most unhappily, a large increase in the number of evictions. The alms of Ireland, and, to some extent, of the United Kingdom, were granted by Parliament to meet the case. And the Government introduced a Bill for the temporary restraint of evictions, much more limited in some respects, though of wider scope in others, than the clause touching eviction for non-payment of rent in the Commons' Bill of 1870. It was confined for its operation to the actual crisis, and was to expire when that crisis would have passed.

This Bill, tenaciously resisted in the House of Commons, was unfortunately thrown out in the House of Lords, by an enormous majority, which included a large detachment of Liberal peers. Under these circumstances, the Land League has found an opportunity which scarcity and distress did not supply, and has, even while under virtual prosecution, started up into very large proportions, paralyzed civil rights, established an extensive terrorism and created an enhanced necessity for speedy legislation, together with a great diminution of that calmness of mind which is necessary in order to direct it wisely.

Let us, then, endeavour for a moment to consider the question of the coming legislation on its merits; postponing the question (not waiving it) whether there is a present necessity for taking other circumstances into view, and making special concessions to feeling.

The case of the Land Act appears to me to be one of general success, partial, and we may almost say local, failure.

It does not seem difficult to mark the causes of the failure: the want of a power to assign; the extreme severity of the forfeiture of all claim for disturbance upon non-payment of rent; the want of adequate provision against unreasonable and frequent changes in rent.

Why should we not give the power to assign; allow the allegation of reasonable causes against the forfeiture of the (assignments) claim for disturbance[1]; and restrain undue changes in rent by a mode the same in principle as that which we made use of in the Land Act to restrain capricious eviction?

In the Session of 1880, amendment of the Land Act seemed to me to be the only demand even of the advanced Home Rulers; not its subversion by a set of principles entirely new.

New feelings, a new temper, have indeed been manifested in Ireland; but what new facts have occurred since the Session of 1880 to show any more radical insufficiency of the Land Act than previous facts may have proved?

If these new feelings are not really related to the facts, and so far are the fruit of a most unscrupulous and almost wicked as well as illegal agitation, I will not say that no account is to be taken of them in our coming legislation; but I can hardly think they ought to be allowed to supply its basis, and to introduce fundamental changes into the nature of property, which might, in their turn, entail claims for compensation upon the people of the United Kingdom, and might next be found difficult to confine to one only of the three Kingdoms.

W. E. G.

December 9, 1880.

I have not referred here to any proprietary and perpetuity clauses, as they lie outside the *knot* of the question.

To W. E. FORSTER, Irish secretary, 9 December 1880.   Add MS 44158, f. 63.

[First letter]

1. I am very glad to receive your account of Law's speech.[2] Should there not be something published to remove the grounds of the attack made by J. MacCarthy in (I think) the D. News.

2. I am extremely sorry the trials cannot be hastened: but I am strongly of opinion that an effort ought to be made to prevent May[3] from sitting. Very probably there would be a reaction after his outburst, & he might be perfectly fair: but nothing can remove the scandal. Surely the Lord Chancellor ought to be able to help in this matter by some friendly intervention. If it is not done, I seriously apprehend a motion in the H. of Commons for an Address: and I, for one, should not know how to meet it. Of course I am proceeding upon the newspaper reports.

3. The state of the Irish community, disclosed in the papers which you send me & in a large further supply which I receive from miscellaneous sources, is indeed deplorable. Is it really quite hopeless to expect that the community itself may do something against the Land League? Can there be no *strong* counter-association to condemn and discountenance a combination aimed at the repudiation of contracts? It is difficult to feel much admiration for those landlords whose Resolutions you sent me; it would not be

---

[1] Gladstone's alteration in ink.

[2] Large bundle of papers sent by Forster, with material on Law, Bessborough, Burke, Judge Fitzgerald etc., Add MS 44158, ff. 39–62.

[3] George Augustus Chichester *May (1815–92, lord chief justice of Ireland 1877–87) on 6 December dismissed contemptuously a submission for postponement of the trial; he later withdrew from sitting for it, being replaced by Mr Justice Fitzgerald.

fair, in their circumstances, to say they only howl and whine; but surely they ought to have gone beyond the scope of mere complaint.

4. As to your sketch of probable course of procedure on the meeting of Parliament, I very much agree with it: reserving however for consideration whether *remedy* might not begin to be dealt with when repression has got (say) through Committee.

5. With regard to the further acceleration of the meeting of Parliament, of course that could only be done by the Cabinet, and hence my Telegraph to you of this forenoon, to which perhaps you mean to reply by post.

[P.S.] Telegram of today to you 'Would you wish to summon Cabinet for an earlier day than Thursday say Monday at three.' Your answer just received 5.15 p.m.

Add MS 44158, f. 64.

[Second letter]

1. I have so many things to touch upon about Ireland today, and so much else to do, that I must be brief, and even abrupt.

2. I feel the necessity of casting the mind forward into the future. There is a sheer panic in Ireland. I must say I think it has a little touched our Commissioners. We must try to proceed, as we shall wish that we had proceeded, first when the current of Irish sentiment is met, in the open daylight of discussion by the counter-currents of English and Scotch opinion, and secondly when, by the lapse of time, and restoration of public tranquillity, this matter shall be viewed in calm retrospect say three or five or fifty years hence.[1]

3 I have this day got from London the terms of reference to the Commission. I hardly think they justify the course taken by the Commissioners. On the main subject, the Land Act, instead of examining and discussing, they are meagre and summary in the highest degree: but perhaps they mean to supply the gap hereafter. Under the name of 'further amendments['] in the law, they really subvert the whole foundations of the law, and make a new law with new foundations.

4. I admit however that we cannot escape a legislative interference with rents: yet I *hope* it may be on the lines of the Land Act, and *once for all*.

5. I admit that you cannot dictate to the Commission, or perhaps press them further. But I think the Cabinet may, and I hope it will, dissuade them from the publication in detail of these most disturbing schemes, and induce them to deal in their report with 'further amendments' in short and simple terms.

6. I am rather amazed, as far as I have gone in the Evidence, at our friend Dowse's questions, which seem almost always to breathe a foregone conclusion.

7. *What of the other Commission?*[2] Ought you not to communicate with the Chairman, perhaps in the first instance with Carlingford, to say that we think legislation necessary, and that we hope for the aid of what they may have to say? I am afraid that if we do not say this they will gladly shirk the responsibility of reporting, and then, not without reason, charge us with having passed them by.

8. Finally I hope that our Commission will be content with the line of recommending amendments in the Land Act, and will be guarded in whatever intimations they may make of a necessity for further changes of a more fundamental kind: and, in any case, I hope you may feel that the Cabinet in its preliminary Resolutions should take the Act for its point of departure, and endeavour as far as may be to build upon it.

[P.S.] I should not like to abandon without further consideration the ideas of Childers' paper. It is ingenious, but he is also practical. I send this round to be copied.

---

[1] This para. in Hammond, 188.

[2] i.e. the Richmond Commission on agricultural distress, set up by the tories.

To Sir C. HERRIES, chairman of the board of inland   Add MS 44544, f. 108.
revenue, 9 December 1880.

Thanks for your very interesting letter.[1]
1. I gather from it that the arrangement for a *Triumvirate* was never actually made [in 1852]. I had always been under the impression that it was made but immediately broken up by Lord B[eaconsfield].
2. It occurs to me that Lord B. took the Chancellorship of the Exchequer because he at once saw that the game of Protection must be abandoned, & that some compensation, real or supposed, must be found for the Landlords out of the Exchequer by financial manipulation. So he determined not unnaturally to keep his hands on the till. No Chancellor of the Exchequer had been Leader except when First Lord also, between Ld. Althorp and Mr D. or before Ld. Althorp as far as I remember.

10. Fr.

Ch 8½ a.m. Wrote to Ld Granville—Mr Childers—Mr Bright—Mr Forster Tel. 1.2.—Mr Hamilton Tel and minutes. Wood cutting with W. Conversation with him—with Mr Godley—Mr Taylor. Worked on Irish Land. Read Irish Land Evidence—Letter to Pr. of Wales.[2]

To H. C. E. CHILDERS, war secretary, 10 December 1880.   Add MS 44544, f. 109.

1. Forster has sent me your plan for Irish County Govt. & land-purchasing operations. Awaiting your details I greatly like your general advice.
2. Ponsonby has sent me the inclosed. But if it is only modesty as in the case of F.M.ship I do not know that I ought to let him suffer.[3]
3. I am afraid you will find the Cabinet very free in mind next week, for the question of further accelerating the Session is now raised by Forster, & the question of land in Ireland is really, I consider, ablaze. The Commissioners have been I think somewhat wild & I now almost hope for something from the other Commission to check them a little. I advise your not taking to the Cabinet anything except the weightiest matters.
4. I do not very well know how if the meeting of Parliament is further hastened you will manage the preparation of your Estimates; unless indeed we were to make it a separate Session.
5. As to the amount of your Estimates, I am sure I may rely upon you to effect every economy you can. We shall probably have to bear a heavy Indian charge, & shall want every shilling.[4]

11. Sat.

Ch 8½ a.m. Wrote to Mr Hamilton Tel.—Mr Barclay M.P.—Ld Monson—Mr G.B. Hill[5]—Sir R. Lingen—Ld F. Cavendish and minutes. Read Barclay on Land[6]—

---

[1] See 7 Dec. 80n.
[2] Possibly W. S. Potter, *Letters from India during . . . the Prince of Wales' visit* (1876).
[3] Offer of constableship of the Tower to Sir W. Codrington; he eventually refused it.
[4] Childers replied, 12 December 1880, Add MS 44129, f. 122: 'I am fighting a heavy battle against the great increase of Estimates called for by Ld Airey's Committee & by H.R.H. If I keep the expenditure at its present level it will be the best, I fear, I can do.'
[5] Thanking George Birkbeck Norman Hill for the *Life* of Sir R. Hill; Add MS 44544, f. 109. See 23 Nov. 80.
[6] J. W. Barclay, M.P., had sent his 'Agricultural distress remedy' (no copy traced); note of thanks at Add MS 44544, f. 109.

Irish Land Evidence—Q. Mary Imprisonment[1] and [blank.] Walk, with Godley & W.H.G. Much thought, much conversation on Irish Land. The perplexities are great; but, as in this mornings Psalm I will call unto the most high God: even unto the God that shall perform the cause that I have in hand.[2] 14 to dinner; conversation on saving crops.

12. 3. S. Adv.

Ch. 11 a.m. & 6½ P.M. Wrote to Ld Hartington—Ld Granville—Ld Vernon—Sir W. Harcourt—Mr Pender—Miss de Lisle—Ld Dufferin—Mr G. Howard—Mr Playfair—Ld Clonmel—Mr W.C. Smith and minutes. Read the New Era—little else; an unSunday like Sunday, Ireland a dark & dreary cloud on the horizon.[3]

To LORD CLONMELL, 12 December 1880.　　　　　　　　Add MS 44544, f. 110.

I return your inclosure; a new testimony added to a state of things which in a portion and an increasing portion of Ireland warrants almost any strength of epithet to describe it.

I will however confess my regret to find that the right-minded portion of the community seems so unable to do any thing for itself by counter-combination against the attempt to drive men into the Land League by exclusive dealing.

In the matter of crime and outrage I quite understand that the orderly and peaceable classes must depend upon the Government, the magistracy, the public force, and in the last resort the Legislature: but how can any or all of these compel men and great masses of men to deal or not to deal with A, B, or C, as customers, labourers, employers, or otherwise?

To Sir W. V. HARCOURT, M.P., home secretary,　　　　　MS Harcourt dep. 8.
12 December 1880.

Many thanks for your letter.[4] The Cabinet meets tomorrow because Forster wishes to propose a further acceleration of the meeting of Parliament. To this I have not yet quite seen my way. But I think the state of the Land question, which is very grave, may make our meeting thus early useful.

Are you not struck with the astounding helplessness of the rightminded part of the community in Ireland—as distinguished from the more personal courage of individuals—in the face of combination for exclusive dealing and the like.

Not all the Governments upon earth can do for a community certain things that it ought to do for itself.

Please let your people communicate with Horace Seymour about the hundred pounds.

To Margaret DE LISLE, 12 December 1880.　　　　　　　Add MS 44544, f. 110.

I must not leave the matter in any doubt about your Father and my pamphlet,[5] as far as I can clear it. Indeed you have it I think pretty clear as to him. You think he encouraged the publication not because he agreed with it but because he thought it would do good in

---

[1] J. D. Leader, *Mary Queen of Scots in captivity* (1880).　　　　　　[2] Psalm lvii. 2.
[3] An echo of his 'cloud in the West' letter of 1845; Bassett, 64.
[4] Of 11 December, Add MS 44196, f. 116, on Scottish business, Ireland, and shipment of English girls to Belgium.
[5] On the Vatican decrees; Miss De Lisle wrote (7 December 1880, Add MS 44467, f. 110): 'I was aware of his having read it but not of his having advised its publication.'

a particular way. Now this is very much my idea. I have never meant to say that he agreed with it, though I think he may have agreed with a good deal that is in it. To this you add that at first he begged me not to publish it and afterwards when he altered his tone that he was moved very much or in part by deference to Lord Acton. Here we part company a little. I think I can say with confidence that if he at any time entertained this adverse opinion he never made it known to me: and further I have no recollection that Lord Acton urged me to publish it.[1]

On the other large subject I have hardly time to say a word. There is no doubt that in connection with the Reformation there grew up what may be called the invisible Church theory, nor would I without much fresh investigation undertake to pronounce upon its origin and limits. But that the authentic acts of the English Reformation only abolished the Pope's ordinary jurisdiction (which is I believe a term of art) is a matter not of opinion but of fact. There was indeed a most violent proceeding taken under Henry VIII in inserting an antipapal clause into the litany: but this was not revived after the reign of Mary. Even that clause shows how much they were acting against the Pope and how little they thought they were doing what of right or of fact severed them from the Western Church at large. Of course the State continuance and the Church continuance are quite separate: but it always appears to me the Roman controversialists are in difficulty when abandoning the generalities of the 'Three conversions' they attempt to show when and how the old Anglican church underwent three corresponding transmutations.

To LORD DUFFERIN, 12 December 1880.   Add MS 44544, f. 110.

I thank you for your paper,[2] which, in a large degree, commands my sympathies. That is to say I am averse to expropriation of the class of Landlords either covert or open, and I have not yet seen in what sense a man is a proprietor who does not ultimately determine, under whatever checks, who shall be the occupier of the land.

On the other hand I do not understand by free sale a sale without any limitations, or a partnership in the land; but only a right, not subject to absolute unconditional veto, of transferring by assignment two things viz. the tenant's improvements and his interest in his occupation as his means of livelihood. Such a right I rather think was recognised in our Land *Bill* of '70; though not in the Act. It may want limitation and restraint but I cannot see that the principle is in its essence bad. I do not now touch cases where it has been bought out.

13. M. [London]

C. & I went off at 8, leaving guests behind us, Downing St at 2.30. Saw Mr Godley—Ld Granville cum Ld Hartington. Then these with Mr Forster—Mr Childers—Ld F. Cavendish. Dined at Lady Lyttelton's. Read 'Pictures from Ireland'. Wrote to Mrs Blake[3]—Mr Holiday—The Queen—W.H.G. (Tel) and minutes. A long & laborious day.

[1] See 29-30 Oct. 74 for de Lisle, Acton and the pamphlet.

[2] See Add MS 44625, f. 40; hostile to the 'Three Fs', but proposing conversion of the rent into a fixed charge or land rate. This letter is in Sir A. Lyall, *The life of . . . Dufferin and Ava* (1905), i. 191; Dufferin was home on leave from the St Petersburg embassy.

[3] Thanking her for *Pictures from Ireland* (1880) by her husband, (Sir) H. A. Blake, pseud. T. MacGrath; Add MS 44544, f. 111.

Cabinet. Dec. 13. 1880 3 p.m.[1]

W.E.G. stated the occasion of summoning Cabinet today *vice* Thursday.[2]

Shall there be coercion? Shall it be the Habeas Corpus?:

Forster emphasised each.

Shall the day of meeting [of Parliament] be altered? and to what day?: No.

Shall the announcement of the basis of a Land measure be postponed? if possible no.

Forster made a *sine quâ non* that he should be empowered to say we would coerce—and that by suspension of *Habeas Corpus*. H[artingto]n was then proceeding to ask opinions of the majority on the alteration of the day for the meeting of Parl[iamen]t. But I said I on my part could not consent to undo the former decision of the Cabinet as to proposing to Parliament our whole policy.

Upon this there was a general acquiescence in the retention of the present day. I am not *sure* that there would have been a *majority* for it: but I think Granville, Kimberley, Bright, Chamberlain, Childers, Harcourt, Dodson, with me. Forster behaved quite well.[3]

Forster: Increase of outrages. Dec 1-11: 295. Violent intimidation greatly increased. Searches[?] by Police, increased from 80 to 119. But the serious matter is the effect of the outrages. Dwelt on Boycotting. Fear of armed collisions. Danger of a rising—not so remote as it seemed some time ago. No fear of punishment for breaking the law. Much fear for keeping it.

Chamberlain: Two things only wd. justify changes. 1) fear of a rising. 2) great increase of homicidal outrages.

W.E.G. Essence of the former decision lay in the *combination* of remedy with repression.

14. Tu.

Wrote to Ld Chancellor—Earl of Derby—The Queen—and minutes. Cabinet 2.5: Irish Land mainly. Saw Earl of Cork—Mr Forster (at great length, on Irish Land)—Mr Childers—Ld Granville: a really composing councillor—Ld Spencer. Dined at Lady S. Spencer's. Read Trevelyan's Fox.[4]

Cabinet. Tues. Dec. 14. 80. 2 p.m.[5]

Mr. Forster opened the subject of Irish Land.

Court for rents largely discussed. Power[?] of evictions.

Virtual expropriation of landlords. Compensation. New principles, or Amendment of the [1870] Land Act?

W.E.G. was requested to print his Resolutions[6] (which were read) and a Mem. of plan founded on amendment of Act of 1870 with quasi Longfield Clauses.[7]

[1] Add MS 44642, f. 108.

[2] At Forster's strong request; see Ramm II, i. 228.

[3] Gladstone thus avoided an early summoning of Parliament, at the price of accepting coercion balanced by a Land Act.

[4] See 18 Nov. 80.

[5] Add MS 44642, f. 112.

[6] Partially drafted on 1 Dec., finalised about this time; see later in this day's entry.

[7] Longfield's scheme for 'parliamentary tenant right' based on seven years' purchase, as alternative to Ulster tenant right, described for Cabinet in mem. of 23 Nov. by J. Naish (Harcourt MSS dep. 106); see 7 Nov. 80.

To LORD SELBORNE, lord chancellor, 14 December   Selborne MS 1867, f. 138.
1880. 'Private'.

I have no doubt you will give your best consideration to the question whether and how far we can strengthen the law or the Government in Ireland by means other than, and probably in addition to the suspension of *Habeas Corpus*. Among other points and indeed principally I am desirous that it should be considered whether apart from the present trials we ought not under the circumstances to have new legislation against a combination [and?] against the Land League.

The *differentia* in the case now before us is that the combination formed at the present time to bring about breach of contract and nonpayment of rent is *dangerous to the public security*.

What I wish to have considered is whether in such a case such a combination does not assume an altogether new character, and whether both its collective proceedings and all acts done in furtherance of its unlawful purposes ought not to be dealt with by more effective and stringent means than the ordinary mode of prosecution for misdemeanour?

This is the question which in haste, at the end of our discussion, I meant to put forward yesterday.

Secret. Draft Resolutions. Irish Land Tenure.

1. That it is expedient to make further provision for the definition and reduction of any exorbitant rents, taken on any ⟨tenancy⟩* agricultural tenancies as from year to year now existing in Ireland* (whereof the valuation does not exceed [   ] pounds).
2. That *without prejudice to the proprietary interest of the landlord ⟨in the just renting value of the soil⟩* it is expedient to secure to the tenant occupiers of land in Ireland the power of selling their interest in their occupation, and to make provision against the defeat of the said power by undue augmentations of the rent upon a vacancy in the holding.
3. That it is expedient to make further provision for the security of tenure in Ireland, and for putting a check upon changes in rent other than such as may be freely agreed on by both parties.
4. That it is expedient further to assist the purchase of small properties in Ireland, and to give to tenants facilities by loan for acquiring a perpetual interest in their holdings, subject to a fixed rent.
5. That it is expedient to establish cheap transfer, ⟨Parliamentary title⟩, and the extension of the powers of limited owners to an equality with those of absolute owners, for the purpose of any Act to be passed for the regulation of Land Tenures in Ireland.[1]

SECRET.   PROVISIONS. IRISH LAND.[2]
                         Summary of Provisions.

1-3. For the adjustment of rents in present holdings, to supply a starting point.
4-6. Establishing right of assignment, or 'free sale.'
7-11. For checking arbitrary and frequent changes in the future rent.
   12. Extending Clauses 8 to 11 to lands under the Ulster, &c., Custom.
13-15. For promotion of perpetual rents and peasant proprietorship.
   16. To exclude leases from the Clauses touching augmentation of rent.
   17. Other amendments of the Land Act to be considered.

[1] Not signed or dated; printed for the Cabinet on 15th December 1880, Add MS 44625, f. 26. Gladstone's additions in ink on the printed paper are marked by asterisks. Draft of 1-4, later amended, dated 'D.1', is at Add MS 44764, f. 165.
[2] Printed for the Cabinet on 15 December; Add MS 44625, f. 19.

Provisions.

1. *In any tenancy existing at the passing of this Act* [*and not exceeding* 100 *l. valuation*] the tenant may allege before the Judge that the rent is exorbitant; and if the Judge be satisfied thereof, and if the landlord shall refuse to reduce the rent accordingly, the exaction of the rent shall be deemed a disturbance.

2. An exorbitant rent, for the purposes of this Act, is such a rent as, in the opinion of the Judge, after hearing all the parties and all the circumstances of the case, a solvent tenant, one year with another, would not undertake to pay.

3. A tenant so disturbed by the landlord may, at his option, claim compensation under the Land Act of 1870, or sell his interest under the provisions of this Act, and in the last-named case shall also receive from the landlord seven times the sum by which the rent shall have been judged to be exorbitant, in addition to the price he may obtain from an incoming tenant.

4. A tenant disturbed or evicted, or wishing to quit his holding, may freely sell his interest therein.

[The fundamental principle of this provision is, that in a country like Ireland, in most parts of which employments are so little diversified as not to leave a real freedom of choice, the occupation of land, upon living terms, is itself money's worth, and is also money's worth of a kind that ought not to be represented in the rent, and that may justly be handled by Parliament as the property of the tenant. Under the Land Act of 1870 this right of occupation was only recognized as a sort of inconvertible property.]

[The landlord should have power to object to the purchaser, as under the Ulster Custom, upon grounds understood to be strictly defined.]

[The tenant selling his interest will of course thereby waive his claim to compensation for disturbance under the Land Act, and for his improvements, which he will have sold to the incoming tenant.]

[By free sale I understand simply a sale not subject to the landlord's absolute *veto*, as opposed to merely permitted sale.]

5. The sum he receives for his interest in his occupation, or for his improvements, or any other sum payable to him by the landlord under the provisions of this Act, shall be subject to reduction by the amount of any legal claims of the landlord against him in respect of rent or otherwise.

6. In any tenancy whatsoever an outgoing tenant may sell his interest to the landlord for a sum to settle all claims by either of them upon the other.

7. The exaction of the rent shall be deemed a disturbance when the landlord demands, and the tenant in possession refuses, an augmentation thereof.

8. The tenant so disturbed quitting his farm and selling his interest in the occupation thereof shall receive from the landlord seven times the amount of the said augmentation, in addition to the price he may obtain from the incoming tenant.

9. No augmentation of rent (except in respect of capital laid out by the landlord under agreement with his tenant) shall be lawful in Ireland until [   ][1] years shall have passed since the last previous augmentation.

[To prevent evasion of the foregoing section by a number of small augmentations.]

10. If—(*a.*) In any tenancy not over 100 *l.* valuation, not existing at the passing of this Act; or (*b.*) In any such tenancy existing at the passing of this Act, except where the tenant shall allege before the Judge that the rent is exorbitant;
the tenant shall demand, and the landlord refuse, a reduction of the rent, the tenant may sell his interest, but shall pay to the landlord out of the price thereof seven times the amount of such reduction.

11. When a tenant voluntarily quitting his farm shall have disposed of his occupation

---

[1] 'Query, 7, 10, 15' printed in the margin.

to an incoming tenant, and the landlord shall demand, and the incoming tenant shall refuse an augmentation of the rent, the incoming tenant shall have the same rights as would have accrued to the outgoing tenant if he had continued in the occupation.

12. The clauses hereinbefore contained (7-11) with regard to changes of rent on which the parties are not agreed shall apply likewise[1] to holdings occupied now under the Ulster Custom, or any custom made legal by the Land Act of 1870.

13. Where a landlord and a tenant shall agree together upon a rent to be paid in perpetuity, and it shall be a condition of the covenant that a sum shall be payable by way of fine to the landlord, there shall be advanced to the tenant, as a first charge upon the holding, a sum not exceeding five times the amount of the rent, nor exceeding three-fourths of the said fine.

14. The tenant who shall thus hold under a perpetual rent shall, except in cases of non-payment thereof, possess all the rights of a proprietor, save that he shall not have any right to divide the holding [into any lot or lots under [blank] acres] until he shall have fully repaid the advances made to him under this Act.

15. Clause to make better provision for encouraging and aiding the formation of a peasant proprietary. [It would be of great advantage that this should be worked through a really representative County Government in Ireland and the responsibility of the County. In this case it would be best to deal with the subject of purchases and perpetuities in a separate Act.(?)]

16. At the termination of any existing lease(?) and of any future lease for thirty-one years or upwards, the tenant may sell his interest, but the landlord, if he shall demand an augmentation of the rent, shall not be liable to the fine on augmentations provided by this Act.

16 A. The landlord and tenant of any holding in Ireland may agree together to refer to the Court of the Assistant Barrister the question what rent shall now and in all future times be payable for the same, with such variation as the Court shall, when appealed to by either of them, determine; with the condition that, subject to the said rent, and to any other fixed stipulations which they may agree on, (1) the said tenant, his heirs and assigns, shall never be disturbed save for breach of the same; and (2) he shall in all cases have the right to assign to another person his interest in his holding, defraying out of the consideration-money the legal claims of the landlord; (3) and the said holding shall thereupon in all respects be taken out of the provisions of the Land Act, 1870.

17. Other points for consideration are:—

(a.) To strengthen the clause as to compensation for improvements. (b.) To strengthen (part of) the scale of compensation for capricious eviction, apart from increase of rent. (c.) To remove or revise the limit of valuation. (d.) To disallow contracting out of the Act. (e.) Whether, and when, to make a new valuation of Ireland.

15. Wed.

Wrote to The Speaker—Mr Forster—Ld Hartington—Ly Hobart[2]—Ld Granville—D of Argyll—Mr Agnew—Ld Northbrook and minutes. Saw Ld Rosebery—Ld F. Cavendish—Ld Granville—Mr Childers—Mr & Mrs Th.—Scotts—General Ponsonby—Priv. Secretaries—The Queen—a long & gracious audience. To Windsor 4.30. Dined with H.M. Read Pictures from Ireland—Enraght's Tract.[3]

---

[1] This word is Gladstone's holograph addition.
[2] Perhaps Lady Georgina Mary Hobart, d. 1900, da. of 6th earl of Buckinghamshire.
[3] R. W. Enraght, 'My ordination oaths' (1880).

To H. B. W. BRAND, the Speaker, 15 December 1880, Brand MSS.
'*Private and confidential*'

As Parliament will meet a month earlier than usual, and as, when it meets, the first demand upon its time will be for the consideration of repressive measures, it is desirable to weigh beforehand, especially in view of the recently developed arts of obstruction, the question what will be the best means of expediting business. Will principle and will precedent warrant or recommend any modification either formal or practical of our ordinary modes of proceeding while we are engaged upon these grave matters, in a month not usually employed upon Parliamentary business? Your judgment and experience will enable you either to examine or to suggest any available proposition on these subjects far better than I can, and I hope you may think the question deserving of all your attention. Probably you could ask the assistance of Sir Thomas May and this letter I need not say is open to his inspection.

Not much has occurred to me that I should even think it worth while to mention, and the other demands upon me are I think the gravest, in connection with Ireland, that I have ever known. But I have asked myself whether it would be possible, until these repressive proposals are disposed of, to give precedence to them, or to subjects in connection with them on all, or on a greater number of days—and also whether something might be gained by a simply practical resolution to have continuous sittings on the several stages of any Bill except the Committee.

But please to receive this letter as an invitation and request for your aid rather than as itself a vehicle of suggestions. The time which has to elapse before the actual meeting will I hope allow you to conduct any communications that may be needful without undue pressure: and I shall not look for any immediate answer to what I have now written.[1]

To W. E. FORSTER, Irish secretary, 15 December 1880. Add MS 44544, f. 111.

I wish to correct an answer I gave you yesterday on a matter of some importance: or rather to enlarge it. You asked[2] me whether I thought wider scope could be given to what are called the Bright clauses; & I replied no. I had in view the difficulties of state purchases, state landlordism, State creditorship against small holders: & the mode in which everybody would conspire against the State in carrying on this new undertaking. But I should give quite a different reply if we can combine this good with another good, namely the establishment of local self government in the Irish counties. The matter would then have in it a healthy principle of life & the impulse of public opinion would measure its operations: all the difficulties & dangers would be got rid of, or at any rate reduced to a minimum. To prevent jobbing there might be some restraining function given to the State. But the main function of the State would then be advancing money, on principles to which we are accustomed more or less, & with such great objects in view I should not be at all inclined to stint this kind of action. Of course the same plan might be applied to the conversion of tenancies into feu-duty proprietorships, & perhaps rather extensively.

To the EARL OF NORTHBROOK, first lord of the admiralty, Add MS 44544, f. 112.
15 December 1880.

I thank you very much for giving me an early intimation as to the character of your Estimates.[3] The announcement however is serious, & it will be requisite, now that we are

---

[1] Brand referred the matter to May, sending his mem. on 22 December 1880; Add MS 44194, ff. 224, 234. [2] Apparently verbally. This reply is in Hammond, 187.
[3] Northbrook's letter untraced, but his pencil note of 16 December, explaining the half-million increase since 1873 largely 'by the increase in the non-effective vote, the increase of pay & naval reserve', is at Add MS 44266, f. 91.

in a condition to draw the various threads together into something like a common result, that the Cabinet should a little consider its position.

Childers has not yet been able to guarantee me a reduction in the army. The civil charges will grow, partly by self acting, partly by exceptional causes; & I fear the growth may be half a million. I doubt if any member of the Cabinet would wish it reduced.

There will be a subvention for India which I take roughly for the year at half a million more—it may exceed this.

Goschen was not a rigid Economist[1]—but the Estimates of this year are I think more than half a million in excess of his. I see they are three quarters.

Can it be necessary that we are to go further? I do not contest what you say on building. I speak of the aggregate. In any case I think you will see there is a case for considering the situation.

16. *Th.*

Prayers at nine. Wrote to the Queen 1.2.—Mr Childers—Mr Cowper MP. and minutes. Audience to Windsor—Council—back to London—Cabinet 2½-6½. Saw Sir W. Harcourt—Mr Childers—Ld Thurlow—Mr Godley—Ld R. Grosvenor—Ld F. Cavendish 1.2. Dined with the F.C.s. Read Irish Land Laws—Pictures from Ireland.

Cabinet. Thurs. Dec. 16. 80. 2($\frac{1}{2}$) p.m[2]

1. Committee on Corrupt Practices Bill and Ballot Act—recited the proceedings of the Committee. Main heads of memn. approved: provisionally.
2. Childers mentioned his questions of Army organisation.[3] Agreed to incl. the two-battalion system keeping the old numbers and titles subject to the territorial titles for the compound body. Promotion to be Major General from Col[onel] shall be by selection in one case of three.
3. Explanations of W.E.G.s land memorandum.
4. Creation of a peasant proprietary. Partial discussion on. Childers, Bright: to print and circulate.[4]
5. Forster inquired whether it might be possible for him to employ in case of necessity any extralegal methods. Various suggestions offered but nothing of very great moment.
6. Preliminary conversation on probable increase of expenditure and Admiralty demand of ½m which I objected to a good deal. A statement to be printed for cons[ideratio]n.[5]

To H. C. E. CHILDERS, war secretary, 16 December 1880.   Add MS 44544, f. 112.

I have read the Duke [of Cambridge]'s paper, which puts his case with a great deal of clearness and I hereby return it.

If I understand the new system right it looks to local recruiting as a new ground for

---

[1] i.e. at the admiralty, 1871-4.
[2] Add MS 44642, f. 113. Undated note, perhaps for Granville, by Gladstone reads: 'Queen very gracious, and well satisfied about Ireland, coercion, and land. I think *F.* has given up the [three] Fs.'
[3] See Childers' mem. of 15 December; PRO CAB 37/4/83 and S. Childers, *Life of H. C. E. Childers* (1901), ii. 33ff.
[4] See Bright's mem. of 17 December; PRO CAB 37/4/86.
[5] May read 'Circ[ulatio]n'; no printed statement found; see exchange with Northbrook on 15 Dec. 80.

harmony and attachment among the men, and of an increased, not a diminished, *esprit de corps*. Of this the Duke takes no account.

I can quite understand however that there may be an advantage in avoiding all breach of tradition and consequently in maintaining or allowing the old designations as subaltern titles of the battalions.

I was greatly struck by the mass of work you have gone through and the mastery you have apparently attained—I speak as one uninitiated—in a short time over a mass of complicated subjects.

At the same time viewing the great increase of our available[?] force, and the fact that the apparent or probable calls upon our army for oversea service are less and not more (as far as there is a change) than when the Tory Govt. framed their last estimates, I trust you will be able to manipulate your plan so as not to exhibit anything like an increase in the number of men.

17. Fr. [*Hawarden*]

Off at 9.30. Reached Hawarden 3.35. Wrote to Ld F. Cavendish—Ld Granville—Mr Forster—Duke of Argyll. Finished Pictures from Ireland. Read Gill's Introduction.[1] Fourteen to dinner.

To W. E. FORSTER, Irish secretary, 17 December 1880.   Add MS 44544, f. 113.

Though I feel very much the difficulty we shall have in the first stages of the Coercion debates before the trials are over, on account of the objection to discussing the deeds or words of persons actually arraigned, yet these stages or at least these debates will far outlast the trials, & in any case I think it would be very desirable that by way of information a collection should at once be made for the Cabinet of the most relevant speeches or parts of speeches of Parnell & the other agitators, as they contribute so vital a portion of the material on which we shall have to work.

I am rather puzzled, and pained, by Mr Blake's last chapter in his 'Pictures from Ireland'. It does not however I should think shake in any particular the credit of Mr Tuke's book.[2]

I hope, even if against hope, that Tuesday's list may have been followed by some other signs of remission in the work of outrage.

[P.S.] I am distressed to see again in the Standard of today the evidence of leakage, as you too will be.

18. Sat.

Ch 8½ a.m. Wrote to Abp of Canterbury—Ld Granville—Mr Childers—Mr Forster—Mr Rogers MP—Provost of Hawick—Mr Coote[3]—Mr Bywater—Mr Lennard—Mr Lowell—Mr Godley Tel. 2.h. walk with E. Wickham, A. Lyttelton, & Geo. Talbot. Saw W.H.G. (mortgage). Read divers Irish Land Pamphlets.—Mrs Gill's Ascension.

[1] Sir D. Gill's introduction to I. Gill, *Six months in Ascension* (1878).
[2] See 13 Dec. 80. J. H. Tuke, *Irish distress and its remedies* (1880); on a visit to Donegal. Tuke was a Quaker.
[3] C. J. Coote, on his Irish property; Add MS 44544, f. 114.

To H. C. E. CHILDERS, war secretary, 18 December 1880.   Add MS 44544, f. 114.

1. I fully appreciate the motive of your letter.[1] But I think you too will see that there is one & only one member of the Government who can really give an opinion on the question whether the Lord Lieutenant is equal to the heavy calls now made upon him. All that you report is negative. Shall I send your letter to Forster?[2] It is obviously disadvantageous that Cowper has been without official experience. But when he was appointed he stood in this respect on a level with Spencer at the date of his appointment, & there was no reason to suppose it might not turn out as well. He certainly has talent, & he is really liberal. He wrote extremely well on the subject of undertaking the trials. The question of administrative vigour is, however, distinct & vital. I know that F. has defended Lord C. & spoken highly of him in conversation with the Queen. I think I can at once go so far as to put a general question to Forster which may in part elicit his mind.

2. With regard to your constituents, there is a topic which requires to be delicately handled, but which also seems to require handling. It is the utter impotence of the Irish landlords to defend themselves, along with the other creditor-classes, I do not say against crime, but against exclusive dealing. Might you not ask Cowper his opinion on this subject.

19. 4. S. Adv.[3]

Wrote to Duke of Westminster—Mr Godley Tel.—Mr A. Peel—Ld Granville— The Speaker—Mr Howard MP.—Mr Ouvry—Mrs Th.—Mr Wilberforce. Worked on Mr W[ilberforce]'s proof sheets *quoad* certain letters of mine. Read Sewell, Xtn Commonwealth[4]—Pearson, Burial Offices[5]—Daniel on the Prayerbook— Eales, Via Crucis.[6]

To H. B. W. BRAND, the Speaker, 19 December 1880.   Brand MSS.

Your letters (of which one was accidentally delayed) reached me today. I thank you very much for your prompt and careful attention.

I will circulate the letter on procedure among my colleagues: that on the case of contempt I have sent to the A. General, for consn. & communication with his brother in Ireland.

As far as my personal disposition goes I have told him that though much disposed to patience in an ambiguous case of obstruction, I would deal with a clear case of contempt in a summary and decisive way.

To A. W. PEEL, undersecretary of the home office,   Add MS 44544, f. 116.
19 December 1880.

I answer in haste your most kind yet not welcome letter.[7] On our official connexion I have always set much value, both for your Father's sake & for our own. I do not at all

---

[1] Of 17 December 1880, Add MS 44129, f. 127: 'Cowper appears to me to be little more than a cypher . . . what I would urge on you is the substitution for Ld Cowper of a real Vice Roy'; Childers suggested Forster.
[2] Childers replied, 19 December, ibid., f. 131, that this was up to Gladstone, who probably thought better of his own suggestion.
[3] News of Boer rising and declaration of a republic reached London this day.
[4] Perhaps W. Sewell, *Christian communism* (1848).   [5] Untraced.
[6] S. J. Eales, *Via Crucis: fourteen sermons* (1880).
[7] Resigning through ill-health; Add MS 44270, f. 329. Harcourt suggested L. H. Courtney as Peel's successor; Gladstone proposed Lord R. Grosvenor's advice be asked first; Add MS 44544, f. 116.

relish being without a Peel in the Government. I hope the measure of precaution which you are wisely adopting may attain its end & may allow you to resume hereafter your official career. Of your personal kindness I have always been very sensible: and though I ought to wish well to your health I am truly glad that your resignation in no degree impairs our political accord.

20. M.

Ch 8½ a.m. Wrote to Ld Hartington—Ld Granville 1 & Tel 1.2.—Duke of Devonshire—Mr Stuart Rendel MP.—Mr Armitstead MP.[1]—Mr Rathbone MP—Ld Coleridge—Sir W. Harcourt and minutes. Saw Mr Mahaffy[2]—E. Wickham & A.L. on Oxford Fellowships. Read Mrs Gill's Ascension—C. Russell on Irish Land[3]—Philae.[4] Worked on Irish Land.

To the 7th DUKE OF DEVONSHIRE, 20 December   Chatsworth MSS 340. 1045.
1880.

I send by Hartington's desire two letters from your Agent in Ireland, with an opportunity of perusing which he has favoured me. I have done it with the painful interest which at this moment attaches to every thing coming from Ireland.

Experience will I suppose reveal to us, after no very long time, what are the respective shares of timidity and cupidity in bringing about, and in maintaining, the present state of things in Ireland.

Let me take this opportunity of offering you my best thanks for a copy, which you have been good enough to send me, of the Catalogue [by Lacaita] of your Library at Chatsworth. Perhaps one may say without being far from the mark that the Library deserves such a Catalogue, and the Catalogue such a Library.

[P.S.] I am told on what should be very good authority that the Duke of Rutland has 200 farms on hand. It can hardly be.

To LORD HARTINGTON, Indian secretary, 20 December   Add MS 44145, f. 165.
1880.

There are one or two things I may as well say on your letter,[5] especially as they need not be polemical.

1. When the prosecution of the chief Land Leaguers was proposed, there was no positive

[1] Stuart Rendel 1834-1913; anglican and liberal M.P. Montgomeryshire 1880-94; cr. Baron Rendel 1894. George Armitstead, 1824-1915; Russian merchant; liberal M.P. Dundee 1868-73, 1880-5; cr. Baron 1906. Rendel agreed, Armitstead declined, respectively to move and second the Address. Both patronised Gladstone in his old age, especially Rendel; see his *Personal Papers*, ed. F. E. Hamer (1931).

[2] See letter to Lefevre, 22 Dec. 80.

[3] *New views of Ireland, or, Irish land: grievances, remedies*, reprinted from the *Daily Telegraph* (1880), sent by the author, (Sir) Charles *Russell, 1832-1900; independent liberal M.P. Dundalk 1880-5, S. Hackney 1885-94; attorney general 1886, 1892-4; Baron Russell of Killowen and lord chief justice 1894. He defended Parnell on the commission of 1888-9.

[4] An early version of *Philae; or the throne of the Priest. A drama of ancient Egypt, in three acts* (1882), sent by the author anonymously.

[5] Long letter of 19 December, Add MS 44145, f. 160, stating his opposition to all aspects of the Cabinet's Irish policy hitherto, save prosecution of the League (though that too slow), and implying resignation if any further concession required from him. Hartington's letter was in part prompted by a strong appeal from the Queen on 12 December (Chatsworth MSS 340, 1037) to his 'loyalty & Straightforwardness' and to his '*firmness* and *determination*'.

decision for it was started by English influences, and pressed on the Irish Government. That Government adopted the present mode of procedure in lieu of the one you anticipated or preferred, because among other reasons, it was greatly more expeditious.

2. So far as I know you need not expect any difficulties in regard to the less or greater stringency of coercion. I am averse generally to meddling with the press; which I think has not been mentioned. But as we have to coerce, the first consideration is to do it effectually; and you will find I have already communicated with the Speaker on the means of expediting its progress through the House of Commons.

3. I am not more sanguine perhaps than you as to the immediate effect in Ireland of any Land measures we can propose; nor at all disposed to mix them with the measures of repression on the principle of pari passu. What I think is requisite is that, in setting out upon the repressive operation, we should in the main know our own minds as to land, and should make known authentically the basis on which we mean to proceed.

4. I will not go back upon the past decisions to which you refer. To me they appear to have involved considerations of great difficulty, upon which men, thoroughly allied in political principles, might not unnaturally differ. From this I own that I rather expect the—not renewal but—revival of the Arms Act; which, after the late Government had virtually dropped renewal, would I believe have been not only useless in Ireland (from incompleteness) but a very serious Parliamentary error.

21. Tu. St Thomas.

Ch (and C.H.) 8½ a.m. Wrote to Sir W. Codrington—Mr Forster—Bp of Ely—Mr Torrens MP.—Dean Bagot—Mr Russell MP.—Mr Welby—Sir Rivers Wilson—Author of Philae—Mr CJ. Herries and minutes. Saw W.H.G. on Estate business. Mr [Scott] Holland—Ch & Univ. matters. Walk with Mr Holland. Finished Philae. Read Pym on Irish Land[1]—Hanno.[2] Thirteen to dinner.

To Sir C. HERRIES, chairman of the board of inland revenue,   Add MS 44544, f. 117.
21 December 1880.

I think that as time does not press you had better hold back your Death Duties Bill until I can have oral comment and explanation upon it.

Also that we may see how far we can go in dealing with the more disputable questions which I suppose to be

1. Ought we to alter or reverse the proceeding of 1853 with respect to leaseholds? On this I do not recollect to have had a report of opinion.

2. What shall we do with regard to reversions? And here (a) I at once adopt your decision to levy the 1 per cent on what you describe as the prevailing form of reversionary bequest which I suppose involves putting the widows on the same footing generally as the children.

(b) I do not wholly give up my notion (it is no more) of charging at once the higher rate or rates upon the residue, with repayment on the falling in of the sum but with no interest: unless I learn from you that estates without a residue would present an insurmountable obstacle.

(c) I put another question. Could we put a fine, so to call it, upon Estates containing reversionary bequests chargeable beyond the One per cent rate? not covering the exact

[1] J. Pim, *The land question in Ireland* (1867); or his *Review of the progress of Ireland since the famine* (1876).
[2] Perhaps *Hanno; a tragedy in five acts* (1853). But see 25 Dec. 80n.

amount but by way of a very rough Composition for it? either (b) or (c) should I think apply to future wills only. But your (a) might run with the Act.

22. Wed.

Ch 8¼ a.m. Wrote to Ld Hartington—The Queen Tel.—Dr Bradley—Ld Chancellor 1.2.—Mr Godley—Mr Lefevre M.P.—Bp of Ely—Rev. D.T. Gladstone—Mr Ouvry and minutes. Saw E. Wickham (Univy) W.H.G. (Mortgages) S.E.G. (Church troubles). Photographed. Read Hanno—Industrial Curiosities[1]—Russell on Ireland.

To LORD SELBORNE, lord chancellor, 22 December 1880.   Selborne MS 1867, f. 156.

1. I suppose Walpole would probably be the best man to have charge of a Patronage Bill in the H. of C.[2] But I should have supposed it ought to begin in the H. of Lords.
2. I return Mr Whiston.[3] No doubt terror (with unmanliness) is doing much in Ireland. But not all. I do not think *terror* makes Railway Companies furnish trains free of charge for Parnell meetings: or leads a London Company to put its Irish Provision Establishments under the League: or a Steam Boat Company to refuse Bence Jones's cattle: or even the Duke of Devonshire's Agent to supply Evergreens free for a local gathering of the League.[4]
3. Thanks for your Christmas greetings, which I return. They cannot be quite so cheery as usual, but may be, I trust, not less hearty.
[P.S.] I am very glad you have framed something against the Land League.

To G. Shaw LEFEVRE, 22 December 1880.   Add MS 44544, f. 118.

You have taken a forward part in the promotion of Tenant Purchase in Ireland at a period when schemes of that kind were less helped by circumstances than they are now. It is probable that you have at this time matured your views, possible that you may even have drawn out the heads, or outlines, or leading principles of a plan. If it be so, I shall be very glad to hear from you. It was not without difficulty that I brought myself to entertain the idea of the purchase of Estates for public account by a Commission, which is of course a very different thing from the disposal of estates coming otherwise than by purchase under the ownership of the State. I was enabled to come up to this point by considering that the very same rules which are needful to guard the public, in such a matter, against the corrupting evils of jobbery & waste, are likewise absolutely required on grounds totally distinct. Mr Mahaffy said to me two days ago, 'whenever you see in Ireland a small holding more wretched than others, you at once know it is a freehold or perpetuity'. But if so these are freeholds or perpetuities not acquired by industry & forethought. I conclude that where we have presumptive evidence of these qualities, we need not on the whole greatly fear. But this evidence, you will, I think, hold, can only be supplied by ability to produce a material portion of the price: & I take it for granted you would only recommend purchase by the State where a large proportion,—say not under ¾

---

[1] A. H. Japp, *Industrial curiosities. Glances here and there in the world of labour* (1880).

[2] For a measure on traffic in church livings; see 1 Dec. 80 and Add MS 44297, f. 112.

[3] Son of the Master of the cathedral school in Rochester, who had forwarded his letter to Selborne; Selborne thought it showed 'simple fear' to be the cause of the Land League's success; Add MS 44297, f. 112.

[4] Selborne's reply (24 December 1880, Add MS 44297, f. 112) still thought all these were manifestations of different types of 'fear'.

in number & value, were prepared to become owners, or perpetuity-men under a moderate free-farm rent. So I hope that the conditions necessary for hopeful settlement would keep the State within the limits of reasonable safety.[1]

23. Th.

Ch 8½ a.m. 11¼–2¼. Duchess of Westminster's funeral at Eccleston. It was simple, in good feeling: many relatives, many of the people. I feel however there is something unspoken, that inwardly I must speak. Saw Argyll—R. Grosvenor—W.H.G. Wrote to Granville—Mrs Th—Mr Chamberlain—Mr Ouvry—Mr A. Mansell[2]—Mr Godley—Mr Bright—Watsons—Mr Forster and minutes. Read Seebohm on Irish Tenures[3]—Murrough OBrien on Irish Land I.[4]

To John BRIGHT, chancellor of the duchy, 23 December 1880.   Add MS 43385, f. 290.

I thank you for your interesting letter,[5] and I will act upon your permission simply to retain and digest it except upon one point—I am, like you, in favour of abolishing limited ownership in land; and, like all the world, aware that limited ownership stands in conflict with much that an adequate Land Bill ought to contain.

On the other hand I am under the impression that a complete law for removal of limited ownership would be a complex business and require some time, more probably than we have to give.

Can we under these circumstances deal with the subject sufficiently for our present purpose on the basis of these two propositions 1. That every act ordered as permitted to be done by an absolute owner under our Bill and the Act of 1870 shall be within the competence of a limited owner. 2. That all money, received in pursuance of such acts, shall be invested, and held subject to the same beneficial interests as those of the limited ownership.

Please to think of this.

With regard to coercion my strong desire has been to keep the mind of the Cabinet fixed mainly on the exigencies of the future i.e. of the Land Question. But, while sensible of the exaggerations and susceptibilities which proceed (how the old Jingoism, now out of work, finds a new congenial occupation in shouting for all sorts of repression in Ireland), I cannot deny that, in my opinion all along, a combination like the Land League, and especially when dangerous to public security, is a fit object for permanent and effective prohibition. As respects other measures, more directly bearing on the restraint of private liberty, I cannot share Forster's very sanguine expectations: but I think that after the concessions he has made a kind of understanding has prevailed in the Cabinet that if offences (even not including those dangerous to life) continued to multiply and the Irish Govern-

---

[1] On 25 December, Lefevre sent a memorandum arguing that if the 1870 Bill had been passed unamended 'the Act would have been a settlement of the question' but that 'no measure merely giving greater effect to the Bright clauses will now suffice', and enclosing copies of letters written at J. Morley's suggestion for the *Pall Mall Gazette* under the *nom de plume* 'an Englishman'; Add MS 44153, f. 56.

[2] *Sic*; probably 'Maunsell' intended; see 25 Dec. 80.

[3] F. Seebohm, 'The historical claims of tenant right', *Nineteenth Century*, ix. 19 (January 1881); article sent in proof by Knowles on 23 December, Add MS 44231, f. 334.

[4] Two articles in *Fortnightly Review*, xxxiv. 409, 576 (October and November 1880).

[5] Of 22 December, Add MS 44113, f. 140, believing violence on the decline in Ireland, doubtful about suspension, and urging a Land Bill 'made out of your views and mine'.

ment demanded extra constitutional powers for the beginning of the Session the Cabinet would be much inclined to give weight to this authority.

The situation is formidable and has need of all the good qualities which good and wise men can bring to our deliberations.[1]

To J. CHAMBERLAIN, president of the board of trade,   Chamberlain MSS 5/34/4. 23 December 1880.

I thank you for your interesting letter and inclosure[2] and for dispensing with my reply: the main matters you touch will of course be for the decision of the Cabinet next week. I have little faith in any plan for breaking up the Parnellite Home Rulers.

24. Fr.

Ch 8½ a.m. Wrote to Mr Knowles Tel.—Ld Kimberley—The Speaker—Sir W. Harcourt—Ly Derby—Mr Courtney MP. Ld Advocate & minutes. Saw Mr Vickers—Ld R. Grosvenor—Mr Salusbury. Arranging private letters. Read Don Quixote.—Imprisonment of Mary Stuart[3]—M. OBrien on Irish Land II.

To LORD KIMBERLEY, colonial secretary, 24 December   Add MS 44544, f. 121. 1880.

I cannot feel surprised that you and Childers should have deemed it necessary to send another regiment to South Africa, though I do not know that the necessity lies on the surface of the case, but you are better judges.

I return your able paper of instructions to Sir H. Robinson,[4] with one or two suggestions on the margin, not I think affecting principle but expression.

Circulation seems hardly necessary but I would I think invite perusal of the paper by Chamberlain or any other colleague who has taken a special interest in any great South African question of the present day.[5] A happy Christmas to you and Lady Kimberley, Ireland notwithstanding.

25. Sat. Xm. Day.

Ch 11 a.m. and H.C.—also 7 P.M. Wrote to Sir H. Ponsonby—Bp of Exeter—Mr Seymour—Mr Forster—Ld Granville—Mr Maunsell—Dr Fairbairn—Mr Dodson—Duke of Argyll—Mr F.C. Thompson[6] and minutes. Read Fairbairn on the Character of our Lord[7]—Imprist. of Mary Stuart.

[1] Bright replied, 24 December 1880, Add MS 44113, f. 146: 'if a good Bill is brought in, there will be no need of "force", and least of all for the "suspension"'.

[2] Chamberlain this day sent a letter by Justin McCarthy (received *via* Labouchere): 'his letter rather confirms the opinion expressed by Labouchere that the majority of the Irish members would be compelled to accept as satisfactory a really strong Land Bill & would leave the Fenians to their own devices afterwards'; Add MS 44125, f. 57.

[3] See 11 Dec. 80.

[4] Sent on 22 December; Add MS 44225, f. 261.

[5] Kimberley circulated the instructions for Cabinet approval; ibid. f. 265. See Schreuder, 93ff., 30 Dec. 80, and *PP* 1881 lxvi.

[6] Had sent 'Hanno'; see Add MS 44544, f. 122.

[7] See 12 Feb. 80.

652 THE GLADSTONE DIARIES

To the DUKE OF ARGYLL, lord privy seal, 25 December   Add MS 44544, f. 122.
1880.

Though God knows I have little time for writing I must not leave you under a grievous misunderstanding which I had hoped to avoid.

'Living terms' are surely terms on which a tenant can live[1]—and these in Ireland have been and are largely worth paying for—& in not a few cases they have been unduly paid for in rent—and they with improvements constitute an interest—and this interest is a fair subject of sale—and its assignment was I believe allowed (it did not require to be enacted) by the Land Bill as we adopted and introduced it.

This is quite apart from Customs, and from Customs bought up.

My doctrine does not in the least interfere with 'full letting' value.

Pray read an article by Seebohm[2] which I have asked Knowles to send you in proof.

I wish there were more men in the Cabinet who had tried to read up the history of Irish Tenures.

I meant to have begun with wishing you a happy Christmas (if Minister can at this time administer such a message of peace). Let me end with it.

To W. E. FORSTER, Irish secretary, 25 December 1880.   Add MS 44158, f. 86.

1. I am exceeding glad that O'Hagan is at work & has hope.[3]
2. The paper that came by mistake seemed to me a strange piece of drafting.[4] I have no doubt you will take care that on the difficult subjects nothing is introduced without *Thring*.
3. I also assume that you will appear on Thursday and with the latest supply of facts.
4. I cannot say that the clouds of any kind are getting thinner. I have no doubt as to the disposition of the large majority of the Cabinet to listen to you & the Irish Govt. about repressive measures: but of some colleagues I feel far from sure. Now I think that when one comes to measures of this class at all, the first requisite is that they should be sufficient. Nevertheless I am sure you will avoid whatever you do not believe to be within the necessity of the case, which is (as we shall find) a very peculiar one, and in some respects novel. That I may exemplify what I mean: I have leaned all along as you know to legislation against the Land League as the main thing. Nevertheless I should be sorry to see that tried merely to meet my wish—unless the propriety & advantage of it are really seen.
5. Again; it will be a great object to be concise & summary. If for example you mean to revive the *provisions* which expired on June 1 without amendment, I should lean to reviving the Act bodily.
6. I do not quite understand what is meant by saying that the Executive has broken down in Ireland. What seems to me much more clear is a. that the judicial system may have broken down, b. that the 'sound' part of society has utterly broken down.
If I do not say 'happy Christmas' I feel it.

26. *S. & S. Stephen.*

Ch 11 a.m. and 6 P.M. Wrote to the Duke of Westminster—Ld R. Grosvenor—
Mr Bass MP.—Ld Granville—Miss Collet—Mr Seymour Tel—Mr Whitworth—

---

[1] Argyll objected to 'living terms' as 'an argument of indefinite elasticity'; letter of 24 December 1880, Add MS 44104, f. 258.

[2] Copy reads 'Irewhen (?)', but F. Seebohm clearly intended; see 23 Dec. 80.

[3] Forster's letter of 23 December, Add MS 44158, f. 82: 'O'Hagan is doing his best about May [see 9 Dec. 80] & I hope he may succeed.'

[4] 'A very early draft', sent in error on 23 December; Add MS 44158, f. 82. Thring may have drafted this version, see Hammond, 189. Thring's memorandum of 23 December is at Add MS 44625, f. 33.

Mr Bryce M.P. and minutes. Read Brahmo S. Year Book[1]—Countess of Northumberland's Devotions[2]—Basis of Spiritualism[3]—Contemp., Jews in Germany—Unconscious Christianity.[4]

27. M. St John.

Ch 8½ a.m. and H.C. Wrote to Sir Jas. Watson—Mr Courtney—Mr Lefevre MP. 1-2.—The Queen—Sir W. Harcourt—Mr G. Howard—Ld Kimberley—Williams & Co—Ld Camperdown—Ld Granville Tel.—Ld R. Grosvenor Tel and minutes. Worked on my yearly statement—in preparation for arr. with W.H.G. Axework with W.H.G. Xm-tree & house rather topsy-turvy. Read Mary Q. of S. in Captivity—Rev. B.W. Smith on Anglo. Israel.[5]

To G. Shaw LEFEVRE, secretary to the admiralty,   Add MS 44544, f. 123.
27 December 1880.

[First letter]   Your opinion on the Irish Land Bill is gratifying, & is also of weight, for your authority on questions of Irish Land is undeniable.

It was for this reason that I wrote to you, alone among the members of the Govt. outside to learn something of your views, before any final decision is taken by the Cabinet.

Forgive me however for suggesting with all frankness, as between friends, that I am a little sorry you should have frustrated that decision by working through the Press on behalf of a particular alternative involving such grave issues.[6]

[P.S.] Lest I should seem to exaggerate let me say that I refer to your letter and not to the general strain & purpose of the letters. It is a pure exception; & I have not forgotten what preceded your Reading Election.

                                                        Add MS 44153, f. 69.

[Second letter] I thank you for your able paper.[7] But I must admit that I think it, as coming from you, a sign of the times. I will note some of the points that occur to me: dismissing your Guarantee Fund (15 and 16) as there is no longer any Church Surplus available.
1. I suppose there is no doubt that *in the main* your plan of the 3 Fs converts the Landlord into an incumbrancer.
2. Do you think that, after doing this, you can keep under a tenure fundamentally different holdings over £100—or grazing farms—or farms improved by the Landlord—or other than agricultural tenancies—or draw a line *by law* to divide between the holdings included in some of these definitions and those excluded.
3. Or that you can constitute a Commission strong enough to take over into its hands the largest and nicest class of private dealings throughout the Irish Agricultural community: and, having put the landlord into the position of an incumbrancer, to put him back 'for other than agricultural purposes' into the position of a landlord? (No. 9)
4. When, under the Ulster Custom, a Court determines rent, how does it come about? What is the position of the parties, which makes them both willing to abide the judgment

---

[1] The annual volume ed. Sophia Collet.

[2] E. Percy, Countess of Northumberland, *Meditations and prayers* (1682), or a privately printed Irvingite work by Louisa, duchess of Northumberland.

[3] Perhaps [E. S. G. Sanders], *Spiritualism. What is it?* (1880?).

[4] In *Contemporary Review*, xxxix. 31, 45 (January 1881).

[5] B. W. Savile, *Anglo-Israelism and the Great Pyramid* (1880).

[6] i.e. in the *Pall Mall Gazette*; see 22 Dec. 80n.

[7] See 22 Dec. 80n.

of the court? The tenant has a power to quit: the landlord, to evict. This is the *ressort* of the whole position. The tenant, rather than quit: the landlord, rather than evict, is willing to go before the court. How can it be an *extension of the Ulster Custom* to create a state of things in which the whole *balance* between the parties is destroyed? The tenant going before the Court retains his power to quit: but the landlord has lost his power to evict. Both will lose their option about *going* before the Court: but the tenant retains another option: the landlord has none.

5. Do you think that the stewards of the taxes of this country can undertake to authorize the purchase for the State of all the Estates in Ireland (I assume that you can make your rule as to terms) whose landlords object to be put under the 3 Fs?

6. Can we effect such a change in Ireland, and be sure that its principle will not struggle for entrance into England & Scotland?

7. The question of existing contracts by lease is a grave one. In 1870 Parliament gave a virtual promise to owners on this subject. There are a multitude of other points. I admit, indeed, that in any form the question bristles with difficulties. I think, however, two propositions indisputable:

1. That a proposal of the 3 Fs would have to be founded on an admission of the total failure of the Land Act.

2. That the determination of rent in Ulster by the voluntary reference of two parties, each having another alternative open to him, cannot be a foundation for a proposal to make the State the universal judge with one party retaining his alternative, & the other deprived of it.

I do not enter upon the large, yet smaller, question of the Bright Clauses: but I am glad you object to the absurd proposal of promoting purchases by handing over the purchase money in a lump to the buyer.

I shall expect only a verbal answer to my queries when we meet. I reserve your pamphlet, for I need not tell you my time is very fully occupied.

To LORD KIMBERLEY, colonial secretary, 27 December   Add MS 44544, f. 123.
1880.

One line to thank and to say there cannot be a doubt as to your proceedings about the military. It may be that these poor fellows gallantly tried to make another Rorke's drift of it.[1] Carnarvon has given Bright an opportunity tempting enough, yet requiring discretion in the use of it. The devil surely found something for his 'idle hands to do'.

28. Tu.

Ch 8½ a.m. Wrote to Messrs Townshend and Barker a letter conveying the arrangment of the Estate receipts & charges. Also separate to Messrs T. & B.—Ld Granville 1 & Tel.—The Queen—Mr Forster—Sir H. Ponsonby—Miss de Lisle—Rev. Dr Bright—W.H.G.—Miss Collet—Mr Caird—Sir H. Thring—Ld Chancellor and minutes. Axework with W.—also conversation with him on the Memorandum and duties consequent.[2] Read Mary Stuart in Captivity and [blank.]

[1] Surprise and surrender at Bronkhorstspruit of British troops advancing on Pretoria, with 56 officers and men killed; see Lady Bellairs, *The Transvaal war* (1885), ch. ii. Kimberley wrote on 25 December 1880, Add MS 44225, f. 265: 'There is nothing disheartening in a military sense in a small body of troops being overpowered by numbers, but a first success is sure to give a great impetus to the rebellion.... I do not think we could possibly take the responsibility of refusing the reinforcements which the general in command declares to be urgently needed.'

[2] See annual accounts, Hawn P, and 1 Jan. 79.

29. Wed. [London]

Birthday. Ch 8½ a.m. A refreshing draught before the plunge. Preparations; off at 10.45. D. St 4.20. Saw Mr Godley. Wrote to Mr Childers—Sir H. Ponsonby 1.2.—Mrs Macgregor. Saw Granville 1.2.

It was a disturbed birthday. Never had I more cause to look back with emotions of thankfulness transcending even shame. But the anxieties connected with the state of Ireland & the pending questions, with the unformed mind which is still observable among my colleagues (& no wonder) drew me away from central thoughts, but made my day I hope a sacrifice in another sense. I must wait for a calmer season before I trust myself to say what a year it has been, and why. The rich & holy words of Scripture are still abundantly ministered to me for support.

30. Th.

Lumbago came on in the night & kept me in bed through the forenoon. Reading up for the Cabinet. Wrote to The Queen 1.2.3. & Tel.—Mr Forster and minutes. Saw Ld Granville—Ld Hartington—Mr Childers—Mr Bright.[1] My No. 3 to The Queen is a long personal explanatory letter referring to hers of the [blank.][2]

Cabinet. Thurs. Dec. 30. 80. 2 p.m.[3]
Prelim.: Corrupt Practices Bill, Bankruptcy Bill: to be ready at the opening of the Session.
1. Mr. Forster produced his [Protection] Bill—with account of Dec[embe]r outrages: 800 & odd to 28th. Also small numbers of committals & convictions compared with outrages for the preceding months.
  Chamberlain disapproved of the Bill but would adhere to the engagement taken in the Cabinet. Bright practically in the same sense: with some amount of *relative* approval to the H.C. Suspension Act.
  General desire for the brevity of the Bill. Some for a single Clause suspending Habeas Corpus Act. Childers *accepts* the H.C. suspension but would have preferred summary powers in the hands of Stip[endiary] Magistrates & a stronger Arms Act. General agreement to work in the sense of the Govt. of Ireland for suspension of H.C. including treasonable practices. To consider thereafter as the other parts & as to union in one Bill. Discussion on the Meeting Clauses.
2. Cabinet at 2 tomorrow. Council on the 4th. [Queen's] Speech Cabinet on the 3rd.
3. Chamberlain proposed a modification in the instructions to Sir H. Robinson.
4. Proposal from the Cape (Merriman) Opposition to send a Comm[issione]r to Transvaal? Declined as unsuitable to the present time.[4]

---

[1] See Walling, *Diaries of Bright*, 452.
[2] Probably on 1841 (see *L.Q.V.*, 2nd series, iii. 167), but Gladstone's 'No. 3' not found in Add MS Loan 73/2 or in Royal Archives.
[3] Add MS 44642, f. 118; undated notes by Granville read: 'Taking coercion first has answered pretty well'; 'H[artingto]n will end by agreeing to your bill, probably requesting some alterations in detail. Forster will make a fight, but we know what that means.' Note by Argyll: 'The "Compensation" scale *may* drive the Landlord to allow sale. *This* was provided for in the Act of 70 and *this* is not open to the objections which lie against a universal power of sale.'
[4] Proposal by John Xavier Merriman, 1841-1926, a leading anti-Confederationalist, that there should be an attempt at negotiation; Goodfellow, 198.

5. Basuto instruction: agreed in the desire to profit by any offer of mediation.
6. Granville mentioned the Greek question: a narrative. His proposed answer was approved.

31. Fr.

Wrote to Ld E. Clinton—Mrs Hope[1]—Mr Ouvry—Sir H. Ponsonby—Mrs Th.— Ld F. Cavendish—Scotts—Sir Thos G—The Queen and minutes.

Cabinet 2¼-5½. Through the tangled wilderness of the Land question we made our way to an important point with hardly any tearing of skin or Clothes. God be thanked. It is a step gained and a singular relief to my mind at least for the present. It teaches me the great lesson 'onward'.

Six to dinner. Saw Ld F.C.—Lord R.G.—Ld Granville—Mr Morley—Ld Kimberley—Mr Dodson—Sir W. Harcourt—Mr Goschen—Mr Childers. Read Burgon's Sermon on Disestablishment of Religion in Oxford.[2]

C. went for a midnight service. I felt too tired & too distracted. The period 29-31 Dec. is for me almost always one of much needed calm & recollection: not what it should be, but yet something. This year I have been quite unable to recover and extricate my mind from the heavy cares of Government and of the state of Ireland in particular. Is not that state a warning & a judgment for our heavy sins as a nation: for broken faith, for the rights of others trampled down, for blood wantonly and largely shed. In our pride we have sinned, and in our pride especially are we punished.

As for myself it is only by moments that I can look back on the sad & continued failings of my life and utter the cry for mercy or of thankful hope. More & more my own thought is concentrated on the desire to bring to an early close the long period of my contentious life. Without this nothing can really avail to give me the attitude which becomes old age. Shakespeare is a great preacher when he likes and nowhere greater than when *he* says (for it can be no other)

O' tis a burden &c.[3]

Farewell old year. I can now even as before cling to thy skirts to catch a parting benediction: in the hand of God I plunge forward into the New.

Cabinet. Frid. Dec. 31. 80 2 p.m.[4]
1. U.K. Alliance Meml.
2. Irish Land. 1. To stand on the principles of the Land Act. 2. To propose measures of self-government.

Chamberlain	Spencer
Bright	Granville
Argyll ═ reserve ab. free sale	Harcourt x
Forster x	Granville [*sic*]
Kimberley	Hartington ═ reserve ab. free sale

[1] Mrs Anne Adele Hope of Deepdene, on assistance for Lady Susan Opdebeck, former wife of 5th duke of Newcastle; Gladstone was retiring as a Newcastle trustee; Add MS 44467, f. 265.
[2] J. W. Burgon, 'The disestablishment of religion in Oxford, the betrayal of a sacred trust' (1881).
[3] *Henry VIII*, iii. 2; see 24 July 80 f. 1.
[4] Add MS 44642, f. 125; note by Forster reads: 'To what does this conversation pledge us?'; Gladstone's reply: 'We are pledged to take Land Act for starting point and develop it. Each man his own interpreter.'

Basis of the Land Act of 1870 adopted. It is to be developed.
The Courtney affair—to persevere.[1]
Duke of Cambridge's remonstrance.[2] Mr. Childers to proceed.

[1] L. H. Courtney succeeded A. W. Peel as undersecretary at the Home Office while reserving his position on the Transvaal and despite the Queen's objections (eventually overcome) to his radicalism; see Bahlman, *Hamilton*, i. 92-6.
[2] To Childers' reforms; see 16 Dec. 80.

APPENDIX

Gladstone's books, pamphlets and articles written in 1875-1880

This list, which does not include political speeches reprinted as pamphlets or letters published in daily newspapers, is in the order of appearance in the diary. The date gives the reference to the footnote describing the work in full; the note is usually placed at the day on which the start of planning or writing is noticed by Gladstone. * indicates anonymity. The following abbreviations are used: *B.Q.R, British Quarterly Review*; *C.R, Contemporary Review*; *C.Q.R, Church Quarterly Review*; *F.R, Fortnightly Review*; *N.C, Nineteenth Century*; *Q.R, Quarterly Review*.

'Vaticanism: an answer to *reproofs and replies*' (February 1875)	2 Jan. 75
*'Speeches of Pope Pius IX', *Q.R* (January 1875)	3 Jan. 75
Rome and the newest fashions in religion (1875)	28 Mar. 75
Ibid., translated into German by Max Lossen	13 Oct. 75
Introductory letter to E. de Laveleye, *Protestantism and Catholicism* (1875)	14 Apr. 75
*Review of volume i of Martin's *Life of the Prince Consort, C.R.* (June 1875)	26 Apr. 75
'Is the Church of England worth preserving?', *C.R* (July 1875)	4 June 75
*'Italy and her Church', *C.Q.R* (October 1875)	16 July 75
Homeric Synchronism (1876)	21 Sept. 75
'Art thou weary', *C.R* (December 1875)	10 Oct. 75
The Church of England and Ritualism (1875)	28 Oct. 75
'Science and Art, Utility and Beauty' (1875)	11 Nov. 75
'Homerology', *C.R* (March, April, July 1876)	23 Feb. 76
*Review of G. O. Trevelyan's *Macaulay, Q.R* (July 1876)	23 Mar. 76
*Review of D. Macleod, *Memoir of Norman Macleod, C.Q.R* (July 1876)	20 Mar. 76
'The courses of religious thought', *C.R* (June 1876)	1 Apr. 76
Biographical sketch of George Lyttelton, *The Guardian* (26 April 1876)	23 Apr. 76
*Notice of N. Loraine, *The church and liberties of England, C.Q.R* (July 1876)	24 June 76
Letter to Schenck of 28 November 1872, *Harper's New Monthly Magazine* (December 1876)	19 Aug. 76
'The Bulgarian Horrors and the Question of the East' (1876)	28 Aug., 5 Sept. 76
'Russian policy and deeds in Turkestan', *C.R* (November 1876)	19 Oct. 76
*Review of volume ii of Martin's *Life of the Prince Consort, C.Q.R* (January 1877)	6 Nov. 76
'The Hellenic Factor in the Eastern Question', *C.R* (December 1876)	13 Nov. 76
Preface to 2nd edition of Mackenzie and Irby, *The Slavonic provinces of Turkey*	14 Dec. 76
*Notice of K. Benrath, *Bernardino Ochino, C.Q.R* (not published)	3 Jan. 77
Review of Sir G. C. Lewis, *Essay on authority, N.C* (March 1877)	8 Jan. 77

'The Sclavonic provinces of the Ottoman Empire', *Eastern Question Association Paper* (1877)	16 Jan. 77
'Lessons in Massacre' (1877)	26 Feb. 77
*Notice of Gopčević, *Montenegro* (not published)	15 Mar. 77
'The Royal Supremacy' (1850, new ed. with preface, 1877)	15 Mar. 77
'Montenegro', *N.C.* (May 1877)	14 Apr. 77
'Piracy in Borneo', *C.R.* (July 1877)	26 May 77
'Rejoiner on authority', *N.C.* (July 1877)	14 June 77
'Aggression in Egypt', *N.C.* (August 1877)	21 July 77
'The Dominions of Odysseus', *Macmillan's* (October 1877)	21 Aug. 77
'The colour sense', *N.C.* (October 1877)	30 Aug. 77
Gleanings of past years (1879)	6 Sept. 77, 6 Nov. 78
Preface to Schliemann's *Mycenae* (1878)	20 Sept. 77
Primer of Homer (1878)	24 Sept., 20 Nov. 77
*Notice of Abbé Valin, *C.Q.R.* (January 1878)	30 Sept. 77
*Notice of d'Eichthal, *C.Q.R.* (January 1878)	3 Oct. 77
'The county franchise, and Mr Lowe', *N.C.* (November 1877)	9 Oct. 77
'Last words on the county franchise', *N.C.* (January 1878)	10 Dec. 77
*Review of volume iii of Martin's *Life of the Prince Consort,* *C.Q.R.* (January 1878)	15 Dec. 77
'The peace to come', *N.C.* (February 1878)	9 Jan. 78
'The paths of honour and of shame', *N.C.* (March 1878)	20 Feb. 78
Preface to pamphlet ed. of 'Paths of honour and of shame' (1878)	9 Mar. 78
'The Iris of Homer', *C.R.* (April 1878)	15 Mar. 78
'Liberty in the East and West', *N.C.* (June 1878)	24 May 78
'A Modern "Symposium"', *N.C.* (July 1878)	15 June 78
'Kin beyond Sea', *North American Review* (September 1878)	21 June 78
'England's Mission', *N.C.* (September 1878)	9 Aug. 78
'The sixteenth century arraigned before the nineteenth', *C.R.* (October 1878)	23 Aug. 78
'The slicing of Hector', *N.C.* (October 1878)	11 Sept. 78
'On epithets of movement in Homer', *N.C.* (March 1879)	8 Oct. 78
'Electoral Facts', *N.C.* (November 1878)	9 Oct. 78
'The friends and foes of Russia', *N.C.* (January 1878)	23 Jan. 79
'Probability as the guide of conduct', *N.C.* (May 1879)	9 Mar. 79
'The evangelical movement', *B.Q.R.* (July 1879)	14 May 79
'Greece and the Treaty of Berlin', *N.C.* (June 1879)	20 May 79
'The country and the government', *N.C.* (August 1879)	9 July 79
'The Olympian system', *N.C.* (October 1879)	15 Aug. 79
Political Speeches in Scotland (1879)	24 Nov. 79
'Dean Hook' (1879)	10 Feb. 79
'Free trade, railways, and the growth of commerce', *N.C.* (February 1880)	16 Dec. 79
'Religion, Achaian and Semitic', *N.C.* (April 1880)	18 Dec. 79
Political Speeches in Scotland, second series (1880)	17 Mar. 80
*'The Conservative collapse', *F.R.* (May 1880)	13 Apr. 80

WHERE WAS HE?
1875–1880

The following list shows where the diarist was each night; he continued at each place named until he moved on to the next. Names of the owners of great houses have been given in brackets on the first mention of the house.

1 January 1875	Hawarden
7 January	London
15 January	Hawarden
12 February	London
27 February	Hatfield House (Salisbury)
1 March	London
24 March	Hagley (Lyttelton)
29 March	London
1 May	The Deanery, Windsor
3 May	London
10 May	Nottingham
11 May	Clumber Park, Worksop (Newcastle)
14 May	Courthey, Liverpool
17 May	Hawarden
24 May	London
28 May	Holmbury (Leveson-Gower)
31 May	London
9 June	Christ Church, Oxford
10 June	London
26 June	Windsor
28 June	London
9 July	Windsor Castle
10 July	London
17 July	Hatfield
19 July	London
7 August	Hawarden
1 September	St Asaph
2 September	Hawarden
23 September	Courthey
24 September	Hawarden
29 September	London
30 September	The Coppice, Henley (Phillimore)
1 October	Oakley Park, Cirencester (Bathurst)
5 October	Hawarden
9 November	London

12 November	Hawarden
18 November	Chatsworth (Devonshire)
30 November	Hawarden
17 January 1876	Hagley
20 January	London
22 January	Hawarden
2 February	London
1 April	Wellington College
4 April	London
8 April	Hawarden
22 April	Hagley
24 April	Hawarden
4 May	Hagley
6 May	London
17 June	Albury Park (Percy)
20 June	London
15 July	Strawberry Hill, Twickenham (Carlingford)
17 July	London
2 August	Hawarden
4 September	London
9 September	Frognall, Foot's Cray, Kent (Sydney)
11 September	Wycombe Abbey, High Wycombe (Carrington)
12 September	Hawarden
20 September	Raby Castle, Darlington (Cleveland)
25 September	Durham
26 September	Ford Castle, Coldstream (Waterford)
2 October	Alnwick Castle (Northumberland)
5 October	Jervaux Abbey (Ailesbury)
7 October	Castle Howard (Lanerton)

11 October	Hawarden	29 October	Powerscourt, Ennis-
24 October	London		kerry (Powerscourt)
28 October	Hawarden	3 November	Carton, Maynooth
17 November	Courthey, Liverpool		(Leinster)
18 November	Hawarden	5 November	Dublin
1 December	Arley Hall, Cheshire	7 November	Abbeyleix, Queen's
	(Egerton-Warburton)		County (De Vesci)
5 December	London	10 November	Woodlands, Consilla
9 December	Hawarden		(Annaly)
		12 November	Hawarden
		3 December	London
17 January 1877	Longleat, Wiltshire	8 December	Hawarden
	(Bath)		
22 January	The Bishop's Palace,	16 January 1878	London
	Wells	18 January	Hawarden
24 January	Dunster Castle	25 January	London
	(Fownes-Luttrell)	30 January	Oxford
27 January	Orchard Neville,	1 February	London
	Somerset	16 February	Brighton
29 January	Bowden Park, Wilt-	18 February	London
	shire	23 March	Latimer (Chesham)
31 January	Savernake, Marl-	25 March	London
	borough (Ailesbury)	13 April	Windsor
5 February	London	16 April	Lysways, Lichfield
10 March	High Elms, Down,		(Forster)
	Kent (Lubbock)	17 April	London
12 March	London	23 April	Keble College, Oxford
2 April	Holmbury, Surrey	26 April	Hawarden
9 April	London	14 May	London
15 May	Hawarden	3 June	On train
31 May	Southbourne, Birming-	4 June	Roseneath, Dumbar-
	ham (Chamberlain)		tonshire (Argyll)
1 June	Hagley	5 June	Sheffield
4 June	London	6 June	Clumber
9 June	Dudbrook, Essex	8 June	Hawarden
	(Carlingford)	12 June	London
11 June	London	6 July	Eton
10 July	On board 'Dublin	8 July	London
	Castle'	7 August	Hawarden
13 July	Exeter	12 September	Bettisfield Park, Whit-
14 July	London		church (Hanmer)
28 July	Hawarden	14 September	Hawarden
24 September	London	1 October	Peveril Hotel, Douglas,
26 September	Bestwood Park, Not-		Isle of Man
	tingham (St Albans)	2 October	The 'Falcon's Nest',
29 September	Hawarden		Port Erin, Isle of Man
17 October	Kilruddery, Bray	3 October	Government House,
	(Meath)		Douglas, Isle of Man
25 October	Royal Fitzwilliam	4 October	Laxley, Isle of Man
	Hotel, Rathdrum	5 October	Government House,
26 October	Coolattin Park, Co.		Douglas, Isle of Man
	Wicklow (Fitzwilliam)	7 October	Hawarden

15 October	London	31 October	Wellington College
19 October	Latimer, Buckingham-shire	3 November	Hawarden
		22 November	Courthey
21 October	Woburn Abbey (Bed-ford)	24 November	Dalmeny House, Edin-burgh (Rosebery)
24 October	Wrest Park, Bedford-shire (Cowper)	1 December	Taymouth Castle, Perthshire (Breadal-bane)
26 October	Cambridge		
30 October	Hawarden	4 December	Glasgow (Sir J. Wat-son)
27 November	London		
20 December	Hawarden	6 December	Dalzell, Motherwell (Carter-Hamilton)
18 February 1879	London	8 December	Hawarden
4 April	Althorp (Spencer)		
8 April	Hawarden	11 January 1880	London
12 April	Worksop	12 January	Cologne
16 April	Newark	22 January	London
17 April	Mentmore (Rosebery)	24 January	Fasque
21 April	London	28 January	Courthey
17 May	York House, Twicken-ham (Grant Duff)	29 January	Hawarden
		23 February	London
19 May	London	16 March	Dalmeny
31 May	Eton	24 March	Edinburgh
2 June	Holmbury	28 March	Dalmeny
7 June	Frant Court, Tun-bridge Wells (Strat-ford de Redcliffe)	30 March	Galashiels (Reay)
		31 March	Edinburgh
		1 April	Dalmeny
9 June	London	6 April	On train
5 July	Eton	7 April	Hawarden
7 July	London	19 April	London
26 July	Hawarden	7 May	Mentmore
20 August	London	12 May	London
23 August	Courthey	15 May	Windsor Castle
25 August	Hawarden	17 May	London
8 September	Arley (Warburton)	19 June	Littleburys, Mill Hill (Aberdeen)
9 September	The Coppice, Henley		
11 September	London	20 June	London
14 September	On ship	3 July	Littleburys
15 September	Cologne	5 July	London
16 September	Munich	17 July	Littleburys
17 September	Tegernsee	19 July	London
24 September	Innsbruck	24 July	Littleburys
25 September	Landro	26 July	London
27 September	Cortina	9 August	Windsor (Wellesley)
29 September	Pieve di Cadore	14 August	Holmbury
30 September	Grand Hotel, Venice	24 August	London
9 October	On train	26 August	Cruising round Britain on 'Grantully Castle'
10 October	Munich		
13 October	On train	4 September	London
14 October	Hotel Bedford, Paris	10 September	Mentmore
21 October	Bettishanger, Kent	13 September	Hawarden
25 October	London	29 September	London

2 October	Holmbury	22 November	London
4 October	London	27 November	Hawarden
12 October	Hawarden	13 December	London
8 November	London	17 December	Hawarden
20 November	Sandringham (Prince of Wales)	29 December	London

LIST OF LETTERS BY CORRESPONDENT,
PUBLISHED IN VOLUME IX

A note on the editing of these letters will be found with the equivalent list in
Volume VII

DRAMATIS PERSONAE, 1875-1880

An index to the whole work will appear in the concluding volume, together with a bibliography of Gladstone's reading as recorded in the diary. Meanwhile readers may be helped by this list of persons mentioned; most of the references refer to the first occasion of mention in the diary. A plain date indicates a first mention in the diary text, usually with a footnote at that date if the person has been identified; a date with 'n' (e.g. 27 Oct. 79n) indicates a mention in a footnote to a person or event noticed by the diarist on that day.

This list covers the years 1875-1880 and must be read together with the lists at the end of volumes two, four, six, and eight. People mentioned in those lists are not repeated here. Readers who wish to identify a person mentioned in the diary, but who is not in this list below, should refer to the four previous lists. The exceptions are names that occur in the first eight volumes but are more fully identified by a footnote in volume nine; these are marked † following their date, in the list below. A few cross-references from this list are to names in previous lists. Names mentioned on the fly leaf of an MS volume of the diary are marked (f.l.) with the nearest date. To increase the list's usefulness as a guide to identification, priests have their initials prefixed by *Rev., bp.* etc., and some other occupations have been briefly indicated.

People with double-barrelled, or particuled, surnames appear under the last part of the name, except that names in M' and Mc are under Mac, Irish names in O' are under O, and D'Aloz, D'Avignon, De Lisle, etc. are under D.

Rulers and royal dukes are given under their regal or Christian names. Other peers, and married women, are listed under their surname, with cross-references from their titles and maiden names.

Abahall, *Mr.*, 21 Apr. 76
Abbot, *Rev.* F. E., 24 Jan. 76
Abbott, *Rev. Dr.* E. A., 8 July 75
Abcarius, J., 24 Aug. 77 (?)
Abel, C., 11 Feb. 78
Ablett, W. H., 25 Feb. 78
About, E. F. V., 14 June 79
Abraham, Ellen, 3 Jan. 75
Abrath, *Dr.* G. A., 28 Feb. 77
Acland, *Sir* A. H. D., *13th Bart.*, 11 June 79
Acland, *Sir* C. T. D., *12th Bart.*, 18 Aug. 79
Acton, F., 23 Mar. 80
Acton, *Lady* M. A., 17 Sept. 79
Adair, *Rev.* T., 20 May 75
Adam, E., 18 Oct. 79n
Adam, F., 17 May 75
Adam, *Madame* J., 18 Oct. 79
Adams, A. W., 2 Mar. 80
Adams, *Miss* E. L. D., 14 Oct. 78 (?)
Adams, *Rev.* J., 20 Oct. 76
Adams, W. B., 24 July 75 (?)
Adams, W. H. D., 27 Mar. 78
Addison, J. H., 22 May 78

Additional Curates Society, 19 May 79
'Adfyer', *see* Hughes, T. J.
Adin, C., 7 Dec. 78
Ady, J. C., 14 Aug. 79
Adye, *Gen. Sir* J. M., 21 Sept. 76
Affghan Committee, secretary, 15 Nov. 78
Agelasto, *Madame*, 5 June 76n (?)
Agnew, *Rev.* P. P., 30 Aug. 79
Agstado, *Madame*, 5 June 76
Ahmed, R. U., 18 Nov. 76
Ainger, A. C., 15 Dec. 77
Ainsworth, *Mrs.* S., 4 Sept. 78 (?)
Aird, *Miss* C., 23 Aug. 76
Aird, R., 6 Apr. 78
Aitken, *Rev.* W. H. M. H., 29 Apr. 75
Akmatoff, *Madame*, 25 Apr. 77
Alagna, G. A., 25 Aug. 75
Albright, *see* Allbright
Alden, H. M., 27 Sept. 76
Aldenham, *Baron, see* Gibbs, H. H.
Alder, *Rev.* G., 14 Nov. 75 (?)
Alderson, *Miss*, 29 June 75
Aldis, W. S., 5 Mar. 80

Atkinson, A., 7 July 77
Atkinson, A., 29 Sept. 76 (?)
Atkinson, J., 28 Nov. 76
Auriemma, F., 4 Nov. 76
Auriemma, T., 13 Jan. 77
Austin, A. G., 23 Dec. 76
Austin, A., 10 Feb. 75
Austin, C. E., 4 Sept. 79
Austin, F. A., 25 Mar. 76
Austin, R. B., 9 Aug. 75
Austrian ambassador, see 1879–88 Karolyi
Aveling, *Rev.* T. W. B., 1 June 78 (?)
Awdry, *Rev. Dr.* W., 13 Dec. 76

Babbage, *Gen.* H. P., 1 Mar. 80 (?)
Babington, *Rev.* C., 5 Aug. 76
Babosa, A., 29 Jan. 77
Bache, *Rev.* K., 3 June 77
Bacon, *Lieut.*, 27 May 75
Bacon, *Rev.* H., 17 Mar. 76 (?)
Bacon, *Sir* N. H., *12th Bart.*, 18 Feb. 79
Bacon, *Rev.* R. B., 20 Nov. 78n
Bacon, *Rev.* T. S., 25 Apr. 79
Bagehot, E., *née* Wilson, 12 June 77
Bagot, *Miss*, 12 Aug. 78
Bagshaw, *Rev.* H. S., 7 June 77 (?)
Bagshawe, *Rev.* J. B., 31 Aug. 79
Bagster, *Miss*, 21 Apr. 79
Bagster, *Messrs.* S., 12 Sept. 79
Bailey, *Messrs.*, 13 Dec. 77
Bailey, *Mrs.*, 20 Nov. 78
Bailey, J. H., 23 Nov. 78
Bailey, S., 22 June 78
Bailey, *Rev.* T. J., 21 June 79 (?)
Bailie, *Mr.*, 29 Aug. 76
Baillie, A. Cochrane-, *see* Vitelleschi
Bain, J., 23 Nov. 76
Bainbrigge, *Gen.* P. J., 1 July 75 (?)
Baird, J. R., 11 Nov. 75
Baker, A. W., 26 Apr. 79
Baker, G., 17 May 77n
Baker, *Rev.* H. R., 12 Jan. 76
Balabanow, M. D., 10 Oct. 76
Balck, *Mr*, 6 Nov. 79
Balfour, A., 11 Aug. 79
Balfour, *Miss* A. B., 10 Aug. 75
Balfour, E. M., *see* Sidgwick
Balfour, F., *née* Campbell, 12 May 79
Balgarnie, *Rev.* R., 1 Dec. 76
Ball, W. J., 13 May 79
Ballasteros, *Mons.*, 17 Aug. 77
Bally, J. G., 12 Dec. 79

Bamford, T. A., 12 July 79
Banbury, *Mr.*, 4 Feb. 76
Bandinel, *Rev.* J., 6 Jan. 78
Bandmann, T., 2 Feb. 78 (?)
Banff, H., 15 July 76
Banfield, E., 29 Jan. 78
Banner, A., 10 Feb. 75
Bannerman, *Sir* A., *9th Bart.*, 17 Mar. 75
Bannerman, *Sir* H. Campbell-, 1 May 80
Barabino, G., 2 Apr. 78
Barbari, *Prof.* P., 28 July 75
Barber, R. F., 1 Nov. 75
Barclay, A. C., 10 Apr. 75
Barclay, J. W., 7 Oct. 75
Barclay, *Canon* J., 30 Jan. 80
Bardoux, B. J. A., 18 Oct. 79
Barfoot, W., 5 Jan. 76n
Baring, E., *1st Baron Cromer*, 28 Oct. 80
Baring, W., 4 July 77 (?)
Barker, R. L., 9 Nov. 75
Barker, T. H., 5 Oct. 77
Barkling, *see* Bartling
Barlow, *Prof.* J. W., 2 Jan. 78 (?)
Barlow, T., 4 Aug. 79
Barnes, B. T., 1 Mar. 80
Barnes, J. W., 12 Feb. 76 (?)
Barnes, S., 14 Nov. 75
Barnes, W., 21 Nov. 79
Barnett, *Lt.-Col.* H. C. B., 13 Nov. 79
Barnett, *Rev.* S. A., 4 Oct. 77
Baron, *Rev.* R. B., 19 Mar. 79
Baronian, *Mr.*, 23 Apr. 80
Barr, J., 20 Mar. 80
Barran, *Sir* J., *1st Bart.*, 13 June 77
Barret, *Rev.* G. T., 12 Apr. 78
Barrett, *Mrs.* E., 13 May 76 (?)
Barrett, *Prof. Sir* W. F., 26 May 77
Barrow, *Gen.* J. L., 23 May 78 (?)
Barry, M. J., 31 July 75
Barry, *Rev.* W. T., 23 Mar. 78
Bartholomew, J. G., 29 Nov. 79 (?)
Bartle, *Rev. Dr.* G., 29 Aug. 77
Bartley, J., 14 Feb. 80
Bartling, *Dr.*, 13 May 76
Barton, *Mr., of Natal*, 1 July 75
Barton, E., 29 Jan. 79
Barton, F. B., 16 Mar. 75
Bashin, *Mr.*, 15 Mar. 78
Bassano, *Duc de, see* Maret
Bassett, *Mr.*, 26 June 79
Batchelor, G. A., 11 Apr. 76 (?)

Bible Echo, ed., see Kellaway, W.
Bickerton, *Alderman*, 16 Sept. 76
Bickford, *Rev.* J., 26 Feb. 79
Bickley, *Mr.*, 30 July 79
Bicknell, W. L., 17 Aug. 78
Bikelas, D., 19 Sept. 76
Billingham, *Mr.*, 19 June 79
Bills, J., 19 July 77
Bingham, *Rev.* W. P. S., 15 Mar. 75
Binns, *Miss*, 14 Oct. 78
Binns, H., 29 May 77
Biograph, editor of, 28 Jan. 79
Bird, *Miss*, 9 May 78
Bird, *Rev.* A., 28 Feb. 77
Bird, J., 14 June 79
Bird, *Rev.* R. J., 8 May 80 (?)
Birdsall, *Mr.*, 7 Jan. 80
Birdwood, *Sir* G. C. M., 2 Nov. 80
Birks, *Mrs.*, 25 Oct. 76
Birmingham, *Dr., see* Burlingham
Birrell, E. *née* Locker, *formerly Mrs. L. Tennyson*, 28 Feb. 78
Biscamp, *Dr.* E., 11 Dec. 78
Bishop, *Mrs., rescue*, 12 July 76
Bishop, *Lady* A., *see* Schultz
Bishop, J., 26 Jan. 78
Bisson, *Capt.* F. S. DeC., 5 Mar. 80
Black, *Rev.* A. H., 25 June 75
Black, W. G., 8 Mar. 78
Blackburn, B., 18 Dec. 77
Blackburn, *Messrs.*, 26 Jan. 76
Blackhorn, *Mr.*, 2 Apr. 78
Blackie, W. G., 17 Apr. 80
Blackmore, *Mr.*, 14 June 78
Blackwell, L., 19 June 78
Blackwood, *Miss* V., 11 Sept. 78
Blades, R. H., 26 Feb. 80
Blades, W., 29 June 77
Blagrove, *Mr.*, 13 May 79
Blaikie, *Prof.* W. G., 16 Mar. 75
Blair, E. Stopford-, 10 Nov. 79 (?)
Blair, F. C. Hunter, 4 Nov. 79
Blair, H. M., 7 Aug. 78
Blair, *Rev.* R. H., 4 July 76 (?)
Blair, *Dr.* W., 29 Dec. 79 (?)
Blake, *Mrs.*, 3 Sept. 76
Blake, *Dr.* C. C., 9 July 79
Blake, *Mrs.* H. A., 13 Dec. 80
Blake, *Rev.* J. L., 27 Feb. 78
Blake, P. J., 12 Mar. 75
Blake, *Rev.* R. J., 19 Oct. 76
Blake, *Rev.* R. T., 27 Apr. 78

Blake, *Dr.* S. L. Jex-, 21 July 77
Blakey, J., 22 Apr. 80
Blakiston, *Rev.* C. D., 26 Feb. 80 (?)
Blanch *& sons*, 30 Aug. 77
Blanch, W. H., 30 Aug. 77
Blantyre, *Master of, see* Stuart
Blarke, B., 2 Jan. 77
Bleck, H., 10 Jan. 80 (?)
Blenkinsopp, *Rev.* E. C. L., 26 May 76
Blennerhassett, *Lady* C., 12 Oct. 79
Block, J. N., 29 Feb. 76
Bloemfontein, Bp. of, see 1870–83 Webb, A. B.
Blomfield, *Mr.*, 29 Sept. 77
Blood, F., 3 Jan. 79
Bloom, *Mr.*, 28 Mar. 78
Blowitz, H. G., 4 June 80
Blumenthal, *Mr.*, 1 Oct. 79
Blyth, B. Hall, 12 Apr. 80
Boardman, E., 6 Feb. 75
Bock, C., 30 June 80
Bockett, *Mr.*, 30 Aug. 77
Bodkin, C., 16 Oct. 78
Boehm, *Sir* J. E., *1st Bart.*, 25 Nov. 79
Bogy, J. S., 9 July 77
Boïelle, J., 17 Mar. 76
Bolam, C., 7 Dec. 78
Boldero, *Rev.* H. K., 30 Mar. 78 (?)
Boldero & Foster, 20 Feb. 78
Bolton, A. J., 20 Mar. 78
Bolton, C., 22 Nov. 79
Bond, *Rev.* J., 24 May 78 (?)
Bond, W. J., 28 Aug. 79
Bonghi, R., 4 Oct. 79
Bonsil, *Mrs.*, 29 June 78
Bony, *Rev.* F., 27 June 78
Book, *Mr.*, 27 Jan. 75
Booth, C. F., 15 May 78
Booth, L., 9 Jan. 80 (?)
Booth, *Rev.* S. H., 4 May 78
Booth, W., 12 Jan. 78 (?)
Boothroyd, *Mrs.*, 25 Jan. 76
Borel, J.-L., 16 Oct. 79 (?)
Borlase, W. C., 29 June 76
Bornford, *Mr.*, 2 July 77
Borowski, *Mons.*, 4 Sept. 77
Boscawen, W. St C., 10 Dec. 75
Bosemworth, *Mr.*, 30 Dec. 79
Bosomerville, *Mr.*, 21 Oct. 78
Botwood, *Mr.*, 25 Apr. 77
Boulay, J. Du, 16 Apr. 75
Bour, *M.*, 25 June 77
Boulting, *Mr.*, 17 July 75

Bude, W., 11 Apr. 78
Budett, H. C., 7 Mar. 76
Budge, *Sir* E. A. T. W., 26 Feb. 78
Bulgarni, R., 6 Dec. 77
Bull, E., 30 Dec. 78
Bullock, *Rev.* N. S., 24 Jan. 75
Bulstrode, *Rev.* G., 5 Nov. 75
Bumpus, J., 24 Apr. 79 (?)
Bunbury, H. M., 17 Nov. 76 (?)
Bunce, J. T., 25 Nov. 75
Bunker, *Mr.*, 4 Feb. 78
Bunn, *Messrs.*, 10 Mar. 76
Bunsen, *Rev.* H. G., 5 June 78
Burbier, J. H., 16 Aug. 78
Burbridge, J., 29 Aug. 76 (?)
Burckhardt, *Mr.*, 14 Mar. 78
Burdon, *Rev.* J., 16 Mar. 78
Burke, *Messrs.*, 24 June 79
Burke, Mrs., *see* Birks
Burke, *Lady* B. F., 10 Nov. 77
Burke, *Sir* J. B., 6 Nov. 77
Burke, U. R., 3 Feb. 78 (?)
Burleigh, J. C., 29 July 79
Burlingham, *Dr.* D. C., 15 Aug. 78n
Burnaby, *Capt.* F. A., 26 July 78
Burnaby, *Rev.* H. F., 15 Jan. 79 (?)
Burnet, R., 18 June 78
Burnett, *Miss*, 5 May 80
Burns, D., 22 July 75
Burns, Sir J., *2nd Bart., 1st Baron Inverclyde*, 10 Jan. 80
Burnstone, *Mr.*, 6 Apr. 78
Burrell, F. W., 9 July 75 (?)
Burritt, E., 19 Oct. 76
Burroughs, W. G., 28 Aug. 79
Burroughs, *Rev.* W. Gore, 28 Aug. 79
Burston, J., 2 July 75
Burt, J., 27 Oct. 79
Burt, T., 27 Feb. 77
Burton, *Rev.* A. B., 3 May 79 (?)
Burton, *Rev.* A. H., 29 Oct. 78
Burton, E. F., 22 Oct. 75
Burton, *Capt.* H., 10 June 75
Burton, *Rev.* J., 1 Aug. 76 (?)
Burton, J. S., 25 Dec. 77
Burton, *Miss* M., 27 Sept. 78
Busbridge, *Mr.*, 4 July 77
Busbridge, *Messrs.* G. F., 31 July 78
Bushell, E., 8 Feb. 78
Bushell, *Rev.* R., 26 Oct. 78
Bushnell, R., 23 Oct. 76
Bussell, *Rev.* F. V., 14 June 78

Bussey, H. F., 3 May 79
Bussy, G. M., 19 Oct. 77
Butler, *Rev.* C. P., 3 Mar. 79
Butler, *Rev.* C. E., 28 Dec. 76
Butler, F., 2 Aug. 77
Butterwick, W. T., 4 June 79
Butti, *Mr.*, 5 Apr. 80
Buttress, *Rev.* A., 29 Sept. 78 (?)
Buxton, *Rev.* T., 16 Apr. 79
Buzacott, *Rev.* A., 19 May 76
Bylandt, *Madame*, 25 May 78
Bylandt, *Count* C., 25 May 78n
Byles, *Sir* J. B., 31 Jan. 76
Byng, *Rev.* F. E. C., *5th Earl of Strafford*, 13 Mar. 79
Byrne, S., 6 Oct. 75
Byrom, E., 19 Feb. 79 (?)
Byron, W., 16 June 75
Byrth, *Rev.* H. S., 1 Apr. 77

Cacha, *Dr.* A., 25 June 79
Cadell, F., 29 Aug. 79
Cadman, *Rev.* W., 3 June 76
Cadogan, G. H., *5th Earl Cadogan*, 22 Jan. 77n
Caesar, J. P., 11 Mar. 78
Caffarelli, F. di, 29 July 76 (?)
Cafflisch, *Mr.*, 22 Nov. 79
Caine, W. S., 12 Mar. 78
Caird, *Principal* J., 17 Nov. 77
Caithbell, *Mrs.*, 29 Dec. 75
Caivano, F., 6 Oct. 76
Calcott, W. H., 25 Aug. 77
Caldburies, *Dr.*, 11 Nov. 76
Calderwood, *Prof.* H., 31 May 79
Caldicott, *Rev.* J. W., 26 Apr. 77 (?)
Callan, P., 14 May 77
Callaway, *Bp.* H., 14 Feb. 78
Callcott, W. H., 23 Apr. 76
Calvert, *Rev.* C. G., 29 Aug. 79 (?)
Cameron, *Dr.* C., 3 June 80
Cameron, *Sir* C., *1st Bart.*, 29 May 76 (?)
Campanella, *Rev.* G. M., 23 Mar. 77n
Campbell, A., *née* Graham, *Lady Breadalbane*, 15 May 76
Campbell, *Rev.* A. B. K., 26 June 76 (?)
Campbell, *Lord* C., 10 Oct. 78
Campbell, D., 15 Feb. 75
Campbell, D. A., 22 Feb. 79 (?)
Campbell, D., 22 June 77
Campbell, G., *6th Earl of Breadalbane, 1st Marquis of Breadalbane*, 15 May 76

Dowland, *Mr.*, 14 Jan. 76
Downie, *Rev.* J. A., 13 June 77
Downes, *Miss*, 29 Oct. 76
Downing, A. M. W., 1 May 75
Downing, W., 9 Jan. 79
Dowser, W. J., 23 Jan. 79
Dowson, T., 15 Sept. 77 (?)
Doyle, H. E., 6 Nov. 77
Doyle, J. B., 24 Oct. 77 (?)
Drake, J. H., 27 Mar. 80
Drake, J. P., 2 Mar. 77
Draper, F., 12 Sept. 79 (?)
Dreyfuss & Teweles, 20 Mar. 79 (?)
Drought, *Mr.*, 30 Oct. 77
Druce, *Messrs.*, 10 Apr. 77
Drucker, L., 6 Feb. 77
Drummond, *Capt.* A. H., 13 Sept. 76
Drummond, *Rev.* R. B., 15 June 76
Drury, E. D., 9 Oct. 78 (?)
Drysdale, *Dr.* C. R., 18 June 77
Du Bled, *Mr.*, 12 Jan. 80
Ducane, *Sir* C., 6 May 80.
Du Champ, M., 2 Mar. 76
Ducie, *Lady, see* Moreton
Dubray, *Miss*, 16 Oct. 78
Duchhayn, *Mr.*, 30 June 80
Dudgeon, W., 30 Dec. 76
Duff, *Rev.* A., 29 Sept. 76
Duff, P., 21 Mar. 79
Duff, *Rev.* W. Pine, 25 Mar. 78
Duggan, *Miss*, 9 Jan. 78
Duffield, A. J., 30 Apr. 78
Duffield, D. B., 8 Oct. 80
Dugdale, W. S., 7 Jan. 78 (?)
Dumbell, G. W., 9 Apr. 79
Dun, F., 4 Dec. 80
Dun, *Rev.* J., 4 Dec. 80n
Dun, T. J. C., 30 Oct. 76
Dunbar, *Mrs.*, 27 June 78
Dunbar, *Dr.* H., 14 Mar. 79
Dunbar, R. H., 16 Jan. 77
Duncan, A., 2 Apr. 79
Duncan, *Rev.* H., 27 Feb. 80
Dundas, *Rev.* R. J., 18 June 76
Dunington, *Rev. Mr.*, 26 Sept. 78
Dunn, A., 14 Nov. 78
Dunn, A. J., 7 Mar. 77
Dunn, R., 28 Jan. 75
Dunne, L., 24 Nov. 77
Dunphie, C. J., 7 May 79
Dunphy, H. M., 29 Aug. 77
Duport, *Rev.* C. D., 2 Mar. 80

Durham, *Earl of, see* Lambton.
Dutton, *Messrs.*, 20 Dec. 79
Dutton, H. B., 12 Dec. 79
Duvergne, *Mr.*, 16 May 78
Dyce, A. S., 3 Nov. 75 (?)
Dyer, *Messrs.*, 28 Mar. 79
Dyer, *Mr.*, 20 July 75
Dyer, G., 15 July 76 (?)
Dyneley, *Rev. Mr.*, 10 Jan. 80

Eardley, *Messrs.*, 1 Apr. 79
Eardley, H., 1 Apr. 79
Earle, J. C., 30 Mar. 76
Earp, H. N., 7 Apr. 79
Earp, T., 20 Nov. 77†
Earwaker, J. P., 2 Apr. 77
Easterly, *Dr.*, 3 Dec. 78
Eastwick, W. J., 28 Feb. 79
Eaton, F. A., 27 Mar. 79
Eaton, *Canon* T., 2 Nov. 75
Eckenbrecher, C. G. Von, 27 July 75
Ecole des Sciences Politiques, *director of*, 24
    July 75
Eddis, A. S., 23 Mar. 78
Eddy, *Mr.*, 19 May 76
Ede, G., 27 Nov. 78
Edge, J. H., 26 Aug. 78
Edgecomb, F. J. S., 19 Mar. 75 (?)
Edmonston & Douglas, 23 Dec. 76
Edwardes, W., *4th Baron Kensington*, 24
    Feb. 75
Edwards, A. A. B., 16 May 76
Edwards, A. R., 3 May 76
Edwards, A., 9 Feb. 77
Edwards, E. A., 22 Nov. 79
Edwards, G. T., 10 Aug. 75
Edwards, *Rev.* H. G., 5 Feb. 75
Edwards, J. W., 14 Nov. 78 (?)
Edwards, R. C., 20 Feb. 79 (?)
Edwards, T., 23 Apr. 75
Edwards, T., 3 Mar. 75 (?)
Edwards, *Rev.* W., 6 May 78
Eklektiké, editor of, 13 Jan. 75n
Elam, *Dr.* C., 29 July 76
Elder, *Mrs.*, 5 May 79
Elder, *Rev.* G., *see, probably*, Alder
Eldred, J. W., 27 Mar. 80
Elford, *rescue*, 16 May 76
Elford, J., 4 Nov. 79
Eliot, *President* C. W., 15 Aug. 78
Elkington, *Rev.* J. J., 19 Feb. 77

Ferrières, *Baron* C. C. A. De, 28 July 79
Festing, *Major* E. R., 4 July 78 (?)
Fetherston, F. M., 27 Jan. 75
Feuerheerd, *Mr.*, 9 Apr. 79
Fewster, C. E., 29 May 78
Fewtrell, *Mr.*, 22 June 77
Ffolliott, *Mrs.* G. C., 21 Nov. 77
Ffolliott, M., 21 Nov. 77n
Ffoulkes, T., 20 Oct. 76
Field, *Miss* K., 22 June 78
Field, R. C., 5 Mar. 80
Fifoot, T., 18 Mar. 76
Figes, T. F., 3 Mar. 76
Finch, *Rev.* F. C., 21 Apr. 76
Finck, H., 20 Mar. 78
Findlay, W. A., 9 Sept. 78
Finlay Brothers, 9 Aug. 76
Finlay, C., 19 May 75
Finlay, F. D., 16 Oct. 77
Finnie, *Mrs.*, 22 Aug. 75
Firman, *Dr.* C. G., 14 Jan. 78 (?)
Fish, L. J., 14 Nov. 79
Fisher, *Rev.* E. R., 19 June 79 (?)
Fisher, J., 4 July 79
Fisher, W., 28 Mar. 77
Fithian, *Sir* E. W., 10 Feb. 80
Fitzgerald, C., *née* Leveson-Gower, *Duchess of Leinster*, 3 Nov. 77
Fitzgerald, *Capt.* M., 15 Sept. 80
Fitzgerald, *Lady* M., 25 June 79
Fitzgerald, *Sir* P. G., '*Knight of Kerry*', *1st Bart.*, 18 Oct. 77
Fitzharry, *Mr.*, 27 July 78
Fitzmaurice, *Lord* E. G. Petty-, *1st Baron Fitzmaurice*, 3 Feb. 78
Fitzpatrick, W. J., 27 Jan. 80
Fitzroy, *Major* C. C., 17 Apr. 79
Fitzroy, *Rev.* S. F., 17 Apr. 80
Fitzwilliam, *Lady* A., 30 Nov. 75
Fitzwilliam, *Lady* A. M., 26 June 75
Fitzwilliams, C. H. L., 30 July 78
Flamdy, *Mr.*, 29 July 76 (?)
Fleischer, R., 21 Sept. 78
Fleming, *Mrs.*, 11 Apr. 78
Fleming, *Rev.* J., 20 July 79
Fleming, R., 10 Sept. 77
Fleming, *Rev.* W. E., 3 Sept. 77
Fletcher, C., 12 June 76
Fleurière, La, *see* De la Fleurière
Flockton, M. J., 12 Dec. 77
Flower, *Rev.* J. E., 21 July 75
Fludye, *Mr.*, 19 Oct. 78

Foecker, *Rev. Herr*, 15 Jan. 80
Fogarty, *Mr.*, 26 Oct. 77
Fogg, W., 20 Jan. 79
Fogge, G., 23 Aug. 78
Foley, J. W., 21 Dec. 75 (?)
Fölkerschamb, *Baron*, 4 Dec. 78
Foot, *Rev.* S. C., 26 Nov. 77
Foote, G. W., 28 Mar. 79
Forbes, A., 23 Nov. 77
Ford, E., 2 Apr. 79
Ford, J., 8 Sept. 76
Ford, T., 20 Aug. 79
Forder, R., 24 May 78
Fordyce, J. D., 10 Mar. 79
Forester, *Rev.* O. W. W., *4th Baron Forester*, 6 Oct. 77
Forjelt, C., 15 Feb. 78
Formby, *Rev.* H., 2 Apr. 78
Forrest, J. A., 28 Aug. 79
Forrest, *Rev.* T. G., 18 Apr. 78
Forrest, T. M., 8 May 78
Forrest, *Rev.* T. G., 18 Apr. 78
Forster, *Capt.* F. B., 2 Nov. 77
Forsyth, W., 6 Apr. 77
Fosbrook, *Mr.*, 10 Nov. 75
Foster, N. T., 20 May 78
Fothergill, *Rev.* E. H., 21 July 78 (?)
Fottrell, *Sir* G., 7 July 79
Fountaine, *Rev.* H. T., 31 Oct. 76 (?)
Fowler, F. H., 11 Jan. 76
Fowler, H. H., *1st Baron Wolverhampton*, 1 June 77n
Fowler, *Rev.* J. T., 25 July 79
Fox, *Lady*, 22 Sept. 77
Fox, G. Lane, 27 Feb. 78
Fox, *Rev.* H. E., 21 Nov. 77
Fox, R. R., 5 Mar. 76
Foxcroft, F., 3 Sept. 77
Foxley, *Rev.* J., 15 July 76
Foy, S. W., 11 Sept. 78
Frampton, *Mrs.*, 16 Sept. 75
Frances, H., 7 Dec. 78
Francis, J. D., 2 Aug. 78
Francis, *Mrs.*, 22 June 78
Franklin, E. A., 22 Oct. 78 (?)
Franzi, *Rev.* C., 3 Oct. 79
Fraser, *Mr., of Dalzell*, 6 Dec. 79
Fraser, *Rev.* D., 26 Dec. 77
Fraser, J. S., 13 July 78
Fraser, *Rev.* J. C. D., 25 Oct. 79
Fraser, R. D., 13 Nov. 77
Fraser, T., 13 July 76

Ginuti, *Cav.*, 26 Dec. 76
Giovanni, *Avvocato de*, 6 Mar. 75
Girdlestone, J., 11 Oct. 77
Girvan, *Mr.*, 26 Jan. 78
Giurlio, *Rev. Cav.* L. Prota-, 11 Oct. 75
Gladstone, *Capt.* C. E., 27 Apr. 78
Gladstone, L. M., *see* Hardy
Gladstone, M. C., *see* Stapleton
Gladstone, Murray, *sen. and jnr.*, 28 Aug. 75†
Gladstone, W. L., 18 Sept. 75
Glanville, E. S., 24 Nov. 77
Glanville, J., 16 Feb. 75 (?)
Glasser, E., 16 May 78
Gledhill, J. T., 12 Jan. 76 (?)
Glendinning, P., 29 Mar. 80
Glennie, J. S. Stuart, 8 July 79
Glover, S. M., 11 Sept. 77
Glover, W. Sutton, 27 Jan. 77 (?)
Gluckstein, L., 6 Oct. 76
Goadby, *Rev.* J. J., 8 Apr. 80
Godden, N., 25 Mar. 76
Godfrey, J. P., 16 May 79
Godley, D., 3 Nov. 77
Godley, G., 27 Dec. 75
Godwin, W. J., 17 Feb. 77
Gomme, *Mr.*, 14 Feb. 78
Gomme, G. L., 26 Feb. 79
Gonzadini, *Sen.* G., 19 May 77
Gonzaga, *Marchese* C. Guerrieri, 21 July 75
Gooch, J., 15 Feb. 75
Goodburn, E., 11 May 76
Goodhew, W. S., 30 June 79
Goodman, E. J., 31 May 79
Goodrich, *Rev.* H. P., 22 July 76
Goodson, A., 25 Feb. 78
Goodwyn, *Gen.* H., 29 Mar. 77
Gool, *Mr.*, 5 Apr. 80
Goolden, W., 13 Nov. 77
Goos, F., 7 Aug. 79
Gopčević, S., 11 Sept. 79
Gordon, A. W., 3 Apr. 80
Gordon, A. L., 27 Jan. 76
Gordon, *Col.* C., 10 Apr. 75
Gordon, *Lady* H., *see* Lindsay
Gordon, *Rev.* R., 25 Mar. 76 (?)
Gordon, *Rev.* W. J., 12 Dec. 79
Gordon, *Rev.* W., 19 Aug. 75 (?)
Gordon, *Capt.* W. E. A., 9 May 75
Gorloff, *General*, 24 Oct. 76
Gorman, *Rev.* T. M., 25 Aug. 76 (?)
Gorringe, H., 27 Feb. 80 (?)

Gostwick, J., 16 Jan. 77
Got, E.-F.-J., 11 Oct. 79
Goulby, *Rev.* J., 11 Mar. 79
Gould, *Rev.* S. Baring-, 1 Jan. 79
Goulden, *Rev.* A. B. B., 7 Feb. 80
Govan, *Mr.*, 2 Oct. 76
Govan, J., 1 Apr. 80
Govier, *Mr.*, 9 Dec. 78
Gower, F. A., 30 Apr. 79
Gower, G. W. G. Leveson-, 3 May 79
Grace, C., 11 May 77
Graf, *Mr.*, 15 Aug. 78
Graff, S. J., 15 Aug. 78 (?)
Graham, C. J., 20 Feb. 75 (?)
Graham, J., 5 Nov. 80
Graham, J. Maxtone-, 29 Jan. 78
Graham, *Rev.* M. R., 25 Mar. 75 (?)
Graham, R. B. Cunninghame, 7 Feb. 79 (?)
Graham, *Lieut.* R. C. Cunninghame, 7 Feb. 79 (?)
Grahame, T., 13 June 76
Grainger, A., 13 Nov. 75
Granby, H., 31 July 77
Grant, D., 29 Mar. 78
Grant, D., 26 Apr. 79
Grant, J. R., 4 Feb. 80
Grant, J., 5 June 77
Grant, R., *& sons*, 18 Nov. 75
Grant, *Lady* S., *née* Ferrier, 28 Nov. 79
Grant, *President* U.S., 5 June 77
Granville, *Dr.* J. M., 20 Apr. 78
Grassis, *Abbé* Portaz-, 5 June 75
Gray, *rescue*, 31 May 76
Gray, E. D., 12 June 78 (?)
Gray, S. O., 11 June 79
Gray, T., 24 Feb. 76
Greave, R., 19 Feb. 77
Greaves, H. H., 1 Dec. 79
Greaves, *Rev.* H. L., 8 Feb. 77
Green, *Mr.*, 6 Nov. 78
Green, B., 14 Sept. 79
Green, B. L., 30 Jan. 79
Green, C. W., 18 Apr. 79
Green, G. W., 22 Nov. 77
Green, J., 4 Oct. 77
Green, J. R., 20 Feb. 77n
Green, T., 30 Oct. 75
Green, *Prof.* T. H., 30 Jan. 78n
Green, W. H., 16 Sept. 76
Green, W. R., 27 Aug. 78
Greene, J. B., 2 Jan. 80
Greenhalg, J. S., 21 Aug. 77

Laurenson, A., 28 Feb. 78

Laurie, *Col.* R. P., 23 June 77

Lavin, M., 16 Jan. 80

Lavis, F., 7 June 77

Law, C., 26 Apr. 79

Law, E., 29 Jan. 77

Law, R., 1 Sept. 76

Law, *Rev.* R. V., 17 Dec. 78 (?)

Law, *Rev.* T. G., 17 Dec. 78

Lawes, *Mrs.*, 8 Dec. 77

Lawley, H., *née* Zaiser, 24 July 77

Lawrence, *Rev.* F., 24 Dec. 77

Lawrence, *Dr.* H. C., 15 May 78 (?)

Lawrence, P. M., 25 Feb. 79

Lawrence, *Rev.* T. J., 29 Sept. 76n

Lawrenson, M., 27 Oct. 77

Lawrie, *Dr.* J. D., 19 Dec. 76 (?)

Lawson, T. E., 28 May 79

Lawton, J., 13 Aug. 79

Layman, *Mr.*, 8 Jan. 75

Layton, C., 17 July 78

Lea, *Sir* T., *1st Bart.*, 17 Dec. 79

Leach, J., 9 Jan. 79

Leahy, *Rev.* T., 31 Oct. 77 (?)

Leake, R., 28 Apr. 78

Learoyd, *Miss*, 21 Dec. 78

Leaver, J., 12 Feb. 80

Leaves, B., 16 Aug. 77

Leathes, *Rev.* S., 29 June 76

Lebey, E. G., 20 Nov. 79

Lechmere, *Lady* L. K., *née* Haigh, 1 Aug. 76

Lechoville, M. de, 5 Feb. 79

Lee, A. F., 15 Nov. 77

Lee, H. W., 11 Feb. 80

Lee, J., 2 Nov. 78

Lee, W. S., 2 Nov. 78

Lee, *Ven.* W., 20 Oct. 77

Leecraft, G. S., 9 Aug. 78

Leedle, *Mr.*, 26 Sept. 78

Leeman, J. J., 28 Oct. 80

Leeman, *Rev.* W. L., 17 Feb. 79

Lees, R., 27 Mar. 80

Lefanu, W. R., 31 Oct. 77

Lefevre, *Messrs.* H. S., 23 Mar. 77

Lefevre, *Mons.*, 21 Mar. 78

Lefevre, G. J. Shaw-, *1st Baron Eversley*, 15 Dec. 78

Legard, *rescue*, 16 June 80

Léger, E., 11 Mar. 78

Legeyt, *Rev.* C. J., 22 Nov. 76

Legge, A. A. K., 6 Jan. 75

Legge, E. H., 20 May 79

Legge, E., *Lady Sherborne*, 21 Oct. 77

Legge, *Rev. Prof.* J., 25 Apr. 78n

Legge, J. H., *3rd Baron Sherborne*, 21 Oct. 77n

Lehmann, R., 20 Mar. 75

Leichenstein, *Dr.*, 14 Jan. 80

Leigh, *Provost* A. Austen, 27 Oct. 78

Leigh, W., 10 Jan. 77

Leinster, *Duke and Duchess of, see* Fitzgerald

Leisk, J. L., 16 Apr. 80

Leith, J. F., 16 Dec. 77

Leith Hospital, 27 Jan. 80

Leitrim, *Earl of, see* Clements

Lennard, *Mr.*, 18 Dec. 80

Lenorègne, *Mr.*, 30 Oct. 77

Lentry, *Mr.*, 11 Feb. 80

Leon, A., 26 Dec. 79

Léon, L., 18 Oct. 79n

Lesciotti, *Sig.*, 12 Dec. 79

Leslie, *Miss*, 29 June 78

Leslie, *Rev.* R. T., 2 July 75

Leslie, W. R., 7 Mar. 76

Lethaby, *Rev.* W., 17 Mar. 76

Leverett & Frye, 16 May 76

Levy, J. H., 16 June 79

Lewin, *Dr.* F., 15 Dec. 76

Lewin, *Miss* J., 19 Dec. 78

Lewis, *Sir* C. E., *1st Bart.*, 30 Apr. 76

Lewis, *Rev.* E., 14 Sept. 75 (?)

Lewis, H. O., 15 July 76

Lewis, J. S., 6 Nov. 78

Lewis, *Rev.* L., 16 Dec. 79 (?)

Lewis, *Rev.* R. T., 31 Jan. 80

Lewis, *Rev.* S. S., 28 Oct. 78

Lewis, *Rev.* T., 22 Apr. 80 (?)

Lewis, W. L., 15 Nov. 78

Leyden, *Countess* De, 12 Oct. 79

Leyden, M., 1 July 78

Liardet, J. E., 5 Feb. 75

Libbey, J. M., 12 July 78

Lichtenberg, G. P., 26 Dec. 78

Lignana, *Prof.* G., 29 Oct. 76

Lilburne, R., 8 Mar. 75

Lilley, E., 28 Apr. 75

Lilley, J., 25 July 77

Lincolnshire, *Marquis of, see* Carrington

Lindley, P., 10 Apr. 77

Lindsay, *Lady* H., *née* Gordon, 8 June 75n

Lindsay, R. J., 23 Mar. 80

Lindsay, T., 21 Dec. 78

Lynian, *Mr.*, 26 May 75
Lyons, *Dr.* R. D., 30 June 80
Lyte, *Rev.* J. Maxwell-, 4 July 76 (?)
Lyttelton, H. M., 12 Jan. 75
Lyttelton, M. S. C., *née* Cavendish, *Lady Cobham*, 19 Oct. 78

Mabbs, G., 10 Apr. 76
Macadam, *Mr.*, 10 June 76
McAll, *Rev.* S., 11 Dec. 75
Macanliffe, *Mr.*, 11 Apr. 79
MacArthur, H., 10 Apr. 79
Macartney, *Dr.* S. H., 19 June 77
Macaulay, *Rev.* G., 3 June 75
Macaulay, G. C., 9 May 77
MacBain, J., 29 June 78
Macbryde, *Mr.*, 1 May 77
McCallan, *Rev.* J. F., 31 Jan. 77
Maccaroni Co., 29 Nov. 77
McCarthy, *Rev.* E. F. M., 1 June 77
McCheane, *Rev.* H. D., 23 May 76
M'Clure, A. C., 27 Mar. 80
MacColl, *Rev.* D., 6 Oct. 77
Maccolla, C. J., 11 Feb. 80
MacConville, *Mr.*, 15 Apr. 80
McCorquodale, *Messrs.*, 24 Nov. 76
McCosh, *Rev. Prof.* J., 19 Oct. 75
M'Coy, *Mr.*, 21 Apr. 75
MacCrie, *Rev.* C. G., 3 Mar. 79
Maccullagh, *Mr.*, 21 Nov. 78
M'Culloch, A., 12 July 76
MacCulloch, *Dr.* J. M., 23 Sept. 75
Macdonald, A., 5 Oct. 77 (?)
MacDonald, *Dr.* D. G. E., 8 Aug. 78
Macdonald, G., 25 Oct. 79 (?)
Macdonald, T., 29 Aug. 78
MacDonald, W., 9 Aug. 77
Macdonnell, J., 12 Mar. 79
Macdonnell, R., 18 July 78
Macdougal, A., 19 Mar. 78
MacDougall, A., 23 Aug. 78
MacDougall, *Messrs.*, 10 Jan. 76
Macdougall, W., 28 Sept. 80
Mace, C. E., 3 Mar. 80
MacElvey, *Mr.*, 16 Oct. 77
Macenter, *Mr.*, 16 May 78
Macewen, W. C., 19 Mar. 80 (?)
Macfarlane, *Sir* D. H., 28 Nov. 80
Macfarlane, *Rev.* W. C., 21 Apr. 79 (?)
Macfie, D. J., *of Borthwickhall*, 29 Mar. 80
MacGreagh, R., 16 July 77 (?)
M'Ghee, *Miss*, 26 May 75

Macghee, R., 23 Jan. 80
MacGitting, *Mr.*, 9 Apr. 80
McGovern, *Rev.* J. B., 18 Nov. 79
MacGregor, *Rev. Principal* D., 15 Aug. 77
Macgregor, E., *rescue*, 14 Mar. 78
Macgregor, *Sir* E., 27 Apr. 80
MacGregor, *Rev. Dr.* J., 4 June 78
Macingo, *Count*, 8 Oct. 79
MacInnes, M., 22 Mar. 80
Macintosh, *Rev.* J., 24 Feb. 77
Macintyre, *Rev.* A., 22 July 78
MacIver, *Col.* H. R. H. D., 25 Oct. 76
Mackay, R., 19 Sept. 75
McKechnie, C., 9 June 75†
Mackee, *Prof.*, H. S., 14 Dec. 77 (?)
Mackenzie, A. C., 10 Apr. 77
Mackenzie, C. J. (F.), 26 Nov. 79 (?)
MacKenzie, *Miss* F. M., 27 Mar. 76
Mackenzie, *Maj.* J. D., 3 May 79
MacKey, *Rev.* D. G., 7 Mar. 79
'Mackie, J. A.', *see* Thompson
Mackie, T., 13 Apr. 78
Mackiewicz, *Rev.* A., 26 July 77
McKinoch, *Mr.*, 28 May 79
M'Konky, *rescue*, 9 July 77
MacKonochie, *Rev.* A. H., 28 June 77
Maclaren, J. W., 24 Mar. 80
Maclauchlin, A., 21 Jan. 78
Maclean, *Rev.* H., 1 Nov. 78 (?)
MacLean, *Sir* J., 21 Apr. 76
Maclean & Pisani, 11 Nov. 75n
Maclehose, J. J., 16 Nov. 77
Macleod, *Rev.* A., 23 Oct. 76
Macleod, M. D., 7 May 78
M'Manny, *Mr.*, 9 Jan. 78
Macmillan, G. A., 3 Apr. 79
MacMordie, H., 30 Dec. 78
MacNab, T., 8 July 75
McNair, J. R., 28 Aug. 77
Macnamara, *Dr.* N. C., 21 Aug. 77
Macnaughton, S., 10 July 79 (?)
Macnee, *Sir* D., 4 Apr. 80
MacNulty, B., 18 Aug. 75
McOscar, *Dr.* J., 22 Apr. 78
McOscar, W., 22 Apr. 78n
Macphail, *Rev.* E. W. St M., 8 June 77 (?)
MacPhail, W. M., 15 Aug. 77
MacPhilpin, *Mr.*, 12 Dec. 79
Macquoid, J. R., 27 Feb. 77
Macrea, J., 2 Sept. 78
Macunslane, *Mr.*, 17 July 78
MacVeigh, *Mr.*, 17 Apr. 76

Momby, J., 4 Nov. 76
Monahan, *Judge* J. H., 14 Aug. 78
Mona's Herald, publisher of, 8 Oct. 78
Moncrieff, J. W., 2 Oct. 76
Moncur, *Baillie*, 4 Dec. 77
Money, W., 29 Jan. 77
Mongan, *Mr.*, 31 May 79
Monk, *Mrs.*, 24 July 75
Monro, *Provost* D. B., 13 Nov. 78
Montagu, *Baron, see* Scott
Montagu, E. G. H., *Lord Hinchinbrook, 8th*
    Earl of Sandwich, 3 May 79
Montenegro, *Prince of, see* Nicolas
Montgomery, A., *née* Ponsonby, 14 Apr. 78
Montgomery, T., 22 June 76
Montmorency, *Miss*, 22 Oct. 80
Monty, *rescue*, 16 Oct. 78
Moody, *Rev.* J. L., 16 Sept. 75
Moon, *Miss*, 4 Mar. 78
Moon, G. W., 15 July 76
Moore, D., 2 Feb. 76 (?)
Moore, *Canon* E., 8 Nov. 79
Moore, R. J., 3 Oct. 78n
Moore, T., 21 Oct. 76
Moore, *Rev.* W. T., 9 Aug. 75
Moran, *Cardinal* P. F., 9 Nov. 77
Morandini, G., 3 Oct. 79
Morell, J. R., 10 Jan. 78
Morelli, *Prof.* L., 11 Oct. 75
Moreton, J., *Lady Ducie*, 5 Apr. 76
Morewood, *Rev.* R. S., 6 June 77
Morgan, *Miss*, 16 Dec. 75
Morgan, A. F., 21 Mar. 78
Morgan, *Rev.* G., 25 Jan. 79
Morgan, J. De, 3 Aug. 76
Morgan, *Rev.* J. H., 29 June 78 (?)
Morgan, *Rev.* J. P., 9 June 76
Morgan, O., *known as* 'Morien', 31 Mar. 75
Morice, B., 4 May 79
'Morien', *see* Morgan, O.
Morison, *Mrs., rescue*, 1 Aug. 75
Morison, J. A. R., 10 May 76
Moritz, E., 6 Dec. 77 (?)
Morley, A., 12 Mar. 79
Morley, J., *1st Viscount Morley of Blackburn*,
    4 Mar. 76 (?)
Morley, W., 29 Jan. 78
Morne, D., 16 May 78
Morris, *Gen.* C. H., 24 Aug. 80
Morris, *Miss* J., 18 July 79
Morris, J. P. R., 22 June 75
Morris, L., 22 Feb. 77

Morris, R. T., 4 Jan. 77
Morris, *Lieut.* W., 1 Sept. 77
Morris, W., 21 Mar. 79
Morrison, J. R., 10 Jan. 78
Morson, W. H., 3 Mar. 79
Mortlock, *Rev.* C., 11 Jan. 76
Morton, *rescue*, 7 Feb. 77
Morton, H. T., 25 Sept. 76
Moscheles, *Mrs.*, 22 Mar. 78
Moseley, W., 24 Aug. 77
Moses, M., 22 Jan. 77
Mot, F., 11 Jan. 78
Mottershead, R., 10 Oct. 76
Mottram, *Rev.* W., 18 Dec. 79
Moulton, *Rev. Dr.* W. F., 22 June 78
Mounet-Sully, J., 17 Oct. 79
Mountain, *Rev.* A. W., 29 July 78
Mountain, *Rev.* J., 19 Jan. 76 (?)
Mountfield, *Rev.* D., 26 Oct. 75
Moxey, *Dr.* D. A., 23 Mar. 80
Moxon, *Rev.* J., 6 Feb. 77
Mudie, *Messrs.*, 25 Apr. 79
Mudie, C. E., 25 Apr. 79n
Muir, T. H., 28 Feb. 80
Muir, *Sir* W., 20 Jan. 79
Mullan, R., 2 Mar. 75
Mulholland, W., 6 Nov. 77 (?)
Mullins, E. R., 14 Dec. 78
Mulock, D., 28 Sept. 79n
Mummery, *Mr.*, 14 Feb. 79
Munday, C. F., 30 Nov. 78
Munday, T., 21 Mar. 79
Mundella, *Miss* M. T., 19 Mar. 77
Munro, A. B., 11 Oct. 78
Munro, L., 20 Feb. 80 (?)
Murdoch, A., 14 Sept. 77
Murdoch, *Rev.* A. D., 2 July 75
Mure, *Col.* W., 20 Nov. 78
Murphy, *Mrs., rescue?*, 8 Mar. 79
Murphy, D. F., 9 Sept. 78
Murphy, E., *rescue*, 18 May 80
Murphy, *Rev.* F. L., 20 May 76
Murphy, H. H., 3 Feb. 75
Murphy, J. J., 15 Aug. 77
Murray, A. G., 23 June 79
Murray, *Lady* E., 9 July 75
Murray, E. C. Grenville, 17 Sept. 77
Murray, H. M., 2 Apr. 78
Murray, J. B., 23 Mar. 78
Murray, W. P., 27 Jan. 79
Musicians, Society of, 20 Jan. 75
Musolini, B., 19 Dec. 77 (?)

Muspratt, E. K., 19 June 78 (?)
Mussalini, *Dr.*, 19 Dec. 77
Mussett, S., 20 Feb. 79
Myers, *Messrs.*, 7 Nov. 79
Myers, *Rev.* A. J., 4 Nov. 78 (?)
Mynott, A., 11 Feb. 80
Myriantheus, *Archimandrite* H., 15 Mar. 75

Naftel, E. L., 28 Nov. 77
Naish, *Rev.* F. C., 15 June 75
Nanson, *Mr.*, 31 May 79
Nash, J., 4 Feb. 75
Nate, *Miss* L., 3 Apr. 78
National Liberal League, 21 Mar. 79n
Nattali, *Mr.*, 15 Apr. 79
Naudet, J., 6 Apr. 77
Neale, C., 16 Oct. 77
Neall, *Mr.*, 13 Oct. 75
Negropontis, M. J., 9 Jan. 77
Neill, *Rev.* E. D., 31 July 75
Neill, W., 13 Jan. 79
Neilson, *Miss* L. A., 24 July 79
Nesbitt, J., 9 Apr. 80 (?)
Nettleton, J. O., 6 Mar. 80
Neuhaus, J. C., 6 Mar. 75 (?)
Neville, R., 7 Feb. 79
Nevin, *Rev. Dr.* R. J., 24 July 78
Nevins, *Rev.* H. W. Probyn-, 22 Mar. 75
Newick, *Rev.* W., 19 Jan. 75
Newman, G., 7 Feb. 75
Newman, *Dr.* J. B., 20 Dec. 79 (?)
Newman, T., 12 July 76 (?)
Newnham, N. J., 8 Oct. 77
Newton, *Sir* E., 16 Oct. 78
Newton, *Rev.* H., 11 Apr. 77
Newton, J., 16 Apr. 80
Newton, T., 27 Aug. 77
Neymarck, A., 15 May 77
Nicholls, J. C., 12 Dec. 77
Nichols, T., 10 Apr. 80
Nichols, *Rev.* W. L., 13 Dec. 75
Nicholson, A., 2 Jan. 77
Nicholson, L. J., 10 Apr. 78
Nicholson, *Rev.* W. T., 16 Jan. 76
Nicol, *Dr.*, 25 Jan. 76
Nicol, D. N., 5 Sept. 79
Nicolas, *Prince, of Montenegro*, 28 Nov. 80
Nikolaides, G., 21 Apr. 80
Nimmo, *Miss* E., 23 Aug. 80
Nisbet, *Messrs.*, 3 Jan. 77
Nixon, A., 1 Mar. 80

Nixon, C. J., 17 Nov. 79
Noble, E., 12 Aug. 78
Noddall, *Messrs.* W. T. & S., 27 Sept. 77
Noel, *Lady* A., 19 Apr. 80
Noel, E., 19 Apr. 80n
Nolan, *Rev.* T., 10 Nov. 77
Noldwatt, *Mr.*, 2 Apr. 79 (?)
Noott, *Rev.* E. H. L., 22 Sept. 77
Norchi & Co., 27 Mar. 79 (?)
Norman, C. B., 23 Jan. 78
Norman, F. J., 6 Apr. 78
Norris, C. A., 26 Dec. 76
Norris, *Ven.* J. P., 22 Feb. 76
North, J. W., 30 Nov. 77 (?)
Northbourne, *Lord, see* James
Norton, *Dr.* A. T., 11 Apr. 78 (?)
Norwood, J., 10 Apr. 78
Nourse, H. D., 11 Apr. 78
Nubar Pasha, 21 June 77
Nublat, M., 4 Dec. 77
Nüth, E. A., 15 June 76
Nuttall, C. G., 11 Feb. 78
Nys, *Prof.* E., 3 July 79

Oakdew, *Mr.*, 3 Sept. 77
Oakeley, *Prof. Sir* H. S., 3 Feb. 80
Oakley, *Rev.* J., 20 Sept. 80
Oates, A., 25 Feb. 80
Oates, W., 13 Dec. 76
O'Brien, E. W., 18 Oct. 75
O'Brien, R. B., 7 Jan. 80
O'Brien, W., 17 Oct. 77
O'Clery, K., 10 May 77
O'Connell, F. D. F., 9 Apr. 80
O'Connor, F., 20 July 77
O'Dell, S. E., 17 Feb. 75
O'Donnell, *Mr.*, 24 Sept. 76
O'Donnell, F. H. O'C., 14 June 80
O'Dwyer, *Father*, 31 Oct. 77
Offer, G., 6 Mar. 78
Officer, *Mr.*, 23 Mar. 80
O'Flanagan, *Rev.* J. R., 3 Feb. 79 (?)
Ogden, H., 1 Apr. 78
Ogilvy, J. T., 27 June 79
Ogilvy, W. S., 23 Sept. 78
Ogilvy, W. T., 23 Sept. 78 (?)
Ogle, *Rev.* J. L., 21 June 78 (?)
O'Hanlon, *Canon* J., 1 Jan. 80
O'Hare, *Rev.* D. V., 21 Apr. 79
O'Hart, J., 18 Jan. 76
Ohlson, *Mr.*, 13 July 76
Olden, *Rev.* T., 23 Apr. 76

Rand, *Rev.* S. T., 28 Aug. 78
Randall, *Ven.* J. L., 1 Nov. 79
Randell, J. S., 15 June 78 (?)
Randolph, *Rev.* F., 10 Jan. 77
Rankin, J., 13 Dec. 79
Ransom, *Messrs.*, 2 Feb. 78
Rathmore, *Lord, see* Plunket
Rawlins, J. H., 12 Aug. 79
Rawlings, S. T., 22 Jan. 77n
Rawnsley, *Rev.* R. D. B., 25 June 77
Rawson, T. W., 4 Oct. 77
Rayner, *Mrs.* R., 22 Feb. 75
Reachman, *Mr.*, 18 Nov. 78
Reade, P., 9 Mar. 76
Reavis, L. U., 3 Mar. 80
Reddish, S., 22 Nov. 78 (?)
Redfern, J., 28 Aug. 79
Redfern, W., 10 Sept. 78 (?)
Redford, G., 17 June 75
Redhouse, *Mr.*, 24 July 79
Redish, *see* Reddish
Reed, A. C., 29 June 77
Reed, C. R., 1 Mar. 76
Reed, G. J., 7 May 79
Reed, J. J., *see* Reid, J. J.
Reed, W. H., 2 Oct. 77
Rees, *Messrs.*, 8 Jan. 79
Rees, A., 19 Mar. 77 (?)
Rees, *Rev.* C. D., 16 Oct. 75 (?)
Reeve, J. E., 24 Mar. 75
Reeves, T., 18 Mar. 80
Reid, A. M., 4 May 78
Reid, *Sir* G. H., 13 July 75
Reid, H., 2 Aug. 78 (?)
Reid, *Sir* H. G., 29 Mar. 78
Reid, J. J., 9 Dec. 79
Reid, S. J., 21 Apr. 79
Reid, *Sir* T. W., 20 May 77
Reinach, S., 4 Nov. 76 (?)
Reiss, C. A., 4 Nov. 79
Relling, F. S., 6 Feb. 75
Renault, E., 22 Feb. 76
Rench, J., 3 Sept. 79
Rendel, S., *1st Baron Rendel*, 20 Dec. 80
Rendell, W., 13 Mar. 79
Restney, A., 7 Feb. 79
Reumert, T., 19 Mar. 78
Reynolds, E. J., 19 Aug. 78
Reynolds, *Rev. Prof.* H. R., 10 June 75
Reynolds, W., 14 June 77
Rhodes, C., 4 Mar. 80 (?)
Rhodes, J., 27 Jan. 75

Rhodocanakis, *Prince* D., 9 May 75
Rhys, D., 20 Feb. 80
Ricardo, *rescue*, 29 May 79
Ricchetti, C., 4 Oct. 79
Rice, C. A. T., 12 Sept. 77
Rice, I. L., 19 Dec. 79
Richards, E. M., 15 June 78
Richardson, R., 16 Mar. 80
Richter, *Herr*, 6 Mar. 77
Ridge, J. J., 30 Aug. 79
Ridsdale case, 16 Dec. 77
Rietti, *Sig.*, 4 Oct. 79
Rigeston, *Mr.*, 19 Dec. 75
Rignold, *Mr.*, 19 Nov. 79
Rimell, *Messrs.*, 10 Mar. 79
Rimmer, A., 31 Aug. 75
Rippin, H. W., 20 Mar. 80
Ritchie, A. J., 15 Mar. 75
Rivers, *Gen.* A. L. Fox Pitt-, 12 July 80
Robb, *Miss*, 26 Dec. 79
Robbins, *Sir* A. F., 22 July 75 (?)
Roberts, A. B., 17 July 77
Roberts, C. A., 26 Feb. 76
Roberts, C. T., 17 Feb. 77
Roberts, *Rev.* C. E. T., 14 Dec. 75
Roberts, F. M., 10 Aug. 77
Roberts, *Rev.* G. R., 9 May 78
Roberts, J., 30 Oct. 79
Roberts, *Rev.* J. T., 3 June 76
Roberts, P. E., 30 Dec. 79
Roberts, *Rev.* W. Page, 2 Nov. 76
Robertson, *Miss*, 15 Mar. 76
Robertson, *Sir* D. B., 25 Sept. 77n
Robertson, *Lady* E., 25 Sept. 77
Robertson, W., 23 Jan. 78
Robertson, *Rev.* W. A. S., 4 Dec. 76
Robins, E. C., 22 Oct. 78
Robinson, *Rev.* J. C., 17 May 79
Robinson, *Rev. Dr.* W. P., 13 Nov. 75
Robjohns, *Rev.* H. J., 5 July 76
Roche, R., 12 Mar. 79
Rochussen, C., 17 May 79 (?)
Rocke, *Mrs.*, 14 Oct. 76
Rodell, *Mr.*, 22 Jan. 79
Roden, W. T., 11 Sept. 77
Rodway, *Rev.* O., 27 July 75
Rodwell, *Rev.* J. M., 10 Mar. 76
Roe, C. S., 26 Apr. 77
Roe, H., 20 Oct. 77
Rogers, *Col.* A. J., 10 May 79
Rogers, *Rev.* J. G., 20 June 76
Rogers, J. D., 11 Dec. 78 (?)

Walker, G., 21 Sept. 78
Walker, G. M., 22 Aug. 76
Walker, J. A., 10 May 76
Walker, *Rev.* J. E., 27 Sept. 78
Walker, *Capt.* O. O., 22 Dec. 76
Walkerston, *Mr.*, 26 July 76
Wall, J., 11 Apr. 80
Wall, *Rev.* J., 6 Mar. 75
Wallace, E., 2 June 75
Wallace, J., 13 Mar. 78
Wallace, *Rev.* W. B., 18 Aug. 75
Wallerstein, H. L., 31 Aug. 78
Wallis, C. W., 24 Feb. 76 (?)
Wallis, H., 31 Oct. 79
Wallop, E., *née* Herbert, *Lady Portsmouth*,
    31 Oct. 79
Wallop, N., *Lord Lymington, 6th Earl of Ports-
    mouth*, 6 Sept. 77
Walmsley, J. V., 2 Oct. 77 (?)
Walmsley, P., 15 Feb. 76
Walpole, J., 13 Nov. 77
Walterer, *Madame*, 3 Aug. 76
Walters, *Rev.* J. V., 19 Sept. 78 (?)
Walters, *Rev.* T., 17 June 79 (?)
Walters, *Rev.* W. C., 18 Apr. 78
Waras, *Mr.*, 10 Aug. 78
Ward, *Sir* A., 12 Nov. 78 (?)
Ward, E. C., 12 Sept. 79
Ward, G. M., 29 Apr. 75
Ward, M. A., *née* Arnold, 29 Apr. 76 (?)
Ward, S., 28 Nov. 79 (?)
Ward, T. H., 29 Apr. 76n
Wardale, *Rev.* C. B., 30 Nov. 76
Wardell, *Dr.* J. R., 13 Nov. 76
Wardrop, *Rev.* J., 2 Apr. 80
Ware, G., 4 Mar. 80
Ware, J., 25 May 77
Waring, C. B., 9 Feb. 76
Wark, A., 12 Sept. 77
Warleigh, *Rev.* H. S., 17 May 75
Warne, T., 26 June 78
Warner, C., 1 Oct. 80
Warner, *Mrs.* M., 24 Apr. 75
Warner, *Mrs.* T., 16 Feb. 78
Warre, *Rev.* E., 6 July 79
Warren, *Rev.* F. E., 4 Nov. 76
Warren, G. W., 25 July 77n
Warren, *Rev.* R. P., 16 July 77
Wash, A., 12 Aug. 76
Washburn, *Rev. Dr.* G., 22 May 80
Wassilieff, *Madame*, 29 Aug. 77

Waterman, T. T., 31 May 78
Waters, E. C., 25 July 77
Waters, E. W., 4 May 76
Waters, E. E., 14 Oct. 76
Waters, *Miss* L., 7 Jan. 76
Waters, *Dr.* T. H., 24 Sept. 75
Waterson, *Messrs.*, 20 Dec. 77
Watherston, E. J., 12 Dec. 77
Watkin, R., 14 Feb. 77
Watkins, F. B., 25 Jan. 75
Watkinson, J., 11 Mar. 78
Watson, *Dr.* A., 18 Jan. 75
Watson, E. H., 23 Apr. 78
Watson, F., 19 July 79
Watson, *Mrs.* M., 16 Mar. 77 (f.l.)
Watson, P. F., 28 May 77
Watson, S. J., 28 Jan. 76
Watson, W. H., 4 Nov. 79
Watson, W. L., 12 Mar. 80n
Watson, W. M., 27 Dec. 77
Watt, *Mrs.*, 7 Aug. 78
Watt, B. H., 5 Jan. 77 (?)
Watt, H., 24 May 79
Watt, R., 16 Mar. 77
Watton, A., 3 May 79n
Watts, *rescue*, 19 June 78
Watts, *Rev.* J. C., 20 June 79
Watts, *Rev.* J., 29 Mar. 75 (?)
Waugh, *Rev.* A. T., 17 Oct. 76
Waugh, F. G., 14 May 77
Way, A., 26 Feb. 80
Wayland, H. L., 11 Jan. 80
Weaver, *Mr.*, 15 Dec. 78
Weaver, B. W., 27 Oct. 77
Webb, *Bp.* A. B., 30 Oct. 78
Webb, E. B., 12 Apr. 77
Webb, G., 7 Sept. 77
Webb, H. C., 9 Oct. 78
Webb, T. H., 12 Jan. 78
Webb, W. T., 22 Feb. 80
Webber, V. A., 1 Sept. 79
Webber, *Rev.* W. T. T., 16 Aug. 79 (?)
Webster, *Rev. Dr.* G., 4 Nov. 77n
Webster, *Dr.* O., 30 Mar. 76
Wed, B., 15 July 76
Wedderburn, *Sir* D., *3rd Bart.*, 30 Mar. 80
Wedgwood, G., 20 Apr. 76
Weeks, A. M., 5 June 76
Weill, *Mr., U.S.A.*, 18 Aug. 76
Weinmann, F. L., 28 Feb. 80
Weir, A. M. C., 5 Apr. 78
Weisenfeld, *Mr.*, 29 May 78